GREAT BRITONS is an illustrated biographical dictionary recording the lives of 645
men and women, all of them British
subjects, who died between 1915 and
1980 and whose mark on their contemporaries and in their chosen careers has
been of exceptional interest and significance. The people represented here come
from all walks of life and span more than
a century of modern British history; also
included are those few 'black sheep'
whose exploits or failures are too firmly
enmeshed in the fabric of the twentieth
century to allow their exclusion.

The information is backed by the
unrivalled authority of *The Dictionary* of
National Biography, supplemented by
unpublished material from *DNB* files as
well as recent biographies and other
modern sources. An index arranged by
occupation or spheres of interest makes it
easy to track down the key figures in any
particular field, and a system of cross-
referencing within the text reveals a web
of relationships and influences that might
not otherwise be immediately apparent.
More than 200 contemporary photographs, cartoons, and drawings evoke the
different moods of the period, put faces
to familiar names, and illustrate the work
of artists featured in the text.

This is a book for the general reader in
search of the immediate British past, for
the student and school-leaver too young
to remember the characters and events of
earlier generations, and for the journalist,
speech-writer, and anyone else needing
a straightforward, reliable, and readable
source of biographical facts.

GREAT BRITONS

Twentieth-Century Lives

GREAT BRITONS

Twentieth-Century Lives

HAROLD OXBURY

Oxford   New York

OXFORD UNIVERSITY PRESS

1985

Oxford University Press, Walton Street, Oxford OX2 6DP

Oxford New York Toronto
Delhi Bombay Calcutta Madras Karachi
Kuala Lumpur Singapore Hong Kong Tokyo
Nairobi Dar es Salaam Cape Town
Melbourne Auckland
and associated companies in
Beirut Berlin Ibadan Mexico City Nicosia

Oxford is a trade mark of Oxford University Press

British Library Cataloguing in Publication Data
Oxbury, Harold
Great Britons: twentieth-century lives.
1. Great Britain—Biography
I. Title
920'.041   DA566.9.A1
ISBN 0-19-211599-5

Library of Congress Cataloging in Publication Data
Oxbury, Harold.
Great Britons.
Includes index.
1. Great Britain—Biography. I. Title.
CT783.093 1985   920'.041   84-27214
ISBN 0-19-211599-5

Printed in Great Britain
at the University Press, Oxford
by David Stanford
Printer to the University

CONTENTS

NOTE TO THE READER

Entries are arranged in alphabetical order with the exception that names beginning with Mc are treated as though they were spelt Mac. Cross-references are indicated by the use of small capital letters: if a name appears in this form on its first appearance in an article, it will be found to have its own entry. There are, however, no cross-references to monarchs or their consorts.

PREFACE

THE idea for this book came originally from Dr Christine Nicholls, Associate Editor of the *Dictionary of National Biography*. Its purpose is to portray the history and character of modern Britain through the lives of those men and women who have left the greatest mark on their time, and to provide a brief, readable, and reliable account of those lives. Only British subjects who died between 1915 and 1980 are included though the coverage is historically broader than this may suggest (George Cadbury was born in 1839) and extends over many fields of endeavour. To bring the work within its allotted compass it has been necessary to exclude a number of names that would otherwise have been included. My final selection will, no doubt, be open to criticism, as it seems unlikely that any two people would make the same choices.

Some of the 'Great Britons' included here, Guy Burgess for example, can hardly be described as great in any commendatory sense; others, like Halifax and Nevile Henderson, were important more for what they failed to do or see than for their achievements. But they appear in this volume not only by virtue of their birth in Great Britain, but also because their influence upon events has seemed to me too profound to ignore. In fact not all of the entrants were born in Britain: some, like Nancy Astor, were American-born; others, such as Wittgenstein, Lucien Pissarro, Weizmann, and Lindemann, came from Europe or elsewhere; but all these became British subjects at a significant stage in their lives, significant enough to allow Britain to claim them as her own. A few, in particular Gandhi, Smuts, and De Valera, were indeed famous citizens of the British Empire, but it was their reaction to this status which singles out the greatness of their contribution to British history.

The book is based mainly on information provided by the *DNB*, but this has been supplemented by material from other works and from my own memory of events and personal acquaintance with a few of the characters. I hope that most readers will find here the essential information they require. If others, and especially young students, having been introduced to the subjects of the book are encouraged to pursue their enquiries further by reference to more detailed biographies, I shall consider my purpose to have been achieved.

I am greatly indebted to Pamela Coote for her invaluable assistance in editing the work, to Dr Nicholls for her help in its preparation, to Phyllis Cooper for her criticism and advice, to Sandra Assersohn for researching the illustrations, and to everyone at Oxford University Press for their co-operation.

HAROLD OXBURY

Huntersmoon
July 1984

LIST OF ABBREVIATIONS

ADC — Aide-de-Camp
AEA — Atomic Energy Authority
AFC — Air Force Cross
ANZUS — Defence treaty signed in 1951 by Australia, New Zealand, and the USA
A.O.C.-in-C. — Air Officer Commanding-in-Chief
ARA — Associate of the Royal Academy
ARCM — Associate of the Royal College of Music
ARCS — Associate of the Royal College of Science
ARP — Air Raid Precautions
ASC — Administrative Staff College, Henley
ASDIC — Anti-Submarine Detection Investigation Committee
ATS — Auxiliary Territorial Service

BA — Bachelor of Arts
B.Ch. — Bachelor of Surgery
BD — Bachelor of Divinity
BEF — British Expeditionary Force
BMA — British Medical Association
BOAC — British Overseas Airways Corporation
BS — Bachelor of Surgery
B.Sc. — Bachelor of Science

CB — Companion of the Order of the Bath
CBE — Companion of the Order of the British Empire
CEMA — Council for the Encouragement of Music and the Arts
CH — Companion of Honour
Ch.B. — Bachelor of Surgery
CI — Order of the Crown of India
CID — Criminal Investigation Department
CIE — Companion of the Order of the Indian Empire
CIGS — Chief of the Imperial General Staff
C.Lit. — Companion of Literature
CM — Master of Surgery
CMS — Church Missionary Society
CND — Campaign for Nuclear Disarmament
CSI — Companion of the Order of the Star of India
CVO — Commander of the Royal Victorian Order

DBE — Dame Commander of the Order of the British Empire
DCL — Doctor of Civil Law
DD — Doctor of Divinity
DFC — Distinguished Flying Cross
DNB — *The Dictionary of National Biography*
DPH — Diploma in Public Health
DSM — Distinguished Service Medal
DSO — Companion of the Distinguished Service Order

EEC — European Economic Community
ENSA — Entertainments National Service Association

FA — Football Association
FAO — Food and Agriculture Organization
FBA — Fellow of the British Academy
FIDO — Fog Intensive Dispersal Operation
FRCM — Fellow of the Royal College of Music
FRCO — Fellow of the Royal College of Organists
FRCP — Fellow of the Royal College of Physicians, London
FRCS — Fellow of the Royal College of Surgeons, England
FRCSE — Fellow of the Royal College of Surgeons of Edinburgh
FRS — Fellow of the Royal Society
FRSL — Fellow of the Royal Society of Literature

GBE — Knight (or Dame) Grand Cross of the Order of the British Empire
GCB — Knight (or Dame) Grand Cross of the Order of the Bath
GCIE — Knight Grand Commander of the Order of the Indian Empire
GCMG — Knight (or Dame) Grand Cross of the Order of St Michael and St George
GCSI — Knight Grand Commander of the Order of the Star of India
G.C.St.J. — Bailiff or Dame Grand Cross of the Order of St John of Jerusalem
GCVO — Knight (or Dame) Grand Cross of the Royal Victorian Order
GHQ — General Headquarters
G.O.C.-in-C. — General Officer Commanding-in-Chief
GWR — Great Western Railway

HAC — Honourable Artillery Company

ICI — Imperial Chemical Industries
ICS — Indian Civil Service
ILO — International Labour Organization
ILP — Independent Labour Party
IRA — Irish Republican Army

JP — Justice of the Peace

KBE — Knight Commander of the Order of the British Empire
KC — King's Counsel
KCB — Knight Commander of the Order of the Bath
KCIE — Knight Commander of the Order of the Indian Empire
KCMG — Knight Commander of the Order of St Michael and St George
KCVO — Knight Commander of the Royal Victorian Order
KG — Knight of the Garter
KRRC — King's Royal Rifle Corps
KT — Knight of the Order of the Thistle

LCC — London County Council
LL B — Bachelor of Laws
LL D — Doctor of Laws
LL M — Master of Laws
LRAM — Licentiate of the Royal Academy of Music
LRCP — Licentiate of the Royal College of Physicians, London
LSA — Licentiate of the Society of Apothecaries
LSE — London School of Economics

MBE — Member of the Order of the British Empire
MC — Military Cross
MCC — Marylebone Cricket Club
MD — Doctor of Medicine
MFH — Master of Fox Hounds
MGM — Metro-Goldwyn-Mayer
MI5 — Counter-Intelligence Service
MI6 — Secret Intelligence Service
Mods. — Moderations (first public examination in some faculties for Oxford BA)
MRC — Medical Research Council
MRCP — Member of the Royal College of Physicians, London
MRCS — Member of the Royal College of Surgeons of England
M.Sc. — Master of Science
M.Sc.Tech. — Master of Science (Technical)

MVO	Member of the Royal Victorian Order	RCM	Royal College of Music
		RDI	Royal Designer for Industry
NATO	North Atlantic Treaty Organization	RE	Royal Engineers
NPL	National Physics Laboratory	RFC	Royal Flying Corps
NUM	National Union of Mineworkers	RGA	Royal Garrison Artillery
		RHA	Royal Horse Artillery
OBE	Officer of the Order of the British Empire	RIBA	Royal Institute of British Architects
OM	(Member of the) Order of Merit	RMC	Royal Military College
OTC	Officers' Training Corps	RNVR	Royal Naval Volunteer Reserve
OUDS	Oxford University Dramatic Society		
		SEATO	South-East Asia Treaty Organization
PC	Privy Counsellor	SHAEF	Supreme Headquarters, Allied Expeditionary Force
PEN	(Authors' club) Poets, Playwrights, Editors, Essayists, Novelists	SIS	Secret Intelligence Service (MI6)
		SOE	Special Operations Executive
Ph.D.	Doctor of Philosophy		
PLUTO	Pipeline under the ocean	TNT	trinitrotoluene
		TUC	Trades Union Congress
QC	Queen's Counsel		
		VAD	Voluntary Aid Detachment
RA	Royal Academician, Royal Artillery	VC	Victoria Cross
RADA	Royal Academy of Dramatic Art		
RAF	Royal Air Force	WRAC	Women's Royal Army Corps
RAFVR	Royal Air Force Volunteer Reserve	WRAF	Women's Royal Air Force
RAM	Member of the Royal Academy of Music	WRNS	Women's Royal Naval Service
RAMC	Royal Army Medical Corps		
RASC	Royal Army Service Corps	YMCA	Young Men's Christian Association
RBA	Member of the Royal Society of British Artists	YWCA	Young Women's Christian Association

A

ABERCONWAY, second BARON (1879-1953). See MCLAREN.

ABERCROMBIE, SIR (LESLIE) PATRICK (1879-1957), architect and professor of town planning, was born on 6 June 1879 at Ashton-upon-Mersey, the son of William Abercrombie, a stockbroker, and his wife, Sarah Ann Heron. He was educated at Uppingham and, after being articled as an architect, was appointed an assistant lecturer at Liverpool School of Architecture (1907-9) and then Research Fellow in town planning and civic design (1909-15). Up to 1914 he travelled widely in Europe studying developments in Paris, Berlin, Vienna, and other cities. In 1909 he married Emilia Maud, daughter of Robert Gordon; they had one daughter and one son.

From 1915 to 1935 he was Professor of Civic Design at Liverpool. During this time he produced numerous reports on regional planning, including studies of Deeside (1923), Sheffield (1924), and the East Kent Coalfield (1925). In 1926, while he was President of the Town Planning Institute, he published a pamphlet which led directly to the establishment of the Council for the Preservation of Rural England.

From 1935 to 1946 he was Professor of Town Planning at University College London and, in addition to dealing with all kinds of planning problems, he campaigned for the Green Belt around London. During the Second World War he was appointed, in association with the LCC architect, J. H. Forshaw, to prepare a plan for post-war rebuilding throughout the county of London. The *County of London Plan* (1943) and the *Greater London Plan* (1944) marked the highlights of his career. He had a hand in the post-war planning of many cities and towns, not only in Britain, but also abroad, and he achieved an international reputation.

He became a Fellow of the RIBA in 1925, and was Vice-President in 1937-9. He was knighted in 1945, and received many other honours and awards. Abercrombie died on 23 March 1957 at Aston Tirrold in Berkshire.

ABRAHAMS, HAROLD MAURICE (1899-1978), athlete and sports administrator, was born in Bedford on 15 December 1899, the youngest of four sons of Isaac Abrahams, a Lithuanian Jewish money-lender, and his wife, Esther Isaacs, of Merthyr Tydfil. Isaac Abrahams, who had changed his name from Klonimus, had been born in Russian-occupied Poland and naturalized in 1902. All of his sons had distinguished careers: the eldest, Adolphe, became a consultant physician at the Westminster Hospital and was knighted in 1939; Sidney (later Sir Sidney) competed in the Olympic Games of 1908 and 1912, served as a colonial Chief Justice and was a Privy Counsellor; and Lionel became Coroner for Huntingdonshire.

Harold was educated at Bedford School, St Paul's, Repton, and Gonville and Caius College, Cambridge. As a small boy he watched his brother compete in the fourth Olympic Games in London (1908), and in 1918 he himself won the public schools' 100 yards race and the long-jump. At Cambridge he won three events in the freshman's sports and won eight times in the annual Oxford-Cambridge sports at the 100 yards, 440 yards, and the long jump (1920-3). He was President of the University Athletics Club in 1922-3.

Abrahams represented Britain in the Olympic Games in Antwerp in 1920 and again in Paris in 1924 when he

Harold Abrahams: Olympic triumph

captained the British team and won the gold medal for the 100 metres, his time of 10.6 seconds equalling the games record. In 1925 he injured a leg in attempting to improve his native long-jump record, and had to retire from athletics.

In 1924 he was called to the Bar (Inner Temple) and practised as a barrister until 1940 when he became a civil servant, for the duration of the Second World War, in the Ministry of Economic Warfare and the Ministry of Town and Country Planning. In 1936 Abrahams had married Sybil Marjorie Evers; they had one adopted son and one adopted daughter. For most of his adult life he wrote articles on athletics for the *Sunday Times* (1925-67), and broadcast for the BBC (1924-74). He was Honorary Treasurer of the British Amateur Athletic Board (1948-68) and Chairman (1948-75). His experience enabled him to redraft the Amateur Athletic Association's rules of competition, and directly influenced changes in the rules of international competition. From 1950 to 1963 he was also Secretary of the National Parks Commission. He was appointed CBE in 1957. His feats on the athletics field have been highlighted in the 1982 award-winning film *Chariots of Fire*.

He wrote many books on training and on the history of athletics; these include *Sprinting* (1925), *Oxford versus Cambridge 1827-1930* (with J. Bruce Kerr, 1931), *The Olympic Games 1896-1952* (1956), and *The Empire and Commonwealth Games 1930-1958* (1958). He died on 14 January 1978 in London.

ADDISON, CHRISTOPHER, first VISCOUNT ADDISON (1869-1951), politician, was born on 19 June 1869, at Hogsthorpe, Lincolnshire, the son of a farmer, Robert Addison, and his wife, Susan, daughter of Charles Fanthorpe, a customs official. There were seven surviving children in the family, he being the youngest of the three boys. He was educated at Trinity College, Harrogate, and Sheffield Medical School, and qualified in 1892 at St Bartholomew's Hospital, London. In 1897, he became Professor of Anatomy at University College, Sheffield, and in 1901 was appointed lecturer in anatomy at Charing Cross Hospital. He published a number of works on anatomy, and edited the *Quarterly Medical Journal*.

Having married in 1902 Isobel Mackinnon, daughter of Archibald Gray, a wealthy merchant, Addison was able, with the money his wife had brought him, to consider abandoning medicine for politics. His main interests, however, continued to be public health and social welfare, and when he was elected Liberal MP for the Hoxton division of Shoreditch in 1910, although no orator, he quickly made his mark in assisting LLOYD GEORGE with the National Health Insurance Bill of 1911 and other welfare measures. He was appointed Parliamentary Secretary to the Board of Education in 1914 and, when Lloyd George became Minister of Munitions in 1915, Addison joined him as Parliamentary Secretary. In that post he carried out the bulk of the detailed administrative work. He became a Privy Counsellor in 1916. When Lloyd George became Prime Minister, Addison in turn was appointed Minister of Munitions. In spite of the fact that Addison was highly successful in this post, which involved control over almost every aspect of war production, Lloyd George replaced him in 1917 with Winston CHURCHILL, and appointed him Minister of Reconstruction. He tackled his new responsibilities with enthusiasm, producing ambitious post-war schemes for social reform; but to the general public he was almost unknown and had not the political influence to put his plans into effect, once the Prime Minister became

heavily involved in the problems of the peace treaties.

As President of the Local Government Board in 1919, he introduced a bill to establish a Ministry of Health, and became the first Minister a few months later. His Housing, Town Planning, etc. Act, enabled local authorities during the next three years to build over 200,000 houses, but the cost was prohibitive, and aroused intense opposition from the Conservatives. In 1921, Lloyd George made him Minister without Portfolio; his housing programme was abandoned and Addison resigned from the Government. He lost his seat in the 1922 election and, after a period of disillusion and frustration, decided to join the Labour party.

He did not get back into Parliament until 1929 when he became Labour MP for Swindon. In the meantime, he published his views on welfare matters in *The Betrayal of the Slums* (1922), *Politics from Within* (2 vols., 1924), and *Practical Socialism* (2 vols., 1926).

In 1930, he became Minister of Agriculture and in that post won the respect and regard of Clement ATTLEE. In the crisis of 1931 Addison refused to support the National Government of MACDONALD and SNOWDEN, and lost his post and his seat. Although he re-won his seat at a by-election in 1934, he lost it again in 1935, and in 1937 was created a baron.

His first wife, by whom he had three sons and two daughters, had died in 1934. Three years later he married (Beatrice) Dorothy, daughter of Frederick Percy Low, a solicitor. He had continued to be an active writer, and published *Four and a Half Years* (2 vols., 1934) and *A Policy for British Agriculture* (1939).

In 1940 he became Leader of the Labour Peers but took no prominent part in politics, until in Attlee's 1945-51 administration he was Secretary of State for the Dominions (1945-7), Lord Privy Seal (1947-51), Paymaster-General (1948-9), and Lord President of the Council (1951). In these posts, this elder statesman, as he had now become, was of great help to the Prime Minister. In 1945 he became a viscount and in 1946 was created KG. He died at Radnage, Buckinghamshire, on 11 December 1951.

ADRIAN, EDGAR DOUGLAS, first BARON ADRIAN of Cambridge (1889-1977), neurophysiologist, was born on 30 November 1889 in London, the son of Alfred Douglas Adrian KC, legal adviser to the Local Government Board, and his wife, Flora Barton. He was a scholar of Westminster School and of Trinity College, Cambridge, where he won a half-blue for fencing and was elected a Fellow in 1913. A year later he qualified at St Bartholomew's Hospital, London, and then became Medical Officer of the Connaught Military Hospital, Aldershot.

After the First World War he returned to Cambridge to work in the physiological laboratory; he was elected FRS in 1923, the year of his marriage to Hester Pinsent. In 1929 he was appointed Foulerton Research Professor of the Royal Society. Like C. S. SHERRINGTON, he concerned himself with the problems of the central nervous system and the brain, and in 1932 they shared the Nobel prize for medicine. In 1937 Adrian was appointed Professor of Physiology at Cambridge. Perhaps the best way for a layman to describe his work is to list the publications for which he was responsible. These include *The Basis of Sensation* (1928), *The Mechanism of Nervous Action* (1932), *The Physical Basis of Perception* (1947), and a number of papers in the *Journal of Physiology* and in *Brain*. These works showed him to be one of the leading physiologists of his time, able to set out with clarity

Max Aitken aboard the *Evening Standard* helicopter, July 1953

and style the results of his experiments, carried out by means of the skilful techniques that he was able to devise.

He was appointed OM in 1942 and received the Copley medal of the Royal Society in 1946. He succeeded G. M. TREVELYAN as Master of Trinity College, Cambridge in 1951 and held that office until 1965. From 1957 to 1959 he was Vice-Chancellor of the University. He was President of the Royal Society from 1950 to 1955, and of the British Association in 1954. In 1955 he was raised to the peerage as Baron Adrian. He was a member of the Commonwealth Fund Fellowships Committee, of the Medical Research Council, and of the University Grants Committee. He also became Editor of the *Journal of Physiology* and Foreign Secretary of the Royal Society (1946–50). He received a large number of academic honours and awards and his wife, by whom he had a son and two daughters, was made DBE in 1965. She died in 1966. From 1957 to 1971 Adrian was the first Chancellor of Leicester University and from 1968 to 1975 he was also Chancellor of Cambridge University. He died on 4 August 1977 and was succeeded in the barony by his son, Richard Hume Adrian.

AITKEN, (WILLIAM) MAXWELL, first BARON BEAVER-BROOK (1879–1964), newspaper proprietor, was born on 25 May 1879 in Ontario, the third son of William Cuthbert Aitken, a Presbyterian minister, and his wife Jane, daughter of Joseph Noble, a storekeeper and farmer. He was educated at a local school, and at the age of sixteen entered a law firm for a short while, then sold insurance. In 1906 he married Gladys Henderson, daughter of Colonel (later General)

Charles William Drury. A few months after his marriage he moved to Montreal and quickly made a fortune on the stock exchange.

In 1910 Aitken came to England, and, with the help of Andrew BONAR LAW, a fellow Canadian, became Conservative MP for Ashton-under-Lyne. In the following year he was knighted. Soon after war was declared in 1914, he became the representative of the Canadian Government at British GHQ in France, and initiated the *Canadian Daily Record* for Canadian troops in Europe. By 1916, however, he was involved in British politics and took an important part in overthrowing ASQUITH and manoeuvring LLOYD GEORGE into 10 Downing Street. The new Prime Minister rewarded him not with a ministerial post as he had hoped but by making him a baron (1917). (He had already become a baronet in 1916.) Later, however, from February to November 1918 he was Minister of Information, having become a Privy Counsellor in March 1918.

In 1916 he had acquired the *Daily Express* when it was losing money and in danger of closing down; by 1934, it had achieved the largest circulation in the world. Meanwhile, in 1918, Beaverbrook had launched the *Sunday Express* and, in 1923, gained control of the *Evening Standard*. He liked to claim that he allowed his newspapers to run themselves but, in practice, he intervened whenever he felt inclined to do so, and used them, sometimes unscrupulously, to pursue his own projects and prejudices.

In 1922, he advised Bonar Law to attend the Carlton Club meeting which brought down Lloyd George's Coalition Government but, when Bonar Law died and Stanley

BALDWIN became Prime Minister, Beaverbrook ceased to have the influence he had previously asserted in the counsels of the Conservative Party. He was not involved in the formation of the National Government of 1931, and appeared to have retired from the political battle. In 1935, through his papers, he supported Samuel HOARE in his pact with Laval over Abyssinia; in 1936 he advised Edward VIII on the action he should take to circumvent Baldwin over the issue of his marriage to Mrs Simpson; in 1938 he approved strongly of Neville CHAMBERLAIN's agreement with Hitler at Munich; and in 1939, the *Daily Express* was proclaiming that there would be no war that year. However, when the war came, Beaverbrook renewed an old friendship with Winston CHURCHILL and, in November 1940, became Minister of Aircraft Production. To the task of producing fighter aircraft quickly he brought all his ruthlessness and vigour, and it was in no small measure due to his efforts that the Battle of Britain was won. This was his greatest achievement during the war; but he was, in succession, Minister of Production, Minister of Supply, and Lord Privy Seal.

He failed to secure the re-election of Churchill in 1945 and he opposed Maynard KEYNES over the settlement of the American loan in 1947. As a constant exponent of imperial preference and British independence, he opposed Harold Macmillan's attempt to enter the Common Market in 1961. Ironically, although he supported the Conservative Party throughout his political life, he never succeeded in winning the trust or confidence of Conservatives.

He wrote voluminously about his own part in great events: his publications include *Politicians and the War* (2 vols., 1928–32), *Man and Power 1917–18* (1956), *The Decline and Fall of Lloyd George* (1963), and *The Divine Propagandist* (1962).

He had two sons and a daughter by his first wife, who died in 1927. In 1963 he married, Marcia Anastasia, daughter of John Christopher and widow of Sir James Dunn. In the meantime, from 1925 to 1945, Mrs Jean Norton had been his most intimate woman friend. He died on 9 June 1964, at his home, Cherkley Court, near Leatherhead.

ALANBROOKE, first VISCOUNT (1883–1963). See BROOKE, ALAN FRANCIS.

ALEXANDER, HAROLD RUPERT LEOFRIC GEORGE, first EARL ALEXANDER OF TUNIS (1891–1969), field-marshal, was born in London on 10 December 1891, the third son of James Alexander, fourth Earl of Caledon, and his wife, Lady Elizabeth Graham-Toler, daughter of the third Earl of Norbury. He was educated at Harrow and Sandhurst, and was commissioned in the Irish Guards in 1911. An accomplished artist, he intended to make a career as a painter but the First World War ended this ambition. He served in France from 1914 to 1919, was twice wounded, awarded the MC (1915) and DSO (1916), and rose from captain to acting brigadier-general in command of the 4th Guards Brigade.

In 1931 he married Lady Margaret Diana Bingham, younger daughter of the fifth Earl of Lucan. They had two sons and a daughter.

In the years between 1919 and 1934 he served on military missions in Eastern Europe, in Turkey, and was posted to the Staff College and the Imperial Defence College. In 1934 he was appointed to command the Nowshera Brigade on the North-West Frontier of India. He was a fine linguist and soon added Urdu to his Russian and German. He was ap-

pointed CSI in 1936 and, in the following year, became major-general, the youngest in the British Army.

In 1939 he took the 1st Division to France, where he was faced with supervising the evacuation from Dunkirk in 1940. Two years later, he was confronted with a second desperate situation when, as a lieutenant-general, he was sent to command the army in Burma. Again, his major task was to organize a retreat, and he himself was almost captured by the Japanese during the evacuation from Rangoon. Later in 1942 CHURCHILL appointed him to succeed Auchinleck as Commander-in-Chief, Middle East. He at once made clear to all in his command that there would be no further retreat in North Africa. In this he had the firm support of General MONTGOMERY and together they prepared for and won the Battle of El Alamein.

Early in 1943 he was present at the Casablanca Conference between Churchill and President Roosevelt, and it was decided to appoint him Deputy Commander-in-Chief to General Eisenhower. In this capacity, he conducted the Tunisian campaign to the point at which the Allies became masters of the whole of North Africa. He next organized the invasion of Sicily and the landings in Italy. The Italian campaign showed him at the height of his powers as strategist and administrator, particularly in his ability to maintain the loyalty of his subordinates and win the confidence of his American allies.

In 1944 he was promoted to field-marshal and appointed Commander-in-Chief, Mediterranean. When the war ended it seemed possible that Alexander would become Chief of the Imperial General Staff, but instead he was appointed Governor-General of Canada, a post which he held from 1946 to 1952. He had become CB in 1938, KCB and GCB in 1942, and now he was made a viscount and GCMG and KG (1946). In 1952, when visiting Ottawa, Churchill invited Alexander to become Minister of Defence. He was not happy in this post as he was unsuited to political life and in 1954 he resigned and retired. He had been created an earl on his return from Canada in 1952.

During the last ten years of his life he served as director of a number of companies and pursued his hobby as an artist. He was Constable of the Tower of London from 1960 to 1965 and Grand Master of the Order of Saint Michael and Saint George. He was President of the MCC in 1955, and was admitted to the Order of Merit in 1959. Alexander died at Slough on 16 July 1969.

ALEXANDRA CAROLINE MARY CHARLOTTE LOUISE JULIA (1844–1925) of Denmark, Queen-Consort of King Edward VII, was born at the Gule Palace, Copenhagen, on 1 December 1844, the eldest daughter of Prince Christian of Schleswig-Holstein-Sonderburg-Glücksburg and his wife, Louise, daughter of the Landgrave William of Hesse-Cassel. The Princess was brought up very simply; she was taught foreign languages, including English, and showed a marked aptitude for music. While Alexandra was still a child, Queen Victoria and her uncle, Leopold, King of the Belgians, were concerning themselves with the problem of finding a suitable bride for the Prince of Wales; Alexandra was favoured by Leopold. In 1861 a meeting was arranged between the Prince and Princess, and Albert, the Prince Consort, wrote to his daughter Victoria, the Crown Princess of Prussia, 'We hear nothing but good of Princess Alexandra: the young people seem to have taken a warm liking to each other.' In 1862 they were betrothed, and in the following year they were married. Queen Victoria, desolated by the untimely death of Albert, took no part in the ceremony, but witnessed the wedding from a seat out of the public eye.

For years after her husband's death, Queen Victoria lived in seclusion, and Edward and Alexandra soon became leaders of English society. At their homes, Marlborough House in London and Sandringham House in Norfolk, they entertained with generous hospitality, and they were not only popular in 'high society', they were regarded with affection by the British public as a whole. The charm and beauty of the Princess, in particular, and her simple manners and dignified demeanour permanently won all hearts, including that of the Prince of Wales, despite his occasional amorous adventures.

In 1863 Alexandra's father became King of Denmark as Christian IX, and her brother, William, was elected King of the Hellenes. But at the end of the year, the Princess's peace of mind was destroyed by the outbreak of war between Denmark and Prussia over the duchies of Schleswig-Holstein which were claimed, not only by her father, but also by Frederick, Duke of Augustenberg, supported by William I of Prussia, the father-in-law of Edward's sister, the Crown Princess of Prussia. Alexandra found herself in an invidious position, her emotions torn between sympathy for her own Danish people and loyalty to her formidable mother-in-law, whose sentiments, echoing those of her late husband, were favourable to Prussia. The humiliations suffered by her parents and her countrymen were bitterly resented by the Princess, though she could not publicly express her feelings and, as soon as the war ended, in August 1864, she and Prince Edward went off to visit Denmark and Sweden. The visit had to be a private one because Queen Victoria had insisted that her son should do nothing that would openly display his sympathy for the Danes.

Earlier in that year Alexandra had given birth to a son, Albert Victor, later Duke of Clarence (who died in January 1892, a blow from which his mother never fully recovered). In June 1865 her second son was born; forty-five years later he was to succeed his father as King George V. The Princess had four other children: Louise (1867), afterwards Duchess of Fife; Victoria (1868); Maud (1869), afterwards Queen of Norway; and John (1871), who died when one day old.

When Disraeli became Prime Minister in 1868, he succeeded in persuading the Queen to allow the first of four visits to Ireland by the Prince and Princess of Wales: they received an enthusiastic welcome. Later in the winter of 1868-9, they undertook a foreign tour together which included a visit to Egypt and Greece. Alexandra was in Denmark when war broke out between Prussia and France in 1870. Queen Victoria insisted that she return to England at once. Alexandra's antipathy to the pretensions of the Prussian monarchy was ill-concealed, particularly since the Queen and her daughter Victoria, the Princess Royal, were glad to see the growing power of Germany which they considered could never be a threat to England. But Alexandra kept silence except when her relatives in Denmark, Greece, or Russia were involved. In 1881 she could not be dissuaded from travelling to St Petersburg, at no little risk to her own safety, to be with her sister, the Empress Marie, after the assassination of her husband Alexander II.

She was at the bedside of her mother-in-law when the old Queen died on 22 January 1901. Despite the contrast in character between the autocratic obstinate Queen and the gentle but determined Princess, they had, over the years, come to have a deep affection for each other and great mutual trust between them. To honour the new Queen-Consort,

Edward, as one of his first acts as King, bestowed upon his wife the Order of the Garter. Alexandra had always been notable for her generous gifts to charity, and her example was certainly an encouragement to wealthy and influential citizens to help in the relief of hardship and poverty. Among the projects to which she gave her name and interest were the Queen Alexandra Imperial Military Nursing Service, set up in 1902, and 'Alexandra Day' on which each year roses were sold in millions and British hospitals benefited by hundreds of thousands of pounds.

On 6 May 1910, King Edward died and Alexandra withdrew into comparative retirement, but the First World War brought her back to do whatever she could to relieve distress and, in particular, to help the wounded. She was a friend of Lord KITCHENER of long standing and, fearing that disaster would befall him, she tried unavailingly to prevent his visit to Russia in 1916. After the tragedy of the *Hampshire*, she immediately placed herself at the head of the appeal for a memorial fund, which soon produced a larger sum than had ever been raised before for a memorial. She also visited Norwich, with her constant companion in her old age, her daughter the Princess Victoria, to unveil a memorial to Edith CAVELL, for whose courage she had great regard.

The last two years of Alexandra's life were spent at Sandringham and there she died quietly as she had lived on 20 November 1925—remembered for her goodness and her beauty.

ALLENBY, EDMUND HENRY HYNMAN, first VISCOUNT ALLENBY OF MEGIDDO (1861-1936), field-marshal, was born on 23 April 1861 at Brackenhurst, Nottinghamshire, the eldest child of Hynman Allenby, a country gentleman, and his wife, Catherine Anne, daughter of the Revd Thomas Coats Cane. He was educated at Haileybury and Sandhurst and, having failed to pass into the Indian Civil Service, was commissioned in the Inniskillings (6th Dragoons) in 1882. He married in 1896, Adelaide Mabel, daughter of Horace Edward Chapman.

After seeing service in Bechuanaland (Botswana) and Zululand, he was promoted in due course to adjutant of the 3rd Cavalry Brigade in 1898, and made a reputation as a capable cavalry commander in the last stages of the Boer War. He became CB in 1902. From that time until the outbreak of war in 1914, he served in England, being promoted to major-general in 1909, and appointed Inspector-General of Cavalry in 1910.

In 1914 he was in command of the Cavalry Division in the retreat from Mons, and commanded the Cavalry Corps in the first Battle of Ypres. He was appointed KCB in 1915. His command of the Third Army during the Battle of Arras in 1917 marked the high point in his military career in Europe. (In the same year, his son, an only child, was killed in action in France.) However, he never felt at ease in his relations with Field-Marshal HAIG, and it was with some relief that he was transferred in the summer of 1917 to command the Egyptian Expeditionary Force in Palestine. His campaign against the Turks, under their German commanders, was highly successful and, having captured Jerusalem, he drove the enemy northwards; then, with the aid of Col. T. E. LAWRENCE and the Arabs, he entered Damascus and Aleppo. The Turks were forced to seek an armistice on 30 October 1918. This was the last campaign in which cavalry were used *en masse*.

During the war, Allenby had been appointed KCB (1915), GCMG (1917), and GCB (1918): in 1919 he was promoted

Allenby received by the Jewish community in Jerusalem, 24 May 1918

to field-marshal and created a viscount. In March 1919, he was appointed Special High Commissioner for Egypt. While holding that office, he persuaded the British Government in 1922 to abolish the protectorate and recognize the independence of Egypt. However, his relations with Austen CHAMBERLAIN, the Foreign Secretary, were never harmonious and in 1925 he resigned, retired to England, and spent his declining years bird-watching and fishing. Allenby died in London on 14 May 1936 and was buried in Westminster Abbey.

AMERY, LEOPOLD CHARLES MAURICE STENNETT (1873–1955), politician and journalist, was born on 22 November 1873 in India. He was the eldest son of Charles Frederick Amery, of the Indian Forest Department, and his wife, Elizabeth Leitner, who was Hungarian. His father left his mother when Amery was three years old, but she contrived to send him to Harrow. He then went on to Balliol College, Oxford, as an exhibitioner and obtained firsts in both Classical Mods. (1894) and Greats (1896). He was also a half-blue for cross-country running. In 1897 he was elected a History Fellow of All Souls.

He had a wide knowledge of languages and, after visiting the Near East for the *Manchester Guardian*, became assistant to the Foreign Editor of *The Times* in 1899. He added to his professional reputation by his organization of the war correspondents of *The Times* during the Boer War; and afterwards spent several years helping to write and edit *The Times History of the War* (7 vols., 1900–9). He had been

called to the Bar (Inner Temple) in 1902, but by 1908 was becoming active in extreme right-wing politics. He refused an offer of the Editor's post of the *Observer*, and four years later in 1912 refused a similar offer from *The Times*.

In 1910 Amery married Adeliza Florence (Bryddie), daughter of John Hamar Greenwood, a Canadian, and sister of Hamar (later Viscount) Greenwood. They had two sons.

Amery was returned unopposed as Conservative MP for South Birmingham (Sparkbrook) in 1911, a seat which he held until 1945. He was always ultra-conservative; he opposed Home Rule for Ireland and the Liberals' free trade policy. During the First World War, he saw service as an intelligence officer in Flanders, the Balkans, and Gallipoli, and in 1916 became joint Political Secretary to Lord MILNER. When Milner became Colonial Secretary in 1919, Amery went with him as Parliamentary Under-Secretary. In 1921 he was transferred to the Admiralty, and when the Conservatives returned to office in 1922 he became First Lord of the Admiralty. In the same year he was sworn of the Privy Council. He was always a zealous advocate of tariff-reform, and when BALDWIN became Prime Minister in 1924 he appointed Amery as Colonial Secretary. Later, in 1925, when a new post of Dominions Secretary was created, Amery held that post too until 1929. Although the Conservatives had failed to introduce imperial preference, he was able, in spite of much opposition, to set up the Empire Marketing Board; and the imperial conference of 1926 produced the definition of dominion status that led to the Statute of Westminster. He was regarded as too extreme to hold office in the National Government, and throughout the thirties he continued to advocate extreme right-wing doctrines. He published *Empire and Prosperity* (1930) and *The Forward View* (1935), and opposed disarmament and appeasement.

In 1940 he ended his anti-CHAMBERLAIN speech in the Commons by quoting Cromwell, when he turned out the Long Parliament, saying 'You have sat too long here . . . In the name of God, go.' Under CHURCHILL he became Secretary of State for India and Burma. He was appointed CH in 1945 but lost his seat in the election and did not stand again. In 1945 his elder son John was executed for treason: an anti-Communist, he had tried to enlist British prisoners of war to fight against Russia. Amery returned to writing, and published *Days of Fresh Air* (1939), *In the Rain and the Sun* (1946), and *My Political Life* (3 vols., 1953–5). He became an honorary Fellow of Balliol in 1946, and was a founder of the Empire (later Commonwealth) Parliamentary Association. His younger son (Harold) Julian entered politics and married the daughter of Harold Macmillan. Leo Amery died in London on 16 September 1955.

ANDERSON, ELIZABETH GARRETT (1836–1917). See GARRETT ANDERSON.

ANDERSON, JOHN, first VISCOUNT WAVERLEY (1882–1958), administrator and politician, was born on 8 July 1882 in Edinburgh, the only surviving son of David Alexander Pearson Anderson, a stationer, and his wife Janet Kilgour, daughter of Charles Briglemen. He was educated at George Watson's College, and Edinburgh University where he graduated B.Sc. and MA in mathematics and natural philosophy (1903). He married, in 1907, Christina, daughter of Andrew Mackenzie, a commercial traveller, and they had one son, who became a doctor, and one daughter, who became Director of the WRAC in 1967.

In 1905 Anderson had passed top into the home Civil

Service and been posted to the Colonial Office. After service in various other departments, he became Chairman of the Board of Inland Revenue from 1919 to 1922, and Permanent Under-Secretary, Home Office, from 1922 to 1932. In that post he chaired the committee controlling emergency preparations for the general strike of 1926, proving himself to be a civil servant of great ability.

From 1932 to 1937 he was Governor of Bengal in a period of particular danger and difficulty. Twice he narrowly escaped assassination, but he was successful in carrying out the transition from diarchy to full provincial authority.

On his return to England, he became Independent Nationalist MP for the Scottish Universities in 1938, a seat which he held until 1950. Neville CHAMBERLAIN appointed him Lord Privy Seal with responsibility for manpower and civil defence, and he was sworn of the Privy Council. In 1940, he entered the War Cabinet as Lord President of the Council with overall responsibility for the organization of civilian and economic resources for total war, including atomic energy. He was also involved in secret work including the development of the atomic bomb. His administrative capacity was of considerable help to CHURCHILL who had great regard for his unselfish loyalty, and in 1943 appointed him Chancellor of the Exchequer.

His first wife had died in 1920, and in 1941 Anderson married Ava, daughter of John Edward Courtenay Bodley, a historian, and widow of Ralph Follett Wigram of the Foreign Office.

Anderson was never a party man, but when a Labour Government came to power in 1945 he was regarded as being aligned with the Conservatives. Nevertheless, from 1945 to 1948, he was Chairman of the committee which led to the establishment of the Atomic Energy Authority in 1954. He never again held ministerial office, but he was Chairman of the Port of London Authority (1946–58) and of the Covent Garden Opera Trust. He became FRS in 1945, and was Romanes lecturer at Oxford in 1946, his subject being 'The Machinery of Government'.

He was appointed CB in 1918, KCB (1919), GCB (1923), GCIE (1932), and GCSI (1937). He became a viscount in 1952, and OM in 1957. Lord Waverley died in London on 4 January 1958, the first civil servant ever to have held high office as a minister. The only other civil servant appointed to such an office was Sir James Grigg who became Secretary of State for War in Churchill's wartime Government.

ANGELL, SIR (RALPH) NORMAN (1872–1967), publicist, was born at Holbeach on 26 December 1872, the youngest child of Thomas Angell Lane, a draper and grocer, and his wife, Mary Ann Brittain. He was educated at the *lycée* in St Omer and Geneva University. After working in a variety of jobs in the USA for seven years, he returned to Europe in 1898, settling in Paris and working as a journalist. In 1904, he was appointed by Lord NORTHCLIFFE as Editor of the *Continental Daily Mail*. He published in 1903 under his real name, Lane, *Patriotism under Three Flags*; subsequently he changed his name to Angell.

In 1909, after it had been turned down by a number of publishers, he himself published *Europe's Optical Illusion*, which in the following year was enlarged and republished as *The Great Illusion*. His determination was vindicated: the book eventually became a best seller and was translated into many languages. It was one of the most influential books of its time; proclaiming that armed aggression would not pay, it was the first practical discussion of the possibility of preventing war. Nevertheless, it created much controversy, and Angell resigned from his post as Editor in 1912 to propagate his ideas through his prolific lectures and writings.

Angell was one of the pioneers of the idea of a League of Nations. He became Labour MP for North Bradford from 1929 to 1931 but was unhappy in his parliamentary activities and particularly in party politics. He was knighted in 1931, and two years later in 1933 was awarded the Nobel peace prize. He died at Croydon on 7 October 1967.

APPLETON, SIR EDWARD VICTOR (1892–1965), physicist, was born in Bradford on 6 September 1892, the eldest child of Peter Appleton, a warehouseman, and his wife, Mary Wilcock. In 1903 he went to Hanson School, Bradford, as a scholar, and in 1910 won the Isaac Holton Scholarship

Sir John Anderson (left) inspects Air Raid Precautions recruiting vans, April 1939

and was awarded an exhibition at St John's College, Cambridge. He obtained a first in both parts of the natural sciences tripos (1913-14) and began to work on the structure of metallic crystals with W. Lawrence BRAGG. On the outbreak of the First World War, Appleton joined the army and worked with the Royal Engineers on the thermionic valve and the problems of radio-wave propagation. During the war, in 1915 he married Jessie, daughter of the Revd John Longson; they had two daughters.

In 1919 he returned to Cambridge as a Fellow of St John's College and in 1920 became an assistant demonstrator in physics at the Cavendish Laboratory, investigating the behaviour of thermionic valves. From 1924 onwards, with the help of Miles Barnett, a New Zealander, he studied the fading of radio waves received from the London broadcasting station and discovered that radio waves are reflected when they hit the ionized part of the upper atmosphere (the ionosphere). In 1924 Appleton was appointed to the Wheatstone chair of physics at King's College, London, where he continued his research on the ionosphere.

He returned to Cambridge in 1936 as Jacksonian Professor of Natural Philosophy, and for a brief period found himself head of the Cavendish Laboratory when Lord RUTHERFORD died suddenly in 1937. Two years later, however, when Lawrence Bragg was appointed Director, Appleton accepted the post of Secretary to the Department of Scientific and Industrial Research. He served in the DSIR for the next ten years, and was closely concerned during the Second World War with the development of radar and work on the atomic bomb.

In 1950 he founded the *Journal of Atmospheric and Terrestrial Physics* of which he remained Editor-in-Chief until he died. He had already, in 1932, published *Thermionic Vacuum Tubes and their Applications* and, up to 1939, was the leading figure in ionospheric research. In 1947 he was awarded the Nobel prize for physics. He was also President of the International Union of Scientific Radio from 1934 to 1952. He became an FRS in 1927 and a KCB in 1941 and GBE in 1946: he received honours and awards from many universities and scientific institutions. In 1949, he was appointed Principal and Vice-Chancellor of Edinburgh University.

His first wife died in 1964, and he married in 1965 Helen Allison, daughter of John Gordon Lennie, who had been his secretary for many years. A month later, on 21 April 1965, he died in Edinburgh.

ASQUITH, EMMA ALICE MARGARET (MARGOT), COUNTESS OF OXFORD AND ASQUITH (1864-1945), was born at The Glen, Peeblesshire on 2 February 1864, the youngest of six daughters of Charles Tennant, later first baronet, and his first wife, Emma, daughter of Richard Winsloe of Taunton. She was educated by governesses and tutors until she was fifteen, when for a short time she went to a finishing school in London, and then went to study in Dresden. She was described by Benjamin Jowett, Master of Balliol, as 'the best-educated ill-educated woman that I have ever met'.

For some time she ran a crèche in Wapping with her sister Laura, the first wife of Alfred Lyttelton, and from 1886, when Laura died, to 1894 she visited women factory-workers whenever she was in London. She was a fearless rider and a provocative conversationalist, and was a member of the group known as the 'Souls', a coterie of intellectuals and aesthetes as well as political celebrities. She was a close friend of Jowett and among her other friends were Gladstone, BALFOUR, ROSEBERY, John MORLEY, and Virginia WOOLF.

In 1894 she married Herbert Henry ASQUITH; she was a shrewd student of politics, but as her stepdaughter, Lady Violet BONHAM CARTER said, 'To her politics meant men not measures.' She could be a most loyal friend or a bitter foe, and became notorious for her caustic criticism of those, such as LLOYD GEORGE, whom she regarded as enemies. Her outspoken attacks were not always of help to her hard-pressed husband during times of crisis.

Her published works include *Autobiography* (2 vols., 1920-2), *More Memories* (1933), and *Off the Record* (1943). She and Asquith had five children only two of whom survived infancy: their daughter, Elizabeth, became Princess Antoine Bibesco, and their son, Anthony, a film director.

Margot Asquith died in London on 28 July 1945, having refused to leave London during the war. It is difficult in a more permissive era to understand the influence which her provocative eccentricity exerted on the social and fashionable life of her time. Perhaps the secret lay in her exciting vitality.

ASQUITH, HERBERT HENRY, first EARL OF OXFORD AND ASQUITH (1852-1928), politician and Prime Minister, was born at Morley in Yorkshire, on 12 September 1852. He was the second son of Joseph Dixon Asquith, a Nonconformist wool-spinner, and his wife, Emily, daughter of William Willans, a wool-stapler of Huddersfield. His father died when he was eight years old, and he was sent to live with relatives in London. He was educated at the City of London School and in 1870 entered Balliol College, Oxford, as a classical scholar. He obtained firsts in Classical Mods. (1872), and Greats (1874), and was awarded the Craven scholarship. He was also President of the Union, and Benjamin Jowett predicted a great career for him. In 1874 he was elected a Fellow of Balliol, and in 1876 was called to the Bar (Lincoln's Inn). He married in the following year Helen, daughter of Frederick Melland, a Manchester physician; and they had four sons and a daughter, Violet (BONHAM CARTER).

Asquith steadily made his name at the Bar, though his main interest was in politics. He was elected Liberal MP for East Fife in 1886, a seat which he held until 1918. His reputation both at the Bar and in the Commons was enhanced when he appeared as junior counsel before the Parnell Commission in 1888. He became a QC in 1890. By this time he was regarded as a formidable debater in Parliament, and Gladstone appointed him Home Secretary and a member of the Cabinet from 1892 to 1895. For the next ten years he was out of office and returned to his law practice, making a considerable income.

His first wife had died in 1891 and in 1894 Asquith married Emma Alice Margaret (Margot ASQUITH), daughter of Sir Charles Tennant, a young woman well-known in London society for her brilliance, mordant wit, and originality of character; they had five children only two of whom survived infancy, a daughter who became Princess Antoine Bibesco and a son, Anthony, who became a film director.

When the Liberals returned to office in 1905, Asquith became Chancellor of the Exchequer, with Campbell-Bannerman as Prime Minister. The 1906 election confirmed the Government in power, with its free-trade policy. Asquith introduced three budgets (1906-8), making, notably, the first provision for old-age pensions. However, in 1908, Campbell-Bannerman became dangerously ill and had to resign, whereupon Asquith became Prime Minister. He appointed LLOYD GEORGE Chancellor of the Exchequer and Winston CHURCHILL President of the Board of Trade. There followed three years of stormy politics. The Government was

Asquith speaking in the Albert Hall, 1911; Margot Asquith is on the extreme right

determined to introduce important social reforms but at the same time the Royal Navy had to be strengthened to meet the threat from the Kaiser's Germany. The budget which Lloyd George introduced in 1909 to raise money for these purposes aroused a serious outcry from the Conservative opposition and led to a constitutional crisis between the Commons and the Lords. Two elections in 1910 confirmed the Government in office; the Lords had to give way and pass the budget. Asquith, however, was determined to bring to an end the power of the House of Lords to reject money bills approved by the Commons, and in 1911 the Parliament Bill was passed for that purpose.

In 1912, the Liberal Government introduced a bill which was intended to give Home Rule to Ireland. This aroused a still more furious controversy. The Ulster unionists, under the leadership of Sir Edward CARSON, organized themselves to resist by force of arms, if necessary, and a group of officers at the Curragh in Dublin made clear that they would resign rather than take part in the coercion of Ulster. The Home Rule Bill was passed in 1914 but, by then, the First World War had broken out and the operation of the Act was suspended for the duration of hostilities.

Meanwhile, Asquith had other problems. The Welsh disestablishment project provoked controversy, and throughout the years from 1906 to 1914 Asquith and other Liberal politicians were the constant target of the suffragettes, who pursued the cause of votes for women with relentless violence, but without success. Overshadowing all these domestic problems was the gathering storm in Europe. Asquith was anxious by all possible means to avoid war with Germany, but he was determined to maintain the strength of the British navy and to maintain an understanding with France. He supported his Foreign Secretary, Sir Edward GREY, in making clear to Germany that Britain would not be a party to any violation of the neutrality of Belgium.

When the German armies invaded Belgium the Cabinet and the country were almost unanimous in their support for the decision to enter the war. The Asquith Government handled the early stages of the war with some skill but, although the appointment of KITCHENER as Secretary of State for War ensured that great strides would be made in strengthening the armed forces, the failure to produce the supply of munitions urgently required for the fighting in France, the disastrous delays in carrying out the Dardanelles campaign, and the ambitious schemes of Lloyd George, combined to concentrate criticism upon Asquith for events over which he had little control. In consequence, he felt obliged, in 1915, to form a Coalition Government with his Conservative opponents. This, however, did not resolve his difficulties: there was bitter dissension in the new Cabinet, with Lloyd George maintaining a running battle with Kitchener for the purpose of changing the whole strategy of the military leaders.

The Dardanelles campaign had to be abandoned; British and French armies became bogged down in the mud of Flanders, and the loss of life in the carnage of trench warfare reached immense proportions. Ireland was still a problem, and in 1916 rebellion in Dublin had to be suppressed with ruthless force. (In the same year, Asquith's eldest son, Raymond, was killed in action.) The brunt of the criticism for these calamities fell upon Asquith. The newspapers, led by

Lord BEAVERBROOK, carried on an unscrupulous campaign to oust the Prime Minister and replace him with Lloyd George. Lloyd George himself brought matters to a head by resigning from the Government and, when Asquith, deserted by the Conservative members of his administration, found himself isolated, he felt bound to resign. Lloyd George became Prime Minister at the end of 1916.

Asquith continued to support the Government for the remaining period of the war, but, when in 1918 Lloyd George called his 'coupon election', Asquith was defeated in East Fife. He returned to Parliament in 1920 as MP for Paisley, and continued to devote much of his activity to the cause of Home Rule for Ireland, until in the following year the policy which he had advocated for so many years was put into effect.

In 1924, he was defeated in the general election and his long period of service in the Commons came to an end. The following year he entered the House of Lords as Earl of Oxford and Asquith and was created KG. For a time he remained leader of the Liberal party but he and Lloyd George were now irreconcilably opposed and in 1926 Asquith resigned. He published accounts of the events in which he had played a part, *The Genesis of the War* (1923), *Fifty Years of Parliament* (2 vols., 1926), and *Memories and Reflections 1852-1927* (2 vols., 1928). He died at The Wharf, Sutton Courtney, Berkshire, on 15 February 1928. He was succeeded in the earldom by his grandson, Julian.

Asquith was a great statesman, more suited to the problems of peace-time politics than to those of war. He had his share of human weaknesses; he drank too much and was fortunate on one occasion to escape the ignominy occasioned by his appearance on the Front Bench intoxicated. His letters to the young Venetia Stanley reveal his dire need at times of crisis in his career for the sympathy which he did not get from the astringent Margot, though she was always loyal and understanding.

ASQUITH OF YARNBURY, BARONESS (1887-1969). See BONHAM CARTER.

ASTOR, JOHN JACOB, first BARON ASTOR OF HEVER (1886-1971), predominant owner of *The Times*, was born in New York on 20 May 1886, the younger son of William Waldorf (later Viscount) Astor, and his wife, Mary Dahlgren Paul, of Philadelphia. His mother died when he was eight; his father became a naturalized Briton five years later. Nancy ASTOR was his sister-in-law. John was educated at Eton and New College, Oxford, joined the 1st Life Guards in 1906, and became ADC to Lord Hardinge of Penshurst, Viceroy of India.

During the First World War he fought in France, was severely wounded, lost his right leg, and was made a Chevalier of the Legion of Honour. In 1927 he was appointed honorary Colonel of the Kent Heavy Brigade, RA, and in 1928 honorary Colonel of the 23rd London Regiment.

His father, on settling in England, had bought Cliveden and given it to Waldorf in 1906, while he himself lived at Hever Castle in Kent. In 1919 he died leaving a large fortune to John who, though he was of a retiring disposition, hoped to play some part in British public life. A year earlier he had also given Hever Castle to John.

In 1922 John Astor was elected Unionist MP for Dover, a seat which he held until 1945. When Lord NORTHCLIFFE died in 1922 it was necessary to find a proprietor for *The Times*, wealthy enough to keep up the circulation of the paper, but self-effacing enough to leave policy to the editorial staff. Almost by chance, it was decided that Astor was such a man, and he agreed to join John Walter, the fifth, in ownership of *The Times*, in the proportion of nine shares to one. Walter had become Chairman of *The Times* in 1910 when his father died, but had soon realized that there was no hope of editorial independence while Northcliffe was associated with the paper.

Walter and Astor now agreed to re-engage Geoffrey DAWSON as Editor in place of Wickham STEED, and from then on the policy of the paper was left entirely in the hands of the Editor without any interference with his judgement. This situation was maintained until *The Times* was eventually transferred to the ownership of Lord Thomson of Fleet in 1966, although in the interim there had been four editors in charge of the paper.

John Astor had many interests besides *The Times*. He and his wife, Lady Violet Mary, daughter of the fourth Earl of Minto, entertained a wide selection of eminent guests at Hever. He was a member of the BBC's General Advisory Council in 1937-9, and was the first Chairman of the Press Council from 1953 to 1955. He was active in local politics, was a JP, and director of a number of City companies. He was also a generous benefactor to the Middlesex Hospital. He was always a keen games player even when handicapped by an artificial leg, and in 1937 he was President of the MCC.

The 1962 Finance Act came as a great blow, because it made liable to estate duty assets held abroad, and therefore applied to the Astor Trust in New York. Astor tried to resign from the Trust but this was legally impossible. To safeguard the inheritance of his children, he decided reluctantly to live abroad, and settled in France until his death at Cannes on 19 July 1971. He was succeeded by Gavin, the eldest of his three sons.

ASTOR, NANCY WITCHER, VISCOUNTESS ASTOR (1879-1964), politician, was born on 19 May 1879 at Danville, Virginia, the younger daughter of Chiswell Dabney Langhorne and his wife, Nancy Witcher Keene. Her father, a Southern gentleman and civil war veteran, had made a fortune in railway development; her mother was of Irish extraction. Her elder sister, Irene, became the wife of Charles Dana Gibson, the artist, who made Irene famous as the original 'Gibson girl'. Nancy herself was attractive, intelligent, and witty. When she was eighteen, she married Robert Gold Shaw by whom she had one son before they were divorced in 1903. He was a heavy drinker.

In 1904 she visited England for the social and hunting seasons and, after rejecting a number of proposals, she married in 1906 Waldorf (later second Viscount) Astor who was also born an American; they had four sons and one daughter. Nancy was by nature religious, and in 1914 she became an ardent Christian Scientist. Her husband had been elected Unionist MP for a Plymouth constituency in 1910, and a year later his father purchased the *Observer* from Lord NORTHCLIFFE. As Lord Astor lived in Italy, Waldorf took over responsibility for the paper. In 1919, when his father died, he inherited the title and in consequence had to resign his seat in the Commons. Nancy contested and won the seat and sat as Conservative MP for the Sutton division of Plymouth from 1919 until 1945. She was the first woman to sit in the House of Commons.

She quickly made her presence felt there and was not in the least over-awed by either her male colleagues or opponents. She became a staunch champion of women's rights and of the temperance cause; she was especially active

Nancy Astor (right) with Lady Cynthia Curzon, Plymouth election campaign, November 1919

on behalf of children, and attempted unsuccessfully, but vigorously, to obtain more generous treatment for the unemployed in the twenties and thirties.

At Cliveden, their magnificent home overlooking the Thames near Taplow, the Astors lavishly entertained influential guests from all walks of life, including the Prime Minister, Neville CHAMBERLAIN, Geoffrey DAWSON, the Editor of *The Times*, and Philip KERR, one of Nancy's life-long friends, who became Lord Lothian, British Ambassador to Washington. The Astors were anti-Nazi but, because they were firm supporters of those, like Chamberlain, who strove to avoid war with Germany, they gained undeserved notoriety as the leaders of the 'Cliveden set', determined upon appeasement at any cost. In 1937 Nancy was appointed CH.

When the war came Nancy and her husband devoted themselves to work in Plymouth, she as one of the city's MPs, and he as Lord Mayor for five successive years. Later, in 1957, she was made an honorary freeman of Plymouth. As it seemed certain that she would lose her seat in the 1945 election, Waldorf persuaded her not to stand again. She missed her active life in Parliament and resented having taken his advice. This clouded, to some extent, the happiness of their relationship in the years up to his death in 1952. She survived him by more than a decade; she died at her daughter's home, Grimsthorpe, in Lincolnshire, on 2 May 1964.

A woman of great courage, generosity, and enthusiasm, she pursued her aims with impetuosity, but was sometimes thwarted by her very inability to act with moderation.

ATTLEE, CLEMENT RICHARD, first EARL ATTLEE (1883–1967), politician and Prime Minister, was born in London on 3 January 1883, the seventh child of Henry Attlee, solicitor, and his wife, Ellen, daughter of T. S. Watson, Secretary of the Art Union of London. He was educated at Haileybury and University College, Oxford, and was called to the Bar (Inner Temple) in 1905. A visit to Haileybury House, a boys' club in Stepney, persuaded him to devote some years of his life to social work in the East End. When his father died in 1908 he inherited a small income, sufficient to enable him to forsake the law and take a number of jobs connected with social work or politics. He

had already become a socialist. He lectured at the London School of Economics, and by 1914 was deeply involved in the Labour movement.

During the First World War he served in Gallipoli, Mesopotamia, and France. In Mesopotamia he was badly wounded. As soon as the war ended, he returned to work in the East End and at the LSE. In 1919 he became Mayor of Stepney, but in 1922, when he was elected Labour MP for Limehouse, he gave up his post at the LSE and became a full-time politician. In the same year he married Violet Helen, daughter of H. E. Millar of Hampstead. They had three daughters and a son.

He became Parliamentary Private Secretary to Ramsay MACDONALD in 1922, and served as Under-Secretary of State for War in the short-lived Labour Government of 1923. From 1927 to 1929, he served on the SIMON Commission devoting his time to the political problems of India. In 1930 he was appointed Chancellor of the Duchy of Lancaster and, in the following year, Postmaster-General. However, when Ramsay MacDonald decided to form a National Government in 1931, Attlee refused to support him, and for the rest of his career considered that MacDonald had perpetrated 'the greatest betrayal in the political history of the country'.

He continued as MP for Limehouse after the 1931 election and was appointed deputy leader of the Parliamentary Labour Party. During the next four years he was constantly involved in debates in the House, and in 1935 succeeded George Lansbury as leader of the party. During the years leading to the Second World War, he concentrated quietly and unobtrusively, but firmly, on trying to hold the party together in the face of fierce dissensions among its members. He published his own views in *The Will and the Way to Socialism* in 1935 and in *The Labour Party in Perspective* in 1937. In 1935 he had asserted the view of most of his socialist colleagues in favour of disarmament and collective security, but gradually his opinions changed as Hitler and Mussolini became increasingly aggressive. He denounced Neville CHAMBERLAIN's Munich agreement as 'a tremendous victory for Herr Hitler', but the party of which he was leader continued to be divided on the whole question of rearmament.

Attlee was ill when the war started but, after the fiasco of the campaign in Norway, it became clear that the Conservative Government would have to form a coalition with Labour. Attlee refused to support Chamberlain, and when CHURCHILL became Prime Minister in 1940 he appointed Attlee as Lord Privy Seal. Attlee served in the War Cabinet in that post until 1942, when he became First Secretary for the Dominions and then, in the following year, Lord President of the Council. He was also, from 1942, Deputy Prime Minister. The day-to-day business of the Government was largely his responsibility and, when Churchill was abroad, Attlee deputized for him at home.

Throughout the war years Attlee supported Churchill with unwavering loyalty and, when Germany was defeated in 1945, he would personally have been prepared to continue the coalition until the Japanese war ended. But party political opinion was opposed to this idea: when the results of the 1945 election were announced, Attlee was surprised by the landslide in favour of Labour which brought him to power as Prime Minister. He appointed his formidable supporter Ernest BEVIN as Foreign Secretary. The other leading figures in the Government, Herbert MORRISON, Stafford CRIPPS, Hugh DALTON, and Aneurin BEVAN were an extremely able, but extremely difficult, team and Attlee needed all his patience and moderation to manage them. Nevertheless, the 1945–51 Labour Government brought about a bloodless revolution in British politics. Key industries were nationalized, the health service was created and the Welfare State es-

tablished; India, Pakistan, and Burma were granted independence, and a beginning was made in preparing the African colonies for self-government. Attlee fully supported Ernest Bevin in his efforts to secure reconstruction and stability in Europe, to take advantage of any assistance that America was prepared to afford, and to hold the line as long as possible against Communist expansion. He was also mainly responsible for the decision that Britain should manufacture her own atomic bomb. The challenge from Russia was met by the Anglo-American Berlin airlift, and NATO was established in 1949.

There continued, however, to be dissensions within the Labour party and, although Attlee and his leading colleagues hoped to win the 1950 election, the result was a disappointment, a majority of ten for Labour. Attlee, who had represented Limehouse since 1922, was now elected for West Walthamstow. The Government remained in office, but was beset with new difficulties, including the Korean war, and a massive rearmament programme which brought inflation and disruption of the balance of payments. In October 1951, Attlee's Government was defeated at the polls, and Churchill returned as Prime Minister. By that time, the Labour party leaders were in sad disarray. Cripps and Bevin had been forced to resign through ill health, and the younger men, GAITSKELL, Bevan, and Wilson, were quarrelling among themselves. When, in another election in 1955, the Conservatives won again, it was clear that Attlee would shortly

Attlee addressing a peace demonstration, Cardiff, August 1936

cease to lead the Labour party. He had already been admitted to the Order of Merit in 1951, and on his resignation at the end of 1955 the Queen conferred an earldom on him. He had been sworn of the Privy Council in 1935, made CH in 1945 and KG in 1956. He was elected FRS in 1947, and had many academic honours. In 1954 he published *As it Happened.* Bevin's tribute to him in 1950 indicated the debt which the Labour party owed to this apparently uninspiring but severely practical politician: 'By God, he's the only man who could have kept us together.' Clement Attlee died in London on 8 October 1967 and was succeeded in the earldom by his son, Martin.

AUDEN, WYSTAN HUGH (1907-1973), poet, essayist, and librettist, was born in York on 21 February 1907. He was the youngest son of Dr George Augustus Auden, a general practitioner, and his wife, Constance Rosalie Bucknell. During the First World War Dr Auden served with the RAMC in Egypt, Gallipoli, and France, and his young son, left fatherless in his formative years, was deeply influenced by his love for his mother, a woman of strong personality. He was educated at St Edmunds, Hindhead (where he met Christopher Isherwood), Gresham's, Holt, and Christ Church, Oxford (1928). While he was at Oxford, he wrote poetry in the style of T. S. ELIOT, whose poem, *The Waste Land,* had been published in 1922; he was also influenced by the work of Gerard Manley Hopkins. He had by this time become a confirmed homosexual.

In 1928 Auden went to Berlin, where, through another Englishman, John Layard, he became interested in the teaching of Homer Lane, an American who believed that all illness was spiritual in origin and that uninhibited love could be a liberating force—a theory which his friend, Christopher Isherwood, told him was nonsense. During 1929 Auden earned his living by giving private tuition in London. For a time, he stayed with Stephen Spender, and in 1930 his play *Paid on Both Sides* was published by T. S. Eliot in the *Criterion.*

From 1930 to 1932 he was a schoolmaster at Larchfield Academy, Helensburgh, and from 1932 to 1935 taught at the Downs School, Colwall, near Malvern. Meanwhile, his work was beginning to influence a new school of poets. His *Poems* (1928) were published privately by Stephen Spender. Then, Faber & Faber published *The Orators* (1932) which one critic described as the most valuable contribution to English poetry since *The Waste Land.* Numerous articles and reviews now appeared, including *New Verse,* and the anthologies, *New Signatures* and *New Country.* In 1935 Auden joined the GPO Film Unit in London and worked with (Sir) William Coldstream, the artist, and John Grierson, the producer. Since 1932 he had been associated with the Group Theatre, and he and Christopher Isherwood wrote *The Dog Beneath the Skin* (1935) and *The Ascent of F6* (1936) for the Group. Isherwood, while living in Amsterdam, had met Erika, daughter of Thomas Mann; she had been marked down as an enemy of the Nazis, and wanted to marry an Englishman to become a British subject. Isherwood, unwilling to marry her himself, put her in touch with Auden, who, without having met her, agreed to marry her: the ceremony took place at Ledbury in June 1935. He was still married to her when she died in 1970.

In 1936, Auden visited Iceland with Louis MacNeice, and in 1937 they published *Letters from Iceland.* In 1937 he went to Spain and drove an ambulance for the republicans. Then, in 1938, he and Isherwood visited China together looking for 'a war of their own' to write about. They saw little of the war in China, but their book *Journey to a War* (1939) contains some of Auden's greatest poetry.

They returned from China via the USA where Erika and the Mann family were now living. The two friends decided to settle in America and become American citizens. In January 1939 they left England together for New York; their decision to remain abroad after the outbreak of war attracted much criticism. During the war Auden made his home in New York with a young poet, Chester Kallman; they were lovers for some years, and remained friends to the end of Auden's life. Auden took up teaching again and taught at a number of American schools and colleges.

In 1940 Auden, who had been a Marxist, became an Anglo-Catholic. In 1941 his new book of verse, *The Double Man,* was published in New York. Later this was published in England by Faber & Faber as *New Year Letter.* Edwin Muir thought it contained some of the author's best work, but other critics were not so complimentary.

After the war, Auden bought a house in the village of Kirchstetten, near Vienna. In 1951 he collaborated with Kallman on the libretto of *The Rake's Progress,* with music by Igor Stravinsky, and a new volume of his poems *Nones* was published in New York. This was followed by *The Shield of Achilles* (1955). In 1956 he was elected Professor of Poetry at Oxford, and until 1961 gave lectures there on a wide range of subjects from Shakespeare to D. H. LAWRENCE, some of which were published in *The Dyer's Hand* (1962).

In 1960 *Homage to Clio* was published in New York, but the reviews of this new volume of verse, both in England and America, were critical of its worth. Auden was now in decline. In 1972, when his old friend Cecil DAY-LEWIS died, Auden's name was mentioned as a possible successor as Poet Laureate, but this was not to be. That year he was granted a 'grace and favour' cottage in the grounds of Christ Church, and he returned to Oxford. His return there was not a success. Oxford had changed since his days as an undergraduate; Auden did not like the changes and his habits did not endear him to the young dons of his college who were not prepared to tolerate his behaviour. Furthermore, he had quarrelled with some of his old friends, including Benjamin BRITTEN.

In 1973 he was in Vienna with Chester Kallman when he died suddenly on 29 September. He was buried at Kirchstetten, and in 1974 a memorial stone was laid in Westminster Abbey.

AUSTIN, HERBERT, BARON AUSTIN (1866-1941), motor manufacturer, was born on 8 November 1866, at Little Missenden, son of Giles Stephen (or Stevens) Austin, a farmer, and his wife, Clara Jane, daughter of Willoughby Simpson, HM Customs officer. He was educated at Rotherham Grammar School and Brampton College, and then in 1884 went out with an uncle to Australia where he became an engineering apprentice at Langlands Foundry, Melbourne. Later he moved to the Wolseley Sheep Shearing Machine Company where he became Manager. In 1887 he married Helen, daughter of James Dron of Melbourne. They had two daughters and a son.

In 1893 he returned to England and continued to work for the Wolseley Company as Production Manager in their Birmingham workshops. The firm made bicycle and machine parts as well as its main product and with growing experience Austin took out a number of patents for his own inventions. In 1911 he became Chairman of the company. He had always been interested in the possibilities of motor vehicles and had produced his first Wolseley car, a three-wheeler, in 1895. In 1901 Vickers Sons and Maxim took over the machine-tool and motor side of the business and Austin became General Manager of the new company.

In 1905, he started his own business at Longbridge as the Austin Motor Company, and speedily increased his work force and output. During the First World War the plant was turned over to the production of munitions, and in 1917, Austin was appointed KBE. His only son was killed in action in 1915. From 1918 to 1924 Austin was Conservative MP for the King's Norton division of Birmingham. After the war he continued his inventive career and became one of the major British car manufacturers.

In 1922 he produced the 'Baby Austin', a 7-horse-power car, which for the first time brought motoring within reach

Herbert Austin in his 1922 'Baby Austin'

of those with modest incomes. This had been preceded by the Austin Twenty (1919), and the Austin Twelve (1921) which was also a popular model: Austin's success continued up to the Second World War when his works were again turned over to meeting military requirements.

As his wealth increased, he paid over large sums of money to philanthropic causes, notably hospitals. He equipped many hospitals with deep-ray therapy, and in 1936 subscribed a quarter of a million pounds to the Cavendish Laboratory at Cambridge. In that year he was created a baron. From 1937 to 1940 he was Chairman of the 'shadow' Aero-Engine Committee.

The foundation of his success was the novelty and efficiency of his designs. Like Lord NUFFIELD, he was a skilled engineer who rose by force of energy, originality, and determination from the workshop floor to management of a large business. The peerage became extinct when Austin died near Bromsgrove on 23 May 1941.

AVON, first EARL OF (1897-1977). See EDEN, (ROBERT) ANTHONY.

AYLWARD, GLADYS MAY (1902-1970), missionary, was born on 24 February 1902 in Edmonton, Middlesex, the eldest of the three children of Thomas John Aylward, a postman, and his wife, Rosina Florence Whiskin, whose father was a bootmaker. She left school at fourteen to become a shop-girl, then a nanny, and finally a parlourmaid. She was brought up as a Nonconformist, and in 1929 was accepted for missionary training by the China Inland Mission. Despite the fact that this organization had as its purpose the training of men and women of poor education, Gladys was soon rejected as a willing but hopeless student. For a time she went to work in the slums of Bristol and Swansea, and seriously damaged her health, but on return to her home at Edmonton she heard that an elderly widow, Jeannie Lawson, member of a small independent mission in North China, needed a helper who would have to pay her own passage to that country.

Once again Gladys Aylward worked as a maidservant to earn sufficient to pay for her fare by the cheapest route—the Trans-Siberian railway. In the autumn of 1932, she eventually joined Mrs Lawson at the mission in Yangsheng, Shansi province. Together they opened an inn for muleteers as a means of evangelism. There she learned Chinese and soon became much loved as a masterly story-teller of simple gospel stories. Known as 'Ai Weh-te', the Chinese version of Aylward, which meant 'the virtuous one', she became a Chinese citizen in 1936.

During the Japanese war with China in 1940 she led a hundred children, through great hardships and perils, to safety beyond the Yellow River. Then she fell ill but, as soon as she recovered, she continued her missionary work among lepers, until in 1949 she returned for a while to England. Her courageous exploits might have remained unknown but for the fact that Alan Burgess, a BBC writer, met her and decided to dramatize her story on radio. Later, in 1957, his fictionalized story *The Small Woman* became a best seller, and two years later it was filmed as *The Inn of the Sixth Happiness* with Ingrid Bergman as Gladys Aylward.

Her last twelve years were spent in Taiwan, where she continued her work, including the running of an orphanage. She died in Taipei on 1 January 1970, and the Chinese buried her in a marble tomb in the hill-top garden of Christ's College, Tamshui.

B

BADEN-POWELL, ROBERT STEPHENSON SMYTH, first BARON BADEN-POWELL (1857-1941), lieutenant-general, and founder of the Boy Scouts and Girl Guides, was born in London on 22 February 1857, the sixth son of the Revd Baden-Powell, Savilian Professor of Geometry at Oxford, and his third wife, Henrietta Grace, eldest daughter of Admiral William Henry Smyth and a great-niece of Nelson. Robert was named after his godfather, Robert Stephenson, the engineer. His father died when he was three; and his mother had to bring up a large family with little means. However, in 1870, he went to Charterhouse, and in 1876 passed second in the cavalry list in the army entrance exam, was excused Sandhurst, and commissioned into the 13th Hussars in India. There he specialized in reconnaissance and scouting, and in 1884 produced a book on the subject, followed by *Cavalry Instruction* in 1885. After fighting in the Zululand campaign in 1888, he was appointed intelligence officer for the Mediterranean in 1891, and years later, in 1915, related his experiences in *My Adventures as a Spy*.

He next served in the Ashanti expedition in 1895-6, and in the Matabele campaign of 1896, and wrote accounts of both. At the age of forty in 1897 he was appointed to command the 5th Dragoon Guards and in 1899 published *Aids to Scouting*. When the Boer War broke out he was in Mafeking, and throughout the siege his ingenuity and confidence sustained the morale of the garrison until the town was relieved on 17 May 1900. Then Sir Alfred MILNER selected him to raise and train the South African Constabulary. He returned to England in 1901 to a hero's welcome and received the CB. In 1903 he was appointed Inspector-General of Cavalry. He held that post until 1907 and, in the following year, commanded the Northumbrian Division of the newly formed Territorials. He had been promoted lieutenant-general in 1907, but in 1910 he retired from the army to devote himself to furthering his greatest interest, the Boy Scouts.

On his return from South Africa in 1903 he had discovered that his book *Aids to Scouting* was being used by teachers; he now decided to re-write the book for boys. *Scouting for Boys* was published in 1908, and became a best seller in Britain and overseas. The Boy Scout movement had got under way in 1907 and, two years later, the Girl Guides were founded. Later, the Wolf Cubs, Sea Scouts, and Rover Scouts were organized. In 1920 Baden-Powell was acclaimed as Chief Scout of the World, and during the next seventeen years 'jamborees', a word which Baden-Powell invented, were held in Denmark, Hungary, and Holland, as well as in England.

He married, in 1912, Olave St Clair, younger daughter of Harold Soames, a retired businessman; they had one son and two daughters. Lady Baden-Powell became Chief Guide in 1918 and was appointed GBE in 1932. Baden-Powell had been appointed KCVO and KCB in 1909, created a baronet in 1922, GCVO in 1923, and GCMG in 1927. In 1929 he became Baron Baden-Powell of Gilwell and in 1937 was appointed to the Order of Merit. He wrote numerous books and illustrated them himself.

Baden-Powell died on 8 January 1941 at Nyeri, Kenya. A stone plaque to his memory was unveiled in Westminster Abbey in 1947.

BAILEY, FREDERICK MARSHMAN (1882-1967), explorer and naturalist, was born on 3 February 1882 at Lahore, India, the elder son of Major (later Lt.-Col.) Frederick Bailey, Royal Engineers, and Florence, daughter of John Clark Marshman, who was one of the founders of the newspaper the *Pioneer of India*. Bailey was educated at Edinburgh Academy, Wellington, and Sandhurst, and was commissioned into the Middlesex Regiment in 1900. He was stationed in the Nilgiri hills in India and there became interested in birds, butterflies, and plants.

In 1903 he secured transfer to the 32nd Sikh Pioneers and went with them to Sikkim; this enabled him to visit Tibet. He was a member of the YOUNGHUSBAND mission to Lhasa in 1903-4 and, after becoming proficient in Tibetan, was sent to report on trade routes between India and Gartok, living for weeks at a height of over 14,000 feet. He applied to be transferred to the political department, and in 1905 went to Gyantse as trade agent, and then to the Chumbi Valley.

In 1911 he set out on an expedition to explore the Tsangpo river and attempted to make his way to the river through Szechuan and Yunnan in China. He did not succeed in reaching the Tsangpo, but returned to India through Mishmi country, and later recounted the journey in *China—Tibet—Assam* (1945). His determination to solve the mystery of the Tsangpo gorges led him in 1913 to set out again with H. T. Morshead, RE, of the Survey of India. Together they entered Tibet from Assam and, after a long and arduous journey, were able to map the course of the Tsangpo from its source to the plains where it became the Brahmaputra. On this expedition, Bailey also discovered the blue poppy (*Meconopsis baileyi*). *No Passport to Tibet* (1957) was his account of this journey for which he was appointed CIE in 1915.

During the First World War he served in France and Gallipoli and was twice wounded. Invalided from the service, he was sent in 1917 to Persia (Iran), and in the following year went to Tashkent to attempt to establish good relations with the Russian authorities there. However, the Bolsheviks were already in power and Bailey had to go underground. Changing his identity, he was able to enlist in the Russian counter-espionage service and spent some months attempting to trace a foreign agent called Bailey! Eventually he escaped into Persia and afterwards recounted his adventures in *Mission to Tashkent* (1946).

In 1921 he married Irena, only child of William Hepburn, second Lord Cozens-Hardy, a barrister. They had no children. From 1921 to 1938 when he retired, Bailey was political officer in Sikkim and Kashmir and British Minister in Nepal, and was able to continue his travels into Tibet. He became a personal friend of the Dalai Lama with whom he could converse freely. After retirement, he joined the Home Guard, and for two years was a King's Messenger in the USA.

He gave his collection of butterflies, birds, and mammals to the British Museum (Natural History). He published papers on many aspects of natural history. Bailey died at Stiffkey, Norfolk on 17 April 1967.

BAIRD, JOHN LOGIE (1888–1946), television pioneer, was born at Helensburgh on 13 August 1888, the youngest child of the Revd John Baird and his wife, Jessie Morrison Inglis, who came of a shipbuilding family in Glasgow. He studied electrical engineering at the Royal Technical College, Glasgow, and worked for the B.Sc. at Glasgow University. Unfit for service in the First World War, he served as a superintendent engineer, but in 1918 set up his own business, though he continued to be dogged by ill health.

After a nervous breakdown he went to live in Hastings in 1922 and decided to concentrate on television research. With the crudest of apparatus he succeeded, in 1924, in transmitting a hazy image for a few feet. He moved to London to continue his work and, despite ill health and poverty, succeeded on 26 January 1926 in giving the world's first demonstration of television to a group of scientists in his attic room in Soho; later that year he demonstrated the use of infra-red rays. In the next year, he demonstrated television over a telephone line between London and Glasgow, and formed the Baird Television Development Company.

Then, in 1928 he made the first transatlantic television transmission between London and New York, and the first demonstration of television in colour and stereoscopic television. The British Broadcasting Corporation inaugurated a service on the Baird system in 1929 and continued to use that system until 1937. In 1931 Baird televised the Derby, and in 1932 gave the world's first demonstration of ultrashort wave television. He married in 1931 Margaret, daughter of Henry Albu, a diamond merchant of Johannesburg; she was a concert pianist. They had one son and one daughter. He continued his colour, stereoscopic, and big-screen experimental work until he died at Bexhill on 14 June 1946.

BAIRNSFATHER, (CHARLES) BRUCE (1888–1959), cartoonist, was born in India on 9 July 1888, the son of Lt. Thomas Henry Bairnsfather; his mother's maiden name was Every. He was educated at the United Services College, Westward Ho! and served for a time in the army, but abandoned army service, initially to study art, but soon became apprenticed as an electrical engineer.

He rejoined the Royal Warwickshire Regiment in 1914 and fought in France. He had kept up drawing as a hobby, and in 1915 his humorous cartoons depicting conditions at the front began to appear in the *Bystander*. His two famous characters were Old Bill, a Cockney private with a walrus moustache, and Bert, a foolish youth with a 'fag' permanently dangling from his mouth. The humour that Bairnsfather contrived to drag from the terrible conditions of trench warfare was exemplified by the cartoon of these two sheltering in a water-logged shell-hole during an artillery barrage with the caption 'Well, if you knows of a better 'ole, go to it' (*Bystander*, 24 November 1915).

Bairnsfather served in France until 1916 when he became officer-cartoonist for the War Office. A play *The Better 'Ole* was produced by (Sir) Charles COCHRAN in 1917. After the war Bairnsfather's humour ceased to appeal to the wide public that had delighted in Old Bill and Bert, but he continued to draw for the *Bystander* as well as for *Life* and the *New Yorker*. In 1921 he married Cecilia Agnes, daughter of William Bruton of Sydney, Australia; they had one daughter.

During 1942–4 he was an official cartoonist to the United States Army in Europe. Bairnsfather died at Worcester on 29 September 1959.

BAKER, SIR HERBERT (1862–1946), architect, was born

Baird with the first television transmitter, March 1925

at Cobham, Kent on 9 June 1862, the fourth of the eleven children of Thomas Henry Baker, a landowner and farmer, and his wife, Frances Georgina, daughter of Robert William Davis of Rochester. He was educated at Tonbridge, and articled to his cousin, an architect, in London. He then studied at the Royal Academy School of Architecture and worked in the office of (Sir) Ernest George, where (Sir) Edwin LUTYENS was a fellow pupil. In 1890 he became an associate of the Royal Institute of British Architects.

Two years later, he went out to South Africa where, by good fortune, he attracted the notice of Cecil Rhodes. They discovered that they both had an interest in the antiquities of Cape Town and, in particular, in examples of the Dutch school of domestic architecture. Rhodes commissioned Baker to restore his house, Groote Schuur, and, when it was later burnt down, Baker in 1896 built the new Groote Schuur, which was to become the official home of the Prime Minister of South Africa. He also built and restored other buildings in Cape Town, and when Cecil Rhodes died in 1902 Baker accepted an invitation from Lord MILNER to help in the reconstruction works in the Transvaal.

In 1904 he married Florence, daughter of Major-General Henry Edmeades; they had three sons and one daughter.

During the next few years, Baker built many magnificent houses in Johannesburg and Pretoria, as well as building parts of the cathedrals in Bloemfontein and Pretoria. He also designed buildings in Rhodesia (Zimbabwe) and Kenya including the nave of the cathedral at Salisbury (Harare) and Government House at Nairobi (1925).

In India, in 1912 and afterwards, Baker collaborated with Lutyens in constructing the new Imperial Delhi—the buildings which Clemenceau, after visiting the ruins of the seven cities of Delhi, is reputed to have said would make 'the grandest ruins of them all'. Lutyens was responsible for the beautiful Viceroy's House, and Baker designed the two massive Secretariat buildings, the Legislative Chamber, and houses for government officials.

In 1913 Baker opened an office in London and, in collaboration with his partner A. T. Scott, designed the new Bank of England (1921), India House (1925), South Africa House (1930), and Church House, Westminster (1934). He was also responsible for the design of many war memorials. At Oxford Baker built Rhodes House, and in 1934 published *Cecil Rhodes by his Architect*, followed by *Architecture and Personalities* (1944). He was knighted in 1926, appointed KCIE in 1930, and elected RA in 1932. He also received many academic honours. Baker died at his home Owletts, Cobham (where he had been born), on 4 February 1946, and was buried in Westminster Abbey.

BALCON, SIR MICHAEL ELIAS (1896-1977), film producer, was born in Birmingham on 19 May 1896, the youngest son of Louis Balcon, a Jewish salesman, and his wife, Laura Greenberg. He was educated at the George Dixon Grammar School, Birmingham. In 1914 he was rejected for military service and went to work with the Dunlop Rubber Company (1914-18).

After the war he joined Victor Saville in a small film distribution enterprise, and in 1922 was successful with *Woman to Woman*. In 1924 he set up Gainsborough Pictures and made a series of silent films at the Islington Studios, including *The Rat* (1925) and *The Lodger* (1926), directed by Alfred HITCHCOCK, and *Blighty* (1927).

In 1924 he married Aileen Freda, daughter of H. Leatherman of Johannesburg; they had a son and a daughter,

Jill, who became an actress and married Cecil DAY-LEWIS.

In 1931 he became producer to the Gaumont-British Picture Corporation as well as Gainsborough and brought out sound films such as *The Good Companions* (1932), *Rome Express* (1932), *The Constant Nymph* (1933), *Jew Süss* (1934), and *Rhodes of Africa* (1936). He also produced further Hitchcock films, *The Man Who Knew Too Much* (1934) and *The Thirty-Nine Steps* (1935), and backed Robert J. Flaherty's *Man of Aran* (1932).

In 1936 he left Gaumont-British and took charge of Metro-Goldwyn Mayer's productions in Britain, but he disliked *A Yank at Oxford* (1938), and returned to partnership with Reginald Baker who had helped him to set up Gainsborough films. Between 1939 and 1945 he produced some notable war films, including *San Demetrio, London* (1943) and, after the war, brought out *The Cruel Sea* (1952) and *The Divided Heart* (1954). He also made the Australian film *The Overlanders* (1946).

Perhaps the Ealing films that will be best remembered are the comedies: *Passport to Pimlico* (1949), *Whisky Galore* (1948), and *The Lavender Hill Mob* (1951). Other films in which (Sir) Alec Guinness took the lead were *Kind Hearts and Coronets* (1949), *The Man in the White Suit* (1951), and *The Lady-killers* (1955); among other notable productions were *The Blue Lamp* (1949) and *Scott of the Antarctic* (1948).

Balcon was knighted in 1948. In 1959 the Ealing Studios closed, but he was by then Chairman of British Lion and became a director of Border Television. He was a Fellow of the British Film Academy and a Governor of the British Film Institute. He was awarded honorary degrees from Birmingham (1967) and Sussex (1975) Universities. In 1969 he published *A Lifetime of Films*. Michael Balcon died at Hartfield, Sussex, on 17 October 1977.

BALDWIN, STANLEY, first EARL BALDWIN OF BEWDLEY (1867-1947), politician and Prime Minister, was born at Bewdley on 3 August 1867, the only son of Alfred Baldwin, ironmaster, and his wife, Louisa, daughter of the Revd George Brown Macdonald, a Wesleyan minister of Highland stock. Louisa's mother was Welsh. This presumably explains why LLOYD GEORGE once said, 'Baldwin is one of us. He is a Celt', although no man could have been less like the mercurial Welshman than Stanley Baldwin who prided himself on being a typical Englishman. Rudyard KIPLING was his cousin.

He was educated at Harrow and Trinity College, Cambridge. In 1888 he entered the family business, became a county councillor and a magistrate, and four years later married Lucy, the eldest daughter of Edward Lucas Jenks Ridsdale, of Rottingdean, a former assay master of the Mint. They had three sons (one stillborn) and four daughters. Alfred Baldwin had been Conservative MP for the Bewdley division of Worcestershire since 1892, and when he died in 1908 Stanley succeeded him, unopposed. He held the seat until he went to the Lords in 1937. During the years before the First World War, he spoke seldom and made no obvious impact on the Commons; but, in 1916, BONAR LAW, who had known his father, made Baldwin his Parliamentary Private Secretary, and a year later he was promoted to joint Financial Secretary to the Treasury. This post he held until 1921, having become a Privy Counsellor in 1920.

At the end of the war, Baldwin had anonymously realized 20 per cent of his capital and purchased £150,000 of War Loan stock for cancellation, appealing under a pseudonym in *The Times* for other wealthy people to do the same and help to reduce the burden of war debt. In 1921 he entered

Lloyd George's Cabinet as President of the Board of Trade, but very quickly became disillusioned with the tactics of the 'Welsh wizard'. At a famous meeting at the Carlton Club in 1922, he made a passionate speech revealing his distrust of Lloyd George and persuaded his Conservative colleagues to bring the Coalition Government to an end. After the subsequent general election Bonar Law became Prime Minister and Baldwin Chancellor of the Exchequer. He was much criticized for the terms on which he arranged settlement of the American debt, contracted during the war; but, when Bonar Law resigned in 1923 through ill health, Baldwin stepped into his shoes as Prime Minister. He was 'a man of the utmost insignificance', said the disappointed Lord CURZON, and Baldwin himself, who had never expected the post, realized that he was inexperienced. The confidence of his supporters was certainly shaken when he called a general election later in the year to obtain for his Government a mandate to introduce protection as a remedy for unemployment. 'I think Baldwin has gone mad', Lord BIRKENHEAD wrote to Austen CHAMBERLAIN. The outcome was unfortunate for the Conservatives: although they still had more seats in the Commons than Labour or the Liberals, they no longer had an overall majority, and Baldwin had to resign. However, his discomfiture was short-lived. The Labour Government of Ramsay MACDONALD lasted for only a few months, and in the autumn of 1924, Baldwin became Prime Minister for the second time.

Now he set himself the task of uniting the country, of diminishing class hatred, and of gaining the confidence of the public, by presenting himself as an unpretentious, pipe-smoking countryman who had no intention of embarking upon ill-considered adventures. It was ASQUITH who coined the phrase 'Wait and see', but it was Stanley Baldwin who put this aphorism into practice. The circumstances of the time were not in his favour. The aftermath of the First World War had brought great hardship for working people, and consequent discontent and resentment. The decision in 1925, taken by CHURCHILL as Chancellor and with the Prime Minister's approval, to return to the gold standard, did nothing to help. In spite of numerous speeches in which Baldwin pleaded for conciliation, the coal-owners' intransigence towards the miners led to a lock-out and, although the Government was able to stave off for a year a wider response by subsidizing the pits, matters came to a head on 3 May 1926 when a general strike began.

Throughout the week of the strike Baldwin did as much as he could to bring it to an end without vindictiveness. His broadcast speeches revealed his determination to resist the unconstitutional actions of the trade unions, but showed also that he had sympathy for the cause of the mineworkers, for whom the other unions had called out their members in misguided support. When the general strike collapsed, however, the miners refused to return to work. For another six months, they and their families held out in the face of dire penury and distress. Baldwin did nothing and, when in the end the mine-owners won and the men had to go back to the pits, they returned nursing a grievance that would be remembered for generations.

In 1928, the Government passed a bill through Parliament, giving the vote to women of twenty-one years and upwards. A number of other comparatively minor pieces of legislation were also enacted, but the major problem of unemployment remained unsolved by this 'torpid, sleepy, barren' Government, as Lloyd George labelled it. At the general election of 1929 the Conservatives were defeated, and Ramsay Mac-Donald returned to office. Meanwhile, another problem caused disagreement in the ranks of the Conservative opposition. In 1925 Baldwin had appointed Lord Irwin (Edward WOOD, later Earl of Halifax) as Viceroy of India, and he was in full agreement with Irwin's policy, in accordance with which in 1929 the Viceroy pledged full Dominion status for India. In June 1930 the Round Table Conference on this matter began; Winston Churchill denounced the proposals as 'absurd', and resigned from the Shadow Cabinet.

The Labour Government, however, was also beset by problems. Unemployment continued to be an insurmountable difficulty, and in 1931 MacDonald and many of his colleagues parted company when the Prime Minister felt bound to form a National Government with Baldwin as Lord President of the Council. At the following general election the National Government secured over 550 seats, of which 471 were held by Conservatives. Ramsay MacDonald, deserted by many of his old supporters, struggled on until June 1935. Meanwhile

'Honest Stan' Baldwin, the pipe-smoker

Baldwin and his friends pushed through an import duties bill which forced Herbert SAMUEL and his free-trade colleagues in the Government to resign. In 1933, Hitler came to power as German Chancellor.

In 1935 Baldwin became Prime Minister for the third time. The Government of India Act was passed in August of that year, but the greatest problem that loomed ahead was the threat to peace from the Fascists and Nazis. At first, the danger came from Mussolini who invaded Abyssinia. After a vigorous speech at Geneva by the Foreign Secretary, Sir Samuel HOARE, it seemed that Britain would impose upon Italy sanctions that might lead to war, but Baldwin was fully aware that the British public was not prepared for war, and he acquiesced when Hoare and Laval, the French Prime Minister, reached an agreement that would have involved the cession of Ethiopian territory to Italy. The British public was appalled. Baldwin hastened to disown his Foreign Secretary and Hoare resigned. During the following year Hitler reoccupied the Rhinelands and, although Baldwin took the first tentative steps towards rearmament, his reactions became more and more ineffectual while the warnings of Winston Churchill, still a back-bencher, went unheeded.

One further crisis had to be dealt with. George V had died in January 1936, and his successor, Edward VIII, was determined to marry a lady who had divorced one husband and was about to divorce another. Baldwin realized at once that public opinion in the country and throughout the British Empire would not accept this situation, and that, if Edward were allowed to have his way, the monarchy would be irretrievably ruined. He therefore refused to countenance any arrangement that would have been agreeable to the King. Edward VIII abdicated, and his more stable brother came to the throne as George VI. Thus, Stanley Baldwin, whatever his failures, and they were many, will be remembered as the Prime Minister who came unexpectedly to that office and carried his country successfully through the general strike and steered the Empire through the royal abdication.

A year later, he resigned. George VI appointed him a Knight of the Garter and created him an earl. Baldwin took no further active part in politics. Lady Baldwin died in June 1945, and Baldwin himself died on 14 December 1947 at his home in Worcestershire, Astley Hall. He was succeeded by his elder son, Oliver, who was a Labour politician. Baldwin was not a great prime minister, but he was a great parliamentarian, and Winston Churchill described him as 'the greatest party manager the Conservatives ever had'.

BALFOUR, ARTHUR JAMES, first EARL OF BALFOUR (1848-1930), politician and Prime Minister, and philosopher, was born at Whittingehame, East Lothian, on 25 July 1848, the eldest son of James Maitland Balfour, a country gentleman, and his wife Lady Blanche Mary Harriet, daughter of the second Marquess of Salisbury. His father died when he was eight, and he was greatly influenced in his youth by the personality of his mother and her friends. He was educated at Eton and Trinity College, Cambridge: his academic performance was moderate but he was keenly interested in scientific developments.

His political career owed much to his uncle, the third Marquess of Salisbury, under whose influence he entered politics as Conservative MP for Hertford, a seat which he held from 1874 to 1885. As the acknowledged leader of the 'Souls'—the smart set of young and sparkling intellectuals and wits, both men and women—Balfour enjoyed enormous social prestige, and entertained lavishly at his home in Scot-

land. In Parliament he was able to mediate between the 'Fourth Party', led by Lord Randolph Churchill, and his uncle, the leader of the Conservatives. His personal life was seriously affected by the death in 1875 of May Lyttelton, to whom he was in effect engaged. Perhaps in consequence of this loss, he never married.

For six months in 1885-6 Balfour was President of the Local Government Board, and at the 1885 election he became MP for East Manchester where he remained until 1906. In 1886 he was appointed Secretary for Scotland and became a member of the Cabinet. Up to this time his political career had not been markedly outstanding but, when in 1887 Lord Salisbury appointed him Chief Secretary for Ireland, he set out on a policy of firm suppression of violence and crime which earned for him the name of 'Bloody Balfour'. His resolute action appeared to succeed and he was able to proceed with more constructive policies such as the Land Purchase Act (1891) which attempted to deal with the problem of the absentee landlord.

In 1891 Balfour became Conservative leader in the Commons and First Lord of the Treasury; now he and his uncle were respectively leaders of their party in both Houses of Parliament. The combination seemed to work well, but Balfour, for all his mastery in debate, was not looked upon as a leader of great authority and industry, and although he continued to lead in the Commons for a second term from 1895 to 1902, his political management was not particularly effective.

In July 1902, when the Boer War had been brought to an end, Lord Salisbury resigned and his nephew became Prime Minister. His period in that office up to 1905 was bedevilled by controversy within his party between the tariff-reformers and the free-traders. He considered that his task was to hold the party together and to keep his options open, but this, to some extent at least, increased the doubts of those who regarded him as indecisive and indolent. In December 1905 he resigned and the Liberal leader, Sir Henry Campbell-Bannerman became Prime Minister. Balfour's Government was not without its achievements. The Committee of Imperial Defence was set up, the Entente with France was established, and the Anglo-Japanese Agreement was renewed after the Russo-Japanese war.

In the general election of January 1906, the Conservatives were disastrously defeated: Balfour himself lost his seat at East Manchester, and his followers in the House were reduced to a small remnant. He returned to Parliament two months later as MP for the City of London, a seat which he held until 1922. As Leader of the Opposition, he attacked many of the proposals of the Liberal Government including LLOYD GEORGE's 'People's Budget' but, when the crisis came between the Government and the House of Lords, he took a leading part in the conference that sought a party truce following the death of Edward VII and accession of George V in 1910. It was through no fault of Balfour's that the attempt to reach a compromise failed and the constitutional battle was resumed, leading eventually to the passage of the Finance Bill through the Lords and the attack upon the Lords' right of veto, which was finally resolved in the Parliament Act of 1911. Because the die-hards in his own party refused to accept his conciliatory advice, he resigned the leadership in November of that year.

At the outbreak of war in 1914, he accepted ASQUITH's invitation to resume his membership of the Committee of Imperial Defence and, when the Coalition Government was formed in 1915, he was appointed First Lord of the Admiralty. Whilst holding that office he succeeded in bringing to an end the dissensions which had endangered the progress of the war at sea; he agreed with the decision to abandon the Gallipoli campaign, was concerned that the Battle of Jutland had not been brought to a more decisive conclusion, and took steps to improve the arrangements for countering the German submarine campaign. He took no part in the manoeuvres to oust Asquith from the office of Prime Minister, but gave his support to Lloyd George when this became a *fait accompli*.

From 1916 to 1919 he served as Foreign Secretary but was inevitably overshadowed by the mercurial Lloyd George. He did, however, achieve one thing which had lasting repercussions. In November 1917 he overcame opposition both within and without the Cabinet and issued the 'Balfour Declaration' in favour of a national home for the Jews in Palestine. He accompanied the Prime Minister to the Peace Conference in 1919 but had little influence over the final terms of the treaties with Germany and Austria. In October of that year he resigned as Foreign Secretary but retained a seat in the Cabinet as Lord President of the Council.

Balfour continued to be interested in foreign affairs. In 1921 he led the British delegation to the Washington Naval Conference; in 1922 he argued strongly in favour of the cancellation of war debts, and was very closely concerned with the economic rehabilitation of Austria under the auspices of the League of Nations.

In 1922 he was appointed KG, accepted an earldom, and continued as Lord President of the Council in BALDWIN'S second Government from 1925 to 1929. He had a hand in the foundation of the Committee of Civil Research intended to co-ordinate scientific investigations throughout the Commonwealth. The 'Balfour Definition' of 1926 prepared the way for the Statute of Westminster (1931).

As a philosopher Balfour published his fundamental views in *A Defence of Philosophic Doubt* (1879) and *Foundations of Belief* (1895). Put as simply as possible, he thought that the foundations of natural science are no firmer than those of theology: 'all men, including all philosophers', he maintained, 'are believers', and all constructive thought must rest on a foundation of faith.

Apart from his other honours Balfour was appointed OM in 1916; he was President of the British Association in 1904, and of the British Academy from 1921 to 1930. He died at Fisher's Hill near Woking on 19 March 1930 and was buried at Whittingehame.

BARBIROLLI, SIR JOHN (GIOVANNI BATTISTA)
(1899–1970), conductor and cellist, was born in London on 2 December 1899, the elder son of an Italian violinist, Lorenzo Barbirolli, and his French wife, Louise Marie Ribeyrol. He was educated at St Clement Dane's School and the Trinity College of Music. Having played the cello from the age of five, he made his public début in a cello concerto at the Queen's Hall in 1911, and he was a scholar of the Royal Academy of Music from 1912 to 1916. During the following two years he played the cello in orchestral concerts, in opera, and in theatres and cinemas.

He served in the Suffolk Regiment in 1918–19 and, on demobilization, resumed his career as a cellist. But he had always intended to become a conductor, and in 1925 was invited to conduct for the British National Opera Company. Four years later he became conductor of the Covent Garden Opera Touring Company and, after a further four years, conductor of the Scottish Orchestra (1933). Then, in 1936, some astonishment was caused in New York when he was

Barbirolli in rehearsal, February 1953

selected to succeed Toscanini as conductor for the Philharmonic-Symphony Society. In spite of some criticism of his interpretation of the works of certain composers, he held that post until 1943 when he was invited to become the permanent conductor of the Hallé Orchestra in Manchester.

In 1932 he had married Marjorie Parry, a soprano; this marriage ended in divorce in 1939; and he then married Evelyn, a celebrated oboist, daughter of R. H. Rothwell, a tea-dealer. There were no children of either marriage.

Barbirolli was faced with a difficult task in recruiting an orchestra in wartime Britain, but soon the players he had succeeded in getting together were being acclaimed as the best orchestra in the country. He was knighted in 1949, and awarded the Royal Philharmonic Society's gold medal in 1950. He continued to accept invitations to conduct as a guest in the USA and in Germany, and from 1961 to 1967 was Conductor-in-Chief of the Houston Symphony Orchestra. But the Hallé was still his major concern, and, after twenty-five years with it, he was appointed Conductor Laureate for life. He was made CH in 1969, and died in London on 29 July 1970, after a day spent preparing for concerts in Japan.

Some of his greatest interpretations were of the music of Mahler, ELGAR, Sibelius, Brahms, and VAUGHAN WILLIAMS. Barbirolli was a complete and accomplished musician with a prodigious capacity for work and possessing a kind of magnetic quality which enabled him to get the best from his players. He was the recipient of many honours and academic awards bestowed upon him both in England and abroad.

BARING, (CHARLES) EVELYN, first BARON HOWICK OF GLENDALE (1903-1973), colonial governor, was born on 29 September 1903 in London, the third son of Evelyn BARING, first Earl of Cromer and the only child of his second wife, Lady Katherine Thynne, daughter of the fourth Marquess of Bath. He was educated at Winchester and New College, Oxford, where he obtained a first in history in 1924.

Baring went out to India in the Indian Civil Service in 1926 and was posted to the United Provinces. In 1929 he was sent to South Africa as Secretary to the Agent of the Government of India in Durban. He returned to India in 1932 only to be assailed by amoebic dysentery, from which he suffered so seriously that he had to retire from the service.

In 1935 he married Lady Mary Cecil Grey, elder daughter of Charles Robert, fifth Earl Grey; they had one son and two daughters.

In England he worked for a short time in the family bank, but he disliked life in the City and soon joined the Sudan Development Company. When the Second World War broke out he was unfit for military service but was employed temporarily in the Foreign Office, and in July 1942, at the age of thirty-eight, was appointed Governor of Southern Rhodesia (Zimbabwe). The country already enjoyed internal self-government so the Governor had no executive power, but throughout his period of office he sought to improve African administration and agriculture.

In 1944 he was appointed British High Commissioner to South Africa and Governor of the protectorates of Basutoland (Lesotho), Bechuanaland (Botswana), and Swaziland. During his period of office, South Africa was visited by King George VI and Queen Elizabeth. J. C. SMUTS was defeated in 1948, and D. F. Malan and the Afrikaner nationalists came to power. In Bechuanaland, Baring had to deal with the problem of the marriage of (Sir) Seretse Khama to an Englishwoman in the face of the opposition of his uncle, the Regent. Both men were for a time banished from the country, and Baring thought that his handling of the matter had damaged his reputation as a proconsul.

In 1952, however, Winston CHURCHILL appointed him Governor of Kenya, and there he had to cope with the Kikuyu problem (Mau Mau). He had to defeat a murderous armed rebellion without losing sight of the important objectives of agricultural development and prosperity for the Africans. When the rebellion was broken in 1956, his policy towards the Africans began to become effective, but the white settlers regarded his agrarian reforms as directly contrary to their own interests.

Baring left Kenya in 1959 to become Chairman of the Colonial (later Commonwealth) Development Corporation, a post he held between 1960 and 1972. He was also Chairman of the Nature Conservancy from 1962 to 1973, President of the Liverpool School of Tropical Medicine (1967-73), Chairman of the British North American Committee (1970-3), and a director of the Swan Hunter Group Ltd.

He was appointed KCMG in 1942, KCVO in 1947, GCMG in 1955, and KG in 1972. In 1960 he received a hereditary barony; he had many honorary degrees, and was an honorary Fellow of New College, Oxford (1960). Baring died in Alnwick on 10 March 1973 and was succeeded by his son Charles Evelyn.

BARING, EVELYN first EARL OF CROMER (1841-1917),

proconsul, diplomat, and administrator, was born at Cromer Hall, Norfolk, on 26 February 1841, the sixth son of the marriage of Henry Baring MP to his second wife, Cecilia, eldest daughter of Admiral William Windham of Felbrigge, Norfolk. His father died in 1848 and Baring was brought up by his mother. He was educated at the Ordnance School, Carshalton, and the Royal Military Academy, Woolwich. In 1858 he was commissioned and went with his battery to the Ionian Islands, where he became ADC to the High Commissioner, Sir Henry Knight Storks. He later accompanied Sir Henry to Malta and Jamaica, and in 1867 returned to England and entered the Staff College.

In 1872 he decided upon a civil career and became Private Secretary to his cousin, Lord Northbrook, Viceroy of India. In 1876 he was awarded the CIE. In the same year he married Ethel Stanley, daughter of Sir Rowland Stanley Errington; they had two sons. Also in 1876, owing to the extravagance of Khedive Ismail, Egypt failed to meet her foreign debts, and the *Caisse de la Dette* was set up to advise her how to meet her liabilities to Egyptian bondholders. Baring was appointed as the first British Commissioner. After two years in this post, he declared Egypt bankrupt and proposed

Evelyn Baring, first Earl of Cromer

liquidation but, as no notice appeared to be taken of his reports, he resigned and returned to England.

In 1879, the Khedive Ismail was deposed in favour of Tewfik; Britain and France reimposed their dual control, and Baring was recalled as British Controller. However, since his views on the action to be taken did not coincide with those of the French, he had to be moved; he was offered and accepted the post of finance member of the Viceroy's Council in India. He served in that post from 1880 to 1883 and retired as KCSI.

Meanwhile, the British Government had assumed full control of affairs in Egypt and Baring was sent there again as Agent and Consul-General. He now represented the only power with military forces occupying the country in strength and, since Egypt was no longer able to control the Sudan, which was being overrun by the Dervishes under the Mahdi, he strongly recommended temporary withdrawal from that area. General Gordon was sent out to put such withdrawal into effect, but allowed himself to be besieged in Khartoum, making no effort to follow his instructions for withdrawal. Baring urged the raising of an international loan to deal with Egypt's economic problems, and the relief of Khartoum, but once again his recommendations were ignored and procrastination in London led to tragedy when in 1885 Khartoum fell and Gordon was murdered.

Baring now insisted on Egyptian withdrawal from all the Sudan provinces except Suakin, and once more directed his attention to the country's economic problems. During the next five years, he succeeded, with the aid of an international loan, in liquidating Egypt's debts. He was now able to improve irrigation and communications, and set in train schemes for revising the system of land taxes and for the more efficient administration of justice and education. He had been gazetted CB in 1885, KCB in 1887, and in 1888 was appointed GCMG. In spite of difficulties caused by the intrigues of the Egyptian ruling class, he continued his work of reform, and undertook further schemes for development including the building of a dam on the Nile which would greatly improve the irrigation system. In 1892 he was created Baron Cromer.

Throughout 1896 and 1897 he supported KITCHENER, who had been appointed Sirdar of the Egyptian army, and protected him from his critics in Egypt and in England during the reconquest of the Sudan which was finally achieved in 1898. Cromer now took steps to ensure that the Sudan did not become the prey of international intrigue, and up till 1907 was able to carry on his great work in Egypt without serious interference. He was created viscount in 1899 and earl in 1901. His first wife died in 1898. In 1901 he married Lady Katherine Thynne, second daughter of the fourth Marquess of Bath; they had one son, (Charles) Evelyn BARING. By 1907 he was worn out physically by the strain of nearly twenty-five years of arduous work in the face of growing nationalism in Egypt and increasing ill health. In spite of Edward VII's personal efforts to dissuade him, Cromer felt that he had no alternative but to retire.

During his retirement he took part in debates in the House of Lords and wrote the books which give his own account of the long period of his stewardship in Egypt. *Modern Egypt* (2 vols.) was published in 1908, followed by *Ancient and Modern Imperialism* (1910) and *Abbas II* (1915). He also published three volumes of *Political and Literary Essays* (reviews of new books written for the *Spectator* from 1912 onwards).

In 1916, in spite of ill health, Cromer agreed to preside over the Dardanelles Commission, but after a meeting in December he collapsed, and on 29 January 1917 he died in London. He was the last great proconsul in the heyday of British imperialism.

BARKER, SIR ERNEST (1874-1960), political scientist and historian, was born at Woodley, Cheshire on 23 September 1874, the eldest child of George Barker, an ex-miner and farm worker, and his wife, Elizabeth Pollitt. He was a scholar at Manchester Grammar School and Balliol College, Oxford, where he obtained firsts in Mods. (1895), in Greats (1897), and in history (1898). He married in 1900 Emily Isabel, daughter of the Revd Richard Salkeld; they had one son and two daughters.

Barker was also a Craven scholar (1895), and a classical Fellow of Merton College from 1898 to 1905. From 1899 to 1909 he was lecturer in modern history at Wadham College. Between 1909 and 1913 he was Fellow and lecturer at St John's College, and from 1913 to 1920 Fellow and tutor of New College. He left Oxford in 1920 to become Principal of King's College, London. His first wife died in 1924, and in 1927 he married Olivia Stuart, daughter of John Stuart Horner, director of an engineering firm; they had a son and a daughter. Then, in 1928, he went to Cambridge as the first Professor of Political Science, and Fellow of Peterhouse until he retired in 1939.

His liberal ideas stemmed from his Congregationalist background, and he particularly appreciated the value of Aristotle's doctrine of the welfare state. He was a great teacher, and at his happiest when discussing political theories with his students, encouraging them to think for themselves rather than to accept doctrines and theses ready-made.

Among Barker's most valuable contributions to the study of political science were his translations from the German writers, Otto von Gierke and Ernst Troeltsch. He was much interested in the concept of political pluralism, largely derived from von Gierke's work, but he fought shy of its conclusion. In particular he sought to reconcile individual liberalism in the tradition of John Stuart Mill with a strong sense of the community. He was also notably fairminded in drawing attention to new ideas. His own publications include *Political Thought of Plato and Aristotle* (1906), *Political Thought in England from Herbert Spencer to Today* (1915), *Reflections on Government* (1942), and *Principles of Social and Political Theory* (1951). He was one of the chief contributors to the Oxford volume *Why we are at War: Great Britain's Case* (1914) and one of the editors of *The European Inheritance* (1954). His autobiographical work *Age and Youth* was published in 1953.

He received many academic honours, was elected FBA in 1947, and knighted in 1944. Barker died in Cambridge on 17 February 1960.

BARKER, SIR HERBERT ATKINSON (1869-1950), osteopath, was born at Southport on 21 April 1869, the only son of Thomas Wildman Barker, a lawyer, and his wife, Agnes Atkinson. Both parents died while he was a schoolboy at Kirkby Lonsdale Grammar School. As a youth he was apprenticed to his cousin, John Atkinson, bone-setter, of Park Lane, London. By the time he was twenty-one Barker was practising on his own, first in Manchester and Glasgow, then in London.

In 1907 he married Jane Ethel, daughter of William Wilson Walker; there were no children.

Barker had no medical qualifications, and was soon in trouble with the medical authorities who were stolidly opposed to anybody practising who had not been trained and qualified from a teaching hospital. Barker, however, was no mean controversialist, and he was prepared for a lifelong fight to secure the recognition of the professional status of bone-setting. In spite of the efforts of the medical profession to discredit his claims, there could be no doubt that Barker succeeded in alleviating the suffering of many people by his skill as a manipulative surgeon, and as he had many friends among journalists, his claims to recognition could not be ignored. In 1922 he was knighted, and the animosity of the doctors gradually faded away.

In 1936 he gave a demonstration of his skill before the British Orthopaedic Association at St Thomas's Hospital; this was later reported in the *Lancet* (27 February 1937). In 1941 he was elected manipulative surgeon to the Noble's Hospital in the Isle of Man.

He died in Lancaster on 21 July 1950, his name a household word, not only for his long battle with the doctors, but because of his remarkable successes in the alleviation of suffering.

BARNES, ERNEST WILLIAM (1874–1953), Bishop of Birmingham, was born on 1 April 1874 at Altrincham, Cheshire, the eldest son of John Starkie Barnes, a schoolmaster, and his wife, Jane Elizabeth Kerry, of Charlbury, Oxfordshire. He was educated at King Edward's School, Birmingham and entered Trinity College, Cambridge, as a scholar in 1893. He was bracketed second wrangler in 1896 and awarded a first in the first division of part ii of the mathematical tripos in 1897. He was also President of the Union in that year. In the following year he was first Smith's prizeman and elected a Fellow of Trinity, becoming assistant lecturer in 1902, junior dean in 1906–8, and tutor from 1908 to 1915. In 1909 he was elected FRS. Although reputedly an atheist when he went to Cambridge, in 1902 he was made deacon, and in 1903 ordained priest.

In 1916 he married Adelaide Caroline Theresa, daughter of Sir Adolphus Ward, Master of Peterhouse, Cambridge; they had two sons.

He was a convinced pacifist during the First World War; from 1915 to 1919 he was Master of the Temple; in 1918 he became Canon of Westminster; and in 1924 Ramsay MAC-DONALD nominated him Bishop of Birmingham where he remained until 1953.

By the time of his appointment to Birmingham he had become a highly controversial figure. In his sermons at the Temple, he not only preached the necessity of substituting for the traditional scriptural outlook, the evolutionary theory accepted by natural science, but also objected to any form of sacramentalism based upon the doctrine of the Real Presence of Christ in the Eucharist. This attitude caused distress to many in the Church of England and was deeply resented.

In Birmingham, where the diocese was largely high church, his behaviour towards Anglo-Catholicism and his continuance of 'gorilla' sermons led to his denunciation as a heretic, and a demand that the Archbishop should bring him to trial. Archbishop DAVIDSON mildly reproved him for his views on sacramentalism; in 1927 Bishop Barnes published his beliefs in *Should Such a Faith Offend?* and for a time the controversy abated.

During the Second World War Barnes again came into prominence when, in 1940, he attacked the Cement Makers' Federation as a ring of monopolists who, to increase their profits, were holding up the supply of cement urgently required for air-raid shelters. The Cement Makers sued the Bishop for slander and were awarded damages but, undismayed, Barnes repeated his allegations in the House of Lords.

In 1947 further fierce opposition to his opinions was aroused by his book *The Rise of Christianity*, in which he precluded the recognition of miracles. In this case, Archbishop Fisher did take the step of condemning the work in an address to Convocation and cautioned its readers against accepting its claims as true. It is clear that Bishop Barnes was a very unusual type of prelate. Although he was a man of great personal charm, he was completely indifferent to the hostility aroused by his unorthodox utterances.

It should be said that he was a mathematician of some note. He was a Fellow of King's College, London (1919), Giffard lecturer at Aberdeen (1926–8), and received a number of honorary degrees. Bishop Barnes died at his home at Hurstpierpoint in Sussex on 29 November 1953, a few months after his resignation from the see of Birmingham.

BARRIE, SIR JAMES MATTHEW (1860–1937), playwright and novelist, was born at Kirriemuir, Forfarshire on 9 May 1860, the youngest son of David Barrie, a hand-loom weaver, and his wife, Margaret, daughter of Alexander Ogilvy, a stonemason. He was educated at Glasgow and Dumfries Academies, and Edinburgh University.

In 1883 he was appointed leader-writer and sub-editor of the *Nottingham Journal*, and had stories, in which Kirriemuir was disguised as 'Thrums', published anonymously in the *St James's Gazette*. Two years later he moved to London; he continued to get articles accepted in magazines and, in 1888, published *Auld Licht Idylls* and *When a Man's Single* under his own name. These were followed by *A Window in Thrums* and *My Lady Nicotine* (1890). His first novel *The Little Minister* was published in 1891 and was an immediate success. His first essays in play-writing were not, however, so successful, until in 1892 *The Professor's Love Story* was staged with acclaim in the United States, and was later successfully produced in London.

In 1894 Barrie married a young actress, Mary, daughter of George Ansell, a licensed innkeeper; they had no children, and the marriage ended in divorce in 1909.

In 1896 Barrie's tribute to his mother, *Margaret Ogilvy*, appeared, and another novel, *Sentimental Tommy* (also in 1896), was followed by *Tommy and Grizel* (1900), his last novel. In 1897 *The Little Minister* was successfully produced as a play in Washington and then in London, where it ran for a year and was very profitable for Barrie. His next successful play was *Quality Street*, staged first at Toledo, Ohio, in 1901, then transferred to New York and, in 1902, brought to London. In that year, too, *The Admirable Crichton* was presented in London with Irene VANBRUGH, (Sir) Gerald du Maurier, H. B. Irving, and Henry Kemble in the cast. Then, in 1904, *Peter Pan*, for which Barrie will always be remembered, was produced for the first time at the Duke of York's Theatre in London, and since then has been revived almost every year to delight generations of young children and provide attractive parts for generations of young actresses.

Barrie wrote many other successful plays including *What Every Woman Knows* (1908), *Dear Brutus* (1917), *Mary Rose* (1920), and *The Boy David* (1936). He also wrote a number of one-act plays such as *The Twelve Pound Look* (1910) and *Shall we Join the Ladies?* (1921).

In 1912 Barrie had erected secretly, at his own expense, in Kensington Gardens, a bronze statue of Peter Pan. Questions were asked about it in Parliament, but the work, by Sir George Frampton, was so clearly an adornment to its environment that authority was glad to permit it to remain.

In 1913 Barrie became a baronet, and in 1922 was appointed to the Order of Merit. He received many honorary degrees and was Chancellor of Edinburgh University in 1930. He died in London on 19 June 1937.

BATEMAN, HENRY MAYO (1887-1970), cartoonist, was born on 15 February 1887 in New South Wales, the only son of Henry Charles Bateman, a farmer, and his wife, Rose Mayo. He was educated in south-east London, the family having returned to England, but left school at sixteen and studied at the Westminster School of Art and the Goldsmith's Institute.

He worked for three years in the London Studio of the Dutch painter, Charles van Havenmaet. His drawings first appeared in 1903 in *Scraps* and then in 1904 in the *Tatler*. He had not really decided whether he wanted to be an artist or a cartoonist until, in 1909, he began to draw people as they felt rather than looked emphasizing, by gesture and facial grimaces, his subjects' emotions. This technique he developed from studying the work of Emmanuel Poiré ('Caran d'Ache') and Henry Ospovat.

After drawing a series of theatrical caricatures for the *Tatler*, he depicted in 1912 'The Missed Putt'. This was the first of 'The Man Who' cartoons, a long series showing the embarrassment of committing some social gaffe or mishap,

H. M. Bateman's 'The man who ate his luncheon in the Royal Enclosure'

such as 'The Guardsman Who Dropped It' and 'The Boy Who Breathed on the Glass at the British Museum'. He also produced a series, the 'Colonels', neat and peppery gentlemen, with gnashing teeth, enraged by some outrage against conventional behaviour.

His first one-man exhibition was held in London in 1911, and further exhibitions were held regularly up to the time of his death and later. His cartoons were published world-wide and he was the most highly paid British cartoonist of his time. Modern advertising also owes him a debt which is repaid by using his technique and making the attribution 'after HMB'.

In 1926 he married Brenda Mary Collison, daughter of Octavius Weir, a country gentleman of Stratford St Mary; they had two daughters, but the marriage was not happy and his wife, who was sixteen years younger than Bateman, left him. In 1933 Bateman retired to Devon and devoted himself to his favourite sport of fly-fishing. He died on the Maltese island of Gozo on 11 February 1970.

BATTENBERG, PRINCE LOUIS OF (1854-1921). See MOUNTBATTEN, LOUIS ALEXANDER.

BAX, SIR ARNOLD EDWARD TREVOR (1883-1953), composer, was born in Streatham on 8 November 1883, the eldest son of Alfred Ridley Bax, of independent means, and his wife, Charlotte Ellen Lea. He could read music from a very early age. In 1898 he studied at the Hampstead Conservatoire, where the Principal at that time was Cecil SHARP. But Bax was not attracted by English folk music and in 1900 he entered the Royal Academy of Music. There, he won many prizes for composition and piano playing.

In 1911 he married Elsita Luisa, a concert pianist, daughter of the Spanish pianist, Carlos Sobrino; they had a son and a daughter.

He made his first public appearance as a composer in 1905. His music was influenced first by Wagner, Richard Strauss, and Debussy, and later by a Celtic mood (largely inspired by the poetry of YEATS), followed by a Nordic one. His tone-poems include *In the Faëry Hills* (1910), *The Garden of Fand* (1916), *Tintagel* (1917), and *The Tale the Pine Trees Knew* (1931). The Symphonic Variations for Piano and Orchestra (1917) and *Winter Legends* (1930) were written for Harriet COHEN. His most important works perhaps are his seven symphonies (1922-39), the Cello Concerto (1932), and the Violin Concerto (1937-8). He also wrote much chamber and choral music. Although he composed ballet and film music, including that for *Malta GC* (1943), he was never interested in the opera.

Bax described himself as a 'brazen Romantic', and his music had a curious mixture of robustness and wistfulness. He possessed private means, so he never needed to seek any paid employment. He was knighted in 1937, and became Master of the King's Music in 1942. He held that post under George VI and Elizabeth II until his death. In 1943 he published his autobiography *Farewell, my Youth*. Ten years later he was appointed KCVO. He died in Cork, in the same year, on 3 October 1953.

BAYLIS, LILIAN MARY (1874-1937), theatrical manager, was born in London on 9 May 1874, the eldest daughter of Edward William Baylis, a singer, and his wife, Elizabeth Cons, who was also a singer and a pianist. She was trained at an early age as a violinist and appeared in public at the

Lilian Baylis (carrying flowers) with the Vic queue in the 1920s

age of seven at the 'Royal Victoria Coffee Music Hall' (the Old Vic), managed by her aunt, Emma Cons.

In 1890 the Baylis family emigrated to South Africa, and for some years Liliantaught music in Johannesburg; but, in 1898, her aunt persuaded her to return to London to assist her in the management of the Royal Victoria Hall. When Emma Cons died in 1912 Lilian Baylis became sole manager of the Old Vic. During her aunt's time this had been a philanthropic temperance venture, but now it was intended to raise the standards of entertainment to be staged there.

The First World War made it possible for the 'Old Vic' to become 'the home of Shakespeare': actors and actresses at that time were eager to belong to a Shakespearean company for modest salaries but with some security of employment. Between 1914 and 1923 all the Shakespeare plays were produced there under Lilian Baylis's management.

In 1931 the Sadler's Wells Theatre in Islington was acquired and rebuilt and, while drama had a home at the Old Vic in south London, opera and ballet now found a home in north London. In spite of inadequate resources which gave Lilian Baylis the reputation of being a hard taskmaster, she was able to inspire great personal loyalty and affection in those who worked for her, and was able to keep her two theatres going by reason of her single-minded devotion to her work, her industry, and determination never to give in, however serious the difficulties she had to face.

She was appointed CH in 1929 and received honorary degrees from Oxford and Birmingham. She died at Stockwell on 25 November 1937.

BEARSTED, first VISCOUNT (1853–1927). See SAMUEL, MARCUS.

BEATON, SIR CECIL WALTER HARDY (1904–1980),

photographer and designer, was born in London on 14 January 1904, the son of Ernest Walter Hardy Beaton, and his wife, Etty Sisson. He was educated at Harrow and St John's College, Cambridge, and whilst at Cambridge rented his first photographic studio and came to the notice of *Vogue* with a photograph of George Rylands as he appeared in *The Duchess of Malfi*. During the twenties, Beaton gradually established himself as a society photographer, helped by his friendship with the Sitwells.

In 1929 he went to America, made photographs of many beautiful women, including Marlene Dietrich, Gloria Swanson, and Mrs Patrick CAMPBELL, and obtained a contract from Condé Nast. In 1930 he held an exhibition of his work at the Cooling Gallery in London for which Osbert SITWELL wrote the introduction. He also published the first of his many books, *The Book of Beauty* (1930). His techniques, particularly that of photographing beautiful women among ruins, began to be copied by other photographers. He became a friend of Mrs Simpson and did a number of studies of her for Edward VIII (1935–6).

During the Second World War he worked for the Ministry of Information, photographing the devastation caused in London by the bombing, and illustrated James Pope-Hennessy's book *History under Fire*. After the war, Beaton was engaged on the design of costumes and scenery for opera, ballets, stage plays, and films in London and New York including *Anna Karenina* (1948), *Gigi* (1958), *Turandot* (1961), and *La Traviata* (1966). He made a name for himself in this field with the film, *My Fair Lady* (1963).

He continued to publish accounts of his work, including *Photobiography* (1951), *Persona Grata* (with Kenneth Tynan, 1954), and *The Best of Beaton* (1968). His one play *The Gainsborough Girls* (1951) was not a success. He was appointed CBE in 1957 and knighted in 1972. He never

Cecil Beaton, by himself

married. He died on 18 January 1980 at Broadchalke, near Salisbury. He had the unique honour of an exhibition of his photographs at the National Portrait Gallery in 1968.

BEATTY, SIR (ALFRED) CHESTER (1875-1968), mining engineer, art collector, and philanthropist, was born on 7 February 1875 in New York, the youngest son of John Cuming Beatty, a banker, and his wife, Hetty, daughter of William Gedney Bull. He was educated at Westminster School, Dobbs Ferry, New York, Columbia University (School of Mines), and Princeton. When he was twenty-eight, he became consulting engineer and Assistant General Manager of the Guggenheim Exploration Company, and helped to develop silver mines in Mexico, copper mines in the USA, and concessions in the Belgian Congo (Zaire).

He married first, in 1900, Grace Madeline, daughter of Alfred Rickard, a mining engineer, of Denver, Colorado; they had a son and a daughter. She died in 1911 and, in 1913, he married Edith, daughter of John Dunn of New York.

In 1913 Beatty settled in England and founded Selection Trust Ltd. responsible, after the First World War, for developing mines in Siberia, West Africa, Serbia, and Northern Rhodesia (Zambia). He had a genius for deciding where to look for minerals, though he personally did not visit the countries in which his geologists and engineers were pros-

pecting, and he acquired valuable concessions in almost every part of the world.

He became a British subject in 1933, and during the Second World War gave valuable service to the British Government in the field of mining. He retired in 1950 and went to live in Dublin.

For many years between the wars he had spent much time in the Middle and Near East and had collected Indian and Persian miniatures, manuscripts and early Bibles; he also acquired the earliest known copy of the *Rubáiyát* of Omar Khayyam. Later, he turned to collecting pictures, rare books, and *objets d'art* from France and Russia. He donated a large collection of Impressionist paintings to the National Gallery in Dublin, and in 1955 handed over a thirteenth-century *Book of Hours* to the Irish nation.

His philanthropic interest was concentrated mainly on cancer research. He created the Chester Beatty Research Institute, which later became the Institute of Cancer Research: Royal Cancer Hospital, London. He received many honours, from those countries in which his firm had developed mineral resources (most of which, in due course, were nationalized). In 1954 he was knighted, and became the first honorary citizen of the Irish Republic.

BEATTY, DAVID, first EARL BEATTY (1871-1936), Admiral of the Fleet, was born at Stapeley, near Nantwich, on

17 January 1871, the second son of Captain David Longfield Beatty, 4th Hussars, and his first wife, Katherine Edith, daughter of Nicholas Sadleir, of Dunboyne Castle, Co. Meath. The Beattys were of old Irish stock and devoted to hunting and training horses.

Set on a career at sea from an early age, at thirteen, Beatty gained entrance to the training ship, *Britannia* and two years later in 1886 was posted to the *Alexandra*, flagship of Prince Alfred, Duke of Edinburgh, Commander-in-Chief of the Mediterranean Fleet. He spent most of the next ten to twelve years in that area, but in 1896 was selected by (Sir) Stanley Colville, commander of the battleship *Trafalgar* to be second-in-command of a small force of gunboats to support KITCHENER's expedition for the recovery of the Sudan. His daring in this campaign was highly praised by Kitchener and he was appointed DSO. In the following year he was again in action on the Nile and commanded a rocket battery ashore at the Battle of Atbara. For these services he was specially promoted commander in 1898.

In 1899 Beatty again joined Colville on the China station in the battleship *Barfleur*. He was wounded in a Boxer ambush, but succeeded in extricating Sir Edward Seymour, the British Commander-in-Chief, from Hsiku where he was completely surrounded by Boxer rebels. In 1900 he was promoted captain at the age of twenty-nine. A year later, he married Ethel, only daughter of Marshall Field of Chicago; they had two sons. During the next ten years he commanded in cruisers and in the battleship *Queen*, and in 1910 was promoted rear-admiral, the youngest flag officer for over a hundred years.

When Winston CHURCHILL became First Lord of the Admiralty in 1911 he selected Beatty to be his Naval Secretary. They were well suited to each other, and in 1913 Beatty was appointed to command the battle-cruiser squadron and, when war broke out in 1914, he was in command of the scouting forces of the Grand Fleet, based at Scapa Flow, under Sir John JELLICOE. The loss of three cruisers in the early months of the war caused Beatty to urge upon Churchill the necessity of equipping Cromarty and Rosyth as operational bases, nearer to the scene of action than Scapa Flow. This was done by the end of 1914.

In the interim, Beatty had made a successful incursion into the Heligoland Bight and thus inhibited the German navy from taking advantage of the position in which the Grand Fleet was placed during the early days of the war. Towards the end of 1914 there were signs that the Germans intended to carry out a tip-and-run raid on the east coast, but Beatty's battle-cruiser squadron was unable, owing to bad weather, to prevent the bombardment of Scarborough, Whitby, and Hartlepool. However, in the following month, Beatty was able to intercept Admiral Hipper near the Dogger Bank. The German battle-cruiser *Seydlitz* was severely damaged and the *Blücher* destroyed, but Beatty's flagship *Lion* was disabled, and, owing to misinterpretation of his signals to the rest of his squadron, the main German force escaped.

In December 1915 Beatty became vice-admiral, and in early summer in the new year he left Rosyth with six battle-cruisers and the fifth battle squadron to join Jellicoe and the Grand Fleet in an attempt to bring the German High Sea Fleet to battle. On the afternoon of 31 May Beatty sighted the German battle-cruisers and reported their position to Jellicoe; a fierce battle followed in which the *Lion*, Beatty's flagship, was repeatedly hit and the *Indefatigable* and the *Queen Mary* blew up. At this point, the main High Sea Fleet was sighted and Beatty retreated northwards hoping to lead

them into the course of the British Grand Fleet. By the evening the main battle fleets were in action but, owing to bad visibility and some misreading of Beatty's signals, the German ships under Admiral Scheer, though they had suffered heavy losses, were able to return to their base under cover of darkness. In this Battle of Jutland Beatty had carried out his part with conspicuous success.

At the end of 1916 Jellicoe became First Sea Lord, and Beatty, at the age of forty-five, was appointed, with the acting rank of admiral, to command the Grand Fleet. He immediately set to work to enforce the lessons of Jutland. He changed 'Battle Orders' so as to encourage senior officers to use their own initiative in putting into effect the general intentions of the Commander-in-Chief, and improved the methods of communication. His main preoccupation, however, was the submarine war, and he organized his own effective convoy system. When the United States entered the war, he worked in harmony with the American admirals. In November 1918 he accepted the surrender of the German High Sea Fleet in the Firth of Forth, and in the following year he became Admiral of the Fleet.

From 1919 to 1927 Beatty was First Sea Lord, a period which spanned the Washington Conference (1921) at which it was agreed that the British fleet and the United States fleet should in principle be on a par. Beatty was anxious, however, that British naval strength should be maintained, and he strongly defended the need for a base at Singapore. He also fought successfully to have control of the Fleet Air Arm transferred to the Admiralty. He played a leading part in the inauguration of the Chiefs of Staffs Committee, and retired in July 1927, not only with the admiration and goodwill of the Navy, but with the congratulations of the Government and the public on a magnificent job, carried out during a period of exceptional difficulty.

His loyalty and devotion to his wartime colleagues were demonstrated when Jellicoe died in 1935. Beatty, against medical advice, rose from a sick-bed to attend the funeral. Four months later, he himself died in London on 11 March 1936, and was buried in St Paul's Cathedral.

His long list of honours include MVO (1905), CB (1911), KCB (1914), KCVO and GCB (1916), GCVO (1917), and OM (1919). He was raised to the peerage as Earl Beatty in 1919 and sworn of the Privy Council in 1927. Throughout hi $naval career he faced ill-informed criticism in silence, and his reputation for courage and daring was matched by his careful judgement and clarity of decision. He was a great sailor in the tradition of Nelson and Rodney.

BEAVERBROOK, first BARON (1879-1964). See AITKEN.

BEECHAM, SIR THOMAS (1879-1961), conductor, was born on 29 April 1879 at St Helens, Lancashire, the elder son of (Sir) Joseph Beecham, a chemist, and his wife, Josephine Burnett. His grandfather, Thomas, had made a fortune from his well-known digestive pills. Beecham was interested in music from an early age; he was educated at Rossall School and Wadham College, Oxford, but went down in 1898 without taking a degree.

His first chance to conduct came somewhat fortuitously, at the age of twenty, when the Hallé orchestra, visiting St Helens, found itself without a conductor. Possibly helped by family influence, Beecham stepped into the breach and led the orchestra through an almost unrehearsed concert.

In 1901 he married Utica ('Utie') Celestia, the daughter of an American diplomat, Charles Stuart Welles of New

York. There were two sons of the marriage, but Beecham and his wife soon separated although they were not finally divorced until 1943. He also had a number of liaisons including a long-standing relationship with Lady Cunard.

After Oxford, he lived in London studying composition and touring with a small opera company as one of its conductors. His ambition, however, was to become a concert pianist but this was thwarted by an injury to his wrist in 1904 and he then concentrated on conducting. At the end of 1905, he gave his first public performance in London with the Queen's Hall Orchestra, and shortly afterwards founded the New Symphony Orchestra (1906–7). He formed a friendship with Frederick DELIUS with whose music his name will always be associated.

In 1910 Beecham mounted his first opera season at Covent Garden, with many works on a grand scale and previously unknown in Britain. They included works of Wagner, Richard Strauss, and Debussy. This enterprise was far too expensive to be a financial success but Beecham had the generous backing of his father. In the following year he presented Diaghilev's Russian ballet, with Nijinsky and, in 1913, presented Chaliapin in a season of Russian opera.

During the First World War Beecham strove to keep music alive and toured his small opera company throughout the country. In 1916 he was knighted, and also succeeded to his father's baronetcy. By 1920, an extravagant opera season at Covent Garden had left him nearly bankrupt and for the next few years he was almost absent from the musical scene. However, in 1929, he presented the first Delius Festival in London, and in 1932, with help from Courtaulds, founded the London Philharmonic Orchestra. Up to the outbreak of the Second World War he presented many excellent concerts with this orchestra, including some in Nazi Germany. From 1939 to 1944 he travelled extensively in the USA and Australia, and his reputation as a wit and raconteur grew as rapidly as his competence as a conductor.

In 1943, he married Betty Thomas, a pianist, who was the daughter of Daniel Morgan Humby, a London surgeon. After his return to London in 1944 he formed the Royal Philharmonic Orchestra, which from 1946 was to be the orchestra with which he had the most lasting association. Between 1950 and 1957 he conducted extensively in London, Paris, and the United States, and his flamboyant conducting and quick wit became widely known throughout the musical world.

His publications include an account of his early years *A Mingled Chime* (1944) and a biography of Frederick Delius (1958). He was made CH in 1957 but the receipt of this honour was clouded by the death of his wife. Two years later he married his personal secretary, Shirley Hudson. In 1960 he was taken ill in the United States and forced to return to London where he died on 8 March 1961.

BEERBOHM, SIR HENRY MAXIMILIAN (MAX) (1872–1956), author and cartoonist, was born in London on 24 August 1872, the youngest child of Julius Ewald Beerbohm, a corn merchant, of a Baltic family, and his second wife, Eliza Draper. (Sir) Herbert Beerbohm TREE was his half-brother. He was educated at Charterhouse and Merton College, Oxford. By the time he left Oxford in 1895 Beerbohm was already celebrated as a gifted, precocious, dandy with a flair as a cartoonist. In 1893 he had met William ROTHENSTEIN, who introduced him to the literary and aesthetic group in London which included Aubrey Beardsley and Oscar Wilde.

Max Beerbohm, *c.* 1943

Beerbohm contributed 'A Defence of Cosmetics' to the first number of the *Yellow Book* in 1894, and other articles to various other periodicals and papers including the *Savoy* and the *Daily Mail*. In 1898 he succeeded Bernard SHAW as drama critic for the *Saturday Review*, a post which he retained until 1910. He was much in demand in the fashionable circles of London as a charming and witty conversationalist. *The Works of Max Beerbohm*, a volume of essays, appeared in 1896, followed by *The Happy Hypocrite* (1897), *More* (1899), and three volumes of drawings produced between 1896 and 1907.

His love affairs ran a peculiarly erratic course, and after engagements to more than one actress, including Constance Collier, he eventually married, in 1910, an American, Florence Kahn, noted for her performances in Ibsen's plays. Together they retired to Rapallo which was to be Beerbohm's main home for the rest of his life. There were no children.

Max continued to draw and to write. His best known works include *Zuleika Dobson* (1911) and *Seven Men* (1919). His drawings were published in a number of volumes, including *A Survey* (1921) and *Heroes and Heroines of Bitter Sweet* (1931). A selection of his dramatic criticisms *Around Theatres* (2 vols.) was published in 1924.

He returned to England from Italy during both world wars, and in 1935 his wife made a return to the stage in *Peer Gynt* at the Old Vic. He also took to broadcasting and was a great success, some of his broadcasts being published in *Mainly on the Air* (1946).

He was knighted in 1939 and made an honorary D. Litt. (Oxford) and an honorary Fellow of Merton College in 1942.

Florence Beerbohm died in 1951, and in 1956 he married Elisabeth Jungmann. He died on 20 May 1956 in Rapallo and his ashes were placed in the crypt of St Paul's Cathedral.

BELL, (ARTHUR) CLIVE HEWARD (1881–1964). See BELL, VANESSA.

BELL, GERTRUDE MARGARET LOWTHIAN (1868–1926), traveller, archaeologist, and civil servant, was born at Washington Hall, co. Durham, on 14 July 1868, the elder child of (Sir) Thomas Hugh Bell, ironmaster, and his first wife, Mary, daughter of John Shield of Newcastle. She was

Gertrude Bell outside her tent at Babylon, 1909

educated at Queen's College, London, and Lady Margaret Hall, Oxford, where she obtained a first in modern history, the first woman to achieve this distinction (1888).

During the next ten years she travelled widely, learned Persian, and became a notable Alpinist. Then, in 1905, she travelled through Syria and Cilicia to Konia in Asia Minor and described this journey in *The Desert and the Sown* (1907). She was already a competent archaeologist, and she now explored the Hittite and Byzantine site at Bin-bir-Kilisse, near Isaura, with Sir W. M. Ramsay. Then, in 1909 and 1911 she explored Ukhaidir, a ruined early Islamic palace, near Kerbela, and published *The Palace and Mosque of Ukhaidir* (1914).

She had always wanted to journey into central Arabia, and set out for this purpose from Damascus in 1913; but the country was too unsettled and she got no further than Hail. By this time she had obtained a unique knowledge of north Arabian personalities and politics, and this was to prove invaluable during the First World War. In 1915 she was appointed to the Arab Intelligence Bureau in Cairo and in 1916 transferred to the military intelligence staff at Basra, where her Arab friendships were valuable in maintaining good relations with the desert tribes. When Sir Percy Cox became Civil Commissioner in Baghdad in 1917 she became Oriental Secretary, and in 1920 prepared a masterly White Paper, a *Review of the Civil Administration of Mesopotamia*.

In 1920–1 she exercised great influence both with Sir Percy Cox, now British High Commissioner in Mesopotamia, and the Emir Faisal, King of Iraq. Meanwhile she continued her interest in antiquities and helped to inaugurate the national museum at Baghdad (1923–6). On the night of 11–12 July 1926 she died in her sleep at Baghdad. Her *Letters* (2 vols.) were published posthumously in 1927. Col. T. E. LAWRENCE, who worked with her, having criticized her for changing direction 'like a weathercock' under the influence of the men with whom she served, wrote finally, 'She was a wonderful person.'

BELL, VANESSA (1879–1961), painter, was born in London on 30 May 1879, the eldest of the four children of (Sir) Leslie Stephen and his second wife, Julia Jackson, widow of Herbert Duckworth. She was educated at home with her sister Virginia (WOOLF) and from 1901–4 studied at the Royal Academy Schools, where she was particularly influenced by the teaching of John Singer Sargent. After the death of her father in 1904, she set up house in Bloomsbury with Virginia and their brothers, Thoby and Adrian. Around them gathered several of Thoby's Cambridge friends and others interested in art and literature, who came to be known as the Bloomsbury group. They included Lytton STRACHEY, John Maynard KEYNES, Desmond MacCarthy, Leonard WOOLF, who married Virginia, and Clive Bell, who married Vanessa. In 1906 Thoby Stephen died suddenly, but the group which he had brought into being by then had its own momentum.

CLIVE BELL, the art critic, was born on 16 September 1881, the son of a civil engineer, William Heward Bell, and his wife, Hannah Taylor Cory. He was educated at Marlborough and Trinity College, Cambridge, where he became friendly with Thoby Stephen. He studied art in Paris for a year after leaving university and married Vanessa Stephen in 1907. They had two sons, Julian and Quentin.

In 1910 Clive Bell met, by chance, the painter and art critic, Roger FRY and, together with Desmond MacCarthy, they searched Paris for suitable paintings for the First Post-Impressionist Exhibition, which was held in the Grafton

Galleries in London that autumn, and which caused a considerable sensation. Four of Vanessa's paintings were exhibited in the Second Post-Impressionist Exhibition in 1912. She collaborated with Fry in the Omega workshops, which he established in 1913. She was also associated with Duncan Grant in his work of mural decoration. Together they showed a close kinship with the decorative aspects of Matisse and were noted particularly for their bold use of colour. In the course of the First World War Vanessa moved away from abstract work to a more representational form and produced many paintings of still life, landscapes, and interiors with figures. She contributed regularly to group exhibitions and had the first exhibition of her own work at the Independent Gallery in 1922.

She and Duncan Grant had meanwhile become lovers, although he was a homosexual, and they lived with Clive in a curiously amicable *ménage à trois*. She and Grant had a daughter, Angelica, who was always known by the surname Bell.

Clive Bell contributed many articles to periodicals and in 1914 the book *Art* was published. Later, he produced *Landmarks in Nineteenth-Century Painting* (1927), *Proust* (1928), and *Enjoying Pictures* (1934). His greatest loves were the Byzantines and modern art post-Cézanne. His theory that appreciation of art is an emotional response to purely formal qualities was vigorously challenged by D. H. LAWRENCE in 1929.

The death of Roger Fry in 1934 was a great blow to Vanessa. Three years later came an even greater disaster when her son Julian was killed in the Spanish Civil War. In 1941 Virginia committed suicide. In spite of these calamities, Vanessa continued to paint throughout the Second World War and for the rest of her life. Painting was her life. Of her children, Angelica Bell married the writer David Garnett and Quentin Bell became a professor of fine art. Vanessa Bell died on 7 April 1961 at Charleston, the farmhouse in East Sussex where she had lived with Duncan Grant for over forty years; Clive Bell died in London just over three years later, on 17 September 1964.

BELLOC, (JOSEPH) HILAIRE PIERRE RENÉ (1870-1953), poet and author, was born at St Cloud, near Paris on 27 July 1870, the son of Louis Belloc, and his wife, Bessie Rayner, daughter of Joseph Parkes, a Birmingham unitarian and historian of the Chancery Bar. Louis Belloc came of a family engaged in the West Indian sugar trade; his mother was Irish. He died in 1872, and his wife brought her son and daughter (who became later the authoress Mrs Belloc Lowndes) to London. The family settled in Sussex.

Belloc was educated at the Oratory School, Birmingham and, after travelling in France and the USA, entered Balliol College, Oxford, where he obtained a first in history in 1895 and was President of the Union. He was disappointed in his hope of becoming an Oxford don but, having married Elodie Agnes, daughter of Joseph Smethwick Hogan, of California, in 1896, he stayed in Oxford, taking pupils and writing books. These included *The Bad Child's Book of Beasts* (1898).

In 1897 he contributed 'The Liberal Tradition' to *Essays in Liberalism* and opposed the Boer War in articles in the *Speaker*, a liberal weekly. In 1899 he left Oxford for London, where he met G. K. CHESTERTON and his brother Cecil; together, in the columns of the *Daily News*, they made biting, satirical attacks upon the Edwardian Establishment. In 1902 he became a naturalized British subject. Meanwhile he was publishing a number of books including *Danton* (1899),

Robespierre (1901), and *The Path to Rome* (1902), and some novels. From 1906 to 1910 he was Literary Editor of the *Morning Post*, and during the same period was Liberal MP for South Salford.

He refused to stand in the second 1910 election because he had become disillusioned with British politics and, in collaboration with Cecil Chesterton, published *The Party System* (1911) which he described as corrupt collusion. In that year he founded his own paper, *Eye-Witness*, which published disclosures regarding the Marconi scandal, implicating some Liberal ministers, including LLOYD GEORGE, who had bought shares in the American Marconi company when the Post Office was awarding a contract to the English company. After a year he handed over his journal to Cecil Chesterton.

Belloc accepted many publishers' commissions, including an American one to complete Lingard's *History of England*; this he carried from 1689 to 1910 (1915). Throughout the First World War he contributed military commentary to *Land and Water*, and in 1915-16 was Lees Knowles lecturer in military history at Trinity College, Cambridge.

Belloc's wife had died in 1914 and his eldest son was killed in the war. He never fully recovered from these blows, but he had two other sons and two daughters to educate, and he went on writing indefatigably, producing *Europe and the Faith* in 1920, and many other books and articles proclaiming and defending the cause of Roman Catholicism, which brought him into controversy with H. G. WELLS, Dean INGE, and the Cambridge historian, Dr Coulton.

The Cruise of the 'Nona' (1925) gave a guarded account of his personal life, but Belloc clearly regarded writing as an unsatisfactory trade and wished to be remembered primarily for his poetry, such as *An Heroic Poem in Praise of Wine* (1932). In his later years he lectured for money in the USA. He had become an honorary LL D Glasgow in 1920, but refused a similar honour from Balliol College, and declined the CH in 1943. In 1941 his youngest son died while serving with the Royal Marines. Belloc himself died in Guildford on 17 July 1953 having been in ill health for some twelve years.

BENN, SIR ERNEST JOHN PICKSTONE, second baronet (1875-1954), publisher and economist, was born on 25 June 1875 at Hackney, London, the elder son of (Sir) John Williams Benn, publisher and Liberal MP, and his wife, Elizabeth, daughter of John Pickstone of Hyde, Cheshire. He was educated at the Lycée Condorcet, Paris, and at the Central Foundation School, London. Then, in 1891 he joined his father's firm, Benn Brothers Ltd., publishers of trade papers. Twelve years later, in 1903, he married Gwendoline Dorothy, daughter of Frederick May Andrews, of Edgbaston; they had three sons and two daughters. During the 1914-18 war he worked in government service in Whitehall and at that time he advocated co-operation between government and business; he was appointed CBE in 1918. However, after the war his views quickly changed and he became a convinced and belligerent individualist.

In 1922 he succeeded his father in the business, but a year later he set up his own book publishing company, Ernest Benn Ltd. He soon became a pioneer in the trade, introducing the Augustan poets and Benn's Sixpenny Library, small volumes on a variety of subjects, forerunners of the paperback. At the same time he interested himself in a number of charitable organizations, and in 1932 became High Sheriff of the County of London.

In 1925 he published the *Confessions of a Capitalist*, his

philosophy being that of a strict Victorian exponent of *laissez-faire*. In 1926, with Sir Hugh Bell, he founded the Individualist Bookshop. During the next twenty-five years, he wrote a succession of books and pamphlets in defence of personal liberty and in opposition to state-planned economy and bureaucratic controls. He took a leading part in founding in 1942 the Society of Individualists. Although he was sounded out by both Liberals and Conservatives he refused to become a candidate for Parliament. He died at Oxted, Surrey, on 17 January 1954.

BENN, WILLIAM WEDGWOOD, first VISCOUNT STANSGATE (1877-1960), politician, was born on 10 May 1877 at Hackney, London, the younger son of (Sir) John Williams Benn, publisher. Ernest BENN was his elder brother. He was educated at the Lycée Condorcet, Paris, and at University College, London, where he obtained a first in French in 1898. After working for a few years in the family publishing business, he became a lifelong radical, being elected Liberal MP for St George's in 1906, a seat which his father had held, and which he held until 1918.

From 1910 to 1914 he was a Junior Lord of the Treasury. Then, in the First World War he fought at Gallipoli with the Middlesex Yeomanry, and in the Royal Naval Air Service. For his war service he was appointed DSO, and awarded the DFC and the Croix de Guerre.

In 1920 he married Margaret Eadie, daughter of Daniel Turner Holmes, Liberal MP for Goran. They had four sons of whom the youngest died at birth.

In 1918 he had been returned as MP for Leith; but, as a devoted supporter of ASQUITH, he became increasingly out of sympathy with LLOYD GEORGE and finally applied for membership of the Labour party in 1927 and resigned his seat. He returned a year later as Labour MP for North Aberdeen, a seat which he held until 1931. From 1929 to 1931 he was Secretary of State for India, with a seat in the Cabinet, and was sworn of the Privy Council. While holding that office he authorized the Viceroy to announce that the legitimate goal of India's hopes was dominion status. Nevertheless, when GANDHI launched his civil disobedience campaign in 1930, Benn ordered his arrest.

Benn refused to join Ramsay MACDONALD's National Government and lost his seat in the Commons. He was out of the House until 1937 when he was returned as Labour member for the Gorton division of Manchester. On the outbreak of the Second World War, he joined the RAF and rose to the rank of air commodore. In 1942 he was raised to the peerage as first Viscount Stansgate. Two years later his eldest son was killed in action. In ATTLEE's Government of 1945 he became Secretary of State for Air; he resigned in 1946, and in 1947 became President of the Inter-Parliamentary Union, a position which he held for the next ten years. He continued to take an active part in debates in the House of Lords where his skills as a parliamentarian were much in evidence. He was taken ill in the Palace of Westminster and died on 17 November 1960.

Benn's second son, Anthony Neil Wedgwood, succeeded his father but, after a long legal struggle, was able to renounce the peerage in 1963, and take his seat in the Commons as Labour MP for Bristol. He was a Minister in the Labour Government of 1964. An outspoken exponent of policies on the far left of the Labour Movement, in 1981 he stood against Denis Healey for the deputy leadership of the party, but was defeated.

BENNETT, (ENOCH) ARNOLD (1867-1931), novelist, playwright, and man of letters, was born on 27 May 1867 at Hanley, Staffordshire, the eldest child of Enoch Bennett, a solicitor, and his wife, Sarah Ann, daughter of Robert Longson, a Derbyshire weaver. He was educated at Burslem Endowed School and the Middle School, Newcastle under Lyme, and also attended a local art school where he learned to paint water-colours. In 1885 he entered his father's office to study law. His family were strict Wesleyan Methodists; they were also musical and artistic and widely read.

When he was twenty-one, Bennett became clerk to a London firm of solicitors, but he was already trying himself out in local journalism and writing sensational novels. He was encouraged by the acceptance of a short story in the *Yellow Book* in 1895 to write *A Man from the North*, which was accepted by John Lane and published in 1898. In 1893 he had become Assistant Editor of *Woman*, a weekly journal and, from 1896 to 1900, he was Editor. He also wrote articles and reviews for the *Academy*.

Then came the first of the novels which made his reputation as an author, *Anna of the Five Towns*, published in 1902 and followed at once by *The Grand Babylon Hotel*. That year he went to live in Paris, but continued to subscribe industriously to British periodicals, including *T.P.'s Weekly*, articles which were later published in book form. In 1908 the appearance of *The Old Wives' Tale* made his name, and put him in the forefront of contemporary novelists with WELLS and GALSWORTHY. This novel was followed by two further successes, *Clayhanger* (1910) and *The Card* (1911). *Hilda Lessways* (1911) and *These Twain* (1916) completed

Arnold Bennett, 1907, from a sketch by Frederick Marriott

the *Clayhanger* trilogy, recounting the turbulent relations between Edwin Clayhanger and Hilda in the background of the Five Towns; these are probably the novels upon which Bennett's lasting reputation as a novelist will be judged. *The Card*, an exuberant story of Denry Machin's rise from poverty to prosperity, followed by *The Regent* (1913), is a less serious picture of the Five Towns.

In 1912 Bennett returned to England, and during the First World War served under Lord BEAVERBROOK, Minister of Information, and wrote powerful articles describing conditions at the front which he visited in 1915. After the war he was able to associate with wealthy men and women, and with those in corridors of power—people whom he satirized in *The Pretty Lady* (1918) and *Lord Raingo* (1926).

In 1907 he had married, in Paris, a Frenchwoman, Marie Marguerite Soulié. They had no children, and they were legally separated in 1921. He then fell in love with an English actress, Dorothy Cheston. In 1926, she and Bennett had a daughter, Virginia. His wife refused to divorce him and Dorothy added Bennett to her name in 1925.

Bennett's plays, *What the Public Wants* (1909), *Milestones* (with Edward Knoblock, 1912), and *The Great Adventure* (1913) had been popularly received by the theatre world, and during the twenties he went into partnership with (Sir) Nigel Playfair and Alistair Tayler in the management of the Lyric Theatre, Hammersmith. He continued to write articles for the press including a weekly literary *causerie* for the *Evening Standard*.

Early in 1931 Bennett contracted typhoid fever, from which he died on 27 March in London. His vast output of articles and books, showing his remarkable versatility, was inevitably uneven in its achievement, but his personal knowledge of life in the Potteries and his ability to describe it vividly and with humour, made a lasting impression upon the English novel.

BENSON, SIR FRANCIS ROBERT (FRANK) (1858–1939), actor-manager, was born at Tunbridge Wells, on 4 November 1858, the third son of William Benson, barrister, and his wife, Elizabeth Soulsby, daughter of Thomas Smith, of Colebrooke Park, Tonbridge. He was educated at Winchester and New College, Oxford, and was one of the founders of the movement which led to the creation in 1884 of the Oxford University Dramatic Society. After acting in private performances, he made his first appearance on the professional stage at the Lyceum Theatre in 1882.

In 1883, Benson became a member of Walter Bentley's Shakespearian company and took over the company when Bentley was in financial difficulties. Soon he had established a sound reputation and his company had become an important influence in the provincial theatre. In 1886 the company was invited to provide the Shakespearian festival at Stratford-on-Avon. Later that year he married Gertrude Constance, daughter of Captain Morshead Fetherstonhaugh Samwell, of the Indian Army. They had a son and a daughter. Gertrude Benson played parts in the company for many years. During the next thirty-three years Benson provided the plays for twenty-eight spring festivals and six summer seasons, in the course of which he presented all Shakespeare's plays except two. He received the freedom of the borough in 1910.

He presented a succession of theatrical seasons at London theatres from 1889 till 1933. He also toured in Canada, the USA, and South Africa. At one time three of his companies were touring Britain simultaneously. At the Shakespeare tercentenary performance at Drury Lane on 2 May 1916, he appeared in the title role of *Julius Caesar* and, after the performance, was knighted by King George V in the royal box. The sword which the King used had come from the 'props.' cupboard.

From 1916 to 1918, although he was nearly sixty, Benson served in France as an ambulance-driver and received the Croix de Guerre. His only son had been killed in action in France in 1916. He made his last stage appearance in London in 1933. Benson died in London on 31 December 1939. He was not a great actor but he was successful in gathering together many capable young actors and actresses who achieved greater fame than he did. His company became the training school for the English stage and, through his efforts, Shakespeare's plays became known throughout the world.

BENTLEY, EDMUND CLERIHEW (1875–1956), writer, journalist, and inventor of the 'clerihew', was born in London on 10 July 1875, the eldest son of John Edmund Bentley, a civil servant, and his wife, Margaret Richardson Clerihew. He was educated at St Paul's School and Merton College, Oxford, where he was President of the Union in 1898. His greatest disappointment was his failure to get a first in history. In 1902 he was called to the Bar (Inner Temple), but he did not practise as a barrister.

While still at school in a science class he thought of the following:

Sir Humphrey Davy
Abominated gravy.
He lived in the odium
Of having discovered Sodium.

This was the first of the clerihews.

Bentley had written regularly for the *Isis* and the *JCR* whilst at Oxford; while studying for his Bar exams he wrote light verse for *Punch*, and by 1900 was a regular contributor to the *Speaker*. In 1901 he decided to be a journalist rather than a lawyer, and joined the staff of the *Daily News*. In 1902 he married Violet Alice Mary, daughter of General Neil Edmonstone Boileau. They had one daughter and two sons, of whom, Nicolas, the younger son, illustrated his father's and many other books. In due course, Bentley became Deputy Editor of the *Daily News* under A. G. Gardiner but, when the paper was amalgamated with the *Morning Leader* in 1912, he joined the *Daily Telegraph* and remained there for the next twenty-two years.

Biography for Beginners by E. Clerihew, illustrated by G. K. CHESTERTON, was published in 1905. Then, after a long interval, came *More Biography* in 1929, and *Baseless Biography* with illustrations by Nicolas Bentley (1939), and *Clerihews Complete* (1951). Bentley also wrote an outstanding detective novel, *Trent's Last Case*, published in 1913 and, after he had returned to the *Daily Telegraph* when the Second World War started, he published *Those Days* (1940). Bentley died in London on 30 March 1956.

BERRY, (JAMES) GOMER, first VISCOUNT KEMSLEY (1883–1968), and his brother **WILLIAM EWERT BERRY**, first VISCOUNT CAMROSE (1879–1954), newspaper proprietors, were born at Merthyr Tydfil on 7 May 1883 and 23 June 1879 respectively, the sons of Alderman John Mathias Berry, an estate agent, and his wife, Mary Ann, daughter of Thomas Rowe, of Pembroke Dock. They were both educated at Merthyr Tydfil and both served their apprenticeship on the *Merthyr Tydfil Times*.

William went to London in 1898 and, after working as a

reporter, launched his own paper, the *Advertising World*, with borrowed money, in 1901. In the following year he was joined by Gomer and the two began a partnership which lasted amicably until 1937. In 1905 they sold the *Advertising World* profitably and bought a publishing business from which they launched a number of periodicals, including *Boxing*.

In 1905 William Berry married Mary Agnes, eldest daughter of Thomas Corns of Bolton St., London; they had four sons and four daughters. Gomer Berry, in 1907, married Mary Lilian, daughter of Horace George Holmes of Brondesbury Park, London. They, too, had a large family of six sons and a daughter.

In 1915 the brothers purchased the *Sunday Times*, and in 1919 the St Clement's Press together with its daily, the *Financial Times*. Other important acquisitions were the Weldon's Group, Kelly's Directories, and the *Graphic* publications. In 1924 they founded Allied Newspapers (later Kemsley Newspapers), which they controlled in partnership with Sir Edward (later Lord) Iliffe, and acquired most of the Hulton papers from Lord ROTHERMERE, including the *Daily Dispatch*, the *Manchester Evening Chronicle*, and the *Sunday Chronicle*. Later, they bought a number of provincial newspapers, together with the *Daily Sketch* and the *Illustrated Sunday Herald*, but their biggest purchase was made in 1926 when they bought the Amalgamated Press from the executors of Lord NORTHCLIFFE.

In 1927 they completed the establishment of this enormous publishing business by purchasing the *Daily Telegraph* from Lord BURNHAM. The brothers now controlled two national and six provincial morning papers, eight provincial evening papers, eight provincial weeklies, and some seventy periodicals. In 1937 they decided to split the large family holding. William retained the *Daily Telegraph*, which in that year had absorbed the *Morning Post*, together with the Amalgamated Press and the *Financial Times*. For a few weeks in 1939, he was controller of press relations in the Ministry of Information. Although a convinced Conservative, he could not support Neville CHAMBERLAIN in his Munich policy; he firmly supported CHURCHILL, of whom he was a close friend. Having become a baron as Lord Camrose in 1929, he was created a viscount in 1941.

Meanwhile, Gomer who had been created Baron Kemsley in 1936, became Chairman of Allied Newspapers, which owned the *Daily Sketch* (later *Daily Graphic*), *Sunday Graphic*, the *Sunday Times*, and a number of provincial papers. He was now the largest newspaper proprietor in Britain. His main interest was in the *Sunday Times* of which he greatly increased the circulation. He staunchly supported the Conservative Government, whether it was headed by Neville Chamberlain, Winston Churchill, or Anthony EDEN. From time to time, he found it necessary to fight libel actions against critics in the Labour party and elsewhere, who accused him of running a gutter press. Throughout the fifties he gradually ran down his empire. In 1952 he sold the *Daily Graphic* to Lord Rothermere. In 1955 he missed a golden opportunity to obtain a footing in commercial television. Finally, in 1959 he sold the whole family share-holding to Roy H. Thompson (later Lord Thompson of Fleet). He was the last of the self-made newspaper barons. In 1945 he became a viscount and he was appointed GBE in 1959. His first wife had died in 1928, and in 1931 he had married Edith, daughter of E. N. Merandon du Plessis of Constance, Flacq, Mauritius. She was appointed OBE in 1953 and was a Commander of the Legion of Honour.

Lord Camrose died in Southampton on 15 June 1954 and was succeeded by his eldest son, John Seymour, who also became Deputy Chairman of the *Daily Telegraph*, while another son, Michael, was its Editor-in-Chief. Lord Kemsley died in Monte Carlo fourteen years later on 6 February 1968. He was succeeded by his eldest son (Geoffrey) Lionel, who had been Deputy Chairman of Kemsley Newspapers Ltd. from 1938 to 1959.

BESANT, ANNIE (1847-1933), theosophist, educationalist, and Indian politician, was born in London on 10 October 1847, the only daughter of William Persse Wood, a business man, and his wife, Emily Mary Roche Morris, who was of Irish descent. Annie was educated by Miss Marryat, a sister of Captain Frederick Marryat RN, the novelist. In 1867 she married Frank Besant, who later became Vicar of Sibsey in Lincolnshire until his death in 1917; they had one son and one daughter. Annie lost her Christian faith, left Sibsey in 1873, and was legally separated from her husband.

In 1874 she joined the National Secular Society and became a close friend of Charles Bradlaugh, the advocate of free thought; she published the *Gospel of Atheism* in 1877 and, in consequence, was deprived by the courts of the custody of her daughter (although both daughter and son returned to her later). She joined the Fabian Society in 1885, and organized the matchmakers' strike and formed their trade union in 1888. Gradually, however, she drifted apart from Bradlaugh and was converted to theosophy.

In 1893 Mrs Besant visited India and soon came to believe that she had often been incarnated in that sacred land. From 1895 onwards, she devoted her energies to reconciling theosophy with the ancient Hindu religion. In 1899, with help from the Maharaja of Benares, she founded the Central Hindu College, and later, in 1904, established a girls' school; these institutions became the nucleus of a Hindu university set up in 1916. Since 1895 she had been an enthusiastic member of the Theosophical Society and was its President from 1907 to 1933; but her standing in the theosophical world was somewhat prejudiced in 1909 by her extraordinary claim that her adopted son, a Madrasi named Krishnamurti, had been revealed to her as a Messiah.

For many years she had advocated the cause of the Indian National Congress which had been founded in 1885. She initiated the Home Rule for India League in 1916 at the height of the First World War, and was interned by the Madras Government on a charge of inflaming racial feeling. When, however, the British Government announced a year later that responsible government would be granted to India by stages, she was released. She was elected President of Congress in 1918, but lost her influence with the more extreme element among Indian politicians when she condemned the violent tactics that had led to the riots and consequent Amritsar tragedy in 1919. She took a stand against revolution and was rejected as President of her own Home Rule League in favour of GANDHI. For a time she retired from Indian politics, but in 1925 she brought a Commonwealth of India Bill to England, where it was twice introduced to the House of Commons and obtained the active support of the Labour party.

In 1931 her health failed and she died at Adyar in India on 20 September 1933 and was cremated by the sea-shore. For a time she had exercised considerable influence on the growth of nationalist feeling in India, but her impact on Indian politics was short-lived because of her opposition to violence at a critical time.

BEVAN, ANEURIN (1897-1960), politician, was born on 15 November 1897 in Tredegar, Monmouthshire, the sixth of ten children of David Bevan, a miner, and his wife, Phoebe, daughter of John Prothero, a blacksmith. He went to the local elementary school, where he was a rebellious pupil, and at thirteen went into the coal-pit. He became an expert both as a miner and as a trouble-maker. By 1916 he was Chairman of his Lodge, unfit for military service, but also violently opposed to the 1914-18 war. In 1919 he was sent to the Central Labour College in London for two years but, on return to Tredegar, found himself unemployed and his family in distress.

In 1926 he became disputes agent for his Lodge, a paid

'Nye' Bevan with Jennie Lee, on his way to the Commons to deliver his resignation speech, 23 April 1951

post, and during that year, which was disastrous for the miners, became recognized as an efficient organizer and a fiery orator. He now saw clearly that only through the Labour party in Parliament could the misery in the coalfields be redressed.

In 1929 he became Labour MP for Ebbw Vale, a seat which he held until his death. His reputation as a stormy petrel, always vehement, sometimes ill-tempered, soon aroused opposition, not only in the House, but in his own party. In 1934 he married Jennie Lee (later Baroness Lee), herself the daughter of a miner and a staunch left-wing member of the party; they had no children. In 1939 he was expelled from the Labour party for a short time but, when readmitted, he continued to support Sir Stafford CRIPPS and from 1942 to 1945 was Editor of the *Tribune*. Throughout the Second World War he opposed the Government and, after coming into conflict with Ernest BEVIN, was in danger of expulsion from the party again.

However, in 1944, he was elected to the national executive, appointed Minister of Health and Housing in the 1945 Labour Government, and became a Privy Counsellor. The passage of the National Health Service Act of 1946 and the painstaking negotiations with doctors and dentists leading to the introduction of the Health Service in 1948 were Bevan's greatest achievements. He was, however, still a problem for the leaders of his party, and his virulent speeches at times did more harm than good.

In January 1951 he moved to the Ministry of Labour, but resigned a few months later, having come into conflict with Hugh GAITSKELL, Chancellor of the Exchequer. The immediate issue was the introduction of charges into the Health Service, but the conflict between the two men was rooted in a fundamental difference in concept of the party. For the rest of his life Bevan was in opposition. He set out his creed in *In Place of Fear* (1952), and 'Bevanism' became the philosophy of the group he led on the left of the movement. In December 1955 he failed to secure the Labour leadership, though winning more votes than Herbert MORRISON. As a member of Gaitskell's Shadow Cabinet, however, Bevan became somewhat more moderate in his attitudes, and was elected deputy leader (1959). His speeches had now become less aggressive, and he was regarded as the best speaker in the House, after CHURCHILL. He died at Chesham on 6 July 1960, and with his death much of the colour went out of politics. He was an indomitable fighter for his beliefs.

BEVERIDGE, WILLIAM HENRY, first BARON BEVERIDGE (1879-1963), social reformer and economist, was born at Rangpur, Bengal, on 5 March 1879, the elder son of Henry Beveridge, an Indian civil servant, and his wife, Annette Susannah Ackroyd, daughter of a Worcestershire business man. He was educated at Charterhouse and Balliol College, Oxford, where he obtained firsts in Mathematical Mods., Classical Mods., and Greats (1898-1901). He then studied law and became BCL in 1903, but decided against the law in favour of social science.

That year he accepted the post of sub-warden at Toynbee Hall, London, and soon came into contact with progressives of all parties. His particular interest was in unemployment, and in 1905 he became leader-writer to the *Morning Post* on social problems. He wrote numerous articles advocating labour exchanges and social insurance, and in 1908 became personal assistant to Winston CHURCHILL at the Board of Trade. In 1909 he published *Unemployment: a Problem of Industry*.

During the First World War he was transferred to the Ministry of Munitions where he came into conflict with the trade unions as the drafter of legislation severely restricting collective bargaining . Then he moved to the Ministry of Food of which in 1919 he became Permanent Secretary and was appointed KCB. But that year he resigned from the Civil Service to become Director of the London School of Economics.

He remained in that post until 1937, and during that time was successful in raising large sums for the LSE and in enhancing its status. As Vice-Chancellor of London University (1926-8), he was largely responsible for the funding of the new Bloomsbury site. He was not, however, on good terms with his colleagues and was regarded as high-handed, so that when he moved to be Master of University College, Oxford, in 1937, his departure was not regretted. In the same year he was elected FBA.

His main preoccupation continued to be the study of unemployment and the history of prices, and when the Second World War broke out he hoped to be put in control of civilian manpower. In 1940 Ernest BEVIN, Minister of Labour, commissioned him to make a survey of manpower requirements, but Bevin had no intention of allowing him to control the manpower programme. In consequence, Beveridge was diverted into the chairmanship of a committee to look into the co-ordination of the Social Services, at the time regarded as a matter of little importance.

Although he was not entirely aware of it, Beveridge had been provided with the opportunity to carry out the most important task of his career. His two reports *Social Insurance and Allied Services* (1942) and *Full Employment in a Free Society* (1944) together represented the 'Beveridge plan', and became best sellers which eventually formed the basis of the post-war Welfare State. The first of these reports was ready for publication in October but, owing to various difficulties, was not published till December. In the meantime Alamein had been fought and won and the new possibility of victory enhanced the welcome for a post-war peace programme.

In 1942 he married his cousin, the widowed Jessy Mair who had been Academic Secretary at the LSE and his intimate for years. There were no children. She died in 1954.

In 1944 Beveridge resigned from University College and was elected Liberal MP for Berwick-upon-Tweed. In 1945, however, he lost his seat and became a Liberal peer. He continued to write. A memoir of his parents *India Called Them* (1947) was followed by *Voluntary Action* (1948) and *Power and Influence* (1953). He himself always regarded *Prices and Wages in England from the Twelfth to the Nineteenth Century* (vol 1, 1939) as his greatest contribution to the study of social problems. He received many academic honours both from British universities and from abroad. Beveridge died on 16 March 1963 in Oxford.

BEVIN, ERNEST (1881-1951), trade-union leader and politician, was born on 7 March 1881 at Winsford on the edge of Exmoor, the illegitimate son of Mercy Bevin, a village midwife. She died when he was eight years old and he never knew who his father was. For a time he lived with his half-sister Mary and attended school in Crediton; but when he was eleven he went to work as a farm boy. He did not take kindly to farm-life, and, between the ages of thirteen and twenty, he lived in Bristol where some ten years earlier Ramsay MacDonald had worked. Bevin had a succession of jobs, kitchen boy, van boy, page boy, and conductor on a horse-drawn tram. Then, in 1901, he became a van driver

with a mineral water firm, and in the comparative security of this employment he married Florence Anne Townley, the daughter of a wine taster at a Bristol wine merchants; they had one daughter.

At this time he was a member of a Baptist chapel and attended discussion and study classes. He even considered the possibility of becoming a minister. But gradually his interests turned from religion to politics: he joined the Bristol Socialist Society and became a keen speaker and organizer. In 1908 he was active in the Right to Work movement which had grown up as a result of mounting unemployment. Two years later, there was a strike in Bristol docks and attempts were made to use the carters and van drivers to load and unload ships. The Dockers' Union appealed to Bevin for help, and a carmen's branch of the union was formed with Ernest Bevin as Chairman; in 1911 he became a full-time official of the Dockers' Union. He had set out on his long and outstanding career in the trades-union movement. By 1913 he had become an assistant national organizer, and, in 1914, one of the union's three national organizers. From the outset he felt strongly the need for centralized authority and the vital importance of having the support of the rank and file in all decisions. He speedily developed great ability as a negotiator, and, although he could be dogmatic, obstinate, and uncompromising, he was also a realist who would prefer to reach agreement rather than provoke confrontation and strife.

During the First World War he had no patience with the pacifism of the politicians of the Independent Labour party, but took an active part in the efforts that were being made to secure the efficient use of manpower. In 1915, for the first time, he represented his union at the Trades Union Congress; and in 1915-16, he went abroad for the first time as a fraternal delegate to the annual convention of the American Federation of Labor. After the war, in 1920, he was appointed Assistant General Secretary to the union, and became a national figure as the 'Dockers' KC' when he persuaded the members of his union to submit their claim for sixteen shillings a day to a court of inquiry under the new Industrial Courts Act. He won their case for them by his powerful arguments which completely demolished those of the experts commissioned by the employers.

He was already working towards the consolidation of the numerous unions representing the transport workers, into one strong organization, and on 1 January 1922 fourteen unions with a membership of 300,000 were merged into the Transport and General Workers' Union with Bevin as its General Secretary. By 1923 the number of unions absorbed had risen to 22, and by 1926 had increased to 27. The failure of the general strike in that year taught him, if the lesson was necessary, that the best hope for improvement of the wages and conditions of working people lay in negotiation from strength rather than in industrial conflict. He had been a member of the general council of the TUC since 1925 and now set himself the task of changing the whole climate of industrial relations. He was also branching out in other directions; he travelled abroad to the ILO conference and to other international conferences. Together with J. M. KEYNES, he was a member of the Macmillan committee on finance and currency and thus acquired a knowledge of international finance and a distrust of the attitude of international bankers to industry and employment. He was a member of the Economic Advisory Council and of the TUC economic committee, and was instrumental in converting the *Daily Herald* into a successful popular newspaper, representing the cause of the trades unions.

In 1936-7 he was Chairman of the TUC and, by now, was recognized as one of the most powerful of Labour leaders. He was quick to see the threat to peace from Nazi Germany and strenuously opposed pacifism in the Labour party and urged at conference after conference the urgent need for rearmament. He was no longer simply concerned with industrial strife; he was by this time very actively concerned with politics. From 1940 to 1950 he was Labour MP for Central Wandsworth, and in 1950-1 member for East Woolwich. With the advent of CHURCHILL to power in the wartime Government of 1940, Bevin was appointed Minister of Labour and National Service and sworn of the Privy Council; thus began the second phase of his remarkable career. He assumed responsibility for all manpower and labour matters and it seems unlikely that the work he did in mobilizing the manpower and the industrial resources of the country could have been done so efficiently by any other man. As a member of the War Cabinet he carried out a vast redeployment of industrial workers with the minimum of discontent and trouble. He achieved this by methods similar to those he had employed as a trade-union leader. Before embarking on such necessary changes as the training of unskilled workers, including women, for jobs previously reserved for skilled men, he sought the agreement of both sides of industry, by establishing, among other consultative arrangements, a Labour Supply Board, to see that working people could be made available wherever they were most needed for the production of war materials. By the middle of 1943 more than three and a quarter million workers had been transferred from less essential industries to those of importance to the war effort.

In May 1945 Churchill, with whom Bevin had much in common, offered him the CH as a reward for his services, but Bevin declined the honour saying that he had merely been doing his job. During the latter part of the war he gave as much time as he could spare to post-war problems of reconstruction and welfare, and when the Labour party came to power in 1945 he would have liked to become Chancellor of the Exchequer and to have been given the opportunity of putting into effect some of his ideas for making the Treasury a positive contributor to economic recovery. In the event,

Ernest Bevin on a tour of the blitzed Humberside, May 1941

ATTLEE invited him to become Foreign Secretary. At first sight, this might appear to be an incongruous decision, but the new Prime Minister, like Churchill, was fully aware that the greatest danger to reconstruction and stability in Europe came from Soviet Russia. He remembered that in 1918 Bevin had led the Council of Action, which successfully prevented the supply of arms to Poland for use against the revolutionary armies in Russia. If, however, he hoped that the Soviet leaders in 1945 would be grateful for Bevin's earlier efforts on behalf of their Bolshevik predecessors, he was soon disabused of this idea, and the Foreign Secretary speedily realized that the Soviets saw in European disorder the best means of achieving their own expansionist ambitions.

In view of Russia's refusal to co-operate in the reconstruction of Europe, Bevin found that his main task was to contain Soviet expansion until the United States could be persuaded to recognize the danger and commit herself to the political and ideological struggle. It was Bevin's influence that persuaded Attlee to give the go-ahead for the manufacture of a British nuclear bomb. He was the first to realize the importance of a speech in which General Marshall offered the European nations economic aid for reconstruction. It was primarily his immediate response to this proposal that led to its practical translation into 'Marshall Aid'. It was Ernest Bevin who set in motion the machinery for co-operation with Britain's continental neighbours which led, in 1947, to the creation of the Organization for European Economic Co-operation; and as he strove to convince the Americans that Britain alone could not be responsible for holding Communist pressure, his efforts finally culminated in the North Atlantic Treaty and the establishment of NATO in 1949.

Inevitably, Bevin made mistakes and had his failures. He tried hard, but without success, to reconcile Jews and Arabs in Palestine, and in the end handed this intractable problem over to the United Nations and withdrew the British administration. But taking his career at the Foreign Office as a whole, and taking account of the difficulties with which he had to contend, there can be little doubt that he proved to be one of the greatest Foreign Secretaries in the history of that office. His officials had enormous respect for his strength of mind and determination. They knew him to be the strong man of the Attlee Government, having a powerful voice in all important decisions, a tower of strength and loyalty in a time of intrigue and dissension.

By 1951, his health was rapidly declining and, within a month of leaving the Foreign Office, he died in London on 14 April 1951. He was buried in Westminster Abbey. This remarkable man who had received little formal education died an honorary Fellow of Magdalen College, Oxford, and the recipient of honorary degrees from Cambridge and Bristol. By sheer strength of character he had made his mark in three widely different fields.

BIRKENHEAD, first EARL OF (1872–1930). See SMITH, FREDERICK EDWIN.

BIRKETT, (WILLIAM) NORMAN, first BARON BIRKETT (1883–1962), barrister and judge, was born at Ulverston, Lancashire, on 6 September 1883, the fourth child of Thomas Birkett, a draper, and his first wife, Agnes, daughter of Moses Tyson, a butcher. He went to school in Ulverston and Barrow, and at thirteen worked in his father's shop, and studied for the Wesleyan ministry. In 1907 he went to Emmanuel College, Cambridge, where he became President of the Union.

He decided to switch from theology to law, and in 1913 was called to the Bar (Inner Temple). He started work in Birmingham where, being medically unfit for army service, he achieved success at the local Bar for the next few years. In 1920 he moved to London and entered the chambers of Sir Edward MARSHALL HALL, acquiring the services as clerk of Edgar Bowker. In the same year Birkett married Ruth, daughter of Emil Nilsson of Sweden; they had a son and a daughter.

Birkett was made KC in 1924, and up to the Second World War made a large income and a famous name, being concerned with many notable cases including those of Clarence Hatry (1930), Maundy Gregory (1933), and the murderers, Rouse (1931), Mancini (1934), and Dr Ruxton (1936). In 1941 he was knighted for services connected with war emergency powers of detention, and became a judge of the King's Bench.

In 1945, he was appointed alternate judge at the Nuremberg war criminals trial, and in 1947 was sworn of the Privy Council. He became a judge of the Court of Appeal in 1950 and six years later retired from the Bench. In 1958 he went to the House of Lords.

During his retirement, he pursued his personal interests, cricket, literature, the City of London, and the preservation of the countryside. He excelled in broadcasting and television, and in 1958 became President of the Pilgrims. He was awarded many academic honours. He died in London on 10 February 1962 two days after making a speech in the Lords opposing a private bill which might have threatened the beauty of Ullswater.

BLACKETT, PATRICK MAYNARD STUART, BARON BLACKETT (1897–1974), physicist, was born on 18 November 1897, the son of a stockbroker, Arthur Stuart Blackett. He entered Osborne and Dartmouth and joined the Royal Navy in 1914 serving at the Battle of the Falkland Islands when he was sixteen and at Jutland at eighteen. When the First World War ended he was sent on a course to Magdalene College, Cambridge, and decided to leave the navy to pursue an academic career. In 1923 he became a Fellow of King's College, Cambridge; he was already working at the Cavendish Laboratory under Sir Ernest RUTHERFORD and had become a friend of Kingsley MARTIN with whose left-wing politics he sympathized. In 1924 he married Constanza Bayon; they had one son and one daughter.

From 1933 to 1937 he was Professor of Physics at Birkbeck College, London, but, whilst at Cambridge, he had made his first great contribution to science by his discovery of the positive electron. He was elected FRS in 1933. In the years before the Second World War his research was mainly directed to the investigation of cosmic rays, and in 1936 Sir Henry TIZARD arranged for him to be a member of the Air Defence Committee. During the war he was scientific adviser to the Anti-Aircraft Command and from 1942 to 1945 Director of Operational Research at the Admiralty.

After the war he took up his post as Langworthy Professor of Physics at Manchester to which he had been appointed in 1937, and continued his work on cosmic rays. In 1948 he was awarded the Nobel prize for physics, and during 1950–2 was Pro-Vice-Chancellor of Manchester University. In 1948 he published his first book on the *Military and Political Consequences of Atomic Energy*, which he followed up in 1956 with *Atomic Weapons and East-West Relations*.

In 1953, Blackett was appointed Professor of Physics at the Imperial College of Science and Technology, London, a post which he held until 1965. From 1961 to 1964 he was

Lord Blackett, bronze by Epstein

Pro-Rector. He was now doing research work on rock-magnetism. For some years he had been advising the Labour party on scientific and technological problems and, when Harold Wilson became leader of the party, Blackett's influence became an important factor in Labour policy and led in due course to the creation of the Ministry of Technology. From 1949 to 1964 he was a member of the Board of the National Research Development Corporation and during those years was closely concerned with many similar organizations dealing with technological developments. He was President of the British Association in 1957–8.

In 1965 he became a CH and in 1967 was appointed OM. In 1965 he was elected President of the Royal Society, and four years later was created a life peer. He also received a large number of academic honours. Blackett died on 13 July 1974.

BLAIR, ERIC ARTHUR (1903–1950). See ORWELL, GEORGE.

BLISS, SIR ARTHUR EDWARD DRUMMOND (1891–1975), composer and Master of the Queen's Music, was born in London on 2 August 1891, the eldest of the three sons of Francis Edward Bliss, an American business man resident in Britain, and his second wife, Agnes Kennard, daughter of James Davis, a Nonconformist minister of Great Yarmouth; she died when Arthur was four years of age. He was educated at Rugby and Pembroke College, Cambridge, where he took his BA and Mus. Bac. in 1913.

For a short time he studied at the Royal College of Music under Sir Charles STANFORD and was tutored by VAUGHAN WILLIAMS and Gustav HOLST; but, soon after the First World War broke out, he enlisted in the army and served with the Royal Fusiliers and the Grenadier Guards on the Western Front and was twice wounded and gassed.

Among his first compositions were *Madam Noy* (1918), *Rhapsody* (1919), and *Rout* (1920), and in the following year he wrote the incidental music for *The Tempest*, produced by Viola Tree at the Aldwych Theatre in London. In 1921 he also composed his large orchestral piece *Mélée Fantasque*, followed in 1922 by *A Colour Symphony*, a commission, secured for him by ELGAR, for the Three Choirs Festival.

From 1923 to 1925 Bliss lived in the USA and in the latter year married Gertrude ('Trudy'), daughter of Ralph Hoffmann, Director of the Natural History Museum at Santa Barbara, California; they had two daughters. After returning to London Bliss composed *Introduction and Allegro for Orchestra* (1926) and *Hymn to Apollo* (1927). Between 1927 and 1933 he also wrote three pieces of chamber music, the Oboe Quintet, the Clarinet Quintet, and the Viola Sonata, together with the symphony, *Morning Heroes* (1930), a combination of chorus, speech, and orchestra composed in memory of his brother Kennard and other comrades killed in the war.

In 1936 Bliss began his work in films by composing the music for H. G. WELLS's *Things to Come*, produced by Alexander KORDA, and in the following year (1937) wrote the music for *Checkmate*, the first of four ballets.

In 1939 Bliss and his family returned to the USA for the first performance of his Piano Concerto and, while he was visiting professor at the University of California, Berkeley, he composed the *Seven American Poems* and his First String Quartet. But Bliss felt bound to return to England to help in the war effort and from 1942 to 1944 he was Director of Music for the BBC, and the ideas which he put forward in that post led eventually to the creation of the Third Programme.

After the war Bliss composed the music for the opera *The Olympians* (with libretto by J. B. Priestley), produced at Covent Garden in 1949. He continued to write a wide variety of other music, including the Violin Concerto and the *Meditations on a Theme of John Blow* (1955). He also composed further music for films and the ballet, and in 1960 wrote the music for *Tobias and the Angel*, with libretto by Christopher Hassall, which was produced for television. Between 1961 and 1974 he composed five cantatas, including *The Beatitudes*, his contribution to the opening ceremony of the new Coventry Cathedral (1962).

Bliss had been appointed Master of the Queen's Music in 1953, and from 1954 he was President of the Performing Right Society. He had been knighted in 1950, and was appointed KCVO in 1969 and CH in 1971. He received many honorary degrees and other awards from the musical world. In 1970 he published his autobiography, *As I Remember*.

Altogether Bliss composed over 150 works, the last of which, *Shield of Faith*, a cantata written for the quincentenary of St George's Chapel, Windsor, he did not live to hear performed. He died in London on 27 March 1975.

In 1982 the Performing Right Society established in his honour an annual postgraduate scholarship in composition.

BLUNDEN, EDMUND CHARLES (1896-1974), poet, teacher, and critic, was born in London on 1 November 1896, the eldest child of Charles Edmund Blunden, a teacher, and his wife, Georgina, also a teacher, daughter of Henry Tyler, secretary to Sir Ralph Verney. He was educated at Christ's Hospital and, after service with the Royal Sussex Regiment (1916-19) in France and Belgium, went to the Queen's College, Oxford, with a scholarship. In 1916 he was awarded the MC. In 1918 he married Mary Daines; they had a son and two daughters.

From 1924 to 1927 he was Professor of English Literature at Tokyo Imperial University. On return to England he wrote for the *Nation* and the *Times Literary Supplement*. From 1931 to 1943 he was a Fellow and tutor of Merton College, Oxford. His first marriage had ended in divorce and in 1933 he married Sylvia Norman. This marriage also ended in divorce, and in 1945 he married Claire Margaret, daughter of John Whitfield Elford Poynting, retired Indian civil servant; they had four daughters. Having spent the years of the Second World War as an instructor in the Oxford University Senior Training Corps, he returned to Tokyo as a lecturer with the UK liaison mission there (1947-50). Then, in 1953, he became a Professor at Hong Kong University, where he stayed for the next decade until he retired to Long Melford in Suffolk in 1964. From 1966 to 1968 he was Professor of Poetry at Oxford.

Blunden was publishing poetry from 1914 till 1965. In 1922 he won the Hawthornden prize for *The Shepherd* which followed *The Waggoner* (1920). His *English Poems* appeared in 1925, followed by other volumes, including *Poems 1914-30* (1930), *Poems 1930-40* (1940), *A Hong Kong House, Poems 1951-1961* (1962), and *Eleven Poems* (1965). The subjects of Blunden's poetry are the celebration of nature, warnings against war, and man's experience of God, love, and time. His inspiration was drawn from the eighteenth century rather than from his own contemporaries.

Like his friend, Siegfried SASSOON, Blunden loathed the chaos and destruction of war, and in *Undertones of War* (1928), his prose description of his war experiences, to which a series of poems was appended, he condemned the inhumanity of the conflict and the devastation it caused. His other prose work was mainly biographical and critical. His first biography *Leigh Hunt* was published in 1930. That was followed by *Charles Lamb and his Contemporaries* (1933) and biographies of Thomas HARDY (1942) and Shelley (1946). He also edited the works of John Clare, Keats, and Wilfred OWEN.

Blunden received many academic awards and prizes. He was appointed CBE (1951) and a Companion of Literature (1962). He was an honorary Litt. D. of Leeds and Leicester. Blunden died at Long Melford on 20 January 1974.

BLUNT, LADY ANNE (1837-1917). See BLUNT, WILFRID SCAWEN.

BLUNT, WILFRID SCAWEN (1840-1922), traveller, politician, and poet, was born at Petworth House on 17 August 1840, the second son of Francis Scawen Blunt, of the Grenadier Guards, of Crabbet Park, Sussex, and his wife, Mary, daughter of the Revd John Flutter Chandler. He was educated at Stonyhurst and Oscott, and entered the Diplomatic Service in 1858, and up to 1869 held a succession of posts in Europe and Latin America.

In 1869 Blunt married LADY ANNE ISABELLA NOEL, only daughter of William, first Earl of Lovelace, and

his first wife, the Hon. Ada Augusta Byron, the only child of Lord Byron. She was born in London on 22 September 1837. In 1872 Blunt inherited the Crabbet estates, and he and his wife set out to travel in the Middle East. They travelled as far as Hail, in the Nedj, and then to Baghdad. At Hail the Emir presented them with brood mares which became the nucleus of the stud they later formed at Crabbet Park.

During the next few years the Blunts also travelled to India and, as a result of what he saw there, Blunt became vehemently anti-imperialist. He published his views in *Ideas about India* (1885), having three years earlier published *The Future of Islam* and denounced the work of Sir Evelyn BARING, and the British occupation of Egypt. When, however, in 1887 he took up the cudgels on behalf of Irish nationalism, he was sent to prison for two months.

His love affairs were no less passionate than his politics. Before his marriage he had a number of affairs, including one with Catherine Walters, the notorious courtesan, 'Skittles', recalled in his poem *Esther* (1892). After his marriage, he continued to philander, and for some years he and Anne lived apart. She was a woman of great character, a fearless horse-woman, a competent musician, and famous among the Arabs for her knowledge of Arabic and the ways of the Bedouin. She published two knowledgeable books, *The Bedouin Tribes of the Euphrates* (2 vols., 1879), and *A Pilgrimage to Nedj* (2 vols., 1881).

Blunt will be remembered for his lyrics and sonnets which W. B. YEATS thought to have an Elizabethan ring. His poetry also had some influence on a younger generation. Among his best-known works are *The Love Sonnets of Proteus* (1880). A collected edition of *Poems* appeared in 1914.

Blunt was a brilliant conversationalist and an agreeable host, and he gathered together as guests at Crabbet Park a diverse coterie of friends, including George Wyndham, Lord CURZON, Oscar Wilde, Lord Alfred Douglas and young poets, such as W. B. Yeats.

Lady Anne Blunt died at Cairo on 15 December 1917, having a few months earlier become Baroness Wentworth. Blunt died at Southwater, Sussex, on 10 September 1922. They had one daughter, Judith Anne Dorothea, who succeeded her mother as Baroness Wentworth.

BONAR LAW, ANDREW (1858-1923), politician and Prime Minister, was born on 16 September 1858, at Kingston, New Brunswick, Canada, youngest son of the Revd James Law, Presbyterian minister, an Ulsterman, and his wife Elizabeth, daughter of William Kidston, a Glasgow iron-merchant. His early childhood was overshadowed by the death of his mother when he was two and the depressions which plagued his father. When he was eleven, Andrew was brought by an aunt to Scotland and educated at Glasgow High School. At sixteen he entered the merchant banking firm of his Kidston relatives and was able to visit the Continent and to learn French and German. He also took over his relatives' Conservative opinions.

In 1885 he joined the Glasgow firm of William Jacks & Co., iron-merchants, and among other business appointments became a director of the Clydesdale Bank. He also received two lucrative legacies from his Kidston aunts. In 1891 he married Annie Pitcairn, daughter of Harrington Robley, of Glasgow; they had four sons and two daughters.

In 1900 he was elected Unionist MP for the Blackfriars and Hutcheson-town division of Glasgow, and in 1902 was appointed Parliamentary Secretary to the Board of Trade. In the following year Joseph Chamberlain launched his scheme of tariff reform and split the Conservative party, which was defeated in the 1905 election. Bonar Law supported tariff reform in alliance with Austen CHAMBERLAIN and, although defeated in 1905, was re-elected as MP for Dulwich in 1906.

Bonar Law was now the most earnest and capable exponent of the views of Joseph Chamberlain, and in 1909 denounced LLOYD GEORGE's 'People's Budget' as 'pure and unadulterated' socialism. At the first 1910 election Bonar Law was returned again for Dulwich but, in the second election of that year, he stood for North-West Manchester and lost. He returned to the House in 1911 as MP for the Bootle division of Lancashire. The Conservatives were still at loggerheads over tariff reform and their different attitudes to ASQUITH's Parliament Bill. Bonar Law supported his leader, Arthur BALFOUR in his decision to accept the *fait accompli* of the Parliament Bill and, when on 8 November 1911 Balfour resigned, Bonar Law was elected Conservative leader, his senior colleagues Walter (later Viscount) Long and Austen Chamberlain accepting him as a compromise selection.

Bonar Law was a close friend of Max AITKEN, who boosted his confidence, particularly after the blow of his wife's death in 1909. During 1911–12 he made some bitter speeches contesting Home Rule for Ireland and advocating tariff reform. In co-operation with Sir Edward CARSON, he succeeded in continually delaying the Home Rule bills and was prepared to sanction unconstitutional means, if necessary, to continue the fight. He took part in the conference at Buckingham Palace in the middle of 1914, which failed to reach agreement on compromise proposals to exclude Ulster from the jurisdiction of Dublin. The Home Rule Bill was passed in September 1914 without the proposed amending bill, which was postponed; and although Bonar Law thought he had been betrayed by Asquith, he offered the Government Unionist co-operation for the conduct of the First World War.

On the resignation of Lord FISHER from the Admiralty over policy in the Dardanelles in 1915, Bonar Law advocated a Coalition Government and, when Asquith agreed, he accepted the post of Colonial Secretary. Later that year, he led the group pressing for the evacuation of the Dardanelles and in 1916, when Asquith resigned, George V invited Bonar Law to become Prime Minister. He, however, advised the King to call upon Lloyd George, and in the new coalition became Chancellor of the Exchequer.

As a loyal supporter of Lloyd George, Bonar Law at the Treasury demonstrated his ability as a financier by successfully issuing a series of war loans and campaigning for national war bonds. In his budgets of 1917–18 he made heavy demands on the public, which were accepted because they coincided with some of the most desperate situations of the war and people realized that there was no effective alternative. During this time, he also suffered the double blow of losing two of his sons, killed on active service.

After the armistice, Bonar Law accepted the continuance of coalition as the only means of ensuring peace abroad and preventing revolution at home. He agreed to the 'coupon' principle of support for coalition candidates at the 1918 election and was himself elected for Central Glasgow. He became Lord Privy Seal and leader of the Commons, and acted as Prime Minister while Lloyd George was attending the peace conferences. He and Lloyd George agreed that Ulster could not be coerced into union with the south, and in 1919 Bonar Law supported a bill to give a parliament to Northern Ireland. He was not, however, a member of

the Government which concluded the Irish Treaty in 1921, since, earlier that year, his health had broken down and he had been forced to resign from leadership of his party.

In 1922 the Chanak crisis convinced the Conservatives that the time to end the coalition had arrived, and at the famous Carlton Club meeting Bonar Law and Stanley BALD-WIN both argued in favour of a break with Lloyd George. In October, Lloyd George resigned, Bonar Law was re-elected Conservative leader in place of Austen Chamberlain and became Prime Minister in a Conservative Government, with a majority of seventy-seven at the ensuing general election.

Bonar Law could hardly have been expected to be a great success as Prime Minister. He was already a sick man and his party was deeply divided. His Cabinet, which contained six peers not including the Lord Chancellor, was the most aristocratic administration of the period. Austen Chamberlain, Balfour, and Lord BIRKENHEAD were not in the Government: they had not accepted the Carlton Club decisions. CHURCHILL called this administration 'a government of the second eleven'.

Bonar Law presided over a conference of Allied Prime Ministers to try to obtain agreement on the problem of reparations by Germany to the Allies. The British and French held markedly divergent views and the conference failed. The Prime Minister sent his Chancellor of the Exchequer, Stanley Baldwin, to the United States with instructions that Britain should only agree to pay her war debts to the extent to which she could recover what was owed to her. Baldwin, advised by Montagu NORMAN, Governor of the Bank of England, did not adhere to this principle, but agreed to terms which appeared to Bonar Law to be unduly harsh. The Prime Minister found himself overruled by his Cabinet colleagues, and reluctantly accepted the terms of the agreement in January 1923.

In May, he was stricken with incurable cancer and resigned. He died in London on 30 October 1923 and was buried in Westminster Abbey. By the time he became Prime Minister he was burnt out by his exertions in 1912–14 on behalf of Ulster and his work as Chancellor of the Exchequer during the war.

BONDFIELD, MARGARET GRACE (1873–1953), trade-union leader and first British woman Cabinet Minister, was born at Furnham, Somerset, the tenth of eleven children of William Bondfield, a lace worker, and his wife, Anne, daughter of George Taylor, a Wesleyan Methodist minister. After a short period of schooling, she taught in a boys' school at the age of thirteen, and at fourteen worked in a drapers' shop.

She joined the National Union of Shop Assistants and worked hard to collect information on the conditions in which shop-girls worked. She joined the Independent Labour party, and in 1898 became Assistant Secretary of her union. She was not a feminist and held out for full adult suffrage when many of her Labour colleagues were prepared to support a bill for limited female emancipation. She helped Mary Macarthur to establish the National Federation of Women Workers (1906), became Assistant Secretary in 1915, and in 1921, when the federation was amalgamated with the National Union of General and Municipal Workers, became the chief woman officer of that union.

She served on the executive of the ILP from 1913 until 1921, and in 1923 became the first woman Chairman of the TUC. That year she became Labour MP for Northampton. In 1924 she was appointed Parliamentary Secretary to the

Margaret Bondfield, the first woman chairman of the TUC, 1923

Ministry of Labour and also worked strenuously for the ILO. From 1926 to 1931 she was MP for Wallsend, and from 1929 to 1931 Minister of Labour, the first woman to be a member of the Cabinet and a Privy Counsellor. She refused to join the National Government of 1931 and lost her seat in the Commons in the subsequent election. From 1939 to 1949 she was Chairman of the Women's Group on Public Welfare, and during the Second World War lectured for the Government in Canada and the USA. Decisive and transparently honest, she could be a powerful speaker when her passions were aroused. She was appointed CH in 1948, and published her autobiography *A Life's Work* in 1949.

Margaret Bondfield died, unmarried, at Sanderstead on 16 June 1953.

BONHAM CARTER, (HELEN) VIOLET, BARONESS ASQUITH of YARNBURY (1887-1969), political figure, was born in London on 15 April 1887, the only daughter and fourth child of Herbert ASQUITH (later Earl of Oxford and Asquith) and his first wife, Helen Kelsall, daughter of Frederick Melland, a physician. Her mother died in 1891. Violet had no English schooling but was 'finished' in Dresden and Paris, and became fluent in German and French.

Her main interest was in public affairs, and she often said that she could not remember a time when she did not hear talk of politics. From an early age she supported her father in his political battles and became his most effective champion. She was also a close friend of Winston CHURCHILL, and in her later years published *Winston Churchill as I Knew Him* (1965). She never forgave LLOYD GEORGE for his treatment of her father.

In 1915 she married (Sir) Maurice Bonham Carter, her father's Principal Private Secretary; they had two sons and two daughters (one of whom married Joseph Grimond, who became leader of the Liberal party). She was never successful in becoming an MP, but in 1964 entered Parliament as a life peeress.

She was President of the Women's Liberal Federation from 1923 to 1925 and from 1939 to 1945, and in the latter year she became President of the Liberal Party Organization, the first woman to do so. Her political views, covering domestic as well as international affairs, were expressed with a combination of passion and clarity. She was an ardent advocate of the League of Nations, serving on its Executive from its foundation until 1941. She was in favour of the National Government in the financial crisis of 1931 and, with Churchill, was one of the earliest to recognize and to speak out against the threat posed by the Nazis.

Her public duties covered a very wide field. She was a Governor of the BBC (1940-6), Vice-Chairman, United Europe Movement (1947), President of the Royal Institute of International Affairs (1964-9), and a member of the Royal Commission on the Press (1947-9), a Governor of the Old Vic (1945), and a trustee of the Glyndebourne Arts Trust (1955). She was the first woman to give the Romanes lecture at Oxford in 1963 when she spoke of *The Impact of Personality on Politics*. She was appointed DBE in 1953. She never gave up fighting for the cause of Liberalism. She died in London on 19 February 1969.

BOOT, JESSE, first BARON TRENT (1850-1931), business man and philanthropist, was born in Nottingham on 2 June 1850, the only son of John Boot, a herbalist, and his second wife, Mary, daughter of Benjamin Wills, of Nottingham. Jesse Boot's grandfather was a farm labourer. His father died when Jesse was ten, and he left school at thirteen to take over his father's shop.

In his spare time he studied pharmacy, and in 1877 opened his first chemist's shop. Nine years later he married Florence Anne, daughter of William Rowe, of St Heliers, Jersey; they had one son and two daughters. In 1888 he turned his business into a limited liability company, and from that time, devoting all his energies to his work and seriously impairing his health as a result, he gradually built up one of the largest retail chemist's organizations in the world.

In 1892 Boot's began manufacturing its own drugs after building large factories in Nottingham. To the sale of drugs and medicines were added circulating libraries, restaurants, and departments offering a large variety of other articles for sale. During the First World War the firm supplied to the forces respirators and pills for the sterilization of water.

In 1920 Jesse Boot sold his Pure Drug Company to the United Drug Company of America; shortly afterwards he retired and his son took over as chairman of his remaining companies. From the early years of the century Boot had been crippled by a form of muscular dystrophy, but this had not deterred him from carrying on and expanding his business or from pursuing those interests that attracted his philanthropy. He made magnificent gifts to the town of Nottingham, including the new University College. In recognition of his munificence he was made a freeman of Nottingham in 1920. He had been knighted in 1909 and in 1929 he became Baron Trent. He owed much to his wife who had remarkable business acumen and was of great value to her husband as confidante and adviser.

Jesse Boot died on 13 June 1931 at Millbrook, Jersey and was succeeded as second baron by his son, John Campbell.

BOWEN, ELIZABETH DOROTHEA COLE (1899–1973), writer, was born on 7 June 1899 in Dublin, the only child of Henry Charles Cole Bowen, a barrister, of Bowen's Court, Kildorrery, Co. Cork, and his wife, Florence Isabella Pomeroy, daughter of Henry Fitz-George Colley of Dublin. She was educated at Harpenden Hall School, Herts., and Downe House, Kent. When she was thirteen her mother died, and she spent her school holidays with her father at their large Georgian house, Bowen's Court, which she later described in her novel, *The Last September* (1929).

In 1923 she married Alan Charles Cameron, Assistant Secretary for Education, Northants. He had won the MC in the First World War, and had been gassed, as a result of which his health was impaired. Elizabeth, from an early age, had a slight stutter. She had many close friends, and although her marriage was childless, it was a happy one.

Elizabeth's first novel *The Hotel* was published in 1927. At that time she and her husband were living in Oxford, and were friends of the Tweedsmuirs (Susan and John BUCHAN), Sir Isaiah Berlin, Lord David Cecil, and Sir Maurice BOWRA. Bowra considered that she had the right presence and authority to have been head of a women's college at Oxford or Cambridge; but she was a creative artist and her writing took up all her time.

In 1935 she published *The House in Paris*, followed by *The Death of the Heart* (1938), *Seven Winters* (1942) set in Dublin in the years before the First World War, and *The Heat of the Day* (1949), probably her finest novel, a tale of espionage in London during 1942–4. After the war she and her husband lived at Bowen's Court, which she had inherited on her father's death in 1930. Alan Cameron died there in 1952 and she was forced to sell the property, although she worked hard lecturing in the USA, and did a great deal of journalism.

Elizabeth Bowen published nearly thirty books including, in addition to the novels, short stories, travel books such as *A Time in Rome* (1960), criticism, and history. Her fame will rest on her novels, the last of which were *A World of Love* (1955), *The Little Girls* (1964), and *Eva Trout* (1969) which was awarded the James Tait Black memorial prize.

She was appointed CBE in 1948 and C.Lit. in 1965. She also received an honorary D.Litt. from Trinity College, Dublin, and from Oxford. She died in London on 22 February 1973.

BOWRA, SIR (CECIL) MAURICE (1898–1971), scholar and academic, was born on 8 April 1898 at Kiukiang, China, the second son of Cecil Arthur Verner Bowra, commissioner in the Chinese Customs Service. Owing to his parents' absence in China, he was brought up by his grandmother and her second husband, the Revd George Mackie. He was educated at Cheltenham College, and won a scholarship to New College, Oxford, but before going there he visited his father in China and went to Russia on the way home (1916). After one term at New College, he was commissioned in the Royal Artillery and fought in the third Battle of Ypres.

He returned to New College in 1919, obtained firsts in

Maurice Bowra at Wadham College, November 1950

Classical Mods. and Greats (1920–2) and was elected to a tutorial fellowship at Wadham College. As an undergraduate he was the leader of a post-war generation firmly opposed to pre-war conventions and critical of the Establishment. For the rest of his life Wadham and Oxford were his home, but he had many friends and contacts in the USA and on the Continent, as well as in Britain.

Bowra wrote some thirty books, and contributed to classical journals. His first book was a translation of Pindar's Pythian Odes (in collaboration with H. T. Wade-Gery, 1928). This was followed by *Tradition and Design in the Iliad* (1930), and other books on Greek literature and lyric poetry.

He was a Fellow and tutor of his college from 1922 to 1938, and in 1938 was elected Warden. His early visit to Russia gave him a lifelong interest in Russian poetry, and as well as Russian he could read French, German, Italian, and Spanish. He was in no sense a pedantic scholar; his interests extended from Pindar to Edith SITWELL and the contemporary young poets of his time. He was renowned as a wit and a conversationalist. His autobiographical *Memories 1898–1939*, published in 1966, gives an eminently readable account, not only of his many friendships, but of his own personality.

His books were not confined to classical scholarship; in 1943 he published *The Heritage of Symbolism*, a study of post-Symbolist poetry, which was followed by a number of books of literary criticism from *The Creative Experiment* (1949) to *Poetry and Politics 1900-1960* (1966). He had no more than a general interest in the world of politics, but his inclinations were radical, and he numbered Hugh GAITSKELL among his friends.

From 1946 to 1951 Bowra was Professor of Poetry at Oxford, and in 1951-4 served as Vice-Chancellor. He sat on the Hebdomadal Council, served the University Chest, and was a Delegate of the University Press. When he retired from the wardenship of Wadham in 1970 he became an honorary Fellow and was invited to continue to live in the College. He was elected FBA in 1938, knighted in 1951, and appointed CH in 1971. He never married. He died at Wadham College on 4 July 1971.

BOYD ORR, JOHN, first BARON BOYD ORR (1880-1971), nutrition expert, was born at Kilmaurs, Ayrshire, on 23 September 1880, a son of R.C. Orr, small property owner, and his wife, Annie Boyd. Like his two brothers, who became ministers, he was intended for the Free Church of Scotland, but while he was studying at Glasgow University he decided against becoming a minister, worked as a school teacher for four years, and then returned to the university to take a medical degree. During his training he was horrified by the malnutrition and disease he saw among slum children and, after research on metabolic disease, obtained his D.Sc.

During the First World War he served with the RAMC in France and won the MC (with bar) and the DSO. He then transferred to the navy and served in 'Q ships'. In 1915 he married Elizabeth Pearson, daughter of John Callum, of West Kilbride; they had two daughters and one son. When the war ended he returned to Edinburgh as Director of Animal Nutrition Research. His work was concerned with the improvement of nutritional standards in the feeding of farm animals, but he had no hesitation in extending his researches to the nutritional requirements of humans. For example, in East Africa, he had inquiries made into mineral deficiencies in the soil as it affected, not only the cattle, but the Masai herdsmen and the Kikuyu. In Scotland he experimented with the feeding of skimmed milk to the children of the unemployed.

In 1932 he was elected FRS, and in 1935 was knighted. In 1936 he published his survey *Food, Health and Income* which aroused concern both in Britain and in many other countries and led eventually to the establishment of the UN Food and Agriculture Organization. During the war, his only son was killed flying with Coastal Command. From 1942 to 1945 Boyd Orr was Professor of Agriculture at Aberdeen University, and in 1945-6 was elected independent MP for the Scottish Universities. He went as the Labour Government's technical adviser to the Quebec Conference in 1945 and was appointed first Director-General of the FAO. In 1946 he was Chancellor of Glasgow University and in 1949 was awarded the Nobel peace prize.

He resigned from his post as Director-General of the FAO in 1948, discouraged by the reluctance of governments to accept his advice. He became a peer in 1949 and received many academic honours. His peace prize was donated to organizations working for peace, and he departed on a world tour visiting the USSR, India, China, the Middle East, and Latin America. His retirement was spent at his farm in Angus. In 1968 he was appointed CH. He continued to publish books such as *Feast and Famine* (1960) and *As I recall* (1966).

Lord Boyd Orr died at his home near Brechin on 25 June 1971.

BRABAZON, JOHN THEODORE CUTHBERT MOORE-, first BARON BRABAZON of TARA (1884-1964), aviator and politician, was born in London on 8 February 1884, the younger son of Lt. Col. John Arthur Henry Moore-Brabazon, of Tara Hall, co. Meath, and his wife, Emma Sophia, daughter of Alfred Richards of Forest Hill. He was educated at Harrow and Trinity College, Cambridge, where he read engineering but did not take a degree.

When he left Cambridge he became an apprentice at the Darracq motor works in Paris, and later an international racing driver. In 1907 he won the *Circuit des Ardennes*. He was the first Briton to pilot a heavier-than-air machine under power in England (1909), and received the first pilot's certificate to be issued by the Royal Aero Club (1910).

He married in 1906 Hilda Mary, daughter of Charles Henry Krabbe, of Buenos Aires; they had two sons.

In the First World War he served with the RFC, was awarded the MC, and became a Commander of the Legion of Honour. From 1918 to 1929 he was Conservative MP for the Chatham division of Rochester, and from 1931 to 1942 was MP for Wallasey. In 1919 he became Parliamentary Private Secretary to CHURCHILL, who was then Secretary of State for War and Air. From 1923 to 1927 he was Parliamentary Secretary to the Ministry of Transport. He strongly supported Churchill's opposition to appeasement, and in 1940 was appointed Minister of Transport and sworn of the Privy Council. A few months later he replaced BEAVERBROOK as Minister of Aircraft Production.

Having at a private luncheon injudiciously expressed the hope that the Russian and German armies would annihilate one another, he had to resign in 1942 and went to the House of Lords. He continued to be closely concerned with aviation. He was President of the Royal Aero Club, and of the Royal Institution, and Chairman of the Air Registration Board. He was appointed GBE in 1953.

A very colourful figure, he was not only a fearless flier, but excelled at a number of sports. Except during the two world wars, he raced down the Cresta run at St Moritz every year from 1907 until his death, and won the Curzon cup three times. He was a member of the Royal Yacht Squadron and Captain of the Royal and Ancient Golf Club in 1952. Brabazon died at Chertsey on 17 May 1964.

BRACKEN, BRENDAN RENDALL, VISCOUNT BRACKEN (1901-1958), politician and publisher, was born at Templemore, co. Tipperary, on 15 February 1901, the younger son of J. K. Bracken, a builder and monumental mason, and his wife, Hannah Ryan. His father died when he was three, and his mother moved to Dublin. He was educated at the Jesuit College, Mungret, near Limerick, but he ran away at the age of fifteen and his mother sent him out to Australia where he went to a sheep station in New South Wales. After working for a time in Sydney he returned to Ireland in 1919 to find that his mother had remarried.

With a small legacy he emigrated to England, spent two terms as a pupil at Sedbergh, and then became a teacher until he had the good fortune to meet J. L. GARVIN who introduced him to the owner of the *Empire Review*, through whom he became interested in the publishing world. At this time, he threw off his Irish Catholic background and represented himself as an orphaned Australian.

Among those he met was Winston CHURCHILL whom he

Brendan Bracken with Churchill, 1940

assisted in his unsuccessful election campaigns at Leicester (1923) and in the Abbey division of Westminster (1924). His attachment to Churchill and Churchill's obvious fondness for him set people gossiping, and there were those who thought Bracken was Churchill's illegitimate son. Certainly Clementine Churchill disliked him and Randolph CHURCHILL resented the influence he appeared to have with his father. But Bracken, revelling in the gossip, became deeply attached to Churchill and was something more than 'the faithful Chela' as Stanley BALDWIN described him.

In 1924 he joined the publishing firm of Eyre & Spottiswoode, and in 1925 was made a director and took over the management of their paper the *Financial News*. In 1929 he joined Sir Henry Strakosch in the control of *The Economist* and acquired the *Investors Chronicle* and the *Practitioner*. His main interest, however, was in the *Financial News*. In 1929, when Churchill was Chancellor of the Exchequer, Bracken was elected Conservative MP for North Paddington, and with Churchill he opposed the India Bill and the appeasement policy of Neville CHAMBERLAIN.

He became Churchill's Parliamentary Private Secretary at the Admiralty in 1939 and stayed with him when he became Prime Minister in 1940. He was sworn of the Privy Council, and in 1941 appointed Minister of Information, where he won the high regard of Fleet Street by defending the press and the BBC from any attack on their freedom and reliability. In Churchill's caretaker Government he was First Lord of the Admiralty.

He lost his seat at the 1945 election, but found another at Bournemouth which he held until 1951. He continued to pursue his business interests and became Chairman of the amalgamated *Financial Times* and *Financial News* and succeeded Strakosch as Chairman of the Union Corporation. When Churchill returned to power in 1951 Bracken declined government office, but in 1952 accepted a viscountcy.

He never married, though at one time he appears to have sought without success to woo two beautiful and influential women. He had many faithful friends and some bitter enemies. Randolph Churchill described him as a mystery man and an expert in the art of make-believe and fantasy. Evelyn WAUGH caricatured him in the character of Rex Mottram in *Brideshead Revisited*. He died in London on 8 August 1958, and bequeathed a large sum of money to Churchill College, Cambridge.

BRADLEY, ANDREW CECIL (1851–1935), literary critic, was born at Cheltenham on 26 March 1851, the youngest son of the Revd Charles Bradley, Vicar of Glasbury, and incumbent of St James's Chapel, Clapham, and his second wife, Emma, daughter of John Linton, a stockbroker, of Clapham. He was a brother of Francis Herbert Bradley, the philosopher, and half-brother of G. G. Bradley, Headmaster of Marlborough, Master of University College, Oxford, and Dean of Westminster. He was educated at Cheltenham and Balliol College, Oxford, where he obtained a first in Greats (1873), was elected Fellow of Balliol (1874), and won the Chancellor's English essay prize in 1875. At Balliol, he was much influenced by the philosophy of T. H. Green. He was appointed college lecturer until, in 1882, he became the first Professor of Literature and History at University College, Liverpool. He was an inspiring lecturer and, after eight strenuous years in Liverpool, moved to Glasgow as Professor of English Language and Literature; but in 1900 he retired to London to concentrate on literary criticism. In 1901, he accepted the chair of poetry at Oxford.

There he produced his masterpiece, one of the great works of English criticism, *Shakespearian Tragedy* (1904), in which he brought out, with reference to a meticulous knowledge of the text of the plays, that Shakespeare was something more than a brilliantly successful Elizabethan playwright. His professorship of poetry at Oxford terminated in 1906 and he spent the rest of his life in London, where he died, unmarried, on 2 September 1935, having received many academic honours. He became FBA in 1907 and was President of the English Association in 1911. He was one of the greatest English critics of Shakespeare's work.

BRAGG, SIR WILLIAM HENRY (1862–1942), physicist, was born on 2 July 1862 at Westward in Cumberland, the eldest son of Robert John Bragg, a farmer. His mother, Mary, daughter of the Revd Robert Wood, died when he was seven. He was educated at King William's College, Isle of Man, and in 1881 entered Trinity College, Cambridge, as a scholar. He graduated as third wrangler in 1884, and in 1886 became Elder Professor of Mathematics and Physics in Adelaide, Australia. In 1889 he married Gwendoline, daughter of (Sir) Charles Todd, FRS, government astronomer of South Australia. They had two sons and a daughter.

He returned to England in 1909 as Cavendish Professor of Physics at Leeds, and from there moved, in 1915, to the Quain professorship at University College, London, a post which he held until 1923. However, the First World War interrupted his academic work and for a period Bragg worked for the Admiralty on the development of the hydrophone used in detecting submarines. At this time he lost his younger son, killed in 1915 at Gallipoli.

His elder son, (William) Lawrence BRAGG became a dis-

tinguished physicist, and together father and son worked on the problems of X-rays, studying ionization, and establishing, for the first time, how atoms are arranged in crystals, thereby founding the modern science of crystallography. In 1915 they were jointly awarded the Nobel prize for physics and published their work in *X-Rays and Crystal Structure*.

In 1923, William Bragg became Fullerian Professor of Chemistry at the Royal Institution and Director of the Davy-Faraday Laboratory, where he remained until his death in 1942. During this time, Bragg became renowned as a lecturer. In 1920, he had published *The World of Sound* and, in 1925, *Concerning the Nature of Things*. His Riddell memorial lectures were published as *Science and Faith* (1941). Elected FRS in 1907, he was President of the Royal Society from 1935 to 1940. He was appointed KBE in 1920 and awarded the OM in 1931. Sir William Bragg died in London on 12 March 1942.

BRAGG, SIR (WILLIAM) LAWRENCE (1890–1971), physicist, was born in Adelaide, Australia, on 31 March 1890, the elder son of William Henry BRAGG. He was educated at St Peter's College and the University of Adelaide, until 1909, when he entered Trinity College, Cambridge, as a scholar. While he was still at college he assisted his father in research on the geometrical arrangement of atoms in crystals of different types as calculated by the diffraction patterns of X-ray beams, and in 1913 published 'X-ray analysis of crystal structure' in the *Proceedings of the Royal Society*. In 1914 he became a Fellow of Trinity College, and lecturer in natural sciences. In the following year he was awarded the Nobel prize for physics, jointly with his father.

From 1915 to 1919 he served as an adviser at GHQ France and was awarded the MC and OBE (1918). After the war he succeeded Sir Ernest RUTHERFORD as Langworthy Professor of Physics at Victoria University of Manchester, where he

W. H. Bragg demonstrates his spectrometer, University College London

remained for eighteen years and built up a research team, many of whose members became famous for their work. He was elected FRS in 1921. He continued his own research on the structures of silicates and of metal crystals. In 1921 he married Alice Grace Jenny, daughter of Albert Hopkinson; they had two sons and two daughters.

During 1937-8 Bragg was Director of the National Physical Laboratory, and in 1938 succeeded Rutherford as Cavendish Professor of Experimental Physics at Cambridge, a post which he held until 1953. From 1953 until 1966 he was, like his father before him, Fullerian Professor of Chemistry, and Resident Professor at the Royal Institution where he worked on the structure of proteins. He was also Director of the Royal Institution from 1954 to 1966. Among his notable publications are *The Crystalline State* (1934) and *Atomic Structure of Minerals* (1937).

Throughout the course of his career Bragg won many medals and received many other academic awards and honours. During the Second World War he was co-ordinator of British, Canadian, and American military research; in 1941 he was knighted, and in 1967 became CH. He served on the Council of the Royal Society (1931-3) and was a member of the BBC General Advisory Council (1952) and of the Scientific Advisory Council (1954). He died on 1 July 1971. His elder son became Vice-Chancellor of Brunel University.

BRAIN, (WALTER) RUSSELL, first BARON BRAIN (1895-1966), physician and medical administrator, was born in Reading on 23 October 1895, the only son of Walter John Brain, a solicitor, and his wife, Edith Alice, daughter of Charles Smith, an architect. He was educated at Mill Hill School and New College, Oxford, where he read history. He joined the Friends' Ambulance Unit in 1915, and obtained experience of X-ray work in London before returning to Oxford to read medicine. In 1920 he entered the London Hospital and qualified BM, B.Ch. (Oxon) in 1922, DM in 1925, and became FRCP in 1931.

In 1920 he married Stella, daughter of Reginald Langdon Langdon-Down, a physician; they had two sons and a daughter. He and his wife became Quakers, joining the Society of Friends in 1931, and were regular attenders of their Meetings.

At the London Hospital he specialized in neurology, and, after a number of years in minor appointments, became physician to Moorfields Hospital from 1930 to 1937. He made important contributions to neurology, including a description of damage to the brain and peripheral nerves in cancer, particularly cancer of the lung. When a unit for the investigation of carcinomatous neuropathies was set up at the London Hospital, he became its Director and held the post up to the time of his death.

He wrote eighteen books and over 150 papers, including *Diseases of the Nervous System* (1933, 9th edn. 1984), *Mind, Perception and Science* (1951), *Speech Disorders* (1961), and *Science and Man* (1966). He edited *Brain* from 1954 to 1966. He was President of the Royal College of Physicians from 1950 to 1957, and of the Association of British Neurologists in 1958. He also served on a large number of committees and royal commissions, proving himself to be a medical statesman of wide experience, foresight, and wisdom. He was knighted in 1952, created a baronet in 1954, and a baron in 1962. He was elected FRS in 1964, and received many academic honours and awards. Brain died in London on 29 December 1966, his last working day having been given to arranging a new issue of *Brain*.

BRIDGES, EDWARD ETTINGDENE, first BARON BRIDGES (1892-1969), civil servant, was born at Yattendon Manor, Berkshire on 4 August 1892, the only son of Robert Seymour BRIDGES, Poet Laureate, and his wife (Mary) Monica, daughter of the architect Alfred Waterhouse. He was educated at Eton and Magdalen College, Oxford, where in 1914 he gained a first in Greats. From 1914 to 1918 he served as an officer in the Oxford. and Bucks. Light Infantry, was wounded on the Somme, and awarded the MC. In 1922 he married Katherine (Kitty) Dianthe, daughter of the second Baron Farmer. They had two sons and two daughters.

After the war he entered the Civil Service and was posted to the Treasury. He was a Fellow of All Souls from 1920 to 1927, but decided to make his career as an administrator. In 1935 he was appointed head of the Treasury division controlling expenditure on the supply and equipment of the armed forces, and in that post showed the quiet determination and efficiency, allied with common sense, which was to distinguish his subsequent career.

In 1938 he succeeded Sir Maurice HANKEY as Secretary to the Cabinet and other committees concerned with the co-ordination of defence; but when CHURCHILL became Prime Minister in 1940, these duties were divided. 'Pug' ISMAY took over responsibility for liaison between the Chiefs of Staff and the Prime Minister, and to Bridges was assigned the task of organizing the intricate machinery of government to serve the war effort. Churchill, who at the outset was inclined to look with suspicion on a Treasury official, soon became aware of the unselfish devotion to duty and the competence of Edward Bridges, to whom he paid tribute in *Their Finest Hour* (vol. ii. of *The Second World War*, 1949). Bridges, for his part, described what it was like to work with Churchill in wartime in his contribution to *Action This Day* (edited by Sir John Wheeler-Bennett, 1968).

During the war Bridges was responsible, not only for the war effort at home, but also for the complicated arrangements for co-operation with Britain's allies, the USA and Soviet Russia, including the preparation of briefs for the British teams at the Yalta and Potsdam Conferences.

After the war, Bridges succeeded Sir Richard Hopkins as Secretary to the Treasury and brought his wide experience of administration to assist the ATTLEE Government in the new conditions of the post-war world. As head of the Government Organization Committee, set up in 1946, he set out to construct an integrated administrative machinery capable of putting into operation the plans of the Labour Government for the Welfare State within the practical limits imposed by Britain's economic and financial restraints. By the time of his retirement in 1956 he had gone a long way to achieving this purpose, quietly and persistently, but none the less effectively.

After his retirement from the Civil Service, Bridges continued his public life in other directions. He was Chairman of the National Institute for Research into Nuclear Energy from 1957, of the Fine Arts Commission from 1957 to 1968, of the British Council from 1959 to 1967, and of the Pilgrim Trust from 1965 to 1968. He also held a number of academic appointments including Chancellor of Reading University and Chairman of the Oxford Historic Buildings Fund. His insistence on the writing of simple English in briefs and minutes was, no doubt, acquired from his father.

He was rewarded with many honours: GCB (1944), GCVO (1946), PC (1953), baron (1957), and KG (1965). He became FRS in 1952, was made honorary Fellow of a number of colleges and societies, and awarded honorary degrees from many universities. Bridges died at Guildford on 27 August 1979.

BRIDGES, ROBERT SEYMOUR (1844–1930), Poet Laureate, was born at Walmer on 23 October 1844, the fourth son of John Thomas Bridges, and his wife, Harriet Elizabeth, daughter of the Revd Sir Robert Affleck. The Bridges family had been yeomen of substance in Thanet since the sixteenth century, and Robert was always a man of independent means. He was educated at Eton and Corpus Christi College, Oxford, where he was a close friend of Gerard Manley Hopkins. When he left Oxford in 1867, he travelled on the Continent and visited Syria and Egypt.

In 1871 he became a medical student at St Bartholomew's Hospital and graduated MB in 1874. During the next seven years he held a number of medical appointments until, in 1881, ill health forced his retirement. He was already writing poetry, and published his first volume in 1873: it was favourably reviewed by Andrew Lang in the *Academy*. After the illness that had caused his retirement from medicine Bridges lived at Yattendon in Berkshire from 1882 to 1904.

In 1884 he married Monica, eldest daughter of the archi-tect Alfred Waterhouse; they had one son, Edward BRIDGES, and two daughters.

He had already published *The Growth of Love* (1876) consisting of twenty-four sonnets, and he now, in collaboration with H. E. Wooldridge, compiled 'The Yattendon Hymnal' (1895–9) which was influential in reviving sixteenth- and seventeenth-century music. At Yattendon he also wrote eight dramas and his long narrative poem *Eros and Psyche* (1885), as well as some influential commentaries on Milton. In 1895 he was invited to stand for election to the chair of poetry at Oxford, but he declined.

In 1907 he built Chilswell House on Boar's Hill overlooking Oxford. He published little there at first apart from a one-volume edition of his *Poems* (1912). Though his work attracted appreciative reviews, he was not known to a wide reaching public so that his appointment to succeed Alfred Austin as Poet Laureate in 1913, in preference to the more popular Rudyard KIPLING, caused some surprise. He wrote some war poems during the period of hostilities, which were published in *October and other Poems* (1920), but they are not generally considered among his best work. He was now keenly interested in English pronunciation and spelling and

Robert Bridges in the 1890s, painting by Charles Wellington Furse

worked on a simplified phonetic script; this led to the foundation of the Society for Pure English, and for the rest of his life Bridges was closely concerned with its activities. In 1916 he published *The Spirit of Man*, a successful anthology, but his greatest work, *The Testament of Beauty*, was not published until 1929 when Bridges was eighty-five.

He was appointed to the Order of Merit in 1929 and died at Chilswell House on 21 April 1930. Sir Henry Newbold described him in *The Times* (22 April) as 'one of the most remarkable figures of his time'. Bridges' own attitude to his work might be revealed by a quotation from *The Testament of Beauty*:

Ah! tho' it may be a simple thing in reach of all,
Best is ever rare, a toilsome guerdon.

BRIDIE, JAMES (1888–1951), playwright, whose real name was Osborne Henry Mavor, was born in Glasgow on 3 January 1888, the eldest son of Henry Alexander Mavor, engineer, and his wife, Janet Osborne. He was educated at Glasgow Academy and studied medicine at Glasgow University, where his lifelong friend, Walter Elliott, was a fellow student. He qualified in 1913 and, during the First World War, served in the RAMC in Flanders, Mesopotamia, and Russia. After the war he became Consulting Physician at the Victoria Infirmary, and Professor of Medicine in Anderson College, Glasgow. In 1923 he married Rona Bremner; they had two sons.

His first play, *The Sunlight Sonata*, was produced in Glasgow in 1928. He wrote forty plays under the pseudonym, James Bridie, including *The Switchback*, presented by Sir Barry JACKSON in Birmingham (1929) and *The Anatomist*, with Henry Ainley in the leading part in London, in 1931. Among his biblical plays were *Tobias and the Angel* (1930), *Jonah and the Whale* (1932), and *Susannah and the Elders* (1937). Bridie also had popular successes with *Mr Bolfry* (1943) with Alastair Sim, and *Daphne Laureola* (1949) with Edith EVANS.

In 1943 Bridie established the Citizen's Theatre in Glasgow, after a brief period of service again in the RAMC in Norway. Soon afterwards, in 1944, one of his sons was killed in France. Bridie was appointed CBE in 1946. He had been awarded the honorary LL D of Glasgow University in 1939.

Bridie died in Edinburgh on 29 January 1951. His surviving son followed his father in the medical profession and also became a drama critic.

BRITTAIN, VERA MARY (1893–1970), writer, pacifist, and feminist, was born at Newcastle under Lyme on 29 December 1893, the only daughter of Thomas Arthur Brittain, a paper manufacturer, and his wife, Edith Mary Bervon. She was educated at St Monica's, Kingswood, and spent her holidays at home at Buxton, where from an early age she chafed against the kind of provincial life enjoyed by her parents and sought means of getting away to a more intellectual milieu. Her chance came when her home was visited by (Sir) John Marriott, a university lecturer, who persuaded the Brittains to allow her to try for a scholarship to Oxford. With his encouragement, but to her own surprise, she was awarded an open exhibition at Somerville in 1914.

Up to that time she had seen little of intellectual company apart from her only brother and his friends, including Roland Leighton (brother of the artist, Clare Leighton), for whom she felt a deep attachment. The war years destroyed her happiness. Before he went away to fight in Flanders, Roland

Leighton and she became engaged. The account of the courtship given in *Chronicle of Youth* (1981), her war diary from 1913 to 1917, reveals an extraordinary concern for the conventions which today appears ridiculous, but there can be nothing but deep sympathy for the shattering blow which Vera received when both Leighton and her brother, and many of her other friends, were killed in France and Italy. Her account of these tragedies, *Testament of Youth* (1933), a poignant story of the horror and misery of war, told with brilliant simplicity, made her name.

While her friends were fighting, Vera served as a VAD in France and Malta, unable to bear what she regarded as the artificial life of the university in wartime. But after the war she returned to Somerville College to read history and met Winifred Holtby, with whom she established a deep friendship and an amicable rivalry as each aspired to be an author. The success of Winifred's novel *South Riding* showed her to have a wider experience and imagination than Vera could at that time command; when Winifred died in 1935 Vera Brittain paid tribute to her in *Testament of Friendship* (1940).

In 1925 she married (Sir) George Catlin of New College, Oxford, but she was determined to pursue her career as a writer and lecturer, and, when her husband went to Cornell and other universities in the USA each year, she remained in England with their son and daughter. Nevertheless, husband and wife never ceased to be united by strong bonds of affection.

By 1936 Vera Brittain had become a socialist. She joined the Peace Pledge Union and spoke widely in support of pacifism. Throughout the Second World War she maintained this position and denounced the bombing of German cities. She never gave up her efforts to convince the world of the futility of war nor her struggle in the cause of feminism.

In 1957 she published a further autobiographical work *Testament of Experience* in which she referred to her children, one of whom, Shirley Williams, was to become a Labour Cabinet minister and a leading Social Democrat. Vera Brittain died in London on 29 March 1970.

BRITTEN, (EDWARD) BENJAMIN, BARON BRITTEN (1913–1976), musician and composer, was born, appropriately on St Cecilia's Day, 22 November 1913 in Lowestoft, the son of Robert Victor Britten, a dental surgeon, and his wife, Edith Rhoda Hockey, secretary of the Lowestoft Choral Society. He was educated at Gresham's School, Holt, and the Royal College of Music. At the age of twelve he began to study music under Frank Bridge and at the Royal College he studied under John IRELAND and Arthur Benjamin. He was already composing songs and carols and had become a competent pianist.

His *Simple Symphony* was first performed in Norwich in 1934, and in 1935 he left the RCM and worked with the GPO Film Unit writing incidental music for documentary films, including *Night Mail*, which had a script by W. H. AUDEN of whom Britten became a close friend. Auden also produced the script for Britten's *Our Hunting Fathers* which was first performed in Norwich in 1936. In the following year, Britten wrote the incidental music to the Auden-Isherwood play *The Ascent of F6*, and his lifelong friendship and collaboration with Peter Pears, the singer, began. His song cycle *On This Island* was also broadcast in 1937.

In 1938 he performed his own Piano Concerto at a Promenade Concert, and in 1939 emigrated to the USA, under the influence of Auden, accompanied by Peter Pears. While he was in America, Britten wrote his first opera, *Paul Bunyan*,

Britten at home in Aldeburgh

with a text by Auden, and there decided to compose *Peter Grimes*, an opera about the fishermen of Suffolk.

Britten was a pacifist but, in 1942, influenced by another of his friends, E. M. FORSTER, he returned with Peter Pears to England to appear before a conscientious objectors' tribunal; he was exempted from military service, and he and Pears undertook concert tours for CEMA. Meanwhile, Britten continued to compose such works as *Hymn to St Cecilia*, *A Ceremony of Carols*, and *Serenade*. In 1945 *Peter Grimes* was first performed in London and this, more than any of his other works, set the seal on his reputation as a composer of outstanding talent.

In 1946 Britten and Pears formed the English Opera Group which became the medium for *The Rape of Lucretia* (1946), and *Albert Herring* (1947). In 1948 the first Aldeburgh Festival took place. At first the festival drew small audiences, but later, as its popularity increased, the appeal was to a much wider public, until in 1967 the large auditorium at the Maltings, Snape, was built, only to be destroyed by fire in 1969, and restored again in 1970.

In 1946 Britten composed *The Young Person's Guide to the Orchestra* and, in 1949, *Let's Make an Opera*. In 1951 the first performance of *Billy Budd* took place at Covent Garden, a work in which Britten had collaborated with E. M. Forster. *Gloriana*, commissioned by Covent Garden for the coronation of Elizabeth II, was first performed there in 1953. In 1955 Britten and Peter Pears went on a successful world tour. *Noye's Fludde*, a setting of the Chester miracle play, appeared in 1958 and his opera *A Midsummer Night's Dream* in 1960. Then, in 1962, *War Requiem*, combining poems of Wilfred OWEN with the text of the Requiem Mass, had its first performance at the consecration of the new Coventry Cathedral.

These are but a few of the works included in Britten's vast output which made him the foremost British composer of his time. In 1953 he was created CH and in 1965 appointed OM. In 1976 he became a life peer. His health had not been good since 1966 but this did not deter him from undertaking exhausting overseas tours and continuing to work incessantly. In 1973 he was seriously ill and had to undergo a heart operation. He began to slow down, composing only small scale works, such as songs for Peter Pears; then, for the Aldeburgh Festival of 1975, he wrote *Phaedra*, a dramatic cantata based on Racine's play, for Janet Baker. He died at the Red House, his Aldeburgh home, on 4 December 1976.

BROGAN, SIR DENIS WILLIAM (1900-1974), historian and student of politics, was born on 11 August 1900 in

Glasgow, the eldest son of Denis Brogan, master tailor, and his second wife, Elizabeth Toner. He was educated at Rutherglen Academy, Glasgow University, and Balliol College, Oxford, where he obtained a first in history (1925). His interest in American history arose from a year at Harvard on a Rockefeller research fellowship.

In 1928 he was appointed lecturer in history at University College, London, and in 1930 lecturer in politics at the LSE. In the following year he married Olwen Phillis Frances, an archaeologist, daughter of William Kendall, physician; they had three sons and one daughter. In 1933 Brogan published his best known work *The American Political System*. A year later, he moved to Oxford as Fellow and tutor of Corpus Christi College, and published *The Development of Modern France, 1870-1939* (1940; revised edition, *1870-1959*, 1967).

During the Second World War Brogan worked in the Ministry of Information and with the overseas services of the BBC; he produced *The English People: Impressions and Observations* (1943), and *The American Problem* (1944).

After the war he was appointed Professor of Political Science at Cambridge and became a Fellow of Peterhouse. His flow of books continued with *The Study of Politics* (1946) and *The Price of Revolution* (1951), and a number of other works on American politics. He also contributed much to the *Times Literary Supplement*. He was elected FBA in 1955 and received many academic honours; he was knighted in 1963. Brogan retired from his chair in 1968 and died in Cambridge on 5 January 1974.

BROOKE, ALAN FRANCIS, first VISCOUNT ALANBROOKE (1883-1963), field-marshal, was born at Bagnères de Bigorre, France on 23 July 1883, the sixth son of Sir Victor Alexander Brooke, third baronet of Colebrooke in co. Fermanagh, and his wife, Alice Sophia, daughter of Sir Alan Edward Bellingham, third baronet of Castle Bellingham in co. Louth. On both sides of the family Irish Protestantism was paramount and service in the army traditional. Brooke was brought up in France, where his mother preferred to live, until at eighteen he entered the Royal Military Academy, Woolwich. He was already a competent French and German speaker.

In 1902 he was commissioned in the Royal Field Artillery and spent the next seven years with that regiment in Ireland and India. In 1909 he transferred to the Royal Horse Artillery, and during the First World War rose from lieutenant to lieutenant-colonel and was awarded the DSO and bar. In 1914 he married Jane Mary, daughter of Col. John Mercyn Ashdall Carleton Richardson; they had a son and a daughter. After the war, Brooke went to the Staff College, where he became an instructor in 1923, and later went to the Imperial Defence College and became an instructor there from 1932 to 1934. By 1935 he was a major-general.

His first wife was killed in 1925 in a car accident and, in 1939, he married Benita Blanche, daughter of Sir Harold Pelly, and widow of Sir Thomas Evan Keith Lees; they had a son and a daughter.

Brooke's experiences in the First World War had led him to attach great importance to fire-power, but by the outbreak of the Second World War, he had come to see that mobility, as well as fire-power, was all-important. In 1938 he took command of the Anti-Aircraft Corps and was responsible for the reorganization of defences which, when he took over, were woefully inadequate. In August 1939 he became Commander-in-Chief, Southern Command, and then Com-

Alan Brooke (right), Commander-in-Chief, Home Forces, on a visit to Scottish Command, June 1941

mander of II Corps in France. His early experiences of life in France made him doubtful of the morale of the French army and he did not entirely agree with the strategy of Lord Gort, the Commander-in-Chief. When it became necessary to evacuate British troops from France and Belgium, Brooke was in charge of the arrangements. He also strongly advised against any attempts to hold a bridgehead in Brittany.

After Dunkirk, he was appointed Commander-in-Chief, Home Forces, and set about the reorganization necessary to repel the expected German invasion. When the RAF made this no longer a danger, Brooke's task was to prepare for overseas operations again. In December 1941 he succeeded Sir John DILL as Chief of the Imperial General Staff and thus became the professional head of the British Army and chief strategic adviser to the War Cabinet as Chairman of the Chiefs of Staff Committee.

In that capacity, Brooke was signally successful, not only in his co-operation with his colleagues, Pound, CUNNINGHAM, and PORTAL, but also in his ability to stand up to CHURCHILL whenever the Chiefs of Staff considered this to be necessary. Unlike some of the military commanders, such as WAVELL who could not convey his views to Churchill clearly and succinctly, or Dill who had not the necessary resilience, Brooke made his points with such clarity and force that the Prime Minister, despite their occasional sharp exchanges, always respected the firm integrity and tenacity of the advice he received. When the USA entered the war, Brooke was able to impress their war leaders with the strength of his character and experience, as he had those under his command in Britain. Brooke controlled the British war effort from the disasters of 1941 to the victories of 1944-5; to Churchill his services were indispensable, and to those who worked with him he was a tower of strength. Throughout this period he was ably assisted by Sir James Grigg, a civil servant, who had been appointed Secretary of State for War when Churchill became Prime Minister. In 1944 Brooke was promoted to field-marshal. He had been created KCB in 1940 and GCB in 1942. In 1945 he became a baron, in 1946 viscount, and in the same year KG and OM. In 1953 he was created GCVO.

Throughout his life Brooke was a keen ornithologist, and was President of the Zoological Society from 1950 to 1954. He was Master Gunner of St James's Park (1946-56), Lord Lieutenant, county of London, and Constable of the Tower in 1950; he was also Chancellor of Queen's University, Belfast, from 1949 to 1963. His war diaries were used by Sir Arthur Bryant for *The Turn of the Tide* (1957), and *Triumph in the West* (1959). Brooke died at Hartley Wintney in Hampshire on 17 June 1963.

BROOKE, RUPERT CHAWNER (1887-1915), poet, was born at Rugby on 3 August 1887, the second of three sons of William Parker Brooke, a master at Rugby School, and his wife, Mary Ruth Cotterill. He was educated at Rugby and King's College, Cambridge, which he entered in 1906. He made his mark at Cambridge by taking a leading part in founding the Marlowe Society, becoming a member of the 'Apostles', winning the Harness prize with an essay *Puritanism in the Early Drama*, and being elected a Fellow of King's in 1912 with a dissertation, *John Webster*.

While still at Cambridge he made himself a home at the Old Vicarage, Grantchester, recalled with nostalgia in his poem of that name. In 1911 he published a volume of *Poems* which aroused considerable interest. Two years later he set out to travel through the USA and Canada to Hawaii, New Zealand, and Tahiti. From Tahiti he sent home poems for publication in *New Numbers*.

In June 1914 he returned to England intending to settle down at Cambridge, but when war broke out he was commissioned in the Royal Naval Division and took part in the Antwerp expedition. Then, in 1915, he was posted to the Dardanelles and, having refused the offer of a staff post, was suddenly attacked by blood poisoning and died at Scyros on 23 April 1915. His *1914 and Other Poems* was published posthumously, as were his *Collected Poems* (1916). The later poems, on which his reputation principally rests, captured that mood of romantic patriotism which was so characteristic of the English people in the early months of the war. Sadly, by his death was lost, not only a brilliant young poet, but a man of great promise. In his poem *Clouds*, he wrote what could be regarded as his epitaph:

They say that the Dead die not, but remain
Near to the rich heirs of their grief and mirth.

BROWNING, OSCAR (1837-1923), schoolmaster and historian, was born in London on 17 January 1837, the third son of William Shipton Browning, a merchant, and his wife, Mariana Margaret Bridge. He was elected a scholar of Eton in 1850, a scholar of King's College, Cambridge in 1856, and a Fellow of King's in 1859. He remained a Fellow of King's until he died. He was President of the Union and was placed fourth in the classical tripos in 1860.

From 1860 to 1875 he was a master at Eton; and his house, supervised by his mother, became the most popular in the school. Browning was a good classical teacher, devoted to the education of intelligent boys. His intimacy with the boys in his charge led to his downfall. He was dismissed from Eton on the basis of charges which were based upon suspicion and could not be substantiated and, in spite of controversial activity on his behalf, by the boys, their parents, and friends, he was not reinstated.

Undeterred, he returned to King's College, Cambridge, resolved to continue his work with young men and to carry on his cantankerous, self-righteous struggle with any who dared to disagree with him. He was appointed lecturer in history at King's in 1880 and in the university in 1883. His ambition was to reorganize his college and create there a small coterie of élite scholars.

His influence with the undergraduates who came within his orbit was considerable. He was a good companion, a genial host, and a man of wide interests, as well as a good teacher. He did not confine his activities to undergraduates. He took a leading part in founding the Day Training College for elementary teachers, of which he was Principal from 1891 to 1908.

He left Cambridge in 1908, considering himself to have been ill-used by some of his colleagues, both at King's and at the training college. His last years were spent in Rome, where he continued to be actively concerned with lecturing and teaching young students. During this time he wrote historical manuals, including *A History of the Modern World 1815-1910* (2 vols., 1912), *A General History of the World* (1913), and *A Short History of Italy 375-1915* (1917). He died in Rome on 6 October 1923 never having married.

BRUCE, CHARLES GRANVILLE (1866-1939), soldier, mountaineer, and traveller, was born in London on 7 April 1866, the younger son of Henry Austin Bruce, later first Baron Aberdare, and his second wife, Norah Creina Blanche, daughter of Lieutenant-General Sir William Napier. He was educated at Harrow and Repton, and commissioned in the Oxford. and Bucks. Light Infantry in 1887.

In 1889 he transferred to the 5th Gurkha Rifles and saw much service on the North-West Frontier of India between that year and 1898, during which time he travelled extensively in the Himalayas. In 1894 Bruce married Finetta Madeline Julia, daughter of Col. Sir Edward Fitzgerald Campbell; their only child, a son, died in infancy. His wife accompanied him on a number of his mountain expeditions and published *Kashmir* (1911). In the First World War Bruce fought and was severely wounded at Gallipoli. On his return to India he served in the Afghan war of 1919. In 1920 he was invalided from the service with the honorary rank of brigadier. In the course of his career with the Gurkhas he became the foremost authority on their language, their customs, and way of life. In his travels he was always accompanied by Gurkhas from his regiment.

He took part in the Karakoram expedition of 1892 and the disastrous attempt to climb Nanga Parbat in 1895. He was the organizer and leader of the Everest expeditions of 1922 and 1924 where his remarkable knowledge of Gurkhas, Sherpas, and Tibetans contributed much to the success of these undertakings, though the latter expedition was marred by the deaths of MALLORY and Irvine near the summit.

He was appointed MVO in 1903 and CB in 1918. He received a number of honours for his achievements as a traveller and climber. In 1923 he was President of the Alpine Club, and he received honorary degrees from several universities. His publications include *Twenty Years in the*

Himalayas (1910), *The Assault on Mount Everest, 1922* (1923), and *Himalayan Wanderer* (1934). His wife died in 1932, and Bruce himself died in London on 12 July 1939.

BRUCE, SIR DAVID (1855–1931), discoverer of the causes of Malta fever and sleeping sickness, was born in Melbourne, Australia on 29 May 1855, the only son of David Bruce, an engineer from Edinburgh, and his wife, Jane, daughter of Alexander Hamilton of Stirling. When he was five his parents settled in Stirling and he went to Stirling High School. After working for seven years in Manchester he entered Edinburgh University to read medicine. He graduated MB, CM in 1881, and in 1883 married Mary Elizabeth, daughter of John Sisson Steele MRCS, general practitioner.

In 1883 Bruce was commissioned in the Army Medical Service and posted in the following year to Malta. Interested in the new science of bacteriology he set out to discover the cause of an obscure fever which claimed many lives in Malta. Within two years he found in the spleens of fatal cases an organism which he called *Micrococcus melitensis* (since renamed *Brucella melitensis*). This he showed to be the cause of Malta fever. Later, in 1904, when he revisited Malta, he proved that the source of infection was goats' milk.

Bruce and his wife left Malta in 1888 and worked together in the laboratory in Berlin of Robert Koch, bacteriologist. Then, from 1889 to 1894, Bruce was Assistant Professor of Pathology in the Army Medical School at Netley. In 1894 he was posted to Zululand, where his researches proved that *Trypanosoma brucei* was the cause of nagana and tsetse fly diseases in cattle.

In 1903 he was seconded by the War Office at the request of the Royal Society to supervise the work of the commission in Uganda studying sleeping sickness. Carefully considering discoveries made by other investigators, he concluded that sleeping sickness was a trypanosome disease transmitted by the tsetse fly. In this work Bruce was always capably assisted by his wife.

In 1912 he was promoted to surgeon-general, and during the First World War was Commandant of the Royal Army Medical College, Millbank. His wife was appointed OBE for her work on trench fever and tetanus. Bruce received many honours for his research work. He was appointed CB in 1905, knighted in 1908, and appointed KCB in 1918. In 1924 he was President of the British Association. He died in London on 27 November 1931, four days after the death of his wife. They had no children.

BRUCE LOCKHART, SIR ROBERT HAMILTON (1887–1970), diplomat and writer, was born on 2 September 1887 in Anstruther, Fife, the eldest of five sons of Robert Bruce Lockhart, headmaster of the Waid Academy, and his wife, Florence Stuart, daughter of John McGregor. He prided himself on being a full-blooded Scot. He was educated at Fettes and in Berlin and Paris, where he learned fluent German and French. From 1908 to 1910 he was a rubber planter in Malaya, but acute malaria necessitated his return to Britain, and in 1912 he joined the Consular Service. In 1913 he married Jean Haslewood, daughter of Leonard Turner, an Australian; they had one daughter who died at birth and a son. He was posted to Moscow as Vice-Consul and was Acting Consul-General during the First World War but was recalled to London in 1917 because of an affair with a Russian Jewess. Early in 1918 he was sent back to Russia as head of a special mission, with a letter from Litvinov to Trotsky, for the purpose of establishing relations with the

Robert Bruce Lockhart at home in Edinburgh, July 1955

Bolsheviks. He was arrested as a spy and imprisoned, but later exchanged for Litvinov.

In 1919 he was appointed Commercial Secretary to the British Legation in Prague, where he became a close friend of Dr Benes and Jan Masaryk. In 1922, because he was living beyond his means, he left the Foreign Service and worked in international banking to restore his fortunes. In 1924 he became a Roman Catholic.

In 1928 he joined the *Evening Standard* as Editor of the Londoner's Diary, a post he held until 1937. In 1932 he published his first book, *Memoirs of a British Agent*, an account of his experiences in Russia. It was an immediate success and was followed by *Retreat from Glory* (1934) and *Return to Malaya* (1936).

At the outbreak of the Second World War, Bruce Lockhart rejoined the Foreign Office and became British Representative with the provisional Czechoslovak Government. In 1941 he was appointed Deputy Under-Secretary of State and Director of the Political Warfare Executive. He was appointed KCMG in 1943 and published his experiences in *Comes the Reckoning* (1947). He published a number of other books, including *My Scottish Youth* (1937) and *My Rod, My Comfort* (1949), all enjoyable reading. In 1973 his *Diaries* for 1915 to 1938 were published. His first marriage ended in divorce in 1938. In 1948 he married Frances Mary, daughter of Major-General Edward Archibald Beck. Bruce Lockhart died in Hove on 27 February 1970.

BRYCE, JAMES, VISCOUNT BRYCE (1838–1922), jurist, historian, and politician, was born in Belfast on 10 May 1838, the eldest son of James Bryce, schoolmaster and geologist, and his wife, Margaret, daughter of James Young of Abbeyville, co. Antrim, merchant. He was educated at Glasgow High School, Belfast Academy, Glasgow University, and Trinity College, Oxford, where he obtained firsts in Classical Mods., Greats, law, and modern history. He was awarded the Craven and the Vinerian law scholarships and became President of the Union. Bryce graduated in 1862 and was a Fellow of Oriel College from 1862 to 1889.

In 1867 he was called to the Bar (Lincoln's Inn) and joined the Northern circuit, but he was not really interested in practising and he gave this up in 1882. In 1863 he had won the Arnold historical essay prize at Oxford with his essay on the *Holy Roman Empire* which he published in 1864. This book has since been translated into German, French, and Italian.

In 1865 and 1866 he was busy in educational inquiries including the development of university education at Manchester. In 1870 he was appointed Regius Professor of Civil Law at Oxford, a post he held until 1893. Some of his important work in this connection was published in *Studies in History and Jurisprudence* (1901). In the mid-seventies he travelled in Russia, visiting the Caucasus and Armenia, and acquired a deep and lasting interest in the Near East and, in particular, in the Armenian nation. An account of his travels, *Transcaucasia and Ararat* was published in 1877. It was largely his interest in the Near East that attracted him to politics. He became Liberal MP for the Tower Hamlets division from 1880 to 1885, and for South Aberdeen from 1885 to 1906.

He married in 1889 Elizabeth Marion, daughter of Thomas Ashton. They had no children.

Meanwhile, he was concerned with the establishment of the *English Historical Review* in 1886, and in 1888 he published *The American Commonwealth*. In 1892 he entered Gladstone's Cabinet as Chancellor of the Duchy of Lancaster and was a member of the committee that prepared the Irish Home Rule Bill. In 1894, he became President of the Board of Trade in Lord ROSEBERY's administration. He was chairman of the Royal Commission on Secondary Education which laid the foundations of a new structure of secondary schools.

Viscount Bryce

In 1895 he visited South Africa: he published *Impressions of South Africa* (1897) and, during the Boer War, his attitude to the Boers made him unpopular in England. In the Liberal Government of 1905 he became Chief Secretary for Ireland and set up a commission on university education in that country.

From 1907 to 1913 Bryce was British Ambassador at Washington, where he wielded a considerable influence in Anglo-American affairs and in Canada. He had refused a peerage in 1907, but on his return to England he was created viscount early in 1914, and became a member of the Hague Tribunal. He was president of the commission which investigated alleged German atrocities and was strongly opposed to reprisals. The rest of his life was devoted to fostering the project of a League of Nations. In 1917 he was chairman of a conference on the reform of the House of Lords, but from that year until 1921 he was mainly engaged on his work *Modern Democracies* (1921).

His honours were many: he received degrees from thirty-one universities. He was appointed FRS in 1893, FBA in 1902, OM in 1907, and GCVO in 1917. Besides those works named above, he wrote many other learned books and articles. Bryce died at Sidmouth on 22 January 1922. Few men of his generation can have surpassed Bryce's wide range of scholarship combined with active participation in political and diplomatic life.

BUCHAN, JOHN, first BARON TWEEDSMUIR (1875-1940), author and Governor-General of Canada, was born at Perth on 26 August 1875, the eldest son of John Buchan, a minister of the Free Church of Scotland, and his wife, Helen, daughter of John Masterton, a farmer. He was educated at Hutcheson's Boys' Grammar School and Glasgow University before entering Brasenose College, Oxford, with a scholarship. In 1899 he obtained a first in Greats and was President of the Union. In the previous year he had won the Newdigate prize for English verse. In 1901 he was called to the Bar (Middle Temple) but earned his living through journalism.

From 1901 to 1903 he was an Assistant Private Secretary to Lord MILNER in South Africa and found that he admired the Boers. Pieter Pienaar became one of the heroes of his adventure stories. On return to London, he resumed work at the Bar, until in 1907 he became 'literary adviser' to T. A. Nelson, the publisher. He had already written half a dozen novels and two books on Africa, and in 1910 he published *Prester John*, the first of the well-known adventure stories.

In 1907 he married Susan Charlotte, elder daughter of Captain Norman de l'Aigle Grosvenor, third son of the first Lord Ebury. They had three sons and a daughter.

When the First World War broke out Buchan was seriously ill, and, from his bed, he started on his *History of the Great War* and wrote *The Thirty-Nine Steps* (1915). When he recovered he joined the staff of *The Times* on the Western Front, and in 1916 joined the army in the Intelligence Corps. Then, during 1917-18 he was subordinate director of the Ministry of Information. *Greenmantle* (1916) and *Mr Standfast* (1919) completed the trilogy begun with *The Thirty-Nine Steps*, recounting the adventures of the redoubtable Richard Hannay.

When the war ended Buchan settled at Elsfield, near Oxford, where he completed his *History of the Great War* (1921-2), and wrote the *History of the Royal Scots Fusiliers* (1925). *Huntingtower* (1922) opened a new series of novels on Glasgow life. He also wrote historical novels such as

Midwinter (1923), and biographical studies including *Montrose* (1928), *Oliver Cromwell* (1934), and *Augustus* (1937).

In 1927 he was elected Conservative MP for the Scottish Universities and held the seat until 1935 when he was raised to the peerage. From 1933 to 1934 he was Lord High Commissioner to the General Assembly of the Church of Scotland. Then, in 1935 he was appointed Governor-General of Canada. In that post he took a special interest in Lower Canada and French-Canadian culture and endeared himself to all Canadians. He also became a friend of President Roosevelt and had a share in maintaining good relations with the USA.

Buchan received many honours, both public and academic. He was sworn of the Privy Council in 1937; appointed CH (1932), GCMG (1935), GCVO (1939); he was elected Chancellor of Edinburgh University in 1937, and an honorary Fellow of Brasenose College in 1934. He died in Montreal on 11 February 1940 and was succeeded by his son John whose wife, as Baroness Tweedsmuir of Belhelvie, was later Minister of State at the Foreign and Commonwealth Office in Edward Heath's Government.

BURGESS, GUY FRANCIS DE MONCY (1911-1963), spy, was born at Devonport on 16 April 1911, the younger son of Commander Malcolm Kingsford de Moncy Burgess RN, and his wife, Evelyn Mary Gillman. He was educated at Eton (1924-5) and, after a spell at the Royal Naval College, Dartmouth (1925-7), returned to Eton, as his defective eyesight debarred a naval career. In 1929 he entered Trinity College, Cambridge, as a history scholar, obtained a first in part i of the historical tripos, and had to take an *aegrotat* in part ii (1934). His Cambridge career was marked by brilliance and dissolute homosexuality. He was a member of the exclusive Pitt Club and became one of the 'Apostles'.

In 1934 he visited the USSR with a friend, Derek Blaikie, and on return to Cambridge disowned the Communist friends with whom he had previously consorted and became the publicity officer of the Anglo-German Fellowship. Lady Rothschild, mother of his friend, Victor, paid him a stipend and he continued to lead a life of drunkenness and disorder, the apparent prototype of bourgeois decadence. In the meantime he was passing to a Soviet agent information about the activities and personalities of the organization for which he was working. He was also supplying the British Secret Service with information gathered from his French friends.

From 1936 to 1938 and from 1941 to 1944 he worked in Bristol as talks producer for the BBC. Then in 1944 he joined the Press Department of the Foreign Office, after a short period as a propaganda expert in the War Office. Nobody could have suspected that he was a spy. His life style was that of a dissolute ruffian. In one instance he was arrested for a homosexual offence, but the case was dismissed. He was sacked from the War Office and taken back by the BBC but refused promotion.

After he joined the Foreign Office he became personal assistant to Hector McNeil, Minister of State, with whom he had long been on friendly terms. From this vantage point he was able to supply the Soviet secret service with much useful information. His drunkenness and bad behaviour continued until Hector McNeil began to tire of him. He was now a permanent member of the Foreign Office staff, and was transferred in 1947 to the Information Research Department, run by (Sir) Christopher Mayhew, Parliamentary Under-Secretary. Mayhew very quickly rid himself of a man he regarded as an idle, disreputable nuisance.

Burgess was again moved to another department, but he was in trouble once more in 1949 through his drunken insolence, and the Personnel Department decided that he must be found an appointment overseas. He was sent to Washington where 'Kim' Philby was installed in the British Secret Intelligence Service (MI6). Donald Maclean was no longer there; he had been blackmailed into spying by Burgess in 1944 when he was working in the Washington Embassy, but by 1949 he was getting himself into trouble in Egypt, and his dependability was being questioned.

Maclean was the weak link in this threesome of spies, and during 1950-1 was under increasing suspicion in London. Philby became aware that Maclean was about to be interrogated, and that he was likely to put all three in jeopardy. He instructed Burgess to return to London and arrange for Maclean's escape to Russia. Burgess secured his recall to London by typically irresponsible behaviour. He was booked three times in one day by the American police for speeding: the Ambassador promptly sent him back to London.

Burgess made contact with Maclean, but dallied sufficiently long about completing the arrangements for Maclean's departure from England for Philby to run the serious risk of implicating himself by sending a cryptic warning telegram.

On 25 May 1951 Burgess and Maclean both escaped from England *en route* to Moscow. For Maclean defection took place in the nick of time, but Burgess was not under suspicion, and by disregarding Philby's instructions and going off with Maclean he put Philby into a serious position which, in spite of his skill in evading detection, aroused much suspicion of his integrity.

For the next twelve years Burgess lived in Moscow which he heartily disliked, working for the Foreign Translations Publishing House, and living with Tolya, a factory worker in his twenties. He never became a Russian citizen and would have liked to be able to return to England. He died in August 1963 in a Moscow hospital.

BURNHAM, VISCOUNT (1862-1933). See LAWSON.

BURNS, JOHN ELLIOT (1858-1943), labour leader and politician, was born in Lambeth on 20 October 1858, the second son and sixteenth child of Alexander Burns, a Scottish engine-fitter, and his wife, Barbara Smith, who came from Aberdeen; she was unable to write. Burns left school at ten and worked variously as a page-boy, and in a candle factory, and in an engineering works till he was fourteen. Then he managed to become apprenticed as an engineer. He was already involved in radical movements and trade-unionism. For one year he worked in West Africa, and then in 1881 drove the first electric tram in England. The following year he tramped through Europe making friends with continental socialists and learning about conditions of labour abroad. Earlier that year he had married Martha Charlotte (Pattie), daughter of John Knight Gale, shipwright; they had one son.

In 1884 he joined the Social Democratic Federation and represented it at the Industrial Remuneration Conference in 1885. He was also active in his trade union, the Amalgamated Society of Engineers. He was a lively speaker and, as a result of his activities in Trafalgar Square, on behalf of the unemployed, he was arrested. This was the first of a number of clashes with authority, one of which in 1887 led to his imprisonment for six weeks.

In 1889 he was elected to represent Battersea on the London County Council and founded the Battersea Labour

League. During that year he also came into prominence as one of the leaders in the London dock strike which secured for the dockers a minimum wage of sixpence an hour. In 1890 he was a delegate to the TUC conference.

He became an MP for the first time in 1892, representing Battersea as a labour member. But he refused to join the Independent Labour party under Keir HARDIE and, although he was re-elected in 1895 as a socialist, he gradually dropped out of the trade union movement and became increasingly associated with the Liberals. He opposed the Boer War but managed to retain his seat in Parliament, and in 1905 was made President of the Local Government Board, in Campbell-Bannerman's Government, with a seat in the Cabinet and became a member of the Privy Council.

He held that post until 1914 and secured the enactment of the Housing, Town Planning Act of 1909—the first of its kind. He became very unpopular with the Labour party because of his actions in the affair of the Poplar board of guardians, who were accused of corruption, and his opposition to Poor Law reform. However, he was twice re-elected for Battersea in 1910 as a Liberal. Early in 1914 he was appointed President of the Board of Trade but, when the First World War broke out, he resigned because he considered that it could have been averted, and he took no further part in public life. He retired from Parliament in 1918, received an annuity under the will of Andrew Carnegie, and spent the rest of his life making a collection of books about old London which was eventually bought by Lord Southwood and presented to the LCC.

Burns died in London on 24 January 1943—the first artisan to become a Cabinet Minister.

BURT, SIR CYRIL LODOWIC (1883-1971), psychologist, was born in London on 3 March 1883, the elder child of Cyril Cecil Barrow Burt, who was at the time a medical student, and later a general practitioner at Snitterfield, Warwickshire, where the geneticist (Sir) Francis Galton and his family were among his patients. Burt's mother was Martha Evans, of Monmouth. He was educated at King's School, Warwick, Christ's Hospital, and Jesus College, Oxford, where he was a classical scholar. His interest in psychology was aroused by his association with the Galton family and by his attendance at the lectures of William McDougall, Wilde Reader in mental philosophy at Oxford.

In 1907 McDougall arranged for Burt to take part in an anthropometric survey sponsored by the British Association, and to investigate some of the psychological tests which it was proposed should be standardized. This work brought him into contact with Charles Spearman, Reader in experimental psychology at University College London, one of the first to advocate statistical methods of measuring intelligence. In the same year (1907) Burt was awarded the John Locke scholarship in mental philosophy at Oxford; this enabled him to spend part of 1908 studying under Oswald Külpe at the University of Würzburg, where he began to realize that British psychological studies were less advanced than those of the German psychologists.

From 1908 to 1913 Burt was a lecturer in psychology in the Department of Physiology under Charles SHERRINGTON at Liverpool University, and continued his researches into various aspects of intelligence, particularly the importance of heredity and the assessment of the weight of genetic and environmental influences.

Then, in 1913, he was appointed part-time psychologist to the LCC, the first post of this kind in Britain. During the next twenty years he combined his duties in this post with similar part-time work in the Cambridge Psychological Laboratory (1912-13), at the National Institute of Industrial Psychology (1922-4), and from 1924 to 1932 at the London Day Training College (later the Institute of Education). In the course of his work for the LCC, Burt carried out a survey of the abilities of a large number of elementary school children, attempting to detect those needing special education whether because they were mentally backward or mal-adjusted, or because they were gifted.

Applying the analytical methods he had developed at Liverpool, he demonstrated the complexity of the factors underlying mental abnormalities in children's capabilities, and the material he collected in the process formed the basis for his published works *The Distribution and Relations of Educational Abilities* (1917), *Mental and Scholastic Tests* (1921), *A Handbook of Tests for Use in Schools* (1923), *The Young Delinquent* (1925), and *The Backward Child* (1937).

In 1932 Burt succeeded Charles Spearman as Professor of Psychology at University College London. In the same year he married Joyce Muriel, daughter of P. F. Woods, a commercial traveller. She was twenty-three and had been one of his students at the London Day Training College; she later trained as a doctor and became a distinguished gynaecologist. At the time of this marriage Burt was more than twice her age. They had no children and the marriage broke down in 1950.

Burt remained at University College until 1950, during which time he pursued his theories of factor analysis and statistical techniques which he publicized in *The Factors of the Mind* (1940) and in the *British Journal of Statistical Psychology*, of which he became the first Editor in 1947 jointly with Sir Godfrey Thomson. In 1946 Burt was knighted; he was elected FBA in 1950, and in the same year also became an honorary Fellow of Jesus College, Oxford.

The twenty years that followed his retirement from University College were attended by disaster. In 1941 he had contracted Ménière's disease (a condition of the inner ear affecting the balance), and his health was seriously impaired. Furthermore much of his research material had been destroyed in the blitz in 1940. He now became more dogmatic in his views, and relations with colleagues, which hitherto had been cordial, became increasingly acrimonious. In particular his views on the inheritance of intelligence came more and more to be questioned. There can be little doubt that in his efforts to justify his theory on the genetic factor in intelligence, he not only fabricated statistical data in respect of a study of fifty-six pairs of identical twins, but also invented mythical assistants supposed to have been employed in the collection of such data.

After his death in London on 10 October 1971 these aberrations were brought to light and, in consequence, Burt's reputation suffered a serious decline. To some extent his almost pathological determination in his later years to overcome opposition to his opinions by any means, however devious, may have been aroused by his poor state of health. In any case this digression from the standards of scientific probity should not entirely detract from his undoubted achievements as a pioneer in the field of educational psychology whose ideas had a lasting influence on the methods of assessment of intelligence in children and on the understanding of the causes of mental abnormality.

BURTON, SIR MONTAGUE MAURICE (1885-1952), multiple tailor, was born of Jewish parentage in Lithuania

Burton's Rotherham branch: the aim to sell good quality clothes at the cheapest possible price

on 15 August 1885, the only son of Charles Judah Burton, a bookseller, and his wife, Rachel Edith Ashe. In 1900 he came alone to England with £100 and took employment as a salesman in a tailor's shop. In 1903 he set up his own business as a general outfitter in Chesterfield. He was a young man of energy and imagination and set out to sell clothes of good quality at the cheapest possible prices. By 1913 he had five men's tailor shops in the north of England with headquarters in Sheffield and his own factories in Leeds.

In 1909 he married Sophia Amelia, daughter of Maurice Marks, dealer in antiques and furniture; they had one daughter and three sons.

During the First World War his business was mainly the manufacture of uniforms, but by 1920 he had re-established his normal business, and by 1929 when the company went public, it had four hundred shops, as well as factories and mills. Although Burton always sought new ways of cutting expenses, he regarded low wages as a false economy, and from the time he entered the industry, when the conditions in the workshops were appalling, he set out to raise conditions in his shops and factories to the highest possible standard. He was one of the first pioneers in the field of industrial welfare. He favoured organized labour and collective bargaining and his business was almost entirely free from strikes.

During the Second World War Burton's supplied a quarter of the total requirements of uniforms for the armed forces and, when the war ended, a third of the demobilization outfits came from Burton's. For the whole of his life Burton had a passion for peace—peace in industry and between nations. He endowed a number of chairs in industrial relations at Leeds, Cardiff (1929), and Cambridge (1930). He also endowed chairs in international relations in Jerusalem (1929), Oxford (1930), London (1936), and Edinburgh (1948).

He was a great traveller, who went round the world four times. He published his experiences in *Globe Girdling* (1936-8) and was delighted when he was elected a member of the PEN Club in 1944. He was a member of the council of Leeds University from 1929, and in 1944 endowed a lectureship there in modern and medieval Hebrew. He was knighted in 1931. A humble and self-effacing man, Burton disliked any kind of personal publicity. At the time of his death he had over six hundred shops, and was still working when he died in Leeds on 21 September 1952 while addressing a meeting of his staff.

BURY, JOHN BAGNELL (1861–1927), classical scholar and historian, was born at Monaghan, now in the Irish Republic, on 16 October 1861, the eldest son of the Revd Edward John Bury, curate of Monaghan, and his wife, Anna, daughter of Henry Rogers of Monaghan. He was educated at Foyle College, Londonderry, and Trinity College, Dublin, where he graduated in 1882 with a double first in classics and mental and moral philosophy. In 1885 he was made a Fellow of Trinity College, and in 1893 was appointed Erasmus Smith Professor of modern history.

In 1885 Bury married Jane, daughter of John Carleton Bury, physician of Mitchelstown, co. Cork; they had one son.

As a student, Bury's main interest was classical philology and philosophy, and his early publications dealt mainly with the interpretation of classical texts. In 1890 he published *The Nemean Odes of Pindar*, and in 1892 *The Isthmian Odes of Pindar*.

Bury was a great linguist: during his classical period as well as studying Hebrew and Syriac he learned Sanskrit; but gradually his interests turned to history, and he then learnt Russian and Hungarian. In 1889 he produced the *History of the Later Roman Empire from Arcadius to Irene* (2 vols.), followed in 1893 by the *History of the Roman Empire from its Foundation to the death of Marcus Aurelius*, and in 1900 by the *History of Greece to the death of Alexander the Great*.

Bury was appointed Regius Professor of Modern History at Cambridge in 1902, and elected a Fellow of King's College in 1903. His output of learned books and articles continued unabated. Between 1896 and 1900 he published an annotated seven-volume edition of Gibbon's *Decline and Fall of the Roman Empire*, and in 1912 a *History of the Eastern Roman Empire from the fall of Irene to the accession of Basil I*. In the realm of philosophical thought, he published a *History of Freedom of Thought* (1914), and *The Idea of Progress* (1920).

For some years, Bury was Editor of the *Cambridge Ancient History* and, altogether, the bibliography of his writings contains nearly 400 entries. Perhaps the most lasting aspect of this vast output lies in his emphasis on the study of public law and administration and the unity and continuity of European

history. He was a Fellow of the British Academy and the recipient of many academic honours. Bury held his chair at Cambridge until his death in Rome on 1 June 1927.

BUTLIN, SIR WILLIAM HEYGATE EDMUND COLBORNE (BILLY) (1899–1980), pioneer of holiday camps, was born in Cape Town on 29 September 1899, the elder son of William Butlin, a cycle-shopkeeper, and his wife, Bertha Hill, daughter of a baker who sold gingerbread at local fairs in Gloucestershire. The marriage broke up; Mrs Butlin brought her sons back to England, travelled the fairgrounds selling gingerbread, married again, and in 1910 emigrated to Canada. Billy left school at twelve, worked in a Toronto department store and, at fifteen, joined the Canadian army as a drummer boy, and saw service in France.

After demobilization he returned to Canada but could not settle there, worked his passage to England on a cattle boat, and sought out his uncles who helped him to become a travelling showman (1921). His business as a fairground showman prospered, but for many years he had in mind the possibility of setting up holiday camps with indoor facilities and amusements to cope with the vagaries of the English weather. In 1936 he opened his first small holiday camp at Skegness. It was a great success, and in the following year he opened another at Clacton.

He was married three times; first, to Dorothy Cheriton of Tiverton, by whom he had a daughter; secondly, to her sister Norah, by whom he had a son and two daughters; and thirdly, to Sheila Devine of Liverpool, by whom he had a son and a daughter.

When the Second World War broke out he had three camps, which were taken over by the Air Ministry and the Admiralty. Butlin himself was appointed by Lord BEAVERBROOK, Minister of Supply, to be Director-General of hostels to the Ministry. For this work he received the MBE (1944). He also became an adviser to Field-Marshal MONTGOMERY

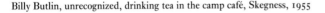

Billy Butlin, unrecognized, drinking tea in the camp café, Skegness, 1955

on the establishment in Belgium and Germany of leave centres for Allied servicemen.

After the war, he regained possession of his camps and, by 1946, had five of them ready to receive holiday-makers. By 1955 he was catering for some 600,000 people. Butlin camps had become a national institution, with their red-coated hosts and hostesses, swimming-pools, dance-halls, children's crèches, and every other facility needed to make highly-organized holidays for families, at prices they could afford. By the 1960s, Butlin camps were visited by a million people a year, and in 1972 Butlin's Ltd. and Butlin Properties Ltd. were sold to the Rank Organization for £43 million. Butlin was a shrewd buyer of pictures by Victorian artists; he liked them large, and never paid more than fifty guineas for one. One of his pictures with a religious subject by William Dyce hung in a holiday camp chapel for thirty years and was sold at auction in 1983 for £125,000.

In 1964 Butlin was knighted and in 1968 he retired to Jersey leaving his son to run the business. He was a man who gave much of his wealth to charities, mainly to help underprivileged children, and was honoured by the Variety Club of Great Britain and the Grand Order of the Water Rats. He died in Jersey on 12 June 1980.

BYNG, JULIAN HEDWORTH GEORGE, VISCOUNT BYNG OF VIMY (1862–1935), field-marshal, was born at Wrotham Park, Barnet on 11 September 1862, the youngest son of the second Earl of Strafford, and his second wife, Harriet Elizabeth, younger daughter of the first Lord Chesham. His grandfather had fought at Waterloo. He was educated at Eton, and in 1883 was commissioned in the 10th Hussars, stationed in India.

He saw action for the first time in the Eastern Sudan against Osman Digna in 1884, and in the Boer War commanded the South African Light Horse (1900–1) and proved himself to be an able leader. In 1902 he married Marie Evelyn, only child of (Sir) Richard Charles Moreton, of Crookham House, near Fleet, Hampshire: they had no

children. After the Boer War, he was appointed to command the 10th Hussars, and held a number of posts up to 1909 when he was promoted to major-general.

When the First World War broke out he was in Egypt, but was brought back to England to command the 3rd Cavalry Division which fought in the first Battle of Ypres (1914). In the following year, he commanded the IX Corps at Suvla and drew up the plan for the successful evacuation of Gallipoli. In 1916–17 he commanded the Canadian Corps in France, winning the confidence and affection of his troops, who distinguished themselves on the Somme and in the capture of Vimy Ridge in April 1917. Later that year, Byng took over command of the Third Army and remained in that post during the fluctuating battles that led to final victory by the Allies in 1918.

Byng was appointed CB in 1906, and KCMG in 1915; in 1919 he was gazetted full general, appointed GCB, and raised to the peerage as Baron Byng of Vimy. He was offered Southern Command but decided to retire from the army.

In 1921 he was appointed Governor-General of Canada and, during his five years there, was very popular in spite of the controversy aroused in 1926 by his refusal to grant a dissolution to W. L. Mackenzie King, the Liberal Prime Minister. Byng refused to consider staying in Canada for a second term but, in 1928, accepted the request of Sir William Joynson-Hicks, Home Secretary, and became Chief-Commissioner of the Metropolitan Police.

During the next three years (1928–31) he reorganized that force, tightening up discipline and introducing a number of reforms which greatly increased efficiency. Although his appointment had been criticized by Labour politicians, the Labour Government of 1929 refused to accept his offer to resign. In 1921 he was appointed GCMG and in 1928 became a viscount. Then, in 1932 he received the honour for which he had always hoped: he was created field-marshal, a most unusual honour for a retired officer. He died suddenly at Thorpe Hall, Thorpe-le-Soken on 6 June 1935 and the peerage became extinct.

C

CADBURY, GEORGE (1839–1922), cocoa and chocolate manufacturer and social reformer, was born at Edgbaston, Birmingham on 19 September 1839, the third son of John Cadbury, founder of the firm of Cadbury Brothers, and his wife, Candia, daughter of George Barrow, merchant and shipowner of Lancaster. He was educated at a Quaker school in Edgbaston, and in 1856, after a brief period of employment in the business of Joseph Rowntree at York, he joined his father's cocoa factory in Bridge Street, Birmingham.

In 1861 John Cadbury died, and George and his elder brother, Richard, took control of the business which appeared to be in decline. After considerable hard work and self-denial on the part of the two brothers, the business began to prosper and, when in 1866, they introduced the first unadulterated cocoa, expansion became the order of the day.

In 1873 Cadbury married Mary, daughter of Charles

Tylor, writer and lecturer, of London; they had three sons and two daughters.

The Cadburys always had great care for the welfare of their employees and were the first in Birmingham to introduce a weekly half-holiday. By 1879 the Bridge Street factory had become too small to cope with the increasing business and the partners decided to move to Bournville, four miles from Birmingham. George Cadbury seized the opportunity to provide good housing for his work people and, after Richard's death in 1899, he founded the Bournville Village Trust providing housing for others as well as his own employees. Cadbury, however, was interested, not only in housing, but also in education; he was a keen worker for the Adult School Movement and hundreds of Birmingham men learnt to read and write under his instruction.

A year after the death of his first wife in 1887, he married

Model Bournville house in the 1880s, part of Cadbury's housing scheme for his workforce

Elizabeth Mary, daughter of John Taylor, a member of the London Stock Exchange; they had three sons and three daughters. He was a Liberal in politics, and in 1901 acquired the *Daily News* and also owned four newspapers in the Birmingham area. In 1903 he handed over his Selly Oak house to the Society of Friends as a settlement for men and women engaged in social or religious work. George Cadbury died in Birmingham on 24 October 1922.

CAMM, SIR SYDNEY (1893–1966), aircraft designer, was born in Windsor on 5 August 1893, the eldest son of Frederick Camm, a journeyman carpenter, and his wife, Mary Smith. After attending the Royal Free School, Windsor, he became an apprentice woodworker and helped to set up the Windsor Model Aeroplane Club.

From model aeroplanes he progressed to man-carrying gliders and powered aircraft, and from 1914 to 1923 worked for the Martinsyde Company at Brooklands studying all kinds of aircraft, both British and foreign. During this period, in 1915 he married Hilda Rose Starnes and they had one daughter. In 1923 he joined the Hawker Engineering Company, and from 1925 to 1966 was their chief designer of aircraft. From 1935 to 1966 he was a member of the board of Hawker Siddeley Aviation.

His first success was with the light biplane, Cygnet, which won a number of prizes in 1925–6 and showed Camm's potential. From 1925 he was concerned with the development of military planes, particularly fighters. He designed the Hawker Hart day bomber and the Fury, a biplane which was sold all over the world.

By 1933 Camm realized that he could carry the design of biplanes no further, and in the following year set out to design a fighter monoplane to meet the operational demands of the Air Ministry. The result was the Hurricane which had a decisive success in the Battle of Britain in 1940, was used in every theatre of war, and was supplied in thousands to Soviet Russia. This was the highlight of Camm's career, but by the time the RAF were flying Hurricanes he was already designing new types such as the Typhoon, Tempest, and Sea Fury. The advent of the jet engine provided a new impetus to Camm's genius and, under his supervision, the Sea Hawk and Hunter aircraft were produced, the latter gaining the world speed record in 1953. During the later years of his career, he was concerned with the design of a vertical take-off and landing fighter.

Camm became a Fellow of the Royal Aeronautical Society in 1932, and was President in 1954–5; he was Chairman of the technical board of the Society of British Aircraft Constructors from 1951 to 1953. He was appointed CBE in 1941 and knighted in 1953. He died at Richmond, Surrey, on 12 March 1966.

CAMPBELL, BEATRICE STELLA (1865–1940), better known as Mrs Patrick Campbell, actress, was born in Kensington on 9 February 1865, the youngest child of John Tanner and his wife, Maria Luigia Giovanna, daughter of Count Angelo Romanini, an Italian political exile. She was educated at Brighton and Hampstead and in Paris, and studied for a short time at the Guildhall School of Music. At the age of nineteen she eloped with Patrick Campbell who held a small post in the City of London. They had one son and one daughter.

She made her first public appearance on the stage in Liverpool in 1888 and appeared in London in 1890. Between 1891 and 1893 she acted in melodrama for the Gattis, but they were dissatisfied with her performances and gave her notice. (Sir) George Alexander, however, engaged her to play the part of Paula Tanqueray in PINERO's *The Second Mrs Tanqueray*. In this play, produced at the St James's Theatre on 27 May 1893, she was an immediate success. Her dark Italian beauty and rich voice took the London audience by storm in the part of a passionate woman that suited her style of acting.

During the years from 1893 to 1911 Mrs Campbell appeared in a number of parts, including the name parts in *Fédora* (1893) and *Magda* (1896), the Rat Wife in Ibsen's *Little Eyolf* (1896), Lady Macbeth (1898), Mrs Daventry in the play *Mr and Mrs Daventry* by Frank Harris (1900), Mélisande in French to the Pelléas of Sarah Bernhardt (1904), and the name parts in *Hedda Gabler* (1907) and *Lady Patricia* (1911).

In 1902 she acted for the first time in New York, and she visited America frequently in later years, spending a whole year there in 1910. Her first husband was killed in the Boer War, and in 1914 she married George Cornwallis West, on the day his divorce from Jenny, Lady Randolph Churchill, was made absolute. He was at least eight years Mrs Campbell's junior and was twenty-one years younger than the wife who divorced him. Three years later, in 1917, Mrs Campbell's son, by her first marriage, was killed in action in France. Her daughter, Stella, also became an actress and often appeared with her mother on stage.

One of Mrs Campbell's last great successes was in SHAW's *Pygmalion*; as Eliza Doolittle, first played at His Majesty's in 1914 and afterwards in the USA, she gave a superb performance. Shaw himself was in love with her, but she avoided his amorous advances. They were, nevertheless, firm friends, as his letters to her reveal in her autobiography *My Life and Some Letters* (1922). Her later performances did not succeed in matching her earlier triumphs but, when she died at Pau on 9 April 1940, James Agate, the well-known theatre critic, said: 'In my life I have seen six great actresses and six only. These are Bernhardt, Réjane, Mrs Kendal, Ellen TERRY, Duse, and Mrs Patrick Campbell.'

CAMPBELL, SIR MALCOLM (1885–1948), racing driver, was born on 11 March 1885 at Chislehurst, the only son of William Campbell, watchmaker and jeweller of Cheapside, and his wife, Ada Westerton. He was educated at Uppingham and in Germany and France, and then worked as a Lloyd's underwriter. He was heir to a fortune from the family business and could afford to indulge his hobby of motor cycles. He also built up a profitable business insuring newspapers against libel actions.

He made his first appearance at Brooklands in 1908 and raced his first car, which he called 'Blue Bird', on the track there. He had his first accident in 1912 when he lost off back and front wheels while travelling at 90 m.p.h. He was luckily unscathed. In 1909 he had built his own aeroplane and became one of the earliest British aviators.

In the First World War Campbell was first a despatch rider and then a ferry pilot and instructor with the Royal Flying Corps. He was awarded the MBE. In 1920 he married Dorothy Evelyn, daughter of Major William Whittall; they had one son and one daughter.

After the war, Campbell returned to motor racing and won over 400 trophies, including the 200-mile race at Brooklands in both 1927 and 1928. By then he had decided to make world speed records his hobby and, in spite of a number of accidents in which he might well have been killed, he became the first man to travel at over 150 m.p.h., a feat he accomplished in 1925. In 1927 he raised this to nearly 175 m.p.h., in 1928 to 207 m.p.h., and in 1931 to 246 m.p.h. Still he was not content: in 1932 he achieved 250 m.p.h. and finally over 300 m.p.h. in 1935. Then he turned to water-speed records, reaching nearly 142 m.p.h. in 1939.

During the Second World War he commanded a motorcycle unit and served on the staff of Combined Operations. His marriage had ended in divorce in 1940.

Campbell contributed to the *Field* and the *Daily Mail* and wrote a number of books on motoring, including *My Thirty Years of Speed* (1935), and *Speed on Wheels* (1949). He was knighted in 1931.

Malcolm Campbell with admirers, July 1925

Campbell died at Reigate on 31 December 1948. His passion for speed was shared by his son, Donald, who raised the water-speed record to 239 m.p.h. in 1957.

CAMROSE, first Viscount (1879-1954). See Berry, William Ewert.

CAPE, (HERBERT) JONATHAN (1879-1960), publisher, was born in London on 15 November 1879, the youngest child of Jonathan Cape, a builder's clerk, and his wife, Caroline Page. At the age of sixteen he became an errand-boy for Hatchard's bookshop and in 1899 worked as a travelling salesman for an American firm of publishers. In 1904 he moved as traveller and then manager to the publishing house of Gerald Duckworth. In 1907 he married Edith Louisa Creak; they had two daughters.

In the First World War Cape served in the Royal Army Ordnance Corps. After the war he returned to Duckworth but in 1920 went as Manager to the Medici Society where he met George Wren Howard. Together they decided to form their own company, Cape finding his share of the capital by acquiring from Duckworth the 'shilling rights' of Elinor Glyn's books. Jonathan Cape was founded in 1921 and its first publication was a re-issue of C. M. Doughty's *Travels in Arabia Deserta*.

Cape's own industry, integrity, and flair for publishing was helped by the shrewdness of Edward Garnett, his reader. T. E. Lawrence's books, *Revolt in the Desert* (1927), *Seven Pillars of Wisdom* (1935), and *The Mint* (1955), were all published by Cape, together with works by Duff Cooper, Mary Webb, H. E. Bates, Ian and Peter Fleming, (Dame) C. V. Wedgwood, Hugh Lofting, and Arthur Ransome. Cape also visited the USA in search of authors, and became the publisher for Ernest Hemingway, Sinclair Lewis, Eugene O'Neill, and others.

His first wife died in 1919 and in 1927 he married Olive Vida James Blackmon; they had a son and a daughter. She in turn died in 1931 and, in 1941, he married Kathleen Webb Wilson; they had one son.

Cape never attempted to move into the field of specialist books; his Travellers' Library, a specially cheap series, set new standards of quality in the period before paperbacks. Publishing was his life, and he died in harness in London on 10 February 1960.

CARDUS, SIR (JOHN FREDERICK) NEVILLE (1889-1975), writer on music and cricket, was born on 2 April 1889 in Manchester, the illegitimate son of a man he never knew and of a girl who died in her twenties. He was educated at a Manchester board school until he was thirteen, when he left to be employed in a series of odd jobs from messenger-boy to clerk in an insurance office. He acquired his elegant style as a writer and his wide knowledge of music and cricket entirely by his own exertions.

From 1912 to 1916 he was assistant to William Attewill, cricket coach at Shrewsbury School; and for a time was secretary to the headmaster, the Revd Cyril Alington who had found him reading Gilbert Murray's *Medea*. By this time he was also contributing articles on music to various journals. During the First World War he was rejected for military service because he was short-sighted, and in 1916-17 worked as secretary to C. P. Scott, Editor of the *Manchester Guardian*. In 1917 he was appointed to the staff of the paper and began writing articles on a variety of topics and assisted Samuel Langford, the music critic. His cricket articles began

in 1919, after he had suffered from ill health and had to spend more time in the open air, and by 1924 he was already publishing books on cricket, such as *Days in the Sun* (1924), followed by *The Summer Game* (1929), and *Good Days* (1934). He lived to see them become classics.

In 1927 Cardus succeeded Langford as music critic of the *Guardian*, and his skilful work in this field brought him the friendship of many eminent musicians, including Kathleen Ferrier, Artur Schnabel, and Thomas Beecham. In 1936 he visited Australia with the England test team, and from 1941 to 1947 wrote articles for the *Sydney Morning Herald* and also gave a weekly broadcast on music. In 1948 he returned to England and during 1948-9 was on the staff of the *Sunday Times*; then, from 1951 onwards, he was the London music critic of the *Guardian*. Altogether his association with the *Guardian* lasted for fifty-eight years.

He published many books on music including *Talking of Music* (1957), *Sir Thomas Beecham, a Portrait* (1961), and *The Delights of Music* (1966). In 1964 he was appointed CBE and in 1967 was knighted. He received a number of awards for his writing on music and cricket. In 1921 he married Edith Honorine King, an art teacher; they had no children. She died in 1968, and Cardus himself died in London on 28 February 1975.

CARSON, EDWARD HENRY, Baron Carson, of Duncairn (1854-1935), Ulster leader, and Lord of Appeal in Ordinary, was born in Dublin on 9 February 1854, the second son of Edward Henry Carson, civil engineer, and his wife, Isabella, daughter of Capt. Peter Lambert of Castle Ellen, co. Galway. He was educated at Portarlington School and Trinity College, Dublin, and called to the Irish Bar (King's Inns) in 1877. In 1879 he married Sarah Annette Foster, the adopted daughter of Henry Persse Kirwan, of Triston Lodge, co. Galway; they had two sons and two daughters.

In 1887 he became junior counsel to the Attorney-General and, two years later, QC at the Irish Bar. In 1892 he was appointed Solicitor-General for Ireland and became MP for Dublin University. Carson was called to the English Bar in 1893 (Middle Temple) and became QC in 1894. His first success was in the libel action brought by Oscar Wilde against the Marquess of Queensberry. Though he made a great deal of money at the Bar he cared nothing for money if it impeded what he regarded as a duty, as he showed in the Archer-Shee case (1910) when he defended, for a nominal fee, a young Osborne cadet wrongly accused of theft. Terence Rattigan later based his play *The Winslow Boy* on this case.

From 1900 to 1905 Carson was Solicitor-General; he was knighted and sworn of the Privy Council. In 1910 he became the leader of the Irish Unionists in the House of Commons, and devoted himself whole-heartedly to the cause of Ulster. In 1912 the Ulster Volunteer Force was raised and the covenant was drafted, making clear that the whole province would resist any attempt to include it in the terms of an Irish Home Rule Bill. As the Liberal Government proceeded with the bill, Carson was the leader of those who were prepared to resist, no matter what the consequences. Winston Churchill in a speech in the spring of 1914 threatened coercion by force, and civil war seemed imminent when the 'Curragh incident', in which British officers threatened to resign, showed how dangerous the situation had become.

Carson's first wife had died in 1913; and in 1914 he married Ruby, elder daughter of Lt.-Col. Stephen Frewen, of Winton and Sigston Castle, Yorkshire; they had one son.

When the First World War broke out a party truce was declared in respect of the constitutional changes in Ireland; the Irish Home Rule Act was passed, but suspended for the period of the war. Carson felt that the British Government had been guilty of a breach of faith in not excluding Ulster from the Act, but he offered the services of the Ulster Volunteer Force for the prosecution of the war against Germany.

In 1915 he took office as Attorney-General in ASQUITH's Government, and accepted LLOYD GEORGE's assurance that the six counties of Ulster would not be included against their will in a Home Rule government. In 1916 he became First Lord of the Admiralty, and entered the War Cabinet. He resigned from Lloyd George's Government in 1917 when he learnt that the Prime Minister intended to introduce a Home Rule Bill for the whole of Ireland. However, Lloyd George and BONAR LAW, on the eve of the 1918 election, gave a pledge that the six counties would be excluded from any bill.

Carson returned to Parliament as MP for the Duncairn division of Belfast (1918-21). He continued to oppose the policy of Home Rule, but did not specifically oppose the 1920 bill, as its defeat would have brought into effect the 1914 Act. When the 1920 bill became law, Carson felt that he should hand over his leadership of the Ulster Unionists to a younger man, and in 1921 he resigned. Three months later he left the House of Commons on appointment as Lord of Appeal in Ordinary with the title of Baron Carson, of Duncairn. He resigned from this office in 1929 and died at Cleve Court, Minster, Kent on 22 October 1935. Carson was one of the most remarkable lawyers ever called to the Bar; he was a great orator and fearless advocate; Ulster will always be indebted to him for his eloquence and courage.

CARTER, HOWARD (1874-1939), archaeologist, was born in London on 9 May 1874, the youngest son of Samuel John Carter, animal painter, and his wife, Martha Joyce Sandys. He was educated privately and trained as a draughtsman by his father. When he was seventeen he went to Egypt as assistant draughtsman on the staff of the Archaeological Survey. In 1892 he joined W. M. Flinders PETRIE at El-Amarna for training in excavation.

From 1893 he was draughtsman to the Egyptian Exploration Fund making line-drawings of sculptures and inscriptions which were published with letterpress by Edouard Naville (1896-1908). In 1899 he was appointed Inspector-in-Chief of the monuments of Upper Egypt and Nubia, and in 1902 began excavations in the Valley of the Tombs of the Kings. In 1903 he was transferred to the inspectorate in Lower Egypt, but shortly afterwards resigned to become a water-colour painter.

In 1908, however, at the request of (Sir) Gaston Maspero, Director-General of the Service of Antiquities of Egypt, he returned to superintend the excavations in the necropolis at Thebes being undertaken by George Herbert, fifth Earl of Carnarvon. Carnarvon was a keen traveller, who some years before had had a serious motoring accident which precluded his entry into public life. He had been attracted by the excitement of archaeology, but he was an amateur at excavation and needed the help of an expert. For the next sixteen years Carter and he worked together.

The First World War interrupted their activities though Carter remained in Egypt and, during this time, discovered the tomb of Amenophis I. Then, in 1922, Carter found the tomb of Tutankhamūn with its wealth of artistic treasures. Lord Carnarvon had decided that 1922 was to be their last season in the Valley of the Kings and was in England, when,

Tomb of Tutankhamūn: Howard Carter examining the doors of the second shrine

after the removal of thousands of tons of rubble, Carter discovered the steps leading into the tomb.

Further excavation by the two archaeologists confirmed that they had discovered the tomb of King Tutankhamūn of Dynasty XVIII, who had ascended the throne about 1350 BC. The inner chamber was then opened in the presence of other archaeologists and officials of the Egyptian Government on 17 February 1923. In the burial chamber was the mummy of the king adjacent to the store-chamber with its treasures of gold and precious stones. The Earl of Carnarvon died soon afterwards in Cairo on 5 April. He had been bitten by a mosquito in the Valley of the Kings in March 1923; the bite had become infected and blood poisoning set in.

Meanwhile, it took Carter ten seasons (1922-32) to record and pack and transport to Cairo the objects found in the tomb. He published *The Tomb of Tut-ankh-Amen* (3 vols., 1923-33, vol. i in collaboration with A. C. Mace). The treasures he described are now to be seen in Cairo. Carter did not live to finish his task of compiling a full catalogue of the objects found. He died in London on 2 March 1939. He had never married.

CASEMENT, ROGER DAVID (1864-1916), British consular official and Irish rebel, was born at Kingstown, co. Dublin, on 1 September 1864, the younger son of Capt.

Roger Casement, third Light Dragoons, and his wife, Anne Jephson of Dublin. His family were Ulster Protestants. He was educated at the Academy, Ballymena and as a young man travelled widely in Africa.

In 1892 he entered the British Consular Service and was appointed Consul at Lourenço Marques (Maputo); six years later he was transferred to Luanda, and then to Boma in the Congo Free State. He was instructed to prepare a report on the conditions in the rubber trade and his report, published in 1903, revealed that the trade was based upon slave labour working under harsh conditions. His findings were confirmed by a Belgian inquiry and were partly responsible for the extinction of the Congo Free State in 1908.

In 1905 Casement was appointed CMG, and in 1906 was moved to Brazil and promoted to Consul-General in Rio de Janeiro in 1909. In the following year, he was asked to inquire into charges of ill-treatment of the natives by agents of the Peruvian Amazon Company. His report accused the agents of atrocious crimes and was not published until 1912 when it created a sensation. Meanwhile, Casement had been knighted in 1911 and retired from the Consular Service to live in Ireland.

Although he was an Ulsterman of Protestant descent, Casement was an extreme Irish nationalist, and from 1904 had been connected with the Gaelic League. He was one of the committee responsible for the formation of the Irish National Volunteers in 1913, and when the First World War broke out, he sought to obtain the help of the Germans in securing Irish independence. He was able to get to Germany in November 1914, and tried to induce Irish soldiers, captured by the Germans, to join an Irish brigade to fight for Germany. He had little success.

He soon ceased to trust the Germans, and became convinced that they would never send an expedition to Ireland and that without it the rebellion planned for Easter 1916 was doomed. Consequently, he persuaded the Germans to allow him to accompany a submarine carrying arms to Ireland, intending to try to convince the nationalists that the uprising would be premature. He was arrested on landing at Tralee on 24 April 1916 and charged in London with high treason, convicted, and hanged at Pentonville on 3 August 1916. His honours were all cancelled. He had been received into the Roman Catholic Church before he died. All those who knew him regarded him as honest and honourable; he died for his misguided extremism in time of war.

CASSEL, SIR ERNEST JOSEPH (1852–1921), financier and philanthropist, was born at Cologne on 3 March 1852, the youngest child of Jacob Cassel, a banker, and his wife, Amelia Rosenheim, both of Jewish descent. He was educated in Cologne, and left school at fourteen to work with a banking firm. During the next few years he worked in Liverpool, Paris, and finally in London with the financial house of Bischoffsheim and Goldschmidt where he quickly showed that he had a special aptitude for finance. In 1874 he was appointed manager.

His own emoluments were increased steadily by the acumen with which he dealt with problems on behalf of his employers, and on his visits to the USA he made contacts which enabled him to invest on his own account in American enterprises. By 1881 Cassel had accumulated a sizeable fortune which he proceeded to expand steadily by shrewd investments. He was soon one of the wealthiest and most powerful financiers in London with a high reputation for integrity and sound judgement. He remained associated with

the Bischoffsheim firm until 1884, and then began to work independently. In 1878 he had become a naturalized British subject. In the same year Cassel married Annette, daughter of Robert Thompson Maxwell, of Croft House, Croft, Darlington, but she died three years later leaving an only daughter.

The vast empire he built up covered the establishment of the Swedish Central Railway on a sound financial basis, the reorganization of the Louisville and Nashville Railway in the USA, the arrangement of the finances of the Mexican Central Railway, and the issue of government loans in Mexico, China, and Uruguay.

From his early years Cassel had been interested in Egypt, and in 1898 he financed the construction of the Nile dams at Aswan and Asyut. He had a hand in the formation of the National Bank of Egypt and in many other schemes for agricultural and industrial development in that country. He was also concerned with the creation of the State Bank of Morocco in 1906 and the National Bank of Turkey in 1909.

His care for British national interests in his activities did not go unrecognized. He became KCMG in 1899, KCVO and PC in 1902, GCMG in 1905, GCVO in 1906, and GCB in 1909. He was also the recipient of many foreign decorations.

He entertained lavishly, and made a valuable collection of old masters, antique furniture, old silver and other *objets d'art*. His interest in horse-racing brought him the close friendship of Edward VII, as Prince of Wales and King, by whom he was held in high esteem, not only because he could provide shrewd financial advice, but because Edward enjoyed his company and his hospitality.

Many of Cassel's public benefactions were made in honour of Edward VII, and they covered a very wide field from

Sir Ernest Cassel in the robes of the Order of St Michael and St George, early 1900s

hospitals and medical research to education and technical training.

During the First World War he had suffered from the attacks of anti-German extremists but he was, in fact, of great value to the British Government in the financial problems arising from the war, and his British patriotism could not be impugned. His enemies were routed by his obvious integrity. At the request of his wife, Cassel became a Roman Catholic, though this was not generally known until he died in London on 21 September 1921.

CATTO, THOMAS SIVEWRIGHT, first BARON CATTO (1879-1959), Governor of the Bank of England, was born on 15 March 1879 at Newcastle upon Tyne, the fifth son of William Catto, a shipwright, and his wife, Isabella, daughter of William Yule, a sea captain. He was educated at Peterhead Academy and Heaton School, Newcastle. At the age of fifteen he worked in the office of the Gordon Steam Shipping Co. and taught himself shorthand and typing. In 1898 he went out to Batoum and Baker where he worked for six years and learnt to speak Russian. Then, in 1904, he joined Mac-Andrews & Forbes, merchants, as Manager of their London office. He became a member of the Baltic Exchange and learnt about the chartering of ships and other business methods in the City.

Catto married in 1910 Gladys Forbes, daughter of Stephen Gordon, a partner in MacAndrews & Forbes; they had one son and three daughters.

In 1906 he went to Smyrna as second in command of the company, and then from 1909 to 1919 worked in New York as Vice-President. From 1915 to 1917 he was British Admiralty representative on the Russian commission to the USA, but when Russia collapsed he was transferred to the British Food Mission, and in 1918 was head of the British Ministry of Food in North America.

From 1919 to 1940 Catto was Chairman of Andrew Yule & Co. in Calcutta, succeeding Sir David Yule. He worked in Calcutta until 1928 when he became a partner in Morgan, Grenfell & Co., although he remained Chairman of Andrew Yule & Co. which, in 1940, became Yule, Catto & Co. He had been appointed CBE in 1918, created baronet in 1921 and in 1936 became a baron.

In April 1940 Catto was appointed a director of the Bank of England but, a fortnight later, succeeded Lord WOOLTON as Director-General, equipment and stores, in the Ministry of Supply. In the following year, he moved to the post of full-time adviser to the Treasury where he worked with John Maynard KEYNES. They were popularly known as 'Catto and Doggo'.

In 1944 he succeeded Montagu NORMAN as Governor of the Bank of England, a post which he held until 1949. Under his control, the Bank was taken into public ownership with the minimum of controversy and the maximum retention of operational independence. He was sworn of the Privy Council in 1947. His eldest daughter, Isabel, was in 1955 elected President of the World YWCA. Catto died at Holmbury St Mary, Surrey on 23 August 1959.

CAVELL, EDITH (1865-1915), nurse, was born at Swardeston, Norfolk, on 4 December 1865, the eldest daughter of the Revd Frederick Cavell, Vicar of Swardeston, and his wife, Louisa Sophia Walming. She was educated at a school in Somerset and in Brussels and, while travelling on the Continent, became interested in nursing. In 1895 she entered the London Hospital as a probationer and, when she was

Edith Cavell Memorial, Brussels, 1918

qualified as a staff nurse, worked in hospitals in London and Manchester.

In 1906 she went to Brussels to assist Dr Depage in establishing a training school for nurses on the British model. A year later, she was appointed the first matron of Depage's Berkendael Medical Institute. She also organized and managed the hospital of St Gilles. In 1914 Dr Depage was called away to set up military hospitals, and Edith Cavell was left in charge of what had become a Red Cross Hospital in which wounded soldiers, both Allied and German, were cared for.

Towards the end of 1914 the Allied armies were compelled to withdraw from Belgium, and many soldiers, having been cut off from their units by the German advance, were refugees seeking shelter wherever they could find it. Many of them went to Nurse Cavell for help, and she assisted large numbers of them to escape from Belgium. In the summer of 1915 the suspicions of the German authorities were aroused; Nurse Cavell was arrested and kept in solitary confinement. The United States Minister in Brussels tried to intervene on her behalf, but found it impossible to persuade the German military regime to allow his legation to make any contact with her. In October 1915 Edith Cavell was brought to trial with thirty-five other persons accused of assisting Allied soldiers to return to the Allied lines to renew their part in hostilities. She was found guilty on the basis of her own confession that she had concealed English and French soldiers and provided them with money and funds to enable them to cross the Dutch frontier. On 12 October she was shot.

In May 1919 her body was brought to Norwich after a memorial service at Westminster Abbey, and she was reburied in a grave outside the south transept of the cathedral. Memorials to her courage were set up in Norwich and elsewhere. To many people she was a martyr who had resolutely done what she regarded as her duty, and her execution by the Germans, however legally justifiable, was a political blunder.

CECIL, (EDGAR ALGERNON) ROBERT GAS-COYNE-, VISCOUNT CECIL OF CHELWOOD (1864-1958), a creator of the League of Nations, was born in London on 14 September 1864, the third son of Lord Robert Arthur Talbot Gascoyne-Cecil, later third Marquess of Salisbury, and his wife, Georgiana Caroline, daughter of Sir Edward Hall Alderson. He was educated at Eton and University College, Oxford where he was President of the Union (1885). He had four brothers who all won distinction in their various fields. He was called to the Bar (Inner Temple) in 1887, took silk in 1899, and became a bencher in 1910. In 1889 he married Lady Eleanor Lambton, daughter of the second Earl of Durham; the marriage was childless. From 1906 to 1910 he was Conservative MP for East Marylebone, but he was a moderate free-trader and a keen supporter of women's suffrage, and in 1910 resigned from the party. From 1911 to 1923 he was independent MP for the Hitchin division of Hertfordshire.

During the First World War he worked for the Red Cross and became Parliamentary Under-Secretary for Foreign Affairs (1915–18), Minister of Blockade (1916–18), and later Assistant Secretary of State for Foreign Affairs (1918–19). Shocked by the horror of war, he prepared a paper for the Cabinet in 1916 making proposals for the avoidance of future wars. This eventually became the basis for the first draft of the Covenant of the League of Nations. After the war, he devoted his life to the maintenance of peace and played a leading part in the debates in Paris which preceded the establishment of the League in 1919. In 1923 Robert Cecil was appointed Lord Privy Seal in Baldwin's Government and put in charge of League affairs. In 1924 he became Chancellor of the Duchy of Lancaster with a similar responsibility but, in 1926, after a number of disagreements with his colleagues, Cecil resigned when the Cabinet refused to take his advice to accept naval parity with the USA. He never again held government office.

Under the Labour Government of 1929, he was made Chairman of a departmental committee on League matters and British representative to the preparatory disarmament commission. But, in 1931, the Disarmament Conference failed and the League failed with it. Cecil hoped to save the League from disintegration by mobilizing public opinion. He was President of the League of Nations Union from 1923 to 1945 and organized the peace ballot of 1934–5. The Abyssinian war proved that he was right in asserting that only strong international organizations to preserve peace could save the world from the devastation of war. In 1937 he was awarded the Nobel peace prize.

He was the recipient of many other honours, both political and academic. He was sworn of the Privy Council in 1915, created viscount in 1923, and CH in 1956. Cecil died in Tunbridge Wells on 24 November 1958; his widow, a person of great intellectual ability who had taken an active interest in his political life, survived him by only a few months.

CECIL, JAMES EDWARD HUBERT GASCOYNE-, fourth MARQUESS OF SALISBURY (1861–1947), was born in London on 23 October 1861, the eldest son of Robert Gascoyne-Cecil, who became third Marquess of Salisbury in 1868, and his wife, Georgiana Caroline, daughter of Sir Edward Hall Alderson. He was educated at Eton and University College, Oxford and from an early age was brought up to be a political figure. He accompanied his father to the Congress of Berlin in 1878, and entered Parliament as Conservative MP for the Darwen division of North-East Lancashire in 1885. He held that seat until 1892, and then

became member for Rochester from 1893 till 1903 when he succeeded his father as fourth Marquess.

In 1887 he married Lady Cicely Alice Gore, daughter of the fifth Earl of Arran. They had two sons and two daughters.

During the Boer War he commanded the 4th Bedfordshire Battalion and was awarded the CB, but he was recalled in 1900 to be Under-Secretary of State for Foreign Affairs in his father's last administration. In 1903 he became Lord Privy Seal in Arthur BALFOUR's Government, and was President of the Board of Trade, briefly, in 1905 until the Liberals came to office. In opposition, he became recognized as the leader of the old Conservatives and played a leading part in opposing the Finance Bill of 1909 and the Parliament Bill of 1911. He fought against the Parliament Bill to the bitter end and, even when it was passed, he continued to argue for the restoration of some of the previous powers of the House of Lords.

In the First World War he became a major-general and from 1916 to 1918 was Chairman of the tribunal to which conscientious objectors could appeal for exemption from military service. He strongly opposed the Irish Treaty of 1921, and took a leading part in bringing the Coalition Government of LLOYD GEORGE to an end in 1922.

In BONAR LAW's, and then BALDWIN's, Cabinets he was Lord President of the Council (1922–4), Chancellor of the Duchy of Lancaster (1922–3), Lord Privy Seal (1924–9), and Leader of the House of Lords (1925–9). In 1931 he resigned as Conservative Leader of the Opposition in the House of Lords and refused to join the National Government of Ramsay MACDONALD. He introduced a bill for the revision of the Parliament Act but the Conservative Party was divided on this issue and the bill was defeated (1934). He strongly opposed the Government of India Bill (1935), was deeply concerned about the lack of preparation for defence, and advocated conscription (1938) and a national government (1939). He supported CHURCHILL in his efforts to persuade the Government to take more serious steps to counter the threat from Hitler.

He was the recipient of many honours including appointment as KG (1917). From 1942 to 1945 he was President of the National Union of Conservative and Unionist Associations. He continued his strenuous defence of Conservative principles and, although he was frequently in disagreement with the leaders of his party, he exercised considerable influence with his fellow peers. In the debate on the King's abdication in 1936 he gave his support to Baldwin. He collapsed while making a speech against post-war materialism and irreligion and died in London on 4 April 1947.

Lord Salisbury had four younger brothers, all of whom had distinguished careers. William became Bishop of Exeter, Robert, VISCOUNT CECIL OF CHELWOOD, was a creator of the League of Nations, Edward was an eminent public servant in Egypt, and Hugh, Baron Quickswood, became Provost of Eton College.

CHADWICK, SIR JAMES (1891–1974), physicist, was born on 20 October 1891 at Bollington, near Macclesfield, the eldest of the three sons of J. J. Chadwick, who owned a laundry business in Manchester. He was educated at Manchester Municipal Secondary School and Manchester University, where he obtained a first in physics in 1911 and an M.Sc. in 1913. At that time Ernest RUTHERFORD was working at Manchester with the German physicist, Geiger, and had announced his nuclear theory of atomic structure.

Chadwick, having followed this work with great interest,

decided to work with Geiger in Berlin, and, when the First World War broke out, he was interned at Ruhleben. However, through the kindness of German scientists such as Planck and Nernst, Chadwick was able to work with Charles Ellis, another British internee, and together, in spite of serious handicaps, they carried out experiments which were later to lead them to the study of radioactive substances.

After the war Chadwick returned to Manchester, but, when in 1919 Rutherford was appointed to the Cavendish Chair of Physics at Cambridge, Chadwick went with him, and with a studentship from Gonville and Caius College, began the research on radioactivity in co-operation with Rutherford which was to occupy his next sixteen years. In 1925 he married Aileen, daughter of H. Stewart-Brown, a Liverpool businessman. They had twin daughters.

In 1921 Chadwick had been elected to a research fellowship, and shortly afterwards was appointed Assistant Director of Research at the Cavendish Laboratory, and became responsible for the detailed organization of research on the artificial disintegration of light elements by alpha particle bombardment, supervised by Rutherford. In his Bakerian lecture in 1920 Rutherford had predicted the existence of the neutron, and in 1932 Chadwick proved its existence. The importance of this discovery arose from the fact that, during the intervening period of twelve years, little advance had been made in the understanding of nuclear structure, and Chadwick's discovery of the neutron was therefore a major landmark in nuclear physics; in 1935 he received the Nobel Prize for Physics.

In that year (1935) Chadwick parted company with Rutherford; they could not agree on Chadwick's view that development at the Cavendish necessitated the construction of a cyclotron. Before this argument between them came to a head Chadwick was offered and accepted the Lyon Jones Chair of Physics at Liverpool, where his marriage had given him many useful contacts. He was able to proceed with his own plans for a cyclotron and the machine was completed in 1939.

During the Second World War, research at Liverpool University was actively concerned with mastering the problem of nuclear fission, and Chadwick was closely involved with the development of the atomic bomb. In 1943 he went to the USA at the head of the British team to co-operate with American scientists on the 'Manhattan Project' and, when that project was successful, Chadwick could see no alternative to using the bomb operationally.

In 1945 he was knighted, and in the following year returned to Liverpool to continue his work there. In 1948 he was appointed Chairman of a committee dealing with the civil application of atomic energy, and its report was influential in deciding the pattern of Britain's nuclear power programme. In the same year Chadwick left Liverpool to become Master of Gonville and Caius College, Cambridge, a post which he held until 1958. In 1970 he was made a Companion of Honour.

Chadwick had become FRS as early as 1927, and he was honoured by many universities and learned societies. Apart from his book *Radioactivity and Radioactive Substances* (1921) and the work he published in collaboration with Rutherford and C. D. Ellis, *Radiations from Radioactive Substances* (1930), he contributed many papers to scientific journals. He died in Cambridge on 24 July 1974.

CHAIN, SIR ERNST BORIS (1906–1979), biochemist, was born in Berlin on 19 June 1906, the son of Dr Michael Chain,

chemist and industrialist of Russian origin, and his wife, Margarete Eisner. He was educated at the Luisengymnasium, and Friedrich-Wilhelm University, Berlin (1930). For three years he did research in Berlin, and in 1933 emigrated to England because of racial persecution. He became a research worker under Sir Frederick Gowland HOPKINS at Cambridge, obtaining his Ph.D. in 1935.

At this time Howard FLOREY, Professor of Pathology at Oxford, was seeking an able biochemist to work with him and, at Hopkins's suggestion, appointed Chain. He set Chain to work on lysozyme, but Chain became interested in other natural anti-microbial products, and in particular in penicillin. He and a group of colleagues at the Sir William Dunn School of Pathology succeeded in extracting and purifying penicillin, and in 1945 Chain shared the Nobel prize for physiology and medicine for this work with FLEMING and Florey. Florey was concerned with the medical uses of penicillin, but Chain was concerned with its biochemical properties, and discovered with E. P. Abraham that the enzyme penicillinase enabled some bacteria to resist penicillin. In 1948 Chain left Oxford for Rome to organize a department of biochemistry and set up a fermentation plant.

In the same year he married Dr Anne Beloff; they had two sons and a daughter. He remained in Rome until 1961 when he returned to England as Professor of Biochemistry at Imperial College, London.

In 1954 he was consulted by the drug firm of Beecham, and as a result of his advice they were able to develop new forms of penicillin which were effective against bacteria which had proved resistant to penicillin in its original form. During the years 1961 to 1973 Chain was able to obtain the money for a new building at Imperial College housing a fermentation plant, and further advances became possible in the development of antibiotics.

Chain became an FRS in 1949, and was knighted in 1969. He received academic honours and awards from all over the world. He died in Ireland on 12 August 1979.

CHAMBERLAIN, (ARTHUR) NEVILLE (1869–1940), politician and Prime Minister, was born at Edgbaston on 18 March 1869, the son of the Liberal and later Conservative politician Joseph Chamberlain, and his second wife, Florence, daughter of Timothy Kenrick of Birmingham. Austen CHAMBERLAIN was his half-brother. He was educated at Rugby, and Mason College, Birmingham, intending to go into business. In 1890 his father bought an estate in the Bahamas and for seven years Neville tried hard to develop this as a sisal plantation, but without success.

He was more successful when he returned to Birmingham to pursue his business career and to take part in local politics as Councillor and Lord Mayor; setting up the first municipal savings bank (1916). In 1911 he married Annie Vere, daughter of Major William Utting Cole, 3rd Dragoon Guards, of Woodhay House, Newbury. They had one son and one daughter. During the First World War he was appointed Director-General of National Service, but LLOYD GEORGE had little confidence in him, and after seven months of frustration Chamberlain resigned and returned to Birmingham.

This experience, however, gave him a taste for national politics and in 1918, when he was nearly fifty, he became Conservative MP for the Ladywood division of Birmingham, a seat which he held for the rest of his life. For four years he supported Lloyd George's Coalition Government in which Austen was Chancellor of the Exchequer; but in 1922 he and Austen parted political company when Neville decided to

Neville Chamberlain, flanked by Hitler and von Ribbentrop, in Munich, September 1938

discontinue his support of Lloyd George. In BONAR LAW's Government Austen refused to take office but Neville became Postmaster-General, then Minister of Health, and during 1923-4 Chancellor of the Exchequer. He was sworn of the Privy Council in 1922. After the brief Labour Government of 1924, Chamberlain refused to return to the Exchequer under Stanley BALDWIN preferring the Ministry of Health, while Austen became Foreign Secretary. As Minister of Health Neville Chamberlain proved himself to be an able administrator. He embarked successfully on an ambitious housing programme and reformed the Poor Law.

In opposition (1929-31) he reorganized the Conservative Central Office, and when the National Government was formed he succeeded Philip SNOWDEN as Chancellor; he held that office till 1937 when he took over from Baldwin as Prime Minister. As Chancellor in 1934 he took a leading part in increasing the air estimates in view of the growing threat from Hitler's Germany. Up to this point in his political career, he had been successful in all the offices of state to which he had been appointed, and none in his party appeared to doubt that he was the obvious choice to succeed Baldwin.

As Prime Minister, however, his policies became a subject of growing controversy, and future historians will for long continue to debate whether or not his unavailing efforts to appease Hitler and Mussolini had any justification. At the time he entered 10 Downing Street, the peace of Europe was already seriously threatened, and neither Britain nor her ally France was prepared for war. Chamberlain himself was in favour of rearmament, but the Opposition were adamantly opposed to it, and the Government were reluctant to reveal the extent of the country's military weakness. The British public as a whole were not ready to fight, though there were

some who saw that Hitler's ambitions must inevitably lead to war. Throughout 1938, after Anthony EDEN had resigned as Foreign Secretary over Chamberlain's readiness to come to terms with Mussolini, and Hitler had invaded Austria and threatened Czechoslovakia, Chamberlain hoped that he could persuade Hitler to moderate his aggressive demands; but, in conference after conference leading finally to Munich, Hitler outwitted him.

When the Prime Minister returned from Munich on 30 September 1938 waving a piece of paper on which Hitler's signature appeared to him to guarantee peace, he was welcomed with acclamation; but his triumph was short-lived, as it soon became obvious that Czechoslovakia had been sacrificed to no purpose, and that a European war to check the aggression of the Nazis had become inevitable. When the war came a year later Chamberlain should have resigned; his policy of appeasement was dead, and he was not the man to lead Britain in a war that would clearly be long and arduous.

The early months of the war were uneventful, but, with the German invasion of Norway in 1940, the first British disaster took place. A coalition government could not be formed with Chamberlain at its head as the Labour leaders, as well as the Liberals under Archibald Sinclair, refused to serve under him. On 10 May he resigned, and Winston CHURCHILL took over as Prime Minister.

Chamberlain joined Churchill's Government as Lord President of the Council but he was already a sick man and on 9 November 1940 he died at Highfield Park, near Reading. He had declined to receive any honour, including the Garter. His ashes were interred in Westminster Abbey. No one could doubt the sincerity of Chamberlain's belief in the absolute necessity of avoiding another European war until there remained no alternative but to fight. His tragedy was that he could not comprehend that any man could be so unreasonable and fanatical as Hitler.

CHAMBERLAIN, SIR (JOSEPH) AUSTEN (1863-1937), politician, was born at Birmingham on 16 October 1863, the son of Joseph Chamberlain and his first wife, Harriet, daughter of Archibald Kenrick, of Berrow Court, Edgbaston. His mother died at his birth. Neville CHAMBERLAIN was his half-brother. He was educated at Rugby and Trinity College, Cambridge, and his father clearly intended that he should become a politician. After spending some time in France, which he loved, and Germany, which he did not, he entered the House of Commons as Liberal Unionist MP for East Worcestershire (1892-1914).

From 1895 to 1900 he was Civil Lord of the Admiralty, and in 1900-2, Financial Secretary to the Treasury. He was sworn of the Privy Council in 1902, and from 1903 to 1905 was Chancellor of the Exchequer, though his father had resigned from BALFOUR's Government in 1903 over the issue of tariff reform.

In 1906 he married Ivy Muriel, daughter of Col. Henry Lawrence Dundas of Datchet; they had two sons and one daughter.

During the years of the Liberal Government, he was one of the die-hards who fought against LLOYD GEORGE's budgets and the Parliament Act of 1911. In November of that year, Balfour resigned from the leadership of the Unionist Party, and Chamberlain and Walter Long (afterwards Viscount Long) were rivals for the succession. However, when it became clear that the contest would be close, they both stood down in favour of BONAR LAW.

In the weeks preceding the First World War Chamberlain used his influence with his Conservative Party colleagues to bring pressure upon ASQUITH to stand by France and Russia. When the Coalition Government was formed in 1915 he became Secretary of State for India, but the mismanagement of the Mesopotamia campaign was felt to be the responsibility of his department and in 1917 he resigned. After the 'coupon election' of 1918, Lloyd George chose Chamberlain to be Chancellor of the Exchequer in his Coalition Government. He produced three sound post-war budgets before resigning from the Treasury in 1921 when he became leader of the Conservative Party on Bonar Law's retirement.

Chamberlain continued to support Lloyd George, in spite of the growing dissatisfaction of the Conservatives with the coalition; but the Carlton Club meeting on 19 October 1922 decided to bring the coalition to an end and, with it, Chamberlain's leadership. He was out of office until, in 1924, BALDWIN asked him to become Foreign Secretary. The Locarno Agreement was largely his work for which in 1925 he was appointed KG and awarded the Nobel peace prize.

Of the various offices held by Chamberlain in the course of his political career, his tenure of the Foreign Office was his most successful. He was the first Foreign Secretary to attend regularly meetings of the Council of the League of Nations, and he took a leading part in the maintenance of peace in Europe, though his policies were not invariably popular with his Conservative colleagues.

In the National Government of 1931 he accepted the post of First Lord of the Admiralty, but his active political career was coming to an end and by then he was concentrating his efforts on ensuring that his half-brother Neville would succeed Baldwin. After 1931 he no longer held office but he continued to be an influence on foreign policy. For example,

he was a severe critic of the Hoare-Laval pact on Abyssinia in 1935, and Baldwin disowned HOARE because he feared the effects of Chamberlain's censure.

During his later years, Chamberlain took on a number of non-political responsibilities: he was Chancellor of Reading University from 1935 to 1937, and Chairman of the Governors of Rugby School. He died suddenly in London on 16 March 1937, two months before Neville became Prime Minister. Winston CHURCHILL once described him as a man who always played the game and always lost.

CHAPLIN, SIR CHARLES SPENCER (1889-1977), comedian, was born on 16 April 1889 in Walworth, London, the son of Charles Chaplin, and his wife, Hannah, daughter of Charles Hill, both music-hall performers. His father was part-Irish, part-French, and his mother, half gypsy, half Spanish. She had been married before and Charlie had a half-brother, Sydney, who changed his name to Chaplin. When Charlie was five the two boys were sent to an orphanage, but two years later they returned to their unfortunate mother and, at the age of seven, Charlie replaced her on the stage at Aldershot. When her voice failed he took over with a clog dance. The two boys continued to live in dire poverty, their father a shiftless drunkard and their mother on the verge of insanity. The father died in 1901, and as he began to earn money Charlie cared for his mother until her death.

By the time he was ten, Chaplin was appearing professionally in music-halls as one of 'The Eight Lancashire Lads'. When he was seventeen he joined Fred Karno's company, and in 1910 went with them as comedian to the USA where he was seen in 1913 by Mack Sennett and was given a comedian's part in a Hollywood film. From Fred Karno Chaplin had learnt the appeal of pathos mixed with comedy, which was the attraction of his type of acting, and he was reluctant to leave the company.

His first films were not successful, but in 1914 he made a name for himself in *Tillie's Punctured Romance*, with Mabel Normand. He continued to work in films for Sennett and Keystone and in 1915 came his masterpiece, *The Tramp*, in which he first appeared in the baggy trousers with the hat and cane that were to make him famous.

In the following year he went to the Mutual Company with whom he made some of his best comedies including *The Floor-walker* and *Easy Street*. Then, he built his own studios and in co-operation with Douglas Fairbanks, Senior, and Mary Pickford formed United Artists. During the twenties he directed his own films, appeared with Jackie Coogan in *The Kid* (1921), and made *The Gold Rush* (1925). He also directed a film, *A Woman of Paris*, with Edna Purviance, who had become his mistress.

Reluctant to take part in talkie films, Chaplin continued to direct and appear in silent films such as *City Lights* (1931) and *Modern Times* (1936), but eventually had to adopt the talkie. He went half-way in *The Great Dictator* (1940) in which most of the film was silent comedy and satire.

Up till this time Chaplin had been uniformly successful in films, but he was now faced with a period of obloquy in America. In 1952 he made *Limelight*, in which the story nostalgically recreates the hardships of his early years in London. Claire Bloom, whom he had picked to be his leading lady, recounts in *Limelight and After* (1982) how Chaplin 'again and again spoke of his London childhood. He described the London parks, that I enjoyed, as places of desolation and despair.'

Charlie Chaplin in *The Gold Rush*, 1925

He was unpopular in America at the time because he was suspected of having Communist sympathies. This was non-sense but, when he left the country for the première of *Limelight* in Europe, the State Department forbade his re-entry; he had never become an American citizen. He and his wife, Oona, found a home in Switzerland. He continued to make films, but without the success of the earlier ones which made him famous. In 1964 he published *My Autobiography*.

In 1972 he was welcomed back in the USA and awarded a special Oscar (award of the Academy of Motion Picture Arts) in recognition of his outstanding contribution to the motion-picture industry. In 1975 he was appointed KBE.

He was married three times before he found permanent happiness. In 1918 he married Mildred Harris; they divorced in 1920. In 1924 he married Lita Grey; they divorced in 1926, after having two sons. In 1936 he married Paulette Goddard, his leading lady in *Modern Times* and *The Great Dictator*; they divorced in 1942. Then, in the following year, he married Oona, the young daughter of Eugene O'Neill. She became a British subject when Chaplin was banned

from America. They had four children, of whom the eldest, Geraldine, followed in her father's footsteps as a successful actress. Oona gave Chaplin the domestic happiness for which he had been vainly looking for years. He died at his home in Switzerland on Christmas Day 1977. Alistair Cooke has expressed the view that throughout the 1920s and into the early 1930s Chaplin was the most famous man on earth.

CHATFIELD, ALFRED ERNLE MONTACUTE, first Baron Chatfield (1873-1967), Admiral of the Fleet, was born in Southsea on 27 September 1873, the only son of Admiral Alfred John Chatfield and his wife, Louisa, eldest daughter of Thomas Faulconer, of Hampstead. He was edu-cated at St Andrew's School, Tenby, and joined the training ship *Britannia* in 1886. During his early years in the Royal Navy he served in sailing ships and specialized in gunnery. In 1909 he married Lillian Emma St John, daughter of Major George L. Matthews; they had two daughters and one son.

In 1909 he commanded *Albemarle* in the Atlantic fleet, and in 1913 was flag-captain in *Lion* with David BEATTY. With

Beatty he took part in the battles of Heligoland Bight (1914), Dogger Bank (1915), and Jutland (1916).

When the First World War ended, Chatfield accompanied Beatty to the Admiralty as Fourth Sea Lord and took a leading part in the Washington Conference of 1921-2. He was promoted to rear-admiral in 1920. After two years in command of the third cruiser squadron in the Mediterranean, he returned to the Admiralty in 1925 as Third Sea Lord and Controller of the Navy. In this post he had to resist the policy of reducing naval strength and came into conflict with the Air Ministry over control of the Fleet Air Arm. He became vice-admiral in 1926, and in 1929 moved to be Commander-in-Chief, Atlantic Fleet. A year later, he rose to admiral and was transferred to the Mediterranean.

In 1933 he achieved his great ambition when he went back to the Admiralty as First Sea Lord. Times had changed, and he was able to set about strengthening the navy and rectifying weaknesses which his previous experiences had revealed. He also won the battle with the Air Ministry and secured naval control of the Fleet Air Arm (1937). In 1935 he was promoted Admiral of the Fleet, and in 1937 was raised to the peerage.

He left the Admiralty in 1938 and was appointed, by Neville CHAMBERLAIN, Minister for Co-ordination of Defence. He was admitted OM and sworn of the Privy Council in the same year. But his membership of the War Cabinet gave him little influence as he had no access to the Chiefs of Staff Committee and had no experience of dealing with politicians. In March 1940 he was asked to resign and his post was abolished.

He was the recipient of many honours and published two autobiographical books, *The Navy and Defence* (1942), and *It Might Happen Again* (1947). Chatfield died at Farnham Common on 15 November 1967. He could claim with justi-fication that he had made revolutionary changes in policy and strategy which transformed the static role of the navy in the First World War to the flexibility and mobility so neces-sary to success in the Second World War.

CHERWELL, VISCOUNT (1886-1957). See LINDEMANN.

CHESTERTON, GILBERT KEITH (1874-1936), poet, novelist, and critic, was born in London on 29 May 1874, the elder son of Edward Chesterton, an auctioneer and estate agent, and his wife, Marie Louise Grosjean, of French and Scottish descent. He was educated at St Paul's School from 1887 to 1892, and then at the Slade School of Art. Although he had a certain talent for drawing he decided to earn his living as a journalist, and by 1899 was working on the *Speaker*. His first published work was a volume of poetry, *The Wild Knight* (1900).

In 1901 he married Frances, eldest daughter of George William Blogg, a London diamond merchant; there were no children. His wife was an Anglo-Catholic and she un-doubtedly influenced his thinking on matters of religion. Among the hundred books that came from Chesterton's pen, many were coloured by his philosophical stance which led him into controversy with other authors such as George Bernard SHAW, H. G. WELLS, and Rudyard KIPLING. *The Napoleon of Notting Hill* (1904), and *Heretics* (1905) dem-onstrated his attitude to imperialists. Studies of *Robert Browning* (1903), and *Charles Dickens* (1906) showed his skill as a literary critic.

In 1908 the Chestertons went to live at Beaconsfield where they remained for the rest of their lives. The first of the Father Brown tales appeared in 1911—detective stories

Conversation piece: Chesterton (left), Belloc (right), and Maurice Baring, by James Gunn, 1932

based on the character of a close friend, Father O'Connor, who in 1922 received Chesterton into the Roman Catholic Church. In 1911 also appeared *The Ballad of the White Horse*, followed in 1912 by *Manalive* and in 1913 by *The Victorian Age in Literature*.

In 1913 Cecil Chesterton, G. K.'s brother, was prosecuted by Godfrey Isaacs for criminal libel for an article published in the *New Witness*. Cecil was found guilty, but escaped with a fine when he had expected to be sent to prison. This was a cause of worry to G. K., and when the First World War broke out he was ill and suffering from strain. He had been opposed to the Boer War, but he had no doubts about the justice of the British cause in this conflict. From Christmas 1914 to Easter 1915 he was desperately ill, but from then onwards he began to recover though he never regained his earlier vigour.

The *New Witness*, a newspaper intended to fight against corruption in public life, had been started by Cecil Ches-terton and Hilaire BELLOC in 1912. When, in 1916, Cecil joined the army, G. K. took over as Editor and, after his brother died in France in 1918, he continued to edit the paper until 1923. It was later revived as *G. K.'s Weekly* from 1925 to 1938.

After becoming a Roman Catholic, Chesterton published *St Francis of Assisi* (1923), *The Everlasting Man* (1925), and *St Thomas Aquinas* (1933). He also travelled widely in the years after the 1914-18 war, lecturing in Europe, the USA, and Canada. He had by then become a legendary figure, obese, absent-minded, good-natured, with large hat, flowing cloak, and sword stick. James GUNN depicted him, typically, in a group painting together with Hilaire Belloc and Maurice Baring. During the last years of his life he gave a series of radio talks for the BBC, which were very popular.

He died at Beaconsfield on 14 June 1936: his wife died two years later. His epitaph could well have been the final lines of his poem *The Rolling English Road*:

But walk with clearer eyes and ears this path that wandereth,
And see undrugged in evening light the decent inn of death;
For there is good news yet to hear and fine things to be seen
Before we go to Paradise by way of Kensal Green.

CHEVALIER, ALBERT (1861–1923), comedian, was born in London on 21 March 1861, the eldest son of Jean Onésime Chevalier, a teacher of languages, and his wife, Ellen Louisa Mathews. He went to St Mary's College, Richmond, to be trained as a priest, but left and took a job as a clerk in a newspaper office. He was interested in the stage from the age of fourteen, and made his first public appearance in 1877. During the next twelve years he appeared in plays in London and on tour.

He sang the coster songs, for which he was to become famous, at the London Pavilion for the first time in 1891. He was immediately successful, and for the next seven years he appeared at London music-halls, occasionally at as many as five halls in a single night. His best known songs, such as 'My Old Dutch' and 'Knocked 'em in the Old Kent Road', were very popular. In 1895 he married Florence, daughter of George Leybourne, another well-known music-hall comedian.

After an unfortunate venture into management, he toured America and Canada in 1896 and was as big a success there as he had been in London. On return to England, he resumed his career in London and in 1902 sang before Edward VII at Sandringham. He also appeared in a number of plays on the London stage including his own play *My Old Dutch* (1920) which was performed nearly 200 times. He appeared for the last time in 1922, and died in 1923 in London.

Chevalier sang over 100 songs 80 of which he wrote himself. He also composed and appeared in monologues, and as his performances were always inoffensive, he helped to raise the standards of entertainment in the music-hall of his time. He published his reminiscences in *Before I Forget* (1901).

CHICHESTER, SIR FRANCIS CHARLES (1901–1972), airman and yachtsman, was born on 17 September 1901 at Shirwell, Devon, the younger son of the Revd Charles Chichester, Vicar of Shirwell, and his wife, Emily Annie, daughter of Samuel Page of London. He was educated at Marlborough, left at seventeen, and emigrated to New Zealand in 1919, where he worked as a land agent and property developer.

He first made a name for himself as an airman. Having learnt to fly, he flew from England to Australia in a Gipsy I Moth in 1929 taking nineteen days for this hazardous solo flight. Later that year, he successfully flew across the Tasman Sea from east to west, an exploit in which he demonstrated his great skill at navigation by making landfall to refuel *en route* at two remote small islands.

In 1923 he married Muriel Eileen, daughter of M. L. Blakiston; they had two sons, the first stillborn; they divorced in 1926, and she died in 1929. In 1937 he married Sheila Mary, daughter of Gerald Craven; they had one son.

By the outbreak of the Second World War, Chichester

Sir Francis Chichester on board *Gipsy Moth IV*, in which he made his solo voyage round the world

had returned to England, but it was not until 1943 that he was able to serve in the RAF as navigation officer at the Empire Flying School. At the end of the war he set up his own firm, publishing maps and guides, took up ocean racing, and in 1960 won the first single-handed transatlantic race. In 1962 he came second. At an age when most people have retired, he then set out to sail solo around the world, a feat which he successfully accomplished, with one stop at Sydney (1966–7).

Chichester was appointed CBE in 1964 and KBE in 1967. He also received a large number of medals and other awards for his achievements as a sailor and navigator. He wrote many books on his experiences, including *Alone Across the Atlantic* (1961), *The Lonely Sea and the Sky* (1964), and *Gipsy Moth Circles the World* (1967). Although he knew that he had cancer he set out on the transatlantic race of 1972, but had to return to Plymouth. He died there on 26 August 1972. Few men could have had more courage and determination.

CHILDERS, ROBERT ERSKINE (1870–1922), author and politician, was born in London on 25 June 1870, the second son of the Pali scholar, Robert Caesar Childers, and his wife, Anna Mary Henrietta, daughter of Thomas Johnston Barton, of Glendalough House, co. Wicklow. He was educated at Haileybury, and Trinity College, Cambridge, and from 1895 till 1910 was a Clerk in the House of Commons.

In the Boer War he fought with the City Imperial Volunteer Battery of the Honourable Artillery Company and recorded his part in the war in *In the Ranks of the CIV* (1900). He also collaborated in the official volume *The HAC in South Africa* (1903).

Childers was a keen yachtsman, and his best-known book *The Riddle of the Sands* (1903) was based upon his experience of the Baltic Coast. It gave a fictional account of German plans to invade Britain. In 1903 Childers visited the USA with the HAC and met Mary Alden Osgood, of Boston; they married in 1904 and had two sons.

He next wrote vol. v of '*The Times*' *History of the War in South Africa* (1907), but from 1908 his whole interest centred in the problems of Ireland. He resigned his post in the Commons in 1910 to pursue the objective of Home Rule, and in July 1914 went so far as to smuggle arms into Ireland for the use of the National Volunteers preparing for armed conflict with the Ulster Volunteers.

During the First World War, however, he served in the RNVR, took part in the Cuxhaven raid, did intelligence work, and received the DSC. In 1919 he went with the Irish republican envoys to Paris to put the claims of Ireland before the Peace Conference. In 1921 he was elected to the republican Dail Eireann and appointed Propaganda Minister. He was principal secretary to the delegation which negotiated the Irish Treaty with LLOYD GEORGE's Government, but he violently opposed Arthur Griffith and Michael Collins who were ready to accept the treaty, which excluded Ulster from the Free State. He joined and served in the Republican army and, on 10 November 1922, Free State troops surrounded his home, Glendalough House, and he was arrested. He was court-martialled in Dublin, condemned, and shot on 24 November 1922. At the time he was branded as a traitor by both Irish and British, but undoubtedly he died for a cause which his conscience dictated that he should fight for.

CHIROL, SIR (IGNATIUS) VALENTINE (1852–1929), traveller, journalist, and author, was born on 23 May 1852 while his parents, the Revd Alexander Chirol, a member of a Huguenot family settled in England, and his wife, Harriet, daughter of the Revd Denny Ashburnham, were abroad. His mother was a Roman Catholic and he was brought up in that faith, and educated mainly in France and Germany; he graduated at the Sorbonne.

He served for four years (1872–6) as a clerk in the Foreign Office; then he abruptly resigned, and spent the next sixteen years travelling in the Near East, India, Persia (Iran), Australia, Egypt, Turkey, and Bulgaria.

In 1892 he was appointed *The Times* correspondent in Berlin, where he gradually came to distrust the ambitions of Kaiser Wilhelm II and the growing animosity towards England. He made no secret of his fears in his dispatches to his paper and for some time was *persona non grata* with the German Foreign Office.

He was recalled to London in 1896 to take charge of the Foreign Department of *The Times*. From 1899 until 1912 he was head of the department. He was consistently in favour of the Anglo-Japanese alliance, the *entente* with France, and the understanding with Russia. He continued to fear the increasing strength of Germany. He also strongly advocated good relations with the USA and was in favour of constitutional reform in India, a country which he visited seventeen times.

The History of the Times—1884–1912 (1947) is somewhat critical of Chirol's relations with his colleagues. It records that, 'He was, in fact, made for another sort of career than journalism and another sort of office than a newspaper's.' Nevertheless, difficult as he might be to work with, he was conscientious, hard working, and fearless in expressing his views. He was knighted in 1912.

During the First World War he worked again for the Foreign Office, taking part in a mission to the Balkans and being present at the Peace Conference in 1919.

He wrote many books, from *The Far Eastern Question* (1896) to *The Occident and the Orient* (1924), including *Indian Unrest* (1910), *India Old and New* (1921), and *India* ('The Modern World' series, 1926).

Part of his difficulties with his colleagues arose from the fact that he suffered ill health for many years. He never married. Chirol died suddenly in Chelsea on 22 October 1929.

CHRISTIE, DAME AGATHA MARY CLARISSA (1890–1976), detective novelist and playwright, was born on 15 September 1890 at Torquay, the youngest child of Frederick Alvah Miller, formerly of New York, and his wife, Clarissa ('Clara') Margaret Boehmer. She had no schooling, but once she had learnt to read she read voraciously. At sixteen she went to Paris to study singing and the piano, but found that she was not suited to a musical career.

In 1914 she married Archibald Christie, an officer in the Royal Flying Corps, while she was with the Voluntary Aid Detachment (VAD) as a nurse. Later, while she was working in a dispensary, she began to write detective stories and conceived the character of Hercule Poirot, a retired Belgian detective, who was to become the infallible hero of many of her novels. In 1920 *The Mysterious Affair at Styles* appeared, followed by similar stories such as *The Murder of Roger Ackroyd* (1926).

In 1926 her mother died, and her husband, Colonel Christie, left her for Nancy Neele. These two disasters led to a breakdown, and to events which have never been satisfactorily explained. Agatha Christie disappeared and for nine days could not be traced. Then, she was discovered in a Harrogate hotel where she had registered under the name of Neele. Naturally, her disappearance was greeted with much publicity and her re-appearance, after she had apparently been suffering from amnesia, with even more publicity, which she did not welcome. In 1928 she divorced Colonel Christie; they had one daughter.

In 1930 she married Max MALLOWAN, whom she had met on a holiday visit to the archaeological site at Ur, where Mallowan was assisting Leonard WOOLLEY. For the rest of her life she was closely associated with archaeological work, and used this as a background for some of the novels including *Death Comes As the End* (1945).

Agatha Christie wrote nearly thirty detective novels in

which the ingenuity of Hercule Poirot was matched by the wisdom of the unassuming Miss Marple, her other investigator; the last novel was *Sleeping Murder* (1976). Her plots were carefully designed to mislead the reader with numerous clues leading into impenetrable dead-ends for everybody except Poirot or Miss Marple. They did not possess the carefully studied backgrounds of Dorothy SAYERS, but were none the less readable. Her novels were translated into 103 languages.

As a playwright Agatha Christie had the unique experience of surpassing all theatrical records with her play *The Mousetrap* (1952) which has run for over thirty years with casts regularly renewed from time to time. She was appointed CBE in 1956 and DBE in 1971. Her *Autobiography* was published in 1977. She died at Wallingford on 12 January 1976.

CHRISTIE, JOHN (1882–1962), founder of Glyndebourne Opera, was born on 14 December 1882, at Eggesford, Devon, the only child of Augustus Langham Christie, a country squire, and his wife, (Alicia) Rosamond Wallop, daughter of the fifth Earl of Portsmouth. He was educated at Eton, Royal Military Academy, Woolwich, and Trinity College, Cambridge. He abandoned a military career, having injured his foot in a riding accident. From 1906 to 1922 he was a master at Eton, except for the years 1914–16 when he served in France with the King's Royal Rifle Corps, and won the MC.

As soon as he obtained legal control of the family estate at

John Christie at the opening of the 1954 Glyndebourne season

Glyndebourne in Sussex, he left Eton to devote himself to the improvement and management of his property. In 1931, he married (Grace) Audrey Laura, daughter of the Revd Aubrey Neville St John-Mildmay (later tenth baronet). She was a talented soprano with the Carl Rosa Opera Company. Together, they planned to present opera at Glyndebourne, and built a small theatre for the purpose.

Their project was greeted with derision, but in 1934 they opened with *Le nozze di Figaro*, conducted by Fritz Busch. The production was an immediate success, and *Così fan tutte*, which followed, was equally successful. Audrey Christie herself took part with great charm, and an evening at Glyndebourne soon became an essential item in the season for the musical and fashionable world.

The first three seasons cost John Christie £100,000, but in 1937 he succeeded in making a small profit. During the Second World War Glyndebourne became a home for evacuated London children, but as soon as the war ended Christie set about obtaining public support for a revival of the opera seasons. In 1946–7 some performances were given including the world premières of Benjamin BRITTEN's *The Rape of Lucretia* and *Albert Herring*, and Gluck's *Orfeo ed Euridice* with Kathleen FERRIER. The company performed at the Edinburgh Festival during 1947–9.

Then in 1950 the support of the John Lewis Partnership enabled Glyndebourne to put on its own season again, and the group, organized as 'The Glyndebourne Festival Society' and registered as a charitable trust, helped to defray the costs of production. Sadly, before the trust could be set up, Audrey Christie died in 1953, leaving a son and a daughter.

John Christie became a CH in 1954, and from that time handed over executive control of the Glyndebourne venture to his son. During his later years Christie had become almost totally blind. He died at Glyndebourne on 4 July 1962. He had succeeded in achieving what at first sight seemed impossible, staging opera of the highest standard at his own country house and attracting audiences from all over the world.

CHURCHILL, RANDOLPH (1911–1968), journalist and author, was born in London on 28 May 1911, the only son of Winston CHURCHILL, and his wife, Clementine Ogilvy, daughter of Col. (Sir) Henry Montague Hozier, and Lady Henrietta Blanche Ogilvy. He was educated at Eton and Christ Church, Oxford, and sought to follow his father, to whom he was always devotedly loyal, by adopting a political career. He stood for Parliament at seven elections, but was faced with insuperable difficulty because, up to the outbreak of the Second World War, his father was at loggerheads with the Conservative Government, first over the policy towards India, and then because of the appeasement of Hitler and the Nazi regime. Randolph had little hope of beating the Conservative party machine. Only when Winston Churchill became Prime Minister in 1940 did his son succeed in getting elected unopposed as Conservative MP for Preston (1940–5). In 1939 he married Pamela Digby, daughter of the 11th Baron Digby, of Minterne, Dorset; they had one son and the marriage ended in divorce in 1946.

During the war he served with the 4th Queen's Own Hussars as an intelligence officer in the Middle East and Yugoslavia, being parachuted into the latter country to join Tito's partisans with his friend, Evelyn WAUGH; they were an ill-assorted pair. Handsome in appearance, arrogant, noisy, argumentative, and often drunken, but witty, lovable, and dauntless, Randolph was handicapped by being the son of a famous man whom he had no chance of emulating though he sought courageously to put on a show of his own. In 1948 he married June, daughter of Col. Rex Osborne, DSO; they had a daughter, and this marriage also ended in divorce (1961).

Churchill became a brilliant journalist, read with interest in both Britain and the United States, and among the most notable of his books are *The Rise and Fall of Sir Anthony Eden* (1959), *Lord Derby*, '*King of Lancashire*' (1960), and *The Fight for the Tory Leadership* (1964). He set out to write the authoritative life of his father, but only succeeded in finishing the first two volumes, vol. i. *Youth, 1874–1900* (1966) and vol. ii. *The Young Politician, 1901–14* (1967). Randolph Churchill died at Stour on 6 June 1968. His son Winston followed family tradition, becoming a writer and politician.

CHURCHILL, SIR WINSTON LEONARD SPENCER (1874–1965), politician and war leader, was born prematurely at Blenheim Palace, his grandfather's home, on 30 November 1874, the elder of the two sons of Lord Randolph Churchill, third son of the seventh Duke of Marlborough, and his wife, Jennie, daughter of Leonard Jerome of New York. He was educated at Harrow and Sandhurst and in 1895 was commissioned in the 4th Queen's Own Hussars. His mother had been widowed in the previous year and, because there was little money to spare, Winston had by some means to earn his own living. This he proceeded to do by journalism, his first efforts being a record for the *Daily Graphic* of fighting, in which he himself took part, with the Spanish forces against the rebels in Cuba. After this adventure, he joined his regiment in India and by 1897 had arranged to cover, for two newspapers, Sir Bindon Blood's campaign against the Pathans on the northern frontier. A few months later he published *The Story of the Malakand Field Force*.

His new ambition was to see service in KITCHENER's campaign to reoccupy the Sudan, and his mother used her influence to overcome the reluctance of Kitchener to accept this pushing young man in a post under his command. Winston was attached to the 21st Lancers and took part in the Battle of Omdurman (1898). He then published *The River War* which appeared in 1899. By this time, he had resigned his commission and set out for South Africa to report on the war there for the *Morning Post*. But within a short time of his arrival at Durban, he was captured in a Boer ambush of an armoured train, escaped with a price on his head, and made his way back to Durban. Returning to England he made a small fortune by publishing two books based upon his experiences in South Africa, *London to Ladysmith, via Pretoria* and *Ian Hamilton's March* (1900).

He had now decided to follow in the footsteps of his father and to seek a career in politics. In 1900 he became Unionist MP for Oldham but, when Joseph Chamberlain introduced proposals for tariff reform, Winston, at that time a convinced free-trader, crossed the floor of the House and joined the Liberals. His Oldham constituents disowned him, but early in 1906 he won North-West Manchester, having become a supporter of Campbell-Bannerman's 1905 administration. He also published *Lord Randolph Churchill* in that year. His first government office was as Parliamentary Under-Secretary for the Colonies, he having refused the offer of a post in the Treasury. He became a Privy Counsellor in 1907. In the following year he published *My African Journey*.

In April of that year LLOYD GEORGE left the presidency of the Board of Trade for the Exchequer, and ASQUITH,

who had succeeded Campbell-Bannerman as Prime Minister, appointed Churchill to that post; he was the youngest Cabinet Minister since 1866. The appointment necessitated a by-election in which Winston was narrowly defeated at North-West Manchester but he was very soon elected as MP for Dundee. Also in that year (1908), he married Clementine, daughter of Lady Blanche and Col. Sir Henry Hozier, Secretary of Lloyd's; she was an elegant, accomplished young lady of twenty-three, who was to devote the rest of her life to assisting her extraordinary husband in his chequered career. In the course of a close relationship which lasted for nearly six decades they had one son, Randolph CHURCHILL, and four daughters, the youngest of whom Mary married the Conservative politician, Christopher (later Lord) Soames and published a biography of her mother in 1979.

From 1908 onwards, Churchill and Lloyd George worked closely together as loyal colleagues of Asquith, aiming to relieve the distress of working people and to bring about a new era in the responsibility of governments for the regulation of the conditions of employment in factory and workshop. The Board of Trade established labour exchanges and introduced an Insurance Bill against unemployment. Later, in 1910 as Home Secretary, Churchill saw through Parliament a Mines Bill to improve safety measures in the coal pits, and a Shops Act to improve the conditions of shop assistants. Meanwhile, Lloyd George, then Chancellor of the Exchequer, was preparing his 'People's Budget', which led to the political crisis of 1910, when the House of Lords threatened to override the will of the majority in the House of Commons, and the Liberals insisted on passing the Parliament Act of 1911. It was during his tenure of the post of Home Secretary that Churchill took part personally in 'the battle of Sidney Street' in which he called out troops to help the police to dislodge a gang from a house in the east end of London. He called out troops again during a riot of miners on strike at Tonypandy in 1910. The riot was put down by metropolitan policemen but support troops arrived as it was ending and Churchill was afterwards accused of having used troops against the miners.

However, as the years passed, the danger of war with Germany became an increasing preoccupation, particularly as the Kaiser set out to build more and more battleships which threatened the safety of Britain at sea. The Agadir crisis of 1911 led Churchill to think seriously of the problems that would have to be faced if war was declared before the Admiralty had made efficient plans to meet such an emergency. In the autumn of that year he assumed the post of First Lord of the Admiralty, and set out to reorganize the Navy Board and to modernize and strengthen the Royal Navy with all the energy and zest with which hitherto he had fought to ameliorate the lot of the poor. 'He talks about nothing but the sea', said David BEATTY, who had become his Naval Secretary. When war came in August 1914, there could be no doubt that, in spite of occasional friction between Churchill and some of his naval colleagues both at the Admiralty and at sea, it was largely due to his determination that the Navy was ready. As Kitchener later told him 'There is one thing . . . they can never take away from you. When the war began, you had the Fleet ready.'

From the outset of the war, Churchill was anxious that the Navy should play a leading role but, as the German admirals refused to risk their capital ships in confrontation with the British and the Allied armies became bogged down in the mud of Flanders, he began to look for some alternative by which the power of the Navy could be brought to bear upon the enemy. This led him to approve a naval attack upon the Dardanelles, despite the fact that Admiral FISHER, whom he had brought in as First Sea Lord, did not support him without misgivings and Kitchener was reluctant to release troops for military support in this venture. The result was disaster, and Churchill, whom the Conservatives had never forgiven for leaving them some twelve years earlier, received most of the blame. When, later in the year 1915, Asquith formed a coalition with BONAR LAW, one condition made by the Conservative leader was that Winston should be removed from the Admiralty. To his dismay and bitter regret, he was forced by Asquith to resign, and for a short time became Chancellor of the Duchy of Lancaster. When Lloyd George replaced Asquith as Prime Minister towards the end of 1916, he looked for an opportunity to give Churchill a further chance to exercise his undoubted talents in the pursuit of victory, in spite of his unpopularity with his Conservative colleagues. In July 1917 Churchill became Minister of Munitions. During the interim, he had rejoined his regiment, the Oxfordshire Hussars, crossed to France with the rank of major, and in 1916 had commanded the 6th Battalion of the Royal Scots Fusiliers.

When the war ended and Lloyd George called his 'coupon election', Winston agreed to stand as a coalition Liberal and was returned as MP for Dundee. In return Lloyd George appointed him Minister for War, and Churchill was responsible for the smooth operation of demobilization while the Prime Minister was busy at the Peace Conference. In 1921 he moved from the War Office to become Colonial Secretary, but his relations with Lloyd George soon deteriorated. When the Conservatives forced the Prime Minister to resign in 1922, Winston was defeated at Dundee in the subsequent general election. For his services during the war he was appointed a Companion of Honour.

He was now in the political wilderness and fought two further elections and suffered defeat in both. Meanwhile, he had bought Chartwell Manor in Kent and published *World Crisis* (1923). A year later he decided to return to the Conservative fold and was elected MP for Epping, a seat which he held until 1945. Stanley BALDWIN was now Prime Minister and, to Winston's surprise, invited him to be Chancellor of the Exchequer. In this post, he brought in five budgets and carried through the return of sterling to the gold standard. Post-war conditions in Britain brought considerable hardship to the working people and consequent industrial strife. Churchill took a leading part in the defeat of the general strike in 1926, during which he edited the government newspaper, the *British Gazette*, which was virulent in its attacks upon the trade unions. When the strike collapsed, however, Winston did what he could to secure a settlement that would take the miners willingly back to work. In the end, however, the miners had to return defeated and resentful.

His partnership with Baldwin ran into trouble when he opposed Ramsay MACDONALD's India Bill which Baldwin was prepared to support. Churchill resigned from the Shadow Cabinet in 1931. In the previous year he had published *My Early Life* and he was now also giving a great part of his leisure hours to painting. *Thoughts and Adventures* appeared in 1932, his four-volume life of his ancestor, the first Duke of Marlborough, in 1933-8, and *Great Contemporaries* in 1937. In the abdication crisis of 1936 he had rather misguidedly supported the cause of Edward VIII but, throughout this period when he was out of office, his main preoccupation was the growing menace from Hitler's Germany and the obvious lack of preparation for war in Britain.

After the temporary euphoria created by the Munich agreement between Neville CHAMBERLAIN and Hitler, Churchill's eloquent warnings in the Commons began to be taken more seriously, but it was not until Germany invaded Poland on 1 September 1939 that Chamberlain invited him to return to the Admiralty. 'Winston is back', the Fleet was informed. At first there were some minor victories at sea, among them the sinking of the battleship *Graf Spee*; but the expedition to Norway was a disaster and, although Churchill himself loyally supported Chamberlain, the Labour members of Parliament demanded a coalition and refused to serve under Chamberlain. The obvious choice as war leader was Winston Churchill and, in May 1940, he became Prime Minister and Minister of Defence. He and Clement ATTLEE, the leader of the Labour party, agreed on the distribution of posts in the Coalition Government which included, in the course of the war, Ernest BEVIN, Sir John ANDERSON, Anthony EDEN, Lord SIMON, Herbert MORRISON, Hugh DALTON, Lord BEAVERBROOK, and Lord WOOLTON. He now set out on the long hard struggle, first to survive and ultimately to achieve victory.

To him the outcome never seemed to be in doubt and, amid the military disasters of 1940, it was his determination and pugnacity that inspired the British people. His 'V for victory' gesture and his inevitable cigar became symbols of resistance to every assault and of the resolution of the public never to surrender. The fall of France was followed by the Battle of Britain in which invasion was thwarted by the RAF. 'Never has so much been owed by so many to so few', said Churchill.

Gradually the tide of war began to turn. Sir Alan BROOKE was appointed Commander-in-Chief, Home Forces; aid from

Churchill 'assists' in pillbox construction during an inspection of defences of the Southern Command, July 1940

the United States was secured by Churchill's close relationship with President Roosevelt; Britain obtained 50 much needed destroyers to assist in the battle of the Atlantic and, when in 1941 the Japanese attacked Pearl Harbor and brought America into the war, Winston knew that final victory was assured. Earlier in that year, he had warned Joseph Stalin of the impending German invasion of Russia, and the naval convoys taking aid to the Soviet Government battled through icy Arctic seas to keep the Russian armies supplied. Nevertheless, there continued to be disasters. The *Prince of Wales* and the *Repulse* were sunk by Japanese aircraft; Singapore was lost and Burma evacuated. In June 1942, Tobruk, the centre of British resistance in North Africa, capitulated with the loss of 25,000 men taken prisoner. Later that year, however, the Eighth Army under General MONTGOMERY won a decisive victory at El Alamein and the final expulsion of the Germans from North Africa had begun.

In 1943 Churchill was gravely ill with pneumonia during a visit to the army in North Africa. Fortunately, he recovered, but as the joint forces of Britain and the USA fought their way through Sicily into Italy, Roosevelt and Churchill began to differ in their approach to the campaign in Europe. Stalin had been pressing, since 1942, for a second front and the recognition of the Russian frontiers of 1941, and Roosevelt was anxious to invade France and push into Germany at the earliest possible date. Winston, however, persuaded by his Chiefs of Staff that the invasion of Europe at that time would be premature and distrusting the post-war ambitions of the Soviets, argued strenuously for diversions in southern Europe. Eventually, General Eisenhower was appointed Supreme Allied Commander in Europe and, in June 1944, the invasion of Hitler's Europe began with the successful landing of Allied armies in Normandy. It was necessary for King George VI to intervene to dissuade Churchill from viewing at close quarters the D-day landings.

When later that year he replied to General SMUTS's congratulations on his seventieth birthday, Churchill admitted that 'it is not so easy as it used to be for me to get things done'. This was true not so much because he was getting old, but because, as an Allied victory became assured, Roosevelt, in their meetings with Stalin at Tehran and Yalta, was more anxious than Churchill to reach agreement with the Russians on post-war policy in Europe. They did, however, agree on the establishment of the United Nations. On 12 April 1945 Roosevelt died suddenly and Harry S. Truman became President. On 8 May the war in Europe came finally to an end.

Churchill proposed to Attlee that the wartime coalition should continue until Japan had been defeated. It was assumed that this would not be achieved for another year and a half. But Attlee, under pressure from his Labour colleagues, refused and, in the subsequent election, Churchill was heavily defeated and a Labour Government took office. Winston was tired but, although he was less forceful than of yore in Parliament, he was forceful enough in his warning of the need for European unity and western co-operation in the 'cold war' with Communism, a phrase he invented in a speech at Fulton, Missouri in 1946.

From 1945 to 1964 he was MP for Woodford, and in 1951 returned to office as Prime Minister; but he was no longer the man he had been and, by the time of his eightieth birthday, it became clear that he could not fight another election as Prime Minister. In April 1953 he was honoured by the Queen with the Garter which, soon after the war ended, he had refused. In 1955 he resigned.

He had continued his voluminous writing throughout the post-war years, including *The Second World War* (6 vols., 1948–54) and *A History of the English-Speaking Peoples* (1956–8). Among his non-political achievements were honorary degrees from over twenty universities and the lord wardenship of the Cinque Ports, which he held from 1941 till 1965; he received the OM in 1946 and the Nobel prize for literature in 1953; he had become a Royal Academician Extraordinary in 1948.

On 24 January 1965 Churchill died at his home at 28 Hyde Park Gate, London, and was given a magnificent state funeral before he was buried at Bladon, near Blenheim Palace. Much will continue to be written about his remarkable character, his mistakes, and his eccentric methods of work which taxed his staff to the utmost limits. But no one will deny that he was a notable orator, a great Englishman, and an indomitable leader in war.

In 1966, his wife, Clementine, was created Baroness Spencer-Churchill of Chartwell. She died in London on 12 December 1977 in her ninety-second year.

COCHRAN, SIR CHARLES BLAKE (1872–1951), showman, was born on 25 September 1872 in Brighton, son of James Elphinstone Cochran, tea merchant, and his wife, Matilda Walton, daughter of a Merchant Navy officer. He was educated at Brighton Grammar School where he shared a study with Aubrey Beardsley.

In 1891 he went to New York hoping to become an actor, but he had no talent for acting and became secretary to the actor-manager, Richard Mansfield, and thus obtained managerial experience. After six years he returned to London and set up as a theatrical agent, promoting boxing and wrestling and music-hall entertainments.

In 1903 he married Evelyn Alice, daughter of Charles Robert Dade, a captain in the Merchant Service; they had no children. In the same year as his marriage, he went bankrupt, having produced two stage failures, but returned to the promotion of roller-skating and circuses. In 1911 he produced Max Reinhardt's *The Miracle* which the praise of the Northcliffe press helped to make a success.

From 1914 Cochran turned to revues and in 1917 had a great success with Bruce BAIRNSFATHER's *The Better 'Ole*. From the end of the First World War Cochran never looked back. He produced a whole string of successful revues, including *Dover Street to Dixie* (1923), *One Dam Thing After Another* (1927) and *Cochran's 1930 Revue*.

In 1925 Cochran went bankrupt again, but nothing could keep him down for long. His promotions included appearances by Sarah Bernhardt, Eleanora Duse, Sacha Guitry, Chaliapin, the Chauve Souris Company and the Diaghilev ballet. He also promoted the Wells–Beckett and Beckett–Carpentier fights. After publishing his first book of memoirs *The Secrets of a Showman* (1925), Cochran used the proceeds to put on cabaret at the Trocadero, and then, in association with Noël COWARD staged *On With the Dance* (1925), *This Year of Grace* (1928), and *Bitter Sweet* (1929). 1930 saw *Private Lives* with Noël Coward and Gertrude LAWRENCE, followed by *Evergreen* with Jessie Matthews, and *Cavalcade* in 1931.

In association with A. P. HERBERT, Cochran staged *Helen* (1932), and that season he produced five other shows, *Dinner at Eight*, *The Cat and the Fiddle*, *Words and Music*, a Sacha Guitry season, and the revival of *The Miracle* with Lady Diana Cooper as the Madonna. In 1933 he was responsible for *Escape Me Never* with Elizabeth Bergner, and Cole

C. B. Cochran's 1932 production of *Helen*, written by A. P. Herbert and designed by Oliver Messel

Porter's *Nymph Errant*; and in 1934 came Noël Coward's *Conversation Piece*.

During the Second World War Cochran had little success with his shows and reverted to writing more memoirs to raise money, but in 1946 he made a come-back with *Big Ben* and *Bless the Bride* by A. P. Herbert and Vivian Ellis. His last spectacular show, however, *Tough at the Top* (1949) was a failure.

Cochran had many side interests; he was President of the Actors' Benevolent Fund, and a Governor of the Shakespeare Memorial Theatre. He was knighted in 1948 and appointed a Chevalier of the Legion of Honour in 1950. Cochran died in London on 31 January 1951, mourned by the stage, the press, the radio, and the public.

COCKCROFT, SIR JOHN DOUGLAS (1897–1967), physicist, was born on 27 May 1897 at Todmorden, the eldest son of John Arthur Cockcroft, millowner, and his wife, Annie Maud Fielden. He was educated at Todmorden Secondary School, Victoria University, Manchester, and St John's College, Cambridge. From 1915 to 1918 he served in the Royal Field Artillery. He obtained his M.Sc. Tech. degree in 1922 and a first in the mathematical tripos, part ii, at Cambridge in 1924.

In 1925 he married (Eunice) Elizabeth, daughter of Herbert Crabtree, of Stansfield Hall; they had four daughters and two sons, one of whom died at the age of two.

From 1925 to 1935 he worked as a research student under Sir Ernest RUTHERFORD at the Cavendish Laboratory, exploring the physics of atomic nuclei. He helped Peter L. Kapitza with his work, and then, in collaboration with E. T. S. Walton, developed a high-voltage particle accelerator machine. Experiments with deuterons were undertaken and in 1933 Cockcroft suggested to Rutherford that the Cavendish should have a cyclotron.

Before this happened, however, Cockcroft had left to take over supervision of the Mond Laboratory which was involved in technical preparations for the coming war. From 1938 Cockcroft worked with Sir Henry TIZARD on the development of radar, and in 1940 became Chief Superintendent of the Air Defence and Research Establishment at Christchurch. Cockcroft was one of the British scientists who thought that Britain should try to produce a nuclear explosive, and in 1943 he went to Canada to take charge of the Montreal laboratory and the building of the NRX heavy-water reactor at Chalk River. When the NRX reactor was almost completed, Cockcroft was recalled to England to direct the atomic energy research station at Harwell. From 1946 to 1959 he worked with Christopher (later Lord) Hinton and W. G. (later Lord) Penney on all aspects of atomic energy, both civil and military. In 1954 the Government created the Atomic Energy Authority and Cockcroft was appointed the first member for research, while remaining Director of Harwell. Under his aegis, major developments were made in fusion research and in such projects as the production of radio-isotopes for biological and industrial use.

He was the recipient of many honours and awards including the CBE (1944), a knighthood (1948), the Nobel prize for physics (with E. T. S. Walton, 1951), KCB (1953), OM (1957), and the Atoms for Peace award (1961). He resigned as a full-time member of the AEA in 1959 to become the first Master of Churchill College, Cambridge, where he remained until his death on 18 September 1967.

COHEN, HARRIET (1896–1967), pianist, was born on 2 December 1896, the eldest daughter of Joseph Verney Cohen, composer and business man, and his wife, Florence, daughter of Benjamin White, a dental surgeon of London. Her father's father was Lithuanian. She was educated at the Royal Academy of Music which she entered in 1909, the

Harriet Cohen, 1928

youngest student ever to hold the Ada Lewis Scholarship. She left the Royal Academy in 1915, having won numerous prizes, to study the piano under Tobias Matthay who was also the teacher of Myra HESS and Irene Scharrer.

In 1922 Harriet joined the Matthay School as a professor and she quickly made a name for herself on the concert platform, specializing in the music of J. S. Bach. In her tours, however, she also took every opportunity to play new music, including the works of Manuel de Falla, Prokofiev, and Shostakovich. The British composers, Arnold BAX, Ralph VAUGHAN WILLIAMS, John IRELAND and Constant LAMBERT, all wrote works for her to play. Arnold Bax was a close friend and she played his music wherever she went in Europe and America.

Her health was never good and in 1925 her career was interrupted by an attack of tuberculosis. Then, in 1948, she lost the use of her right hand in an accident at the Cheltenham Festival. Two years later, she gave the first performance of *Concertino for Left Hand* which Bax had composed for her. She won many honours; she was created CBE in 1938, became a Freeman of the City of London (1954), and received an honorary doctorate from the National University of Ireland (1960). Her autobiography *A Bundle of Time*, published posthumously in 1969, after her sudden death in London on 13 November 1967, quotes extensively from the letters of her wide body of friends, including those from the world of music such as Sir Edward ELGAR and celebrities from other walks of life, including George Bernard SHAW, H. G. WELLS, Arnold BENNETT, Ramsay MACDONALD, and Albert Einstein.

COLE, GEORGE DOUGLAS HOWARD (1889–1959), university teacher, writer, and socialist, was born in Cambridge on 25 September 1889, the son of George Cole, a jeweller, and his wife, Jessie Knowles. He was educated at St. Paul's School and Balliol College, Oxford, where he achieved firsts in Mods. (1910) and Greats (1912) and was elected to a prize fellowship at Magdalen College. As an undergraduate he became a convinced socialist and joined the Fabian Society and the ILP, though in the years between 1911 and 1914 he was strongly critical of the close links between the Labour and Liberal parties.

His panacea for the ills of society was a form of guild socialism, and he had no sympathy for the bureaucratic approach of Sidney and Beatrice WEBB or for Communism. In 1915 Cole became honorary research adviser to the Amalgamated Society of Engineers with a brief to advise on wages, prices, and the wartime dilution of labour and enjoying an influence without precedent in trade-union history. From 1916 to 1924 he was Honorary Secretary of the Fabian (later Labour) Research Department. There, on the permanent staff, he met **MARGARET ISABEL POSTGATE** whom he married in 1918. She was the daughter of the classical scholar, J. P. Postgate, and had herself gained a first in classics at Girton College, Cambridge, in 1914. Spurred on by the imprisonment of her brother Raymond as a conscientious objector in 1916, she had resigned from her teaching post at St Paul's Girls' School to work full time for the labour movement. She and her husband had a son and two daughters.

Meanwhile books on socialist topics poured from Cole's pen, including *The World of Labour* (1913), *Self-Government in Industry* (1917), and *Guild Socialism Re-stated* (1920). From 1921 to 1925 he worked as the first full-time class tutor in London University and made valuable contributions to the Workers' Educational Association. Margaret Cole collaborated in this work for education also, making a major contribution in her own right over many years.

In 1925 Cole became Reader in economics at Oxford. There, in their home, the informal weekly discussion meetings of undergraduates, eventually known as the Cole group, had considerable influence on young men who later became well known in many walks of life; they included Hugh GAITSKELL, Michael Stewart, W. H. AUDEN, and (Sir) John Betjeman. From 1939 to 1944 Cole was a faculty Fellow of Nuffield College, which had been founded two years earlier. In 1940 he assisted William BEVERIDGE in an inquiry into manpower and war production, and this led to his appointment as Chairman and Director of the Nuffield College Social Reconstruction Survey; from 1942 to 1944 he was Sub-Warden of the college. Then, in 1944, he became Chichele Professor of Social and Political Theory at Oxford, a post which he held until 1957.

Throughout his years at Oxford the flow of books continued: in particular he made a major contribution to the rethinking of socialist policy which followed the collapse of Ramsay MACDONALD's Labour Government in 1931. *The Intelligent Man's Guide through World Chaos* appeared in 1932, followed by many other works, including *Practical Economics* (1937), *British Working Class Politics, 1832–1914* (1941), *Chartist Portraits* (1941), and *Socialist Thought* (4 vols., 1953–8). From 1930 Margaret Cole was publishing almost as freely as her husband. She collaborated with him in *The Intelligent Man's Review of Europe Today* (1933), *A Guide to Modern Politics* (1934), and *The Condition of Britain* (1937). As a sideline, between 1923 and 1942 they published together twenty-nine detective novels. On her own she published *The New Economic Revolution* (1937) and *Marriage Past and Present* (1938). After the Second World War her *Makers of the Labour Movement* (1948) appeared, followed by a memoir on Beatrice Webb and the *Diaries* (2 vols., 1952, 1956), and *The Story of Fabian Socialism* (1961).

Over the years the Coles' relations with the Fabian Society blew hot and cold, but Cole was Chairman for two periods, 1939–46 and 1948–50, and President from 1952 to 1959. In 1947 he also became a director and, in 1956, Chairman of the *New Statesman* for which he had been writing since 1918.

From 1931 Cole suffered from diabetes, and his general health was not good. He died in Oxford on 14 January 1959 before a volume of essays in his honour, intended to be presented on his seventieth birthday, could be produced. Margaret Cole described him as 'a strong Tory in everything but politics'. In 1971 she published *The Life of G. D. H. Cole*, having already written her autobiography in two volumes, *Growing Up Into Revolution* (1949) and *Servant of the County* (1956). In 1970 she was made DBE. She died at Goring-on-Thames on 7 May 1980, one day after her eighty-seventh birthday.

COLE, DAME MARGARET ISABEL (1893–1980). See COLE, GEORGE DOUGLAS HOWARD.

COLEBROOK, LEONARD (1883–1967), bacteriologist, was born in Guildford on 2 March 1883, the third son of May Colebrook, farmer and Nonconformist preacher, and his second wife, Mary Gower. He was educated at Guildford Grammar School, Westbourne High School, Bournemouth, and Christ's College, Blackheath. In 1900 he began to study medicine at the London Hospital Medical College, went on to St Mary's Hospital with a scholarship, and qualified MB, BS (London) in 1906.

Under the influence of Sir Almroth WRIGHT he went to the Inoculation Department of St Mary's as an assistant, and worked on Wright's vaccine therapy, and then in 1911 with Alexander FLEMING on the treatment of syphilis with salvarsan.

In 1914 he married Dorothy, daughter of John Scarlett Campbell, of the Indian Civil Service. During the First World War, Colebrook joined the RAMC and worked on wound infections. In 1919 he was appointed to the staff of the Medical Research Council and worked on dental caries. However, in 1922 he rejoined Almroth Wright at St Mary's and from him he derived his skill as a bacteriologist. He published a biography of Wright in 1954.

He began the study of puerperal fever, found that Wright's vaccine therapy was ineffective and that treatment with arsenicals was of little use. When in 1930 he became honorary Director of the research laboratories of Queen Charlotte's Maternity Hospital he carefully studied the origins of infection in the wards and strongly advocated an aseptic regimen. Then, in 1935, he read in a German medical paper that prontosil could cure infection with virulent haemolytic streptococci. He found, by experiment, that this claim was justified and, after the use of sulphanilamides, the death rate in the isolation block of the hospital fell from 30 to 4 per cent.

In 1938 Colebrook rejoined the RAMC as bacteriological consultant to the British Expeditionary Force and realized the danger of infected burns in mechanized warfare. In 1940 he proved that such infection could be controlled by sulphanilamides and, later, by penicillin. From 1942 to 1948 he was Director of the Burns Investigation Unit of the MRC.

By the time of his retirement the Burns Investigation unit had acquired an outstanding reputation. Throughout these years, he fought with determination, and considerable success, for Government measures to prevent burns to children and old people; the Fireguard Act was passed in 1952 and other safety regulations in 1964 and 1967.

His first wife had died in 1941; and in 1946 he married Vera Scorell, daughter of Thomas James Locke, a civil servant. There were no children of either marriage. Colebrook became an honorary Fellow of the Royal College of Obstetricians and Gynaecologists in 1944, and FRS in 1945. He received many other honours. He made few original discoveries, but his readiness to make use of the discoveries of others in chemotherapy certainly saved lives and spared large numbers of his patients from sickness and pain.

COMPTON-BURNETT, DAME IVY (1884–1969), novelist, was born at Pinner, Middlesex, on 5 June 1884, the eldest of the seven children of Dr James Compton Burnett and his second wife, Katharine, daughter of Rowland Rees, a Mayor of Dover. She was educated at Addiscombe College, Hove, Howard College, Bedford, and the Royal Holloway College. Her father had had five children by his first wife and they did not get on with their stepmother; even within the second family there was little unity. Dr Burnett died in 1901 and Mrs Compton-Burnett (who added the hyphen), became an invalid and died from breast cancer in 1911.

Ivy was very attached to her brother, Guy, who was only

Ivy Compton-Burnett in the 1950s

a year younger than herself, and it was a severe blow to her happiness when he died in 1905. To some extent, his place was taken by her other brother, Noel, who was three years younger than she was, but in 1906, when Ivy was expected by her mother to act as governess to her four younger sisters, family life at Hove was anything but agreeable.

After the death of Mrs Compton-Burnett, Ivy was in charge of the family. Her sisters were musical, and two of them, Vera and Judy, were taught the piano by Myra HESS. Ivy, who was already trying to write, found their constant practising disturbing and forbade them to play. Naturally, her attitude did little to endear her to her sisters and, in 1915, they insisted on living apart from her and moved to London, where they shared a flat with Myra Hess. Then, in 1916 Noel was killed on the Western Front, and in 1917 Ivy's two youngest sisters, Topsy and Primrose, committed suicide.

Meanwhile, in 1911, while she was living at Hove, Ivy had published her first novel *Dolores*. It was not a success, and later she claimed that much of it had been written by Noel. Within three years of its publication, her publishers were proposing to dispose of their stock as a remainder since there was no demand for the work.

Ivy, despite her inclination towards a solitary, almost secret life, had one friend, Margaret Jourdain, who was herself a writer and had published in 1910 a *History of English Secular Embroidery*. She was eight years older than Ivy, had been educated at Lady Margaret Hall, Oxford, and was typically a 'new woman'. In 1919 the two friends decided to share a flat and they lived together until Margaret died in 1951.

About this time, Ivy began to write again. Her novel *Pastors and Masters* was published in 1925 at Ivy's own expense. Unexpectedly, it turned out to be a masterpiece, and from 1929 she produced a new novel nearly every two years. Among her twenty novels were *Brothers and Sisters* (1929), *Daughters and Sons* (1937), *Parents and Children* (1941), and *Mother and Son* (1955; awarded the James Tait Black memorial prize). The main inspiration for her books was clearly her own experiences, particularly those during her unhappy family life up to 1919. She herself said that she didn't have 'any real or organic knowledge of life later than about 1910'. For many years her novels were read and enjoyed by only a small number of people, but gradually they came to reach a wider public and became more popular.

Ivy Compton-Burnett was appointed CBE in 1951, DBE in 1967, and received the honorary D.Litt. of Leeds in 1960. She died unmarried in London on 27 August 1969.

CONAN DOYLE, SIR ARTHUR (1859–1930), author, was born in Edinburgh on 22 May 1859, the eldest son of Charles Altamont Doyle, a clerk in the Board of Works and an artist, and his wife, Mary Foley. His family were Irish Roman Catholics. His grandfather was John Doyle, the portrait painter, and his uncle, Richard Doyle, the black and white artist. Arthur Conan Doyle was educated at Stonyhurst and Edinburgh University. He qualified MB (1881) and MD (1885) and practised at Southsea from 1882 to 1890. He married, in 1885, Louise, daughter of J. Hawkins, of Minsterworth; they had one son and one daughter.

In 1887 he published his first novel *A Study in Scarlett* in which he introduced Sherlock Holmes, probably the most famous figure in detective fiction. From 1891 to 1893 *The Adventures of Sherlock Holmes* appeared month after month in the *Strand Magazine*, until towards the end of 1893 Conan

Doyle appeared to have allowed his great detective to fall over the Reichenbach Falls in fatal conflict with his arch-foe, Moriarty. The author himself was tired of Holmes but such was the outcry from the reading public that, in 1903, Conan Doyle felt bound to explain that Holmes had in fact escaped with his life; and a new succession of stories about his exploits continued to appear.

The character of Sherlock Holmes may have been based on that of an eminent Edinburgh surgeon under whom Conan Doyle had worked as a student. He is supposed to have emphasized the importance in medicine of close observation of details and the intelligent interpretation of their significance. Many stories were published, recounting the course of investigations carried out by Holmes, and related by his less perceptive companion, Dr Watson. Such was the popularity of the series that the memory of Sherlock Holmes has been kept alive by a society named after him whose members could not be more serious about his activities if he had really lived instead of being the invention of an author.

During the Boer War, Conan Doyle was senior physician in a field hospital, and was knighted for his services (1902). He published a pamphlet *The War in South Africa. Its Cause and Conduct* (1902) in which he sought to justify the actions of Britain as a counter to criticism on the Continent. He was a strong supporter of the policy of Joseph Chamberlain advocating tariff reform and colonial preference, but he failed to get into Parliament.

His wife died in 1906; and a year later Conan Doyle married Jean, daughter of James Blyth Leckie, of Blackheath; they had two sons and one daughter.

He championed the cause of Oscar Slater, convicted of murder in 1909; he was convinced that Slater was the victim of mistaken identity, and published a criticism of the judgement in 1912. The result of an official inquiry was confirmation of the verdict but, years later, fresh evidence came to light and the sentence was quashed in 1928.

Conan Doyle was writing adventure novels for nearly forty years. From *The White Company* in 1890 to *The Lost World* in 1912 he produced a large number of best sellers including his stories of another hero, Brigadier Gerard, the flamboyant adventurer of the Napoleonic wars. During the First World War, he wrote a *History of the British Campaign in France and Flanders* (6 vols., 1916–20).

In his later years Conan Doyle became a convinced spiritualist, and wrote and lectured much on the subject. He died at Crowborough on 7 July 1930. Conan Doyle considered his best work to be his historical novels; he thought that the Holmes stories were not to be taken seriously, but whether he would like it or not, it is for Sherlock Holmes that Conan Doyle is remembered.

CONNOLLY, CYRIL VERNON (1903–1974), author, literary editor, and journalist, was born in Coventry on 10 September 1903, the only son of Major Matthew Connolly, a conchologist, of Bath, and his Irish wife, Muriel Vernon. He was educated at Eton and Balliol College, Oxford, and was a scholar of both. In 1925 he obtained a third in modern history, but he had by then acquired a devotion to the classical authors upon whom he modelled his own prose style.

After leaving Oxford, Connolly worked as secretary to Logan Pearsall Smith, man of letters, whose sister, Alys, was the first wife of Bertrand RUSSELL. Pearsall Smith not only provided Connolly with the means of becoming a writer but helped to develop his individual standards of precise expression. Connolly liked to travel, but only to places where he could live in civilized fashion. His first book was a novel set in the south of France, *The Rock Pool* (1936). In 1930 he married Frances Jean Bakewell, of Baltimore, USA; this marriage ended in divorce; and he then married Barbara Skelton, and this also ended in divorce.

His second book, *Enemies of Promise* (1938) included a candid account of his time at Eton. During the Second World War he published, under the pseudonym of Palinurus, *The Unquiet Grave* (1944, revised edn. 1945), a book of aphorisms of his own and of his favourite authors and of nostalgia for the pleasures of peacetime and his lost youth.

In 1939 Connolly founded, with Peter Watson and Stephen Spender, the literary journal *Horizon* which he edited until 1950, and in which appeared George ORWELL's essays, Evelyn WAUGH's *The Loved One*, Mary MacCarthy's *Oasis*, and Augustus JOHN's autobiography. In 1953 he published *The Golden Horizon*, an anthology of the best of the contributions to the magazine in poetry, fiction, and criticism. Between 1942 and 1943 Connolly was Literary Editor of the *Observer* and later became a book reviewer for the *Sunday Times*. His contributions in this field of literary criticism were collected into *The Condemned Playground* (1945), *Ideas and Places* (1953), *Previous Convictions* (1963), and *The Evening Colonnade* (1973). He claimed that writing ephemeral articles about books had for him taken the place of the epic poetry or classical novel that he would have preferred to write but found impossible.

In 1959 he married Deidre, daughter of Major (Patrick William) Dennis Craig, son of the first Viscount Craigavon. She was the former wife of Jonathan Craven. By this marriage Connolly had a son and a daughter.

In 1965 he published *The Modern Movement*, a discussion of one hundred key books written from 1880 to 1950. The first editions of these books were included in an exhibition mounted by the University of Texas in Connolly's honour. Connolly was a Chevalier of the Legion of Honour, FRSL, and was appointed CBE and C. Lit. in 1972. He died in London on 26 November 1974.

CONRAD, JOSEPH (1857-1924), novelist, was born, Teodor Josef Konrad Korzeniowski, near Mohilow in Poland on 3 December 1857, son of Joseph Theodore Apollonius Korzeniowski, a man of letters, and his wife, Evelina, daughter of Joseph Bobrowski. His parents were banished to Russia in 1862, and his mother died in 1865 and his father in 1869. He was educated in Cracow, living with an uncle who had become his guardian. But his ambition was to go to sea and, in 1874, he joined the French merchant marine and spent the next four years either at sea or in Marseilles. In 1878 he joined the crew of an English ship and set foot in England for the first time. From that year until 1886, he continued to work hard as a seaman, earning his mate's certificates and finally becoming 'ship's master'. He became a naturalized British subject—and took the name Joseph Conrad—in 1886. During 1887 and 1888 he sailed in the Malay Archipelago, and then found his way up the Congo River, until in 1890 he went to visit his uncle in the Ukraine, a part of the world he had not been in for nearly twenty years.

He had begun writing in 1889. His father, who had translated Shakespeare and Victor Hugo into Polish, had given his son a love of the English language as well as a deep knowledge of French. In 1894, Conrad decided to leave the sea and to devote his energies to writing. This was a risky undertaking, since at the time he had published nothing. However, he was fortunate because Edward Garnett, reader

for T. Fisher Unwin, recommended publication of his first story *Almayer's Folly*. The book came out in 1895, and was followed by *An Outcast of the Islands* (1896), and *The Nigger of the 'Narcissus'* (1897). These novels, based upon Conrad's experiences at sea, were welcomed by a small number of people who appreciated the author's remarkable command of English, but it was to be several years before they came to the attention of a wider public.

Meanwhile, Conrad and Jessie, daughter of a bookseller, Alfred Henry George, whom he had married in 1896, lived an impecunious existence in various places in the south of England. Two sons were born and the need to earn sufficient to keep his family was not helped by the fact that Conrad was in poor health and suffered from bouts of deep depression. He continued to write. *Lord Jim* (1900) was followed by *Nostromo* (1904), *The Mirror of the Sea* (1906), *The Secret Agent* (1907), and *Under Western Eyes* (1911).

But it was only with the publication in New York in 1914 of *Chance* that Conrad became recognized as one of the great novelists of his day. From that time until his death in 1924 he was a celebrity. During the First World War he worked hard to raise funds for the relief of Polish refugees and in 1916 went to sea for a short time in a 'Q' ship for trapping submarines. He died at Bishopsbourne near Canterbury on 3 August 1924. That a Pole, who did not visit England until he was twenty-one, could write books with such a consummate command of English and the most vivid descriptions of scenes and characters derived from his seafaring experiences is one of the most extraordinary phenomena in twentieth-century English literature.

CONSTANTINE, LEARIE NICHOLAS, BARON CONSTANTINE (1901-1971), cricketer and West Indian politician, was born on 21 September 1901 at Diego Martin, Trinidad, the son of Lebrun Constantine, foreman of a cocoa plantation and cricketer, and his wife, Anaise Pascal, the daughter of a former slave. He was educated at St Ann's Roman Catholic School, Port of Spain, until he was fifteen, but his main interest was in cricket in which he was encouraged by his father who had played for the West Indies. In 1927 he married Norma Agatha Cox, of Port of Spain; they had one daughter.

After playing in only three first-class matches, Constantine was selected for the West Indies tour to England in 1923 and again in 1928. He was a good all-round cricketer who excelled as a fielder. From 1929 to 1940 he was a professional cricketer in England, the first coloured man to play for Nelson in the Lancashire League. Nelson won the league title eight times in ten seasons and in 1963 Constantine was given the freedom of the borough. Altogether, he played in only eighteen test matches, but in 1929-30 his bowling was an important factor in the West Indies' first victory in a test match. In 1934-5 he helped them to win the series against England; and in his last test at the Oval in 1939 his batting gave his team a first innings lead.

During the Second World War he stayed in England, and in 1942-7 was a welfare officer employed by the Ministry of Labour. He was appointed MBE in 1945. He was always prepared to fight for the rights of West Indians and a determined opponent of any colour prejudice. In 1954 he was called to the English Bar (Middle Temple). He returned to Trinidad and worked as a legal adviser to the Trinidad Oil Company. He entered local politics, became MP for Tunapuna, and in 1956 became Minister of Works and Transport. From 1962 to 1964 he was High Commissioner for Trinidad

Learie Constantine at the wicket, 1939 test series

and Tobago in London, and made his name as a highly respected representative of his Government. He was knighted in 1962, and elected honorary Master of the Bench in 1963. He became a Governor of the BBC, Rector of St Andrews University, a member of the Race Relations Board and of the Sports Council. In 1969 he was created a life peer, the first negro to be so honoured.

He published a number of books in co-operation with his friend, C. L. R. James, including *Cricket and I* (1933) and *Cricket in the Sun* (1949). He also contributed to the *Listener* and other journals. Learie Constantine died in England on 1 July 1971. His wife died two months later.

COOK, ARTHUR JAMES (1883–1931), miners' leader, was born at Wookey, Somerset, on 22 November 1883, the eldest son of Thomas Cook and his wife, Selina Brock. Thomas Cook was a soldier, and Arthur and his two brothers and seven sisters were all born in English or Irish barracks. At the age of twelve, Arthur ran away from the Curragh, boarded a vessel bound for Bristol, and, after working for a short time on a farm, became a miner in the coal pits of South Wales. There he spent twenty-one years working underground. As a lad of sixteen he was a preacher conducting

singing missions among the Baptists. In 1906 he married Annie Edwards and had one son and two daughters.

In 1905 he had joined the Independent Labour party and six years later the South Wales Miners' Federation awarded him a scholarship to study Marxist economics at the Central Labour College. He never became a Communist and, after filling various minor offices in the miners' trade union, he was appointed agent for Rhondda No. 1 district and a member of the South Wales Federation executive in 1919. He also represented the Welsh miners on the Miners' Federation of Great Britain, and in 1924, was elected Secretary of the Federation and also Secretary of the International Miners' Federation. In the interim, he had been sent to prison in 1918 and 1921 during disputes in the mining industry in the course of which he was charged with incitement to rioting.

1924 was a critical year in the coal-mining industry. The miners had secured from the owners an increase in wages, but competition from coal pits in Germany and Poland undercut prices in Britain and the owners decided to reduce wages and impose longer hours. Cook refused to make any concession on the part of the miners' union, and succeeded in obtaining the support of the TUC. In the summer of 1925 the mine owners demanded a sharp reduction in wages and, when the union refused to agree, the owners threatened a lock-out. The TUC, in turn, threatened to place an embargo on the movement of coal from the pits. The Government reluctantly intervened and offered to subsidize the industry for nine months whilst a royal commission under Sir Herbert SAMUEL was set up to inquire into the difficulties of the mining industry. The lock-out was postponed.

Meanwhile, the Conservative Government took steps to deal with the eventuality of a general strike should peace in the mines not be maintained. The royal commission made its report in March 1926. Sir Herbert Samuel and his colleagues made a number of proposals for reorganizing the industry, but also recommended that the miners should accept reductions in wages. The coal owners refused to agree to any reorganization and demanded longer hours; Arthur Cook on behalf of the miners said, 'Not a penny off the pay: not a minute on the day.' On 1 May the miners were locked out, and on 3 May the general strike began in their support. The strike was a fiasco. The TUC accepted further suggestions from Sir Herbert Samuel, which involved reductions in miners' wages on condition that the owners accepted the royal commission's recommendations for reorganization. The general strike ended on 12 May. Cook himself, in spite of his reputation for intransigence, opposed the continuation of the strike without the support of the TUC but accepted the majority decision of his colleagues and the miners continued their strike for another six months. Throughout that period they refused to make any concession, either to the owners or the Government. But their obdurate resistance cost them dear: after half a year of distress and poverty they were forced to return to work and accept the coal owners' terms to save their families from starvation. They have never forgotten this bitter conflict.

In 1927 Cook was elected to the General Council of the TUC, and for another four years did what he could to make the public understand the terrible conditions under which the miners had to work. He himself had been injured during his early years underground, and in 1931 had to have a leg amputated. He went on working but, within a few months, he died in hospital at Hampstead on 2 November, 1931.

COOPER, (ALFRED) DUFF, first VISCOUNT NORWICH

(1890–1954), politician, diplomat, and author, was born in London on 22 February 1890, the only son of (Sir) Alfred Cooper, a surgeon, and his wife, Lady Agnes Duff, sister of the first Duke of Fife. He was educated at Eton and New College, Oxford, and in 1913 entered the Foreign Office. Many of his friends were killed during the early years of the First World War, and in 1917 he obtained permission to join the Grenadier Guards. He saw service in France and was appointed DSO.

On demobilization he returned to the Foreign Office, and in 1919 married Lady Diana Manners, daughter of the eighth Duke of Rutland, and one of the most beautiful women of the period. Cooper's ambition was to become a politician, but he was handicapped by lack of means. In 1923 Lady Diana accepted a lucrative offer to play the Madonna in *The Miracle* in New York, and in the following year her husband was elected Conservative MP for Oldham.

In 1928 he was appointed Financial Secretary to the War Office, but in 1929 lost his seat. Out of Parliament, he set about writing *Talleyrand*, a biography which brought him acclaim when it was published in 1932. In 1931 he returned to the Commons as MP for St George's, Westminster, a seat which he held until 1945. He resumed his post at the War Office until, in 1934, he went to the Treasury. In the following year he became Secretary of State for War and a Privy Counsellor.

When Neville CHAMBERLAIN succeeded Stanley BALDWIN in 1937 he appointed Duff Cooper as First Lord of the Admiralty. Meanwhile, Cooper had published *Haig* (2 vols., 1935–6). In his new post, he did what he could to strengthen the Royal Navy in readiness for war, but he was never on easy terms with the Prime Minister. When in 1938 Chamberlain returned in triumph from Munich, Duff Cooper resigned and, in an impressive speech in the Commons, argued strongly against the agreement made with Hitler.

Out of office, he wrote a weekly article for the *Evening Standard* and lectured in the USA. When CHURCHILL took over from Chamberlain in 1940, Duff Cooper became Minister of Information until he was appointed Chancellor of the Duchy of Lancaster from 1941 to 1943. During 1941–2 he went out to Singapore as Resident Cabinet Minister there. Then, early in 1944, he went to Algiers as British representative with the French Liberation Committee under General de Gaulle. While he was there, he and Lady Diana entertained Churchill and did what they could to heal the breach between him and de Gaulle. Later in the year, Duff Cooper became British Ambassador in Paris.

He and his wife worked hard to obtain the good opinion of de Gaulle and the French, despite the continued antipathy of the General and Winston Churchill. In March 1947 a treaty of alliance between France and Britain was signed, and Duff Cooper felt that his objective had been achieved. He left Paris later that year, was appointed GCMG in 1948, and became Viscount Norwich in 1952.

In retirement, among other books, he wrote a remarkable autobiography, *Old Men Forget* (1953), and a few weeks after publication, on 1 January 1954, he died while on a voyage to the West Indies. He was succeeded by his son, John Julius. 'Life has been good to me', he wrote in his autobiography, 'and I am grateful.'

COOPER, DAME GLADYS CONSTANCE (1888–1971), actress and theatre manager, was born at Lewisham on 18 December 1888, the eldest daughter of Charles William Frederick Cooper, journalist and editor of *Epicure*, and his wife,

Gladys Cooper with Ivor Novello in *Enter Kiki!*, Playhouse, 1923

Mabel, daughter of Capt. Edward Barnett of the Scots Greys. She was educated at home by a French governess and from the age of seven became a photographic model.

In 1905 she was auditioned and offered the title role of *Bluebell in Fairyland* by Seymour HICKS and started to tour with this play on her seventeenth birthday. A year later she joined the George Edwardes Company and appeared in singing and dancing roles in musicals. But she aspired to be a straight actress.

In December 1908 she married Herbert John Buckmaster, and in July 1910 their daughter, Joan, was born. When she returned to the stage Gladys Cooper played in straight theatre, first at the Royalty, and then in a revival of *The Importance of Being Earnest* at the St James's (1911). This was followed by a part in *Milestones* by Arnold BENNETT and Edward Knoblock at the Royalty (1912). She was already recognized by the public as a beauty whose picture was sold freely on postcards and calendars. In 1913 she began her association on the stage with (Sir) Gerald du Maurier in *Diplomacy* at Wyndham's. Then came the First World War. Her husband went to France with the Royal Horse Guards and she also visited the Front with a Seymour Hicks concert party. Her second child, John, was born in 1915. In 1917 she began her career as manager in partnership with Frank Curzon at the Playhouse Theatre. She and Lilian BAYLIS at the Old Vic were the only women to run theatres up to 1939. She produced four Somerset MAUGHAM premières, *Home and Beauty*, *The Letter*, *The Sacred Flame*, and *The Painted Veil*, and revivals of *My Lady's Dress*, *The Second Mrs Tanqueray*, and *Magda*.

When her husband returned from the war they agreed to an amicable divorce (1921) and remained good friends. In 1928 she married Sir Neville Arthur Pearson, second baronet, and her last child, Sally, was born. This marriage ended in divorce in 1937. She was now less successful with her plays in London, and the success on Broadway of Philip Merivale, who was to become her third husband, persuaded her to try her luck in New York. She married Merivale in 1937 and made the USA her home. They made a brief appearance together in London in *Dodsworth* (1938) but returned to New York in Dodie Smith's *Spring Meeting*.

In 1939 Alfred HITCHCOCK offered her a part in his first Hollywood film *Rebecca*; she went to California for three weeks and stayed for nearly thirty years. Between 1940 and 1967 she played in thirty films with MGM, of which the best were *Now Voyager*, for which she was nominated for an Oscar in 1943, *Separate Tables* (1958), and *My Fair Lady* (1964). Philip Merivale died in 1946, but she continued to live in California until the sixties when she returned to England. She had paid visits to London to appear in Noël COWARD's *Relative Values* (1951), *The Chalk Garden* (1955), and the revival of *The Sacred Flame* (1967).

In 1967 she was appointed DBE and she died at home in Henley on 17 November 1971. Both her daughters had married actors: Joan married Robert Morley in 1940, and Sally married Robert Hardy in 1961. Gladys Cooper was one of the most beautiful women and most remarkable actresses of her time.

COURTAULD, SAMUEL (1876-1947), art patron and industrialist, was born at Braintree, Essex, on 7 May 1876, the second son of Sydney Courtauld, a silk-weaver, and his wife, Sarah Lucy, daughter of William Sharpe. He was educated at Rugby School, and in 1896 went to Krefeld in Germany to study silk weaving. The family business which had been founded in 1816, expanded rapidly after 1904 with the purchase of the British rights to manufacture rayon yarn, and its registration as a public company. Courtauld became General Manager of the textile mills in 1908, joined the board of directors in 1915, and by 1921 had become Chairman.

A man of great foresight and practical sense, he was deeply concerned with problems of management and industrial relations, laying an emphasis on spiritual values and the worth of the individual worker which was unusual in the industrial context. He was a member of many committees concerned with managerial problems, and a Visiting Fellow and Trustee of Nuffield College, Oxford.

His greater fame, however, shared with his wife, Elizabeth Theresa Frances, daughter of Edward Kelsey, whom he married in 1901, was as a patron of the arts. His own collection of paintings contained a number of outstanding works, particularly of the French Impressionist School, including major works by Van Gogh, Renoir, and Manet. In 1923 he gave £50,000 for the purchase of Impressionist and Post-Impressionist paintings for the Tate Gallery. When his wife died in 1931 he presented a considerable part of his collection to London University, and provided a capital sum to found the Courtauld Institute of Art. Courtauld was also largely responsible for bringing the Warburg Institute to London when it was displaced from Hamburg. He was also Chairman of the Trustees of the National Gallery and a Trustee of the Tate.

His services to art were recognized by the conferring of an honorary D.Lit. of London University (1931) and his appointment as an Officer of the Legion of Honour. His book *Ideals and Industry* (1949) was published posthumously. He died in London on 1 December 1947 leaving one daughter.

COWARD, SIR NOËL PEIRCE (1899-1973), actor and playwright, was born on 16 December 1899 at Teddington, Middlesex, the son of Arthur Sabin Coward, clerk, and his wife, Violet Agnes, daughter of Capt. Henry Gordon Veitch, RN. Both parents were musical. He went to the Chapel Royal Choir School, Clapham, for a short while in 1909 and started his professional career as a child actor early in 1911. In 1913 he appeared with the young Gertrude LAWRENCE and began a friendship that lasted till her death nearly forty years later.

He continued to play small parts until 1918. However, in 1916 he wrote the words and music for his first song and by 1917 had written three plays. In 1918 he spent nine months in the army, an experience which he found extremely disagreeable. Two years later he made his first appearance in London in a play of his own which was not a success, but he was encouraged to persevere by George Bernard SHAW, and in 1923 was part-author and composer of *London Calling*, in which he played the lead with Gertrude Lawrence.

His first important success came in 1924, with *The Vortex*, in which he shocked some of the critics with a play realistically portraying drug addiction. This was followed in 1925 by *On With the Dance*, in which Coward began his long association with Charles COCHRAN, *Fallen Angels* with Tallulah Bankhead, and *Hay Fever* with Marie TEMPEST. Later that year, *The Vortex* was a triumph in New York.

In 1926 Coward was in bad health and his sudden success suffered a reverse; but in 1928 he made a comeback with *This Year of Grace*, followed, in 1929, by *Bitter Sweet*. Then, in 1930, he appeared with Gertrude Lawrence in the play that will probably be revived more often than any of his other successes, *Private Lives*. Sophisticated, witty, and mock-sentimental, this play caught the carefree spirit of the era of which Coward had become the most representative British playwright. In *Cavalcade* (1931), he turned to a pageant of patriotism which some critics thought could not be serious. Later, he showed by *This Happy Breed* and the film *In Which We Serve* (1942), the story of his friend Louis MOUNTBAT-TEN's destroyer *Kelly*, that he could deal seriously with serious subjects.

Among his other plays and films, mention must be made of *Design for Living* (1932), *Conversation Piece* (1934), and *Blithe Spirit* (1941). However, between the end of the Second World War and the early sixties, his work was less successful. In 1948 he built a house in Jamaica and stayed there with Graham Payn who had joined him in the previous year. *Present Laughter*, with French dialogue, was a failure in Paris.

In 1951 Coward started a new career in cabaret, singing, in his distinctive voice, his own songs at the Café de Paris in London, and later in Las Vegas. This, together with television and film engagements, restored his fortunes, and persuaded him to take refuge from the tax authorities, first in Bermuda, and later in Switzerland. In 1953 he appeared with great acclaim as King Magnus in Shaw's *The Apple Cart*. In

Noël Coward and Gertrude Lawrence in *Private Lives*, Phoenix, September 1930

1964 he directed Dame Edith EVANS in *Hay Fever* at the National Theatre.

Among his most successful films, one cannot forget *Brief Encounter* with Celia Johnson and Trevor Howard, and, among his publications, his autobiographical *Present Indicative* (1937), and *Future Indefinite* (1954).

His seventieth birthday was celebrated by an emotional tribute from his friends and fellow professionals. In 1970 he was knighted, and received in the USA a special award for his services to the theatre. He never married, being a homosexual; he did not pretend to be otherwise, but he always behaved with dignity and discretion. He died in Jamaica on 26 March 1973. *The Noël Coward Diaries*, edited by Graham Payn and Sheridan Morley, were published in 1982.

CRAIG, (EDWARD HENRY) GORDON (1872–1966), artist and stage designer, was born on 16 January 1872 at Stevenage, the only son of Edward William Godwin, an architect, and the actress Ellen TERRY. His parents were unmarried. When Ellen Terry and Godwin parted company in 1875 she married Charles Clavering Wardell. Craig was

known at first as Edward Wardell, and under that name went to a school near Tunbridge Wells in 1883. In 1886 he went to Bradfield College and, later, to a school in Heidelberg.

Meanwhile, in 1885, while touring with his mother in the USA, he had acted in a small part at Chicago in (Sir) Henry Irving's production of *Eugene Aram*. After he had left school he was engaged by Irving at the Lyceum where he played in *The Dead Heart* (1889), and continued to act until 1896–7. He adopted Craig as a stage name—after the island Ailsa Craig. Then, he started a magazine, *The Page*, in which he published some of his earliest wood-engravings. He married an actress, May Gibson, in 1893 but, four years later, though they had four children, they were on bad terms and Craig embarked upon a long series of liaisons.

In 1900 he designed and directed Purcell's *Dido and Aeneas*, followed by *Acis and Galatea* two years later. His stagings marked a breakthrough in theatrical design, particularly in the use of lighting and colour and the departure from pictorial realism. In 1905 he was working in Berlin and, from that time, rarely returned to England. He was now living with Elena Meo, a violinist, by whom he had a son and daughter; but in this year (1905) Craig began his affair with Isadora Duncan, the dancer; she had a daughter by him.

In 1907 he settled in Florence and began a theatre magazine *The Mask*. His most influential book *On the Art of the Theatre* appeared in 1911, at about the time he was designing *Hamlet* at the Arts Theatre, Moscow. During the First World War, he lived for a while in Rome, drawing, writing, and engraving. For his staging of Ibsen's *The Pretenders* in Copenhagen (1926) he received the Order of the Knights of Dannebrog in 1930, the year in which his designs were published by the Oxford University Press.

From 1930 he concentrated on his books, writing biographies, including *Henry Irving* (1930), and *Ellen Terry and Her Secret Self* (1931), and his memoirs, published in 1957 under the title *Index to the Story of My Days (1872–1907)*. He had not married Elena Meo but, when she died in 1957 in England, her daughter went out to live with him at Vence. In 1938 Craig was appointed RDI of the Royal College of Art; in 1958 he became CH, and in 1964 was President of the Mermaid Theatre, London. He died at Vence on 29 July 1966 aged ninety-four, having lived to see many of his revolutionary ideas for the design and staging of plays become general practice in the theatre.

CRIPPS, SIR (RICHARD) STAFFORD (1889–1952), politician and lawyer, was born in London on 24 April 1889, the fifth child of Charles Alfred Cripps (later Lord Parmoor) and his wife, Theresa Potter. His mother, who was the sister of Beatrice WEBB, died when he was four. He was educated at Winchester and University College London, where he was part-author of a scientific paper read before the Royal Society when he was only twenty-two. He could have become an

Stafford Cripps lectures newsmen, New York, October 1948

eminent chemist but chose to be called to the Bar (Middle Temple) in 1913.

Unfit for military service, he worked as a driver for the Red Cross in France in 1914 until recalled to be assistant superintendent of the explosives factory at Queensferry, which he made one of the most efficient munitions factories. His hard work in this post exacerbated the ill health which dogged him for the rest of his life.

Returning to the Bar in 1919 Cripps made a name for himself by his ability to master the details of complicated issues and to present his cases clearly and precisely. He became KC in 1927. Much of his time was spent on the World Alliance to promote international friendship.

In 1929 he joined the Labour party, and in 1930 became Solicitor – General and was knighted. He was Labour MP for East Bristol from 1931 to 1950. Almost at once he moved to the extreme left of the Labour party; he refused to join the National Government of 1931, and was a leading member of the militant group, the Socialist League, which favoured abolition of the House of Lords and revolutionary politics.

He was a prime mover in the United Front which, in 1936, aimed to combine Labour, Liberal radicals, Independent Labour, and Communists in one organization. A year later, he helped to launch the *Tribune* of which Aneurin BEVAN later became Editor (1942). In 1938 Cripps proposed a Popular Front to overthrow Neville CHAMBERLAIN. This would include Conservatives, something that the executive of the Labour party could not accept. When Cripps refused to withdraw, he was expelled from the party and remained outside it until 1945.

In 1939 Cripps visited India and Russia, and in 1940 accepted CHURCHILL's invitation to become Ambassador to Moscow. He soon became disillusioned about Russian Communism, but he organized a pact of mutual assistance between Britain and the Soviet Union in 1941. In the same year he was sworn of the Privy Council. On his return to England he was appointed by Churchill leader of the House of Commons and Lord Privy Seal, with a seat in the War Cabinet. Then, from 1942 to 1945, he was Minister of Aircraft Production.

In the post-war Labour Government Cripps became President of the Board of Trade and, in 1946, went on the abortive mission to India to try to get Congress and the Muslim League to agree to a united India. In 1947 he was appointed Minister for Economic Affairs and, when Hugh DALTON's budget indiscretion led to his resignation, Cripps took over as Chancellor of the Exchequer.

It was in this office that Cripps earned his unenviable reputation for austerity, but the condition of the country's economy was such that he had no alternative, and by his personal authority he succeeded in securing restraint, both in respect of wage demands and dividends, in the years 1948–9. His health, however, would not stand up to the strain and in 1950 he had to resign.

For all of his public life he was sustained by the support and constant companionship of his wife, Isobel, daughter of Commander Harold William Swithinbank, of Denham Court, Bucks. They had married in 1911 and had three daughters and one son. Cripps was a Fellow of University College London (1930), Rector of Aberdeen University (1942–5), elected FRS (1948), and appointed CH (1951). His wife was appointed GBE in 1946. Cripps died at his home in the Cotswolds on 21 April 1952.

CROMER, first EARL OF (1841–1917). See BARING, EVELYN.

CROMPTON, RICHMAL (1890–1969), author, whose real name was Richmal Crompton Lamburn, was born on 15 November 1890 at Bury, Lancs., the second of the three children of the Revd Edward John Sewell Lamburn, schoolmaster and curator, and his wife, Clara Crompton. She was educated at St Elphin's Clergy Daughters' School, Warrington, at Darley Dale, Derbyshire, and the Royal Holloway College, London. She won a university scholarship in 1912 and the Driver scholarship in classics in 1914, the year in which she obtained her BA (London).

From 1915 to 1917 she taught at her Darley Dale school and was classics mistress at Bromley High School from 1917 to 1924. She began to write short stories and had one published in *Home Magazine* in which William Brown, a schoolboy based on her memories of the childhood of her brother John and that of a nephew, featured as a tough, mischievous youngster.

In 1922 George Newnes published a selection of her stories about this lad under the titles *Just William* and *More William*. Richmal Crompton aspired to write serious adult novels and did succeed in producing thirty-nine of them, but if her 'William' books had not become so popular she might have remained virtually unknown. As it was, she published nearly forty 'William' books; millions of them were sold, and translations made into almost every European language. Four 'William' films were made and two television series produced.

In 1923 Richmal Crompton contracted poliomyelitis, lost the use of her right leg, and had to give up teaching. This enabled her to devote more time to her writing. During the Second World War she volunteered to work in the Bromley fire service. She spent most of her adult life in Kent, supported a number of charities and, although she loved young children, she never married. She continued to write about William until shortly before she died at Farnborough Hospital, Kent, on 11 January 1969.

CROSLAND, (CHARLES) ANTHONY RAVEN (1918–1977), politician and writer, was born on 29 August 1918 at St. Leonard-on-Sea, the only son of Joseph Beardsel Crosland, under-secretary at the War Office, and his wife, Jessie Raven, lecturer in Old French at Westfield College, London University. He was educated at Highgate School and Trinity College, Oxford, where he was a scholar (1939). During the Second World War he served in the Royal Welch Fusiliers and the Parachute Regiment in North Africa, Italy, France, and Austria. He returned to Oxford in 1946, obtained a first in philosophy, politics, and economics, and was appointed lecturer and Fellow in economics at Trinity College (1947–50). He was Treasurer of the Union in 1940 and President in 1946.

In 1950 Crosland was elected Labour MP for South Gloucestershire, a seat he held until 1955. He gave up his academic career, and in the House of Commons became a close friend and assistant of Hugh GAITSKELL while the latter was Shadow Chancellor of the Exchequer. Crosland failed to get returned to Parliament in 1955 and took seriously to writing. In 1953 he had published *Britain's Economic Problem*. Three years later, he published *The Future of Socialism*, an important contribution to socialist theory, based on the assumptions of the success of Keynesian economics, the lessening of the class struggle, and the continuance of economic growth; it was a challenge to bureaucratic socialism and strongly egalitarian in the liberal tradition.

In 1952 he had married Hilary Anne, daughter of Henry

Anthony Crosland as Foreign Secretary shortly before his death

Sarson of the vinegar family but the marriage was dissolved after five years.

In 1959 Crosland was elected MP for Grimsby, a seat which he held until his death in 1977. He supported Gaitskell in the 'clause four' controversy on nationalization and in his opposition to unilateral disarmament. He disagreed with Gaitskell, however, about entry to the European common market which at that time he favoured and Gaitskell opposed.

In Harold Wilson's administration he was appointed Minister of State in the Department of Economic Affairs (1964–5), and after three months was promoted to Cabinet rank and sworn of the Privy Council as Secretary of State for Education and Science. He was an efficient administrator of his department, but his public impact was unspectacular; furthermore he was sometimes confused with Richard CROSSMAN. After two and a half years in the Department of Education, Crosland became President of the Board of Trade (1967). He was disappointed in his hopes of being appointed Chancellor of the Exchequer and, in the last four months of the Labour Government, he was Secretary of State for Local Government and Regional Planning.

In opposition, he published *Socialism Now* (1974), a successor to his collection of political essays entitled *The Conservative Enemy* (1962). Later, when Harold Wilson returned to power in 1974, he was appointed Secretary of State for the Environment.

In March 1976, when Wilson resigned as Prime Minister, Crosland was a candidate for the succession. He came bottom of the poll but, undeterred, accepted appointment as Foreign Secretary under James Callaghan. He held the post for only ten months which, with his previous inexperience of international affairs, gave him little time to make his mark. As before, he would have preferred to be Chancellor of the Exchequer but this ambition was never realized. In February 1977 he had a massive cerebral haemorrhage and died at Oxford six days later on 19 February 1977. His widow, formerly Mrs Susan Barnes Catling, the daughter of Mark Watson, of Baltimore, USA, whom he had married in 1964, was a prolific author of articles and essays, written under the name of Susan Barnes. She had two daughters by a previous marriage.

CROSSMAN, RICHARD HOWARD STAFFORD (1907–1974), politician, journalist, and diarist, was born on 15 December 1907 in London, the third of six children of (Sir) (Charles) Stafford Crossman, a barrister and later judge, of Buckhurst Hill House, Essex, and his wife, Helen Elizabeth, daughter of David Howard, DL. He was a scholar of Winchester and of New College, Oxford, where he obtained firsts in Classical Mods. and Greats and, in 1930, was elected to a fellowship.

In 1931 Crossman spent a year in Germany, where he acquired an interest in politics and a wife, Erika Simon (née Landsberg) a twice-married German Jewess. Back at Oxford, he quickly earned a reputation as a lecturer and tutor and published *Plato Today* (1937), *Socrates* (1938), and *Government and the Governed* (1939). From 1936 to 1940 he led the Labour group on the Oxford City Council.

Crossman left Oxford in 1937, having married, as his second wife, the divorced wife of one of his New College colleagues, Inezita Hilda Baker (née Davis). By this time he had become actively involved in Labour politics and had fought unsuccessfully a Parliamentary by-election. He became Assistant Editor of the *New Statesman* in 1938, and two years later his friend Hugh DALTON enlisted him into the Ministry of Economic Warfare. During 1944–5 he was assistant chief of the Psychological Warfare Division, Supreme HQ Allied Expeditionary Force (SHAEF). He was appointed OBE in 1945.

From 1945 to 1974 Crossman was Labour MP for Coventry East, but his early career in the House of Commons was unspectacular, and he had the misfortune to make an enemy of Ernest BEVIN. In 1952, however, he was elected to the party's national executive committee, and was a firm adherent of Aneurin BEVAN until Bevan resigned from the Labour Shadow Cabinet in 1954, when Crossman transferred his allegiance to Harold Wilson.

When Wilson was elected to the leadership of the party in 1963, Crossman became opposition spokesman on higher education and science, but when the Labour Government came to office in 1964 he was appointed Minister of Housing and Local Government when, according to his *Diaries of a Cabinet Minister* (3 vols., 1975, 1976, and 1977), he fought a continuous battle with Dame Evelyn (later Baroness) Sharp, his Permanent Secretary. In 1964, the year in which he became a Privy Counsellor, he wrote a controversial introduction to a new edition of Walter Bagehot's *The English Constitution*.

In 1966 he became Lord President of the Council and Leader of the House of Commons, where he did good work in originating the departmental select committees but failed to get his scheme for the reform of the House of Lords accepted. From November 1968 to June 1970, Crossman was Secretary of State for the Department of Health and Social Security.

He had been Assistant Editor of the *New Statesman* up to 1955, and he now became Editor, but he held that post for only twenty-one months during which time he consistently disagreed with his staff until, in the end, the *New Statesman's* board dismissed him (March 1972).

From the early 1950s when he was a back-bencher to the time when he was a Cabinet Minister (1964–70), Crossman kept a political diary recording his own reactions to his colleagues and opponents and his reflections on the whole range of Parliamentary business. His second wife died in 1952 and, two years later, he married Anne Patricia, daughter of Alexander Patrick McDougall, a farmer. Living happily on the Oxfordshire farm, inherited from his father-in-law, he now set out to prepare his diaries for publication. When the first volume was ready it was published serially in the *Sunday Times*, arousing considerable interest. Then, when the Labour Attorney-General sought an injunction to prohibit publication in book form, this was refused. The three volumes duly appeared, followed by an addition *The Backbench Diaries of Richard Crossman* (1981). One critic described the diaries as 'the most important book on British government to have appeared since the war', and another described them as 'a unique account, uncommonly detailed, uncommonly lively, uncommonly thoughtful and uncommonly outspoken, of what a cabinet minister does.'

Crossman did not live to see the success of this work. He died at his home in Oxfordshire, Prescote Manor, on 5 April 1974. He and Anne had a son and a daughter; there were no children by his earlier marriages.

CROWTHER, GEOFFREY, BARON CROWTHER (1907–1972), economist, journalist, and business man, was born on 13 May 1907 in Leeds, the eldest son of Charles Crowther, scientist and university teacher, and his wife, Hilda Louise Reed. He was educated at Leeds Grammar School, Oundle, and Clare College, Cambridge, which he entered as a scholar, and where he obtained a double first and became President of the Union (1928). With a Commonwealth scholarship, he studied at Yale and Columbia Universities (1929–31).

In 1932 he joined the staff of *The Economist*. In the same year, he married Margaret, daughter of E. H. Worth, of Claymont, Delaware, USA; they had two sons and four daughters. By 1938 he was Editor of *The Economist*, a post which he held until 1956. The clear concise style of his articles set the pattern for the paper, which under his leadership increased its circulation more than five-fold and became one of the most influential economic journals in the world. In 1941 he published *An Outline of Money*.

During the Second World War he carried on as Editor, also working in the Ministry of Supply (1940–1), the Ministry of Information (1941–2), and the Ministry of Production (1942–3). After the war, he went into business, succeeded Lord LAYTON as Chairman of The Economist Newspaper Ltd., and became Deputy Chairman of Commercial Union Assurance. He created the British Printing Corporation and was Chairman of Trust Houses when it merged with Forte Holdings in 1970. He then became Chairman of the new company but, within two years, was forced to resign because of boardroom disagreements which he failed to control.

In 1957 he was knighted and was created a life peer in 1968. His public duties included the chairmanship of the Central Advisory Council for Education (1956–60), which produced the Crowther Report, and the chairmanship of the Committee on Consumer Credit (1968 and 1971). He was also Chancellor of the Open University in 1969, and Chairman of the Commission on the Constitution. He also had a number of honorary degrees. He died suddenly at Heathrow Airport on 5 February 1972.

CUNNINGHAM, ANDREW BROWNE, VISCOUNT CUNNINGHAM OF HYNDHOPE (1883–1963), Admiral of the Fleet, was born in Dublin on 7 January 1883, the son of Daniel John Cunningham, a professor of anatomy, and his wife, Elizabeth Cumming, daughter of the Revd Andrew Browne, of Beith, Ayrshire. He was educated at Edinburgh Academy, and Stubbington House, Fareham, and entered the training ship *Britannia* in 1897. During the years before the First World War, he made his way in the service, and by 1911 was in command of the destroyer *Scorpion*. He held this command until 1918, fighting in the Dardanelles campaign and in the Dover Patrol under Roger (later Lord) Keyes and taking part in the raid on Zeebrugge. He was appointed DSO in 1915 and added bars in 1919 and 1920. In 1929 Cunningham married Nona Christine, daughter of Horace Byatt, schoolmaster; they had no children.

After further service in destroyers, he became flag captain and chief staff officer to (Sir) Walter Cowan, Commander-in-Chief, North America and West Indies station in 1926 and, in 1929, commanded the battleship *Rodney*. After a period of service ashore, Cunningham was appointed in 1933 rear-admiral (destroyers) in the Mediterranean. He was appointed CB in 1934 and promoted to vice-admiral in 1936. During 1937–8 he commanded the Battle-Cruiser Squadron.

In September 1938 he became Deputy Chief of Naval Staff at the Admiralty, and in 1939 was promoted temporarily to admiral and appointed KCB and Commander-in-Chief, Mediterranean. During the Second World War his task was to keep the Mediterranean clear of hostile ships to ensure, as far as possible, the security of the lines of communication with the troops in North Africa. After the fall of France, he was able to immobilize the French fleet in Alexandria without resort to fighting. He made a successful night attack on Taranto harbour in 1940, putting many Italian warships out of action. In 1941, a few months after his confirmation as admiral, he defeated the Italian fleet off Cape Matapan.

From June to October 1942 Cunningham was with the Combined Chiefs of Staff in Washington heading the British Admiralty delegation. He made an excellent impression on the Americans and was selected to be 'Allied Naval Commander Expeditionary Force' under Eisenhower. In that capacity, he successfully covered the 'Torch' landings in North Africa in 1942 and the convoying of the Allied armies to Sicily and Salerno in 1943.

Later that year he succeeded Sir Dudley Pound as First Sea Lord. He had been promoted to GCB in 1941 and created a baronet in 1942; in 1945 he was created KT and, at the end of the war on his retirement from the post of First Sea Lord became a viscount and was appointed OM. In 1951 he published his memoirs *A Sailor's Odyssey*. He was Lord High Commissioner of the General Assembly of the Church of Scotland in 1950 and again in 1952, Lord Rector of Edinburgh University from 1945 to 1948, and President of the Institution of Naval Architects from 1948 to 1951. He received many other honours.

He died in London on 12 June 1963. Lord ALEXANDER OF TUNIS considered him to be one of 'the great sea commanders of our island race' famed for his skill in holding the Mediterranean with a small fleet at a time when Britain was fighting the war alone.

CUNNINGHAME GRAHAM, ROBERT BONTINE (1852–1936), traveller, scholar, and Scottish nationalist, was born in London on 24 May 1852, the eldest son of William Cunninghame Bontine, a major in the Scots Greys, and his wife, Anne Elizabeth, daughter of Admiral Charles Elphinstone Fleeming. By an entail of 1770, the eldest son had

R. B. Cunninghame Graham at a Heinemann garden party, 1932

to bear the surname Bontine during the lifetime of his father. Cunninghame Graham was educated at Harrow and in Brussels. When he was seventeen he paid the first of several visits to Latin America and rode with the gauchos, and became a friend of 'Buffalo Bill' in Mexico.

From 1886 to 1892 he was Liberal MP for North-West Lanarkshire and was said to have been the first member suspended for using the word 'damn' in the House of Commons. He was always emotionally on the side of the underdog; he became an ardent devotee of Parnell, and then a keen socialist friend of William Morris and John BURNS. In 1887 he was sent to prison after a riot in Trafalgar Square. When the National party of Scotland was founded in 1928 he was elected its first President.

His grandmother, with whom he lived when young, was Spanish; she taught him the language and instilled in him an understanding of Spanish ways. He wrote numerous historical and biographical studies, including *Portrait of a Dictator* (1933), an account of the life of Francisco Solano Lopez, and many volumes of stories, essays, sketches, and verse, including *Thirteen Stories* (1900), *Success* (1902), and *Charity* (1912). He also wrote an account of a dangerous journey through southern Morocco, *Mogreb-el-Acksa*. W. H. HUDSON considered him to be the only European writer who could reveal some of the colour of a way of life in South America which was rapidly disappearing.

In 1879 he married Gabriela, daughter of Don Francisco José de la Balmondière, who was born in Chile, of a French father and Spanish mother, and was a poet, water-colourist, botanist, and mystic. She died, childless, in 1906, and Cunninghame Graham himself dug her grave on the island of Inchmahome in the Lake of Menteith, Scotland. He died at Buenos Aires on 20 March 1936 and was buried beside his wife. In his honour a new city in Argentina was named Don Roberto.

CURRIE, SIR WILLIAM CRAWFORD (1884-1961), shipowner, was born in Calcutta on 4 May 1884, the elder son of William Currie, East India merchant and his wife, Jessie. Both parents were Scottish. His father was a partner of Mackinnon, Mackenzie & Co., managing agents of the British India Steam Navigation Co. (BISN) which in 1914 was merged with the Peninsular and Orient Steam Navigation Co. (P & O). Currie was educated at Glasgow Academy, Fettes College, and Trinity College, Cambridge, where he gained a rugby blue (1905).

After qualifying as an accountant in 1910, he joined Mackinnon, Mackenzie & Co., in Calcutta as an assistant. In 1918 he became a partner and took a prominent part in public life in India. He was Sheriff of Calcutta (1921-2) and a member of the Bengal Legislative Council (1921-5). In 1924 he was Chairman of the Bengal Chamber of Commerce. He was appointed a member of the Council of State for India and knighted in 1925.

He then returned to Britain and became a partner in the Inchcape family firm, Gray, Dawes & Co., and served for four years (1926-30) on the Imperial Shipping Committee. He was also President of the Chamber of Shipping of the United Kingdom (1929-30).

In 1932 Currie was appointed Deputy Chairman and Managing Director of the P & O and BISN companies and, six years later, he became Chairman. Throughout the Second World War he was a member of the Advisory Council of the Ministry of War Transport, and in 1942 became Director of the Liner Division of the Ministry. In 1947 he was appointed

GBE and in 1953 a Commander of the Legion of Honour.

In 1958 he became a director of Inchcape & Co. Ltd. He was President of the Institute of Marine Engineers during 1945-6, High Sheriff of Buckinghamshire in 1947, and Prime Warden of the Worshipful Company of Shipwrights in 1949. Currie had many other business interests and was concerned with a number of committees connected with shipping and seamen.

In 1914 he had married Ruth Forest Dods of Edinburgh; they had two sons, the elder of whom was killed in Burma in 1944. Currie died at Aylesbury on 3 July 1961.

CURTIS, LIONEL GEORGE (1872-1955), public servant, was born at Coddington, Ledbury, on 7 March 1872, the youngest child of the Revd George James Curtis, and his wife, Frances Carr. He was educated at Haileybury, and New College, Oxford. On leaving Oxford he began studying law and set out to gain experience of the working of the Poor Law by becoming a tramp, begging, and sleeping in workhouses. He was later called to the Bar (Inner Temple) in 1902. Meanwhile, he enlisted as a private and fought in the Boer War. Then, in 1900 he became secretary to Sir Alfred MILNER and worked on a plan for a new Johannesburg municipality. He recounted his experiences as a member of Milner's 'kindergarten' in *With Milner in South Africa* (1951). He was the main author of the 'Selbourne memorandum' (1907), aimed at uniting the four South African colonies, and resigned from government service to organize 'closer union' societies throughout South Africa.

On return to England in 1909, Curtis and some of his South African friends founded the *Round Table*, a quarterly review of which Philip KERR became Editor. In 1912 Curtis was Beit lecturer on colonial history at Oxford and from 1911 to 1916 was mainly concerned with advocating a closer unity of the British Commonwealth.

In 1916-17 he took a prominent part in the discussions aimed at advancing India towards self-government, and in 1920 published *Dyarchy*. He attended the Paris Peace Conference as a member of the League of Nations section of the British delegation. It was through his efforts that the (Royal) Institute of International Affairs (Chatham House) was founded and endowed (1920-1). In 1921 he became a research Fellow of All Souls and, as adviser to the Colonial Office, assisted in framing the Irish constitution.

In 1920 he married Gladys Edna (Pat), daughter of Prebendary Percy Richard Scott of Tiverton; they had no children.

From 1924 to 1934 he was busy on his book *Civitas Dei* (3 vols., 1934-7), in which he set out his hopes for world unity through democratic institutions. During the Second World War he worked in the foreign research and press service housed in Balliol College. He exercised a lasting influence on many young Oxford men, and helped to found the Oxford Society and the Oxford Preservation Trust. He received many honorary degrees and became CH in 1949. Curtis died at Kidlington on 24 November 1955. His achievements, little known to the public, were his share in the creation of the Union of South Africa, in the progress of India towards self-government, and in the Irish Treaty of 1921.

CURZON, GEORGE NATHANIEL, MARQUESS CURZON OF KEDLESTON (1859-1925), politician, was born at Kedleston Hall, Derbyshire, on 11 January 1859, the eldest of eleven children of the Revd Alfred Nathaniel Holden

Curzon, fourth Baron Scarsdale, Rector of Kedleston, and his wife, Blanche, daughter of Joseph Pocklington Senhouse, of Netherall, Maryport, Cumberland. After an unhappy childhood and a precociously brilliant career at Eton, he went up to Balliol College, Oxford, in 1878 and, having obtained a first in Mods., was disappointed at getting only a second in Greats. He was, however, Secretary of the Canning Club and President of the Union, and in 1883 became a Fellow of All Souls.

From the age of nineteen he was handicapped by spinal curvature, which for the rest of his life caused him much discomfort and pain and, to some extent, explained the peculiar tension and rigidity of his temperament. On leaving Oxford, he was forced to supplement the meagre allowance from his father by writing and, as he travelled abroad, he sent back to England articles on political and current affairs.

From 1886 to 1892 he was Conservative MP for the Southport division of Lancashire, and when he was in England was a convivial member of the 'Souls' and Wilfrid Scawen BLUNT's Crabbet Club. From 1887 to 1894 he made a succession of travels through North America, Russia, the Near and Far East, India, Afghanistan, and Persia (Iran), recounted the story of these journeys in *Russia in Central Asia* (1889), *Persia and the Persian Question* (1892), and *Problems of the Far East* (1894), and made a reputation for himself as a leading authority on Asiatic affairs.

In 1895 Curzon married Mary Victoria Leiter, the daughter of an American millionaire and a woman of great beauty and charm, whose fortune relieved him of any further monetary problems. From 1895 to 1898 he was Under-Secretary for Foreign Affairs, but his relations with Lord Salisbury were not comfortable as the Prime Minister, who also retained the portfolio of the Foreign Office, was apt to ignore him and they did not always see eye to eye about policy, particularly in respect of countries which Curzon had visited. Furthermore, lacking any special expertise on Europe, Curzon was inclined to underestimate the European dimension in foreign policy. However, as the spokesman on foreign affairs in the Commons, he became a public figure.

Then, in 1898 at the age of thirty-nine, he was appointed Viceroy of India and created Baron Curzon. He had insisted on an Irish rather than an English peerage so that he would not be debarred from the Commons. For the next seven years he was able to live in great splendour, exercising immense authority over the affairs of a sub-continent. At the beginning his policies were successful; he was determined to administer even-handed justice to the different nationalities under his control whilst maintaining a cautious approach to some of the age-old problems of the frontier. He was able to settle the Berar question in a treaty with the Nizam of Hyderabad (1902).

The Durbar of 1903 was the high-water mark of Curzon's splendour as Viceroy, but even before it took place he was engaged in controversy with the Secretary of State and the home Government over a number of matters, and when Lord KITCHENER arrived in India as Commander-in-Chief, two masterful personalities came into conflict over the control of the armed forces in India. This disagreement was eventually resolved by a compromise, but Curzon did not take kindly to compromise and, when he found himself being overruled by the India Office on another matter, he resigned (1905).

For the next eleven years Curzon felt embittered by what he regarded as public neglect of his achievements in India. In 1906 Lady Curzon died, and to anger and humiliation were added grief and despair. His unhappiness was relieved to some degree by his election as Chancellor of Oxford University, and by his absorption in work for the Royal Geographical Society and the National Gallery.

In 1911 he was created Earl Curzon of Kedleston, and once again came into public prominence. During the First World War he was a member of the Coalition Government, as Lord Privy Seal in 1915 and, after the fall of ASQUITH, as Leader in the House of Lords, Lord President of the Council (1916), and a member of LLOYD GEORGE's War Cabinet. He was also appointed KG. In 1917 he married Grace, daughter of Joseph Monroe Hinds, another American, and his loneliness, which had been alleviated by his liaison with Elinor Glyn, the novelist, gave way once more to a social life.

In 1919 Curzon succeeded Arthur BALFOUR as Foreign Secretary, but once again he found himself in a frustrating

Lord Curzon salutes the guard of honour at the Durbar, 1903

position since Lloyd George was apt to conduct his own foreign policy without consulting his Foreign Secretary. Eventually the Prime Minister's anti-Turkish policy convinced Curzon that he could no longer endure to be a member of the 'coupon' Government. When the Conservatives overthrew Lloyd George and BONAR LAW became Prime Minister in 1922 Curzon remained Foreign Secretary. The Lausanne Conference on Graeco-Turkish matters was a failure, but Curzon dominated its deliberations and restored British prestige in Turkey.

Bonar Law resigned in 1923 and Curzon confidently expected to be summoned to be Prime Minister, but Stanley BALDWIN was preferred and, once again, Curzon had to hide his chagrin. He soldiered on at the Foreign Office until 1924 when he became Lord President of the Council. He died on 20 March 1925 in London. He had been created a marquess in 1921; he had three daughters by his first wife, but no son, so on his death, the marquessate became extinct.

Curzon's career was the story of a man of brilliant potential, who held high office but failed to reach the highest post open to him, not because he lacked ability, but because his lofty manner, grandiloquence, and intransigence in a period of great political fluidity were insupportable to his contemporaries.

D

DALE, SIR HENRY HALLETT (1875-1968), physiologist-pharmacologist, was born in London on 9 June 1875, the third son of Charles James Dale, the manager of a manufacturing firm, and his wife, Frances Ann, daughter of Frederick Hallett, a furniture-maker. He was educated at the Leys School and Trinity College, Cambridge, where he obtained firsts in both parts of the natural sciences tripos (1896-8). He qualified at St Bartholomew's Hospital, London and gained his B.Ch. (Cambridge) in 1902. In 1904, the year of his marriage to a first cousin, Ellen Harriet, daughter of F. W. Hallett, he was appointed to a research post at the Wellcome Research Laboratories. Within two years he had become Director, remaining there until 1914, when he became Director of the Department of Biochemistry and Pharmacology of the projected Institute for Medical Researches. This became the National Institute in 1920, and Dale was its Director from 1928 to 1942. From 1942 to 1946 he was Director of the Royal Institution and Fullerian Professor of Chemistry. He was Chairman of the Wellcome Trust from 1938 to 1960; he was Secretary of the Royal Society from 1925 to 1935, and President from 1940 to 1945.

During the years in which Dale held these offices, he was responsible with his co-workers for fundamental discoveries in pharmacology, including the effects of histamine and acetylcholine, and made a great contribution to therapeutics by his work for the acceptance of international standards for hormones, vitamins, and drugs. In 1936 he was awarded the Nobel prize for physiology and medicine (with Otto Loewi).

Throughout these years, he also carried a heavy administrative burden and, during the Second World War, he had secret advisory duties and was chairman of a confidential scientific committee advising the War Cabinet. He was a member of the Medical Research Council from 1942 to 1946, and was concerned with many other organizations such as the Royal Society of Medicine and the British Council. He received many academic honours and prizes; he became FRS (1914), CBE (1919), was knighted in 1932, and became GBE in 1943, and OM in 1944. Dale died in Cambridge on 23 July 1968. All three of his children, two daughters and a son, studied either physiology or medicine.

DALTON, (EDWARD) HUGH JOHN NEALE, BARON DALTON (1887-1962), politician, was born at Neath, Glamorganshire, on 26 August 1887, the eldest child of Canon John Neale Dalton, and his wife, Catharine Alicia, elder daughter of Charles Evan-Thomas, DL, of Neath. He was educated at Eton and King's College, Cambridge, where he read maths and economics and was taught by both Arthur PIGOU and John Maynard KEYNES. At that time he became a close friend of Rupert BROOKE. He was called to the Bar (Middle Temple) in 1914 and, in the same year, he married Ruth, daughter of Thomas Hamilton-Fox, a business man. Their only child, a daughter, died aged four and a half.

During the First World War he served with the army in France and Italy, and recorded his experiences in *With British Guns in Italy* (1919). After the war, he became a lecturer in economics at the LSE, obtained his D.Sc. in 1921, and was Reader in economics at London University from 1925 to 1936. In 1923 he published *Principles of Public Finance*, based on orthodox pre-Keynesian economics, and followed by *Practical Socialism for Britain* (1935).

He was Labour MP for Peckham (1924-9), and for Bishop Auckland (1929-31). He was Parliamentary Under-Secretary to Arthur HENDERSON at the Foreign Office (1929) but refused to serve in the National Government of 1931. During the next four years he travelled extensively visiting Russia, Italy, France, Germany, and Australia.

In 1935 he was elected again for Bishop Auckland and held the seat until 1959. Convinced of the danger from Hitler, he was consistently in favour of re-armament. He supported Winston CHURCHILL and became his Minister of Economic Warfare and PC in the Coalition Government of 1940. It was his task to set up the SOE, the secret organization for subversion and sabotage in aid of the resistance movements in Europe. In 1942 he moved to the Board of Trade, where he was instrumental in the establishment of a Ministry of Fuel and Power and a National Coal Board.

He held his seat in the 1945 election, and in the Labour Government was Chancellor of the Exchequer (1945-7) with Lord Keynes, to whose economic theories he had become an ardent convert in 1937, as personal adviser. Under his aegis

Dalton attending the International Socialist Conference on the Marshall Plan, Selsdon Park, Surrey, 1948

DARBISHIRE, HELEN (1881-1961), scholar, critic, and Principal of Somerville College, Oxford, was born in Oxford on 26 February 1881, the elder daughter of Samuel Dukinfield Darbishire, a physician, and his wife, Florence Eckersley. She was educated at Oxford High School, and Somerville, where she was a Pfeiffer scholar and gained a first in English (1903).

After a short time as lecturer at the Royal Holloway College, London, she returned to Somerville in 1908 as English tutor; she remained there for thirty-seven years, as a Fellow in 1922, university lecturer in 1927-31, Principal from 1931-1945, and honorary Fellow in 1946.

Her main interests were in Wordsworth and Milton. In 1914 she published *Wordsworth's Poems published in 1807* and, in 1952, the completed edition of the Clarendon Wordsworth (5 vols.) which she took over from Ernest de Selincourt (who had been her teacher at Oxford) when he died in 1943. In 1931 appeared *The Manuscript of Paradise Lost, Book I*, followed by *The Early Lives of Milton* (1932).

During her long tenure as Principal, a post which could not have been welcome to one of so reserved a nature, she supervised many new developments, particularly in respect of additional buildings, including the east quadrangle, named after her, and the chapel.

In retirement she continued her work on Milton and Wordsworth, including a new and, to some extent, controversial text of *Paradise Lost* (1952) and the complete poems of Milton in the Oxford Standard Authors series (1958); she also published *The Poet Wordsworth* (1950), and a new edition of the *Journals of Dorothy Wordsworth* (1958).

Her many honours included FBA (1947) and CBE (1955). From 1943 to her death she was Chairman of Dove Cottage, Grasmere, and greatly improved its facilities as a centre of study. She died at Shepherds How, overlooking Grasmere, on 11 March 1961.

DARWIN, BERNARD RICHARD MEIRION (1876-1961), essayist and sports writer, was born at Downe, Kent, on 7 September 1876, the only son of (Sir) Francis Darwin, botanist, and his first wife, Amy, daughter of Lawrence Ruck, of Pantlludw, Machynlleth, North Wales. He was the grandson of Charles Darwin, author of the *Origin of Species*. He was educated at Eton and Trinity College, Cambridge, where he played golf for the university for three years (1895-7) and was Captain in 1897. In 1903 he was called to the Bar (Inner Temple) but his heart was in writing rather than in the law.

In 1907 he contributed occasional articles to the *Evening Standard*, *Country Life*, and *The Times*, but from 1908 concentrated on writing about golf. His weekly golf articles in *The Times* were a regular feature for forty-three years and he continued to write for *Country Life* almost to the time he died. In 1913 he covered for *The Times* the appearance of Harry Vardon and Edward Ray in the US Open Championship which was won by Francis Ouimet, an event which marked the advent of American ascendancy in the game.

After the First World War, in which he served in the Royal Army Ordnance Corps, Darwin played for the British amateurs in the first Walker Cup match against the United States in America (1922). Two years later he won the President's Putter, and in 1934 was elected Captain of the Royal and Ancient Golf Club.

When Darwin began to write, golf reporting was little more than a few statistics in a sports column, but by the time he retired it had become a branch of literary journalism in which he quoted fully from his favourite authors. It was no

the Bank of England was nationalized (1946), but in 1947 he ran into trouble with heavy falls in the stock market and a fuel crisis. In the autumn a sterling crisis forced him to produce a second budget, and he inadvertently leaked the details of his proposals to a journalist before he had revealed them to the Commons. They appeared prematurely in an evening paper, and Dalton felt obliged to resign for his indiscretion.

He rejoined the Cabinet in the following year as Chancellor of the Duchy of Lancaster, and served on the Council of Europe for which he was well equipped as he was fluent in French and Italian. In 1950 he was Minister for Town and Country Planning and helped to develop new towns and national parks.

He did not stand for election in 1959, and in 1960 accepted a life peerage. In spite of his emotional approach to politics and a tendency to be over-confident, he contributed much to the Labour party, particularly by his practical socialism and his assistance to many younger men in the party.

His memoirs were published in three volumes, *Call Back Yesterday* (1953), *The Fateful Years* (1931-1945) (1957), and *High Tide and After* (1962). He also received many academic honours. Dalton died in London on 13 February 1962.

surprise when he was selected to write the foreword to the *Oxford Dictionary of Quotations* (1941). Among his own publications were *The Tale of Mr. Tootleoo* (1926), a book for children, illustrated by his wife, Elinor Mary, daughter of William Thomas Monsell, whom he had married in 1906. He also published books on English public schools (1929), on London clubs, and on W. G. GRACE (1934), as well as his autobiographical *Green Memories* (1928), *Pack Clouds Away* (1941), and *The World that Fred Made* (1955). He was appointed CBE in 1937.

Darwin died at Denton, Sussex on 18 October 1961. He had three children, two daughters and a son, Robin, who became Principal of the Royal College of Art from 1948 to 1967 and was knighted in 1964.

DAVIDSON, RANDALL THOMAS, BARON DAVIDSON OF LAMBETH (1848–1930), Archbishop of Canterbury, was born in Edinburgh on 7 April 1848, the eldest child of Henry Davidson of Leith, a merchant, and his wife, Henrietta, daughter of John Campbell Swinton, of Kimmerghame, co. Berwick. Both parents were Presbyterians. He was educated at Harrow, and Trinity College, Oxford, where he read law and modern history. During the three years from 1871 to 1874 he divided his time between travel abroad and training for holy orders. In 1874 he was ordained deacon, and in 1875, priest.

From 1877 to 1882 he was resident chaplain to Archbishop Tait, whose daughter, Edith, he married in 1878. They had no children. When Tait died, Davidson was consulted by

Randall Davidson, Archbishop of Canterbury, February 1922

Queen Victoria about a successor and, after the appointment of Dr Benson as Archbishop, he became Dean of Windsor and the Queen's domestic chaplain. He was now the confidant of both Queen and Archbishop. In 1891 he became Bishop of Rochester, and, four years later, Bishop of Winchester. When Archbishop Benson died in 1896, the Queen wished Davidson to succeed him, but Lord Salisbury thought otherwise, and Dr TEMPLE was appointed. During these years at Winchester, Davidson took an active part in public affairs and was one of BALFOUR's principal advisers on educational matters. On 19 January 1901 he was called to Osborne, which was in his diocese, and he remained with the Queen until she died.

In 1902 Temple died and Davidson succeeded him as Archbishop of Canterbury. The twenty-five years during which he served in that office were a time of controversy, and Davidson was faced with the task of maintaining the unity of the Church of England in the face of wide differences over ritual and revision of the Prayer Book. He was a member of the Royal Commission on Ecclesiastical Discipline in 1904; he opposed the Education Bill (1906) and the Deceased Wife's Sister Marriage Act (1907); he presided over the fifth Lambeth Conference of bishops of the Anglican communion (1908); he also took a keen interest in the work of missions abroad, and did what he could to maintain Anglo-German good relations. He officiated at the coronation of George V in 1911 and played an important part behind the scenes in the controversy leading to the Parliament Act; he also strongly resisted the legislation for the disestablishment of the Welsh church, and had a moderating influence on the disagreements over ecumenism in the Church which came to a head in 1914.

Throughout the First World War, whilst believing firmly in the justice of the Allied cause, he spoke out against the use of poison gas and air reprisals, and in 1916 authorized the National Mission of Repentance and Hope. He also gave public support to proposals for a League of Nations. After the war, he supported the Church of England Assembly (Powers) Act of 1919 which was intended to strengthen the ability of the Church to carry on its work; he also took a keen interest in the movement for greater unity of the Christian churches, and won the confidence and trust of the leaders of the Free Churches.

During the general strike of 1926 he appealed for a settlement in a spirit of co-operation and, although his action was criticized in some quarters, the sympathy he had shown in calling for concessions by the Government and the mine owners as well as appealing for the strike to be called off, was appreciated by the labour leaders. Naturally, he was closely concerned with the movement for the revision of the Prayer Book, and was deeply disappointed when the House of Commons rejected the measure in 1928.

On 12 November 1928 Davidson resigned and was created baron. He had been Archbishop longer than any of his predecessors since William Warham (1504–32). He died at Chelsea on 25 May 1930, and was buried in Canterbury Cathedral. Having served as primate during a difficult period he had proved to be an able administrator and a moderating influence on the warring elements in his charge.

DAVIES, WILLIAM JOHN ABBOTT (1890–1967), rugby player, was born on 21 June 1890 in Pembroke, the eldest child of William George Davies, a shopkeeper, and his wife, Florence Meyrick Davies. He was educated at Pembroke Dock Grammar School, the Royal Naval College, Keyham, and the Royal Naval College, Greenwich. He was a Pembroke

Dock apprentice in 1905, and went to Greenwich in 1910.

He took up rugby by chance at twenty, played with the United Services Club, Portsmouth and, within three years, was capped for England; he played for England five times in 1913.

During the First World War he served in the *Iron Duke* and *Queen Elizabeth*, and in 1919 returned to Admiralty work at Portsmouth as an assistant constructor and was appointed OBE. He then began his famous partnership at half-back with C. A. Kershaw. They played together for England for four seasons, and England never lost a match in which they played. When Davies retired from international rugby at the end of the 1922–3 season, he had never been in a losing side. He was capped twenty-two times. He captained the Royal Navy and Hampshire, and became an England selector (1923–6).

Between 1935 and 1938 Davies was attached to the staff of the Commander-in-Chief, Mediterranean Fleet, and in 1939 became chief constructor. Between 1942 and 1950 he was Assistant Director of warship production, Superintendent of warship production on the Clyde, and Director of merchant shipbuilding and repairs. He was President of the Civil Service Football Club from 1937 to 1966, and in 1951 became a liveryman of the Royal Company of Shipwrights. He wrote two books, *Rugby Football* (1923), and *How to Play Rugby Football* (1933).

In 1923 he had married Margaret Bleecker, daughter of Major Ernest Glanville Waymouth, RA; they had a son and a daughter, both of whom became doctors. Davies died in Teddington on 26 April 1967. He was one of the best flyhalves who have ever played for England.

DAVIS, JOSEPH (1901–1978), billiards and snooker player, was born on 15 April 1901 at Whitwell, Derbyshire, the eldest son of Fred Davis, publican, and his wife, Ann-Eliza Clark. He went to school at Newbold, but spent all his spare time practising on the billiard table in his father's public house. He won a local billiards amateur championship when he was thirteen, and in 1922 won the Midland Professional championship. In 1921 he married Florence Stevenson; they had a son and a daughter.

When he entered for the World Championship he was beaten three years running by Tom Newman, but he won the title every year from 1928 to 1932. Then, in 1933 and 1934, he was defeated by Walter Lindrum. By this time the enormous breaks, including Lindrum's world record of 4,137, were spoiling billiards for the spectators, and in 1926–7 Joe Davis won the first world professional snooker title which he continued to hold until 1946. He made his first public snooker break of 100 in 1928 and by 1938 had increased this to 138. In 1955 he achieved his ambition of making a break of 147, the first time this maximum possible had been reached.

During the Second World War he raised large sums of money for war charities by appearing in the variety stage in exhibitions of trick shots and other forms of snooker skill. He won his last snooker world title in 1946. The only other player to win the world title at both billiards and snooker was his youngest brother, Fred. His first marriage having ended in divorce, in 1945 Davis married June Malo, a singer and daughter of William Warren Triggs. Although he was no longer champion, Joe continued to play, and was chairman of the professionals' association. In 1976 he published *The Breaks Came My Way*; he also wrote books on the technique of the game. In 1963 he was awarded the OBE. He died on 10 July 1978 at Grayshott, at a time when snooker was again

Joe Davis in action, Leicester Square Hall, 1951

becoming popular with the public through the televising of professional tournaments, and the prizes were such as Joe Davis could hardly have dreamt of.

DAWSON, BERTRAND EDWARD, VISCOUNT DAWSON OF PENN (1864–1945), physician, was born at Croydon on 9 March 1864, the fourth son of Henry Dawson, architect, and his wife, Frances, daughter of Obadiah Wheeler, of Perivale. He was educated at St Paul's School and University College, London, and qualified at the London Hospital, becoming B.Sc. (1888), and MRCS (England), MD, MRCP (London), and FRCP between 1890 and 1903. In 1900 Dawson married Ethel, daughter of the shipbuilder, (Sir) Alfred Fernandez Yarrow; they had three daughters.

He became assistant physician at the London Hospital in 1896, the year in which he also began private consultancy work, and was physician from 1906 to 1945. In 1907 he was appointed physician-extraordinary to the King, a post he held until 1914 when he went to France as consulting physician with the rank of major-general. Although mainly engaged on hospital administration, he found time to publish papers on infectious diseases, and reached the conclusion that the general standard of fitness was low and that a national health service was required. He was Chairman of the Ministry of Health Consultative Council on Medical Services (1919–20) whose report foreshadowed this requirement. He was opposed to a full-time salaried medical service, but recognized that the profession should co-operate in future developments of medical care. However, the Dawson Report did not lead to legislation at this stage.

In 1920 Dawson was created a baron, and became the spokesman of the medical profession in the House of Lords. He held numerous hospital appointments; among other responsibilities, he was Chairman of the Army Medical Advisory Board (1936–45), President of the Royal Society of

Medicine (1928-30), of the BMA (1932 and 1943), and of the Royal College of Physicians (1931-8).

During the grave illness of George V in 1928 Dawson attended the King, and in 1929 became a Privy Counsellor. He was also with the King in his last illness. He was promoted to viscount in 1936, and remained in the household of both Edward VIII and George VI. He was the recipient of many academic honours as well as KCVO (1911), CB (1916), GCVO (1917), KCMG (1919), and KCB (1926).

When war broke out in 1939 he was concerned with the organization of the Emergency Medical Service and was a member of the commission set up by the BMA to consider a national health service. Before he was able to complete his efforts to reconcile the claims of the profession with those of the public interest he died in London on 7 March 1945.

DAWSON, (GEORGE) GEOFFREY (1874-1944), Editor of *The Times*, was born at Skipton-in-Craven, Yorkshire, on 25 October 1874, the eldest child of George Robinson, banker, and his wife, Mary, daughter of William Mosley Perfect. He assumed the name Dawson on succeeding his aunt in the estate of Langcliffe Hall, Settle in 1917. He was educated at Eton, where he was a King's scholar, and Magdalen College, Oxford, where he obtained firsts in Classical Mods. and Greats (1895-7). He was elected a Fellow of All Souls in 1898, and entered the Civil Service.

In 1899 he was posted to the Colonial Office under Joseph Chamberlain to whom he became assistant private secretary in 1901, and later that year he went out to South Africa to serve Lord MILNER in the same capacity. He served in the famous 'kindergarten' until 1905, and then became Editor of the Johannesburg *Star* and correspondent of *The Times*. Like Lionel CURTIS, he was a strong supporter of the movement which led to the Union of South Africa in 1910.

In 1911 he returned to England to work on *The Times* and, in the following year, Lord NORTHCLIFFE, the proprietor, appointed him Editor in succession to G. E. Buckle, and invited him to get away from the traditional attitudes of the paper and to give it freshness and life. Throughout the difficult period up to the end of the First World War he was able to work harmoniously with Northcliffe, but when peace came Northcliffe insisted on interfering with editorial policy and Dawson resigned.

In 1919 he married Margaret Cecilia, daughter of Sir Arthur Lawley (later sixth Baron Wenlock); they had one son and two daughters.

He returned to Oxford, became Secretary of the Rhodes Trust (1921-2), and for a time edited the *Round Table*. When John Jacob ASTOR became chief proprietor of *The Times* in 1923, he recalled Dawson to the editorship and gave him a free hand over editorial policy, which in the main, for Dawson, meant support for the government of the day. Until he resigned in 1941 he wielded considerable influence in the corridors of power, being an intimate of Stanley BALDWIN and a supporter of Neville CHAMBERLAIN, throughout the years leading to the Second World War. Like Philip KERR, who had also been a member of Milner's 'kindergarten', he was firm in his approval of appeasement, and went to great lengths to justify this policy.

After his resignation from *The Times*, Dawson again edited the *Round Table* until he died in London on 7 November 1944.

DAY-LEWIS, CECIL (1904-1972), Poet Laureate, was born on 27 April 1904, at Ballintubbert, Queen's County,

co. Laois, the only child of the Revd Frank Cecil Day-Lewis, and his wife, Kathleen Blake, daughter of William Alfred Squires, civil servant. He was educated at Sherborne and Wadham College, Oxford, where he met W. H. AUDEN and they collaborated in *Oxford Poetry 1927*.

During 1927-8 he was an assistant master at Summer Fields preparatory school, Oxford, during 1928-30 taught at Larchfield, Helensburgh, near Glasgow, and during 1930-5 at Cheltenham Junior School. From 1935 to 1938 he was a political activist and a member of the Communist party. During what Isaiah Berlin has called 'the dark and leaden thirties', he and Auden and Stephen Spender were echoing the troubles of the time in their poetry. Day-Lewis published *Beechen Vigil* (1925) followed by *Country Comets* (1928), *From Feathers to Iron* (1931), *The Magnetic Mountain* (1933), *A Time to Dance* (1935), *Noah and the Waters* (1936), and *Overtures to Death* (1938). In 1935 he began to publish detective novels under the name of Nicholas Blake, his first, *A Question of Proof*, set in a prep. school.

He married in 1928 (Constance) Mary, daughter of Henry Robinson King, a Sherborne master; they had two sons. In 1938 they settled in Devon and Day-Lewis produced his translation of Virgil's *Georgics* (1940), his own verse collections *Word Over All* (1943) and *Poems 1943-47* (1948). By this time the influence of Thomas HARDY's work was apparent in his poetry, though the voice was unmistakably his own. During 1941-6 he worked at the Ministry of Information, but his private life was becoming complicated; after a passionate affair with Edna Elizabeth ('Billie') Currall, the wife of a neighbour in Devon, which resulted in the birth of a son, he began a relationship with Rosamond Lehmann, the novelist, which lasted until 1949. Then he fell in love with an actress, Jill Angela Henriette, daughter of the film producer, Sir Michael BALCON. In 1951 his first marriage ended in divorce and he married Jill; they had a son and a daughter.

In 1946 he was Clark lecturer at Cambridge, and in 1951 was elected Professor of Poetry at Oxford. In that year his translation of Virgil's *Aeneid* was broadcast by the BBC. From 1946 he had been a senior reader for Chatto and Windus Ltd. and subsequently became a director of the company. He continued to publish detective novels and poetry, though lecturing and work for such organizations as the Royal Society of Literature and the Arts Council claimed much of his time.

In 1968 he succeeded John MASEFIELD as Poet Laureate. His final volumes of poetry, *Pegasus* (1957), *The Gate* (1962), *The Room* (1965), and *The Whispering Roots* (1970) were not received with the acclaim of his earlier work. In 1960 he published his autobiography *The Buried Day*.

He received many academic honours, including an honorary Fellowship of Wadham College, Oxford. He died on 22 May 1972 at Hadley Wood, Herts. in the home of Elizabeth Jane Howard and Kingsley Amis, with whom he and Jill were staying.

DEAKIN, ARTHUR (1890-1955), trade-union leader, was born at Sutton Coldfield on 11 November 1890, the illegitimate son of a domestic servant, Annie Deakin. At the age of thirteen he became a steel worker in South Wales. In 1914 he married Annie, daughter of Robert George of Connah's Quay, Flintshire; they had two sons. In 1911 he had joined the Dock, Wharf, Riverside, and General Workers' Union, and by 1919 had become a full-time official of the union. Three years later he was assistant district secretary for the North Wales area, when his union became part of the Transport and General Workers' Union.

In 1932 Deakin moved to London, and in 1935 was appointed Assistant General Secretary by Ernest BEVIN. He worked closely with Bevin during the years leading up to the Second World War, which were difficult ones for the union. When Bevin became Minister of Labour in CHURCHILL's wartime Government, Deakin took over the running of the union, though effective control of it remained in Bevin's hands. However, when Bevin resigned as General Secretary in 1946, Deakin succeeded him.

In many ways he modelled himself upon Ernest Bevin and, after the resignation of (Sir) Walter Citrine from the TUC, he became the dominant figure in the trades union movement. During the period of the ATTLEE Government, he loyally supported the administration, urging the members of his union to increase productivity and to exercise restraint in their wage demands. By some he was regarded as dictatorial, but he was always careful to secure the support of the majority of members of his union for the policies which he thought to be right. He became a determined opponent of Communism, helped to set up the International Federation of Free Trade Unions in 1949, and persuaded his own union to ban Communists from office.

Although he gave an impression of a flamboyant personality in public, in fact he lived simply, was a teetotaller, and a member of the Primitive Methodist Church. He twice refused a knighthood but was appointed CBE in 1943, CH in 1949, and PC in 1954. He died in office at Leicester on 1 May 1955 while he was addressing a May Day rally.

DE HAVILLAND, SIR GEOFFREY (1882-1965), aircraft designer and manufacturer, was born at Wooburn, Bucks. on 27 July 1882, the second son of the Revd Charles de Havilland, curate of Hazlemere, and Alice Jeanette, daughter of Jason Saunders. After attending St Edward's School, Ox-

ford, he was trained in mechanical engineering at the Crystal Palace Engineering School (1900-3). He was apprenticed to Willans and Robinson of Rugby and in 1905 became a draughtsman, first with the Wolseley Tool and Motor Car Co., Birmingham, and then with the Vanguard Omnibus Co. His first important design was for the Blackburn motor cycle.

In 1908-9 he designed his own aeroplane and engine, and taught himself to fly; this was one of the first half dozen British-built aircraft. Between 1912 and 1914 he evolved an important range of aeroplanes, and during the First World War designed and flew eight military planes, including the DH4.

In 1920 de Havilland founded the de Havilland Aircraft Co. He supplied airliners to three airlines, and pioneered the light aeroplane movement with the Moth, in which many long-distance flights were made by Amy JOHNSON and others. The Tiger Moth trainer, developed in 1931, was used by the RAF throughout the Second World War. In 1927 the first de Havilland aero-engine appeared and during the 1930s several airliners were developed all with de Havilland engines. The de Havilland Comet racer won the Mac-Robertson International England to Australia race in 1934 and, during the war, de Havillands produced the Mosquito, the fastest aircraft of the time.

After the war the company entered the jet field with the Vampire fighter, followed by other planes designed for the navy and air force. In 1949 their Comet became the first jet airliner to cross the Atlantic with fare-paying passengers. The Trident followed the Comet.

In 1909 de Havilland had married Louie, daughter of Richard Thomas of Chepstow; they had three sons. The youngest died in an air collision and the eldest, who was the chief test-pilot responsible for the entire flight development of the Mosquito, was killed in 1946. Three years later Louie died. In 1951, de Havilland married Joan Mary, the widow of Geoffrey Mordaunt, and daughter of E. P. Frith. He

De Havilland looks apprehensive aboard an early aeroplane of his own design, September 1912

retired in 1955; during his career 45,000 aeroplanes bearing his name were produced. Natural history was his hobby, and he made some excellent films of wild life; he was a council member of the Fauna Preservation Society. His honours included the OBE (1918), Air Force Cross (1919), CBE (1934), and OM (1962); he was knighted in 1944. He died on 21 May 1965 at Stanmore, Middlesex.

DE LA MARE, WALTER JOHN (1873-1956), poet, novelist, and anthologist was born on 25 April 1873 at Charlton, Kent, the sixth child of James Edward de la Mare, an official of the Bank of England, and his wife, Lucy Sophia Browning. He was educated at St Paul's Cathedral Choristers' School, and then worked for the Anglo-American Oil Co. until 1908.

He published his first book of poems, *Songs of Childhood*, in 1902, and followed this by a large output of poems, stories, novels, books for children, and anthologies. His first prose work was *Henry Brocken* (1904), followed by *The Return* (1910), *The Three Mulla-Mulgars* (1910), and *Memoirs of a Midget* (1921).

His book of poetry, *The Listeners* (1912), reached a wide public, and his poems for children *Peacock Pie* were very popular. His anthologies included *Come Hither* (1923), *Behold, This Dreamer* (1939), and *Love* (1943).

De la Mare's poetry has a strange fascination; there is 'The Scarecrow':

I lift void eyes and scan
The skies for crows, those ravening foes,
Of my strange master, Man.

and Old 'Nod', the shepherd:

Walter de la Mare, by Norman Parkinson, 1951

Wrinkled with age, and drenched with dew,

The Traveller (1946) is a synopsis of his philosophy with its curious mixture of the obscure and the bizarre. His poetry reflects a relentlessly inquisitive imagination creating a mosaic of dreams and reality, peopled by fairies and ghosts as well as natural beings, and with an element of horror never very far from the surface.

De la Mare received many academic honours; in 1948 he was appointed CH, and in 1953 OM. In 1899 he married Constance Elfrida, daughter of Alfred William Ingpen; they had two daughters and two sons, the elder of whom became Chairman of Faber & Faber Ltd., publishers. Walter de la Mare died at Twickenham on 22 June 1956 and was buried in St Paul's Cathedral.

DELIUS, FREDERICK (1862-1934), musician, was born at Bradford on 29 January 1862, the second son of Julius Delius, a wool merchant, and his wife, Elise Pauline, daughter of Christian Kroenig, of Bielefeld, Westphalia; both parents were German born, and Julius Delius had become a naturalized Englishman in 1850. Frederick was educated at Bradford Grammar School, and the International College at Isleworth. He wished to make music his career but his parents opposed this plan and sent him out to Florida to plant oranges.

There he met T. F. Ward, a Brooklyn organist, who encouraged him to play the piano and gave him instruction. In 1885 Delius set himself up as a teacher of piano and violin. A year later his parents relented and sent him to study at the Leipzig Conservatorium. There he met the composer Grieg who went with him to London and persuaded his parents that he had a future as a musician. He had always preferred the music of Grieg to that of Mozart and Beethoven and their friendship now encouraged a lasting affection for Scandinavian life and literature.

In 1888 Delius became a full-time composer, living in France, first in Paris, then at Grez-sur-Loing, near Fontainebleau, where he met and married Jelka Helen (von) Rosen. Except for a short period during the First World War Delius lived there composing his music until he died. At first, his music was recognized only in Germany, where it became very popular: 'Sea Drift', a cantata, was performed at Essen in 1906, and his opera *A Village Romeo and Juliet* at Berlin in 1907, and, in a single year (1910), 'Brigg Fair' was played by thirty-six different orchestras.

He had given a concert, conducted by Alfred Hertz in London in 1899, including the tone poem 'Over the Hills and Far Away', but the critics were puzzled by the apparent formlessness of his music, and it was not until 1910, when Thomas BEECHAM discovered its charm, that Delius became known in England. Beecham directed the recording of all his main works.

In 1924 Delius lost his sight and the use of his limbs, as a result of a disease he had contracted in Paris in the 1890s; but four years later, he gratefully accepted the offer of Eric Fenby, a Yorkshire musician, to be his amanuensis. Fenby described this relationship in *Delius as I Knew Him* (1936).

From 1926 onwards, helped by the conducting of Sir Thomas Beecham, Delius soon became a popular success in England. In 1929 a six-day Delius Festival was held at the Queen's Hall, London, in the presence of the composer in his bathchair. In the same year he was appointed CH.

Apart from those pieces already mentioned, his best-known works include *A Mass of Life* (with text from Nietzsche's

Delius (right) with Percy Grainger, *c.* 1923

Also sprach Zarathustra), 'On Hearing the First Cuckoo in Spring', 'A Song of Summer', 'In a Summer Garden', 'Paris: the Song of a Great City', and 'Songs of Farewell' (five settings of Walt Whitman for double chorus and orchestra).

He died at Grez-sur-Loing on 10 June 1934 and was buried at Limpsfield in Surrey. His wife was buried there too, a few days later. They had no children.

DERBY, seventeenth EARL OF (1865–1948). See STANLEY.

DESBOROUGH, BARON (1855–1945). See GRENFELL, WILLIAM HENRY.

DE VALERA, EAMON (1882–1975), Prime Minister and President of Eire, was born in New York on 14 October 1882, the only child of Vivion Juan de Valéra, a Spanish artist, and his wife, Catherine (Kate), daughter of Patrick Coll, an Irish farm labourer. His father died when he was two, and his mother took him to Ireland, where he was brought up by Patrick Coll, his uncle, and went to school in Charleville and Blackrock College, Dublin, and to University College, Blackrock, and the Royal University of Ireland. In 1893 he became a teacher, and in 1904 Professor of Mathematics at the training college of Our Lady of Mercy, Carysfort, Blackrock. In 1910 he married Sinead, daughter of Laurence Flanagan of Carbery, co. Kildare; they had five sons and two daughters.

In 1913 De Valera joined the Volunteers, the response of southern Ireland to the Ulster Volunteer Force, and in 1916 took part in the Easter rising, was captured, and was sentenced to imprisonment for life, the only volunteer commandant to escape the death penalty. He was released in the general amnesty in 1917, and won a by-election in East Clare, professing a policy of complete independence for an Irish republic. He was elected President of the Sinn Fein movement, and in 1918 was rearrested and incarcerated in Lincoln prison, from which he escaped in 1919, and went to the United States to raise funds for the cause to which he was now fully committed.

Meanwhile, there was civil war in Ireland, the Irish Re-

publican Army (IRA) under Michael Collins fighting a guerrilla war against the British army and police, reinforced in 1920 by the Black and Tans. Sinn Fein refused to recognize the constitution provided by LLOYD GEORGE's Government of Ireland Act though Ulster accepted it; and when King George V opened the first Stormont Parliament in 1921 he made a personal plea for peace, and the British Prime Minister invited De Valera to London for talks. Lloyd George offered dominion status, but Sinn Fein and De Valera held out for a republic. The fighting continued but, when the IRA were on the verge of complete defeat, a truce was arranged which brought the conflict to an end (July 1921). De Valera took no part in the subsequent negotiations leading to the 1921 Treaty which gave Southern Ireland dominion status. He felt bound to repudiate the agreement made by Michael Collins and Arthur Griffith, but the Dáil accepted the treaty, and De Valera ceased to be President of Sinn Fein. A renewed civil war broke out and he had to go into hiding but was caught and imprisoned in 1923–4. His political career appeared to be at an end.

However, in 1926 he launched a new party, Fianna Fáil, which by 1932 was in a sufficiently strong position to form a coalition government with the Labour party. Although he had overcome his objections to taking the oath of allegiance to the British Crown, De Valera continued to be opposed to the terms of the 1921 Treaty and now aimed at what he described as 'external association' with Britain. In 1937 he brought in a new constitution which gave force to this idea, changed the Irish Free State into Eire, reduced the office of Governor-General to a sinecure, and created a separate Irish citizenship.

In an agreement with the government of Neville CHAMBERLAIN he obtained an important concession, the renunciation by Britain of the right under the 1921 Treaty to maintain naval and air facilities in certain Irish ports; and, when the Second World War broke out, he declared Irish neutrality, a stance which he maintained resolutely during the next six years, in spite of pressure from the British, Germans, and French. Partition of Ireland had become reinforced by the stress of war, and in 1948 De Valera was defeated, and a new government of Eire cut the last link with the Commonwealth by repealing the External Relations Act. He returned to office in 1951 but was again in opposition from 1954 to 1957. In 1959 he retired from politics, and for fourteen years was President of his country. His greatest regret was his failure to unite Ireland north and south. De Valera died in Dublin on 29 August 1975.

DICEY, ALBERT VENN (1835–1922), jurist, was born at Claybrook Hall, near Lutterworth, on 4 February 1835, the third son of Thomas Edward Dicey, proprietor of the *Northampton Mercury*, and his wife, Anne Mary, daughter of James Stephen, master in chancery. He was educated at King's College School, London, and Balliol College, Oxford, where he gained firsts in Classical Mods. and Greats (1856–8), and was President of the Union.

In 1860 he became a Fellow of Trinity College, and won the Arnold prize for an essay on the Privy Council. He was called to the Bar (Inner Temple) in 1863, and was appointed junior counsel to the Commissioners of Inland Revenue (1876). As well as practising at the Bar, he contributed to the *Spectator* and the New York *Nation*.

In 1872 he married Elinor Mary, daughter of John Bonham-Carter (MP for Portsmouth from 1830 to 1841); they had no children.

From 1882 to 1909 Dicey held the Vinerian chair of English Law at Oxford with a fellowship at All Souls. During his tenure of this post, he published three important contributions to the history of English law, *Introduction to the Study of the Law of the Constitution* (1885), *Digest of the Law of England with Reference to the Conflict of Laws* (1896), and *Lectures on the Relation between Law and Public Opinion in England during the Nineteenth Century* (1905), based on lectures Dicey gave at Harvard in 1898. These works not only elucidated, with brilliant clarity, what was acknowledged to be one of the most complex branches of the law, but also had considerable influence on its subsequent development.

During this period Dicey took a prominent part in political controversy. He was strongly opposed to Home Rule for Ireland and was keenly interested in social problems, holding the post of Principal of the Working Men's College in London from 1899 to 1912. He became QC in 1890 and did not retire from law practice until 1916, when he was over eighty.

He received many academic honours. Dicey died at Oxford on 7 April 1922.

DICK, SIR WILLIAM REID (1878–1961). See REID DICK.

DILL, SIR JOHN GREER (1881–1944), field-marshal, was born on 25 December 1881 at Lurgan, co. Armagh, the only son of John Dill, a bank manager, and his wife, Jane, daughter of George Greer of Woodville, near Lurgan. He was educated at Cheltenham, and the Royal Military College, Sandhurst, and in May 1901 went with the Leinster Regiment to South Africa.

In 1907 he married Ada Maud, daughter of Col. William Albert Le Mottée; they had one son.

Between the Boer War and the First World War he led the normal life of an army officer, having a spell at the Staff College; and in 1914 went to France as brigade-major of the 25th Brigade (8th Division) and fought at Neuve Chapelle and Aubers Ridge. In the course of the war he became a capable staff officer, was wounded, and awarded the DSO (1915) and appointed CMG (1918).

After the war, he was appointed army instructor at the Imperial Defence College (1926–9), and then went to India as chief general staff officer, Western Command, with the rank of major-general. From 1931 to 1934 he was Commandant of the Staff College, and from 1934 to 1936 Director of Military Operations and Intelligence at the War Office. He moved again in 1936 to command the forces in Palestine; he was now a lieutenant-general. From 1937 to 1939 he was G.O.C.-in-C., Aldershot.

Up to this point in his career his promotion had been rapid, and he hoped to be the next Chief of the Imperial General Staff, but in this he was disappointed preference being given, first to Lord Gort, and then to Sir Edmund (later Lord) Ironside. When the Second World War broke out Dill went to France in command of I Corps with the rank of general, whilst Gort was in command of the Expeditionary Force. He was not happy serving under Gort whom, despite his undoubted courage and integrity, Dill found lacking in strategic sense. However, he did not have to endure this situation for long because in April 1940 he was brought back to the War Office as Vice-Chief of the Imperial General Staff and, a month later, succeeded Ironside as CIGS.

He came to this post at a difficult time since German arms appeared to have succeeded in causing the collapse of the whole Allied military structure, and Dill, the practical sol-

dier, found difficulty in meeting the more bellicose demands of Winston CHURCHILL; the Prime Minister, in turn, saw him as over-cautious and obstructive. Dill did not possess the reserves of strength required to sustain the arduous labours called for by the Churchill regime, and the serious illness and death of his wife in 1940 further weakened his health.

In 1941 he visited the Eastern Mediterranean and at first opposed sending British troops to Greece, but later changed his mind: the Greek campaign was not a success and led to disaster in Crete and defeat of the depleted troops in North Africa. Churchill decided on a change; Dill was succeeded by Sir Alan BROOKE, promoted to field-marshal, and appointed Governor-Designate of Bombay.

However, when Japan entered the war, Dill went to the USA with Churchill and remained there as the senior British representative on the Combined Chiefs of Staff Committee in Washington. In 1943 he attended the Casablanca Conference, and afterwards flew to India and China to confer with WAVELL and Chiang-Kai-shek. In Washington Dill reached the height of his career. His tact and skilful diplomacy gained the respect of the Americans; he became a personal friend of General Marshall and Admiral King, the US chiefs of the army and navy, and won the confidence of the President. His friend, Alanbrooke, paid tribute to the part Dill played in securing the agreement of the British and American leaders over the action to be taken to achieve success against the Germans and the Japanese. Roosevelt also spoke of him as 'the most important figure' in reaching accord on the combined operations of the Allies.

On 4 November 1944 Dill died in Washington; he was buried in Arlington Cemetery. He had been appointed CB (1928), KCB (1937), and GCB (1942), and was awarded posthumously the American DSM. His second wife whom he married in 1941 was Nancy, daughter of Henry Charrington, brewer, and widow of Brig. Dennis Walter Furlong.

DOLMETSCH, (EUGENE) ARNOLD (1858–1940), musician and musical craftsman, was born at Le Mans, France, on 24 February 1858, the eldest son of Rudolph Arnold Dolmetsch, piano maker, and his wife, Marie Zelie Guillouard. He was early apprenticed to the craft of instrument making. In 1877 he married Marie Morel of Namur; they had one daughter. After the death of his father, he attended the Brussels Conservatoire and the Royal College of Music, London (1883) and made a study of early English instrumental music in the British Museum (1889).

His life-work became the study of early music and how to play it, and the making of lutes, virginals, clavichords, harpsichords, recorders, and viols. His researches brought to light a school of English composers including John Jenkins (1592–1678) and William Lawes (1602–45), and he re-established the recorder as an instrument of popular music. In 1915 he published *The Interpretation of the Music of the Seventeenth and Eighteenth Centuries*.

He settled at Haslemere with his second wife, Mabel, daughter of John Brookes Johnston of London, whom he married in 1903 after the death of Marie. They had two sons and two daughters. There he established workshops, and inaugurated in 1925 an annual summer festival of chamber music performed by pupils, and his sons and daughters, all of whom became versatile performers. In particular, his daughter by his first marriage was a fine viol player.

In 1928, in honour of his seventieth birthday, the Dolmetsch Foundation was formed for the encouragement of the revival of early instrumental music. In 1931 he became naturalized, and in 1937 was granted a civil pension. He was a Chevalier of the Legion of Honour (1938) and received the honorary degree of D.Mus. (Durham, 1939). He died at Haslemere on 28 February 1940.

DONOGHUE, STEPHEN (1884-1945), jockey and trainer, was born on 8 November 1884 at Warrington, the eldest son of an ironworker, Patrick Donoghue, and his wife, Mary Mitchell. He was determined to be a jockey, and at fourteen walked from Warrington to Chester racecourse to see John Porter, a famous trainer, who took him on as an apprentice.

After a year, he returned to Warrington and, after getting involved in a fight, mistakenly thought he had killed a man. He ran away with his younger brother and took employment with a northern trainer, Dobson Peacock, in Yorkshire. Later, the boys made their way to Newmarket where Donoghue joined the stables of Alfred Sadler junior. He had his first experience of racing in France where he won a race at Hyères in 1905. Then he went to Ireland to ride for P. Behan's stable, finishing third in the Derby of 1910. He became Champion Jockey in Ireland and, on return to England, rode for H. S. Persse. Major Dermot McCalmont's The Tetrarch, one of the fastest racehorses of all time, unbeaten on the racecourse, made Donoghue's name as a jockey.

'Steve' as he was known to the public won two wartime Derbys on Pommern (1915) and Gay Crusader (1917), and then four in five years: on Humorist (1921), Captain Cuttle (1922), Papyrus (1923), and Manna (1925). Later, in partnership with Brown Jack, Sir Harold Wernher's horse, he won the Queen Alexandra Stakes at Ascot in six successive years (1929-34).

He married, in 1908, Bridget, daughter of the Irish trainer, P. Behan; they had two sons and a daughter but the marriage ended in divorce. Then, in 1929, he married a music-hall artiste, Ethel, daughter of Michael Finn, an American barrister. His book *Just my Story* was published in 1923. Donoghue retired from racing in 1937 and became a trainer. On 23 March 1945 he died suddenly in London. He had been Champion Jockey for ten years in succession from 1914 to 1923. He had the rare ability to get the best out of a horse with his hands, not his whip.

DOUGHTY, CHARLES MONTAGU (1843-1926), poet and traveller, was born on 19 August 1843 at Theberton Hall, Suffolk, the younger son of the Revd Charles Montagu Doughty, a landowner, and his wife, Frederica, daughter of the Hon. Frederick Hotham, Rector of Dennington, Suffolk. He was prepared for the Royal Navy, but rejected as medically unfit. He took his degree at Gonville and Caius College, Cambridge in 1865 having in the meanwhile spent nine months alone in Norway studying glaciers. He was keenly interested in sixteenth-century literature, and his ambition was to become a poet reviving the diction of Chaucer and Spenser.

In 1870 he set out on his travels as a poor student, visiting Holland, France, Italy, Spain, North Africa, and Greece. He climbed Vesuvius to witness the eruption in 1872. He then went on to Palestine, Syria, and Egypt and, after visiting Petra, decided to study the geology and life of Arabia.

Adopting the guise of an Arab Christian, he settled in Damascus for a year to learn Arabic. Then, in 1876, he joined a caravan making a pilgrimage to Mecca, and travelled to Medain Salih, Hail, Kheybar, and the Kasim in Central Arabia and, after much hardship and danger, eventually reached Jiddah twenty-one months later. In the course of this journey, he gathered much new information about the geography and geology of north-western Arabia, and gained a valuable insight into the Arab character and the nomadic way of life. His account of his experiences, *Travels in Arabia Deserta*, was published in 1888 by the Cambridge University Press after it had been refused by four other publishers. In this work Doughty used Elizabethan English as his medium, and it was not until 1908 when Edward Garnett, Doughty's and Joseph CONRAD's friend, issued an abridgement called *Wanderings in Arabia*, that the book reached a wide public, and not until 1921, when a new edition was published, that it was recognized as a classic.

In 1886 he married Caroline Amelia, daughter of Gen. Sir William Montagu Scott McMurdo; they had two daughters. For the rest of his life Doughty devoted his time to poetry; he regarded his verse as more important than his prose; and his publications include *The Dawn in Britain* (6 vols., 1906-7), *Adam Cast Forth* (1908), *The Cliffs* (1909), *The Clouds* (1912), *The Titans* (1916) and *Mansoul* (1920). But the public reception of his poetry could not match that of his one work in prose. Doughty received honorary degrees from Oxford and Cambridge, and became an honorary FBA. He died on 20 January 1926 at Sissinghurst. His *Travels in Arabia Deserta* is one of the outstanding classics of exploration, but admiration for Doughty's poetry was limited to a discerning few, such as Robert BRIDGES and Edward THOMAS.

DOUGLAS, (WILLIAM) SHOLTO BARON DOUGLAS OF KIRTLESIDE (1893-1969), Marshal of the Royal Air Force, was born in Oxford on 23 December 1893, the second son of the Revd Robert Langton Douglas, and his first wife, Margaret Jane, daughter of Percival Cannon, a printer. He was educated at Tonbridge and Lincoln College, Oxford, but his studies were interrupted by the First World War; he joined

Steve Donoghue on Captain Cuttle, on his way to winning the 1922 Derby

the Royal Field Artillery, and within a few months was in France. In 1915 he transferred to the Royal Flying Corps. By 1916 he was in command of No. 43 Squadron, which suffered heavy losses, but Douglas led a charmed life and, in command of No. 84 Squadron of fighters, he was engaged in further air combats in four tours of operations on the Western Front. By the end of the war he had survived nearly four years, and won the MC (1916) and the DFC (1919).

After the war he worked for a time as an airline pilot with the Handley Page Aircraft Co., but in 1920 rejoined the air force with a permanent commission as squadron-leader. From 1920 to 1936 he served in flying schools, staff posts, and at the Imperial Defence College. By 1938 he was an air vice-marshal at the Air Ministry. He became Assistant (in 1940 Deputy) Chief of Air Staff responsible for training and new equipment. Like DOWDING who commanded Fighter Command, he had to fight senior officers and politicians to convince his superiors of the importance of radar and other aerial devices; he watched with despair while the disasters in France and Norway caused serious losses in the strength of the RAF.

As a trained fighter pilot, he was not entirely in agreement with the cautious policy of Dowding and, since his views carried weight with the air staff, he was appointed to succeed Dowding with the rank of air-marshal and a KCB (1941). In that post he rebuilt Fighter Command from its weak position after the Battle of Britain to the strength it attained two years later. He had the advantage of being an old friend of Sir Alan BROOKE, CIGS.

By 1942 he was air chief marshal and Commander-in-Chief, Middle East and, in spite of disagreements and dis-appointments, by the time he returned to England in 1944 North Africa and Sicily had been occupied and Italy knocked out of the war. He was now posted as Commander-in-Chief, Coastal Command, and in that capacity was concerned with the Battle of the Atlantic and the invasion of Normandy. In 1945 he became Commander-in-Chief, British Air Forces of Occupation, and a year later was promoted GCB and Marshal of the RAF. At the same time he was asked to succeed MONTGOMERY as C.-in-C., British Forces in Germany and Military Governor of the British zone. He would have pre-ferred to retire, but he accepted responsibilities which were extremely distasteful to him, among them the duty of confirm-ing the executions of German war criminals. He was glad when in November 1947 he was allowed to resign.

In the following year he was awarded a peerage and took his seat in the Lords as a Labour supporter. In 1949 he became Chairman of the British European Airways, an ap-pointment which he held until 1964.

In 1919 Douglas had married Mary Howard; the marriage ended in divorce in 1932, and in 1933 he married Joan Leslie, daughter of Col. Henry Cuthbert Denny; this marriage also ended in divorce. In 1955 he married Hazel, daughter of George Eric Maas Walker, and widow of Capt. W. E. R. Walker; they had one daughter. Douglas died at Northampton on 29 October 1969, an honorary Fellow of Lincoln College, and an honorary Companion of the Royal Aeronautical Society. He published *Years of Combat* (1963) and *Years of Command* (1966).

DOVER WILSON, JOHN (1881-1969), Shakespeare scholar, was born at Mortlake, Surrey on 13 July 1881, the eldest child of Edwin Wilson, an engraver, and his wife, Elizabeth Dover. He was educated at Lancing College and Gonville and Caius College, Cambridge, and in 1904 won

the Harness prize for an essay on *John Lyly*, which led to his being commissioned to write two chapters of the *Cambridge History of English Literature*. After teaching for a year at Whitgift Grammar School, he became English Lektor at Hel-singfors (Helsinki), from 1906 to 1909, and then returned to England as lecturer in English literature at Goldsmith's College, London. In 1906 he married Dorothy Mary, daughter of Canon Edward Curtis Baldwin, Vicar of Hars-ton, near Cambridge; they had one son and two daughters.

In 1911 he published his anthology, *Life in Shakespeare's England*. In the following year he became an inspector for the Board of Education, and for the next twelve years was busily engaged on the problems of evening schools and the teaching of English. In 1924 he was appointed Professor of Education at King's College, London, and in 1926 began the *Journal of Adult Education*.

He had now, however, become a keen Shakespeare scholar, and in 1919 joined Sir Arthur QUILLER-COUCH in editing the New Cambridge Shakespeare (1921-66). He produced commentaries on *Hamlet* (1934-5), and *The Essential Shake-speare* (1932) and, when Quiller-Couch retired on completion of the comedies, Dover Wilson went on to tackle the histories and completed the work with the sonnets before, in the end, he became blind. In 1943 he published *The Fortunes of Falstaff*, followed in 1962 by *Shakespeare's Happy Comedies*.

He was elected FBA in 1931 and appointed CH in 1936. He received many academic awards. From 1935 to 1945 he held the regius chair of rhetoric and English literature at Edinburgh. During the Second World War, he lost his only son, killed on active service in 1944. His first wife died in 1961, and in 1963 he married his widowed cousin, Dr Elizabeth Wintringham, daughter of Sir Joseph Arkwright, the bacteriologist. Dover Wilson died at Balerno, near Edinburgh, on 15 January 1969.

DOWDING, HUGH CASWALL TREMENHEERE, first BARON DOWDING (1882-1970), Air Chief Marshal, was born at Moffat, Dumfriesshire, on 24 April 1882, the eldest son of Arthur John Caswall Dowding, a schoolmaster, and his wife, Maud Caroline, daughter of Major-General Charles William Tremenheere, Chief Engineer, Public Works De-partment, Bombay. He was educated at Winchester and the Royal Military Academy, Woolwich. Up to 1913 he served as a gunner in the RGA, but in that year he learnt to fly, obtained a pilot's certificate and, when the First World War broke out, was appointed Commandant of the RFC Dover Camp.

In 1915 he commanded No. 16 Squadron in France, and two years later was promoted to brigadier-general. In 1919 he was appointed CMG, and became a permanent officer in the RAF. In the previous year he had married Clarice Maud Vancourt, daughter of Capt. John Williams of the Indian Army, but she died in 1920 leaving an infant son.

Dowding was able to take part in active flying again when in 1924 he became chief staff officer to Air HQ in Iraq. During the war his career had been affected by disagreements with H. M. TRENCHARD, but his work in Iraq was appreciated by Trenchard, and in 1930 he was made a member of the Air Council. In this post he had frequent clashes with colleagues and experts, but he was partly responsible for some rev-olutionary developments in the design and construction of military aircraft.

In 1936 he was appointed A.O.C.-in-C., Fighter Command, and was concerned, not only with the preparation of the air defences of Britain, but also with the creation of

Dowding (centre) talking to Battle-of-Britain 'veterans' before take off, September 1945; Group Captain Douglas Bader is on his left

the new squadrons of Spitfires and Hurricanes, which proved their value in the Battle of Britain. But for the resolute determination of Dowding to husband his resources, it is possible that victory in that battle might have gone to the Germans, despite the heroism of the 'Few'. When France was on the verge of surrender Dowding fought successfully to resist the despatch of any more fighter squadrons to the French and, when battle was joined, Dowding by his skilful deployment of his forces and his constant consideration of the essential requirements of reserves of aircraft and personnel, made an invaluable contribution to the outcome of the struggle.

His defensive strategy had, however, made him unpopular in some quarters and on 25 November 1940 Dowding was replaced at Fighter Command by Air Marshal Sholto DOUGLAS. In 1941–2 he had a post in the Air Ministry but in July 1942 he retired at his own request, his book *Twelve Legions of Angels* being suppressed until 1946. In retirement he wrote books and articles on spiritualism and theosophy.

In 1951 Dowding married Muriel, widow of Pilot Officer Maxwell Whiting, RAF, and daughter of John Albino. He was appointed CB (1928), KCB (1933), GCVO (1937), and GCB (1940). A barony was conferred on him in 1943; he died in Kent on 15 February 1970, and was buried in Westminster Abbey.

DU CROS, SIR ARTHUR PHILIP (1871–1955), pioneer of the pneumatic tyre industry, was born in Dublin on 26 January 1871, the third of seven sons of (William) Harvey du Cros, and his first wife, Annie Jane, daughter of James Roy, a small landowner. The family was of Huguenot origin. In 1888, JOHN BOYD DUNLOP patented his pneumatic rubber tyre, and in the following year Harvey du Cros was appointed Chairman of the company formed to exploit this invention. Dunlop had been born in Scotland in 1840, but migrated to Belfast in 1867 and established a successful veterinary practice. He had become a friend of Harvey du Cros

and, although he continued for some years to take an interest in the business, he gradually handed over responsibility to du Cros, who steered the business through many difficulties including the problems which arose from the claim that the pneumatic principle had been discovered in 1845 by another inventor and that this invalidated the Dunlop patent.

Arthur du Cros was educated in Dublin and at fifteen entered the Civil Service, but in 1892 he joined his father and brothers in the tyre company, and in 1896 became joint Managing Director. In 1901 he founded the Dunlop Rubber Co. at Coventry, and in the next twenty-five years became an expert on motor transport and played a leading part in the development of the tyre industry.

In 1908 he was elected Conservative MP for Hastings, succeeding his father in the seat, and together they urged the Government to recognize the importance of the military use of motor transport and aviation. During the First World War du Cros worked for the Ministry of Munitions, financed three motor-ambulance convoys, and raised an infantry battalion of which he became the honorary Colonel. He was created a baronet in 1916, and in 1918 became coalition Unionist MP for Clapham. In his heyday du Cros was very wealthy and was both a public and a private benefactor. He helped to prevent the Countess of Warwick, to whom he had lent a large sum of money, from publishing intimate letters written to her by Edward VII, and in 1929 he lent his house near Bognor Regis to George V for his convalescence.

Dunlop himself, whose invention had led to the establishment of the company that bore his name, had died in Dublin on 23 October 1921. In 1923 his daughter, Jean McClintock, published her father's reminiscences as *The History of the Pneumatic Tyre*. However, it was the hard work of du Cros which was the means of making the name Dunlop renowned world-wide, and it was through no fault of his that the Dunlop Rubber Co. failed in the financial crisis at the end of the 1920s. He lost much of his fortune

John Dunlop (centre), inventor of the pneumatic tyre

when this happened. He recorded the history of the pneumatic tyre industry in *Wheels of Fortune: a Salute to Pioneers* (1938).

He married in 1895, Maude, daughter of William Gooding, of Coventry; they had two sons and two daughters; that marriage ended in divorce in 1923 and in 1929 he married Florence May Walton, daughter of James Walton King; she died in 1951 and he married, later that year, Mary Louise Joan, daughter of Wilhelm Bühmann, a German railway official. Du Cros died at Oxhey on 28 October 1955.

DUNLOP, JOHN BOYD (1840-1921). See DU CROS.

DUVEEN, JOSEPH, BARON DUVEEN (1869-1939) art dealer, patron, and trustee, was born at Hull on 14 October 1869, the eldest of the ten sons of (Sir) Joseph Joel Duveen, and his wife, Rosetta, daughter of Abraham Barnett, of Hull. He was educated privately, and at seventeen entered his father's business which dealt mainly with oriental porcelain and *objets d'art*. He soon realized the possibilities of buying pictures by the great masters in Europe and selling them in the USA. His success in this venture, which often involved the purchase of whole collections, brought him a

fortune, and eventually supplied public galleries and museums in America with important paintings.

In 1899 he married Elsie, daughter of Gustav Salamon of New York; they had one daughter.

His art benefactions to English galleries were on a princely scale. He not only donated to the Tate Gallery valuable pictures, including works by Correggio, Hogarth, J. S. Sargent, and Augustus JOHN, but also financed several galleries for modern art; he donated funds for similar galleries to the National Gallery, the National Portrait Gallery, and the British Museum. In 1931 he endowed a chair for the history of art at London University.

He was a Trustee of the Wallace Collection from 1925, of the National Gallery from 1929 to 1936, and of the National Portrait Gallery from 1933. He was a member of many committees and commissions, and received a number of foreign decorations. He was knighted in 1919, created a baronet in 1927, and became Baron Duveen, of Millbank in 1933. The peerage became extinct on his death in London on 25 May 1939.

DYER, REGINALD EDWARD HARRY (1864-1927), brigadier-general, was born at Murree in the Punjab, India, on 9 October 1864, the youngest son of Edward Dyer, the manager of a brewing firm, and his wife, Mary Passmore, of Barnstaple. He was educated at Middleton College, co. Cork, and the Royal Military College, Sandhurst. In 1885 he was commissioned in the Queen's Royal Regiment, and in 1888 transferred to the Indian Army. In the same year he married Anne, daughter of Col. Edmund Pippon Ommaney, Indian Staff Corps; they had two sons. He saw active service in several campaigns, including the Burma war (1886-7); and during the First World War served in Persia (Iran) and

Sir Joseph Duveen (centre) with King Geoge V and Queen Mary, examining a group portrait by Sargent at the opening of the new wing of the Tate Gallery, 26 June 1926

was appointed CB. In 1917 he met with a serious riding accident which incapacitated him for a year and left him subject to severe headaches and gradual impairment of the muscles of his legs. However, he returned to India and took up his command as brigadier-general at Jullundur in 1918.

On 10 April 1919 a mob in Amritsar, within Dyer's jurisdiction, killed five Englishmen and seriously injured a lady missionary. Dyer arrived on the scene the following day and took action to restore order, the civil authority having handed over control. Three days later, a dense crowd of several thousand, contrary to the general's orders, assembled in the confined space of the Jalianwala Bagh. He took a small force of rifles and opened fire without warning, killing some 380 of the panic-stricken crowd and wounding about a thousand, including innocent spectators. On 19 April Dyer ordered that any Indian passing along the street in which the missionary had been wounded must go on all fours, and on the spot where the assault occurred he had six men whipped before they had been tried for this crime.

Dyer's action certainly succeeded in suppressing disorder for some weeks, but the massacre at Amritsar inevitably aroused violent racial animosity throughout the Punjab and was a cause of political violence for many years afterwards. The Government of India set up a committee of inquiry and, although the Lieutenant-Governor of the Punjab, Sir Michael O'DWYER, defended him, Dyer was severely reprimanded for his actions and forced to resign from the service (1920). Whatever Dyer's motives for his behaviour in Amritsar may have been, the results of his actions were disastrous in uniting responsible opinion in India in opposition to the Government.

After his resignation, Dyer's health failed rapidly, and he died at Long Ashton, near Bristol on 23 July 1927.

DYSON PERRINS, CHARLES WILLIAM (1864-1958), collector and benefactor, was born at Claines, near Worcester, on 25 May 1864, the only son of James Dyson Perrins, of Lea & Perrins, makers of Worcester sauce, and his wife, Frances Sarah, daughter of Charles Perrins. He was educated at Charterhouse and the Queen's College, Oxford, and between 1888 and 1892 served with the 4th Battalion of the Highland Light Infantry. In 1889 he married Catherine Christina, daughter of Alexander Allan Gregory, corn merchant of Inverness; they had two sons and two daughters.

After his army service he gave his attention to the family business and to public life. In 1897 he was Mayor of Worcester and in 1899 High Sheriff of Worcestershire. Between 1900 and 1920 he was busy using his wealth to make a magnificent collection of books, manuscripts, and art treasures, about which a number of works were published, including a *Descriptive Catalogue* of his illuminated manuscripts by Sir George Warner, and a catalogue of his early Italian books by A. W. Pollard.

His first wife died in 1922, and a year later he married Frieda, daughter of John Milne, of Belmont, Cheadle.

In 1946 Dyson Perrins decided to sell his printed books in order to save the Royal Worcester Porcelain Factory from closure. He had for many years been interested in this factory and had a unique collection of its wares. He had, for a time, after the First World War taken over its management to keep it running during a period of financial difficulty. After the Second World War the sale of his books enabled the factory to be re-equipped and to continue production to its very high standards of excellence.

Dyson Perrins was a discriminating benefactor to the Victoria and Albert Museum, the National Gallery, and the Ashmolean and British Museums. To Malvern he donated a hospital and public library (in conjunction with the Carnegie Trust) and his own house and gardens. To Oxford he gave funds for the study of organic chemistry and a laboratory which was named after him. He was a life Governor of Birmingham University, and DCL (Oxford). He died in Malvern on 29 January 1958.

E

EASTON, HUGH RAY (1906-1965), stained-glass artist, was born in London on 26 November 1906, the younger son of Frank Easton, a medical practitioner, and his wife, Alice Muriel, daughter of William Howland, and granddaughter of Sir William Howland, Lieutenant-Governor of Ontario. He was educated at Wellington College and the University of Tours. He had a natural aptitude for drawing and painting, and his hobby was brass-rubbing. He received training as a craftsman with the firm of Blacking of Guildford.

After service during the Second World War with the RNVR as naval adviser in the censorship division of the Ministry of Information, he set up a workshop at Harpenden, and in due course designed over 250 windows. His work with stained glass was influenced by the designs of (Sir) J. Ninian Comper, the church architect, who designed the great window in West-minster Hall (1952) and windows in Westminster Abbey, where he also designed the Warriors' Chapel.

Easton designed windows for the cathedrals of Canterbury, Durham, Winchester, Ely, and Exeter, for Westminster Abbey and Romsey Abbey, and for a large number of churches. His windows are also to be found in barracks, hospitals, town halls, and colleges, including Clare College, Cambridge, and schools, including St Edward's School, Oxford, Clifton, and Bedford Modern School. His most important work was the 'Battle of Britain' window at the east end of Westminster Abbey.

Easton's work had critics because he was not prepared to follow the current fashion for abstract design, but he pursued his own ideas, disregarding criticism, particularly in his practice of placing his figures on a background of clear glass which contributed to their vivid beauty.

Easton never married. He died in London on 15 August 1965.

EDDINGTON, SIR ARTHUR STANLEY (1882-1944), mathematician and astrophysicist, was born at Kendal on 28 December 1882, the only son of Arthur Henry Eddington, headmaster of the Friends' School, Kendal, and his wife, Sarah Ann Shout, of Darlington. The Quaker background remained an important influence for the whole of his life. He was educated at Owens College, Manchester, and Trinity College, Cambridge. At Manchester he graduated B.Sc. with a first in physics (1902); at Cambridge, he was senior wrangler in part i of the mathematical tripos (1904), and awarded a first in the first division of part ii (1905).

In 1906 he succeeded (Sir) F. W. Dyson, as chief assistant to the Astronomer Royal at Greenwich, a post which he held until 1913, and in which he studied stellar proper-motions and star-drifts and devised a mathematical method for analysing these motions which he made the subject of a Smith's prize essay and dissertation for a fellowship at Trinity College (1907).

Eddington succeeded Sir George Darwin as Plumian Professor of Astronomy at Cambridge in 1913, and in the following year became Director of the Observatory, and published his first book *Stellar Movements and the Structure of the Universe*. In 1916 he became deeply interested in Einstein's theory of general relativity, and prepared a report for the Physical Society which was later published as *The Mathematical Theory of Relativity* (1923). His contribution to the theory made his name as a pure mathematician, and was important in the development of differential geometry.

Apart from his great interest in relativity, Eddington in 1916 was researching into the internal constitution of the stars, and this led to the discovery of the mass-luminosity relation, and made possible the modern theory of stellar evolution. Another problem he solved was the nature of the stars known as 'white dwarfs'. The results of these investigations were published in *The Internal Constitution of the Stars* (1926).

The last sixteen years of his life Eddington devoted to the discovery and development of new principles in physics and constructed a comprehensive doctrine combining and transcending the theories of quantum-mechanics and relativity; his final systematic presentation was set out in *Fundamental Theory* (published posthumously in 1946).

Eddington was elected FRS in 1914, knighted in 1930, and appointed to the Order of Merit in 1938. He was President of the Royal Astronomical Society (1921-3), of the Physical Society (1930-2), and of the International Astronomical Union from 1938 to the end of his life. He also received many academic honours and prizes. He died, unmarried, at Cambridge on 22 November 1944.

EDEN, (ROBERT) ANTHONY, first EARL OF AVON (1897-1977), politician and Prime Minister, was born at Windlestone Hall, near Bishop Auckland, on 12 June 1897, the third son of Sir William Eden and his wife, Sybil Frances, daughter of Sir William Grey. He was educated at Eton and in 1915 left school to fight with the King's Royal Rifle Corps; he was awarded the MC in 1917. It was a particularly difficult time for his family: his eldest brother was killed in 1914, another brother was interned in Germany, his father died in 1915, and his younger brother was killed at the Battle of Jutland.

In 1919 he entered Christ Church, Oxford, and obtained a first in 1922, having read Persian and Arabic. In 1923 he became Conservative MP for Warwick and Leamington and held the seat until 1957. In 1923 he married Beatrice Helen, daughter of Sir Gervase Beckett, banker, and Chairman of the *Yorkshire Post*. In 1926 he was appointed Parliamentary Private Secretary to Sir Austen CHAMBERLAIN, the Foreign Secretary, and subsequently Parliamentary Under-Secretary to Lord READING and later to Sir John SIMON. He was appointed Lord Privy Seal in 1933, and met Hitler in Berlin and Mussolini in Rome to discuss proposals for disarmament. Then in 1935 he visited Moscow and, when BALDWIN became Prime Minister, he appointed Eden a member of his Cabinet as Minister for League of Nations Affairs. He supported Sir Samuel HOARE in trying to reach a compromise with Mussolini over Abyssinia but, when the Hoare-Laval plan was formulated giving the Duce most of Abyssinia, Hoare was forced to resign and Eden became Foreign Secretary (1935).

During the next two years he saw Mussolini triumphant in Abyssinia, Hitler's reoccupation of the Rhineland, and the outbreak of the Spanish Civil War. In 1937, when Neville CHAMBERLAIN succeeded Baldwin, Eden agreed with the new Prime Minister's anxiety to preserve peace in Europe, but took offence at Chamberlain's interference with his work as Foreign Secretary, particularly when he agreed that Lord HALIFAX should visit Hitler at Berchtesgaden, and later when Chamberlain, without consulting him, rejected a proposal from President Roosevelt to launch an international peace plan. He also discovered that the Prime Minister was secretly conducting his own negotiations with Mussolini, and in 1938 Eden resigned.

When the Second World War broke out he accepted the post of Dominions Secretary without a seat in the Cabinet but, when CHURCHILL took over in 1940, Eden became Secretary for War, and later that year, when Lord Halifax went to Washington as Ambassador, he returned to the Foreign Office, where he remained until 1945. He also became a member of Churchill's War Cabinet. Although he did not always agree with Churchill (for example, he was vehemently against the Morgenthau plan which would have destroyed all German industry), he supported him throughout the years of the war, accompanied him to the conferences at Cairo, Tehran, Quebec, and Moscow, and was in accord with the policy of saturation bombing of German cities. At this time Eden was a party to a War Cabinet decision for which he has been severely criticized. To placate Stalin, Russians captured in German uniforms were returned to certain death in the Soviet Union. Eden went with Churchill to the Yalta Conference in 1945, but neither of them could do anything effective to thwart the determination of the Soviet leaders to dominate Eastern Europe.

In 1945 his elder son, a pilot officer, was killed in Burma, and in 1946 he and his wife parted company. Throughout the life of the ATTLEE Government Eden lent his support to Ernest BEVIN, the Foreign Secretary, but, when Herbert MORRISON succeeded Bevin, Eden was less amenable and, in particular, attacked Morrison for his failure to resist Mussadeq's nationalization of British Iranian oil interests.

In 1951 Churchill, at the age of seventy-seven, returned to office, and Eden became leader of the House as well as Foreign Secretary, but some months later the two offices were separated. His main concern now was the maintenance of British interests in the Middle East. In 1953 Mussadeq was overthrown, but by that time Col. Nasser had become the ruler of Egypt, in which country a new nationalism had arisen. In Europe, however, Eden succeeded in saving NATO from the threat of disunity. Unfortunately his own health had become precarious. His divorce had been granted in 1950, and in 1952 he married (Anne) Clarissa, daughter of Major John Strange Spencer-Churchill, Winston's niece; in 1953 he had to undergo three major operations and was a sick man when the Prime Minister suffered a stroke.

Churchill recovered, but his health had been seriously impaired, and in 1955 he resigned, and Eden at last became Prime Minister. A general election confirmed his position in power, but the Government was soon in trouble, and some personal criticism of Eden was led by Randolph CHURCHILL. Eden's main interest continued to lie with foreign affairs. He had agreed in 1954 to the British evacuation of the Suez base, but this had failed to satisfy the ambitions of Nasser. The American and British Governments agreed to help to finance the Aswan high dam to deal with the Nile irrigation problems, but Nasser was in no hurry to accept their help. In 1956 King Hussain of Jordan summarily dismissed General (Sir) John Glubb, commander of the Arab Legion, and Eden saw the hand of Nasser in this affront to Britain.

Later that year John Foster Dulles, the American Sec-

retary of State, without consulting London, withdrew from the Aswan dam project and Nasser, seizing upon this as an excuse, announced an Egyptian take-over of the Suez Canal Company. Eden and the French Premier, Guy Mollet, decided that this breach of international law must be opposed, by force of arms, if necessary. Dulles gave them no support, nor would he agree to the matter going to the Security Council of the United Nations, but the British and French ignored him on this point.

What happened at this stage has, so far, never been clearly revealed, but it appears that the British and French agreed with the Israeli Government that the latter would make an incursion in the direction of the canal and that British and French forces would occupy the canal zone, ostensibly to enforce a cease-fire. The Israelis played their part; Eden issued an ultimatum to Nasser which he repudiated, and British and French forces landed at Port Said. This action led to uproar in the British Parliament, two of Eden's junior ministers resigned, the Government had little support from the Commonwealth, and the attitude of the USA forced Eden

Anthony Eden speaking in support of the Tory candidate for Uxbridge, general election campaign, May 1955

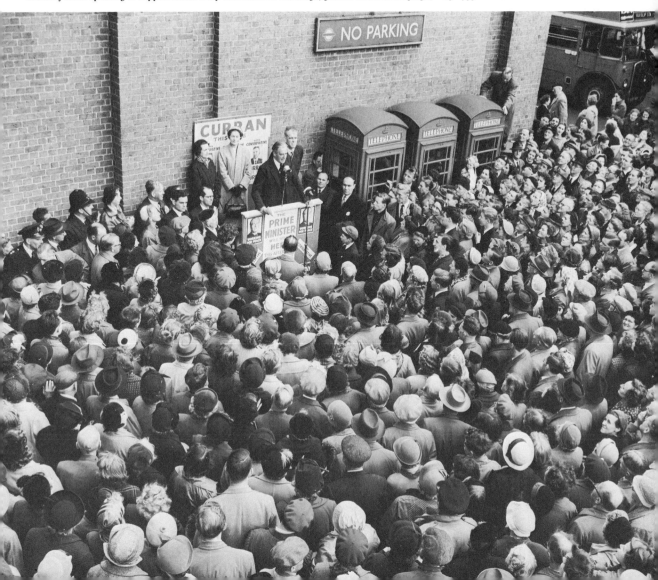

to call a halt to the military operation. He had little alternative in view of the fact that there was a run on the pound and the Chancellor of the Exchequer was opposed to further action without American support. Eden, in any case, was a very sick man and, early in 1957, he resigned and was succeeded by Harold Macmillan.

In spite of his ill health he lived for another twenty years. In 1961 he became Earl of Avon, having published the first of his three volumes of memoirs *Full Circle* (1960). *Facing the Dictators* and *The Reckoning* appeared in 1962 and 1965, and *Another World 1897-1917* in 1976. He was sworn of the Privy Council in 1934 and appointed KG in 1954. He had many academic honours and other distinctions. He died at Alvediston, Wiltshire on 14 January 1977, and was succeeded by his younger son, Nicholas.

EDWARD VIII (1894-1972), King of Great Britain, Ireland, and the British Dominions beyond the seas, Emperor of India, was born at White Lodge, Richmond Park on 23 June 1894, the eldest son of the Duke and Duchess of York (later King George V and Queen Mary). His baptismal names were Edward Albert Christian George Andrew Patrick David; he was always known to his family as David. When he was thirteen he went to Osborne and in 1909 went on to Dartmouth. At the age of sixteen he was created Prince of Wales (1911). His educational achievements were negligible apart from the fact that he spoke fluent German, French, and Spanish. In 1912 he entered Magdalen College, Oxford. His early years had not been very happy; he feared the discipline which his father attempted to impose.

When the First World War broke out he wished to go into the front line with his regiment, the Grenadier Guards, but this was out of the question for the heir to the throne, and he spent the war as a staff officer, who visited the troops when he could and was very popular, not only with the British tommies but also with Canadians and Australians. In 1919 he visited Canada and the USA where he received a welcome which induced in him an affection for Americans. In 1920 he visited Australia and New Zealand, and in 1921-2 toured India, Burma, and the Far East. He enjoyed travelling abroad although his unconventional behaviour did not always please the Establishment. In 1925 and 1931 he toured South America.

In England his favourite sport was steeplechasing and he had numerous well-publicized falls. He was also tireless on the dance floor. But in his official duties he showed great sympathy for the plight of the unemployed. From 1929 he made Fort Belvedere, near Windsor Castle, his favourite home, but while his brothers married, he remained single finding happiness in the company of married women including Mrs (Freda) Dudley Ward and Lady (Thelma) Furness.

Through Lady Furness, he met Wallis Simpson, the daughter of Teakle Wallis Warfield of Baltimore, USA; she had been married to Lt. Earl Winfield Spencer, US Navy, but he had become an alcoholic and the marriage ended in divorce. When she met the Prince of Wales she was married to Ernest Simpson, who had a shipping business in England, and for a time both of them were friends of the Prince. It soon became clear, however, that Edward was determined to marry Wallis, and her husband was faced with the problem of divorce.

On 20 January 1936 George V died and Edward ascended the throne. Later that year he and Wallis Simpson went on a cruise together in the Mediterranean, and the press abroad, in the USA and elsewhere, gave considerable publicity to their trip. The press in Britain kept silence. In October the Simpson divorce suit was to be heard and the Prime Minister, Stanley BALDWIN, tried to persuade the King to advise Wallis to withdraw the case. The King refused. The decree *nisi* was granted at the end of the month, and in November the King informed Baldwin that he intended to marry Mrs Simpson. Baldwin told him that the country and the dominions would not approve and that a morganatic marriage would be unconstitutional. Clement ATTLEE, Leader of the Opposition, and most leading politicians, with the exception of Winston CHURCHILL, agreed that such a marriage was out of the question, and that if the King persisted in such a course there was no alternative to his abdication. The King wished to appeal to the country in a broadcast but this, he was told, would also be unconstitutional.

On 10 December the King signed an instrument of abdication and made a farewell broadcast to the nation. Mrs Simpson was already in France; he joined her there and, when her decree was made absolute in June 1937, they were married. Edward's brother, George VI, conferred the title of Duke of Windsor on the ex-king, but the title of Royal Highness was expressly denied to the Duchess, his wife, and their descendants. In the event they had no children. The Windsors lived in France until 1940. In October 1937 they unwisely visited Hitler and provided the Nazis with a propaganda gift.

When France fell in 1940 they escaped to Madrid and Winston Churchill, who had become Prime Minister, offered the Duke the governorship of the Bahamas. In this post Edward was popular, though the Windsors' frequent visits to the USA were unwelcome to the authorities in London. In 1945 they returned to France and the Duke undertook to write his memoirs with the help of ghost writers. *A King's Story* (1951) became a best seller and was made into a film. The Duke made infrequent visits to England, the Duchess never. He died in Paris on 28 May 1972 and was buried at Frogmore. The Duchess attended the funeral as the guest of Queen Elizabeth II.

The abdication passed into history as an incident which in no way affected the British crown, thanks to the integrity and devotion to duty of George VI and his Queen, Elizabeth.

ELGAR, SIR EDWARD WILLIAM (1857-1934), composer, was born at Broadheath, near Worcester, on 2 June 1857, the eldest surviving son of William Henry Elgar, organist and music salesman, and his wife, Ann, daughter of Joseph Greening, of Weston, Herefordshire. Edward succeeded his father as organist at St George's RC church in Worcester (1885-9), and also learnt to play the violin. In 1877 he saved sufficient money to take violin lessons from Adolf Pollitzer, but gradually decided to become a composer rather than a solo violinist.

In 1889 he married Caroline Alice, only daughter of Sir Henry Gee Roberts, who had been his pupil for three years. She encouraged him to devote his whole time to composition. For the 1890 Three Choirs Festival at Worcester he produced the *Froissart* overture, and in 1896 completed his first oratorio *The Light of Life*, and a choral work *Scenes from the Saga of King Olaf*.

It was not until his orchestral composition, the 'Enigma Variations', was played under Hans Richter (1899) that the musical world recognized that Elgar was a great composer. His genius was confirmed by his oratorio *The Dream of Gerontius*, a setting of Newman's poem, first performed in

Elgar, *c.* 1900

Birmingham in 1900 under the baton of Richter. In that year Cambridge University conferred on Elgar the honorary degree of doctor of music.

The next twenty years, up to the time of his wife's death, were Elgar's most creative period. W. H. Reed, who was leader of the London Symphony Orchestra and one of Elgar's closest friends at this time, has spoken of the decisive influence she had on Elgar's work. He produced songs and marches as well as full-scale orchestral and choral works. The oratorios *The Apostles* (1903) and *The Kingdom* (1906) were interspersed with orchestral works such as the four *Pomp and Circumstance* marches (1901–7), the first of which included 'Land of Hope and Glory' without which, in later years, no last night at the Promenade concerts would be complete.

Some critics would say that Elgar's best work was still to come with his violin concerto, dedicated to Fritz Kreisler, who was the soloist in its first performance in 1910, and his two symphonies (in A flat, 1908, and in E flat, 1911), together with the cello concerto (1919), and the symphonic study *Falstaff* (1913). Among the chief elements in his music are the harmonic legacy of Brahms and Schumann combined with a mastery of orchestral technique and choral effect. He possessed a rare ability to render serious ideas in a popular form.

In 1924 Elgar was appointed Master of the King's Music, an office which he held until his death but, after his wife died in 1920, Elgar composed little. He received many academic honours, was knighted in 1904, appointed OM in 1911, and created baronet in 1931, as well as KCVO in 1928, and GCVO in 1933.

On the occasion of his seventy-fifth birthday (1932) it was announced that the BBC had commissioned him to write his third symphony, but this work was not completed when he died at Worcester on 23 February 1934. He was survived by his only child, a daughter.

ELIOT, THOMAS STEARNS (1888–1965), poet, playwright, critic, editor, and publisher, was born in St Louis, Missouri on 26 September 1888, the youngest son of Henry Ware Eliot, an industrialist, and his wife, Charlotte Chauncy Stearns, a writer. He was educated at Smith Academy, St Louis (1898–1903), Milton Academy, Massachusetts (1905), and Harvard University where he received his BA (1909). Intending to become a professor of philosophy, he entered Harvard Graduate School, took his MA (1910), and then went to the Sorbonne for a year.

On return to Harvard he started on a doctoral dissertation on the philosophy of F. H. Bradley, and studied Sanskrit and Pali. He also wrote 'The Love Song of J. Alfred Prufrock' in 1910. In 1914 he entered Merton College, Oxford, on a travelling fellowship and, under the supervision of Harold Joachim, studied Bradley's *Appearance and Reality*. Later that year, he decided to give up philosophy in favour of poetry and to reside in England; in this he was advised by Ezra Pound, who also helped to get 'Prufrock' published in 1915. That year Eliot married Vivian Haigh Haigh-Wood, an Englishwoman; the marriage was not happy, and this found reflection in some of Eliot's verse. Furthermore, the ruin of his domestic life seemed to echo the international ruin which he perceived all around him.

Eliot's parents were opposed to his settling in England, and he was faced with the necessity of earning a living. For a time he taught at High Wycombe Grammar School, and at Highgate Junior School, but he could not settle to teaching, and in 1917 accepted a post in Lloyds Bank in London where he worked until 1925. When the United States entered the First World War he was rejected for military service as medically unfit. Working at night he wrote reviews and essays and a few poems. In 1917 he published *Prufrock and Other Observations*, in 1919 *Poems*, and in 1920 *Ara Vos Prec*. In that year he also published his prose pieces as *The Sacred Wood*.

Overwork and his wife's neurotic illness brought Eliot to the verge of a breakdown, and he was forced to take leave from the bank to convalesce in Switzerland. There he completed *The Waste Land* on which he had been working since 1919 and which was to establish him as the leading exponent of modern verse. Late in 1922 it was published on both sides of the Atlantic and caused something of a stir. Of London he wrote:

> Unreal City,
> Under the brown fog of a winter dawn,
> A crowd flowed over London Bridge, so many,
> I had not thought death had undone so many.

In 1927 Eliot became a member of the Church of England and a British subject. He became active in church affairs, and an exponent of Christian religious ideas, exemplified in his poems 'The Hollow Men', 'Journey of the Magi', and 'Ash-Wednesday', and later in his book *The Idea of a Christian Society* (1939).

From 1922 he was giving much of his time to editing and publishing. He founded a new quarterly review, the *Criterion* but, as he was still employed by Lloyds Bank, he edited this review anonymously until, in 1925, he left the bank and became a director of Faber & Gwyer (later Faber & Faber), publishers. In the thirties he began his work on poetic drama

T. S. Eliot

of which the most outstanding examples are *Murder in the Cathedral* (1935), a play about Thomas Becket, and *The Family Reunion* (1939) followed in later years by *The Cocktail Party* (1949), *The Confidential Clerk* (1953), and *The Elder Statesman* (1958).

He continued to publish verse. In 1944 *Four Quartets* was published, a collection of four poems which had been previously published separately as *Burnt Norton* (1935), *East Coker* (1940), *The Dry Salvages* (1941), and *Little Gidding* (1942). In the last of these he wrote:

We shall not cease from exploration
And the end of all our exploring
Will be to arrive where we started
And know the place for the first time.

A garden in the Cotswolds, a village in Somerset and another in Huntingdon, and the seashore of New England were the sources of inspiration in these poems.

As a critic, Eliot wrote essays on the Elizabethan dramatists and Milton and Dante, as well as on his contemporaries, JOYCE, Pound, and LAWRENCE. His works in this field included *After Strange Gods* (1934), *On Poetry and Poets* (1957) and *To Criticize the Critic* (1965). In 1948 Eliot received the Nobel prize for literature and the Order of Merit. He also received many academic honours and became an officer of the Legion of Honour. Vivien Eliot died in 1947, and ten years later he married (Esmé) Valerie, daughter of James Fletcher, of Leeds. He died in London on 4 January 1965, and a stone to his memory was placed in Westminster Abbey. His work was translated into many languages, but he was, above all else, a man of letters writing for the English-speaking world.

ELLIS, (HENRY) HAVELOCK (1859–1939), pioneer in the scientific study of sex, thinker, critic, essayist, and editor, was born at Croydon on 2 February 1859, the only son of Edward Peppen Ellis, sea captain, and his wife, Susannah

Mary, daughter of John Wheatley. He was educated at private schools in Merton and Mitcham; then at the age of sixteen, for the sake of his health, he went on his father's ship to Australia. He decided to stay there, and for four years taught at a school in a lonely place in the bush of New South Wales. Influenced by the writings of James Hinton, author of *Philosophy and Religion* (1881), he planned to write a book on religion, but then decided to study sex instead.

He returned to England and was a medical student at St Thomas's Hospital from 1881 to 1889 but, while he was studying, he was also writing for reviews, and editing the 'Mermaid' series of dramatists contemporary with Shakespeare, and the 'Contemporary Science' series. In fact, he did little medical practice.

Meanwhile, he was having passionate love affairs simultaneously with two women: Olive Schreiner, the authoress, who wrote *The Story of an African Farm*, and Edith Mary Oldham, only daughter of Samuel Oldham Lees, a landed proprietor. Ellis first met Olive Schreiner in 1884, and their relationship continued until she died in 1920, although in the meantime he married and she married. In 1890 he met Edith Lees, and they were married in the following year. She was an independent young woman who had no objection to her husband's attachment to another woman provided that he allowed her to go her own way. Both were enthusiastic devotees of Hinton's teaching on sex. Edith died in 1916, and Olive Schreiner attended her funeral.

Meanwhile Ellis was engaged on his life's work *Studies in the Psychology of Sex* (6 vols., 1897–1910). A seventh volume appeared in 1928, and in 1936 he rearranged the whole in four volumes. His earliest volume *Sexual Inversion* was the subject of a prosecution, but the defendant was a bookseller, not Ellis, and the problem of continuing the series was solved by publishing them in the United States. They were addressed not to the general public but to doctors and psychologists, and have since been translated into many languages.

At the same time, Ellis poured forth a spate of books for the general reader including *Man and Woman* (1894), *The Erotic Rights of Women* (1918), and *Little Essays of Love and Virtue* (1922). His autobiography *My Life* was published posthumously in 1940, including a long account of his marriage which is of great interest. He died, childless, on 8 July 1939 at Hintlesham in Suffolk.

ELVIN, SIR (JAMES) ARTHUR (1899–1957), founder of Wembley Stadium, was born in Norwich on 5 July 1899, the son of John Elvin, a police officer, and his wife, Charlotte Elizabeth Holley. He was educated at an elementary school, and in 1914 joined the Royal Flying Corps, became an observer, and was shot down and taken prisoner. He escaped but was recaptured because he could not speak French or German and was unable to swim. This gave him the idea of building a public swimming-pool some day.

After the war he was employed by a firm which purchased war stores in France and he learnt a good deal about metals. Later he became a cigarette salesman at the 1924 British Empire exhibition at Wembley. He noticed that the window frames of his kiosk were made of real bronze; this encouraged him to tender for a demolition contract. Other contractors wanted payment for the job, but he offered to pay for the materials after demolition, and was awarded the contract.

He married in 1925 Jean, daughter of William Charles Harding, and widow of William Heathcote Dolphin; they had no children.

At that time the Wembley Stadium was used only once a year for the FA cup final. Elvin thought that it could be profitably used for greyhound racing. He floated a private company, bought the stadium, and held the first greyhound meeting there in 1927. A considerable area of land was attached to the stadium, and Elvin decided to realize his early ambition by building a swimming-pool. To make this pay he covered over the pool with a floor which could be used for ice skating, ice hockey, and boxing. He also introduced dirt-track cycle racing in the stadium.

During the Second World War the Wembley Pool was used as a hostel for Gibraltarians, but as soon as the war was over Elvin set about organizing for the Olympic Games to be held at Wembley. This took place in 1948, and is believed to have been the first occasion on which the games were held without financial loss and without a government subsidy. In 1966 the world cup in football was staged at Wembley, and international matches have been played there regularly.

In 1945 Elvin became an honorary freeman of the borough of Wembley and was appointed MBE; in 1946 he was knighted. His hard work to achieve success involved his being at the stadium day and night six days a week. As a result, his health suffered and in 1957 he had to take a sea voyage to South Africa to recuperate; he died *en route* and was buried at sea on 4 February 1957.

EPSTEIN, SIR JACOB (1880–1959), sculptor, was born on 10 November 1880 in New York in the Jewish quarter near the Bowery, the third son of Max and Mary Epstein, a merchant family of orthodox Jewish immigrants from Tsarist Russia and Poland. As a boy he was interested in drawing and made sketches of the many types of people near his home. He also learned bronze casting in a foundry, and studied modelling at evening classes. He illustrated a book on life on the East Side of New York (1902), and with his earnings travelled to Paris and studied sculpture there.

Epstein at work on a bust of Anna Neagle, 1952

In 1905 he settled in London and, in the following year, he married Margaret Gilmour Dunlop; they had one son and one daughter. In 1911 Epstein was naturalized. He became one of the New English Art Club circle, with Francis Dodd, (Sir) Muirhead Bone, and Augustus JOHN; Dodd introduced him to Charles Holden, the architect, who invited him to decorate his new building for the BMA in the Strand. Epstein carved eighteen over-life-size nude figures symbolizing human life from birth to death. These figures caused an outcry and, later, the officials of the Southern Rhodesian Government, who took over the building, had them destroyed.

These were not the only examples of Epstein's sculpture causing controversy. His carving for the tomb of Oscar Wilde in Paris (1912) and his memorial to W. H. HUDSON in Hyde Park (1925) were attacked by outraged critics, in particular Roger FRY and John GALSWORTHY. His work was defended, however, by his friends of the New English Art Club and by (Sir) Matthew Smith and Walter SICKERT.

Epstein was a member of the London Group, but he was refused membership of the Royal Society of British Sculptors and of the Royal Academy. The National Portrait Gallery refused his original casting of his bust of Joseph CONRAD, and his *Lucifer* was refused by the Fitzwilliam Museum, Cambridge, the Victoria and Albert Museum, and the Tate Gallery. It went to the Birmingham City Art Gallery.

It was only late in his life that Epstein's work received recognition. In particular, his portrait bronzes, principally in the baroque tradition, were at first more readily appreciated than his stone carvings which were rooted in primitive sculpture. During the Second World War he was commissioned by the Ministry of Information to make portrait bronzes of service chiefs, and after the war he made one of Winston CHURCHILL. In 1948 his *Lazarus* was not well received, but in 1952 it was bought for New College, Oxford and placed in the ante-chapel there. From then onwards he obtained many important commissions, including the *Madonna and Child* for the Holy Child Convent, *Christ in Majesty* for Llandaff Cathedral, and *St Michael and the Devil* for Coventry Cathedral.

Epstein was also successful in his popular picture exhibitions, including Paintings of Epping Forest (1933) and Flower Paintings (1936 and 1940), but his book illustrations were less well received.

In 1938 he received an honorary LL D from Aberdeen, and in 1953 an honorary DCL from Oxford. A year later he was appointed KBE. His first wife had died in 1947, and in 1955 he married Kathleen Esther, daughter of Walter Chancellor Garman, a surgeon. He was still working when he died in London on 19 August 1959.

EVANS, SIR ARTHUR JOHN (1851-1941), archaeologist, was born at Hemel Hempstead on 8 July 1851, the eldest son of the archaeologist and numismatist (Sir) John Evans, and his first wife, Harriet Ann, daughter of John Dickinson, the paper-maker. He was educated at Harrow, and Brasenose College, Oxford, where he gained a first in modern history (1874). He studied for a year at Göttingen, and then travelled in Finland, Lapland, and the Balkans, and from 1876 to 1882 studied languages, customs, and antiquities at Ragusa (Dubrovnik). In the latter year he was arrested for his support of the Slavs during an insurrection and condemned to death by the Austrians, but later was reprieved and expelled. He collected vases and coins in Italy and Sicily, and pre-

historic seal-stones in Crete, which aroused his curiosity and led to his determination to excavate in the island.

In 1890 he lectured on British pre-historic antiquities, but he was not a good lecturer. He excavated a Roman villa at Frilford, near Oxford, and the late Celtic urnfield at Aylesford in Kent (1891). In 1878 he had married Margaret, daughter of the historian, Edward Augustus Freeman. She died in 1893. In the following year he was appointed Keeper of the Ashmolean Museum at Oxford, a post which he held until 1908.

As a young man he had been influenced by the work of Heinrich Schliemann, and in 1894 Evans acquired a share of an estate at Kephála, near Candia, the classical Knossos, where 'Mycenaean' remains had been found in 1878. He excavated there from 1899 to 1907 and found an elaborate palace of the late Bronze Age with many clay tablets inscribed in Linear script, superimposed on earlier buildings, with 'Kamárais' pottery, brilliant frescoes, and imported Egyptian and Babylonian objects. Skilful and extensive reconstruction of this palace of Knossos was carried out, and in 1926 when he could no longer supervise the work personally, Evans conveyed the property in trust to the British School of Archaeology at Athens. He published accounts of these discoveries in *Scripta Minoa* (2 vols., 1909-52), and *The Palace of Minos at Knossos* (4 vols., 1921-35).

Evans resigned from his post at the Ashmolean in 1908, and offered himself as a Liberal candidate for Oxford University, but subsequently withdrew. He was elected FRS in 1901 and a founder of the British Academy in 1902. From 1916 to 1919 he was President of the British Association. He received many academic awards, and in 1911 was knighted. He died at Youlbury on 11 July 1941, thinking that the Germans had destroyed Knossos. In fact, they had been careful to preserve it. Later archaeologists have been critical of the extensive reconstruction at Knossos carried out under Evans's instructions, and of his theories accounting for the disappearance of the Minoan civilization. His own great disappointment was his failure to decipher the Linear script. Twelve years after his death, Michael Ventris announced that the language was an ancient Greek dialect. Sir Arthur Evans had been on the wrong track. C. M. BOWRA who knew him at Oxford in his old age said that sometimes Evans had been deceived by clever forgeries.

EVANS, DAME EDITH MARY (1888-1976), actress, was born in London on 8 February 1888, the daughter of Edward Evans, a civil servant, and his wife, Caroline Ellen. She was educated at St Michael's Church of England School, Pimlico, and at fifteen was apprenticed as a milliner. In 1910 she appeared on the stage as an amateur, and in 1912 made her first professional appearance for William Poel under whose direction she played Cressida in *Troilus and Cressida* for the Elizabethan Stage Society.

In the course of a career spanning over sixty years she played over 150 parts. She made her name in plays by George Bernard SHAW, particularly in *Back to Methuselah* (1923), *The Apple Cart* (1929) and *The Millionairess* (1940). She also appeared as Mrs Millamant in *The Way of the World* (1924), Rosalind in *As You Like It* (1926 and 1936), and the Nurse in *Romeo and Juliet* (1932, 1934, and 1961). Probably the part for which she will be best remembered was that of Lady Bracknell in *The Importance of Being Earnest* (1939), and nobody who heard it could forget her cry of haughty astonishment 'In a hand-bag!' at the young man's account of his discovery as a baby.

Edith Evans as the Nurse with the young Peggy Ashcroft, in *Romeo and Juliet*, 1935

She appeared in her first silent film in 1915, but it was not until 1948 that she made a new reputation in Emlyn Williams's *The Last Days on Dolwyn* and in Thorold Dickinson's *The Queen of Spades*. She also played Lady Bracknell for the films and Mrs St Maugham in Enid Bagnold's *The Chalk Garden*. For Mrs Ross in *The Whisperers* (1966) she received awards from Berlin and the United States, as well as Britain. Those who had the good fortune to hear her play will always remember her voice, which was different from that of any other actress.

Her last appearance on the West End stage took place in 1974 when she was eighty-six years of age. In 1946 she was appointed DBE; she received honorary degrees from London, Cambridge, Oxford, and Hull. She was a Christian Scientist, and at her death left a large sum for the benefit of the Actors' Charitable Trust.

In 1925 she married George ('Guy') Booth; they had no children, and he died in 1935. She died at Kilndown, Kent, on 14 October 1976.

EVANS, EDWARD RATCLIFFE GARTH RUSSELL, first BARON MOUNTEVANS (1880–1957), admiral, was born in London on 28 October 1880, the second son of Frank Evans, a barrister, and his wife, Eliza Frances Garth. His adventurous career started in his youth: he often ran away from home, and was expelled from Merchant Taylors' School for truanting. He entered the navy from the mercantile marine training ship, *Worcester*.

In 1902 he was selected to be second officer of the *Morning*, the ship sent to the relief of (Sir) Robert Scott's first Antarctic expedition; after locating the *Discovery* stuck fast in the ice, he revictualled her, but had to leave her until the following year when he returned and *Discovery* was able to break free. Seven years later, Evans was chosen by Scott to be second-in-command of the second Antarctic expedition, and in 1912 he accompanied Scott to within 150 miles of the Pole, where he had to turn back, a victim of scurvy. After a short convalescence in England he returned to the Antarctic in the *Terra Nova*, only to discover that Scott and his companions had perished.

In 1914 he served in the Dover Patrol and became famous as 'Evans of the *Broke*' when, in 1917, he was in a counter-attack on six German destroyers, which had shelled Dover harbour, and rammed one of the destroyers with his ship the *Broke*. He was appointed DSO and promoted to captain.

From 1926 to 1928 he commanded the battle-cruiser *Repulse* and in the latter year became a rear-admiral in command of the Australian squadron.

From 1933 to 1935, as vice-admiral, he was commander-in-chief, African station, and while acting as High Commissioner, in the absence of Sir Herbert Stanley, suspended Tshekedi, Regent of the Bamangwato tribe in Bechuanaland (Botswana), who had ordered the flogging of a European accused of assault and seduction of African women. Although after a few weeks Evans reinstated Tshekedi, he was criticized for the ostentatious way in which he had taken action when his objective could have been achieved with less publicity.

Evans was promoted to admiral in 1936, and served as Commander-in-Chief at the Nore from 1935 to 1939. During the Second World War he was Regional Civil Defence Commissioner in London and served throughout the blitz on London, though he retired from the navy in 1941. He had received the freedom of Dover in 1938. His other honours included the CB (civil, 1913, military, 1932), KCB (1935), and a peerage as Baron Mountevans in 1945. He wrote a number of books including *South with Scott* (1921), *Adventurous Life* (1946), and *Happy Adventurer* (1951).

He was twice married; first, in 1904 to Hilda Beatrice, daughter of Thomas Gregory Russell, barrister, of Christchurch, New Zealand; they had no children, and she died in 1913. In 1916 he married Elsa, daughter of Richard Andvord, *statshauptman* of Oslo; they had two sons. Mountevans died at Golaa in Norway on 20 August 1957. He was not typical of the 'silent service'; he loved publicity, but he had great skill as a seaman and was popular with both officers and men of the ships in which he served.

EVANS, HORACE, BARON EVANS (1903–1963), physician, was born at Dowlais, near Merthyr Tydfil, on 1 January 1903, the elder son of Harry Evans, musician, and his wife, Edith Gwendolen Rees. He was educated at Liverpool College, City of London School, and London Hospital Medical College. He qualified in 1925, obtained his MB, BS, in 1928, and MD and MRCP in 1930, and was made FRCP in 1938. He trained under (Sir) Arthur Ellis who recognized his capacity although his academic ability was not outstanding.

In 1929 he married Helen Aldwyth Davies, daughter of a former high sheriff of Glamorgan; they had two daughters.

Evans was appointed Assistant Director of the Medical Unit in 1933, and Assistant Physician to the London Hospital in 1936. He became full Physician in 1947, and was Consulting Physician to the Royal Navy, and to the Royal Masonic and other hospitals.

In 1946 he succeeded Lord DAWSON of Penn as physician to Queen Mary, became physician to George VI in 1949, and to Queen Elizabeth from 1952 until his death. He received many honours, KCVO (1949), GCVO (1955), and was created a baron in 1957. He was a general physician of great skill and personality at a time when medicine was becoming more and more highly specialized.

He had little time to devote to research and he published little. However he made an intensive study of Bright's disease and embodied this in his Croonian lectures for 1941 (published in the *Lancet*, 1942). He was President of the Medical Society of London, a founder member of the British Heart Foundation, and Vice-President of the Royal College of Physicians. He died in London on 26 October 1963.

F

FABER, SIR GEOFFREY CUST (1889–1961), publisher, was born in Malvern on 23 August 1889, the second son of the Revd Henry Mitford Faber, housemaster at Malvern College, and his wife, Florence Ellen, daughter of George Nathaniel Colt, a barrister. He was educated at Rugby, where his friends included Philip Guedalla, Maurice Collis, and Michael Sadleir, and at Christ Church, Oxford, where he obtained a first in Classical Mods. and Greats (1910–12).

In 1913 he joined the Oxford University Press. During the First World War, while serving on the Western Front with the London Regiment (Post Office Rifles), he published two volumes of verse, *Interflow* (1915), and *In the Valley of Vision* (1918). He became a prize Fellow of All Souls in 1919, and joined the board of Strong & Co, a brewing firm with which he had family connections. In 1920 he married Enid Eleanor, daughter of Sir Henry Erle Richards, Chichele Professor of International Law and Diplomacy at Oxford; they had two sons and one daughter. He was awarded the Eldon law scholarship, and called to the Bar (Inner Temple) in 1921.

Two years later Faber had abandoned brewing and the law, and was negotiating a partnership with (Sir) Maurice Gwyer, whose wife owned a publishing firm issuing a successful weekly paper, the *Nursing Mirror*, and medical books. Their aim was to enter the field of general publishing. After joining the Gwyers, he became chairman of the firm, Faber & Gwyer Ltd. Shortly afterwards, he invited T. S. ELIOT to become a member of the board, and four years later when he bought out the Gwyers, the firm became Faber & Faber (1927).

Within a few years, not only was Faber & Faber distinguished for its assistance to promising young writers, particularly poets, but Faber himself had become a prominent figure in the publishing world. In 1934 he was a member of the council of the Publishers' Association, and from 1939 to 1941 its President. When Sir Kingsley Wood, Chancellor of the Exchequer, introduced purchase tax in 1940, Faber was able to mobilize sufficient influential opinion to persuade the Government to exempt books from the operation of the Act. In 1944, he helped to establish the National Book League, and became its first Chairman (1945).

Publishing was not Faber's sole interest. In 1923 he succeeded Geoffrey DAWSON as Estates Bursar of All Souls, an office which he held until 1951, and in which time important developments and a significant increase in the income of the college took place.

Faber continued to write poetry, and in 1941 published *The Buried Stream*, but his prose works are likely to prove the more important; they include his work on the Oxford Movement *Oxford Apostles* (1933) and *Jowett* (1957), and an edition of John Gay in the Oxford Poets Series (1926), published by the Oxford University Press. He resigned as Chairman of Faber & Faber in 1960 and was appointed President of the company. He had been knighted in 1954. Faber died at Midhurst on 31 March 1961.

FAIRLEY, SIR NEIL HAMILTON (1891–1966), physician, was born in Inglewood, Victoria, Australia, on 15 July 1891, son of James Fairley, a bank manager, and his wife, Margaret Louise Jones. He was one of four sons who became doctors. He was educated at Scotch College, Melbourne, and Melbourne University, where he qualified with first class honours in 1915. In 1916 he was commissioned in the Australian Army Medical Service and served in Egypt. In 1919 he married Violet May Phillips; they had one son.

After the First World War, he worked in the Lister Institute in London and obtained his MRCP (London), and DPH (Cambridge). On his return to Australia in 1920 he worked in the Eliza Hall Research Institute, Melbourne, for two years, and then was appointed medical research officer at the Bombay Bacteriological Laboratory. There he studied worm infections in man and beast, and devised methods of treating sprue (a chronic inflammation of the bowel and ulcerated mucous membrane), but could not find its cause. After an attack of sprue from which he recuperated in Britain, he returned to Melbourne and studied snake venoms.

His first marriage ended in divorce in 1924; and in 1925 he married Mary Evelyn, daughter of Herbert R. Greaves, of Bombay; they had two sons.

In 1929 Fairley settled in London, working in the Hospital for Tropical Diseases and lecturing at the London School of Hygiene and Tropical Medicine. He discovered that severe hepatitis in sewer workers was an infectious, preventable disease, contracted from rats. He also visited a malaria research unit in Salonika to study blackwater fever.

In 1940 he was appointed consultant to the Australian troops in Middle East Force, and in Cairo was able to show that sulphaguanidine was a specific cure for acute bacillary dysentery. When Japan entered the war, Fairley went out to the South Pacific area as brigadier and Director of Medicine in the Australian Medical Service. He quickly realized that the most acute medical problem was malaria and, after further study, decided that mepacrine was effective in preventing malaria provided that it was taken daily without fail. When orders were issued enforcing the daily dose the result was dramatic. Malaria ceased to be a problem with the forces.

After the Second World War Fairley resumed teaching in London. He was appointed Wellcome Professor of Tropical Medicine and held the chair from 1946 to 1949. He became FRS in 1942, and having been appointed OBE in 1918 and CBE in 1941, was promoted KBE in 1950. He received many academic honours, was honorary Secretary of the Royal Society of Tropical Medicine and Hygiene from 1930 to 1951, and President from 1951 to 1953. Neil Fairley died in Sonning on 19 April 1966. His youngest son, Gordon Hamilton Fairley, an authority on oncology, was killed by a bomb placed under his car in London by a dissident group who mistook his car for somebody else's.

FARJEON, ELEANOR (1881–1965), writer, was born in London on 13 February 1881, the daughter of Benjamin Leopold Farjeon, a prolific Victorian novelist of Jewish descent, and his wife, Margaret, daughter of the celebrated American actor, Joseph Jefferson. She had no formal education but was brought up in the company of actors, writers, and musicians.

She became established as an author when (Dame) Rebecca West perceptively reviewed her romantic fantasy *Martin Pippin in the Apple-Orchard* (1921). She had published a volume of poems *Pan-Worship* in 1908, and *Nursery Rhymes of London Town* (1916), and from 1921 onwards children's verses, songs, and stories poured from her pen. As 'Tom Fool' she wrote a topical verse a day for thirteen years for the *Daily Herald* and a weekly poem throughout the twenties for *Time and Tide*. An important element in her development as a writer was her friendship with the poet, Edward THOMAS,

Eleanor Farjeon

and his wife. She later wrote about this period in *Edward Thomas: The Last Four Years* (1958).

She wrote novels, operettas, and plays, including *The Glass Slipper* (St James's, 1944), and *The Silver Curlew* (Arts, 1949), but her most notable works were her books for children. The finest of her short stories are in *The Little Bookroom* (1955). *Silver-Sand and Snow* (1951) and *The Children's Bells* (1957) contain the best of her poetry. In 1959 she was awarded the American Regina medal for her work for children. Eleanor Farjeon never married, but she was one of the best writers for children of her generation. She died in Hampstead on 5 June 1965.

FAWCETT, DAME MILLICENT (1847–1929), better known as MRS HENRY FAWCETT, leader of the women's suffrage movement, was born at Aldeburgh on 11 June 1847, the daughter of Newson Garrett, a merchant, and his wife, Louisa, daughter of John Dunnell. Her elder sister was Elizabeth GARRETT ANDERSON. She was educated at a school in Blackheath. The difficulties which Elizabeth met when she was trying to get qualified in medicine led to Millicent's determination to work for an improvement in the position of women.

In 1867, she married Henry Fawcett, the blind Professor of Economics at Cambridge and Liberal MP for Brighton. This brought her into contact with John Stuart Mill and other radical thinkers of the day. It was in the Fawcett home in Cambridge that the scheme was launched which eventually led to the foundation of Newnham College. Her main objective, however, was the achievement of women's suffrage without which she did not think that much progress could be made in improving the status of women in society. In 1867 she joined the first women's suffrage committee and, in spite of ridicule and opposition, tried by every possible means to bring the subject before the public.

She also worked to secure for married women the right to their own property, a cause which eventually led to the Married Women's Property Act of 1882. She was interested in the protection of young girls, but became more and more convinced that to secure progress women must have the right to vote. In 1897 she was elected President of the National Union of Women's Suffrage Societies, which became an efficient and determined political force. She did not, however, join the Women's Social and Political Union formed by Emmeline PANKHURST and her daughter Christabel, and did not approve of the militant activities of the suffragettes.

During the First World War she suspended the propaganda issued by her own movement and encouraged women to enter war work, and when in 1918 the first women's suffrage victory was won, she retired from the presidency of the National Union.

Her husband had died in 1884; they had one child, a daughter. Millicent Fawcett was appointed DBE in 1925; she was made an honorary LL D of St Andrews University in 1905. She died in London on 5 August 1929 and a memorial to her was placed in Westminster Abbey in 1932.

FERRIER, KATHLEEN MARY (1912–1953), singer, was born on 22 April 1912 at Higher Walton, near Preston, the daughter of William Ferrier, headmaster, and his wife, Alice, daughter of James Murray. She was educated at Blackburn High School, but left at fourteen to become a Post Office telephonist. She showed early ability as a pianist and passed her ARCM and LRAM examinations at eighteen. In 1935

Kathleen Ferrier in *The Rape of Lucretia*, Glyndebourne, 1946; Britten wrote the part of Lucretia specially for her

she married Albert Wilson, a bank clerk, but the marriage was annulled in 1947. There were no children.

After her marriage Kathleen lived near Carlisle, and in 1937 won the Rose Bowl at the Carlisle festival for both singing and pianoforte. She was advised to study singing, and from 1939 to 1942 she did so under Dr Hutchinson of Newcastle. She made public appearances with the Council for the Encouragement of Music and the Arts (CEMA), and was heard by Malcolm SARGENT who introduced her to the Tilletts, the London concert agents.

In 1942 she moved to London and spent four years in intensive training of her voice with Roy Henderson, with whom she was associated for the rest of her life. Joint recitals with him gave her experience in a variety of songs, and she did broadcasts and made records. Benjamin BRITTEN wrote the name part of his opera *The Rape of Lucretia* for her and she performed in this work at Glyndebourne in 1946, and in the following year was superb in Gluck's *Orfeo ed Euridice*.

Rudolf Bing, the Glyndebourne manager, asked Bruno Walter to hear her, and Walter decided that she was the ideal Mahler singer for whom he was seeking. Concert tours, opera singing, and choral works were now undertaken by Kathleen Ferrier in many European countries. She sang in the Salzburg, Edinburgh, and English festivals, and toured in the USA and Canada. In some of her recitals she was accompanied by Bruno Walter, but her favourite accompanist was Gerald Moore. She had now become a world-famous singer, loved not only for her rich contralto voice, but for her warm personality, gaiety, and charm.

Then tragedy struck. In 1951 she had to undergo a serious operation for cancer. Regular visits to hospital for deep X-ray treatment did not deter her from singing, but her days were numbered. The disease could not be contained. Her last triumphant appearance took place in 1953 at Covent Garden in *Orpheo* conducted by her great friend, John BARBIROLLI. She sang in great pain, but her voice was as lovely as it had ever been. She died in London on 8 October 1953, having been appointed CBE, and awarded the Royal Philharmonic Society's gold medal earlier in the year. The musical world was thus deprived of a great artiste, and the public mourned her loss. She is remembered in the Kathleen Ferrier scholarships for young singers. She was the most beloved singer of her time and is not forgotten thirty years after her death.

FIELDS, DAME GRACIE (1898–1979), music-hall artiste and film star, was born in Rochdale, Lancashire, on 9 January 1898, the eldest of four children of Fred Stansfield, an engineer, and his wife, Sarah Jane Bamford. She went to school in Rochdale until she was thirteen, her mother doing all she could to encourage her to make a career on the stage. Appearing in local music halls and with amateur groups, she adopted the name of Gracie Fields, and by the time she was fifteen had set out on a professional career as a singer and *comédienne*.

In 1916 she joined Archie Pitt (whose real name was Selinger) who had formed a company to perform his own revues. Gracie toured the music-halls with him for the next eight years, and from him she learnt the rudiments of the profession: dancing, singing, mimicry, and acting. Pitt was ruthless in his efforts to drill into her a dedication to her work and an urge to excel in it. In 1923 they married; Gracie was so much under the influence of Pitt that she agreed to marry him as a means of furthering her career. They had no children.

In 1924 Pitt's company, with Gracie as leading lady, appeared in London in *Mr Tower of London*; the production was a success and Gracie Fields was acclaimed by the critics as a new star on the West-End stage. From that time up to the outbreak of the Second World War she became famous as 'Our Gracie', appearing in revues, cabaret, and in films, singing her unforgettable songs, some highly sentimental, others extremely comical, all the individual contribution of the lass from Lancashire.

Her film, *Sally in Our Alley* (1931), including the song of that name, which Gracie came to find tedious but always in demand, was an immediate success, but until her films came under the direction of the Italian, Monty Banks (Mario Bianchi), they had little distinction as films. However, under the direction of Banks there was a marked improvement, and in 1938 Gracie began to appear in Hollywood films and became one of the highest paid stars of the screen. She was also honoured with a CBE.

In 1939 she had to undergo an operation for cancer, causing great anxiety to the vast number of people who followed her career with affection and admiration. In 1940 she divorced her first husband and married Monty Banks, who, as an Italian, was liable to be interned in England, and for this reason Gracie and her new husband lived in the United States throughout the war. Although she was indefatigable in her appearances for the entertainment of the troops, her popularity in Britain suffered a marked decline.

After the war, however, she soon returned to favour, but her appearances in Britain were much less frequent than before. In 1950 Monty Banks died, and in 1952 Gracie married Boris Alperovici, a Bessarabian radio engineer, who was living in Capri, where she had made her home. This marriage was a very happy one.

Gracie Fields continued to make occasional appearances on television to the delight of millions. Her only prop was a headscarf, which she put on her head, while singing such popular comic songs as 'The Biggest Aspidistra in the World', in a raucous voice completely dissimilar from the emotional strains in which she sang such serious works as 'Ave Maria'. She never ceased to hold her audiences, up to the time of her death in Capri on 27 September 1979.

She gave large sums of money to charity, having endowed in 1935 the orphanage, named after her, at Peacehaven, Sussex. In 1937 she received the freedom of Rochdale and in 1979 was appointed DBE. She made some 500 recordings of her songs and appeared eleven times in Royal Variety performances. Her autobiography *Sing As We Go* was published in 1960.

FISHER, HERBERT ALBERT LAURENS (1865-1940), historian, politician, and Warden of New College, Oxford, was born in London on 21 March 1865, the eldest son of Herbert William Fisher, and his wife, Mary Louisa, daughter of John Jackson, a physician in the service of the East India Company. His father was a barrister, who became Private Secretary to the Prince of Wales and was the holder of the office of Vice-Warden of the Stannaries. H. A. L. Fisher was educated at Winchester and New College, Oxford, where he obtained firsts in Classical Mods. and Greats (1886-8). He was elected a Fellow of New College in 1888. After studying modern history at Göttingen and Paris, he returned to Oxford to teach and write. In 1899 he married Lettice, daughter of the parliamentary draftsman Sir Courtenay Ilbert; they had one daughter.

In 1898 he published *The Medieval Empire*, followed by other books including several on Napoleon, of which the short life in the Home University Library series (1913) was described by a French writer as the best in any language. He contributed Volume V (1485-1547) to Longman's *Political History of England* (1906), published a biography of his brother-in-law, Professor Frederic William Maitland, and edited Maitland's lectures on *The Constitutional History of England* (1908), and his *Collected Papers* (3 vols., 1911).

From 1912 to 1917 Fisher served on the Royal Commission on the Public Services in India, and in the latter year was elected Vice-Chancellor of Sheffield University. In this office he did much to develop the activities of the young university, including the encouragement of the application of science to industry and, during the First World War, the adaptation of the cutlery industry to the requirements of war.

In December 1916 LLOYD GEORGE invited Fisher to join his Cabinet as President of the Board of Education; it was realized that much needed to be done in the field of national education. Fisher was responsible for the Education Act of 1918 which established state scholarships to the universities, improved the salaries and pensions of elementary school teachers, and introduced the School Certificate. He also recommended part-time continuation schools up to the age of eighteen, but this recommendation, though included in the Act, was not put into effect. It was, however, a proposal which was taken into consideration years later in the Butler Act of 1944.

From 1916 to 1918 Fisher was Liberal MP for the Hallam division of Sheffield, and from 1918 to 1926 member for the combined universities. He left the Cabinet when Lloyd George ceased to be Prime Minister in 1922. In 1925 he was appointed Warden of New College, Oxford, and for the next fifteen years devoted himself once more to academic affairs. He produced biographies of *James Bryce* (2 vols., 1927), and *Paul Vinogradoff* (1927) and, besides publishing lectures on a number of subjects, he published his most serious work the *History of Europe* (3 vols., 1935).

He had been elected FBA in 1907, and became President of the Academy from 1928 to 1932. He was elected FRS in 1920, and appointed OM in 1937. He received honorary degrees from many universities and was a Trustee of the British Museum. He died in London on 18 April 1940, having been involved in an accident and knocked down by a lorry while on his way to preside at the appeal tribunal on conscientious objectors to military service.

FISHER, JAMES MAXWELL McCONNELL (1912-1970), ornithologist, was born in Clifton, Bristol on 3 September 1912, the eldest son of Dr Kenneth Fisher, a master at Clifton College, who later became headmaster of Oundle, and his wife, Constance Isabel, daughter of James Boyd, yarn agent, of Altrincham, Cheshire. He was educated at Eton, where he was a King's scholar, and Magdalen College, Oxford. He went as ornithologist on the Oxford University expedition to Spitzbergen in 1933, and won the OU Challenge Sculls in 1934. After graduation in 1935, he taught for a short time at Bishop's Stortford College, and during 1936-9 was Assistant Curator at the Zoological Society, London. In 1936 he married Margery Lilian Edith, daughter of (Sir) Henry S. E. Turner, a civil servant; they had three sons and three daughters.

Fisher's uncle, Arnold Boyd, a former editor of *British Birds*, encouraged his interest in ornithology. From 1938 to 1944, he was honorary Secretary of the British Trust for Ornithology. In co-operation with Julian HUXLEY he set up the Trust's Hatching and Fledging Enquiry (later the Nest Record Scheme). With other young ornithologists he carried

James Fisher, photographed in Holland, 1970

out a survey of the breeding populations of the North Atlantic Gannet, and in 1938-9 studied the Fulmar, publishing the results of his research in *The Fulmar* (1952).

From 1940 to 1946 Fisher worked in Oxford, studying the food of the Rook, and wrote a number of books on birds including *Birds as Animals* (1939, reissued 1954), *The Birds of Britain* (1942), and *Bird Recognition* (3 vols., 1947, 1951, and 1955). His *Watching Birds* (1940, revised by Jim Flegg, 1978) became a Pelican paperback best seller. Fisher's main interest was always in sea-birds, and he visited many of the islands of Britain and Northern Europe where sea-birds nest, including Rockall, on to which he was lowered by helicopter in 1955. This exploit was the subject of his book *Rockall* (1956).

Disappointed at not being made Director of the Edward Grey Institute of Field Ornithology at Oxford, he concentrated on publishing and from 1946 to 1954 was natural history editor at Collins and one of the founders of their New Naturalist Library. With his wife, he wrote a life of Sir Ernest H. SHACKLETON, published in 1957. He also made over a thousand broadcasts, of which two hundred were on television, lecturing on ornithology and natural history, and explaining the importance of conservation. From 1968 to 1970 he was Deputy Chairman of the National Parks (later Countryside) Commission. He was a Fellow of the Royal Geographical Society, Linnean Society, Geological Society, and Zoological Society. He won a number of awards for his work. Fisher died in a car accident at Hendon on 25 September 1970.

FISHER, JOHN ARBUTHNOT, first BARON FISHER (1841–1920), Admiral of the Fleet, was born on 25 January 1841 in Ceylon (Sri Lanka), the elder son of Capt. William Fisher, of the 78th Highlanders and 95th Foot, and his wife, Sophia, daughter of Alfred Lambe of London. He entered the navy in 1854, and served as a naval cadet in the Baltic fleet during the Crimean War and as a midshipman in China during the war of 1859-60.

During the next twenty-two years he saw no fighting, but pursued the career of a naval officer in peacetime, qualifying in gunnery and being concerned with the development of the torpedo. He rose to the rank of captain. Then, in 1882, in command of the *Inflexible*, the greatest battleship of the time, he was again in action at Alexandria and was awarded the CB for his services against Arabi Pasha.

For the next fourteen years Fisher served ashore. From 1883 to 1886 he was Captain of the Gunnery School, Portsmouth, and from 1886 to 1890, Director of Ordnance and Torpedoes at the Admiralty. In 1890 he was promoted to rear-admiral and, from 1892 to 1897, was Third Sea Lord and Controller of the Navy. During this time he superintended the building of the battleship *Royal Sovereign*, and was responsible for the programme of ship-building authorized by the Naval Defence Act (1889). In 1894 he was promoted KCB and, two years later, became vice-admiral. He was Commander-in-Chief, North America and West Indies station in 1897, and commanded the Mediterranean fleet from 1899 to 1902. He was promoted to admiral in 1901, and appointed GCB in 1902.

In 1902 Fisher was called to the Admiralty as Second Sea Lord with charge of the personnel of the fleet. He was now well known to be an outstanding officer who, without regard for outworn traditions and naval customs, was determined to improve training and efficiency and prepare the navy for its twentieth-century role and, in particular, to face up to the growing threat from Germany. In his new post he introduced important administrative reforms, including a common entry for training officers at the new school at Osborne, and the replacement of the *Britannia* training ship with a college of the same name at Dartmouth. Necessarily, his enthusiasm for innovation aroused hostility among officers of the older school, but Fisher's determination rode roughshod over all opposition to his schemes.

After a short period as Commander-in-Chief, Portsmouth, during which he also served as a member of a War Office reconstruction committee, Fisher entered on his long and important period as First Sea Lord from 1904 to 1910. He received the OM in 1904. He and Lord Selbourne and Lord Cawdor, who took over from Selbourne as First Lord of the Admiralty in 1905, set out to reorganize the distribution of the Royal Navy, which had hardly been changed since the Crimean War. Fisher's object was to concentrate the strength of the navy in home waters, and for this purpose he reorganized the Mediterranean, Atlantic, and Channel fleets, and abolished a number of ships of out-dated design. He had for some time advocated the building of the *Dreadnought* type of battleship, and the first of these was launched in 1906.

The advent of a Liberal Government in 1906 made it difficult for a time for Fisher and his colleagues at the Admiralty to go ahead with their schemes, and the postponement of the construction of the new dockyard at Rosyth and the abandonment of the programme of building four capital ships a year, was a matter of acute anxiety to Fisher, and threatened to give the Germans a great opportunity to secure a lead in the naval rivalry between the two countries. By 1908, however, it had become obvious that the policy of the Campbell-Bannerman Government had failed, and that the Kaiser, far from modifying his own schemes for naval supremacy, was going ahead with his building programme relentlessly. After a bitter contest in the Cabinet, it was decided to build eight new battleships during 1909-10, and to hasten the construction of the Rosyth dockyard.

Unfortunately, during this time of stress, Fisher became less and less prepared to face criticism, and Lord Charles Beresford, Commander-in-Chief of the Channel fleet, who found himself disagreeing with the Admiralty on certain points of detail, became the object of Fisher's vindictive rancour in a feud which lasted until Fisher's retirement and resulted in the termination of Beresford's command in 1909. In that year Fisher was raised to the peerage as Baron Fisher, of Kilverstone, and in 1910 he retired.

Fisher, however, did not lose his concern with naval affairs; in 1912 he sat as Chairman of the royal commission which resulted in the adoption of oil-fuel for all new ships, and in October 1914, after the outbreak of the First World War, CHURCHILL, as First Lord of the Admiralty, invited Fisher to return as First Sea Lord when Prince Louis of BATTENBERG resigned.

At first, this combination worked well. Fisher's initial task was to redress the loss of Sir Christopher Cradock's squadron at Coronel, destroyed by Admiral von Spee; he dispatched two battle-cruisers, under the command of Admiral Sturdee, to intercept von Spee and destroy his ships. As a result of Fisher's insistence on the necessity for speed in this operation, von Spee was found at the Falkland Islands and four of his five ships were sunk (1914). This was Fisher's last success. He reluctantly agreed to the naval action that ended in disaster at the Dardanelles because, although he feared it would fail, he was reluctant to disagree publicly with Churchill. When it became obvious that the strength of the Channel fleet would be weakened by the dispatch of more ships to Gallipoli, Fisher resigned on 15 May 1915. His resignation resulted in the removal of Churchill from the Admiralty, as the price of BONAR LAW's agreement to a Coalition Government, but Fisher was not invited to return by BALFOUR, the new First Lord.

When the war ended, Fisher published his reminiscences *Memories* (1919), and *Records* (1919). In 1866 he had married Frances, only daughter of the Revd Thomas Delves Broughton; they had one son and three daughters. Lady Fisher died in 1918. He died two years later on 10 July 1920 and was given a public naval funeral in London. He was one of the most remarkable personalities of his time; his career extended from the Crimean War to the First World War, and he was one of the most outstanding administrators in the history of the Royal Navy.

FLECK, ALEXANDER, BARON FLECK (1889-1968), industrial chemist and business man, was born in Glasgow on 11 November 1889, the only son of Robert Fleck, a coal merchant, and his wife, Agnes Hendry, daughter of James Duncan, a coal clerk. He was educated at Saltcoats Public School, and Hillhead High School, but he had to leave school at fourteen. His ambition was to be a scientist, and he found work as a laboratory boy at Glasgow University. There he came to the notice of Frederick SODDY who encouraged him to study at evening classes and then to become a full-time student. He gained an honours degree in chemistry, at twenty-two, but Soddy could hardly have foreseen that, one day, Fleck would be chairman of ICI.

In 1911 Fleck joined the teaching staff of the university and continued to work on the chemistry of the radioactive elements, which foreshadowed the later conception of isotopes. In 1916 he was awarded a D.Sc. for a thesis on this subject. In 1913 he had joined the staff of the Glasgow Radium Committee with his own laboratory for radiological work on cancer.

The First World War took him away from an academic career. In 1917, the year of his marriage to Isabel Mitchell Kelly, a farmer's daughter, he became Chief Chemist to the Castner Kellner Alkali Co. Two years later, he was Works Manager and, when his firm and others were incorporated in Imperial Chemical Industries in 1926, he was put in charge of the planning of the new chemical works at Billingham and the successful transfer there of workers and their families from the Clyde and the Tyne.

In 1931 Fleck became Managing Director of the General Chemicals Division at Liverpool and, six years later, he returned to Teesside as Chairman of the Billingham Division. There, he kept this great centre of chemical manufacture working throughout the heavy bombing, which it had to undergo, during the Second World War. In 1944 he was appointed to the ICI board. When the war ended he was mainly concerned with the company's organization for marketing agricultural products, and from 1947 to 1951 he was Chairman of Scottish Agricultural Industries.

He became Deputy Chairman of ICI in 1951 and from 1953 to 1960 he was Chairman, an office in which he was highly successful, not only because of his business acumen, but because of his understanding of his colleagues and staff. He was also busy in other directions. He was Chairman of the Coal Board Organization Committee (1953-5); he was Chairman of the Prime Minister's Committee on the Windscale Accident (1957-8), and of the Scientific Advisory Council (1958-65). He chaired a government committee on the fishing industry, and in 1958 was President of the British Association for the Advancement of Science. He received a large number of honorary degrees, was elected FRS in 1955, and was Vice-President of the Royal Society in 1960. After retirement from ICI in 1960, he was President of the Society of Chemical Industry (1960-2), Chairman of the Nuclear Safety Advisory Committee (1960-5), and President of the Royal Institution (1963). He was also a director of the Midland Bank (1955). Fleck was appointed KBE in 1955, and created baron in 1961. He died childless on 6 August 1968 in London.

FLEMING, SIR ALEXANDER (1881-1955), bacteriologist, was born on 6 August 1881, the third of four children of Hugh Fleming, a farmer of Lochfield in Ayrshire, and his second wife, Grace Morton, daughter of a neighbouring farmer. He was educated at Darvel, near his home, at Kilmarnock Academy, and at the Polytechnic Institute, Regent Street, London. For a time he worked as a clerk in a shipping office, but in 1901, having received a small legacy, he became a student at St Mary's Hospital Medical School. There he won a number of scholarships and prizes, qualified in 1906, became MB, BS of London University in 1908 with honours, and FRCS in 1909.

As soon as he had qualified, Fleming was appointed an assistant bacteriologist in the inoculation department of the hospital (which later became the Wright-Fleming Institute in Microbiology). In this post he served his apprenticeship under Almroth WRIGHT, who ably directed the general research of the department, and Fleming's ingenuity and

Alexander Fleming in 1943; by then the value of penicillin, which he had discovered fifteen years earlier, was evident

originality of mind soon became obvious to all who came into contact with his work. He was appointed lecturer in bacteriology at St Mary's in 1920, and in 1928 was given the title of Professor of Bacteriology at London University.

During the First World War he served in the RAMC working with Almroth Wright in France on the treatment of war wounds. In this capacity he made some important contributions to knowledge of the bacteriology and treatment of septic wounds. He realized that the soldiers' uniforms were infected and warned of the danger of severe infection from *Streptococcus pyogenes*, which occurred after the patient had been admitted to hospital indicating the likelihood of hospital cross-infection with this organism.

In 1922 Fleming made what he regarded as his most important discovery when he found lysozyme, an antimicrobial substance produced in the body in mucus, tears, saliva, etc., which he described as the body's natural protection against infection. Then, in 1928, he made his name famous by an observation that would in time lead to a new era in the treatment of disease by antibiotics. While he was studying colony variation in the staphylococcus, he noticed that 'around a large colony of a contaminating mould the staphylococcus colonies became transparent' and were obviously disintegrating. The perception of this phenomenon

led directly to the discovery of penicillin which Fleming recognized as having potential value as a new and remarkable addition to the treatment of infections. He did not have available, however, the means to develop this new substance, and it was not until 1941–2 that the Oxford team of CHAIN and FLOREY were able to demonstrate the effectiveness of treatment by penicillin on patients at the Radcliffe Infirmary.

Although this discovery was Fleming's most outstanding contribution to medical science, there were many other sides to his work, in all of which he combined intuitive and original observation with great technical skill and inventiveness. He became a Fellow of the Royal Society in 1943, a Fellow of the Royal College of Physicians in 1944, and in the same year received a knighthood. Together with Chain and Florey, he was awarded the Nobel Prize for Medicine in 1945. During 1946–1954 he was Principal of the Wright–Fleming Institute. Throughout his career academic honours were bestowed upon him, and his services were in great demand, for example, as a Member of the Medical Research Council and of the Senate of London University.

He was twice married; first, in 1915 to Sarah Marion McElroy, an Irish girl who was a trained nurse; she died in 1949. In 1953 he married Amalia Voureka Coutsouris, daughter of a Greek doctor, and herself a medically qualified bacteriologist. There was one son of the first marriage who became a general practitioner. Fleming died suddenly at his home in Chelsea, London on 11 March 1955. He was buried in St Paul's Cathedral.

FLINT, SIR WILLIAM RUSSELL (1880–1969), artist, was born in Edinburgh on 4 April 1880, the eldest son of Francis Wighton Flint, commercial artist, and his wife, Jane Purves. He was educated at Daniel Stewart's College, and at fourteen was apprenticed as a lithographic artist to a printing firm. In the evenings he studied at the Royal Institution School of Art. In 1900 he became an illustrator to medical publications in London, and then moved to a part-time job with Dickinson's, the paper makers, and also studied at Heatherleys. From 1903 to 1907 he worked as staff artist on the *Illustrated London News*.

He now became a freelance illustrator of books, including an edition of the *Imitation of Christ* (1908), classics for the Medici Society, and the *Morte d'Arthur*, for which in 1913 he won a silver medal at the Paris Salon. From 1905, the year of his marriage to Sibylle, sister of (Sir) Murray Sueter, he exhibited water-colours at the Royal Academy, but he also painted in oils, and held many successful one-man shows.

In 1917 he became a member of the Royal Society of Painters in Water-Colours, of which he was President from 1936 to 1956. In 1910 he had been elected to the Royal Institute of Oil Painters, and he became ARA in 1924 and RA in 1933. He was knighted in 1947, and in 1962 a retrospective exhibition of his work was held at the Royal Academy.

His work became widely known, largely through reproductions of many of his pictures of nudes and semi-nudes and of landscapes of water, sand, and trees, characteristically set in Spain or the South of France. Throughout his life he remained detached from the experimental currents in twentieth-century art.

Flint died in London on 27 December 1969. His son Francis Murray Russell Flint became a well-known artist.

FLOREY, HOWARD WALTER, BARON FLOREY (1898–1968), experimental pathologist and the main creator of penicillin therapy, was born in Adelaide on 24 September 1898, the only son of Joseph Florey, an Oxfordshire shoemaker who had emigrated in 1885, and his second wife, Bertha Mary Wadham, an Australian. He was educated at Kyre College and St Peter's Collegiate School, Adelaide, and in 1916 entered Adelaide University Medical School qualifying MB, BS, in 1921. In that year he was awarded a Rhodes scholarship and worked his passage to England as a ship's surgeon.

He entered Magdalen College, Oxford, and studied in the Physiology Department under Sir Charles SHERRINGTON, and in 1923 obtained a first. Sherrington invited him to stay on to do research on the blood flow in the capillaries of the brain but, after a year, having spent the summer vacation with the Oxford University Arctic Expedition, Florey moved to Cambridge to study at the Pathology Department. There he continued his research on blood-flow changes in inflammation and thrombosis, and for his work in this subject earned his B.Sc. (Oxford, 1925). That year he was awarded a Rockefeller fellowship to learn micro-surgical techniques in Philadelphia. He then went to Chicago to study mucus secretion, a subject in which he was now very interested, since he personally suffered from indigestion diagnosed as a mucous infection.

In 1926 Florey returned to England as a research Fellow at the London Hospital, and married Dr Mary Ethel Hayter Reed, daughter of an Adelaide bank manager, whom he had known as a medical student. Neither liked London, and in the next year Florey accepted the Huddersfield lectureship in pathology at Cambridge and a fellowship at Gonville and Caius College. Another thesis, on blood and lymph flow, obtained for him his Ph.D. (1927).

During the next four years, together with various collaborators, he published twenty scientific papers, his most important work being his study of lysozyme which Alexander FLEMING had discovered in 1922. Florey took up the study of this agent in mucoid secretions because he thought it might explain an antibacterial action he had noticed, and might also be the reason for the natural immunity of some animals. He published two papers on this subject in 1930, and was determined to discover the nature of lysozyme and how it worked.

In 1932 Florey was appointed Joseph Hunter Professor of Pathology at Sheffield. While he was there he worked on the control of spasms in tetanus by curare combined with mechanical artificial respiration—the basis of modern treatment, but his main interest continued to be lysozyme.

On the death of Georges Dreyer, Florey was appointed to the chair of pathology at Oxford (1935). Within a few years, with the help of Dr Beatrice Pullinger and Jim Kent, his laboratory assistant, he made the Sir William Dunn School of Pathology among the best in the world, in spite of difficulties caused by lack of finance. He and a number of young postgraduates pursued various lines of research, but his own work leading to the practical use of penicillin was the most important.

E. A. H. Roberts, a biochemist, had purified lysozyme in 1937. Florey asked another young biochemist, Ernst CHAIN, to discover how lysozyme dissolved bacteria. Chain read Fleming's 1929 paper describing his discovery of a penicillium mould that dissolved bacteria, and Chain was interested because penicillin attacked a wider range of bacteria than lysozyme. He was fortunate enough to find an actual culture of Fleming's mould in the School of Pathology. Florey had not been particularly interested in penicillin; he was concerned more with antibacterial substances produced by the body itself than with those produced by moulds. But he now agreed with Chain that he should pursue his research on penicillin, as work on lysozyme had reached a dead end.

The Rockefeller Foundation made a substantial grant for this research, and the Florey team, working together on all aspects of the matter, decided in May 1940 to try out the effects of penicillin on mice infected with virulent streptococci. The experiment was completely successful. Florey now tried to persuade British drug firms to produce penicillin with which to treat human cases, but with so little success that he decided to manufacture penicillin in his own laboratory. In 1941, under the direction of Dr C. M. Fletcher, it was tried in the Radcliffe Infirmary, Oxford, on patients who had apparently hopeless infections. The results proved that penicillin could overcome infections against which any other treatment was powerless. In 1943 Florey with Hugh Cairns tried out penicillin in the treatment of war wounds in North Africa, and success in this field led to further discoveries at the School of Pathology on other antibiotics. In 1949 a complete account of this work was published as *Antibiotics* (2 vols.) by Florey and six of his collaborators.

Florey was elected FRS in 1941, knighted in 1944, and in 1945 shared the Nobel Prize for Medicine with Chain and Fleming. In the mid 1950s he returned to his early interests in new research on mucus secretion and vascular changes which can cause thrombosis. He continued to undertake responsibilities outside his scientific work; he was President of the Royal Society in 1960, became Provost of the Queen's College, Oxford in 1962 and was Chancellor of the Australian National University in 1965. He had been a Fellow of Lincoln College since 1935, and he received many other academic honours and awards. In 1965 he was created a life peer and a member of the Order of Merit. His wife Ethel, by whom he had a son and a daughter, died in 1966, and a year later he married the daughter of the third Baron Cottesloe, Dr Margaret Augusta Fremantle, who had worked with him in the School of Pathology since 1936. Florey suffered from angina and died suddenly of a heart attack in Oxford on 21 February 1968.

His remarkable ability as a scientist, his industry and determination, his capacity for obtaining the best from his colleagues, and the enormous extent of his research are revealed by the textbook *General Pathology* (1954), edited by Florey and published in four editions. His work marked an important step forward in the history of medical treatment with the development of antibiotics, a potent aid to the general practitioner as well as to the hospitals.

FOOT, ISAAC (1880–1960), politician, was born in Plymouth on 23 February 1880, the fourth son of Isaac Foot, a builder and undertaker, and his wife, Elizabeth Ryder. He was educated at Plymouth Public School and the Hoe Grammar School, and articled for five years to a Plymouth solicitor, Frederick Skardon. He was admitted as solicitor in 1902, and set up the firm of Foot and Bowden. From 1907 to 1927 he was a member of Plymouth City Council; he was Deputy Mayor in 1920, and Lord Mayor in 1945.

His parliamentary career was remarkable in that he was defeated in seven elections between 1910 and 1945 and sat in the House of Commons for only eight years, during which time he made his name as a natural orator. He fought his first election in 1910 and was defeated. In 1919 he was defeated by Lady ASTOR who became a lifelong friend. However, he became Liberal MP for Bodmin in 1922 and held the seat until 1924, and again from 1929 to 1935. On the formation of the National Government in 1931 he became Parliamentary Secretary for Mines, and was also an active member of the India Round Table Conference but, when the Government introduced protection after the Ottawa Conference of 1932, he resigned and as a result was never in office again, although in 1937 he was sworn of the Privy Council.

His outstanding gift as an orator, his sense of history, and his wide general knowledge acquired from his enormous personal library, made him a notable Lord Mayor of Plymouth. He was a voracious reader and late in life taught himself Greek in order to be able to read his New Testament in that language. He was an eloquent local preacher of the Methodist Church.

In 1904 he married Eva, daughter of Angus Mackintosh MD; they had two daughters, and five sons, who were all indebted to their father for their own careers. Dingle, named after his mother's grandfather, William Dingle, became Solicitor-General in the Labour Government of 1964 and was knighted; Hugh, after a distinguished career in the Colonial Service, was made a life peer as Baron Caradon; Michael, who succeeded Aneurin BEVAN as Labour MP for Ebbw Vale, became Leader of the Labour party; Dingle and Michael were both Presidents of the Oxford Union and Hugh was President of the Cambridge Union. The other two sons,

John and Christopher carried on the family business as solicitors in Plymouth, and John was made a life peer in 1967. Their mother died in 1946, and in 1951 Isaac Foot married Catherine Elizabeth Taylor.

He had been President of the Liberal party in 1947, Vice-President of the Methodist Church in 1937–8, and President of the Cromwell Association for many years. He was also Chairman of the Cornwall quarter-sessions from 1953 to 1955. He died at Callington, the family home in Cornwall, on 13 December 1960.

FORBES, (JOAN) ROSITA (1890–1967), traveller and writer, was born on 16 January 1890 at Riseholme Hall, Lincoln, the eldest of six children of Herbert James Torr, landowner, and his wife, Rosita, daughter of Duncan Graham, of Willaston, Cheshire. She had a conventional upbringing, enjoying reading and riding. In 1911 she married Col. Ronald Foster Forbes; they were divorced in 1917.

In 1919 she travelled round the world; the journey ended in North Africa and there Rosita Forbes first came into contact with the Arab world. She met leading personalities in Cairo, Damascus, and Beirut, and acquired an interest in the Arabs which lasted for the rest of her life. She described her journey in *Unconducted Wanderers* (1919).

Rosita Forbes in characteristic disguise, March 1923

She planned to go in the winter of 1920-1 across the Libyan desert to the oasis of Kufra which lay within the territory of Sayed Idris el Senussi (later King Idris of Libya). Only one European, Gerhard Rohlfs, had visited Kufra; that was in 1879. Rosita disguised herself as a Muslim, taking the name of Khadija, but her Arabic was not as good as Lady Anne BLUNT'S had been, and she felt bound to invent a Circassian mother to account for its defects. She travelled with an Egyptian scholar and explorer, Ahmed Hassanein Bey, whose knowledge and expertise were vital to the success of the venture. Their journey by camel was arduous and, at times, dangerous. Rosita Forbes's account of the expedition *The Secret of the Shahara: Kufara* (1921) substantiates her claims as a serious explorer.

In 1921 she married Col. Arthur Thomas McGrath, but continued to use Rosita Forbes as her professional name and went on travelling as before. In 1922, again disguised as Khadija, she visited the Yemen and planned to explore Southern Arabia with St John PHILBY, but the arrangements were held up while she visited el-Raisuni, a Moroccan brigand in the Atlas mountains, whose life she wrote in *El Raisuni, the Sultan of the Mountains* (1924). Her plans to go into Southern Arabia with Kim Philby's father were thwarted, as the Aden authorities thought the journey would be too dangerous. As an alternative, she trekked through Ethiopia, with Harold Jones, a photographer, and together they made a film. She also produced *From Red Sea to Blue Nile* (1925). Another visit to the Middle East gave her the material for *Conflict: Angora to Afghanistan* (1931). Then in 1936 she travelled from Kabul to Samarkand.

She and her husband travelled much together, and when they were in London entertained extensively. During the First World War she drove ambulances in France, and during the Second World War she supported the war efforts by lecturing in America. In her later years she and her husband settled in the Bahamas. She died in Bermuda on 30 June 1967. She had never acquired the influence in the Arab world of Gertrude BELL, but she was a resourceful traveller whose adventurous life was recorded in two autobiographies, *Gypsy in the Sun* (1944) and *Appointment with Destiny* (1946), which were reissued as *Appointment in the Sun* (1949).

FORD, FORD MADOX (1873-1939), author and critic, was born Ford Hermann Hueffer at Merton, Surrey, on 17 December 1873, the elder son of Francis Hueffer, and his wife, Catherine, daughter of the artist Ford Madox Brown. His father, music critic of *The Times*, had come to England from Germany, and his mother's sister was the artist, Lucy Madox Rossetti, wife of W. M. Rossetti. Ford was educated at University College School, London.

His first book *The Brown Owl* (1892) was a fairy story he had made up to amuse his sister, Juliet. This was followed by *Ford Madox Brown* (1896) and *Rossetti* (1902) and a series of essays, poems, and novels. He also collaborated with Joseph CONRAD in three books, including *Romance* (1903). Conrad had already written *Almayer's Folly*, *The Outcast of the Islands*, and *The Nigger of the 'Narcissus'* and it is not easy to see why he collaborated with Ford.

Ford's most notable achievement was the production in 1908 of the *English Review* which, during the short time he was Editor, became an outstanding literary periodical to which articles were contributed by Thomas HARDY, Tolstoy, Henry JAMES, H. G. WELLS, Arnold BENNETT, and John GALSWORTHY. He had a genius for detecting the potentialities of writers, and was the first to recognize that D. H. LAW-

RENCE would be a great author. Ford ceased to be Editor when financial difficulties forced him to sell the *Review*.

From 1915 to 1919 he served in the Welch Regiment in France and was seriously gassed. In 1915 one of his best novels *The Good Soldier*, which had been written some years earlier, was published. After the First World War he changed his name from Hueffer to Ford and took up farming, but in 1922 he moved to Paris where he became a friend of Ezra Pound and Ernest Hemingway and published their work in the *Transatlantic Review* which he set up in 1924. Between 1924 and 1928 he wrote a series of war novels around the character of Tietjens, *Some Do Not* (1924), *No More Parades* (1925), *A Man Could Stand Up* (1926), and *Last Post* (1928). He spent much of his time in the USA and in 1937 was appointed lecturer in comparative literature at Olivet College, Michigan.

In 1894 he married Elsie, daughter of William Martindale, an analytical chemist. They had fallen in love while he was a schoolboy, but her father who was a successful pharmacist disapproved, and Elsie ran away from home and married Ford without her parents' consent. They had two daughters, but Ford was promiscuous and became involved with Violet Hunt, a novelist. Elsie was reluctant to divorce him, and in 1931 she sued the *Throne* newspaper for describing Violet Hunt as Mrs Ford Madox Hueffer. She won the case and the publicity did not help Ford's reputation.

Ford died at Deauville in France on 26 June 1939.

FORMBY, GEORGE (1904-1961), comedian, was born in Wigan on 26 May 1904, the son of James Booth, and his wife, Eliza Hoy. James Booth, a music-hall comedian, had adopted the stage name of George Formby. His son was born blind, but at the age of two, a fit of sneezing restored partial sight. George left school at seven, and went to work in a racing stable as he wanted to be a jockey; he grew up, and remained for the rest of his life, almost totally illiterate.

In 1921 James Booth died. His son, who had become too big to be a jockey, saw a show at the Victoria Palace, London, in which a comedian was doing his father's act with success. He decided that he could imitate his father better than anybody else, and calling himself George Hoy, made his first appearance on the stage at the Hippodrome, Earlestown. He would not use the name Formby until he topped the bill. This he achieved two years later, and from 1923 he was known as George Formby Junior.

In 1925 he played a ukulele on the stage for a bet, and his act with catchy tunes and saucy lyrics was a great success. Formby stopped impersonating his father and put on his own show.

During the thirties he went in to films, first with Ealing Studios, and later with Columbia Pictures. He made some fifteen to twenty films that established him as an international star. His simple form of comedy had a great appeal for the Russians when Ealing Studios released his films in the Soviet Union, and Formby was awarded the Order of Lenin in 1943. For his work in entertaining British troops during the Second World War he was appointed OBE (1946). Then, in 1952, while he was enjoying a great success in the London production of *Zip goes a Million*, a severe heart attack forced him into partial retirement.

Formby married in 1924, Beryl Ingham, a fellow music-hall performer; she gave up her career to manage Formby's and made a great success of the job. They had no children, and she died on 25 December 1960. Formby later became engaged to a schoolteacher, Pat Howson, but three weeks before the

George Formby entertaining the troops in a French farmyard, March 1940

wedding he had another heart attack, and died at Preston on 6 March 1961. Formby was a natural, a born entertainer in the style most enjoyed perhaps by northern audiences, to whom his accent and humour would be most familiar, but his songs and his ukulele made him a favourite with a much wider audience, not only in England, but abroad as well. Among his most popular songs one calls to mind, 'Oh Mr Wu, what shall I do?', 'I'm leaning on a lamppost at the corner of the street', and 'When I'm cleaning windows'.

FORSTER, EDWARD MORGAN (1879-1970), novelist and man of letters, was born in London on 1 January 1879, the only son of Edward Morgan Llewellyn Forster, architect, and his wife, Alice Clara ('Lily'), daughter of Henry Whichelo. His great-grandfather was Henry Thornton, philanthropist and member of the Clapham Sect, and his great-aunt Marianne Thornton, left him sufficient money to enable him to go to Cambridge, and to be able to live as a writer. Forster's father died while he was a child and he was brought up by his mother and his maiden aunts, Emily and Laura. In 1895 he went to Tonbridge as a day boy, and hated it, and in *The Longest Journey* (1907) savagely described the snobbery and venality of the masters at Sawston, a school which he modelled on Tonbridge. Forster had no use for public schools, and little liking for their products.

In 1897 he went as a classical exhibitioner to King's College, Cambridge where, although he did not shine academically, he received encouragement to write from his supervisor, Nathaniel Wedd, and from G. Lowes Dickinson, a Fellow of King's, who had published *The Greek View of Life* in 1896. Through Lowes Dickinson Forster became a member of the 'Apostles', and met young friends, who later formed the Bloomsbury set, with Leonard and Virginia

WOOLF, Roger FRY, and others, to whom he often seemed aloof. At Cambridge he was also patronized by that eccentric self-centred don, Oscar BROWNING. Forster enjoyed his years at King's as he also recorded in *The Longest Journey*, the story of a young man who wanted to write, but in order to marry became a schoolmaster, and entered on a life he found detestable.

On leaving Cambridge with a degree in classics and history, Forster travelled in Italy and Greece, where his natural diffidence seemed less oppressive, and where the life-style of the people he met seemed more congenial to him than the middle-class conventionality of society at home. He began to write short stories, and in 1905 published his first novel *Where Angels Fear to Tread* in which his dislike of British upper-class complacency and insensitive reaction to unhappiness in others is contrasted with the genuine feeling of an Italian, Gino, a ne'er-do-well, who refuses to give up his son to his dead wife's wealthy English relatives. The book was well received, but Forster had not yet arrived as a novelist. *The Longest Journey* (1907), was followed by *A Room with a View* in 1908 and *Howards End* in 1910.

A Room with a View begins in Italy, providing Forster with an opportunity to describe the behaviour of British people abroad as it centres on a group of visitors living in a pension in Florence. The heroine, Lucy Honeychurch, is the vehicle through which Forster demonstrates his attitude to the changing social values of his time.

With *Howards End* Forster came to be recognized as a leading English novelist. The novel is written around the strange characters of two women, Helen and Margaret Schlegel, whose contrasted attitudes to life portray Forster's own understanding of the complexity of human behaviour. He wrote: 'The world would be a grey bloodless place were it entirely composed of Miss Schlegels. But the world being what it is, perhaps they shine out of it like stars.' This novel marked a turning point in his career. From the time of its successful publication, Forster gradually overcame his emotional dissatisfaction with his own achievements and began to regard himself as a novelist of standing who would not take kindly to criticism of his work.

In 1912 Forster went to India with Lowes Dickinson but during this period of his life his home was with his mother at Weybridge. He was unhappy that she did not approve of *Howards End* possibly because she shrank from the description of Helen's seduction. He dared not reveal to her that he was now writing a novel in which he described the difficulties of a young homosexual, who eventually found happiness in contradiction of all the probabilities. His friend Hugh Meredith, who was in Forster's mind when he wrote the book, was disgusted with it when he saw it in manuscript; Forster felt hurt and almost abandoned it. In any case, it could not be published at the time, and was not in fact published until 1971.

During the First World War Forster served with the Red Cross in Alexandria and in 1921 returned to India and became Private Secretary to the Maharaja of Dewas State Senior. His experiences in India, in particular the failure of understanding between East and West, produced what is regarded as his masterpiece, *A Passage to India* (1924), for which he was awarded the Femina Vie-Heureuse and James Tait Black memorial prizes. This novel, like ORWELL's *Burmese Days*, is biased against the British sahibs and memsahibs and was resented by some of those British officials and merchants who had made careers in India, but Forster's respect and sympathy for the aspirations of Indians endeared him to Hindu and Muslim alike, and had some influence on those concerned with political developments in that country.

Besides these novels, Forster wrote literary criticism, essays, and biographies, as well as broadcast talks. His Clark lectures at Cambridge were published as *Aspects of the Novel* (1927) and his essays and talks collected in *Abinger Harvest* (1936), and *Two Cheers for Democracy* (1951). He also helped Eric Crozier to write the libretto of Benjamin BRITTEN's opera *Billy Budd*.

Since his Cambridge days he had taken an interest in the Working Men's College, founded by F. D. Maurice in 1854, and he was twice President of the National Council for Civil Liberties, a cause to which he was deeply attached. He had lived with his mother since 1925 at Abinger and, when she died in 1945, he was invited to return to King's College, Cambridge, as an honorary Fellow. He lived there, admired and loved by many friends, until shortly before his death. He had met a young policeman, Bob Buckingham, in 1930 to whom he became very attached, and although the young man married, he and Forster remained close friends and Forster grew to be fond of the wife, May. He died in their home at Coventry on 7 June 1970.

He refused a knighthood offered by Clement ATTLEE, but in 1953 he became CH and on his ninetieth birthday was admitted to the Order of Merit. His books were translated into twenty-one languages. He once said that he was not a great novelist, but since his death this has been belied by critics and the reading public alike.

FOWLER, HENRY WATSON (1858–1933), author of *Modern English Usage*, was born on 10 March 1858 at Tonbridge, Kent, the eldest son of the Revd Robert Fowler, Fellow of Christ's College, Cambridge, and a schoolmaster, and his wife, Caroline, daughter of Humphry Watson, a tenant farmer. He was educated at Rugby, and Balliol College, Oxford, where he was a scholar, but failed to get a first in either Mods. or Greats (1881).

For seventeen years (1882–99), he was a master at Sedbergh, and resigned when the headmaster, H. G. Hart, insisted that he should prepare boys for confirmation despite the fact that Fowler, who was not a professing Christian, could not do so conscientiously. As he had inherited a small legacy, he was able to make a fresh start in London; he read voraciously, and wrote literary essays, which helped to eke out his small income. Throughout his life he always lived simply, and did not require large earnings.

In 1903 he went to live in Guernsey, with his brother, Francis George Fowler (1870–1918), scholar of Peterhouse, Cambridge, and together they produced a translation of Lucian (4 vols., 1905), published by the Oxford University Press. 'Who are the Fowlers?' the *New York Times* asked. The Press found some difficulty in deciding what the brothers' next book should be called, but eventually the title agreed upon was *The King's English*; published in 1906, it was intended to be a guide to correct English, and did not hesitate to criticize the language used not only by Marie Corelli, but also by George Borrow and Dickens. The two brothers were next commissioned by the Press to produce *The Concise Oxford Dictionary* which appeared in 1911.

In 1908 Henry married Jessie Marian, daughter of Richard Sydenham Wills, a nursing sister. Then came the First World War. Henry enlisted at the age of fifty-six, having subtracted thirteen years from his age and deceived the authorities by his physical fitness; Frank followed his example. But neither could fool the authorities for long, and neither of them reached the front line. Henry's letters to his wife, telling of their experiences, are preserved in the library of St John's College, Cambridge. Frank died in 1918 of tuberculosis.

The Pocket Oxford Dictionary was published in 1924, having on its title page the names of both brothers. By then Henry was at work on the book which was published in 1926 as *Modern English Usage*; it was reprinted four times in that year, and 50,000 copies were issued for the market in the USA. In his preface to the second edition, Sir Ernest GOWERS wrote 'This was indeed an epoch-making book in the strict sense of that overworked phrase. It made the name of Fowler a household word in all English-speaking countries.' In spite of many changes in our language since the book was published it has held its place unchallenged as a guide to modern usage.

Henry Fowler continued to work as a lexicographer for the Oxford University Press, helped by another brother, A. J. Fowler, and Colonel Le Mesurier, but the death of his wife in 1930 was a grievous loss; his physical health deteriorated, his eyesight was seriously impaired, and on 26 December 1933 he died at Hinton St George, Somerset, where he and his wife had settled in 1925.

FOYLE, WILLIAM ALFRED (1885–1963), bookseller, was born on 4 March 1885 in Shoreditch, London, the seventh child of a seventh child of a seventh child, and his daughter Christina says that 'to this he attributed his remarkable visionary and intuitive gifts'. He was the son of William Henry Foyle, a wholesale grocer, and his wife, Deborah Barnett. He was educated at Dame Alice Owen's School, Islington. Having failed the entrance examination for the Civil Service, he became a clerk to Edward MARSHALL HALL, KC, in 1902.

Foyle's interest was in books and he started trading as a bookseller in 1903 by opening a second-hand bookshop in Islington with his brother Gilbert. He bought books wherever he could and, in one shop he visited, he met Christina, daughter of William Tulloch, and Helen Gifford. Christina became his partner and his wife in 1907.

Foyle was an earnest searcher after unusual or rare books and would take much trouble to track down what a customer wanted. His reputation grew, and in 1907 he took larger premises in the Charing Cross Road, where he stocked books on every subject. Foyles became a mecca for book-lovers. In 1912 he began to trade in new books and a further extension had to be made to the premises.

Foyle had many Bohemian friends with whom he started the First Edition Club. He introduced Foyles literary lectures at which the SITWELLS, CONAN DOYLE, Walter DE LA MARE, and other famous authors could be heard. He also began the Book Club in 1937.

Before he died Foyle had gone far to achieve his ambition of being the biggest bookseller in the world. He had foreseen that the demand for books would increase considerably as education became more extensive, and when this happened after the Second World War, he was prepared to take advantage of it. He himself had a passion for collecting rare books and formed a great library at his home, the Abbey of Beeleigh, Maldon, Essex.

He died there on 4 July 1963, and his work was carried on by one of his two daughters, Christina, who had understudied her father and was ready to step into his shoes. As a director of the business she introduced the literary luncheons which made her name.

FRANCIS-WILLIAMS, BARON (1903-1970). See WILLIAMS, EDWARD FRANCIS.

FRASER, HUGH, first BARON FRASER OF ALLANDER (1903-1966), draper, company chairman, and philanthropist, was born in Glasgow on 15 January 1903, the only son of Hugh Fraser, a drapery warehouseman, and his wife, Emily Florence McGown. He was educated at Glasgow Academy and Warriston School, Moffat. He left school at sixteen and entered his father's drapery business; he learnt the business from the bottom with such success that his father made him Managing Director in 1924 when he was only twenty-one.

In 1931 he married Kate Hutcheon, daughter of Sir Andrew Jopp Williams Lewis, shipbuilder; they had a daughter, and a son.

Fraser had become Chairman of the business on the death of his father in 1927. His ability and integrity enabled him to borrow funds for expansion, and in 1936 he acquired other stores in Glasgow. After the Second World War he was able to float the House of Fraser Ltd. as a public company (1948). His success was due to his thorough knowledge of the drapery business and his use of a device for raising capital by selling the freeholds of his shops and obtaining leases of the property on reasonable terms.

In 1957 he acquired the John Barker group in London, and in 1959, after keen competition, took over Harrods. But, although he had extensive interests in England, Fraser's headquarters remained in Glasgow. In 1964 he acquired the *Glasgow Herald* to ensure that its control should continue to be centred in Glasgow. He also set out to expand the tourist industry in the Scottish Highlands by creating the facilities for skiing and other sports at Aviemore. In 1960 he created, in memory of his mother, the Hugh Fraser Foun-

Hugh Fraser and son, outside Harrods after the acquisition of the store, 1959

dation, and gave power to the Trustees to make charitable payments at their sole discretion whether in Scotland or elsewhere. He was an honorary LL D of St Andrews (1962), was created baronet in 1961, and baron in 1964. Hugh Fraser died at his home near Glasgow on 6 November 1966. His son Hugh, who disclaimed the barony, succeeded him as Chairman of the House of Fraser.

FRAZER, SIR JAMES GEORGE (1854-1941), social anthropologist, was born at Glasgow on 1 January 1854, the elder son of Daniel F. Frazer, partner in a firm of chemists, and his wife, Katherine, daughter of John Brown, merchant. He was educated at Glasgow University and Trinity College, Cambridge, of which he was a scholar, and where he obtained a first in the classical tripos in 1878 and became a Fellow in 1879. In 1882 he was called to the Bar (Middle Temple), but never practised. In 1896 he married Elisabeth (Lilly) Johanna, widow of Charles Baylee Groves, master mariner, and daughter of Sigismund Adelsdorfer, merchant; they had no children. Lady Frazer wrote books on the teaching of French and contributed the volume on *Dancing* to the Badminton Library.

Frazer's interest in anthropology was aroused by reading *Primitive Culture* by (Sir) E. B. Tylor (1871), and *Lectures on the Religion of the Semites* by William Robertson Smith (1889); these books led him to the study of undeveloped races and their customs and religions. In 1888 he contributed articles on 'Taboo' and 'Totemism' to the *Encyclopaedia Britannica* (9th edition). As an anthropologist Frazer collected and classified phenomena from all parts of the world, and worked out, by deduction, a continuous development in human institutions based on the concept of survival as a link between the successive stages of magic, religion, and science. Later anthropologists have found his theories less reliable than his facts.

His great work *The Golden Bough* first appeared in 1890 with succeeding editions in 1900 and 1915 but, as his studies widened and his accumulation of facts became overwhelming, Frazer decided to publish his findings in separate volumes. He began these with *The Magic Art* and *Taboo and the Perils of the Soul* (1911) and concluded them with *The Scapegoat* and *Balder the Beautiful* (1913), published under the general title of *The Golden Bough* to which he added in 1936 a supplement, *Aftermath*.

Frazer was Professor of Social Anthropology at Liverpool from 1907 to 1922, but he could not settle to the duties of the post, and eventually returned to Trinity College, Cambridge to resume the production of his numerous books. Among these are *Psyche's Task* (1909), reissued as *The Devil's Advocate* (1928), *Totemism and Exogamy* (4 vols., 1910), *The Worship of Nature* (1926), and *The Fear of the Dead in Primitive Religion* (3 vols., 1933–6).

He did not confine his work to anthropology. He produced an edition of Pausanias's *Description of Greece* (1898), and of the *Fasti* of Ovid (1929); he also published an edition of *The Letters of William Cowper* (1912) and *The Gorgon's Head* (1927).

Frazer was a recluse who hated the limelight, but in 1914 he was knighted and in 1925 appointed to the Order of Merit. Honorary degrees and other academic honours were bestowed upon him by many institutions and colleges. He was elected FBA in 1902 and FRS in 1920. He died at Cambridge on 7 May 1941 and Lady Frazer died a few hours later.

FRENCH, JOHN DENTON PINKSTONE, first EARL OF YPRES (1852–1925), field-marshal, was born on 28 September 1852 at Ripple, Kent, the only son of Commander John Tracy William French, RN, and his wife, Margaret, daughter of William Eccles of Glasgow. Both parents died when he was a child and he was brought up by his sisters. He was educated at Eastman's Naval Academy, Portsmouth, and entered the training ship *Britannia* in 1866. But French wanted a military career: in 1870 he joined the Suffolk Artillery Militia and four years later was transferred to the 19th Hussars.

In 1880 French married Eleanora, daughter of Richard William Selby-Lowndes, of Elmers, Bletchley, Bucks.; they had two sons and one daughter.

His career in the army followed the normal pattern until 1884, when he saw service with the column under Sir Herbert Stewart, sent in vain to relieve General Gordon in Khartoum. In 1888 he was appointed to command the 19th Hussars, and for a short time served in India. In 1893 he was placed on half pay and his career appeared to have come to a dead end, but Sir Redvers Buller, having in mind French's work in the Sudan, gave him an appointment in the War Office where he produced a new *Cavalry Manual*.

The outbreak of the Boer War gave French a new opportunity for active service. In 1899 he was sent to command the cavalry under Sir George Stuart White in Natal and then in the Cape Colony which he virtually cleared of Boer invaders. Under the command of Lord Roberts, French relieved Kimberley and secured the surrender of the Boers at Paardeberg. Before the war ended, he was promoted to major-general and created KCB; he spent two further years in South Africa and, on his return to England in 1902, became a lieutenant-general and KCMG.

From 1902 to 1907 French was Commander-in-Chief, Aldershot. He was then promoted general and created GCVO, and appointed Inspector-General of the Forces. In 1912 he succeeded Field-Marshal Lord Nicholson as Chief of the Imperial General Staff, and in the following year was promoted to field-marshal. He was one of the signatories of the document drawn up by the War Office assuring the officers at the Curragh that they would not be employed against Ulster, and when the Cabinet repudiated this undertaking, he resigned.

None the less, when the First World War broke out French was appointed Commander-in-Chief of the British Expeditionary Force sent to France. Under instructions from Lord KITCHENER he was to go to Maubeuge to link up with the French armies opposing the German advance through Belgium. French, like the troops that made up the BEF, was fully competent to fight in conditions such as had been encountered in South Africa, but he and his armies were ill-equipped for the kind of trench warfare in which they soon found themselves involved. Reaching Maubeuge on 20 August they were able to push on to Mons, where they were faced with powerful German forces and had to beat a hasty retreat, marching 200 miles in 13 days. French was appalled at the losses he had suffered and decided to pull out of the line to refit, but Kitchener ordered him to stand and fight with the French under Joffre. For a time the Germans retreated, but on the Aisne they dug in, the Anglo-French forces were brought to a halt and trench warfare began in earnest.

The BEF was then transferred to Flanders. In November, when the first Battle of Ypres took place, the casualties were enormous; in the three months since the BEF landed in France more than half of French's command had become casualties. A line of trenches ran from the Swiss border to the sea and the war had reached deadlock.

In the following spring (1915), French was involved in further heavy fighting and consequent heavy losses, and the battles raged throughout the summer, up to the Battle of Loos in September, without any success having been achieved. French himself was under great strain, and the authorities in England were becoming more and more concerned at the course the war was taking. Excuses can be made for him: he had never been provided with the shells and equipment essential for such a campaign, but the fact remains that French was not, either by temperament or by experience, equal to such a struggle. On 4 December 1915 he resigned, and was succeeded by Sir Douglas HAIG. He had received the Order of Merit in 1914; in 1916 he was created Viscount French of Ypres and appointed Commander-in-Chief, Home Forces.

At Easter 1916 the Irish rebellion took place in Dublin, and French dispatched two divisions to suppress the rising. In May 1918 he was appointed Lord-Lieutenant of Ireland, where during the next two years conditions went from bad to worse, outrages and reprisals becoming widespread. In December 1919 an attempt was made to assassinate him; it was unsuccessful, but French felt himself helpless to impose law and order. After the passage of the Government of Ireland Act in 1921, he resigned and retired into private life. In 1922 he was created Earl of Ypres. He died three years later on 22 May 1925 at Deal, Kent.

FRY, CHARLES BURGESS (1872–1956), sportsman, was born at Croydon on 25 April 1872, the eldest child of Lewis John Fry, a civil servant, and his wife, Constance Isabella White. He went to Repton as an exhibitioner in 1885 and quickly made his mark as an all-round athlete, captaining the football and cricket elevens, and twice winning the individual prize for athletics. Entering Wadham College, Oxford as a scholar in 1890, he was placed senior to F. E. SMITH (later Earl of Birkenhead) and became a triple blue at association football, cricket and athletics, and gained an international cap for England at football.

In 1898 he married Beatrice Holme, daughter of Arthur Sumner; they had one son and two daughters.

After Oxford, he played football for years for the

Corinthian team and won another international cap in 1901. A year later he achieved the remarkable feat of playing for Southampton in the FA cup final on a Saturday and scoring 82 runs against Surrey on the following Monday. He first played cricket for Sussex in 1894, and in 1899 opened the innings for England against the Australians at Nottingham. In 1912 he was Captain of the England test side, having in the meantime moved from Sussex to Hampshire in 1909. Ranjitsinhji, another great batsman, thought that C. B. Fry was the greatest batsman of his time on any type of wicket.

For a few years (1896–8) he was a master at Charterhouse, but he found that he had a flair for sporting journalism and that this gave him greater leisure to play cricket. Apart from being Athletics Editor of the *Captain*, a boys' monthly magazine, and Editor and Director of *Fry's Magazine*, he also wrote *Great Batsmen* (with George W. Beldam, 1905), *Great Bowlers and Fielders* (with George W. Beldam, 1906), and *Batsmanship* (1912).

From 1908 to 1950 Fry was Director of the training ship *Mercury* and helped to turn out generations of boys destined for the Royal and Merchant Navies; for this service he was made an honorary Captain of the Royal Naval Reserve. He published his autobiography *Life Worth Living* in 1939. Fry died in London on 7 September 1956.

FRY, ROGER ELIOT (1866–1934), art critic and artist, was born at Highgate on 14 December 1866, the younger son of (Sir) Edward Fry, judge, and his wife, Mariabella, daughter of John Hodgkin, barrister. Both parents were Quakers. Margery FRY was his sister. He was educated at Clifton, and King's College, Cambridge, where he obtained firsts in both parts of the natural sciences tripos, and was a member of the 'Apostles' (1887–8). He became an intimate friend of the Stephen sisters, Virginia (WOOLF) and Vanessa (BELL), and other members of what became known as the Bloomsbury group. J. H. Middleton, Slade Professor of Fine Art, encouraged his interest in art, but Fry's father was anxious that he should follow a scientific career.

In 1891, Fry gave up biology and went to Italy. For a short time he studied at the Académie Julian in Paris, but his interest in Italian Renaissance art made it difficult for him to paint in the modern 'idiom' and his paintings were rejected by the New English Art Club. In 1894 he again visited Italy and studied the history of art. During the next two years he lectured in the subject and became recognized as the most exciting lecturer of his time. In 1896 he married Helen, daughter of Joseph Coombe; they had a son and a daughter, but she became permanently insane.

In 1901 Fry was appointed art critic of the *Athenaeum*, and for some years was engaged on ephemeral writing until, in 1905, he produced his erudite edition of Sir Joshua Reynolds's *Discourses*. He had now established his reputation as a scholar and expert, and he took an active part in the establishment of the *Burlington Magazine* and the foundation of the National Art Collections Fund in 1903. In 1904 he stood for the Slade professorship at Cambridge but was rejected. He was invited by John Pierpont Morgan, whom he had advised as a collector, to become Director of the Metropolitan Museum of Art in New York. Fry hoped to become Director of the National Gallery, but in 1905 he accepted the post in New York, and then was offered the post in London when it was too late. He stayed at the Metropolitan until 1910.

At this time Fry was regarded as an expert on the painting of the old masters, but with little interest in modern painting.

The situation changed when in 1906 he saw the work of Cézanne for the first time, and began to be absorbed in similar artists such as Gauguin, Van Gogh, and Matisse. In November 1910 he organized the first exhibition of the Post-Impressionists at the Grafton Galleries. He was abused for his pains, but from then onwards he ceased to be an expert on the old masters and became the exponent of modern art, and an important influence on young artists such as Vanessa Bell and Duncan Grant.

In 1910 he applied for the Slade chair at Oxford, but was unsuccessful. He had for some time been impressed by the need to re-introduce art into daily life, and in 1913 he founded the Omega workshops for the manufacture of well-designed articles; chairs, tables, pottery, and other goods for household use were designed by young artists who brought into interior decoration a new boldness of colour and style. As he developed his affection for the moderns Fry's own painting was more successful; he contributed regularly to the London Group of which he was a founder.

In 1920 his articles in the *Burlington Magazine* were published as *Vision and Design*, and another collection appeared in 1926 as *Transformations*; in 1927 he published *Cézanne* and in 1930 *Henri Matisse*. In 1927 he applied again for the Slade professorship at Oxford. One Oxford don thought that Fry was an obvious candidate, an inspiring lecturer, who had done more than anyone in the country to make known French painting of the Impressionist and Post-Impressionist periods. He was rejected by the electors, 'not, as some of them pretended, because his views on art were unsound, but because he was said to be living with a woman not his wife' (*Memories: 1898–1939* by C. M. BOWRA).

However, Cambridge was more tolerant, and in 1933 Fry became Slade Professor there. He died in London on 9 September 1934 before he could complete his planned course of lectures on *Art-History as an Academic Study*. His biography, written by Virginia Woolf, was published in 1940.

FRY, (SARA) MARGERY (1874–1958), social worker and Principal of Somerville College, Oxford, was the sixth daughter of (Sir) Edward Fry, and his wife, Mariabella, and the sister of Roger FRY. She was born at Highgate on 11 March 1874. She was educated at home until she was seventeen, and then for a year went to the school at Brighton that later became Roedean. Encouraged by Roger, she wished to go to Newnham College, Cambridge, but her Quaker parents objected, and it was not until 1894 that she entered Somerville College, Oxford, to read mathematics. There she met Eleanor RATHBONE, who became a lifelong friend.

From 1899 to 1904 she was Librarian of Somerville, and became concerned with young people and their problems. In 1904 she accepted the post of Warden of a hall of residence for women students at Birmingham University. She remained there until 1914, engaged in a wide range of social projects. Then during the First World War she worked in France with her sister, Ruth, with the Friends' War Victims Relief Committee.

When the war ended she lived in London with Roger Fry and his children, and came to know his artist friends. From 1919 to 1948 she was a member of the University Grants Committee, and from 1919 to 1926 Secretary of the Penal Reform League (from 1921 the Howard League). In 1921 she became one of the first women magistrates, and in 1922 the first educational adviser to Holloway prison.

In 1926 she succeeded (Dame) Emily Penrose as Principal of Somerville College. There she enjoyed fresh opportunities for contacts with young people but, despite all her charm and persuasiveness, she failed to prevent Congregation from restricting the number of women to be in residence at the university (1927).

She was deeply involved in the campaign for the abolition of capital punishment and, when she retired from Somerville in 1931 and resettled in London, she became increasingly occupied with the international aspects of penal reform. She was now known abroad for her work in this field, and lectured in China, the USA, and other countries on the subject.

During the thirties she discovered that she enjoyed broadcasting and was good at it. She took part in 'Any Questions?', and in 1942 became a member of the 'Brains Trust'. She was also a Governor of the BBC. Her books include *The Future Treatment of the Adult Offender* (1944) and *Arms of the Law* (1951).

For the rest of her life she continued to be deeply interested in all aspects of crime and punishment, and anxious to alleviate the misery of poverty, hardship, and old age. She never married. She died in London on 21 April 1958.

G

GAITSKELL, HUGH TODD NAYLOR (1906–1963), politician, was born in Kensington on 9 April 1906, the younger son of Arthur Gaitskell, of the Indian Civil Service, and his wife, Adelaide Mary, daughter of George Jamieson, who had been Consul-General in Shanghai. He was educated at Winchester and New College, Oxford, where he obtained a first in philosophy, politics, and economics in 1927. As a young man at Oxford, Gaitskell had a wide circle of friends and was completely lacking in class-consciousness. His rad-

ical views led him naturally to the Labour party. During the general strike of 1926, when most undergraduates were volunteering as bus drivers and special constables, Gaitskell was helping the strikers.

On leaving Oxford, he went to Nottingham as tutor in charge of extra-mural classes, but in 1928 moved to London as a lecturer in political economy at University College, where in 1938 he became head of the department. In the previous year he had married Anna Dora, daughter of Leon

Hugh Gaitskell canvassing in his Leeds constituency, October 1959

Creditor; they had two daughters. During the Second World War he served in the Ministry of Economic Warfare and at the Board of Trade, and proved his administrative ability. He was appointed CBE in 1945.

In that year he became Labour MP for South Leeds, a seat which he held until his death in 1963. In 1946 he became Parliamentary Secretary at the Ministry of Fuel and Power, taking over as Minister in 1947 when he was sworn of the Privy Council. Then in 1950 he joined the Treasury as Minister of State for Economic Affairs and, during the illness of Sir Stafford CRIPPS, prepared the measures necessary for devaluation of sterling. When Cripps had to resign, Gaitskell was appointed to succeed him as Chancellor of the Exchequer.

It was at this point in his career that he came into conflict with Aneurin BEVAN. Baroness Lee (Bevan's wife) has written that the gap between them was unbridgeable. They had grown up in different worlds and from their political experiences they drew very different conclusions. Gaitskell was convinced that socialism was about social justice, and completely rejected the idea that socialism was synonymous with nationalization. He was a pragmatist, in favour of rearmament in alliance with the United States. Bevan, who had been an unemployed miner when Gaitskell was at Oxford, opposed him on both counts. Gaitskell regarded the struggle between them as 'a fight for the soul of the Labour party'.

Their rivalry came to a head when Gaitskell insisted on the levy of health service charges, and Bevan, disillusioned with the trade unions and his inability to persuade his colleagues to accept his left-wing views, resigned from his post of Minister of Labour (1951). In 1954 and 1955 Gaitskell defeated Bevan for the treasurership of the party, and in December 1955, when Clement ATTLEE resigned, Gaitskell was elected leader of the Labour party, after a three-cornered contest with Bevan and Herbert MORRISON.

He patched up his differences with Bevan who became deputy leader and Shadow Foreign Secretary. In 1959 they visited Russia together. In that year Gaitskell hoped to become Prime Minister, but the Labour party was defeated at the general election. During the next few years Gaitskell was engaged in a bitter struggle within his party, first on the subject of nationalization and then on unilateral disarmament. Differences within the party led to bitter recriminations and, more than once, Gaitskell's leadership was in jeopardy. But he survived, and in 1962 led the party to oppose British entry into the EEC. It now seemed certain that he would be the next Prime Minister, but he died suddenly in London on 18 January 1963. His wife was created a life peeress within a year of his death.

Bevan once described him as a desiccated calculating machine, and certainly in his speeches his appeal was to reason rather than emotion, but he was a man of deep convictions who was prepared, as he once said, 'to fight, fight, and fight again' for what he believed in. His own attitude is revealed in his diary for the years 1945-56 published in 1983, edited by Philip M. Williams.

GALLACHER, WILLIAM (1881-1965), agitator and politician, was born in Paisley on 25 December 1881, the fourth of seven children of an Irish labourer, John Gallacher, and his Scottish wife, Mary Sutherland. His father died when he was seven. When he was nine he refused to go to a Catholic school any longer; at ten he did a milk round before going to board school, and at twelve left school to become a grocer's delivery boy. When he was fourteen, he was apprenticed as a brass-finisher and later became an engineer, but from 1909 to 1910 he was a ship's steward. In 1913 he married Jean Miller, daughter of John Roy; they had two sons who died at birth.

In 1906 he had joined the Social Democratic Federation, and up to 1914 was active in organizing the shop stewards' movement in Scotland. During the First World War he was Chairman of the Clyde Workers' Committee and took an important part in the anti-war campaign, organizing strikes. In 1916 he was sentenced to a year's imprisonment for sedition, and in 1919 to three months for rioting.

He welcomed the Russian revolution of 1917 and became an active supporter of the Soviet Union. Up to 1920 he was a firm believer in 'direct action' to overthrow the capitalist system and did not hope for any progress through parliamentary legislation. In 1919 he published, with J. R. Campbell, *Direct Action* but, when a year later he visited Moscow for a congress of the Communist International, he met Lenin who persuaded him that his attitude was mistaken. Thereupon he changed his views and helped to found the British Communist Party. He served three months in prison in 1921 for sedition, and in 1925 was sentenced to twelve months for 'seditious libel'. He was in prison at the time of the general strike.

He contested Dundee in 1922 and 1923 and West Fife in 1929 and 1931 unsuccessfully, but in 1935 was elected Communist MP for West Fife and held the seat for fifteen years. In Parliament he was very active in support of Communism and the Soviet Union. He protested in a speech in the Commons when the House congratulated Neville CHAMBERLAIN on his achievement at Munich in 1938.

During the Second World War, both of his adopted sons, who were in fact nephews, were killed while serving with the armed forces.

He lost his seat in the 1950 general election but continued to be Chairman of the Communist party, a post to which he had been elected in 1943; in 1956 he became its President. He wrote four books of memoirs, *Revolt on the Clyde* (1936 and 1949), *The Rolling of the Thunder* (1947), *Rise like Lions* (1951), and *Last Memoirs* (1966). He also wrote a number of pamphlets and articles including *The Case for Communism* (1949). He was a man of selfless devotion to the principles in which he believed and of complete integrity.

Gallacher died in Paisley on 12 August 1965.

GALSWORTHY, JOHN (1867-1933), novelist and playwright, was born at Kingston Hill, Surrey on 14 August 1867, the elder son of John Galsworthy, solicitor, and chairman and director of several companies, and his wife, Blanche Bailey, daughter of Charles Bartleet, needlemakers of Redditch. He was educated at Harrow and New College, Oxford. He was called to the Bar (Lincoln's Inn) in 1890 and took up marine law. For experience he travelled in merchant ships to the Far East and, on a voyage in 1893, met Joseph CONRAD who became his friend for life.

From 1897 until 1904 Galsworthy wrote stories and novels under the pseudonym John Sinjohn, but in the latter year he published *The Island Pharisees* under his own name. As in his later better-known novels, this was critical of the upper-class British. It was followed in 1906 by *The Man of Property*, the first of the *Forsyte Saga* sequence. This novel is the story of Irene, wife of Soames Forsyte, who leaves her wealthy, conventional husband for Bosinney, an impecunious young architect employed by Soames, with whom she falls recklessly in love. In the end Bosinney is killed, but Soames never forgives his wife.

The character of Irene is modelled on that of Ada Pearson, adopted daughter of Emanuel Cooper, MD, of Norwich, an eccentric doctor; her mother was Anna Julia Pearson. Ada was the wife of Galsworthy's cousin Arthur John Galsworthy and for some ten years Galsworthy had been living secretly with her. He was anxious that *Man of Property* should not be published until they could marry. When Ada's husband divorced her in 1905, they were able to marry and the novel was published shortly afterwards.

The Man of Property established Galsworthy as a novelist comparable with his contemporaries, E. M. FORSTER and Joseph Conrad; and the other novels making up the *Saga*, which appeared from 1918 to 1921, were equally successful. They were followed in 1924 by *The White Monkey* and two other novels, republished as a trilogy *A Modern Comedy* in 1929. In these Galsworthy related the problems which confronted Fleur, Soames' daughter by his second wife, who fell in love with Jon, Irene's son by her second husband; however, this part of the story is set in a post-war society in which a younger generation has become more tolerant than the generation to which Soames Forsyte belonged.

Galsworthy was not only a successful novelist, whose work gradually deteriorated as his success became more marked; he was also a competent playwright, whose straightforward, unsubtle works, such as *The Silver Box* (1906), *Justice* (1910), and *The Skin Game* (1920), were acclaimed when they were produced on the London stage, and as propaganda were instrumental in bringing about some social reforms.

In his later years Galsworthy became the respectable, conventional Englishman of the type he had described with little sympathy in his earlier books and plays. He became the first President of the PEN club and was President of the English Association in 1924. His *Collected Plays* appeared in 1929, by which time his work was successful in Europe as well as in England.

He refused a knighthood in 1918, but he accepted a number of honorary doctorates; he was appointed to the Order of Merit in 1929, and awarded the Nobel prize for literature in 1932. He and Ada had no children. He died at Hampstead on 31 January 1933. His *Collected Poems* were published in 1934. More than thirty years after his death *The Forsyte Saga* was screened as a successful television series.

GANDHI, MOHANDAS KARAMCHAND (1869–1948),

Indian political leader and social reformer, was born in Porbandar on 2 October 1869, the third son by his fourth wife of Karamchand Uttamchand Gandhi, chief minister in Porbandar. His family belonged to the sub-caste of banias or merchants. His mother tongue was Gujerati. He was married according to custom at the age of thirteen to Kasturbai, daughter of a Porbandar merchant. At the age of nineteen he went to England to study law. He was called to the Bar (Inner Temple) in 1891. In England he tried to conform to English standards and ways, but soon gave this up for a life of extreme frugality. He studied religious books including the *Bhagavad Gita* and the New Testament.

Returning to India, he appeared to have little aptitude for legal practice, and in 1893 accepted a post as legal adviser to an Indian firm in Natal. There, coming into contact for the first time with acute racialism, he became the champion of his countrymen's rights, and his legal practice prospered. In the Boer War he formed an ambulance unit to serve with the British forces and received a war medal. He received another medal for similar service in the Zulu War (1906).

During this campaign, his custom of self-discipline, now habitual, led him to take a vow of complete sexual abstinence. His first child had died at birth, but he had four other sons. His experiences in South Africa led him to evolve the technique of passive resistance or 'Satyagraha' (truth-force) as a weapon against oppression. Its efficacy was demonstrated by the agreement of General SMUTS to a compromise over the legislation restricting the rights of Indians.

In 1914, Gandhi was in England, and raised an Indian ambulance unit. On return to India he received the Kaisar-i-Hind gold medal. With the end of the First World War, Indian nationalism increased in force and Gandhi took an active part in the work of Congress. He was most concerned with social reform but had come to believe that this was not possible under an alien government. When the Government of India took new security powers against disorder, Gandhi called a *hartal*, a general strike with prayer and fasting, and inaugurated a policy of non-co-operation with the authorities. This led directly to violence, including conflict between Hindus and Muslims. Gandhi was arrested and sentenced to six years imprisonment, but was released after two years on grounds of ill health (1922–4).

For a time he abandoned civil disobedience and concentrated on his crusade for social reform, advocating Hindu-Muslim unity, the abolition of untouchability, and the adoption of hand spinning in the villages. He also adopted the white loin-cloth, white shawl, and sandals with which he would become associated, not only in India but in the West also. He was now known throughout India as the Mahatma—the great soul.

In 1924 he undertook his first fast unto death as a means of bringing pressure—in this instance pressure for Hindu-Muslim unity. For a brief period it seemed that Hindu-Muslim differences might be ameliorated.

In 1928 the SIMON Commission visited India, and in 1929 the Viceroy, Lord IRWIN, announced dominion status for India. Congress wanted independence, and civil disobedience was resumed. Gandhi emerged again and defied the Government by publicly manufacturing salt which was against the excise laws. He was imprisoned again, but released in 1931 to go to England to attend the second Round Table conference. The discussions were abortive, and Gandhi returned to India and undertook further fasting and underwent more imprisonment, until he was released when his life was in danger.

When in 1937 Congress accepted office under the new constitution, Gandhi was busy with his campaign on behalf of the untouchable caste. He was in poor health, and did not realize the extent of the rift developing between Congress and the Muslim League. During the Second World War he adopted a pacifist posture, took part in further civil disobedience moves which led to riots, was again imprisoned, and again released after fasting.

He tried to reach agreement with M. A. Jinnah, the leader of the Muslim League, for the solution of the Hindu-Muslim problem, but Jinnah was determined upon the partition of India and, in spite of his enormous influence in the country, Gandhi could not prevent what he regarded as an unmitigated evil. When deadlock was reached in 1947 the Viceroy, Earl MOUNTBATTEN, announced the acceptance of partition by the British Government. Congress would rule India and the Muslim League Pakistan. When India became independent in 1947, Gandhi undertook new and prolonged fasts to obtain communal harmony. He was unsuccessful. The two communities in India and Pakistan were now at each others' throats and thousands were being massacred in both countries. Gandhi's efforts to preserve peace merely aroused the hostility of militant Hindus who blamed him for partition and on 30 January 1948 he was shot dead by one of them as he was leading people to prayer in Delhi.

Historians will for a long time to come have divergent views on this enigmatic figure who to a multitude of Indians was a saint and to others merely a consummate politician. Few, however, will deny that he had a leading part in changing the course of Indian history. In 1982 Sir Richard Attenborough directed an award-winning film of the Gandhi epic.

GARRETT ANDERSON, ELIZABETH (1836-1917), physician, was born in London on 9 June 1836, the second daughter among the seven children of an Aldeburgh merchant, Newson Garrett and his wife, Louisa Dunnell. One of her younger sisters became well known as Millicent FAW-CETT. She was educated at a school in Blackheath. From an early age she was determined to train as a medical practitioner but it was not until 1865 that, having managed to secure the necessary training, she forced the Society of Apothecaries to allow her to take their examinations and she was granted their licence to practise.

In the following year she opened a dispensary in Marylebone for women and children, which was soon converted

Elizabeth Garrett Anderson, the first woman member of the BMA

into a hospital, the New Hospital for Women, later renamed the Elizabeth Garrett Anderson Hospital — she had married James George Skelton Anderson of the Orient Steamship line in 1871.

In 1873 she became the first woman to be elected to the BMA. Her pioneering work in improving the status of women at last began to bear fruit. In 1874 the London School of Medicine for Women was founded by Dr Sophia Louisa Jex-Blake. Elizabeth Garrett Anderson lectured there on medicine from 1875-97 and was Dean from 1883-1903. She was also senior physician at the New Hospital for Women from 1866-92.

She and her husband had a son, Sir Alan Garrett Anderson, KBE, and a daughter, Dr Louisa Garrett Anderson, who organized the first hospital managed by women at the front during the First World War. Elizabeth Garrett Anderson died at Aldeburgh on 17 December 1917.

GARROD, HEATHCOTE WILLIAM (1878-1960), scholar, was born at Wells on 21 January 1878, the fifth of six children of Charles William Garrod, a solicitor, and his wife, Louisa Ashby. He was educated at Bath College and Balliol College, Oxford, where he gained firsts in Mods. and Greats (1899-1900), and won the Hertford and Craven scholarships, the Gaisford and Newdigate prizes, and was elected to a prize fellowship at Merton College.

He was elected to a tutorial fellowship in 1904 and, with a few short breaks, lived in Merton until he died. Up to 1922 he was concerned with classical scholarship. He published an edition of Statius (1906) and of the second book of Manilius' *Astronomicon* (1911) and the *Oxford Book of Latin Verse* (1912).

His work on Manilius was severely criticized by A. E. HOUSMAN, probably the greatest Latinist of his generation but an acerbic critic of other classical scholars. The *Oxford Book of Latin Verse* was widely acclaimed, however, as was Garrod's edition of the *Letters of Erasmus* (completing the work of P. S. Allen in collaboration with Allen's widow 1938-47).

During the First World War Garrod was a civil servant who showed exceptional ability in the Ministry of Munitions (1915-18), and towards the end of the war in the Ministry of Reconstruction. He was appointed CBE (1918).

In 1925 he resigned his tutorship for a research fellowship in English, and from 1923 to 1928 was Professor of Poetry. His chief contribution to English scholarship came with the publication in 1939 of his edition of Keats in the Oxford English Texts (second edition, 1958), but he also published *Wordsworth: Lectures and Essays* (1923), *The Profession of Poetry* (1929), and *Poetry and the Criticism of Life* (1931). In his lecture on A. E. Housman, included in *The Profession of Poetry*, he retaliated for the Cambridge don's criticism of his Manilius by describing scornfully 'the false pastoralism' of *A Shropshire Lad*.

Garrod himself wrote poetry and published *Oxford Poems* (1912), *Poems from the French* (1925), and *Epigrams* (1946). He lived the life of an unmarried Oxford don for more than fifty years; at Merton College he was the presiding genius, the friend of dons and undergraduates alike; in Oxford he was a character, well known for his frequent visits to Blackwell's bookshop and for walking his dogs in the meadows. In the *DNB* he is described as 'one of those rich, uncommon personalities who have added an imperishable part to the Oxford heritage'. He received honorary degrees from Durham and Edinburgh. He was elected FBA in 1931, and an honorary

Fellow of Merton in 1955. He died in Oxford on 25 December 1960.

GARVIN, JAMES LOUIS (1868–1947), editor of the *Observer*, was born at Birkenhead on 12 April 1868, the younger son of an Irish immigrant, Michael Garvin, and his wife, Catherine Fahy. His father died when he was two. He left school at twelve and worked as a clerk in Newcastle upon Tyne. He taught himself French, German, and Spanish, and began writing for newspapers, advocating Irish Home Rule and defending Parnell.

In 1891 he was contributing regularly to *United Ireland*, and later that year joined the *Newcastle Chronicle*, first as a proof-reader, and then as a journalist. He began contributing to the *Fortnightly Review* in 1895 and, up to the First World War as 'Calchas' in that paper, he advocated military preparedness for possible war with Germany and supported Joseph Chamberlain's campaign for tariff reform.

In 1908 Lord NORTHCLIFFE appointed him Editor and Manager with a fifth share of the *Observer*, and in two years Garvin made the paper profitable and an important supporter of the Tory party. He opposed the LLOYD GEORGE budget

J. L. Garvin, *Vanity Fair* cartoon by Alick P. F. Ritchie; the correspondence in the wastepaper basket carries the initials of A. J. Balfour

of 1909 and urged the Lords to reject the Parliament Bill.

In 1911 he came into conflict with Lord Northcliffe over food taxes but, when W. W. ASTOR bought the *Observer* on the advice of his son Waldorf, Garvin was retained as Editor, and also became Editor of the evening paper, the *Pall Mall Gazette* from 1912 to 1915. During the First World War he strongly supported the Lloyd George war policy, but criticized the Treaty of Versailles and advocated a League of Nations which would include Germany as an equal. In the inter-war years he favoured negotiation with Hitler, but only from strength by rearmament, particularly in the air. Shortly after the Munich agreement, he became convinced that Hitler was determined upon aggression and insisted that no further concessions should be made.

In 1942 Garvin and Waldorf Astor disagreed over the Editor's overt defence of Winston CHURCHILL'S continuance as Minister of Defence; there had been earlier disagreements which had been patched up, but this time Garvin had to resign. He had been Editor of the *Observer* for thirty-four years and had made the paper a strong political force.

He continued to work as a journalist, writing for the *Sunday Express* (1942–5), and for the *Daily Telegraph* (1945–7). He also edited the supplementary volumes, making up the 13th and 14th editions of the *Encyclopaedia Britannica*, and wrote three volumes of a projected *Life of Joseph Chamberlain* (1932–4) but was unable to finish the work.

He held a number of offices in the press world and received honorary degrees from Durham and Edinburgh. He declined a knighthood from Lloyd George, but in 1941 became CH.

In 1894 Garvin married Christina Ellen, daughter of Robert Wilson, superintendent of police; they had one son, who was killed in the First World War, and four daughters, one of whom, Viola, was Literary Editor of the *Observer* (1926–42), and another, Una, became a consultant physician. Christina died in 1918, and Garvin married in 1921 Mrs Viola Woods, daughter of Harry Ashworth Taylor, King's messenger. Garvin died on 23 January 1947 at Beaconsfield. As Editor of the *Observer* he pioneered a new pattern of Sunday journal, which not only exercised strong political influence but was also a first-class newspaper giving full coverage of the arts.

GASQUET, FRANCIS NEIL (in religion Dom Aidan) (1846–1929), cardinal and historian, was born in London on 5 October 1846, the third son of Raymond Gasquet MD and his wife, Mary Apollonia, daughter of Thomas Kay, of York. The Gasquets were of Provençal origin, and Gasquet's grandfather, a vice-admiral, was a royalist refugee at the time of the French revolution. In 1862 Gasquet went to Downside School, and in 1866 entered the Benedictine novitiate at Downside Priory.

From 1870 to 1878 he taught history and mathematics at Downside; he was ordained priest in 1874. In 1878 he was appointed Prior at the age of thirty-two. He took steps to modernize the school and to enlarge the outlook and growth of the priory. This was a turning point in the history of the school, but his exhaustive activity impaired his health and forced his resignation in 1885.

As relaxation he took to writing, working in London for two years on his *Henry VIII and the English Monasteries* (2 vols., 1888–9), a work which put him in the forefront of English historians. This was followed by a succession of other works which made him a leading authority on the ecclesiastical history of England in the later Middle Ages and Tudor period.

In 1899 Pope Leo XIII appointed him Chairman of the papal commission for the reorganization of the English Benedictine Congregation; in 1900 he was elected Abbot President, and held this office until 1914.

In 1907 Pope Pius X appointed Gasquet to be President of the papal commission for revising the text of the Vulgate; this necessitated his residing in Rome. On 25 May 1914 he was created cardinal deacon.

During the First World War the work on the Vulgate was suspended, and Gasquet found himself with a new Pope, Benedict XV who, at the outset, was strongly influenced by pro-German elements. Gasquet took a leading part in the appointment of a British minister to the Vatican in December 1914, and was successful in countering anti-Allied propaganda in Rome throughout the war.

When the war ended, work on the Vulgate text was resumed under his supervision, and in 1919 he was appointed Librarian of the Holy Roman church. He became the leading figure in the English community in Rome and in 1924 received George V and Queen Mary and showed them the Vatican library's treasures. In that year he was appointed cardinal priest.

He lived and worked in Rome for twelve years and died there on 5 April 1929. He was buried in the abbey church at Downside, where a memorial designed by Sir Giles Gilbert SCOTT was erected over his grave.

GEORGE V (1865–1936), King of Great Britain, Ireland, and the British Dominions beyond the seas, Emperor of India, was born at Marlborough House on 3 June 1865, the second son of the Prince and Princess of Wales, later King Edward VII and Queen Alexandra, and was baptized George Frederick Ernest Albert. He joined the training ship *Britannia* with his elder brother, the Duke of Clarence, in 1877 and followed a naval career until 1892 when the Duke of Clarence died. Whilst serving in the Royal Navy he visited North and South America, South Africa, Australia, Japan, China, and the Mediterranean, and when he retired had reached the rank of Commander.

In 1892 he was created Duke of York, and in the following year became engaged to Princess Victoria Mary (May) of Teck, who had been engaged to his elder brother six weeks before he died. They were married, with the blessings of Queen Victoria, on 6 July 1893. When the Queen died in 1901, George became Duke of Cornwall and his public duties increased. He and Princess Mary toured Australia and New Zealand and opened the new Commonwealth Parliament in Melbourne, and visited South Africa and Canada (1901). In that year he was created Prince of Wales.

The relations between Queen Victoria and her eldest son had been uniformly difficult, but those between George and Edward VII were uniformly harmonious. The King had complete confidence in the integrity and good sense of his son and, in contrast with Queen Victoria's behaviour, encouraged him to study state papers and to prepare himself for his future responsibilities. The Prince of Wales, unlike his father, maintained a lofty standard of family life and a rigid rectitude in his own moral outlook. Six children were borne by his wife: Edward (1894), Albert (1895), Mary (1897), Henry (1900), George (1902), and John (1905). The Prince and Princess paid several visits to the courts of their relations in Europe, made an extensive tour of India in 1905–6, and visited Canada in 1908.

The Prince of Wales became George V on the death of his father (6 May 1910) and was crowned in Westminster Abbey

on 22 June 1911. He received the fleet at Spithead and, after visits to Ireland and Wales, he and Queen Mary paid a state visit to India. In a magnificent durbar at Delhi he announced that the seat of government was to be transferred there from Calcutta.

His accession to the throne, however, had been clouded by the constitutional impasse that had been reached in the dispute between the Commons and the Lords over LLOYD GEORGE's 'People's Budget' and the Parliament Bill. Before he died, Edward VII had indicated to the Liberal Prime Minister that he would not be prepared to intervene until two general elections had confirmed that the country was behind the Government. In January 1910 the Liberals returned to power with a smaller, but still effective, majority in the Commons. The Lords accepted the budget but were still opposed to the Parliament Bill which would restrict their powers to interfere with money bills passed by the lower house. There was a short truce when George V became King. He suggested a conference between the opposing parties; the conference lasted for nearly five months but ended in disagreement. ASQUITH called a second general election and in December, when this took place, the result was almost identical with that of the previous January. The Government reintroduced the Parliament Bill and it passed through the Commons. The leaders of the opposition in the Lords were informed that, to avoid a third general election, the King was prepared, if necessary, to create new peers to give the Government a majority in the House of Lords. The Lords gave way and passed the Bill (10 August 1911).

Meanwhile, the danger of war with Germany increased, and Ireland presented grave problems. The Liberal Government unwillingly increased its expenditure upon new battleships and pursued its policy of Home Rule for Ireland, in spite of the danger that Ulster would resist by force of arms. The Commons again came into conflict with the Lords when the upper house twice rejected the Government's Home Rule Bill. Once again the King called a conference and again the conference failed to reach agreement. Asquith expressed his admiration for the patience, tact, and judgement exercised by the King in his efforts to end the crisis. This dispute was overtaken by the outbreak of the First World War, which compelled the conflicting parties to postpone the struggle.

During the war the royal family remained at Buckingham Palace and the King insisted that the royal household should observe the strict rationing regulations to which his people were subjected. In 1917 he adopted the name of Windsor for his family.

When the war ended the controversy over Ireland was renewed and George V again appealed to all concerned for conciliation, and was praised by the Prime Minister, Lloyd George, for his efforts to secure acceptance of the Irish Treaty. In 1923, when BONAR LAW resigned, the King sent for Stanley BALDWIN rather than Lord CURZON, whose claims to succeed were prejudiced by the fact that he was not a member of the House of Commons. When Ramsay MACDONALD became the first Labour Prime Minister, the King assured him of his full support, and in 1931, when MacDonald was faced with crisis within his own party, George V urged him to consider leading a National Government.

Each Christmas Day from 1932 to the time of his death, the King broadcast to the nation a personal message, a procedure that has since been consistently followed by his son and granddaughter. In 1935 he celebrated his silver jubilee amid great rejoicing and the acclamation of his people.

On 20 January 1936 he died at Sandringham after a short

illness. He was buried at Windsor. His character was shaped by his long period of service in the Navy; conscientious, mistrustful of any form of extremism, keenly interested in the fighting services, a strict but devoted father, and in private life, keen on his hobbies of stamp collecting, shooting, sailing, and tennis.

GEORGE VI (1895-1952), King of Great Britain, Ireland, and the British Dominions beyond the seas, was born at York Cottage, Sandringham on 14 December 1895, the second son of the Duke and Duchess of York, afterwards King George V and Queen Mary. He was baptized Albert Frederick Arthur George. Like his father, he served in the navy (1909-1917) and, in spite of the fact that he was handicapped by a stammer and indifferent health, he was able to visit the West Indies and Canada and take part as a sub-lieutenant in the Battle of Jutland.

In 1917 his weak health forced him to give up his naval career, and in 1919 he overcame his dislike of flying to qualify as a pilot in the RAF. In 1919-20 he spent a year with his younger brother, Henry, at Trinity College, Cambridge. He then took on an increasing number of public engagements, became President of the Industrial Welfare Society, and inaugurated the scheme of camps for boys from public schools and industry, which he personally attended with obvious enjoyment. In 1920 he was created Duke of York and, on 26 April 1923, married Lady Elizabeth Angela Marguerite Bowes-Lyon, daughter of the fourteenth Earl of Strathmore and Kinghorne. Two daughters were born: Princess Elizabeth Alexandra Mary (21 April 1926), and Princess Margaret Rose (21 August 1930). In 1927 the Duke and Duchess toured Australia and New Zealand and were present at the opening of Parliament at Canberra, the new capital of Australia.

In 1926 he consulted the speech therapist Lionel Logue, who in time was able to help him to overcome his stammer so that public speaking became less of an ordeal. The devoted support of his wife, Elizabeth, was also of great assistance to him.

As a boy he had always been overshadowed by his more extrovert brother, Edward, Prince of Wales, who in 1936 succeeded his father as Edward VIII. A year later, frustrated in his determination to make a twice-divorced American, Mrs Wallis Simpson, his consort, Edward VIII abdicated and, to his dismay, the Duke of York found himself King as George VI. His mother, Queen Mary, remarked, 'The Yorks will do very well.' The coronation took place in Westminster Abbey on 12 May 1937. Many people thought that the abdication of Edward VIII would weaken the monarchy, but George VI, in spite of his frail health and inexperience, was able, with the help of Queen Elizabeth, to set such a high example, especially during the Second World War, that the Crown came to hold a higher place than ever in the regard and affection of the British public.

Throughout the war, the royal family remained in London. Queen Elizabeth said, 'The children can't go without me. I can't leave the King, and, of course, the King won't go.' Buckingham Palace was repeatedly hit by bombs, and this only helped the King and Queen to speak from experience when they consoled their subjects in the blitzed areas of London and other cities. In 1940 the King created the George Cross and the George Medal for civilian heroism.

When CHURCHILL expressed his intention of visiting Normandy on D-day, only the King could deter him, by announcing that, if his Prime Minister went, he would go too.

In 1945 when Churchill was defeated at the general election and Clement ATTLEE became Prime Minister, it was the King's suggestion that Ernest BEVIN should be appointed Foreign Secretary. In 1947 the King and Queen and the two princesses visited Southern Africa and the King opened Parliament in Cape Town. In 1948 the royal pair celebrated their silver wedding. They hoped to visit Australia and New Zealand in 1949, but on 12 March of that year the King had to undergo a right lumbar sympathectomy. He appeared to make a good recovery, and on 3 May 1951 opened the Festival of Britain. Later, in September, he underwent an operation for the removal of his left lung.

On 31 January 1952 the King went to London airport to see Princess Elizabeth and Prince Philip, whom she had married in 1947, begin their flight to East Africa. Six days later, on 6 February 1952, George VI died in his sleep at Sandringham. He was buried in St George's Chapel, Windsor. He had come to the throne unexpectedly and without experience but, by his devotion to duty and his courage in adversity, and with the help of his Queen, he set an example to his people which stood his daughter in good stead when she ascended the throne as Elizabeth II.

GERALDO (1904-1974), dance-band leader, whose real name was Gerald Walcan-Bright, was born in London on 10 August 1904, the twin son of Isaac Walcan-Bright, a master tailor, and his wife, Frances Feldman. He was learning to play the piano at five years of age and, later, trained at the Royal Academy of Music. His first professional job was that of pianist at a cinema showing silent films. His first band was formed in 1924 to play at the Metropole in Blackpool.

For five years he was musical director at the Hotel Majestic, St Anne's on Sea, and his orchestra was the most popular

Geraldo and his orchestra, 1954

dance band in the north of England. In 1929 he spent some time in Argentina and Brazil studying Latin-American rhythms. He then formed his Gaucho Tango orchestra which played at the Savoy Hotel, London from 1930 to 1933, during which time he changed his professional name to Geraldo. In 1933 he formed a new orchestra, continuing to play at the Savoy, broadcasting, and appearing in films. In that year his orchestra appeared at the royal command performance.

At the outbreak of the Second World War, Geraldo became Supervisor of the bands division of the Entertainments National Service Association (ENSA) and Director of Bands for the BBC. His orchestra became the most popular in Britain, and included a number of musicians who, later, had their own orchestras, including Ted Heath, Leslie Hutchinson, and Nat Temple. They entertained the forces in the Middle East, North Africa, and Europe.

After the war, as well as conducting his own orchestra, the first to appear on British television, Geraldo became an entrepreneur, supplying orchestras to dance-halls, theatres, restaurants, and liners (such as Cunard). He was a founder-director of Harlech television and Musical Director of Scottish TV. In 1948 he married Alice Plumb; they divorced in 1965, and he married Marya, daughter of Leopold Detsinyi, a Hungarian textile manufacturer. From 1969, he returned to conducting concerts at the Royal Festival Hall, and made his last appearance at Eastbourne shortly before he died on holiday in Vevey, Switzerland, on 4 May 1974.

GIBB, SIR ALEXANDER (1872–1958), engineer, was born at Broughty Ferry on 12 February 1872, the eldest son of Alexander Easton Gibb and his wife, Hope Brown Paton. His forebears for four generations had been civil engineers. He was educated at Rugby and, after a year at University College London, was articled to (Sir) John Wolfe-Barry and Henry Marc Brunel. After two years he joined his father's firm, Easton Gibb & Son, and remained with them for sixteen years, during which time he married, in 1900, Norah Isobel, daughter of Fleet-Surgeon John Lowry Monteith, RN. One of his major responsibilities was the accelerated construction of Rosyth naval base, which was brought into use during the First World War.

In 1916 he became Chief Engineer, Ports Construction to the British armies in France and Belgium. Then in 1918 he was appointed Civil Engineer-in-Chief to the Admiralty. To counter German submarines, he designed 'mystery towers' to be sunk in the English Channel, but the war ended before they could be used. In 1919 Gibb became Director-General of Civil Engineering, Ministry of Transport, and was concerned with the design of a Channel tunnel and the Severn Barrage. For his services, he was appointed CB and KBE in 1918 and GBE in 1920.

In 1921 he set up the firm of Sir Alexander Gibb & Partners, consulting engineers, and undertook the design of the aquarium for the London Zoo, and the first designs for Barking power-station. Among his other achievements were the Kincardine Bridge, the Guinness brewery at Park Royal, the Captain Cook graving dock at Sydney and the Singapore naval base. In 1936 he collaborated with C. H. Mertz and William McLellan on the Galloway hydro-electric scheme, the first major work of its kind and, during the Second World War, he collaborated in the design of the Mulberry harbour for the D-day landings in Normandy.

When, in 1929, he was consulted about the danger of the port of Rangoon being silted up, he built a hydraulic model to study the problem and was able to reassure the authorities that the danger would pass without any expensive remedy being required. This proved to be the case.

Gibb was elected FRS in 1936, was President of the Institution of Civil Engineers (1936–7), and received honours from many academic and professional bodies. He died at Hartley Wintney on 21 January 1958. He had three sons, the eldest of whom, Alistair, succeeded his father after the Second World War as head of the firm, but died after an accident in 1955.

GIBSON, GUY PENROSE (1918–1944), airman VC, was born in Simla, India on 12 August 1918, the younger son of Alexander James Gibson, of the Indian Forest Service, and

September 1944 photograph of a Mulberrry Harbour for the D-day landings, co-designed by Sir Alexander Gibb

his wife, Nora Mary Strike. He was educated at St Edward's School, Oxford, and joined the RAF in 1936. As a pilot in No. 83 (Bomber) Squadron, he took part in the first attack of the Second World War, on the Kiel Canal, and in 1940 was awarded the DFC. In the same year, Gibson married Evelyn Mary Moore; there were no children. He gained a bar to his DFC as a night fighter, shooting down at least four enemy aircraft.

In 1942 he became commander of No. 106 Squadron of Bomber Command, took part in the first 1000-bomber raid, and was appointed to the DSO. His most famous exploit took place when he commanded No. 617 Squadron, formed for the attack on the Möhne and Eder Dams. After a period of special training with the unusual bombs invented by Barnes WALLIS, Gibson led the squadron on the successful night attack, in which the dams were seriously damaged. For his heroism in this action he was awarded the VC.

In June 1944 he was in No. 5 (Bomber) group, and as 'master bomber' in a Mosquito, directed an attack on a German target on the night of 19–20 September. On its way back to base, his aircraft crashed in Holland and he was killed. In 1946 his book *Enemy Coast Ahead* was published.

GILL, (ARTHUR) ERIC ROWTON (1882–1940), stonecarver, engraver, typographer, and author, was born at Brighton on 22 February 1882, the eldest son of Arthur Tidman Gill, a minister of the Calvinist Methodist association known as the Countess of Huntingdon's Connexion, and his wife, Cicely Rose King. From 1897 to 1899 he studied at Chichester Art School; he then moved to London and studied architecture and masonry, and lettering under Edward Johnston.

In 1904 he married Mary Ethel, daughter of Henry Holding Moore, head verger of Chichester Cathedral; they had a son and three daughters.

In 1909 he made his first sculptured figure carved direct from stone, and was encouraged by Roger FRY and Augustus JOHN to continue. In 1913 he became a Roman Catholic and was commissioned to carve the Stations of the Cross in Westminster Cathedral, a task that occupied him until 1918. From 1919 onwards, he executed a number of war memorials and sculptures for churches and colleges. He was also making engravings and drawings at this time. His most important sculptures include *Mankind* (1928, acquired by the Tate Gallery), *Deposition* (1925, at King's School, Canterbury), those at Broadcasting House, London, and the *Creation of Adam* at the League of Nations building, Geneva.

In 1924 he acquired the disused nineteenth-century monastery of Llanthony at Capel-y-Ffin in the Black Mountains. There with two other families, he set up his workshops and established a small community, giving expression to his belief in the inter-relation of art, craft, and work.

During this time he was engraving for the Golden Cockerel Press and designing the first two of his ten printing types 'Perpetua' (1925), and 'Gill Sans-Serif' (1927). His lettering in stone was now accepted as the finest that had been seen for centuries. Late in 1928, he moved to Buckinghamshire and, in the following year, published his first full-length book *Art-Nonsense* and this was followed in 1931 by *Essay on Typography*.

In the early thirties Gill produced his brilliant illustrations for the *Canterbury Tales* and the *Four Gospels*. His other books are *The Necessity of Belief* (1936), and his *Autobiography*, published posthumously in 1940. He became an honorary ARIBA (1935), ARA (1937) and honorary LL D

Eric Gill at work on his sculpture *Christ giving sight to Bartemus*, Moorfields Eye Hospital, 1934

Edinburgh (1938). When he died at Harefield Hospital on 17 November 1940 he was carving a reredos for a chapel in Westminster Cathedral.

The *Engravings of Eric Gill* were published by Gill's nephew, Christopher Skelton in 1983.

GOLLANCZ, SIR VICTOR (1893–1967), publisher, was born in London on 9 April 1893, the son of orthodox Jews, Alexander Gollancz, a jeweller of Polish descent, and his wife, Nellie Michaelson. His uncles were Sir Hermann Gollancz, Semitic scholar, and Sir Israel Gollancz, Shakespearian scholar. He was educated at St Paul's School and New College, Oxford, where he was a scholar, won the Chancellor's Latin essay prize (1913), and obtained a first in Mods. (1914).

Without taking his degree, he was commissioned in the Northumberland Fusiliers, and seconded to Repton School as a master (1916–18). His civics class was thought to be too anti-war in attitude, and he was posted to Singapore.

In 1919 he married Ruth, artist daughter of Ernest D. Lowy; they had five daughters.

He began publishing in 1920 with Benn Brothers and, as Managing Director of the book department, introduced the Players' Shakespeare and *The Sleeping Princess*, with designs by Bakst, as well as Benn's Sixpenny Library. In 1928 he founded his own firm with Stanley MORISON as typographer. Together they created an individual house style with book jackets, printed in black and magenta on yellow paper, easily recognizable to their customers.

Their first success was R. C. SHERRIFF's play, *Journey's End*, and their list of authors included Daphne du Maurier, Elizabeth BOWEN and Dorothy SAYERS. In 1936 Gollancz founded the Left Book Club, to resist the rise of Fascism and Nazism. Although he was a clever business man, he would never bring out a book that put forward ideas which challenged his own convictions. In 1945, much as he had hated the Nazis, he started the Save Europe Now movement to relieve starvation in Germany. For this work he was awarded the grand cross of the German Order of Merit (1953), and the Peace prize of the German Book Trade (1960).

Gollancz was a brilliant public speaker in support of nuclear disarmament and the abolition of capital punishment and other causes in which he believed. He published *A Year of Grace* (1950), *From Darkness to Light* (1956), and *Reminiscences of Affection* (1968).

He made an indelible mark on British publishing, and in 1965 was knighted. His eldest daughter, Livia, continued to run the publishing company after her father's death in London on 8 February 1967.

GOOCH, GEORGE PEABODY (1873–1968), historian, was born in London on 21 October 1873, the third son of Charles Cubitt Gooch, a merchant, and Mary Jane, daughter of the Revd Edmund Blake, rector of Bramerton, Norfolk. He left Eton at the age of fifteen and moved to King's College, London, and then to Trinity College, Cambridge, where he obtained a first in the historical tripos (1894), the Members' English essay prize, and the Lightfoot scholarship (1895). For three years he studied in Berlin and Paris, and, failing to get a fellowship at Trinity, he taught at Mansfield House,

G. P. Gooch, 1943

at the Working Men's College, and at Toynbee Hall.

He was a Liberal in politics, anxious to get into Parliament, and distressed by the Boer War, on the justice of which Liberals were divided. From 1906 to 1910 he was Liberal MP for Bath, but failed to get elected in either of the 1910 elections. He was critical of the foreign policy of Sir Edward GREY. In 1911 he became joint Editor with J. Scott Lidgett of the *Contemporary Review* and remained Editor until 1960, setting out to make the *Contemporary* the leading monthly on foreign affairs.

Since his four years at Trinity College, he had been developing as a historian and, with encouragement from Lord Acton, he published in 1898 *English Democratic Ideas in the Seventeenth Century*. One of his most important works, *History and Historians in the Nineteenth Century*, was published in 1913.

The outbreak of the First World War was distressing to Gooch, not only because he was attached to German scholarship, but because in 1903 he had married a German art student, Sophie Else Schön. They had two sons. Gooch blamed Sir Edward Grey for his pre-war policy and thought that the conflict with Germany could have been avoided.

In 1919 he edited (jointly with Sir Adolphus Ward) the *Cambridge History of British Foreign Policy* (3 vols., 1922–3), and in 1920 he published *Germany and the French Revolution*. In 1924 Ramsay MACDONALD invited him to edit the *British Documents on the Origins of the War 1898–1914*. Gooch insisted on having H. W. V. Temperley as fellow editor, and the thirteen volumes were published between 1926 and 1938. His other works included *Before the War: Studies in Diplomacy* (1936–8), and *Frederick the Great* (1947). He had tried hard to make Englishmen understand Germany after the First World War, but he modified his views about Sir Edward Grey as more evidence came to light, and he must have been deeply distressed by the rise of Hitler and Nazism.

He was elected FBA in 1926, and elected to an honorary fellowship at Trinity College, Cambridge in 1935. He also received an honorary doctorate from Oxford, was appointed CH in 1939, and OM in 1963. In 1958 he published *Under Six Reigns*. He died at Chalfont St Peter on 31 August 1968. His colleague, Harold Temperley, had been elected Master of Peterhouse in 1938 and died at Cambridge on 11 July 1939.

GORE, CHARLES (1853–1932), bishop, and militant churchman, was born at Wimbledon on 22 January 1853, the youngest son of Charles Alexander Gore (son of the second Earl of Arran), commissioner of forests and woods, and his wife, Lady Augusta Lavinia Priscilla, daughter of John William Ponsonby, fourth Earl of Bessborough, and widow of William Thomas Petty-Fitzmaurice, Earl of Kerry. He was educated at Harrow and Balliol College, Oxford, where he was a scholar and obtained firsts in Classical Mods. and Greats (1872–5). In 1875 he was elected a Fellow of Trinity College.

He was ordained deacon (1876) and priest (1878) and, up to 1880, taught at Trinity College. In that year he became Vice-Principal of Cuddesdon College, where for three years he exercised considerable influence on young clergymen. From 1884 to 1893 he was Principal Librarian of Pusey House. Through his sermons, lectures, books and personal relations, he was a strong influence on the religious life of the university. He was active on behalf of the Christian Social Union, and from 1892 till 1902 was Superior of the

Community of the Resurrection at Mirfield, a brotherhood of celibate priests.

Throughout these years, Gore was heavily engaged in controversy on behalf of Anglo-Catholic doctrine and practice. In 1889 he published in *Lux Mundi* an essay on 'The Holy Spirit and Inspiration' in which his 'free thinking' led him to the conclusion, to the dismay of his friends, that the true humanity of Christ entailed certain limitations of consciousness. Unhappy at the reaction of his friends, he was ready to explain but not to retract his beliefs.

After refusing the offer of appointment as Dean of Winchester in 1894, he accepted a canonry of Westminster, and his sermons and lectures drew crowds to the Abbey. He was now recognized as a power in the Church, and Lord Salisbury offered him the bishopric of Worcester in 1902. The see was split in 1905 and Gore moved over to the new see at Birmingham, to which he had contributed almost the whole of his private fortune. There he established good relations with the civic authorities and Free Churchmen, and took a keen interest in the Workers' Educational Association. In politics he was a Liberal and supported LLOYD GEORGE's 'People's Budget' of 1909.

He left Birmingham in 1911 to become Bishop of Oxford where determined adherence to his personal beliefs continued to involve him in perpetual controversy. His inquiry into the Benedictine community at Caldey led to most of its members becoming Roman Catholics. He paid two visits to the troops in France (1914–15) and another to America to lecture on war aims (1918). Objections to Gore's appointment to Worcester in 1902 had been raised on doctrinal grounds, and in 1917 Gore raised similar objections to the appointment of Hensley HENSON as Bishop of Hereford. In both cases the objections were over-ruled. He resigned from Oxford, ostensibly because the Representative Church Council decided to make baptism (without confirmation) the qualification for a vote for electors to the Church Assembly, but he was now sixty-six, and exhausted by his struggles to check what he regarded as disloyalty to the creeds of the Church.

From 1924 to 1928 he was Dean of the Theological Faculty at King's College, London, and devoted himself to his writing. His publications at this period included *The Reconstruction of Belief* (1926), *The New Commentary on Holy Scripture* (1928), *Christ and Society* (1928), and *Jesus of Nazareth* (1929). He supported the attempted revision of the Prayer Book (1927–8). He was an honorary Fellow of Balliol and Trinity Colleges, Oxford, and of King's College, London, and received many honorary degrees. He died in London on 17 January 1932.

GOSSE, SIR EDMUND WILLIAM (1849–1928), poet and man of letters, was born in Hackney on 21 September 1849, the only child of Philip Henry Gosse, a zoologist, and his first wife, Emily, a religious writer, daughter of William Bowes, of Boston, Massachusettes. Both parents were devout Plymouth Brethren, and Gosse's reading as a boy was confined to religious literature, his only knowledge of other books being gained surreptitiously.

From 1865 to 1875 he worked in the catalogue section of the British Museum, and made up for his lost time by the study of literature and by learning French, German, Italian, and Swedish. In 1870 he and John Blaikie published jointly *Madrigals, Songs, and Sonnets*. After a visit to Trondheim, he studied Ibsen in Norwegian and translated *Hedda Gabler* (1891), and *The Master-Builder* (with William Archer, 1893)

and, in articles and reviews, introduced Ibsen to the English public.

In 1875 Gosse was appointed translator to the Board of Trade. In the same year, he married Ellen, daughter of George Napoleon Epps, and sister-in-law of Sir Lawrence Alma Tadema; they had one son and two daughters. He published a number of books of literary criticism, as well as a life of Gray in the 'English Men of Letters' series (1883), a *Life of William Congreve* (1888), *Life and Letters of Dr. John Donne* (1899), *Coventry Patmore* (1905) and a *Life of Sir Thomas Browne* (1905). In 1884–5 he lectured in the USA and was offered the chair of English literature at Harvard. He declined and, on return to England, became Clark lecturer at Trinity College, Cambridge, a post he held until 1890, publishing his lectures as *From Shakespeare to Pope* (1885). In 1904 Gosse was appointed Librarian to the House of Lords, a post which gave him security and which he held for ten years.

In 1907 he published, anonymously, his classic work *Father and Son* describing his childhood passed in the restricted atmosphere prescribed by his religious parents. Now at the height of his powers, he continued to contribute articles and reviews, including a weekly series in the *Sunday Times* covering a wide range of literary topics. His *Collected Essays* were published in five volumes in 1913. He excelled in literary portraiture, and numbered among his friends Swinburne, Thomas HARDY, R. L. Stevenson, George A. MOORE and Henry JAMES. He has been criticized, however, for an unscholarly proclivity for inaccuracy. He was the recipient of many honours including CB (1912), a knighthood (1925), and a number of honorary degrees. He died in London on 16 May 1928.

GOWERS, SIR ERNEST ARTHUR (1880–1966), public servant, was born in London on 2 June 1880, the younger son of (Sir) William Richard Gowers, physician, and his wife, Mary, daughter of Frederick Baines of Leeds. He was educated at Rugby and Clare College, Cambridge, where he was a scholar and obtained a first in the classical tripos (1902). In that year he entered the Civil Service. In 1905 he married Constance, daughter of Thomas Macgregor Greer, a solicitor, of Ballymoney, Co. Antrim; they had one son and two daughters. He was called to the Bar (Inner Temple) in 1906. In 1911 he was Principal Private Secretary to the Chancellor of the Exchequer, LLOYD GEORGE, and filled a number of other important posts, including Permanent Under-Secretary for mines (1920), and Chairman of the Board of Inland Revenue (1927–30). He retired from the Civil Service in 1930.

He continued in public service as Chairman, Coal Commission (1938), Chairman, Manpower Subcommittee of Committee of Imperial Defence, and Senior Regional Commissioner for Civil Defence (1941). He was Chairman of a number of other commissions and committees, and of the National Hospitals for Nervous Diseases, Queen Square, London, of which his father had been a pioneer.

Gowers was one of the greatest public servants of his day, but is likely to be remembered mainly for his contribution to the propagation of simple and direct English and his attack upon officialese, which unfortunately in spite of his efforts, has continued to plague and bewilder the British public. In 1948 at the invitation of Edward BRIDGES, head of the Civil Service, he wrote a little booklet *Plain Words: a Guide to the Use of English*: it was intended as a guide to entrants to the Civil Service in the writing of clear, unambiguous English.

Sir Ernest Gowers

He followed this, at the request of the Oxford University Press, with a revision of Henry FOWLER'S *Modern English Usage* (1965). In his introduction to this edition, he quoted Swift: 'Proper words in proper places make the true definition of a style.' Both Fowler and Gowers knew this to be true.

Gowers received many honours: he became an honorary D. Litt. of Manchester and an honorary ARIBA. He was appointed CB (1917), KBE (1926), KCB (1928), GBE (1945), and GCB (1953). He died at Midhurst on 16 April 1966.

GRACE, WILLIAM GILBERT (1848–1915), cricketer, was born on 18 July 1848, the fourth of five sons of Henry Mills Grace, a doctor of Downend, near Bristol, and his wife, Martha, daughter of George Pocock, of Bristol. He was educated at Bristol Medical School, and St Bartholomew's and Westminster Hospitals, London. After qualifying MRCS and LRCP he practised as a surgeon in Bristol (1879). In 1873 he married Agnes Nicholls Day; they had three sons and one daughter.

Both his father and his uncle, Alfred Pocock, were keen cricketers, and he and his brothers were coached in every branch of the game. In 1865, when he was sixteen, he played for the Gentlemen against the Players at the Oval and at Lords. He won fame mainly as a remarkable batsman, but he was also a good medium pace or slow bowler and an excellent fielder. In 1866 he made 224, not out, for England against Surrey and this was the first of a long series of innings in which he scored an extraordinary number of runs. In 1876 he scored 400 in one match and in three consecutive first-class matches made 344, 177, and 318, not out.

He became a member of the MCC in 1869 and in 1870, with two of his brothers, started the Gloucestershire side, composed entirely of amateurs. In 1880 he made 152 in the first match to be played against Australia in England. He visited Australia twice, first in 1873, and then, eighteen years later, in 1891. In 1895 in one county match between Gloucestershire and Kent, he opened the first innings and was out last and was in the field for all three days of the match. In that season he reached one thousand runs by 30 May. He played for England for the last time in 1899, at the age of fifty-one.

Statistics mean very little as conditions have changed so considerably since the heyday of Dr Grace, or 'W.G.' as he was known to the public. In modern cricket many more first-class matches are played, there are many more professionals, and pitches are prepared with much greater skill. However, for the record, in his career of forty-three years, Grace made 126 centuries, scored nearly 55,000 runs, and took 2,876 wickets. His greatest claim to fame is that he created the art of batsmanship with a variety of strokes that cricketers throughout the years since he died have striven to emulate.

Grace practised medicine in Bristol from 1879 to 1899, but he also put his cricketing skill to advantage by demanding and getting his share of the proceeds which his participation in a match ensured. His burly figure and thick black beard were familiar to the public far beyond the cricket field; he was one of the best-known men in England and became a legend in his own lifetime. He died at Eltham on 23 October 1915, and the MCC erected an entrance gateway in his memory in 1923.

GRAHAM, ROBERT BONTINE CUNNINGHAME (1852–1936). See CUNNINGHAME GRAHAM.

GRAHAME, KENNETH (1859–1932), author, was born in Edinburgh on 8 March 1859, the second son of James Cunningham Grahame, an advocate, and his wife, Bessie, daughter of John Ingles, of Hilton, Lasswade. He was educated at St Edward's School, Oxford, and then spent two years in the Westminster office of his uncle, a parliamentary agent.

In 1879 he entered the Bank of England as a clerk, and in his spare time wrote verse and trained with the London Scottish. In 1886 he was encouraged by Frederick Furnivall, founder of the Shelley Society, to write prose for the reviews rather than persist with his verse. William Henley, Editor of the National Observer, accepted some of his essays and suggested that he leave the Bank; but Grahame had more sense and remained in a job he disliked, though he continued writing. In 1893 he published his first book *Pagan Papers*. From 1894 to 1897 he wrote for the *Yellow Book* and published *The Golden Age* (1895), which showed a remarkable understanding of the child mind and was praised by Swinburne.

In 1898 Grahame became Secretary of the Bank of England and a year later married Elspeth, daughter of Robert William Thomson of Edinburgh, and step-daughter of Lord Moulton. They had one son but the marriage was not happy. *Dream Days* appeared in 1898, but it was not until 1908, the year of his retirement from the Bank, when *The Wind in the Willows* was published, that its author was recognized as a master in the writing of children's books. It portrays an idyllic world, endangered by industrial encroachments. The book became a classic and made him a fortune. Its famous characters,

1900 edition of Kenneth Grahame's *The Golden Age*, described by Swinburne as 'too praiseworthy for praise'

Mole, Badger, Rat, and Toad, appeared in A. A. MILNE'S dramatization of the work as *Toad of Toad Hall* in 1929. *The Wind in the Willows* was written in part as letters to Grahame's young son, Alastair, who was born in 1900. At the age of twenty, Alastair, who was handicapped, killed himself, run over by a train near Oxford. Grahame died suddenly at Pangbourne on 6 July 1932.

GRANVILLE-BAKER, HARLEY GRANVILLE (1877–1946), actor, producer, dramatist, and critic, was born in Kensington on 25 November 1877, the only son of Albert James Baker, an architect, and his wife, Mary Elizabeth Bozzi Granville, well known as an elocutionist and reciter, of Italian descent. As a child he assisted at his mother's recitals, and first appeared publicly in 1891. In 1895 he toured with (Sir) Phillip Ben Greet, and acted and produced for the Stage Society.

He became a close friend of G. B. SHAW and in producing plays such as *Candida* and *Mrs Warren's Profession*, he made Shaw's name as a playwright. Granville-Baker was keen to raise the standards of English acting, and in 1904 drew up, with William Archer, *A Scheme and Estimates for a National Theatre*, but this was not made public till 1907.

From 1904 to 1907 he made his own name as a director in partnership with John E. Vedrenne at the Court Theatre. As well as Shaw's plays, those of GALSWORTHY and MASE-FIELD were staged, together with works of Ibsen and Maeterlinck. Galsworthy's first play *The Silver Box* was staged at the Court. The Barkers and the Galsworthys became firm friends. Lillah McCarthy joined the company in 1905 to play in Shaw's *John Bull's Other Island* and *Man and Superman* and, in 1906, she and Granville-Barker were married.

When the Vedrenne-Barker partnership moved to the Savoy Theatre in 1907, their successes ceased to be financially viable, and in 1910 Barker became repertory producer for Charles Frohman. Among plays that were outstanding successes were Galsworthy's *Justice* and Barker's own *The Madras House*.

In 1912 Granville-Barker, with the backing of Lord Howard de Walden, staged at the Savoy Theatre Shakespeare's *The Winter's Tale* and *Twelfth Night*, followed in 1914 by *A Midsummer Night's Dream*. These productions set a new standard in the presentation of Shakespeare and had a profound influence on future productions. He was equally successful with Shaw's *Fanny's First Play* (1911) and Arnold BENNETT's *The Great Adventure* (1913).

The First World War came when Granville-Barker was at the height of his powers and brought his career as a producer virtually to an end. In 1915 he produced *A Midsummer Night's Dream* in New York, and fell in love with Helen, the wife of Archer Huntington, a millionaire. In 1918 he and Lillah McCarthy were divorced, as were the Huntingtons, and he married Helen. There were no children of either of his marriages. Helen was wealthy and insisted that her new husband should no longer work in the theatre and should break off his connection with Bernard Shaw.

From 1919 to 1932, Granville-Barker was Chairman of the British Drama League, and from 1923 to 1946 edited 'The Players' Shakespeare' and continued, when the series was abandoned, to write invaluable prefaces to the plays. In 1930 he became Clark lecturer at Trinity College, Cambridge, and in 1937 was Romanes lecturer at Oxford. From 1937 to 1939 he was Director of the British Institute in Paris. His own best-known play was a comedy *The Voysey Inheritance*. He died in Paris on 31 August 1946.

GREGORY, ISABELLA AUGUSTA, LADY GREGORY (1852–1932), playwright and poet, was born at Roxborough on 15 March 1852, the youngest daughter of Dudley Persse, a landowner of Roxborough, co. Galway, and his second wife, Frances, daughter of Col. Richard Barry. She was educated privately, and in 1880 became the second wife of Sir William H. Gregory who was Governor of Ceylon (1871–7). Her husband died in 1892.

In 1898 Lady Gregory met W. B. YEATS in London and, becoming interested in the theatre decided, in collaboration with Yeats and George A. MOORE, to found the Irish Literary Theatre, and produced Yeats's *The Countess Cathleen* in May 1899. At first, English actors were imported, but later Irish amateurs formed a company.

In 1904, with Yeats and J. M. Synge, the Irish dramatist, Lady Gregory opened the Abbey Theatre, Dublin. About this time she became interested in Gaelic, learnt the language, and published some of the sagas in English. She was herself a playwright of considerable skill and wrote twenty-seven plays, including *The Image* (1910), *The Golden Apple* (1916), *The Dragon* (1920), and *Sancho's Master* (1928).

In 1918 her only son, Robert, who was a distinguished painter, was killed in action in Italy. Robert Gregory is the subject of Yeats's elegy 'An Irish Airman Foresees his Death'. Lady Gregory remained a director of the Abbey

Theatre, Dublin, until she died at Coole Park, Gort, co. Galway on 22 May 1932. Without her energy and enthusiasm the Abbey Theatre could not have survived the struggle of its early years.

GRENFELL, JOYCE IRENE (1910–1979), actress, entertainer, and broadcaster, was born in London on 10 February 1910, the only daughter of Paul Phipps, an architect, and his wife, Nora Langhorne, an American and sister of Nancy ASTOR. She was educated at the Christian Science School, Clear View, South Norwood and a finishing school in Paris, and studied at the Royal Academy of Dramatic Art. In 1929 she married Reginald Pascoe Grenfell, a chartered accountant.

From 1936 to 1939 she was radio critic of the *Observer*, and began her career as an entertainer in Herbert Farjeon's *Little Revue* (1939), followed by *Diversion* and *Light and Shade*. During the Second World War she entertained with ENSA, and in 1946 was appointed OBE. At this time she also worked with Stephen POTTER on a series of satirical radioprogrammes.

In 1945 she appeared in Noël COWARD's *Sigh No More* and later in *Tuppence Coloured* (1947) and *Penny Plain* (1951). She also appeared in a number of films including *Genevieve*, *The Happiest Days of Your Life*, *The Million Pound Note*, and *The Yellow Rolls-Royce*.

In 1954 she had her own show, *Joyce Grenfell Requests the Pleasure* with which she toured all over the world from Switzerland to Australia and the USA. The versatility of her monologues and songs was unmatched by that of any other entertainer except, possibly, her friend Ruth Draper. She captivated her audiences with her gaiety and humour and her acute observation of the foibles of those around her.

She revealed her knowledge of music to the viewing public in 'Face the Music', a TV quiz programme, in which she appeared with Bernard Levin. In 1976 she published *Joyce Grenfell Requests the Pleasure*, and in 1979 *In Pleasant Places*.

Like her aunt, Nancy Astor, of whom in her girlhood she stood in awe, she was a committed Christian Scientist, and on occasions lectured on religion and metaphysics and contributed to the BBC's 'Thought for the Day'. She held honorary degrees from Cambridge and Manchester and was a member of the Winston Churchill Memorial Fellowship Trust.

She died, childless, in London on 30 November 1979.

GRENFELL, WILLIAM HENRY, BARON DESBOROUGH (1855–1945), all-round sportsman and public servant, was born in London on 30 October 1855, the eldest son of Charles William Grenfell MP, of Taplow Court, Bucks., and his wife, Georgiana Caroline, daughter of William Saunders Sebright Lascelles, son of the second Earl of Harewood. He was educated at Harrow and Balliol College, Oxford, where he was President of both the University Boat and Athletic Clubs, a unique feat. In 1877 he rowed in the dead-heat race against Cambridge.

From 1880 to 1882 and from 1885 to 1886 he was Liberal MP for Salisbury and from 1892 to 1893 MP for Hereford; he resigned rather than support Gladstone's Irish Home Rule Bill. In 1905 he became Baron Desborough. For thirty-two years he was Chairman of the Thames Conservancy Board, and was also President of the London Chamber of Commerce.

However, it will be for his athletic prowess that he will be remembered. He won the Thames punting championship for three successive years (1888–90); he stroked an eight across the Channel; he rowed in the Grand Challenge Cup at Henley. He twice swam Niagara; he ascended the Matterhorn by three different routes, and achieved many other climbing

Joyce Grenfell working at home with Stephen Potter, *c.* 1940

feats in the Alps and Rockies. He was a big-game hunter and fisherman in many parts of the world; and hunted, and rode in point-to-points.

He was President of the Amateur Fencing Association, of the 1908 Olympic Games, the MCC, and the Law Tennis Association. He was also President of the Bath Club and Chairman of the Pilgrims of Great Britain. In 1887 he married Ethel Anne Priscilla, daughter of Julian Henry Charles Fane; they had three sons and two daughters. All three of his sons died prematurely: the eldest, Julian the poet, and the second son were both killed in action in 1915; his youngest son died in a motor accident in 1926. His elder daughter married Sir John Salmond, Marshal of the RAF, and the younger became Viscountess Gage.

Desborough was appointed CVO (1907), KCVO (1908), GCVO (1925); in 1928 he was appointed KG. He died at Panshanger, Herts. on 9 January 1945.

GREY, SIR EDWARD, VISCOUNT GREY OF FALLODON (1862–1933), politician, was born in London on 25 April 1862, the eldest son of Col. George Henry Grey and his wife, Harriet Jane, youngest daughter of Lt.-Col. Charles Pearson. He was a direct descendant of the second Earl Grey of the 1831 Reform Bill. He was brought up at Fallodon, Northumberland, and from his early years was a keen birdwatcher and fly fisherman. He was educated at Winchester and Balliol College, Oxford, from which he was sent down for incorrigible idleness in 1884.

Back at his Fallodon estate, which he had inherited from his grandfather, together with a baronetcy, in 1882, his own father having died in 1874, he came under the influence of Mandell Creighton, the rector of the parish, who was writing his *History of the Papacy*. Creighton instilled into Grey his own brand of Liberalism and a sense of public duty. In 1884 Grey became Private Secretary to Sir Evelyn BARING, and in 1885 was elected Liberal MP for Berwick-on-Tweed, a seat which he held until he was raised to the peerage in 1916. In 1885 he married (Frances) Dorothy, daughter of a local squire, Shalcross FitzHerbert Widdrington and, as she cared little for politics, Grey might have retired permanently to Fallodon but for the influence of his political friends, As-QUITH and HALDANE. The Liberals being out of office from 1886 to 1906 except for the years 1892–5, Grey and his wife had a chance to enjoy their quiet life at Fallodon and at their cottage on the Itchen in Hampshire.

From 1892 to 1895 Grey served his apprenticeship at the Foreign Office as Parliamentary Under-Secretary. In 1895 he made the 'Grey declaration' warning France that encroachment on the upper waters of the Nile would be regarded as an 'unfriendly act'. He disagreed with the more radical members of his party and approved of the Boer War, but, later in 1905, warmly supported Campbell-Bannerman's policy in granting self-government to South Africa.

When the Liberals returned in power in 1905, Grey was reluctant to accept the office of Foreign Secretary, thinking that Campbell-Bannerman should retire to the House of Lords; but Asquith and Haldane persuaded him to take it and he soon found himself in complete accord with the Prime Minister, particularly in respect of his policy of friendship with France and his distrust of the ambitions of Germany. Two months after Grey became Foreign Secretary, Lady Grey was killed in a carriage accident; but for this tragedy it is possible that Grey would not have been prepared to stay in office for the next eleven years.

In the winter of 1905–6 Grey let both France and Germany know that, in his view, England would fight to defend France in a case of German aggression, though he could give no absolute pledge until the circumstances arose. He continued the 'military conversations' with France, initiated by his predecessor, and in 1906 the Algeciras conference on Morocco induced Germany to accept a compromise because of England's support of France. Grey also took the initiative in reaching agreement with Russia (1907) as a means of avoiding hostilities in Tibet, Afghanistan, and Persia (Iran), and to prevent Russia from aligning herself with Germany. He has been criticized for not having made firm alliances with France and Russia which might have deterred Germany from entering the First World War. G. M. TREVELYAN, writing in the *DNB*, defended Grey from this criticism on the grounds that he had no power to make formal alliances, which would not have been supported by his colleagues or the public, and he also feared that such alliances might encourage France and Russia to provoke Germany into war. At the same time, he was prepared to make concessions to Germany, as his greatest hope was to preserve peace. In 1911 he renewed the alliance with Japan, which dated from 1902. In 1911 he was faced with the Agadir crisis: France and Germany were again at loggerheads over Morocco, and Germany sent a warship to the Moroccan port. LLOYD GEORGE entered the fray with a speech at the Mansion House in London in which he made clear that Britain would be united in support of France if she were attacked. Once again peace was maintained, though the situation in Europe continued to be alarmingly unsettled.

In 1912, still seeking peace, Grey agreed to the Haldane mission to Germany to attempt to persuade the Kaiser that limitation of the rapid growth of the German navy was essential to better relations with Britain. The mission was a failure; naval rivalry continued. After the Serbian defeat of Turkey, backed by Russia, there was a further danger of a European war in 1912, but Germany, France, and Britain were agreed on this occasion, and Grey succeeded in averting Armageddon.

In 1914 he failed. This time Germany supported Austria, and Russia and France backed Serbia, while the British cabinet was divided about supporting France. Grey had no doubt what should be done, and the outcome became clear when Germany showed plainly that she would attack through Belgium. On 4 August 1914 the war began; this was a tragic day for Grey, but the country was united, and opinion in the United States was largely pro-Allies. Grey had been at pains to maintain good relations with the USA, and continued to do so through his personal friendship with Walter Page, the American Ambassador in London, and Col. House, President Wilson's adviser. In 1915 he concluded a secret treaty with Italy to prevent her from joining Germany and Austria.

His health was deteriorating and his eyesight going, but he soldiered on. In 1916 he became Viscount Grey of Fallodon and, when Lloyd George succeeded Asquith as Prime Minister, Grey resigned as Foreign Secretary. In 1918, although almost totally blind, he became President of the League of Nations Union. From 1928 to 1933 he was Chancellor of Oxford University, from which forty-four years earlier he had been sent down for idleness. He had been PC since 1902; he became KG in 1912 and FRS in 1914.

In 1922 he married again; Pamela Adelaide Genevieve was the daughter of Percy Scawen Wyndham, and widow of Edward Priaulx Tennant, first Lord Glenconner; in 1928 she died. In the years between the end of the First World War and his death at Fallodon on 7 September 1933 Grey

Sir Edward Grey (left), Winston Churchll (centre), and Lord Crewe on their way to a Cabinet meeting, 1910

produced his books; he told the story of his public career in *Twenty-five Years, 1892-1916* (2 vols., 1925), helped in his blindness by his friend, John Alfred Spender. This monumental work was followed by *The Fallodon Papers* (1926) and *The Charm of Birds* (1927).He had written *Fly Fishing* in 1899. These books on nature place Grey in the front rank of English writers in the subject, comparable with Izaak Walton, Gilbert White of Selborne, and his friend W. H. HUDSON, whom he had helped when Hudson was hard pressed financially. He died childless, and his peerage became extinct. He left Fallodon to Capt. Cecil Graves, son of his eldest sister.

GRIEVE, CHRISTOPHER MURRAY (1892-1978). See MacDIARMID.

GUINNESS, EDWARD CECIL, first EARL OF IVEAGH (1847-1927), philanthropist, was born at St Anne's, Clontarf, co. Dublin on 10 November 1847, the youngest son of the brewer Sir Benjamin Lee Guinness, of Dublin, and his wife, Elizabeth, daughter of Edward Guinness of Dublin. He was educated privately and at Trinity College, Dublin (1870). His father having died in 1868, Edward Guinness after his graduation, took part in the management of the famous brewery of which in 1855 his father had become sole proprietor.

He also played a part in Dublin municipal life, and was High Sheriff of the city in 1876 and of the county in 1885. In the latter year he was created a baronet. In 1873 he had married his cousin, Adelaide Maud, daughter of Richard Samuel Guinness MP, of Deepwell, co. Dublin. They had three sons.

When the Dublin brewery was incorporated as a public company in 1886, Guinness became Chairman, but resigned from active management in 1889. To mark his retirement he placed a large sum of money in trust to erect workmen's houses in London and Dublin, and made another large gift to Dublin for the purpose of slum clearance. He also contributed to the Lister Institute of Preventive Medicine in London, for the endowment of bacteriological research.

In 1891 he became Baron Iveagh and, during the Boer War, set up and maintained a field hospital. In 1905 he became a viscount. He was then living at Elveden Hall in Suffolk, a well-known sporting estate, where he entertained Edward VII and George V. In 1908 he was elected Chancellor of Dublin University. The disturbances in Ireland after the First World War caused him much distress, but after the 1922 settlement he continued his benefactions to the Irish Free State. He became Earl of Iveagh in 1919. In March 1925, when the Ken Wood preservation committee came to the end of their resources, he purchased the remainder of the Ken Wood estate in Hampstead and bequeathed it to the nation together with a valuable collection of pictures. He was elected FRS in 1906 and received honorary doctorates from Dublin and Aberdeen. He died in London on 7 October 1927.

GUINNESS, RUPERT EDWARD CECIL LEE, second EARL OF IVEAGH (1874–1967), philanthropist, was born in London on 29 March 1874, the eldest son of Edward Cecil GUINNESS, and his wife, Adelaide Maud Guinness. He was educated at Eton and Trinity College, Cambridge, and while there won the diamond sculls (1895 and 1896), and the Wingfield sculls (1896) at Henley. In 1903, with his yacht *Leander*, he won the King's Cup at Cowes.

Having become a director of Arthur Guinness, Son & Co. Ltd. in 1899, he went to South Africa in the following year and worked in the hospital which his father had donated to the war effort. He was appointed CMG in 1901. In 1903 he married GWENDOLEN FLORENCE MARY ONSLOW, born on 22 July 1881, the elder daughter of William Hillier Onslow, fourth Earl of Onslow, and his wife, Florence Coulston, daughter of the third Baron Gardner. She was keenly interested in politics and shared her husband's work when from 1908 to 1910 he was Conservative MP for Haggerston, Shoreditch.

Out of Parliament from 1910 to 1912, he and his wife visited Canada and, on return to England, they set up schemes for providing opportunities for young men and women to emigrate to Canada. Guinness was appointed CB in 1911 and elected MP for S.E. Essex (later Southend) in 1912. He held that seat until 1927, when he succeeded his father as Earl of Iveagh. From 1912 to 1927 he was Governor of the Lister Institute of Preventive Medicine, endowed by his father. He was a close friend of Almwroth WRIGHT and Alexander FLEMING and became Chairman of the Wright–Fleming Institute of Microbiology. He also financed research into the production of clean milk at Rothamsted.

During the First World War he commanded the London division of the RNVR which he himself had raised between 1905 and 1914. In 1916 he was ADC to the King. His wife was appointed a member of the National Prisoners of War Fund and in 1920 became CBE.

After the war Guinness continued to be interested in the production of clean milk; he produced tuberculin tested milk on his Pyrford farm, and in 1920 was the first Chairman of the Tuberculin Tested Milk Producers Association, and worked closely with the Research Institute in Dairying at Reading University.

In 1926 he and his wife visited India where her brother-in-law, Lord IRWIN, was Viceroy and in the following year, when the first Earl of Iveagh died, he inherited the great Elveden estate and became Chairman of the Guinness Company. Still interested in farming, Lord Iveagh now set out to turn Elveden into an efficient, economic farming unit with tuberculin-free herds on a large scale.

Lady Iveagh succeeded her husband as MP for Southend from 1927 to 1935; she became Chairman of the National Union of Conservative and Unionist Associations and was a most competent speaker and broadcaster. Shortly before the Second World War, Lord Iveagh presented his Dublin town-house to the Republic of Ireland and it became the Department for Foreign Affairs. The Guinness Company built the Park Royal brewery in London and this was able to keep the supply of stout going throughout the war. During the war Elveden increased its production of food. The

Iveaghs suffered a shattering blow when their only son, Arthur, a major in the 55th Suffolk and Norfolk Yeomanry, was killed on active service.

Lord Iveagh's achievements were recognized by his appointment to the Order of the Garter in 1955; he was elected FRS in 1964, and was Chancellor of Trinity College, Dublin until 1963. He resigned from the chairmanship of the Guinness Company in 1959. Lady Iveagh died at Pyrford on 16 February 1966 and Lord Iveagh died there on 14 September 1967. They were survived by three daughters; their grandson (Arthur Francis) Benjamin succeeded to the title and became Chairman of the Guinness Company.

GUNN, SIR JAMES (1893–1964), painter, was born in Glasgow on 30 June 1893, the son of a tailor, Richard Gunn, and his wife, Thomasina Munro. He was educated at Glasgow High School, Glasgow School of Art, Edinburgh College of Art, and the Académie Julien, Paris. His life as a painter was interrupted by the First World War in which he served with the Artists' Rifles and the 10th Scottish Rifles.

In 1919 he married Mary Gwendoline Charlotte, daughter

James Gunn, 1953, with a sketch of Queen Elizabeth II made in 1947, and in the background his unfinished painting of King George VI and Queen Elizabeth arriving for the opening of the Festival of Britain

of Capt. H. E. Hillman, RN; they had three daughters. In 1929 he married, secondly, (Marie) Pauline, daughter of A. P. Millar; she was the model for some of his best-known paintings; they had a son and a daughter.

In 1932 he painted the conversation piece of BELLOC, CHESTERTON, and Baring, and in 1939 the portrait of Lord Crawford, both of which are in the National Portrait Gallery. He also painted a famous portrait 'Pauline in the Yellow Dress' and a portrait of DELIUS in Bradford (1933).

He was influenced, particularly in his early work, by the paintings of Velazquez. He used broad tonal designs with colours close together, often capturing a likeness with great skill, without seeking to mask the severity of expression of some of his sitters. When he had become well known, Gunn painted portraits of prime ministers, field-marshals, judges, dons, and bankers as well as writers and artists. He painted George VI and his family at Windsor and the state portrait of Elizabeth II (1956), which is generally considered to be disappointing.

In 1953 he followed Augustus JOHN as President of the Royal Portrait Society and became ARA. He was appointed RA in 1961, and knighted in 1963; he also received honorary degrees from Manchester and Glasgow. Gunn died in London on 30 December 1964.

H

HAGGARD, SIR (HENRY) RIDER (1856–1925), novelist, was born on 22 June 1856, at West Bradenham Hall, Norfolk, the sixth son of William Meybohm Rider Haggard, a barrister, and his wife, Ella, elder daughter of Bazett Doveton of the East India Company's service. He was educated at Ipswich Grammar School and by private tutors, and at the age of nineteen went out to South Africa as secretary to Sir Henry Bulwer, Governor of Natal. In 1878 he became a Master and Registrar of the High Court of the Transvaal. Returning to England in the following year, he married in 1880 an heiress, Mariana Louisa, daughter of Major John Margitson of Ditchingham House, Norfolk. They had one son (who died young) and three daughters.

Haggard was called to the Bar (Lincoln's Inn) in 1884, but decided to make his career not in the law, but in writing. In 1882 he had published *Cetawayo and his White Neighbours*, and this was followed by a succession of novels, published between 1885 and 1905. The best-remembered of these are *King Solomon's Mines* (1885), *She* (1887), *Allan Quartermain* (1887), and *Ayesha* (1905), all very readable, romantic stories, based on Rider Haggard's knowledge of Southern Africa.

Apart from his writing of romances, he was keenly interested in agriculture. In 1899, he published *The Farmer's Year Book* and, in 1902, *Rural England* (2 vols.), describing the results of his researches into the condition of agriculture and the rural population in England. He was also much concerned with matters dealing with welfare throughout the British Empire. From 1912 to 1917 he travelled widely as a member of the Dominions Royal Commission. He was knighted in 1912 and created KBE in 1919.

From 1914 to 1925, Rider Haggard kept a diary which was published in 1980. It revealed his close friendship with Rudyard KIPLING and his anxiety about his friend's ill health. In fact, Kipling outlived him by over ten years.

Rider Haggard died in London on 14 May 1925, and the story of his life *The Days of my Life: An Autobiography* was published in 2 vols. in 1926, edited by C. J. Longman.

HAIG, DOUGLAS, first EARL HAIG (1861–1928), field-marshal, was born in Edinburgh on 19 June 1861, the youngest son of John Haig, of Cameron Bridge, Fife, and his wife, Rachael, daughter of Hugh Veitch, of Stewartfield, Midlothian. He was educated at Clifton, Brasenose College, Oxford, and Sandhurst (1883–4). In 1885 he was gazetted to the 7th Hussars in India where he played polo for the regi-

Rider Haggard on the steps of Ditchingham House, 1893

Sir Douglas Haig (left) and Marshal Foch inspecting the guard of honour of the Pipes and 'C' Company, 6th Gordon Highlanders, four days after the armistice

ment. He spent his leaves in France and Germany studying the languages. In 1896 he entered the Staff College, and the good impression he made there brought him to the notice of KITCHENER.

In 1898 Haig served in the Omdurman campaign in the Sudan, and then in the following year went to South Africa as staff officer to FRENCH who commanded the cavalry division. Throughout the Boer War Haig served with distinction, and at the end of hostilities was made CB and aide-de-camp to the King. During 1903–6 he served as Inspector-General of Cavalry under Kitchener in India. He was promoted to major-general in 1904.

While he was staying as the guest of Edward VII at Windsor in 1905, he met the Hon. Dorothy Vivian, daughter of Hussey Crespigny, third Baron Vivian, and one of the Queen's ladies-in-waiting; they were married in the private chapel of Buckingham Palace, the first couple not of royal blood to be married there. Haig's friendship with royalty was to stand him in good stead during the First World War.

In 1906 he was appointed a Director on the general staff at the War Office, and assisted R. B. HALDANE, the Secretary of State for War, in creating the Imperial General Staff and drafting the first British field service regulations. In 1909–11 he returned to India as Chief of Staff to Sir O'Moore Creagh. He was created KCVO in 1909 and promoted to lieutenant-general in 1910.

When the First World War broke out, Haig went to France with I Army Corps. Like Kitchener, he believed that the war would be a long one. During 1914 and 1915 when the British forces were ill equipped for trench warfare, he conducted the retreat from Mons, the first Battle of Ypres, and the Battles of Neuve Chapelle and Loos, after which it became clear that Lord French was incapable of continuing

as Commander-in-Chief, and Haig replaced him on 19 December 1915.

In spite of several attempts to supersede him, he remained in that post for the rest of the war, thanks to the support of King George V and the leaders of the Unionist party, who agreed to support LLOYD GEORGE's claim to be Prime Minister in 1916 on condition that CHURCHILL was kept out and that Haig stayed in command. Haig was almost certainly the ablest officer available; he was resolute, determined, loyal to his subordinates, undeterred by defeats, and always confident that in good time he could win the war. Even the Battle of the Somme from July to November 1916, in which 19,000 British troops were killed, mown down by German machine guns, and 57,000 wounded in a single day, did not upset his habitual calm, and he persevered with his offensive for weeks of further slaughter until it petered out in the mud with no advantage having been attained for all the carnage.

A similar performance was repeated at Passchendaele in the summer of 1917 but, throughout the winter of 1917–18 when the Germans in their turn tried to break through the British and French armies, Haig's courage and resolution inspired his troops to resist successfully, and in 1918, profiting from his earlier mistakes, he was able to lead his armies to victory at last. On New Year's Day 1917 the King had promoted him to field-marshal.

He returned to England in 1919 to take up the post of Commander-in-Chief, Home Forces and to supervise demobilization. The King created him Earl Haig and conferred on him the Order of Merit. He was already GCB, GCVO, and KT. He retired from his command in 1921, and devoted himself to the cause of ex-servicemen, uniting the various ex-service organizations into the British Legion of which he became President. In 1921 he was presented with Bemersyde, the ancestral home of the Haigs, purchased by public subscription.

He died suddenly in London on 30 January 1928; he left one son and two daughters.

HAILEY, (WILLIAM) MALCOLM, Baron Hailey (1872–1969), public servant, was born in Newport Pagnell on 15 February 1872, the third son of Hammett Hailey, medical practitioner, and his wife, Maria Coelia, daughter of John Clode. He was educated at the Merchant Taylors' School and Corpus Christi College, Oxford, where he was a scholar, and obtained firsts in Classical Mods. and Greats (1892–4).

In 1894 he entered the Indian Civil Service and in 1895 was posted to the Punjab. In the following year he married Andreina Alessandra, daughter of Count Hannibale Balzani of Italy. After being colonization officer for the Jhelum Canal Colony, he was posted to the secretariat in 1907, first to the Punjab, and then in 1908 to the Finance Department of the Government of India. In 1912 he was appointed first Chief Commissioner to the new province of Delhi, and in 1919 became finance member of the Viceroy's Executive Council. In 1922 he became home member and leader of the government bloc in the Legislative Assembly. He was appointed KCSI (1922).

He attached great importance to the principle of diarchy under which subjects such as education and local government became the responsibility of Indian ministers. He was wholly committed to constitutional progress. In 1924 he was appointed Governor of the Punjab, and in that post succeeded in preserving peace between Muslim, Sikh, and Hindu. In 1928 he was appointed Governor of the United Provinces, attended the Round Table Conference of 1930–1, and played an important part in the discussions which led to the Government of India Act of 1935. He was appointed GCIE in 1928 and GCSI in 1932.

Hailey left the United Provinces in 1934. He had always taken his leaves in India. He was raised to the peerage in 1936, and became director of a comprehensive survey of Africa which had been suggested by J. C. Smuts in his Rhodes lecture of 1929. *An African Survey* was published in 1938. It contained expert opinion on politics, administration, education, irrigation, soil erosion, and the improvement of crops. Hailey carried out a journey of 22,000 miles in discussing all aspects of its compilation.

Hailey believed that the Africans should and would take over political power and that the 'indirect rule' introduced by Lord Lugard in Northern Nigeria was only a temporary stage in constitutional development.

During the Second World War, Hailey undertook missions to Britain's African colonies and the Belgian Congo. In the course of the war he lost his only son, and his only daughter died a few years later in 1922. In his retirement he served on many committees concerned with colonial affairs. He was sworn of the Privy Council in 1949 and admitted to the Order of Merit in 1956. He was a Rhodes Trustee in 1946–66 and, up to the time of his death, he never ceased trying to further the interests of retired members of the Indian Civil Service, who owed a great deal to his efforts. His last book *The Republic of South Africa and the High Commission Territories* was published in 1963. He received numerous academic honours including an honorary fellowship of Corpus Christi College, Oxford. Hailey died in Putney on 1 June 1969. Few men contributed so much to the transition from bureaucratic rule to democracy in India; few so much to the peaceful transfer of power in Africa.

HAILSHAM, first Viscount (1872–1950). See Hogg.

HALDANE, JOHN BURDON SANDERSON (1892–1964), geneticist, was born on 5 November 1892 in Oxford, the only son of John Scott Haldane, physiologist, and his wife, Louisa Kathleen, daughter of Coutts Trotter of Dreghorn; both parents came from Scottish families, his mother being a passionate feminist. R. B. Haldane was his uncle and his younger sister was to become well known as the writer, Naomi Mitchison. He was educated at Eton and became a mathematical scholar of New College, Oxford, where he obtained firsts in Mathematical Mods. (1912) and Greats (1914).

In the First World War he served in the Black Watch and was twice wounded, once in France and later in Mesopotamia. He finished the war lecturing at a bombing school in India, and then returned to New College as a Fellow, researching in physiology, in which subject as a boy he had been much helped by his father. In 1922 he was appointed Reader in biochemistry at Cambridge under F. Gowland Hopkins. Three years later he was dismissed from his post because he had been cited as co-respondent in a divorce case, but he appealed against dismissal and was reinstated in 1926. In that year he married Charlotte Burghes, née Franken, a journalist. This marriage ended in divorce in 1945.

Whilst holding his readership, Haldane was also officer in charge of genetical investigations at the John Innes Horticultural Research Station from 1927 to 1936 and also held the Fullerian Professorship of Physiology at the Royal In-

J. B. S. Haldane in the Department of Biochemistry, Cambridge, 1920s

stitute from 1930 to 1932. In 1933 he resigned from his Cambridge post to become Professor of Genetics and then of Biometry at University College London. He served in that post until 1957.

In 1945 he had married Helen Spurway, a former student who became a lecturer in his department, and in 1957 they went out to India together where Haldane became a member of the Biometry Research Unit at the Indian Statistical Institute, Calcutta. Four years later, they both became Indian citizens and, in 1962, he was appointed head of the Laboratory of Genetics and Biometry at Bhubaneswar.

Haldane was a remarkable man, with scientific interests covering a very wide field and strong political views that coloured his whole outlook. He was an eccentric who thought nothing of demonstrating the logic of his physiological theories by experimenting upon himself. His main contribution to science was in uniting the Darwinian theory of evolution with Mendelian genetics and in re-establishing natural selection as the accepted mechanism of evolutionary change. He did much to encourage the development of human genetics, and an understanding of animal behaviour and of the physiology of deep-water diving. In connection with this latter work he investigated the disaster to the submarine *Thetis*, in which civilian workmen had been killed. Subsequently during the Second World War, he worked for the Royal Navy on the physiological effects of gases at high pressures, and also undertook physiological research for the RAF.

His great gift as a scientist was his ability to reduce complex problems to simple terms, and his capacity for lucid and vivid exposition. He was a most effective popularizer of science, as was shown by his books *Daedalus* (1924), *Possible Worlds* (1927), and the *Inequality of Man* (1932).

Haldane's political views were strongly influenced by his reactions to the rise of Hitler. He had been a socialist whilst at Oxford but, in the thirties, he inclined more and more towards Communism. He visited Spain three times during the civil war and advised the Spanish Government about defence against gas attacks and air raids. This led to the publication in 1938 of his book *A.R.P.* From 1940 to 1950 he was Chairman of the editorial board of the *Daily Worker* to which he contributed weekly articles. He resigned from the Communist party, however, in 1950, giving as his reason Stalin's interference with science. Nevertheless, he continued to maintain that there was some positive content to the theories of the Russian geneticist, Lysenko, although he was fully aware that, in many of his claims, Lysenko was wrongly attempting to justify ideas which were ideologically acceptable to his Soviet masters.

Haldane spent his final years in India teaching and encouraging research in biometry and genetics. He was honoured by numerous prizes and other academic honours from universities at home and abroad. He died in India on 1 December 1964. He had no children.

HALDANE, JOHN SCOTT (1860–1936), physiologist and philosopher, was born in Edinburgh on 3 May 1860, the fourth son of Robert Haldane, writer to the Signet, of Auchterardar, Perthshire, and his second wife, Mary Elizabeth, daughter of Richard Burdon-Sanderson, of West Jesmond and Otterburn Dene, Northumberland. He was a brother of Richard Burdon HALDANE and Elizabeth Sanderson Haldane, the first woman to be made a JP in Scotland. He was educated at Edinburgh Academy and University and at Jena. He graduated in medicine in 1884, and was appointed demonstrator in physiology at University College, Dundee.

In 1887 he moved to Oxford to be demonstrator to his uncle (Sir) John Burdon-Sanderson, Waynflete Professor of Physiology. He was elected a Fellow of New College in 1901 and was Reader in physiology at Oxford from 1907 to 1913. He became associated with the mining industry through his research into the physiological action of carbon monoxide. Between 1892 and 1900 he introduced new methods for investigating the physiology of respiration, and blood and gas analysis, the most important of which were described in the *Journal of Physiology* (vol.xxxii, 1905). In 1907, after studying the problems of deep-sea diving, he developed a detailed method of 'stage decompression' by which divers could be brought safely to the surface.

During the First World War he worked on the identification of poison gases and methods of treatment of their effects. From 1912 to 1936 he was Director of a mining research laboratory founded by Doncaster colliery owners and was concerned with ventilation, rescue apparatus, fires underground, illumination at the coal face, and pulmonary diseases caused by coal dust. In 1921 he became honorary Professor of Mining at Birmingham University. From 1924 to 1928 he was President of the Institution of Mining Engineers.

He left a record of his work in *Respiration* (1922, 2nd ed. 1935). He was also interested in philosophy and developed his theories in this field in *The Sciences and Philosophy* (1929), *The Philosophical Basis of Biology* (1931), and *The Philosophy of a Biologist* (1935). He received many honorary degrees, was elected FRS in 1897 and appointed CH in 1928.

He married in 1891 Louisa Kathleen, daughter of Coutts Trotter, of Dreghorn; they had one son, J. B. S. HALDANE, FRS, and one daughter, the novelist, Naomi Mitchison. Haldane died at Oxford on the night of 14–15 March 1936, shortly after returning from a visit to Persia (Iran) to investigate heat-stroke in oil refineries.

HALDANE, RICHARD BURDON, VISCOUNT HALDANE, of Cloan (1856–1928), politician, lawyer, and philosopher, was born in Edinburgh on 30 July 1856, the second son of Robert Haldane, writer to the Signet, and his second wife, Mary Elizabeth, daughter of Richard Burdon-Sanderson, of West Jesmond and Otterburn Dene, Northumberland. J. S. HALDANE was his younger brother. He was educated at Edinburgh Academy, and Göttingen and Edinburgh Universities, where he obtained a first in philosophy and graduated MA in 1876.

He was called to the Bar (Lincoln's Inn) in 1879, and in 1882 became junior to Horace (later Lord) Davey and distinguished himself in a number of cases before the Privy Council and the House of Lords. From 1885 to 1911 he was Liberal MP for East Lothian. He took silk in 1890 and dealt with many important appeals before the Privy Council.

From 1905 to 1912 Haldane was Secretary of State for War in the Liberal Governments of Campbell-Bannerman and ASQUITH. In that post, fully cognizant of the growing danger from German militarism, he used his knowledge of Germany, and particularly of the German army, to redevelop the whole military organization in Britain with a view to creating an efficient army capable of meeting the requirements of modern war. Despite the indifference of most of his colleagues, he persuaded the House of Commons to pass legislation necessary to give effect to his reforms, which included the creation of the Imperial General Staff, the formation of the militia into a special reserve, the creation of Officers' Training Corps, the improvement of medical and nursing services, and the building up of an Expeditionary Force. His reforms, though unwelcome to some of his political friends, were well received by most of the senior officers at the War Office. It was primarily due to Haldane's work that, when the First World War broke out, it was possible to mobilize quickly the forces required to go to the aid of Belgium and France.

From 1912 to 1915 Haldane was Lord Chancellor, and in that office he was able to secure an increase in the number of lords of appeal and gave to the Privy Council a status from which it commanded increasing confidence in Britain and in the dominions. In 1912 he went on an abortive mission to Germany to try to persuade the authorities there to limit the expansion of the German navy which Britain regarded as a serious threat to its security. His experience of the Germans provided an embarrassment when war broke out because he, like Prince Louis of BATTENBERG, was labelled pro-German without any justification, and in 1915, when Asquith and BONAR LAW formed a Coalition Government, Haldane was excluded from office.

After leaving office, Haldane became more and more estranged from the Liberal party and, when the Labour party came to power in 1924, he resumed his seat on the Woolsack. From 1925 to 1928 he led the small number of Labour peers who formed the official opposition in the upper house.

For the whole of his adult life Haldane was keenly interested in philosophy. His Giffard lectures at St Andrews University in 1902-3 were published as *The Pathway to Reality* (1903). In a later book, *The Reign of Relativity* (1921), he showed his intensive interest in the theories of Einstein. He also discussed the new ideas of modern science in *The Philosophy of Humanism* (1922), and *Human Experience* (1926). He received numerous honorary degrees, was elected FRS in 1906, and FBA in 1914. In 1911 he was made a viscount. His other honours included PC (1902), KT (1913) and OM (1915). He never married; he died at Cloan on 19 August 1928, and the peerage became extinct.

HALIFAX, EARL OF (1881-1959). See WOOD, EDWARD FREDERICK LINDLEY.

HALL, SIR EDWARD MARSHALL (1858-1927). See MARSHALL HALL.

HAMILTON, CHARLES HAROLD ST JOHN (1876-1961). See RICHARDS, FRANK.

HAMMOND, WALTER REGINALD (1903-1965), cricketer, was born at Dover on 19 June 1903, the son of William Walter Hammond, a corporal (and later a major) in the RGA, and his wife, Charlotte Marion Crisp. After spending his early years in Malta and in China, he went to Cirencester Grammar School, and played his first match for Gloucestershire at the age of seventeen. He became a regular member of the side in 1923 and, two years later, scored 1,818 runs and took 68 wickets and 65 catches in the season, thus establishing himself as a promising all-rounder.

In 1925 he went to the West Indies with the MCC, and made 238 not out in his first representative match. For a year he was out of cricket with an illness, but returned in 1927 and became the first player since W. G. GRACE, in 1895, to score 1,000 runs in May. In the winter he played in all five tests in South Africa. In the summer of 1928 he made 139 and 143 against Surrey, took the wicket of Jack HOBBS, and set up a world record of ten catches in the match.

During the 1928-9 tour in Australia, he made 251 runs at Sydney, 200 at Melbourne, and 119, not out, and 177 at Adelaide, a total of 905 runs in the test matches, with an average of over 113. In 1933 he headed the English averages with an aggregate of 3,323, and he continued to head the averages in every season, except one, for the rest of his career. In 1934 he was less successful in Australia but in his final test match innings in 1938, he scored 240 in six hours after three English wickets had fallen for 31. In that year he ceased to be a professional cricketer and, as an amateur, captained Gloucestershire and England.

In the Second World War he served in the RAF in the Middle East and South Africa. He was now troubled with fibrositis and, when he took an England side to Australia in 1946-7, the tour was a disaster. All the test matches were lost, and Hammond, struggling against ill health, was a failure as captain. At the end of the tour he announced his retirement.

In 1929 Hammond had married Dorothy, daughter of a wool merchant, Joseph Barker Lister; this marriage ended in divorce; and in 1947 he married Sybil Ness-Harvey, of Durban. Hammond settled in South Africa and, after losing his money in an unwise venture, became coach and groundsman to Natal University. He died in Durban on 1 July 1965.

In his heyday few English cricketers, other than Jack Hobbs or Leonard Hutton, could rival Hammond as a batsman, and he was also a bowler who took wickets, and a fielder in the slips who missed very few chances. In his career he made 50, 493 runs, with 167 centuries, took 732 wickets, and made 819 catches. In his book *My Life Story*, Hobbs described Hammond as 'a really great bat', 'a good change bowler', and 'a brilliant fielder anywhere'.

HANCOCK, ANTHONY JOHN (TONY) (1924-1968), comedian, was born at Small Heath, Birmingham, on 12 May 1924, the second son of John Hancock, hotelier, and his wife, (Lucy) Lilian Thomas. He was educated at Durlston Court, Swanage, and Bradfield College, Reading. Much of his youth was spent in Bournemouth where, in his father's hotel, he met many people from the world of entertainment.

During the Second World War he enlisted in the RAF, and in 1942 toured with ENSA. From 1946 to 1948 he appeared at the Windmill Theatre, but his success came not on the stage, but in radio. He started out in 'Workers' Playtime', 'Variety Bandbox', and 'Educating Archie', and in 1954 made an immediate success with his own programme 'Hancock's Half-Hour'.

With a script produced by Alan Simpson and Ray Galton, and supported by Sid James, Bill Kerr, and Kenneth Williams, Hancock appeared as a misanthropic, pretentious snob, in situations in which the whole world was at fault except Anthony Aloysius St John Hancock in his incongruous East Cheam milieu. The series was very funny indeed, and in 1956 it was transferred to television where the sight of the heavy-jowled, seedy-looking Hancock, impatient with the stupidity of all around him, made him more popular than ever with his audience. One calls to mind the radio ham, receiving a mayday call, shouting with frustrated annoyance at the caller that he must wait until he could find a pencil. Together with Sid James, Hancock was involved in constant disaster of one sort or another, and their audience enjoyed every moment.

Then, bored with this kind of success, Hancock parted company with Sid James and with Galton and Simpson. He made three poor films and took part in a television series

Tony Hancock, 'Television's funniest man of 1959', uses his trophy as a stage prop

which was not a success. He took to drinking heavily. The resentment against life, which he had expressed so lugubriously on the screen, became the real thing. In the end he committed suicide in Sydney, Australia on 25 June 1968.

In 1950 he married Cicely Romanis; this marriage ended in divorce in 1965, and he married 'Freddie' Ross, his public relations agent, in the same year. This second marriage also ended in divorce, a week before he died.

HANDLEY, THOMAS REGINALD (TOMMY) (1892–1949), radio comedian, was born in Liverpool on 17 January 1892, the son of John Handley, a cowkeeper, and his wife, Sarah Anne Pearson. On leaving school, he worked for a short time as a salesman but was determined to go on the stage. In 1917 he joined the Royal Naval Air Service and became a member of a concert party. After the war, he worked with Jack HYLTON, the band leader, and toured with a music-hall sketch, which reached the London Coliseum and was part of a royal command variety performance in 1924.

In 1929 he married a singer, Rosalind Jean, daughter of Robert Allistone, a jeweller; she had been the wife of William Henshall; they had no children.

From 1925 he worked in radio with his own revues and also appeared in a film, but his great success arrived in 1939 when, for the next ten years, he became the leading actor in ITMA (It's that man again), a weekly programme of nonsense, which became more familiar to radio audiences than any other throughout the Second World War. The catch phrases, such as Mrs Mopp's 'Can I do you now, sir', and the bibulous Colonel's 'I don't mind if I do', repeated week after week, never seemed to pall, and sustained the sense of humour of wartime audiences, avid for something to laugh at. The script writer was Ted Kavanagh, but it was Tommy Handley who made the show live.

In 1942 it made history by being the first radio programme to be selected for a royal command performance. After the war, the series continued without losing its appeal but, when Handley died suddenly in London on 9 January 1949, the show died with him.

HANDLEY PAGE, SIR FREDERICK (1885–1962), aircraft designer and manufacturer, was born on 15 November 1885 at Cheltenham, the second child of Frederick Joseph Page, master upholsterer, and his wife, Eliza Ann Handley. He was educated at Cheltenham Grammar School and Finsbury Technical College.

In 1906 he was appointed chief electrical designer at Johnson and Phillips Ltd., Charlton, and in 1907 joined the (Royal) Aeronautical Society and helped to construct an automatically stable aeroplane. After constructing several aeroplanes and a glider, he registered Handley Page Ltd. in 1909 and flew his first monoplane in the following year. He joined the Northampton Polytechnic Institute (later the City University) as lecturer in aeronautics and installed a wind tunnel. In 1911 he flew his first passenger-carrying monoplane across London. His first biplane was demonstrated in 1914, and during the First World War he produced a large twin-engined bomber followed, in 1918, by a four-engined bomber. Planes of these types were the first to fly from England to India. He was appointed CBE in 1918, and in that year married Una Helen, daughter of John Robert Thynne; they had three daughters.

In 1919 Handley Page promoted airlines in Europe, India, South Africa, and Brazil and, between 1922 and 1939, his aeroplanes carried thousands of passengers over Imperial Airways' routes to India and Africa. Meanwhile, the firm was producing bombers for the Royal Air Force, automatic wing-tip slots having been adopted to eliminate 'stall-and-spin' accidents. Handley Page was knighted in 1942. His transport aircraft assisted in the Berlin air-lift of 1948–9, and equipped the African routes of the British Overseas Airways Corporation.

He was a pioneer in technological education, became a Fellow of the City and Guilds of London Institute in 1939, and Chairman of its council ten years later. He helped to set up the College of Aeronautics at Cranfield in 1946; he was Chairman of the Society of British Aircraft Constructors and its first President (1938–9); he was also Vice-Chairman of the Air Registration Board, and President of the Institute of Transport (1945–6) and the Royal Aeronautical Society (1945–7). He was an Officer of the Legion of Honour and received a number of other honours.

Handley Page died in London on 21 April 1962. He is remembered by the annual Handley Page memorial lecture, first given in 1963 by Prince Philip, Duke of Edinburgh.

Illustration, p. 152.

HANKEY, MAURICE PASCAL ALERS, first BARON

Handley Page in the glider he designed for himself, 1909

HANKEY (1877–1963), Secretary to the Cabinet, was born at Biarritz, France on 1 April 1877, the third son of Robert Alers Hankey, who had been a sheep farmer in Australia, and his wife, Helen, daughter of William Bakewell, a lawyer, of Adelaide. He was educated at Rugby, and joined the Royal Marine Artillery in 1895, was awarded the sword of honour at the Royal Naval College, and from 1899 to 1902 served in *Ramillies* on the Mediterranean station.

In 1903 he married Adeline Hermine Gertrude Ernestine, daughter of Abraham de Smidt, Surveyor-General in the Cape Colony; they had three sons and one daughter.

In 1902 he went to the Naval Intelligence Department at the Admiralty and, after a further short period of service at sea in 1907, was appointed in 1908 Assistant Secretary to the Committee of Imperial Defence, and in 1912 became Secretary.

The outbreak of the First World War led to Hankey's making for himself a unique career, beginning as Secretary of the War Council, the Dardanelles Committee, and the War Committee. In 1916 he was instrumental in establishing the War Cabinet Secretariat of which he became the chief. The War Cabinet met almost every day, and Hankey prepared the agenda, kept the minutes, and took the responsibility of seeing that decisions were put into effect by the department concerned. BALFOUR once said that without Hankey 'we would have lost the war'.

When the war ended, Hankey combined the posts of Secretary to the Cabinet and the Committee of Imperial Defence with that of Clerk of the Privy Council. He held all three of these posts from 1923 to 1938. In addition, he was Secretary to the British delegation at the Paris peace conference (1919), and Secretary to the Council of Four (LLOYD GEORGE, Cle-

menceau, Orlando, and Woodrow Wilson). He was British Secretary at the Washington conference (1921), the Genoa Conference (1922), and the Imperial Conferences of 1921, 1923, 1926, 1930, and 1937. He was also Secretary-General of the conferences on German reparations in London (1924), and Lausanne (1932), the Hague Conferences of 1929 and 1930, and the London Naval Conference (1930).

As a public servant, Hankey was unrivalled. He served successfully leaders as dissimilar in character as ASQUITH, Lloyd George, BONAR LAW, BALDWIN, Ramsay MACDONALD, and Neville CHAMBERLAIN. When Bonar Law ousted Lloyd George as Prime Minister in 1922, he intended to abolish all his predecessor's innovations including the Cabinet Secretariat, but he quickly changed his mind and retained the Secretariat with Hankey as Secretary, and the Cabinet continued to function efficiently.

In 1939 Hankey was created a baron and joined Neville Chamberlain's War Cabinet as Minister without Portfolio. When CHURCHILL became Prime Minister in 1940, he appointed Hankey as Chancellor of the Duchy of Lancaster and subsequently, in 1941, Paymaster General. But Churchill and Hankey were unlikely to get on well together as colleagues. In Cabinet, Hankey had been silent as a Secretary, as a Minister he talked too much. He was a strict exponent of 'muscular Christianity', spartan in his habits, temperate in food and drink, a persistent advocate of the virtues of physical exercise, attributes which were mostly anathema to the cigar-smoking Prime Minister. In 1942 Hankey was dismissed, but in retirement he became Chairman of the Cabinet's Scientific Advisory Committee and other committees which he chaired at the request of Ernest BEVIN.

He also prepared his memoirs of the First World War, but

the publication of these was banned by Churchill, ATTLEE, and Macmillan and, having been revised for security reasons, did not finally appear until 1961 as *The Supreme Command 1914–1918* (2 vols.). In 1945 he published his Lees Knowles lectures on *Government Control in War*, in 1946 *Diplomacy by Conference*, and in 1951 his Romanes lecture on *The Science and Art of Government*.

Hankey had many honours:CB (1912), KCB (1916), GCB (1919), GCMG (1929), and GCVO (1934). He was sworn of the Privy Council in 1939. He held many honorary degrees. He died at Limpsfield on 26 January 1963.

HARARI, MANYA (1905–1969), publisher and translator, was born at Baku (USSR) on 8 April 1905, the youngest daughter of Grigori Benenson, a Jewish financier, and his wife, Sophie Goldberg. In 1914 the family emigrated to London, and Manya was educated at Malvern Girls' College, and Bedford College, London, graduating in 1924.

In 1925 she visited Palestine, where she met and married Ralph Andrew Harari, a leading member of Egypt's Anglo-Jewish community and a merchant banker and art scholar. Shocked by social conditions in Egypt, she undertook welfare work. In 1932 she became a Roman Catholic, and in London was associated with Cardinal Hinsley's Sword of the Spirit movement, for the encouragement of Christian principles in public and private life in Europe.

In 1940 she worked on the *Dublin Review* and then edited her own periodical, *Changing World*. When publication ceased in 1942 she became a translator in the Political Warfare Department.

In 1946 she and Marjorie Villiers founded the Harvill Press, publishing books on religion, metaphysics, the arts, and psychology. When it became a subsidiary of Collins in 1954, she and her partner continued as directors. Manya became widely known when, in collaboration with Max Hayward, she translated and published Boris Pasternak's *Dr Zhivago* (1958). She and Marjorie Villiers also published the works of other Russian authors, such as Alexander Solzhenitsyn, Ilya Ehrenburg, and Yevgeni Yevtushenko.

In 1948 she went to Palestine as a reporter and in 1955, 1956, and 1961 revisited Russia. She and her husband were noted for their generosity in their London home. He was a great collector of French paintings and Japanese art, and an authority on Persian art. He died on 26 May 1969 and Manya died in London on 24 September 1969, four months after her husband, while working on her autobiography, *Memoirs*, published posthumously in 1972. They left one son.

HARDIE, (JAMES) KEIR (1856–1915), socialist and labour leader, was born at Legbrannock, Lanarkshire, on 15 August 1856. His father was a ship's carpenter and his mother, Mary Keir, had been a domestic servant. They were very poor. At seven Hardie became a messenger boy and, at ten, went to work in a Lanarkshire coal mine. He was a miner for twelve years, but went to evening school and became active in the temperance movement. In the late seventies, he began to try to organize the miners; this cost him his job and he was black-listed by the coal-owners. In 1879 he married Lillie, daughter of Duncan Wilson, a collier; they had two sons and two daughters, one of whom died in infancy.

In 1878 he opened a stationer's shop at Low Waters and became local correspondent for the *Glasgow Weekly Mail*. For the next eight years, he worked hard to organize miners' unions, earning a living by journalism, and in 1886 the Ayrshire miners' union was formed, with Hardie as unpaid secretary. In 1888 he broke with the Liberal party and stood as

Keir Hardie addressing an anti-war demonstration, Trafalgar Square, 1914

a Labour candidate at the Mid-Lanark by-election; he also became Founding Chairman of the Scottish Labour party, the first independent labour political party in Britain.

In 1889 he founded the *Labour Leader*, published monthly till 1894 and, thereafter, weekly. This paper became the mouthpiece of the new socialist movement. In 1892 Hardie was elected to Parliament as Independent Labour member for South West Ham; he was fortunate in having Liberal support in what became a straight contest with the Unionists when the Liberal candidate died shortly before the election. He held the seat until 1895 with John BURNS who was returned for Battersea. In 1893 the Independent Labour party was formed with Keir Hardie as Chairman.

He was severely criticized for his opposition to the Boer War, but in 1900 he was elected MP for Merthyr Burghs, a seat he held until his death in 1915. In 1906 he became the leader in the House of Commons of the first Labour group of MPs, and in 1913 became Chairman of the Independent Labour party for a second time. He was shocked by the impotence of labour organizations to prevent the First World War to which he was strongly opposed and his health broke down soon after the outbreak of war. He died on 2 September 1915. Keir Hardie is recognized as the creator of the British political Labour movement.

HARDINGE, ALEXANDER HENRY LOUIS, second BARON HARDINGE OF PENSHURST (1894-1960), Private Secretary to King Edward VIII and King George VI, was born in Paris on 17 May 1894, the younger son of Charles Hardinge (later first Baron Hardinge of Penshurst) and his wife, Winifred Selina Sturt, daughter of the first Baron Alington, of Crichel. At the time, his father was head of chancery in the Paris embassy, and later became Viceroy of India (1910-16).

Alexander Hardinge was educated at Harrow and Trinity College, Cambridge, and in 1915-16 was aide-de-camp to his father in India; the Viceroy had recently lost both his wife and elder son. In 1916-18 Hardinge served in France and Belgium with the Grenadier Guards, was wounded, and awarded the MC.

In 1920 he became Assistant Private Secretary to King George V, being trained by Lord Stamfordham and Clive (later Lord) Wigram. In the following year he married Helen Mary, only daughter of Lord Edward Cecil, and his wife, the Viscountess Milner; they had two daughters and one son.

In May 1936 Edward VIII appointed him Principal Private Secretary. On 27 October 1936 Mrs Simpson obtained a divorce from her second husband, and Edward VIII now saw no impediment to his intention to marry her. At no time did the King take his Private Secretary into his confidence, but Hardinge thought that his duty necessitated warning Edward of the constitutional difficulties he was likely to meet if he persisted in his desire for this marriage. When the divorce was imminent, Hardinge urged the Prime Minister, Stanley BALDWIN, to see the King; he himself informed Edward of growing opposition to the proposed marriage building up in the dominions, while the British press kept silence. Finally, Hardinge warned the King in writing that, whatever popular sympathy there might be for Edward's predicament, the attitude of the Establishment made it inevitable that his determination to marry Mrs Simpson would bring about a constitutional crisis very damaging to the Crown. The King, while carrying on normal business with Hardinge, ignored his warnings, and made no use of his services in the negotiations that led finally to the abdication.

Hardinge continued as Private Secretary to George VI from 1936 to 1943. He was sworn of the Privy Council in 1936 and succeeded his father as Baron Hardinge in 1944. In 1955 in an article in *The Times*, he refuted the allegations that there had been a conspiracy to bring about Edward VIII's abdication and argued that everything possible had been done to keep him on the throne.

In 1943 ill health forced his resignation. He received many honours; MVO (1925), CVO (1931), CB (1934), GCVO and KCB (1937), and GCB (1943). Hardinge died at Penshurst on 29 May 1960.

HARDWICKE, SIR CEDRIC WEBSTER (1893-1964), actor, was born on 19 February 1893 at Lye in Worcestershire, the only son of Edwin Webster Hardicke, a medical practitioner, and his wife, Jessie Masterston. He was educated at King Edward VI Grammar School, Stourbridge, and Bridgnorth School. At first it was intended that he should become a doctor, but he wanted to be an actor and in 1913 joined the (Royal) Academy of Dramatic Art.

In 1913 he toured with Frank BENSON's Shakespeare Company to South Africa and Rhodesia (Zimbabwe), and in 1914 was in the Old Vic Company; but he had shown no special acting talent and, from the end of 1914 to 1921, he served in the army.

He restarted his acting career in 1922 with (Sir) Barry JACKSON's Birmingham Repertory Company, and in 1924 went to the Court Theatre, London, with Jackson and was successful as Churdles Ash, the sharp-tongued old farm labourer, in *The Farmer's Wife*, which had a long run (1925). This success was followed, in 1926, by a similar triumph as the old misogynist in *Yellow Sands*. In 1929 Hardwicke appeared as King Magnus in *The Apple Cart* and in 1930-1 as Edward Moulton-Barrett in *The Barretts of Wimpole Street*.

Hardwicke was now recognized as a star. In 1932 at the Malvern Festival he played Abel Drugger in *The Alchemist* and this success was followed by *Tovarich* (1935) and *The Amazing Dr Clitterhouse* (1937).

In 1934 he was knighted, and two years later gave the Rede lecture at Cambridge on 'The Drama Tomorrow'.

In 1938 Hardwicke went to America where, after playing in *Shadow and Substance* on the New York stage, he went on to Hollywood and appeared in several films. He returned to London in 1944, but continued to have engagements in New York and, after playing with the Old Vic Company again, returned finally to New York where he died on 6 August 1964.

He was married twice; first, to an English actress, Helena Pickard, and secondly to an American actress, Mary Scott. Both wives divorced him; he had a son by each. He published *Let's Pretend* in 1932, and *A Victorian in Orbit*, an autobiography, in 1961.

HARDY, GODFREY HAROLD (1877-1947), mathematician, was born at Cranleigh, Surrey on 7 February 1877, the only son of Isaac Hardy, a master at Cranleigh School, and his wife, Sophia Hall. He was educated at Cranleigh, Winchester, and Trinity College, Cambridge, where he was a scholar, fourth wrangler in 1898, first wrangler in 1899, and elected to a prize fellowship in 1900.

Immersing himself in mathematical research, he wrote the first of 350 original papers which were his life's work. In 1908 he wrote *A Course of Pure Mathematics* which has been translated into many languages. He was elected FRS in 1910 and Cayley lecturer in mathematics at Cambridge in 1914.

In an autobiographical book, *A Mathematician's Apology* (1940), Hardy wrote that he had never done anything 'useful'; he regarded mathematics as purely an intellectual exercise; and in his introduction to the book C. P. SNOW recalled that, in conversation with Hardy, J. Maynard KEYNES once said, 'If you studied the share prices with as much diligence as you study the cricket scores you would be a rich man.' In 1908, however, Hardy made a contribution to genetics that in the textbooks became 'Hardy's law'. In a letter to *Science* (vol. xxviii, new series), he settled the argument about the proportions in which dominant and recessive Mendelian characters would be transmitted in a large mixed population. His work is important in the study of Rh-blood groups and the treatment of haemolytic disease of the new-born. This, at least, was an exception to his general rule that his work, much of it done with collaborators, contributed only to pure mathematics, solutions to problems and theories of interest to mathematicians alone. From 1912 he worked with (Professor) J. E. Littlewood, and in 1934 they published, with Professor George Pólya, their book *Inequalities*, the culmination of a series of papers.

In 1914 Hardy began his collaboration with the Indian mathematician, Srinivasa Ramanujan, an account of which is given in the introduction to Ramanujan's collected works, which Hardy edited, and in Hardy's book *Ramanujan* (1940). Hardy was a disciple of Bertrand RUSSELL and sympathised with his opposition to the First World War.

He became Savillian Professor of Geometry at Oxford in 1920. He not only lectured on geometry but also on 'mathematics for philosophers', to which lectures he drew a large audience of Oxford philosophers. In 1928 he gave the Rouse Ball lecture at Cambridge on 'Mathematical Proof'.

From 1931 to 1942 Hardy held the Sadleirian chair of pure mathematics at Cambridge, and published four volumes in the series of Cambridge Mathematical Tracts, *An Introduction to the Theory of Numbers* (1938, with Professor E. M. Wright), and *Divergent Series* (1949). He was twice President of the London Mathematical Society, on the council of which he served from 1905 to 1945. He received many academic honours, and was generally recognized as the leading English mathematician of his time.

He never married. He died at Cambridge on 1 December 1947.

HARDY, THOMAS (1840–1928), poet and novelist, was born on 2 June 1840 at Higher Bockhampton, near Stinsford, Dorset, the eldest child of Thomas Hardy, a builder, and his wife, Jemima, daughter of George Hand, of Melbury Osmund. Both parents came of native Dorset stock, both were musical, and Hardy's childhood was spent in rural surroundings among people who carried on the crafts and trades of the countryside and celebrated harvest-home and other anniversaries with traditional songs and dances. After a year at the village school, he went at the age of nine to a private school in Dorchester, where he learnt some Latin and French, to which he later added some German and Greek.

In 1856 he went as a pupil to John Hicks, a church architect in Dorchester; he continued to study Latin and Greek, and made the acquaintance of the Revd William Barnes, the Dorset poet, a selection of whose verse he later edited (1908). Under the direction of Hicks, he undertook restoration work on old churches and became a sufficiently accomplished architect to seek work in London, where from 1862 to 1867 he was employed by (Sir) Arthur William Blomfield as a Gothic draughtsman. In 1863 he won the essay prize offered by the Royal Institute of British Architects.

His literary interest at this time was centred on poetry and he tried without success to get magazines to accept some of his verse, which many years later would be published as *Wessex Poems*.

Ill health forced him to return to Dorchester in 1867 and to resume work with Hicks, but his mind was now set upon writing. His first effort was a novel *The Poor Man and the Lady*, which was accepted for publication in 1869 but, on the advice of George Meredith, the publishers' reader, he withdrew the book.

When John Hicks died, his successor sent Hardy to do some survey work in Cornwall and, while there, he met Emma Lavinia, daughter of John Attersoll Gifford, a Plymouth lawyer; she became his first wife in 1874. Meanwhile, in 1871, he had paid a publisher to bring out *Desperate Remedies* anonymously; it had little success, but it was followed in 1872 by *Under the Greenwood Tree*, which was more successful and attracted the attention of (Sir) Leslie Stephen, Editor of the *Cornhill* magazine. After the considerable success of *A Pair of Blue Eyes* (1873), *Far from the Madding Crowd* appeared (still anonymously) in the *Cornhill* (1874). It was at once recognized as a remarkable work.

For the next twenty years, Hardy continued to produce his novels, including *The Return of the Native* (1878), *The Trumpet Major* (1880), *A Laodicean* (1881), *Two on a Tower* (1882), *The Mayor of Casterbridge* (1886), *The Woodlanders* (1887), *Tess of the D'Urbervilles* (1891), and *Jude the Obscure* (1895). *Tess* enjoyed an unprecedented success, earning Hardy a considerable fortune. However, the publication of *Jude* caused an outcry among the critics who saw it as an obscene attack on morality and religious belief. Thereafter, Hardy turned solely to poetry which he had always regarded as being of greater importance than his novels. In any case, with *Jude the Obscure*, he appeared to have exhausted the possibilities of the novel as the medium for his artistic and intellectual output. There was some justification for the jibe of Max BEERBOHM, 'Mr Hardy writes no more novels because he has no more novels to write.' But not all the critics were so unkind: many, including Swinburne, were full of praise for his work, and regarded his Dorsetshire novels, in particular, as a treasure-house of ideas and images.

By 1885 he had settled near Dorchester at Max Gate, a house he had built for himself. Now he devoted himself to his poetry, and published *Wessex Poems* (1898), *Poems of Past and Present* (1901), and his dramatic epic on the Napoleonic theme *The Dynasts* (1903, 1906, 1908), which few of his critics appeared to comprehend at first, but which gradually came to be accepted as one of his greatest achievements. Many of the poems published at this time were works that he had composed and revised at a much earlier period. Among these were *Time's Laughingstocks* (1909), *Satires of Circumstance* (1914), and *Moments of Vision* (1917). There was also the mummers play of Tristran and Iseult, *The Famous Tragedy of the Queen of Cornwall* (1923).

In 1912 Emma Hardy died. The marriage had not been happy but now Hardy was filled with intense remorse which found expression in hundreds of poems, some of them among the finest he ever wrote:

> Woman much missed, how you call to me, call to me,
> Saying that now you are not as you were
> When you had changed from the one who was all to me,
> But as at first, when our day was fair.

Thomas Hardy (with bicycle), Emma Hardy, and the gardener, at Max Gate, 1900

In 1914, though he continued to be obsessed with Emma, Hardy married Florence Emily, daughter of Edward Dugdale, of Enfield; she was at that time an elementary schoolteacher in her mid-twenties; she devoted herself to his welfare for the remaining fourteen years of his life, and after his death fiercely defended his reputation. Hardy had no children.

In 1910 he received the Order of Merit and the freedom of Dorchester. In 1909 he succeeded Meredith as President of the Society of Authors. He received a number of honorary degrees, and was an honorary Fellow of Magdalene College, Cambridge and the Queen's College, Oxford. He died at Max Gate on 11 January 1928, and his ashes were buried in Westminster Abbey.

HARMSWORTH, ALFRED CHARLES WILLIAM, VISCOUNT NORTHCLIFFE (1865–1922), journalist and newspaper proprietor, was born on 15 July 1865 at Chapelizod, near Dublin, the eldest son of a barrister, Alfred Harmsworth, and his wife, Geraldine Mary, daughter of William Maffett, a land agent in co. Down. He went to Stamford Grammar School (1876–8), but he was largely self-educated as at fifteen he became head of the family and had to help to give his brothers a start in life.

From 1880 he was reporting for newspapers and writing articles for boys' and girls' magazines. In 1882 he wrote as a free-lance journalist for the *Globe*, *Morning Post*, and the *St James's Gazette*. Owing to ill health, he had to leave London and, from 1885 to 1887, gained practical experience with a publishing firm in Coventry, Iliffe & Sons.

Returning to London in 1887, he used his savings to form a general publishing business with his brother Harold HARMSWORTH. The company published periodicals, including the well-known *Answers*, and became the nucleus of

the Amalgamated Press. In 1894 they acquired the derelict *Evening News*, and two years later founded the *Daily Mail*, which opened a new epoch in Fleet Street, in presenting news to the public and, in particular, women readers, in a concise, interesting style, employing skilful writers, and using advertisements and competitions to encourage invention, and to finance schemes of exploration and enterprise. The *Daily Mail* was firmly established by 1900 and during the Boer War a duplicate edition was issued in Manchester. Unlike previous newspapers, the *Mail* made a profit under the skilful management of Harold, the financier of the duo.

By this time Alfred Harmsworth owned *Answers*, a magazine for women called *Home Chat*, two comic papers for boys, *Comic Cuts* and *Illustrated Chips*, *Marvel*, a magazine of adventure stories, and a number of other weeklies. They all made money. There was no radio or television to compete with them.

In 1903 the *Daily Mirror* was founded and, from 1905 to 1912, the *Observer* was under Harmsworth control. From 1900 onwards, Harmsworth was at the zenith of his career, rich and powerful, entertaining a stream of influential British and foreign visitors at his homes in London and Surrey with his wife, Mary Elizabeth, daughter of Robert Milner, of Kidlington, Oxfordshire, whom he had married in 1888. He was created a baronet in 1903 and became Baron Northcliffe in 1905. In 1908 he became the chief proprietor of *The Times*.

The *Daily Mail* had the largest circulation of any daily paper. It was popular, 'written by office-boys for office-boys' Lord Salisbury sneered. Harmsworth intended *The Times* to be different. This also had to pay its way, but it was to become the vehicle for Northcliffe's opinions and prejudices. Unassociated with any political party it would continue to be the national voice but the voice would be Northcliffe's. He was anxious to breathe fresh air into the stuffy atmosphere of Printing House Square and in 1912 replaced George Buckle with Geoffrey DAWSON as Editor, and, to quote *The History of the Times 1884–1912*, 'Now that the paper had an editor of his own choice he would bid him lighten the paper, make it easier to read, by concentrating upon news.'

The First World War made Northcliffe a public figure. He conducted his own campaigns for the prosecution of the war, heading the popular movements of the moment: advocating the removal of Lord HALDANE from Whitehall, later, criticizing KITCHENER for the shortage of shells, supporting the creation of the coalition governments, and then condemning their errors. Necessarily, he provoked hostility. He visited the Western Front and later published some of his dispatches in *At The War* (1916).

In 1917 at the request of LLOYD GEORGE, he undertook a British war mission to the USA and, on his return, was created a viscount as a reward for his services. He refused an invitation to become Secretary of State for Air. After the war, however, Northcliffe's relations with Lloyd George changed drastically. The Prime Minister refused to appoint him an official delegate to the peace conference and castigated his baneful influence in a speech in the Commons. Northcliffe's megalomania, which had steadily increased during the war years, may have been caused to some extent by growing

Alfred Harmsworth, caricature entitled 'Imperial Alfred' by Faustin, February 1905

ill health. However, through the *Daily Mail* and *The Times*, he still had influence, and he used it to bring about the Irish Treaty of 1921.

In that year he went on a long projected world tour, and a series of articles he sent back to London were collected and published as *My Journey Round the World* (1922). This was his last great effort. He died on 14 August 1922 in London, and his title became extinct. Northcliffe was a consummate journalist who changed the whole course of British journalism. Lord BEAVERBROOK, in *Politicians and the War* (2 vols., 1928–32), described him as 'the greatest figure who ever strode down Fleet Street'.

HARMSWORTH, HAROLD SIDNEY, first VISCOUNT ROTHERMERE (1868–1940), newspaper proprietor, was born at Hampstead on 26 April 1868, the second son of Alfred Harmsworth, and younger brother of Alfred HARMSWORTH (later Viscount Northcliffe). He was educated at St Marylebone Grammar School, but left at an early age to become a clerk in the Inland Revenue Office. He married in 1893 Mary Lilian, daughter of George Wade Share.

In 1888 he had joined the publishing firm of his brother Alfred and, with the purchase of the *Evening News* in 1894, they both embarked on careers that would make them multi-millionaires. From 1900 to 1914 Harold ran the financial side of the business and made the *Daily Mail* and the *Daily Mirror* highly profitable enterprises.

He was a shy man, and had no wish to attract the public attention paid to his brother. In 1910 he was created a baronet, and began a series of public benefactions, including the founding of a chair at Oxford and two at Cambridge. In 1914 he became Baron Rothermere and started a new and more public phase of his career. In 1917 he was appointed Minister for Air, but soon after his appointment his eldest son died of wounds received in battle. His second son had been killed in 1916, and this further blow for a time overwhelmed the grief-stricken father and he retired from the public eye.

In 1919 he was created a viscount, and resumed his activities with newspapers. He had sold his *Daily Mail* interest in 1910, but still owned the *Daily Mirror*, the *Sunday Pictorial*, a Glasgow paper the *Record*, and the *Leeds Mercury*.

His brother's death in 1922 added to his responsibilities. He took over control of Associated Newspapers, owning the *Daily Mail*, *Evening News*, and the *Sunday Dispatch*. He sold *The Times* to John J. ASTOR, and the Amalgamated Press to the BERRY brothers. Although he still shunned appearing in public, Rothermere was not averse from publicly airing his views. In 1929 he joined with Lord BEAVERBROOK in crusading for Empire Free Trade, which caused Stanley BALDWIN to denounce them both as wanting power without responsibility. Rothermere also campaigned for a strong Air Force, though he had admiration for Hitler and Mussolini and was in sympathy with Sir Oswald MOSLEY.

His excursions into foreign affairs were less important than his benefactions. He made gifts to the Middle Temple, which elected him an honorary bencher, and he saved the Foundling Hospital; he also contributed pictures to municipal galleries. In 1940 he was asked by Lord Beaverbrook, then Minister of Aviation, to undertake a mission to the United States. His health failed and he died in Bermuda on 26 November 1940. He was succeeded by his youngest and only surviving son, Esmond Cecil.

HART, SIR BASIL LIDDELL (1895–1970). See LIDDELL HART.

HARTLEY, ARTHUR CLIFFORD (1889–1960), engineer and inventor, was born in Hull on 7 January 1889, the elder son of a surgeon, George Thomas Hartley, and his wife, Elizabeth Briggs. He was educated at Hymers College, Hull, and the City and Guilds College, London, where he obtained his B.Sc. (Eng.) in 1910. He then undertook practical work in Hull and London.

He served in the Royal Flying Corps during the First World War and was awarded the OBE (1918). He joined the armaments section of the Air Board and was responsible for the development of the Constantinescu gear, which enabled fighter pilots to fire the Vickers machine-gun directly through the propeller blades.

In 1920 he married Dorothy Elizabeth, daughter of Gavin Wallace, a marine engineer, of Shanghai; they had two sons; she died in 1923, and he married in 1927 Florence Nina, daughter of William Egerton Hodgson, a merchant of Doncaster; they also had two sons.

In 1924 Hartley joined the Anglo-Persian (Iranian) Oil Company and in 1934 became Chief Engineer. At the outbreak of the Second World War, he was seconded to the Ministry of Aircraft Production and helped to develop the automatic bomb-sight which was used to sink the *Tirpitz*, and also FIDO, the fog dispersal unit which was used on runways to assist bombers returning to base during foggy weather.

His most important contribution to the war effort was PLUTO (Pipeline under the Ocean), a high-pressure petrol pipeline to provide vital supplies after the Normandy landings, which had to be constructed secretly to avoid destruction by the Germans. Many of these lines were laid down, and a million gallons of petrol a day were pumped to the advancing armies making for the Rhine.

In 1944 Hartley was appointed CBE and in 1946 received the US Medal of Freedom. He retired from the Anglo-Iranian Oil Co. in 1951 and became a consultant. In 1959 his invention of a hoisting device for loading oil tankers, where no berthing facilities were available, was successfully used for the first time by the Kuwait Oil Co.

In 1951 he was President of the Institution of Mechanical Engineers and in 1959 of the Institution of Civil Engineers. He received many professional honours. Hartley died in London on 28 January 1960.

HASTINGS, SIR PATRICK GARDINER (1880–1952), lawyer, was born in London on 17 March 1880, the younger son of Alfred Gardiner Hastings, an unsuccessful solicitor, and his wife, Kate Comyns Carr, a pre-Raphaelite painter. He spent two years at Charterhouse, but his youth was affected by the variations in the family fortunes. For a time he held a post as a mining engineer and then, with his elder brother, served with the Suffolk Imperial Yeomanry in the Boer War.

He had always wanted to be a barrister and, in spite of his very limited means, succeeded in reading for the Bar, and was called by the Middle Temple in 1904. He was fortunate to be able to enter the chambers of (Sir) Horace Avory, from whom he learnt a great deal. He married in 1906, Mary Ellenore, daughter of Lt.-Col. Frederick Leigh Grundy; at the time he and his wife had £20 between them. However, his fortunes soon began to improve. Having been rejected as medically unfit for service in the First World War, in 1919 he took silk.

He was now recognized as a successful advocate and, having become Labour MP for Wallsend in 1922, was appointed Attorney-General by Ramsay MacDonald in 1924 and knighted. Hastings's occupation of this office was memorable for the so-called Campbell case, which led to the downfall of the first Labour Government.

Campbell was an ex-serviceman with a good war record who, in 1924, was acting Editor of the *Workers Weekly* when the paper published an appeal to soldiers not 'to turn your guns on your fellow workers'. The Director of Public Prosecutions decided to bring a case against Campbell for sedition. Sir Patrick Hastings decided to drop the prosecution which both he and the Prime Minister regarded as ill-advised. The Communists claimed, and the opposition to the Government complained, that this was political interference with the course of justice. MacDonald would have preferred Hastings to resign, but the controversy brought about the defeat of the Government and, at the subsequent election, Hastings was again returned for Wallsend. He resigned in 1926 as overwork was endangering his health.

From 1926 to 1948 Hastings shared the leadership of the Common Law Bar with his friend Norman Birkett. He appeared in some sensational cases, including the action between Dr Marie Stopes and Dr Sutherland, the action for libel brought by Harold Laski, and the Savidge tribunal. His brilliance in cross-examination and his incisive appeals to juries were sufficient to win cases without the histrionics of some of his predecessors.

After his retirement in 1948 he published his *Autobiography* (1948), *Cases in Court* (1949), and *Famous and Infamous Cases* (1950). He also wrote some successful plays, including *The River* (1925), *Scotch Mist* (1926), and *The Blind Goddess* (1947).

He and his wife had two sons and three daughters. Their younger son was killed in the Second World War, and in 1950, on a visit to his other son, who was farming in Kenya, Hastings suffered a stroke from which he never recovered. He died in London on 26 February 1952.

HATTON, SIR RONALD GEORGE (1886–1965), horticultural scientist, was born in Hampstead on 6 July 1886, the youngest child of Ernest Hatton, barrister, and his wife, Amy, daughter of William Pearson KC. He was educated at Brighton College, Exeter School, and Balliol College, Oxford (1906–10). He then worked as a farm labourer and in 1912 went to study agriculture at Wye College in Kent. A year later his book, *Folk of the Furrow*, was published under the name of Christopher Holdenby.

In 1914 he married Hannah Rachel, daughter of Henry Rigden of Ashford, Kent; they had one son. In the year of his marriage he became Acting Director of the East Malling Research Station and in 1918 Director. During the next thirty years he developed East Malling into the leading fruit research institute in the world. His own research work was mainly in the classification and standardization of the rootstocks of apples, pears, and plums. With the help of his staff he transformed fruit-growing from folklore to a science. He also worked on the control of pests and diseases, particularly in liaison with the John Innes Horticultural Institute, and the Institute of Plant Physiology of the Imperial College of Science, London.

Many students came to East Malling from all over the world and, up to his retirement in 1949, Hatton visited a number of countries to advise on fruit growing. He published many papers, and was the founder in 1919 of the *Journal of Pomology*, which in 1948 became the *Journal of Horticultural Science*. He was the first Director of the Imperial (later Commonwealth) Bureau of Horticulture and Plantation Crops (1929), and its journal, *Horticultural Abstracts*, begun in 1931, became the standard source of information on fruit crops.

In 1952 Hatton was elected a Vice-President of the Royal Horticultural Society; he was elected FRS in 1944, and a Fellow of Wye College in 1949. He was appointed CBE in 1934 and knighted in 1949. Hatton died in Benenden on 11 November 1965.

HAWTHORN, (JOHN) MICHAEL (1929-1959), racing motorist, was born in Mexborough, Yorkshire on 10 April 1929, the only son of Leslie Hawthorn, a motor engineer and racing motor-cyclist, and his wife, Winifred Mary Symonds. He went to school at Ardingly and, when he left in 1946, was apprenticed to Dennis Brothers, commercial vehicle builders at Guildford. He then went to Kingston Technical College and the College of Automobile Engineering at Chelsea intending to join his father's business.

He found that he preferred driving to engineering, and began with motor-cycle racing. In 1951 he had his first season as a racing motorist driving a pre-war Riley. In the following year, he was invited by a friend of the family to race with a new Cooper-Bristol and had an immediate success at Goodwood in competition with world-class drivers. Enzo Ferrari invited him to drive for Ferraris in 1953 and he won the French Grand Prix from Fangio, the reigning champion. At the end of the season he was awarded the gold star of the British Racing Drivers' Club.

In 1954 he had a bad crash in the Syracuse Grand Prix and his legs were saved by the devoted nursing of some nuns

in Sicily; he was in hospital in Rome for some time. On recovery, he was on his way to take part in the Le Mans 24-hour race, when he heard that his father had died in a motor accident. In spite of these troubles, he won the Spanish Grand Prix that year.

In 1955 he won the Le Mans race for Jaguar, beating Fangio in a Mercedes-Benz and setting up a lap record. In this race there was an accident in which eighty spectators were killed by a German car. In 1957 he returned to Ferrari, and in the following year won the French Grand Prix and became the first British world champion. He was awarded the British Automobile Racing Club's gold medal.

He intended to get married and retire from motor racing in 1959, but he was killed in a motor accident near Guildford on 22 January 1959. Mike Hawthorn published two accounts of his exploits, *Challenge Me the Race* (1958), and *Champion Year* (1959).

HAYWARD, JOHN DAVY (1905-1965), anthologist and bibliophile, was born in London on 2 February 1905, the younger son of John Arthur Hayward, a surgeon, of Wimbledon, and his wife, Rosamund Grace, daughter of George Rolleston, a physician. He was educated at Gresham's School, Holt, and King's College, Cambridge (1923-7). From an early age he suffered from muscular dystrophy, and the greater part of his adult life had to be spent in an invalid chair. Fortunately, he had a private income and was able to follow a career as author, editor, critic, and book-collector.

He was a friend of T. S. ELIOT, Geoffrey FABER, and F. V. Morley and, from 1946, he and Eliot lived together in Cheyne Walk, Chelsea, an association which ended only with

Mike Hawthorn with his Ferrari, before the start of the 1954 Syracuse Grand Prix in which he narrowly escaped death

Eliot's second marriage in 1957. Among the offices which Hayward held were those of Editorial Adviser to the Cresset Press, Editorial Director of the *Book Collector*, and Vice-President of the Bibliographical Society. He was appointed CBE in 1953.

His industry was remarkable. He edited the *Collected Works* of Rochester (1926), and published the *Complete Poetry and Selected Prose of John Donne* (1929), *The Letters of Saint-Evremond* (1930), Swift's *Gulliver's Travels* (1934), and Swift's *Selected Prose Works* (1949). He also compiled anthologies, including *Nineteenth Century Poetry* (1932), *Silver Tongues* (1937), *Love's Helicon* (1940), *T. S. Eliot: Points of View* (1941), *Seventeenth Century Poetry* (1948), *Dr. Johnson* (1948), *Donne* (Penguin Poets, 1950), *T. S. Eliot: Selected Prose* (1953), *The Penguin Book of English Verse* (1956), *The Faber Book of English Verse* (1958), *Herrick* (Penguin Poets, 1961), and *The Oxford Book of Nineteenth-Century English Verse* (1964).

Hayward never married. He died in Chelsea on 17 September 1965. He left his collection of books and letters from authors, including T. S. Eliot, to King's College, Cambridge, where there is a Hayward Room in the library.

HEATH ROBINSON, WILLIAM (1872–1944), cartoonist and book illustrator, was born in London on 31 May 1872, the son of Thomas Robinson, principal illustrator on the

A typical 'Heath Robinson contraption': the multi-movement tabby silencer

Penny Illustrated Paper, and his wife, Eliza Ann, daughter of William Heath, a publican. He was educated at Islington schools, and studied at the Islington School of Art (1887) and the Royal Academy Schools (1890).

He then worked in his father's studio and became an illustrator of books, including *Don Quixote*, a Hans Andersen, an *Arabian Nights*, and the poems of Edgar Alan Poe (1897-1902), followed in later years by *Twelfth Night*, a Rabelais, and the *Water Babies* (1908-15).

In 1903 he married Josephine Constance, daughter of John Latey, art and literary editor of the *Penny Illustrated Paper*; they had four sons and one daughter.

He also did advertising work and a number of theatrical commissions, but he will be remembered for his humorous drawings of jerry-built machinery and apparatus, constructed in a highly complicated design, for completely ridiculous purposes. His work added a new phrase to the language, 'a Heath Robinson contraption for any unpractical, imaginary piece of apparatus, designed to carry out some simple task in the most complicated way. These humorous caricatures appeared in the *Sketch*, *Bystander*, *Strand Magazine*, and *Illustrated London News*, and by 1914 Heath Robinson's reputation was world-wide. He published *My Line of Life* in 1938. He died in London on 13 September 1944. Advertising agents continue to make use of his ideas labelled 'after Heath Robinson'.

HEINEMANN, WILLIAM (1863–1920), publisher, was born at Surbiton on 18 May 1863, the eldest son of Louis Heinemann, German-born and naturalized in 1856, and his wife, Jane Lavino, of Manchester. He was educated in Dresden and then had a tutor in England. He intended to become a musician but decided that his talent was not sufficient to warrant a career in music.

As he was keenly interested in books, he trained as a publisher, and in 1890 set up his own business. The first of his publications was (Sir) Hall Caine's *The Bondman* (1890) which was a best seller. He also published J. M. Whistler's *Gentle Art of Making Enemies* (1890) and the Pennells' *Life of Whistler*. From 1895 to 1897, he published *The New Review* edited by W. E. Henley.

Heinemann married in 1899 Donna Magda Stuart Sindici, a young Italian whose first novel *Via Lucis* he had published; they divorced in 1904.

The most notable aspect of Heinemann's publishing was his fiction list, which included among its authors R. L. Stevenson, Rudyard KIPLING, Sarah Grand, Flora Annie Steel, Israel Zangwill, Max BEERBOHM, John MASEFIELD, John GALSWORTHY, Somerset MAUGHAM, and H. G. WELLS. He also published plays, including those by Sir Arthur PINERO, Somerset Maugham, Israel Zangwill, Henry Davies, and Charles Haddon Chambers.

Heinemann spoke French, German, and Italian fluently and knew some Spanish. His firm produced, under the editorship of Edmund GOSSE, the International Library of translations from leading works of European fiction, commissioned Mrs Constance Garnett's translations of Dostoevsky, Turgenev, and Tolstoy, and launched in England the works of Ibsen, Björnson, and Romain Rolland. In partnership with an American, Dr James Loeb, he produced the Loeb classical library of translations of classical authors.

He was one of the founders of the Publishers' Association in 1896 and was President from 1909 to 1911. He died suddenly in London on 5 October 1920.

HENDERSON, ARTHUR (1863-1935), labour leader and politician, was born in Glasgow on 13 September 1863, the younger son of David Henderson, a Scottish cotton-spinner, who died when Henderson was nine. His mother re-married and moved to Newcastle upon Tyne. He left school at twelve and was apprenticed as a moulder at the local locomotive and foundry works. He learnt to make speeches as a Wesleyan lay preacher and at eighteen joined the Ironfounders' Union. In 1888 he married Eleanor, daughter of William Watson, of Newcastle; they had three sons and a daughter.

In 1892 he became a member of the Newcastle city council. He was at that time a supporter of Gladstone, but in 1899 he attended the London conference of socialists and trade unionists, which set up the Labour Representation Committee, and in 1903 he became its Treasurer. In that year he was elected Independent Labour MP for Barnard Castle, a seat which he held until 1918. Subsequently he was MP for Widnes (1919-22), East Newcastle (1923), Burnley (1924-31), and Clay Cross (1933-5). In 1903 he was working closely with Keir HARDIE and Ramsay MACDONALD and presided over the conference in 1906 which established the Labour party, of which he was Secretary from 1911 to 1934.

Unlike MacDonald, he supported the Government during the First World War and held War Cabinet office in both ASQUITH'S and LLOYD GEORGE'S Governments as adviser on labour. He was sworn of the Privy Council in 1915. A year later he lost his eldest son, killed in action. In 1917 he visited Russia, and resigned from the Government when Lloyd George rejected his advice to send delegates to a conference of international socialists at Stockholm. He refused to accept the CH.

The Stockholm conference gave Henderson an international outlook, but this did not preclude his working to strengthen and broaden the Labour party organization. He held the office of Chief Whip in 1914, 1921-3, and 1925-7, and was largely responsible for the statement of the party's aims in *Labour and the Nation* (1928). In the first Labour Government, he was Home Secretary (1924), and in the 1929 Government was Foreign Secretary.

During his tenure of the Foreign Office, he strove to establish British leadership in seeking secure foundations for international peace through the League of Nations. To reach agreement on Egyptian independence, he forced the resignation of Lord LLOYD, the High Commissioner and, in pursuance of good relations, sent the first British Ambassador to Soviet Russia. When Stresemann, the German Chancellor, died in October 1929, Henderson became the dominant figure in the League of Nations. He was trusted by both France and Germany and, when in 1932 a world disarmament conference met, he was elected President.

By the time the conference was held, Henderson had ceased to be Foreign Secretary. When the economic crisis hit the Labour Government and MacDonald decided to form a National Government, Henderson resigned and in the 1931 general election was defeated. From 1932 to 1935, however, he continued to preside over the disarmament conference at Geneva, and in 1934 was awarded the Nobel peace prize. 'Uncle Arthur', as he was known to his contemporaries, died in London on 20 October 1935.

HENDERSON, SIR NEVILE MEYRICK (1882-1942), diplomat, was born at Horsham on 10 June 1882, the second son of Robert Henderson, manager of the family business of R. & I. Henderson, and his wife, Emma Caroline, daughter of John Hargreaves of Lyndhurst. He was educated at Eton and abroad, and entered the diplomatic service in 1905.

He served in the Foreign Office and at St Petersburg (Leningrad), Tokyo, Rome, Nish, Paris, and Constantinople (Istanbul) between 1905 and 1920. He was promoted to Counsellor in 1922, and in 1924 posted to Cairo, where he disagreed with the policy of Lord LLOYD, the High Commissioner, and would have made concessions to Egyptian nationalism. In 1928 he became Counsellor-Minister in Paris.

From 1929 to 1935 he was Minister Plenipotentiary at Belgrade and formed a close friendship with King Alexander of Yugoslavia, a dictator, whom Henderson greatly admired. After a short period as Ambassador at Buenos Aires (1935-6), he was posted as Ambassador to Germany in 1937.

Henderson had served in the Foreign Office for a very short time in his career, and was to some extent cut off from the main stream of opinion in England, rigidly adhering to his own views, which were critical of the French, isolationist as far as Britain's involvement in Europe was concerned, and sympathetic to the claims made by Hitler. How he could serve in Germany and ignore what was being done there by the Nazi regime is almost incomprehensible. He attended the Nuremberg rallies of 1937 and 1938 and, having no prejudice against authoritarian government, thought that he was destined to reconcile Britain and Germany, despite the obvious growth of Nazi militarism and the threat which Hitler posed to the peace of Europe. His reports to London were consistently in favour of compromise with the increasing demands of the Führer, and provided no warning to Neville CHAMBERLAIN of the dangers of appeasement. He acquiesced in the anschluss incorporating Austria into Germany and supported those who sought appeasement throughout the Czechoslovak crisis and up to and beyond the Munich agreement of 1938.

Disillusion set in only when Hitler occupied Czechoslovakia in March 1939 and Henderson was recalled to London. On return to Germany, he undertook the thankless task of persuading Hitler not to attack Poland and risk war with France and Britain. On the outbreak of war he returned to Britain, and ill health prevented him from being offered any further employment. He tried to justify his actions in Berlin and those of the British Government in *Failure of a Mission* (1940) which was followed by *Water under the Bridges*, published posthumously in 1945.

Henderson was appointed CMG (1923), KCMG (1932), and GCMG (1939); he was sworn of the Privy Council in 1937. He never married. He died in London on 30 December 1942.

HENSON, HERBERT HENSLEY (1863-1947), bishop, was born in London on 8 November 1863, the fifth son of Thomas Henson, a business man, and his first wife, Martha Fear. His mother died when he was six, and he was brought up by his German stepmother, who encouraged his reading. He was educated at a private school in Broadstairs, and his father, who was a strict non-conformist, was persuaded by his second wife to allow the boy to go to Oxford as a non-collegiate student (1881). He obtained a first in modern history (1884) and was elected to a fellowship at All Souls.

In 1887 he was ordained deacon and became head of Oxford House, Bethnal Green; in 1888 he was ordained priest and appointed to an All Souls living in Barking. He was already becoming opposed to Anglo-Catholic opinions, and from 1895, when he accepted the chaplaincy of Ilford Hospital, became a highly controversial figure in the Church of

England, writing and preaching in favour of the liberal views of churchmen who thought as he did. He was an eloquent preacher attracting huge congregations.

In 1902 he married Isabella Caroline, only daughter of James Wallis Dennistoun of Dennistoun; they had no children. Two years earlier he had become a Canon of Westminster Abbey and Rector of St Margaret's, which provided new opportunities for carrying on the struggle in the many fields of his interest and influence. As a proctor in Convocation (1903-12) he was a lively critic of the episcopate and a fierce advocate of closer relations with the Free Churches. Charles GORE, Bishop of Birmingham, forbade him to preach in a Congregational church in the city, but Henson defied him and went on denouncing Anglo-Catholicism.

He was appointed Dean of Durham in 1912, and in 1917 was nominated to the see of Hereford. Bishop Gore and other Anglo-Catholics strongly opposed the appointment, stressing their doubts about his orthodoxy, but Henson was able to convince Archbishop DAVIDSON that his views had been misrepresented or misunderstood. As a bishop he endeared himself to his people in Hereford, and there was much regret when in 1920 he was translated to Durham.

He remained at Durham until 1939, continuing to engage in controversy. When Parliament rejected the revised Prayer Book, he advocated disestablishment; his outspoken objection to socialist remedies to cure the prevalent unemployment aroused some hostility among the miners, but his obvious humanity and his active efforts to relieve distress endeared him even to those who were violently opposed to his opinions.

In 1935-6 he delivered the Gifford lectures on 'Christian Morality'. He also published *Ad Clerum* (1937), *Bishoprick Papers* (1946), and his autobiography *Retrospect of an Unimportant Life* (3 vols., 1942-50). Henson died on 27 September 1947 at Hintlesham near Ipswich to which he had retired in 1939.

HEPWORTH, DAME (JOCELYN) BARBARA (1903-1975), sculptor, was born on 10 January 1903 at Wakefield, the daughter of H. R. Hepworth, CBE, a civil engineer, and his wife, Gertrude Johnson. She studied at Wakefield Girls' High School, Leeds School of Art, and the Royal College of Art (1920-4). She went to Italy with a scholarship in 1924 and met a fellow sculptor, John Skeaping, whom she married a year later. Their first joint exhibition was held at the Beaux Arts Gallery, London in 1928.

In 1938, after divorce from John Skeaping, Barbara Hepworth married Ben Nicholson, with whom she had been working since 1931; they had triplets, a son and two daughters. She also had a son by her first marriage. He was killed while serving with the RAF in Malaya in 1953. She and Nicholson exhibited together at the Lefevre Gallery, London, and were both active members of groups such as 'Unit One', concerned with abstract art. In 1939, a few weeks before the outbreak of war, they left London for St Ives and became part of a colony of artists there. One recalls visiting her home which was decorated with stones and shells from the beach, artistically arranged, and which seemed to be full of young children, while Barbara herself was sitting in the garden, surrounded by her monolithic works in stone, industriously chiselling at an enormous block of wood, which, in due course, would become one of those enigmatic, but strangely beautiful, abstractions for which she became famous.

By the end of the fifties her work was winning prizes

Barbara Hepworth at work on her monolithic sculptures for the Festival of Britain, 1951

abroad from São Paulo to Tokyo. Her commissions included the bronze 'Single Form' for the UN building in New York and the large bronze abstract for State House, Holborn. Permanent collections of her work are to be seen in the Tate Gallery and in galleries and museums all over the world.

She received many academic honours and awards. In 1958 she was appointed CBE and in 1965 DBE, by which time her reputation was probably greater than that of any other woman sculptor. A film of her work *Figures in a Landscape* was made in 1952-3, and much has been written about her art. She and Ben Nicholson were divorced in 1951. She died at St Ives in a fire at her studio on 20 May 1975.

HERBERT, SIR ALAN PATRICK (1890-1971), author and wit, was born on 24 September 1890, the eldest son of Patrick Herbert Herbert of Ashtead, Surrey, a civil servant, and his wife, Beatrice Eugénie, daughter of Sir Charles Jasper Selwyn, a lord justice of appeal. He was educated at Winchester and New College, Oxford, where he obtained a first in jurisprudence. He was already writing light verse while still at school, and while he was at Oxford became a contributor to *Punch*.

During the First World War he enlisted as a seaman in the RNVR, was commissioned in 1915, and served at Gallipoli and in France. In 1917 he was wounded and, during convalescence, wrote *The Secret Battle* (1919). In 1914 he had married Gwendolen Harriet, daughter of Harry Quilter, artist and art critic; they had three daughters and a son. The composer Roger Quilter was his wife's nephew.

In 1918 he was called to the Bar (Inner Temple) but, after two years as Private Secretary to Sir Leslie Scott, KC, MP, joined the staff of *Punch* (1924). Over the initials APH, he used his knowledge of the law to satirize its absurdities and anomalies in a series of amusing articles on 'Misleading Cases' which were published as a book in 1927. Later in *Holy Deadlock* (1934), he mercilessly exposed the crudities of the English divorce laws.

Meanwhile, his revue *Riverside Nights* (1926) was put on at the Lyric Theatre, Hammersmith, followed by his operettas, including *La Vie Parisienne* (1929), *Tantivy Towers* (1931), and *Derby Day* (1932). In 1930 he published a novel about canal people, *The Water Gipsies*. Numerous amusing letters to *The Times* also helped to bring him to public notice. One of them dated 21 March 1961 included a letter in verse to the Inland Revenue which provoked a reply in the same medium.

In 1935 he was elected independent MP for Oxford University, a seat which he held until the university franchise was abolished in 1950. His private member's bill was passed as the Matrimonial Causes Act in 1936. In 1940 he fought in the House of Commons to prevent purchase tax being applied to books. He won. During the Second World War he served with the Royal Naval Auxiliary Patrol. In 1945 he was knighted.

After the war, he returned to writing for the stage, and his musical *Bless the Bride* (1950) was an outstanding success, as was the COCHRAN revue, *Home and Beauty*. He continued to fight for causes in which he was keenly interested, such as a public lending right for authors and the construction of a Thames barrage. His book *Independent Member* (1950) defended the case for private members of the Commons. In 1970 he published *A.P.H., his Life and Times*.

Herbert served on many organizations. He was a Trustee of the National Maritime Museum, President of the London Corinthian Sailing Club, President of the Society of Authors, and Vice-President of the Performing Rights Society. He was appointed CH in 1970, and DCL Oxford in 1958. He died in London on 11 November 1971.

HESS, DAME (JULIA) MYRA (1890–1965), pianist, was born in London on 25 February 1890, the youngest child of Frederick Solomon Hess, a textile merchant, and his wife, Lizzie, daughter of John Jacobs, a shopkeeper and moneylender, of London. She grew up in a typical Jewish family, receiving only a superficial education; but from the age of five she was given piano and cello lessons. She studied the piano at the Guildhall School of Music and at the Royal Academy of Music to which she went in 1903 with the Ada Lewis scholarship. There she studied under Professor Tobias Matthay for five years.

Her début took place on 14 November 1907 at the Queen's Hall in London with Thomas BEECHAM conducting. At the time he was almost unknown and was notoriously unsympathetic to female soloists. But, though nervous, she successfully played concertos by Saint-Saëns and Beethoven. Her first solo recital was given at the Aeolian Hall two months later. However, at this time, she had few engagements and depended to a large extent upon teaching.

Her first great success came in 1912 in Holland when she played with the Concertgebouw Orchestra conducted by Willem Mengelberg. After this, her engagements steadily increased in England. The First World War made it im-

possible for her to tour abroad and, while it lasted, she lived in London, sharing a flat with the sisters of Ivy COMPTON-BURNETT.

In 1922 she made a successful début in the USA at the Aeolian Hall, New York. From that time, she toured North America each year in the winter and gave concerts in England and Holland in the spring and autumn. She played contemporary music in the early part of her career, but gradually came to prefer the classical repertoire. She enjoyed chamber music and regularly played with the London String Quartet at this time. Later, in the 1930s, she played in Britain and the USA with Jelly D'Aranyi, the Hungarian violinist, with whom she enjoyed a close friendship.

When the Second World War broke out, she cancelled an American tour and stayed in London, where she organized, with the assistance of Sir Kenneth (later Lord) Clark, a remarkable series of daily chamber-music concerts at the National Gallery, which ran for six and a half years. When the series ceased she resumed her tours abroad. Myra Hess made a number of recordings although she much preferred playing before a live audience. She was well known for her piano transcription (1926) of the chorale-setting from Bach's Cantata No. 147, known as 'Jesu, Joy of Man's Desiring'.

For her services to music, Myra Hess was appointed CBE (1936) and DBE (1941); she also received honorary degrees from a number of universities. Sadly, during her later years,

Myra Hess performing in a wartime music festival at the Stoll Theatre, April 1943

she became troubled by arthritis in her hands. Her last concert appearance was on 31 October 1961 at the Royal Festival Hall, London, with Sir Adrian Boult. She died, unmarried, in London on 25 November 1965.

HICKS, SIR (EDWARD) SEYMOUR GEORGE (1871-1949), actor-manager and author, was born at St Helier, Jersey, on 30 January 1871, the son of Lieut. (later Major) Edward Percy Hicks, of the 42nd Highlanders, and his wife, Grace Seymour. He was educated at Prior Park College, near Bath, and Victoria College, Jersey, and first appeared on the stage at the age of sixteen. He then spent two years in England and the USA with W. H. and (Dame) Madge Kendal, taking small parts in the early plays of Arthur PINERO and other period classics.

Recommended by Irene VANBRUGH, he obtained the part of Andrew McPhail, the young Scottish medical student, in James BARRIE's *Walker, London*, in which he was a great success (1892). In the following year he married Mary Ellaline Lewin, daughter of William Terriss, actor, who, as Ellaline Terriss, became a talented actress; they had a son, who died at birth, and a daughter. During the next ten years Hicks appeared in a number of successful plays in London and in America. He was best known as an extremely versatile comic actor but also played some tragic roles, in particular the title-role in *Edmund Kean* in which he was enormously successful. In 1901 he wrote and acted in *Bluebell in Fairyland*. This was followed in 1903 by his *The Cherry Girl*, with Ivan Caryll's music, and in 1904 by *The Catch of the Season*, which he wrote with Cosmo Hamilton and which ran until 1906.

In 1905 Hicks built the Aldwych Theatre and in 1906 the Hicks, which later became the Globe. His successes during the next few years included *The Beauty of Bath*, which he also wrote with Cosmo Hamilton, *The Gay Gordons* (1907), with music by Guy Jones, and *The Dashing Little Duke* (1909), with music by Frank E. Tours.

During the First World War he organized a concert party and gave a series of performances to the troops in France. After the war he had a number of successes, adapting French plays for the English stage, including *The Man in Dress Clothes* (1922) in which he played the lead, and *You're Telling Me* (1939), in which he appeared with Sacha Guitry.

Hicks was appointed a Chevalier of the Legion of Honour in 1931 for his services to French drama, and in 1935 was Life (1910) and *Me and My Missus—Fifty Years on the Stage* (1939). Seymour Hicks died at Fleet, Hants, on 6 April 1949.

HILL, ARCHIBALD VIVIAN (1886-1977), physiologist, was born in Bristol on 26 September 1886, the son of Jonathan Hill, a timber merchant, and his wife, Ada Priscilla, daughter of Alfred James Rumney, a draper. His sister became a biochemist and married Dr T. S. Hele, who was later Master of Emmanuel College, Cambridge. His parents' marriage broke up when Hill was three years of age and, although his father lived till 1924, Hill never knew him. He was educated at Blundell's School, Tiverton, from which he went to Trinity College, Cambridge with a scholarship. In 1907 he was third wrangler in the mathematical tripos, but he decided to desert mathematics for physiology and obtained a first in the natural sciences tripos in 1909. In the following year he was elected a Fellow of Trinity College.

J. N. Langley, Professor of Physiology, suggested that Hill should investigate 'the efficiency of the cut-out frog's muscle as a thermodynamic machine', and Hill thus started on the research which was to be his main interest throughout a long career. For a few months during 1911 he visited Germany and studied the work on myothermic techniques of Karl Bürker, a fellow physiologist. On his return to Cambridge he experimented with new apparatus for measuring heat production during the passage of nerve impulses through muscles, and published two papers with the co-operation of his sister Muriel suggesting that his calorimetric apparatus could be developed and applied to mammals.

In 1913 Hill married Margaret Neville, daughter of Dr John Neville Keynes and sister of John Maynard KEYNES, the economist; they had two sons and two daughters. When war broke out in 1914 Hill joined the Cambridgeshire Regiment, and was seconded to direct the Anti-Aircraft Experimental Section of the Munitions Inventions Department. While he was carrying out research in this field he was elected FRS in 1918.

In 1919 he returned to his work in Cambridge on the problems of heat production in muscles and the chemical processes involved; but in the following year he accepted the post of Brackenbury Professor of Physiology at Manchester University. After three years in Manchester, he moved to London as Jodrell Professor of Physiology at University College and in the same year (1923) was awarded, jointly with Otto Meyerhof of Kiel, the Nobel prize for physiology and medicine.

In 1924 Hill visited the United States to lecture at Johns Hopkins Medical School. For the next two years he and his colleagues at University College continued their study of the metabolic effects of muscular exercises in man and related lines of research. Then, in 1926, the year in which he delivered the Croonian Lecture, he accepted the invitation of the Royal Society to become Foulerton Professor, a chair which he held until 1951. He continued to publish papers on his neurothermal experiments, and was also one of the Chief Editors of the *Journal of Physiology*.

In 1935 Hill became a member of the TIZARD Committee but resigned in the following year with other members including Patrick BLACKETT, in protest at the intervention of Professor LINDEMANN. During the Second World War Hill's laboratory was closed, and he was elected as an Independent MP, representing the University of Cambridge from 1940 to 1945. In 1940 he visited the USA again as Supernumerary Air Attaché at the British Embassy in Washington, as part of a move to establish liaison with American scientists prior to America's entry into the war. On his return to London he served on a number of scientific committees concerned with the war effort. During 1943-4 he also visited India to advise the Indian Government on scientific and industrial research.

After the war was over he returned to research, reorganizing his laboratory and making it a centre for important bio-physical research which attracted many able students of physiology. As Foreign Secretary of the Royal Society he did much to revive post-war scientific activity in Europe. In 1955 he was elected President of the Marine Biological Association; he had for many years been closely associated with the work at their laboratory in Plymouth.

Hill received many academic awards and honours; he was appointed OBE in 1918 and CH in 1946. His publications include *Living Machinery* (1927), *The Ethical Dilemma of Science* (1960), *Trails and Trials in Physiology* (1965), and *First and Last Experiments on Muscle Mechanics* (1970). He died in Cambridge on 3 June 1977.

HINSHELWOOD, SIR CYRIL NORMAN (1897–1967), physical chemist and biochemist, was born in London on 19 June 1897, the only child of Norman Macmillan Hinshelwood, a chartered accountant, and his wife, Ethel Frances Smith. His father died in 1904 and his mother settled in Chelsea where she and her son had their London home for the rest of their lives. His mother died in 1959. He was educated at Westminster City School and won a Brackenbury scholarship to Balliol College, Oxford, in 1916. But he first worked as a chemist in the Explosives Supply Factory at Queensferry from 1916 to 1919 and became assistant chief laboratory chemist.

In 1919 he went up to Balliol and, before he had even taken his degree, three papers he had written at Queensferry on the decomposition of solids were published by the Chemical Society. He was elected to a research fellowship at Balliol in 1920, and from 1921 to 1937 was a tutorial Fellow of Trinity College. During this time his researches were done in the cellars of Balliol and the outhouses of Trinity.

His first book, *Kinetics of Chemical Change in Gaseous Systems* (1926), was a milestone in chemical literature. It was based upon five years of intensive research, starting from a study of the work of Clerk Maxwell and the *Dynamical Theory of Gases* of (Sir) James Jeans (1904), and going on, with the help of his pupils, to investigate a wide range of gaseous reactions of various types.

Hinshelwood proceeded to consider the theories of contemporary scientists such as F. A. LINDEMANN, Nernst, Christiansen, and Semenov, and the problems posed by their work on photochemical reactions and the complexities of the reaction of gases under various conditions.

In 1937 he succeeded Frederick SODDY as Dr Lee's Professor of Physical and Inorganic Chemistry. He moved from Trinity to Exeter College, and in 1941 Lord NUFFIELD provided him with a Physical Chemistry Laboratory which soon became an important centre of research, used at one time by nine Fellows of the Royal Society. In 1936 Hinshelwood had taken up a new subject of research, the study of the chemical kinetics of living cells, and in 1946 published the results of ten years of investigation in *The Chemical Kinetics of the Bacterial Cell*.

In 1964 he moved to London to become senior research Fellow at Imperial College, and in 1966 published his last book, *Growth, Function and Regulation in Bacterial Cells* (with A. C. R. Dean).

Hinshelwood became a Fellow of the Royal Society in 1929 and was President from 1955 to 1960. He was also President of the Chemical Society (1946–8). He was knighted in 1948, and in 1956 shared a Nobel prize with Semenov for their work on chemical kinetics. He was appointed OM in 1960, and in 1964–5 was President of the British Association. From 1934 he was a Delegate of the Oxford University Press. He was an honorary Fellow of four Oxford colleges.

Apart from his achievements as a scientist, Hinshelwood was a brilliant linguist, proficient in French, German, Italian, Spanish, Russian, and Chinese. He was a keen collector of Chinese porcelain and Eastern carpets, and a competent painter in oils. He was a Trustee of the British Museum and member of a number of advisory committees, including the education committee of the Goldsmiths' Company.

He never married. He died in his Chelsea flat on 9 October 1967.

HITCHCOCK, SIR ALFRED JOSEPH (1899–1980), film director, was born on 13 August 1899 at Leytonstone, London, the youngest of the three children of William Hitchcock, a greengrocer and poulterer, and his wife, Emma Jane Whelan. He was educated at Catholic schools in London, leaving St Ignatius's College, Stamford Hill, on the death of his father, when Alfred was fourteen. After studying at the School for Engineering and Navigation, he became a draughtsman and advertising designer with a cable company, until in 1920 he obtained work at the Islington Studios and embarked on his career in the film industry. During the next five years he gained experience in all branches of the business at Gainsborough Pictures.

In 1925 Michael BALCON engaged him to direct his first picture, *The Pleasure Garden*, and Hitchcock began his rise to fame as a director of thrillers. In the following year he directed *The Lodger*, and for the first time made a brief personal appearance which was to become his signature in the films under his direction. In the same year he married Alma Reville, a script girl, who assisted her husband with many of his films. The early films were silent, but in 1929 Hitchcock directed his first British 'talkie', *Blackmail*. He now began to specialize in thriller films, directing *The Man Who Knew Too Much* (1934), followed by *The Thirty-Nine Steps* (1935), *Sabotage* (1936), *The Lady Vanishes* (1938), and *Jamaica Inn* (1939).

Attracted by the greater opportunities presented by the American film industry, Hitchcock began to work for David O. Selznick in 1939, and his first film in Hollywood, Daphne du Maurier's *Rebecca* (1940), won an Oscar for the best film of the year. For the next thirty years Hitchcock continued to work in Hollywood though most of his films still provided opportunities for British actors and actresses and many were set in Britain. In 1955 he became an American citizen.

His notable Hollywood films include *Rope* (1948), *Strangers on a Train* (1951), *I Confess* (1952), *Dial M for Murder* (1954), *The Wrong Man* (1957), and his well-known horror films, *Psycho* (1960) and *The Birds* (1963). During these years Hitchcock was also making a name for himself, particularly in France and the United States, as a psychologist and Catholic moralist. He received a number of honorary doctorates and the Irving C. Thalberg memorial award (1972) from the American Film Academy, together with other similar honours; and finally in 1980 became a KBE.

He was planning a new film when he died in Los Angeles on 29 April 1980. His wife died two years later. Their only child, Patricia, trained at RADA in London and acted in some of her father's films.

HOARE, SIR SAMUEL JOHN GURNEY, VISCOUNT TEMPLEWOOD (1880–1959), politician, was born in London on 24 February 1880, the elder son of (Sir) Samuel Hoare (later first baronet), of Sidestrand Hall, Norfolk, and his wife, Katharin Louisa Hart, daughter of Richard Vaughan Davis, commissioner of audit. He was educated at Harrow and New College, Oxford, where he obtained firsts in Classical Mods. and modern history, and represented the university at rackets and lawn tennis (1901–3).

From 1907 to 1910 he served on the London County Council. He was elected Conservative MP for Chelsea in 1910 and held the seat until 1944. He succeeded to the baronetcy in 1915.

During the First World War he served in the military mission to Russia (1916–17) and later to Italy (1917–18). In 1917 he was appointed CMG. He gave an account of his experiences in Russia in *The Fourth Seal* (1930).

Hoare was one of the Conservative MPs who brought

about the downfall of the LLOYD GEORGE Coalition Government in 1922, and was appointed Secretary of State for Air by BONAR LAW. He was sworn of the Privy Council, and was at the Air Ministry from 1922 to 1929 except for the short period of the Labour Government in 1924. Sir Hugh (later Viscount) Trenchard was Chief of Air Staff and, together, he and Hoare co-operated in shaping the RAF to the necessary post-war requirements, whilst at the same time Hoare did all he could to encourage the development of civilian air communications. He related the story of this work in *Empire of the Air* (1957). He and his wife, Lady Maud Lygon, daughter of the Earl of Beauchamp, whom he had married in 1909, went on the first civil air flight to India in 1927. In that year she was appointed DBE and he was appointed GBE.

In the National Government of 1931, Hoare was Secretary of State for India and, during the next four years, tried hard to reach agreement with GANDHI, without success. He took a leading part in the joint select committee on the Indian Constitution (1933–4) and, in spite of intransigent opposition from Winston CHURCHILL and some other Conservative back-benchers, steered the Government of India Bill through the Commons until it eventually received the royal assent in 1935. In the previous year he had been appointed GCSI.

In 1935 BALDWIN succeeded Ramsay MACDONALD as Prime Minister and appointed Hoare Foreign Secretary. He would have preferred to go to India as Viceroy. At the Foreign Office it was a time of great difficulty. The armed forces had been run down, whilst Germany and Italy under their dictators were becoming increasingly aggressive. The League of Nations was mainly concerned with the interminable disarmament discussions at Geneva. The pacifist movement was gaining strength in Britain, and any policy of re-armament would have been highly unpopular. Hoare decided that time was required to restore the country's capacity to resist aggression, and that, in the meantime, he must go along with the French and try to keep Italy out of the arms of Germany.

His test came with Italy's invasion of Abyssinia (Ethiopia). The French made it clear that they would take no military action against Mussolini. There seemed to be only one recourse, to arouse the League to put collective security into effect by taking collective action. In a speech at Geneva on 11 September 1935, Hoare gave a pledge that Britain would fulfil her obligations to defend 'the collective maintenance of the Covenant'. His speech got wide publicity, but little action followed, and Mussolini went ahead with his invasion, regardless of the League. Hoare seems to have been ready to impose sanctions on Italy which would have included oil, but France was not prepared to take the risk of war, and the British Cabinet was divided on the issue.

In December, Hoare, on his way to Switzerland to recuperate from an illness, broke his journey in Paris to discuss further action with Laval, the French Foreign Minister. Laval persuaded him to agree to a plan for peace under which Italy would have been permitted to take over a large area of Abyssinia in return for some minor concessions. The Hoare-Laval plan was leaked to the French press, and violently criticized in the British press as a complete reversal of the policy enunciated by Hoare in his Geneva speech.

The Cabinet, having at first approved the plan, quickly revised its attitude. Baldwin asked Hoare to withdraw his approval of the plan. Hoare refused. A number of members of the Cabinet, including the influential Lord HALIFAX, decided that 'Sam should be asked to resign'. Iain MACLEOD, in his

Neville Chamberlain, quotes from CHAMBERLAIN's diary that 'Halifax carried most weight when he said that, unless Sam went, the whole moral force of the Government would be gone.' So, Sam went, his reputation with the British public irreparably damaged.

In June 1936 Baldwin took Hoare back into the Government as First Lord of the Admiralty and, in the following year when Neville Chamberlain took over from Baldwin, Sir Samuel became Home Secretary. During his short period in this office, he sought to introduce penal reforms which in the event were frustrated by the outbreak of the Second World War. In 1938 Hoare, together with Halifax and Sir John SIMON, became a member of the small inner Cabinet which supported the Prime Minister in his efforts to maintain peace with Hitler's Germany. Hoare backed the Munich agreement without reservation, maintaining that Britain could not stand alone against Germany until progress had been made with rearmament.

On the outbreak of war, Hoare became Lord Privy Seal, and in April 1940 became Secretary of State for Air once more. However, he did not survive the changes made when Churchill became Prime Minister and Minister of Defence. His career as a minister ended, but he accepted appointment as Ambassador to Spain, where he remained until 1944 striving to maintain good relations with the Spanish Government.

In 1944 he was created Viscount Templewood and retired from public life, living quietly on his Norfolk estate. He wrote prolifically, publishing *Ambassador on Special Mission* (1946), and *Nine Troubled Years* (1954), as well as books on his forebears and on his objections to capital punishment. He was President of the Howard League for Penal Reform from 1947 till he died. He was also President of the Lawn Tennis Association (1932–56), Chancellor of Reading University (1937–59), and received many academic awards and foreign decorations.

He died in London on 7 May 1959 and, as he and his wife were childless and his younger brother had pre-deceased him, the titles became extinct.

HOBBS, SIR JOHN BERRY (JACK) (1882–1963), cricketer, was born at Cambridge on 16 December 1882, the eldest of the twelve children of John Cooper Hobbs, a labourer, and his wife, Flora Matilda Berry. His father became a professional at Fenner's, the university ground, and later groundsman at Jesus College, and Jack, who went to the local Church of England boys' school, from an early age would get up early in the morning to practise on Parker's Piece. He never had any formal coaching but by 1902 he was playing cricket for Cambridgeshire, and in 1903 was given a trial by Surrey.

From 1905 until he retired from professional cricket in 1934, Hobbs was always associated with Surrey. He scored a century in his first championship game against Essex and, after he had gained experience as an opening batsman with Tom Hayward during his first three seasons, he was selected for the England tour of Australia in 1907–8. He was left out of the first test, but made 83 runs in the second and, from that time until his test career ended in 1930, he was never omitted from an England team when he was available.

In 1909 he made prolific scores in the county championship, and in 1909–10 went with the England side to South Africa where he learnt to master spin bowlers on their native matting. He put this experience to good use in 1911–12 when England won the rubber in Australia, having lost the first test, and Hobbs and Wilfred RHODES set up a record

Jack Hobbs at the wicket, Surrey Cricket Club, *c.* 1934

score of 323 for the first wicket. His Australian opponents regarded him as the best batsman ever produced by England. He played in 41 tests against Australia, and in 71 innings made 3,636 runs, at an average of over 54. It should be remembered that he was an opener with the task of blunting the edge of the fast bowlers' attack. One recalls nostalgically the pleasurable anticipation with which one watched Hobbs, and his partner, Herbert Sutcliffe, walking out to the wicket to open an England innings against the Australians at Lords or the Oval.

In the summer of 1914, Surrey were champions for the only time in Hobbs's career; he made 11 centuries that season. He was now recognized as the best batsman in the world, having scored an aggregate of nearly 26,000 runs, made 65 centuries, and played in 28 test-matches. The First World War interrupted his cricketing career but, when it was over, he resumed where he had left off. In 1925 he overtook W. G. GRACE's record of 126 centuries and, when he retired from professional cricket in 1934, he had accumulated over 60,000 runs and scored 197 centuries, 98 of them after his fortieth birthday.

Hobbs's skill was not confined to batting. He was a brilliant fielder at cover point and woe betide the batsman who was foolish enough to try to take a quick run when Hobbs was going for the ball. Above all, he was a great sportsman who would never wittingly take advantage of an umpire's mistake.

In 1934 the Surrey club made him a life member, and in 1949 the MCC paid him the same tribute. In 1953 he was honoured with a knighthood, the first professional cricketer to achieve this distinction. After his retirement he continued for many years to be active in his sports shop in Fleet Street, London. He died at Hove on 21 December 1963, a few months after the death of his wife, Ada Ellen, daughter of Edward G. Gates of Cambridge, whom he had married in 1906; they had three sons and a daughter. His memory is kept alive by the Hobbs Gates at the Oval. Douglas JARDINE, captain of England, named him as the greatest batsman of his time: 'he was so good on bad pitches'.

HOGG, DOUGLAS McGAREL, first VISCOUNT HAILSHAM (1872–1950), politician and Lord Chancellor, was born in London on 28 February 1872, the eldest of the three sons of the philanthropist, Quintin Hogg, and his wife, Alice, daughter of William Graham, MP. He was educated at Eton, and then entered his father's firm of sugar merchants, Hogg, Curtis, Campbell & Co., and gained an experience of commerce which would be useful in his later career.

During the Boer War he served as a trooper with the Lothian and Berwick Yeomanry and narrowly escaped being killed. In 1902 he was called to the Bar (Lincoln's Inn), and made rapid progress, dealing with commercial and common law cases. In addition, when his father died in 1903, he took over the work his father was doing for the Polytechnic Institute in London. He took silk in 1917, became a bencher of Lincoln's Inn in 1920, and was appointed Attorney-General to the Prince of Wales (1920–2).

When LLOYD GEORGE's Coalition Government was defeated in 1922, BONAR LAW appointed Hogg as Attorney-General although he still had to be elected to Parliament. He became Conservative MP for St Marylebone, and held the seat until 1928. He was sworn of the Privy Council and knighted (1922). When BALDWIN succeeded Bonar Law, Hogg remained as Attorney-General, until, in 1928, he was appointed Lord Chancellor with the title of Baron Hailsham. In the following year he became a viscount.

Throughout 1930–1 he led the Conservative opposition in the House of Lords. In the National Government of 1931, he served as Secretary of State for War and made a start with the task of rearming the Services. When in 1932 Neville CHAMBERLAIN brought forward his Import Duties Bill, which was unacceptable to the Liberal members of the Government, Hailsham, pledged to free trade, made the suggestion that members of the Cabinet should agree to differ, thus postponing the inevitable break up of the Government until after the Ottawa Conference. Hailsham attended that conference and the World Economic Conference (1933).

When Baldwin formed his third administration in 1935, Hailsham returned to the Woolsack and remained in office until 1938. He presided at the trial of Lord de Clifford for manslaughter, the last trial of a peer by his peers. In 1938 he succeeded Lord HALIFAX as Lord President of the Council but held this office for only a few months, his health having broken down. He was President of the MCC in 1933, and received a number of honorary doctorates. He died at his Sussex home, Carter's Corner Place, on 16 August 1950.

He was married twice; first in 1905 to Elizabeth, daughter of Judge Trimble Brown, of Nashville, Tennessee, and widow of the Hon. Archibald John Marjoribanks; they had two sons. Elizabeth died in 1925; and Hailsham married in

Douglas Hogg, Lord Chancellor, in procession from Westminster Abbey for the opening of the Law Courts in the new legal year, October 1935

1929 Mildred Margaret, widow of the Hon. Alfred Clive Lawrence. He was succeeded by his elder son, Quintin McGarel, who in 1970 would follow in his father's footsteps as Conservative Lord Chancellor.

HOLDSWORTH, SIR WILLIAM SEARLE (1871–1944), lawyer, was born at Beckenham, on 7 May 1871, the eldest son of Charles Joseph Holdsworth, a solicitor, and his wife, Ellen Caroline Searle. He was educated at Dulwich College and New College, Oxford, where he obtained firsts in history and jurisprudence (1893–4). He was called to the Bar (Lincoln's Inn) in 1896, but decided to pursue an academic career, and in 1897 accepted a fellowship at St John's College, Oxford. In 1903 he married Jessie Anne Amelia Gilbert, daughter of Gilbert Wood of Bickley, Kent.

In 1910 he became All Souls' Reader in English law, and in 1922 Vinerian Professor of English Law, a post which he held for the next twenty-two years. Between 1903 and 1952 he published his monumental *History of English Law* (13 vols.), which put him in the same class of legal historians as Sir William Blackstone and Professor F. W. Maitland. He wrote many other books, including *Sources and Literature of English Law* (1925), *Some Lessons from our Legal History* (1928), and *Charles Dickens as a Legal Historian* (1928). He also contributed to the publications of the Selden Society.

In addition to his busy career as an academic, Holdsworth carried out public duties as a member of the Indian States Inquiry Committee (1928) and of the Committee on Ministers' Powers (1929–32). He lectured in the USA, and in India where, in 1938, he was Tagore Professor at Calcutta.

The death of his only child on active service with the RAF in 1942 was a great blow. Richard Holdsworth had gained a first in law, rowed for Oxford against Cambridge three times, and become Stowell Civil Law Fellow at University College.

Holdsworth was knighted in 1929 and appointed to the Order of Merit in 1943. He was elected FBA in 1922 and honorary Fellow of St John's College in 1926. He received many honorary degrees from universities at home and abroad. He died at Oxford on 2 January 1944.

HOLLAND, SIR HENRY TRISTRAM (1875–1965), eye surgeon, missionary, and philanthropist, was born in Durham on 12 February 1875, the second son of Canon William Lyall Holland, and his wife, Mary Gertrude, daughter of the naturalist, Canon Henry Baker Tristram. He was educated at Loretto School and Edinburgh University Medical School, where he became MB and CHB in 1899. He decided to become a medical missionary, and in 1900 joined the Punjab Mission of the Church Missionary Society. He spent the next forty-eight years in that part of the world.

In 1910 he married Florence Ethel, daughter of the Revd J. Tunbridge; they had two sons and a daughter.

His main centre was the CMS hospital at Quetta where he soon established a reputation for cataract surgery. In 1907 he became FRCSE. He performed over 60,000 operations for cataracts, and visitors came to him from all over the world. In the Quetta earthquake disaster in 1935, the CMS hospital was destroyed; Holland was buried in the ruins, but was rescued by his son, and lived to be responsible for the construction of bigger and better hospital buildings in Quetta.

He also operated every year at a hospital at Shikapur, Sind, built in 1911 by a Hindu philanthropist on condition that Holland and his team would spend six weeks a year there carrying out eye operations.

Holland was a founder-member of the Royal Commonwealth Society for the Blind. He was appointed CIE in 1929 and knighted in 1936.

After Holland retired from the CMS in 1948 he and his wife frequently returned to the North-West Frontier at the invitation of local chieftains, and he continued to perform eye operations at Quetta and Shikapur. Both of his sons were also eye specialists.

In 1960 he and his son Ronald were honoured with the Ramon Magsaysay award by the Philippines. The citation stated that father and son had saved the sight of some 150,000 people. Holland regarded his surgical achievements as only part of his work as a missionary. He was an honorary member of the Ophthalmology Section of the Royal Society of Medicine, and Vice-President of the Pakistan Society. He died at Farnham, Surrey on 19 September 1965.

HOLMES, SIR GORDON MORGAN (1876–1965), neurologist, was born in Dublin on 22 February 1876, the son of Gordon Holmes, an Irish landowner and farmer, and his wife, Kathleen, daughter of John Morgan. He was educated at Dundalk Educational Institute and Trinity College, Dublin. He qualified in medicine in 1898, and for two years studied neuroanatomy at Frankfurt; in 1901 he became house-physician at the National Hospital for Nervous Diseases, Queen Square, London, where he became MD in 1903, and FRCP in 1914. From 1911 to 1914 he worked with (Sir) Henry Head (1861–1940), studying the part played by the human cerebral cortex in sensory perception.

During the First World War Holmes was consulting neurologist to the British Army and was able to publish a number of studies dealing with the effects of cortical lesions on vision and on somatic sensation, and the effects of war wounds involving the nervous system. He was appointed CMG in 1917 and CBE in 1919.

In 1918 he married Rosalie, daughter of Brigade Surgeon William Jobson. They had three daughters.

In 1922 he succeeded Head as Editor of *Brain*, a post which he held until 1937. He became FRS in 1933 and, during his years as Editor of *Brain*, made important contributions to neurological teaching, particularly with reference to the physiology of the cerebral cortex, thalamus, and cerebellum. In 1935 he was President of the International Congress of Neurology when it met in London. He retired from the post of consulting physician at the National Hospital in 1941, and was knighted in 1951. In 1946 he published the *Introduction to Clinical Neurology* and in 1954 wrote a short history of the National Hospital. In 1956 his *Selected Papers* were edited by Sir F. M. R. Walshe, who had taken over as Editor of *Brain* in 1937. Holmes died at Farnham, Surrey on 29 December 1965.

HOLST, GUSTAV THEODORE (1874–1934), composer, originally Gustavus Theodore von Holst, was born at Cheltenham on 21 September 1874, the elder son of Adolph von Holst, a music teacher, and his wife, Clara, daughter of Samuel Lediard, a solicitor, of Cirencester. The von Holst family came originally from Sweden. Holst began to learn the violin and the piano at an early age and, at Cheltenham Grammar School, started to set Macaulay's 'Horatius' to music, but was discouraged by his father who wanted him to be a virtuoso pianist. However neuritis made this impossible.

In 1892 he obtained his first professional engagement as organist of Wyck Rissington, Gloucestershire, and in 1893 his music for an operetta was performed at Cheltenham.

Because of this success, his father sent him to the Royal College of Music to study composition with C. V. STANFORD. Grieg had been his favourite composer and he never lost a love of Bach, but now Wagner's music became his passion. He was later influenced by English folk-music and his attraction to mysticism goes some way to explain the visionary quality of his music.

To earn a living, Holst played the trombone in a dance band, but in 1895 the Royal College awarded him a small scholarship and he was able to continue his studies, though he had to live frugally. His neuritis got worse and his eyesight deteriorated. In 1898 he became a trombone player with the Carl Rosa Opera Company and then with the Scottish Orchestra. In the following year he learnt sufficient Sanskrit to make translations of the Vedic hymns for musical setting. In 1903 he decided to give up the trombone and write music. But he found that he had to earn a living by other means and he became a music teacher. In 1901 he had married Isobel, daughter of an artist, Augustus Ralph Harrison; they had one daughter.

In 1905 he was appointed Director of Music at St Paul's Girls' School, Hammersmith. He was to retain this appointment for the rest of his life. In 1913 a sound-proof music room was built at the school, and here he composed the *St*

Gustav Holst (left) on a walking tour with Ralph Vaughan Williams, *c.* 1920

Paul's Suite for strings (1913). His most famous work, *The Planets* suite, was begun in 1914 and completed in 1917. During the First World War Holst tried to enlist, but he was medically unfit and went out instead to Salonika to organize music for the troops. It was at this time that he dropped the 'von' from his name.

The Planets was publicly performed for the first time at the Queen's Hall in 1919, followed there by his choral work *The Hymn of Jesus* in 1920. In the years 1919 to 1927 he also composed the 'Ode to Death' (a setting of a poem by Whitman), the operas *The Perfect Fool* and *At the Boar's Head*, the 'Keats' choral symphony, and the tone-poem *Egdon Heath*, written as a tribute to Thomas HARDY.

From 1919 to 1924 Holst was Professor of Composition at the Royal College of Music and simultaneously held a similar post at Reading University (1919–23). He made three visits to the USA between 1923 and 1932 and lectured at Harvard and conducted his own music at Boston.

In Holst's later years, his daughter Imogen, who became a composer and teacher, was his constant companion. He died in London on 25 May 1934. His lifelong friend, Ralph VAUGHAN WILLIAMS, writing in the *DNB*, said, 'Holst's music has been called cold and inhuman: it is only cold from its burning intensity.'

HOPKINS, SIR FREDERICK GOWLAND (1861–1947), biochemist, was born on 20 June 1861 at Eastbourne, the only son of Frederick Hopkins, and his wife, Elizabeth Gowland. His father, a first cousin of the poet Gerard Manley Hopkins, died when Frederick was an infant. He was educated at the City of London School, and articled to a consulting analyst for three years. With a small legacy he was able to study at South Kensington and University College London (1881). He then became assistant to (Sir) Thomas Stevenson, Home Office analyst, and read for the B.Sc. (London). In 1888 he entered Guy's Hospital as a medical student,

graduated in 1890, and qualified in 1894. In 1891 he published his first piece of research, a method for determining uric acid in urine.

From 1894 to 1898 Hopkins was assistant in the Department of Physiology at Guy's Hospital and carried on his research work. In 1898, the year of his marriage to Jessie Anne, daughter of Edward William Stevens, of Ramsgate, he became lecturer in chemical physiology at Cambridge, but had to supplement his income with tutorial work at Emmanuel College. He continued his research into the nature of the amino-acids and the necessity in diet of unknown substances later identified as vitamins.

In 1902 his lectureship became a readership. However, after a serious illness in 1910 due to overwork, he was offered a praelectorship with no formal duties by Trinity College, which he held until 1921. In 1914 he was appointed Professor of Biochemistry and began to build up a school of young scientists which had a far-reaching influence on the development of biochemistry at Cambridge. In 1921 he became the first Sir William Dunn Professor of Biochemistry, a post which he held until 1943. He was awarded a Nobel prize in 1929 jointly with the Dutch scientist, Eijkman, for his work on the chemistry of intermediary metabolism which led, during his lifetime, to the identification of the part played by vitamins in the chemistry of the life process.

He was elected FRS in 1905 and was a member of the first Medical Research Committee appointed in 1913. He was knighted in 1925 and appointed OM in 1935. He was President of the Royal Society (1930–5), and of the British Association (1933). He also received many honorary degrees.

Hopkins died in Cambridge on 16 May 1947. He and his wife had a son and two daughters, one of whom married J. B. Priestley and became well known as the author Jacquetta Hawkes.

HORDER, THOMAS JEEVES, first BARON HORDER

Gowland Hopkins at the School of Biochemistry, Cambridge, shortly before his retirement, 1943

(1871-1955), physician, was born on 7 January 1871, at Shaftesbury, the youngest child of Albert Horder, a draper, and his wife, Ellen Jeeves. He was educated at Swindon High School and, for reasons of health, worked on his uncle's farms for two years (1886-7). He then took a correspondence course in biology, and H. G. WELLS, who corrected his papers, is said to have noted that Horder was not suited to research. Wells later became one of his patients.

In 1891 Horder went with a scholarship to St Bartholomew's Hospital. He graduated B.Sc. in 1893, and qualified in medicine in 1896, obtaining his MB, BS (London) in 1898 and MD in 1899. He became a member of the Royal College of Physicians in 1899 and a Fellow in 1906. In 1902 he married Geraldine Rose, daughter of Arthur Doggett, of Newnham Manor, Baldock; they had two daughters and one son.

His resident hospital experience began as house-physician to Samuel Gee, at Bart's, from whom he learnt much, particularly about medical diagnosis. He had not yet decided whether to pursue biology, physiology, or medicine, but Gee helped to clarify his mind, and from 1904 to 1911 he served in a number of posts in Bart's and other hospitals in London. In 1912 he was appointed Assistant Physician at Bart's, and from 1921 to 1936 was Senior Physician.

While still a junior, he built up a successful private practice, making a reputation for his skill in combining acute observation at the bedside with careful examination of laboratory investigations. His outstanding ability was recognized when he was called into consultation to see King Edward VII and made a correct diagnosis. He eventually became the foremost clinician of his time, numbering among his patients George V, George VI, Elizabeth II, BONAR LAW and Ramsay MACDONALD.

He was chairman of the Empire Rheumatism Council (1936-53), medical adviser to London Transport (1940-55), and first Chairman of the Fellowship for Freedom in Medicine (1948). In 1953 he published *Fifty Years of Medicine*. Horder was knighted in 1918, created a baronet in 1923, and a baron in 1933. He was appointed KCVO (1925) and GCVO (1938). He held a number of honorary degrees. Horder died suddenly at Petersfield on 13 August 1955.

HORE-BELISHA, (ISAAC) LESLIE, BARON HORE-BELISHA (1893-1957), politician, was born in London on 7 September 1893, the only son of Jacob Isaac Belisha, an insurance company manager, of Sephardic Jewish descent, and his wife, Elizabeth Miriam, daughter of John Leslie Miers. His father died when he was less than a year old, and in 1912 his mother married (Sir) (Charles Fraser) Adair Hore and Belisha added his stepfather's name to his own. He was educated at Clifton College, and St John's College, Oxford, but his education was interrupted by the First World War during which he served in the ASC in France and Salonika.

He returned to Oxford in 1919 and became President of the Union. He earned a living for a time by journalism, and in 1923 was called to the Bar (Inner Temple). From that year until 1945 he was Liberal MP for Devonport, and continued to work as a journalist. In 1931 he organized the Liberal National party supporting the National Government, and during 1931-2 was Parliamentary Secretary at the Board of Trade. As Financial Secretary to the Treasury, he helped Neville CHAMBERLAIN to pilot the Ottawa agreements through the Commons (1932-4).

In 1934 he was appointed Minister of Transport, and in that post obtained much publicity by extending the use of pedestrian crossings, and introducing 'Belisha beacons', driving tests, and other measures which improved road safety. In 1935 he was sworn of the Privy Council, and in 1936 entered the Cabinet.

When Neville Chamberlain succeeded BALDWIN as Prime Minister in 1937, he appointed Hore-Belisha Minister of War with the specific task of making drastic changes to bring the military machine up to date. Within a few months the new War Minister had introduced an extensive programme of reforms, covering conditions of service, training, mechanization, and improvement of the status of the Territorial Army. Inevitably his personality and methods aroused hostility from the generals and some of his Cabinet colleagues, but the Prime Minister supported him, describing him as the best War Minister since HALDANE.

When the Second World War broke out, there was friction between Hore-Belisha and Lord Gort, the Commander-in-Chief of the British Expeditionary Force; Gort's annoyance at the War Minister's criticism of the state of the defences at the front was communicated to the Prime Minister through (Lord) Ironside, the CIGS, and the King. Chamberlain visited France to see for himself, and returned convinced that the Minister of War had been tactless in his dealings with Gort and would have to go. Chamberlain would have transferred him to the Ministry of Information, but Lord HALIFAX objected to this appointment, and Hore-Belisha was offered the Board of Trade. He refused and, as he could not state publicly the reasons for his resignation because this would have given valuable information to the Germans, he retired to the back benches until, in CHURCHILL's 'caretaker' Government in 1945, he became Minister of National Insurance for a few months.

In 1944 he married Cynthia, daughter of Gilbert Elliot, of Hull Place, Sholden, Kent; they had no children. He lost his seat at Devonport in 1945. He then joined the Conservative party but, when in 1950 he stood for Coventry South, he was defeated, and in 1954 accepted a peerage. He died suddenly on 16 February 1957 when leading a parliamentary delegation to France.

HORNER, ARTHUR LEWIS (1894-1968), miners' leader, was born on 5 April 1894 in Merthyr Tydfil, the eldest of the seventeen children of James Horner, a railwayman, and his wife, Emily Lewis, who ran the first Merthyr Co-operative Stores. Eleven of her children died at birth or in their infancy. Arthur Horner left school at eleven to become a railway clerk. He was a remarkable boy preacher, and at seventeen entered a Baptist college, but was more interested in becoming a politician than a minister.

Having joined the ILP of which James Keir HARDIE was the leader, he soon became known as an agitator and could only obtain work in the mines under an assumed name. In the First World War he was a conscientious objector and absconded to Ireland; on return, he was arrested and imprisoned. In 1920 he became a leading member of the British Communist party and went frequently to Soviet Russia and other communist countries.

In 1921 he was imprisoned again for unlawful assembly. He was a close friend and collaborator of A. J. COOK, the national Secretary of the Miners' Federation, but in 1930 Horner was expelled from the South Wales branch for standing as a Communist candidate for Parliament against the official miners' candidate.

He re-entered the union in 1934, and two years later was elected President of the South Wales Miners' Federation. In

1937 he negotiated a coalfield wages structure for the region with the colliery owners. His political views, however, precluded his election to the General Council of the TUC in spite of his obvious ability. In January 1945 he played a leading part in the formation of the National Union of Mineworkers, and in 1946 became national Secretary and was closely concerned with the discussions leading to nationalization of the coal industry.

When he retired in 1959 he received the freedom of Merthyr. In 1960 he published his autobiography *Incorrigible Rebel*. In 1916 he had married Ethel Mary Meyrick; they had three daughters. Horner died at Wembley on 4 September 1968.

HORSBRUGH, FLORENCE GERTRUDE, BARONESS HORSBRUGH (1889–1969), politician, was born in Edinburgh on 13 October 1889, the youngest daughter of Henry Moncrieff Horsbrugh, a chartered accountant, and his wife, Mary Harriet Stark Christie. She was educated at Lansdowne House, Edinburgh, and St Hilda's, Folkestone.

From 1931 to 1945 she was Conservative MP for Dundee. She was always interested in child welfare, and as a private member introduced the bill which became the Adoption of Children (Regulation) Act of 1939. From 1939 to 1945 she was Parliamentary Secretary to the Ministry of Health and did much preparatory work on the scheme which eventually became the National Health Service. In the 'caretaker' Government of 1945 she was Parliamentary Secretary to the Ministry of Food, but in the 1945 election she was defeated.

She returned to the House of Commons as MP for the Moss Side division of Manchester in 1950; in 1951 Winston CHURCHILL appointed her to be Minister of Education, and in 1953 she became the first woman to hold a Cabinet post in a Conservative Government. She resigned in 1954 and was created GBE, having been appointed MBE in 1920 and CBE in 1939. She was sworn of the Privy Council in 1945. In 1959 she was made a life peer. She died in Edinburgh on 6 December 1969.

HOUSMAN, ALFRED EDWARD (1859–1936), classical scholar and poet, was born at Fockbury, Catshill, Worcestershire, on 26 March 1859, the eldest child of Edward Housman, a solicitor, and his wife, Sarah Jane Williams. With his younger brother Laurence, who became a well-known writer, he was educated at Bromsgrove School and St John's College, Oxford, which he entered as a scholar and where he gained a first in Classical Mods. but failed to do so in Greats. (1879–81). From 1882 to 1892 he worked as a clerk in the Patent Office in London. There he found time to study the classics, and in 1882 published a paper on Horace in the *Journal of Philology*, followed in 1883 by a note on Ovid's *Ibis*, and in 1887 by an article in the *Classical Review* on Sophocles and Euripides.

In 1889 Housman became a member of the Cambridge Philological Society and the high quality of his studies of classical textual problems began to attract notice. In 1892 he was appointed Professor of Latin at University College London, and from that time, apart from a few minor contributions to Greek studies, he confined his published work to Latin authors. He remained, however, one of the leading scholars of Greek.

During his tenure of the chair in London, which he held until 1911, Housman published four masterly papers on the manuscripts of Propertius, edited Ovid's *Ibis* (1894), began his meticulous study of the works of Manilius, and edited

A. E. Housman, from a drawing by Francis Dodd, 1926

the text of Juvenal. In his preface to Book I of Manilius, Housman asserted his opinions not only on his own methods of scholarship, but on those of other scholars, some of whom he criticized with ruthless sarcasm. He was undoubtedly the greatest Latinist of his age; he was a perfectionist, and castigated any other scholar who did not maintain his own high standards of textual analysis.

In 1896 he showed another unexpected aspect of his character by publication of *A Shropshire Lad*, a set of sixty-three lyrical poems, which he had written for the most part in 1895, some in earlier years.

In 1911 Housman was appointed Professor of Latin at Cambridge, and became a Fellow of Trinity College where he lived until his death in 1936. He continued to publish his work on Manilius and continued to show his contempt for the work of earlier scholars. In 1926 he published an edition of Lucan.

In 1922 he published *Last Poems*, and in 1932 became Leslie Stephen lecturer at Cambridge and published his lecture on *The Name and Nature of Poetry*. He died at Cambridge on 30 April 1936. He never married. His brother, Laurence, published *More Poems* that year, and *The Collected Poems of A.E. Housman* appeared in 1939.

Housman refused to accept honours, including the Order of Merit, but he accepted an honorary fellowship at St John's College, Oxford (1911). He wrote his own epigraph in *More Poems*:

They say my verse is sad; no wonder,
Its narrow measure spans
Tears of eternity and sorrow.
Not mine, but man's.

HOUSTON, DAME FANNY LUCY (1857-1936), eccentric philanthropist, was born in London on 8 April 1857, the daughter of Thomas Radmall, a warehouseman, and his wife, Maria Isabella Clarke. She was a beautiful young woman who for a time was an actress. In 1883 she married Theodore Francis Brinckman, later third baronet; she divorced him in 1895. In 1901 she married George Frederick William, ninth Lord Byron; he died in 1917. In 1924 she married Sir Robert Paterson Houston, baronet, MP for the West Toxteth division of Liverpool (1892-1924), owner of the Houston Shipping Line. He died in 1926 and left Lady Houston a large fortune.

She was a strong advocate of women's rights, and in 1917 was appointed DBE for her work for nurses during the First World War. Her inheritance from her third husband led to litigation with the Inland Revenue, and in 1927 and 1933 Lady Houston made large *ex gratia* payments to the Treasury although denying any legal liability.

She was a warm-hearted woman, determined to get her own way and, as owner of the *Saturday Review*, was able to air her views demonstrating her extreme patriotism, strident but none the less sincere. Her contributions to charity covered a wide field, but she will be remembered chiefly for her gift of £100,000, which enabled a British team to compete for the Schneider trophy in 1931. The race was won by a super-marine Rolls-Royce S6, the direct predecessor of the Spitfires and Hurricanes which won the Battle of Britain in 1940. Lady Houston also financed the expedition which flew over Mount Everest in 1933, at that time an extremely hazardous enterprise and one which assisted in the ultimate conquest of Everest by providing new maps of the area.

In 1932 she offered money for the air defence of London; this offer was refused, as was a similar offer to salvage the Finnish barque *Herzogin Cecilie* to be used as a training ship. She had now become noted mainly for her eccentricity.

Lady Houston had no children and died intestate in London on 29 December 1936.

HOWARD, SIR EBENEZER (1850-1928), originator of the garden city movement and founder of Letchworth and Welwyn garden cities, was born in London on 29 January 1850, the only son of Ebenezer Howard, a confectioner, and his wife, Ann Tow, of Colsterworth, Lincolnshire. He was educated at private schools at Sudbury, Cheshunt, and Ipswich. After leaving school he became a clerk in the City of London and taught himself shorthand.

In 1872 he went to the USA and worked in Chicago as a stenographer. While he was in America he came under the influence of Emerson, J. R. Lowell, and Walt Whitman. In 1877 he returned to London and was employed as shorthand writer to the official reporters to the Houses of Parliament and also carried on his own business as shorthand writer to the Law Courts. Two years later he married Elizabeth Ann, daughter of Thomas Bills, of Nuneaton; they had one son and three daughters.

Another influence on Howard's thought was Edward Bellamy's *Looking Backward*, a Utopian vision, published in America in 1888. This led him to write *Tomorrow. A Peaceful Path to Real Reform* (1898), which was republished in 1902 as *Garden Cities of Tomorrow*. Howard sought some remedy for the problems of overcrowding in urban areas and depopulation of the countryside; his solution was the creation of garden cities, containing buildings for both industrial and residential purposes, well planned, within a green belt which gave the townspeople access to the countryside and the farmers access to a market for their produce.

Howard had no money himself; he was always dependent upon his business as a shorthand writer. He set to work, however, to get backing for his ideas, and in 1899 formed the Garden City Association. By 1903 he had obtained sufficient support to purchase an estate at Letchworth and to organize the development of the first garden city, which by 1934 was a flourishing town with over 15,000 inhabitants. In 1919 Howard raised sufficient money to buy another estate at Welwyn; he formed a company to develop the site as another garden city and appointed Louis de Soissons as planner.

Howard's first wife died in 1904, and in 1907 he married Edith Annie, daughter of William Knight, of Wellingore, Lincoln. From 1909 to 1928 he was President of the International Garden Cities and Town Planning Association. *Garden Cities of Tomorrow* was translated into many languages and Howard's ideas gained acceptance, not only in Britain, but also in many other countries. Although it is unlikely that garden cities will in future be developed exactly on the lines laid down by this pioneer of the movement, he certainly had a marked influence on modern town planning. He was appointed OBE in 1924 and knighted in 1927. Howard died in Welwyn Garden City on 1 May 1928.

HOWARD, LESLIE (1893-1943), actor, producer, and film director, was born, Leslie Howard Steiner, in London on 3 April 1893, the eldest son of Ferdinand Steiner, a stockbroker's clerk, and his wife, Lilian Blumberg. He was educated at Dulwich, and became a bank clerk.

His early interest in the theatre developed still further during the First World War when he served in the Northamptonshire Yeomanry. While the war was still on he adopted the surname Howard. In 1916 Howard married Ruth Evelyn, daughter of Henry William Martin, a laundry manager, of Colchester. In the same year he left the army and made his first appearance as a professional actor in 1917. From then until 1920, he appeared on the London stage in a number of plays including *The Freaks*, by Sir Arthur PINERO, *Our Mr. Hepplewhite*, and *Mr. Pim Passes By*. He first appeared in New York in 1920 in *Just Suppose*, and for the next five years built up a successful career in a number of plays in the USA. Subsequently, he divided his time between London and New York, played Peter Standish in *Berkeley Square* in both cities, and played the leading part of Alan Squier in *The Petrified Forest* in New York (1935).

Howard first appeared in films in 1930, and it was as actor, producer, and director of films that he became well known. He had notable successes in *Outward Bound*, *Berkeley Square*, *The Scarlet Pimpernel*, *The Petrified Forest*, *Pygmalion*, *Gone With the Wind*, *49th Parallel*, and many other films.

During the Second World War he produced and acted in some of the best British war films, including *Pimpernel Smith*, *The First of the Few*, and *The Lamp Still Burns*. He was an attractive actor with a quiet manner, clear voice, and pleasant personality, without flamboyance or robustness; in his prime he was very popular.

He was killed on 1 June 1943 when the aeroplane in which he was returning to England from a visit to Spain and Portugal was shot down, possibly because the enemy wrongly thought that some military or political figure was aboard.

Illustration, p. 174.

HOWICK OF GLENDALE, first BARON (1903-1973). See BARING, (CHARLES) EVELYN.

Leslie Howard with Vivien Leigh in *Gone with the Wind*, 1939

HUDSON, WILLIAM HENRY (1841-1922), naturalist and writer, was born near Buenos Aires on 4 August, 1841, the third son of Daniel Hudson, and his wife, Catherine Kemble, both Americans. Daniel Hudson's father came from Devon, and Catherine was a descendant of one of the pilgrim fathers. William was brought up on the farms and ranches of the Rio de la Plata; he had little schooling: in his own words he 'ran wild in a wild land'. The story of his first eighteen years is told in *Far Away and Long Ago* (1918) in which he describes his life in Argentina. Unfortunately he contracted typhus fever at the age of fifteen, and this was followed by rheumatic fever, which affected his heart and forced him into a more sedentary kind of life during which he read widely. He spent some time travelling in South America, collecting bird-skins for the Smithsonian Institute in Washington and the Zoological Society in London. In 1869 he came to England where he spent the rest of his life.

Hudson lived in London for some years, lonely and impecunious. In 1876 he married his landlady, Emily Wingrave, who was some fifteen years older than he was, but this did not improve his situation; together they moved from one part of London to another, always beset by poverty and debts. During these years from 1876 to 1892, Hudson wrote a great

deal, but his work did not find a wide public. One of his best books *The Purple Land that England Lost: Travels and Adventures in the Bandu Oriental* was published in 1885 but was not a success. His first book on bird life, in which he specialized, was an *Argentine Ornithology* (written in collaboration with Dr P. L. Sclater in 2 vols., 1888-9). In addition to books on natural history, he tried his hand at romantic novels, but with conspicuous lack of success.

Hudson had a natural ability to write about birds and other wild life and could graphically describe his own experiences in studying animals in their natural habitat. The first of his books to meet with moderate success was *The Naturalist in La Plata* (1892), which he followed up with *Birds in a Village* (1893). In 1901 his circumstances were improved when Arthur BALFOUR, probably at the suggestion of Edward GREY, himself a bird-lover, granted him a civil list pension, which enabled him to get away from London and to study natural scenery and country life in the provinces. He continued to write voluminously. Little is known of his life at this time, since he was at pains to keep it private.

From 1900 his books met with greater appreciation. These include *Hampshire Days* (1903), *Afoot in England* (1909), and *A Shepherd's Life* (1910), one of his best works, depicting

W. H. Hudson photographed in the New Forest in the early 1900s

life on the Wiltshire Downs. Edward Garnett helped to make his work more widely known and Edward Grey wrote of his peculiar gifts of observation and clarity of description. He died in London on 18 August 1922. *Idle Days in Patagonia* was published in 1923. Hudson is commemorated by Jacob EPSTEIN's memorial to him set up in Hyde Park in 1925 for the Royal Society for the Protection of Birds—a creation which at the time it was unveiled caused much controversy.

HUMPHREYS, SIR (RICHARD SOMERS) TRAVERS CHRISTMAS (1867–1956), judge, was born in London on 4 August 1867, the fourth son of Charles Octavius Humphreys, a solicitor, and his wife, Harriet Ann Grain. He was educated at Shrewsbury and Trinity Hall, Cambridge, and was called to the Bar (Inner Temple) in 1889. In 1895 he appeared as junior counsel in the case which led to the conviction and imprisonment of Oscar Wilde.

In 1896 he married Zoë Marguerite, daughter of Henri Philippe Neumans, the artist, of Antwerp; they had two sons.

Humphreys mainly concentrated on criminal cases, and in 1908 was appointed junior counsel for the Crown at the Central Criminal Court, and became a senior counsel in 1916. In 1910 he took part in the trial of Dr Crippen for the murder of his wife, and in 1912 appeared in the trial of F. H. Seddon for poisoning Eliza Barrow. In 1915 he appeared with (Sir) Archibald Bodkin at the trial of G. J. Smith, the murderer of the 'Brides in the Bath'. In all these cases the murderer was convicted. In 1916 he was one of the team that prosecuted Sir Roger CASEMENT for treason. In the following year his elder son was killed on active service.

Humphreys was Recorder of Chichester, from 1921 to 1926 when he became Recorder of Cambridge. He was elected a bencher of his Inn in 1922 and knighted in 1925. In 1922 he secured the conviction of Horatio Bottomley for fraudulent conversion, and assisted the Solicitor-General in the prosecution of Frederick Bywaters and Edith Thompson for the murder of her husband. In 1925 he led for the Crown in the case against W. C. Hobbs, who had blackmailed Sir Hari Singh.

In 1928 Humphreys was appointed judge of the King's Bench Division, and remained in that office until 1951. He was sworn of the Privy Council in 1946. As a judge he presided over the trial of a number of criminals in cases that attracted wide publicity. He was always a courteous and attentive listener to the evidence submitted in his court and a master of the art of summing up and directing juries. Among the cases he tried were those of Leopold Harris, convicted of arson and fraud (1933), that of Mrs Rattenbury and George Stoner for the murder of her husband (1935), and that of J. G. Haigh, the acid-bath murderer (1949).

By the time he retired Humphreys was acknowledged to be a master of the criminal law. In 1946 he published his reminiscences *Criminal Days*, and in 1953 *A Book of Trials*. Mr Justice Humphreys died in London on 20 February 1956. His younger son (Travers) Christmas Humphreys followed his father as criminal lawyer and judge.

HUSSEY, CHRISTOPHER EDWARD CLIVE (1899–1970), architectural historian and contributor to *Country Life*, was born in London on 21 October 1899, the only son of Major William Clive Hussey, RE, and his wife, Mary Anne, eldest daughter of the Very Revd George Herbert, Dean of Hereford. His grandfather was Edward Hussey of Scotney Castle, Kent. He was educated at Eton and Christ Church, Oxford, but before going up to the university he

served in 1918 in the Royal Field Artillery. While he was an undergraduate (1919–21) he wrote his first country house articles for *Country Life*.

In 1920 he joined the editorial staff, and during the next fifty years contributed some 1,400 articles (and from 1933 to 1940 was Editor), concentrating on planning, landscape, historic towns, and modern movements in architecture, as well as descriptions of country houses and their history. In 1936 he married Elizabeth Maud, daughter of Major P. Kerr Smiley; they had no children.

His publications include *Eton College* (1922), *Petworth House* (1926), *English Country Houses: Early Georgian* (1955), *Mid Georgian* (1956), and *Late Georgian* (1958). He also wrote *The Picturesque* (1927) and *English Gardens and Landscapes 1700-1750* (1967).

Hussey was an admirer of the work of Sir Edwin LUTYENS whose *Life* he published in 1950. He took an active part in public work, particularly for the National Trust and the Historical Buildings Council for England. He was President of the Society of Architectural Historians in 1964-6. He was an honorary ARIBA (1935), FSA (1947), and was appointed CBE in 1956.

In 1952 Hussey inherited Scotney Castle, and in subsequent years spent much effort on the maintenance and improvement of the property. When he died at Scotney on 20 March 1970 he left the estate to the National Trust.

HUXLEY, ALDOUS LEONARD (1894–1963), man of letters, was born at Laleham, near Godalming, on 26 July 1894, the third son of Leonard Huxley, an assistant master at Charterhouse and later Editor of the *Cornhill Magazine*, and his first wife, Julia Frances Arnold, granddaughter of Thomas Arnold of Rugby, and niece of Matthew Arnold. Julian HUXLEY was his eldest brother; they were grandsons of T. H. Huxley, the naturalist. Aldous Huxley went to Eton with a scholarship in 1908, and the death of his mother shortly afterwards was a great shock to him. Two years later, he contracted an eye infection which left him almost blind, and he had to leave Eton. He taught himself to read braille, to type, and to play the piano, continuing his education with tutors. In October 1913 his sight, although irreparably damaged, improved sufficiently for him to go up to Balliol College, Oxford, where he obtained a first in English literature in 1916 and won the Stanhope prize.

He was a young man of great charm, modest and gentle, with an immense intellectual curiosity. His enjoyment of life at Oxford was ended by the outbreak of the First World War and the suicide of his elder brother, Trevenen. While he was an undergraduate he began to write poetry and short stories and, at the Garsington home of the Morrells, met many of the young writers and painters of the day. It was at Garsington that he met Maria Nys, who came from a well-to-do Flemish family who had come to England as refugees. Three years later they were married (1919). Meanwhile, Huxley taught at Repton and Eton and earned money by journalism, but at the time of his marriage his income was very small. He also suffered from bouts of manic depression.

His first novel, *Crome Yellow*, appeared in 1921; Lady Ottoline MORRELL complained bitterly that it was a travesty of life at Garsington. It was followed by *Antic Hay* (1923), *Those Barren Leaves* (1925), and *Brave New World* (1932). These were all stories that satirized contemporary society and the last of them was a terrifying forecast of a world in which humanity had been annihilated by science. In between the novels, Huxley published short stories and essays,

Aldous Huxley, November 1948

including *Mortal Coils* (1922), *Little Mexican* (1924), *Two or Three Graces*, and *Jesting Pilate* (1926).

In 1928 he published *Point Counter Point* which was a best seller both in Britain and the USA. As his income improved, he and his wife were able to travel abroad, visiting India and the Far East, as well as European countries and South America. In Italy they became close friends of D. H. LAWRENCE, whose *Letters* Huxley edited in 1932.

After visiting the USA in 1937, the Huxleys decided to settle there in 1938. He tried a new American method of improving impaired eyesight, and this appears to have worked because, by the middle of 1939, he was able to read and write without spectacles. He published this experience in *The Art of Seeing* (1942). His writing changed from satire to a new philosophical appreciation of the potential of human capability. Included in these new works are *The Perennial Philosophy* (1945), *Science, Liberty and Peace* (1946), *Themes and Variations* (1950), and *Brave New World Revisited* (1958). His later novels also had a different tone from those of his earlier days. These include *After Many a Summer* (1939), which was awarded the James Tait Black memorial prize, *Time Must Have a Stop* (1944), *Ape and Essence* (1948), and *The Genius and the Goddess* (1955).

In 1953 Huxley, who was already interested in hypnosis, also became interested in the therapeutic uses of drugs such as mescalin and LSD. He published his views on this subject in *The Doors of Perception* (1954) and *Heaven and Hell* (1956), and laid himself open to the charge of encouraging young people to take these psychedelic drugs.

Early in 1955 his wife, Maria, died of cancer; they had one son. In 1956 Huxley married Laura Archera, an Italian concert violinist and psychotherapist, but in 1960 he contracted cancer. In 1961 he had another misfortune; his Los Angeles home was completely destroyed by fire. He died in Los Angeles on 22 November 1963; his ashes were buried in his parents' grave at Compton cemetery, Surrey.

HUXLEY, SIR JULIAN SORELL (1887–1975), biologist,

was born on 22 June 1887, the eldest son of Leonard Huxley, Editor of the *Cornhill Magazine* and Julia Frances, daughter of Thomas Arnold and sister of Mrs Humphrey Ward. Aldous HUXLEY was his youngest brother. He was a scholar of both Eton and Balliol College, Oxford, where he gained a first in zoology and a scholarship to study in Naples (1909); he also won the Newdigate prize for poetry (1908). He returned to Balliol in 1910 as lecturer in zoology and, from 1912 to 1916, was Research Associate and Assistant Professor at the Rice Institute, Houston, Texas.

After service as a staff lieutenant in Italy, in 1918 he returned to Oxford as Senior Demonstrator in Zoology and a Fellow of New College (1919–1925). In 1919 he married (Marie) Juliette Baillot, of Neuchâtel, Switzerland; they had two sons. In 1921 he went on the university expedition to Spitzbergen. During 1925–7 he was Professor of Zoology at King's College, London, but resigned so that he could devote himself to research and to writing. He held the post of Fullerian Professor of the Royal Institution during 1926–9. In *New Bottles for New Wine* (1957), he explains that he felt himself impelled to explore, by reference to the discoveries of the twentieth century, the place of man in nature, his relations with the rest of the universe, and his role in the universal cosmic process.

Huxley wrote scores of scientific papers and books and was a pioneer in the fields of ornithology and animal behaviour. In 1932 he published *Problems of Relative Growth*, followed in 1942 by *Evolution, the Modern Synthesis*; he also published *Evolution in Action, Man in the Modern World* (1947), and many other similar works.

In 1929 he visited East Africa to advise on education; this led to *Africa View*, published in 1931, and later he was a member of the general committee for Lord HAILEY's 'African Survey'. He was elected FRS in 1938. From 1946 to 1948 he was the first Director-General of UNESCO.

This brief outline of his activities can give little indication of the wide extent of his interests or the influence he exerted in the field of popular science. From 1935 to 1942 he was

Secretary of the Zoological Society of London and, during the Second World War, became well known as a broadcaster on the BBC's 'Brain's Trust'. He was an ardent supporter of the work of Nature Conservancy, not only in Britain, but world-wide. He received many academic honours from all over the world and was knighted in 1958.

Huxley died on 14 February 1975. His elder son, Anthony, became a horticulturist and botanist, and his younger son, Francis, an anthropologist.

HYLTON, JACK (1892–1965), dance-band leader, and impresario, was born in Bolton on 2 July 1892, the son of George Hilton, a millhand, and his wife, Mary Greenhalgh. He was educated at the higher grade school in Bolton and learnt to play the piano as a child. His first professional engagement was at Rhyl in 1905 as assistant pianist with a pierrot troupe. He later changed his name to Hylton.

In 1913 he became cinema organist at the Alexandra, Stoke Newington, and in 1920 was working as a double act with Tommy HANDLEY at the Bedford Music Hall. He joined the Queen's Hall roof band, became its leader, and made his first records with the band for 'His Master's Voice' in 1921. In the following year he opened an office in London and placed first-class dance-bands at the Piccadilly Hotel and the Kit-Cat Club, while touring with his own band which was now recognized as the best show-band in Britain.

From 1927 to 1938 he appeared with his band in a number of musical shows at the London Hippodrome, the Palladium, and Prince's. He also toured Europe with great success, but was unable to take his band to the USA because of restrictions imposed by the American Federation of Musicians. However, he visited the States in 1935 and conducted an American band for six months.

In 1935 he appeared in the film *She Shall Have Music* and, after he disbanded his band in 1940 because of difficulties arising from the war, he went into the theatre business, and between 1941 and 1946 presented a number of West-End successes including *Lady Behave* (His Majesty's, 1941), *The Merry Widow*, revived at the same theatre in 1943, and *Follow the Girls*, also at His Majesty's in 1945.

Hylton also composed many popular songs. He was very helpful to young musicians and composers and presented many well known stage personalities, including Arthur Askey, Stanley Holloway, George FORMBY, Tommy Handley, and Leslie Sarony. He also launched the careers of some performers who later became well known, including Jack Jackson, Ted Heath, 'Chappie' d'Amato, and Billy Ternent. Jack Hylton appeared in six royal command performances, and received the Légion d'Honneur. In 1922 he married Florence Parkinson (Ennis Parkes), revue artiste; this marriage ended in divorce as did his second marriage to Friederike Kogler. In 1963 he married Beverley Prowse. Hylton had two daughters and a son. He died in London on 29 January 1965.

Jack Hylton (left) and his band in the 1930s

I

INCHCAPE, first EARL OF (1852–1932). See MACKAY.

INGE, WILLIAM RALPH (1860–1954), Dean of St Paul's, was born on 6 June 1860 at Crayke, Yorkshire, the elder son of William Inge, curate (later Provost of Worcester College, Oxford), and his wife, Susanna Mary, daughter of Edward Churton, archdeacon and theologian. His childhood was spent at Crayke, being taught by his parents, and in 1874 he became a scholar of Eton, and in 1879 a scholar of King's College, Cambridge, where he obtained firsts in both parts of the classical tripos (1882–3), was awarded the Bell, Porson, and Craven scholarships, and was senior Chancellor's medallist. In 1885 he was Hare prizeman.

For four years he was a master at Eton but was not suited to life as a schoolmaster, being subject to bouts of severe melancholia and also afflicted with deafness. In 1888 he was elected Fellow and tutor of Hertford College, Oxford. He was also ordained deacon, but did not take priests' orders until four years later. In 1899 he was Bampton lecturer, his subject being *Christian Mysticism*; this lecture was published that year and became widely read and had a considerable influence on theological thinking.

In 1905 Inge became Vicar of All Saints, Ennismore Gardens, and married Mary Catharine, daughter of Henry Maxwell Spooner, Archdeacon of Maidstone, and niece of W. A. SPOONER, the famous Warden of New College, Oxford, who gave the word 'spoonerism' to the English language. Two years later, the brief experience Inge had of life as a parish priest ended with his appointment as Lady Margaret's Professor of Divinity at Cambridge and Fellow of Jesus College. In 1909 he became BD and DD. At Cambridge he resumed his studies of Christian mysticism and Platonism, and published *Personal Idealism and Mysticism* (1907), and *Faith and its Psychology* (1909).

In 1911 Inge became Dean of St Paul's, an office which he held until 1934. His preaching attracted large congregations, but increasingly it was his writing that brought Dean Inge, 'the gloomy dean' as he was nicknamed, the attention of the public. His weekly articles in the *Evening Standard* (1921–46) were widely discussed. In them he attacked what he regarded as the superstitions of his day, criticized the notion of 'a war to end wars' and the facile optimism of a belief in progress as inevitable. Two volumes of *Outspoken Essays* (1919–22) elucidated clearly and forcibly his views on theological and ideological problems.

He continued to demonstrate his interest in classical scholarship and mystical devotion in the Gifford lectures on 'The Philosophy of Plotinus', published in two volumes in 1918. He also published *Personal Religion and the Life of Devotion* (1924) with a remarkable chapter on 'Bereavement' commemorating his daughter, Margaret, who died in childhood. *God and the Astronomers* (1933) gave his views on scientific cosmologies and their relation to theology. His last public lecture was on the faith of St Paul (Westminster Abbey 1951).

Inge was appointed CVO in 1918 and KCVO in 1930. He was elected FBA in 1921 and received a number of honorary degrees.

He had three sons and two daughters; the youngest son was killed in active service with the RAF in 1941. His wife died in 1949, and he died at Wallingford on 26 February 1954.

IRELAND, JOHN NICHOLSON (1879–1962), composer, organist, and pianist, was born at Inglewood, Dunham Massey, Cheshire on 13 August 1879, the youngest child of Alexander Ireland, Editor and part-owner of the *Manchester Examiner*, and his second wife, Annie Ireland, biographer of Jane Welsh Carlyle. He was educated at Leeds Grammar School, and studied the piano and organ at the Royal College of Music, London. When he was fifteen both his parents died, but a year later he was awarded a fellowship of the Royal College of Organists and, at the age of seventeen, was appointed Assistant Organist and Choirmaster of Holy Trinity Church, Sloane Street (1896).

From 1897 to 1901 he studied with Charles STANFORD, and in 1904 was appointed Organist and Choirmaster of St Luke's, Chelsea; there he remained for the next twenty-two years. In 1908 he became Mus. B. (Durham). While at St Luke's, he composed most of his church music, and his other works of this period include the Phantasy Trio in A minor (1909), the Violin Sonata in D (1910), the Second Violin Sonata (1917), and the piano suite *Decorations* and the orchestral *The Forgotten Rite* (1913).

John Ireland at Rock Mill, Sussex

In 1923 Ireland was appointed Professor of Composition at the Royal College of Music and, in the following year, became FRCM and honorary RAM. Four years after his appointment to the chair of composition, he married Dorothy Phillips, a piano student at the college; but the marriage was annulled soon afterwards. He held his chair until 1939, during which period his pupils included E. J. Moeran, Alan Bush, Humphrey Searle, Benjamin BRITTEN, and Geoffrey Bush. During these years, his principal compositions were a Cello Sonata, a Piano Sonatina, the Piano Concerto in E flat, *Legend* for piano and orchestra, *A London Overture*, and the choral work *These Things Shall Be*, commissioned by the BBC for the coronation of King George VI in 1937.

In 1939 he retired to Guernsey but was forced to return to England when the Germans invaded the Channel Islands. During the war he composed one of his finest pieces, *Sarnia*, the Channel Island sequence for piano. This was followed by the overture *Satyricon*, and the music for the film *The Overlanders*. After his eightieth birthday the John Ireland Society was formed to propagate his music (1959). Ireland's output of major works was comparatively small, but he produced many song tunes in the settings of English poets from Shakespeare and William Blake to Thomas HARDY and A. E. HOUSMAN.

In the last decade of his life he settled at Rock Mill, a converted windmill near the Chanctonbury Ring in Sussex, where he was cared for devotedly by his friend Mrs Norah Kirby. He died there on 12 June 1962.

IRWIN, first BARON (1881–1959). See WOOD, EDWARD FREDERICK LINDLEY.

ISAACS, ALICK (1921–1967), virologist, was born in Glasgow on 17 July 1921, the eldest of three sons of Louis Isaacs, a shopkeeper, and his wife, Rosine, daughter of Jacob Lion, a Jewish leather merchant of London. His father's father, Barnet Galinsky, had emigrated from Lithuania and taken the name Isaacs. Alick was educated at Pollokshields Secondary School and at Glasgow University where in 1944 he obtained his MB and Ch.B.

He soon decided that clinical medicine was not his *métier* and began the study of bacteriology; in 1947 he was awarded a Medical Research Council scholarship to study at Sheffield. There he began work on the influenza virus which was to become his main interest. A year later he went to Melbourne, Australia, with a Rockefeller travelling fellowship, and in 1949 married Susanna Gordon, a paediatrician, daughter of Herbert James Foss, pianist and composer; they had twin sons and a daughter. They returned to England in 1951 so that Isaacs could work at the National Institute for Medical Research at Mill Hill, London.

While he was in Melbourne, he had produced a number of papers, in collaboration with Margaret Edney, on the 'interference phenomenon': the ability of one virus, live or inactivated, to suppress the growth in the cell of another virus. Working in London, with Dr. J. Lindenmann of Zurich, Isaacs discovered that there was an active agent which stimulated interference and produced fresh interfering activity with viruses thus providing an entirely new defence mechanism, not only against the virus by which it had been activated, but also against many viruses of other kinds. Isaacs and Lindenmann named the active agent 'interferon', and interferon was soon being studied by scientific workers, both in Britain and abroad, in the hope that it would provide a natural chemotherapeutic agent of great potential value in medicine. These hopes could not be realized immediately as the process of producing interferon was found to be extremely complicated and expensive; but the rapid advances in genetic engineering in the fifteen years following Isaacs's death have made it possible to overcome this difficulty.

Isaacs also did valuable work with the World Influenza Centre under the World Health Organization, studying the various strains of influenza virus and the constant changes in their antigenic composition. In 1955 he was awarded the MD with honours at Glasgow University; in 1962 he received a similar honour from the Catholic University of Louvain, Belgium. He was elected FRS in 1966.

In his later years he suffered from serious bouts of intense depression. He had been appointed head of the virus division at Mill Hill in 1961, but the attacks of depression continued, and on 26 January 1967 he died in University College Hospital, London.

ISAACS, RUFUS DANIEL, first MARQUESS OF READING (1860–1935), Lord Chief Justice, Ambassador to USA, and Viceroy of India, was born in London on 10 October 1860, the fourth of the nine children of Joseph Michael Isaacs, a Jewish fruit merchant, and his wife, Sarah, daughter of Daniel Davis of London. He had little schooling, but spent a short time in Hanover learning German, and at fifteen entered his father's business. He found this work uncongenial, and during 1876–7 he went round the world as ship's boy on a sailing-ship, the *Blair Athole*. On return he rejoined the fruit business, but in 1880 gave this up to become a jobber on the Stock Exchange, and in 1884 was 'hammered' when he could not meet his commitments.

His mother, a strong-minded woman, now decided that he should study law. In 1887 he was called to the Bar (Middle Temple) and his remarkable career began in earnest. In that year he married Alice Edith, daughter of Albert Cohen, a City merchant. In 1898 he took silk. For the next ten years he handled successfully a number of cases dealing with commercial law and the trade unions, including the Taff Vale litigation (1902), and the prosecution of Whitaker Wright for fraud (1904). He was not an erudite lawyer, but his previous experience of the City and his good sense made him a very effective advocate. In 1898 he took silk.

In 1904 Isaacs became Liberal MP for Reading, and in 1910 was appointed Solicitor-General and, a few months later, Attorney-General. He made an excellent law officer, in 1911 leading for the prosecution in a case in which the defendant was convicted of criminal libel for alleging that George V was already at the time of his marriage married to Queen Mary. He also secured the conviction of the poisoner F. H. Seddon in 1912 and, though he was in favour of women's suffrage, he prosecuted Mrs Emmeline PANKHURST and other militant suffragettes for conspiracy. In 1911 he was sworn of the Privy Council and appointed KCVO. In 1912 he was the first Attorney-General to become a member of the Cabinet, but was bitterly disappointed that he had not been made Lord Chancellor, Lord HALDANE being appointed instead.

Unfortunately, the career of Rufus Isaacs was marred by one episode that cannot be ignored. In March 1912 Herbert SAMUEL, the Postmaster-General, accepted an important tender from the British Marconi Company for the construction of a chain of wireless stations. One of Isaacs's brothers was a managing director of the company. A French newspaper alleged that Samuel and Isaacs, the Attorney-General, had corruptly influenced this transaction. The paper was sued for libel and at once retracted its story. The House of Commons, however, set up a select committee to enquire into the matter, and it was revealed that Isaacs and LLOYD GEORGE, then Chancellor of the Exchequer, had purchased shares in the American Marconi Company, but had had nothing to do with Samuel's agreement with the British company. The shares had been purchased through another brother of Isaacs and, although the Attorney-General was exonerated from any charge of corruption, he and Lloyd George had to admit to the House that they had shown a serious error of judgement in purchasing the shares and in concealing the fact from the House. The House voted by a majority to accept the apologies of the Ministers, acquitted them of acting otherwise than in good faith, and rejected the insinuations of corruption. ASQUITH, the Prime Minister, had no hesitation a year later in offering the post of Lord Chief Justice to Isaacs.

Isaacs was appointed Lord Chief Justice in 1913 and became Baron Reading in 1914. His activities during the First World War, however, went far beyond the limits of the law courts. In 1915, having been appointed GCB, he led the Anglo-French mission to the USA and succeeded in securing a loan of $500m for the war effort. He became a viscount in 1916 and, when a year later America entered the war against Germany, he returned to the States as High Commissioner for Finance in Canada and the USA. Early in 1918 he became British Ambassador to Washington and his work there considerably accelerated the supply of food and the rapid deployment of troops to Europe.

He returned to his judicial duties in 1919, but in 1921 vacated the office of Lord Chief Justice to become Viceroy of India. For the next five years he held this post with distinction in a time of great difficulty. His task was to apply the Montagu-Chelmsford reforms embodied in the 1919 Act and he set about this work in a spirit of patience and conciliation; but he was eventually forced, by the boycott by Congress and the increasing violence, to resort to harsh measures, including the imprisonment of GANDHI (1922). His difficulties with Indian extremists had not been surmounted when he left the country in 1926 and was created a marquess. He had been appointed GCSI and GCIE in 1921 and GCVO in 1922.

On return to England he became President of Imperial Chemical Industries. He played a prominent part in the Round Table Conference of 1930, and from August to October 1931 was Foreign Secretary in the National Government of Ramsay MACDONALD. In 1934 he was appointed Lord Warden of the Cinque Ports.

In 1930 Lady Reading died and, in 1931, Lord Reading married Stella, daughter of Charles Charnaud, who had been his secretary for many years. Reading died in London on 30 December 1935. His only child, a son by his first marriage, followed him in the legal profession.

ISMAY, HASTINGS LIONEL ('PUG'), BARON ISMAY (1887–1965), general, was born at Naini Tal, India on 21 June 1887, the younger son of (Sir) Stanley Ismay, a member of the Viceroy's Legislative Council, and his wife, Beatrice Ellen, daughter of Col. Hastings Read. He was educated at Charterhouse and the Royal Military College, Sandhurst.

He entered the Indian Army in 1905, and served in India until 1914, when he was seconded to the King's African Rifles. He served during 1917–19 with the Somaliland Indian Contingent, and during 1919–20 with the Camel Corps, winning the DSO. In 1921 he passed through the Staff College, Quetta, with distinction. In the same year he married Laura

Kathleen, daughter of Henry Gordon Clegg, of Wormington Grange, Gloucestershire; they had three daughters.

After a short period at the RAF Staff College at Andover, Ismay served from 1925 to 1930 as Assistant Secretary to the Committee of Imperial Defence under Sir Maurice HANKEY. Then, having been appointed CB in 1931, he returned to India as Military Secretary to the Viceroy, Lord Willingdon. He came back to London two years later and served in the War Office until 1936. From 1936 to 1938 he was Deputy Secretary to Hankey and, when Hankey retired in 1938, Ismay became Secretary to the Committee of Imperial Defence.

When in 1940 Winston CHURCHILL became Prime Minister and Minister of Defence, he kept Ismay as his chief staff officer, heading a small secretariat of carefully selected staff, and acting as an essential link between Churchill and the Chiefs of Staff. Throughout the Second World War Ismay was in his own words 'in the middle of the web', an essential part of the military and administrative machine, responsible for dealing with Churchill's draft orders and minutes, the repository of most secret matters, ready to depart at short notice on important missions abroad, and burdened with the difficulties of working the eccentric hours that the Prime Minister demanded of his subordinates. Resilient, imperturbable, reliable, and indefatigable, Ismay survived, becoming a lieutenant-general in 1942 and full general in 1944.

In 1945 he became CH, but in 1946 Clement ATTLEE, the new Prime Minister, thought that his services had not been sufficiently recognized and Ismay was created a baron. In 1946 he retired from the army but, when Lord Louis MOUNTBATTEN was appointed Viceroy of India, he insisted on having Ismay as his Chief of Staff. For three years Ismay worked with Mountbatten, but he did not enjoy this time in India as he was out of sympathy with the policy of partition, although he accepted that it was inevitable. Furthermore, he did not feel the same attachment to Mountbatten that he had felt to Churchill. He declined the grand cross of the Star of India.

When Ismay returned to England in 1948, Attlee ap-

Wartime conversation between Ismay (right) and the Lord Chancellor, Sir John Simon, c. 1942

pointed him Chairman of the Council for the Festival of Britain, and Churchill, on returning to office in 1951, appointed Ismay Secretary of State for Commonwealth Relations. Ismay held this office for only a few months and then was selected to be the first Secretary-General of NATO, a post which he held successfully until 1957. He was sworn of the Privy Council in 1951, and appointed KG on his retirement (1957).

He assisted Churchill with *The Second World War* (1948-53), and in 1960 published his own *Memoirs* which, according to Lord MORAN, gave the ageing Churchill great enjoyment.

Known to all as 'Pug', Ismay's eventful life ended at Wormington Grange on 17 December 1965.

IVEAGH, COUNTESS OF (1881-1966). See GUINNESS, RUPERT.

IVEAGH, first EARL OF (1847-1927). See GUINNESS, EDWARD.

IVEAGH, second EARL OF (1874-1967). See GUINNESS, RUPERT.

J

JACKSON, SIR BARRY VINCENT (1879-1961), theatre director, was born in Birmingham on 6 September 1879, the youngest child of George Jackson, a wealthy provision merchant who founded the Maypole Dairies, and his wife, Jane Spreadborough. He was educated by a tutor and encouraged to go to the theatre. After working for five years in an architect's office, he decided at the age of twenty-three that the theatre was to be his vocation.

In 1907 he and some friends, including John Drinkwater, founded the Pilgrim Players. Six years later, this developed into the Birmingham Repertory Company, opening with *Twelfth Night* (1913). Soon afterwards, Jackson gave up acting himself and concentrated on directing. His money kept the Birmingham theatre going although the response of the public was slow.

During the First World War, while Jackson was in the Royal Navy, John Drinkwater kept the theatre active with plays which included his own *Abraham Lincoln* (1918). When Barry Jackson returned, he produced a number of plays including *The Immortal Hour* (1921), *Cymbeline* in modern dress (1923), and *Back to Methuselah* (1923). Jackson and George Bernard SHAW became close friends.

Disappointed by the apathy of the Birmingham public, Jackson closed the theatre for a time and moved to London, where he produced *The Farmer's Wife* by Eden Phillpotts at the Royal Court Theatre. In 1925 he leased the Kingsway as well as the Royal Court and presented *Hamlet* in modern dress. In that year he was knighted for his services to the stage. The Birmingham Rep. reopened and gave a start to a number of actors and actresses who later became well known, including Gwen Ffrangcon-Davies, Cedric HARDWICKE, Ralph Richardson, and Laurence Olivier. In 1929, besides his activities in London, Jackson organized the Malvern summer festival, and continued to do so for the next nine years.

In 1935 he left London to concentrate on the Birmingham theatre. He had spent a considerable sum of money on its productions during the past twenty-two years and he now transferred his interest to a local trust which, in effect, meant giving the theatre to the city.

From 1946 to 1948 he worked for three seasons reorganizing and restoring the fortunes of the Shakespeare Memorial Theatre at Stratford-upon-Avon, in the course of

Barry Jackson in exuberant spirits, February 1954

which Paul Scofield became established as an actor and Peter Brook as a director.

From 1948 to the time of his death, he withdrew to Birmingham again, staging among other successes *Henry VI* (1953), *Caesar and Cleopatra* (1956), and *Antony and Cleopatra* (1961).

He wrote, translated, and adapted a number of plays. He received several honorary degrees and was a director of the Royal Opera House from 1949 to 1955. He never married. He died in Birmingham on 3 April 1961.

JAMES, ALEXANDER WILSON (1901–1953), footballer, was born at Mossend, Bellshill, Lanarkshire on 14 September 1901, the son of Charles James, a railwayman, and his wife, Jane Ann Barrie Wilson. After leaving school, he played football for junior sides until 1922–3 when he played for Raith Rovers in the Scottish League. He was then transferred to Preston North End and played with them for seven years in the second division of the English League. During that time he was capped four times for Scotland, and in 1928 scored two goals when Scotland beat England at Wembley 5–1.

In 1928 Herbert Chapman, the shrewd manager of the Arsenal club, obtained Alex James from Preston for what was then a record fee of £9,000 and, until the end of the 1936–7 season, he was an Arsenal player. During that time Arsenal won the League championship four times and the FA cup twice. James also played four more times for Scotland.

James was a genius. One recalls his stocky figure, in baggy shorts well below his knees and with flapping sleeves, twisting and turning with the ball, as if it were glued to his boots, while opponents unavailingly attempted to tackle him, until, when he saw the moment was ripe, he was able to pass the ball with pin-point accuracy to an unmarked member of his side in a scoring position.

Inevitably he was often the object of rough tactics and was frequently injured. He retired from playing in 1937 when he found that he could no longer recover from injury quickly.

During the Second World War, James served in the Maritime AA Regiment and, when the war ended, became an Arsenal coach. He died in London on 1 June 1953.

JAMES, HENRY (1843–1916), novelist, was born in New York on 15 April 1843, the second son of Henry James, religious philosopher, and his wife, Mary Walsh, daughter of a wealthy cotton merchant. Henry James, the elder, was a restless traveller, who took his family backwards and forwards between the USA and Europe, and Henry the younger, and his three brothers and sister were sent to schools in New York, London, Paris, and Geneva. In 1862 Henry entered the Harvard Law School, but he quickly discovered that he preferred writing stories to following the legal profession.

From 1865 he began to make a living by writing reviews, sketches, and short stories for American magazines. His first novel *Watch and Ward* was serialized in 1871 when James was writing for the *Atlantic* and the *Nation*. *Roderick Hudson* followed, being published in Boston in 1876, the story of a young American who visits Italy, gets into trouble, and dies mysteriously in Switzerland. The numerous visits to Europe during his boyhood had given James a feeling for the old world which he never lost and, after he had made trips to

Alex James (second left) playing for Arsenal against his former club, Preston, 26 October 1935

Europe again in 1869 and 1872, he decided that he must make his home in Europe. At first, he planned to live in Paris, where he met many French writers, including Guy de Maupassant, Edmond de Goncourt, Emile Zola, and Alphonse Daudet, and became a friend of Turgenev, the Russian novelist, whose work he greatly admired.

In 1876, however, James decided to settle in London, and lived there until 1898, when he moved to Rye, where he stayed until he died. But, although he had determined to settle and work in England, he did not seek British citizenship until 1915, as a patriotic gesture during the First World War. Once settled in London, James made friends with writers such as Robert Louis Stevenson and, although he considered English culture in many ways extremely insular, he sought by keen observation to discover the intricacies of English character and behaviour, and to collect material for new novels based on the society in which he now found himself.

To begin with he studied the impact of American life on the cultured society of the old world. *The American* (1877), *Daisy Miller* (1879), *Washington Square* (1880), and *The Portrait of a Lady* (1881) were all derived from this idea. In the last of these, the story of a young American girl's adventures in Europe, the character of his heroine, Isabel Archer, was probably based on that of his cousin, Minny Temple, who died young. In spite of having sought out for himself a way of life that suited him, James never lost his affection for his family, and particularly for his sister, Alice. His brother William once said of him, 'He is a native of the James family, and has no other country.'

It has often been asked why a man with James's affectionate nature never married. This mystery has never been solved. In his youth he suffered some kind of injury which may have incapacitated him, and he frequently suffered from bouts of ill health and nervous depression. He was easily moved by the deaths of his relatives and friends to moods in which he felt stricken for days.

During his early years in London he was feeling his way towards an understanding of the British character and way of life, but his experience was always limited to the society in which he moved, to the people he met at dinner parties and other social occasions or during weekends at country houses. Apart from a few intimate friends, including Robert Louis Stevenson, Burne Jones, George du Maurier, and J. R. Lowell, he held himself aloof from most of his acquaintances; but gradually he absorbed something of English social, political, and artistic life. His experience of the upper middle class society in London during the nineties gave him the inspiration for *The Tragic Muse* (1890), *The Spoils of Poynton* (1897), *What Maisie Knew* (1897), *The Awkward Age* (1899), and a large number of short stories.

In *The Wings of the Dove* (1902), *The Ambassadors* (1903), and *The Golden Bowl* (1904), James returned once more to his obsession with the clash of American and European character and its consequences. His work in these later years became more and more intricate and involved and his stories tended to be lost in the lengthy, involved descriptions of the peculiarities and sensitivities of his characters. In particular, he employed the method which he described as an alternation of drama and picture, whereby the action is interspersed with reflections on life in the mind of one of the characters.

James had many disappointments. In 1895 he had high hopes of his play *Guy Domville*, which George Alexander produced at the St James's Theatre. On the first night James went to see Oscar Wilde's *An Ideal Husband* at the Hay-

Henry James, Beerbohm cartoon, *c.* 1904

market, unable to bear the strain of watching his own play. Its reception was a disaster and it took James some time to recover from the shock. During 1907-9 he worked on a 24-volume collection of *The Novels and Tales of Henry James*. It was not greeted with the success for which he hoped. His friend, Edith Wharton, persuaded her publishers, who were also James's, to pay him her royalties concealed as an advance of his own.

In 1914 he began work on two further novels, *The Ivory Tower* and *The Sense of the Past*; they were unfinished when he died. During his last years at Lamb House, Rye, James's home was near to those of Joseph CONRAD, Ford Madox FORD, and H. G. WELLS, but he appears to have seen little at this time of these fellow authors. He suffered constantly from deep depression, and at one time consulted Sir William OSLER, Regius Professor of Medicine at Oxford. The First World War was a staggering blow to one whose admiration for the culture of Europe had persuaded him to give up his own country. In 1916 he was appointed to the Order of Merit; he died soon afterwards on 28 February 1916. A collection of the letters of this enigmatic man was published in 1920. During his lifetime, his reputation as a writer never reached the heights at which he aimed, and it was not until some thirty years later, after another world war, that the depth of his knowledge of character and his psychological insight into human behaviour began to be understood and appreciated by the reading public, and films of some of his works achieved success.

JAMES, MONTAGUE RHODES (1862–1936), biblical scholar, antiquary, and palaeographer, was born on 1 August 1862 at Goodnestone, Kent, the third son of Herbert James, curate, and his wife, Mary Emily, daughter of Admiral Joshua Sydney Horton. As a scholar at Eton, besides learning classics and French, he taught himself Italian and also studied the early Western manuscripts in the college library. At King's College, Cambridge, he became a Bell scholar (1883) and a Craven scholar (1884), and obtained firsts in both parts of the classical tripos (1884–5).

In 1886 he was appointed Assistant Director of the Fitzwilliam Museum, and in the following year became a Fellow of King's College for a dissertation on *The Apocalypse of St Peter*. During 1887–8 he visited Cyprus and helped in the excavation of the Temple of Aphrodite at Paphos. In the following year he was appointed lecturer in divinity and a year later Dean of King's College. There his profound knowledge of Christian iconography enabled him to reconstruct some of the stained glass disarranged by earlier restorers in the windows of the chapel when they had to be re-leaded. Later he performed a similar service for the Priory Church at Great Malvern.

In 1893 James was appointed Director of the Fitzwilliam Museum, and two years later brought out the first of a long list of descriptive catalogues of the Western manuscripts at Cambridge and elsewhere. Between 1895 and 1932 he catalogued the manuscripts at Eton, Lambeth, Westminster Abbey, all the Cambridge colleges, the Fitzwilliam Museum and the University Library, as well as those at Manchester and St Andrews.

He wrote extensively on the arts and literature of the Middle Ages, adding Danish, Swedish, and Coptic, with some Hebrew and Syriac, to his knowledge of languages. In 1924 he published his *Apocryphal New Testament*. From 1900 to 1902 he was a tutor of King's College, and in 1905 was elected Provost. He held this post for the next thirteen years, and from 1913 to 1915 was Vice-Chancellor of Cambridge University. From 1918 to 1936 he was also Provost of Eton.

His vacations were spent bicycling in France, Denmark, and Sweden, and he claimed that he had visited 141 of the 143 French cathedrals. Among his other amusements was the writing of ghost stories. He published *Ghost Stories of an Antiquary* (1905) and *Collected Ghost Stories* (1931). He became FBA in 1903, received many honorary degrees, and in 1930 was appointed to the Order of Merit. He died unmarried at Eton on 12 June 1936.

JARDINE, DOUGLAS ROBERT (1900–1958), cricketer, was born at Bombay on 23 October 1900, the only son of Malcolm Robert Jardine, a barrister, who had played cricket for Oxford and Middlesex, and his wife, Alison, daughter of Robert Moir MD. He was educated at Winchester and New College, Oxford, where he was a cricket blue and also played tennis for the university in 1921.

Jardine qualified as a solicitor in 1926, and his professional commitments precluded him from playing county cricket regularly. However, when he was available, he was sure of a place in the Surrey side and he became one of the best amateur players of the period between the wars. In 1927 and 1928 he headed the English averages.

Jardine (centre) leads the England side onto the field, second test at Melbourne, January 1933

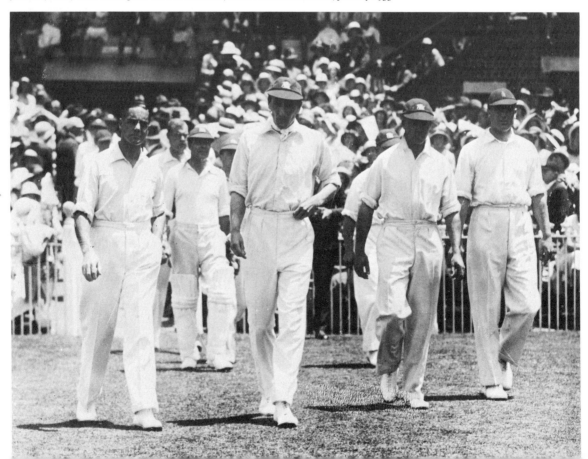

In 1928-9 he was selected to go to Australia with the England test team led by A. P. F. Chapman, another gifted amateur. With him in the side as batsmen were HOBBS, Sutcliffe, HAMMOND, Hendren, and Leyland. He played in all five tests. Hobbs in his book, *My Life Story*, said of Jardine: 'As a batsman he was a wonderful fighter. England never had a better number five: you could put him in when things were going wrong and be almost certain that he would stop the rot.' In a stand of 262 with Hammond at Adelaide, a new record was established for England's third wicket against Australia.

During the next two seasons, Jardine was unable to play much cricket, but in 1932 he captained England against India, and was invited by the MCC to lead the team which visited Australia in 1932-3. This series was the most controversial that has ever taken place between the two countries. England had two fast bowlers, Larwood and Voce, who were not only fast but deadly accurate, and Jardine used these two to attack the leg stump of the Australian batsmen, including (Sir) Donald Bradman. England won the first test, lost the second, and won the remaining three and the rubber. The Australians described this fast bowling as 'body-line' and protested to the MCC; it took some time for the controversy to die down. The Australian crowds were extremely hostile to Jardine, forgetful of the fact that in earlier years their own Warwick Armstrong had used two equally menacing bowlers, MacDonald and Gregory, against English batsmen.

Jardine led the England team to India in 1933-4, but his business commitments necessitated his giving up cricket at the age of thirty-three when he was in his prime. He had played in 22 test matches, 15 as captain; in tests he made 1,296 runs, with an average of 48. He continued his interest in the game as an occasional journalist and wrote two books about it, *In Quest of the Ashes* (1933) and *Cricket* (1936).

During the Second World War he served in France, Belgium, and India with the Royal Berkshire Regiment. In 1934 he married Irene Margaret, daughter of Sir William Henry Peat; they had a son and three daughters. Jardine died in Switzerland on 18 June 1958.

JARVIS, SIR JOHN LAYTON (JACK) (1887-1968), racehorse trainer, was born at Newmarket on 28 December 1887, the youngest son of William Arthur Jarvis, racehorse trainer, and his wife, Norah, daughter of James Godding, also a racehorse trainer. He was educated at Cranleigh and, when he left school, became an apprentice jockey with his father and rode the winner of the Cambridgeshire Handicap at the age of sixteen. He soon became too heavy to ride as a jockey and in 1914 became a trainer. In the same year he married Ethel Edina, daughter of Thomas Leader, another Newmarket trainer; they had one daughter.

His first important success did not come until after the First World War, when in 1921 he won the Two Thousand Guineas with Ellangowan. He won the same race in 1928 with Flamingo and in 1939 with Blue Peter. He also won the One Thousand Guineas three times, in 1924 with Plack, in 1934 (Campanula), and 1953 (Happy Laughter). He won the St Leger in 1931 with Sandwich, and the Derby twice in 1939 (Blue Peter) and 1944 (Ocean Swell).

Jarvis trained from 1922 until his death for the fifth and sixth Earls of Rosebery and, while on a visit to South Africa, found a young jockey, John Gorton, who rode for Lord Rosebery and won the Epsom Oaks on Sleeping Partner (1969).

Jarvis set himself the highest standards and had a deep understanding of racehorses. He was also interested in hare-coursing, and won the Waterloo Cup and the Barbican Cup. Another of his interests was pigeon fancying. In 1967 he was knighted for his services to horse racing. His autobiography *They're Off* was published in 1969. Jarvis died at Newmarket on 19 December 1968.

JEANS, SIR JAMES HOPWOOD (1877-1946), mathematician, physicist, astronomer, and popular writer on physics and astronomy, was born on 11 September 1877 at Birkdale, Southport, the only son of William Tulloch Jeans, a parliamentary journalist, and his wife, Martha Ann Hopwood. He was a precocious child, educated at Merchant Taylors' School and Trinity College, Cambridge, where he was a scholar, and was bracketed second wrangler in 1898. He obtained a first in mathematics (part ii) and an Isaac Newton studentship in astronomy and optics (1900). In the following year he was a Smith's prizeman and became a Fellow of Trinity College.

He wrote his book *Dynamical Theory of Gases* in 1904 while he was in a sanatorium recovering from tuberculosis of the joints. In 1940 he rewrote this work as *An Introduction to the Kinetic Theory of Gases*. From 1904-5 he was a university lecturer in mathematics at Cambridge, from 1905 to 1909 Professor of Applied Mathematics at Princeton, USA, and during 1910-12 returned to Cambridge as Stokes lecturer.

While he was at Princeton, he published *Theoretical Mechanics* (1906) and *The Mathematical Theory of Electricity and Magnetism* (1908). He married in 1907 Charlotte Tiffany, daughter of Alfred Mitchell, explorer, of New London, Connecticut; they had one daughter. Charlotte was wealthy, and from 1912 it was unnecessary for Jeans to hold any university post. From 1912 to 1918 they lived in London, during which time he gave the Bakerian lecture before the Royal Society (1917). In 1919 he published *Problems of Cosmogony and Stellar Dynamics*. He had become FRS in 1906, and from 1919 to 1929 was an honorary Secretary of the society. He was also President of the Royal Astronomical Society (1925-7). In 1928 he was knighted, and he received many honorary degrees and other academic awards.

When he ceased to be honorary Secretary of the Royal Society, Jeans set out on a new career as a successful writer of popular science. He produced in quick succession *Eos, or the Wider Aspects of Cosmogony* (1928), *The Universe Around Us* (1929), *The Mysterious Universe* (1930), *The Stars in their Courses* (1931), *The New Background of Science* (1933), and *Through Space and Time* (1934).

Apart from science, his main interest was music, and he often played the organ for three or four hours a day. His first wife died in 1934, and in 1935 he married the concert organist Susanne (Susi), daughter of Oskar Hock, of Vienna; they had two sons and a daughter. Jeans became a director of the Royal Academy of Music in 1937 and, in the same year, published *Science and Music*, dedicated to his wife.

In 1934 he was President of the British Association meeting at Aberdeen, and in 1935 the Royal Society set up a chair of astronomy, to which he was elected annually until 1946. In 1939 he was appointed to the Order of Merit, and in 1941 became an honorary Fellow of Trinity College, Cambridge. His last book *Physics and Philosophy* was published in 1942.

He died at Dorking on 16 September 1946.

JELLICOE, JOHN RUSHWORTH, first EARL JELLICOE (1859-1935), Admiral of the Fleet, was born at Southampton on 5 December 1859, the second of four sons of John Henry Jellicoe, a captain in the merchant service, and his wife, Lucy Henrietta, daughter of John Rushworth Keele, of Southampton. His mother's family had a strong naval tradition. In 1872 he entered the training ship, *Britannia*, and in 1874 passed out top of his term and was posted to the frigate *Newcastle*. The ship was at sea for two and a half years visiting ports in the Far East and South America.

From 1877 to 1884 Jellicoe served in the Mediterranean Fleet and in the latter year, after specializing in gunnery, was appointed to the staff of the *Excellent* gunnery school under Captain J. A. FISHER. In 1889 he assisted Fisher, by then Director of Naval Ordnance, at the Admiralty. He rejoined the Mediterranean Fleet in 1892 as a commander and in the following year narrowly escaped drowning when the *Camperdown* ran down and sank the *Victoria* with the loss of her admiral and nearly 400 men. In 1897 he was promoted to captain, and posted to the China station and, after converting Wei-hai-wei into a naval base, was Chief of Staff with the International Naval Brigade advancing on Peking against the Boxer rebels, when he was seriously wounded in the left lung. He was evacuated and returned to England in 1901.

In 1902 Jellicoe married Florence Gwendoline, daughter of Sir Charles William Cayzer (later first baronet); they had one son and five daughters.

Shortly before his marriage he had become the first naval assistant to the Controller with the task of inspecting all new ships under construction, and in 1905 he served again under Fisher, now First Sea Lord, as Director of Naval Ordnance. In 1907 he became rear-admiral, was appointed Second-in-Command of the Atlantic Fleet and KCVO. He had been appointed CB in 1900 and CVO in 1906. In 1908 he returned to the Admiralty as Controller and Third Sea Lord, responsible for new naval construction. In this post he strongly argued the case for the construction of eight battleships in 1909-10 and the improvement of British armour-piercing shells.

In 1910, as vice-admiral, Jellicoe hoisted his flag in the *Prince of Wales* in command of the Atlantic Fleet, but, two years later, was again recalled to the Admiralty as Second Sea Lord, responsible for discipline and manning of the Fleet. Then, when the First World War broke out, he was posted as Commander-in-Chief, Grand Fleet, with the acting rank of admiral, flying his flag in the *Iron Duke*. Scapa Flow, where the Grand Fleet was based was, in 1914-15, wide open to attack by German submarines, and Jellicoe felt bound to keep his ships continually at sea; casualties and necessary repairs inevitably reduced the effective strength of the fleet, but fortunately the German High Seas Fleet stayed in harbour, apart from brief raiding sorties in which they attacked seaside towns in Yorkshire.

In 1916, however, the appointment of Admiral Scheer to the German command made their High Seas Fleet more venturesome and, led by battle-cruisers under Admiral Hipper, they sought to bring British ships to battle, hoping to lead the British vanguard towards the German dreadnoughts and to annihilate them before they could escape. Jellicoe, owing to defective communications, had no warning that the German ships had left port, but BEATTY'S squadron, sailing in advance of the main force under Jellicoe, made contact with Hipper's battle-cruisers. Beatty suffered severe losses from the greater accuracy of the German gunners but, when he realized that he was being led into a trap, he turned northwards to lead the Germans into the more formidable

battle array under Jellicoe's command. The two main fleets were engaged in a brief exchange of gun fire, and then the German admiral turned away, firing torpedoes. Jellicoe, in turn, turned away to avoid the torpedoes, and for a time the German ships were out of sight. But the British fleet was between them and their home ports. The German ships briefly reappeared, there was a further exchange of shots, and in the gathering mist and darkness the Germans disappeared once more. Jellicoe lost them and the Battle of Jutland was over.

When the news of the battle was received in London, it appeared to have been a defeat for the Grand Fleet. Their losses had been more severe than those of the Germans; British ships appeared to have been more vulnerable to German shell-fire, and the Germans had escaped. CHURCHILL'S comment was that Jellicoe was the only man who could have lost the war in an afternoon, but Jellicoe's justification for his apparent failure was that the German High Seas Fleet never again effectively challenged the Grand Fleet during the rest of the war.

In 1916 Jellicoe was appointed to the Order of Merit, and towards the end of the year became First Sea Lord. By that time the U-boat menace to British merchant shipping had become the Admiralty's most serious problem. Early in 1917 ships were being lost at the rate of one in every four leaving British ports, and there seemed to be no effective method of improving the situation. Jellicoe did all he could to speed up the arming of the merchant fleet, but he and his staff were slow in accepting the need for a convoy system. LLOYD GEORGE, bitterly conscious of the heavy losses being sustained, felt compelled to seek some scapegoat for what he regarded as the Admiralty's inefficiency. Determined to take matters into his own hands, he forced the convoy system on his reluctant admirals, and Jellicoe was dismissed from his post of First Sea Lord in December 1917.

In January 1918 he was raised to the peerage as Viscount Jellicoe, of Scapa. In 1919 he was promoted Admiral of the Fleet. During 1919-20 he toured the Commonwealth to advise on naval defence and made proposals for a naval base at Singapore and the establishment of the Royal India navy and a New Zealand naval division. From 1920 to 1924 he was Governor-General of New Zealand, and in 1925 became Earl Jellicoe.

During the last eleven years of his life he took on various responsibilities, including the Presidency of the British Legion from 1928 to 1932. He died on 20 November 1935 in London and was buried in St Paul's Cathedral beside Nelson and Collingwood.

JENNINGS, SIR (WILLIAM) IVOR (1903-1965), constitutional lawyer, was born in Bristol on 16 May 1903, the son of a carpenter, William Jennings, and his wife, Eleanor Jane Thomas. He was educated at Bristol Grammar School, and St Catharine's College, Cambridge, where he obtained firsts in part i of the mathematical tripos (1923) and in both parts of the law tripos (1924-5), and was Whewell scholar in 1925. He was appointed Holt scholar of Gray's Inn in 1925, and Barstow scholar in 1926, and called to the Bar in 1928. In the same year he married Helena Emily, daughter of Albert Konsalik, of London; they had two daughters.

In 1925-9 Jennings lectured in law at Leeds University; he then moved to the London School of Economics and in 1930 was appointed lecturer in English law, a post which he held for the next ten years. In 1936 he published *Cabinet Government* and in 1939 *Parliament*, both of which were at the time authoritative works. He also published *The Law and the Constitution* (1933), *Parliamentary Reform* (1934), and *A Federation for Western Europe* (1940).

In 1940 Jennings was appointed Principal of University College, Ceylon (Sri Lanka), and two years later, when the college became a university, he was its first Vice-Chancellor. His services as an adviser on constitutional law and practice were sought by Pakistan in 1954-5, and by Malaya, where he was a member of the constitutional commission (1956-7).

In 1954 Jennings was appointed Master of Trinity Hall, Cambridge. He served as Vice-Chancellor of the university from 1961 to 1963, and during this time became Downing Professor in the laws of England (1962).

His interest in the British Commonwealth led to the publication in 1938 (in collaboration with C. M. Young) of a casebook on the *Constitutional Laws of the British Empire*, and in 1956 he published *The Approach to Self-Government*.

Jennings was knighted in 1948, appointed QC in 1949, and KBE in 1955, the year of his election to the British Academy. He became a bencher of Gray's Inn in 1958, and also received a number of honorary degrees. His *Party Politics* (3 vols. 1960-2) was considered not up to the standard of his earlier works. He died at Cambridge on 19 December 1965.

JEROME, JEROME KLAPKA (1859-1927), novelist and playwright, was born at Walsall on 2 May 1859, the younger son of Jerome Clapp Jerome, colliery proprietor, and his wife, Marguerite Jones, daughter of a Swansea solicitor. When the colliery business failed, Jerome senior moved to London and became a wholesale ironmonger. Jerome was educated at Marylebone Grammar School until he was fourteen, when he went out to work as a railway clerk, and later as a schoolmaster, actor, and journalist.

In 1888 he married Georgina Henrietta Stanley, daughter of Lieut. Nesza, of the Spanish army, and in the same year he published his first book *On the Stage and Off*. This was followed in 1889 by *The Idle Thoughts of an Idle Fellow* and *Three Men in a Boat*. The latter was a great success, was translated into a number of languages, and had a wide circulation, particularly in Russia. This is the one book of J. K. Jerome that is likely to survive.

In 1892, with Robert Barr and George Brown Burgin, Jerome founded *The Idler* a monthly illustrated magazine to which Mark Twain, Israel Zangwill, Eden Phillpotts, and W. W. Jacobs contributed. In the following year, Jerome founded a weekly paper *Today*, in which he constantly attacked the ambitions of the German Kaiser. An expensive law suit brought this to an end in 1897.

Jerome wrote a number of plays, of which the most successful was *The Passing of the Third Floor Back*, produced at the St James's theatre with Sir Johnston Forbes-Robertson in the lead (1908). He also wrote many other novels and sketches and a volume of reminiscences *My Life and Times* (1926).

During the First World War Jerome served as an ambulance driver on the Western Front. He and his wife had one daughter. Jerome died at Northampton on 14 June 1927 and his ashes were buried in the churchyard of Ewelme, Oxfordshire.

JESSOP, GILBERT LAIRD (1874-1955), cricketer, was born at Cheltenham on 19 May 1874, the son of Henry Edward Jessop, a surgeon, and his wife, Susannah Radford Hughes. He was educated at Cheltenham Grammar School

and Christ's College, Cambridge but, as his father died when he was fifteen, he had to earn his own living, and for six years worked as a schoolmaster and did not enter college until 1896. He had played cricket for Gloucestershire since 1894 and for the next four years played for the university, captaining the team in 1899.

He succeeded W. G. GRACE as captain of Gloucestershire in 1900, having already played for England in 1899. Since he was only 5 feet 7 inches in height, his stooping stance at the wicket earned for him the nickname of 'the Croucher'. He was a very fast scorer of runs, hitting the ball to every corner of the field with a great variety of strokes. In a match against the Professionals of the South at Hastings in 1907, he reached his 50 in 24 minutes, 100 in 42, 150 in 63, and altogether scored 191 in 90 minutes. Even allowing for the fact that the Hastings ground was not the size of the Oval or Lords and that at the time overs were bowled more quickly than nowadays, this was no mean feat.

Jessop played in 18 test matches, and is best remembered for his innings at the Oval in 1902 against the Australians. When he went in to bat, England had scored 48 for 5 on a rain-damaged wicket, and were needing 263 to win. Jessop scored 104 out of 139 in 75 minutes, and England won the match. Altogether, Jessop hit 53 centuries, six of them in less than an hour. He was also a good fast-bowler and four times took eight wickets in an innings. Jack HOBBS described him as 'about the best cover-point ever seen on a cricket field'.

Jessop was an all-round sportsman, was invited to play as a hockey goalkeeper against Oxford, played soccer for the Casuals, and rugby for Gloucester; he was also a good athlete and a scratch golfer. At the age of forty, he enlisted in 1914 in the Manchester Regiment and was invalided out with a damaged heart in 1918.

He published two books, *A Cricketer's Log* (1922) and *Cricket and How to Play It* (1925). In 1902 he married Millicent Osborne of New South Wales; they had one son, the Revd G. L. O. Jessop, who was also a county cricketer. It was at his vicarage at Fordington, near Dorchester, that Jessop died on 11 May 1955.

JOHN, AUGUSTUS EDWIN (1878-1961), artist, was born on 4 January 1878 at Tenby, Wales, the third child of Edwin William John, a solicitor, and his wife, Augusta, daughter of Thomas Smith, a plumber, of Brighton. Augusta died when John was six and his childhood was unhappy. He attended schools at Tenby and Clifton and studied art at Tenby and the Slade School, London (1894).

In 1897 he injured his skull diving into the sea on holiday in Wales and his work at the Slade at once appeared completely transformed. Whereas his previous work had been described by Henry TONKS as 'methodical', it now achieved brilliance. In 1898 he visited Amsterdam for a great Rembrandt exhibition, having won the summer composition prize with *Moses and the Brazen Serpent*.

John held his first one-man exhibition in 1899. This was sufficiently successful to enable him to travel abroad with other artists, including Charles Conder, William ORPEN, and William ROTHENSTEIN.

In 1901 he married a fellow student at the Slade, Ida, eldest daughter of John Trivett Nettleship, animal painter; they had five sons, including (Sir) Caspar, who became First Sea Lord. Ida died in 1907 but, four years earlier, John had met Dorothy (Dorelia), daughter of William George McNeill, a mercantile clerk and, before Ida's death, Dorelia had borne him a son. They subsequently had two daughters, and she remained with him until he died, in spite of his frequent infidelities. (He had two more illegitimate daughters and a son between 1915 and 1935).

In 1901-2 John was an art instructor at Liverpool University, but in 1903 he moved with his family to Essex. For most of his life he was constantly on the move in England and abroad. From 1902 till 1920 he produced a succession of masterly works, mainly portraits and landscapes, including portraits of George Bernard SHAW, Arthur Symons and Matthew Smith. He achieved enormous fame while still a young man, perhaps as much on account of his romantic appearance and Bohemian way of life, as for his undoubted talent. Yet, he seemed continually conscious of a sense of inadequacy, claiming: 'I am just a legend; not a real person at all.' After 1920 his work gradually deteriorated, as he forsook his earlier style for large imaginative compositions, in which he could make no use of his brilliant powers of observation. In 1932 T. E. LAWRENCE wrote: 'John is in ruins.'

His work appeared in many exhibitions, the most important of which were the retrospective at the Royal Academy in 1954, and two at the National Portrait Gallery in 1975. John was fascinated by gypsies, and he made contributions to the *Journal of the Gypsy Lore Society*; he also wrote *Chiaroscuro, Fragments of Autobiography* (1952), and *Finishing Touches* (1964).

He became an RA in 1928 and was appointed to the Order

Augustus John camping at Cambridge, summer 1909

of Merit in 1942. He died on 31 October 1961 at Fordingbridge, Hampshire. His sister, Gwen, also became a notable painter, thought by some critics to be more talented than her brother. She died in 1939.

JOHNSON, AMY (1903-41), airwoman, was born at Kingston-upon-Hull on 1 July 1903, the eldest daughter of John William Johnson, a herring importer, and his wife, Amy, granddaughter of William Hodge, Mayor of Hull. John Johnson's father was a Dane who married a Devonshire woman. Amy was educated at the Boulevard Secondary School, Hull, and Sheffield University, where she graduated BA in 1925. She then worked as a secretary with a firm of solicitors in London and spent all her leisure time at the London Aeroplane Club.

Amy was the first woman in Britain to be granted an Air Ministry's ground-engineer's licence and she obtained a full navigation certificate. She had never flown further than from London to Hull, when on 5 May 1930 she started out to fly solo to Australia in a Moth with a Gypsy engine. She arrived at Karachi six days later, breaking the record for that distance, but she had difficulties from there onwards, including a forced landing near Rangoon. She did not arrive at Darwin until 24 May and, flying on to Brisbane, wrecked the machine when trying to land. The flight aroused great interest and enthusiasm; she was appointed CBE, and the *Daily Mail* presented her with £10,000.

This flight to Australia was the first of several long-distance flights, including a record breaking flight across Siberia to Tokyo and back in 1931. In the following year, she broke the record for a solo flight to Cape Town and back.

In 1932 she married James Allan, son of Hector Alexander Mollison, a consultant engineer, of Glasgow. In 1934 they made a record flight together to Karachi, and in 1936 Amy made another record solo flight to Cape Town and back.

In 1938 she and Mollison were divorced; they had no children. She resumed her maiden name, and in 1939 joined the Air Transport Auxiliary. She was lost over the Thames estuary on 5 January 1941 when ferrying an aeroplane with material for the Air Ministry from Blackpool to Kidlington, Oxon. No one knows why she was more than 100 miles off course or what caused her plane to crash. Her death was presumed in the Probate Court in December 1943.

JOHNSON, HEWLETT (1874-1966), the 'Red Dean', was born in Manchester on 25 January 1874, the third son of Charles Johnson, wire manufacturer, and his wife, Rosa, daughter of the Revd Alfred Hewlett. He was educated at Macclesfield Grammar School and the Owens College, Manchester, where he obtained a B.Sc. in 1894, and won the geological prize. In 1898 he became an associate member of the Institute of Civil Engineers. However, his religious upbringing and his experience of the Manchester slums led him to offer his services to the Church Missionary Society. In 1904 he gained a second in theology at Wadham College, Oxford, where he captained the college rowing.

The CMS regarded him as unsuitable for their work and, having been ordained deacon in 1905 and priest in 1906, he became a curate at Altrincham. He was already well known for his outspoken, radical opinions, but he was an eloquent preacher, and in 1919 became an honorary Canon of Chester, and in 1922 Rural Dean of Bowden.

From 1905 to 1924 Johnson edited a theological magazine *The Interpreter* and continued his studies, obtaining his BD

Amy Johnson at the London Aeroplane Club, Stag Lane, Edgware, after her Australian flight, 1930

(Oxford) in 1917, and the DD in 1924 for his work on the Acts of the Apostles. In 1924, when Ramsay MACDONALD was Prime Minister, Johnson was appointed Dean of Manchester. He was assisted in this office by his much-loved wife, Mary, daughter of Frederick Taylor, merchant, of Broughton Park, Manchester, whom he had married in 1903. In 1931 she died, and in the same year, he was moved to Canterbury.

Johnson had a passion for overseas travel and visited many European countries, but did not go to Russia until 1937. The rise of Fascism in Germany and Italy and his sympathy for the Republican government in Spain disposed him to favour what he saw in the Soviet system. After his visit to Russia, he became a convinced Communist, stubbornly disregarding the more unpleasant aspects of Stalinism, and obtaining wide sales for his books on the Soviets, translated into many languages, in particular *The Socialist Sixth of the World* (1939). He was also an indefatigable speaker for the Left Book Club.

In 1932 he had visited China, and after the Second World War he paid four more visits to that country as well as visiting the countries of Eastern Europe, the USA, Canada, Australia, and Cuba. In 1951 he was awarded the Stalin peace prize. His activities in the cause of Communism, which earned him the name of the 'Red Dean', were inevitably extremely embarrassing to the Establishment of the Church of England. In 1947 the Archbishop of Canterbury issued a statement disclaiming any responsibility for the Dean's speeches and opinions, and the Canons of Canterbury for many years disassociated themselves from his political utterances. In 1963 he resigned.

Although he aroused criticism for his views, the Dean was a gifted man and preacher, who was admired for his wide culture and many acts of personal kindness. Towards the end

of his life, he returned to psychical research, in which he had been interested as a young man, and explained his personal beliefs in his autobiography *Searching for Light* (1968).

In 1938 he married Nowell Mary, daughter of his cousin, the Revd George Edwards; they had two daughters. He died in Canterbury on 22 October 1966.

JONES, SIR HAROLD SPENCER (1890–1960). See SPENCER JONES.

JOYCE, JAMES AUGUSTINE (1882–1941), poet, novelist, and playwright, was born in Dublin on 2 February 1882, the eldest son of John Stanislaus Joyce, a well-known Dublin character, a fine singer, and a bibulous companion, who produced a family, but was improvident and feckless. His wife, Mary Jane, daughter of John Murray, an agent for wines, of Longford, was a brilliant pianist and the backbone of the family. Joyce was educated at Belvedere College, Dublin, a Jesuit school, and University College, Dublin, where he specialized in languages and studied the works of Aristotle and St Thomas Aquinas. While still an undergraduate, he published in the *Fortnightly Review* an essay on 'Ibsen's New Drama' (1900).

In 1902, when he was nineteen, Joyce left Dublin for Paris, living precariously on loans and small sums begged from his younger brother, Stanislaus, and friends. Before he left Dublin, he had thought of becoming a medical student, but in Paris he found this to be impossible. By 1904 he was back in Dublin, having borrowed the money to attend his mother's funeral. While there, he met Nora Barnacle, a young woman, working in Dublin, who was ready to give herself to the impecunious young man, whose whole life appeared now to be wrapped up in his urge to write. Together, they went to Zurich and then to Trieste, where for a time, Joyce taught English in the Berlitz school.

As he acquired a family, a son and a daughter, his financial difficulties necessarily increased, but Nora stood by him through all adversity. His first book of poems, *Chamber Music*, was published in 1907 and *Dubliners*, a book of short stories, in 1914.

Joyce and Nora spent most of the First World War in Zurich, and his ability as a writer of unusual merit came slowly to be recognized. Their monetary difficulties were eased when the British Prime Minister, Herbert ASQUITH was persuaded by Edmund GOSSE and others to grant Joyce £100 from the privy purse. In 1917 Harriet Shaw Weaver, the spinster Editor of the *Egoist* magazine, came to his assistance by settling a sizeable sum of money on him, thus ensuring his financial independence.

His first full-length work, *The Portrait of the Artist as a Young Man*, was published in the USA in 1916 and in England in 1917. This was an autobiographical novel, based on the experiences of himself and Stanislaus in their early days in Dublin, graphically describing the Jesuit teachers he knew at school and the many Dublin characters that he met through his father and his father's friends.

From 1920 till 1940 Joyce and his family lived in Paris. In 1931 he married the patient and devoted Nora, and in 1940 they returned to Zurich. His daughter suffered from serious mental illness, and Joyce himself, throughout his adult life, was a sick man, partially blind, and afflicted by a stomach ulcer, which no doctor appeared to be able to cure. In his later years Joyce underwent many painful and ineffective operations for cataract.

His most important work, *Ulysses*, was published in Paris in 1922 but, because of the language used in certain passages, was banned in the United States until 1934 and in Britain until 1936. This highly original record of a day in Dublin in 1904 took Joyce seven years to write. In both language and style it was revolutionary, striking an entirely new note in English prose literature, and showing remarkable insight into human feelings and behaviour. As in *The Portrait of the Artist*, it drew heavily upon the life of Dublin, nostalgically recalled, and Joyce's father figures prominently in both works. Unlike Stanislaus, Joyce appears never to have lost his affection for his father, whose personality had made a deep impression upon him as a young man in spite of his egotism and other failings. *Ulysses* was a classic, which influenced, in its style and technique, many young writers in the period between the two world wars, though Joyce was

James Joyce (left) with Ezra Pound (standing), Ford Madox Ford, and John Quinn (right), Paris, 1923

an isolated example of a literary genius, whose work could not be imitated.

Ulysses was followed in 1939 by *Finnegans Wake*, a fantasy based on a dream during a night in Dublin, in which Joyce not only used the same devices as he had employed in *Ulysses*, describing 'the stream of consciousness' in the minds of his characters, but also created a language of his own, based on his knowledge of the classics and Italian and French, which was so esoteric as to be almost incomprehensible.

In 1918 Joyce wrote a play, *Exiles*, showing the influence of Ibsen in whose work he had been interested as a young man. In 1927 appeared a second slight volume of poems, *Pomes Penyeach*, written mainly between 1912 and 1924, short lyrical verses, less savage than some of his other work. Stanislaus Joyce, quoting his diary in the introduction to his book, *My Brother's Keeper* (1958), said of Joyce 'His great

passion is a fierce scorn of what he calls "the rabblement" — a tiger-like, insatiable hatred.' This aspect of Joyce is revealed in his poem 'The Holy Office' which begins:

> Myself into myself will give
> This name, Katharsis Purgative

and ends:

> And though they spurn me from the door
> My soul shall spurn them evermore.

having, in between, pilloried his contemporary Irish writers from W. B. YEATS through J. M. Synge to AE.

Joyce died in Zurich on 13 January 1941, described by ELIOT as 'the greatest master of English since Milton'.

K

KEMSLEY, first VISCOUNT (1883-1968). See BERRY, GOMER.

KENNINGTON, ERIC HENRI (1888-1960), artist, was born in London on 12 March 1888, the younger son of Thomas Benjamin Kennington, artist, and his Swedish wife, Elise Nilla Steveni. He was educated at St Paul's School, and then studied at the Lambeth School of Art and the City and Guilds School, Kennington. He first came to notice with his paintings of cockney types and London scenes, and from 1908 exhibited at the Royal Academy and the Leicester Galleries. One of the best-known of his works of this period is *Costermongers*, painted in 1913 and presented to the Musée de Luxembourg, Paris.

During the First World War Kennington enlisted as a private in the 13th London Regiment, the Kensingtons, and served in France and Flanders until 1915 when he was invalided out of the army. His war painting *The Kensingtons at Levantie*, depicting ten exhausted soldiers, including himself, in a battered village, was exhibited at the Goupil Gallery in 1916. He painted many other expressive war pictures, many of which, like this one, were painted on glass. From 1915 to the end of the war he was an official war artist.

In 1920 he met T. E. LAWRENCE and they became friends. He went out to the Near East and returned with a collection of portraits of the Arab leaders, which was exhibited at the Leicester Galleries in 1921. Some were used to illustrate the 1926 edition of Lawrence's *Seven Pillars of Wisdom*.

In 1922 he married Edith Celandine, daughter of Lord Francis Cecil; they had a son and a daughter.

Kennington took up sculpture and carved the stone figures of three infantrymen erected in Battersea Park as a memorial to his regiment. He then went on to create the British memorial at Soissons, France, in 1927-8, the carvings in the School of Hygiene and Tropical Medicine, Gower Street, the bronze memorial head of Thomas HARDY at Dorchester (1929), and the decorations on the façade of the Shakespeare Memorial Theatre, Stratford-upon-Avon. In 1939 he created the recumbent effigy of T. E. Lawrence in Arab dress to be

seen in St Martin's Church, Wareham, and a bronze head of Lawrence in the Tate Gallery.

During 1940-5 Kennington was again an official war artist, and made scores of pastel portraits of soldiers, from privates to generals, and naval personnel, from able seamen to admirals, and also members of the RAF. Many of these were reproduced in *Drawing the RAF* (1942) and *Tanks and Tank Folk* (1943), as well as in John Brophy's *Britain's Home Guard* (1945).

Kennington was elected ARA in 1951 and RA in 1959. There are many examples of his work in the Tate Gallery and the Imperial War Museum. He died in Reading on 13 April 1960.

KENSWOOD, first BARON (1887-1963). See WHITFIELD.

KENT, DUCHESS OF (1906-1968). See MARINA.

KERR, PHILIP HENRY, eleventh MARQUESS OF LOTHIAN (1882-1940), journalist and politician, was born in London on 18 April 1882, the elder son of Major-General Lord Ralph Drury Kerr, and his wife, Lady Anne, sixth daughter of Henry Granville Fitzalan-Howard, fourteenth Duke of Norfolk. He was a nephew of Schomberg Henry Kerr, ninth Marquess of Lothian, and of Lord Walter Talbot Kerr, Admiral of the Fleet. He was educated at the Oratory School and New College, Oxford, where he obtained a first in modern history in 1904.

Leaving Oxford, he went out to South Africa as Private Secretary to the Lieutenant-Governor of the Transvaal and became the youngest of Lord MILNER's 'kindergarten' and a colleague of Lionel CURTIS. He felt strongly the need for federation of the South African colonies, and during 1908-9 edited *The State*, a monthly review founded for the promotion of that aim.

After the Union constitution came into operation in 1909, he returned to England and became the first Editor of the *Round Table*, a quarterly aiming at the organic union of the British Commonwealth. As Editor, he frequently drew attention to the danger of aggression from Germany. In 1916 the Prime Minister, LLOYD GEORGE, appointed Kerr as his Private Secretary and, throughout the remainder of the war and the peace negotiations, he was an indispensable aid to Lloyd George and played an important part in dealing with the Dominions, India, and the USA. He was largely responsible for the document forming the preface to the Treaty of Versailles.

In 1921 Kerr resigned from his post with Lloyd George, and for a year was a director of United Newspapers. Having given that up, he spent much time writing on imperial politics and, in collaboration with Lionel Curtis, published *The Prevention of War* (1923). In 1925 he accepted the post of Secretary to the Rhodes Trustees, an office which he held until 1939. In 1930 he succeeded his cousin as eleventh Marquess of Lothian.

He was not ambitious to be a politician, but in 1931 held the office of Chancellor of the Duchy of Lancaster as a Liberal member of MACDONALD's National Government. After a few months, he became Under-Secretary of State for India, and in 1932 was Chairman of the Indian Franchise Committee; but he parted company with the Government later that year, when the Ottawa Conference led to tariff proposals which he, as a convinced free-trader, could not accept.

For the next seven years, he was one of the influential people who became notorious, as the 'Cliveden set', for their determined advocacy of appeasement and obstinate refusal to recognize that Hitler was aiming at the hegemony of Europe, by war, if necessary. As a close friend of Nancy ASTOR, Lord Lothian was in complete sympathy with the views of the group the Astors represented, in opposition to what they regarded as the intransigence of Winston CHURCHILL and his few friends. Years earlier he had renounced his Roman Catholic faith and, like Lady Astor, had become a convinced Christian Scientist.

In 1939 Neville CHAMBERLAIN appointed him British Ambassador to the United States and, for a little over a year, until his death in 1940, he showed remarkable ability as a persuasive advocate of the justice of the British cause and of the danger to the United States if Hitler succeeded in gaining control of western Europe and the Mediterranean sea and the Atlantic ocean. It is possible that, had he been prepared to have recourse to normal medical aid, his life could have been prolonged, but this was an expedient that his rigid adherence to Christian Science practices precluded him from adopting. He died in Washington on 12 December 1940. He never married.

He had been appointed CH in 1920 and PC in 1939; he was designated KT in 1940, but was never actually invested with the insignia. He received a number of honorary degrees. In his will he left Newbattle Abbey to Edinburgh for educational purposes and his beautiful Elizabethan house, at Blickling in Norfolk, to the National Trust.

KEYNES, JOHN MAYNARD, BARON KEYNES (1883–1946), economist, was born in Cambridge on 5 June 1883, the elder son of John Neville Keynes, lecturer in moral science and Registrar in the university, and his wife, Florence Ada, daughter of the Revd John Brown; she was an early student of Newnham College who became a JP, alderman, and Mayor of Cambridge. Keynes was a scholar of Eton and King's College, Cambridge, and was twelfth wrangler and

President of the Union in 1905; he was also a member of the 'Apostles' and later of the Bloomsbury group.

In 1906 he entered the home Civil Service and was posted to the India Office, where he became interested in Indian currency and finance. In 1908, however, he accepted the offer of a lectureship in economics at Cambridge, was elected a Fellow of King's College in 1909, and appointed Editor of the *Economic Journal* in 1912, a post which he held until 1945. He served as Secretary of the Royal Economic Society in 1913, and was a member of the Royal Commission on Indian Finance and Currency in 1913–14.

During the First World War, Keynes worked in the Treasury and in 1917 was appointed CB in recognition of his services there. He was the principal Treasury representative at the Peace Conference in 1919, but shortly afterwards resigned as he disagreed with the proposals for the realignment of frontiers and the exaction of reparations, and foresaw that these would inevitably lead to future problems. His own views on these matters were set out in *The Economic Consequences of the Peace* published in 1919. His ideas on the reconstruction of post-war Europe aroused considerable controversy, but he continued to publish pamphlets and articles in justification of his arguments. His close friends, Duncan Grant and Vanessa BELL, who were pacifists, were very critical of his activities during the war, but thoroughly approved of the reasons for his resignation in 1919.

In 1923 he became Chairman of the *Nation and Athenaeum* (forerunner of the *New Statesman*), and was a member of the Macmillan committee on finance and industry from 1929 to 1931. He set out his revolutionary theories on the cure of unemployment and the relation of savings and investment to rising and falling prices in *A Treatise on Money* (2 vols., 1930) and the *General Theory of Employment, Interest and Money* (1936). In these books he explained lucidly and concisely why he disagreed with accepted economic thought of his time. His main point was the importance of investment by the Government in a time of recession, even if this involved increasing national indebtedness.

Meanwhile, he was appointed Second (1919), and then First (1924–6) Bursar of King's College, Cambridge. By shrewd investment of capital, he considerably increased the income of the college, and his own. He was a keen collector of books and paintings, and built and financed the Arts Theatre, Cambridge. He served as chairman of CEMA (later the Arts Council), and was appointed Chairman of the National Mutual Life Assurance Society in 1921. Later, he published *Essays in Persuasion* (1931) and *Essays in Biography* (1933).

In 1925 he married the Russian ballerina, Lydia Lopokova, daughter of Vassili Lopokoff and Constanzia Douglas of Leningrad. She had danced solo parts with the Imperial Ballet in St Petersburg (Leningrad) and later performed with Diaghilev's *Ballet Russe*. They had no children.

On the outbreak of the Second World War Keynes returned to the Treasury, and was created a baron in 1942. He played a leading part at the Bretton Woods Conference (1944) from which emerged the International Monetary Fund and the International Bank, on both of which he was the first British governor. During 1944–5 he was engaged on Lease-Lend negotiations with the USA and arranged for an American loan to post-war Britain on conditions for which he was criticized in Parliament in 1945. On return to England, worn out by his efforts to persuade the Americans of the dire needs of the British economy, he died suddenly at Tilton, Sussex on 21 April 1946. He had been elected FBA

Maynard Keynes and his wife, Lydia Lopokova, by William Roberts, *c.* 1932

in 1929 and D.Sc., Cambridge in 1946; he was a Trustee of the National Gallery and a director of the Bank of England.

Keynes was a generous friend, a man of immense vitality and original thought. His views for which he fought almost alone in the thirties were raised to the level of orthodoxy in the years following the Second World War during which was created the Welfare State. In more recent times there has been further questioning of the validity of his 'Keynesian economics', but his ideas, like those of Karl Marx, have been accepted or rejected by many who did not fully understand them.

KING, SIR (FREDERIC) TRUBY (1858–1938), pioneer of mothercraft, was born at New Plymouth, New Zealand, on 1 April 1858, the third son of Thomas King, a bank manager, and his wife, Mary Chilman. He was educated at New Plymouth and Edinburgh University, where he was awarded the Ettles scholarship, and became MB, CM in

1886. In the following year he married Isabella Cockburn, daughter of Adam Millar, of Edinburgh; they had one daughter. In 1907 he founded the Royal New Zealand Society for the Health of Women and Children (the Plunket Society). From 1921 to 1927 he was Director of Child Welfare for New Zealand.

In 1918 he was sent to England by the Government of New Zealand and founded in London the Plunket Society Training Centre for teaching the rudiments of infant welfare, from which centre, his ideas and methods spread all over the English-speaking world, and his books were translated and read in Russia, Poland, and China. These books, which were the first authentic works on the subject of mothercraft, included *Feeding and Care of Baby* (1913), and *The Expectant Mother and Baby's First Month* (1924); later revised by his daughter Mary, as *Mothercraft* (1934).

In New Zealand the results of Truby King's advice to mothers were very striking. Between 1905 and 1934, the annual mortality of infants in their first year was reduced from 8 per cent to 3.16 per cent. His teaching, based upon common sense, was eventually accepted generally and in due course became commonplace.

He was appointed CMG in 1917 and knighted in 1925. He died at Wellington, New Zealand, on 9 February 1938.

KING-HALL, (WILLIAM) STEPHEN RICHARD, BARON KING-HALL (1893-1966), writer, and broadcaster on politics and international affairs, was born in London on 21 January 1893, the only son of (Admiral Sir) George F. King-Hall, and his wife, Olga, daughter of Richard Ker, diplomat and MP for Downpatrick. Both father and son were lifelong teetotallers. King-Hall was educated in Lausanne and at Osborne and Dartmouth. He entered the Royal Navy and served in *Southampton* at the battle of Jutland in 1916.

While in Cape Town as a midshipman, he met (Amelia) Kathleen, daughter of Francis Spencer, an associate of Cecil Rhodes. He married her in 1919 and they had three daughters.

After the First World War he served in the Admiralty before passing through the Royal Naval Staff College and being posted to the China station. During 1925-6 he was intelligence officer to Sir Roger (later Lord) Keyes in the Mediterranean. In 1928-9 he worked on the naval staff at the Admiralty, but in 1929 resigned from the Royal Navy to take a research post in the Royal Institute of International Affairs (Chatham House).

For some years he had been writing for the press under a pseudonym and in 1924 had produced his first book under his own name, *Western Civilization and the Far East*, followed by *Imperial Defence* (1926). His financial circumstances were assured when in 1930, in collaboration with Ian Hay, his naval comedy *The Middle Watch* was a great success.

While he was at Chatham House between 1929 and 1935, he made his name as a liberal-minded internationalist who foresaw clearly the increasing danger from Fascism and put forward his views with great directness and clarity. From 1930 to 1937 he broadcast weekly on current affairs in the BBC's 'Children's Hour', attracting an adult audience as well, and when he left Chatham House he became a radio celebrity, a widely-published journalist, and was in demand as a lecturer at home and abroad. He published some forty books, including *Our Own Times* (1934-5), a contemporary history which went through four editions.

In 1936 he undertook a new and original venture, the *King-Hall News Letter* which, to begin with, went to 600 subscribers, but in three years became a financial success with 60,000 subscribers. He continued to warn his public of the threat from Hitler's Germany and contrived to get a German version of his warning into the Reich.

From 1939 to 1945 he was National Labour MP for Ormskirk, but he was not as successful in the Commons as he was outside and, having resigned from the party in 1942, lost his seat to Harold (later Lord) Wilson in 1945 and failed as an independent candidate at Bridgwater in 1950. In 1944 he founded the Hansard Society.

After the Second World War he argued vigorously for European union and was in favour of unilateral nuclear disarmament, but he no longer had the influence which his earlier broadcasting and writing had enjoyed. In 1954 he was knighted, and in 1966 received a life peerage. His last years were saddened by the death of his wife in 1963, and he died in London on 2 June 1966.

KINGDON-WARD, FRANCIS (FRANK) (1885-1958), plant collector, explorer, and author, was born on 6 November 1885 in Manchester, the only son of Harry Marshall Ward, lecturer in botany at the Owens College, and his wife, Selina Mary Kingdon. He was educated at St Paul's School, London, and Christ's College, Cambridge, where he graduated in 1906.

In 1907 he became a master at the Shanghai Public School, and in 1909, accompanied by an American zoologist, made his first exploratory journey in China, travelling to Szechuan and Kansu, collecting botanical specimens. In 1911 he became a professional plant collector working for Bees of Liverpool, the horticulturists.

In 1923 he married Florinda Norman-Thompson, daughter of a landed proprietor in Ireland; they had two daughters, and the marriage ended in divorce in 1937. In 1947 he married Jean, daughter of Sir Albert Sortain Romer Macklin, a retired Indian judge.

For nearly fifty years Kingdon-Ward was engaged on botanical exploration, disappearing into the unmapped territory on the borders of Burma, India, and China, searching for new plants, and frequently travelling in these remote areas for months on his own. In these expeditions he succeeded in collecting large numbers of plants, new to the gardens of Britain and America, including rhododendrons, primulas, poppies, gentians, and lilies of wide varieties and species.

Altogether, he undertook some twenty-five expeditions, including one in which he set off into the northernmost tracts of Burma just before the Japanese war led to the invasion of that country in 1942. On other journeys he visited South-East Tibet, the remoter regions of Assam north of Ledo, French Indo-China (Vietnam), and East Manipur.

These expeditions and their botanical finds were described in twenty-five books and innumerable articles in magazines and scientific journals, and included *The Land of the Blue Poppy* (1913), *In Farthest Burma* (1921), *Plant Hunting on the Edge of the World* (1930), and *Return to the Irrawaddy* (1956). His works contributed much to an understanding of the conditions in which plant-life flourished in the unexplored regions into which his searches led him. His best-known introduction to European gardens was probably the *Meconopsis betonicifolia* (baileyi), which Frederick BAILEY had discovered in 1913. Kingdon-Ward, having rediscovered this beautiful blue poppy, collected the seed, which in 1926 became available in England and was planted in Hyde Park, London.

He received many honours from organizations such as the Royal Geographical and the Royal Horticultural Societies. In 1952 he was appointed OBE. Kingdon-Ward died in London on 8 April 1958.

KINGSFORD SMITH, SIR CHARLES EDWARD (1897-1935), airman, was born at Brisbane on 9 February 1897, the youngest son of William Charles Smith, a bank manager, and his wife, Catherine Mary Kingsford. He was educated at Sydney Cathedral School and Sydney Technical College, and in 1915 served as a dispatch-rider in Egypt and Gallipoli. In 1916 he joined the Royal Flying Corps, and then became an instructor in the Royal Air Force. He was awarded the MC in 1917.

After demobilization, he returned to Australia and founded an air taxi service. In 1927 he flew round Australia in ten days. His main claim to fame arose in the following year (1928), when he made the first flight across the Pacific in the *Southern Cross*. In 1929 he flew from Australia to England,

and in 1930 completed his flight, circling the globe at its greatest circumference. He was appointed KBE in 1932. He made a number of other pioneer flights during 1930-5, and on 7 November 1935 passed over Calcutta on a flight from England and was never seen again.

In 1921 he married Thelma McKenna; this marriage ended in divorce in 1930, and in that year he married Mary, daughter of Arthur Powell, a merchant, of Melbourne; they had one son. Kingsford Smith published *The Old Bus* (1932), the story of the *Southern Cross*, and, posthumously, *My Flying Life* (1937).

KIPLING, (JOSEPH) RUDYARD (1865-1936), author, was born in Bombay on 30 December 1865, the only son of John Lockwood Kipling, an architectural sculptor in the Bombay School of Art, and his wife, Alice, daughter of George Browne Macdonald, a Wesleyan minister of Wolverhampton. One of his mother's sisters was the mother of Stanley BALDWIN, and another married Sir Edward Burne-Jones. In 1871 Rudyard Kipling was sent home to England, and spent five years with a family at Southsea in what he came to describe as the 'House of Desolation', but his Christmas holidays were spent happily with the Burne-Jones family. Then in 1877 his mother returned to England, rescued him from Southsea, and in the following year sent him to the United Services College, Westward Ho!, which later became the background for *Stalky and Co.* (1899). There he acquired a wide knowledge of the English classics and of French literature.

In 1882 he returned to India and joined the staff of the Lahore *Civil and Military Gazette*, and was soon writing verses, sketches, and short stories which brought him fame while he was still a young man. Among these were *Departmental Ditties* (1886), *Plain Tales from the Hills, Soldiers Three, The Story of the Gadsbys, In Black and White, Under the Deodars, The Phantom Rickshaw*, and *Wee Willie Winkie* (all 1888). In London his work was praised by such critics as Edmund GOSSE and Andrew Lang, but there were also those who were revolted by his realism, not least Max BEERBOHM, who admitted his genius but was repelled by his style and matter.

In 1889, Kipling left India and returned to England via Japan and the USA. He settled in London and in 1891 published his novel *The Light that Failed*. He now spent much of his time travelling in America, Australia, and South Africa. He became a close friend of Wolcott Balestier, an American journalist of French origin, with whom he collaborated in *The Naulahka* (1892). When Balestier died suddenly in 1891, Kipling was very distressed and his decision to marry Balestier's sister, Caroline, in 1892, was deeply involved with his affection for her brother. After their marriage the Kiplings went to America and settled for the next four years on the Balestier estate at Brattleboro, Vermont.

Kipling was not happy in the USA and a local quarrel hastened his return to England. Meanwhile he had published *Many Inventions* (1893), and the two *Jungle Books* (1894-5) and drafted *Captains Courageous* which was published in 1897. He was now at the height of his fame. Between *Barrack-Room Ballads* (1892) and *The Seven Seas* (1896), he had become the exponent and prophet of a philosophy of nationalism and imperialism which his readers either revelled in or hated. In 1897 he wrote the 'Recessional', which he regarded as his best poem and, although *Kim* (1901), *Puck of Pook's Hill* (1906), and *Rewards and Fairies* (1910) were

still to come, Kipling was never again so universally popular as in the years immediately before the Boer War.

In 1899 his six-year-old daughter, Josephine, died; this was the first of some shattering blows that were to disturb Kipling's career; she was his eldest child for whom the *Just So Stories for Little Children* (1902) were intended. The early British disasters in the Boer War gave rise to a wave of anti-imperialist sentiment, which made it possible for young intellectuals to denigrate the popular patriotic fervour with which Kipling's early work had been greeted. But Kipling continued writing undeterred by adverse criticism, and during this period produced some of his most durable poetry, including 'The Glory of the Garden' and 'If'.

In 1902 he and his family settled at Bateman's at Burwash in Sussex. In 1907 he was awarded the Nobel prize for literature. In 1916 Robert BRIDGES, describing him as 'the greatest living literary genius that we have', recommended that he should be appointed to the Order of Merit, but Kipling declined the honour and continued to do so when it was offered again in 1921 and 1924. He had refused to become Poet Laureate as long ago as 1895.

From his fiftieth year until his death, Kipling suffered constant and often acute pain from a duodenal ulcer and his friend, Rider HAGGARD, confided to his private diary that he feared for his life. His writing became more cryptic and involved. He saw the danger from Germany growing year by year, and during the First World War poured out letters and articles on war topics. He also wrote the history of his only son's regiment, *The Irish Guards in the Great War* (2 vols., 1923). The boy was killed in action on the Western Front in 1915.

Kipling's study at Bateman's is as he left it

In the post-war period many honours were bestowed upon Kipling. In 1922 he was elected Lord Rector of St Andrew's University; in 1926 he was awarded the gold medal of the Royal Society of Literature; in 1932 he became an honorary Fellow of Magdalene College, Cambridge, and received many honorary degrees from universities at home and abroad.

His unfinished autobiography *Something of Myself* was published posthumously in 1937. Kipling died in London on 18 January 1936 and was buried in Westminster Abbey. He left one surviving child, Elsie. His widow bequeathed Bateman's to the National Trust.

Kipling's work has continued to be popular with some, anathema to others. George ORWELL in 1942 wrote: 'At his worst . . . in poems like 'Gunga Din' or 'Danny Deever' Kipling is almost a shameful pleasure, like the taste for cheap sweets that some people secretly carry into middle life', and C. S. LEWIS, in his essay 'Kipling's World', wrote: 'I have never at any time been able to understand how a man of taste could doubt that Kipling is a very great artist.'

KITCHENER, HORATIO HERBERT, first EARL KITCHENER, of Khartoum (1850–1916), field-marshal, was born in co. Kerry on 24 June 1850, the second son of Lt.-Col. Henry Horatio Kitchener and his first wife, Anne Frances, daughter of the Revd John Chevallier, MD. He was educated in Switzerland and at the Royal Military Academy, Woolwich, during 1868–70. In 1871 he was commissioned into the Royal Engineers and, subsequently, carried out surveys in Palestine (1874), Cyprus (1878), and the Sinai Peninsula (1883).

In 1884–5 he served with the Egyptian army in (Lord) Wolseley's belated expedition for the relief of General Gordon. He resigned his commission in the Egyptian army in 1885 and was appointed to the joint commission to delimit the territory of the Sultan of Zanzibar. He was Governor-General of the Eastern Sudan during 1886–8 and then, in the latter year, was appointed adjutant-general of the Egyptian army and commanded the cavalry at the defeat of the dervishes at Toski. He was appointed CB in 1889, and succeeded Sir Evelyn BARING as Sirdar of the Egyptian army in 1892. From then until 1896 he prepared for the reconquest of the Sudan; he was appointed KCMG in 1894.

In 1896 he led the River War campaign and was promoted to major-general and KCB. He annihilated the Khalifa's army at Omdurman in 1898 and reoccupied Khartoum. Also in that year, he secured the withdrawal of a French expedition under Major Marchand at Fashoda. By now a popular hero, he was made a baron on his return to England. In the following year, he was appointed Governor-General of the Sudan but, on the outbreak of the Boer War, became Chief of Staff to Lord Roberts. He succeeded Roberts as Commander-in-Chief in 1900, and organized the blockhouse system and concentration camps to defeat the Boers' guerrilla tactics. When the war ended in 1902, he became a viscount and OM.

As Commander-in-Chief, India from 1902 to 1909, he overcame the opposition of the Viceroy, Lord CURZON, to the abolition of the system of dual control of the army in India, and introduced reforms in administration and training, including the establishment of a Staff College. He was promoted to field-marshal in 1909, and was British Agent and Consul-General in Egypt from 1911 to 1914. He was given an earldom in 1914, and on the eve of the First World War ASQUITH appointed him Secretary-of-State for War.

In this post, he was handicapped by his ignorance of the organization of the War Office and of the army in Britain but

Kitchener in the Sudan, 1896 watercolour

realizing, unlike many of his colleagues, that the war would be a long one, he made immediate plans for the expansion of the armed forces, and by 1916 had increased army strength to seventy divisions, three million men having voluntarily enlisted. The poster, seen throughout the country, calling young men to serve their king and country, made his appearance familiar to millions. In 1915 his outstanding service was rewarded by the King: he was appointed KG.

Although he was extremely popular with the public, he had no political support and when, in 1915, Asquith formed a Coalition Government, Kitchener found himself opposed by LLOYD GEORGE and lost much of his influence with the Cabinet. He visited the Near East and advised abandonment of the Dardanelles campaign, and he undertook to visit and advise the Russian Government on more effective co-operation in the conduct of the war. He sailed in HMS *Hampshire* on 5 June 1916 and died with most of those aboard when *Hampshire* was sunk off the Orkneys. He never married. His death was mourned by the British people as a great calamity, but his important work had been completed. His resolution in the face of criticism had never wavered, and it was largely due to his determination that Britain survived the disasters of the first two years of the war.

KNIGHT, HAROLD (1874–1961). See KNIGHT, DAME LAURA.

KNIGHT, DAME LAURA (1877–1970), painter, was born on 4 August 1877 at Long Eaton, Notts., the youngest of the three daughters of Charles Johnson, and his wife, Charlotte

Bates. Johnson deserted his family when he discovered that his wife's father's lace factory was failing, and Charlotte brought up her daughters by teaching art in Nottingham. Laura was educated at Brincliffe School, and at St Quentin in northern France, where she lived with an aunt. At the age of fourteen, she entered the Nottingham School of Art and met a fellow student, HAROLD KNIGHT, born in Nottingham on 27 January 1874, the eldest son of an architect, William Knight. They were married in 1903.

In 1905 they exhibited together at the Leicester Galleries in London and sold sufficient paintings to spend some time in Holland. A year later they both had pictures accepted by the Royal Academy. They then settled at Newlyn in Cornwall, where Laura became a close friend of A. J. MUN-NINGS, who made his name as a painter of horses. In 1909 her painting *Daughters of the Sun* was exhibited at the Royal Academy, but did not sell as she had set her price too high.

Laura and Harold Knight were poles apart in their attitude to painting. He was not interested in experiment, admired the old masters, particularly Vermeer, was less emotional than Laura, and was intent on mastering the technique of his medium; she loved painting out of doors, depicting the effects of sun and light in an opulent and flamboyant style. By 1912 Harold had begun to obtain commissions as a portrait painter, and during the First World War, being a conscientious objector, worked as a farm labourer, while Laura continued to increase her reputation as an artist of unusual subjects.

When the war ended, they settled together in London and Harold established himself as a skilful, meticulous painter of portraits, and Laura was able to work behind the scenes of Diaghilev's Ballet Company. In 1927 she was elected ARA. Munnings introduced her to Bertram Mills, the circus owner, and soon she was producing studies of clowns, acrobats, jugglers, and other circus characters, including the animals. Her large canvas *Charivari* was exhibited at the Royal Academy in 1929.

Harold was elected ARA in 1928, and in 1929 Laura was appointed DBE. She was now painting scenes of gypsy life at Epsom and Ascot racecourses. Harold continued to paint excellent portraits of celebrities, such as the Bishop of Truro and W. H. Davies, the poet. In 1936 Laura became the first woman to be elected RA and Harold was elected RA a year later.

During the Second World War Laura worked for the War Artists' Advisory Committee and did some notable paintings for them. Then in 1946 she went to Nuremberg to paint pictures of the war criminals' trial, one of which is in the Imperial War Museum, London. Harold was in failing health and he died in Colwall, Cornwall on 3 October 1961.

Laura exhibited his paintings and arranged further exhibitions of her own work. She was given a retrospective exhibition at the Royal Academy in 1965 and '75 years of Painting' at the Upper Grosvenor Galleries in 1969. Both she and her husband were honoured by many artistic and academic organizations. She died in London on 7 July 1970; the marriage was childless. Her paintings can be seen in many public collections, including the Royal Academy, the National Portrait Gallery, the Tate, and the British Museum. Her books *Oil Paint and Grease Paint*, *A Proper Circus Omie*, and *The Magic of a Line* were published in 1936, 1962, and 1965 respectively.

KNOX, RONALD ARBUTHNOTT (1888-1957), Roman Catholic priest and translator of the Bible, was born on 17 February 1888 at Kibworth, Leicestershire, the youngest of

six children of the Rector, the Revd Edmund Arbuthnott Knox, later Bishop of Manchester, and his first wife, Ellen Penelope, daughter of Thomas Valpy French, Bishop of Lahore. His eldest brother, E. V. Knox (Evoe), became Editor of *Punch*. Knox was educated at Eton, where he was a senior scholar from Summer Fields, Oxford. He was also a scholar of Balliol College, Oxford. While still a schoolboy, he gained a reputation as a composer of witty verses in English, Latin, and Greek, by publishing *Signa Severa*. At Oxford he won the Hertford (1907), Ireland (1908), and Craven (1908) scholarships, and the Gaisford Greek verse (1908), and Chancellor's Latin verse (1910) prizes; he obtained a first in Greats (1910). He was also President of the Union in 1909, renowned for his satire and wit.

He was ordained Anglican deacon (1911) and priest (1912) and appointed Fellow (1910) and Chaplain (1912) of Trinity College, Oxford. Unlike his father, who was a leader of the Low Church party, Knox was an Anglo-Catholic, who played a prominent part in claiming that the Church of England was a branch of the Catholic Church. He wrote two brilliant works defending his position, *Absolute and Abitofhell* (a parody of Dryden), and *Reunion All Round*, a parody of Swift (1913-14).

During the First World War Knox taught for a time at Shrewsbury and then worked at the War Office (1916-18). He had become more and more disillusioned about his position in the Church of England, and in 1917 he was received into the Roman Catholic Church. In the following year he published *A Spiritual Aeneid*, explaining why he had taken this decision. He took Roman Catholic orders in 1919 and from 1918 to 1926 taught at St Edmund's College, Ware.

From 1926 to 1939 he was Chaplain to Roman Catholic students at Oxford and, during that time, wrote a number of books, not only on religious subjects but also detective stories. In 1926 he received a certain notoriety by a broadcast announcement of the outbreak of revolution in London, which was intended as a joke but was taken seriously by some listeners. He also published in 1939 *Let Dons Delight*, a series of imaginary common-room conversations at intervals of fifty years from the time of Elizabeth I up to 1938.

His great ambition, to which his responsibilities at Oxford were a hindrance, was to translate a new version of the Bible. He therefore resigned his position at Oxford in 1939 and devoted himself to this task until it was completed in 1955. He also wrote *Enthusiasm* (1950), which he intended to be a polemical attack on those who regarded themselves as having a special individual revelation of God's will, but with age his thoughts had mellowed and this book was more objective than controversial, as he had come to doubt the value of religious disputation. In his later years he composed a translation of the *Autobiography* of Saint Thérèse of Lisieux (1958) and began a translation of the *Imitation of Christ* which he did not complete.

In 1936 he was created monsignor; in 1951 he became protonotary apostolic, and in 1956 was elected to the Pontifical Academy. He was made an honorary Fellow of Trinity (1941) and of Balliol (1953), and in 1957 delivered the Romanes lecture at Oxford on the subject of 'English Translation'. It was obvious to his audience that he had not long to live and he died at Mells in Somerset on 24 August 1957.

KORDA, SIR ALEXANDER (1893-1956), film producer, was born on 16 September 1893 in Hungary. His original name was Alexander Laszlo Kellner, and he was the eldest

Korda (centre) directs Michael Wilding on the set of *An Ideal Husband*, 1947

of three sons of Henry Kellner, land agent, and his wife, Ernestine Weisz. He was educated at schools in Nagykoros and Kecskemet and at a commercial school in Budapest. His father died when he was thirteen; at seventeen he became a newspaper reporter in Budapest and published a novel under the name of Alexander Korda.

His first introduction to films was as translator of sub-titles from French into Hungarian, and in 1912 he started a film magazine, the first of its kind to appear in Budapest. In 1913 he began to direct short films. Poor eyesight excused him from call-up in the First World War, and in 1918 his first full-length film *The Man of Gold* was a great success.

In 1919, after being arrested in connection with political unrest and then released, he fled to Vienna, where he produced *The Prince and the Pauper* (1920) and *Samson and Delilah* (1922). In 1923 he moved to Berlin and in 1926 to Hollywood. There he made *The Private Life of Helen of Troy* (1927). He returned to Europe in 1930 and in Paris made the classic film, *Marius* (1931).

In 1931 Korda settled in London and directed *Service for Ladies*, which was an outstanding success and marked a turning point in his career. He formed his own company, London Film Productions, and built the Denham studios and laboratories (1937). Meanwhile, he had some spectacular successes with films such as *The Private Life of Henry VIII* (1933), *The Ghost Goes West* and *The Scarlet Pimpernel* (1935), *Knight Without Armour* (1936), *Elephant Boy* (1936-

7), *Fire Over England* (1937), and *The Four Feathers* (1939).

Korda was now recognized as one of the leading personalities in the film world, able to attract to his studios stars of the English stage and screen, including Robert Donat, Charles Laughton, Leslie HOWARD, and Vivien LEIGH. He did not have the reputation of Samuel Goldwyn for memorable *bons mots*, or of Alfred HITCHCOCK for psychological drama; he made straightforward films with a good story and was superbly equipped technically for the task he set himself. Among his assistants were his talented brothers, Zolta and Vincent.

In 1939 financial difficulties necessitated giving up the Denham studios, but he continued to make films, including *The Thief of Baghdad* (1939-40), *Lady Hamilton* (1941), and *The Jungle Book* (1941). After the Second World War, he was able to revive London Films and built studios at Shepperton. There he produced *An Ideal Husband* (1947), *The Fallen Idol* and *The Third Man* (1949), *The Wooden Horse* (1950), *Sound Barrier* (1952), and *Richard III* (1955).

Korda became naturalized in 1936, and was knighted in 1942, and made an Officer of the Legion of Honour in 1950. In 1921 he married Maria Farkas, a Hungarian film actress, known as Maria Corda; they had one son. They divorced in 1931, and in 1939 he married Merle Oberon, a well-known Hollywood film star; that marriage also ended in divorce in 1945, and in 1953 he married Alexandra Irene Boycun, a Canadian. Korda died in London on 23 January 1956.

L

LAMBERT, CONSTANT (1905–1951), composer and musician, was born in London on 23 August 1905, the younger son of the Australian artist, George Washington Lambert, ARA, and his wife, Amelia Beatrice Absell. His brother was Maurice Lambert, the sculptor. He was educated at Christ's Hospital and the Royal College of Music, where he studied under Ralph VAUGHAN WILLIAMS, and was commissioned by Diaghilev, while still a student, to write the ballet *Romeo and Juliet*, first performed in 1926 at Monte Carlo.

He became a close friend of the Sitwells, and in 1922 and 1923 shared with Edith SITWELL the speaking part in *Façade*, poems which she had written with music by (Sir) William Walton. He was staying with the Sitwells when he composed his second ballet *Pomona* in 1926. In 1927 he composed *Music for Orchestra* which was followed by *The Rio Grande*, a setting of (Sir) Sacheverell Sitwell's poem for piano, chorus, and orchestra, which contained jazz effects. Lambert was interested in jazz, and his Piano Sonata and Concerto for piano and nine instruments showed this influence.

In 1931 he married Florence Chuter; they had one son.

In 1930 he had become conductor of the Camargo Society from which developed the Vic-Wells Ballet and the Sadler's Wells Ballet. He was the first Musical Director until 1947, after which he remained as artistic adviser. His choral masque *Summer's Last Will and Testament* was first performed at the Queen's Hall in 1936, conducted by Lambert himself. His third ballet, *Horoscope* was performed at Sadler's Wells in 1938 with choreography by (Sir) Frederick Ashton, and his last ballet, *Tiresias* was performed at Covent Garden in 1951. The décor for this ballet was produced by his second wife, Isabel Delmer, whom he had married in 1947 after his divorce from his first wife.

In 1940 while he was with the Sadler's Wells Ballet in Holland, he narrowly escaped capture by the Germans. As director of Sadler's Wells, he made arrangements for them of the music of many composers. He also did much conducting at the promenade concerts and was associate conductor on the BBC Third Programme during 1945–6. He frequently conducted at Covent Garden.

In 1934 he published his *Music Ho!* on music of the twenties; he wrote musical criticism for the *New Statesman*, *Figaro*, and the *Sunday Referee* and contributed articles to *Lilliput* and other magazines. He died in London on 21 August 1951, shortly before his forty-sixth birthday.

LAMBURN, RICHMAL CROMPTON (1890–1969). See CROMPTON, RICHMAL.

LANE, SIR ALLEN (1902–1970), publisher, was born Allen Lane Williams in Bristol on 21 September 1902, the eldest of the four children of Samuel Allen Gardiner Williams, a municipal architect, and his wife, Camilla Matilda Lane. He was educated at Bristol Grammar School, and in 1919 joined the Bodley Head publishing house of John Lane, a kinsman of his mother, who stipulated that he should change his name to Lane (1919).

He learnt the book trade in all its aspects from errand boy and packer to traveller, and for some time lived with John Lane and his American wife. When John died in 1925, the firm was in serious financial difficulty and, first as director and later as chairman, Allen Lane failed to persuade the board to venture into paperback reprints. He therefore decided to take action on his own with the help of his brothers, and in 1935 published the first ten Penguins at sixpence each. He had to pay Jonathan CAPE a large advance for six of the titles, as experienced publishers expected the venture to fail, but Woolworth's placed a large order and the public made a success of what was in fact a revolution in bookselling. In 1936 Lane set up Penguin Books and resigned from the Bodley Head, which was on the verge of bankruptcy.

In 1937 the first Penguin Shakespeares were launched, and later that year the first group of Pelicans appeared. Then came the Penguin Specials, which were a great success, and gradually Lane ceased to be a publisher of reprints and more and more books were specially commissioned, and many distinguished authors were glad to be on Lane's paperback list. In 1946 *The Odyssey* appeared as the first of the Penguin Classics, followed by the Pelican History of Art, and (Sir) Nikolaus Pevsner's *The Buildings of England* (over 40 vols., 1951–74).

In 1936 the Bodley Head had published the first British edition of James JOYCE's *Ulysses*, and Lane was a party to the decision to take this chance, although by the time of publication he had left the firm. Years later, in 1960, he took a similar risk in publishing the unexpurgated text of D. H. LAWRENCE's *Lady Chatterley's Lover* and, with the help of Gerald (later Lord) Gardiner, won the court case at the Old Bailey aroused by his decision.

In 1941 he married Lettice Lucy, daughter of Sir Charles William James Orr, KCMG; they had three daughters. Lane was knighted in 1952 and appointed CH in 1969. He was the recipient of many academic awards and honours.

Penguin Books was turned into a public company in 1960, and in 1967 Lane retired from the post of joint Managing Director. In 1969 he celebrated fifty years in publishing with the first British paperback edition of *Ulysses*. He was already a victim of cancer, and died near London on 7 July 1970. His career as a publisher introduced a new epoch in the production of books which brought pleasure and interest to a wider public than ever before.

LANE, LUPINO (1892–1959), comedian and theatre manager, was born in London on 16 June 1892, the elder son of Harry Lupino and his wife, Charlotte Sarah Robinson. He assumed the name Lane from his great-aunt, Sarah Lane, who had made a fortune from the management of the Britannia Theatre, Hoxton. His family were acrobats, dancers, and clowns with a long record in the music-hall and circus world. He made his first public appearance at the age of four in Birmingham, and in 1903 made his debut at the London Pavilion as 'Nipper' Lane, a comedian with an endearing Cockney personality, who quickly captured the attention of his audience.

In 1917 he married an actress, Violet, daughter of John Propert Blyth, a sea captain; they had one son.

In 1915 he had appeared at the Empire in *Watch Your Step*, and from then on he was always in demand in Manchester, London, or New York as a professional funny man.

In 1925 he appeared in New York as Ko-Ko in *The Mikado*, and his reputation was established on both sides of the Atlantic.

His greatest success came when the part of Bill Snibson, an irrepressible cockney, was created for him in *Twenty to One*, a musical by L. Arthur Rose and Frank Eyton, with music by Billy Mayel. This was put on at the London Coliseum in 1935 jointly by Lupino Lane and Sir Oswald STOLL and ran for nearly a year before it went on tour. A second Snibson play, *Me and My Girl*, by L. Arthur Rose and Douglas Furber with music by Noel Gay, was directed and presented by Lupino Lane at the Victoria Palace in 1937, and had a run of over 1,600 performances. This was the musical in which 'The Lambeth Walk' was first seen and heard. This cockney stomp was for years a popular item in all dance-halls in England and abroad. Both the Snibson plays were revived several times, and *Me and My Girl* was filmed as *The Lambeth Walk*.

Lane had become a rich man, and in 1946 he bought the Gaiety Theatre with which his family had been connected for a hundred years. But his success did not last, he failed to get the financial backing he needed, and resold the theatre in 1950. Lupino Lane died in London on 10 November 1959.

LANG, (WILLIAM) COSMO GORDON, BARON LANG OF LAMBETH (1864–1945), Archbishop of Canterbury, was born on 31 October 1864 at Fyvie Manse, Aberdeenshire, the third son of the Revd John Marshall Lang and his wife, Hannah Agnes, daughter of the Revd Peter Hay Keith, of Hamilton. He was educated at Edinburgh University and Balliol College, Oxford, where he was Brackenbury scholar, and President of the Union, a founder of the OUDS, and undergraduate-secretary of Toynbee Hall. Benjamin Jowett warned him that his task in Oxford was 'not to reform the East End of London' but to get a first in Greats. In fact, he got a second, but obtained a first in modern history in 1886.

After leaving Oxford he studied for the Bar, but in 1888 was elected a Fellow of All Souls and decided to enter the Church. He was ordained deacon in 1890 and priest in 1891, and went as curate to Leeds. Two years later he was elected Fellow of Magdalen College, Oxford, and appointed Dean of Divinity. In the following year he became Vicar of the university church of St Mary the Virgin, but after a further two years went to the vicarage of Portsea. He was also appointed one of Queen Victoria's chaplains at Osborne and, after her death, he conducted a service on board the *Alberta*, at which Edward VII and the Kaiser were present.

In 1901 Lang was appointed to a canonry at St Paul's and became Suffragan Bishop of Stepney. He renewed his activities for the people of the East End and travelled all over the country, preaching in aid of the East London Church Fund. Many were surprised when in 1909 he was appointed Archbishop of York. As a high churchman, he had to show tact and diplomacy in dealing with bishops who were predominantly low church. In the Lords, he supported the Liberal Government's 1909 Budget and the Parliament Bill, risking the wrath of many Conservatives.

Early in the First World War, he aroused considerable animosity by referring to his 'sacred memory' of the Kaiser when Queen Victoria died. At the time he was in poor health, but was able to visit the Grand Fleet in 1915 and the Western Front in 1917. He also went on a preaching tour in the USA and made a lasting friendship with John Pierpont Morgan. In 1921 his mother, to whom he was deeply attached, died.

Lang was a close friend and able supporter of Randall DAVIDSON, Archbishop of Canterbury, and took a leading part in the discussions on the revision of the Prayer Book. He wound up the debate in the House of Lords and achieved a large majority in favour of revision. When the Commons rejected the measure for the second time in 1928, Davidson promptly resigned, and Lang was appointed to succeed him as Archbishop of Canterbury.

His early years in this office were clouded by ill health, but gradually he recovered, helped by a cruise in the Mediterranean in Pierpont Morgan's yacht. His visit to the Near East enabled him to make contact with the Churches of the East and revitalized his lasting ambition to bring about the unity of all Christian Churches. He had already, when he was at York, had discussions with the Free Churches and the Roman Catholics. From 1930 onwards he organized a number of conferences to further this objective and hoped that the Lambeth Conference of 1940 would endorse the work he had undertaken, but the Second World War put an end to his hopes and there was no conference in 1940. At home, he took part in debates in the Lords, was a member of the joint committee on Indian constitutional reform in 1933, and a principal Trustee of the British Museum. He lived at Lambeth during the war, until bombing in 1941 rendered the palace uninhabitable.

He was always a close friend of George V and Queen Mary. However, his relations with Edward VIII were difficult, since he felt strongly about the King's intention to marry Mrs Simpson, and his broadcast after the abdication was widely criticized. He resumed his friendship with the royal family when George VI succeeded his brother.

Cosmo Gordon Lang, Archbishop of Canterbury, arriving at Church House, Westminster, for the Assembly of the Upper and Lower Houses, November 1930

He never married. He received many academic honours and was appointed GCVO in 1937. In 1942 he resigned as Archbishop and went to live at Kew, helped financially by the generosity of Pierpont Morgan, who made him a gift of £15,000. He was also given a peerage and continued to attend the House of Lords. He died suddenly on 5 December 1945.

LANSDOWNE, fifth MARQUESS OF (1845–1927). See PETTY-FITZMAURICE.

LASKI, HAROLD JOSEPH (1893–1950), political theorist and university teacher, was born in Manchester on 30 June 1893, the second son of Nathan Laski, a Jewish cotton shipping merchant, and his wife, Sarah Frankenstein. He was educated at Manchester Grammar School and University College London, where he studied genetics. In 1911, the year of his marriage to Frida, daughter of Francis John Kerry, a farmer and landowner, of Acton Hall, Suffolk, he went to New College, Oxford, with an exhibition, and in 1914 obtained a first in modern history. He was rejected for military service on medical grounds, and became a lecturer at McGill University, Montreal, during 1914–16. He then joined the staff of Harvard University and, while there, became a close friend of several eminent American lawyers, including Oliver Wendell Holmes. He was attacked in 1919 for his sympathetic attitude to the Boston police strikers, which also lost him any chance of promotion at Harvard. In 1920 he became a lecturer at the London School of Economics and, in 1926, Professor of Political Science, a post which he held until he died in 1950.

As a teacher, Laski was a great success; he was a brilliant lecturer and generous and popular with his students. His earliest publications were mainly concerned with the theoretical problems of sovereignty and the nature of the State. *Studies in the Problem of Sovereignty* was published in 1917 and *Authority in the Modern State* in 1919. These were followed in 1925 by *A Grammar of Politics*. At this time, Laski favoured the pluralist doctrine in which the State, if the most powerful, was but one of many organizations in society, and in 1927 in *Communism* he explained his objections to Marxist theories.

In 1931, however, his views underwent a radical change, possibly because of the economic depression and the split in the Labour party when Ramsay MACDONALD set up a National Government. Laski now came to the conclusion that socialist policies could not become effective under the existing system of parliamentary democracy. In *The Crisis and the Constitution 1931 and After* (1932), *Democracy in Crisis* (1933), and *Parliamentary Government in England* (1938), he examined British institutions and decided that the social revolution, which he believed to be inevitable, could only be brought about by radical change and the resort to violence if necessary. He continued to reject the Russian style of government and hoped instead to be able to adapt Marxism to British requirements.

He was a member of the Executive Committee of the Fabian Society from 1921 to 1936 and of the Labour party from 1936 to 1949. He was closely associated with Victor GOLLANCZ and John STRACHEY in the formation of the Left Book Club, for which the books chosen usually had a Marxist bias. In 1945 he was Chairman of the Labour party and became the bogy man of the general election, condemned by the Conservatives as the advocate of revolution. When ATTLEE and his party won the election, Laski toured Europe arguing for co-operation between social democrats and Communists, but opposing any suggestion of joining the Communist bloc. His criticism of Communist tactics appeared in *The Secret Battalion* (1946).

Laski continued to be a close friend of Oliver Wendell Holmes, and their correspondence, published after his death, covered a period of nearly twenty years. He wrote two books on America, *The American Presidency* (1940) and *The American Democracy* (1948); the latter caused considerable controversy on account of its Marxist interpretation of American history. He died in London on 24 March 1950, leaving one daughter.

LAUDER, SIR HARRY (1870–1950), comedian, was born in Portobello, near Edinburgh, on 4 August 1870, the eldest of seven children of John Lauder, a potter, and his wife, Isobella Urquhart Macleod, daughter of Henry MacLennan, of the Black Isle, Ross-shire. His father died when he was eleven and he had to go out to work, at first part-time in a flax-mill and then as a miner. He was soon well known locally as an amateur entertainer, and then became a professional with concert-parties. In 1890 he married Annie, daughter of James Vallance, a mine-manager.

He was thirty when he first appeared in London, but he quickly became 'top of the bill' at the Tivoli, Oxford, and the London Pavilion, singing such favourites of music-hall audiences as 'Tobermory' and 'The Lass of Killiecrankie'. He made his name with popular songs, many of which he composed himself, interspersed with comical, and sometimes more serious, patter. As a Highlander, in fantastic tartans, carrying his twisted cromach, he captured his audiences with ease in such songs as 'Roamin' in the Gloamin' ', 'A Wee Deoch-an-Doris' and 'Glasgow Belongs to Me'.

He liked to end his performances with serious songs of which the favourites were 'Rocked in the Cradle of the Deep' and 'The End of the Road'. At the height of his fame, he sometimes played four houses a night and made a great deal of money. From 1907 onwards, he toured the Dominions and the United States annually, in successful appearances. He gave a command performance before Edward VII in 1908.

During the First World War, in which he lost his only son, killed in action, he undertook concerts for the troops, both at home and on the Western Front. He was knighted for this work in 1919, and received the freedom of Edinburgh in 1927. During the Second World War he also gave his services to entertain the troops, but he had ceased to have the immense popularity he had enjoyed in his heyday.

He published his memoirs in *Harry Lauder at Home and on Tour* (1907), *A Minstrel in France* (1918), and *Roamin' in the Gloamin'* (1928). He died at Strathaven on 26 February 1950.

LAVERY, SIR JOHN (1856–1941), painter, was born in Belfast, the second son of Henry Lavery, a publican, and his wife, Mary Donnelly. The exact date of his birth is not known, though, for convenience, he used 17 March, St Patrick's Day; he was baptized on 26 March 1856. His father was drowned in 1859, while emigrating to America on the *Pomona*, and his mother died shortly afterwards. He was brought up by an aunt and uncle until, at seventeen, he was employed as apprentice to a painter-photographer in Glasgow. By some means, he managed to pay to be a student at the Glasgow School of Art.

In 1876 he sold his first water-colour painting in a public-house raffle and, having become an independent artist in 1879, was able, from insurance money collected as a result of a fire in his studio, to study at Heatherley's School of Art and the Académie Julian in Paris. He exhibited in the Paris Salon and in 1886 his *Tennis Party* was shown at the Royal Academy. From that time onwards, he pursued a successful career as a painter, being commissioned to paint the state visit of Queen Victoria to the Glasgow Exhibition in 1888.

In 1890 he married Kathleen MacDermott, who died after giving birth to a daughter. In 1897 he became Vice-President, with J. A. McN. Whistler as President, of the International Society of Sculptors, Painters, and Gravers, and his early work was perceptibly influenced by Whistler. But as he became more successful, his own individual style asserted itself, particularly in such portraits as *Mrs. Lavery Sketching* (Municipal Gallery of Modern Art in Dublin).

Lavery was at his best in his portraits of women; although less successful with men, he did paint portraits of contemporary politicians, particularly those concerned with the setting up of the Irish Free State, and presented collections of these to public galleries in Dublin and Belfast. Some of his paintings of scenes which had some personal significance for him were among his best, including his *High Treason Trial, 1916* and *The Jockeys' Room at Epsom* (1924), and *St Patrick's Purgatory* (1930). He also accomplished some pleasing conversation pieces such as those of Lady Cunard in her drawing-room with George MOORE, and Ramsay MAC-DONALD in his sitting-room at Lossiemouth.

In 1910 Lavery married Hazel, daughter of Edward Jenner Martyn of Chicago, and widow of Dr Edward Livingstone Trudeau, of New York. In 1918 he was knighted and became RA in 1921. He received many other honours, and his paintings are represented in galleries all over the world. A painting of him by Winston CHURCHILL is reproduced in Lavery's autobiography, *The Life of a Painter* (1940), written in his eighty-fourth year. His second wife died in 1935, and Lavery died in Kilkenny on 10 January 1941.

LAW, ANDREW BONAR (1858–1923). See BONAR LAW.

LAWRENCE, DAVID HERBERT (1885–1930), poet, novelist, and essayist, was born on 11 September 1885 at Eastwood, near Nottingham, the third son and youngest child of John Arthur Lawrence, and his wife, Lydia Beardsall. His father was a 'butty'—a middleman between mine-proprietor and miners. His mother had been a teacher. Lawrence was not raised in the dire poverty that one associates with the coal-miner of the period, but as a young man he sympathized with much of the hardship and distress of the mining community in which he lived, as can be seen from his poem 'The Collier's Wife'. His misfortune was that as a child he had pneumonia and became subject to tuberculosis.

His knowledge of the conditions in which his neighbours lived impelled him to a bitter loathing of industrialism but, fortunately, he could escape on country walks, drawing inspiration for his poetical imagination from the wonder and beauty of natural scenery. He longed for 'the fine, fine wind that takes its course through the chaos of the world'.

When he was thirteen he won a scholarship to Nottingham High School, and at eighteen went to University College, Nottingham, graduated, and became a schoolteacher. His mother had encouraged him to use his ability to the best advantage; she had helped in his years as a schoolboy and student, and Lawrence never ceased to be grateful to her and to show her a passionate devotion that had in it elements of the lover as well as the son, as is revealed in the semi-autobiographical *Sons and Lovers*, which he was writing during his mother's long, last illness.

Lawrence was teaching in a school in Croydon when his first sweetheart, Jessie Chambers, sent some of his poems to the *English Review*, and Ford Madox FORD, who had a genius for spotting literary potentiality, published these poems and helped Lawrence to get his first novel, *The White Peacock*, published in 1911. Edward Garnett, publishers' reader and a friend of Joseph CONRAD and many other authors, also recognized that Lawrence was capable of becoming a gifted writer of great originality, and gave him invaluable advice on the technicalities of his work whilst encouraging him to continue writing. In 1911 Lawrence took the plunge, gave up teaching, and devoted himself to writing. *The White Peacock* was followed in 1912 by *The Trespasser*, a love story based upon the confidences of a fellow teacher. In the following year (1913) *Sons and Lovers* was published and also *Love Poems and Others*.

There can be little doubt that Lawrence's character and the nature of his work as a novelist were formed partly by his deep attachment to his mother and partly by his love for the capricious Frieda, who became his wife. He met her when he revisited Nottingham. For twelve years she had been the wife of Ernest Weekley, Professor of Languages, and she had borne him a son and two daughters. She was a German, the daughter of Baron von Richthofen, the Military Governor of Metz. To the dismay of her husband, she and Lawrence fell deeply in love at first sight, and went off together to Germany, leaving her children behind. After Weekley, with marked reluctance, had divorced her, she and Lawrence were married on their return to England in 1914. Whatever impression might be given by his novels, Lawrence, with his strict upbringing and his devotion to his mother, was not unfaithful to his wife with other women, though he had passionate attachments to men, such as John Middleton MURRY. Frieda, however, was instinctively casual and always ready to seek the sexual satisfaction that, possibly, after marriage she did not find with Lawrence. Nevertheless, her infidelities seem to have done little to spoil the marriage for Lawrence. It was from Frieda that Lawrence learned about Freud's theory of the Oedipus complex and perhaps to her also he owed much of his sensitive insight into the intricate pattern of female emotions.

By the time the First World War broke out, Lawrence had won a reputation as an author and was accepted by his contemporary writers as one of them. He was never a member of the Bloomsbury set, but Lady Ottoline MORRELL invited him with Frieda to Garsington Manor and there he met E. M. FORSTER, and criticized the paintings of Duncan Grant. The war, however, brought him extreme distress. Because Frieda was a cousin of the famous German fighter pilot, they were constantly harassed by the police and, when they left London and took refuge at Zennor in Cornwall, they were ordered to leave and forbidden to enter any prohibited area (1917). His novel *The Rainbow* (1915), in which he denounced war, was condemned as indecent, a rebuff which he felt very keenly. Towards the end of 1919 Lawrence left England and, except for brief visits, never returned.

Women in Love was published in New York in 1920 and in London in 1921. For a time, Lawrence lived in Italy, plagued by ill health, but still able to enjoy the countryside. There he produced *Aaron's Rod* (1922). In 1916 he had written the first of his travel books *Twilight in Italy*; he now published *Sea and Sardinia* (1921). He continued to write incessantly. *Psychoanalysis and the Unconscious* appeared in

Birthplace of D. H. Lawrence: 8a Victoria Street, Eastwood

1921, followed by *Fantasia of the Unconscious* in 1922.

In 1922 he left Italy for the United States and Mexico. In 1923 another set of poems, *Birds, Beasts, and Flowers* was published and *Studies in Classical American Literature* appeared. His experiences in Mexico led to the strange novel *The Plumed Serpent* (1926) and to his book *Mornings in Mexico* (1927). In 1925 he was forced by a bout of malaria, from which he nearly died, to leave Mexico and return to Italy, where he settled near Florence. There, laboriously, he wrote *Lady Chatterley's Lover*.

His last years were a time of frustration and distress. A police prosecution was set in train against his last and most notorious novel, the original manuscript of his poems *Pansies* (1929) was confiscated by the police, an exhibition of his paintings was condemned as obscene, and the book containing reproductions of these was suppressed. However, a private edition of *Lady Chatterley's Lover* was more profitable than any of his earlier works. The original version was banned from publication in England until in 1960 Allen LANE courageously faced prosecution and brought out the first edition to be published in London.

During his last years near Florence, Lawrence was often seriously ill and in 1930 while he was living near Toulon he died in a clinic at Vence on 2 March 1930. After his death, the revealing *Letters* were published (1932). In *Apocalypse* (1931) he explained his attitude to life and, in *Last Poems* (1932), revealed the sad record of his feelings and thoughts as he faced up to the imminence of death:

And if tonight my soul may find her peace
in sleep, and sink in good oblivion,

and in the morning wake like a new-opened flower
then I have been dipped again in God, and new-created.

LAWRENCE, GERTRUDE (1898–1952), actress, was born in London on 4 July 1898, Gertrud Alexandra Dagmar Lawrence, daughter of Arthur Lawrence Klasen, music-hall singer, a Dane, and his wife, Alice Louise Banks, an English actress. Her parents divorced while she was an infant and she was brought up first by her mother, then by her father.

She made her first appearance in pantomime in 1910; Noël COWARD saw her in 1913 as a child-performer and noted that she was not pretty but was 'tremendously alive'. She became the foremost of his leading ladies. Her first manager was André Charlot and her first success *London Calling* (1923), a revue written by Noël Coward. In 1929 he wrote *Bitter Sweet* for her but her voice was too light to sustain the leading part. Then Coward wrote *Private Lives* (1930), in which they played together and had an immense success both in London and New York.

Gertrude Lawrence was praised not only by the English theatre critic, James Agate, for her skill and artistry as a mimic and her captivating sense of fun, but also by the American, George Jean Nathan, who for many years praised her glamour and effervescence on Broadway in plays, including *Lady in the Dark*, *Pygmalion*, and *The King and I*.

In his *Present Indicative* (1937), Noël Coward described her personality with her 'quick humour, insane generosity, and loving heart', as well as her considerable ability as an actress. He also described her vitality and style in *Future Indefinite* (1954) in equally glowing terms.

Gertrude Lawrence in *Nymph Errant*, Adelphi Theatre, 1933

In 1917 Gertrude Lawrence married Francis Xavier Howley, playwright and producer; they had a daughter. The marriage ended in divorce and in 1940 she married Richard Stoddard Aldrich, an American. She published her reminiscences *A Star Danced* in 1945. She died in New York on 6 September 1952, and a film of her life, entitled *Star*, was made in 1968, with Julie Andrews in the leading role.

LAWRENCE, THOMAS EDWARD (1888–1935), known as 'Lawrence of Arabia', was born at Tremadoc, North Wales on 15 August 1888, the second of five sons of Thomas Robert Chapman, who had assumed the name Lawrence after leaving his wife to live with the governess of their four daughters, Sarah Madden, the illegitimate daughter of a Sunderland engineer. Chapman later succeeded to a baronetcy, but never claimed it. Lawrence's mother held strong religious beliefs, and after the death of his father in 1919 went out to China as a missionary. She and Chapman had never married as his wife was an Irish Catholic. By the time he was ten Lawrence knew that he was illegitimate.

He was educated at Oxford High School and Jesus College, Oxford, of which he was an exhibitioner; he obtained a first in modern history in 1910. From 1911 to 1914 he went on a British Museum expedition to the Hittite city of Carchemish, assisting Leonard WOOLLEY, learning some Arabic, and wearing Arab clothes and eating Arab food. Early in 1914 they carried out an archaeological survey of

the Negeb and, on the outbreak of the First World War, Lawrence served for two years in the Arab Bureau in Egypt.

In 1916 Lawrence went with (Sir) Ronald Storrs, Oriental Secretary, Cairo, to meet Sharif Abdullah, second son of Husain, Grand Sharif of Mecca, and also Faisal, his third son, who was fighting a losing battle with the Turks in the Hejaz. Lawrence was appointed adviser to Faisal, won his confidence, and set about the organization of his tribal levies. Together, he and Faisal attacked the Hejaz railway and brought the country south of Aqaba (except Medina, where the Turks had 10,000 troops) under their control.

Sir Edmund ALLENBY, Commander-in-Chief, put half a million pounds at Lawrence's disposal to raise Arab levies as a mobile right wing to the British Expeditionary Force against the Turks, and Lawrence and the Arabs became so effective at train-wrecking that the Turks in Medina were isolated. Later, the Arabs defeated the Turks east of the river Jordan and took Damascus on 1 October 1918.

Towards the end of 1917, Lawrence was captured by the Turks at Deraa, but was not recognized, though a large reward had been offered for his seizure. What actually happened to him, before he escaped, will never be known with certainty. Lawrence himself gave differing accounts of the experience. It seems likely that he had to submit to some form of sexual assault but, whatever the details, it seems that the outrage affected his whole future attitude to life.

After the war, Lawrence returned to England, and in 1919 was elected to a research fellowship at All Souls, Oxford. He strove fanatically to serve the cause of Faisal and the Arabs in the peace negotiations and was bitterly disappointed at what he considered to be a humiliating failure in the face of political machinations, which he was powerless to circumvent. But in 1921, when Winston CHURCHILL appointed him political adviser to the Middle Eastern Department of the Colonial Office, Faisal had become King of Iraq and his brother Abdullah ruler of Trans-jordan (Jordan). Lawrence attended the Cairo Conference where he and Gertrude BELL warmly supported the views of Sir Hugh TRENCHARD, Chief of the Air Staff, against those of Sir Percy Cox, the British High Commissioner in Baghdad. In 1922, when Lawrence, feeling that his debt to the Arabs had been paid, insisted on release from the Colonial Office, Trenchard assisted him in enlisting in the ranks of the Royal Air Force under the name of J. H. Ross, which he changed in the following year to T. E. Shaw.

Truth and legend have become so inextricably mixed, regarding Lawrence, that it is almost impossible to comprehend why he sought in 1922 to hide himself away in anonymity. Colonel Richard Meinertzhagen, with whom he had served in the Middle East, wrote that Lawrence craved to be famous, but had a horror of being known to like being known, and it seems that, although Lawrence changed his identity, he was hurt if he was not recognized as Lawrence. When it became public property that Shaw was in fact Lawrence, he had to leave the RAF and joined the Tank Corps for a time, but was able to rejoin the RAF in 1925 and, for some years, happily worked testing, supervising, and even designing high-speed and power motor-craft at Plymouth and on the Solent. His service expired in February 1935 and he settled in a cottage at Clouds Hill in Dorset, but on 13 May was seriously injured in a motor-cycle accident and died in Bovington Camp Hospital on 19 May 1935. He never married.

(Sir) Ronald Storrs, writing in the *DNB*, expressed the view that 'Unique in kind as were Lawrence's exploits, their chance of historic survival would have been uncertain had he not himself recorded them in his brilliant and arresting *Seven Pillars of Wisdom.*' This account Lawrence had written and rewritten in 1919-20; in 1926 he issued privately some hundred copies; the abridged version *The Revolt in the Desert* was published in 1927, but the original book was not published till 1935 after Lawrence's death. He also wrote an account of his experiences in the RAF, entitled *The Mint*, and forbade publication until 1950 (though a sale of fifty copies was arranged in the USA in 1926). In 1938 David Garnett selected and edited *The Letters of T. E. Lawrence* and these, covering his relations with friends as diverse as E. M. FORSTER, Lady ASTOR, Hugh Trenchard, Robert Graves, G. B. SHAW, and Thomas HARDY, are perhaps the most revealing evidence of the versatility and complexity of his enigmatic character.

T. E. Lawrence alias Shaw in RAF uniform, sketch by A. John, 1935

LAWSON, SIR HARRY LAWSON WEBSTER LEVY-, VISCOUNT BURNHAM (1862-1933), newspaper proprietor, was born in London on 18 December 1862, the elder son of Edward Levy-Lawson, first Baron Burnham, and his wife, Harriette Georgiana, daughter of the actor-manager, Benjamin Nottingham Webster. He was educated at Eton and

Balliol College, Oxford, where he obtained a first in modern history in 1884 and was Secretary of the Union. In that year he married Olive, eldest daughter of General Sir Henry Percival de Bathe, fourth baronet; they had one daughter.

Lawson was elected Liberal MP for West St Pancras from 1885 to 1892, lost the seat in that year, and was MP for Cirencester in 1893-5. Having resigned from the Liberal party on the Home Rule issue, he became Unionist MP for the Mile End division of Tower Hamlets during 1905-6 and 1910-16. He succeeded to the barony in 1916.

In 1891 he was called to the Bar (Inner Temple); he served on the LCC from 1889 to 1892 and from 1897 to 1904, and was Mayor of Stepney in 1907-9. He took over the management of the *Daily Telegraph* from his father in 1903 and continued this work until 1928; during this period he declined any offer of a ministerial post as he did not wish to compromise the independence of the paper. He became a leading figure in the London newspaper world, and was President of the Imperial Press Conferences in Ottawa and Melbourne in 1920 and 1925.

He used his influence to further the cause of Anglo-Belgian friendship and to support the Territorial Army. On the outbreak of the First World War he rejoined the Royal Bucks. Hussars, the regiment he had commanded from 1902 to 1913. He played a leading part in training the second reserve regiment and for these services he was made a viscount in 1919, having been CH since 1917. He was appointed GCMG in 1927.

He served on a number of public committees and commissions and his most outstanding work of this kind was done as Chairman of the Standing Joint Committee representing teachers and local education authorities which in 1920 formulated new scales of pay for teachers in state schools. In later disputes he acted as arbitrator and established the 'Burnham scales', which became the basis of teachers' pay.

His last public service was membership of the Indian Statutory Commission (1927-30). He died in London on 20 July 1933.

LAYTON, WALTER THOMAS, first BARON LAYTON (1884-1966), economist, editor, and newspaper proprietor, was born in London on 15 March 1884, the son of Alfred John Layton and his wife, Mary, FRCO, daughter of Walter Johnson, a schoolmaster. She was a gifted organist. He was educated at King's College School, London, Westminster City School, University College London, and Trinity College, Cambridge, where he obtained firsts in both parts of the economics tripos (1906-7).

In 1908 with J. M. KEYNES, he was appointed lecturer in economics, being elected a Fellow of Gonville and Caius College (1909-14); from 1909 to 1912 he was also Newmarch lecturer at University College London. In 1910 he married (Eleanor) Dorothea, daughter of Francis Beresford Plumptre Osmaston, of Limpsfield, Surrey; they had three sons and four daughters.

During the First World War he worked for the Ministry of Munitions and was a member of the MILNER mission to Russia (1917) and the BALFOUR mission to the USA (1917). He was appointed CBE in 1917 and CH in 1919.

His main interest was in statistics, and after the war he was a member of the Consultative Economic Committee of the League of Nations and Director of the Economic and Financial Section of the League. In 1920 he published *An Introduction to the Study of Prices.*

From 1922 to 1938 he was Editor of *The Economist.* He

reorganized and refashioned the paper and, with the help of the Cadbury family, arranged for its purchase from the Bagehot sisters in 1928. In that year, in co-operation with Keynes and H. D. Henderson, he published the *Liberal Yellow Book*. He was also appointed Editorial Director of the *News Chronicle*, while maintaining his post with *The Economist*. In this work he was ably assisted by Geoffrey CROWTHER who eventually succeeded him as Editor of *The Economist*. From 1945 to 1953 Layton was also a director of Reuters.

During the Second World War he worked in the Ministry of Supply and the Ministry of Production, and he and Crowther both returned to their papers when the war ended. *The Economist* continued to flourish but the *News Chronicle* and the evening paper, the *Star*, of which he became Editor in the thirties, eventually had to be closed down.

Layton, unlike Keynes, never belonged to the Bloomsbury set; he was a shy man, handicapped to some extent by a stammer. His main achievement was to pass on something of the values he cherished to younger men. He was knighted in 1930, created a baron in 1947, and was a member of the Legion of Honour. He became an honorary Fellow of Gonville and Caius in 1931. Lady Layton died in 1959 and Layton published a biographical memoir *Dorothy* (1961). He died in London on 14 February 1966.

LEACH, BERNARD HOWELL (1887-1979), potter, was born in Hong Kong on 5 January 1887, the only son of Andrew John Leach, a puisne judge in the Straits Settlements, and his wife, Eleanor née Sharpe. He was educated at Beaumont College and the Slade School of Art, where he studied under Henry TONKS, and then attended the London School of Art to study etching under Frank Brangwyn.

In 1909, having tried and decided that he would never be happy as a banker, he went out to Japan and studied the art of pottery under Kenzan VI, until in 1913 Kenzan built a kiln for him and he began to make his own pottery. Leach made friends of Tomimoto, a young Japanese architect, Soetsu Yanagi, who later became a Director of the National Craft Museum, and Shoji Hamada, another Japanese potter; they all helped him to gain an understanding of oriental values in art. During 1916-18 Leach visited Peking to learn something of Chinese art, and he then set up a pottery in Tokyo.

In 1920 he returned to England with his family. In 1909 he had married his cousin, Edith Muriel, daughter of Dr William Evans Hoyle, Director of the National Museum of Wales; they had two sons and three daughters. He founded his pottery at St Ives, with Hamada as his assistant. At first Leach had to face serious financial difficulties but, as his reputation grew, he was able to teach students his new ideas, and his two sons joined him in his work.

In 1934-5 he revisited Japan and Korea and found Hamada, who had returned home after three years at St Ives, well-established as a potter in his own country. Leach's work was by this time being exhibited in England and abroad, and in 1940 when he published *A Potter's Book*, it made his name in the USA as well as in Britain. After the Second World War he lectured in America, both north and south, and his work was exhibited in many parts of the world. More books were published, including *A Potter's Portfolio* (1951), and *A Potter in Japan 1952-1954* (1960). Through his own work and that of his pupils, Leach exercised an important influence on the development of the potter's art.

After his first marriage had ended in divorce, he married

Vase by Bernard Leach, from his St Ives Workshop *c.* 1934, shows clearly the oriental influence in his art

Laurie Cookes in 1936. This marriage also did not last, and in 1955 he married an American potter, Janet Darnell, who took over the management of the St Ives pottery. Leach was appointed CBE in 1962 and CH in 1973. He died on 6 May 1979 and was buried at St Ives.

LEAKEY, LOUIS SEYMOUR BAZETT (1903-1972), archaeologist, anthropologist, and human palaeontologist, was born on 7 August 1903 at Kabete, Kenya, the third child of Canon Harry Leakey, and his wife, Mary Bazett, daughter of a colonel in the Indian Army. Both parents were missionaries with the CMS and Louis spent his first sixteen years at Kabete, freely associating with Kikuyu youths. He was later educated at Weymouth College, and St John's College, Cambridge, where he obtained firsts in the modern languages tripos (French and Kikuyu), and in the archaeology and anthropology tripos (1925-6).

In 1923 he was a member of a British Museum East African Expedition to Tanganyika (Tanzania), and between 1926 and 1935 led four archaeological expeditions to East Africa, in which important discoveries were made about the prehistory of that part of the continent. He described these discoveries in *The Stone Age Cultures of Kenya Colony* (1931), *The Stone Age Races of Kenya* (1935), and *Stone Age Africa* (1936).

In 1928 he married Henrietta Wilfrida, daughter of Henry Avern; they had a son and a daughter. In 1930 he became a Ph.D., and from 1929 to 1934 was Leverhulme Research Fellow at St John's College, Cambridge. In 1936 he also published *Kenya: Contrasts and Problems* and in 1937 *White African*, the first volume of his autobiography.

During the Second World War, he was in charge of a special branch of the CID in Nairobi and worked for the department as a handwriting expert until 1951. After the war, from 1945 to 1961 Leakey was Curator of the Coryndon Memorial Museum at Nairobi, and from 1947 to 1951 Secretary of the Pan-African Congress on Prehistory, which he had founded. From 1955 to 1959 he was its President. In 1950 he warned the Kenya Government of the danger of a Mau Mau rising, and two years later wrote *Mau Mau and the Kikuyu*, followed in 1954 by *Defeating Mau Mau*. At the trial of Jomo Kenyatta Leakey was the court interpreter.

In 1936 his first marriage had ended in divorce. He then married Mary Douglas Nicol, who had been working with him for some time. They had three sons, and a daughter who died in infancy. In 1942 he and his wife discovered the Acheulian of Olorgesailie in the Rift Valley, in 1959 Mary Leakey found the skull of *Australopithecus* (*Zinjanthropus*) *boisei*, and in 1960 their son, Jonathan, discovered the first remains of *Homo habilis*, a hominid dated at 1.7 million years. The Leakeys also found in 1960 the skull of one of the makers of the Acheulian culture at Olduvai, to which Leakey gave the name *Homo erectus*. These discoveries are described in a series of books entitled *Olduvai Gorge*.

Leakey and his family thus made an enormously valuable contribution to the discovery of early man and his culture, and revolutionized palaeolithic archaeology. Just before Leakey's death, his son Richard, a distinguished archaeologist and palaeontologist in his own right, showed him human remains, found on the shores of Lake Rudolf, dated at 2.6 million years. It must be said, however, that some of his discoveries were the subject of much controversy.

Leakey received many academic awards and was elected FBA (1958). He died on 1 October 1972 when flying to London. The second part of his autobiography *By the Evidence: Memoirs, 1932-1951* was published two years later. The Louis Leakey Memorial Institute for African Prehistory was set up in Kenya after his death and a Leakey Foundation was established in California to promote his work.

LEAVIS, FRANK RAYMOND (1895-1978), literary critic and teacher, was born on 14 July 1895 in Cambridge, the elder son of Harry Leavis, a salesman of musical instruments, and his wife, Kate Sarah Moore. He was educated at the Perse School, and Emmanuel College, Cambridge, where he was a scholar and obtained a first in the English tripos in 1921. Between school and college he served with the Friends' Ambulance Unit on the Western Front.

In 1924 he became a Ph.D. for his research into the relationship of journalism to literature; at this time his views on literary criticism were influenced by I. A. RICHARDS and Mansfield Forbes. In 1927 he was appointed a probationary faculty lecturer in English, and in 1929 married Queenie Dorothy, daughter of Morris Roth, master draper, and his wife, Jenny Davis; she had obtained a first in English in 1928, being a scholar of Girton College. At the time of her marriage she was working for a Ph.D.; this she achieved in 1932 for a thesis on *Fiction and the Reading Public*, published in the same year.

Meanwhile, Leavis was already acquiring a reputation as a teacher, and published, also in 1932, *New Bearings in English Poetry*, in which he emphasized the importance of the modern poets, Gerard Manley Hopkins, YEATS, T. S. ELIOT, and Ezra Pound, as in earlier work he had argued for James JOYCE, and D. H. LAWRENCE. His veneration for Lawrence, as a critic as well as a writer, was a distinguishing feature of his literary standpoint. Leavis's lectureship had been terminated in 1931, and in the following year he became Director of Studies in English at Downing College, and he and his wife helped launch the literary quarterly, *Scrutiny*, which for the next twenty-one years would gain a reputation for the high standards of its criticism, its pioneering attitude to new writers, and its articles on education, music, and culture generally.

In 1933 Leavis and his wife, with the collaboration of Denys Thompson, published *Culture and Environment*, a follow up to Leavis's book *Mass Civilization and Minority Culture* (1930). But much of their effort to publicize their conception of the role of literature in education was concentrated on their articles and reviews in *Scrutiny*; these had considerable influence on students and teachers of English. In 1963, after the journal had ceased publication, the complete collection of its articles was republished by the Cambridge University Press.

Leavis dedicated his *Revaluation* (1936) 'to those with whom I have discussed literature as a teacher' and it is his teaching that constitutes Leavis's main claim to fame. He had been appointed a university lecturer in English in 1936, and it was not until 1959 that he became Reader. Throughout these years he taught at Downing College until in 1962 he retired from his university readership and was appointed an honorary Fellow of the college. He continued teaching practically to the end of his life. He was Chichele lecturer at Oxford in 1964, and in the following year, visiting professor at York University; in 1967 he gave the Clark lectures at Cambridge, published in 1969 as *English Literature in Our Time and the University*. In the same year he published *Lectures in America* which he and Queenie had delivered there in 1968. In 1969 Leavis was appointed visiting professor at the University of Wales; and in 1970 he held a similar appointment at Bristol.

Apart from his reputation as a teacher Leavis was noted for his readiness to indulge in controversy. A notorious example of this was his virulent attack upon C. P. SNOW's *Two Cultures* (1959), which Leavis castigated in '*Two Cultures?' The Significance of C. P. Snow* (1962). He resigned from his honorary fellowship of Downing College in 1964 because he disagreed with the decision of the college to make changes in the policies he had pursued as an English teacher there. In his later years he was embittered by the thought that Cambridge, far from recognizing his merit, had treated him badly. This feeling no doubt contributed to the acrimony with which he engaged in combat with those who did not accept his views without reservation. He never relented, remaining to the end of his life the self-appointed arbiter of literary merit. Of this his *Nor Shall My Sword* (1972) bore witness, together with *The Living Principle* (1975), and *Thought, Words and Creativity* (1976).

In 1978 he became a Companion of Honour; he died in Cambridge on 14 April in that year. His wife continued after his death to lecture and write on English literature until she died in Cambridge on 17 March 1981, survived by their two sons and a daughter.

LEE, ARTHUR HAMILTON, VISCOUNT LEE OF FAREHAM (1868-1947), politician, benefactor, and patron of the arts, was born on 8 November 1868 at Bridport, the youngest child of the Revd Melville Lauriston Lee, and his wife, Emily Winter, daughter of Thomas Dicker, a banker, of Lewes, Sussex. He was educated at Cheltenham College and the

Royal Military Academy, Woolwich, and in 1888 joined the Royal Artillery.

After service in China, he became Professor of Military History at the Royal Military College, Kingston, Canada, until in 1898 he was appointed Military Attaché with the US army in Cuba and became a close friend of Theodore Roosevelt. In the following year, he became Military Attaché at the British Embassy in Washington. He also married Ruth, daughter of John Godfrey Moore, a leading New York banker.

From 1900 to 1918 Lee was Conservative MP for the Fareham division of Hampshire; in 1903 he was appointed Civil Lord of the Admiralty, and from 1906 to 1914 was opposition spokesman on naval affairs in the Commons. When the First World War broke out, he rejoined the army and served in France, but in 1915 LLOYD GEORGE invited him to become Parliamentary Military Secretary at the Ministry of Munitions, and then his personal Military Secretary at the War Office. In 1916 he was appointed KCB.

In 1917 Lee was appointed Director-General of Food Production and in this post took an important part in safeguarding the country from acute food shortages. He was appointed GBE and became a peer as Baron Lee in 1918. He joined Lloyd George's Cabinet in 1919 as President of the Board of Agriculture and Fisheries and was sworn of the Privy Council. Two years later he returned to the Admiralty as First Lord and went with Arthur BALFOUR to the Washington Naval Conference, where he achieved a great reputation as an exponent of British views, but failed in his attempt to secure the banning of submarine warfare. He resigned in 1922 and was promoted to viscount.

Out of political office, he carried on in public service and chaired three important royal commissions between 1923 and 1928. He became GCB in 1929. In January 1921 he and Lady Lee had presented the Chequers estate to be held in trust for the use of successive Prime Ministers, appropriately furnished, with a collection of works of art, and an endowment of £100,000 for its upkeep.

Lee then began a new collection of paintings, which he bequeathed to the Courtauld Institute of Art which, with help from Samuel COURTAULD, was financed and opened in 1932. With Courtauld, he also arranged for the transfer of the Warburg Institute and libraries from Hamburg to London. He was a Trustee of the Wallace Collection, and Chairman of the National Gallery and the Royal Fine Art Commission.

He and his wife had no children. He died on 21 July 1947 at his Gloucestershire home at Avening.

LEE, SIR SIDNEY (1859–1926), Shakespearian scholar and Editor of *The Dictionary of National Biography*, was born in London on 5 December 1859, the elder son of Lazarus Lee, a merchant, and his wife, Jessie Davis. He was originally named Solomon Lazarus, but in 1890 changed to Sidney. He was educated at the City of London School and Balliol College, Oxford, graduating in 1882. While still an undergraduate, he published two articles on Shakespeare in the *Gentleman's Magazine* (1880).

In 1882 he was appointed Sub-Editor to (Sir) Leslie Stephen, when George Smith founded the *DNB*. He became Assistant Editor in 1883, Joint Editor in 1890, and sole Editor from 1891 to 1901 and from 1910 to 1912; from 1901 to 1916 he retained general oversight of the Dictionary. During his period as Editor 63 volumes of the Dictionary and

the First Supplement (3 vols.) were completed in 1901, and the Second Supplement appeared in 1912.

Lee wrote two articles which were subsequently expanded and published as his *Life of William Shakespeare* (1897) and *Queen Victoria, a biography* (1898). The *Life* passed through thirteen editions (1925) in Lee's lifetime and a fourteenth appeared in 1931. In this work, he showed the influence of foreign literature on Shakespeare's plays and sonnets and the extent to which Shakespeare borrowed from Ovid, Petrarch, and Ronsard, as well as from contemporary English writers.

In 1901–2 Lee was Clark lecturer in English literature at Trinity College, Cambridge, and made a successful tour of American universities, publishing his lectures as *Great Englishmen of the Sixteenth Century* (1904). He edited between 1907 and 1910 the *Renaissance Shakespeare*, a work which was reissued in 1910 as the *Caxton Shakespeare*.

He was President of the Elizabethan Literary Society at Toynbee Hall (1890) and he and Frederick Rogers developed it into a centre of Elizabethan study. The Society later moved to King's College, London in 1913. He was also a founder of the English Association and in 1917 its President. From 1913 to 1924 he was Professor of English Language and Literature at East London College.

Lee's last important work was his *Life of King Edward VII*, undertaken at the request of George V. The first volume was published in 1925, and the second, completed by (Sir) S. F. Markham, appeared in 1927. Lee was elected FBA in 1910 and knighted in 1911. He wrote a number of other books besides those referred to above. He was never married. He died in London on 3 March 1926.

LEIGH, VIVIEN (1913–1967), actress, was born Vivian Mary Hartley in Darjeeling, India, on 5 November 1913, the only surviving child of Ernest Richard Hartley, a junior partner in a firm of exchange brokers, Calcutta, and his wife, Gertrude Robinson Yackje. In 1920 she came to England with her parents and went to school at the Convent of the Sacred Heart, Roehampton, until she was thirteen, and then travelled on the Continent learning French, German, and Italian. By the time she was eighteen, her beautiful green eyes, chestnut hair, classic features, and flawless complexion made her uniquely qualified for a career in the limelight.

While studying at the Royal School of Dramatic Art, however, she met and married in 1932 a young barrister, Herbert Leigh Holman, and gave birth to a daughter, Suzanne, in 1933. A year later she had her first small part in a film and decided upon the stage name of Vivien Leigh. In 1935 she played a leading part in *The Mask of Virtue* at the Ambassadors' Theatre and, in spite of her inexperience, was acclaimed as 'a star of unusual promise'.

She was immediately placed under contract to Alexander KORDA, and in 1937 played in *Fire Over England* with Laurence (later Lord) Olivier. She fell hopelessly in love with him and determined to marry him despite the fact that they were both married. In Denmark, in the same year she played Ophelia to Olivier's Hamlet and, learning all the time, strove to rival the artistry of the man who was already renowned for his acting. From Elsinore she wrote to tell her husband that she was in love with Olivier and would not return to him. Olivier's wife, Jill (Esmond), by whom he had two children, saw what was happening, but was helpless. Vivien Leigh and Laurence Olivier, as soon as their divorces were settled, married in California in 1940.

Meanwhile, David O. Selznick had spent two years without success looking for an actress who could fit the part of

Vivien Leigh as Blanche in the film version of *A Streetcar named Desire*, 1951, for which she won an Oscar

Scarlett O'Hara in Margaret Mitchell's *Gone with the Wind*. When he met Vivien Leigh he took one look at her and knew she was right for the part. So, in 1939, the film was made and Vivien won an Oscar for her performance, and attained international status as a film star.

She and Olivier made the film *Lady Hamilton* in 1941, and then returned to England. He served in the Royal Navy, and Vivien returned to the stage in *The Doctor's Dilemma* in 1942 and, in the following year, went on a tour of North Africa with Beatrice Lillie. In 1945 she appeared as Sabina in Thornton Wilder's *The Skin of Our Teeth*. Two years later Laurence Olivier was knighted. In 1948 they went together on an exhausting ten-month tour with the Old Vic Company to Australia and New Zealand.

Vivien had now reached the height of her powers as an actress. In 1949-50 she appeared as Blanche in *A Streetcar Named Desire*, both in London on the stage, and in a film performance which earned her another Oscar. In 1951 she appeared with Olivier, under his direction, in *Caesar and Cleopatra* by SHAW and *Anthony and Cleopatra* by Shakespeare on alternate nights. In 1955 they did a season together at Stratford-upon-Avon, leading up to a production by Peter

Brook of *Titus Andronicus*, and in 1957 they appeared together, for the last time, in a film of the same play.

Sadly, Vivien had for years been subject to recurrent bouts of depression, followed by manic outbursts in which she became physically violent, and no amount of treatment relieved the severity of these attacks. Neither she nor Olivier had been faithful; he was in love with Joan Plowright, whom he later married, and she was having an affair with Jack Merivale, stepson of Gladys COOPER. In 1960 they divorced; they had no children; Vivien had had two miscarriages.

Vivien Leigh continued to act successfully, but for her life had lost its zest and radiance. She appeared in *Duel of Angels* by Jean Giraudoux in London (1958) and in New York (1960), and made a name for herself in a new departure, the musical *Tovarich* in New York (1963). Her physical condition, however, was deteriorating, and her attempts to drive herself were only making things worse. In her last months she was helped by her first husband; they had never ceased to be friends. She died of tuberculosis in London on 8 July 1967, and that night the exterior lights of the West End theatres were darkened for an hour.

LEIGH-MALLORY, SIR TRAFFORD (1892-1944). See MALLORY, G. L.

LEIPER, ROBERT THOMSON (1881-1969), professor of helminthology (the study of parasitic worms), was born on 17 April 1881 in Kilmarnock, the eldest of three children of John Leiper, a tailor, and his wife, Jessie Aird. He was educated at Warwick School, Leamington Technical College, Mason College, Birmingham, and Glasgow University. For a time he worked at the Millport Marine Station. In 1904 he graduated in medicine, but his interest was in helminthology, and in 1905 he was appointed by Sir Patrick MANSON as helminthologist to the London School of Tropical Medicine.

This appointment led to a period of field work, in which he travelled to many parts of the tropics. In 1905 he went to Accra to study 'Guinea worm' which caused an ulcerated skin condition. His researches proved that the infection was spread by drinking water, contaminated by the water flea which became infected with a helminth contaminated by sores on the legs of infected humans. In 1912 he detected the cause of Calabar swelling, another infectious disease in West Africa, and in the following year went to Egypt to study the cause of schistosomiasis, which affected a third of the population there. He was able to confirm that Japanese research on water snails in rice fields was on the track of the disease and that the snails carried the worm that caused the infection. Leiper became D.Sc. Glasgow in 1911 and MD in 1917. During the First World War he was in charge of a Bilharzia mission in Egypt and was able to indicate what steps should be taken to protect British troops from the disease.

In 1919 Leiper was appointed Professor of Helminthology, London; from 1919 to 1921 he was Director of the Prosectorium of the London Zoological Society; and from 1924 to 1945 was Director of Parasitology at the London School of Hygiene and Tropical Medicine. In 1923 he became FRS. In the same year he founded the *Journal of Helminthology*. He set up the Institute of Agricultural Parasitology, near St Albans, in 1925, and from 1929 to 1958 was founder and Director of the Commonwealth Bureau of Helminthology. He was elected FRCP in 1936 and appointed CMG in 1941.

In 1908 he married Ceinwen Saron Jones, a dentist; they

had one son and two daughters. Leiper died in St Albans on 21 May 1969.

LEJEUNE, CAROLINE ALICE (1897–1973), film critic, was born on 27 March 1897 in Manchester, the youngest child of Adam Edward Lejeune, a cotton merchant, and his wife, Jane Louisa MacLaren. Her father, descended from a Huguenot family which settled in Germany, came to England from Frankfurt as a young man; her mother was the daughter of a Nonconformist minister. Caroline was educated at Withington Girls' School, but decided against going to Oxford and studied at home for a degree in English at Manchester University.

C. P. SCOTT was a close friend of the family, and encouraged her as a young woman to write for the *Manchester Guardian*, and later, when she was twenty-four, suggested that she should move to London and become a film critic. She took this advice, and in 1921 moved to London with her mother (her father had died when she was an infant). She began writing a regular column for the *Guardian* called 'The Week on the Screen'. In 1925 she married Edward Roffe Thompson, who at one time edited *John Bull*; for her professional work she retained the name C. A. Lejeune.

In 1928 J. L. GARVIN invited her to become film critic of the *Observer*. With the approval of C. P. Scott, she accepted and stayed with the paper for the rest of her career, over thirty years. She also wrote for many other journals and came to be recognized as the doyen of film critics, noted for her integrity, her keen observation, and the elegance of her writing. She was the friend of film actors, such as Peter SELLERS, and of the great directors of British films, including Alexander KORDA and Michael BALCON.

After the Second World War she reviewed television drama as well as films, and adapted for television some of her favourite books, such as the Sherlock Holmes stories. She retired from the *Observer* in 1960, and gave up visiting the cinema. In 1964 she published her autobiography *Thank You For Having Me*. She also published collections of her reviews, *Cinema* (1931) and *Chestnuts in Her Lap* (1947). She died on 1 April 1973, leaving one son, Anthony Lejeune.

LENNON, JOHN WINSTON (1940–1980), pop musician and composer and one of the 'Beatles' group, was born in Liverpool on 9 October 1940, the only child of Alfred Lennon, a ship's steward, and his wife, Julia Stanley. His parents separated while he was an infant and he was brought up by his aunt and uncle, Mimi and George Smith. He attended the Quarry Bank High School but did not excel, being a natural rebel. His headmaster, however, helped him to gain admission to Liverpool College of Art where he was no more studious than at school. With help from his mother, with whom he had been reunited, he learnt to play the banjo and formed a skiffle group, a type of popular music which needed little technical knowledge.

In 1957 this group, the Quarrymen, was joined by Paul McCartney and, a few months later, by George Harrison. Later, in 1962, Ringo Starr replaced Pete Best as the drummer and the group that later won fame as the Beatles was complete. Lennon and McCartney composed the songs for the group though neither of them could read or write music. In 1958 Lennon had the distressing experience of losing his mother in a street accident. From the time the group became the Beatles in 1960, they played in the Cavern club in Liverpool and the 'Mersey sound', which they introduced, soon

became locally popular as a new version of the 'rock 'n' roll' type of music.

Their first professional appearances took place in the Reeperbahn and other nightclubs in Hamburg, and it was a song they recorded there that brought them to the notice of Brian Epstein, who ran a record department in Liverpool. He eventually secured for them in 1962 an audition with George Martin of Parlophone and the first single, 'Love Me Do', was produced, and entered the charts. Early in 1963 it reached the top, to be followed by a series of records which took the pop music world by storm. Throughout 1963, the Beatles' distinctive style became increasingly popular, not only in Britain, but also abroad, and the phenomenon known as Beatlemania was born. When the group made a personal appearance, hordes of young people shrieked and swooned hysterically, and their records of songs, such as 'She Loves You' and 'I Want To Hold Your Hand', sold in millions of copies. In 1964 the group were equally successful in the USA, where six of their records reached the top of the charts in one year. The Beatles had become the leading recording act in the world, their records being publicly broadcast in

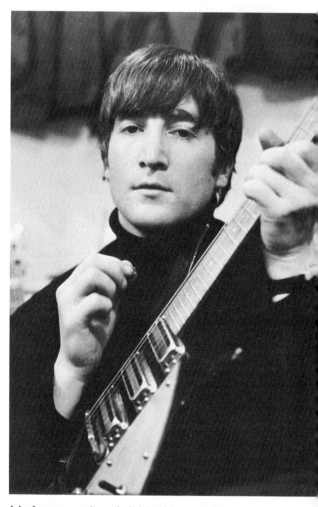

John Lennon, *c.* 1964, at the height of the Beatles' fame

such unlikely places as the main square in Warsaw. And all their material was their own, Lennon and McCartney composing the songs, and the group putting them together to their own distinctive rhythms. In many ways, John Lennon was the most important member of the group. In 1965 each of them received the MBE in recognition of the fame they had brought to their type of British music and the foreign exchange it had earned.

Success, however, in some of its aspects, was not entirely agreeable to John Lennon, who continued to be a rebel at heart. When, in 1966, the group ceased to tour, he cut himself off from the rest of them and, although they came together for recording sessions, he became more and more involved in transcendental meditation, drugs, and mystical religion. In 1962 he had married Cynthia, daughter of Charles Edwin Powell, a commercial traveller, and they had a son. In 1968 Lennon met Yoko, daughter of Eisuke Ono, of the Yokohama specie bank, Tokyo; she was a film producer and avant-garde artist, and they were soon on intimate terms. Lennon's first marriage ended in divorce in 1968, and in 1969 he married Yoko. In 1971 the Beatles partnership was ended in the High Court and each member of the group went his separate way. Paul McCartney continued to write successful music with a new group, and Lennon made solo recordings, of which the best known is probably 'Imagine' (1971).

Meanwhile, he had become increasingly involved in left-wing causes. In 1969 he returned his MBE as a protest against British policy in respect of Nigeria and Vietnam. He also found himself in trouble with the immigration authorities in the USA, but in 1972 he and Yoko were granted permission to live there. They had a son and Yoko managed the business side of Lennon's very lucrative estate. On 9 December 1980 John Lennon was shot dead outside his New York apartment leaving an enormous fortune. His stories and drawings had been published as *In his own Write* (1964), and *A Spaniard in the Works* (1965). For some years before his murder, he had lived in seclusion, but at the time of his death he had just produced, with his wife, a new album, *Double Fantasy*, which appeared to mark a new beginning for his unusual genius.

LEVER, WILLIAM HESKETH, first VISCOUNT LEVER-HULME (1851–1925), soap manufacturer, was born in Bolton, on 19 September 1851, the elder son of James Lever, a grocer, of Bolton, and his wife, Eliza, daughter of William Hesketh, a cotton-mill manager, of Manchester. He went to school at the local Church Institute and, at the age of sixteen, entered the family business. He became a junior partner in 1872. In 1874 he married Elizabeth Ellen, daughter of Crompton Hulme, a linen-draper of Bolton; they had one son.

In 1884 Lever decided to set up his own business, specializing in soap. His brother joined him in this enterprise. They chose the name 'Sunlight' for their product, which was made largely from vegetable oils instead of tallow. In 1885 they purchased the soapworks of Winser & Co. at Warrington and began to manufacture their own soap. The demand grew rapidly and in 1888–9 Lever founded Port Sunlight, a new town in Cheshire, where his soap could be manufactured and his work-people housed. In 1890 Lever Brothers became a limited company, and in 1894 the company went public with William Lever as major shareholder and Chairman.

The business continued to expand, amalgamating with other soap manufacturers, until at the beginning of the twentieth century Lever occupied the leading position in the industry. In 1907 he won a libel action against the NORTH-CLIFFE press, which had accused him of fraudulent trading and bad treatment of his workers. With the proceeds of the damages, settled out of court, he purchased the old Blue Coat School in Liverpool and gave the balance to Liverpool University to endow a School of Tropical Medicine.

From 1906 to 1909 Lever was Liberal MP for the Wirrall division of Cheshire, but he found that he could not combine politics with his business responsibilities. During the First World War he supported the Government in some important committee-work and became honorary Treasurer of the Star and Garter Home for disabled soldiers at Richmond.

In 1910 the firm had set up crushing mills in Nigeria to process palm oil with modern machinery, and after the war Lever extended this side of his business, purchasing the shares of the Niger Company. He spent much time and energy on the improvement of facilities at Port Sunlight, but failed with an experiment in the islands of Lewis and Harris to develop the fishing industry and improve the lot of the crofters.

He was a keen collector and a great public benefactor. He purchased Stafford House, St James's, and presented it to the public as Lancaster House. He gave generously to Liverpool University and to his home town, Bolton, of which he was Mayor (1918–19).

Lever was created a baronet in 1911, and became Baron Leverhulme in 1917. The title was a combination of his own name and that of his wife, who had died four years earlier. He was created viscount in 1922. Leverhulme died in London on 7 May 1925 and was succeeded by his son.

LEVERHULME, first VISCOUNT (1851–1925). See LEVER.

LEWIS, CLIVE STAPLES (1898–1963), writer and scholar, was born in Belfast on 29 November 1898, the younger son of Albert James Lewis, a solicitor, and his wife, Florence (Flora) Augusta, daughter of the Revd Thomas Hamilton. His mother died when Lewis was nine, a tragedy for a sensitive boy. He was educated at Campbell College, Belfast and Malvern College, and won a classical scholarship to University College, Oxford, in 1917. However, during 1917–18, he served in France with the Somerset Light Infantry and was wounded in the Battle of Arras. He returned to Oxford in 1919, obtained firsts in Classical Mods. and Greats, and in English language and literature (1920–3), and won the Chancellor's English essay prize.

His personal life, apart from his university activities and his many academic friends, took a strange course. While he was recovering from his war wound he became intimate with Mrs J. K. Moore, mother of one of his friends who had been killed in the war. He set up home with her and her daughter while he was still an undergraduate in Oxford. As time passed she became more and more possessive and demanding, and Lewis's brother, Warren, wrote bitterly of this woman's hold over him. However Lewis continued to look after Mrs Moore until her death in 1951.

After a short time as a lecturer in philosophy, in 1925 he became Fellow and tutor of Magdalen College, teaching Anglo-Saxon, philosophy, political theory, and English literature. In 1926 he published a long narrative poem *Dymer*, under the pseudonym Clive Hamilton. At Oxford he had arrived as an agnostic, but he gradually and reluctantly accepted theism and eventually became a Christian evangelical. In 1933 he published his first allegorical work *The Pilgrim's Regress*, based upon his experience of conversion. This was followed in 1936 by *The Allegory of Love*, a study of medieval allegory, 'courtly love', and a critical analysis of the work of Chaucer, Gower, and Spenser, which won the Hawthornden prize.

Lewis also published lectures, in which he showed his readiness to enter into controversy regarding the teaching of English. In 1942 he produced *The Screwtape Letters*, a Christian apologia, in which an elderly devil writes letters of advice to a junior devil with many suggestions, all useless, for reclaiming the soul of a convert to Christianity. This publication and his broadcast talks on religious topics made Lewis an international figure, well known, particularly in America. During the Second World War he also wrote a trilogy of allegorical, space, science fiction stories, and in 1948 began the popular series of seven Narnia books for children; he was awarded the Carnegie medal for *The Last Battle* (1956), the final story of the overthrow of evil. In *The Problem of Pain* (1940), he set out to demonstrate, in simple terms, the Christian doctrine explaining the existence of pain and sorrow in the world.

In 1946, despite the popularity of his lectures, Lewis was passed over for the Merton chair of English literature and in 1950 missed appointment to the chair of poetry. But in 1944 his Clark lectures at Cambridge had been a great success and in 1954 they were published as *English Literature in the Sixteenth Century*. In the same year he was invited to become Professor of English Medieval and Renaissance Literature at Cambridge and, when he accepted this offer, was elected a Fellow of Magdalene College. When the Merton chair at Oxford again fell vacant, it was impossible to persuade him to accept it.

He resigned his Cambridge chair in 1963 because of failing health. In 1955 he had been elected FBA, but he declined appointment as CBE.

In 1953 he had met an American couple, the Greshams; Mrs Gresham was Jewish, and by 1955 she was in England with her two sons, having divorced her husband. She was now known as Joy Davidman and did secretarial work for Lewis in Cambridge. He married her in 1956 so that she could remain in England. When it appeared that she had a terminal disease, they remarried with the blessing of the Anglican church; but she miraculously recovered for a time, and she and Lewis spent a happy two years together. When she died in 1960, he described his deep sense of loss in *A Grief Observed* (1961). Lewis himself died in Oxford on 22 November 1963.

LEWIS, JOHN SPEDAN (1885–1963), shopkeeper and industrial reformer, was born in London on 22 September 1885, the elder son of John Lewis, a draper, and his wife, Eliza, daughter of Thomas Baker, also a draper, of Bridgwater. He was educated as a Queen's scholar at Westminster School, and left at nineteen to join his father in the Oxford Street shop, which John Lewis had acquired in 1864. In 1910 Lewis had a riding accident which permanently impaired his health and, during his convalescence, he conceived the idea of profit-sharing with his employees.

In 1914 he took charge of the business Peter Jones Ltd., purchased by his father some years earlier. In 1916, after a disagreement with his father, he took over this business and gave up his partnership in the Oxford Street shop. In 1920 he reconstructed the company and distributed preference shares to his workpeople. Trade declined for some years and in 1924, after he and his father had patched up their disagreement, he resumed his partnership at Oxford Street,

J. S. Lewis, *c.* 1950

until in 1928 his father died and he became sole owner, having bought out his brother who was an MP.

In 1923 he had married Sarah Beatrice Mary, daughter of Percy Hunter of Teddington; she was a graduate of Somerville College, Oxford, whom Lewis had engaged for a senior post in the business; she later became Deputy Manager; they had two sons and a daughter.

In 1929 Lewis formed the public company, John Lewis Partnership Ltd., covering both his shops, transferring all the equity capital to trustees on behalf of his employees. He was a very efficient business man and, under his management, the company rapidly expanded; but, whilst sharing the profits, he retained the management in his own hands. He did, however, keep his employee partners fully informed about the business through a house journal, which from 1918 was published weekly.

In 1950 he completed the legal arrangements for the equity of the business to be held permanently in trust on behalf of the employees and, when he retired in 1955, the Partnership had over 12,000 members and annual sales amounted to more than £25 million.

Lewis had wide interests besides his business. In 1956–7 he was President of the Classical Association; he also served on the council of the Zoological Society. Lewis published *Partnership for All* in 1948 and *Fairer Shares* in 1954. He died at Longstock in Hampshire on 21 February 1963.

LEWIS, ROSA (1867–1952), hotel owner, was born on 26 September 1867 at Leyton, Essex, the fifth of the nine children of William Edwin Ovenden, a watchmaker and undertaker, and his wife, Eliza, daughter of John Cannon, a jeweller. Leaving a Leyton board school at twelve, Rosa became a general servant and, at sixteen, was employed in the home of the exiled Comte de Paris. She worked her way up to head kitchenmaid and, after a period in the household of the Duc d'Aumale at Chantilly, was put in charge of the kitchen of the Duc d'Orleans at Sandhurst.

Having acquired the skill of French cooking, she started going out to cook in private houses in 1887 and was employed by Lady Randolph Churchill, the Saviles, the Asquiths, and Capt. Charles Duff, a prominent member of the Marlborough House set. Edward VII first met her at Sheen House and was charmed, not only by her cooking, but also by her personality; for the next twenty years she was in demand by hostesses entertaining the King.

In 1893 Rosa married a butler, Excelsior Tyrel Chiney Lewis, and they ran a lodging house, but he was a drunkard and in 1903 she divorced him. Meanwhile, she continued her business of cooking in private houses, now able to take a team of cooks with her, though she was careful to see that her standards were fully maintained. She also gave lessons to the cooks of wealthy households.

In 1902 Rosa bought the Cavendish Hotel in Jermyn Street and maintained it as a fashionable hotel, to which only guests of whom she approved were admitted, the more distinguished the better, with a few presentable wealthy Americans. Up to the time of the First World War, the Cavendish was highly regarded by many well-known aristocrats and country gentlemen, and Rosa continued to be highly popular in the kitchens of the London houses of fashionable hostesses.

During the war, private entertaining on a grand scale ceased and Rosa had only the Cavendish to keep her busy. She was immensely generous to young officers, who could not afford to meet her charges, and she became notorious for the way in which she allowed the impecunious young men to stay without paying their bills and recouped her losses from the more wealthy. In her later years, she became a legend. Evelyn WAUGH described her in *Vile Bodies* (1930) as a 'warm-hearted, comic, and totally original woman', and she was fortunate in retaining into old age some of the beauty that had made her attractive as a young woman. She died at the Cavendish on 29 November 1952.

LIDDELL HART, SIR BASIL HENRY (1895–1970), military historian and strategist, was born in Paris on 31 October 1895, the younger son of the Revd Henry Bramley Hart, a Wesleyan minister, and his wife, Clara, daughter of Henry Liddell. He was educated at St Paul's School, London, and Corpus Christi College, Cambridge. After a year at college, he joined the King's Own Yorkshire Light Infantry, was wounded in France in 1915 and 1916 and, as adjutant of training units of the Volunteer Force in 1917–21, evolved new methods of instruction and battle drill. He helped to compile the post-war *Infantry Training* manual. From 1921 to 1927 he served in the Army Educational Corps, but in the latter year was invalided out. In 1918 he married Jessie Douglas, daughter of J. J. Stone; they had one son.

Liddell Hart's experiences on the Western Front had given him definite views on the best methods of conducting modern warfare. He was severely critical of the inflexible attitude of Field-Marshal HAIG, and advocated mobility and surprise. He published his views in *Strategy—The Indirect Approach* (1929). He was closely concerned with the inter-

war pioneers of British armoured development and, as military correspondent of the *Daily Telegraph* (1925–35) and correspondent and defence adviser of *The Times* (1935–9), he consistently tried to further the efforts of the advocates of mechanization.

He backed up his ideas with studies of military history. He wrote over thirty books, including studies of Scipio Africanus (1926), Sherman (1930), Foch (1931), and T. E. LAWRENCE (1934). These were supplemented by *The Real War* (1930, enlarged and reissued as *A History of the World War*, 1934), a controversial indictment of Haig as a general, and *The Ghost of Napoleon* (1933).

In 1937–8 Liddell Hart was unofficial adviser to the War Minister, Leslie HORE-BELISHA, but neither of them was very popular with the military establishment, though they introduced some useful reforms. Throughout the Second World War he was excluded from any position of influence. He was a consistent opponent of 'total war', and had the frustrating experience of seeing German generals putting into effect some of his pre-war theories.

After his first marriage had ended in divorce, in 1942 he married Kathleen, daughter of Alan Sullivan, of Toronto, and widow of Henry Philbrick Nelson, FRCS.

After 1945, his relations with surviving German commanders enabled him to write *The Other Side of the Hill* (1948), and to edit *The Rommel Papers* (1953), followed by *The Tanks* (2 vols., 1959). His *History of the Second World War* was published posthumously in 1970. He was prescient in his warning that the existence of nuclear weapons would not preclude non-nuclear warfare and that preparation would be necessary to combat guerrilla activity. In 1967 the Israelis affirmed their debt to his theories.

His *Memoirs* (2 vols.) were published in 1965. He received a number of academic honours and awards, including an honorary fellowship of Corpus Christi College, Cambridge. He was knighted in 1966. Liddell Hart died at Medmenham on 29 January 1970.

LINDEMANN, FREDERICK ALEXANDER, VISCOUNT CHERWELL (1886–1957), scientist, politician, and adviser to Winston CHURCHILL, was born on 5 April 1886 at Baden Baden, the second of three sons of Adolphus Frederick Lindemann, whose family was of Catholic French Alsatian origin, and his wife, Olga Noble, the American daughter of a British-born engineer, and widow of a rich banker named Davidson. She was a Protestant and insisted on her children being brought up as Anglicans. Adolphus Lindemann had become a naturalized British subject, after emigrating to Britain in his twenties. He was a scientist and astronomer and a wealthy man.

Lindemann was educated at Blair Lodge, Polmont, Scotland, at the Real-Gymnasium and the Hochschule, Darmstadt, and at the Physikalisch-Chemisches Institute in Berlin, where he gained his Ph.D. in 1910. He was a wealthy student, a vegetarian, non-smoker, and teetotaller, and a first-class tennis player. Between 1910 and 1924, he worked on low temperature physics and, with his brother Charles, invented a glass transparent to X-rays; he also wrote papers on the use of photo-electric cells in astronomical photometry. In 1919 he co-operated with F. W. Aston on the possibility of separating isotopes. These and other scientific activities indicated his facility for simplifying complicated problems and explaining them in non-technical terms. He was elected FRS in 1920.

Unsuccessful in his attempts to gain a commission, in 1915

he joined the Royal Aircraft Factory at Farnborough, where he learned to fly and evolved a theory to deal with piloting a stalling aircraft, a cause of fatal disasters to many pilots. To prove his theory, he deliberately put a machine into a nose dive and demonstrated his mathematical conclusion, that to land safely it was necessary to increase speed to a maximum in a vertical dive. Those watching expected him to crash to certain death, but his theory worked and he landed his plane intact.

In 1919 Lindemann was elected Dr Lee's Professor of Experimental Philosophy (physics) at Oxford, with a fellowship at Wadham College. He was also, in 1921, elected to a studentship of Christ Church and, from 1922 onwards, he lived there until he died. During this period of his life, he made the Clarendon Laboratory, which had been regarded as of little importance, into the foremost physics department in Britain, attracting not only some of the leading physicists among British research workers, but also many refugee scientists of high calibre. He had many clashes, however, with his academic colleagues, and his comparative wealth did not endear him to many of those with whom he worked.

In 1921 he met and became a close friend of Winston Churchill. Like Churchill, he was quick to recognize the danger from Hitler, and was gravely disturbed by the inadequacy of Britain's air defences. In 1934 he pressed for a high-level committee to look into this matter. The Air Ministry had already decided to set up a committee under the chairmanship of Henry TIZARD, who had been a colleague of Lindemann in Berlin. Lindemann was appointed to this committee and proceeded to make his criticisms so hostile that the friendship between him and Tizard soon turned into

Lindemann, 'the Prof', with Admiral of the Fleet Sir Roger Keyes, 1941

bitter recrimination. The committee resigned *en masse*, and was re-formed without Lindemann. He had not ceased to be a close confidant of Churchill and one cause of dissension arose from his unscrupulous use of Churchill to get his own way.

For some years his efforts brought only frustration, but, when the Second World War broke out, he became Churchill's personal assistant at the Admiralty and, later, his most influential scientific adviser, when Churchill became Prime Minister in 1940. In 1941 he was made a peer as Baron Cherwell, of Oxford, in 1942 he became Paymaster-General, and in 1943 a Privy Counsellor. There can be no doubt that, in spite of his controversial attitude to many of the leading scientists engaged on war work, Cherwell was invaluable to the Prime Minister because, in addition to his facility for examining critically any scheme put forward by other experts, he could make imaginative proposals of his own and could interpret in simple terms, often by an easily understandable graph, highly complicated scientific ideas, which it was essential that Churchill should be able to grasp easily and quickly. Inevitably he made mistakes: he overestimated the effects of massive area bombing and underestimated the capacity of the Germans to produce devastating rocket bombs. But throughout the war, in some 2,000 minutes, he supplied Churchill with acute assessments of proposals put forward by the departments, and encouraged research into new weapons, such as microwave radar, and improvements in old ones, which directly affected the progress of the war. In his book, *Churchill: The Struggle for Survival*, Lord MORAN wrote of Cherwell: 'I believe that historians will agree that without the Prof. a war that was won by science might have gone differently.'

In 1945 Cherwell went back to the Clarendon Laboratory at Oxford; he returned to Churchill's 1951 administration as Paymaster-General, but resigned in 1953 and was made CH. In 1956 he was created a viscount. In the same year, he resigned his Oxford post, but continued to live in Christ Church. He never married. He died at Oxford on 3 July 1957. Henry Tizard, with whom he frequently crossed swords, regarded him as 'one of the cleverest men I ever met'.

LINDSAY, ALEXANDER DUNLOP, first BARON LINDSAY OF BIRKER (1879–1952), educationalist, was born in Glasgow on 14 May 1879, the eldest of the three sons of the Revd Thomas Martin Lindsay, historian of the Reformation. He was brought up in a Calvinist family, and educated at Glasgow University and University College, Oxford, where he was a scholar, obtained firsts in Classical Mods. (1900) and Greats (1902), and was President of the Union.

In 1907 Lindsay married Erica Violet, daughter of Francis Storr; they had a daughter and two sons.

Between 1902 and 1906 he was successively Clark Philosophy Fellow at Glasgow, Shaw Philosophy Fellow at Edinburgh, and Assistant Professor of Philosophy at Manchester. In 1906 he was elected Fellow and classical tutor at Balliol College, Oxford. There he remained until 1922, except that during the First World War he served with labour battalions in France, and was appointed CBE. At Oxford, where he earned a great reputation as a tutor, he published a translation of Plato's *Republic* (1907), a book on *The Philosophy of Bergson* (1911), *The Philosophy of Immanuel Kant* (1913), and an introduction to Hobbes's *Leviathan* (1914).

For a short while (1922–4), he was Professor of Moral Philosophy at Glasgow and then, from 1924 to 1949, was

Master of Balliol College, Oxford. He was one of the few academics who supported Archbishop DAVIDSON's appeal for a negotiated settlement of the general strike in 1926. He was keenly interested in the Workers' Educational Association and did much to help the transition, in the thirties, of educational opportunities at Oxford from the monopoly of the wealthy to a wider spectrum of the social classes. He was also eager to serve publicly in such causes as the improvement of higher education in India. He visited that country for four months in 1930 and became a friend of GANDHI.

From 1935 to 1938 he was Vice-Chancellor of Oxford University, and did much to improve the financial and administrative structure of the university. He took a leading part in setting up the new Clarendon Laboratory and in establishing Nuffield College. Meanwhile, he did not lose his interest in public affairs and was outspoken in his condemnation of the Munich agreement (1938). During the Second World War, he took an active part in organizing the education of the forces, and in 1945 was created a baron by the ATTLEE Government.

After the war, he worked for the establishment of a university college in North Staffordshire where, for over twenty years, he had assisted with adult education. When he retired from Balliol at the age of seventy in 1949, he became the first Principal of the new University College, Keele, and set out to make the college curriculum broadly based and not so specialized as the courses at the older universities. He was always interested in social welfare and the problems of the under-privileged, an interest which was firmly underpinned by his Christian principles. He published *The Essentials of Democracy* (1929), *The Modern Democratic State* (1943), and *Religion, Science, and Society in the Modern World* (1943). He died at Keele on 18 March 1952 and was succeeded in the title by his elder son, a specialist in Chinese economics.

LIPTON, SIR THOMAS JOHNSTONE (1850–1931), grocer, yachtsman, and philanthropist, was born in a tenement house in Glasgow on 10 May 1850, the only surviving child of Thomas Lipton, an Irish labourer, who left Ireland at the time of the potato famine, with his wife, Frances, daughter of Frank Johnstone of Kilrid, Clones. After working in Glasgow, the two opened a small grocer's shop, and, by the age of nine, Thomas was also working in this shop. At the age of fifteen, he emigrated to the United States and worked on a tobacco plantation in Virginia and in rice-fields in South Carolina. He then stowed away on a ship to New York and worked there in a grocer's shop until, at the age of twenty, he saved sufficient to return to Glasgow.

For a year he worked in his father's shop and, on his twenty-first birthday (1871), opened his own shop in Glasgow. By hard work, shrewd buying, integrity, and enterprise, he prospered and at twenty-four opened his second shop. He was a pioneer in skilful advertising and, by 1889, was able to transfer his headquarters to London. By the age of thirty, he was a millionaire, running his own paper-bag factory, and owning pork factories in Chicago and a tea plantation in Ceylon (Sri Lanka).

By 1897 Lipton was giving part of his wealth to charity and pursuing his passion for yacht-racing. He assisted the Princess of Wales in financing meals for the poor and met the whole cost of £100,000 for a restaurant for the indigent. In 1898, the year of his knighthood, he formed the limited liability company of Lipton Ltd. He also purchased the steam yacht, *Erin*, on which he entertained lavishly many eminent people including King Edward VII.

He issued his first challenge for the America's cup in 1899 with *Shamrock I* and, for the next thirty years, made many attempts to win the cup with a number of *Shamrocks*, but never succeeded in achieving this ambition. In 1930 the Americans presented him with a gold cup in recognition of his fine sportsmanship. He was appointed KCVO in 1901 and created a baronet in 1902. During the First World War his yacht *Erin* was used in the Mediterranean to carry medical supplies, until she was sunk by a submarine.

Lipton was one of the most successful businessmen of his time, a great sportsman, a genial host (though an abstainer from alcohol and tobacco), and a friend of many of the most distinguished people of the Edwardian age. He never married and, when he died in London on 2 October 1931, he bequeathed most of his large fortune to Glasgow charities.

LLOYD, GEORGE AMBROSE, first BARON LLOYD (1879–1941), public servant, was born near Solihull, Warwickshire on 19 September 1879, the youngest son of Samuel Lloyd, a business man, and his wife, Jane Emelia, daughter of Thomas Lloyd, a director of Lloyds Bank. He was educated at Eton and Trinity College, Cambridge, and coxed the winning Cambridge boat in 1899 and 1900. He left the university without a degree, probably because of the death of his parents, and travelled in the East. On return, he entered his father's firm, Lloyd & Lloyd, steel-tube manufacturers, but in 1905 left the company on appointment as honorary attaché at Constantinople (Istanbul). In 1907 he undertook a mission of inquiry into the future of British trade in the Near East.

In 1911 he married Blanche Isabella Lascelles, a maid of honour to Queen Alexandra, and daughter of Frederick Canning Lascelles, commander RN and cousin of the sixth Earl of Harewood. They had one son.

From 1910 to 1918 he was Conservative MP for the West Staffordshire division, but during the First World War he served in the army and was engaged on special missions in the Near East, which included landing in the Dardanelles with the Australians and visiting the Russian High Command. During 1916–17 he was attached to the Arab Bureau for special duties connected with the Arab revolt led by T. E. LAWRENCE. In 1917 he was appointed CIE and DSO.

From 1918 to 1923 Lloyd was Governor of Bombay. It was a time of political agitation and post-war economic problems but, in this difficult atmosphere, he achieved the setting up of the Bombay development scheme and the erection of the Lloyd barrage across the Indus. In 1924 he received the GCSI, having received the GCIE in 1918. He was also sworn of the Privy Council.

He re-entered Parliament as MP for Eastbourne in 1924 but, in the following year, was created a baron and appointed to succeed ALLENBY as High Commissioner in Egypt. His period of office there was not a success, mainly on account of his imperialistic view of his responsibilities, which caused disagreements with the Foreign Office. In 1929 Arthur HENDERSON forced him to resign and he was able to overcome criticism in the Commons by pointing out that Lloyd had had similar disputes with his predecessor, Sir Austen CHAMBERLAIN. Lloyd published his version of the controversy in *Egypt since Cromer* (2 vols., 1933–4).

Although he was out of favour with the Government, Lloyd continued to work strenuously in the public interest, especially in support of imperial causes. He was instrumental in the establishment of the British Council, designed to publicize abroad British achievements in education and other fields of enterprise; he became its first Chairman in 1937, and was indefatigable in pursuing its aims during the Second World War. By some means, however, probably because of a disagreement on tariff policy, Lloyd caused offence to Lord BEAVERBROOK, and for many years the British Council had to suffer the hostility of the Beaverbrook press, which during Beaverbrook's lifetime was unrelenting in its antagonism to the organization Lloyd had created.

In 1940 Winston CHURCHILL appointed Lloyd Secretary of State for the Colonies. Soon afterwards, he flew to Bordeaux to attempt to persuade the French Government not to agree to an armistice with the Germans; however, in this, he failed. He died suddenly in London around midnight on 4-5 February 1941.

LLOYD, (JOHN) SELWYN BROOKE, BARON SELWYN-LLOYD (1904-1978), politician, was born on 28 July 1904 in West Kirby, Wirral, the third child and only son of John Wesley Lloyd, MRCS, LRCP, a dentist, and his wife, Mary Rachel Warhurst. He was educated at Fettes and Magdalene College, Cambridge, where he was President of the Union in 1927. He began his political career as a Liberal but, converted to the need for a protective tariff, he later became a Conservative.

He was called to the Bar (Gray's Inn) in 1930, practised on the Northern Circuit, and became Chairman of the Hoylake Urban District Council (1936). In 1939 he enlisted as a private in the RHA, was commissioned, and promoted to lieutenant-colonel by 1942. He was a successful staff officer, rose to brigadier, being appointed OBE (1943) and CBE (1945).

In 1945 he was elected Conservative MP for Wirral, took silk in 1947, and was Recorder of Wigan (1948-51). In 1949 he was a member of the BEVERIDGE Committee on the organization of the BBC and, in a minority report, recommended a competitive TV system. In 1951 he was appointed Minister of State at the Foreign Office, under Anthony EDEN, and sworn of the Privy Council. In 1954 he became Minister of Supply, and in 1955 entered the Cabinet as Minister of Defence. In December of that year he succeeded Harold Macmillan as Foreign Secretary.

In July 1956 Col. Nasser nationalized the Suez Canal Company and Selwyn Lloyd organized a conference in London of the principal users of the canal. However, without American support, the conference resolutions could not be implemented; and, when John Foster Dulles, the US Secretary of State, refused to refer the crisis to the UN Security Council, the French Premier, Mollet, secretly put forward to Eden a plan for military action in collaboration with Israel. Eden appears to have taken the lead in this matter but Selwyn Lloyd accompanied him to Paris for talks with Mollet, at which it was agreed that Franco-British forces would intervene if Israeli forces reached the canal. Lloyd appears not to have been aware of the secretly arranged plan for Franco-British collusion with Israel, but the whole British Cabinet knew of the intention to intervene by force. Lloyd continued to press the British case at the United Nations, but at the same time was concerned with the planning of the military operation, and was disturbed at the resignation of his Minister of State, (Sir) H. Anthony Nutting, who disagreed with the course being taken. Lloyd's frustration was increased when the Cabinet accepted the advice of the Chancellor of the Exchequer (Macmillan) and ordered a cease-fire on 6 November 1956.

When, after the Suez débâcle, Eden resigned as Prime Minister, Selwyn Lloyd remained as Foreign Secretary in Macmillan's Government, and helped to restore Anglo-American relations. In 1959 he went with the Prime Minister to the Soviet Union for talks with Khrushchev. He also opened negotiations for Britain's entry to the European Economic Community.

In 1960 he became Chancellor of the Exchequer; his 'pay pause' was ineffective, but he was responsible for setting up the National Economic Development Council. His efforts to curb wage increases were unpopular, and in July 1962 he was one of the victims of Macmillan's Cabinet reshuffle, known as 'the night of the long knives'. He very much resented the treatment. He was created CH, and in 1963 became Deputy Lord Lieutenant of Chester.

When Macmillan's ill health caused his retirement in 1963, Selwyn Lloyd supported the claims of the Earl of Home (later Sir Alec Douglas Home and then Lord Home of the Hirsel), and became leader of the House of Commons. After the Conservative defeat in 1964, he remained in the Shadow Cabinet and became Conservative spokesman on Commonwealth affairs. In 1966 he resigned from the Shadow Cabinet and took up a number of directorships in the City.

In 1971 he was elected Speaker of the House of Commons, and served in that office until 1976, when he was created a life peer. That year he published *Mr. Speaker Sir*, followed by *Suez 1956* (1978). He received a number of academic honours.

In 1951 he had married his secretary, Elizabeth ('Bay'), daughter of Roland Marshall, a solicitor of West Kirby; they had one daughter, but were divorced in 1957. He died at Preston Crowmarsh, Oxfordshire, on 17 May 1978.

LLOYD GEORGE, DAVID, first EARL LLOYD-GEORGE OF DWYFOR (1863-1945), politician and wartime Prime Minister, was born in Manchester on 17 January 1863, the elder son of William George, a schoolmaster, and his wife, Elizabeth, daughter of David Lloyd, of Llanystumdwy, Caernarvonshire. William George died in 1864, and his widow went to live with her brother, Richard Lloyd, a master-shoemaker. The young David was much influenced by this radical Welsh dissenter who brought him up. He changed his surname to Lloyd George. He went to the local church school, but this did nothing to change his hostility to privilege and ardent adherence to Welsh nationalism.

In 1884 he qualified as a solicitor, and soon established a high reputation as an eloquent advocate, both in magistrate's courts and in Baptist chapels. He also engaged actively in local politics and in 1890 was elected Liberal MP for Caernarvon Boroughs, a seat which he held until 1945.

In 1888 he married Margaret, daughter of Richard Owen, a farmer of Criccieth; they had two sons and three daughters. One of the daughters, Mair Eiluned, died in 1907. Margaret was a loyal supporter of her husband but she preferred to bring up her family in Criccieth rather than to reside permanently in London, particularly as Lloyd George became notorious among his political contemporaries for his philandering.

While his younger brother, William, kept the legal business going, David entered with gusto into the hurly-burly of politics, concentrating at first on the hardships, real or imagined, of the Welsh. His fervour in the Welsh cause led in 1896 to his being suspended by the Speaker. During the Boer War he earned notoriety by his unpopular support of the Boers, and in 1901 had to escape from a meeting in Birmingham, disguised as a policeman.

In 1905 he was appointed President of the Board of Trade and sworn of the Privy Council and his energies were diverted, to some extent, from the Welsh cause into other channels. His reputation as an eloquent speaker was enhanced by his success as an adroit debater and a patient negotiator. During the three years he held this office, he promoted the Merchant Shipping Act (1906), the Patents and Designs Act (1907) and the Port of London Act (1908).

In 1908, when Herbert ASQUITH became Prime Minister, Lloyd George succeeded him as Chancellor of the Exchequer, and set out on his campaign to improve the living conditions of the under-privileged by imposing new methods of taxation upon the wealthier classes. His 'People's Budget' of 1909 was bound to arouse the serious opposition of the House of Lords, as it proposed the levy of taxes on unearned increment in land values and thus affected every landowner. Lloyd George did nothing to pacify the opposition. In his speeches in Limehouse, he went out of his way to be provocative and to arouse the public against the aristocrats who opposed his policy. The budget was rejected by the Lords, and was only passed when a general election in January 1910 returned the Liberals to power.

Throughout 1910 controversy raged over the Parliament Bill which was designed to remove from the House of Lords their power to amend or reject finance bills passed by the Commons. The bill was passed after a second general election in December 1910. In 1911 Lloyd George demonstrated another aspect of his strongly held views by warning Germany, in a speech on the appearance of the German gunboat *Panther* at Agadir, that Britain would not tolerate any interference with her international interests and responsibilities. But his main preoccupation continued to be the alleviation of poverty, and in this year, 1911, he brought in his contributory scheme of health and unemployment insurance, the first of its kind.

His reputation was endangered, however, by the Marconi scandal of 1912, in which he was involved by his purchase of shares in the American company, when the British company had recently been granted a lucrative contract by his colleague, Herbert SAMUEL, the Postmaster-General. He was one of those who had to apologize to Parliament for his failure to disclose his interest in the matter, but his embarrassment was temporary and he was cleared of personal dishonesty.

When war became imminent in July 1914, Lloyd George was not prepared to intervene until Germany's invasion of Belgium violated a treaty to which Britain was a party. Then, his whole-hearted support for Asquith's decision to fight made him more determined than most of his colleagues to wage war until victory could be achieved. Within a few months of the outbreak of hostilities, he was concerned about the inefficiency with which the Allies appeared to be conducting operations, objecting strongly to the static war situation on the Western Front and anxious, most of all, that the realities of 'total war' should be realized and active steps taken to prepare for a lengthy period of hostilities and to repair the shortages in shells and the deficiencies in the mobilization of labour.

When, in May 1915, Asquith formed a Coalition Government, Lloyd George became Minister of Munitions and set out urgently to remove the obstacles to a vastly increased output of guns and shells, including the restrictive practices which defended the interests of the trade unions; and, by his eloquent speeches explaining to the workers the serious situation of the armed forces, he was able to ensure that, when the bloody battle of the Somme took place, the British army at least had the assurance that their supplies of arms and ammunition would be adequate for their needs.

In July 1916 Lloyd George became Secretary of State for War at a time when the British forces were suffering terrible losses, the submarine war at sea was imposing an intolerable burden on British shipping, and the Russian armies were being overrun by the Germans for want of adequate equipment. In November 1916 Lord LANSDOWNE suggested to the Cabinet that the Government should consider a negotiated peace. Lloyd George became increasingly critical of Asquith's conduct of the war and found himself more and more in sympathy with the views of the Conservatives, BONAR LAW and CARSON. He hoped to be given the authority to lead a small War Cabinet and, when Asquith refused to accept this proposal he resigned, thus precipitating a crisis which forced the Prime Minister to resign. To Asquith's dismay, the Conservative and Labour leaders agreed to support Lloyd George and, on 7 December 1916, he took over as Prime Minister.

As soon as he became head of the Government, he embarked on his war policy with renewed vigour, set up a small War Cabinet of five, summoned the ministers from the dominions, such as J. C. SMUTS, to an Imperial War Conference and War Cabinet, and forced a reluctant Admiralty to embark upon the convoy system for protecting British merchant shipping from submarine attacks. On the Western Front he strongly advocated a more united opposition by the Allies to German offensives and in 1917 secured the establishment of a Supreme War Council and the appointment of the French general, Foch, as Commander-in-Chief of the Allied armies on the Western Front.

When the Americans decided to join the Allies, the German generals sought to achieve victory with a massive attempt to break the British and French lines on the Western Front before American troops could reach the battlefield. They failed and, on 11 November 1918, the armistice was signed. Lloyd George's determination had been a major influence in the Allied victory. At the end of the war, he was at the height of his power and authority. The King, in 1919, appointed him to the Order of Merit; the French awarded him the Grand Cordon of the Legion of Honour.

Together, he and Bonar Law appealed to the country, in what came to be known as the 'coupon election', and the coalition obtained 526 seats out of 707, with the Conservatives predominating, the Liberal party split in two, and Lloyd George entirely dependent upon the good will of Bonar Law and Austen CHAMBERLAIN. The Prime Minister went off to Paris for five months, negotiating the peace treaties with President Wilson, a sick man, preoccupied with his fourteen points which nobody else took very seriously, and Clemenceau, realistically determined to see that Germany did not regain her strength sufficiently to make a further attack on France. Lloyd George himself was genuinely concerned to see Europe revived and peace secured by agreements which would be moderate and practical and likely to be kept. He failed. The Treaty of Versailles of 1920 contained within its terms potential causes of a future war.

The Prime Minister was more successful in his efforts to achieve peace in Ireland. After rebellion and outrages, revenged by the reprisals of the Black and Tans, British forces who met atrocity with atrocity, Lloyd George, by patience and skilful diplomacy, succeeded in persuading the Irish leaders to sign the Treaty of 1921. Meanwhile, post-war problems in Britain were causing discontent and hardship.

Lloyd George's downfall, however, came about from an

Lloyd George practising the art of water divining

unusual set of circumstances. The Turks under their new leader, Mustapha Kemal, attempted to invade the neutral zone at Chanak, established by the Treaty of Sèvres, to which Kemal had not been a party. British troops, under Sir Charles Harrington, were in danger of embroilment with the Turks. In the event, confrontation was avoided, but there was anxiety lest Lloyd George should plunge the country into a new war and this gave his opponents their chance. At a Carlton Club meeting in October 1922, the majority of the Conservatives, led by Stanley BALDWIN, decided to end the coalition, and Lloyd George was forced to resign. At the subsequent election, he found himself the leader of fifty-five 'National Liberals'.

He had at his disposal a large party fund, believed to have been accumulated by the sale of honours, and he added to this by his journalistic work and skilful management of the *Daily Chronicle*. His manipulation of this fund caused controversy, but part of it was put to good use by promoting expert investigation into post-war social problems. The decision of the Conservatives to introduce protection temporarily united the Liberals in 1923, but not for long, and differences between Lloyd George and Asquith led to the eclipse of the party as a political force. By 1931, Lloyd George was leader of a family party of four, including his son, Gwilym, and his daughter, Megan.

He declined to stand again for the party leadership and retired to his estate at Churt, where he wrote *The Truth About Reparations and War-Debts* (1932), *War Memoirs* (6 vols., 1933–6), and *The Truth About the Peace Treaties* (2 vols., 1938). As he grew older, Lloyd George became increasingly critical of French foreign policy and sympathetic

towards Germany's post-war problems. In 1936 he visited Hitler but, as the aggressive policies of the Nazis developed, he recognized the danger to European peace and advocated co-operation with Russia. He vehemently opposed appeasement and helped to bring down Neville CHAMBERLAIN. But when, in 1940, Winston CHURCHILL invited him to join his Cabinet, he declined, as he did not feel strong enough physically to stand the strain of office. He also refused the post of Ambassador at Washington.

For many years he lived with his faithful secretary, Frances Louise, daughter of John Stevenson and his wife Louise Augustine Armanino, who was half-French and half-Italian. Frances was twenty-five years younger than Lloyd George. In 1911 she became private tutor to Megan, his youngest daughter. Soon, she became his personal secretary and mistress and, by 1913, was indispensable to him. Although Margaret, his wife, preferred to stay in North Wales, from time to time she descended upon Downing Street, and Frances had to stay in the background. Although it was clear to her that Lloyd George would never separate from Margaret, she remained his loyal supporter and close confidante throughout the war and the period of the Coalition Government (1918–22) and, when Bonar Law became Prime Minister, she refused his offer of a permanent post in the Civil Service. She and Lloyd George had a daughter, born in 1929.

Margaret Lloyd George died in 1941, and in 1943 Frances and Lloyd George were married. For a time they lived together at Criccieth. He became Earl Lloyd-George of Dwyfor in January 1945. Less than three months later, on 26 March 1945, he died, and was buried on the bank of the river Dwyfor. In 1967 Frances, Countess Lloyd-George, published her reminiscences, *The Years that are Past*. She died at Churt on 5 December 1972. She had been appointed CBE in 1918.

Lloyd George was succeeded by his elder son, Richard. His younger son, Gwilym, became a Conservative politician, and after serving under Churchill and EDEN was created first Viscount Tenby. Lady Megan Lloyd-George, who was never reconciled to her father's marriage to Frances Stevenson, was Liberal MP for Anglesey from 1929 to 1951 and in 1955 joined the Labour party.

LOCKHART, SIR ROBERT HAMILTON BRUCE (1887-1970). See BRUCE LOCKHART.

LONGHURST, HENRY CARPENTER (1909-1978), journalist, essayist, and television commentator on golf, was born on 18 March 1909 at Bedford, the only child of William Henry Longhurst, the owner of a furnishing business, and his wife, Constance Smith. He went to Charterhouse with a scholarship and then to Clare College, Cambridge, where he played golf for the university for four years, becoming Captain in 1931. He won the German amateur championship and was runner-up in the Swiss.

In the early thirties he began writing on golf for the *Sunday Times*, and continued to do so for over forty years, contributing more than a thousand articles. He also wrote, for the *Tatler* and the *Evening Standard*, articles which, though different in style from those of Bernard DARWIN, had a similar literary quality.

It was, however, his skill as a television commentator that made him well known with a wider public. He began his broadcasting career in 1939, and after the Second World War, when the televising of golf tournaments became a normal practice, Longhurst's expertise in the art of commentary came into its own. In 1965 he became the first Englishman to work regularly on the American TV networks, and in 1973 won the Walter Hagen award for his success in fostering golfing ties between Britain and the USA.

During the war he was an anti-aircraft gunner, and from 1943 to 1945 Conservative MP for Acton. In 1972 he was appointed CBE, and in 1976 elected an honorary member of the Royal and Ancient Golf Club, St Andrews. He published a dozen books on golf, including *Candid Caddies* (1936), *Round in Sixty-Eight* (1953), and *My Life and Soft Times* (1971).

In 1938 he married Claudine Marie Berthé Sier; they had a son and a daughter. Longhurst died on 21 July 1978.

LONSDALE, fifth EARL OF (1857-1944). See LOWTHER.

LOTHIAN, eleventh MARQUESS OF (1882-1940). See KERR.

LOW, SIR DAVID ALEXANDER CECIL (1891-1963), cartoonist and caricaturist, was born in Dunedin, New Zealand on 7 April 1891, the youngest son of David Brown Low, a business man, and his wife, Jane Caroline Flanagan. He went to Christchurch Boys' High School up to the age of eleven and then taught himself to draw and determined to make a living as an artist. Before he was twelve, he had a drawing published in the Christchurch *Spectator*. Modelling his work on that of Phil May, which he had discovered in some old copies of *Punch*, he had many sketches accepted by local papers and soon became political cartoonist on the *Spectator* and on the *Canterbury Times*.

In 1911 he moved to Australia, as political cartoonist on

the Sydney *Bulletin*, and made his name by his caricatures of William M. Hughes, who became Prime Minister in 1915. His cartoons, ridiculing Hughes and his policies, were published as *The Billy Book* (Sydney, 1918). His work was now also becoming known in England, and in 1919 Low accepted a post on the Liberal paper, the *Star*, and proceeded to lambaste LLOYD GEORGE's Coalition Government unmercifully, representing the Prime Minister astride the 'coalition ass', a double-headed donkey, symbolizing the stupidity of coalition policies.

In 1920 he married Madeline Grieve Kenning, a New Zealander; they had two daughters.

In 1926 Lord BEAVERBROOK persuaded Low to join the *Evening Standard* and undertook to give him a free hand. In the years leading up to the Second World War, Low remorselessly pilloried Hitler and Mussolini, deriding all forms of totalitarianism to such effect that Goebbels protested to Lord HALIFAX, and the *Evening Standard* was banned from Germany and Italy. During these years also, the pipe of Stanley BALDWIN and Neville CHAMBERLAIN's umbrella became familiar symbols of Low's mockery.

In 1949 Low resigned from the *Evening Standard* and in 1950 joined the *Daily Herald*. During the next three years, the public became familiar with the heavy, blundering carthorse representing the TUC. Perhaps, however, Low's most famous caricature was the character of 'Colonel Blimp', a muddle-headed, elderly gentleman, often clad only in a towel, bald and fat, delivering nonsensical, reactionary views with a pompous complacency.

Collections of Low's cartoons appeared in *Lloyd George & Co* (1921), *Low's Political Parade* (1936), and *Low Visibility: a Cartoon History, 1945-1953* (1953); his other publications include *British Cartoonists, Caricaturists, and Comic Artists* (1942) and *Low's Autobiography* (1956). He also did illustrations for H. G. WELLS's *The Autocracy of Mr Parham*

David Low at home in Golders Green, 1950, shortly after joining the *Daily Herald*

(1930), and water-colour illustrations for *The Modern Rake's Progress*, for which (Dame) Rebecca West wrote the words.

Low was knighted in 1962. He died in London on 19 September 1963. Winston CHURCHILL described him as 'the greatest of our modern cartoonists'.

LOWRY, LAURENCE STEPHEN (1887-1976), artist, was born in Manchester on 1 November 1887 the only child of Robert Stephen McAll Lowry, an estate agent's clerk, and his wife, Elizabeth, daughter of William Hobson, a hatter; she was an accomplished pianist. Lowry left the Victoria Park School when he was fifteen to become a clerk (1904) but, from 1905 for the next ten years, he studied at evening classes in the Manchester Municipal College of Art, where he was taught by Adolphe Valette.

In 1910 he was employed as a rent collector by the Pall Mall Property Company and worked with this firm until his retirement in 1952, but he always tried to hide the fact that he was not a man with private means, presumably because he did not wish to be regarded as an amateur painter, but also because he took some delight in mystifying people about his private life. After leaving the Manchester Art College in 1914, he studied for another five years at the Salford School of Art.

He was rejected for military service in the First World War, and was already producing paintings, such as *The Mill Worker* (1912) and *Selling Oil Cloth in Oldham Road* (1914). He had his first exhibition in Manchester in 1921, together with the work of two water-colourists; and Bernard Taylor, the art critic of the *Guardian*, spoke highly of his industrial scenes. For the first time, Lowry received encouragement in his highly individual approach to the Manchester settings of his work. It was Taylor, too, who criticized the bleakness of his dark backgrounds; this led Lowry to adopt a white background, without shadows, for his industrial scenes (though Taylor tried to persuade him to put in the shadows).

Many of Lowry's finest pictures were painted by artificial light and, although he made factual sketches on location, his paintings were always composed to suit his own convenience and imagination. In many of his pictures, for example, among his stick-like figures and curious dogs, he would introduce the figure of a handicapped person. In 1930 he sold his painting, *An Accident* (1926), to the Manchester Art Gallery, but it was not until 1938 that his work came to the notice of A. J. McNeil Reid of the Lefevre Gallery, London, and Lowry had his first one-man exhibition there (1939). He was, however, already exhibiting in Paris, and in 1934 had become a member of the Royal Society of British Artists.

After his father's death in 1932, Lowry patiently nursed his sick mother, until she died in 1939. He continued to live in her house in Manchester until, in 1948, he moved to Mottram in Cheshire, to a house which he always said he loathed but nevertheless stayed in until he died. Lowry was a secretive eccentric who never married and, unlike his contemporary, Stanley SPENCER, appears to have had no sex life. In his later years, when his work had become recognized and was fetching high prices, he continued to live the life of a poor man. He collected a notable series of portraits of girls by Dante Gabriel Rossetti, and became a close friend of Sheila Fell, an accomplished young artist, and of Ann Helder, who became the model for his 'single figure' paintings. He also befriended a young girl, Carol Ann Lowry, whose mother claimed to be a relative of Lowry and, although he did not think this was genuine, he became very fond of the girl and left the bulk of his estate to her in his will.

Lowry was elected ARA in 1955 and RA in 1962. In 1967 the GPO issued a postage stamp depicting one of his industrial scenes. He refused the honour of a knighthood and also the CH. He held an honorary degree from Manchester University; the main collection of his work went to the City Art Gallery, Salford. He died on 23 February 1976 at Glossop.

LOWTHER, HUGH CECIL, fifth EARL OF LONSDALE (1857-1944), sportsman, was born in London on 25 January 1857, the second son of Henry Lowther (later third Earl of Lonsdale), and his wife, Emily Susan, daughter of St George Francis Caulfield, of Donamon, Roscommon. He was educated at Eton, and from the age of nine showed great prowess as a rider to hounds. Later, he became Master in turn of the Woodland Pytchley, Blankney, Quorn, and Cottesmore hounds, and noted for his authoritative bearing as an MFH.

In his teens he toured with a circus in Switzerland and became a life-long admirer of circus folk. In his early thirties he spent a year in the Arctic and confirmed that there was gold in the Klondike in northern Canada. He was a leading expert on horses and dogs, but he had little success as a race-horse owner, the only classic race he won being the St Leger in 1922. He won the Waterloo cup for coursing. He was a notable boxer as a young man and was a sparring partner of John L. Sullivan, the world heavy-weight champion. The Lonsdale Belts of the National Sporting Club keep his memory alive in the boxing world. He was also a keen yachtsman, and in 1896 raced his yacht against the Kaiser's *Meteor*, winning seventeen prizes in twenty-two races. The Kaiser was a personal friend and Lonsdale refused to denounce his friendship during the First World War.

Lonsdale was one of the last of the great aristocratic sportsmen; in the eyes of the public he was the epitome of grandeur and glamour on the racecourse and at other sporting events. His friendships ranged over a broad sweep of society from the royal family to the pearly kings and queens, whose patron he was. From the age of twenty-one he kept a resolution never to play cards for money or bet on a horse.

In 1878 he married the daughter of the tenth Marquess of Huntly, Lady Grace Cecilie Gordon, who shared his great passion for sport. Four years later he succeeded his brother as fifth earl. He and his wife entertained lavishly at Lowther Castle and at Barley Thorpe, Rutland though, in spite of his immense inherited wealth, his last ten years were spent with 'straightened means'. In 1925 he was appointed GCVO and in 1928 became KG. From 1917 to 1944 he was Lord Lieutenant of Cumberland. The 'Lonsdale Library of Sports, Games, and Pastimes', which he edited with Eric Parker, began publication with its first three volumes in 1929.

He died at Barley Thorpe on 13 April 1944, and was succeeded by his brother, since he and his wife had no children.

LUGARD, FREDERICK JOHN DEALTRY, BARON LUGARD (1858-1945), soldier, administrator, and author, was born at Fort St George, Madras, on 22 January 1858, the eldest son of the Revd Frederick Grueber Lugard, senior chaplain, and his third wife, a missionary, Mary Jane, daughter of the Revd John Garton Howard, Vicar of Stanton-by-Dale, Derbyshire. He was educated at Rossall School and the Royal Military College, Sandhurst.

In 1878 he was commissioned in the 9th Foot (the Norfolk Regiment) and served in India until 1885 when, having transferred to the Military Transport Service, he was sent to Suakin in support of the Sudan campaign for the relief of Khartoum. In the following year, he took part in the operations in Upper Burma. He was awarded the DSO in 1887.

In 1888-9 he led a small force, sent by the African Lakes Company to defend Karongwa on Lake Nyasa against Arab slave traders. In the following year he went to Uganda to secure the interests of the Imperial British East Africa Company and, having made a treaty with the Kabaka of Buganda, restored order in his territory and the neighbouring chiefdoms. Further disorder, however, broke out, and the British Company withdrew; Lugard returned to England to further the efforts of the missionary and anti-slavery societies to persuade the Gladstone Government to undertake responsibility for the administration of Uganda. In 1894 Uganda was declared a British protectorate. Lugard's views on the development of East Africa were set out in his book, *The Rise of Our East African Empire* (2 vols., 1893).

In 1894 Lugard was engaged by the Royal Niger Company to assist in obtaining treaties with the local chieftains before the French could do so. He succeeded in this task, and in 1895 was appointed CB. In 1897 he was called upon by Joseph Chamberlain to undertake further work in West Africa and was appointed Commissioner for the hinterland of Nigeria. In 1900, when the British Government declared a protectorate over Northern and Southern Nigeria, Lugard was appointed High Commissioner of Northern Nigeria and given the temporary rank of brigadier-general. He was appointed KCMG in 1901. For six years he worked in Northern Nigeria, bringing the area under administrative control with the minimum use of force and with a realistic appreciation of the relations between his administration and the chiefs, as dependent rulers to be advised and controlled. In 1902-3, however, he had to resort to force against the Fulani tribe in spite of Colonial Office opposition and in 1906 he resigned.

In the following year, he became Governor of Hong Kong, was largely responsible for the foundation of Hong Kong University in 1911, and was appointed GCMG in that year. Then from 1912 to 1914 he became Governor of North and South Nigeria and, when the two protectorates were amalgamated in 1914, was made Governor-General of Nigeria, a post he held until 1919. While he held this office, Lugard gave substance to the policy with which his name will always be associated: the system of indirect rule. He believed firmly that administration of territories in West Africa and elsewhere should be based on the development of the traditional institutions of the native peoples, and that these institutions should be used to prevent the disintegration of native society and to educate the people for self-government.

After Lugard retired, he was sworn of the Privy Council in 1920 and two years later published *The Dual Mandate in British Tropical Africa*, a work which established him, both in Britain and abroad, as an authority on colonial government. From 1922 to 1936 he was a member of the Permanent Mandates Commission of the League of Nations, and in 1926 became Chairman of the International Institute of African Languages and Cultures. In 1928 he was raised to the peerage as Baron Lugard, of Abinger, Surrey.

Lugard's wife, Flora Louise Shaw, whom he had married in 1902, was also a colonial specialist. She had become well known as the head of the Colonial Department of *The Times* and in 1905 published a history of Northern Nigeria, *A Tropical Dependency*. She was appointed DBE in 1918. They had no children. Lugard had many honours and academic awards. He died at Abinger on 11 April 1945.

LUNN, SIR ARNOLD HENRY MOORE (1888-1974), pioneer of skiing, was born in Madras on 18 April 1888, the eldest son of (Sir) Henry Simpson Lunn, a medical missionary, and his wife, Ethel, daughter of Canon Thomas Moore. He was educated at Harrow and Balliol College, Oxford, where he was Secretary of the Union, edited the *Isis*, and founded the University Mountaineering Club and the Alpine Ski Club.

From 1908 he explored the high Alps and became expert on skis. A serious fall in 1909 on Cader Idris did not deter him, although it resulted in the permanent shortening of his right leg. During the First World War he worked in France with a Quaker ambulance unit and in Switzerland with Allied internees. In 1922 at Mürren he invented the modern slalom and obtained international and Olympic recognition of downhill and slalom racing and in 1924 he made the first ski ascent of the Eiger. He organized the first world championships in 1931 and introduced the skiing events to the Olympics in 1936, at which his elder son captained the British ski team. He represented Great Britain on the Federation Internationale de Ski (1928-49).

Lunn wrote a number of books on skiing, including *Alpine Skiing* (1921) and *The Story of Skiing* (1952). He also edited the *British Ski Year Book* from 1919 to 1971. During the Second World War he was a press correspondent in the Balkans, Chile, and Peru and was attached to the Ministry of Information.

Apart from his large number of publications on mountaineering and skiing he was also much concerned with the polemics of religious controversy in which he debated with such noteworthy opponents as J. B. S. HALDANE, G. G. Coulton, and Ronald KNOX. His publications in this field include *Roman Converts* (1924), *Science and the Supernatural* (1935), and *Is the Catholic Church Anti-Social?* (1946).

In 1952 Lunn was knighted and he received many honours from France, Switzerland, and Spain. An annual lecture is held in his memory under the auspices of the Ski Club of Great Britain and the Alpine Ski Club.

In 1913 he married Lady Mabel, daughter of the Revd the Hon. John Stafford Northcote, and sister of the third Earl of Iddesleigh; they had a daughter and two sons. Lady Mabel died in 1959, and in 1961 Sir Arnold married Phyllis, daughter of Oliver Needham Holt-Needham, who cared for him during the declining years of his life. He died on 2 June 1974 in London.

LUTYENS, SIR EDWIN LANDSEER (1869-1944), architect, was born in London on 29 March 1869, the eleventh of fourteen children of Capt. Charles Henry Augustus Lutyens of the 20th Foot, and his wife, Mary Gallway, who declined Sir Edwin Landseer's offer to adopt her eleventh child, but consented to him bearing the artist's names. Capt. Lutyens was a well-known painter of horses, whose great-grandfather had come to England from Schleswig-Holstein and acquired British nationality. A delicate child, 'Ned' was educated at home and there taught himself the elements of building and learnt to draw. At sixteen he studied at the school which was later to become the Royal College of Art, South Kensington, and in 1887 became the pupil of (Sir) Ernest George. He became a close friend of Herbert BAKER and came to admire the work of R. Norman Shaw, who designed houses in the Tudor and Jacobean styles. However, the principal influences on his work came from Renaissance architecture, with its dedication to mathematical relationships and the classical orders.

In 1897 he married Lady Emily, daughter of the first Earl of Lytton; they had one son and four daughters.

In 1896 Lutyens had built for Gertrude Jekyll a house in Surrey, Munstead Wood, and through her brother he was commissioned to design the British pavilion at the Paris Exhibition of 1900. The successful Munstead Wood was the first of many clever designs for country houses throughout Britain and for the restoration of a number of buildings. With Gertrude Jekyll's collaboration, he designed some beautiful gardens, which gave him the experience that he later put to good use in the design of the gardens of the Viceroy's House, New Delhi, where he incorporated Persian and European concepts of the garden to produce something wholly original.

Lutyens was elected FRIBA in 1906, and in 1908-9, as consulting architect to Hampstead Garden Suburb, he designed the churches and houses in the Square. In 1909-11 in South Africa he designed the Rand war memorial and the Johannesburg Art Gallery. His most notable work, however, was achieved when, in 1912-13, he became the architect for the government buildings in New Delhi. At his own suggestion, Herbert Baker was associated with him in this project and this ultimately resulted in the end of their friendship. The Viceroy, Lord Hardinge of Penshurst, selected Raisina Hill as the site for the viceregal house and, on Baker's advice, this hill was also accepted as the site for the secretariat buildings, in consequence of which the site for the house had to be moved back some distance. The outcome was that Lutyens's elegant building was obscured by the massive buildings which Baker designed to house the government

Lutyens (centre) and fellow members of the Delhi Town Planning Committee, Herbert Baker (right) and G. S. C. Swinton, survey the scene

offices and legislative assembly. In Lutyens's opinion this spoilt the whole aesthetic perfection of the original plans, and it became the cause of intense bitterness between him and Baker. Nevertheless, the Viceroy's House was one of the most beautiful creations in modern architecture and a brilliant blending of classical Renaissance style with Indian elements.

In 1917 Lutyens was appointed architect to the Imperial War Graves Commission and designed the basic war memorial adopted for many cemeteries; in 1919 he designed the Cenotaph erected in Whitehall. During the twenties he designed some fifty war memorials, including that to 'the Missing of the Somme' at Thiepval and the Mercantile Marine Memorial on Tower Hill, London.

It is impossible within the compass of this article to describe the many buildings designed by Lutyens. They include Brittanic House, Finsbury Circus (1920-2), the Midland Bank, Poultry (1924-37), the British Embassy, Washington (1926-9), and Campion Hall, Oxford (1934). He also collaborated in the construction of large blocks of flats in London including Grosvenor House, Park Lane. His magnificent design for Liverpool Catholic Cathedral (1929-45) could not be put into effect in post-war conditions and had to be modified.

Lutyens was elected ARA in 1913, RA in 1920, and was President from 1938 to 1944. He was knighted in 1918, appointed KCIE in 1930, and OM in 1942. He received many academic and other honours. Lutyens died in London on 1 January 1944 and his ashes were placed in St Paul's Cathedral. His third daughter, Elizabeth, became a successful composer, and his youngest daughter, Mary, a writer of fiction and biography.

LYTTON, SIR HENRY ALFRED (1865-1936), actor and doyen of the D'Oyly Carte Opera Company, whose original name was Henry Alfred Jones, was born in London on 3 January 1865, the only son of a jeweller, Henry Jones, and his second wife, Martha Lavinia Harris. He was educated at St Mark's School, Chelsea but ran away to become a professional actor.

In 1882 he made his first appearance at the Philharmonic Theatre, Islington, in the *Obstinate Bretons*, in the cast of which was his future wife, Louie, daughter of William Webber, her stage name being Louie Henri. Through her influence, he secured in 1884 an engagement with the D'Oyly Carte Company in the chorus of *Princess Ida*, appearing under the name of H. A. Henri. He and Louie were married in that year.

Early in 1887 he became understudy to George Grossmith, the elder and, a week after the opening of *Ruddigore*, had his chance as Robin Oakapple because Grossmith fell ill. He had a great success and, as a result, (Sir) W. S. Gilbert suggested that he should adopt the name Lytton. He then toured with the Company for several years until 1897, when he succeeded Grossmith as Ferdinand the Fifth in *His Majesty* at the Savoy Theatre.

From 1897 to 1899 he appeared in a number of revivals of Gilbert and Sullivan operas and made a name for himself in leading parts. After a brief but unsuccessful venture as a manager, he returned to the Savoy in 1899, and remained there until 1903, playing in several operas, including *The Pirates of Penzance* (1900) and *Iolanthe* (1901).

Then, from 1903 to 1908, Lytton appeared in a number of other plays in a variety of London theatres but, after he returned again to the Savoy in 1908, he played exclusively in Gilbert and Sullivan operas up to the time of his retirement in 1934. He was now the mainstay of the D'Oyly Carte Company and played leading parts in all the famous operas, from Ko-Ko in *The Mikado* to Jack Point, his favourite part, in *The Yeomen of the Guard*. Apparently Lytton could not read a note of music and his songs were learnt with the help of his wife, who played them over and over again until he had mastered them.

In 1930 he was knighted and, after the celebration of his stage jubilee in 1932, received a national testimonial signed by many famous names. He and Louie had two sons and two daughters. One son died in 1917 serving with the Royal Flying Corps.

In 1922 Lytton published *The Secrets of a Savoyard*, followed in 1933 by *A Wandering Minstrel*. He died in London on 15 August 1936.

M

Rose Macaulay, March 1958, photograph by Cecil Beaton

MACAULAY, DAME (EMILIE) ROSE (1881–1958), author, was born at Rugby on 1 August 1881, the second of the seven children of George Campbell Macaulay, an assistant master at Rugby, and his wife, Grace Mary, daughter of the Revd William John Conybeare. Her early years were spent in Italy, until in 1894 she went with two sisters to Oxford High School, and in 1900 to Somerville College, Oxford.

The first of her twenty-three novels, *Abbots Verney*, was published in 1906 and by 1914 she had written six more including *The Lee Shore*, which won first prize in a Hodder & Stoughton novel competition in 1912. She also published

books of poems. During the First World War she lived in London and did various wartime jobs, but also found time to write other novels, including *What Not* (1918).

Her reputation as a novelist was made, however, in the decade after the war, with a series of books which poked fun, with gentle irony, at the absurdities of post-war life. Among these are *Potterism* (1920), *Dangerous Ages* (1921), which won the Femina Vie Heureuse prize, *Told by an Idiot* (1923), *Orphan Island* (1924), *Crewe Train* (1926), and *Keeping up Appearances* (1928).

At this time, she was also writing lively articles for the press, and books of essays such as *A Casual Commentary* (1925), and *Catchwords and Claptrap* (1926). Later, she wrote more serious works, including *Some Religious Elements in English Literature* (1931), a biography of Milton, an anthology *The Minor Pleasures of Life* (1934), and *The Writings of E. M. Forster* (1938).

During the Second World War she served as a part-time ambulance driver in London and, when the war was over, began writing travel books, including *They Went to Portugal* (1946), *Fabled Shore* (1949), and *Pleasure of Ruins* (1953). In 1956 her final novel *The Towers of Trebizond* was awarded the James Tait Black memorial prize. During these years she also wrote prolifically for the *Times Literary Supplement*, the *Spectator*, the *New Statesman*, the *Observer*, and the *Listener*.

In 1951 she became an honorary Litt.D., Cambridge, and in 1958 was appointed DBE. She died suddenly in London on 30 October 1958. Three volumes of her letters were published posthumously.

MacCARTHY, SIR (CHARLES OTTO) DESMOND (1877–1952), literary and drama critic, was born on 20 May 1877 at Plymouth, the only son of Charles Desmond MacCarthy, sub-agent to the Bank of England, and his wife, Louise Joanne Wilhelmine von Chevallerie. He was educated at Eton and Trinity College, Cambridge where he was one of the 'Apostles' and graduated in 1897. He was a friend of G. E. MOORE, G. M. TREVELYAN, and Virginia and Vanessa Stephen (Virginia WOOLF and Vanessa BELL).

After leaving Cambridge, MacCarthy became what he described as a literary journalist, first as a freelance, and then in 1903 as drama critic of the *Speaker*. In this capacity, he covered the Vedrenne-Barker seasons at the Court Theatre and saw many of SHAW's plays. His reviews of these plays were collected in *The Court Theatre 1904-1907* (1907), and years later, in 1951, the notices on Shaw's plays were re-published as *Shaw*.

In 1906 he married Mary, daughter of F. W. Warre-Cornish, Vice-Provost of Eton; they had two sons and a daughter.

From 1907 to 1910 MacCarthy edited the *New Quarterly*, and in 1913 became drama critic of the *New Statesman*, a post which he held until 1928, combining it from 1920 to 1927 with that of Literary Editor. During the First World War he served with the Red Cross and was attached to the French Army. His impressions were published as *Experience* (1935).

In 1928 he succeeded Sir Edmund GOSSE as senior literary critic on the *Sunday Times* and continued to contribute reviews to that paper up to his death; his reviews were read and appreciated by a wide public. They were always based upon a thorough study of his subject, even where this involved careful research up to the last possible moment before publication. Lord David Cecil, in his preface to *Humanities* (1953), wrote that MacCarthy's 'greatest gift was the capacity to understand and expound some new, fresh vision of reality'. Above all else, he was eminently readable.

His portraits of Samuel Butler, Meredith, Henry JAMES, Shaw, CONRAD, and Ruskin are among his best works. From 1928 to 1933 he edited *Life and Letters*. Seven volumes of his collected works were published during his lifetime, including *Portraits* (1931), and after his death three more volumes were published in England and the USA.

MacCarthy was President of the PEN club in 1945; he was an honorary LL D of Aberdeen University (1932) and honorary Litt.D. (Cambridge, 1952); he was knighted in 1951. Lady MacCarthy was herself an able writer, who published *A Nineteenth Century Childhood* (1924) and a novel, *A Pier and a Band* (1918). Their daughter, Rachel, married Lord David Cecil. Desmond MacCarthy died in Cambridge on 7 June 1952.

MacDIARMID, HUGH (1892–1978), poet and author, whose real name was Christopher Murray Grieve, was born on 11 August 1892 at Langholm in Dumfriesshire, the elder son of James Grieve, a postman, and his wife Elizabeth, daughter of Andrew Graham, a farm labourer of Waterbeck. He was educated at Langholm Academy and began to write poetry while in his teens. He trained as a teacher in Edinburgh, but decided to leave teaching for journalism and, up to the outbreak of the First World War, worked on newspapers in Scotland and South Wales. He also joined the ILP and the Fabian Society and contributed articles to *New Age*.

He enlisted in 1915 and was sent out to Salonika a year later in the RAMC but was sent home with malaria in 1918. In that year he married Margaret Cunningham Thompson Skinner (Peggy); they had a son and a daughter. After demobilization in 1919 he resumed work as a journalist in Scotland, for a time on the *Montrose Review*. In 1923 he published *Annals of the Five Senses* consisting, for the most part, of verses written during the war.

In 1920–2 he edited three anthologies of contemporary Scottish poetry entitled *Northern Numbers*, and from 1920 onwards he became interested in the movement to revive Scots as a literary language and for his own work adopted the pen-name Hugh MacDiarmid. In this medium he published *Sangschaw* (1925), *Penny Wheep* (1926), and *A Drunk Man Looks at the Thistle* (1926).

MacDiarmid was one of the founders of the National Party

of Scotland in 1928, but was expelled from the party in 1933 and joined the Communist party a year later, only to be expelled from that party also in 1938, primarily because his main political interest was Scottish nationalism. However, he later rejoined the Communist party in 1954 and was Communist candidate for Kinross in 1964.

In 1932 MacDiarmid's first marriage ended in divorce; he already had a son by Valda Trevlyn Rowlands, and in 1934 they were married. During the years up to the outbreak of the Second World War, he and his wife lived in the Shetlands, and two volumes of poems including the two 'Hymns to Lenin' were published in 1931 and 1935.

During the war he was called up to work first in a factory, and later in the merchant navy; in 1945 he stood as an Independent Scottish Nationalist for Kelvingrove but was not elected. He had published the first of his autobiographical studies *Lucky Poet* in 1943; this included a 'Third Hymn to Lenin', and in 1950 he visited the Soviet Union. In the same year he was also granted a Civil List pension. He was now living at Biggar, Lanarkshire.

In 1957 he was awarded an honorary LL D by Edinburgh University; he was also honorary RSA. His *Collected Poems* appeared in 1962, and a further autobiographical study, *The Company I've Kept*, in 1966. He died in Edinburgh on 9 September 1978. A Sassenach can obtain some idea of his 'Scots' style from his poem 'Old Wife in High Spirits: In an Edinburgh Pub' which begins:

An auld wumman cam' in', a mere rickle o' banes, in a faded black dress
And a bonnet wi' beads o' jet rattlin' on it;

and ends:

A' I ken is weel-fed and weel-put-on though they be
Ninety per cent o' respectable folk never hae
As muckle life in their creeshy carcases frae beginnin' to end
As kythed in that wild auld carline that day!

MacDiarmid was the most talented Scottish dialect poet of his time.

MacDONALD, JAMES RAMSAY (1866–1937), politician and Prime Minister, was born at Lossiemouth, Morayshire, on 12 October 1866, the son of Anne Ramsay, a farm worker, and John MacDonald, a head ploughman. His mother and father never married. He went to the local school and, when he was sixteen, became a pupil teacher. Having a free run of the 'dominie's' bookshelves, he read avidly the works of Shakespeare, Carlyle, Ruskin, and Henry George, including his *Progress and Poverty*.

In 1885 he obtained employment in Bristol, where he became a member of the Social Democratic Federation. In 1886 he worked in London as an invoice-clerk, spending all his spare time on study, until, overworked and underfed, he was forced to return home when his health broke down. In the meantime he had joined the Fabian Society. From 1888 till 1891 he was private secretary to Thomas Lough, Gladstonian parliamentary candidate for West Islington, and in 1894 he became a member of the ILP and stood as Independent Labour candidate for Southampton in 1895, but was decisively defeated. He was now no longer poverty-stricken and liable to be unemployed, but able to earn a living by journalism.

In 1896 he married Margaret Ethel, daughter of John Hall Gladstone, FRS, a great-niece of Lord Kelvin; she and her father were active social workers. The marriage brought

MacDonald financial independence and enabled him to travel abroad with his wife. Through her, he also made new friends. In 1900 he became Secretary of the Labour Representation Committee (later the Labour party) and he held this post until 1912, when he became Treasurer. From 1901 to 1904 he was also a member of the LCC.

From 1906 to 1918 MacDonald was Labour MP for Leicester. He had already in the previous year published *Socialism and Society*, and in 1907 *Socialism* appeared; this established him as a theorist of the movement, with an authoritative preference for moderation rather than for, what he considered, the outdated tenets of Marxism. In 1911 he became Chairman of the Parliamentary Labour Group, but also in that year he had to face the tragedy of his wife's death, a loss which seriously affected his outlook, making him more introspective and aloof.

In the years leading up to the First World War there was considerable industrial strife, as well as international tension and political controversy. In the Commons, MacDonald strenuously defended the case for the workers, though he continued to counsel moderation, often at the expense of severe criticism from the extremist elements in the Labour movement. In 1912 he visited India as a member of the Royal Commission on the Public Services and his findings found a place later in *The Government of India* (1919).

MacDonald was opposed to Britain's entry into the First World War and he resigned his chairmanship of the Labour party when his colleagues refused to oppose the Liberal Government's demand for a war credit. However, once the country was involved, he thought every effort must be made to win. He was not a pacifist, but his attitude was grossly misunderstood and misrepresented, and he became increasingly unpopular and distrusted. For a short time in 1914-15 he was a member of a British ambulance unit attached to the Belgian army. He welcomed the first Russian revolution in 1917, and would have visited the provisional government of Kerensky and the moderates, but the crew of the ship, which would have taken him to Russia, refused to sail with him on board, and a contact that might possibly have strengthened the hand of the Russian moderates could not be made.

In August 1917 Arthur HENDERSON resigned from LLOYD GEORGE's War Cabinet and, for a time, Henderson and MacDonald worked together. In the 1918 election MacDonald was heavily defeated at West Leicester, but he continued to work for moderation in his party, and in 1920 succeeded in persuading the annual conferences of both wings of the party to reject Communism. In 1921 he was narrowly defeated in a by-election at East Woolwich, but in 1922 returned to Parliament as MP for the Aberavon division of Glamorganshire. He was at once re-elected Chairman of the Parliamentary Party.

After the general election of 1923, the Labour party had more seats than the Liberals and together they outnumbered the Conservatives. MacDonald, with no previous experience of ministerial office, was sworn of the Privy Council and became Prime Minister and Foreign Secretary. In spite of his lack of administrative experience, he proved to have considerable executive ability and, in the world of diplomacy, he demonstrated his skill in mediation by securing the acceptance by France and Germany of the Dawes plan for the settlement of the reparations problem. He also attended the League of Nations Assembly, the only British Prime Minister to do so. He was less successful in his negotiations with Soviet Russia and laid himself open to attack by both Liberals

and Conservatives by agreeing to a treaty which included a loan to Russia.

The first Labour Government was brought down by a muddle of which its opponents were able to take advantage. Under MacDonald's orders, the Attorney-General dropped the prosecution of J. R. Campbell for incitement to mutiny arising from his letter in the *Workers' Weekly* urging the army not to shoot. The prosecution need never have been undertaken but the opposition were able to attack the decision to withdraw it as political interference with justice. The Government was defeated and, at the ensuing election, the suspicion that Labour was sympathetic to Communism was further exacerbated by the publication of a letter allegedly written by Zinoviev, President of the Communist International, to the British Communist party, suggesting a number of seditious activities. The Conservatives, led by BALDWIN, had an overwhelming victory.

MacDonald's own reputation did not suffer. In fact, his influence with his party was increased, and in 1925 the Labour party conference once more emphatically repudiated Communism. In 1926 he did what he could to prevent the general strike, but felt bound to support the strikers when he failed to avert 'direct action'. He played a leading part in drafting the party manifesto *Labour and the Nation* (1928) and, in the 1929 general election, was returned as MP for the Seaham division of Durham and his party, with 287 seats, was for the first time the strongest party in Parliament.

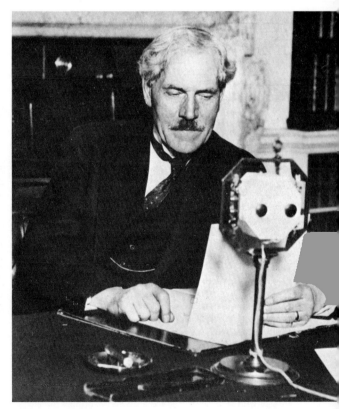

Ramsay MacDonald broadcasting from the Cabinet Room, 10 Downing Street, August 1931

Although Arthur Henderson now became Foreign Secretary, MacDonald's main interest continued to be foreign affairs. After meeting President Hoover, the first British Prime Minister to visit the United States, he succeeded in reviving the idea of a naval conference and, when it was held in London in 1930, an agreement was reached between Britain, the USA, and Japan which appeared to promise genuine disarmament. He also presided over the first Indian Round Table Conference of 1930.

In domestic affairs, however, his Government was beset by economic problems. Confronted by a serious financial crisis, it was necessary to make severe cuts in public expenditure; the Cabinet could not agree on a proposal to reduce payments to the unemployed, and MacDonald resigned. George V, after consultation with Sir Herbert SAMUEL and Baldwin, asked him to reconsider this decision, and MacDonald agreed to form a National Government with the support of the two other parties. Some of his colleagues, notably Philip SNOWDEN and J. H. THOMAS, supported him but the bulk of the Labour party rejected MacDonald's lead and he was at once superseded as party leader by Arthur Henderson.

The National Government won support at the general election of 1931 but, within a few months, the administration, headed by MacDonald, had become, in effect, Conservative. The main body of the Labour party, particularly its younger leaders such as Aneurin BEVAN, never forgave him for his subservience to his political opponents. Snowden left the coalition in 1932, when the Government reached preferential tariff agreements at the Ottawa Conference. The Prime Minister continued to be mainly concerned with foreign affairs, and Stanley Baldwin and Neville CHAMBERLAIN really decided domestic policy. MacDonald, personally, was put under considerable strain by the growing menace of Fascism and Nazism and he had a hand in drafting the 1935 White Paper on National Defence, which heralded a programme of rearmament. His former colleagues in the Labour party continued to attack him remorselessly and, in the summer of 1935, he resigned the premiership and became Lord President of the Council in a Government led by Stanley Baldwin.

He was defeated at Seaham in November 1935 but returned in January 1936 as MP for the Scottish Universities. He died suddenly on a sea voyage on 9 November 1937. He received a number of academic honours but, although he was on very good terms with King George V, he consistently refused any national honour. He was survived by two sons and three daughters. His younger son, Malcolm, had a distinguished political career, and held a number of ministerial and other posts in the public service.

McGOWAN, HARRY DUNCAN, first BARON McGowan (1874–1961), business man, was born in Glasgow on 3 June 1874, the only son of Harry McGowan, a brass fitter, and his wife, Agnes, daughter of Richard Wilson. He was educated at Hutchesontown School and Allan Glen's School, Glasgow, and at fifteen joined Nobel's Explosives Company as an office boy. Without influence, training, or capital, he worked his way up to professional manager. In 1903 he married Jean Boyle, daughter of William Young, of Paisley; they had two sons and two daughters.

Between 1909 and 1911 he played a leading part in constructing Canadian Explosives Ltd., which eventually became the largest chemical business in Canada. During the First World War he carried out a merger of almost the entire British explosives industry, and was closely concerned in a similar comprehensive merger of the British dyestuffs indus-

try. In 1918 he became Chairman and Managing Director of Explosives Trade Ltd. (later, in 1920, Nobel Industries Ltd.). In 1919 he joined the board of the British Dyestuffs Corporation.

His aim in forming Nobel Industries was to move resources out of explosives into more profitable peace-time investments. In 1926 he succeeded in agreeing with Sir Alfred MOND upon a merger which brought into existence Imperial Chemical Industries Ltd. When Mond (Lord Melchett) died in 1930, McGowan became Chairman and sole Managing Director of ICI.

In 1937 his dictatorial methods antagonized his board and they tried to supplant him with the second Lord Melchett, but Melchett had a heart attack and McGowan in consequence seemed indispensable; he remained Chairman until 1950. His most important contribution to the British chemical industry was to see what needed doing and to have the courage and nerve to do it.

He was appointed KBE in 1918 and created a baron in 1937. McGowan died in London on 13 July 1961.

McINDOE, SIR ARCHIBALD HECTOR (1900–1960), plastic surgeon, was born in Dunedin, New Zealand, on 4 May 1900, the second of the four children of John McIndoe, a printer, and his wife, Mabel Hill. He was educated at Otago High School and University, qualifying MB, Ch.B, in 1924. In that year he married Adonia, daughter of Thomas Aitken; they had two daughters. After studying as a post-graduate at the Mayo Clinic and obtaining his MS (Rochester), he came to London in 1930 and joined his cousin, Sir Harold Gillies, who had gained a remarkable reputation as a plastic surgeon during the First World War. He passed his FRCS (England) in 1932.

In the same year, McIndoe was appointed General Surgeon to the Hospital for Tropical Diseases and, by the time the Second World War broke out, he was recognized as a plastic surgeon of great promise, who had published a number of papers on his speciality. At the time, Sir Harold Gillies was consultant to the Royal Air Force, as well as plastic surgeon to a number of London hospitals. He arranged for McIndoe to become consultant in plastic surgery to the RAF, and McIndoe organized a centre at Queen Victoria Hospital, East Grinstead, which soon became a model to the rest of the country.

At East Grinstead, hundreds of badly burned airmen had their wounds treated, and were not only restored to bodily health, but were rehabilitated psychologically. The hospital was so well known that airmen going into action had the certainty that, however seriously injured they might be, there was a first-class medical service, which would do everything possible to assist them to recover. Patients at East Grinstead founded their own club 'McIndoe's Guinea Pigs', which continued to meet annually after the war.

McIndoe was appointed CBE in 1944 and knighted in 1947; he also received many foreign decorations. He was Vice-Chairman of the Royal College of Surgeons in 1957–9 and raised a huge sum of money for the college. His staff at East Grinstead helped to train plastic surgeons from all over the world. With Gillies he helped to found the British Association of Plastic Surgeons, and became its President in 1949. He received honorary doctorates from many countries and was much admired in the USA, where he was a frequent visitor.

In 1954, he and his first wife having been divorced, he married Mrs Constance Belchem, daughter of John Hutton,

Archibald McIndoe (seated, centre) celebrates Christmas with patients and staff, Queen Victoria Hospital, East Grinstead

a member of Lloyd's. McIndoe died in London on 12 April 1960 and his ashes were buried in the RAF church of St Clement Danes, an honour unique to a civilian.

MACKAY, JAMES LYLE, first EARL OF INCHCAPE (1852–1932), shipowner, was born at Arbroath, Tayside, on 11 September 1852, the youngest son of James Mackay, a shipowner, and his wife, Deborah, daughter of Alexander Lyle, a Canadian. When he was ten, his father was drowned at sea, and his mother died two years later. He went to school at Elgin Academy and left at fourteen to work first in a lawyer's office and then as apprentice to a rope-maker. When he was nineteen, he went to London and worked with a firm concerned with shipping interests.

In 1874 he was appointed to the staff of Mackinnon Mackenzie & Co., Calcutta, and four years later was posted to Bombay as agent for the British India Steam Navigation Co. There he obtained wide experience of shipping and commerce in the Persian Gulf and East Africa and became a partner in the firm. In 1883 he returned to Calcutta, and in the same year married Jane Paterson, daughter of James Shanks, a leading Scottish engineer; they had one son and four daughters. In due course, he became senior partner in Mackinnon Mackenzie & Co. By mergers with other companies, he became a leading entrepreneur in the jute, tea, and coal industries of Bengal, the cotton and wool trade of Madras, and the seaborne trade between India and Burma, and the Persian Gulf and East Africa. From 1890 to 1893 he was President of the Bengal Chamber of Commerce, served on the Legislative Council during 1891–3, and was closely concerned with the problem of stabilizing the Indian currency.

In 1893 Mackay returned to take charge of the London office of the British India Co. and was soon taking a leading part in the management of a number of other companies, which led to mergers with many shipping companies and the establishment of the P & O Co. as the pre-eminent shipping company controlling commerce with the East. He was three times President of the UK Chamber of Shipping (1903, 1918, 1919).

He was also concerned with work on behalf of the British Government: he negotiated a commercial treaty with China

(1901–2), served on the Council of India (1897–1911), the Imperial Defence Committee (1917) and the Geddes Economy Committee (1921–2), and carried out, for the Exchequer, the difficult task of selling off the fleet of ships acquired during the First World War.

Mackay was appointed KCIE in 1894, GCMG in 1902, and KCSI in 1910. In 1911 he was raised to the peerage as Baron Inchcape, became a viscount and GCSI in 1924, and was advanced to earl in 1929. The most prominent figure of his time in British shipping, he was an ardent advocate of free trade and deeply resented any encroachment by the state into the life of the individual. In 1928 his third daughter died in an attempt to fly the Atlantic. Lord Inchcape died on board his yacht *Rover* at Monaco on 23 May 1932.

McKENNA, REGINALD (1863–1943), politician and banker, was born in London on 6 July 1863, the fifth son of William Columban McKenna, a civil servant, and his wife, Emma, daughter of Charles Hanby. He was educated in France and Germany, at King's College School, London, and Trinity Hall, Cambridge, where he was a scholar, senior optime in the mathematical tripos of 1885, and a rowing blue. In 1887 he was called to the Bar (Inner Temple).

From 1895 to 1918 McKenna was Liberal MP for North Monmouthshire, and when Campbell-Bannerman became Prime Minister in 1905, he appointed McKenna Financial Secretary to the Treasury. Within a year, he was sworn of the Privy Council and became President of the Board of Education (1907–8). His administrative ability was impressive, and in 1908 the new Prime Minister, ASQUITH, appointed him First Lord of the Admiralty. A few weeks later, he married Pamela, younger daughter of Sir Herbert Jekyll; they had two sons.

His early education abroad had convinced him of the likelihood of war between France and Germany and the possible embroilment of Britain. In co-operation with FISHER, the redoubtable First Sea Lord, he fought in the Cabinet and won the battle for the construction of eight *Dreadnoughts* in 1909 and five each year in 1910–11. The Agadir crisis, however, brought him into conflict with Lord HALDANE and the War Office, regarding the strategy to be followed in case of war and, when he refused to give way, Asquith removed him from the Admiralty and appointed him Home Secretary. From 1911 to 1915 McKenna was concerned with such problems as the disestablishment of the Welsh Church and the intransigence of the militant suffragettes. When the First World War broke out, he was responsible for internal security and served on the munitions committee set up in October 1914.

When Asquith was compelled to form a coalition with the Conservatives in 1915, McKenna succeeded LLOYD GEORGE as Chancellor of the Exchequer, and held that office during the most critical years of the war. In his first budget, he increased income tax, imposed an excess profits tax, and imposed duties on articles such as motor cars, clocks, and watches, which were regarded as luxuries. These, the famous McKenna duties, were intended to be temporary, but they were continued when the war ended. McKenna also invoked a patriotic campaign for investment in war loans, and was able to obtain American contracts for war supplies, by guaranteeing payment through handing over a large sum in insurance company securities and gold from the Bank of England. In his second budget, he further increased income tax and imposed an amusements tax.

McKenna was opposed to conscription on the ground that the country could not afford to maintain an army of the size envisaged, and offered to resign when Asquith and the Cabinet decided against him. He was persuaded to stay on at the Treasury until Asquith was superseded by Lloyd George in the leadership of the Coalition Government. McKenna and Lloyd George had been bitter opponents for years and McKenna could not agree to serve under the 'Welsh wizard'. In the 1918 election he was defeated and retired from political life.

He now embarked upon a new career in the City of London, and in 1919 became Chairman of the Midland Bank. When in 1922 BONAR LAW offered to appoint him again as Chancellor, he refused the invitation and, although he would have accepted when the offer was renewed in 1923, he could not find a safe seat in Parliament. He strenuously opposed, as did Maynard KEYNES, the settlement of Britain's war debt to the USA on the terms negotiated by Stanley BALDWIN and Montagu NORMAN. He enjoyed his work as a banker and made a reputation as a skilful exponent of his views on monetary policy. He always refused to write a treatise on the subject, but a selection of his speeches was published in 1928 as *Post-War Banking Policy*. He died in London on 6 September 1943.

MACKENZIE, SIR (EDWARD MONTAGUE) COMPTON (1883-1972), writer, was born on 17 January 1883 at West Hartlepool, the eldest child of Edward Compton (Mackenzie), actor-manager of the Compton Comedy Company, and his wife, Virginia, daughter of Hezekiah Linthicum Bateman, an actor-manager, of Baltimore. Fay Compton, the actress, was one of Compton Mackenzie's three sisters. He was educated at St Paul's School, and Magdalen College, Oxford. As a youth, he travelled with his parents, meeting actors, artists, and writers. He could have become an actor himself, but he preferred to write, and was encouraged to do so by Logan Pearsall Smith.

In 1905 he married Faith, daughter of the Revd Edward Daniel Stone, of Abingdon; they had no children.

His first book of poems was published in 1907, followed by his novel *Carnival* in 1912 and *Sinister Street* in 1913. In 1900-1, he served in the 1st Hertfordshire Regiment and in

1915 was with the Royal Naval Division at the Dardanelles. He was invalided, and in 1916 was Military Control Officer in Athens and, in the following year, Director of the Aegean Intelligence Service. His war service was the subject of *Gallipoli Memories* (1929), *Athenian Memories* (1931), and *Greek Memories* (1932). The last had to be withdrawn as it offended against the Official Secrets Act; it was reissued in 1940. He also satirized the Secret Service in *Water on the Brain* (1933).

Mackenzie was a great lover of islands. In 1927 *Vestal Fire* appeared, followed in 1928 by *Extraordinary Women*; these were based on Capri and the other writers among whom he was living there. From 1931 to 1935 he was literary critic of the *Daily Mail*, and from 1923 to 1961 Editor of the *Gramophone*. During the Second World War, Mackenzie lived on the island of Barra and published in 1947 *Whisky Galore*, an exciting and hilarious account of the wreck of a ship loaded with thousands of cases of whisky. This story was made into a very successful film (1948).

Mackenzie wrote many other novels and some delightful children's books, as well as plays and his autobiography *My Life and Times* (10 vols., 1963-71). He was a cat-lover and was Life President of the Siamese Cat Club. He was also President of the Croquet Association (1954-66), the Songwriters' Guild (1956), the Poetry Society (1961-4), and the Dickens Fellowship (1939-46). From 1931 to 1934 he was Rector of Glasgow University.

He was appointed OBE in 1919, knighted in 1952, and held a number of honorary degrees. In 1962, after the death of his first wife two years earlier, he married Christina, daughter of Malcolm MacSween, of Tarbert, Harris; she died in 1963, and in 1965 he married her younger sister, Lilian (Lily). Mackenzie died in Edinburgh on 30 November 1972.

MACKINTOSH, HAROLD VINCENT, first VISCOUNT MACKINTOSH OF HALIFAX (1891-1964), business man and public servant, was born in Halifax on 8 June 1891, the eldest of the three sons of John Mackintosh, owner of a confectionery business, and his wife, Violet, daughter of James Taylor of Halifax. He was educated at Halifax New School, and left in 1909 to work in the family's factory in Germany.

During the First World War, in which he served in the RNVR, he married in 1916 Constance Emily, daughter of Edgar Cooper Stoneham, a civil servant; they had a daughter and a son. On the death of his father in 1920, he became Chairman of the family business—it flourished, primarily because Mackintosh insisted on good quality in its products, but also because he was an advocate of large-scale advertising. After they had taken over the chocolate business of A. J. Caley in Norwich, Mackintosh decided to make his home in Norfolk.

He had very wide interests besides his business. He was keenly interested in the savings movement and was involved in the negotiations which led to the amalgamation in 1928 of two building societies into 'The Halifax'. Throughout the Second World War he was active in the war savings campaign, handling the publicity side in particular and introducing War Savings Weeks. In 1943 he became Chairman of the National Savings Committee, and in 1946 its President.

Mackintosh was also a staunch Methodist, and in 1924-5 was President of the National Sunday School Union; he was also a Vice-President of the National Council of the YMCA. In 1926 he became secretary of a campaign in Yorkshire for cancer research and in 1936 was chairman; he helped to raise the funds for setting up Cancer Research Centres at Leeds and Sheffield Universities.

As a recreation, he took up farming and won many prizes with his Jersey cows. He was President of the Yorkshire Agricultural Society in 1928-9 and of the Royal Norfolk Agricultural Society in 1960.

He was active in promoting the new University of East Anglia and would have been its first Chancellor but died before he could be officially installed. He was a collector of early Staffordshire pottery and of paintings, particularly works of the Norwich school. In 1938 he published *Early English Figure Pottery*. From 1959 to 1964 he was a member of the Arts Council.

He was appointed a JP in 1925 and Deputy Lieutenant for the West Riding in 1945. He was knighted in 1922, created a baronet in 1935, baron in 1948, and viscount in 1957. Mackintosh died in Norwich on 27 December 1964.

McLAREN, HENRY DUNCAN, second BARON ABER-CONWAY (1879-1953), industrialist and creator of Bodnant Garden, was born in Barnes on 16 April 1879, the eldest child of Charles Benjamin Bright McLaren, later first Baron Aberconway, and his wife, Laura Elizabeth, daughter of Henry Davis Pochin, of Bodnant, Denbighshire. He was educated at Eton and Balliol College, Oxford and in 1905 was called to the Bar (Lincoln's Inn) but, unlike his father, he never practised.

In 1906 he was elected Liberal MP for West Staffordshire and until 1910 was Parliamentary Private Secretary to LLOYD GEORGE. He was defeated in the January 1910 election but in December was elected for the Bosworth division of Leicestershire, which he represented until 1922. Also in 1910, he married Christabel Mary Melville, daughter of Sir Melville Leslie Macnaghten, chief of the Criminal Investigation Department; they had two daughters and three sons.

During the First World War he was a Director at the Ministry of Munitions and, after the war, succeeded his father as Chairman of John Brown & Co. He had many other business interests including directorships of the National Provincial Bank and the London Assurance. His main business interest, however, was in his grandfather's family firm, H. D. Pochin & Co., producers of china clay. In 1932 he arranged for the amalgamation of a number of china clay companies and became Chairman of English Clays Lovering Pochin & Co. Ltd. In 1934 he succeeded to the peerage on the death of his father.

Aberconway was a man of many hobbies; he was a keen and knowledgeable collector of antique furniture, ornaments, and pictures. But his greatest interest was in gardening, and at Bodnant, with the help of his mother, he created one of the finest and most beautiful gardens in the British Isles, laid out with consummate artistry, taking advantage of the superb site with a small stream at the bottom of a deep ravine. In 1949 he gave the garden to the National Trust and it gives pleasure to thousands of visitors every year. Extremely knowledgeable as a plantsman as well as a designer, he was between the wars one of the pioneers among hybridists of rhododendrons. From 1931 until his death he was President of the Royal Horticultural Society.

Lord Aberconway died at Bodnant on 23 May 1953. He was succeeded by his eldest son, who shared his father's great love of horticulture, following him in the running of Bodnant for the National Trust and later in the presidency of the RHS.

MACLEOD, IAIN NORMAN (1913-1970), politician, was born at Skipton, Yorkshire, on 11 November 1913, the eldest son of Norman Macleod, a general practitioner, and his wife, Annabel, daughter of Rhoderick Ross, a doctor on the Isle of Lewis. He was educated at Fettes, and Gonville and Caius College, Cambridge, where he formed the university Bridge Club and became its President (1935).

For a time he worked with Thomas de la Rue, but made more money at the bridge table, and in 1939 he joined the Royal Fusiliers as a private, was commissioned in the Duke of Wellington's Regiment, and badly wounded in France. After recovering he landed in France again on D-Day and served there until the end of the war.

After demobilization in 1946, Macleod joined the Conservative Parliamentary Secretariat and specialized in home affairs in the research department. He continued to earn a living by his skill at bridge, writing a weekly bridge column for the *Sunday Times*. In 1950 he was elected MP for Enfield West, a seat which he held until his death. He made a deep impression on Winston CHURCHILL and his colleagues when he vigorously attacked a speech made by Aneurin BEVAN on the National Health Bill in 1952. Six weeks later, the Prime Minister appointed him Minister of Health, and he was sworn of the Privy Council.

In 1941 he had married Evelyn Hester, daughter of the Revd Gervase Vanneck Blois, Rector of Hanbury, Worcestershire, whose first husband, Mervyn Charles Mason, had been killed in 1940; they had a son and a daughter. Shortly after Macleod became a minister, his wife was struck down by meningitis and polio but, partially recovering, continued to help him in his political work. Macleod's own health was poor as he was suffering from a form of rheumatoid arthritis, aggravated by his war wound.

In April 1955 Anthony EDEN became Prime Minister; in his December Cabinet reshuffle, he appointed Macleod to be Minister of Labour and National Service. In this post he had every opportunity of demonstrating his skill as a negotiator and he became a national figure when he crossed swords with Hugh GAITSKELL and defeated Frank Cousins in the bus strike of 1958.

Harold Macmillan became Prime Minister in 1959 and transferred Macleod to the Colonial Office. There, in spite of violent opposition from the Conservative right wing, Macleod set about speeding up the move towards independence of the African colonies. He released Dr Banda and Jomo Kenyatta from gaol and stuck to his progressive policy, although he fully understood that his persistence would probably damage his own political career. In consequence, it can be said that Britain's peaceful withdrawal from her colonial responsibilities in Africa was his greatest achievement.

Macmillan, however, perturbed at the dissension being aroused within his party, particularly by the problems of Northern Rhodesia (Zambia), decided in 1961 to move Macleod again and he became leader of the House of Commons and Chairman of the Conservative party. He showed himself to be a most effective leader of the House but, when Douglas-Home took over from Macmillan, Macleod refused to serve under him as he had supported R. A. Butler's claims to the office and committed himself not to accept office from Douglas-Home.

He filled the hiatus in his political career by becoming Editor of the *Spectator* from 1963 to 1965. After the 1964 election he agreed to join the Shadow Cabinet but he appears to have decided at some time before Douglas-Home resigned in 1965 that he would not enter the lists for the succession.

Iain Macleod, by Vicky

He supported the claims of Edward Heath, who appointed him Shadow Chancellor of the Exchequer and, after the 1970 election, he held that office for only two weeks before he was taken ill with appendicitis; he died of a heart attack in No. 11 Downing Street a few weeks later on 20 July 1970.

In 1952 he published *Bridge is an Easy Game* and in 1961 his life of *Neville Chamberlain*. R. A. (Lord) Butler, who was a close colleague of Macleod, felt that 'by his death the people of this country suffered a rather more terrible loss than they imagined'.

MacNEICE, (FREDERICK) LOUIS (1907–1963), poet and writer, was born in Belfast on 12 September 1907, the youngest of three children of the Revd John Frederick Mac-Neice, then Rector of Holy Trinity, Belfast, and his wife, Elizabeth Margaret, daughter of Martin Clesham, of Galway. He was educated at Marlborough College, where he was a scholar, and Merton College, Oxford, where he obtained firsts in Classical Mods. in 1928 and Greats in 1930. He also edited *Oxford Poetry* with Stephen Spender, and published his first book of poems, *Blind Fireworks*.

From 1930 to 1936 he was lecturer in classics at Birmingham University and, although he carried out his duties conscientiously, his main interest was in writing. He made a number of friends at Birmingham who influenced his later career, including Professor E. R. Dodds, who later became Professor of Greek at Oxford, and R. D. Smith with whom he was later associated in the BBC. His second volume of *Poems* was published in 1935 and his translation of Aeschylus' *Agamemnon* in 1936.

In 1930 he married Giovanna Marie Thérèse Babette (Mariette) Ezra, stepdaughter of (Sir) John Beazley. Five years later she suddenly left him. Disconsolate, he visited Spain with Anthony Blunt in 1936, and later that year took a post as lecturer in Greek at Bedford College, London, and then went to Iceland with W. H. Auden, a venture about which they subsequently wrote in *Letters from Iceland* (1937).

Although MacNeice had left-wing sympathies, he was never a Communist. While working in London he published, in 1938, another volume of poems, *The Earth Compels*, two prose works, *I Crossed the Minch* and *Zoo*, a critical book, *Modern Poetry*, and began his *Autumn Journal*, published in 1939, a long lyrical meditation on his childhood and formative years.

Early in 1940 MacNeice became a lecturer at Cornell University in the USA, but he returned to England, was rejected for active service, and joined the BBC Features Department in 1941. He produced a series of notable programmes and radio plays, and, in the course of the war, published three more books of poetry, *The Last Ditch* (1940), *Plant and Phantom* (1941), and *Springboard* (1944). He also wrote *The Poetry of W. B. Yeats* (1941).

In 1942 he married Hedli Anderson, the actress and singer. His son by his first marriage came to live with him, and in 1943 a daughter was born. He continued to work for the BBC after the war, and undertook a number of assignments abroad. He published more poems *Holes in the Sky* (1948) and *Collected Poems 1925–1948* (1949). In 1950 he took leave from the BBC and spent some months as Director of the British Institute in Athens.

He continued to publish poetry and other works. In 1952 appeared *Ten Burnt Offerings*, in 1954 *Autumn Sequel*. This last poem reflected his growing melancholy and restlessness at the passage of time and his deep distress at the death of his close friend Dylan Thomas. He published nothing further until 1957 when *Visitations* appeared. In 1960 his second wife left him, and in 1961 he left the BBC. He delivered the Clark lectures in 1963, published as *Varieties of Parable* in 1965. His autobiography *The Strings are False* was published posthumously in 1965. In 1958 he was appointed CBE. He died in London on 3 September 1963.

MAFFEY, JOHN LOADER, first Baron Rugby (1877–1969), public servant, was born at Rugby on 1 July 1877, the younger son of Thomas Maffey, a commercial traveller, and his wife, Mary Penelope, daughter of John Loader, of Thame. He was educated at Rugby and Christ Church, Oxford, where he was a scholar. He entered the Indian Civil Service in 1899, transferred to the Political Department in 1905, and had a distinguished career on the North-West Frontier. In 1907 he married Dorothy, daughter of Charles Long Huggins, of Hadlow Grange, Sussex; they had two sons and a daughter.

In 1908 he served with the Mohmand field force; from 1909 to 1912 he was Political Agent, Kyber, during 1914–15 Deputy Commissioner, Peshawar, and in 1919 Chief Political Officer with the forces in Afghanistan. During 1915–16 he was Deputy Secretary in the Foreign and Political Department of the Government of India, and from 1916 to 1920 Private Secretary to the Viceroy, Lord Chelmsford. Writing in the *DNB*, Sir Gilbert Laithwaite, who at one time held the same office, described Maffey's tact and experience as of great importance when E. S. Montagu, Secretary of State for India, visited the country to consider proposals which led to constitutional reforms (1918). Maffey was also Chief Secretary to the Duke of Connaught during his visit in 1920–1.

While Maffey was Chief Commissioner, North-West Frontier Province (1921–4), he had to deal with the capture of Mollie Ellis, a girl held to ransom by marauding tribesmen who had killed her mother. Knowing that an attempt to secure her release by force might lead to her murder, he asked Lilian Agnes Starr, of the Peshawar Medical Mission, to negotiate with the kidnappers. Miss Starr was successful in getting the girl released without payment of any ransom.

In 1924 the advice of Maffey, as an expert on frontier problems, was overruled by the British Government, although it had been accepted by the Governor-General's Council and the Commander-in-Chief, India. In consequence Maffey resigned from the ICS.

In 1926 he was appointed Governor-General of the Sudan, and for the next seven years guided the country through a period of development, which included the Gezira Scheme. From 1933 to 1937 Maffey served as Permanent Under-Secretary of State for the Colonies and, on the outbreak of the Second World War, was appointed the first British Representative in Eire. Throughout the war and up to 1949, he held this onerous post with great success, steering a tactful course between Dublin and Belfast, and earning the friendship of DE VALERA without sacrificing the respect of Ulster.

Maffey was appointed CIE (1916), CSI (1920), KCVO (1921), KCMG (1931), KCB (1934), and GCMG (1935). He was raised to the peerage in 1947. Maffey, Lord Rugby, died at Bungay, Suffolk, on 20 April 1969.

MALLORY, GEORGE LEIGH (1886–1924), mountaineer, was born at Mobberley, Cheshire, on 18 June 1886, the elder son of the Revd Herbert Leigh Mallory, Rector of Mobberley, and his wife, Annie Beridge Jebb. He was educated as a scholar at Winchester and an exhibitioner of Magdalene College, Cambridge. While at Cambridge he abandoned his intention of taking holy orders and decided to become a schoolmaster. In 1909 he published a study of James Boswell, and a year later was appointed assistant master at Charterhouse. In 1914 Mallory married Ruth, daughter of an architect, Hugh Thackeray Turner, of Godalming; they had two daughters and a son.

During the First World War he served in the army; he returned to Charterhouse in 1919, but in 1923 accepted a post at Cambridge as lecturer and Assistant-Secretary for the Board of Extra-Mural Studies.

While he was still a schoolboy, Mallory had become an ardent climber, both on rock in England and Wales, and on snow and ice in the high Alps. By 1920 he was recognized as one of the leading mountaineers of his day and was invited to be in the first party to attempt to climb Mount Everest in 1921. The main reconnaissance and survey of the approaches to the mountain were made by Mallory and G. H. Bullock with native porters, and it was Mallory who first saw and named the 'western cwm'.

In 1922 Mallory was one of the party who attempted to reach the summit by the route he had pioneered in the previous year. In company with E. F. Norton and Dr H. T. Somervell, he reached the record height of 26,985 ft., but the party were then forced to return by the onset of the monsoon.

In his third attempt on Everest in 1924, Mallory was again one of a party who carefully prepared for the expedition, but found the weather a formidable obstacle. High winds and storms swept the mountain, and twice the whole party had to retire to their base-camp. It was decided, however, to make further attempts, and on the first effort to reach the summit,

Mallory and Norton on Mallory's last Everest expedition, May 1924

Mallory, together with Norton and Somervell, reached 28,126 ft. before they had to retreat. Four days later, on 8 June, Mallory set out again with a young climber A. C. Irvine, of Merton College, Oxford, to make a final attempt. They were seen at a point some 800 ft. below the summit. Then clouds hid them from sight and they were never seen again.

Mallory will always be remembered by other climbers as the man who, when asked why he wanted to climb Everest, answered, 'Because it's there'.

His younger brother, SIR TRAFFORD LEIGH-MALLORY was born at Mobberley, Cheshire, on 11 July 1892. He was educated at Haileybury and Magdalene College, Cambridge, and served with the Royal Flying Corps during the First World War. He was granted a permanent commission, and by 1937 was commanding No. 12 (fighter) group of the RAF, a group which gained great distinction in the decisive 'Battle of Britain' in 1940. In 1943 Leigh-Mallory was appointed Air Chief Marshal and KCB, and on 15 October 1944 was killed when the aeroplane in which he was travelling to take up a new appointment as Allied Air Commander-in-Chief, South East Asia Command, crashed in the mountains west of Grenoble.

MALLOWAN, SIR MAX EDGAR LUCIEN (1904–

1978), archaeologist, was born on 6 May 1904 in London, the eldest son of Frederick Mallowan, formerly in the Austrian Horse Artillery, and his wife, Marguerite Duvivier of Paris, a poetess. He was educated at Lancing and New College, Oxford. The warden, H. A. L. FISHER, recommended him to C. Leonard WOOLLEY as an assistant at the excavations at Ur of the Chaldees. While working there with Woolley, he met Agatha CHRISTIE, and in 1930 they married.

After five years at Ur (1925-30), he spent two years (1931-2) on the staff of the British Museum expedition to Ninevah. During the next six years he directed excavations on behalf of the Museum and the British School of Archaeology at Arpachiyah, Iraq, at Chagar Bazar in North Syria, and at Brak and other sites in the Balikh Valley, where he discovered the third millennium shrines called the Eye Temple and the Palace of Naram-Sin.

During the Second World War he served with RAFVR, and was posted to the British Military Administration in Tripolitania (1943-4). In 1947 he returned to Iraq as Director of the British School of Archaeology, a post which he held until 1961. His most important work at Nimrud revealed a wealth of art treasures and inscriptions, which he described in his classic *Nimrud and Its Remains* (2 vols., 1966). In 1947 he also became Professor in Western Asiatic Archaeology at London University. In 1962 he gave up this post and was elected a Fellow of All Souls, Oxford. He became FBA in 1954. His book, *Twenty-five Years of Mesopotamian Discovery, 1932-1956* was published in 1956.

Mallowan was President of the British Institute of Persian Studies (1961), Vice-President of the British Academy (1961-2); he was appointed CBE in 1960, and knighted in 1968. He was a Trustee of the British Museum (1973-8), Editor of *Iraq* (1948-71), Advisory Editor of *Antiquity*, and Editor of Penguin Books Near Eastern and Western Asiatic series (1948-65).

His wife Agatha Christie, the detective novelist, died in 1976 and in 1977 he married Barbara, daughter of Capt. R. F. Parker, RN; she had been his assistant in Iraq. He died on 19 August 1978 at Greenway House, Churston Ferrars, Devon, the home he and Agatha had bought in 1939. *Mallowan's Memoirs* were published in 1977.

MANSFIELD, KATHERINE (1888-1923), writer, whose real name was Kathleen Beauchamp, was born at Wellington, New Zealand, on 14 October 1888, the third daughter of (Sir) Harold Beauchamp, a banker and company director, and his wife, Annie Burnell, daughter of Joseph Dyer, secretary of a provident society. Her early childhood was passed at Karori, a village near Wellington. Her first short story was published when she was nine. In 1903 she became a student at Queen's College, Harley Street, London. There she edited the college magazine, in which she included some of her own short stories.

She returned to New Zealand in 1906, but was unhappy there and began the tragic succession of love affairs, including one with a Maori girl, Maata Mahupuku. Her father reluctantly agreed to her return to England in 1908 and made her a small allowance. While she had been at Queen's College, she and another girl, Ida Baker, had become intimate friends and, on return to London, she renewed this friendship, but she also made the acquaintance of George Bowden, a teacher, and in 1909 they were married. The day of the marriage, she left her husband without any explanation.

For the next two years she contributed stories and articles for the *New Age*, a weekly paper edited by Alfred Orage, to which G. K. CHESTERTON, H. G. WELLS, and Arnold BENNETT also contributed. In 1911 her first collection of short stories, *In a German Pension*, was published under the pseudonym of Katherine Mansfield. About this time she met John Middleton MURRY, an impecunious young man who, with the financial assistance of his friends, launched *Rhythm* and, later, *The Blue Review*, periodicals to which Katherine Mansfield transferred her contributions from the *New Age*. From 1912 she and Murry were living together, though neither of them believed in fidelity, and she was still married to Bowden. During the early days of the war, after Murry had been rejected for military service, they became very friendly with D. H. LAWRENCE and his wife, Frieda and, from time to time, visited Garsington to stay with Philip and Ottoline MORRELL. Katherine also maintained a curious love-hate relationship with Virginia WOOLF. During 1915 she compiled and edited, with the help of Murry and Lawrence, a magazine called *The Signature*.

Her physical constitution throughout her life was always precariously weak and she was subject to recurrent pleurisy. In 1915 she lost her only brother, Leslie Heron Beauchamp, killed in action in France. Thinking nostalgically of her childhood, Katherine now published collections of short stories based on her early years, including *Prelude* (1918) and *Je ne parle pas français* (1919). In 1918 she was divorced from George Bowden and married Murry. A year later Murry became Editor of the *Athenaeum*, and Katherine wrote reviews of current novels for the magazine, which were later collected and published as *Novels and Novelists* (1930).

Katherine Mansfield's reputation as a short-story writer *par excellence* was established by *Bliss* (1920) and *The Garden Party* (1922). By this time, however, she was a very sick woman, suffering from tuberculosis, and travelling sadly from place to place in Italy, Switzerland, and the South of France, in search of a warm climate. In 1922 she entered the Institute, near Fontainebleau, set up by the Russian mystic George Gurdjieff; she died there on 9 January 1923.

Other collections of her short stories, including *The Doves' Nest* (1923) and *Something Childish* (1924), were published posthumously. Her *Poems* were collected in 1923, her *Journal* was published in 1927 and her *Letters* in 1928. She demonstrated her skill as a writer by breaking away from the older tradition of story-telling. When she died, Virginia Woolf wrote in her diary that Katherine's was 'the only writing I have ever been jealous of'. Virginia mourned her death, though in life they had often been jealous rivals.

MANSON, SIR PATRICK (1844-1922), physician and parasitologist, was born on 3 October 1844, the second son of John Manson, of Oldmeldrum, Aberdeenshire, a bank manager, and his wife, Elizabeth, daughter of Patrick Blaikie. He was educated at the Gymnasium and West End Academy, Aberdeen and at Aberdeen University, where he graduated MB and CM (1865) and MD (1866).

In 1866 he was appointed Medical Officer for Formosa in the Chinese Imperial Maritime Customs. From 1871 to 1882 he worked in Amoy in charge of a missionary society's hospital. There he was particularly concerned with elephantiasis, the cause of which was unknown. Learning of the discovery in Calcutta that *micro-filariae* had been found in the blood of elephantiasis victims, he carried out research in this aspect of the disease and discovered that the *filaria* was to be found in mosquitoes. He did not, however, find out how the filarial larva was transmitted to humans.

In 1875 he married Henrietta Isabella, daughter of Captain

James Ptolemy Thurburn, RN; they had three sons and three daughters.

In 1883 Manson settled in Hong Kong, and set up a school of medicine which subsequently became the University and Medical School of Hong Kong. He left China in 1889, and in 1892 became physician to the Seamen's Hospital Society in London. While in this post he made certain observations on the malaria parasite, which had been discovered by A. Laveran in 1880. From his earlier work he inferred that the mosquito might carry the parasite and, although he carried his researches no further, his work provided the clue from which (Sir) Ronald Ross was able to trace the aetiology of the malaria parasite through the anopheles mosquito.

In 1897 Manson was appointed Physician and Adviser to the Colonial Office. The foundation in 1899 of the London School of Tropical Medicine was based on a scheme drawn up by him in 1897. He was a busy lecturer and published a number of works on his research, including *Tropical Diseases: a Manual of the Diseases of Warm Climates* (1898) and other books on the same subject.

He became an FRS (1900), was created KCMG (1903) and GCMG (1912). Manson died on 9 April 1922, recognized in the medical profession as 'the father of tropical medicine'.

MARINA, DUCHESS OF KENT (1906–1968), was born in Athens on 13 December 1906, the youngest of three daughters of Prince and Princess Nicholas of Greece. Her father was the third son of King George I of Greece and her mother the Grand Duchess Helen, daughter of Grand Duke Vladimir, uncle of Tsar Nicholas II. She and her sisters were brought up in Athens with an English governess and Marina became fluent in English and French. Her parents were twice exiled, once in 1917, and again in 1922. The family settled in Paris and Marina went to a finishing school there.

In 1934 she married Prince George, fourth son of King George V and Queen Mary and became Duchess of Kent. Her eldest son, Prince Edward was born in 1935; Princess Alexandra was born in 1936, and Prince Michael in 1942. The Duke and Duchess lived at Coppins, near Iver, Buckinghamshire and in London in Belgrave Square, where they entertained a wide circle of actors, authors, and artists, and people concerned with the charitable organizations in which the Kents were interested. The Duchess was renowned for her elegance and charm.

In 1942 the Duke was killed in a flying accident while serving with the RAF, but the Duchess carried on with her public duties, undertaking many of those previously the responsibility of her husband. During the war she was mainly concerned with the WRNS, of which she became Chief Commandant. She was also President of the Royal National Lifeboat Institution.

In 1952 she undertook a tour of the Far East, visiting Malaya, Sarawak, and Hong Kong. She represented the Queen in 1957 at the independence celebrations of Ghana and in 1966 at those of Botswana and Lesotho. She was probably best known by the public as President of the All England Lawn Tennis Club and for her attendance at the Wimbledon Championships.

Towards the end of her life she was Chancellor of the new University of Kent. She was also a patron of the National Association for Mental Health, and Colonel-in-Chief of the Queen's Own Royal West Kent Regiment and the Corps of Royal Electrical and Mechanical Engineers.

She was appointed CI and GBE in 1937 and GCVO in 1948. She died at Kensington Palace, London on 27 August 1968.

MARKS, SIMON, first BARON MARKS OF BROUGHTON (1888–1964), retailer and business innovator, was born in Leeds on 9 July 1888, the only son of Michael Marks, a Jewish immigrant from Poland, and his wife, Hannah Cohen. Michael Marks began with a market stall, but in 1894 went into partnership with Thomas Spencer and set up a chain of Marks & Spencer penny bazaars. Simon Marks was educated at Manchester Grammar School and, after studying languages on the Continent for two years, joined his father's business in 1907, became a director in 1911 and Chairman in 1916.

At school he met Israel (later Lord) Sieff, who, in 1910 married his sister, Rebecca; in 1915 Marks married Sieff's sister, Miriam, and Sieff joined the board of Marks & Spencer.

During the First World War Marks joined the Royal Artillery, but, following the Balfour Declaration, in 1917 was seconded to Chaim WEIZMANN to set up the Zionist headquarters in London. By 1916 he was also in full command of Marks & Spencer, and in 1926 the firm became a public company and Sieff became Joint Managing Director.

In 1928 'St Michael' was registered as the brand name of the firm and a reputation for good quality at reasonable prices was established, particularly in respect of clothing and food stuffs. To the fullest extent possible, the goods sold in 'Marks and Sparks' shops were produced in Britain. Marks was a genius at business management and was concerned not only for his customers but also for his staff, in whose welfare he showed great interest.

During the Second World War he served as Deputy Chairman of the London and South Eastern Regional Production Board, and as adviser to the Petroleum Warfare Department. He was also one of the first directors of British Overseas Airways. He was a public benefactor, contributing generously to the Royal College of Surgeons, University

Simon Marks (left) and Israel Sieff in their twenties

College London, the British Heart Foundation, and Manchester Grammar School. He was always a firm supporter of the Zionist cause and was Vice-President of the Zionist Federation.

He received a number of honorary degrees and other academic awards. He was knighted in 1944 and raised to the peerage in 1961. He and his wife had one son and one daughter. Marks died in London on 8 December 1964 at the head office of Marks & Spencer.

MARQUIS, FREDERICK JAMES, first EARL OF WOOLTON (1883-1964), business man and politician, was born in Salford on 23 August 1883, the only child of Thomas Robert Marquis, a saddler, and his wife, Margaret Ormerod. He was educated at Manchester Grammar School and University and obtained his B.Sc. in 1906.

From 1906 to 1910 he was mathematics master at Burnley Grammar School and became a Research Fellow in economics at Manchester University in 1910 and MA in 1912. In that year he was appointed Warden of the David Lewis Hotel and Club Association, a social settlement in Liverpool dockland; he was soon also Warden of Liverpool University settlement, assisted by his wife, Maud Smith, an old Lancashire friend, whom he married in 1912. They had a daughter and a son. During the First World War he worked for the War Office, became Secretary of the Leather Control Board, and civilian boot controller.

After the war he became Secretary of the new Federation of the Boot Industry and a free-lance journalist, then went to the USA, accompanied by (Sir) Rex Cohen, who had recently graduated from Cambridge and joined the family business, Lewis's, the highly successful department store in Liverpool, Manchester, and Birmingham. Marquis drafted their report on the stores they visited in the United States and, although Lewis's was an exclusively Jewish firm, he was rewarded with a seat on the board of the company. In 1928 he became joint Managing Director and in 1936 Chairman, a post which he held until 1951.

His activities with Lewis's were not his only work; Marquis had always been interested in social welfare and he became a member of the advisory councils to the Overseas Development Committee (1928-31), the Board of Trade (1930-4), and the Post Office (1933-47). From 1930 to 1933 he was President of the Retail Distributors Association and became Chairman in 1934. In 1935 he was knighted and in 1939 created Baron Woolton.

From 1936 onwards Marquis was engaged on important work preparing for the coming war. He served on a committee concerned with civilian defence against heavy bombing, on another group dealing with the aircraft industry, and in April 1939 undertook the task of clothing the army.

When war broke out he accepted the post of Director-General of the Ministry of Supply until in 1940 he undertook the onerous duties of Minister of Food, and was sworn of the Privy Council. By diplomacy and efficiency, he secured the confidence of the public, cut bureaucratic corners and, in spite of the severe shortages caused by submarine warfare, contrived to ensure that essential supplies were maintained and fairly distributed. In 1942 he was appointed CH.

From 1943 to 1945 Lord Woolton was Minister of Reconstruction and a member of the War Cabinet but, as the end of the war approached, politics took over and his task became impossible. In the caretaker Government of Winston CHURCHILL he was Lord President of the Council. When the Labour party won the 1945 election, Woolton joined the

Conservative party and, a year later, accepted Churchill's invitation to become Chairman of the party. His reorganization was to some extent responsible for the Tory recovery and in 1951-2 he served again as Lord President of the Council and in 1952-5 as Chancellor of the Duchy of Lancaster. During 1953-4 as Minister of Materials he wound up the ministry.

Woolton was created a viscount in 1953 and an earl in 1956. He was honoured with a number of academic degrees and in 1944 was appointed Chancellor of Manchester University. His first wife died in 1961 and in 1962 he married Dr Margaret Eluned Thomas. Lord Woolton died at Walberton on 14 December 1964.

MARSH, SIR EDWARD HOWARD (1872-1953), civil servant, scholar, and patron of the arts, was born in London on 18 November 1872, the only son of Frederick Howard Marsh, surgeon and later Master of Downing College, Cambridge, and his second wife, Jane, daughter of Spencer Perceval, and granddaughter of the Prime Minister, assassinated by a madman in 1812. Marsh was educated at Westminster and Trinity College, Cambridge, where he obtained a first in both parts of the classical tripos (1893-5) and was awarded the Senior Chancellor's medal. He was a member of the 'Apostles', a friend of G. E. MOORE and Bertrand RUSSELL, and, through Maurice Baring, joined the literary circle in London of Edmund GOSSE; he wrote his first essays in criticism as an ardent admirer of Ibsen.

In 1896 Marsh joined the Colonial Office and in 1905 became Private Secretary to Winston CHURCHILL and thus began their long association. He went with Churchill to the Board of Trade (1908-10), Home Office (1910-11), and Admiralty (1911-15) and, after a short break while Churchill was in the army and Marsh was Assistant Private Secretary to ASQUITH, he rejoined Churchill at the Ministry of Munitions (1917), War Office (1919-21), and Colonial Office once more (1921-2).

He remained at the Colonial Office, serving under the Duke of Devonshire (1922-4) and J. H. THOMAS (1924), and then was with Churchill for the last time at the Treasury (1924-9). In 1929 he returned to serve again under J. H. Thomas and moved with him to the Dominions Office in 1930, and there remained until his retirement in 1937, working from 1935 as Secretary to Malcolm MacDonald.

Marsh began collecting paintings in 1904 but it was not until 1911 that he began buying modern paintings, beginning with Duncan Grant and going on to John and Paul NASH and Stanley SPENCER, so that by 1914 he possessed one of the most valuable collections of modern art in private hands.

He was also a patron of poets, becoming a close friend of Rupert BROOKE, and other young poets, whose work he edited under the title *Georgian Poetry* (5 vols., 1912-22). After Rupert Brooke's untimely death, Marsh became his literary executor. Other poets whose work appeared in *Georgian Poetry* included J. E. Flecker, Lascelles Abercrombie, W. H. Davies, Walter DE LA MARE, D. H. LAWRENCE, Siegfried SASSOON, Robert Graves, and Edmund BLUNDEN. Marsh also published Brooke's *Collected Poems* in 1918.

Another of Marsh's interests was translation. In 1931 he published the Fables of La Fontaine in two volumes, and these were followed by translations of the *Odes* of Horace and two works by the Princess Marthe Bibesco, *The Sphinx of Bagatelle* (1951) and Proust's *Oriane*. He also published in 1939 a book of reminiscences, *A Number of People*.

Winston Churchill was indebted to 'Eddie' Marsh for the

Sir Edward Marsh, champion of the Georgian poets

painstaking work he did on the correction of the proofs of Churchill's books, from *Marlborough* (4 vols., 1933-8) up to the first volume of the *History of the English-Speaking Peoples* (1956). Marsh also undertook similar work for sixteen of the books of Somerset MAUGHAM.

Marsh was a Trustee of the Tate Gallery and a Governor of the Old Vic and was Chairman of the Contemporary Art Society from 1936 to 1952. He was appointed KCVO in 1937. He never married. He died in London on 13 January 1953.

MARSHALL HALL, SIR EDWARD (1858-1927), lawyer, was born at Brighton on 16 September 1858, the youngest of ten children of Alfred Hall, a general practitioner, and his wife, Julia Elizabeth, daughter of James Sebright, a postal official. He was educated at Rugby and, after a short period as a clerk in a tea merchant's office, entered St John's College, Cambridge (1880-2). He was called to the Bar (Inner Temple) in 1883.

On the South-Eastern circuit and Sussex sessions, his commanding personality attracted many clients, but he first came into the public eye when he secured a manslaughter verdict in the Rex v. Hermann murder case with (Sir) Charles Mathews and (Sir) Archibald Bodkin prosecuting (1894).

He was married twice; first, in 1882 to Ethel, daughter of Henry Moon, MD, of Brighton; she died in 1890; and he married in 1896, Henrietta, daughter of Hans Kroeger, of Altona, Schleswig-Holstein; they had one daughter.

At the age of thirty-nine he took silk and soon became a fashionable leader. From 1900 to 1906 Marshall Hall was Conservative MP for Southport division, Lancashire and,

from 1910 to 1916, for East Toxteth division, Liverpool, but he had no success in the House of Commons, his knowledge of politics being superficial.

His success in the courts led to a certain irresponsibility, and in 1901, in a libel case against the *Daily Mail*, he secured judgement for a young actress by a dubious tactic which was severely criticized in the Court of Appeal. This temporarily had an adverse effect on his practice, but in 1907 he re-established his reputation with the successful defence of a young artist accused of murder. Once again he became famous for his appearance in sensational cases, and in 1923 achieved a brilliant victory in the Russell divorce case. The Hon. John Russell queried the paternity of a son born to his wife and sued for divorce. At the first hearing the jury could not agree and the case was dismissed. Hall was brought into the second trial, and although Russell's wife resolutely withstood his cross-examination for four hours, he won the case, and won on appeal, but lost on a point of law in the House of Lords.

In 1916 Marshall Hall had become Recorder of Guildford and in 1917 he was knighted. He died suddenly at Brook, near Godalming on 23 February 1927 and his death was a great loss to the Bar.

MARTIN, (BASIL) KINGSLEY (1897-1969), editor, was born at Hereford on 28 July 1897, the second of the four children of the Revd David Basil Martin, Nonconformist minister, and his wife, Charlotte Alice Turberville. He was educated at Mill Hill School and Magdalene College, Cambridge. During 1917-18, as a conscientious objector, he served in France with the Friends' Ambulance Unit. He entered Cambridge in 1919 and obtained a first in both parts of the historical tripos (1920-1), then spent a year as a visiting scholar at Princeton, and returned to Magdalene College as a Fellow.

In 1924 he became assistant lecturer in politics at the London School of Economics and became a close friend of Harold LASKI, but was soon on bad terms with the Director, W. H. BEVERIDGE. In consequence, in 1927 he accepted appointment as a leader writer on the *Manchester Guardian*, but his contract was not renewed in 1930 as he was in conflict with the Editor, C. P. SCOTT.

On his return to London, J. M. KEYNES, who controlled the *New Statesman*, appointed him Editor, and shortly afterwards that paper absorbed the *Nation*. Later the *Week-End Review*, which had been started by Gerald Barry, was also taken over (1934). Kingsley Martin remained Editor of these papers until 1960 and, under his editorship, the *New Statesman and the Nation* increased its circulation, its advertising revenue, and had a wide influence with intellectual radicals. A. J. P. Taylor said of Martin in his *English History 1914-1945*, 'No man expressed better the confused emotions of the nineteen-thirties—collective security and pacifism, hostility to the German Nazis and hatred of war all in the same parcel.'

In his political views, Kingsley Martin was always unpredictable, but he was always readable, and he typified the bewilderment of the intellectual left wing during a period of great difficulty and menace. The editorship of the *New Statesman and the Nation* was his real life-work, but he was also a co-founder, with W. A. Robson, of the *Political Quarterly*, and published two books *The Triumph of Lord Palmerston* (1924) and *French Liberal Thought in the Eighteenth Century* (1929). After his retirement he also published two volumes of autobiography, *Father Figures* (1966), and *Editor* (1968).

David Low cartoon of Kingsley Martin, *c*. 1930

In 1926 he married Olga Walters, but she left him in 1934, and they were divorced in 1940. At this time he was living with Dorothy Woodman, but their association precluded neither of them from other amorous adventures. They remained together, however, until Kingsley Martin's death in Cairo on 16 February 1969.

MARY, (VICTORIA MARY AUGUSTA LOUISE OLGA PAULINE CLAUDINE AGNES) (1867-1953), Queen Consort of King George V, was born on 26 May 1867 at Kensington Palace, London, the eldest child of Francis, Prince (after 1871 Duke) of Teck, and his wife, Princess Mary Adelaide, younger daughter of Adolphus, Duke of Cambridge, first cousin of Queen Victoria. She was popularly known until her marriage as Princess May. Her father had no private fortune and the family were comparatively poor. Mary was brought up in a household dominated by her popular mother and three brothers but, with the help of her Alsatian governess, Hélène Bricka, she contrived to educate herself, to learn French and German, and acquire a knowledge of political and social life, particularly in the principalities of her German relatives.

In 1891 she was engaged to marry the Prince of Wales's eldest son, the Duke of Clarence, but he died shortly afterwards, and in 1893 she became engaged to his brother, the Duke of York. They were married on 6 July 1893. Their children were Edward (later Edward VIII), born in 1894; Albert (later George VI), born in 1895; Mary (later Princess Royal), born in 1897; Henry (later Duke of Gloucester), born in 1900; George (later Duke of Kent), born in 1902; and John, born in 1905 who died in 1919.

The Princess and her husband led a quiet family life very different from that of George's father, the Prince of Wales, but George was always on very good terms with his father. Having been trained in the Royal Navy, he expected his family to observe strict discipline, and his children, especially his eldest son Edward, sometimes found this irksome. Princess Mary did what she could, without disloyalty to her husband, to temper the rigour of his control. But there were periods when the parents had to be away from their children. In 1901 they visited Australia for the first opening of the federal Parliament, and in 1905-6 they toured India.

In 1910 Edward VII died and Princess Mary became Queen Mary. In 1911-12 she and the King paid their second visit to India for the durbar. The First World War brought the Queen new and arduous duties, which took her into close touch with the leading women in the Labour movement; she also became the patron of the Women's Army Auxiliary Corps, and in 1917 accompanied the King to France. In 1918 they celebrated their silver wedding amid proofs of public respect and affection. The advent of the first Labour Government was met with great consideration and tact by George V, but the King was already a sick man. In 1928 he was desperately ill, and the Queen's fortitude sustained her husband through the last years of his life, which she knew were numbered. George V died in 1936, and the Queen immediately signalled her loyalty to his successor, her eldest son. She moved into Marlborough House, but continued to carry out her public engagements untiringly.

Throughout the abdication crisis of 1936 she maintained a dignified attitude to events, while strongly disapproving of the failure of Edward VIII to put his duty to the country and the crown before his personal desires and, when he decided to go, she transferred her loyalty to the new King George VI saying, 'The Yorks will do it very well'. Meanwhile, she pursued her interests in her collection of works of art and continued to appear in public on such occasions as the British Industries Fair and the Wimbledon Tennis championships.

In 1939 she had a car accident, in which her eyesight was permanently impaired and, when the Second World War came, she reluctantly moved out of London to Badminton. She was saddened by the tragic death of her favourite son, the Duke of Kent, in 1942 and at once went to comfort her daughter-in-law, Princess Marina, and attended the funeral at Windsor.

When the war ended, she returned to London and resumed her public duties, which she continued to carry out until after the death of George VI in 1952. She died on 24 March 1953 at Marlborough House and was buried beside her husband in St George's Chapel, Windsor. She was a great Queen-Consort.

MASEFIELD, JOHN EDWARD (1878-1967), Poet Laureate, was born at Ledbury on 1 June 1878, the son of George Edward Masefield, a solicitor, and his wife, Caroline Louisa Parker. His parents died while he was young and he was brought up by relatives. He was educated at King's School, Warwick, and at thirteen entered the *Conway* to learn seamanship. For some years he worked in the USA doing menial jobs and obtaining experience of the lot of the under-privileged.

In 1897 he was back in England, and up till 1906 was contributing to the *Outlook*, the *Academy* and the *Speaker*.

In 1902 he published his *Salt Water Ballads*. In 1903 he married Constance, daughter of Nicholas de la Cherois Crommelin and, in the same year, published *Ballads*, a further volume of poems based on his seafaring experiences. This was followed by *Ballads and Poems* (1910), in which his debt to KIPLING is perhaps most evident. In 'Sea Fever' he wrote: 'I must go down to the seas again, to the vagrant gypsy life', but, in fact, he had settled in London, and in 1907 began to work on the *Manchester Guardian*.

He continued to produce work based on his own experiences of hardship and frustration in *The Everlasting Mercy* (1911) and *Dauber* (1913), but in 1919 he produced his masterpiece *Reynard the Fox*, a narrative in which he vividly described the English countryside as he had known it before he went to sea—'the stables alive with din' and 'the harness-room, that busy scene'.

Masefield was not only a poet; he wrote naval histories and works of criticism, such as his *William Shakespeare* (1911). He also published novels, including *Lost Endeavour* (1910) and *The Bird of Dawning* (1933). There were children's books too—*The Midnight Folk* (1927) and *The Box of Delights* (1935). He was very keen on drama and staged amateur dramatics in a little theatre at his home but his own

John Masefield in his early twenties

plays, apart from religious drama, such as *Good Friday* (1916) and *The Coming of Christ* (1928) were less successful than his other work.

Masefield was appointed Poet Laureate in 1930 and OM in 1935. He took his laureate duties seriously, lecturing frequently in the USA and in Europe. In 1941 he wrote a short prose work *The Nine Days Wonder*, the story of the Dunkirk evacuation, to which his own experiences in the Red Cross in the Dardanelles during the First World War added point. A year later his only son was killed in action.

He was honoured with academic degrees, and was President of the Society of Authors (1937), and of the National Book League (1944-9). His only daughter, Judith, illustrated some of his books. Masefield died at his home near Abingdon on 12 May 1967.

MAUGHAM, (WILLIAM) SOMERSET (1874-1965), writer, was born in Paris on 25 January 1874, the youngest son of Robert Ormond Maugham, legal adviser to the British Embassy, and his wife, Edith Mary, daughter of Major Charles Snell, of the Indian Army. His brother Frederick became Lord Chancellor. His parents were both dead by the time he was ten. Up till then he was brought up in France, and French was his first language. Then he went to his uncle in Kent and was educated at King's School, Canterbury, and spent a year at Heidelberg University. In 1892 he became a medical student at St Thomas's Hospital, London, and five years later qualified MRCS, LRCP.

In the same year (1897) he published *Liza of Lambeth*, a novel, which was sufficiently successful to enable him to abandon medicine for writing. He now travelled abroad in Spain and France, and published more books which were not so successful, and wrote plays which made little impression until, in 1907, *Lady Frederick* was staged at the Court Theatre and was such a success that soon Maugham had four plays running at the same time in the West End.

In 1915 he published his second novel *Of Human Bondage*, on which he had been working since 1911. During the First World War he was, first, a driver in an ambulance unit in France and, then, in 1915 joined the Intelligence Department and served in Geneva and in Russia. His experiences in this role became the basis for his Ashenden espionage stories.

Of Human Bondage, which had sold some ten million copies by 1965, was followed by *The Moon and Sixpence* (1919), *The Painted Veil* (1925), and *Cakes and Ale* (1930), which the critics regarded as a malicious satire on Thomas HARDY and Hugh WALPOLE. As an impecunious young man, Maugham had been a keen student of the work of de Maupassant, and probably his most lasting work will be his collections of short stories. These were derived from his extensive travels, some of the best of them, such as *Rain* and *The Letter*, from his travels in South-East Asia. These stories were filmed several times.

In 1940, after the fall of France, Maugham had to leave his home, the Villa Mauresque, at St Jean, Cap Ferrat, and settle in the United States until, when the war ended, he was able to return. In 1944 he published his last notable novel, *The Razor's Edge*, a philosophical study of a young American whose life-style was regenerated by Indian mysticism. This also was made into a film. Maugham was now a rich man, with influential friends, accepted as a leading English author whose books had sold over sixty-four million copies. *The Summing Up* (1938) and *A Writer's Notebook* (1949) described his skill in developing his technique and his affection for his own epigrams. In the *Notebook*, he admitted that few

Somerset Maugham at 84, in 1958

of the characters in his stories were imaginary. He put people he had met on his travels into situations of dramatic interest. Some of them could be recognized by their friends and acquaintances.

Somerset Maugham, in spite of all his success, was not a happy man. In 1917 he married Gwendoline (Maude) Syrie Wellcombe, daughter of Thomas John Barnardo, having been cited as co-respondent in her divorce from (Sir) Henry Wellcombe. They had one daughter, Elizabeth Mary (Liza) who had been born in 1915. The marriage was not a success, Maugham knowing, before he married, of his wife's lovers, and she knowing that he was a homosexual. The marriage ended in divorce in 1927. While he was serving with his ambulance unit during the First World War, Maugham met a young American adventurer, Gerald Haxton, who became his secretary, companion, and lover, until he died in 1944. Alan Searle then took his place and looked after Maugham in his old age. In 1962 Maugham published *Looking Back* in which he traduced his ex-wife Syrie who had died in 1955; he had already quarrelled publicly with his daughter, who tried to prevent the publication of this book.

Maugham was appointed CH in 1954 and C.Lit. in 1961; he was also a Commander of the Legion of Honour and had a number of honorary degrees. In 1947 he founded the Somerset Maugham Award to encourage young writers. He died in Nice on 15 December 1965. His nephew, Robin, son of Frederick, Viscount Maugham, published *Somerset and all the Maughams* (1966).

MAURICE, SIR FREDERICK BARTON (1871-1951), major-general, was born in Dublin on 19 January 1871, the eldest son of (Major-General Sir) John Frederick Maurice. He was educated at St Paul's School and the RMC, Sandhurst, and commissioned in the Derbyshire Regiment in 1892.

He served in the Tirah campaign of 1897-8 and the Boer War and held a number of staff appointments. In 1899 he married Helen Margaret, daughter of Frederick Howard Marsh (later Master of Downing College, Cambridge) and sister of Edward MARSH; they had one son and four daughters.

In 1913 he became an instructor at the Staff College under Sir William Robertson with whom he formed a close friendship. During the First World War he served again under Robertson, at first in France, where he was appointed CB (1915), and later at the War Office as Director of Military Operations when Robertson was Chief of the Imperial General Staff. He was appointed KCMG in January 1918.

The military leaders had, for some time, been in disagreement with LLOYD GEORGE about the prosecution of the war, and in February 1918 Robertson was replaced by Sir Henry Wilson; in April Maurice was forced to resign. Disregarding the regulations imposed upon senior army officers, he wrote to *The Times* on 7 May accusing Lloyd George of deceiving the House of Commons about the strength of the British forces in France in January 1918. In the subsequent debate, the Prime Minister was able to claim that the figures he had used had been supplied by Maurice himself. Lloyd George was able to refute the allegations made by Maurice and from that time to the end of the war, was unassailable.

Maurice did not know until later that the original figures supplied by the War Office had included the British forces in Italy and that they had later been amended. It seems probable that Lloyd George received these amended figures before the debate but ignored them. This allegation, however, has never been proved. Whether Maurice was right or not, his breach of discipline could not be condoned. He was retired from the army and refused an inquiry.

The political result of this episode was the decisive division of the Liberal party into two groups, one supporting Lloyd George, and the other remaining loyal to ASQUITH.

Maurice subsequently sought a career in the academic world. From 1922 to 1933 he was Principal of the Working Men's College, London; in 1927 he became Professor of Military Studies in London University, and from 1933 to 1944 he was Principal of East London College (later Queen Mary College). He was a member of the University Senate, an honorary LL D (Cambridge) and Lees Knowles lecturer at Trinity College in 1925-6.

He published a number of historical works, including biographies of Robert E. Lee, Lord Wolseley, Lord HALDANE and Lord Rawlinson; a *History of the Scots Guards* (2 vols., 1934), and *The Armistice of 1918* (1943). He was also military correspondent for the *Daily Chronicle* and the *Daily News* and a contributor to the *Cambridge Modern History*.

Maurice died in Cambridge on 19 May 1951. One of his daughters, Joan Robinson, became Professor of Economics at Cambridge.

MAVOR, OSBORNE HENRY (1888-1951). See BRIDIE, JAMES.

MAXTON, JAMES (1885-1946), politician, was born in Pollockshaws, near Glasgow on 22 June 1885, the elder son of James Maxton, a schoolteacher, and his wife, Melvina

Purdon, who had also been a schoolteacher. His younger brother, John, became Director of the Institute of Agrarian Affairs, Oxford from 1941 to 1951. Maxton was educated at Hutchinson's Grammar School, Glasgow, and Glasgow University, where he obtained his MA in 1909. At the university he joined the Conservative Club and the 1st Lanarkshire Rifle Volunteers, but moved to the Independent Labour Party in 1904, after hearing a speech by Philip SNOWDEN. He was then working as a teacher.

Maxton rapidly made a name for himself as an orator and rebel, though not a Marxist. In 1916 he went to prison for a year for a speech at Glasgow, condemned as seditious. On release he worked as a labourer in a shipyard. After the First World War he became an organizer for the ILP, having failed to get elected for Parliament in 1918.

In 1919 he married Sarah Whitehead, daughter of John McCallum, but she died in 1922, a blow from which Maxton took years to recover.

At the general election of 1922 he was elected MP for Bridgeton, and in 1926 became Chairman of the ILP, a post he held until 1931 and again from 1934 to 1939. He held Bridgeton in every election between 1922 and 1945 and was a popular member of the House of Commons, both with his friends and his opponents. He and his ILP group, however, had little influence after the formation of Ramsay MAC-DONALD's National Government in 1931. In 1932 the ILP was disaffiliated from the official Labour party.

Jennie (Baroness) Lee, in her book *My Life with Nye*, said that BEVAN could not take Maxton seriously as a leader. Jennie, who had known Maxton all her life, wrote that 'he had charisma and compassion. He loved everyone. He was a man of deep feeling, but there was no hard metal in him.' In 1938 Maxton supported Neville CHAMBERLAIN in his efforts to come to terms with Hitler.

In 1935 he married his secretary, Madeline Grace, daughter of George Henry Brougham Glasier, an estate agent. Maxton published *Lenin* (1932) and *If I were a Dictator* (1935). He died at Largs, Ayrshire on 23 July 1946.

MAXWELL, GAVIN (1914–1969), writer and conservationist, was born on 15 July 1914 at Elrig, Wigtown, the youngest son of Lt.-Col. Aymer Edward Maxwell, and his wife, Lady Mary Percy, daughter of the seventh Duke of Northumberland and sister of Lord Eustace Percy (later Lord Percy of Newcastle). His father died of wounds in October 1914. Gavin Maxwell was educated at Stowe and Hertford College, Oxford, and from his boyhood had a strong interest in all aspects of natural history.

After leaving Oxford in 1937 he set out to travel but, after the outbreak of war, served in the Scots Guards and in the Special Operations Executive. Invalided from the army in 1944, he started a shark fishery on the island of Soay, off Skye. This venture failed but it gave him the material for his first book *Harpoon at a Venture* (1952). Between 1949 and 1952 he tried to earn a living as a portrait painter in London, and then decided to travel and write.

In 1953 he went to Sicily and from his researches there produced *God Protect me from my Friends* (1956), and *The Ten Pains of Death* (1959). Then, in 1956, he went to Southern Iraq, after which he published a study of the marsh Arabs, *A Reed Shaken by the Wind* (1957). In 1960 he produced his most famous book, *Ring of Bright Water*, a poignant account of a man's relationship with otters. This was made into a successful film. It was followed by *The Otter's Tale* (1962) and *The Rocks Remain* (1963). Maxwell

wrote two further books, *The House of Elrig* (1965), which was autobiographical, and *Lords of the Atlas* (1966), a history of the Moroccan house of Glaoua.

In 1962 he married Lavinia Jean, daughter of Sir Alan Frederick Lascelles; the marriage ended in divorce two years later; Maxwell was, in fact, bisexual. He had affairs with women but preferred the company of boys and men. He was President of the British Junior Exploration Society, a Fellow of the Royal Society of Literature, the Royal Geographical Society, and the Royal Zoological Society (Scotland).

In 1968 his highland home was mysteriously destroyed by fire and he had to move. Later he was found to have an inoperable cancer; he died at Inverness on 7 September 1969.

MELBA, DAME NELLIE (1861–1931), prima donna, whose real name was Helen Porter Mitchell, was born on 19 May 1861 in Melbourne, Australia, the daughter of David Mitchell, a business man, and his wife, Isabella Ann Dorn. Both parents were natives of Forfarshire. From her earliest years, Nellie was encouraged to sing; she went to the Presbyterian Ladies' College in Melbourne and her voice was trained by a competent music teacher. Her father was opposed to her wish to adopt singing as a profession but, after her marriage in 1882 to Charles Nesbitt Frederick Armstrong and the birth of a son, her father relented and, the marriage

Melba

having broken down, paid her passage to England. She and Armstrong were divorced in 1900.

In 1886 Nellie arrived in London, but her few professional appearances were not successful and she decided to go to Paris to study under Mme Mathilde Marchesi, a famous teacher, to whom she had a letter of introduction. Mme Marchesi was confident that Nellie would become a star singer and, after a year's training, 'Melba', as she now called herself in tribute to Melbourne, appeared as Gilda in Verdi's *Rigoletto* in Brussels and was acclaimed as a great success (1887).

Soon she was appearing in Italian opera at Covent Garden, making her début there as Lucia in Donizetti's *Lucia di Lammermoor* (1888). In the next year she made her first appearance at the Paris Opéra as Ophélie in Ambroise Thomas's *Hamlet*. She also studied with Gounod, and received great help from Sarah Bernhardt in the finer points of acting. Her beautiful soprano voice, with its compass of two and a half octaves, was now near to perfection, and during 1889 Melba was persuaded to return to Covent Garden. There she appeared in the first performance of Gounod's *Roméo et Juliette* in French and, from then onwards, she took part in every Covent Garden season.

Her position was now assured and she appeared in a number of countries, including Russia and the USA (1891-3). In Italy Verdi went through the music of *Otello* with her, and in 1893 she fulfilled a promise to Leoncavallo by introducing Nedda in *Pagliacci* to the British public. She studied *La Bohème* with Puccini and sang it first in Philadelphia in 1894 and later at Covent Garden. Saint-Saëns composed the title-role of *Hélène* for her, which she sang in Monte Carlo in 1904.

Melba was received rapturously when she revisited Australia in 1902. Despite her world-wide fame as a prima donna, she never forgot Australia and she settled there after her retirement in 1926. In 1918 she was appointed DBE, and in 1927 GBE. During the First World War she raised over £100,000 for the Red Cross. In 1922-3 she gave encouragement to the British National Opera Company, which aimed at the production of opera in English; she appeared with them in London. She retired while her voice was still wonderfully fresh and her technique superb. In 1925 she published *Melodies and Memories*. She died at Sydney on 23 February 1931.

MELCHETT, first BARON (1868-1930). See MOND.

MELLANBY, SIR EDWARD (1884-1955), medical scientist and administrator, was born at West Hartlepool on 8 April 1884, the youngest son of John Mellanby, a shipyard manager, and his wife, Mary Isabella Lawson. His elder brother, John, became Waynflete Professor of Physiology at Oxford. He was educated at Barnard Castle School and Emmanuel College, Cambridge, where he obtained a first in part ii of the natural sciences tripos (physiology) in 1905. From 1905 to 1907 he worked as a research student under (Sir) Frederick Gowland HOPKINS. In 1909 he qualified in medicine at St Thomas's Hospital, London, during 1909-11 was demonstrator in physiology there, and in 1910-12 held a Beit memorial fellowship for medical research.

In 1914 Mellanby married May, eldest daughter of George Tweedy, of London; they had no children; she was herself a research worker in physiology and was Mellanby's lifelong colleague.

From 1913 to 1920 he was lecturer in and later Professor of Physiology at King's College for Women, London. In 1914, at the request of the Medical Research Committee, he investigated the cause of rickets and established the main cause to be deficiency of vitamin D. For the rest of his career he undertook important research into biochemical and physiological problems. In 1915 he became MD (Cambridge).

In 1920 Mellanby was appointed to the new chair of pharmacology at Sheffield and honorary Physician to the Royal Infirmary. He held these posts until 1933, when he succeeded Sir Walter Fletcher as Secretary of the Medical Research Council and became Fullerian Professor of the Royal Institution (1936-7). He was closely concerned with the planning of the new Institute of Medical Research at Mill Hill, opened in 1950.

While he was at Sheffield, Mellanby was Chairman of an international conference for the standardization of vitamins (1931) and took part in further such conferences in 1934 and 1949. During the Second World War he was actively concerned with schemes for wartime diet and the welfare of personnel, both military and civilian. After his retirement from the MRC in 1949, he undertook missions abroad, in an advisory capacity, to India and Australia and New Zealand.

He was elected FRS (1925), FRCP (1928), and honorary FRCS Ed. (1946). He was appointed KCB in 1937, and GBE in 1948, and received many prizes and other academic honours. He gave a large number of public lectures including the Linacre and Reed lectures at Cambridge and the Croonian lecture of the Royal Society. He died, while working in his laboratory at Mill Hill, on 30 January 1955.

MENZIES, SIR STEWART GRAHAM (1890-1968), head of the Secret Intelligence Service, was born in London on 30 January 1890, the second son of John Graham Menzies, and his wife, Susannah West, daughter of Arthur Wilson, a shipowner, of Tranby Croft. He was educated at Eton, in 1909 joined the Grenadier Guards, and in 1910 transferred to the Life Guards.

In 1914 he served in France, and in 1915, after recovering from a gas attack, was given an intelligence assignment at GHQ. His knowledge of European languages was a great asset in this post and, since he was good at the work, he was selected in 1919 to be military liaison officer with the SIS (MI6). He ended the First World War with the DSO and MC.

Menzies remained in intelligence work for the next thirty-two years, retiring from the Life Guards in 1939. Three months later he took over command of the SIS as 'C' and continued to control the service until 1951, when he retired. Of necessity, little publicity was given to his work during these years, but it is known that during the Second World War he was successful in reorganizing the service and guiding it through the complications of inter-Allied and inter-Service relations. Under his supervision, the Government Code and Cipher School succeeded in breaking the German 'Enigma' enciphering machine, which the Germans believed to be impenetrable. The secret of this achievement was kept until the end of the war. Some forty years later, it is still impossible to estimate the importance of this work in the conduct of the war to final victory.

During the war years, Menzies was in close touch with the Prime Minister, Winston CHURCHILL, and played an important part in the shaping of military policy. After the war he had to deal with all the complications arising from the 'cold war' and the highly sophisticated developments in the techniques of espionage and counter-espionage.

He was appointed CB in 1942, KCMG in 1943, KCB in 1951, and received a number of foreign decorations. In 1918 he married Lady Avice Ela Muriel Sackville, daughter of the eighth Earl De La Warr; in 1931 they divorced, and in 1932 he married Pamela Thetis, daughter of Rupert Evelyn Beckett, and divorced wife of James Roy Notter Garton. She died in 1951, and in 1952 he married Audrey Clara Lilian, daughter of Sir Thomas Paul Latham. He had one daughter by his second wife. He died in London on 29 May 1968.

MERCER, CECIL WILLIAM (1885–1960). See YATES, DORNFORD.

MESSEL, OLIVER HILARY SAMBOURNE (1904–1978), artist and stage designer, was born in London on 13 January 1904, the younger son of Lt.-Col. Leonard Charles Rudolph Messel, member of the London Stock Exchange, and his wife, Maud Frances, daughter of Edward Linley Sambourne, cartoonist. Before the First World War, his parents inherited Nymans in Sussex, where they developed and preserved one of the finest gardens in England. Oliver Messel was educated at Eton, and studied under Henry TONKS at the Slade School of Art.

In 1925 he held an exhibition of head masks in which he had specialized; this led to his first commission, to devise masks for a scene from *Zephyr and Flora*, the ballet directed by Georges Braque at the London Coliseum. In 1926 he also created masks for *Cochran's Revue* at the London Pavilion, and went on to design costumes and scenery for a number of C. B. COCHRAN's productions, including the revival of *Helen*, directed by Max Reinhardt, and *The Miracle* (1932). In 1933 he wrote *Stage Designs and Costumes*. By this time, Messel was recognized as one of the foremost stage designers in Britain, and designed the settings in opera for *The Magic Flute* (1947), *The Queen of Spades* (1950), and the Glyndebourne production of *Der Rosenkavalier* (1959). In ballet he made outstanding designs for the scenery of *Francesca da Rimini* (1937) and *The Sleeping Beauty* (1946). He also designed settings and costumes for films, including *Romeo and Juliet* (1936), *Caesar and Cleopatra* (1945), and *Suddenly Last Summer* (1959).

Between them, Oliver Messel and his friend, Rex Whistler, succeeded in raising the standards of theatre design to a very high level, and Messel's collection of designs, masks, and costumes was lent by his nephew, Lord Snowdon, to the Victoria and Albert Museum for display (1982).

During the Second World War, Messel served in the army. He never married, and his last years were spent in Barbados, where he died on 13 July 1978.

MILFORD HAVEN, first MARQUESS OF (1854–1921). See MOUNTBATTEN, LOUIS ALEXANDER.

Oliver Messel working on a design for *The Infernal Machine*, 1940; on the wall are some of the head masks in which he specialized

MILLS, BERTRAM WAGSTAFF (1873-1938), circus proprietor, was born in London on 11 August 1873, the son of Halford Lewis Mills, and his wife, Mary Fenn Wagstaff. His father was a coach builder and owned two small farms. When he was fourteen, Mills entered the business, learnt to ride horses, and exhibited his father's coaches at shows all over Europe.

In 1901 Mills married Ethel, daughter of William Notley of Thorndon, Suffolk; they had two sons.

During the First World War he served in the RAMC, and after the war, with little coach-building in prospect, he started up a circus business, and from 1920 to 1937 put on an annual circus show at Olympia at Christmas time. In 1929 he extended the business with a touring tented circus.

He and his sons travelled all over the world seeking new turns for the circus, and the Bertram Mills Circus became a famous popular entertainment and a profitable enterprise. The fifth Earl of LONSDALE became a great friend of Mills and accepted the presidency of the company in 1921.

Mills was also a prominent figure and a successful competitor at the Richmond Horse Show for many years. He was President of the Showmen's Guild from 1934 until his death. From 1928 to 1938 he was a member of the LCC. He died at Chalfont St Giles on 16 April 1938 and, in accordance with his wish, the circus was carried on by his sons.

MILNE, ALAN ALEXANDER (1882-1956), author, was born on 18 January 1882 in London, the youngest son of John Vine Milne, headmaster of a private school, and his wife, Sarah Maria, daughter of Peter Heginbotham, a manufacturer. He went with a scholarship to Westminster and then to Trinity College, Cambridge, where he became Editor of the *Granta* (1903).

In 1906 he was appointed Assistant Editor of *Punch* under Owen SEAMAN and soon made a reputation for light, witty articles. In 1913 Milne married Dorothy (Daphne), daughter of Martin de Sélincourt, a City merchant. During the First World War he served with the Royal Warwickshire Regiment, but in 1917 was able to stage *Wurzel-Flummery*, followed in 1920 by his successful comedy *Mr Pim Passes By*.

Milne left *Punch* in 1919 to concentrate on stage comedy and, encouraged by the success of *Mr Pim*, went on to produce for the stage some notable plays, including *The Truth About Blayds* (1921), *The Dover Road* (1922), *The Great Broxopp* (1923), *To Have the Honour* (1924), *The Fourth Wall* (1928), *Michael and Mary* (1930), and *Other People's Lives* (1932).

His famous dramatization of *The Wind in the Willows*, by Kenneth GRAHAME, was produced in 1929 as *Toad of Toad Hall*. By that time, Milne had already made a lasting reputation through his verses for children, including *When We Were Very Young* (1924), delightful poems dedicated to his four-year-old son, Christopher Robin, followed in 1927 by *Now We Are Six*.

Equally well-known were his prose stories for young children, *Winnie-the-Pooh* (1926) and *The House at Pooh Corner* (1928), with enchanting illustrations by E. H. SHEPARD. These were translated into foreign languages which included Japanese and Bulgarian.

A. A. Milne died at Hartfield, Sussex, on 31 January 1956. His son later wrote about his childhood in *The Enchanted Places* (1974).

MILNER, ALFRED, VISCOUNT MILNER (1854-1925), colonial administrator and politician, was born at Giessen,

A. A. Milne with Christopher Robin and bear in the early 1920s

Hesse-Darmstadt, on 23 March 1854, the only son of Charles Milner, MD, and his wife, Mary Ierne, daughter of Major-General John Ready, and widow of St George Cromie. He spent three years at the Tübingen Gymnasium, his grandmother being German; but, when he was fifteen, his mother died and, by her wish, he continued his education in England at King's College, London. He won a scholarship to Balliol College, Oxford, where he obtained a first in Classical Mods. and Greats (1874-6), won the Craven, Eldon, and Derby scholarships, and became President of the Union (1875). In 1876 he was elected a Fellow of New College.

In the company of his Oxford friends, including H. H. ASQUITH and Arnold TOYNBEE, Milner developed a keen interest in social work and public service. In 1881 he was called to the Bar (Inner Temple), but briefs were scarce, and to earn a living he took to journalism, joining the staff of the *Pall Mall Gazette*. He continued to be interested in social work and took part in the activities of the University Extension Society and co-operated in the foundation of Toynbee Hall, named after his friend who died in 1883.

In 1884 Milner became Private Secretary to G. J. (later Viscount) Goschen, who was also concerned with social experiments such as Toynbee Hall; Milner assisted him in the formation of the Liberal Unionist Association. When Goschen succeeded Lord Randolph Churchill as Chancellor of the Exchequer in 1886, he again appointed Milner as his Private Secretary, and found in him an invaluable assistant in financial matters.

In 1889 Milner was appointed Director-General of accounts in Egypt, and six months later became Under-Secretary to the Finance Ministry and won the respect and admiration of his chief, Sir Evelyn BARING. Milner described the complications of Egyptian administration and justified the British position in Egypt in *England and Egypt*, published in 1892. In that year Goschen recalled him to England to take over as Chairman of the Board of Inland Revenue, in which post Milner served until 1897, being created CB in 1894 and KCB in 1895.

Joseph Chamberlain, Colonial Secretary, had met Milner in Egypt and been impressed with his ability; he now appointed him High Commissioner in South Africa, and Milner set out on his most difficult task and most lasting achievements. He began with an open mind regarding the controversy between the Boers and the Uitlanders, which had been exacerbated by the Jameson raid of 1895; he learnt Dutch and Afrikaans, and tried to reach cordial relations with President Kruger and his Transvaal Government. But, within twelve months, he came to the conclusion that the Boers would not extend to the Britons in the Transvaal the constitutional rights that the Boers enjoyed in Cape Colony and that, failing such reforms, war was inevitable.

In 1899 matters came to a head when he forwarded to the Queen a petition from 20,000 people on the Rand and informed the British Government of his views that intervention in their support was a matter of urgency. Joseph Chamberlain was reluctant to accept this advice and Milner tried to reach agreement with Kruger on a compromise at a conference in which they met at Bloemfontein in the summer of 1899. They could not agree and, when Milner presented an ultimatum to the Boer President, he replied with what was, in effect, a declaration of war.

At the outset of the Boer War, Milner was faced with grave anxieties, which were only allayed with the arrival of Lord Roberts in January 1900 and the campaign which ended with the capture of Pretoria. Later that year, while the guerrilla war continued, he became Administrator of the Orange River Colony and the Transvaal, the two Boer states annexed by Britain, and on a brief visit to London was made a baron.

When peace was finally declared in 1902, he was promoted to viscount and assumed full powers as High Commissioner and Governor of the Transvaal and the Orange River Colony; and with the help of his 'kindergarten', young men such as Lionel CURTIS and Philip KERR, mostly recruited from Oxford, he set out to rehabilitate the economy of the country and to reorganize its administration. He immediately set about the task of repatriating Boer prisoners of war and re-establishing them on their farms; he also took steps to encourage British farmers to settle in South Africa. To provide the labour required, to get the mines operating again, he introduced Chinese workers to South Africa, a controversial measure which aroused considerable opposition from Liberal opinion in England and was one of the issues that led to the Conservative débâcle in the 1906 general election.

Throughout this arduous work, Milner's great ambition was to convert South Africa into a viable component of the British Empire but, when he retired to England in 1905, although he had succeeded in restoring the economy of the country and repairing the damage caused by the war, he had failed to overcome the intractable hostility of the Afrikaans population and to reconcile them to his ideas of British education and culture.

For some time after his return to London, he took little part in politics but, to repair his own fortunes, undertook remunerative work in the City and carried out congenial public work, such as the organization of the Rhodes Trust. In the House of Lords he opposed LLOYD GEORGE's budget of 1909 and the Parliament Bill of 1911. He was strongly opposed to Home Rule for Ireland as he had been to the grant of full responsible government to South Africa.

When, however, the First World War broke out, he took up new public duties with fresh enthusiasm. During the first year of the war, he presided over a committee to increase food production, and in 1916 became a member of Lloyd George's War Cabinet. During the dark days of the war, when the Allies were suffering terrible reverses, he staunchly supported the Prime Minister in his difficulties with the military leaders. He was mainly responsible for the inclusion in the War Cabinet of J. C. SMUTS and other leaders from the Dominions. In the spring of 1918, when the German offensive had broken through the British defences near Amiens and cut them off from the French, he went to the front to report on the state of affairs, and at a conference at Doullens with Clemenceau, the French Premier, took the responsibility for agreeing to the appointment of General Foch to take supreme command of the Allied armies on the Western Front.

Later that year, Lloyd George appointed Milner to be Secretary of State for War but, when he supported the idea of an armistice, he was denounced by his political opponents as pro-German. When the Government was reconstructed after the 1918 election, Milner was moved to the post of Colonial Secretary, but he was a tired man who had become increasingly disenchanted with Lloyd George, and early in 1921 he resigned and was created KG.

Later in that year he married Violet Georgina, daughter of Admiral Frederick Augustus Maxse, and widow of Lord Edward Herbert Gascoyne-Cecil. He continued to work in the City and to write on social and imperial questions. In 1925 he published *Questions of the Hour* and became Chancellor-elect of Oxford University. He died, however, before he could take up this office, on 13 May 1925 at his home Sturry Court, near Canterbury. He was a great public servant, but his ideas of beneficent imperialism were out of tune with liberal opinion from 1906 onwards.

MITCHELL, SIR PETER CHALMERS (1864–1945), zoologist, was born at Dunfermline on 23 November 1864, the eldest son of the Revd Alexander Mitchell, DD, and his wife, Marion Hay, daughter of the Revd Peter Chalmers, DD. He was educated at Dunfermline High School and Aberdeen Grammar School, and graduated MA from King's College, Aberdeen (1884). That year he entered Christ Church, Oxford, as an exhibitioner, and obtained a first in natural science (1888).

For the next three years he was university demonstrator in comparative anatomy and assistant to the Linacre Professor; then he spent another two years as organizing secretary for technical instruction under the Oxfordshire County Council, and also contributed articles to the *Daily Chronicle*. In 1893 Mitchell married Lilian Bessie, daughter of the Revd Charles Pritchard, Savilian Professor of Astronomy at Oxford. They had no children.

In 1892 he was appointed lecturer in biology at Charing Cross Hospital Medical School, and in 1894 lecturer at the London Hospital Medical College. Meanwhile, he worked on the anatomy of mammals and birds at the London Zoo. He made frequent visits to France and Germany and translated into English a number of French and German books on scientific subjects.

From 1903 to 1935 Mitchell carried out his most important work as Secretary of the Zoological Society of London. Under his guidance, the Society became the foremost institution of its kind in the world, the Zoo in Regent's Park was considerably improved, the number of visitors increased threefold, and Whipsnade Zoological Park was created.

During the First World War Mitchell was attached to the

department of military intelligence at the War Office, and was mainly responsible for the distribution of propaganda behind the German lines. For this work he was created CBE, and in 1929 was knighted. He was elected FRS in 1906, and from 1923 to 1927 was President of the Society for the Preservation of the Fauna of the Empire. He was Biological Editor of the eleventh edition of the *Encyclopaedia Britannica* and scientific correspondent of *The Times*. He published a biography of T. H. Huxley (1900).

Mitchell received many academic honours and awards, including an honorary LL D (Aberdeen). In 1937 he published his autobiography *My Fill of Days*. He died in London on 2 July 1945 as the result of a street accident.

MITFORD, NANCY FREEMAN- (1904–1973), novelist and biographer, was born in London on 28 November 1904, the eldest child of David Bertram Ogilvy Freeman-Mitford, the second Baron Redesdale, and his wife, Sydney, daughter of Thomas Gibson Bowles, MP. Her grandfather, the first baron, was a distinguished diplomat, traveller, and gardener, the close friend of King Edward VII, Sir Richard Burton, and Thomas Carlyle. Through her grandmother, Lady Clementine Ogilvy, she was related to the Stanleys, and edited two volumes of their correspondence, *The Ladies of Alderley* (1938) and *The Stanleys of Alderley* (1939).

Her father became second Baron Redesdale in 1916 and for three years Nancy was brought up at Batsford Park; later, the family moved to Asthall Manor and then to Swinbrook Manor, all in the Cotswolds. She had no formal education as her father did not believe in sending his daughters to school, but she devoured the books in her grandfather's library, particularly biographies, memoirs, letters, and diaries. Although her grandfather had been noted for his books, such as *Tales of Old Japan* (1871) and *The Bamboo Garden* (1896), her father took pride in being a low-brow; she deftly caricatured him as 'Uncle Matthew' in her novels.

After a short spell at the Slade School of Art, Nancy went to Paris, where she found life delightful; she then returned to London and made friends with a group of young men, including Evelyn WAUGH, Robert Byron, John Sutro, and (Sir) Harold Acton, who were charmed by her intelligence, gaiety, and beauty. For five years she was engaged to James Alexander (Hamish) St Clair-Erskine, but nothing came of that.

In 1928 she went to live in London with Evelyn Waugh and his first wife, but the 'two Evelyns' parted company, and she had to fend for herself, writing articles for *Vogue* and *Harper's Magazine*. Her first novel *Highland Fling* was published in 1931, followed by *Christmas Pudding* (1932) and *Wigs on the Green* (1935).

In 1933 she married Peter Murray Rennell Rodd, son of the first Baron Rennell, but the marriage was unhappy; there were no children, and she left him and agreed to a divorce in 1958. Meanwhile, during the Second World War, she became an ARP driver and worked with immigrant refugees. In 1940 she published *Pigeon Pie*, and in 1942 went to work in Heywood Hill's bookshop, where she made herself an expert and in 1946 became a partner in the firm.

Her fifth novel *The Pursuit of Love* (1945) was an immense success and gave stability to her precarious financial position. It revealed the most important event in her life, her love affair with the 'Colonel', Gaston Palewski, a member of the Free French forces, who appeared in the book as Fabrice de Sauveterre. This experience confirmed her love of France, and after the war she settled there with her faithful maid,

Nancy Mitford at home in Paris, 1954

Marie. Her reputation as a satirical, humorous writer was confirmed by *Love in a Cold Climate* (1949) and *The Blessing* (1951).

Next, she turned to biography, producing the readable *Madame de Pompadour* (1954), *Voltaire in Love* (1957), *The Sun King* (1966) and *Frederick the Great* (1970). Among her other works are *Noblesse Oblige* (1956) and *The Water Beetle* (1962), a collection of short essays.

Her only brother, Thomas David, was killed in action in Burma in 1945; her six sisters all became well known, some for their eccentric behaviour, others for their success as authors and broadcasters. In 1972 Nancy was awarded the Légion d'Honneur and appointed CBE. She died at her home in Versailles on 30 June 1973, and was buried in Swinbrook churchyard beside her misguided sister, Unity.

MOFFATT, JAMES (1870–1944), theologian, was born at Glasgow on 4 July 1870, the eldest son of George Moffatt, a chartered accountant, and his wife, Isabella Simpson, daughter of Robert Starret Morton, a general merchant, of Edinburgh. He was educated at Glasgow Academy and University, where he graduated with honours in classics (1890). He studied theology in the Glasgow College of the Free Church of Scotland, and in 1896 was ordained minister of the Free Church in Dundonald, Ayrshire. In the same year he married Mary, daughter of Archibald Reith, MD of Aberdeen; they had three sons, one of whom died in boyhood, and a daughter.

In 1901 he published *The Historical New Testament* and in consequence became DD (St Andrews) in 1902. From 1907 to 1911 he was minister of the United Free Church at Broughty Ferry, and in 1911 published *Introduction to the*

Literature of the New Testament and began his quarterly survey of current religious books in the *Hibbert Journal*, which he continued up to the year of his death.

From 1911 to 1915 he was Professor of Greek and New Testament at Mansfield College, Oxford, and in 1913 published his translation of the New Testament, which was followed in 1924 by a translation of the Old Testament. These two works made the results of biblical scholarship available to the public throughout the English-speaking world.

In 1915, having become DD Oxford, he returned to Glasgow as Professor of Church History and, up to 1927, was writing, preaching, and lecturing there. In that year he went to the United States as Washburn Professor of Church History in the Union Theological Seminary, New York, and held that chair until 1939, during which time he published *The First Five Centuries of the Church* (1938). He also wrote introductions to works on Shakespeare and George Meredith and a series under the title of 'The Moffatt New Testament Commentary'.

James Moffatt died in New York on 27 June 1944.

MONCKTON, WALTER TURNER, first VISCOUNT MONCKTON OF BRENCHLEY (1891–1965), lawyer and politician, was born on 17 January 1891 at Plaxtol, Kent, the elder son of Frank William Monckton, a paper manufacturer, and his wife, Dora, daughter of William Golding. He was educated at Harrow and Balliol College, Oxford, where he was President of the Union in 1913. In 1914 he married Mary Adelaide Somes, daughter of Sir Thomas Colyer Colyer-Fergusson; they had a son and a daughter.

During the First World War, in spite of defective eyesight, he served with the Queen's Own West Kent Regiment in France and won the MC in 1919. In the same year, he was called to the Bar (Inner Temple) and soon had a flourishing practice. In 1930 he took silk; from 1930 to 1937 he was Recorder of Hythe; he was Chancellor of the diocese of Southwell (1930–6), and Attorney-General to Edward, Prince of Wales, whom he had known at Oxford (1932–6).

From 1933 to 1936 Monckton was constitutional adviser to the Nizam of Hyderabad and the Nawab of Bhopal. When the Government of India Act was passed in 1935 the princes had to decide whether or not to join the proposed federation of All-India. Monckton tried to persuade his most important client, the Nizam, of the wisdom of joining the federation, but the Nizam delayed until the opportunity had passed, anxious to retain his independence, and in the event his principality was taken over by force.

As Attorney-General to the Duchy of Cornwall Monckton was closely concerned with the crisis which arose when Edward VIII determined to marry Mrs Simpson (later Duchess of Windsor). As the King's closest adviser, he tried to convince Edward that constitutionally the marriage was out of the question and that the King could not broadcast his case to the nation over the heads of his Government. Monckton worked tirelessly as go-between for the King at Fort Belvedere and Stanley BALDWIN and his colleagues in Whitehall and, when Edward decided to abdicate, Monckton drove down to Portsmouth with him and bade him farewell as he left his kingdom (1938). Throughout the crisis, Monckton remained sympathetic to Edward, but firmly correct in his attitude to the constitutional problem. As soon as the crisis was over, George VI created him KCVO and Monckton continued to act for the new King in matters which concerned him and his brother (the Duke of Windsor).

In 1940 Monckton was appointed Director-General of the

Walter Monckton as Director-General, Ministry of Information, 1940

Ministry of Information and in 1942 acted as Minister of State in Cairo, but his affair with a lady aroused the indignation of some of his colleagues and, after a difference of opinion with Winston CHURCHILL, he returned to the Bar for a short time. In 1944, however, he returned to favour and in the caretaker Government of 1945 was appointed Solicitor-General, although he had no seat in Parliament.

After the 1945 election, Monckton resumed his legal career and visited India again to try to rescue the Nizam of Hyderabad from the consequences of his own obstinacy. His efforts, however, were unsuccessful, and in 1948 the state was occupied by the Indian Army.

His first marriage ended in divorce in 1947. In the same year, Monckton married Bridget Helen, daughter of the ninth Lord Ruthven, and divorced wife of the eleventh Earl of Carlisle; they were married by the Resident of Hyderabad.

In 1951 Winston Churchill persuaded Monckton to stand for Parliament and he was elected Conservative MP for Bristol West, and appointed Minister of Labour, much to his surprise as he had expected to become a law officer of the crown. The fact that until 1951 he had never been in the House of Commons was an asset in this post, which he held for four difficult years of industrial disturbance. His non-political outlook helped in the process of conciliation in dealing with recalcitrant railwaymen and other trade unionists.

When Anthony EDEN succeeded Churchill, he appointed Monckton Minister of Defence and Monckton found himself involved in the Suez crisis. Although he served the Prime Minister loyally through this débâcle, he was personally opposed to military action, and in 1956 retired to the post of

Paymaster-General and, in the following year, resigned from the Government and was appointed viscount.

From 1957 to 1964 he was Chairman of the Midland Bank, and from 1958 to 1965 Chairman of the Iraq Petroleum Company. In 1957 he was President of the MCC. In 1958 he undertook to chair the Monckton Commission on the constitution of the Federation of the Rhodesias and Nyasaland, but the report which followed was not well received and, tired out by the strain of this work, Monckton's health broke down, and he had to retire.

In 1963 he became the first Chancellor of Sussex University. He was appointed KCMG in 1945, PC in 1951, and GCVO in 1964. Monckton died at Folkington on 9 January 1965. In his book *The Art of Memory* (1982) Lord Butler described him as 'a very able man of infinite patience. Thoughtful, sensitive and deeply courteous to all those he met, I believe I can say that he never hurt anybody.'

MOND, ALFRED MORITZ, first BARON MELCHETT (1868-1930), industrialist, financier, and politician, was born at Farnworth, Lancs. on 23 October 1868, the younger son of Ludwig Mond, who emigrated from Cassel to England and with (Sir) John Tomlinson Brunner founded Brunner, Mond & Co., the great chemical industry. Mond's mother was Frida, daughter of Adolph Meyer Löwenthal, of Cologne. He was educated at Cheltenham College, St John's College, Cambridge, and Edinburgh University. He was called to the Bar (Inner Temple) in 1894 and practised as a lawyer, intending to go into politics. In the same year he married Violet Florence Mabel, daughter of James Henry Goetze, coffee merchant of London; they had one son and three daughters.

In 1895 he entered the family business, became a director and then Managing Director, and began to extend the business, believing firmly, at that time, that success in industry depended on creating larger and larger units but securing the co-operation of workers by the development of profit-sharing and the avoidance of industrial disputes. In 1926, by a process of amalgamations, he created Imperial Chemical Industries Ltd. He was also Chairman of Amalgamated Anthracite Collieries, the Mond Nickel Company, and a number of other firms, including the Industrial Financial Investment Corporation.

In 1906 he entered the House of Commons as Liberal MP for Chester, from 1910 to 1923 represented Swansea, and from 1924 to 1928 Carmarthen. From 1916 to 1921 he was first Commissioner of Works in LLOYD GEORGE'S Government, and in 1921-2 was Minister of Health. The First World War and its aftermath had an important influence on Mond's views about the economics of industry and trade. His earlier faith in free trade gave way to advocacy of imperial preferences, and his belief in big business did not go so far as to induce him to accept the socialist doctrine of nationalization. In Parliament he vigorously opposed socialism.

In 1926 he joined the Conservative party and in his book *Imperial Economic Unity* in 1930 strongly advocated trade co-operation within the British Empire. Mond was created a baronet in 1910, PC in 1913, and became Baron Melchett in 1928. He was elected FRS in 1918 and received a number of honorary degrees. He was always an enthusiastic Zionist and contributed generously to the cause for settling Jews in Palestine.

He died in London on 27 December 1930.

MONTAGU, EDWIN SAMUEL (1879-1924), politician,

was born in London on 6 February 1879, the second son of Samuel Montagu, first Baron Swaythling, a banker, and his wife, Ellen, daughter of Louis Cohen. He was educated at Clifton, the City of London School, and Trinity College, Cambridge where he was President of the Union and graduated in 1902.

Montagu was elected Liberal MP for the Chesterton division of Cambridgeshire in 1906 and held the seat until 1922. He was appointed Private Secretary to H. H. ASQUITH, then Chancellor of the Exchequer. From 1910 to 1914 he was Parliamentary Under-Secretary of State for India and in 1912 paid a visit to India. During 1914-16 Montagu was Financial Secretary to the Treasury, and in 1915 was sworn of the Privy Council and entered the Cabinet. In 1916 he was appointed Minister of Munitions but, when Asquith was superseded by LLOYD GEORGE, he resigned.

In 1915 he married the Hon. (Beatrice) Venetia, daughter of Edward Lyulph Stanley, fourth Baron Sheffield; they had one daughter. Venetia Stanley was a close friend of Violet Asquith (later BONHAM CARTER) and for two or three years, up to the time of her marriage, she had been an intimate correspondent of Herbert Asquith, the Prime Minister.

In 1917 Montagu rejoined the Government as Secretary of State for India, an office he held until 1922. Although he was a Jew he did not support the Zionist cause and was opposed to the Balfour Declaration of 1917. The fact that he was a Jew, however, helped him to understand and to win the confidence of Indians. On behalf of the Coalition Government, he declared on 20 August 1917 that the goal of British policy was the 'progressive realization of responsible government' in India. From November 1917 to May 1918 he toured India with a delegation, which produced its *Report on Indian Constitutional Reforms* (Cmd. 9109 of 1918). This led to the Government of India Act of 1919, thanks in no small degree to the determination and resilience with which Montagu argued the case in the House of Commons. This legislation gave to India the beginnings of responsible self-government, hedged around though it was by safeguards.

In 1922, when Lloyd George took the side of the Greeks against the Turks, the Government of India, fearing the resentment of their Muslim subjects, protested against the Treaty of Sèvres and Montagu supported them in their protest. Lord CURZON, the Foreign Secretary, expressed his indignation at this unconstitutional behaviour and Lloyd George asked for Montagu's resignation.

This spelt the end of Montagu's political career. He lost his seat in the 1922 election and, leaving politics, took up financial positions in the City until he died in London on 15 November 1924.

MONTGOMERY, BERNARD LAW, first VISCOUNT MONTGOMERY OF ALAMEIN (1887-1976), field-marshal, was born on 17 November 1887, the son of the Revd Henry Montgomery, and his wife, Maud, daughter of Frederic Farrar, Dean of Canterbury and author of *Eric, or Little by Little*, a Victorian children's book. He spent his early years in Tasmania, where his father became Bishop when his son was two. His upbringing was very strict, his mother being a harsh disciplinarian. His parents returned to England in 1901, and Montgomery and his brother went to St Paul's School, London as day-boys. He did not distinguish himself at his studies but was a good athlete and captain of rugby. He passed into the RMC, Sandhurst, at the age of nineteen, and in 1908 was commissioned in the 1st Royal Warwickshire Regiment and posted to the North-West Frontier of India.

Montgomery enters Paris for the first time since the Normandy landings, 1945

In 1912 his regiment returned to England; Montgomery passed out top of a musketry course and played hockey for the army. During the First World War he served at the Battles on the Marne and the Aisne, was seriously wounded at the first Battle of Ypres, and awarded the DSO, and the Croix de Guerre. In 1920 he went to the Staff College and, after service in Ireland, returned to Camberley as a member of the staff in 1926. In 1927 he married Betty Carver, whose first husband had been killed at Gallipoli; they had a son, and Montgomery suffered a bitter blow when she died in 1937 from septicaemia.

Up to the time of the Second World War he served with his regiment in the Middle East and India, and from 1934 to 1937 was Chief Instructor at the Staff College, Quetta. In 1938 he was promoted to major-general to command a division in Palestine. On the eve of the war, he became Commander of the 3rd Division of the British Expeditionary Force under Alan BROOKE. After Dunkirk, he was appointed C.-in-C. South-Eastern Command, and in this post built up his reputation as a strict disciplinarian, who disapproved of smoking, drinking, and other vices, which he had himself eschewed, but also earned a certain popularity with the troops for his eccentric foibles.

In 1942 he was appointed to command the Eighth Army in North Africa, which had been driven back to its defensive position at El Alamein and was faced by a new attack launched by Rommel, the German Commander. This assault was defeated but, despite pressure from CHURCHILL and the War Cabinet, Montgomery refused to mount a counter-attack until he had built up his forces sufficiently to ensure success. When the battle came, Montgomery's victory was decisive, one of the most decisive victories of the war, and it began the advance that cleared the Germans out of the whole of North Africa. Montgomery's reward was the KCB.

The invasion of Sicily followed, in which Montgomery had to work in co-operation with the Americans, under General Eisenhower, the Supreme Allied Commander. He remained with the Eighth Army during the fighting in Italy and then returned to England as Commander of the 21st Army Group, in preparation for the invasion of north-west Europe in 1944. He was given command of all British and American forces for the landings and the consolidation of a bridgehead, on the understanding that, when this had been achieved, Eisenhower would assume command and Montgomery would revert to Commander of the British Army Group. The landings were successful, the bridgehead secured, and the advance to the Seine began, not without some bitter battles and some set-backs. When he thought the time was ripe, Eisenhower took over, much to Montgomery's disappointment, particularly since he and the American Commander-in-Chief were not agreed as to the next steps to be taken in the campaign.

The British forces pushed forward through Belgium into Holland and captured Antwerp. Uncharacteristically 'Monty', as he was now known to all his troops, allowed himself to be hurried into an attempt to secure bridges over the Rhine by a parachute attack in advance of his main forces; the attack at Arnhem failed; the land forces could not reach the assault troops in time. Meanwhile, the Americans were making slow progress to the Rhine, and in December 1944 the Germans made a last desperate counter-attack in the Ardennes and the Americans, taken by surprise, were forced to give way. Eisenhower called upon Montgomery to take command of the American units north of the salient made by the Germans. Montgomery attacked when he knew that the enemy had outrun their strength and was completely successful in pushing back the Germans, but he was unsuccessful in his relations with his American allies because his self-confidence and vanity in his achievements made him intolerable to his American colleagues.

When the German surrender finally came, Montgomery was appointed C.-in-C. of the British Forces of Occupation until in 1946 he succeeded Alanbrooke as Chief of the Imperial General Staff. In that year he had become a viscount and KG. He had already been promoted from KCB to GCB in 1945 and become field-marshal. He remained as CIGS for only two years and then took up an international appointment as Military Chairman of the Western Union Commanders'-in-Chief Committee, and in 1951 became Deputy-Supreme Commander under Eisenhower of the Allied forces of NATO in Europe, a post which he held until 1958.

After his retirement, he published his controversial memoirs *The Memoirs of Field-Marshal the Viscount Montgomery of Alamein KG* (1958), which aroused critical comment in the USA, but 'Monty' was nothing if not a controversialist, who believed in stating his opinions and prejudices with clarity, regardless of other people's reactions. In 1959 he visited the Soviet Union and in 1960 India and China. He also toured Africa and Central America, and published his account of these travels in *Three Continents* (1962). Among his other publications was the *History of Warfare* (1968).

By the time of his death he had mellowed, but he will always be remembered as a great soldier who had no nonsense about modesty and, as Lord Moran has said, 'made plain at the very beginning that he was not at all like other people', but was able to inspire in those under his command a new confidence in the certainty of victory. He died on 24 March 1976.

MOORE, GEORGE AUGUSTUS (1852–1933), novelist, was born at Ballyglass, co. Mayo, on 24 February 1852, the eldest son of George Henry Moore, an Irish politician, and his wife, Mary, daughter of Maurice Blake, of Ballinafad, co. Mayo. Like his father, he was educated at Oscott College, Birmingham, but unlike him he rejected Roman Catholicism. His father died in 1870, and in 1873 Moore went to Paris, wishing to become an artist, but was unsuccessful as a painter and by 1880 was in London, struggling to earn a living as a writer.

His first novel *A Modern Lover* was published in 1883, followed by *A Mummer's Wife* (1885) and *Confessions of a Young Man* (1888), together with two volumes of essays which brought him to notice. In 1894 he produced *Esther Waters*, the first of his novels of any literary value.

In 1901, under the influence of W. B. Yeats, he left London for Dublin and published a volume of Irish stories *The Untilled Field* (1903) and the three volumes of his highly individualist and candid autobiography, *Hail and Farewell: Ave, Salve, and Vale,* which appeared in 1911, 1912, and 1914.

From 1911 to his death, Moore lived in London at 121 Ebury Street and, like Henry James, sought to write with a keen sense of the importance of style. His new range of books included *Conversations in Ebury Street* (1924), and *Celibate Lives* (1927), a theme with which he had been concerned as far back as 1895, when he published *Celibates.*

Perhaps his greatest achievements were his novel on the Christian story, *The Brook Kerith* (1916), and his epic, *Héloïse and Abelard* (1921). For part of his life, Moore was regarded as a scandalous writer who disregarded the current Victorian prejudices, but in his later years he came to be respected as 'a master of English literature'. He never married. Nancy Cunard loved him as an old man, knowing that he had been her mother's lover. He died in London on 21 January 1933.

MOORE, GEORGE EDWARD (1873–1958), philosopher, was born in London on 4 November 1873, the third son of Daniel Moore, MD, and his wife, Henrietta Sturge. He was educated at Dulwich College and Trinity College, Cambridge, where he was a scholar and obtained firsts in part i of the classical tripos (1894) and part ii of the moral sciences tripos (1896), won the Craven scholarship (1895), and was elected a Fellow of Trinity (1898).

Among his friends at Cambridge was Bertrand Russell; both were taught by the Hegelian philosopher, J. M. E. M'Taggart, but both later rejected Hegelianism. Each of the friends influenced the thinking of the other; Russell wrote that he had derived his position on fundamental questions from Moore, and Moore wrote that he had been influenced by Russell more than any other philosopher. Moore published his *Principia Ethica* (1903) in the same year as Russell published *The Principles of Mathematics.*

From 1911 to 1925 Moore was lecturer in moral science at Cambridge, and from 1925 to 1939 Professor of Philosophy. From 1921 to 1947 he was Editor of *Mind.* His other published works were *Ethics* (1912), *Philosophical Studies* (1922), and *Some Main Problems of Philosophy* (1953).

Moore's philosophy was based fundamentally upon 'common sense'; he was one of the first to ask what is the meaning of any philosophical statement, and his emphasis on analysis led directly to the modern school of logical positivists. In his autobiography Leonard Woolf wrote that Moore 'had a genius for seeing what was important and what was unimportant'.

He was a brilliant lecturer who had a great influence on generations of Cambridge undergraduates by his obvious sincerity and clarity of exposition. He was elected FBA in 1918 and appointed to the Order of Merit in 1951.

In 1916 he married Dorothy Mildred, daughter of George Herbert Ely, of Croydon; they had two sons. He died in Cambridge on 24 October 1958.

MORAN, first BARON (1882–1977). See WILSON, CHARLES MCMORAN.

MORGAN, CHARLES LANGBRIDGE (1894–1958), novelist, critic, and playwright, was born at Bromley, Kent on 22 January 1894, the younger son of (Sir) Charles Langbridge Morgan, a civil engineer, and his wife, Mary, daughter of William Watkins. He entered the Royal Navy in 1907 and served in the Atlantic and on the China station in the *Good Hope.* In 1913, encouraged by his friend (Commander) Christopher Arnold-Forster, Morgan resigned from the navy intending to write. He was entered at Brasenose College, Oxford, but rejoined the service in 1914 and took part in the disastrous Antwerp expedition.

After the fall of Antwerp, he escaped into Holland and was interned until 1917. There he was able to write *The Gunroom*, based on his early naval experiences. In 1919 he went up to Oxford and became President of the OUDS. In 1921 he joined the staff of *The Times* and, on the death of A. B. Walkley in 1926, became principal drama critic, a post he held until 1939.

In 1923 Morgan had married the novelist, Hilda Vaughan, daughter of Hugh Vaughan Vaughan, of Builth, a solicitor; they had one son and one daughter.

My Name is Legion was published in 1925 and *Portrait in a Mirror* (1929), brought him the Femina Vie Heureuse prize (1930). In 1932 *The Fountain*, a love story set in the Holland of 1915, won the Hawthornden prize (1933) and became a best seller in England, on the Continent, and in America. *Epitaph on George Moore* (1935), about whose life Morgan also wrote in the *DNB*, was followed in 1936 by *Sparkenbroke*, another love story, set in Italy.

In 1938 Morgan was successful with a play *The Flashing Stream* with (Sir) Godfrey Tearle and Margaret Rawlings in the leading parts. Then, in 1940, he won the James Tait Black memorial prize with *The Voyage*. During the Second World War Morgan served in the Admiralty and lectured in the United States, but he found time to write a series of weekly articles for the *Times Literary Supplement* and to publish *Reflections in a Mirror* (1944-6). Articles written by Morgan were circulated in occupied France and he was one of the first English civilians to enter liberated Paris in 1944. *The River Line* (1949), later made a play (1952), was a study of life under enemy occupation. His last play, *The Burning Glass*, was produced in 1953, and the last of his novels, *Challenge to Venus*, was published in 1957.

Although to a later generation of young readers Morgan's novels appeared dated, his books were translated into nineteen languages and were highly regarded on the Continent. He was an Officer of the Legion of Honour, and in 1949 was elected to the Institute of France, up till then an honour accorded to only one other English novelist, Rudyard KIPLING. From 1953 to 1956 he was President of the International PEN. Morgan died in London on 6 February 1958.

MORISON, STANLEY ARTHUR (1889-1967), typographer, was born at Wanstead, Essex, on 6 May 1889, the only son of Arthur Andrew Morison, a commercial traveller, and his wife, Alice Louisa, daughter of Charles Cole, a clerk. He was educated at Owen's School, Islington, but left school at fourteen and sought work because his father had deserted his family. From 1905 to 1912 he worked unhappily as a clerk with the London City Mission. In 1908 he became a Roman Catholic.

Having suddenly developed an interest in the study of printing and typography, he became an assistant with *Imprint* in 1913, and the following year was taken on to his staff by Wilfred Meynell, Managing Director of Burns & Oates, Roman Catholic publishers. During the First World War he was a conscientious objector, was imprisoned, and then worked on a farm. In 1916 he married Mabel Williamson, a schoolteacher, seventeen years older than he was, though he did not know that at the time.

After the war, he was temporarily re-employed by the Meynells until, in 1921, he became typographer to the Cloister Press, near Manchester. This firm became bankrupt in 1922, and Morison then became a free-lance consultant to a number of publishers. He made his name as typographical adviser to the Monotype Corporation, a post he held from 1922 till 1954. During this time, he prepared the specifications for twelve new typefaces which became predominant in book-printing in Britain. As adviser to *The Times* (1930-64), he recommended many typographical changes for the better; in particular, in 1932 his new typeface *The Times New Roman* was first used.

He published a number of erudite articles on the history of type in the *Fleuron* (1923-30), founded in co-operation with Oliver Simon. His 'First Principles of Typography' was reprinted as a book (1936) and had much influence on experts concerned with book production. He also published *Blackletter Text* (1942). From 1923 to 1959 he acted as typographical adviser to the Cambridge University Press.

Morison's services to *The Times* extended beyond typography. He edited *The History of The Times* (4 vols., 1935-52) and during 1945-7 was Editor of the *Times Literary Supplement*. He became a member of the editorial board of the *Encyclopaedia Britannica* in 1961. He remained in London during the Second World War and suffered disaster when his rooms, his books, and his work in progress were destroyed in an air raid.

During 1956-7 he was James P. R. Lyell Reader in Bibliography at Oxford. He received the degree of Litt.D. from Cambridge in 1950 and was awarded other academic honours. He was elected FBA in 1960 and three times declined a knighthood. He was appointed Royal Designer for Industry in 1960.

Stanley Morison, 1952

In 1926 he and his wife separated. For the rest of his life he lived with the American typographer, Beatrice Lamberton Warde in a relationship which was chaste though loving; she was by his bedside when he died in London on 11 October 1967.

MORLEY, JOHN, VISCOUNT MORLEY OF BLACKBURN (1838–1923), politician and man of letters, was born at Blackburn on 24 December 1838, the second son of Jonathan Morley, a surgeon, and his wife, Priscilla Mary Donkin, who came from a shipowning family in North Shields. He was educated at Cheltenham College and Lincoln College, Oxford, where he was a scholar, but left with only a pass degree after quarrelling with his father.

Morley began his career as a man of letters by working from 1860 to 1863 as a free-lance journalist in London and as an ill-paid hack worker, until he was commissioned to write for the *Saturday Review*. On its staff was (Sir) Leslie Stephen, who became a lifelong friend. He also became acquainted with George Meredith, Frederick Augustus Maxse, and John Stuart Mill. In 1866 he reviewed in *Macmillan's Magazine* one of George Eliot's novels and she also became his friend.

In 1867, having made a reputation as a writer, he was appointed Editor of the *Fortnightly Review* and, with the help of Frederic Harrison, set out to make that journal a highly influential organ of liberal opinion to which many brilliant writers such as Anthony Trollope, T. H. Huxley, Herbert Spencer, and Matthew Arnold contributed. He was Editor for fifteen years, during which time he published articles which had a great impact upon the thought of the day, such as Huxley's article on the *Physical Basis of Life*, which appeared in 1869, substituting evolution for the Book of Genesis. Morley's own work included essays on Burke, published in book form in 1867, followed by *Voltaire* (1871) and *Rousseau* (1873), the *Life of Cobden* (1881), *Walpole* (1889), *Oliver Cromwell* (1900), and his *Life of Gladstone* (3 vols., 1903). In 1880 he became Editor of the *Pall Mall Gazette* and turned it from a conservative to a radical paper.

In 1870 he married Mary, daughter of Thomas Ayling; they had no children.

He was already keenly interested in politics, but was disappointed in his attempts to enter Parliament in 1868–9 and 1880. His interest in the programme for secular education brought him into alliance with Joseph Chamberlain, and from 1873 onwards he co-operated with Chamberlain and Sir Charles Dilke in their radical aims to secure disestablishment, secular education, land reform, and progressive taxation, objectives with which Gladstone was not in sympathy. From 1875 the *Fortnightly* came to be regarded as the medium of political radicalism.

In 1882 Morley resigned his post as Editor of the *Fortnightly*, and in 1883 succeeded in getting elected to Parliament as Liberal MP for Newcastle upon Tyne. In 1885 he fell out with Joseph Chamberlain who had changed his views on conciliation in Ireland. Morley was always opposed to coercion and, when Gladstone returned to office in 1886, he appointed Morley Chief Secretary for Ireland. The opposition of Chamberlain and other Liberal-Unionists, however, brought down the Government within six months. In opposition, Morley concentrated on his condemnation of the policy of coercion, pursued with persistent determination by Lord Salisbury and Arthur BALFOUR, who had succeeded Morley as Chief Secretary.

In 1892 Morley became Chief Secretary for the second time and concentrated his efforts on helping Gladstone to prepare and steer through the Commons his second Home Rule Bill which was defeated in the Lords (1893). When Gladstone retired in 1894, Morley transferred his allegiance to Lord ROSEBERY until the Government was defeated again in 1895. At the general election Morley lost his seat, but early in 1896 was elected for the Montrose Burghs, a seat which he held until 1908.

In opposition again, Morley continued to oppose the imperialist policies of the Conservatives, demonstrated in the re-conquest of the Sudan and the Boer War. In 1902 he was appointed to the Order of Merit. When the long period of Conservative rule ended in 1905, the new Prime Minister, Campbell-Bannerman, appointed Morley Secretary of State for India. In that office, which he held until 1910, he was able to secure the passage through Parliament of the Indian Councils Bill (1909), which made the Legislative Councils in India partly elective and enlarged the Executive Councils by the appointment of a few Indians. These measures were not really designed to lead to self-government but they proved in effect to be the first tentative steps to that end.

When ASQUITH became Prime Minister in 1908, Morley was raised to the peerage as Viscount Morley of Blackburn. In 1910 he resigned from the India Office, but remained in the Cabinet as Lord President of the Council. He helped to conduct through the House of Lords the controversial Parliament Bill.

Throughout the years leading to the First World War, Morley was anxious that Britain should not commit herself to support Russia and France against Germany and Austria, and when the war came he refused to accept any responsibility for a conflict which he thought would be disastrous; he resigned from the Government. In his retirement he concerned himself closely with the affairs of Manchester University, of which he had been elected Chancellor in 1908. Morley died in London on 23 September 1923.

MORRELL, LADY OTTOLINE VIOLET ANNE (1873–1938), was born in London on 16 June 1873, the only daughter of Lieutenant-General Arthur Cavendish-Bentinck, and his second wife, Augusta Mary Elizabeth, daughter of Henry Montague Browne, Dean of Lismore. She was brought up by her widowed mother at Welbeck Abbey, the home of her half-brother, who in 1879 became Duke of Portland. At an early age, she rebelled against the class-consciousness of her brothers and the traditional habits of her home, a brilliant but uneducated, eccentric and passionate young woman.

In 1902 she married Philip Edward Morrell, Liberal MP for South Oxfordshire from 1906 to 1910 and for Burnley from 1910 to 1918; they had a son, who died in infancy, and a daughter. The Morrells settled in London where Ottoline, despite her lack of formal education, soon became London's leading hostess for a Bohemian and intellectual circle of young authors and artists, which included Duncan Grant, Virginia WOOLF, Aldous HUXLEY, D. H. LAWRENCE, Augustus JOHN, Lytton STRACHEY, and many others well known in the world of art and literature. Bertrand RUSSELL was among her lovers.

In 1913 the Morrells moved to Garsington Manor in Oxfordshire, and there she continued her generous patronage of young authors. Some of them, notably D. H. Lawrence and Aldous Huxley, used the house and its delightful gardens as a setting for their novels, and Lady Ottoline was deeply affronted by the portrait of herself which she recognized in

Ottoline Morrell (second right) with
Bertrand Russell (right), Lytton
Strachey, and Faith Bagenal, c. 1916

Hermione in *Women in Love*. Although some amendments were made, she said in her memoirs that its publication was 'the end of her intimacy' with Lawrence. Later she had a similar quarrel with Huxley for his description of Garsington in *Crome Yellow*.

During the First World War the Morrells, who were both confirmed pacifists, made Garsington a refuge for conscientious objectors and, when the war was over, continued to entertain a new generation of budding genius in their home which, from 1924 onwards, was in Gower Street, London. Whether she was behind the scenes at the theatre congratulating the ballerina Lydia Lopokova, who married her friend Maynard KEYNES, or writing numerous letters to young authors and artists, she was always her eccentric self, dressed in her own individual fashion, unprepossessing, but fascinating by the intensity of her passion for whatever she thought was beautiful or creative in art and literature.

Lord David Cecil in the *DNB* described her as 'a figure of the first importance in the literary and artistic history of her time'. She died at Tunbridge Wells on 21 April 1938. Her memoirs were published posthumously in two volumes in 1963 and 1974.

MORRIS, WILLIAM RICHARD, VISCOUNT NUFFIELD (1877–1963), industrialist and philanthropist, was born in Worcester on 10 October 1877, the eldest of a family of seven, of whom only his sister survived with him beyond infancy. His father was Frederick Morris, a draper's assistant, his mother Emily Ann, daughter of Richard Pether, a farmer of Headington. His father returned to Oxford when Morris was three and he was brought up at Cowley, where he went to the village school. He set up his own bicycle business when he was sixteen with a capital of £4. In 1904 he married an Oxford girl, Elizabeth Maud, daughter of William Jones Anstey; they had no children.

In 1902 he had designed a motor-cycle and by 1910, although he had no formal training as an engineer, was repairing motor cars and had become a garage owner. At the 1912 Motor Show he exhibited his Morris-Oxford car which was an immediate success. His Longwall garage in Oxford was now no longer suitable for large-scale production and he acquired buildings at Cowley, including what had once been Hurst's Grammar School, where his father had received his schooling. In 1914 he produced the Morris-Cowley with components made in the USA.

During the First World War the Morris works were turned over to munitions, and in 1917 Morris was appointed OBE. In 1919 Morris Motors Ltd. was incorporated, but in 1921 the firm was involved in the post-war slump. Morris met this situation by a drastic reduction in the price of his Morris-Cowley car, and by 1926 he was responsible for about a third of the national output of cars and had established himself as the major producer of popular cars.

In that year he set up the Pressed Steel Company at Cowley to supply car bodies to the industry, and Morris Motors (1926) Ltd. was formed as a public company, but Morris himself retained personal control. In 1927 Morris acquired the Wolseley Company and the SU Carburettor Company, which became Morris Industries Ltd. In 1930 he registered the MG Car Company which produced the famous sports car. The first small car, the Morris-Minor, appeared in 1931.

In 1937 the Morris Companies began the manufacture of tanks, and in 1938 of aircraft. During the Second World War Cowley became the headquarters of the Civilian Repair Organization.

William Morris, Lord Nuffield, arriving at the works in his own Wolseley, 1947

After the war the manufacture of cars was resumed, and in 1951 the two-millionth Morris car came off the assembly line. Then in 1952 Morris Motors was merged with the Austin Motor Co. to form the British Motor Corporation, of which Morris became the first Chairman. Six months later he retired.

Morris had begun his career as a generous benefactor in 1926 when he endowed a chair of Spanish studies at Oxford. During his lifetime he donated some £30 million to causes for the alleviation of human suffering. In 1936 he endowed the Medical School at Oxford. He also provided the means to set up a residential college for the Royal College of Surgeons and donated large sums to a number of hospitals in London and the Midlands. He provided the capital for the Nuffield Orthopaedic Centre at Oxford, the Nuffield Fund for Cripples, the Nuffield Provincial Hospitals Trust, and the Nuffield Foundation to promote research. In 1937 he founded Nuffield College, Oxford, for the study of social, economic, and political problems.

In 1929 he was created a baronet; in 1934 he became Baron Nuffield, and four years later was promoted to viscount. He was appointed GBE in 1941 and CH in 1958. He was elected FRS in 1939; he was awarded honorary degrees and elected an honorary Fellow of several Oxford colleges. He died at Nuffield Place on 22 August 1963.

MORRISON, HERBERT STANLEY, BARON MORRISON OF LAMBETH (1888–1965), politician, was born in London on 3 January 1888, the youngest of seven children of Henry Morrison, a police constable, and his wife, Priscilla Caroline Lyon, daughter of an East-End carpet fitter. He became blind in his right eye while a baby. He went to a Board school and left at fourteen to become an errand boy. He then worked as a shop assistant and switchboard operator. By the time he was eighteen he was already involved in the Labour movement and from 1912 to 1915 was employed as circulation manager for the Labour paper, the *Daily Citizen*. He was also instrumental in the decision to form the London Labour party, of which he became part-time secretary in 1915. He shepherded his party through the First World War, to which he was opposed, and in 1919 won a majority in sixteen London boroughs. This was achieved largely through his powers of organization and his ability to find and train candidates in the art of winning elections and running local government. Morrison became Mayor of Hackney, and in 1922 a member of the London County Council; he held his seat until 1945.

In 1923 Morrison was elected Labour MP for Hackney South; he lost the seat in 1924, but was re-elected in 1929, was appointed Minister of Transport by Ramsay MAC-DONALD, and became a member of the Cabinet. He was now leader of the Labour group on the LCC and as Minister was responsible for the 1930 Road Traffic Act and for the London Passenger Transport Bill of 1931. He did not support Ramsay MacDonald's National Government of 1931, and again lost his seat in the House.

He continued his work with the LCC, and this was in many ways one of his finest achievements. When in 1934

Labour gained control, the LCC, under his guidance, re-formed public assistance, kept Poor Law officers out of the hospitals, built the new Waterloo Bridge, introduced the green belt, and went ahead with slum clearance and school building.

In 1935 he was again elected MP for Hackney South, but his absence from Parliament during 1931 to 1935 affected his subsequent career because Clement ATTLEE, who had been his junior in the Labour party, was now elected leader. Morrison, however, was one of those who took effective action to oust Neville CHAMBERLAIN in 1940, and in CHUR-CHILL's Government that year he became Minister of Supply and then Home Secretary and Minister of Home Security. He created the National Fire Service, instituted fire watching to minimize as far as possible the effects of the blitz on London, and co-ordinated Civil Defence. While Churchill was busy with the problems of winning the war, Morrison, with the help of William BEVERIDGE was actively preparing for the problems of peace. His blueprints for post-war re-construction played a notable part in engineering the Labour victory at the 1945 election.

In that election, Morrison became MP for Lewisham East. He was undoubtedly ambitious to become Prime Minister, but Attlee forestalled him, and Ernest BEVIN, the powerful trade-unionist, supported Attlee. Attlee appointed Morrison Lord President of the Council. In 1947 there was further disunion among the leaders of the party. Sir Stafford CRIPPS was in favour of Bevin's taking over from Attlee and tried to secure Morrison's support, but Morrison would not help to promote Bevin, and the plan to oust Attlee failed. Attlee did not trust Morrison, and Bevin went further; he detested Morrison. When somebody is alleged to have said to Bevin, 'You know, Ernie, Herbert is his own worst enemy', Bevin is reputed to have replied, 'Not while I'm alive, he aint.'

From 1947 to 1951 Morrison was Leader of the House of Commons. In 1951 he was appointed CH. When Bevin had to resign from his post at the Foreign Office through ill health, Attlee felt bound to appoint Morrison to that office, but foreign affairs were a closed book to him and, in the affair in which Mossadeq nationalized the British-owned oil wells at Abadan, Attlee vetoed Morrison's intention of intervening by force. Morrison's political standing was not enhanced by his short spell at the Foreign Office.

After the 1951 election Morrison continued to hold his Lewisham seat and continued to be deputy leader of the Labour party, a position he had held since 1945 but, when Attlee decided to retire in 1955, the party decided in favour of a younger man than Morrison and Hugh GAITSKELL was elected. Morrison, in his bitter disappointment, refused to continue as deputy.

In 1959 he became a life peer, and in 1960 was appointed President of the British Board of Film Censors. He published a number of books on his activities on behalf of the Labour party, including *Socialization and Transport* (1933), *Government and Parliament, a Survey from the Inside* (1954), and *An Autobiography* (1960).

In 1919 he married Margaret, daughter of Howard Kent, a clerk at Euston Station; they had one daughter. Margaret died in 1953, and in 1955 he married Edith, daughter of John Meadowcroft, of Rochdale.

Morrison died at Sidcup on 6 March 1965; his ashes were scattered on the Thames in London. He was a great parliamentarian, and a master of administrative detail, but, as Attlee said of him, 'Herbert cannot distinguish between big things and little things', and this was his Achilles' heel.

MOSLEY, SIR OSWALD ERNALD (1896-1980), poli-tician and Fascist leader, was born in London on 16 November 1896, the eldest son of Oswald Mosley (later fifth baronet) and his wife, Katharine Maud, the daughter of Capt. Justinian Edwards-Heathcote, of Longton Hall, Stoke on Trent. His father and mother separated when he was five, and he was brought up by his mother and his grandfather. He was educated at Winchester and Sandhurst.

In 1914 he joined the 16th Lancers, then transferred to the RFC, but was sent back to the 16th Lancers. In 1916 he was invalided out of the forces owing to the serious de-terioration of an earlier injury to his ankle in a plane crash. He spent the rest of the war in the Ministry of Munitions and the Foreign Office. In 1918 he became Conservative MP for Harrow, and in 1920 married Lady Cynthia Blanche, daughter of Sir George Nathaniel CURZON, who brought him a large fortune.

He soon found himself disagreeing with his party over military expenditure and their Irish policy; in 1922 he joined the opposition, and was returned to Parliament as an In-dependent in the general election that year. He continued to hold his Harrow seat in 1923, and in 1924 joined the Labour party. He was defeated at Birmingham Ladywood by Neville CHAMBERLAIN in 1924 but elected in 1926 as Labour MP for Smethwick.

In 1928 he succeeded to the baronetcy. In the following year he was returned for Smethwick while his wife became Labour MP for Stoke on Trent. In the new Labour Govern-ment he became Chancellor of the Duchy of Lancaster and was deputed to help J. H. THOMAS, Lord Privy Seal, to deal with the problem of unemployment. He was the only member of the Government to put forward constructive proposals for the direction of industry, control of foreign trade, and a systematic programme of public works. However, his views conflicted with the orthodox policies of Philip SNOWDEN and Thomas and, when his proposals were rejected, he resigned (1930).

Mosley was an outstanding orator, but his arrogance was resented by his colleagues; his proposals were defeated at the Labour party conference, and in 1931 he launched his 'New Party'. The result was disastrous; all twenty-four candidates were defeated in the October election. He now became dis-satisfied with the Parliamentary system and, after a visit to Mussolini's Italy in 1932, set about creating a British Fascist movement. At first he received some Conservative support, but by 1934 Mosley and his blackshirts had become identified with violence, extremism, and anti-semitism.

In 1936 the movement became the British Union of Fascists and National Socialists, and Mosley's Keynesian policies of 1930 were replaced by totalitarianism and chauvin-istic racialism. In 1933 his wife had died, and in 1936 he married, in Berlin, the Hon. Mrs Diana Guinness, daughter of the second Baron Redesdale, and sister of Jessica, Unity, and Nancy MITFORD. From 1936 Mosley was pro-Nazi, and mounted a peace campaign, which he continued after the Second World War had started. In 1940 he and his wife were detained under Regulation 18B; they were released in 1943 because of Mosley's state of health.

After the war he sought to justify his actions in *My Answer* (1946) and *My Life* (1968). From 1948 to 1966 he led the Union movement, aiming at European unity, based on racial ideas. He was defeated in Parliamentary elections in 1959 and 1966. He died at his home at Orsay in France on 3 December 1980. Potentially Mosley was a brilliant politician, but his arrogance and lack of judgement led him into

Mosley (centre) at the Blackshirt Rally, Hyde Park, September 1934

situations which drove him into extremism that could only end in disaster. By his first wife he had two sons and a daughter, and by his second two sons.

His eldest son, Nicholas, published a biography of his parents *The Rules of the Game* (1982) and *Beyond the Pale, Sir Oswald Mosley 1933-80* (1983). In the first of these he reveals his mother's distress at the relation between his father and Diana Guinness, though this was but one of Mosley's infidelities.

MOUNTBATTEN, EDWINA CYNTHIA ANNETTE, COUNTESS MOUNTBATTEN OF BURMA (1901-1960), was born in London on 28 November 1901, the elder daughter of Col. W. W. Ashley, PC, MP (later Baron Mount Temple), of Broadlands, Romsey, and Classiebawn Castle, co. Sligo (both inherited from Lord Palmerston). Her mother was Amalia Mary Maud, only child of Sir Ernest CASSEL, friend and confidant of Edward VII. She was the great-granddaughter of the seventh Earl of Shaftesbury. Her mother died in 1911, and her father married again. When she was sixteen, unhappy at her home at Broadlands, she went to live with her grandfather in London, and assisted him with his social responsibilities.

She was nineteen when Sir Ernest died and left an immense fortune to her and her sister, Mary. In 1921 she met Lord Louis MOUNTBATTEN, RN, younger son of Admiral the Mar-

quess of Milford Haven, formerly Prince Louis of BATTENBERG, and his wife, Victoria, granddaughter of Queen Victoria. They were married in 1922 at a grand wedding, attended by George V, Queen Mary, and Queen Alexandra, with Edward, Prince of Wales as best man.

For the rest of that year they travelled in Europe and America, and made friends with a number of film stars in Hollywood, including Charles CHAPLIN and the Fairbanks. Back in London, they entered upon a hectic social life. In 1924 Patricia, their first daughter, was born, but this did not deter Edwina from accompanying her husband, with the Prince of Wales, when they visited the USA that summer.

During the following year Mountbatten was on a signals course at Portsmouth, and for a time it appeared that he and Edwina were settling down to the domestic routine appropriate to an ambitious naval officer and his wife. But Edwina soon became restless and dissatisfied with this life, and in 1925 she set off on the first of her travels on her own. On this occasion, she visited the South Seas. In 1926 Mountbatten was posted to the Mediterranean fleet, and he and Edwina took up residence in Malta early in 1927. Life in Malta did not content Edwina for long, and soon she was on her travels again, visiting Persia and returning to Hollywood. In 1929 her second daughter, Pamela, was born.

In 1932 *The People* published a piece of gossip about a rich society hostess who was alleged to have had an affair with a coloured man. It appeared that this could only refer to Edwina, and the Mountbattens sued Odhams newspapers for libel and forced the defendants to make an unqualified apology; Edwina refused damages, but this case, which aroused much publicity, did harm to her reputation, which no one could claim to be entirely above reproach.

The Second World War gave both Mountbattens the chance to make a name for themselves. Edwina entered upon a distinguished career with the Order of St John. After working in London during the worst of the air raids, she was appointed Superintendent-in-Chief of the St John Ambulance Brigade in 1942. Later, when Lord Louis became Supreme Allied Commander, South East Asia, she worked indefatigably for the welfare of released Allied prisoners of war and internees.

During 1947–8 Mountbatten was the last Viceroy and first Governor-General of independent India. From the outset, the Viceroy sought to win the confidence of Indian leaders such as Nehru and GANDHI, and in this he was ably assisted by Edwina. She charmed all the Indian leaders, and Nehru, a lonely widower, adored her. When independence was accompanied by riots and massacres Lady Mountbatten again worked tirelessly to organize the welfare activities needed to bring some relief to the bereaved and homeless.

On their return to England, she continued her work and became Chairman of the St John and Red Cross Services Hospitals Welfare Department, and in 1950 was appointed Superintendent-in-Chief of the St John Ambulance Brigade Overseas. She also continued to make exhausting tours abroad and, while on one of these, she died in her sleep at Jesselton, North Borneo, on the night of 20–21 February 1960. Her body was flown home, and she was buried at sea off Portsmouth.

Her elder daughter, Patricia, married the film producer John Knatchbull, seventh Baron Brabourne, and her younger daughter, Pamela, married the designer David Hicks.

Mountbatten was created viscount in 1946 and earl in 1947. Edwina was appointed GC St. J (1945), DCVO (1946), CI (1947), and GBE (1947). Jawaharlal Nehru wrote her epitaph when he said she had 'the healer's touch'.

MOUNTBATTEN, LOUIS ALEXANDER, first MARQUESS OF MILFORD HAVEN, formerly Prince Louis Alexander of Battenberg (1854–1921), Admiral of the Fleet, was born at Gratz, Austria, on 24 May 1854, the eldest son of Prince Alexander of Hesse, and his wife, Countess Julia Theresa von Haucke. His mother was a close friend of Princess Alice, daughter of Queen Victoria. Prince Louis was brought up in England, naturalized, and entered the Royal Navy in 1868.

In 1884 he married his cousin, Princess Victoria, daughter of Louis IV of Hesse-Darmstadt and Princess Alice; they had two sons and two daughters.

The Mountbattens with GANDHI, New Delhi, 1947

He saw service as a lieutenant during the Egyptian War (1882) and was promoted commander in 1885. In 1892 he was posted to the Admiralty and from 1902 to 1905 was Director of Naval Intelligence; he was promoted to rear-admiral in 1904. From 1908 to 1910 he commanded the Atlantic Fleet; he became vice-admiral in 1910, and returned to the Admiralty as Second Sea Lord in 1911.

Winston CHURCHILL, then First Lord of the Admiralty, selected Prince Louis to be First Sea Lord in 1912 and it was primarily due to Prince Louis's initiative that, when the First World War was declared, the navy was in a state of readiness. This did not, however, protect him from criticism on account of his German birth. In October 1914 he resigned.

When the war ended he was promoted to Admiral of the Fleet. In 1917, at the request of King George V, he relinquished his German titles and assumed the name Mountbatten; he was raised to the peerage as Marquess of Milford Haven.

He died in London on 11 September 1921 and was succeeded by his elder son, George. His younger son, Lord Louis MOUNTBATTEN, had a distinguished career in the navy and became Viceroy of India.

MOUNTBATTEN, LOUIS FRANCIS ALBERT VICTOR NICHOLAS, first EARL MOUNTBATTEN OF BURMA (1900–1979), Admiral of the Fleet, was born at Frogmore House, Windsor on 25 June 1900, the younger son of Prince Louis of Battenberg (later MOUNTBATTEN). He entered Osborne in 1913 and Dartmouth in 1914; in 1916 he was posted as midshipman to BEATTY's flagship HMS *Lion* and in the following year served in the *Queen Elizabeth*. At this time his father took the family name of Mountbatten. In 1919–20 Lord Louis spent a year at Christ's College, Cambridge, and was invited to accompany Edward, Prince of Wales, his cousin, on a tour of Australasia. This was followed in 1921–2 by a similar royal tour to India and Japan.

In 1922 he married Edwina Ashley; they had two daughters. From 1923 to 1938 he pursued his naval career, specializing as a signals officer, serving in destroyers. During this period, he earned a reputation as a playboy, which was not regarded with favour by the Establishment, and Edwina MOUNTBATTEN also attracted some adverse publicity. The abdication of his friend, Edward VIII, however, caused him much distress.

On the outbreak of the Second World War he became captain of the 5th Destroyer Flotilla. The war provided him with the opportunity to make a name for himself. In HMS *Kelly*, immortalized by Noël COWARD's film, *In Which We Serve*, Mountbatten succeeded in evacuating Carton de Wiart and Allied troops from Norway, and survived the sinking of his ship off Crete. In 1942 he was appointed Chief of Combined Operations, with the acting rank of vice-admiral; and in this capacity planned the attack on the dry dock at St Nazaire and the costly Dieppe raid. He was also directly concerned with the plans for the invasion of Normandy. It is possible that he could claim some credit for the decision to make the attack in that area rather than in the Pas de Calais. Years later (1966–7) in the television saga 'The Life and Times of Lord Mountbatten', he claimed to have been responsible for the Mulberry harbour (floating port) and PLUTO (Pipe Line under the Ocean), which contributed to the success of the landings. It seems probable that his support for these unconventional projects helped to get them accepted as an important element in the planning of the invasion.

In 1943 Mountbatten attended the Quebec Conference and was selected as acting admiral and Supreme Commander, South-East Asia. He took over his new responsibilities at a time when Allied prospects of success against the Japanese were at a low ebb. His appointment was not welcomed by some of those under his command nor by the American, General Stilwell ('Vinegar Joe'), his deputy. Mountbatten was in favour of an amphibious operation, aimed at the recapture of Rangoon, whilst Stilwell was solely concerned with reopening the road between northern Burma and China. These differences were resolved by the Japanese, who in 1944 tried to force a way into India via Imphal in the western hills of Burma. The battle for Imphal was won by General SLIM and the 14th Army, and later, with Slim's capture of Meiktila in central Burma, the way was opened to the recapture of Rangoon by land (1945). Mountbatten's contribution to this success was the heightening of morale which he induced in the troops under his command.

He attended the Potsdam Conference in July 1945 and was informed about the atomic bomb. On 12 September he received the formal surrender of the Japanese at Singapore, but he was still faced with the problems of restoring law and order and providing relief in the vast areas of South-East Asia, which the enemy had occupied. His own inclinations favoured the new nationalist movements, given increased impetus in Burma and Malaya by the initial defeat of the colonialist regimes. In Burma, for example, he accepted the co-operation of Aung San and his young followers, who had supported the Japanese and then changed their allegiance when they saw that the Japanese would be on the losing side. This created problems when civil government was restored in 1946, and led to the assassination of Aung San and all his Cabinet through the connivance of one of the older pre-war Burmese politicians U Saw. Mountbatten's critics have argued that his support of the nationalists in Malaya also led to future troubles there. However, the fact remains that, once the military forces were withdrawn from these countries by demobilization, the upsurge of nationalism could not have been subdued.

In 1946 Mountbatten left South-East Asia, hoping to return to the navy but, towards the end of that year, he was persuaded by Clement ATTLEE to replace Lord WAVELL as Viceroy of India. It was clear by the time he arrived in Delhi that the principle of a united India, for which the CRIPPS mission to India had striven, was no longer practicable and that division between India and Pakistan had become inevitable. Mountbatten and his wife, Edwina, soon gained the respect and confidence of Nehru, but Jinnah remained intractably hostile. In mid-1947 the Viceroy announced that independence would be granted on 15 August and on that date he became Governor-General of India, but not of Pakistan. The sub-continent erupted into violence and disorder. Some quarter of a million people were killed in racial massacres and there was little that Mountbatten could do about it. Early in 1948, with the help of GANDHI, he persuaded the Indian Government to release large sums due to Pakistan and thus avoided a dangerous crisis between the two countries. A few weeks later Gandhi was assassinated. In June 1948 the Mountbattens left India, having succeeded in gaining the affection of millions and having maintained good relations between the newly independent Government and Britain.

Lord Louis returned to the navy as rear-admiral commanding the 1st Cruiser Squadron in the Mediterranean. He was promoted vice-admiral in 1949 and in 1950 became Fourth Sea Lord. In 1953 he was promoted to admiral and returned to the Mediterranean, where he was appointed Supreme Allied Commander of the new NATO command. Then, in 1955, he achieved his lifelong ambition by becoming First Sea Lord, and set out to reorganize the navy to meet the post-war conditions which demanded serious changes. The Suez crisis of 1956 found him disagreeing with the Prime Minister, Anthony EDEN, about the planning of the landings in the canal zone, and he offered his resignation which was refused. Later that year, he was promoted Admiral of the Fleet. In 1959 he took over as Chief of Defence Staff and, with the agreement of Harold Macmillan, attempted to secure closer co-ordination of the three Services. In spite of considerable opposition, he succeeded in 1964 in strengthening the role of the CDS, though his hopes of centralizing control of defence were not realized because his ideas were unacceptable to the Chiefs of Staff. He believed firmly that Britain must have an independent nuclear deterrent and was in favour of the Polaris missile.

Edwina died in 1960, and Lord Louis agreed to stay on as CDS until 1964, and then until 1965. After his retirement, he undertook public service of a different kind. For example, in 1966 he reported to the Home Secretary on prison security. He also became Governor of the Isle of Wight and Colonel of the Life Guards. Mountbatten was always a great favourite of the royal family; he received many honours and decorations. He was appointed MVO (1920), KCVO (1922), GCVO (1937), DSO (1941), CB (1943), KCB (1945), viscount (1946), KG (1946), PC (1947), earl (1947), GCSI (1947), GCIE (1947), GCB (1955), and FRS (1966). He was also an honorary DCL (Oxford) and held honorary degrees from many other universities.

Every summer he went for a family holiday to Classiebawn Castle, co. Sligo, which Edwina had inherited. On 27 August 1979 a bomb, planted by the IRA, exploded in a fishing boat as Lord Louis and his party were setting out to collect lobsters. He was killed instantly, together with Lady Brabourne, his son-in-law's mother, his grandson, Nicholas, and a local Irish boy. He was succeeded by his elder daughter, Patricia, by special remainder.

MOUNTEVANS, first BARON (1880-1957). See EVANS, EDWARD RATCLIFFE GARTH RUSSELL.

MUIR, EDWIN (1887-1959), writer and poet, was born in Deerness in the Orkneys on 15 May 1887, the youngest of six children of James Muir, a farmer, and his wife, Elizabeth, daughter of Edwin Cormack. He was brought up on farms in the Orkneys and on the mainland near Kirkwall, and went to Kirkwall Grammar School. When he was fourteen his family moved to Glasgow, and within five years his father, mother, and two brothers were dead. He found work as office-boy and clerk. When war broke out he volunteered for the army but was rejected as physically unfit.

In 1919 he married Wilhelmina (Willa) Johnstone, daughter of Peter Anderson, a draper, of Montrose; together they left Glasgow for London, where Muir became assistant to A. R. Orage, Editor of the *New Age*, a weekly review to which he had contributed some verses in 1913. During the next few years he earned his living as a critic, with the help of his wife as a translator. Together they made the works of Kafka and Hermann Broch available to the British public, as well as Feuchtwanger's *Jew Süss*. He also wrote a life of John Knox (1929) and published *Scottish Journey* (1935). His criticism was published in a thousand articles which were collected and republished in book form. T. S. ELIOT thought

his 'the best criticism of our time'. He also continued to write poetry, much of it based on his early memories of life on a Scottish farm, and the best of it written when he was over fifty. He was not an innovator and tried to portray what he saw, clearly and simply. His *Collected Poems 1921-51* were published in 1952 and *1921-58* in 1960.

From 1942 to 1950 Muir worked for the British Council in Edinburgh, Prague, and Rome, and from 1950 to 1955 was Warden of Newbattle Abbey, an adult education college, near Edinburgh. Then during 1955-6 he went to Harvard as Charles Eliot Norton Professor. He was appointed CBE in 1953, and received a number of honorary degrees. He published his *Autobiography* in 1954, and died at Cambridge on 3 January 1959; he and Willa had one son.

MUNNINGS, SIR ALFRED JAMES (1878-1959), artist, was born on 8 October 1878 at Mendham Mill, Suffolk, the second of the four sons of the miller, John Munnings, and his wife, Ellen, daughter of William Ringer, a farmer. He was educated at the village school, the grammar school at Redenhall, and Framlingham College, but left school at fourteen to become an apprentice with Page Brothers, lithographers of Norwich. In the evenings he studied at the Norwich School of Art.

Munnings designed posters for Caley's chocolates and crackers and was taken abroad by the manager, Shaw Tomkins, to visit art galleries. In 1898 he had the misfortune to lose the sight of his right eye in an accident. He was obsessed by his love of horses and, during his early career as an oil painter in Norfolk, he mostly painted gypsies and their animals. In 1911 he moved to Newlyn in Cornwall and became one of the group which included Harold and Laura KNIGHT and Lamorna Birch. In 1912 he married Florence Carter-Wood, who died in 1914.

During the First World War he was rejected for military service but became a war artist with the Canadian Cavalry Brigade. His first outstanding success came with his portrait of General J. E. B. Seely (later Lord Mottistone) on his horse, Warrior. This was followed by a number of equestrian portraits, including those of Lord Harewood and the Princess Royal, and Lord BIRKENHEAD. After the war he achieved notable success and financial independence with his studies of gypsies and horses on Epsom Downs. In 1919 he moved to London. In 1920 he married Violet McBride, widowed daughter of Frank Golby Haines, a riding master; she took over the business side of his career and capably managed the large sums he received for some of his paintings; they had no children.

He now became the finest painter of animals of his time. In 1924 he visited the United States, and in 1926 Spain, where he was aghast at the treatment of horses, particularly in the bullring. He was elected ARA in 1919 and RA in 1925. He immortalized many famous racehorses including Humorist, Hyperion, and Brown Jack.

In 1944 Munnings was knighted and became President of the Royal Academy. It was his idea that Winston CHURCHILL should be made an honorary academician in 1949. He was bitterly antagonistic to all modern art and he resigned as President of the Royal Academy in 1949. In 1947 he was appointed KCVO. He published his autobiography in three volumes, *An Artist's Life* (1950), *The Second Burst* (1951), and *The Finish* (1952). A successful exhibition of his work was held at the Royal Academy in 1956. Munnings died at Castle House, Dedham on 17 July 1959.

MUNRO, HECTOR HUGH (1870–1916), author under the pseudonym Saki, was born on 18 December 1870 at Akyab, Burma, son of Col. Munro, Inspector-General of Police. His mother died when he was young, and he was brought up in Devon, with his brother and sister, by his grandmother and two aunts whose authoritarian ways he heartily disliked. He went to school in Exmouth and then to Bedford Grammar School. In 1893 he returned to Burma and, like George ORWELL at a later date, joined the police. Also like Orwell, he did not stay long in Burma; after fifteen months he resigned through ill health.

He began writing as a political satirist for the *Westminster Gazette* and his sketches were published as *The Westminster Alice* (1902). In the same year he published the *Not So Stories*. He had already produced in 1900 a history of Russia, *The Rise of the Russian Empire*, and in 1904 he went to Russia as correspondent for the *Morning Post*. In 1908 he was in Paris working for that paper.

In 1910 he returned to London and continued to contribute political essays to a number of papers. His first collection of short stories, *Reginald*, was published in 1904, followed by similar unconventional stories including *Reginald in Russia* (1910), *The Chronicles of Clovis* (1911), and *Beasts and Super-Beasts* (1914). *The Unbearable Bassington* (1912) was a novel in the same satirical vein as the short stories. All these were published under the pseudonym, Saki, the name of the cup-bearer in *The Rubáiyát* of Omar Khayyám.

In 1914 Munro enlisted. He was sent to the front in France in November 1915 and was killed near Beaumont Hamel a year later on 14 November 1916. *The Toys of Peace* (1919) and *The Square Egg* (1924) were published posthumously; the latter of these includes a biography of Munro by his sister.

MURRAY, (GEORGE) GILBERT AIMÉ (1866–1957), classical scholar and internationalist, was born in Sydney on 2 January 1866. His father, (Sir) Terence Murray, was President of the Legislative Council of New South Wales and his mother was a cousin of (Sir) W. S. Gilbert of Gilbert and Sullivan fame. His brother, Hubert, became Governor of Papua. His innate sympathy for the oppressed was nurtured in Australia by what he saw of the treatment of the aborigines. When he was eleven his father died and his mother took him to England. He was educated at Merchant Taylors' School and St John's College, Oxford, where he won the Hertford and Ireland scholarships in 1885, and obtained a first in Greats and a fellowship of New College in 1888.

When he was appointed Professor of Greek at Glasgow at the age of twenty-three, he was described by Sir Richard Jebb as 'the most accomplished Greek scholar of the day'. He had to begin the day's work with prayers but, although he had been brought up as a Roman Catholic, he had now become an agnostic and satisfied his conscience by giving the Lord's Prayer in Greek. He was a natural teacher with a beautiful voice and his students were charmed by his lectures. He left Glasgow in 1899 after ten years because of ill health, and during the next few years he lived at Churt in Surrey; but also visited Berlin to study Greek under Ulrich von Wilamowitz-Moellendorff.

He was already writing plays and, at the request of his friend George Bernard SHAW, published some of his translations of Greek plays in 1902. Shaw put him into *Major Barbara* as Cusins (1905).

In 1905 Murray returned to Oxford as a Fellow of New

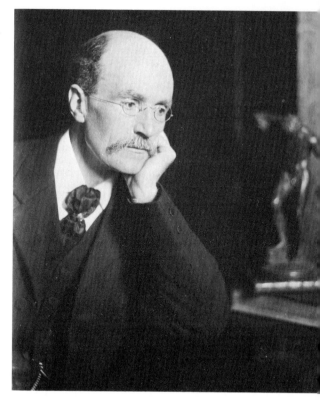

Gilbert Murray

College; in 1908 he was appointed Regius Professor of Greek and in 1910 was elected FBA. He had already edited Euripides for the Oxford Classical Texts (3 vols., 1901–9) and translated Euripides into English verse, followed by translations of Aeschylus and Sophocles. In these he adopted a style based on Swinburne and William Morris. When he tackled Aristophanes, he used for the *Frogs* and the *Knights* the language of W. S. Gilbert. T. S. ELIOT wrote: 'as a poet Mr Murray is merely a very insignificant follower of the pre-Raphaelite movement', and objected to the fact that Murray would add to his script words that were not in the original Greek text. This was true, but his translations had an appealing liveliness and were intended to be used for the stage. A. E. HOUSMAN, who could be a harsh critic, accepted that Murray, with consummate scholarship, was always careful to preserve the meaning of the original text in his more scholarly work. In 1907 he published the *Rise of the Greek Epic* and in 1912 *Four Stages of Greek Religion* (extended in 1925 to *Five Stages*).

In 1889 Murray married Lady Mary Howard, daughter of the ninth Earl of Carlisle, who was beautiful and eccentric and, like her husband, was a radical who hated oppression and was a generous friend of refugees. Murray had disapproved of the Boer War and advocated votes for women, but he changed his attitude to war as the danger of German aggression increased after 1910. He personally admired ASQUITH and GREY, and his *Foreign Policy of Sir Edward Grey* (1915) temporarily estranged him from close friends such as Henry Brailsford and Bertrand RUSSELL.

He was, however, essentially a man of peace, and from

1919 to his death strove to make effective the organizations intended to outlaw war. He was a founder (and Chairman 1923-38) of the League of Nations Union, and after the Second World War Joint President (1945-7, 1949-57) and sole President (1947-9) of the United Nations Association. To some extent, his energetic pursuit of these activities impaired his work as Professor at Oxford though he would have indignantly denied this, and in 1923 told the Vice-Chancellor of Oxford, 'I care far more for teaching Greek than for any other pursuit in life.'

He retired from the regius professorship in 1936 and was appointed to the Order of Merit in 1941. He and his wife had three sons and two daughters. She died in 1956 and he died at his home on Boar's Hill on 20 May 1957 in his ninety-second year. One of his Oxford colleagues wrote, 'It was impossible to know him without loving him, or to see him without being revived and encouraged and inspirited.'

MURRAY, SIR JAMES AUGUSTUS HENRY (1837-1915), first Editor of *The Oxford English Dictionary*, was born at Denholm, near Hawick, Roxburghshire, on 7 February 1837, the eldest son of Thomas Murray, a men's outfitter of Hawick, and his wife, Mary, daughter of Charles Scott, a linen manufacturer. He was educated at Cavers and Minto schools, and when he was seventeen became assistant master at Hawick Grammar School. He meanwhile continued his own education: to the Latin, Greek, and French which he had learned at school he now added other languages while also studying science and local antiquities. At the age of twenty Murray was appointed Headmaster of the Subscription Academy, Hawick (1857).

In 1862 he married Maggie Isabella Sarah Scott, of Belfast. Owing to her ill health, they moved to London where he took a job as a bank clerk, but in 1864 she died. Three years later Murray married Ada Agnes, daughter of George Ruthven, of Kendal; they had six sons and five daughters. In 1870 Murray became a master at Mill Hill School and three years later became BA (London).

Soon after his arrival in London Murray had become a member of the London Philological Society which had been planning since 1857 the compilation of a new English dictionary based on historical principles, for which Herbert Coleridge, grandson of the poet, had been collecting material, until his premature death in 1861. Murray took an active part in keeping the scheme alive, but no publisher could be found who was willing to sponsor the enterprise until, in 1879, the Delegates of the Clarendon Press agreed to undertake publication of the dictionary and Murray was appointed Editor. He retained his post at Mill Hill School and, in the interim, had already published his *Dialect of the Southern Counties of Scotland* (1873) and written the article on the English language in the *Encyclopaedia Britannica* (1878).

For some years Murray worked at Mill Hill selecting from and organizing material sent to him by voluntary workers, many of them in the USA, and the cards on which he noted this information had risen to some five million by 1885 when, in order to concentrate full time on his tremendous task, he moved to Oxford. The first section of the dictionary, covering *A-Ant*, had been published in the previous year. At the time the Clarendon Press undertook to publish the dictionary it was hoped that the work could be completed in ten years. In fact, when Murray died in 1915, he had been working indefatigably for thirty-five years, but had only been able to complete half the project covering A-D, H-K, O, P, and T.

However, it was Murray who established the principles

upon which the dictionary was to be compiled, and it was fortunate for this vast undertaking that he was available to carry out the first and most difficult part of the work. To honour his achievement he received a number of degrees and was elected to a number of learned societies. He was President of the London Philological Society three times, was an original Fellow of the British Academy, and in 1908 received a knighthood. He died at Oxford on 26 July 1915.

MURRAY, MARGARET ALICE (1863-1963), Egyptologist, was born in Calcutta on 13 July 1863, the younger daughter of James Charles Murray, a business manager, and his wife, Margaret Carr, who had gone to India as a missionary. Margaret Murray received private education in England and Germany but never went to school. She wanted to become a nurse, and in 1883 worked in Calcutta General Hospital, but returned to England in 1886 and found that she could not become a professional nurse as she was too small. All her life she was an ardent feminist.

In 1894 she became a student of Egyptology under Flinders PETRIE at University College London. She quickly learnt to decipher Egyptian hieroglyphs and became the first woman Egyptologist. In 1902 she assisted Petrie with his excavations at Abydos, but her lecturing and teaching in London restricted her opportunities for field work.

In 1899 she was appointed junior lecturer at University College, and was promoted to assistant (1909), lecturer (1921), senior lecturer and Fellow (1922), and assistant professor (1924-35), being appointed D.Lit. in 1931. She also became interested in anthropology and ethnology.

She excavated in Malta (1920-3), Minorca (1930-1), and at Petra (1937), and in 1938 joined Petrie's expedition to Tell El Ajjul, ancient Gaza, and worked specially on the Hyksos cities. She published over eighty books on ancient Egypt, including *Ancient Egyptian Legends* (1904), *Saqqara Mastabas* (2 vols., 1905-37), *Elementary Egyptian Grammar* (1905), *Index of Names and Titles in the Old Kingdom* (1908), *Egyptian Temples* (1931), *The Splendour that was Egypt* (1949), and *The Genesis of Religion* (1963).

Margaret Murray was also deeply interested in witchcraft and folklore, and was a Fellow of the Royal Anthropological Institute (1926) and President of the Folklore Society (1953-5). In 1921 she published *The Witch-Cult in Western Europe*, an authoritative work on the subject. She also wrote an autobiography, *My First Hundred Years* (1963). She was a woman of great courage and strong personality who took an active interest in the welfare of her students. She died in London on 13 November 1963, aged 100.

MURRY, JOHN MIDDLETON (1889-1957), author and literary critic, was born in London on 6 August 1889, the elder son of John Murry, a clerk in the Inland Revenue Department, and his wife, Emily Wheeler. The family was poor and Murry obtained his education at Christ's Hospital and Brasenose College, Oxford through scholarships. He went up to Brasenose in 1909, obtained a first in Mods. (1910), and later that year went to Paris, where he came under the influence of Bergson and returned reluctantly to Oxford to take his degree with a second in Greats (1912). Together with his friend, Michael Sadleir, he started a new periodical which they called *Rhythm*. He also met Katherine MANSFIELD, became her lodger and, later, her lover.

During 1912-13 he wrote for the *Westminster Gazette* and the *Times Literary Supplement*. Unfit for military service, he got a job in 1916, with the help of Eddie MARSH, in the

John Middleton Murry and Katherine Mansfield, 1913

Political Intelligence Department of the War Office, and in 1919 was appointed Chief-Censor. Meanwhile, in 1918 he had married Katherine Mansfield. From 1919 to 1921 he was Editor of the *Athenaeum* and became one of the leading post-war literary figures, an intimate friend of D. H. LAW-RENCE and Ottoline MORRELL, but also a bitter opponent of other authors whose work he severely criticized. Under his control the *Athenaeum* lost money, and in 1921 was merged with the *Nation*.

Katherine Mansfield, from 1919 to the time of her death, was a very sick woman; during the winter of 1919–20 she was in a sanatorium, and in 1920 she wrote her last review for the *Athenaeum*. After the merger of the paper with the *Nation*, Murry resigned as Editor. Soon after Katherine's death in 1923 Murry founded the *Adelphi* which he managed until 1948. In 1924 he married again, but his second wife, Violet le Maistre, by whom he had a son and daughter, died, as Katherine had done, from tuberculosis (1931). His son, Colin, considered that their love for each other was based on an illusion: Murry saw in her the reincarnation of Katherine.

As early as 1916 Murry had produced a critical study of Dostoevsky, and this was followed by similar works on Keats, D. H. Lawrence, William Blake, and Shakespeare. His writing was interrupted by political and social activities, which included lecturing on a variety of subjects. His reputation depends, however, on his critical work, and his books on authors such as Lawrence were followed years later by *Jonathan Swift* (1954), *Unprofessional Essays* (1956), and *Love, Freedom and Society* (1957). He described his early life up to the time of his marriage to Katherine Mansfield in *Between Two Worlds* (1935).

His third marriage was to Elizabeth Ada, daughter of Joseph Cockbayne, a farmer (1931); they had a son and a daughter, but the marriage was unhappy and, when Elizabeth died in 1954, Murry married Mary, daughter of Henry Gilbert Gamble, an architect, with whom he had lived since 1941.

In 1920 Murry was appointed OBE. He died at Bury St Edmunds on 13 March 1957.

MURRY, KATHLEEN (1888–1923). See MANSFIELD, KATHERINE.

N

NAMIER, SIR LEWIS BERNSTEIN (1888–1960), historian, was born on 27 June 1888 at Wola Okrzejska, to the east of Warsaw, the only son of Joseph Bernstein, advocate and landowner, and his wife, Ann, daughter of Maurice Theodor Sommerstein. Both parents were Polish Jews. Namier, born Ludwik Bernstein, was educated at Lwow and Lausanne Universities, the London School of Economics, and Balliol College, Oxford. He obtained a first in modern history (1911) and shared the Beit prize (1913). He took British nationality in 1913 and changed his name by deed poll.

In the same year he took a business appointment in the United States and also undertook research into eighteenth-century parliamentary history. On the outbreak of the First World War he volunteered and served as a private in the Royal Fusiliers until, in 1915, his knowledge of eastern Europe led to his employment in the Foreign Office on propaganda and political intelligence.

In 1917 he married Clara Sophie Edeleff, the widowed daughter of Alexander Poniatowski, doctor of medicine.

During 1920–1 he was a tutor at Balliol College. He wanted to pursue research, but first had to earn the money for the purpose; so he again entered business, as representative of a firm of Manchester cotton manufacturers with his headquarters in Czechoslovakia. He was also a correspondent for the *Manchester Guardian*.

From 1924 to 1929 he returned to historical research, aiming to produce a multi-volumed study of the British Parliament during the period of the American revolution. He published two works which formed part of this project, *The Structure of Politics on the Accession of George III* (1929) and *England in the Age of the American Revolution* (1930). These books were notable for their meticulous attention to detail, and for the attempt to build up a graphic picture of the parliamentary history of the period from a careful study of the individuals concerned, their backgrounds and interests, with elaborate footnotes, chasing side-issues, wherever they might lead to further clarification. Unfortunately, Namier in these two studies did not reach the American revolution.

In 1929 he became Political Secretary to the Jewish Agency for Palestine, but in 1931 was appointed Professor of Modern History at Manchester and held the chair until 1953. In 1939 he was adviser to Chaim WEIZMANN at the Palestine Conference, and during 1940-5 was working full time on political work with the Jewish Agency. When he, later, became a Christian, Weizmann ceased to be his friend.

His first marriage, which had not been happy, came to an end with the death of Clara in 1945. Two years later he married Iulia de Beausobre, widowed daughter of Mikhail Kazarin, barrister at the Russian Law Court. Namier had no children of either marriage.

He was elected FBA in 1944, and gave the Raleigh lecture, which was expanded and published as *1848: The Revolution of the Intellectuals* (1946). He also published his researches into the origins of the Second World War in *Diplomatic Prelude* (1948), *Europe in Decay* (1950), and *In the Nazi Era* (1952). He had little respect for Karl Marx.

In 1951 he returned to what had always been his main historical interest; he was appointed to the editorial board for producing a history of Parliament, and given responsibility for the period 1754-90. He did not live to see this work completed. He died suddenly in London on 19 August 1960 and the work was finished by his chief assistant, John Brooke, and published in three volumes in 1964.

Namier as a historian exerted considerable influence over other historians of his generation and brought a new perspective to the period about which he wrote. Much of his work took the form of essays and book reviews, some of which were collected in book form. He became an honorary Fellow of Balliol College in 1948 and received a number of honorary degrees. In 1952 he was knighted. Isaiah Berlin has described him as 'one of the most distinguished historians of our time'.

NASH, PAUL (1889-1946), artist, was born in London on 11 May 1889, the elder son of William Harry Nash, Recorder of Abingdon, and his first wife, Caroline Maude, daughter of Capt. John Milbourne Jackson, RN. He was educated at St Paul's School, the Chelsea Polytechnic, and the Slade School of Fine Art where he studied during 1910-11.

Unlike some of his contemporaries such as Stanley SPENCER and Ben Nicholson, he was not influenced by the Post-Impressionist Exhibition staged by Roger FRY in 1910. Advised by Sir William Richmond, who had been Slade Professor at Oxford, to 'go in for Nature', Nash adopted a highly individual style which is illustrated in his monoliths and monster trees.

He had his first one-man exhibition of water-colours at the Carfax Gallery in 1912, and shared an exhibition with his brother John Northcote Nash at the Dorien Leigh Gallery in 1913.

In 1914 Nash married Margaret Theodosia, daughter of the Revd Naser Odeh; they had no children. At the outbreak of the First World War he enlisted in the Artists' Rifles and saw active service in France until in 1917 he was invalided home. He then returned to the front as a war artist and produced paintings, the most famous of which *The Menin Road*, is in the Imperial War Museum.

In the post-war years he illustrated books, designed scenery, fabrics, and posters, and became established as a water-colourist, famous for his series of pictures of Dymchurch beach and his studies of trees. In 1933 he founded the 'Unit

Paul Nash, by Helen Muspratt, 1933

One' group, held exhibitions at the Redfern and Leicester Galleries, and in 1938 exhibited at the Venice Biennale.

In 1930 he began his illustrations for Sir Thomas Browne's *Urne Buriall* and *The Garden of Cyrus*. During the Second World War he worked for a time in Oxford and then again became a war artist, employed by the Air Ministry and the Ministry of Information. One of his paintings of this period, *Totes Meer*, portraying damaged German aeroplanes on a dump at Oxford, is in the Tate Gallery. He died at Boscombe on 11 July 1946.

NEVINSON, HENRY WOODD (1856-1941), essayist, philanthropist, and journalist, was born at Leicester on 11 October 1856, the second son of George Nevinson, a solicitor, and his wife, Mary Basil Woodd. He was educated at Shrewsbury, where he was a scholar, and Christ Church, Oxford. After leaving Oxford in 1879, he taught Greek at Westminster and then studied German at Jena. In 1884 he published *Herder and his Times*, followed in 1889 by a book on Schiller. Also in 1884 he married Margaret Wynne, daughter of the Revd Timothy Jones, Vicar of St Margaret's, Leicester; they had a daughter and a son.

His main interest at this time was the study of military

history, though he came to hate war. On return from Germany, he worked at Toynbee Hall and lectured at Bedford College. He was also Secretary of the London Playing Fields Committee.

In 1897 H. W. Massingham, Editor of the *Daily Chronicle*, appointed him correspondent in the Graeco-Turkish War; he also reported the Boer War for that paper, and was in Russia during the abortive revolution of 1905-6. In 1907-8 he went to India for the *Manchester Guardian*, and was with the Bulgarians during the first Balkan War. During the First World War, he was a reporter on the Western Front and at the Dardanelles, where he was wounded. He published *The Dardanelles Campaign* in 1918. In 1926 he went to Palestine, Syria, and Iraq for the *Manchester Guardian*.

Nevinson was always a supporter of the cause of the oppressed or suffering. He helped to organize relief for the Macedonians (1903) and the Albanians (1911) and to found the Friends' Ambulance Unit in Flanders (1914). After an arduous journey of investigation, he conducted a crusade single-handed, and ultimately successfully, against the atrocities of slavery in Portuguese Angola (1904-5) and wrote *A Modern Slavery* (1906). In 1909 he resigned a post on the *Daily News* in protest at the paper's attitude to women's suffrage. He also protested against the outrages committed by the Black and Tans in Ireland.

From 1907 to 1923 he contributed articles to the *Nation* during Massingham's editorship, and these were collected in several volumes, including *Essays in Freedom* (1909), and *Essays in Rebellion* (1913). His best work was published after his death in *Essays, Poems, and Tales of Henry W. Nevinson* (1948). He also wrote three volumes of autobiography which were republished as *The Fire of Life* by Ellis Roberts in 1935.

In 1938 he was President of the PEN club and he also received a number of academic honours. Margaret Nevinson died in 1932 and in 1933 Nevinson married Evelyn, daughter of John James Sharp, a slate merchant; she was an authoress and suffragette; they had no children. Nevinson died at Chipping Campden on 9 November 1941. His son Christopher (1889-1946) became an artist, notable for his war paintings, many of which are in the Imperial War Museum and other museums and galleries at home and abroad.

NICKALLS, GUY (1866-1935), oarsman, was born on 12 November 1866, the third son of Tom Nickalls, of Horton Kirby, Kent, an original member of the London Rowing Club, and his wife, Emily Quilhampton. He was educated at Eton and Magdalen College, Oxford; at Eton he was in the crew that won the Ladies' Plate in 1885, and he rowed five years for Oxford (1887-91) and was in the winning crew of 1890-1. In 1898 he married Ellen Gilbey, daughter of Henry Gold, JP, of Hedsor, Bucks; they had two sons.

His successes at the Henley Regatta are unlikely to be surpassed. He won 67 races out of the 81 in which he took part. His victories included 5 Diamond Sculls, 6 Goblets in pair-oared races, 7 Stewards' Cups in fours, 4 Grand Challenge cups, and 1 Olympic eight, in which he rowed when he was approaching forty-two years of age.

From 1891 to 1922 he was a member of the Stock Exchange. During the First World War he joined the army at the age of forty-seven and served in France as superintendent of physical and bayonet training. In his later life he worked in aid of the Worcester College for the Blind.

His elder son, Guy, was a member of the Oxford winning crew in 1923, President of the Oxford University Boat Club, and created a record by winning the Grand Challenge cup

seven times; his younger son, Rodney, was Captain of the Boats at Eton. Nickalls died at Leeds as the result of a motoring accident on 8 July 1935; his wife died a month later.

NICOLSON, SIR HAROLD GEORGE (1886-1968), author and diplomat, was born in Tehran on 21 November 1886, the third son of (Sir) Arthur Nicolson (later Lord Carnock), and his wife, Katharine Rowan Hamilton. At the time, his father was chargé d'affaires in the British Embassy. His early years were spent abroad with his father and at his mother's home in Ireland. He was educated at Wellington and Balliol College, Oxford, where he did not distinguish himself; but in 1909, to his father's surprise, he passed successfully into the Diplomatic Service.

For the next twenty years Nicolson served in a number of posts overseas, in Madrid, Constantinople (Istanbul), Paris, Tehran, and Berlin. During the First World War he worked in the Foreign Office in London, and in 1919 attended the Paris Peace Conference. He was appointed CMG in 1920. In 1927 he was posted to Berlin but did not care for his work there. His uneasiness was partly caused by the fact that his wife, who had visited him from time to time in his foreign posts but had never lived permanently with him overseas, loathed Berlin.

In 1913 he had married Victoria Mary (Vita) SACKVILLE-WEST, only child of Lionel, third Lord Sackville, and his wife, Victoria. They began what, in its early years, was a normal, happy, married life, but later became a curious relationship between two bisexual people who continued to have a mutual understanding and affection, in spite of Vita's infatuation with Violet Trefusis and other women friends, and Harold's aberrations with men. Their younger son, Nigel, has told this story in *Portrait of a Marriage* (1973).

Nicolson's book, *Some People*, depicting delightful cameos of some of his diplomatic colleagues without malice but with considerable humour, was published in 1927, and was not pleasing to some of his senior colleagues. However, when he was posted to Berlin, he appeared to be on the way to a distinguished career in his chosen profession. Then in 1929, to the dismay of his friends, he resigned from the Diplomatic Service, although at the time he was not well off financially.

For a short time in 1930-1 he contributed to the 'Londoner's Diary' of the *Evening Standard* and, although he was busy writing some of the books that made his name, he also sought to enter politics as a supporter of Sir Oswald MOSLEY. But when Mosley's party became the British Union of Fascists, Nicolson broke away and for a while concentrated on his writing.

Between 1921 and 1926 he had published books on *Paul Verlaine* (1921), *Tennyson* (1923), *Byron* (1924) and *Swinburne* (1926). From 1930 to 1939 he published his major works *Lord Carnock* (1930), *Peacemaking 1919* (1933), *Curzon, the Last Phase* (1934), *Dwight Morrow* (1935) and *Diplomacy* (1939). During these years he was also doing broadcasts, at which he excelled, and at the time of the Munich crisis he fearlessly condemned the policy of trying to appease Nazi Germany.

From 1935 to 1945 Nicolson was National Labour MP for West Leicester but, although he loyally supported Winston CHURCHILL, his only political appointment was as Parliamentary Secretary to the Ministry of Information under Duff COOPER during 1940-1. From 1941 to 1946 he was a Governor of the BBC. His experience of foreign affairs always secured for him the respect of the House when he chose

Harold Nicolson, by Howard Coster

to speak, but his more important contributions to the war effort were his weekly 'Marginal Comment' articles in the *Spectator* (1939-52), book reviews in the *Daily Telegraph*, and a Penguin Special *Why Britain is at War* (1939), which sold 100,000 copies in a few months.

In the 1945 election he was defeated, and in 1947 joined the Labour party, contested North Croydon in 1948, and was again defeated. He continued to write prolifically. *The Congress of Vienna* appeared in 1946, followed by *The English Sense of Humour* (1947), *King George V: His Life and Reign* (1952), *Good Behaviour* (1955), *The Age of Reason* (1960), and *Monarchy* (1962). From 1949 to 1963 he was also contributing weekly book reviews to the *Observer*.

In 1953 he was appointed KCVO, and became an honorary Fellow of Balliol College, Oxford. He was chairman or trustee of a number of organizations including the National Trust, the London Library, and the National Portrait Gallery.

In 1930 he and his wife took over Sissinghurst Castle, near Cranbrook in Kent, and there, to his design, they created one of the most beautiful and well-known gardens in England, which is now the property of the National Trust and visited by thousands every year. Nicolson died there on 1 May 1968. His *Diaries and Letters 1930-62* (3 vols., 1966-8) were edited and published by Nigel Nicolson. He and Vita had another son, Lionel Benedict, elder brother of Nigel; he became editor of the *Burlington Magazine*.

NORMAN, MONTAGU COLLET, BARON NORMAN (1871-1950), Governor of the Bank of England, was born in London on 6 September 1871, the elder son of Frederick Henry Norman, a partner in Martins Bank, and his wife, Lina Susan Penelope, daughter of (Sir) Mark Wilks Collet, sometime Governor of the Bank of England. He was educated at Eton and King's College, Cambridge, which he left after one year to learn German in Leipzig.

In 1892 he returned to England and pursued a banking career in London and New York until the outbreak of the Boer War, in which he served for two years. He was appointed to the DSO but was eventually invalided back home. In 1907 he was elected to the Court of the Bank of England, but a nervous breakdown kept him from work during 1913-14.

He resigned from his own bank in 1915 and joined the Bank of England full-time, becoming Deputy Governor in 1918, and Governor in 1920. Departing from traditional practice, he was re-elected to that office until 1944. He was confronted in 1920 with inflation, unstable exchanges, unsettled war debts, and the threat of central European economic collapse. His policy was one of orthodox finance, balanced budgets, foreign loans to save currencies from collapse, and the establishment of new central banks.

Together with BONAR LAW, the Prime Minister, he originally hoped that the USA would cancel war debts, but he was convinced by his American banking friends that this was impossible. Consequently, when he went with Stanley BALDWIN to negotiate a settlement with the USA, he persuaded the Chancellor of the Exchequer to accept terms which were very unpopular in England and which Bonar Law was reluctant to accept.

Three years later (1925) when Winston CHURCHILL was at the Treasury, Norman advised him that the time had come to return to the gold standard, and this was done at the old parity in the interest of maintaining cheap imports of food and raw materials, although some economists, notably J. M. KEYNES, warned that at the old parity high British export prices would make it difficult to compete abroad. By 1929 the drain of funds abroad was threatening the gold standard, and the world depression of 1931 threatened the security of currencies throughout Europe. Norman's efforts to defend sterling led to another breakdown in health but, on his return to work, his advice to the National Government was useful in restoring confidence in sterling and helping to maintain industries of national importance.

In 1933 he married Priscilla Cecilia Maria Worsthorne, daughter of Major Robert Reyntiens of the Belgian Artillery, and Lady Alice Reyntiens, daughter of the seventh Earl of Abingdon; they had no children.

Norman was able to reorganize the Bank of England as a central bank with responsibility for leadership in the financial world and, although he supported the Government of the day, his orthodox attitude to economics led him to resist the rising tide of Government intervention in business affairs. He intended to retire in 1939, but the advent of another European war led him into the planning of war finance, purchasing, and exchange control. In 1944 he was again struck down by illness and forced to retire.

He had refused a peerage in 1923, when he was sworn of the Privy Council, but now he accepted the honour. He took no further part in public affairs, and died in London on 4 February 1950.

NORTHCLIFFE, VISCOUNT (1865-1922). See HARMS-WORTH, ALFRED CHARLES WILLIAM.

NORWAY, NEVIL SHUTE (1899–1960). See SHUTE, NEVIL.

NORWICH, first VISCOUNT (1890–1954). See COOPER, ALFRED DUFF.

NOVELLO, IVOR (1893–1951), actor-manager, playwright, and composer, was born David Ivor Davies, in Cardiff on 15 January 1893, the only son of David Davies, a rate collector, and his wife, Clara Novello Davies, a well-known musician and music teacher. He was educated in Cardiff and Gloucester, and went to Magdalen College School, Oxford as a choral scholar. He was soon composing songs, and in 1910 scored a success with 'The Little Damozel'.

For a time, he taught the piano in Cardiff, but later went with his mother to London, where he haunted the theatres and wanted to join the chorus at Daly's, but his mother dissuaded him from doing so. He continued to compose music, some of which took him to New York, where he composed his first musical, *The Fickle Jade*, which was never produced.

When the First World War broke out, he produced the patriotic song 'Keep the Home Fires Burning', which made him a fortune; and, from that time onwards, he wrote songs in revues and musicals which were a big success. Meanwhile, he served in the Royal Naval Air Service but, after two bad crashes, was relegated to clerical work in the Air Ministry.

After the war, he visited the USA and was successful as an actor in a number of films. In 1921, back in England, he appeared on the London stage, at first in small parts, but later in larger roles. In 1924 he wrote *The Rat*, staged it himself at the Prince of Wales's Theatre, and played the lead with Constance Collier. This marked the beginning of his career as actor-manager and playwright. In 1927 he adopted the name of Ivor Novello. Between 1928 and 1951 he wrote thirteen comedies; most were successful, including *The Truth Game*, *Murder in Mayfair*, and *We Proudly Present*.

In 1935, he had a notable triumph at Drury Lane with the musical *Glamorous Night*, which was followed there by *Careless Rapture* (1936), *Crest of the Wave* (1937), and *The Dancing Years* (1939). The latter was brought back to the Adelphi Theatre in 1942 and was the outstanding success of the war years.

In 1944 he was imprisoned for a month for evading the petrol restrictions, but he returned to the theatre to win further acclaim with *Perchance to Dream* (1945) and *King's Rhapsody* (1949). While playing in *King's Rhapsody* at the Palace Theatre on 6 March 1951, he died suddenly. He never married. His songs gave much pleasure to many people and have become a part of the repertory of theatre music.

NOYCE, (CUTHBERT) WILFRID FRANCIS (1917–1962), mountaineer and writer, was born at Simla on 31 December 1917, the elder son of (Sir) Frank Noyce, Indian civil servant, and his wife, Enid Isabel, daughter of W. M. Kirkus, of Liverpool. He was educated at Charterhouse and King's College, Cambridge, where he was a scholar and obtained firsts in the classical tripos (part i, 1939), and in the preliminary examination for part ii of the modern languages tripos (1940).

Ivor Novello with Fay Compton in his own comedy, *Murder in Mayfair*, Globe Theatre, 1934

In 1939 he joined the Friends' Ambulance Unit and in 1940 enlisted in the Welsh Guards, was commissioned in the KRRC and spent 1942-6 in India, first in intelligence, and then as Chief Instructor at the Aircrew Mountain Centre in Kashmir. Noyce was by then a fine mountain climber and, while he was in India, reached the summit of Pauhunri in Sikkim (23,385 ft.) with Sherpa Antharkay.

In 1950 he married Rosemary, daughter of Henry Campbell Davies; they had two sons. From 1946 to 1950 he was an assistant master at Malvern and then taught for the next ten years at Charterhouse, until he retired from teaching in 1961.

He was a member of the 1953 Everest expedition led by Sir John (later Lord) Hunt. In his book *The Ascent of Everest* (1953), Hunt records how, at a critical stage in the ascent, Noyce and Sherpa Annulla opened the route to the South Col. 'It was a great moment for them both and it was shared by all of us who watched them. Their presence there was symbolic of our success in overcoming the most crucial problem of the whole climb.'

In 1957, Noyce attempted Machapuchare (*c.* 23,000 ft.) in western Nepal but was defeated by bad weather. In 1960 he led an expedition to Trivor (25,370 ft.) in the Karakoram and was one of the two who reached the summit. He not only climbed mountains; he wrote about them. In 1947 he published an autobiography, *Mountains and Men*. His other books about mountaineering include *South Col* (1954), *Climbing the Fish's Tail* (1958), and *To the Unknown Mountain* (1962). He also published poems, a novel, a study of historic figures who loved mountains, *Scholar Mountaineers* (1950), and *They Survived* (1962), a study of the will to survive in dangerous situations.

In 1962 Noyce joined an expedition to the Pamirs to promote friendship between British and Russian climbers. He was killed in the USSR on 24 July 1962 when he and a companion fell, descending from the summit of Garmo Peak (*c.* 21,500 ft.).

NOYES, ALFRED (1880-1958), poet, was born at Wolverhampton on 16 September 1880, the eldest son of Alfred Noyes, a grocer, and his wife, Amelia Adams Rowley. He was educated at Aberystwyth and Exeter College, Oxford.

He published his first book of verse *The Loom of Years* in 1902. This was followed by *The Flower of Old Japan* (1903), *Poems* (1904), *Forty Singing Seamen* (1907), and an epic, *Drake* (2 vols., 1906-8). In 1913 he gave the Lowell lectures at Boston, USA, on 'The Sea in English Poetry', and from 1914 to 1923 was Professor of Modern English Literature at Princeton. He returned to England to work at the Foreign Office and in France for a time during the First World War, and was appointed CBE in 1918.

In 1927 he became a Roman Catholic, and *The Torch-Bearers*, an epic in three volumes (1922-30), dealt with science and the Christian faith. This work was followed by *The Unknown God* (1934) and *Voltaire* (1936), in which he again defended Christianity against agnosticism. He was a determined controversialist, who crossed swords with W. B. YEATS, among others. Together with G. K. CHESTERTON and Lord Dunsany, he ridiculed the eccentricities of modern verse and was intractably opposed to any who contravened his moral code in the name of art.

In 1907 he had married Garnet, daughter of Col. B. G. Daniels, of the United States Army; she died in 1926, and in 1927 he married Mary Angela, widow of Richard Shirburne Weld-Blundell; they had one son and two daughters. During the Second World War he took his children to Canada and lectured there and in the United States. He was gradually becoming blind. In 1949 he returned to his home in the Isle of Wight and wrote his autobiography *Two Worlds for Memory* (1953). He received many honorary degrees, and is remembered at Exeter College, Oxford by a window in the Hall. In his later years he showed great sympathy for the blind. In his poem *Spring, and the Blind Children* he wrote:

> They did not leap or dance or run
> Only, at times, without a word or smile
> Their small blind faces lifted to the sun.

He died in the Isle of Wight on 28 June 1958. A final collection of his poems was published in 1963.

NUFFIELD, VISCOUNT (1877-1963). See MORRIS.

O

O'CASEY, SEAN (1880-1964), Irish dramatist and author, was born in Dublin of Protestant parents on 30 March 1880, the youngest child of Michael and Susanna Casey. His real name was John Casey. He lived in poverty in a tenement of the Dublin slums with his mother and a brother, his father who had been a clerk, having died when the boy was six. O'Casey suffered from an eye disease which kept him from school, but he taught himself to read, especially the Bible.

Up to the age of thirty, he worked as a casual labourer, often unemployed and in poor health. He involved himself in Irish politics, joining a number of organizations, including the Irish Republican Brotherhood and Irish Citizen Army but, after 1916, he took to writing plays, while still working as a day labourer.

His first three plays were rejected by the Abbey Theatre, but *The Shadow of a Gunman* was a great success there in 1923 and, after his next success, *Juno and the Paycock* (1924), his masterpiece, he turned professional. He was awarded the Hawthornden prize for *Juno* in 1926 and his third play, produced at the Abbey, *The Plough and the Stars*, dealing with civilian reactions to the 1916 Easter rising, gave great offence in Dublin, and O'Casey decided to emigrate to England. However, he never found the satisfaction he needed in the London theatre, partly because he did not possess the

Sean O'Casey (right), with Eithne Dunn and producer Sam Wanamaker, watching a rehearsal of his play, *Purple Dust*, London, May 1953

technical skill required for success on the English stage, in spite of his genius. His anti-war play *The Silver Tassie*, rejected by the Abbey Theatre but produced in London in 1929, did not attract the play-going public, although it was praised by the critics. *Within the Gates*, set in London, was also a failure. *Red Roses for Me* (1946) was a little more successful.

Between 1939 and 1954 O'Casey wrote his autobiography in six volumes. At that time he had settled in Devon, but he was an unhappy, disappointed, and embittered man, who could never come to terms with what he regarded as his rejection by his own country. A play intended for the Dublin International Theatre Festival of 1958 had to be withdrawn and O'Casey then withdrew all his plays from production in Dublin.

In 1927 he married Eileen Reynolds, an actress under the name of Eileen Carey, who was of Irish Roman Catholic parentage; they had two sons and one daughter. The younger son died in 1957, and O'Casey died at Torquay on 18 September 1964.

O'DWYER, SIR MICHAEL FRANCIS (1864–1940), Indian administrator, was born on 28 April 1864 at Barronstown, co. Tipperary, the sixth son of John O'Dwyer and his wife, Margaret, daughter of Patrick Quirk, of Toom, Tipperary. He was educated at St Stanislaus College, Tullamore, and Balliol College, Oxford, where he obtained a first in jurisprudence.

In 1885 he entered the Indian Civil Service and was posted to the Punjab. In 1896 he married Una, daughter of Antoine Bord, of Castres, France; they had one son and one daughter.

He rose rapidly in the service, and from 1901 to 1908 was Revenue Commissioner of the new North-West Frontier Province, and from 1913 to 1919 Lieutenant-Governor of the

Sir Michael O'Dwyer

Punjab. He was warned by the Viceroy, Lord Hardinge, that there was a danger of a serious outbreak of violence in the province; during 1914-16 widespread disturbances were threatened, but avoided by O'Dwyer's firmness and moderation. He had been appointed KCSI in 1913, and in 1917 was created GCIE.

In 1916, however, the 'home rule' agitation intensified under the leadership of B. G. Tilak and Annie BESANT, and the Government of India passed legislation which led to GANDHI's civil disobedience campaign in 1919. This led to riots in the Punjab, and the tragedy of the Jalianwala Bagh at Amritsar, when Brigadier-General DYER ordered his troops to fire on a dense crowd of several thousands, assembled contrary to his orders; some 380 people were killed and over 1,000 wounded.

O'Dwyer, under the impression that Dyer could not have avoided this massacre in which many innocent spectators were killed, approved the action taken and, in the subsequent inquiry set up by the Government of India, attempted to defend General Dyer, but without success, as Dyer was forced to resign, and O'Dwyer himself had to fend off accusations of involvement, by fighting a libel action in which his integrity was confirmed (1924).

After his retirement in 1919, O'Dwyer continued to maintain an interest in Indian problems. He was opposed to the 1919 and 1935 constitutions and made his convictions clear with fearless energy and tenacity. In 1925 he published *India as I Knew It, 1885-1925*. At a meeting of the Royal Central Asian Society in London on 13 March 1940 he was shot in the back and killed by an Indian assassin.

OGDEN, CHARLES KAY (1889-1957), linguistic psychologist and originator of Basic English, was born on 1 June 1889 at Rossall School, Fleetwood, the elder son of Charles Burdett Ogden, a housemaster, and his wife, Fanny Hart. He was educated at Rossall and Magdalene College, Cambridge, where he was a scholar and obtained a first in the classical tripos, part i (1910). In 1912 he founded the weekly *Cambridge Magazine*, which became an organ of international opinion to which well-known authors such as G. B. SHAW, Thomas HARDY, and Arnold BENNETT contributed. He also founded the Heretics Society, and between 1911 and 1914 papers read by Shaw, G. K. CHESTERTON, G. M. TREVELYAN, and other writers were published.

After visiting the Continent to investigate methods of language teaching, Ogden published, with R. H. Best, *The Problem of the Continuation School* and *The Schools and the Nation* (1914), a translation from the German. In 1923 he and I. A. RICHARDS published *The Meaning of Meaning*. In 1922 Ogden was appointed Editor of *Psyche* and, with F. P. Ramsey, translated and introduced to the British public Ludwig WITTGENSTEIN's *Tractatus Logico-Philosophicus*. He also planned and edited two series, 'The History of Civilisation' and 'The International Library of Psychology, Philosophy, and Scientific Method'.

Between 1925 and 1927, he worked on Basic English as an auxiliary international language with a small vocabulary of essential words and verbs restricted to fundamentals. In 1930 he published *Basic English*, followed by *The Basic Vocabulary* (1930), *Debabelization* (1931), and *The Basic Words* (1932).

Winston CHURCHILL took steps to develop Basic English as an international and administrative language (1944), and in 1946 Ogden assigned his copyright to the Crown and was compensated by £23,000. The Basic English Foundation was established in 1947.

Ogden was an enthusiastic book collector, and in 1953 University College London bought his manuscripts and early printed books, as well as his collection on Jeremy Bentham and Brougham. The rest of his library was bought by the University of California when he died in London on 20 March 1957. He never married.

OMAN, SIR CHARLES WILLIAM CHADWICK (1860-1946), historian, was born at Mozufferpore, India, on 12 January 1860, the only child of Charles Philip Austin Oman, an indigo planter, and his wife, Anne, daughter of William Chadwick, a railway constructor. He was educated at Winchester and New College, Oxford, of both of which he was a scholar; he obtained firsts in Greats (1882) and modern history (1883) and was elected Fellow of All Souls (1883). In the following year he won the Lothian prize for an essay on 'The Art of War in the Middle Ages', and in 1898 published an enlarged edition.

In 1902 he produced the first instalment of the *History of the Peninsular War*, which appeared in seven volumes between 1902 and 1930. From 1905 to 1946 he was Chichele Professor of Modern History at Oxford, and from 1919 to 1935 sat in Parliament as burgess for Oxford University. He taught history at Oxford, while producing further works including *The Great Revolt of 1381* (1906), and *England before the Norman Conquest* (1910). His travels abroad were recorded in *Things I have Seen* (1933).

During the First World War he worked for the Press Bureau and the Foreign Office, and in 1920 was appointed KBE. He was elected FBA in 1905 and an honorary Fellow of New College in 1936. He received a number of honorary degrees.

In 1892 he married Mary Mabel, daughter of General Robert Maclagan; they had a son, who became an authority on metalwork, and two daughters, one of whom, Carola, became well known as a biographer. Sir Charles died at Oxford on 23 June 1946.

ONIONS, CHARLES TALBUT (1873-1965), lexicographer and grammarian, was born in Birmingham on 10 September 1873, the eldest son of Ralph John Onions, designer in metal, and his wife, Harriet, daughter of John Talbut, a locksmith. He was educated at King Edward VI's School, Birmingham, and Mason College, Birmingham.

In 1895 he was invited by J. A. H. MURRAY to join the staff of the English Dictionary at Oxford, and from 1906 to 1913 prepared various parts of the work including the final entry. In 1911 he produced his *Shakespeare Glossary*, a notable survey of Shakespearian usage.

He married in 1907 Angela, daughter of the Revd Arthur Blythman, Rector of Shenington; they had seven sons and three daughters.

After the death of William Little in 1922, he was commissioned by the Clarendon Press to complete Little's work on a *Shorter Oxford English Dictionary*, which appeared in 1933, and was revised by him until 1959. Similarly, on the death of Sir Sidney LEE, he completed the editing of *Shakespeare's England* (1916).

In 1918 he worked in the Naval Intelligence Division of the Admiralty, and on his return to Oxford became university lecturer in English (1920) and Reader in English Philology (1927-49). In 1922 he revised the *Anglo-Saxon Reader*. He was elected a Fellow of Magdalen College in 1923, and from 1940 to 1955 was Librarian of the College.

From 1932 to 1956 he was Editor of *Medium Ævum*, the journal of the Society for the Study of Medieval Languages and, during the last twenty years of his life, compiled the *Oxford Dictionary of English Etymology* (1966). He also contributed the chapter on English language to *The Character of England* (1947), edited by Sir Ernest BARKER.

From 1929 to 1933 Onions was President of the Philological Society; he was elected FBA in 1938. The universities of Oxford, Leeds, and Birmingham conferred honorary degrees on him on the completion of the Oxford Dictionary (1933). He was appointed CBE in 1934. He died at Oxford on 8 January 1965.

OPPENHEIMER, SIR ERNEST (1880–1957), financier, was born in Friedberg, Germany on 22 May 1880, the fifth son of Eduard Oppenheimer, a cigar merchant, and his wife, Fanny Hirschhorn. He went to school in Friedberg and at sixteen became a junior clerk in the London firm of Dunkelsbuhler & Co. He was naturalized in 1901, and in 1902 went as the firm's representative to Kimberley, South Africa, where he became Mayor in 1912–15. In 1906 he married May Lina, daughter of Joseph Pollak, a London stockbroker; they had two sons.

In 1917, with the help of Herbert Hoover, the American mining engineer who later became President of the USA, and J. P. Morgan & Co., Oppenheimer founded the gold mining concern, The Anglo-American Corporation of South Africa Ltd. Then, he went into the diamond mining industry, eventually became Chairman of the De Beers Company in 1929, and went on to unify the diamond industry throughout Africa.

He also developed the copper mining industry in Northern Rhodesia (Zambia) and set up Rhodesian Anglo-American Ltd. (1928). He then opened up the Orange Free State goldfield and created the Orange Free State Investment Trust (1944).

He was knighted in 1921 and from 1924 until 1938 represented Kimberley in the Union Parliament, supporting J. C. SMUTS. He was a generous benefactor who believed in African advancement within the Commonwealth. He was influential in raising a loan of £3 million for the creation of African housing in Johannesburg. He made a large grant towards the establishment of Queen Elizabeth House at Oxford and contributed to medical and scientific research in Britain and South Africa. His benefactions were continued after his death through the Ernest Oppenheimer Memorial Trust.

May Oppenheimer died in 1934, and in 1935 Oppenheimer married Caroline Magdalen, widow of his nephew, Sir Michael Oppenheimer. He died in Johannesburg on 25 November 1957, and was succeeded as head of the Anglo-American Corporation by one of his sons.

ORPEN, SIR WILLIAM NEWENHAM MONTAGUE (1878–1931), painter, was born at Stillorgan, co. Dublin on 27 November 1878, the youngest son of Arthur Herbert Orpen, a solicitor, and his wife, Anne, daughter of Charles Caulfeild, Bishop of Nassau. The Orpens were a well-known Protestant family. William was educated at the Metropolitan School of Art, Dublin. He then studied at the Slade School of Fine Art, London, where, with the encouragement and critical guidance of Henry TONKS, he became one of the best students in a brilliant group, which also included Augustus JOHN.

In 1900 he was elected to the New English Art Club, where exhibitions of his realistically detailed interiors with figures attracted immediate attention. His choice of subject may have owed something to his brother-in-law, William

William Orpen (seated), war artist at work, Amiens, August 1918

ROTHENSTEIN, but the influence of the seventeenth-century Dutch masters and of the English tradition of Wilkie was also apparent. Although Orpen had connections with the pre-Raphaelites, having married in 1901 Grace, daughter of Walter John Knewstub, the friend and assistant of Dante Gabriel Rossetti, his style was totally different from theirs. Orpen also painted pictures of scenes in Ireland and visited Dublin to give life-classes at the school where he had been trained when he was young. In 1908 he exhibited a portrait at the Royal Academy, and in 1910 became ARA.

During the First World War he went to France as an official war artist and produced a large number of striking paintings and drawings which were exhibited at Agnews in 1918 and then presented to the Imperial War Museum. Orpen was appointed KBE in 1918 and elected RA in 1919. He attended the Peace Conference in Paris and painted the scene in the Hall of Mirrors at Versailles depicting the leaders of the Allied powers. He also produced *To the Unknown British Soldier in France*. After the war he was in growing demand as a fashionable portrait painter of high technical ability, and produced altogether some 600 portraits.

He published two books *An Onlooker in France, 1917–1919*, (1921), and *Stories of Old Ireland and Myself* (1924). The Orpens had three daughters. He died in London on 29 September 1931.

ORR, JOHN BOYD (1880–1971). See BOYD ORR.

ORTON, JOHN KINGSLEY (JOE) (1933–1967), playwright, was born in Leicester on 1 January 1933, the eldest child of William Orton, a gardener, and his wife, Elsie, a machinist and charwoman. He was educated at a primary school, took a secretarial course at Clark's College, Leicester and, after a number of office jobs, went to RADA with a scholarship.

After working with the Ipswich Repertory Company, he decided that he would never make a career as an actor, and accepted the advice of Kenneth Leith Halliwell (1926–67), a fellow student, that he should write. Halliwell, with whom Orton lived for the rest of his life, was the better-educated of the two, and together they wrote a series of worthless novels. They eked out an existence on Halliwell's small inheritance by doing odd jobs.

By 1957 Orton had begun to write novels and plays on his own, mostly those of an angry young man. In 1959 he took to defacing public library books, and he and Halliwell deliberately set out to shock public opinion. In 1962 they were arrested and sent to prison for six months. Prison appears to have assisted Orton in his writing, and in 1963, after ten years, of failure, a radio play *The Ruffian on the Stair*, was accepted by the BBC and broadcast.

During the next four years, he became a playwright of international repute and 'Ortonesque' became a word for scenes of macabre outrage. Among his full-length plays were *Entertaining Mr. Sloane* (1963), *Loot* (1965), and *What the Butler Saw* (1967). He also wrote a number of one-act plays. Films were made of *Sloane* (1969) and *Loot* (1970), which also won the *Evening Standard* award for the best play of the year (1966). He was adept at combining terror and elation in farcical comedy and anarchy.

His end was as sensational as his plays. His homosexual companion, Halliwell, jealous of Orton's success and his frequent promiscuity, murdered him and then committed suicide on 9 August 1967.

ORWELL, GEORGE (1903–1950), author, was born at Motihari in Bengal on 25 June 1903. His real name was Eric Arthur Blair and he was the only son of Richard Walmesley Blair, of the Bengal Civil Service, and his wife, Ida Mabel Limouzin. He was a scholar of Eton, and on leaving school in 1921 joined the Indian Police Service. He was posted to Burma which was then a province of India. He soon found that he did not enjoy life in an up-country station in Burma, as is obvious from *Burmese Days*, his first novel, published in 1935. After five years in the police, he resigned and, after returning to Europe, deliberately sampled the life of a down-and-out first by working as a dish-washer in Paris, and

George Orwell

then by living as a tramp in England. These experiences he chronicled in *Down and Out in Paris and London* (1933). Later, he worked as a bookseller's assistant and schoolmaster. In 1936 he married Eileen Maud, daughter of Laurence O'Shaughnessy of the Inland Revenue. His ambition was to become an author and in 1939 he published another novel *Coming up for Air*, a story of big business.

During the Spanish civil war, he was severely wounded fighting against the forces of General Franco. This experience coloured his attitude to life. He hated autocracy in any form, Fascist, Socialist, or Communist, and made this clear in the books for which he is best known: *The Road to Wigan Pier* (1937), *Homage to Catalonia* (1938), *Animal Farm* (1945), and *Nineteen Eighty Four* (1949), satirical, polemical diatribes against any form of tyranny. Orwell was preeminently a propagandist, whose power of expression arose from his personal knowledge of the subjects about which he wrote. He had had Communist sympathies and could write *Animal Farm* from an inside knowledge of the movement. His satirical books are the works on which his reputation as an author will rest, but he also published more traditional literary essays on authors and their works in which he expressed more moderate views and less trenchant criticism.

After the death of his first wife in 1945, he married, in 1949, Sonia Mary, daughter of Charles Neville Brownell, a business man in India. Orwell died of consumption in London on 21 January 1950.

OSLER, SIR WILLIAM (1849-1919), Regius Professor of Medicine at Oxford, was born at Bond Head, Ontario, on 12 July 1849, the sixth son of a missionary, the Revd Featherston L. Osler, and his wife, Ellen Free Pickton. He was educated at Trinity College School, Weston, and Trinity College, Toronto, where he studied medicine before going on to McGill University, Montreal, and graduating in 1872. After two years post-graduate study in Europe, Osler was appointed Professor of the Institutes of Medicine at McGill (1874). For ten years he lectured on physiology and pathology at McGill and on helminthology at the Veterinary College.

In 1884 he became Professor of Medicine at the University of Pennsylvania and spent the next twenty years in the United States. In 1889 he moved to the chair of medicine at Johns Hopkins University, Baltimore. There he organized a clinical unit which was unique at that time, and under his training teachers went to the leading medical schools in North America, and his work revolutionized medical education in the USA and Canada.

Osler made frequent trips to Europe and his work was recognized in Britain by his election as FRCP in 1884 and FRS in 1898. In 1904 he became Regius Professor of Medicine at Oxford, where he remained until his death. In the more leisurely atmosphere of Oxford, he found time for literary and antiquarian studies. He was a Curator of the Bodleian Library and a Delegate of the Clarendon Press, as well as Master of the ancient almshouse at Ewelme. In 1919 he was President of the Classical Association. He was one of the founders of the Association of Physicians and of the historical section of the Royal Society of Medicine, and Senior Editor of the *Quarterly Journal of Medicine*. He was created a baronet in 1911, and received many academic honours.

He published a number of monographs and lectures and a textbook *The Principles and Practice of Medicine* (1891) which was republished many times and translated into a number of languages, including Chinese.

In 1892 he married Grace, daughter of John Revere, a Boston manufacturer, and widow of Dr S. W. Gross of Philadelphia; they had two sons, one of whom died in infancy. Their second son was killed in Flanders in 1917. Osler himself died two years later on 29 December 1919 in Oxford; he bequeathed his valuable library to McGill University.

OWEN, WILFRED EDWARD SALTER (1893-1918), poet, was born at Oswestry on 18 March 1893, the eldest child of Tom Owen, clerk to the Great Western Railway, Oswestry, and his wife, Susan Shaw. He was educated at Shrewsbury Technical College. He began writing poetry while still a young boy. His early love of Keats developed and remained the principal influence on his work. In 1911 he became lay assistant and pupil of the Revd Herbert Wigan, Vicar of Dunsden, who was to coach him for the university entrance examination. He never sat the examination and instead became an English teacher at the Berlitz School in Bordeaux.

In 1915 Owen joined the Artists' Rifles, and in 1916 fought in the Battle of the Somme in which 19,000 British troops were killed in one day, 57,000 casualties sustained, and the slaughter was maintained for months. In 1917 Owen returned from the front with shell shock and nervous exhaustion. While he was recuperating in an Edinburgh hospital he met Siegfried SASSOON, who was considered to be in need of medical attention, after he had protested about the way the war was being conducted. With the encouragement of Sassoon, who had already published a volume of war poems,

Wilfred Owen with Arthur Newboult, the son of Edinburgh friends, July 1917

Owen's work now matured and lost some of its early luxuriance of style. Both these men, so different in their outlook and backgrounds, wrote unforgettable poems condemning the horrors of modern war.

Owen recovered and returned to France, fought with the 2nd Manchesters and was awarded the MC. He was killed on the Sambre Canal on 4 November 1918, within a week of the armistice.

Owen was one of the greatest of the war poets. His well-known poem *Anthem for Doomed Youth* ends:

> The pallor of girls' brows shall be their pall;
> Their flowers the tenderness of patient minds,
> And each slow dusk a drawing-down of blinds.

Perhaps the most vivid expression of the horror of being maimed is found in *Disabled* which begins:

> He sat in a wheeled chair, waiting for dark

and ends:

> Tonight he noticed how the women's eyes
> Passed from him to the strong men that were whole.
> How cold and late it is! Why don't they come
> And put him into bed? Why don't they come?

These extracts, however, can give but little understanding of the depth of feeling expressed in his poetry by this courageous, gentle, and lovable young man who was only twenty-five when he died. His work, *The Collected Poems*, was edited by Cecil DAY-LEWIS and published in 1963.

OXFORD AND ASQUITH, COUNTESS OF (1864-1945). See ASQUITH, EMMA ALICE MARGARET (MARGOT).

OXFORD AND ASQUITH, first EARL OF (1852-1928). See ASQUITH, HERBERT HENRY

P

PAGE, SIR FREDERICK HANDLEY (1885-1962). See HANDLEY PAGE.

PANKHURST, EMMELINE (1858-1928) and DAME CHRISTABEL HARRIETTE **PANKHURST** (1880-1958), leaders of the suffragette movement, were mother and daughter. Emmeline was born at Manchester on 4 July 1858, the eldest daughter of Robert Goulden, owner of a calico printing and bleach works, and his wife, Sophia Jane Craine. She was educated in Manchester and Paris, and in 1879 married Richard Marsden Pankhurst LL D, a barrister and prominent advocate of women's suffrage. They had five children, two sons and three daughters, of whom Christabel was the eldest born in 1880. Dr Pankhurst died in 1898 leaving his family in straightened circumstances. For a time Mrs Pankhurst worked as registrar of births and deaths at Rusholme.

Christabel, attractive and intelligent, gained a first in law at Manchester but was refused admission to Lincoln's Inn because she was a woman. In 1903 she and her mother founded the Women's Social and Political Union (WSPU), and two years later Christabel and her friend Annie Kenney interrupted a meeting addressed by Sir Edward GREY, caused a disturbance, were arrested, and went to prison rather than pay a fine for assault. This was the first of many disturbances made in the cause of women's suffrage, not only by the interruption of political meetings, but by many other forms of propaganda.

In 1908 Emmeline Pankhurst was arrested for 'conduct likely to cause a breach of the peace', convicted, and imprisoned for three months. In 1909 the campaign was carried on with increased violence and there were more arrests with prisoners adopting a policy of hunger-striking, which the authorities countered with forcible feeding. In 1910 a Women's Suffrage Bill was introduced into Parliament and Mrs Pankhurst called a temporary truce to the militancy of her movement. But, when the ASQUITH Government called a second general election in November 1910, they promised nothing to placate the suffragettes and the campaign was renewed with still further violence.

Christabel was the leader of the new militancy, which drove from the movement less militant supporters such as the PETHICK-LAWRENCES; and, from the safety of Paris, she organized a campaign of crime, in which the suffragettes set fire to houses and public buildings such as schools, slashed pictures in public galleries, cut telephone wires, and raised false fire-alarms. More arrests were made and more hunger strikes followed. Mrs Pankhurst was frequently sent to prison, and in 1913 was sentenced to three years' penal servitude for incitement to violence. During that year Parliament passed the 'Cat and Mouse' Act under which hunger strikers could be released but re-arrested to serve out their sentences. Under this system, Mrs Pankhurst was re-arrested twelve times in twelve months. Meanwhile, in Paris Christabel was editing a new paper *The Suffragette*.

With the outbreak of the First World War the campaign for women's suffrage ended. Mrs Pankhurst turned her energies to recruiting for the army, and went to the USA and Russia on propaganda missions. Christabel returned to England and also undertook public service in the cause of the war. After the war, neither of them was prepared to renew the struggle and both went to the USA where Christabel decided to stay. In 1918 a bill was passed granting limited suffrage to women.

Emmeline returned to England in 1926 and joined the Conservative party. She died in London on 14 June 1928, just after the Act was passed which gave full and equal suffrage to men and women. In 1936 Christabel was appointed DBE; she died in Los Angeles on 13 February 1958.

Emmeline's second daughter (Estelle) Sylvia, born in 1882,

Mrs Pankhurst (centre) and Christabel (on her right) are welcomed by supporters, February 1908

was also active in the suffragette movement and went to prison a number of times. Unlike her mother, she opposed the war, enthusiastically supported the Bolshevik revolution, and, later, took up the cause of Abyssinian independence. She died in Addis Ababa on 27 September 1960.

The youngest daughter, Adela Constantia Mary, born in 1885, worked for a short time with Emmeline for the WSPU, but later emigrated to Australia, where she organized the Women's Party and the Australian Socialist Party. She published *Put up the Sword* during the First World War and was interned during the Second World War. She died in Australia on 23 May 1961.

There is a memorial statue of Emmeline Pankhurst in Victoria Tower Gardens, London.

PARRY, SIR (CHARLES) HUBERT HASTINGS (1848–1918), composer, teacher, and musical historian, was born at Bournemouth on 27 February 1848, the second son of Thomas Gambier Parry, an authority on decorative painting and frescoes, and his first wife. He showed an interest in music from an early age and showed a precocious aptitude while at school at Eton. When he was at Exeter College, Oxford, he founded the University Musical Club.

In 1872 he married Lady Elizabeth Maude Herbert, second daughter of Sidney, first Lord Herbert of Lea; they had two daughters. In the year after his marriage he settled in London, became a member of Lloyd's and, in spite of his keen interest in music, did not intend to make a professional career in that field. He studied the piano under Edward Dannreuther, who encouraged his efforts at composition and became a close friend. Parry went to Bayreuth in 1876 and came under the spell of Wagner. In his compositions at this

Sir Hubert Parry, by E. C. Hoppé

time, he concentrated mainly on instrumental music. He also collaborated with Sir George Grove as Assistant Editor of the *Dictionary of Music and Musicians*.

His musical compositions covered a very wide field. After 1880, when his Piano Concerto, written for Dannreuther, was performed at the Crystal Palace, he enjoyed considerable success. Also in that year *Scenes from Shelley's Prometheus Unbound* for solo voices, chorus and orchestra, was given at the Gloucester Festival, and this led to a number of commissions, particularly for choral works. In 1887 the most famous of his works, a setting for double choir and orchestra of Milton's ode 'At a solemn Music', *Blest Pair of Sirens*, was performed by the Bach Choir. His first oratorio *Judith* was performed in Birmingham in 1888, followed by *Job* (1892), and *King Saul* (1894). In 1903 the Royal Choral Society produced in London *War and Peace*, a symphonic ode for solo voices, chorus, and orchestra. Many other works were produced which have gone into the repertoire of English music.

In 1883 Parry became Professor of Music at the Royal College of Music, and in 1895 was appointed Director of the college. He held this post for the rest of his life. In 1884 he also became Choragus at Oxford, and from 1899 to 1908 was Professor of Music at the University. He was knighted in 1898 and appointed baronet in 1902. Parry's publications include *The Art of Music* (1893), *The Oxford History of Music* (vol. iii, 1902), and *Style in Musical Art* (1911). He also wrote a study of J. S. Bach (1909).

The First World War effectively destroyed his world. One of his last works, written in 1916, was the unison setting of Blake's 'Jerusalem' which afterwards achieved the status of a national song. Parry died at Rustington in Sussex on 7 October 1918 and was buried in the crypt of St Paul's Cathedral.

PARSONS, SIR CHARLES ALGERNON (1854–1931), engineer and scientist, was born in London on 13 June 1854, the youngest of the six sons of William Parsons, third Earl of Rosse, and his wife, Mary, daughter of John Wilmer Field, of Heaton Hall, Yorkshire. He was brought up in Ireland and taught privately by distinguished scientists. His father was an astronomer. From the age of seventeen Parsons spent two years at Trinity College, Dublin, before entering St John's College, Cambridge in 1873 and graduating as eleventh wrangler in mathematics in 1877.

For the next four years he trained as an engineer with Sir William Armstrong & Co. and Messrs. Kitson & Co. of Leeds. In 1884 he became head of the electrical department of Clarke, Chapman & Co., of Gateshead, and set out to produce a steam turbine: in the same year he constructed the first Parsons turbo-dynamo, which was the prototype of machines at first used mainly in ship-lighting.

In 1889 Parsons formed his own firm, C. A. Parsons & Co., with works at Heaton, near Newcastle upon Tyne, and installed the first turbo-generating plant in the world in the electrical power station at Newcastle. Other public lighting companies quickly followed Newcastle's lead. Early power stations generated electricity at some 2,000 volts and increased the pressure, when necessary, by transformers. By 1905 Parsons had succeeded in raising the voltage to 11,000 volts, and by 1928 he had raised it to 36,000 volts, dispensing with expensive transformers.

From the outset, Parsons had seen the potential of the steam turbine as a means of propelling ships. In 1894 the Parsons Marine Steam Turbine Co. was formed and three years later his turbine-equipped vessel, *Turbinia*, created a

sensation by its speed of thirty-four knots at the naval review held to celebrate Queen Victoria's diamond jubilee. During the years from 1897 to 1905 Parsons continued to demonstrate the advantages of turbines in warships, and in the latter year the Admiralty decided that in future turbines should be used exclusively in all classes of warship, including the new dreadnoughts.

In the same year, the Cunard Co. adopted turbines for their liners, and they were installed in the *Carmania*, *Lusitania*, and *Mauritania*, the last of which held the 'Blue Riband of the Atlantic'—for the fastest crossing—for nearly twenty-five years.

Parsons did not confine his interests to turbines; he was also concerned with optical developments. In 1889 he began production of searchlight reflectors, and after the First World War he set up the Parsons Optical Glass Co. (1922), which produced a hundred different kinds of glass for optical use, and manufactured large astronomical telescopes including a 36-inch reflecting telescope for Greenwich Observatory and 74-inch ones for Toronto and Pretoria.

In 1883 Parsons had married Katherine, daughter of William Frogatt Bethel, of Rise Park, East Yorkshire; their son was killed in action in 1918; their daughter became a member of the Institution of Naval Architects. Parsons was appointed CB in 1904, and KCB in 1911, and admitted to the Order of Merit in 1927. He was elected FRS in 1898 and was President of the British Association in 1919. He received a number of academic and civic honours. When he died on board the *Duchess of Richmond* at Kingston, Jamaica, on 11 February 1931, he was considered to be the most original British engineer since James Watt.

PARSONS, SIR JOHN HERBERT (1868–1957), ophthalmologist and physiologist, was born in Bristol on 3 September 1868, the youngest child of Isaac Jabez Parsons, a grocer, and his wife, Mary Goodhind Webb. He was educated at Bristol Grammar School, University College, Bristol, and University College London, where he graduated B.Sc. with honours in physiology (1890). He completed his medical studies at St Bartholomew's Hospital, becoming MB in 1892. Two years later he married Jane Roberta, daughter of John Hendrie of Uddington, near Glasgow; they had a son and a daughter.

Taking up ophthalmology, he became clinical assistant at Moorfields Eye Hospital, acquired his FRCS in 1900, and in 1904 was appointed Consultant Surgeon to the Moorfields and University College Hospitals, a post which he held until 1939.

By 1908 Parsons had become a world authority on the diseases of the eye. In the meantime he had published *Elementary Ophthalmic Optics* (1901), *The Ocular Circulation* (1903), *The Pathology of the Eye* (1904–8), and *Diseases of the Eye* (1907). He then went on to study the psychology of vision and perception and produced *An Introduction to the Study of Colour Vision* (1915), *An Introduction to the Theory of Perception* (1927), *Mind and the Nation: A Précis of Applied Psychology* (1918), and *The Springs of Conduct* (1950).

During the First World War he was Ophthalmic Consultant to the Home Forces and Adviser to the Army, Navy, and Royal Air Force. In 1919 he was appointed CBE. He was elected FRS in 1921 and knighted in 1922.

He had many honorary appointments and received a number of honorary degrees. He was President of the Royal Society of Medicine (1936–8), and Chairman of the Editorial Committee of the *British Journal of Ophthalmology* from 1917 to 1948. He took a prominent part in the improvement of lighting in factories, and was a leader in the expansion of knowledge of ophthalmology internationally.

Parsons died in London on 7 October 1957.

PASSFIELD, Baron (1859–1947). See Webb.

PEAKE, MERVYN LAURENCE (1911–1968), artist and author, was born at Kuling, China on 9 July 1911, the younger son of a medical missionary, Ernest Cromwell Peake, MD, and his wife, Amanda Elizabeth Powell. He was educated at Tientsin Grammar School, Eltham College, Kent, and the Royal Academy Schools, where he won the Hacker prize in 1931. After two years in an artists' colony on Sark in the Channel Islands, he obtained a post at the Westminster School of Art and taught life drawing from 1935 to 1939.

In 1937 he married Maeve, daughter of Owen Eugene Gilmore, MD; they had two sons and a daughter. His wife was also an artist whom he had met at the Westminster School.

During the Second World War Peake served in the Royal Artillery and the Royal Engineers but was invalided out of the army in 1943 and worked for two years in the Ministry of Information. In 1946 he, with his family, went back to Sark, but the need to find employment forced his return to England three years later. He became a part-time teacher at the Central School of Art, Holborn, where he remained for the next eleven years.

Between 1946 and 1959 Peake wrote three novels, *Titus Groan*, *Gormenghast*, and *Titus Alone*, strange works which can hardly be adequately described as fantasies, centred on Titus, the Earl of Groan, the crushing atmosphere of his ancestral home, Gormenghast, and his struggle to find escape in a new land. The novels attracted attention only after Peake was dead. In 1957 his one West End play *The Wit to Woo* was a failure, and from that time he became increasingly incapacitated by Parkinson's disease.

Although after his death Peake's reputation was made by the trilogy of 'Titus' novels, during his lifetime he was better known as an artist and illustrator. Examples of his work as an illustrator are Lewis Carroll's *The Hunting of the Snark* (1941) and the *Alice* books (1946 and 1954), Coleridge's *The Rime of the Ancient Mariner* (1943), and Stevenson's *Dr. Jekyll and Mr. Hyde* (1948) and *Treasure Island* (1949). He also illustrated his own books for children.

He published collections of his sketches, including *The Craft of the Lead Pencil* (1946) and *The Drawings of Mervyn Peake* (1949). He also demonstrated his versatility with the publication of collections of his poems, including *Shapes and Sounds* (1941), *The Glassblowers* (1950), and *A Reverie of Bone* (1967), as well as nonsense verse and poems for children.

In 1951 he became an honorary fellow of the Royal Society of Literature. He died at Burcot, Berkshire on 17 November 1968. After his death new interest in his work as an artist was aroused by the publication in 1974 of his *Writings and Drawings* and *Drawings*.

PERRINS, CHARLES WILLIAM DYSON (1864–1958). See Dyson Perrins.

PETHICK-LAWRENCE, FREDERICK WILLIAM, Baron Pethick-Lawrence (1871–1961), social worker and politician, was born on 28 December 1871 in London, the younger son of Alfred Lawrence, a builder, and his wife,

Mary Elizabeth, daughter of Henry Ridge, and granddaughter of Robert Brook Aspland, a well-known preacher. His father died when he was three, and his mother brought him up as a Unitarian. He was educated at Eton and Trinity College, Cambridge, where he obtained firsts in the mathematical tripos, part i, and the natural sciences tripos, part i (1894–5). He was Smith's prizeman for mathematics and Adam Smith prizeman for economics (1896–7) and President of the Union. He was elected a Fellow of Trinity (1897–1903), but decided to forego an academic career for social work.

He was called to the Bar (Inner Temple) in 1899, and worked at Mansfield House, the university settlement in Canning Town. When his elder brother died in 1900, he inherited a fortune. In 1901 he married a fellow social worker, Emmeline, daughter of Henry Pethick, and prefixed her name to his own. Together, they continued to work in the East End, and ran an evening half-penny newspaper, the *Echo*, until it failed to pay and ceased publication in 1905.

As a result of his sympathy for three suffragettes whom he defended in the courts, he and his wife took up the cause of women's suffrage, became joint editors of *Votes for Women* (1907), and worked with the Pankhursts' Women's Social and Political Union. He and his wife were both imprisoned with Emmeline Pankhurst in 1912, went on hunger strike, and were released. They quarrelled with Mrs Pankhurst, however, and were expelled from the WSPU because they were in favour of a more moderate policy than the militants were prepared to accept.

During the First World War Pethick-Lawrence, a conscientious objector, worked on the land, and tried to get elected to Parliament as a 'peace by negotiation' candidate. He failed, and failed again in 1922, but in 1923 became Labour MP for West Leicester, defeating Winston Churchill in a bitterly contested election. He was re-elected in 1924, and in 1929 was appointed Financial Secretary to the Treasury under Philip Snowden, Chancellor. He refused to support Ramsay MacDonald's National Government and was defeated in 1931.

He was re-elected in 1935 for East Edinburgh, and in 1937 became a Privy Counsellor. When Clement Attlee formed his 1945 Government he appointed Pethick-Lawrence Secretary of State for India and Burma; and a barony was conferred on him. In 1946 he led the mission to India, with Stafford Cripps, and A. V. (later Earl) Alexander, with the aim of persuading Congress and the Muslim League to agree on a united India. In spite of indefatigable efforts by Cripps and Pethick-Lawrence as well as Lord Wavell, the Viceroy, the mission failed, and when, in 1947, the Government decided to fix a definite date for the transfer of power in India and to replace Wavell with Lord Mountbatten of Burma, Pethick-Lawrence, exhausted by the labour and frustration of his office, resigned and went into retirement. He continued, however, in the Lords to support the Government's policy of granting independence to India and Burma.

In 1942 he published his autobiography *Fate has been Kind*; his wife, who in 1938 had published *My Part in a Changing World*, died in 1954; they had no children. In 1957 Pethick-Lawrence married Helen Millar, widow of Duncan McCombie, and daughter of Sir John George Craggs, a chartered accountant; they had been friends for over forty years since the time when Helen had been a militant suffragette. He died in London on 10 September 1961.

PETRIE, SIR (WILLIAM MATTHEW) FLINDERS

Frederick Pethick-Lawrence, newly appointed Secretary of State for India, in his local village shop, Shere, Surrey, December 1945

(1853–1942), Egyptologist, was born at Charlton, Kent on 3 June 1853, the only child of William Petrie and his wife, Anne, daughter of Capt. Matthew Flinders, RN, the surveyor of the southern coasts of Australia. Ill health prevented him from going to school, but his father, who was a chemist, engineer, and surveyor, and his mother, who was a geologist and collector of ancient coins, were admirable teachers, and by the age of sixteen the boy was fully familiar with the galleries of the British Museum, particularly with the Egyptian collections. His father encouraged him to carry out practical work in surveying the earthworks in southern England and Stonehenge.

The two had intended to visit Egypt together but, in the event, Flinders Petrie went there alone, and in 1883 published *The Pyramids and Temples of Gizeh*, sponsored by the Royal Society. His meticulous methods led him to deplore the haphazard work done by previous excavators and, in this respect, he attracted the attention of Amelia Edwards, one of the founders of the Egypt Exploration Fund, for which he worked from 1883 to 1885. During that time he discovered the Greek trading-station of Naucratis in the delta of the Nile where, although no buildings survived, he was able to piece together historical information through the careful examination of the broken pottery he found there.

A feature of Petrie's work was the ingenious system of 'sequence-dating' of Egyptian pottery by reference to the approximate age of the geological strata in which it was found; by this means he was able to provide a chronological framework for his discoveries from prehistoric periods for which there was no other method of determining the age. From 1896 he worked on his own, financed by popular subscriptions to a fund which he managed personally and which eventually became the British School of Archaeology in Egypt. His discoveries included the early royal tombs at Abydos, the Merenptah inscription mentioning the Hebrews in Palestine, and the Hyksos and Sinaitic monuments and inscriptions indicating early Greek contacts with Egypt. His work was meticulously documented and every year he published the results of his field-work so that other scholars could benefit without delay.

In 1897 he married Hilda Mary Isabel, daughter of Richard Denny Urlin, of Worthing, and she became of great assistance to him in his work of excavation and the management of the British School of Archaeology in Egypt. They had one son and one daughter.

From 1892 to 1933 Petrie was Professor of Egyptology at London University, a chair established by funds provided in the will of Amelia Edwards and to which she expressed the hope that he would be appointed. The Edwards Library, in which he housed his remarkable collection of Egyptian artefacts, became the centre for teaching of all aspects of Egyptology. In 1904 he published *Methods and Aims in Archaeology*, followed by numerous other publications which were invaluable to students and field-workers.

In 1926 Petrie, dissatisfied with the situation in Egypt, went to Palestine, where he remained for the rest of his life. He was knighted in 1923. He had been elected FRS in 1902 and FBA in 1904. He was honoured by many universities and learned societies both in England and abroad. He died in Jerusalem on 28 July 1942. He could justly claim to have been the creator of the science of Egyptology.

PETTY-FITZMAURICE, HENRY CHARLES KEITH, fifth MARQUESS OF LANSDOWNE (1845-1927), was born at Lansdowne House, London on 14 January 1845, the elder son of the fourth Marquess, Henry Thomas, and his second wife, Emily Jane Mercer Elphinstone de Flahault, Baroness Nairne, daughter of the Comte de Flahault and the Baroness Keith and Nairne. He was educated at Eton and Balliol College, Oxford, where he came under the influence of Benjamin Jowett. In 1866 he succeeded his father and became one of the largest landowners in the country.

From 1868 to 1880 he held minor posts in Gladstone's Governments, including those of Under-Secretary of State for War and Under-Secretary of State for India. In 1869 he married Lady Maud Evelyn Hamilton, the youngest daughter of James, first Duke of Abercorn. They had two daughters and two sons. In 1880 he resigned as he could not support Gladstone's Irish policy, but three years later Gladstone appointed him Governor-General of Canada. During his period of office (1883-8) he saw the completion of the Canadian Pacific Railway. The dispute between the USA and Canada about the Newfoundland fisheries remained unresolved when he returned to England, but the rebellion led by Louis Riel was successfully put down.

From 1888 to 1894 Lansdowne was Viceroy of India during a period without serious incident, in which he ensured the stabilization of the currency. He was created KG and honorary DCL, Oxford, in 1894. When Lord Salisbury came to office as Prime Minister in 1895 Lansdowne became Secretary of State for War and helped Lord Wolseley to carry out some administrative reforms in the army, but was blamed for the early failures of British forces in the Boer War (1899).

In 1900 he was appointed Secretary of State for Foreign Affairs, a post which he held until 1905, and in which he successfully negotiated a treaty with Japan (1902) and the Anglo-French *Entente* of 1904. He was keen to reach agreement with Germany, but in this he was unsuccessful, and the rivalry between that country and Britain continued. He also had difficulties with the USA over the European blockade of Venezuela and the arbitration in respect of American claims to Alaska (1903). When Arthur BALFOUR succeeded Salisbury as Prime Minister in 1903 Lansdowne became leader of the Conservatives in the House of Lords.

Throughout the period of Liberal Government from 1905 to the outbreak of the First World War, Lansdowne led the Conservative opposition in the Upper House. He successfully opposed the Education Bill of 1906 and took a leading part in the opposition to LLOYD GEORGE's 'People's Budget' and the Parliament Bill. When, after the second 1910 general election, it was known that the Government could rely upon the creation of sufficient peers to overcome the Lords' opposition, he abstained from voting and the bill became law (1911).

Lansdowne continued to have considerable influence, which was unimpaired when BONAR LAW succeeded Balfour in 1912. On 2 August 1914 Bonar Law and Lansdowne and a few other colleagues met at Lansdowne House and pledged their party to support France in the war with Germany. Their decision helped to persuade ASQUITH to decide on supporting France. After the first few months of the war Lansdowne's younger son was killed in action.

In May 1915 Lansdowne joined the first Coalition Government as a member of the War Cabinet and Minister without Portfolio. In 1916, on Asquith's invitation, he set out in a private memorandum his views on the possibility of a negotiated peace with Germany. Lloyd George was not prepared to consider this proposal and, when he ousted Asquith as Prime Minister, Lansdowne had no place in the new Government.

Lansdowne grew more and more uneasy as the war seemed to have reached stalemate on the Western Front, and on 29 November 1917 the *Daily Telegraph* published a letter in which he again set out the views he had earlier propounded in his memorandum. The letter was violently repudiated by the Government and the press, and brought upon Lansdowne's head accusations of disloyalty to the Allied cause. He resented the failure of his Conservative colleagues to support him and continued to advocate peace. When the war ended, he was incapacitated by ill health and retired to Bowood.

In 1922 his house in Ireland was destroyed by fire, but by 1925 it had been rebuilt and, on his way there in 1927, he died suddenly at Newtown Anner, Clonmel, the home of his younger daughter, on 3 June 1927.

PHILBY, (HARRY) ST JOHN BRIDGER (1885-1960), explorer and orientalist, was born in Ceylon (Sri Lanka), on 3 April 1885, the second son of Henry Montague Philby, a tea planter, and his wife, May Beatrice, daughter of General John Duncan. He was educated as a scholar both at Westminster and Trinity College, Cambridge, where he obtained a first in the modern languages tripos and passed into the Indian Civil Service in 1907. In 1910 he married Dora, daughter of Adrian Hope Johnston of the Indian Public Works Department; they had three daughters and one son.

Philby was posted to the Punjab, where he became proficient in Urdu and Persian but did not commend himself to his seniors. As a proficient linguist, he was posted as Assistant Political Officer, Mesopotamian Expeditionary Force, from 1915 to 1917 and was appointed CIE (1917). He was still out of favour with his seniors, and in 1917 was attached to a mission to Abdul Aziz Ibn Saud (later King of Saudi Arabia), whose help the Government sought against the Turks. The mission was successful and Philby, with Ibn Saud's assistance, travelled across Arabia to Jedda, the first time the crossing had been made. This journey convinced him that the Sharif Hussain (King Hussain of the Hejaz) was not a suitable candidate for ruler of liberated Arabia and that the future rested with Ibn Saud.

Philby returned to Riyadh and made another remarkable journey to the Wadi Duwasir before returning to England on leave. He was then asked by Sir Percy Cox to join his staff in Baghdad but, when Faisal, son of Sharif Hussain, was nominated King of Iraq by the British Government, he resigned. In 1921 he was appointed chief British Representative to Trans-Jordania (Jordan) in succession to T. E. LAWRENCE, but he resigned this post in 1924 and, after trying to mediate between Ibn Saud and Sharif Hussain and again incurring the disapproval of his seniors, he resigned from the Indian Civil Service in 1925.

Philby now went back to Jedda and became adviser to Ibn Saud. In 1930 he became a Muslim. He spent much of his time in exploration and, as he was a skilled cartographer, naturalist, and botanist, he contributed much to a wider knowledge of Arabia, particularly in the field of archaeology.

In 1939 he was in England again and, after failing to get elected to Parliament as an anti-war candidate of the British

St John Philby (centre) in his mud house in Riyadh, with J. Ryckmans (left) and Professor Ryckmans, *c.* 1920

People's Party, he returned to Arabia and strongly advised Ibn Saud against involvement in the war; but Ibn Saud was annoyed by the bitterness of his attacks on his own country and Philby had to leave Arabia. He took ship from Karachi for the USA but was arrested by security men, brought back to England, and detained under Section 18B of the Defence of the Realm regulations (1940).

After five months, his case was reconsidered and he was completely exonerated, some of his friends, including E. M. FORSTER, J. M. KEYNES, and Dennis Robertson, having protested against his imprisonment. He signalled his release by using his influence to obtain for his son Kim a post with the Secret Intelligence Service, thus unwittingly furthering Kim's career as a spy for the Soviet Government.

Philby returned to Arabia when the war ended, but became increasingly disenchanted with the extravagance and inefficiency of the Saudi regime, and in 1955 was banished and moved to Beirut. The old King Ibn Saud had died in 1953 and, although Philby was reconciled with his successor in 1956, he stayed in Beirut completing his memoirs, and died there on 30 September 1960.

He was a prolific author and published a number of books on his Arabian exploits, including the *Heart of Arabia* (2 vols., 1922), *Sheba's Daughters* (1939), and *Arabian Highlands* (1952). His autobiography *Arabian Days* appeared in 1948. He received honours from the Royal Geographical Society and the Royal Asiatic Society. Harold (Kim) Philby was in Beirut when his father died, and later escaped to the USSR.

PIGOU, ARTHUR CECIL (1877–1959), economist, was born on 18 November 1877 at Hyde, Isle of Wight, the son of Clarence George Scott Pigou, a retired army officer, and his wife, Nora, daughter of Sir John Lees. He went to Harrow and to King's College, Cambridge, with scholarships, and obtained firsts in the historical tripos and part ii of the moral sciences tripos (1899–1900); he was President of the Union in 1900. He also won the Chancellor's medal for English verse in 1899 and the Burney prize in 1900.

In 1901 he began to lecture on economics and in the following year was elected a Fellow of King's College. In 1904 he became Girdler's lecturer in economics and in 1908 succeeded Alfred Marshall as Professor of Political Economy and held that post for thirty-five years.

He was a devoted pupil and exponent of Marshall's ideas; he made no great contribution of original ideas to economics, but trained a number of students in the techniques and disciplines of economic reasoning. His first book *Principles and Methods of Industrial Peace* (1905) was an expansion of an essay that had won him the Adam Smith prize in 1903. His *magnum opus, Wealth and Welfare*, was published in 1912, and later editions were entitled *The Economics of Welfare*. He was a humanist who believed profoundly in equality and made this clear in his work.

During the First World War he was a conscientious objector and worked at the front as a driver for the Friends' Ambulance Unit. He later joined the Board of Trade, but showed little aptitude as a civil servant. After the war, he served on the Cunliffe Committee (1918–19) and the

Chamberlain Committee (1924-5) and advocated an early return to the gold standard. In 1927 he was elected FBA. He then resumed academic economics. When Keynes published his *General Theory* in 1936, attacking the ideas of traditional economics and those of Marshall and Pigou in particular, Pigou naturally disagreed with him and wrote a strongly critical review of the work. However, he later had the courage to admit that he had not appreciated some of the important things that Keynes had said.

He had continued to publish books including *A Study in Public Finance* (1928), *The Theory of Unemployment* (1933), and *Employment and Equilibrium* (1941), and showed himself to be the last of the great classical school of economists in the tradition of Henry Sidgwick and Alfred Marshall. He died unmarried at King's College, Cambridge on 7 March 1959.

PINERO, SIR ARTHUR WING (1855-1934), playwright, was born in London on 24 May 1855, the only son of John Daniel Pinero, a solicitor, who came of a family of Portuguese Jews, and his wife, Lucy Daines. He had little education, and at the age of ten went into his father's office, but the law had no attraction for him and, when he was nineteen, he became an actor. He played in a number of small parts until,

Pinero, depicted by Scotson Clark, September 1901

in 1884, he decided that he would never succeed as an actor. In the previous year he had married Myra Emily Wood (an actress under the name of Myra Holme), daughter of Beaufroy A. Moore, and widow of Capt. John Angus Lushington Hamilton. He had no children but was deeply attached to his step-daughter.

In 1877 he had begun to write plays, but he attracted little attention until he wrote farces such as *The Magistrate*, which was staged in 1885. From farce he graduated, under the influence of Ibsen, to more serious plays and had a big success with *The Second Mrs. Tanqueray* (1893), with Mrs Patrick CAMPBELL in the leading part. Pinero found Mrs Campbell, and was the first playwright to start a new vogue by selecting players of the type required, physically and intellectually, for the parts to be played.

Among Pinero's other successes were *Trelawny of the 'Wells'* (1898), *The Gay Lord Quex* (1899), *Letty* (1903), *His House in Order* (1906), *Mid-Channel* (1909), and *The Enchanted Cottage* (1922). He was knighted in 1909. In fifty-five years he wrote fifty-four plays, and until George Bernard SHAW took his place, he was the leading English playwright of his generation. He died in London on 23 November 1934.

PISSARRO, LUCIEN (1863-1944), painter, wood-engraver, and book-printer, was born in Paris on 20 February 1863, the eldest son of Camille Jacob Pissarro, Impressionist painter, and his wife, Julie Vellay. His father was of Spanish-Jewish stock and his mother was French. He grew up in France until in 1883 his father sent him to England to learn English. He planned to study painting at the Slade School of Fine Art but was dissuaded by his father and Degas, and in 1884 returned to France. There he worked with his father and got to know painters including Van Gogh, Gauguin, and Seurat, whose *pointillisme* influenced his style.

In 1890 he returned to London, and in 1892 married Esther, daughter of Jacob Samuel Levi Bensusan, a London merchant. He had for some time been interested in wood-engraving and, with the help of his wife, he established his own press, the Eragny Press. From 1896, using the Vale type of Ricketts, he printed a number of books with his own wood-cuts. He was now settled in London, and in 1902 designed his own type which he called Brook type, and became one of the most attractive and original book designers of his time.

He was also painting. In 1906 he joined the New English Art Club. He held his first one-man show at the Carfax Gallery in 1913. In 1916 he became a naturalized British subject. In 1920 he founded the Monarro Group. His style was a modified form of *pointillisme*, and his painting did much to interpret the French Impressionists to English artists and art critics. His wife presented her valuable collection of paintings to the Ashmolean Museum, the National Gallery, the Tate, and other galleries. She and her husband had one daughter, Orovida, also a painter.

Pissarro died at Southchard, Chard, Somerset on 10 July 1944.

POLLITT, HARRY (1890-1960), Chairman of the British Communist party, was born in Droylesden, Lancashire, on 22 November 1890, the second of six children of Samuel Pollitt, a blacksmith's striker, and his wife, Mary Louisa Charlesworth, who was a foundation member of the Independent Labour party and the British Communist party. She was her son's political mentor, having taken him at the age of thirteen to a socialist lecture by Philip SNOWDEN on the overthrow of capitalism. Pollitt left his local elementary school at twelve and worked in a weaving mill. At fifteen he was apprenticed to a locomotive-building firm, and at night school studied mathematics, machine-drawing, shorthand, and economics.

In 1912 he became a member of the Boilermakers' Society, having joined the ILP in 1909. Up to 1914 he gained a reputation as a socialist speaker throughout Lancashire and Yorkshire. He opposed British participation in the First World War, and in 1919 became Secretary of the London district of the Boilermakers' Society. In 1920 he became a founder member of the British Communist party and in 1921 visited the Soviet Union and met Lenin. In 1924 he became Secretary of the National Minority Movement which aimed to bring the trade unions under Communist control.

In 1925 he was sentenced to twelve months' imprisonment for seditious libel and incitement to mutiny. In 1929 he was elected General Secretary of the British Communist party. He stood several times unsuccessfully for Parliament. When the Second World War broke out, he immediately wrote a pamphlet *How to Win the War*. He was embarrassed when the party refused to support the war effort and for about two years ceased to be leader but, when Russia was invaded, he was reinstated. From 1956 to his death he was Chairman of the party. His wife, formerly Marjory Edna Brewer, whom he had married in 1925, was a Communist parliamentary candidate in 1950. They had a daughter and a son, who became President of the Oxford Union. Pollitt died on 27 June 1960 on the *Orion* returning from Australia. He was an orator, agitator, and warm-hearted opponent of poverty and hardship, the epitome of the British revolutionary movement in the radical politics of the first half of the twentieth century.

POLLOCK, SIR FREDERICK (1845-1937), jurist, was born in London on 10 December 1845, the eldest son of Sir William Frederick Pollock, second baronet, and his wife, Juliet, daughter of Henry Creed, Vicar of Corse, Gloucestershire. He was educated at Eton, where he was a King's scholar, and Trinity College, Cambridge, where he was also a scholar, came second in the classical tripos (1867), and was sixth of the senior optimes in the mathematical tripos (1867). He was elected a Fellow of Trinity in 1868 and called to the Bar (Lincoln's Inn) in 1871. In 1873 he married Georgina Harriet, younger daughter of John Deffell, an East India merchant, of Calcutta; they had a daughter and a son. In 1888 he succeeded his father as third baronet.

He practised rarely, but concentrated on producing a series of important works on English law. Among these were *Principles of Contract at Law and in Equity* (1876), *The Land Laws* (1883), and *The Law of Torts* (1887).

In 1883 Pollock was appointed Corpus Professor of Jurisprudence, Oxford, a post which he held until 1903. In 1890 he published *Introduction to the History of the Science of Politics*, followed by *First Book of Jurisprudence for Students of the Common Law* (1896). He was Professor of Common Law in the Inns of Court from 1884 to 1890, and in 1894 visited India to deliver the Tagore law lectures, which were published as *The Law of Fraud, Misrepresentation and Mistake in British India* (1894).

Pollock lectured at Harvard in 1903 and at Columbia University in 1912. These lectures led to *The Genius of the Common Law* (1912) and *Essays in the Law* (1922). He was a friend of F.W. Maitland, with whom he collaborated in the *History of English Law before the Time of Edward I* (2 vols., 1895, second edn. 1898).

From 1885 to 1919 Pollock edited the *Law Quarterly Review*, and from 1895 to 1935 was Editor-in-Chief of the *Law Reports*. He was also a close friend of Oliver Wendell Holmes, the American lawyer, and their correspondence was published as *The Holmes-Pollock Letters . . . 1874-1932* (1942).

Pollock was interested in philosophy as well as law and published a life of Spinoza (1880); he also contributed to the Badminton Library volume on *Mountaineering* (1892). He was elected FBA in 1902 and sworn of the Privy Council in 1911. He received many academic honours, and in 1914 was appointed Admiralty Judge of the Cinque Ports. In 1933 he published, among other works in a lighter vein than usual, *For my Grandson. Remembrances of an Ancient Victorian*. Pollock died in London on 18 January 1937.

PORTAL, CHARLES FREDERICK ALGERNON, first VISCOUNT PORTAL OF HUNGERFORD (1893-1971), Marshal of the Royal Air Force, was born on 21 May 1893 at Hungerford, the younger son of Edward Robert Portal, who was of Huguenot descent. His elder brother was Admiral Sir Reginald Portal. He was educated at Winchester and Christ Church, Oxford and joined the army in 1914 as a dispatch rider. In 1915 he was seconded to the RFC, at first as observer, and later as a pilot. His courage and skill as a pilot earned for him the MC (1917) and the DSO with bar (1918). In 1919 he was permanently commissioned as a squadron leader and in that year married Joan Margaret, daughter of Sir Charles Glynne Earle Welby; they had two daughters.

In the years leading to the Second World War he attended the RAF Staff College, worked as a staff officer in the Air Ministry, commanded No.7 (Bomber) Squadron, and served in India and Aden. In 1936 he was Instructor at the Imperial Defence College and in 1937 was promoted to air vice-marshal and appointed Director of Organization at the Air Ministry. In 1939 he was appointed to the Air Council and made a CB.

When the war began he became Acting Air Marshal, and in 1940 was appointed A.O.C.-in-C., Bomber Command, and later that year Chief of the Air Staff, the post he retained until 1 January 1946. Portal was remarkable for his imperturbability and for his success in dealing with the officers under his command, some of them difficult to control. Winston CHURCHILL once said that 'he had everything', and Lord TRENCHARD considered him as good a pilot as he was staff officer, an unusual combination.

In 1940 he was appointed KCB, and in 1942 GCB; in 1944 he became Marshal of the Royal Air Force, in 1945 was created a baron, and in 1946 viscount and OM. Later that year he was appointed KG. From 1946 to 1951 he was Controller of Atomic Energy, Ministry of Supply; he refused to become Minister of Defence in Churchill's last administration. In 1960 he was appointed Chairman of British Aircraft Corporation. He retired from this post in 1968. He was President of the MCC (1958-9). Portal died on 22 April 1971.   *Illustration p. 280.*

POTTER, (HELEN) BEATRIX (1866-1943), writer and illustrator of children's books, was born in London on 28 July 1866, the elder child and only daughter of Rupert Potter, a barrister, and his wife, Helen, daughter of John Leech of Dukinfield, Cheshire. Both parents had inherited fortunes from Lancashire cotton. Beatrix did not go to school, but was educated by governesses, one of whom encouraged her to draw and to study natural history. A lonely child, she spent much time drawing flowers, and small animals, of which

Sir Charles Portal inspecting members of a Spitfire squadron, Malta, February 1943

Beatrix Potter, in her late twenties, with her brother Bertram

she carefully studied the anatomy. In her London home she made pets of rabbits, mice, bats, frogs, snails, and a tame hedgehog.

At the age of twenty-seven, still living with her parents in South Kensington, she began writing letters to the sick child of a former governess, illustrating them with drawings of her pets. In 1900 she had the story of Peter Rabbit privately printed and in 1902 she did the same with *The Tailor of Gloucester*. She then became associated with the publishers Warne & Co., and during the next thirty years they published twenty-four of her little books for children with her own illustrations.

At the age of thirty-nine she became engaged to Norman Warne, disregarding the opposition of her parents; they never married because he died a few months later. From the tales of Peter Rabbit, Jemima Puddle-Duck, Mrs Tiggy-Winkle, Squirrel Nutkin, and Mr Jeremy Fisher, she had made sufficient money by 1913 to buy herself a small farm in the Lake District. She continued to write, while learning to be a farmer. The books she wrote at Sawrey are illustrated with her charming water-colour paintings of the Lakeland countryside.

In 1913 at the age of forty-seven, again acting against the advice of her parents, she married William Heelis, a solicitor of Ambleside. For the next thirty years she and her husband developed their farm, acquiring more land and rearing sheep, and they became very successful breeders. Beatrix Potter died at Sawrey on 22 December 1943. She was a passionate conservationist and bequeathed her property in the Lake District to the National Trust. Her illustrations for *The Tailor of Gloucester* are in the Tate Gallery. Her books have remained popular with small children long after her death.

POTTER, STEPHEN MEREDITH (1900–1969), writer and radio producer, was born on 1 February 1900 in London, the only son of Frank Collard Potter, a chartered accountant, and his wife, Elizabeth (Lilla) Reynolds. He was educated at Westminster and Merton College, Oxford, which he entered in 1919 after a short period of service in the Coldstream Guards.

After working as secretary to the playwright, Henry Arthur Jones, he was appointed lecturer in English at Birkbeck College, London (1926–38). In 1930 he published a study of D. H. LAWRENCE, and in 1933 edited the Nonesuch Press *Coleridge* and Mrs Coleridge's letters to Thomas Poole in *Minnow among Tritons* (1934). These were followed by *Coleridge and S.T.C.* (1935) and *The Muse in Chains: a Study in Education* (1937).

In 1938 Potter joined the British Broadcasting Corporation's Features Department and later became Editor of Features and Poetry. Up to 1943 he was concerned with literary features and war documentaries. Then, with Joyce GRENFELL, he wrote a series of satirical 'How' programmes, including 'How to talk to children', 'How to woo', and 'How to listen to radio'.

In 1945 he became theatre critic of the *New Statesman and Nation* and in 1946 book critic of the *News Chronicle*. He also took part in BBC 'Critics' programmes. In 1947 there appeared the first in the series of books in which he gave a new word to the language: *The Theory and Practice of Gamesmanship; or the Art of Winning Games Without Actually Cheating*. This was followed by *One-Upmanship* (1952) and *Supermanship* (1958). From 1949 to 1951 he was Editor of the *Leader*.

Potter was himself an obsessive games player—squash,

tennis, golf, croquet, and snooker, and in 1968 published *The Complete Golf Gamesmanship* among several other books from *Potter on America* (1956) to *Steps to Immaturity* (1959), an autobiography.

His first wife was the distinguished painter Mary Potter, formerly Marian Anderson, daughter of John Arthur Attenborough. They were married in 1927 and had two sons. In 1955 this marriage ended in divorce, and in that year he married Mrs Heather Jenner, daughter of Brigadier C. A. Lyon, DSO; they had one son, who died at the age of sixteen. Potter died in London on 2 December 1969.

POWELL, CECIL FRANK (1903–1969), physicist, was born in Tonbridge on 5 December 1903, the only son of Frank Powell, a gunsmith, and his wife, Elizabeth Caroline Bisacre. He was educated at Sir A. Judd's Commercial School (later the Judd School), Tonbridge, and Sidney Sussex College, Cambridge, where he obtained firsts in both parts of the natural sciences tripos (1924–5).

He became a research worker in the Cavendish Laboratory under C. T. R. WILSON until in 1928 he moved to be research assistant to Professor A. M. Tyndall in the H. H. Wills Physics Laboratory at Bristol. In 1931 he became lecturer, in 1946 Reader, and from 1948 to 1963 Melville Wills Professor of Physics, and Director of the Physics Laboratory (1964–9). During 1964–7 he was Pro-Vice-Chancellor of Bristol University. He was elected FRS in 1949 and awarded the Nobel prize for physics in 1950. He was President of the Association of Scientific Workers in 1954 and of the World Federation of Scientific Workers in 1957.

Powell played a leading part in the establishment of the European Centre for Nuclear Research (CERN) at Geneva and was Chairman of its Scientific Policy Committee from 1961 to 1963. He was also involved in setting up the Pugwash Conferences on Science and World Affairs in 1957 and was elected Chairman in 1967, having been Deputy Chairman from their inception. From 1965 to 1968 he was also Chairman of the Nuclear Physics Board of the British Science Research Council.

His research work was described in many scientific papers and books, including *Nuclear Physics in Photographs* (with G. P. S. Occhialini, 1947) and *The Study of Elementary Particles by the Photographic Method* (with P. H. Fowler and D. H. Perkins, 1959). He received many academic awards and honours.

He married in 1932 Isobel Therese, daughter of Johann Artner, Austrian business executive; they had two daughters. Powell died from a heart attack on 9 August 1969 at Lago di Como, Italy, eight days after his retirement from Bristol.

POWYS, JOHN COWPER (1872–1963), author, was born on 8 October 1872 at Shirley, Derbyshire, the eldest of eleven children of the Vicar, the Revd Charles Francis Powys, and his wife, Mary Cowper, daughter of the Revd William Cowper Johnson, Rector of Yaxham, Norfolk. He was educated at Sherborne and Corpus Christi College, Cambridge.

In 1896 Powys married Margaret Alice Lyon; they had one son. From 1898 to 1909 he lectured for the Oxford University Extension Delegacy. In 1905 he made his first lecture tour to the United States, where from 1909 to 1934 he spent much of each year, and became an influential and popular lecturer. He published his first novel, *Wood and Stone*, in New York (1915). This received little notice, but his later novels were published both in New York and in London and made his reputation. These included *Wolf*

Solent (1929), *A Glastonbury Romance* (1933), *Owen Glendower* (1941), *Atlantis* (1954), *The Brazen Head* (1956), and *All or Nothing* (1960).

Powys also published philosophical essays, including *The Meaning of Culture* (1930) and *The Art of Happiness* (1935), as well as literary studies such as *Dostoievsky* (1947) and *Rabelais* (1948). His *Letters to Louis Wilkinson* (1958) contain shrewd comments on modern authors. His masterpiece, however, was his *Autobiography* (1934), which J. B. Priestley called 'one of the greatest autobiographies in the English language'.

His two brothers, Theodore Frank and Llewelyn, were also authors, and all three were steeped in the love of the West Country and Wales. His son, who became a Roman Catholic priest, died in 1954. Powys died in Wales at Blaenau Ffestiniog on 17 June 1963.

PRIMROSE, ARCHIBALD PHILIP, fifth EARL OF ROSEBERY (1847–1929), Prime Minister and politician, sportsman, and author, was born in London on 7 May 1847, the elder son of Archibald Primrose, Lord Dalmeny, and his wife, Catherine Lucy Wilhelmina, only daughter of Philip Henry Stanhope, fourth Earl Stanhope. His grandfather was Archibald John Primrose, fourth Earl of Rosebery. His father died when he was three and he was educated at Eton and Christ Church, Oxford, as Lord Dalmeny. He succeeded his grandfather as fifth Earl in 1868. He was already an owner of racehorses and left Oxford without a degree because the authorities objected to an undergraduate figuring on the racecourse. He was elected to the Jockey Club in 1870.

From time to time Rosebery made outstanding speeches in the House of Lords, notably in 1872 when, in the debate on arbitration between Britain and the USA for damage done in the American Civil War, he urged that care should be taken to maintain good relations between the two countries.

In 1878 he married Hannah, heiress of Baron Meyer Amschel de Rothschild, who, on the death of her father in 1874 and mother in 1877, became the owner of Mentmore and its treasures. They had two sons and two daughters. When in 1879 Gladstone set out on his Midlothian campaign, Rosebery invited him to make Dalmeny his headquarters but, when Gladstone offered him a post in his new ministry, Rosebery declined the offer. He pressed, however, for the appointment of a Minister for Scottish affairs. In 1881 he became Under-Secretary in the Home Office, but in 1883, dissatisfied with the progress made on Scottish affairs, he resigned. Eventually the Scottish Office was set up, but he declined to become the first Minister.

In 1883 he and Lady Rosebery visited Australia and New Zealand and he made a number of speeches emphasizing his view of the Empire as a Commonwealth of Nations, a theme to which he attached great importance. Another of his political aims was the reform of the House of Lords for the purpose of increasing its efficiency, but his eloquence in this respect fell upon deaf ears.

In 1885 he accepted the office of Lord Privy Seal with a seat in the Cabinet, and in the following year became Foreign Secretary, 'the only good appointment' in Gladstone's third administration, said Queen Victoria. Rosebery had clear ideas about foreign policy which differed little from those of Lord Salisbury. He distrusted Russia, regarded friendship with France as essential, and emphasized the common interests of Britain and Germany and, although he held this office for less than six months, he enhanced his reputation as a statesman.

Archibald Primrose, Earl of Rosebery, talking to the Countess of Arran at a Dublin horse show, August 1913

In opposition, he continued to press his views on imperial relations and the reform of the House of Lords, and in 1889–90 became Chairman of the new London County Council. In 1890 Lady Rosebery died and for eighteen months, shocked by his loss, Rosebery withdrew from politics. However, in 1892, encouraged by the Queen, he again accepted the office of Foreign Secretary and was created KG.

Between 1892 and 1894 he had the chance to put into effect his imperial aims by setting up a protectorate in Uganda and Kenya and supporting Lord CROMER in his policy in Egypt. These measures brought him into conflict with Sir William Harcourt, the first of many occasions on which Gladstone's Cabinet was divided. In 1893 he succeeded in bringing coal owners and miners to the negotiating table and ending the great strike of that year.

In March 1894 Gladstone, threatened with blindness, resigned, and Queen Victoria, on her own initiative, sent for Rosebery, disregarding the claims of Sir William Harcourt to succeed as premier. But Rosebery as Prime Minister, in spite of his popularity in the country, was at a disadvantage; his Liberal following was divided into two warring camps, and the Nonconformist element in the party instinctively distrusted him as a successful racehorse owner. His Government lasted for only sixteen months. His political fortunes were not improved by the fact that twice during that period his horses won the Derby. In 1895 the Government was defeated on a 'snap' vote of censure and Rosebery resigned. The Liberals were defeated at the subsequent election; Rosebery ended his official connection with Harcourt, and in 1896, angered by Gladstone's return from retirement to fulminate against the Turks for the Armenian massacres, he resigned as leader of the Liberal party, feeling that he could not acquiesce in a policy which might lead to war.

His resignation did not bring about union in the party; its dissension was increased by the Boer War, and in 1902 Rosebery became President of one wing, the Liberal League, supported by Herbert ASQUITH and Sir Edward GREY. When, however, the Liberals returned to power in 1905 and Asquith and Grey decided to serve under Campbell-Bannerman, Rosebery severed his connection with official Liberalism.

In the years up to the First World War he saw, with misgivings, the Anglo-French *entente* of 1905, the failure to reform the House of Lords, the impact of LLOYD GEORGE's 'People's Budget' of 1909, and the Parliament Act of 1911, which he at first opposed but later accepted as of less conse-quence than the creation of a large number of peers so as to secure its passage. When war broke out, however, he supported the Government; he was offered an appointment in the second coalition but refused (1916). His younger son was killed in action in 1917, and in 1918 Rosebery became a permanent invalid. He died at his home in Epsom on 21 May 1929.

He will be remembered not only as a statesman and a sportsman, whose horses won the Derby three times, but also as an author. His publications include *William Pitt* (1891), *Sir Robert Peel* (1899), *Oliver Cromwell* (1899), *Napoleon: the Last Phase* (1900), *Lord Randolph Churchill* (1906), *Chatham: his Early Life and Connections* (1910), and *William Windham* (1913). He was elected Lord Rector of Aberdeen University in 1878 and of Edinburgh University in 1880.

Q

QUILLER-COUCH, SIR ARTHUR THOMAS ('Q') (1863-1944), man of letters, was born at Bodmin on 21 November 1863, the eldest child of Thomas Quiller Couch, a medical practitioner, and his wife, Mary, daughter of Elias Ford, yeoman, of Abbots Kerswell, near Newton Abbot. The Quillers and Couches had been Cornish for generations. He was educated at Newton Abbot and Clifton Colleges, and Trinity College, Oxford, where he wrote for the *Oxford Magazine* under the pseudonym 'Q'. After a year as lecturer in classics, he left Oxford for London in 1887 to be a journalist. Two years later Quiller-Couch married Louisa Amelia, daughter of John Hicks, of Fowey; they had one son and one daughter. In 1890 he became Assistant Editor of the *Speaker*, to which he also regularly contributed short stories and articles until 1899.

In 1888 he published *The Astonishing History of Troy Town*, Troy being Fowey, the small Cornish port to which he was much attached and where he made his home in 1892. During the next twenty years he published some sixty books, mostly romantic novels, but also many other works, including anthologies, notably *The Oxford Book of English Verse* (1900).

In 1910 he was knighted, and in 1912 appointed King Edward VII Professor of English Literature at Cambridge. In this post, which he held until 1944, he succeeded in establishing an independent honours school in his subject, and had the satisfaction from 1917 onwards of seeing large numbers of students reading for the English tripos. His lectures, which were very popular, were published under such titles as *On the Art of Writing* (1916) and *On the Art of Reading* (1920). He received numerous academic honours.

Just after the end of the First World War he lost his only son, who died on active service in 1919. Although he lived in Cambridge at Jesus College during term time, Quiller-Couch never ceased to be a Cornishman. In 1937-8 he was Mayor of Fowey, and he died there on 12 May 1944.

Quiller-Couch, 1943

R

RALEIGH, SIR WALTER ALEXANDER (1861-1922), critic and essayist, was born in London on 5 September 1861, the only son of Alexander Raleigh, a Congregational minister, and his wife, Mary Darling, daughter of James Gifford, of Edinburgh. He was educated at Edinburgh Academy, University College School, University College London, and King's College, Cambridge, where he was Editor of the *Cambridge Review* and President of the Union (1884).

During 1885-7 he was Professor of English Literature at the Mohammedan Anglo-Oriental College, Aligarh, India, and in 1888-9 lectured for the Oxford University Extension Delegacy before being appointed Professor of Modern Literature at University College, Liverpool, succeeding A. C. BRADLEY (1890). In that year he married Lucie Gertrude, daughter of Mason Jackson, art editor of the *Illustrated London News*; they had four sons and one daughter. While at Liverpool, he published *The English Novel* (1894), *Robert Louis Stevenson: an Essay* (1895), *Style* (1897), and *Milton* (1900).

In 1900 he was appointed Professor of English Language and Literature at Glasgow, again succeeding Bradley. In 1903 he published *Wordsworth*, but his lectures gave him little time for writing.

In 1904 he became the first holder of the chair of English literature at Oxford. He then published *The English Voyages of the Sixteenth Century* (Hakluyt's *Voyages*, 1906), *Shakespeare* (1907), and *Six Essays on Johnson* (1910). In 1911 he was knighted; and in 1912 produced an edition of the *Complete Works of George Savile, first Marquess of Halifax*. In 1914 his chair was reconstituted as the Merton chair of English literature and Raleigh became a Fellow of Merton College. During the First World War he wrote a number of pamphlets on the war and English character collected as *England and the War* (1918).

After the war he wrote the first volume of *The War in the Air* (the official history of the Royal Air Force, 1922). He contracted typhoid fever in the Near East while preparing the second volume and died in Oxford on 13 May 1922.

RAMSAY, SIR WILLIAM (1852-1916), chemist, was born on 2 October 1852 in Glasgow, the only child of William Ramsay, a civil engineer, and his wife, Catharine Robertson. He was educated at Glasgow University (1866-9) and at Tübingen, where he obtained his Ph.D. (1871). Returning to Glasgow in 1872, he was appointed assistant in the Young Laboratory of Technical Chemistry and, from then until 1880, did research in organic chemistry and established a close relationship between the alkaloids, quinine, cinchonine, and pyridine.

In 1880 he was appointed Professor of Chemistry at University College, Bristol, and in 1881 became Principal. In that year he married Margaret, daughter of George Stevenson Buchanan; they had a son and a daughter. Ramsay spent seven years at Bristol, his research being concerned with physical chemistry, and he published a series of papers, dealing with vapour densities and connected problems.

From 1887 till 1913 he held the chair of general chemistry at University College London, and it was during these years that his most important work was done—the discovery of the chemically inert elementary gases, argon, helium, neon, krypton, and xenon. Argon was discovered in 1894 in collaboration with Lord RAYLEIGH. For their work together they jointly received the Nobel prize in 1904.

Ramsay was elected FRS in 1888 and appointed KCB in 1902. After the discovery of argon, he continued to work with his colleagues with a view to finding further inert elements and, in due course, the other inert gases were discovered. In co-operation with Dr F. SODDY, Ramsay proved that the emanation of radium produces helium during its atomic disintegration. His experiments and his findings were of great importance to the advance of chemical and physical science, leading to the discoveries of Sir Ernest RUTHERFORD and others. Ramsay was the foremost chemical discoverer of his time, and was able to build up a great school of chemical research at University College. A collection of his lectures was published as *Essays and Addresses*.

After retirement he set up a small private laboratory at his home near Hazlemere, Bucks, and he was doing war work there when he died on 23 July 1916.

RANK, (JOSEPH) ARTHUR, first BARON RANK (1888-1972), industrialist and builder of a British film organization, was born on 22 December 1888 in Hull, the youngest child of Joseph Rank, a wealthy miller, and his wife, Emily Voase. He was brought up as a strict Methodist and, after going to the Leys School, Cambridge, was apprenticed to the flour business and worked in his father's firm in London. During the First World War he served in France. In 1917 he married Laura Ellen Marshall, daughter of Baron Marshall of Chipstead; they had two daughters.

As a teacher in a Methodist Sunday school, he recognized the value of films as an educational medium, and in 1933 founded the Religious Film Society. A year later he formed a small company, British National Films, and made a film, *Turn of the Tide*, which was not a success because of lack of interest among distributors. This brought home to Rank the importance of distribution and he decided that he would enter this side of the business.

After his father died in 1943, Rank undertook, in addition to his responsibilities towards Rank's Hovis McDougall Ltd., to challenge the grip of Hollywood on the British film industry and to secure for the Rank Organisation control of the industry in Britain. He bought the film studios at Denham and Pinewood and those owned by Gainsborough and Gaumont-British, and acquired control of the Gaumont-British and Odeon circuits. The organization turned out a succession of films of variable quality and for some years had a monopoly of British talent. Rank did not interfere in film making; he left that to his able producers, directors, writers, and actors. It was, however, Rank's business acumen and determination that led the way in the creation of a viable British film industry. In 1957 he was created a peer. He died on 29 March 1972.

RANSOME, ARTHUR MICHELL (1884-1967), journalist and author, was born in Leeds on 18 January 1884, the eldest child of Cyril Ransome, professor of history, and his wife, Edith, daughter of Edward Baker Boulton, who had been a sheep farmer in Australia. He was educated at Rugby where he was taught by Dr W. H. D. Rouse, later Headmaster of the Perse School, Cambridge, a remarkable scholar in Sanskrit and Pali as well as Latin and Greek. Ransome went on to Yorkshire College, Leeds, but left the college for London when he was seventeen and worked for Grant Richards, the publishers.

For the next twelve years he led a Bohemian life, the friend of writers, actors, and artists, making a frugal living as a journalist. In 1909 he married Ivy Constance, daughter of George Graves Walker; they had one daughter; but the marriage was unhappy and ended in divorce. In 1912–13 he was involved in a libel case over a book on Oscar Wilde, and although judgement was given in his favour he found it a worrying experience. In 1913 he went to Russia to study Russian folklore, and in 1916 published *Old Peter's Russian Tales*, which was a great success. He was in Russia throughout the revolution, and in 1919 published *Six Weeks in Russia in 1919*, followed by *The Crisis in Russia* (1921), in which he defended the revolution. In 1924 Ransome married Evgenia, daughter of Peter Shelepin, with whom he had been living in Estonia in 1921.

In that year (1924) he became a correspondent of the *Manchester Guardian* under C. P. Scott, and during 1925–6 went to Egypt and China for the paper. Then, in 1929, he began the series of books that made his reputation with *Swallows and Amazons*, an account of four children camping and sailing in the Lake District, followed by *Swallowdale* (1931) and *Peter Duck* (1932). These books were based on the adventures of the Altounyan children, sons and daughters

Arthur Ransome with a friend, leaving the Court during the libel case brought against him by Lord Alfred Douglas, April 1913

of an old Armenian friend. Ransome also wrote books about bird-watching and fishing, including *Rod and Line* (1929), *Coot Club* (1934), and *Mainly about Fishing* (1959). For his *Pigeon Post* (1936) he received the Library Association's Carnegie medal for the best children's book of the year. He was appointed CBE in 1953. He died in Manchester on 3 June 1967.

RATHBONE, ELEANOR FLORENCE (1872–1946), social reformer, was born in London on 12 May 1872, the daughter of William Rathbone, a Liverpool social reformer, and his second wife, Emily Acheson Lyle. She was brought up in an atmosphere of social reform in Liverpool and politics in London, as her father was an MP (1868–95). She was educated at Kensington High School and Somerville College, Oxford.

An inquiry into the position of widows under the Poor Law led her to formulate the case for family allowances, of which she became the leading advocate, publishing *The Disinherited Family* in 1924, and *The Case for Family Allowances* in 1940. She was also a firm supporter of the women's suffrage movement and succeeded Millicent FAW-CETT as President of the National Union of Women's Suffrage Societies (1919). As an independent member of Liverpool City Council (1909), she concerned herself with the problems of housing.

In 1929 she was elected Independent MP for the Com-bined English Universities and retained the seat until her death. From 1928, when women in Britain achieved equal voting rights with men, she concentrated on the plight of Indian women, publishing in 1934 *Child Marriage: The Indian Minotaur*. Her work was recognized by the conferment of honorary degrees from Liverpool and Oxford. She was opposed to the appeasement policies of the Governments from 1931 to 1939 and expounded her views in *War Can Be Averted* (1937). When the war came, she was indefatigable in organizing schemes for the relief of refugees. She was active in the problems of Palestine when she died suddenly in London on 2 January 1946.

RATTIGAN, SIR TERENCE MERVYN (1911–1977), playwright, was born in London on 10 June 1911, the younger son of a diplomat, (William) Frank Arthur Rattigan, and his wife, Vera Houston. He was educated as a scholar at Harrow and Trinity College, Oxford. A short stay in France led to *French Without Tears*, the comedy staged at the Criterion Theatre (1936), which made his name.

During the Second World War Rattigan served with the RAF, and produced *Flare Path* in 1942, followed by *While the Sun Shines* in 1943. After the war he had further outstanding success with the more serious themes of *The Winslow Boy* (1946), *The Browning Version* (1948), *The Deep Blue Sea* (1952), and *Separate Tables* (1954).

Many of these were made into films directed by Anthony

Terence Rattigan on stage with the cast of *Separate Tables*, (l. to r.) Celia Johnson, Trevor Howard, Deborah Kerr, and Wendy Hillier, at the performance to celebrate his sixtieth birthday, 1972

Asquith. It was Rattigan who first coined the term 'Aunt Edna' to indicate the ordinary, unsophisticated playgoer who is not interested in experimental theatre. Rattigan did not take part in the avant-garde movement of the post-war playwrights, and in consequence suffered from the criticism of some reviewers, but his plays were popular, and his last, *Cause Célèbre* (1977), showed that he had not lost his touch.

In 1953 his collected plays were published in two volumes. In 1958 he was appointed CBE, and in 1971 knighted. He was a homosexual and never married. He died in Bermuda on 30 November 1977.

RAYLEIGH, third BARON (1842–1919). See STRUTT.

READ, SIR HERBERT EDWARD (1893–1968), writer, critic, and poet, was born on 4 December 1893, the eldest son of Herbert Read, of Muscoates Grange, Kirbymoorside, Yorkshire, and his wife, Eliza Strickland. He was educated at the Crossley and Porter Endowed School for Orphans, Halifax, and Leeds University.

In 1914 he was commissioned in the Green Howards and won the DSO and MC. In 1919 he married Evelyn May Roff; they had one son. From 1919 to 1922 he worked at the Treasury, but by then his interest in the arts was becoming predominant. From 1923 to 1931 he was Assistant Keeper at the Victoria and Albert Museum, and was Watson Gordon Professor of Fine Art, Edinburgh (1931–3). He then edited the *Burlington Magazine* (1933–9), during which time he published *The Innocent Eye*, a fragment of autobiography (1933), *Art Now* (1933), *Art and Industry* (1934), and *Art and Society* (1937).

In 1936 he championed the Surrealist Exhibition, and in 1947 founded, with Roland Penrose, the Institute of Contemporary Arts. He was a convinced pacifist and, with Bertrand RUSSELL, demonstrated against the nuclear bomb. In 1953, however, he was knighted.

In 1930 he gave the Clark lectures on *Wordsworth* and in 1936 wrote *In Defence of Shelley*, opposing the criticism of his friend, T. S. ELIOT. His other publications include *Education Through Art* (1943), *Modern Painting* (1959), and *Modern Sculpture* (1964), and a novel, *The Green Child* (1935). A poem, *Moon's Farm*, written for radio, was published in 1951. For some years he was a director of Routledge & Kegan Paul. He also spent much time abroad as a speaker at international congresses.

He and his first wife were divorced in 1936, when he married Margaret Ludwig; they had three sons and a daughter. He died at Stonegrave, near his birthplace, on 12 June 1968.

READING, first MARQUESS OF (1860–1935). See ISAACS, RUFUS DANIEL.

REED, AUSTIN LEONARD (1873–1954), men's outfitter, was born at Newbury on 6 September 1873, the eldest son of William Bilkey Reed, hosier and hatter, of Reading, and his wife, Emily Florence Bowler. He was educated at Reading School and joined his father's business in 1888. He then visited the USA to study the business methods of Wanamaker's in Philadelphia and Chicago and, at the age of twenty-seven, set up his own business in Fenchurch Street, London (1900). In 1902 he married Emily, daughter of Alfred Wilson, a Reading butcher; they had two sons and four daughters.

By 1908 he had three shops in the City of London, and in 1911 the first West-End branch was opened in Regent Street. Two years later, the business was extended to Birmingham and in 1914 to Manchester. By 1930 there were branches in most large cities in Britain, and in 1929 a shop was opened on the *Aquitania*, followed by shops on the *Queen Mary* and the *Queen Elizabeth*.

In 1920 Reed's firm became a public company, Austin Reed Ltd., and he set out to provide the man of limited means with a 'Savile Row suit'; in 1926 he opened a new Regent Street shop, where changing rooms and bathrooms were provided. Customers could join the Austin Reed club, a form of credit before the days of credit cards.

Reed was a founder member of the Regent Street Association and its Chairman in 1927. He was also a founder member of the National Association of Outfitters, a President of the City of London Trade Association, and Master of the Glovers' Company. During the Second World War, his younger son, a fighter pilot, was killed. Reed died at Gerrard's Cross on 5 May 1954.

REID DICK, SIR WILLIAM (1878–1961), sculptor, was born in Glasgow on 13 January 1878, the son of Francis Dick, a journeyman engine-fitter, and his wife, Elizabeth Reid. He served a five-year apprenticeship as a stone-mason's assistant, and in 1906–7 studied at the Glasgow School of Art. In 1907 he settled in London, and in the following year exhibited at the Royal Academy. In 1914, he married Catherine, daughter of William John Treadwell, of Northampton; they had a son and two daughters. He served in the army in France and Palestine (1916–18), and after the war made his name with the *Pieta*, an altar panel, and the recumbent figure of Lord Kitchener in St Paul's Cathedral (1922–5); he followed these with the *Lion* above the Menin Gate in Ypres (1927), and the *Eagle* surmounting the RAF memorial on the Thames embankment.

He designed memorials to Lord LEVERHULME at Port Sunlight (1930), to Lord IRWIN and Lord Willingdon at New Delhi (1932–6), to David Livingstone at Victoria Falls (1931–3), and to President Roosevelt in Grosvenor Square, London (1948). In 1938 he chiselled the recumbent figure of George V for the tomb in St George's Chapel, Windsor, designed by Sir Edwin LUTYENS and also one for Queen Mary. He was the sculptor of the statue of George V (c.1941) alongside the east end of Westminster Abbey, of which Sir Gilbert SCOTT was the architect.

He produced many other important works, including a bas-relief of *Children* for Selfridges in Oxford Street (1928), two large groups of shire horses for Unilever House, near Blackfriars Bridge (1932), and a bronze statue of Lady Godiva for Coventry (c.1950). He received many commissions for portrait busts including Harry LAUDER (1911), Lady Diana Cooper (1922), George VI (1942), Winston CHURCHILL (1943), and Princess Elizabeth (1947).

Reid Dick was elected ARA in 1921, RA in 1928, was President of the Royal Society of British Sculptors (1933–8), a member of the Royal Fine Art Commission (1928) and of the Royal Mint Advisory Committee (1934–5). He was appointed KCVO in 1935, and was King's (later Queen's) Sculptor in Ordinary for Scotland.

He died in London on 1 October 1961; there is a memorial to him in St Paul's Cathedral.

REITH, JOHN CHARLES WALSHAM, first BARON REITH (1889–1971), first Director-General of the BBC, was born on 20 July 1889 at Stonehaven, Kincardineshire, the youngest of the seven children of the Revd George Reith, a minister of the Free Church of Scotland, and his wife, Adah Mary, daughter of Edward Weston, a London stockbroker. He was educated at Glasgow Academy, Gresham's School, Holt, and the Royal Technical College, Glasgow. In 1908 he was apprenticed as an engineer and in 1914 was employed at the Royal Albert Dock extension in London.

During the First World War he served in France with the 5th Scottish Rifles, was wounded at the Battle of Loos (1915) and during 1916–17 worked for the Ministry of Munitions. In 1920 he was, briefly, General Manager of William Beardmore & Co. at Coatbridge. In the following year he married Muriel Katharine, daughter of John Lynch Odhams, head of Odhams' press, whom he had met during the war; they had a son and a daughter.

In 1922 he was appointed General Manager of the British Broadcasting Company. He at once set about creating an organization that would reflect the 'best in every department of human knowledge, endeavour, and achievement', and with uncompromising fanaticism insisted, not only on the propriety of the programmes, but also on the clean living of his staff. No whisper of scandal must impair the image of broadcasting. When, in 1926, the Company became the British Broadcasting Corporation, Reith, as its first Director-General, was its main architect and dictator. His views on his responsibilities were set out in *Broadcast Over Britain* (1924): education, religion, and culture were essential ingredients as well as information and entertainment. And Reith's training as an engineer ensured that he would aim at the highest technical efficiency.

His ruthless Calvinistic temperament did not invariably endear him to his colleagues; he had trouble with his Board of Governors until J. H. Whitley (former Speaker of the Commons) became Chairman in 1930. Meanwhile, Reith had succeeded in keeping the Corporation out of trouble during the general strike of 1926, and in 1927 had been knighted.

Lord Reith: his temperament did not invariably endear him to his colleagues

In 1932 he inaugurated the Empire Service, the first venture into international broadcasting, and persuaded King George V to give the first royal Christmas broadcast to the nation and the Commonwealth. In 1936 he inaugurated British television.

In 1938 he decided to leave the BBC, and became Chairman of Imperial Airways, and in 1939 the first Chairman of BOAC. However, he was not happy in this work and regretted that he had left the BBC. Early in 1940, Neville CHAMBERLAIN appointed him Minister of Information and he was elected National MP for Southampton. When Winston CHURCHILL succeeded Chamberlain, he transferred Reith to the Ministry of Transport and, towards the end of 1940, appointed him Minister of Works; in the same year he became the first Baron Reith. Reith, however, could never co-operate with politicians; Churchill dismissed him shortly afterwards, and incurred his virulent and lasting dislike.

During 1943–4 Reith worked at the Admiralty, planning the movement of supplies, war materials, and transport for the invasion of Europe. He was appointed CB (military) for this work. In 1943 he joined Cable and Wireless, and between 1946 and 1959 held important posts with the Commonwealth Telecommunications Board, the New Towns Committee, and the Colonial Development Corporation. He also held a number of commercial appointments. In 1967–8 he was Lord Commissioner of the General Assembly of the Church of Scotland and was appointed Knight of the Thistle (1969).

His later years were those of a disappointed man, who resented that full use had not been made of his capabilities. He received many honours including GBE (1934), GCVO (1939), PC (1940). He was awarded a number of academic honours, and was Lord Rector of Glasgow University from 1965 to 1968.

Reith died in Edinburgh on 16 June 1971 and his wife unveiled a memorial to his memory in Westminster Abbey in 1972. His war diaries, *Wearing Spurs*, were published in 1966, and *The Reith Diaries*, edited by Charles Stuart, in 1975.

RHODES, WILFRED (1877–1973), cricketer, was born at Kirkheaton, Yorkshire, on 29 October 1877, the son of a miner, Alfred Rhodes, and his wife, Elizabeth Holliday. He was educated at the Spring Grove school, Huddersfield, and left at sixteen to work on the railways. He had inherited from his father a capacity and enthusiasm for cricket and, after playing in his village team, he had two years as a professional at Galashiels. In 1893 he joined the Yorkshire side as a slow left-arm bowler and played with George Hirst who had also come from Kirkheaton.

In 1899 Rhodes married a Kirkheaton girl, Sarah Stancliffe; they had one daughter. In that same year he played for England against Australia in the first test match, the last in which W. G. GRACE appeared. In the first test of the tour to Australia in 1902, Rhodes and Hirst bowled the Australians out for 36 runs, Rhodes taking 7 for 17 off 11 overs. In the fifth and last match of that series, there occurred the legendary situation in which Rhodes went in as last man to bat with Hirst at the other end, England needing 15 runs to win. Hirst is supposed to have said to Rhodes, 'Don't worry, Wilf, we'll get 'em in ones'. Whether this story is true or not they certainly succeeded in getting the runs.

Gradually Rhodes established himself in the England side, not only as a bowler, but also as a batsman. On the 1903–4 tour to Australia with Pelham WARNER's side, he shared a record last-wicket partnership of 130 runs with R. E. Forster.

By 1911-12 he was sharing an opening partnership with Jack HOBBS of 323 runs in the Melbourne test, a record which stood for thirty-five years. From then onwards he and Hobbs became famous as 'the Old Firm', the regular openers for England, noted for their uncanny understanding of each other's minds, each completely confident of the other, keeping their opponents in a state of continual anxiety by their flair for stealing quick singles. As Hobbs himself wrote of Rhodes, 'Nobody with whom I ever batted exceeded him as a run-stealer'.

As a bowler Rhodes was noted for his deceptive flight and spin and, bowling off a short run, he could carry on for long spells, unchanged, without losing his accuracy or cunning. In the second test on the 1903-4 tour to Australia he bowled throughout both Australian innings and took 15 wickets for 124 runs. In his professional career of thirty-two years he took over 4,000 wickets and made nearly 40,000 runs. He took 100 wickets in a season twenty-three times and during sixteen of them also made 1,000 runs. He had 58 caps for England, 41 of them in tests against Australia.

During the First World War Rhodes worked in a munitions factory at Huddersfield and, when peace came, returned to cricket for Yorkshire and England. In 1926, in his forty-ninth year, he played at the Oval in his last test match and, amidst great excitement, in Australia's second innings took 4 wickets for 44 runs and thus helped England to victory both in that match and in the series; England had recovered the Ashes after a fourteen-year interval.

He continued to play in his early fifties, but his eyesight was beginning to fail. When he retired, he was appointed cricket coach at Harrow school, but in 1945 he was found to be suffering from glaucoma and in 1952 he became totally blind. In that year his wife died and he went to live with his daughter. He continued to go to cricket matches with his friends, although he could no longer see. He died on 8 July 1973 at Broadstone, Dorset. As a cricketer he was one of the greatest of all-rounders and has been described in the *Guinness Book of Cricket* as 'the greatest wicket-taker of all time'.

RICHARDS, FRANK (1876-1961), writer, whose real name was Charles Harold St John Hamilton, was born on 8 August 1876 at Ealing, the sixth child of John Hamilton, a journalist, and his wife, Marian Hannah Trinder. Little is known of his early years and he himself was reticent on the subject. He claimed to have received his first cheque for a story when he was seventeen.

He concentrated on boys' papers, writing voluminously for the *Gem* and the *Magnet*. In the latter, he wrote about Greyfriars School and its 'Famous Five' of the Remove, which included Harry Wharton, Frank Nugent, and Hurree Jamset Ram Singh, together with Billy Bunter, the fat scrounging tuck-hunter, always waiting for a postal order which never arrived. Richards continued writing these stories for over thirty years, and in 1952 wrote scripts about Bunter for television.

The Second World War put an end to the *Gem* and the *Magnet*, but Bunter continued to appear in hardbacks when the war was over. Richards created other schools, including Rookwood in the *Boys' Friend*, and Cliff House School with Bessie Bunter in the *School Friend*. Altogether, he appears to have created some thirty schools.

George ORWELL and others criticized his stories because of their snobbery and their attitude to foreigners, but Richards was undeterred, and threatened legal action to prevent his work being discussed in a book provisionally titled *The Penny Blood*. It is unlikely that any contemporary of Richards exceeded his output which was estimated to be equivalent to a thousand ordinary novels.

He never married. He died at his home near Broadstairs on 24 December 1961. His autobiography, which he published in 1952, was remarkable for its evasion of any real facts about his personal life. *Billie Bunter of Greyfriars School* edited by Kay King was published in 1982.

RICHARDS, IVOR ARMSTRONG (1893-1979), literary critic, was born at Sandbach, Cheshire, on 26 February 1893, the youngest son of William Armstrong Richards, an engineer, and his wife, Mary Ann, daughter of George Haigh, a wool manufacturer. He was educated at Clifton College and Magdalene College, Cambridge; but for two years (1915-16) was incapacitated by tuberculosis and had to recuperate in north Wales.

Returning to Cambridge in 1917, he was appointed to lecture for the English tripos and soon acquired a reputation as a teacher, his specialities being the theory of criticism and the modern novel. His first book *The Foundations of Aesthetics* (1922) was written in collaboration with C. K. OGDEN, the inventor of Basic English, and James Wood. That was followed by *The Meaning of Meaning* (1923), also written in collaboration with Ogden, and *Principles of Literary Criticism* (1925), which inaugurated the modern critical movement.

In 1926 he was elected to a fellowship at Magdalene, and produced *Science and Poetry*, of which a second, revised edition was published in 1935. He showed great originality in his teaching and set out his methods in *Practical Criticism* (1929), which was followed by *Coleridge on Imagination* (1934), and *The Philosophy of Rhetoric* (1936).

Richards was an accomplished mountaineer, who made several Alpine first ascents and pioneered new routes. In 1926 he married Dorothy Eleanor, daughter of John J. Pilley, a science master; they had no children. They often climbed together, and Dorothy Richards described some of their most memorable exploits in *Climbing Days* (1935).

Richards was also a traveller. In 1927 he visited China, and in 1929-30 was Visiting Professor at the Tsing Hua University at Peking. In 1932 he published *Mencius on the Mind*, which discussed the difficulties of translating Chinese. In 1936-8 he was again in China working for Basic English at the Orthological Institute, Peking. He was now more interested in elementary education than in specialist teaching, and in 1937 published *Interpretation in Teaching*. He had visited Harvard in 1931, and from 1944 till 1963 was a Professor of Harvard University where, although he continued to lecture on poetry, much of his time was devoted to Basic English. This led to his *How to Read a Page* (1943), *Basic English and its Uses* (1943), and many other books. He also worked in radio and television and edited booklets on the learning of languages.

In his later years, he published poetry, including *Goodbye Earth, and Other Poems* (1958). He also wrote plays, some of which with his collected poems were published in *Internal Colloquies* (1972). He became an honorary Fellow of Magdalene and was appointed CH in 1964. He also received other academic distinctions and awards. In 1979 he visited China again to teach in the universities and to promote Basic English. He became ill, was flown home, and died at Cambridge on 7 September 1979.

ROBEY, SIR GEORGE EDWARD (1869-1954), comedian, was born in London on 20 September 1869, the elder son of George Wade, a civil engineer, and his wife, Elizabeth Mary Keene. Much of his youth was spent moving about in England and abroad, on account of his father's work. Consequently, he was educated at Dresden and Leipzig University, where he was wounded in a duel. When the family returned to England, he found employment as a clerk in Birmingham and also appeared as an amateur comedian, with increasing success.

He changed his name to Robey and made his first professional music-hall appearance in London at the Oxford in 1891. His red nose, heavily blackened eye-brows, down-at-heel respectability in long frock-coat with battered hat and cane, soon made him very popular with audiences and critics. He rapidly established his name as 'the prime minister of mirth'.

As the single appearance became less popular, he played in revues, notably *The Bing Boys are Here*, with Alfred Lester and Violet Loraine, during the First World War. After the war, he appeared in operetta, and in 1935 played successfully the part of Falstaff in *Henry IV, Part I* at His Majesty's Theatre — the first music-hall star to appear in Shakespeare. He had refused a knighthood, but accepted a CBE in 1919.

In 1908 he published *My Life Up Till Now*, and in 1933 *Looking Back on Life*. He was knighted in 1954.

George Robey, 'the prime minister of mirth', 1915

In 1898 Robey married a musical-comedy actress, Ethel, daughter of Thomas Haydon, of Melbourne; they had a son and a daughter, but this marriage ended in divorce in 1938; and Robey married in that year Blanche, daughter of F. R. Littler, theatrical manager.

Robey died at Saltdean, Sussex on 29 November 1954.

ROBINSON, WILLIAM HEATH (1872–1944). See HEATH ROBINSON.

ROGERS, SIR LEONARD (1868–1962), pioneer of tropical medicine, was born at Hartley House, near Plymouth on 18 January 1868, the seventh son of Capt. Henry Rogers, RN, and his first wife, Jane Mary, daughter of John Samuel Enys, of Enys. He was educated at Tavistock Grammar School, Devon County School, and Plymouth College. He then entered St Mary's Hospital in 1886 and obtained his FRCS and MB, BS in 1892.

He joined the Indian Medical Service in 1893, obtained the MD London (1897) and MRCP (1898), and then was seconded to the Veterinary Department for Research at Múktesar, where he carried out important work on the control of rinderpest and surra in horses and camels.

In 1900 he was posted to the Bengal Civil Medical Department and acted for the Professor of Pathology, Calcutta, for six years until, in 1906, he was confirmed as Professor. During his service in Calcutta, he made many discoveries regarding the nature and treatment of tropical diseases, including the cause of kala-azar and its cure, the effects of sea-snake venom, and the differentiation of amoebic from bacterial dysentery and the value of emetine in the treatment of the amoebic variety. He also saved innumerable lives by his treatment of cholera with sterile salt solution and made notable contributions to the study of leprosy.

He played a leading role in the foundation of the Calcutta School of Tropical Medicine and the British Empire Leprosy Relief Association (1923). In 1921 he retired from the IMS and was appointed lecturer at the London School of Tropical Medicine; in 1928 he became President of the India Office Medical Board.

In 1914 Rogers married Una Elsie, daughter of Charles Niven McIntyre North, an architect; they had three sons. He was appointed CIE (1911), knighted (1914), created KCSI (1932); he was elected FRS (1916); he was President of the Indian Science Congress (1919) and of the Royal Society of Tropical Medicine and Hygiene (1933–5). He published his autobiography, *Happy Toil*, in 1950.

ROSEBERY, fifth EARL OF (1847–1929). See PRIMROSE.

ROSS, SIR RONALD (1857–1932), discoverer of the cause of malaria, was born at Almora in India on 13 May 1857, the eldest child of (General Sir) Campbell Claye Grant Ross, Indian Army, and his wife, Matilda Charlotte, daughter of Edward Merrick Elderton, a London lawyer. He was educated at Springhill, near Southampton, and St Bartholomew's Hospital, where he obtained the MRCS (1879) and LSA (1881) and joined the Indian Medical Service.

During the years from 1881 to 1894, Ross served with the army in Madras and Burma. In 1889 he married Rosa Bessie, daughter of Alfred Bradley Bloxam; they had two sons and two daughters. He was on leave in England in 1894 when he met Patrick MANSON and became interested in the cause of malaria. Two years after his return to India, he found traces of the malaria parasite in the anopheles mosquito (1897) and, a year later, discovered that a parasite in the blood of birds closely resembled the parasite of human malaria. He realized that since this was transmitted by the anopheles, it was likely that human malaria was transmitted by the same agent.

In 1899 Ross became a lecturer in the Liverpool School of Tropical Medicine, and from 1902 to 1912 was Professor. His activities were now mainly concentrated on the elimination of the anopheles mosquito, as a means of preventing malaria. From 1912 to 1917 he was Physician for Tropical Diseases at King's College Hospital, London, and also Professor of Tropical Sanitation at Liverpool. In 1917 he became consultant in malaria to the War Office. He had recently lost his elder son, who was reported missing in 1914. When, in 1933, the Ross Institute and Hospital for Tropical Diseases was founded in his honour, he became its first Director-in-Chief.

Ross always acknowledged his debt to Manson and, although he did not work out the details of the cycle in human malaria, he definitely disproved the view that malaria was contracted from air or water, and in the latter part of his life added materially to the knowledge of malarial epidemiology. His publications include *Prevention of Malaria* (1910) and his *Memoirs* (1923). From 1913 to 1932 he edited *Science Progress*.

He was elected FRS in 1901, received the Nobel prize for medicine in 1902, was appointed CB in 1902 and KCMG in 1911. He received many honorary degrees. Ross died at the Ross Institute, Putney on 16 September 1932.

ROTHENSTEIN, SIR WILLIAM (1872-1945), painter, was born at Bradford, Yorkshire, on 29 January 1872, the second son of Moritz Rothenstein, a cloth merchant, of German birth and naturalized in 1867, and his wife, Bertha, daughter of William Dux, of the Hildesheim banking family. He was educated at Bradford Grammar School, and studied at the Slade School of Fine Arts (1888) and the Académie Julian in Paris (1889), where he was helped by Degas and Fantin-Latour.

He returned to England in 1893, was commissioned by John Lane to make lithographs of eminent Oxford characters and, between that time and 1925, executed a remarkable series of over 750 portrait drawings and 135 lithographs. In 1910 he visited India and in 1912 the United States. In 1917 he was appointed Professor of Civic Art at Sheffield University. During the First World War he was an official war artist making pictures of the Western Front.

From 1920 to 1935 Rothenstein was Principal of the Royal College of Art, which he radically reorganized. From 1927 to 1933 he was a Trustee of the Tate Gallery, and from 1931 to 1938 a member of the Royal Fine Art Commission. He published his memoirs *Men & Memories* (2 vols., 1931-2), and *Since Fifty* (1939). During the Second World War he was an unofficial artist to the Royal Air Force.

He was knighted in 1931 and made an honorary D. Litt. (Oxford) in 1934. A number of his works are in the Tate and the National Portrait Gallery; others are in galleries throughout the country.

In 1899 Rothenstein married the actress, Alice Kingsley, in private life, Alice Mary, daughter of Walter John Knewstub, a friend of Dante Gabriel Rossetti; they had two sons and two daughters, the elder son becoming Director of the Tate Gallery and the younger a painter.

Rothenstein died on 14 February 1945 at Far Oakridge, his Cotswold home.

ROTHERMERE, first VISCOUNT (1868-1940). See HARMSWORTH, HAROLD SIDNEY.

ROUND, HENRY JOSEPH (1881-1966), radio pioneer, was born on 2 June 1881 at Kingswinford, Staffordshire, the eldest child of Joseph Alfred Round, registrar of births and deaths, and his wife, Gertrude Rider. He was educated at Cheltenham Grammar School and the Royal College of Science, London, where he became ARCS (mechanics) in 1901.

In 1902 he joined the Marconi Company and worked in the USA and South America until 1912. He redesigned two stations on the upper reaches of the Amazon, deliberately giving them different wave lengths for day and night, the first time this expedient was used to minimize heavy signal attenuation.

Back in England in 1913-14, he patented improved valves and transmission systems. During the First World War he worked with military intelligence, setting up a network of valved direction-finding stations, and was instrumental in detecting radio signals from the German navy, which warned the Admiralty of German intentions and led to the Battle of Jutland in 1916. In 1918 he was awarded the MC.

His newly designed valves were used in 1919 for the first European radio-telephone crossing of the Atlantic, and in 1920 the first radio-telephony news service was installed. Round also designed the transmitter for 2LO, the first radio station to be taken over by the BBC (1922). In 1921 he was appointed Chief of the Marconi Research Group and continued to invent new improved transmitters and receivers for ships, public address systems, and recorded sound.

In 1931 he became a private consultant, between 1941 and 1950 worked on ASDIC and echo-sounding, and between

The young William Rothenstein, sketch by John Singer Sargent, 1897

1950 and 1962 patented a number of other devices for the improvement of radio. In all, his patent applications numbered 117 and the electronics industry owed much to his prolific inventions.

In 1911 he married Olive Wright, daughter of John Evans, a saddler; they had two sons and five daughters; the elder son, a Spitfire pilot, was killed in the Second World War and awarded the DFC. Olive died in 1958, and in 1960 Round married Evelyn Baise. He died at Bognor Regis on 17 August 1966.

ROWNTREE, JOSEPH (1836–1925), cocoa manufacturer and philanthropist, was born at York on 24 May 1836, the second son of Joseph Rowntree, Quaker educationalist, and his wife, Sarah, daughter of Isaac Stephenson, of Manchester. He was educated at Bootham School, York, and at fifteen joined his father's grocery business.

In 1869 he entered into partnership with his elder brother, Henry Isaac, who had acquired a cocoa-manufacturing business. Henry died in 1883, and Joseph became sole owner of H. I. Rowntree & Co., which in 1897 became a limited company.

Joseph Rowntree took the view that his employees were fellow workers in a great industry. By the creation of charitable social service and village trusts, he consulted his workpeople about conditions and provided for housing, unemployment insurance, and pensions. The eight-hour day was introduced in 1896, a pension scheme in 1906; a works doctor was appointed in 1904. 'Social helpers' were recruited to deal with the problems of women employees, and Works Councils were set up in 1919.

Rowntree was an enthusiastic temperance reformer; he did much to promote adult education. He was also a strong supporter of the League of Nations. The firm gave to the city of York, Rowntree Park, in memory of their workmen who died in the First World War. Rowntree also published a number of books on sociological problems.

In 1862 Rowntree married Julia Eliza, daughter of Benjamin Seebohm; they had a daughter who died in infancy. Julia died in 1863, and Joseph married in 1867 Emma Antoinette, daughter of Wilhelm Seebohm, and cousin of Julia; they had four sons and two daughters. Benjamin Seebohm, the second son, assisted his father in the welfare side of the business and succeeded him as Chairman of the company. Rowntree died at York on 24 February 1925.

ROYCE, SIR (FREDERICK) HENRY (1863–1933), engineer, was born at Alwalton, near Peterborough on 27 March 1863, the younger son of James Royce, a flour miller, and his wife, Mary, daughter of Benjamin King, a farmer. Owing to his father's death when he was ten, he had to earn his own living: he was a newspaper boy, messenger boy, and then apprentice to the locomotive works at Peterborough. He was unable to complete his apprenticeship for lack of funds, and in 1881 went to work in a tool factory at Leeds. In 1882 he became a tester with an electrical company, studied at night school, and was soon appointed chief electrical engineer. In 1893 he married Minnie Grace, daughter of Alfred Punt, of London; they had no children.

In 1884 he had founded F. H. Royce & Co., manufacturers of arc lamps, dynamos, and electric cranes, in Manchester. His experience with an early motor car led him to decide to design and make motor cars himself, and in 1904 he produced his first 10 h.p. two-cylinder Royce car. Its silence, smoothness, and flexibility were of such interest to C. S. Rolls, who had a selling agency for cars in London, that he and his partner undertook to buy the whole output of Royce cars and to sell them as Rolls–Royce.

Sir Henry Royce with prototype 'Phantom I', Elmstead, 1925

In 1906 the two firms were combined, Royce becoming engineer-in-chief, and Rolls technical managing director. Royce had no intention of producing a wide range of models; he sought to perfect one type of vehicle and, by the end of 1906, he had manufactured the 40-50 h.p. 'Silver Ghost', which remained the prototype until 1925, when it gave way to 'Phantoms' and 'Wraiths'. In 1908 the motor section of the firm was transferred to Derby.

In 1910 Rolls was killed in a flying accident. He had often tried to persuade Royce to design an aero-engine, but Royce did nothing about this until the First World War. Then, he produced the 'Eagle' engine, which played an important part in the conflict. This was followed by the 'Falcon', 'Hawk', 'Condor', and 'Merlin' engines, the last of which was extensively used in the Second World War. Rolls-Royce entered the Schneider cup competitions and won the trophy in 1929 and 1931, setting up a world speed record of 408 m.p.h.

Royce was appointed OBE in 1918 and created a baronet in 1930. He died at West Wittering on 22 April 1933.

ROYDEN, (AGNES) MAUDE (1876–1956), preacher, was born on 23 November 1876 at Mossley Hill, near Liverpool, the youngest daughter of (Sir) Thomas Bland Royden, shipowner and later first baronet, and his wife, Alice Elizabeth, daughter of Thomas Dowdall, a stockbroker. Her brother was Thomas (later Lord) Royden. She was educated at Cheltenham Ladies' College and Lady Margaret Hall, Oxford (1899).

She spent three years as a social worker in Liverpool and then as a parish worker at South Luffenham, where the Vicar was the Revd George William Hudson Shaw. She became a lecturer in English literature for the Oxford University Extension Delegacy, and from 1908 to 1914 obtained experience as a public speaker in the cause of women's suffrage; she also edited the *Common Cause* (1913-14).

She never ceased to regard herself as an Anglican. But, since women were not permitted to preach in the Church of England, in 1917 she became assistant preacher at the City Temple, London and soon made a reputation as a preacher of great force, covering a wide range of subjects, including current international and political issues. In 1920, however, she left the Nonconformist Church for an inter-denominational pulpit, through the 'Fellowship Services' at the Guildhouse in Eccleston Square. She continued to preach there for the next sixteen years, delivering her sermons without notes, and drawing eloquently upon her extensive knowledge of theology, literature, and social history. She also made many preaching tours abroad to the USA, Australia, New Zealand, India, and China.

Both in the pulpit and on radio, her voice had a peculiar charm. She was, however, handicapped all her life by a dislocated hip. In 1936 she resigned from the Guildhouse to devote her time to the cause of peace, but during the Second World War she renounced her former pacifism.

In 1930 she was appointed CH and she held honorary degrees from Glasgow and Liverpool. In October 1944 she married the Revd Shaw whom she had known and loved for forty-three years since she worked with him at South Luffenham. He died two months later. Maude Royden died in London on 30 July 1956.

RUGBY, first BARON (1877–1969). See MAFFEY.

RUSSELL, BERTRAND ARTHUR WILLIAM, third EARL RUSSELL (1872–1970), philosopher, mathematician, and pacifist, was born at Trelleck in Monmouthshire on 18 May 1872, the younger son of Viscount Amberley (eldest son of the first Earl Russell), and his wife, Kate, daughter of the second Baron Stanley of Alderley. Both parents were eccentric, and both died before Russell was four. The atheist guardians appointed by them to bring up their children were set aside by the courts and the children were placed under the guardianship of their grandmother, Lady Russell. Russell was brought up in the home of his grandmother and maiden aunts, until he went up to Trinity College, Cambridge in 1890.

Then the Spartan regime of his life at Pembroke Lodge was exchanged for the freedom and intellectual excitement of the university, where his genius as a mathematician was recognized by Alfred North WHITEHEAD. He became an 'Apostle' and made numerous friends including G. E. MOORE, the first influence upon his philosophical thinking. He was placed seventh wrangler in part i of the mathematical tripos (1893), and obtained a first in the moral sciences tripos (1894).

In that year he married Alys Whitall, daughter of Robert, and sister of Logan Pearsall Smith; she was a Quaker, five years older than Russell. In 1895 he was elected a Fellow of Trinity for a dissertation published in 1897 as *An Essay on the Foundations of Geometry*. In 1896 he and Alys travelled on the Continent and to the United States; Russell studied the works of Marx and Engels, and later that year lectured at the London School of Economics. He was already set upon the path which he would follow for the rest of his life. His *Autobiography* (3 vols., 1967-9) begins: 'Three passions, simple but overwhelmingly strong, have governed my life: the longing for love, the search for knowledge, and unbearable pity for the suffering of mankind.'

In 1899 Russell began to be recognized as a professional philosopher. Professor M'Taggart persuaded him to take his place as a lecturer at Cambridge while he was abroad, and Russell, not content to echo the master, gave a brilliant reinterpretation of the ideas which they had once shared but which Russell had since repudiated. He was now working on his book *The Principles of Mathematics*, which was published in 1903; he was influenced in his mathematical thinking by Giuseppe Peano and Gottlob Frege, who were working on the same lines as Russell, aiming at reducing mathematics to logic.

In 1902, while the Russells and the Whiteheads were sharing a house in Grantchester, Russell suddenly discovered that he was no longer in love with Alys and caused her great distress by bluntly telling her so. At that time, he and Whitehead were planning together the mathematical masterpiece, the *Principia Mathematica*, and Russell was in love with Evelyn Whitehead, who was a sick woman, worried by her husband's extravagance and, what seemed to her, his mental aberration. In his *Principles of Mathematics*, Russell had set out to prove that mathematics could be defined within the language of symbolic logic. A further volume of the work was discussed with Whitehead and they agreed to work together on the project. This was the genesis of *Principia Mathematica*, the first volume of which appeared in 1910, followed by two later volumes in 1912 and 1913. A fourth volume which was to have been written by Whitehead was never completed.

During the years from 1902 to 1911 Russell and Alys lived together in the same house in Bagley Wood, near Oxford, a life in which both were tortured by Russell's inability to reciprocate his wife's devotion. In 1909 her brother, Logan

Pearsall Smith, brought Lady Ottoline MORRELL to visit them, and thus began for Russell an infatuation, which blossomed into the first of his many extra-marital love affairs.

In 1910 Russell was appointed lecturer in the principles of mathematics at Trinity College, Cambridge, and made a friend of Ludwig WITTGENSTEIN, whom he described as 'the most perfect example I have ever known of genius'. In 1912 he published *The Problems of Philosophy*. He also met Joseph CONRAD through Ottoline Morrell and became a great admirer of the man as well as of his novels.

In 1914 Russell delivered the Lowell lectures at Harvard and met T. S. ELIOT and his wife Vivienne with whom he later had one of his amorous interludes. By 1915 he was becoming heavily involved in opposition to the First World War; he joined the No-Conscription Fellowship and was dismissed from his Cambridge lectureship. Then, in 1916, he met both Dora Black, daughter of Sir Frederick Black, and Lady Constance Malleson (the actress Colette O'Niel), who was the wife of Miles Malleson. His affair with Lady Ottoline was coming to an end and he was now having an affair with a young American, Helen Dudley. Russell was anxious to beget a child, and soon discovered that Dora Black was willing to bear his child, whether they were married or not.

In 1918 Russell was sentenced to six months' imprisonment for sedition and, while he was incarcerated, wrote his *Introduction to Mathematical Philosophy* (1919). His life returned to something like normality when, in 1919, Trinity

College, Cambridge reinstated him, but he was now obsessed with the desire to beget a family. In 1920 he and Dora Black visited Russia together, where he formed a conviction of the ruthlessness and bigotry of the Bolshevik regime, which he described in *The Practice and Theory of Bolshevism* (1920). They also travelled to China. Then, in 1921, having resigned his Cambridge post, Russell and Alys were at last divorced and he married Dora, who later that year gave birth to a son.

From 1921 up to the time of the Second World War, Russell concentrated on earning a living by writing and journalism, publishing a number of books such as the *ABCs of Atoms* (1923), *Marriage and Morals* (1929), and *Religion and Science* (1935). He also carried out lucrative lecture tours in the United States. His need for money was increased by the cost of Beacon Hill School, near Petersfield, which he and Dora started in 1927, and which created a number of problems for him until, in 1935, he and Dora parted company. They had had another child, a daughter, but Dora had also had two children by an American, and Russell had fallen in love with his children's governess, Marjorie Helen Spence, daughter of Harry Evelyn Spence, who changed her name to Patricia ('Peter').

He and Dora divorced in 1935 and he married 'Peter' in 1936. In 1931 Russell had inherited the title from his brother Frank, and in 1937 he and Peter had a son. Russell would have liked to return to Cambridge, but this was not possible; he therefore turned to the USA and, with financial help from George Santayana, took up visiting lectureships in Chicago, Los Angeles, and New York.

In 1944 he was once more invited to rejoin Trinity College, Cambridge. His work *A History of Western Philosophy*, published in 1945, was a success on both sides of the Atlantic and secured his financial position for the rest of his life. He also became popular as a broadcaster, particularly in the BBC's 'Brains Trust'. His Reith lectures on radio were published as *Authority and the Individual* (1949). In 1949 he was admitted to the Order of Merit and in 1950 awarded the Nobel prize for literature.

His ardent amorous adventures continued unabated. His marriage to 'Peter' collapsed in 1949 and, after another divorce, he married in 1952 Edith, daughter of Edward Bronson Finch, of New York, whom he had met during the war. In 1958 he became the first President of the Campaign for Nuclear Disarmament, and in 1961 he and his wife took part in a demonstration which led to a prison sentence, but they were released after a week owing to his age and ill health. During these years, the books he wrote were, for the most part, about himself, such as *Portraits from Memory* (1956), *My Philosophical Development* (1959), and his autobiography.

He died on 2 February 1970 at his home, Plas Penrhyn in Merioneth, to which he had gone with his last wife Edith in 1955. His uninhibited opinions and his maverick life-style provoked much criticism at certain times during his life, but in his old age he was admired for his lucidity and eloquence and regarded as the most influential philosopher of his generation as well as the co-author of a work, the *Principia Mathematica*, for which he will always be remembered.

RUSSELL, SIR THOMAS WENTWORTH (1879–1954), Pasha, Director, Egyptian Central Narcotics Intelligence Bureau, was born on 22 November 1879 at Wollaton Rectory, the third son of the Revd Henry Charles Russell, grandson of the sixth Duke of Bedford, and his wife, Leila Louisa Millicent Willoughby, daughter of the eighth Baron Middle-

Bertrand Russell, 1916

ton. He was educated at Cheam, Haileybury, and Trinity College, Cambridge.

In 1902 he entered the Egyptian Civil Service, and in 1903 was appointed Provincial Sub-Inspector; he then served as Inspector in every Egyptian province, thus acquiring unrivalled local knowledge. In 1906 a police camel corps was formed on his initiative and was the means of eliminating bedouin brigands. In 1911, the year of his marriage to Evelyn Dorothea Temple, daughter of Francis Moore, a stockjobber, he became Assistant-Commandant of the Alexandria police and conducted extensive anti-contraband operations; in 1917 he was appointed Commandant of the Cairo city police with the title of Pasha. Egypt was then a British protectorate and Russell had to deal with demonstrations, which always threatened to flare into violence.

Egypt became independent in 1922 and, between then and 1946, Russell served under twenty-nine Ministers of the Interior. He was increasingly concerned with the drug traffic and, when in 1929 the Egyptian Central Narcotics Intelligence Bureau was formed, he became its first Director. By 1939 he had succeeded in destroying most of the European bases from which supplies reached Egypt. In that year he was elected Vice-President of the League of Nations Advisory Committee on the Opium Trade. In 1946 he retired, the last British officer in Egyptian service. He was appointed OBE (1920), CMG (1926), and KBE (1938). He also held a number of foreign decorations. His reminiscences were published as *Egyptian Service* in 1949. He and his wife had one son and one daughter. Russell died in London on 10 April 1954.

RUTHERFORD, ERNEST, Baron Rutherford of Nelson (1871–1937), physicist, was born at Spring Grove, near Nelson, New Zealand, on 30 August 1871, the second son of James Rutherford, a farmer, and his wife, Martha, daughter of Charles Edwin Thompson. Rutherford was brought up on the family farm, went to local schools, and to Canterbury College, Christchurch (1890), where he obtained firsts in mathematics and physics (1893) and a scholarship to Trinity College, Cambridge.

There he worked under (Sir) J. J. Thomson, who in 1897 proved the existence of the electron, whilst in 1895 Röntgen had discovered X-rays and in 1896 Antoine Henri Becquerel had found that uranium compounds emit radiations similar to X-rays. Rutherford continued the work he had started in New Zealand on the transmission and detection of electromagnetic waves, and then studied the conduction of electricity through gases. He devised simple and ingenious equipment for measuring the velocity and rate of recombination of gaseous ions, and proved that uranium radiation is different in nature from X-rays and consists of two types of radiation, which he distinguished as alpha and beta, the latter being less effective but more penetrating. This research was described in five papers, which were published before Rutherford left Cambridge in 1898.

In that year, at the early age of twenty-six, he was appointed to the Macdonald research professorship of physics at McGill University, Montreal. In 1899 he published a paper on 'Thorium and Uranium Radiation' and, during the next few years, attracted young scientists to his laboratory and became the leader of a team of willing co-operators. Together with one of these, Frederick Soddy, he investigated the chemistry of radioactive material and discovered the cause of radioactivity. Their theory that radioactivity is a phenomenon accompanying the spontaneous transformation of the atoms of radioactive elements into different kinds of matter—

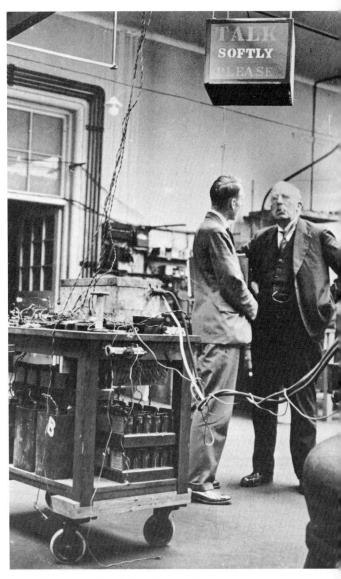

Ernest Rutherford with J. A. Ratcliffe in the Cavendish Laboratory, 1935; the notice was intended to protect the delicate electrical tracking equipment against Rutherford's very loud voice

the disintegration theory—was published by the London Chemical Society in 1902 and elaborated in Rutherford's book *Radio-activity* (1904). This theory, which completely contradicted the accepted view that matter is indestructible, was at first received with scepticism, but Rutherford was elected FRS in 1903, and by 1907, before he left Montreal, the theory was generally accepted.

In 1907 he was appointed Langworthy Professor of Physics at Manchester and set out on the final stages of his research into the nature of 'alpha particles', until in 1908 he proved the alpha particle to be helium. In that year he was awarded the Nobel prize for physics. At Manchester, as at McGill, he gathered round him an enthusiastic group of young scientists and in 1911, in a paper in the *Philosophical*

Magazine, propounded the nuclear theory of the atom. In 1914 he visited the USA, Australia, and New Zealand, lecturing on his discoveries. He was also knighted.

In 1915–17 he was engaged in Admiralty work connected with anti-submarine warfare, and in 1917 visited the USA again to give American scientists information about the new methods of detecting submarines and devising new means of dealing with them. In 1919, working alone in his Manchester laboratory, he provided evidence of the artificial transmutation of matter and published his findings in the *Philosophical Magazine*.

In 1919 he was elected to the Cavendish chair of experimental physics at Cambridge in succession to J. J. Thomson. There he remained until 1937, continuing for some time his own researches, discovering that long-range particles from nitrogen are hydrogen nuclei, and speculating on the existence of the neutron. In the main, however, his activities were concentrated on the reorganization of the Cavendish Laboratory and the furtherance of work on the constitution of the nucleus, by the installation of elaborate electrical machinery. In 1925 he was appointed OM and elected President of the Royal Society, and in 1931 became Baron Rutherford of Nelson.

From 1930 to 1937 he was Chairman of the Advisory Council of the Department of Scientific and Industrial Research. In 1937 he published *The Newer Alchemy*, an account of the work carried out by his colleagues, James CHADWICK, John COCKCROFT and others in the transmutation of elements. Sir Henry TIZARD, in the *DNB*, has expressed the view that 'In the whole course of the history of science no one has surpassed Rutherford in his influence on his contemporaries.'

In 1900 he married Mary Georgina, daughter of Arthur Charles Newton, of Christchurch, New Zealand; they had one daughter. Rutherford received innumerable academic honours. He died in Cambridge on 19 October 1937 and was buried in Westminster Abbey.

Vita-Sackville-West at Long Barn, 1924

S

SACKVILLE-WEST, VICTORIA MARY (VITA) (1892–1962), writer and gardener, was born at Knole near Sevenoaks, Kent on 9 March 1892, the only child of Lionel Sackville-West (later third Baron Sackville) and his wife and cousin, Victoria Sackville-West. She was brought up at Knole, a Tudor palace, one of the largest houses in England, and she was bitterly disappointed that, as a woman, she could not inherit the estate. She was educated at home by governesses, and travelled abroad in France, Italy, Russia, Poland, Austria, and Spain.

In 1913 she married Harold NICOLSON and they lived for a short while at Constantinople, where he was Third Secretary at the Embassy. For a time, their marriage was normal and happy, and in 1914 their first son, Lionel Benedict, was born. On return to England they lived at Long Barn, near Knole. In 1915 a son was born dead, and in 1917 a third son, Nigel, was born. The subsequent story of this marriage has been told by Nigel in *Portrait of a Marriage* (1973).

From 1918 to 1921 Vita had a passionate love affair with Violet Trefusis, with whom she would go off from time to time, returning to her husband when it suited her to do so. Harold, himself, was a homosexual, but for the rest of their lives together they had a mutual understanding and affection which clearly surmounted the unorthodox nature of their union.

Vita was a prolific writer, and between 1922 and 1937 she published *Knole and the Sackvilles* (1922), a long poem *The Land* (1926), for which she was awarded the Hawthornden prize in 1927, *Twelve Days* (1928), a book about a visit to Persia (Iran), *Sissinghurst*, another lyric poem, a novel *All Passions Spent* (1931), *Family History* (1932), *Collected Poems* (1933), *Saint Joan of Arc* (1936), and *Pepita* (1937), a life of her Spanish grandmother.

From time to time, Vita visited her husband while he was serving abroad in the diplomatic service but she never lived permanently with him until he decided to retire in 1929. In the following year they bought Sissinghurst Castle in Kent. Harold was very concerned when Vita revealed to him that she had a deep affection for Virginia WOOLF, who in 1928 wrote *Orlando*, in which she made clear that she was equally in love with Vita. Their friendship endured until Virginia took her own life in 1941 to the deep distress of Vita.

After they had purchased Sissinghurst, Harold and Vita spent much time and effort on designing and creating one of the most unusual and beautiful gardens in England. During the Second World War Vita managed to keep Sissinghurst going and worked for the Women's Land Army. She wrote more books, including *The Eagle and the Dove: St Teresa of Avila, St Thérèse of Lisieux* (1943) and *The Garden* (1946), another long poem. In 1948 she was appointed CH. In 1959 she published *Daughter of France*, a biography of La Grande Mademoiselle, Duchesse de Montpensier, and in 1961 *No Signposts in the Sea*, her last novel.

From 1946 to 1961 she wrote a gardening column for the *Observer*, and in 1955 was awarded the Veitch memorial medal by the Royal Horticultural Society. In 1961 she became seriously ill with cancer and died at Sissinghurst on 2 June 1962. Sissinghurst passed to the National Trust, and thousands of people visit it every year to see the gardens and the room in the tower where Vita wrote her books.

SAKI (pseudonym) (1870–1916). See MUNRO, HECTOR HUGH.

SALISBURY, FRANCIS OWEN (FRANKO) (1874–1962), painter, was born on 18 December 1874 at Harpenden, a son of Henry Salisbury, a plumber and glazier, and his wife, Susan Hawes. At fifteen, he was apprenticed to the stained-glass works of his eldest brother at St Albans. As he displayed a talent for painting, his brother sent him to Heatherley's and from there he won a scholarship to the Royal Academy Schools.

He first exhibited at the Royal Academy in 1899 and, although he afterwards exhibited regularly, he was never elected a member. In 1901 he married Alice Maude, daughter of C. Colmer Greenwood; they had twin daughters, who provided inspiration for Salisbury's paintings of children. Heraldry and pageantry were also among his interests and he painted a number of pictures of historic events including *The Burial of the Unknown Warrior* and the coronation of George VI. He painted many murals for the House of Lords, the Royal Exchange, and elsewhere.

His portraits in oil included those of five presidents of the USA, five British prime ministers, three archbishops of Canterbury, and many other celebrities. He also painted a number of religious pictures and worked in stained glass. Some 200 of his paintings were exhibited at the Royal Institute Galleries in 1953.

He was appointed CVO in 1938, and was Master of the Worshipful Company of Glaziers in 1933–4. He published his memoirs, *Portrait and Pageant*, in 1944, and a revised version was published as *Sarum Chase* in 1953. He died in London on 31 August 1962.

SALISBURY, fourth MARQUESS OF (1861–1947). See CECIL, JAMES EDWARD HUBERT GASCOYNE-.

SALT, DAME BARBARA (1904–1975), diplomat, was born in California on 30 September 1904, the younger daughter of a banker, Reginald John Salt, and his wife, Maud Fanny Wigram. Shortly after her birth, her parents returned to England and settled at Oxford. She was educated at The Downs School, Seaford, and Munich and Cologne universities. She worked as a secretary from 1933 to 1938, and then joined the Special Operations Executive (SOE), and from 1942 to 1946 served in Tangier, becoming head of the SOE office there (1944–6).

In 1946 she joined the Foreign Office, in 1950 was First Secretary (Commercial) in Moscow, and from 1951 to 1955 First Secretary in Washington, being promoted to Counsellor *sur place* in 1955. She stayed in Washington until 1957, and then moved to the British Embassy in Tel Aviv. In 1960 she was promoted to Minister and appointed Deputy Head of the United Kingdom Combined Disarmament and Nuclear Tests Delegation at Geneva. Then, in 1961, she became United Kingdom Representative to the Economic and Social Council of the United Nations.

In 1962 she was appointed Ambassador-Designate to Israel, but this appointment had to be cancelled owing to her serious illness, in which both legs had to be amputated (1963). Between 1963 and 1966, however, she led UK delegations in financial negotiations with Israel, the USSR, and Romania. From 1966 to 1973, when she retired, she was engaged in historical research on the Second World War.

She was the first woman in the Diplomatic Service to become Counsellor, Minister, and Ambassador-Designate. She was appointed MBE (1946), CBE (1959), and DBE (1963).

She died in London on 28 December 1975, after enduring her disability with indomitable spirit.

SAMUEL, HERBERT LOUIS, first VISCOUNT SAMUEL (1870–1963), politician, was born on 6 November 1870, in Liverpool, the youngest son of Edwin Louis Samuel, a banker, and his wife, Clara, daughter of Ellis Samuel Yates, a Liverpool business man. Both parents came of Jewish stock. He was educated at University College School and Balliol College, Oxford, where he obtained a first in history (1893) and was President of the Russell, the University Liberal Club. In 1897 he married his first cousin, Beatrice Miriam, daughter of Ellis Abraham Franklin, another banker; they had three sons and one daughter.

Samuel assisted his brother in his political work in the East End of London and became involved with a political club for Liberals and Socialists. He published *Liberalism: its Principles and Proposals* in 1902. In that year he was elected Liberal MP for the Cleveland division of Yorkshire, a seat he held until 1918. He was appointed Under-Secretary of State at the Home Office in 1905, where he was closely associated with a wide range of legislation for social reform. He became a PC in 1908, and Chancellor of the Duchy of Lancaster and Cabinet Minister in 1909. In 1910, when he was Postmaster-General, he was inadvertently involved, with LLOYD GEORGE and Sir Rufus ISAACS, in the Marconi scandal, but was exonerated from any blame or misconduct.

Early in 1914, he was appointed President of the Local Government Board but, in ASQUITH's Coalition Government, ceased to be a member of the Cabinet, until in 1915 he became Postmaster-General and Chancellor of the Duchy again, and was restored to cabinet rank. In 1916 he was appointed Home Secretary but, when Lloyd George superseded Asquith, Samuel, out of loyalty, refused to serve under the new Prime Minister. In 1918 he lost his seat in the 'coupon election', and the Liberal party was split into rival factions.

From 1920 to 1925 he served as the first High Commissioner in mandated Palestine and was appointed GBE. In that post, he conscientiously attempted to create a multinational commonwealth. On retirement, he was refused permission to settle in Palestine. His next public service involved presiding over the Royal Commission on the Coal-Mining Industry (1925-6). Its recommendations were acceptable neither to the owners nor to the miners, but in 1926 Samuel's negotiations with the TUC brought the general strike to an end, though the coal strike continued.

In 1926 he was appointed GCB, and in 1929 returned to the Commons as Liberal MP for Darwen. When the 1931 financial crisis came, Lloyd George was seriously ill. As acting Liberal leader Samuel advocated a National Government, with Ramsay MACDONALD continuing as Prime Minister. He served briefly in this administration as Home Secretary (1931-2). He resigned in 1932 when BONAR LAW made the Ottawa agreements ending free trade. In 1935 he was defeated at Darwen, and in 1937 was created Viscount Samuel, becoming leader of the Liberals in the House of Lords.

In his later years, he concentrated on philosophical studies and became well known as a broadcaster in the BBC 'Brains Trust' programmes. He was honoured with degrees from a number of universities. In 1949 he was elected Visitor of Balliol College, Oxford, and in 1958 became OM.

Lady Samuel died in 1959, and Samuel died in London on 5 February 1963.

SAMUEL, MARCUS, first VISCOUNT BEARSTED (1853-1927), joint-founder of the Shell Transport and Trading Company, was born in London on 5 November 1853, the second son of Marcus Samuel, a London merchant, and his wife, Abigail, daughter of Abraham Moss, of London. He began his commercial career as a trader in shells, general produce, and rice. After visiting Japan on business, he set out to ship oil from Russia to the Far East. He overcame the difficulty of carrying freight on the return journey by cleaning out the hull with steam, and loading his ships with rice and other cargo.

In 1881 he married Fanny Elizabeth, daughter of Benjamin Benjamin; they had two sons and two daughters.

In 1897 he established the Shell Transport and Trading Company, taking the name from his earliest business. A serious rival to this organization was the Dutch Petroleum Company, which obtained oil from Java and Borneo. Samuel and his colleagues turned their attention to Borneo and in 1907, to avoid further competition, the two interests were merged in one large oil-producing, refining, and distributing organization.

In 1898 two of Shell's tugs salvaged HMS *Victorious*, aground off Port Said, and Samuel was knighted. During the First World War the services of his firm were of inestimable value to the Allies, not only in the supply of oil, but also in the manufacture of the high explosive TNT, for which Samuel set up a factory near Bristol.

In 1891 he became an alderman of the city of London; in 1894 he was Sheriff, and in 1902-3 Lord Mayor. He was Chairman of the committee which formulated the scheme for the Port of London Authority. At the end of his term as Lord Mayor, he was created a baronet.

He was a great benefactor to hospitals, and other philanthropic enterprises, and turned his home near Maidstone into a hospital for the wounded during the First World War. During the war, his younger son was killed. In 1921 he became Baron Bearsted and in 1925 a viscount. He received honorary degrees from Cambridge and Sheffield. Samuel's

wife died on 16 January 1927 and he survived her by only a few hours, dying in London on 17 January 1927.

SARGENT, SIR (HENRY) MALCOLM WATTS (1895-1967), conductor, was born in Ashford, Kent, on 29 April 1895, the only son of Henry Edward Sargent, a Stamford coal merchant, and his wife, Agnes Marion Hall, daughter of a Hertfordshire landscape gardener. His father was a keen amateur musician who encouraged the boy's musical talents while he was at Stamford School. On leaving school in 1912, Sargent was articled to Haydn Keeton, organist of Peterborough Cathedral.

In 1914 he was appointed organist of Melton Mowbray, had piano lessons from Moiseiwitch and conducted a Leicester orchestra sufficiently well to be invited by Sir Henry WOOD to conduct in the 1921 Promenade Concert season. In 1923 he moved to London and took a post at the Royal College of Music as teacher of conducting. In the following year he married Eileen Laura Harding Horne; they had a son and a daughter.

From that time, Sargent conducted for a number of organizations, including Robert Mayer concerts, the Diaghilev Ballet, the Royal Choral Society, the British National Opera Company, and the D'Oyly Carte Company. He conducted the first performances of *Hugh the Drover* by Ralph VAUGHAN WILLIAMS and *Belshazzar's Feast* and *Troilus and Cressida* by (Sir) William Walton.

In 1932 Sargent suffered a complete breakdown of health, including a tubercular infection, which necessitated two years absence from the rostrum; but, when he returned, he did so with his old flair and enthusiasm. The death of his daughter, however, from polio in 1944 was a shattering blow and he was under further strain when his marriage ended in divorce two years later.

In 1950 he succeeded Sir Adrian Boult as conductor of the BBC Symphony Orchestra and, from then until his death, he was accepted as a great conductor and musician to whom British music owed a considerable debt, as he made it known in concert halls in many parts of the world. Sargent was awarded many musical honours, including the hon. D.Mus. (Oxford) in 1942. He was knighted in 1947.

During these years, his appearance on the BBC 'Brains Trust' made him well known to millions, and his conducting in the Promenade Concerts was appreciated by hordes of young music-lovers, who showed their appreciation of his brilliance and good humour in his farewell performance a few days before his death in London on 3 October 1967.

SASSOON, SIEGFRIED LORAINE (1886-1967), poet and author, was born on 8 September 1886 at Weirleigh in Kent, the second son of Alfred Ezra Sassoon, and his wife, Georgina Theresa, daughter of the sculptors, Thomas and Mary Thornycroft. He was brought up by his mother and educated at Marlborough College and Clare College, Cambridge. Leaving the university without a degree, he lived as a country gentleman, hunting, playing cricket, and writing poems, which he published privately (1906-12).

During the First World War he enlisted as a trooper in the Sussex Yeomanry and in 1915 was commissioned in the Royal Welch Fusiliers. He served in France, was awarded the MC, and wounded in 1917. While convalescing in England, he was befriended by Ottoline MORRELL and made a declaration opposing the continuance of the war, which he expected to result in court-martial, but his friends, Robert Graves and Edward MARSH, persuaded the authorities that

Siegfried Sassoon (seated) with Mark Gertler

Dorothy Sayers, with a penchant for mystery both in fiction and in real life

he needed treatment for shell-shock and he was sent to the Craiglockhart Hospital, near Edinburgh, where he met Wilfred OWEN, a fellow poet.

In 1918 he was ready to fight once more, was posted to Palestine, and then rejoined his regiment in France. He was wounded again, shot by mistake by one of his own NCOs, as he returned from a patrol. His war poems *The Old Huntsman* (1917) and *Counter-Attack* (1918) established his reputation as a poet. Like Thomas HARDY, to whom the first of these was dedicated, he made brilliant use of direct speech—in a savage attack on hypocrisy and incompetence. In 1919, for a short time, he was the Literary Editor of the *Daily Herald* and became a friend of Edmund BLUNDEN. During the next few years, he enjoyed hunting in Gloucestershire, evaded the charms of Ottoline Morrell, and produced more poetry, including *Selected Poems* (1925), *Satirical Poems* (1926) and *The Heart's Journey* (1927).

In 1928 he published his elegy for a vanished pastoral way of life, *Memoirs of a Fox-Hunting Man*, which was an immediate success and won the Hawthornden and James Tait Black memorial prizes. This account of his early life was followed by *Memoirs of an Infantry Officer* (1930) and *Sherston's Progress* (1936). He continued his prose writing with *The Old Century and Seven More Years* (1938), *The Weald of Youth* (1942), and *Siegfried's Journey* (1945). His *Collected Poems* appeared in 1947, and in 1948 he published a critical biography of George Meredith. He was appointed CBE in 1951.

In 1933 he married Hester, daughter of Sir Stephen Herbert Gatty, Chief Justice of Gibraltar; they had one son and the marriage ended in separation. In 1957 Sassoon was received into the Roman Catholic Church. He died at Heytes-

bury in Wiltshire on 1 September 1967. His *Diaries 1915-18* and his collected *War Poems* edited by Rupert Hart-Davis were published in 1983.

SAYERS, DOROTHY LEIGH (1893-1957), writer, was born in Oxford on 13 June 1893, the only child of the Revd Henry Sayers, Headmaster of Christ Church Choir School, and his wife, Helen Mary Leigh. She was educated at the Godolphin School, Salisbury and Somerville College, Oxford, where she was a scholar and obtained a first in modern languages in 1915. From 1916 to 1931 she worked as an advertiser's copywriter with S. H. Benson Ltd. and, with (Sir) John Gilroy the artist, was responsible for the famous advertisements 'My goodness; my Guinness!'. In 1926 she married Capt. Oswald Atherton Fleming, a war correspondent; he was a permanent invalid during most of their marriage up to the time of his death in 1950; they had no children. Dorothy before her marriage had borne a son by a lover whose name was kept secret and the boy was brought up by her cousin, Ivy Shrimpton. Later, Dorothy 'adopted' him.

Her earliest publications were in verse *Op. 1* (1916) and *Catholic Tales* (1918), but she made her reputation as a writer of detective stories centred on the private detective, Lord Peter Wimsey. These began with *Whose Body?* (1923) and ended with *Gaudy Night* (1935) and *Busman's Honeymoon* (1937). In *Strong Poison* (1930), Lord Peter cleared a young woman of a murder charge, fell in love, and married her. One important aspect of these novels was the care with which Dorothy Sayers studied her backgrounds and the technicalities involved in her subjects. For example, in *The Nine Tailors* (1934), the plot turns on the intricacies of bell-ringing. Her stories also had a pleasant literary flavour.

Leaving her detective stories in 1937, Dorothy Sayers embarked on works with a religious content. *The Zeal of Thy House* (1937) and *The Devil to Pay* (1939) were plays written for the Canterbury Festival. They were followed by the successful radio play *The Man Born to be King* (1941) and other similar pieces. In 1940 she published a translation of Dante's *Inferno*, followed in 1955 by a translation of the *Purgatorio*. She was at work on Dante's *Paradiso* when she died at Witham, Essex, on 17 December 1957.

SCHOLES, PERCY ALFRED (1877–1958), musical writer and encyclopedist, was born at Leeds on 24 July 1877, the third child of Thomas Scholes, a commercial agent, and his wife, Katharine Elizabeth Pugh. His education was limited by ill health, but he was a keen student of music and, after teaching music at Kent College, Canterbury (1901) and in South Africa (1904), he became an extension lecturer for Manchester University, and in 1908 obtained his B. Mus. at St Edmund Hall, Oxford. In that year he married Dora Wingate, daughter of Richard Lean, a civil engineer; they had no children.

From 1908 to 1921 he edited *The Music Student* (later *The Music Teacher*), and from 1913 to 1920 was music critic of the *Evening Standard*. He was also an extension lecturer for Cambridge, Oxford, and London universities. During the First World War he worked for the YMCA 'music for the troops' in France, leading to the publication in 1919 of his *Listener's Guide to Music*.

In 1920 he became music critic of the *Observer*, a post which he held until he became musical director of the *Radio Times* (1926–8). In 1928 he moved to Switzerland, where he planned more ambitious books, such as *The Oxford Companion to Music* (1938), a biography of Dr Charles Burney (2 vols., 1948, James Tait Black memorial prize), *The Concise Oxford Dictionary of Music* (1952), and *The Oxford Junior Companion to Music* (1954).

Scholes received many honorary degrees and was appointed FSA in 1938 and OBE in 1957. He died at Vevey, Switzerland on 31 July 1958.

SCOTT, CHARLES PRESTWICH (1846–1932), journalist, was born in Bath on 26 October 1846, the eighth child of Russell Scott, a partner in a coal business, and his wife, Isabella Civil, daughter of Joseph Prestwich, a wine merchant. He was educated partly at Clapham Grammar School and partly privately for reasons of ill health; he graduated from Corpus Christi College, Oxford (1866–9) with a first in Greats.

His cousin, John Edward Taylor, owned the *Manchester Guardian*, and he offered Scott a post on the paper; less than a year later, in 1872 Scott became Editor, a position which he held until 1929. In 1874 he married Rachel, daughter of John Cook, Professor of Ecclesiastical History at St Andrews. She was one of the original students at Girton College, Cambridge; they had three sons and a daughter.

Scott held Liberal views in politics and strongly supported Gladstone's Home Rule policy and was opposed to the Boer War. From 1895 to 1905 he was Liberal MP for the Leigh division of Lancashire. At first, Taylor had encouraged Scott's political ambitions but the financial strain imposed on the paper by the pursuit of the unpopular anti-Boer War policy encouraged a belief that Scott was neglecting his work on the *Guardian*. When Taylor died in 1905, Scott did not inherit the paper as he had expected but was obliged to purchase it, having some difficulty in raising the money.

Shortly afterwards he suffered the blow of his wife's death, a calamity, not only because of their constant affection, but because of her acumen and keen involvement in the interests of the newspaper.

During the fifty-seven years that he edited the *Manchester Guardian* Scott raised it to a leading place among the world's newspapers, giving it considerable influence in the political field and in the world of the arts and literature. His impact was particularly strong on the course of Liberal policies; he maintained close contact with ministers in the Liberal Governments of Campbell-Bannerman and ASQUITH, although he did not always agree with their views.

He was critical of the foreign policy of Sir Edward GREY, leading to British involvement in the First World War but, once the country was embroiled, he steadily supported the efforts of LLOYD GEORGE to bring the conflict to a successful conclusion. When peace came, however, he was critical of the Prime Minister's 'coupon' election of 1918 and of the Black and Tans' activities in Ireland. He used his influence to bring about the Irish Treaty in 1921. In the years that followed he watched the decline of the Liberal party with growing sadness.

In 1921 he received an honorary degree of LL.D. from Manchester University, and in 1930 became a freeman of the city; in 1923 he was elected an honorary Fellow of Corpus Christi College, Oxford. He declined a knighthood on more than one occasion.

Scott died in Manchester on 1 January 1932. His eldest son had died in 1908; his second son became Manager of the *Guardian* in 1905, and succeeded his father as Editor in 1929, but was accidentally drowned shortly after his father's death. Scott's daughter married C. E. Montague, himself a journalist of distinction.

SCOTT, SIR GILES GILBERT (1880–1960), architect, was born in London on 9 November 1880, the son of George Gilbert Scott, and his wife, Ellen King-Sampson. He was a grandson of Sir George Gilbert Scott, creator of the Albert Memorial. He was educated at Beaumont College, and in 1898 became a pupil of Temple Moore. While working with Moore, at the age of twenty-two, he won the competition for the new Anglican Cathedral, Liverpool, for which the first contract was placed in 1903.

This success led to further commissions for the design of churches and chapels notably those of Charterhouse School, Ampleforth Abbey, Oban Cathedral, and the Carmelite church, Kensington. His university buildings include the University Library, Cambridge, the extension to the Bodleian Library, Oxford, and the addition to Clare College, Cambridge. Most of his designs were broadly within the idiom of Gothic revival, but the extension for Clare College revealed his ability also to handle neo-Georgian styles with complete success.

In 1932 he was appointed architect for the new Waterloo Bridge, opened in 1945; he also designed the Battersea Power Station, the rebuilding of the House of Commons (1948–50), and the restoration of the Guildhall, London.

He was elected ARA (1918) and RA (1922). In 1924 he was knighted, and in 1944 appointed OM. He received honorary degrees from Oxford, Cambridge, and Liverpool.

In 1914 he married Louisa Wallbank Hughes; they had two sons. Scott died in London on 8 February 1960.

SCOTT, PAUL MARK (1920–1978), author, was born on 25 March 1920 at Palmer's Green, London, the younger son backgrounds and published *The Bender* and *Corrída at San Feliú*.

Scott had left David Higham Associates in 1960 and in 1964 he revisited India: the fruits of his visit were the quartet of novels about that country—his best known work, particularly following its successful adaptation as a television series in 1982. The first of these volumes, *The Jewel in the Crown* (1966), sets the scene and describes the event which reverberates through all the books. This central event is the rape of an unsophisticated English girl, who is engaged in a love affair with a westernized young Indian who cannot speak his own language. The liaison ends in tragedy for both, a tragedy which Scott uses to describe and reveal the other characters in the four books, retelling the event and its consequences from different points of view over a shifting time-scale, and changing the focus of interest at each retelling.

The other novels of the quartet are *The Day of the Scorpion* (1968), *The Towers of Silence* (1971), and *A Division of the Spoils* (1975). They were published in one volume as *The Raj Quartet* in 1976. All have as their background the uneasy tensions in India during the war with Japan in which Indian prisoners of war were being cajoled or forcibly persuaded to join the Indian National Army, recruited by Subhas Chandra Bose, an ex-President of Congress in exile. The analogy of India as the jewel in the crown is never far from the surface but underlying it is the suggestion, though never made explicit, that the rape itself has a wider symbolism. An attendant theme is Scott's fascination with people who do not belong in their own society and the effect this has on the individuals themselves and on those who have to live with them. Throughout the series, Scott is deeply concerned with the relationship between the British sahibs and memsahibs and the Indian subjects of the Raj. However, like E. M. FORSTER before him, his imaginative work is inclined to portray his English characters with less understanding than he gives their Indian counterparts.

His final novel, *Staying On* (1977), is a masterly study of two minor characters from the Raj Quartet, a retired British army officer and his unfortunate wife, who have chosen to live in penury in an Indian hill-station rather than return to England after Independence. For this novel, Scott was awarded the Booker prize in 1977. At the time he was Visiting Professor at the University of Tulsa, Oklahoma, having just undergone surgery for cancer. He died in London on 1 March 1978 shortly after returning from the USA. *Staying On* was also adapted for television (1980).

Paul Scott, 1970

of Thomas Scott, a commercial artist, and his wife, Frances Mark. He was educated at Winchmore Hill Collegiate School, and trained as an accountant. He enlisted in the army in 1940, and a year later married Nancy Edith, daughter of Francis Percival Avery, a Conservative political agent; they had two daughters.

Scott was commissioned in 1943, and served in India, Burma, and Malaya, until he was demobilized in 1946. For the next four years he was employed by the Falcon Press and the Grey Walls Press, but in 1950 he joined a literary agency and in due course became a director of David Higham Associates.

His first novel, *Johnnie Sahib*, based on his war-time experiences in India, was published in 1952, having been rejected by many publishers. India remained the chief source of inspiration for most of his novels from then onwards. *The Alien Sky* appeared in 1953; then six years later came *The Mark of the Warrior*, in which the central character, whose second-in-command has died of wounds while both are retreating from the Japanese through the Burmese jungle in 1942, later finds himself responsible for training the dead man's son in jungle warfare. Two other novels based in India were *The Chinese Love Pavilion* (1960) and *The Birds of Paradise* (1962). Scott had meanwhile experimented with a non-Indian scenario in *A Male Child* (1956), set in London. Then in 1963 and 1964 he turned again from his Indian

SEAMAN, SIR OWEN (1861–1936), Editor of *Punch*, was born in London on 18 September 1861, the only son of William Mantle Seaman, a dressmaker, and his wife, Sarah Ann Balls. He was educated at Shrewsbury and Clare College, Cambridge, where he was a Porson prizeman (1882), and obtained a first in part i of the classical tripos (1883). He was called to the Bar (Inner Temple) in 1897. During his time as a schoolmaster at Rossall (1884) and Professor of Literature at Durham College of Science, Newcastle upon Tyne (1890–1903) he produced light verse of high quality.

As a consequence, in 1902 he was invited to become Assistant Editor of *Punch*; from 1906 to 1932 he was Editor. From his undergraduate days, he wrote brilliant parodies of contemporary poets, and during the Boer War produced political satire of wit and style. Later, during the First World War, he composed verses of dignity and serious content.

As Editor, he gave great encouragement to authors who

contributed to *Punch*. His own publications included *In Cap and Bells* (1899), *Borrowed Plumes* (1902), *A Harvest of Chaff* (1904), *War-Time* (1915), and *Interludes of an Editor* (1929). In 1934 he wrote a prologue for the performance of Milton's *Comus* at Ludlow Castle. He frequently lectured on Browning.

He received a number of honorary degrees, was knighted in 1914 and created a baronet in 1933. He died unmarried in London on 2 February 1936.

SELFRIDGE, HARRY GORDON (1858-1947), business man, was born on 11 January 1858 at Ripon, Wisconsin, USA, the only son of Robert Oliver Selfridge, dry goods merchant, and his wife, Lois Frances Baxter. He was brought up by his mother, a teacher, and at fourteen became a bank clerk.

In 1879 he joined the mail-order firm of Field, Leiter & Co., and became a valuable assistant to Marshall Field, travelling on behalf of the firm in the USA and Europe. In 1890 he became a junior partner, but in 1904 left the company, and in 1906, with a small fortune, arrived in London to set up his own business.

In 1909 Selfridge & Co. Ltd. opened in Oxford Street, London, with 130 departments, a library, rest-rooms, and a roof-garden—all of which was backed by a strong advertising programme. After the First World War the business flourished and was able to acquire a number of suburban and provincial shops. Selfridge, however, by 1939, was heavily indebted to the company, owing to his personal extravagance. He resigned from the board, and became honorary President of the company. In 1937 he had become a naturalized British subject. His attitude to business is revealed in his book *The Romance of Commerce* (1918).

Peter Sellers as Inspector Clouseau

He accumulated fine collections of orchids and bookbindings.

In 1890 he married Rosalie Buckingham, of Chicago; they had three daughters and a son. Selfridge died in London on 8 May 1947.

SELLERS, RICHARD HENRY ('PETER') (1925-1980), comic actor, was born in Portsmouth on 8 September 1925, the only child of William Sellers, a pianist, and his wife, Agnes ('Peg') Marks, an entertainer, and great-granddaughter of Daniel Mendoza, the boxer. Peg was Jewish, but her son was educated at St Aloysius College, Highgate. He left school at fourteen and did odd jobs in the theatre.

For a time he was a drummer in a dance band, but at eighteen he entered the RAF, despite the efforts of his mother, with whom he was very close, to get him exempted on medical grounds. He was soon recruited to the Ralph Reader Gang Show, where he became an adept impersonator, entertaining the troops in South-East Asia.

After the war he worked for a time at the Windmill Theatre, and then obtained a part in a BBC radio programme by hoodwinking the producer, imitating, over the telephone, the voices of Kenneth Horne and Richard Murdoch, two popular entertainers. Soon he was engaged in a number of radio shows, including 'Ray's a Laugh' and 'Workers' Playtime'. In 1951 he joined Harry Secombe, Spike Milligan, and Michael Bentine in 'The Goon Show', which ran for nine years. During these years, he was also appearing in variety and in films.

His first major success in films came in 1959 with *I'm All Right Jack*, the Boulting Brothers film, in which Peter Sellers played the part of Jack Kite, the shop steward. His achievement in this film was followed by success in *The Millionairess*, when he played opposite Sophia Loren (1960), *Mr Topaze* (1961), and *Doctor Strangelove* (1962). In the following year, 1963, he had what was probably his most outstanding triumph as the hapless Inspector Clouseau in *The Pink Panther*, the first of a series of 'Pink Panther' films which made him a large fortune.

Throughout most of his adult life Sellers suffered from a heart condition, which made him liable to sudden heart attacks, but he did not allow these to inhibit his career as a superb entertainer. In 1959 he won the British Film Academy award as the Best Actor; he won other awards of the same kind, including in 1975 the *Evening News* Best Actor of the Year prize. In 1966 he was appointed CBE.

In 1951 he married Anne Howe, a young Australian actress; they had a son and a daughter, but the marriage ended in divorce in 1964. That year he married Britt Ekland, the Swedish film actress; they had one daughter, and the marriage was dissolved in 1969. In 1970 he married Miranda, daughter of Richard St John Quarry and Lady Mancroft; they had no children and the marriage broke up in 1974. Finally, in 1977 he married Lynne Frederick; they had no children. Up to the time of her death, 'Peg', his mother, exercised a curious influence over Peter Sellers from which he never completely broke away. He died in London on 24 July 1980.

SELWYN-LLOYD, BARON (1904-1978). See LLOYD, (JOHN) SELWYN BROOKE.

SHACKLETON, SIR ERNEST HENRY (1874-1922), explorer, was born at Kilkee, co. Kildare, on 15 February 1874, the eldest son of Henry Shackleton, MD, and his wife, men, crossed 800 miles of stormy seas to reach South Georgia and, later, at the third attempt, rescued the rest of his *Endurance* party (1916). He gave an account of this expedition in *South* (1919). He was awarded the OBE (1919).

He spent the winter of 1918-19 organizing winter equipment with the North Russian expeditionary force. In 1921 he sailed in the *Quest*, on a new attempt to explore another area of Antarctica, but died suddenly on South Georgia, on 5 January 1922.

Shackleton is remembered by Mount Shackleton in the Canadian Rockies, Shackleton Inlet and Shackleton Ice Shelf in the Antarctic, and Mount Shackleton in East Greenland.

SHARP, CECIL JAMES (1859-1924), collector and arranger of English folk-songs and dances, was born in London on 22 November 1859, the eldest son of John James Sharp, a slate-merchant, and his wife, Jane Bloyd. He was educated at Uppingham and Clare College, Cambridge, and in 1882 went to Adelaide to take up a legal post. During 1889-91 he was Co-Director of the Adelaide College of Music. Returning to England in 1892, in the following year he married Constance Dorothea, daughter of Priestley Birch, of Woolston, Devon; they had a son and three daughters. From 1893 to 1910 he was music master of Ludgrove School, and from 1896 to 1905 Principal of the Hampstead Conservatoire of Music.

Attracted by the revival of interest in traditional music, he joined the newly-formed Folk-Song Society and began to make systematic collections of folk-dances and folk-songs. In 1902 he published *A Book of British Song* followed in 1904 by *Folk-Songs from Somerset* and in 1907 *English Folk-Song: some Conclusions*. In 1911 he founded the English Folk-Dance Society, and from 1912 to 1924 was its Director. During 1916-18 he visited the Appalachian Mountains in the USA in search of songs of English origin. In all, he discovered nearly five thousand folk-tunes, about one third of which he found in America.

He was also a pioneer in research into morris-, sword-, and country-dances, and between 1907 and 1914 published over three hundred dances with their tunes.

Sharp died in London on 23 June 1924, and in 1930 Cecil Sharp House in Regent's Park Road was erected 'in memory of Cecil Sharp who restored to the English people the songs and dances of their country'.

SHAW, GEORGE BERNARD (1856-1950), playwright, was born on 26 July 1856 in Dublin, the son of George Carr Shaw, a miller, and his wife, Lucinda Elizabeth, daughter of Walter Bagnall Gurly, an impoverished country gentleman. George Shaw was a feckless drunkard and his wife, a singer, left him and settled in London with her two daughters and a musician named Lee. In 1867 Shaw went to the Wesley Connexional School, Dublin, but his education consisted mainly of musical appreciation from his mother and her friends, and study of his father's books and the pictures in the National Gallery of Ireland.

In 1871 he became a clerk in an estate agent's, and from 1872 to 1876 was cashier, still living at the time with his father. In 1876 he left Dublin to live with his mother in London. During 1878-83 he worked in a number of jobs, recovered from smallpox in 1881, and wrote, but failed to publish, five novels, including *Immaturity*, *Love Among the Artists*, and *Cashel Byron's Profession*.

In 1884 he joined the Fabian Society and became a friend

Ernest Shackleton, *c.* 1909

Henrietta Letitia Sophia, daughter of Henry John Gavan, Inspector-General of Police, Ceylon. He was educated at Dulwich College (1887-90), and then went to sea as an apprentice in a sailing ship of the White Star line. From 1890 to 1901 he served in ships of the White Star, Shire, and Union Castle lines, and in a book, *OHMS* (1900, in collaboration with Dr W. McLean), described his experiences in carrying troops to the Boer War.

In 1901 he served under Commander Robert Falcon Scott in the *Discovery* and accompanied Scott on the Antarctic expedition which journeyed over the Ross barrier. From 1904 to 1905 he was Secretary to the Royal Scottish Geographical Society and during this time (1904), he married Emily Mary, daughter of Charles Dorman, of Wadhurst, Sussex; they had two sons and a daughter. But, by 1907, he was planning to explore the Ross barrier and, if possible, reach the South Pole. He sailed in the *Nimrod*, reached the barrier in 1908, and sent parties to the South Magnetic Pole and the summit of Mount Erebus. Rewarded with the CVO and a knighthood, he met the costs of the expedition by lecturing in Europe and America, and published *The Heart of the Antarctic* (1909).

He set out again for Antarctica in 1914 in the *Endurance*. His ship was crushed in the ice, and Shackleton, with five of William Archer and Sidney WEBB. In 1885 Archer obtained work for him as a book-reviewer for the *Pall Mall Gazette* and later, from 1886 to 1889, secured for him the post of art critic on the *World*. During 1888–90 Shaw, as Corno di Bassetto, was music critic of the *Star* and in 1890 joined the *World* in the same capacity. In 1889 he edited *Fabian Essays in Socialism*, and in 1891 published *The Quintessence of Ibsenism*. In 1897 he joined the Society of Authors, and for the rest of his life fought against publishers and censorship.

His first efforts as a playwright were no more successful than his novels. *Widowers' Houses* (1892) and *The Philanderer* (1893) were failures, and *Mrs Warren's Profession* was banned by the Lord Chamberlain until 1925. *Arms and the Man*, *Candida*, and *You Never Can Tell* were, at the outset, no more successful. In 1895 he appeared to accept that he was a failure as a playwright by taking the post of drama critic of the *Saturday Review*.

His plays marked a break from the prevailing fashion in English theatre, in their appeal to the intellect rather than the emotions of his audience. The dialogue was witty and often eloquent. In 1894 *Arms and the Man* and in 1897 *The Devil's Disciple* met with success in New York, and Shaw

could look forward to further triumphs. Success, however, did not come immediately in London. *The Man of Destiny* and *You Never Can Tell* were a further disappointment, and Ellen TERRY, with whom he was corresponding at this time, refused to play the part of Lady Cecil Waynflete, which he had written for her in *Captain Brassbound's Conversion*.

Shaw had converted himself from a shy young man into a capable speaker on public platforms, and during 1897–1903 was a vestryman and later a borough councillor of St Pancras. In 1904 he published *The Common Sense of Municipal Trading*. In 1898 he suffered a physical breakdown, and was nursed back to health by Charlotte Frances, daughter of Horace Payne-Townshend, an Irish barrister. In the same year they were married.

In 1899 the tide turned. *Caesar and Cleopatra* was produced with Mrs Patrick CAMPBELL as Cleopatra. *Man and Superman* was written during 1901–3, *John Bull's Other Island* in 1904 and *Major Barbara* in 1905. All three were produced at the Royal Court Theatre during the Vedrenne-Barker seasons. The last play at the Court was *The Doctor's Dilemma* in 1906, and *Getting Married* (1908) was put on at the Haymarket, *The Shewing-up of Blanco Posnet* at the Abbey Theatre, Dublin (1909), *Misalliance* (Duke of Yorks,

Shaw (right) rehearsing Granville-Barker and Lillah McCarthy in *Androcles*, 1913

1910) and *Fanny's First Play* (Little Theatre, 1911) with Lillah McCarthy.

In 1913 came *Androcles and the Lion* at the St James's Theatre, and in 1914 *Pygmalion* at His Majesty's, with Mrs Patrick Campbell as the flower-girl and Sir Herbert TREE as the professor. Shaw was at the height of his success when the First World War put an end, temporarily at least, to his popularity. The Germans were quick to exploit his *Commonsense about the War* (1914), which brought him much severe criticism and even hatred.

After the war, however, *Arms and the Man* was revived with marked success in 1919 in London, and *Heartbreak House* was produced in 1920 in New York, and in 1921 in London. These were followed by *Back to Methuselah* (New York, 1922, Birmingham Repertory, 1923), and *Saint Joan* (New York, 1923, London, with Sybil THORNDIKE, 1924). St John Ervine in the *DNB* wrote: 'Shaw was now beyond question the most famous living dramatist in the world.' In 1925 he was awarded the Nobel prize, and with the money he established the Anglo-Swedish Literary Foundation.

He now resumed political writing with *The Intelligent Woman's Guide to Socialism* and *Capitalism* (1928), followed by *The Adventures of the Black Girl in Her Search for God* (1932) and *Everybody's Political What's What?* (1944). His collected plays were published in 1931 and the collected prefaces in 1934.

The Malvern Festivals, started by Sir Barry JACKSON were the venue for Shaw's later plays *The Apple Cart* (1929), *Too True to be Good* (1932), *Geneva* (1938), and *In Good King Charles's Golden Days* (1939). New fame and fortune came to him with the film productions of *Pygmalion*, *Major Barbara*, and *Caesar and Cleopatra*.

His wife died in 1943; they had no children. Shaw had lived at Ayot St Lawrence since 1906 and he died there on 2 November 1950. The house was left to the National Trust and the residue of the estate was left to set up a British alphabet of at least forty letters, and to endow the National Gallery of Ireland, the British Museum, and the Royal Academy of Dramatic Art. Shaw was a prolific letter writer and, apart from his correspondence with Ellen Terry, which was published in 1931, he corresponded with Mrs Patrick Campbell, GRANVILLE-BARKER, CUNNINGHAME GRAHAM, Gilbert MURRAY, H. G. WELLS, Lord Alfred Douglas, and others. He was a vegetarian and teetotaller and idiosyncratic in his clothes.

SHEPARD, ERNEST HOWARD (1879–1976), painter and illustrator, was born in London on 10 December 1879, the younger son of Henry Donkin Shepard, an architect, and his wife, Jessie Harriet, daughter of William Lee, a water-colour painter. He was educated at St Paul's School, and studied at Heatherleys Art School and the Royal Academy Schools, where he was taught by John Singer Sargent. (Sir) Frank Dicksee was a friend of the family. In 1899 Shepard won the Landseer and British Institution scholarships; he was already contributing drawings to magazines.

He began his career as an illustrator by providing drawings for *David Copperfield*, *Tom Brown's Schooldays*, *Aesop's Fables*, and *Henry Esmond*, in 1906 had drawings accepted by *Punch*, and by 1914 had become a regular contributor to that magazine. During the First World War he served on the Western Front in the Royal Artillery and won the MC. His elder brother was killed in the war.

In 1921 he became a member of the *Punch* staff, and in

E. H. Shepard's original design for the jacket of *Drawn from Memory*

1924 became a regular exhibitor at the Royal Academy, his first painting having been accepted as early as 1901. Also in 1924, he began his association with A. A. MILNE, which brought fame to both of them with *When We Were Very Young*. *Winnie the Pooh* (1926), *Now We Are Six* (1927), and *The House at Pooh Corner* (1928) followed, all of which gave immense pleasure to generations of young children, for whom Christopher Robin and Pooh became intimate friends.

His other work as an illustrator included drawings for *Everybody's Pepys* (1926), *Everybody's Boswell* (1930), *Everybody's Lamb* (1933), and for Kenneth GRAHAME's *The Wind in the Willows* (1931) and Laurence Housman's *Victoria Regina* (1935). From 1935 to 1953 he held the post of second cartoonist at *Punch*. In 1957 he wrote his autobiographical *Drawn from Memory*, followed in 1961 by *Drawn from Life*. In 1972 he was appointed OBE.

In 1904 he married a fellow student, Florence Eleanor, daughter of James Hopper Chaplin, a gem expert; they had a son, who died in 1943, and a daughter, who married E. V. Knox. Florence died in 1927, and in 1944 Shepard married Norah, daughter of J. C. Carroll, of Australia; she was a hospital nurse. He died at the age of ninety-six at Midhurst on 24 March 1976.

SHERIDAN, CLARE CONSUELO (1885–1970), sculptor, was born in London on 9 September 1885, the only daughter of Moreton Frewen, a landowner, and his wife, Clara, eldest of the three daughters of Leonard Jerome, of New York.

Clare Sheridan in madonna-like pose, by Bertram Park; through the deaths of two of her children she found her vocation as a sculptor

Jennie, Lady Randolph Churchill, was her aunt and Winston CHURCHILL, her cousin. She became fluent in French and German but learnt little of English literature until she met William (Wilfred) Frederick Sheridan, a stockbroker, son of Algernon Thomas Brinsley Sheridan, great-grandson of Richard Brinsley Sheridan. In 1910 she and Sheridan were married; they had two daughters.

When her younger daughter died in 1914, Clare, in her distress, modelled an angel for the child's grave and discovered that she wanted to be a sculptor. In 1915 her husband was killed on the Western Front, a few days after the birth of her son.

She studied under William REID DICK and her first exhibition aroused considerable interest, leading to commissions from ASQUITH, F. E. SMITH, and Winston Churchill, among others.

In 1920 she was invited to Moscow by Kamenev, head of a Soviet trade delegation to London. There she did busts of Lenin and Trotsky and other leading Russians, much to the annoyance of Churchill, who was then Secretary of State for War and pressing for intervention against the Bolsheviks. In 1921 she published her Russian diaries, entitled *Mayfair to Moscow* in the USA and *Russian Portraits* in England.

She then visited the USA, where she became a friend of Charles CHAPLIN, and in 1922 she returned to Europe as correspondent for the New York *World*. She obtained many scoops for the paper, including interviews with Ataturk, Mussolini, and Queen Marie of Romania. In 1924 she toured southern Russia with her brother on a motor-cycle, and in 1925 published *Across Europe with Satanella*.

That year she went with her children to Istanbul and later to Algeria, and published *A Turkish Kaleidoscope* (1926) and *Nuda Veritas* (1927). In 1936 she published *Arab Interlude*. Then, in 1937, her son died and, in her grief, she took up wood carving and produced a memorial for the young man, a great oak madonna which can be seen in Brede church. She spent some time in an art colony on a Red Indian reservation in the Rockies and, on return, put on an exhibition of Indian heads carved in wood; she also published *Redskin Interlude* (1938).

She continued to model, producing a bronze head of Churchill in 1942. After the war, she became a Roman Catholic. Her last book of memoirs, *To the Four Winds*, was published in 1957.

Clare Sheridan died on 31 May 1970 at Brede Place, Sussex. Her works are scattered throughout England and

Ireland; her bust of Asquith is at the Oxford Union and her head of Churchill at Harrow.

SHERRIFF, ROBERT CEDRIC (1896-1975), author, was born on 6 June 1896 at Hampton-Wick, Surrey, the only child of Herbert Hankin Sherriff, an insurance clerk, and his wife, Constance, daughter of Charles Winder of Iver, Bucks. He was educated at Kingston Grammar School, joined the London staff of the Sun Insurance Office in 1914, was an officer in the East Surrey Regiment in 1917, and was severely wounded at Ypres. After the war he returned to the insurance office, and began to write plays.

In 1929 he achieved an outstanding success with *Journey's End* which, after a number of rejections and a production by the Stage Society, began a long run at the Apollo Theatre. Set in a dug-out in the front line on the eve of the great spring offensive of 1918, it gave a straightforward, honest account of the horrors of trench warfare and the reactions of the varied characters among the officers to the terrors of bombardment and their misery and privation in Flanders mud. It was highly commended by James Agate, the influential theatre critic, was translated and performed throughout Europe, and was immensely successful in the USA.

Sherriff wrote another nine stage plays, including *Badger's Green* (1930), *Windfall* (1933), and *St. Helena* (with Jeanne de Casalis, 1935). During 1931-3 he studied history at New College, Oxford, and in 1937 founded a scholarship there. In 1948 *Miss Mabel* was staged in the West End, followed in 1950 by *Home at Seven*, a play of suspense in which (Sir) Ralph Richardson played the lead. Between 1953 and 1960 Sherriff wrote four more plays which had less success than *Home at Seven*.

He wrote a number of film scripts, including *Goodbye Mr. Chips* (from the book by James Hilton, 1936), *The Four Feathers* (from the novel by A. E. W. Mason, 1938), *Lady Hamilton* (1941), *Odd Man Out* (1945), *No Highway* (1950), and *The Dam Busters* (1955). One of his best novels was *The Fortnight in September* (1931). His memoirs *No Leading Lady* were published in 1968. He never married. He died at Kingston upon Thames on 13 November 1975.

SHERRINGTON, SIR CHARLES SCOTT (1857-1952), physiologist, was born on 27 November 1857 in London, the son of James Norton and Anne Brookes Sherrington, of Great Yarmouth. He was educated at Ipswich Grammar School and Gonville and Caius College, Cambridge, where he was a scholar and obtained firsts in both parts of the natural sciences tripos (1881-3). He qualified at St Thomas's Hospital, London, MRCS (1884), LRCP (1886), Cambridge MB (1885), MD (1892), and Sc. D. (1904). In 1891 he married Ethel Mary, daughter of John Ely Wright, of Preston Manor, Suffolk; they had one son.

In 1887 he was elected a Fellow of his college and a lecturer in systematic physiology at St Thomas's. In 1891 he was appointed Professor Superintendent of the Brown Animal Sanatory Institution, London. He was elected FRS two years later, and in 1895 appointed Holt Professor of Physiology at Liverpool. There, he carried out extensive research into the nervous system of animals, and in 1904 gave the Silliman lectures at Yale, which were published in 1906 as *The Integrative Action of the Nervous System*. Lord ADRIAN, with whom in 1932 he shared the Nobel prize for medicine, described Sherrington's work as opening up 'an entirely new chapter in the physiology of the central nervous system'.

From 1913 to 1935 he was Waynflete Professor of Physiology at Oxford and a Fellow of Magdalen College. During the First World War, he studied industrial fatigue for the War Office and during 1914-17 was Fullerian Professor of Physiology at the Royal Institution. He was President of the Royal Society from 1920 to 1925 and of the British Association in 1922. He was appointed GBE (1922) and OM (1924).

In 1937-8 he gave the Gifford lectures at Edinburgh, published in 1940 as *Man on his Nature*, and in 1946 published *The Endeavour of Jean Fernel*. Sherrington died at Eastbourne on 4 March 1952; in 1948 the Sherrington lectures were founded in his honour at Liverpool University.

SHORTER, CLEMENT KING (1857-1926), journalist and author, was born in London on 19 July 1857, the youngest son of Richard Shorter, a carrier between London and Cambridge, and his wife, Elizabeth Clemenson. The railway ruined Richard Shorter and he emigrated to Australia and died while Clement was still young. Clement went to school at Downham Market (1863-71), and was then employed by various booksellers and publishers in London.

From 1877 to 1890 he was a clerk at Somerset House. In 1890, after spending a short time in Germany, he began work as an editor, issuing a selection of Wordsworth's poems. He was also writing a books' column for the *Star* and the *Queen*. In 1890-1 he became Editor of the *Illustrated London News*, and of the *English Illustrated Magazine*; in 1893 he founded and edited the *Sketch*. By 1897 he was editing five papers, but in 1900 left the *Illustrated London News* and its connected papers to found the *Sphere*, which he edited up to the time of his death. In 1901 he founded the *Tatler*.

His work as a journalist was supplemented by work as an author. His publications include *Charlotte Brontë and her Circle* (1896), *The Brontës: Life and Letters* (2 vols., 1908), *Napoleon and his Fellow-Travellers* (1908), and *George Borrow and his Circle* (1913). He also wrote many other works on books and bookmen and *C.K.S., an Autobiography*, which was published posthumously in 1926.

He married in 1896 Dora, daughter of George Sigerson, MD, of Dublin; she died in 1918, and in 1920 he married Annie Doris, daughter of John Banfield, a shipowner of Penzance; they had a daughter.

Shorter died at Great Missenden on 19 November 1926.

SHUTE, NEVIL (1899-1960), novelist and aeronautical engineer, whose full name was Nevil Shute Norway, was born in Ealing on 17 January 1899, the younger son of Arthur Hamilton Norway, assistant secretary of the General Post Office, and his wife, Mary Louisa Gadsen. From an early age, he was fascinated by model aircraft and the problems of aeronautics. He was educated at the Dragon School, Oxford, and Shrewsbury. During the First World War he passed into the Royal Military Academy, but failed to get into the Royal Flying Corps because of a bad stammer. He served, however, as a private in the Suffolk Regiment.

In 1919 he went up to Balliol College, Oxford, and studied engineering science, working during the vacations at an aircraft factory. In 1922 he joined de Havillands, and learnt to fly and gained experience as a test observer. Two years later, he became Chief Calculator to the Airship Guarantee Co., and in 1929 was appointed Deputy Chief Engineer under Barnes WALLIS. He worked on airships until he was disillusioned by the inefficiency with which the R101 was constructed and the subsequent disaster, in which it was wrecked with the loss of many lives.

In 1931 he married Frances Mary Heaton; they had two daughters. From 1931 to 1938 he managed Airspeed Ltd. which he had founded as an aeroplane construction company but, when the work became routine, he decided to give it up for writing novels, with which he had been experimenting since leaving Oxford. Two of his novels had already been accepted by the film industry.

On the outbreak of the Second World War, Norway joined the Royal Naval Volunteer Reserve and experimented with secret weapons, until he was sent by the Ministry of Information to witness the Normandy landings in 1944 and to be a war correspondent in Burma in 1945. After the war, he emigrated to Australia, and there continued to produce best-selling novels, under the name of Nevil Shute, and to make a reputation for stories which made excellent films.

Among these are *No Highway* (1948), the story of an inarticulate engineer's attempt to warn against metal fatigue in a passenger aircraft, *A Town Like Alice* (1950), the grim and poignant story of women and children captured by the Japanese in Malaya, *Round the Bend* (1951), about a half-caste aeronautical engineer, who taught his men religion through the medium of work efficiently performed, and *On the Beach* (1957), the story of a submarine crew faced with the horror of the consequences of a nuclear war. Many other novels written between 1939 and 1955 were equally successful, some of them as films.

In 1954 Norway published *Slide Rule* (written under his full name), an account of his life in the aircraft industry. He died in Melbourne on 12 January 1960.

SICKERT, WALTER RICHARD (1860–1942), painter, was born in Munich on 31 May 1860, the eldest son of Oswald Adalbert Sickert, a Danish painter, and his wife, Eleanor Louisa Moravia Henry, of mixed Irish and English blood. His father became a naturalized British subject after moving to London in 1868. Sickert was educated at a private school and at King's College, London.

For a short time he worked as an actor before going in 1881 to the Slade School of Fine Art where he studied under Alphonse Legros. He then became apprenticed to J. A. McN. Whistler, who reinforced his inclination towards the use of subdued colours. Of even greater significance for Sickert, however, were Whistler's links with the French Impressionists. In 1883 in Paris Sickert first met Degas, later to become a close and much admired friend, who shared his interest in the theatre and influenced him in his preference for working from drawings, memory, or photographs rather than live models. He spent his summer holidays at Dieppe where he met several leading French writers as well as the artists Renoir, Monet, and Pissarro.

In 1885 he married Ellen, daughter of Richard Cobden, but they divorced in 1899 and, after quarrelling with Whistler, Sickert settled at Dieppe.

By 1884 he was showing his pictures with the (Royal) Society of British Artists; then in 1888 he joined the New English Art Club and a year later, in association with P. Wilson Steer and Frederick Brown, held an exhibition under the name of the London Impressionists. However, although Sickert was becoming known as a painter in Paris, he was making little money, and in 1905 he returned to London. At this time, under the influence of Camille Pissarro, he adopted a new style and technique using more compact design and applying the paint more thickly, in patches almost like mosaic.

His paintings were mainly of unfashionable suburban interiors with figures, often set in Camden Town. Together with others, dissatisfied with the New English Art Club, he helped form the Camden Town Group which in 1913 merged with the London Group. Members of the group included Lucien PISSARRO (son of Camille Pissarro), Augustus JOHN, Spencer Gore, and Harold Gilman. Sickert also sponsored the Allied Artists' Association which held annual no-jury exhibitions.

In 1908 Sickert took a teaching appointment at the Westminster Technical Institution, and two years later opened a private school called Rowlandson House. He married in 1911 one of his pupils, Christine Drummond, daughter of John Henry Angus, a Scottish leather merchant; they had no children. He continued to exhibit at the New English Art Club, the London Group, the Carfax Gallery, and the Royal Academy. He also exhibited etchings, but these were never so important as his oil paintings, notable for their craftsmanship and mastery of technique.

After the First World War, Sickert and his wife went back to Dieppe and she died there in 1920. Six years later he married Thérèse, daughter of Jules Lessore, a watercolourist. She was herself a painter whose work Sickert had long admired. They settled at Bath. In his writing on art subjects, as in his teaching, Sickert fought for recognition of the revolution in style deriving from the French Impressionists. He was elected ARA in 1924 and RA in 1934; he was President of the London Group in 1926 and of the Royal Society of British Artists in 1928. He held honorary degrees from Manchester and Reading Universities.

He died in Bath on 22 January 1942. His work can be seen in the Tate Gallery, in provincial galleries in England, and abroad at Dieppe, Rouen, Boston, USA, and in many countries of the Commonwealth. A volume of his writings, edited by Sir Osbert SITWELL, was published posthumously in 1947 as *A Free House!*.

SIDGWICK, ELEANOR MILDRED (1845–1936), Principal of Newnham College, Cambridge, was born at Whittingehame, East Lothian, on 11 March 1845, the eldest daughter of James Maitland Balfour, and his wife, Lady Blanche Harriet, daughter of the second Marquess of Salisbury. Arthur BALFOUR was her brother and J. W. STRUTT her brother-in-law.

In 1876 she married Henry Sidgwick, praelector on moral and political philosophy at Trinity College, Cambridge (and later Professor of Philosophy). Together they were pioneers for the higher education of women and, by their efforts, Newnham College was founded. From 1880 to 1882 Eleanor Sidgwick was its Vice-Principal and from 1892 to 1910 its Principal. She and her husband were generous benefactors of the college. In 1894 she was the first woman to serve on a royal commission, that on secondary education.

Her husband died in 1900; they had no children. In 1916 she left Cambridge and, from then until her death, lived with her brother Gerald, second Earl of Balfour, and his wife. Both she and her brother were deeply involved in the study of psychical phenomena. From 1907 to 1932 she was honorary Secretary of the Society for Psychical Research and in 1908 was elected President.

She contributed to the *Proceedings* of the Society; and received honorary degrees from Manchester, Birmingham, Edinburgh, and St Andrews. She died at Fisher's Hill, near Woking on 10 February 1936.

SILLITOE, SIR PERCY JOSEPH (1888–1962), policeman and head of MI5, was born in London on 22 May 1888, the second son of Joseph Henry Sillitoe, and his wife, Bertha Leontine Smith. He was educated at St Paul's Choir School, and from 1905–7 worked for the Anglo-American Oil Company. In 1908 he became a trooper in the British South Africa Police in Southern Rhodesia (Zimbabwe), and in 1911 was commissioned and transferred to the Northern Rhodesian Police. He took part in the campaign in German East Africa and, from 1916 till 1920, served as a political officer in Tanganyika (Tanzania). During 1920–2 he served in the Colonial Service in East Africa but, after a serious illness, resigned and returned to England.

In 1920 he married Dorothy Mary, daughter of John Watson of Elloughton, Yorkshire. His father-in-law advised him to apply for a post as chief constable. At first he was unsuccessful, but in 1923 he was appointed Chief Constable of Chesterfield. After two years there, he moved to the East Riding of Yorkshire and then, in 1926, to Sheffield. In all these posts he acquired a reputation as a capable administrator, and in 1931 was appointed Chief Constable of Glasgow, a post almost as onerous as that of the head of the Metropolitan Police. He was appointed CBE in 1936 and knighted in 1942. From 1943 to 1946 he was in command of a new Kent force co-operating with the army and other fighting services. He continued to make his mark as a capable organizer, who was always ready to introduce modern methods and equipment.

From 1946 to 1953 Sillitoe was Director-General of MI5, a post in which he himself was not happy and for which his experience as a policeman did not entirely meet the needs of difficult situations, in which people of some eminence were reluctant to give evidence against their colleagues and friends, and Sillitoe and his staff were faced with many frustrating problems. During these years, Alan Nunn May and Klaus Fuchs were brought to trial and Pontecorvo, Guy BURGESS, and Donald MacLean defected. The disappearance of Burgess and MacLean at a time when MacLean was about to be arrested was particularly damaging to MI5 and, to add to Sillitoe's uneasiness, he and his senior colleagues were not on good terms. His most valuable contribution in this MI5 post was his collaboration with dominion and colonial authorities in their security problems. However, in spite of criticism of his competence in this post, he had the confidence and support of Clement ATTLEE as Prime Minister, and in 1950 was appointed KBE.

On retirement from MI5, Sillitoe was appointed head of De Beers International Diamond Security Organization, in which post he met with some success in the suppression of diamond smuggling. In 1957 he became Chairman of Security Express Ltd. His autobiography *Cloak without Dagger* was published in 1955.

He died at Eastbourne on 5 April 1962. He and his wife had a daughter and two sons.

SIMON, JOHN ALLSEBROOK, first VISCOUNT SIMON (1873–1954), politician and Lord Chancellor, was born in Manchester on 28 February 1873, the only son of the Revd Edwin Simon, a Congregational minister, and his wife, Fanny, daughter of William Pole Allsebrook, a farmer. He was educated at Bath Grammar School, Fettes, and Wadham College, Oxford, where he obtained a first in Greats and was President of the Union (1896). He was elected a Fellow of All Souls (1897) and called to the Bar (Inner Temple) in 1899. In that year he married Ethel Mary, daughter of

Gilbert Venables. She died in 1902, and Simon became a widower before he was thirty and thereafter was increasingly shy and reserved.

From 1900 to 1906 he made steady progress at the Bar, but he regarded this as a stepping-stone to politics, and in 1906 was elected Liberal MP for Walthamstow, a seat which he held until the 'coupon election' of 1918. In 1910 he was appointed Solicitor-General and knighted; in 1912 he became a PC; and in 1913 succeeded Rufus ISAACS as Attorney-General with a seat in the Cabinet. He refused the office of Lord Chancellor in 1915 and went to the Home Office, but he resigned in 1916 on the issue of conscription. For the next fifteen years, he was out of office and, after war service with the RFC, applied himself again to his legal career.

From 1922 till 1940 Simon was MP for Spen Valley, and after the First World War identified himself with the Liberals who were opposed to LLOYD GEORGE. He attracted notice during the general strike of 1926 by declaring the strike to be illegal. In 1927 he became Chairman of the Indian Statutory Commission which was to recommend future constitutional progress. Before he could make his report, the Viceroy, Lord IRWIN, speaking for the Labour Government, made a public promise of dominion status for India (1929), and the huge report, which had been so carefully compiled, became merely a historical document when it was published in 1930.

In 1931 Simon became the leader of the National Liberals pledged to support the National Government, and from 1931 to 1935 was Foreign Secretary. He had little success in this office, for which he was temperamentally unsuited. His legal approach to the difficult problems of disarmament and aggression justified, to some extent, the gibe of Lloyd George that Simon had sat on the fence for so long that the iron had entered his soul.

In 1935 BALDWIN moved him back to the Home Office, and in 1937 CHAMBERLAIN made him Chancellor of the Exchequer. Throughout the period of 'appeasement', he loyally supported the Prime Minister, even after the Nazi occupation of Prague but, when he saw that war was inevitable, he was among those ministers who pressed upon Chamberlain the obligation to delay no further.

When in 1940 CHURCHILL became Prime Minister, Simon, who had always been on good terms with him, accepted the office of Lord Chancellor and became a viscount. He was not a member of the War Cabinet and had little influence on the conduct of the war. He was undoubtedly more successful as a lawyer than he had been as a politician. After the Labour victory of 1945 he continued to take an active part in the business of the House of Lords. He was appointed KCVO in 1911, GCSI in 1930, and GCVO in 1937. He was High Steward of Oxford University in 1948.

He had one son and two daughters by his first wife. In 1917 he married Kathleen, widow of Thomas Manning and daughter of Francis Eugene Harvey of Kyle, co. Wexford; she was appointed DBE in 1933; they had no children. Simon died in London on 11 January 1954.

SITWELL, DAME EDITH LOUISA (1887–1964), poet and critic, was born at Scarborough on 7 September 1887, the eldest child of Sir George Reresby Sitwell, fourth baronet, and his wife, Lady Ida Emily Augusta Dennison, daughter of the Earl of Londesborough. Though she was very fond of her home, Renishaw Hall, near Chesterfield, her interests were not those of her parents, and her childhood was unhappy until, in 1903, Helen Rootham became her governess, won her affection, and encouraged her artistic

tastes. Her mother was more concerned with the shape of Edith's nose than her education. From 1914 to 1938 she and Helen lived penuriously together, at first in London, then in Paris.

Her first volume of poems, *The Mother*, appeared in 1915. In 1916 she published, in collaboration with her brother, Osbert SITWELL, *Twentieth-Century Harlequinade* and an anthology of new poems, *Wheels*, which appeared annually till 1921, and in 1919 included Wilfred OWEN's war poems. In 1923 the critics were stirred by *Façade*, a brilliantly innovative concert piece, with Edith's verse and (Sir) William Walton's music, which caused an outcry when it was first performed, but soon became popular especially with young music-lovers. Her other poems were published in *The Sleeping Beauty* (1924), *Troy Park* (1925), and *Gold Coast Customs* (1929).

During her time in Paris, Edith had an unhappy relationship with Pavel Tchelitchew, a white Russian homosexual artist, who painted her several times; she also had to cope with the terminal illness of Helen Rootham, which made great demands on her time and energy. Helen died in 1938 and after some years of silence, Edith published further poems in *Street Songs* (1942), *Green Song* (1946), and the *Shadow of Cain* (1947). The last was a sombre, rather macabre, poem unlike her earlier work, such as *The Sleeping Beauty*. Among her prose works are *The English Eccentrics* (1923), and *Fanfare for Elizabeth* (1946). In addition to *Wheels*, she produced other anthologies such as *A Poet's Notebook* (1943) and *The Atlantic Book of British and American Poetry* (1959).

She was awarded honorary doctorates and appointed DBE in 1954. In appearance she was striking rather than beautiful, and her strong personality was emphasized by the unique quality of her dress. She was photographed by Cecil BEATON and painted by many artists. Virginia WOOLF was fascinated by the beauty of her hands. In 1953 Edith became a Roman Catholic. She died in London on 9 December 1964. Her autobiography *Taken Care Of* was published posthumously (1965).

SITWELL, SIR (FRANCIS) OSBERT SACHEVERELL (1892–1969), writer, was born in London on 6 December 1892, the elder son of Sir George Reresby Sitwell, fourth baronet, and his wife, Lady Ida Emily Augusta Dennison, third daughter of the Earl of Londesborough. He was educated at Eton (1906–9), and in 1911 was commissioned in the Sherwood Rangers, and in 1912 transferred to the Grenadier Guards, with whom he served in the First World War. In 1916, in collaboration with his sister Edith SITWELL, he published *Twentieth-Century Harlequinade*.

Osbert Sitwell was pre-eminently a satirist as he showed in his novels *Before the Bombardment* (1926), *The Man Who Lost Himself* (1929), and *Miracle on Sinai* (1933). His verses were published in *England Reclaimed* (1927) and *On the Continent* (1958).

His most outstanding work, however, was his autobiography *Left Hand, Right Hand* (5 vols., 1939–50) supplemented by *Tales My Father Taught Me* (1962), dominated by his father, an odd character, whose eccentricity Osbert highlights. Osbert himself was a joyful, sometimes malicious controversialist. In particular, he would attack anything which he considered even remotely philistine. He succeeded his father as fifth baronet in 1943, and was appointed CBE in 1956 and CH in 1958. He held honorary degrees, and was a Trustee of the Tate Gallery (1951–8). His companion for

some thirty years was David Horner, but his secretary, Frank Magro, cared for him in his last years of decline when he had Parkinson's disease. He died on 4 May 1969 at Montegufoni, the medieval castle near Florence, which his father had bought and renovated. He was succeeded in the baronetcy by his brother Sacheverell, the poet and critic. The Sitwells were notable for the generosity with which they proffered assistance to any young writer, artist, or musician who appeared to them to show promise and need help.

SLIM, WILLIAM JOSEPH, first VISCOUNT SLIM (1891–1970), field-marshal, was born in Bristol on 6 August 1891, the younger son of John Slim, an iron merchant, and his wife, Charlotte, daughter of Charles Tucker, of Burnham, Somerset. He was educated at King Edward's School, Birmingham. He wanted to be an army officer but his parents could not afford to send him to Sandhurst, so he took a job and managed to get accepted for the Birmingham University OTC.

In 1914 he joined KITCHENER's army and was commissioned in the Royal Warwickshire Regiment, served in the Dardanelles, and was badly wounded. On recovery, he was posted to Mesopotamia, where he was again wounded and awarded the MC. In 1917 he transferred to the Indian Army and served at HQ until in 1920 he was posted to the 1/6th Gurkha Rifles.

In 1926 he married Aileen, daughter of the Revd John Anderson Robertson, minister at Corstorphine, Edinburgh; they had one daughter and one son.

During the years up to the outbreak of the Second World War, Slim entered the Staff College, Quetta, then, in turn, became Indian Army Instructor at the Staff College, Camberley, and commanded first the 2/7th Gurkhas and then the Senior Officers School at Belgaum. In 1940 he commanded the 10th Indian Infantry Brigade in Eritrea, fought against the Italians, and was wounded again. In 1941 he commanded the 10th Indian Division in Iraq and Syria with the rank of major-general.

In 1942 he began his Burma career, when he was able to evacuate 'Burcorps' to India and was given command of XV Corps. He was appointed CBE (1942). In 1942–3 he was involved in the closing stages of the disastrous campaign in Arakan, and in 1943 took command of the newly formed 14th Army, with which his name will always be associated. He was also awarded the DSO.

The Japanese launched an offensive in 1944, which they intended to take them victoriously into India. They suffered a disastrous defeat with heavy losses and were driven back from Imphal and Kohima to the Chindwin river. Slim earned the CB and KCB. During this campaign, he was the only British commander from whom 'Vinegar Joe' Stilwell, the American general, was prepared to take orders and they were able to co-operate without difficulty. Slim, however, had to acquiesce in the 'Chindit' raids into Japanese-occupied territory, organized by Major-General Orde WINGATE, although he was not in agreement with this exploit.

In 1945 Slim's strategy completely outwitted the Japanese by cutting the main line of their communications at Meiktila, when they thought that his main offensive was directed at Mandalay. Their failure to retake Meiktila sealed the fate of their army in Burma, and on 5 May the 14th Army marched into Rangoon, from which the Japanese forces had retired without a fight.

In 1944 when the Allied Land Forces South East Asia (ALFSEA) had been formed Sir Oliver Leese was given command of the new group. He and Slim had not always seen eye to eye and, after the recapture of Rangoon, Leese proposed to relieve Slim of his command of the 14th Army. Slim threatened to resign and the CIGS, Lord ALANBROOKE, intervened and cancelled Sir Oliver's orders, much to the relief of the 14th Army, who attributed their success in the struggle from retreat to victory to the leadership of their general. Slim was promoted to full general and superseded Leese as Commander-in-Chief of ALFSEA.

From 1946 to 1948 he was Commandant of the Imperial Defence College, and from 1948 to 1953 Chief of the Imperial General Staff with the rank of field-marshal. He was appointed GCB (1950) and GCMG (1952). In 1953 he was appointed Governor-General of Australia, and he and Lady Slim spent six successful years there. In 1954 he was made GCVO, in 1959 KG and in 1960 created viscount. After his return to England Slim received many honours from universities and regiments. He was made a freeman of the City of London and Constable and Governor of Windsor Castle. His book *Defeat into Victory* (1956) was a great success, as were *Courage and other Broadcasts* (1957) and *Unofficial History* (1959).

Slim died in London on 14 December 1970. Winston CHURCHILL, who did not always respect his generals, greatly admired Slim for his ability to distinguish between great and small events. 'I can work with him,' he said.

SMART, WILLIAM GEORGE (BILLY) (1893–1966), circus proprietor, was born on 23 April 1893 in London, the son of Charles Smart, a fairground owner, and his wife, Susan. At fifteen he began work in his father's business at Slough. In 1914 he married Nellie, daughter of Harry Digby, and set up his own fairground business, at first without success, and was forced to become a rag-and-bone merchant, until gradually he became more successful and by the time of the Second World War owned one of the largest fairground concerns in the country.

The war was a set-back but, when it ended, he put all his money into a travelling circus. This soon became well known as one of the most entertaining shows in the country and was helped, when from 1957 it became established as a favourite programme on television. The permanent headquarters of the circus were set up with a zoo at Winkfield, Berkshire, but it travelled the length and breadth of the British Isles.

Billy Smart and his wife had six daughters and four sons and the business was able to carry on after Smart died on 25 July 1966 while conducting the band at his circus at Ipswich.

SMITH, SIR CHARLES EDWARD KINGSFORD (1897–1935). See KINGSFORD SMITH.

SMITH, FREDERICK EDWIN, first EARL OF BIRKENHEAD (1872–1930), politician and Lord Chancellor, was born at

Mr and Mrs Billy Smart with three of their sons, Birmingham, 1971

Birkenhead on 12 July 1872, the eldest son of Frederick Smith, an estate agent, and his wife, Elizabeth, daughter of Edwin Taylor. He was educated at Birkenhead School and Wadham College, Oxford, and was a contemporary of J. A. SIMON and C. B. FRY. He obtained a first in jurisprudence (1895) and was President of the Union (1893). In 1896 he was awarded the Vinerian scholarship, elected a Fellow of Merton College, and during 1897-9 taught law at Oriel College.

In 1899 he was called to the Bar (Gray's Inn) and set up practice in Liverpool. In 1901 he married Margaret Eleanor, daughter of the Revd Henry Furneaux, Fellow of Corpus Christi College, Oxford; they had one son and two daughters.

Between 1902 and 1906 he appeared in some notable cases, first as the defender of Goudie, a bank clerk who pleaded guilty to a charge of fraud and for whom Smith pleaded eloquently for the mitigation of sentence, and later, in the litigation between the Imperial Tobacco Company and an American combine (1902-6).

In 1906 he was elected Conservative MP for the Walton division of Liverpool and moved to London. He appeared in the cases brought in 1907 by LEVER Brothers against the Northcliffe newspapers and successfully defended Ethel le Neve, the mistress of Dr Crippen (1910). His maiden speech in the House, remarkable for its invective and wit, made his parliamentary reputation at the outset. His extravagant way of life, his love of cards and horses, appeared irresponsible to many, and made him enemies as well as friends, his most lasting friendship being with Winston CHURCHILL. In speech after speech, he opposed the liberal policies of the ASQUITH Government, particularly LLOYD GEORGE's 'People's Budget', but when the Finance Bill was passed in the Commons he foresaw the consequences of opposition in the Lords and tried to persuade his party to accept the *fait accompli*. He failed but, throughout the controversy over the Parliament Bill, advised compromise and conciliation. He was in favour of a party truce and the formation of a National Government.

Meanwhile, he carried on his extensive practice at the Bar and took silk in 1908. When BONAR LAW became leader of the Conservative opposition, Smith was sworn of the Privy Council. From 1910 to the outbreak of the First World War, he was heavily engaged in the political struggle against the Home Rule Bill, identifying himself with the resistance of Ulster, to the point of assisting Sir Edward CARSON to prepare for armed conflict. Throughout the early part of 1914 however, he worked for a compromise that would exclude Ulster from the bill.

During the war he became active on behalf of the Government's war efforts until, on the formation of the first Coalition in 1915, he was appointed Solicitor-General, and, within a few months, Attorney-General. In his legal work, he was primarily concerned with the law of prize but he was also a member of the Cabinet until the war ended. In 1918 he became a baronet, and in the general election was returned for the West Derby division of Liverpool; in 1919 he became Lord Chancellor. He held this office until 1922 and his tenure was notable for the legislation relating to the transfer of land, culminating in the Law of Property Act of 1922. The problems of Ireland continued to occupy his attention, and he worked for and supported the treaty of 1921. He was promoted to baron in 1919 and viscount in 1921.

He still continued to advocate a National Government, and was bitterly disappointed when Lloyd George's Coalition Government fell in 1922. In that year he was created Earl of Birkenhead. He refused to join Bonar Law's Government and had little respect for Stanley BALDWIN's first administration, but in 1924, when the Labour Government was defeated, he agreed to accept office as Secretary of State for India. He persuaded Sir John Simon to chair the royal commission to consider constitutional developments, but left office in 1928 before the commission made its report. He was created GCSI (1928). He died in London on 30 September 1930. He was described by Lord BEAVERBROOK as 'the cleverest man in the kingdom'.

SMUTS, JAN CHRISTIAN (1870-1950), South African politician and Prime Minister, was born in Cape Colony on 24 May 1870, the second son of Jacobus Abraham Smuts, a Boer farmer, and his wife, Catharina Petronella de Vries, also of Dutch origin. He was educated at a school in Riebeck West and Victoria College, Stellenbosch (1891). Having won the Ebden scholarship, Smuts entered Christ's College, Cambridge, where he obtained firsts in both parts of the law tripos (1894) and was offered a teaching post, which he refused.

Returning to South Africa in 1895, he worked as a lawyer and journalist, and defended Cecil Rhodes. But the Jameson raid brought him disillusion and caused him, in 1896, to go to Johannesburg and gain admission to the Transvaal Bar. In the following year he married Sybella Margaretha, daughter of Japie Krige, a farmer; they had two sons and four daughters.

In 1898 he became State Attorney and, throughout 1899, during the Anglo-Boer negotiations, worked unsuccessfully for peace. He expounded the Boer case in the pamphlet *A Century of Wrong*. During 1901-2 he was leader of a raiding party into Cape Colony until he was summoned to the Vereeniging Conference and succeeded in persuading the Boer leaders to accept the peace terms. On the formation of the Het Volk (the People's party) he was sent to England to seek responsible government and, when this was granted to the Transvaal in 1906 and the Orange River Colony in 1907, he returned to be Colonial Secretary and Minister of Education in Louis Botha's Government of the Transvaal.

In 1910 he pressed his plan for union and, when Botha was elected premier of the Union, Smuts became Minister of Mines, Defence, and the Interior. He built up a South African Defence Force, and used it in 1914 to suppress a general strike on the Rand. During the First World War Botha and Smuts suppressed rebellion at home and in 1915-16 successfully defeated the Germans in South-West Africa (Namibia). In 1917 he went to London to represent South Africa in the Imperial War Cabinet and accepted the invitation of LLOYD GEORGE to join the British War Cabinet. He was now becoming recognized as a statesman of world stature.

He was one of the first to work for a British Commonwealth of Nations and for a League of Nations. He was also the leading advocate of a mandates system. He was disappointed that the peace treaties were not more lenient, and returned to South Africa in 1919 protesting against them.

In that year Smuts succeeded Botha as Prime Minister, and found himself faced with difficult, post-war problems of dissension and unrest, culminating in another Rand strike in 1922. In 1924 his Government was defeated and he was out of office until 1933. He used that period to set out his philosophy in *Holism and Evolution* (1926), lectured at Oxford and in the USA, and in 1931 presided at the centenary meeting of the British Association.

From 1933 to 1939 he entered a coalition as Deputy Prime Minister under J. B. M. Hertzog, and in 1934 their two parties were united as the United South Africa National Party. This alliance did not survive the outbreak of the Second World War since Hertzog was pro-German and proposed a policy of neutrality which Smuts rejected. Hertzog resigned, and from 1939 to 1948 Smuts was Prime Minister again.

In 1941 he was appointed a British field-marshal, and South African forces played an important part in the war in North Africa and Italy. His friend, Winston CHURCHILL, frequently sought his advice. When the war ended, reaction set in in South Africa as it had in 1919. Smuts's Government was defeated in 1948, and he died on 11 September 1950 on his farm at Irene, near Pretoria.

He was rewarded with many honours. He was sworn of the Privy Council in 1917 and appointed CH. In 1947 he was appointed OM. He became a KC in 1906 and FRS in 1930. He received many academic honours, was Chancellor of Cambridge University (1948), and the Smuts chair of British Commonwealth history was founded there in 1953. A statue of Smuts by Jacob EPSTEIN was unveiled in Parliament Square, London, in 1956.

SMYTH, DAME ETHEL MARY (1858–1944), composer, author, and feminist, was born on 23 April 1858 at Sidcup, the daughter of Lt.-Col. (later Major-General) John Hall Smyth, CB, and his wife, Emma, daughter of Charles Struth. She was educated in Putney, and from the age of twelve wanted to be a musician. A musical career was furiously opposed by her father, but in 1877 she got away from home to study at the Conservatorium, Leipzig, where she was helped by Elizabeth, the wife of Heinrich von Herzogenberg under whom she studied.

Ethel Smyth, 1921; nine years earlier she had conducted the 'March of the Women' with a toothbrush from the window of her Holloway cell

Her early chamber works, in the German romantic style, were performed in Germany; but she first attracted attention in England with her Mass in D, performed at the Albert Hall in 1893 and revived in 1924. Her operas, *Fantasio*, *Der Wald*, and *Der Strandrecht*, were all performed in Germany between 1898 and 1906. In 1909 *Der Strandrecht* was first performed in English as *The Wreckers*, conducted by Sir Thomas BEECHAM. The First World War prevented *The Boatswain's Mate* (after the story by W. W. Jacobs) from appearing in Germany, and it had its première in London in 1916. *Fête Galante* was produced in Birmingham in 1923 and *Entente Cordiale* at Bristol in 1926.

Ethel Smyth was an indefatigable crusader, not only to become the first woman to gain recognition as a composer of operas, oratorios, and concertos, but also in the cause of women's suffrage, for which she went to prison. 'The March of the Women' was composed as the battle-song of the suffragettes.

Her ebullience and eccentricity are amply revealed in her autobiographical books, *Impressions that Remained* (2 vols., 1919), *Streaks of Life* (1921), *A Final Burning of Boats* (1928), *Beecham and Pharaoh* (1935), *As Time Went On . . .* (1936), and *What Happened Next* (1940).

She was the first woman to receive an honorary degree at Oxford (1926); she received similar degrees from other universities, and in 1922 was appointed DBE. She died, unmarried, at Woking on 9 May 1944.

SNOW, CHARLES PERCY, BARON SNOW (1905–1980), author and controversialist, was born in Leicester on 15 October 1905, the second of four sons of William Edward Snow, FRCO, a clerk in a shoe factory, and his wife, Ada Sophia Robinson. He won a scholarship from a local elementary school to Alderman Newton's Grammar School, Leicester, studied at University College (later the University of Leicester), where he obtained a first in chemistry and an M.Sc. in physics (1928), and went on with a scholarship to do postgraduate research at the Cavendish Laboratory in Cambridge. In 1930 he became a Ph.D. and Fellow of Christ's College. He was tutor of the college from 1935 to 1945.

His research in infra-red spectroscopy failed, since the results of experiments did not confirm his theories but, although he could not claim to have succeeded as a scientist, his interest in chemistry and physics remained undiminished, and he undertook the task of explaining the achievements of his contemporaries to the world. His reputation was made, however, as a publicist and a novelist.

In 1932 he published his first novel *Death under Sail*, and in 1934 *The Search*, followed by the series which began with *Strangers and Brothers* (1940), in which the leading character, Lewis Eliot, an academic lawyer, involved with dons and civil servants, is a mirror image of the man that Snow himself would have liked to be. The series contained a number of novels, woven around the same characters, including *The New Men* (1954), dealing with the early efforts to develop the atomic bomb, *The Affair* (1960), and *The Corridors of Power* (1964), in which the author drew upon his knowledge of the workings of Whitehall departments. In between came *The Masters* (1951), probably Snow's best work, in which he recounted the intrigues of dons involved in the election of a new head of a college. For *The New Men* and *The Masters* Snow was awarded the James Tait Black memorial prize. Some of these novels were produced as plays, notably *The Affair* (1961–2) and *The Masters* (1963–4), both adapted by Ronald Millar.

Snow was a public servant as well as a writer. In 1939 he became concerned with the deployment of scientific manpower, in 1942 he was appointed Director of Technical Personnel at the Ministry of Labour, and from 1945 till 1960 was a Civil Service Commissioner, recruiting scientists to government posts. He was appointed CBE in 1943, knighted in 1957, and became a life peer in 1964. His excursion into politics was not successful. He accepted appointment as Parliamentary Secretary to the Ministry of Technology, set up by the 1964 Labour Government, but this experiment was a failure and he retired in 1966. He was, however, a popular figure in the House of Lords, where his ungainly figure and heavy jowled features seemed to give weight to his ponderous utterances.

In 1950 Snow married his fellow novelist, Pamela Hansford Johnson, daughter of R. Kenneth Johnson, who had previously been married to Gordon Stewart; she and Snow had one son, Philip, who became a scholar at Eton.

In his post-war years, Snow became increasingly concerned with what he saw as the vital importance of understanding between scientists and artists and humanists. He had acquired an extensive knowledge of European literature, including the works of Russian authors, and had retained his early interest in scientific progress. In his Rede lectures at Cambridge in 1959, *The Two Cultures and the Scientific Revolution*, he argued that the ignorance of humanists about science was as harmful as the ignorance of scientists about art and literature. These views brought him into conflict with the professional scholars of English literature, led by F. R. LEAVIS, University Reader in English at Cambridge.

He made a further excursion into controversy with his 1960 Godkin lectures at Harvard, published as *Science and Government* (1961) and *Postscript* (1962). In these he declaimed against the influence of 'the Prof', F. A. LINDEMANN, who was scientific adviser to Winston CHURCHILL during the Second World War. Lindemann had disagreed with the views of Sir Henry TIZARD on the development of radar and the value of saturation bombing of German towns. Snow's sympathies were with Tizard.

He was also keenly concerned with the effort required to achieve some understanding between the Soviet Union and the West, especially in the field of books, and in this respect supported the Anglo-Russian activities of the British Council. In his later years, however, Snow became increasingly disillusioned with a world in which his hopes seemed doomed to disappointment, and rationalism and good sense appeared to be overridden by violence and extremism. He died in London on 1 July 1980, having been awarded many academic honours by British and Russian universities.

SNOWDEN, PHILIP, VISCOUNT SNOWDEN (1864-1937), politician, was born at Ickornshaw, near Keighley, Yorkshire, on 18 July 1864, the only son of John Snowden, a weaver, and his wife, Martha, daughter of Peter Nelson. He was brought up as a radical and a Wesleyan Methodist, educated at the local elementary school, and at fifteen went to work as a clerk, until at twenty-two he became a minor civil servant. This career was cut short in 1891 when he was permanently crippled in a cycle accident. During his convalescence he became a socialist and, on recovery, worked for the Independent Labour party as the Editor of a local paper, and from 1903 to 1906 as National Chairman of the party. In 1905 he married Ethel, daughter of Richard Annakin, of Harrogate; they had no children.

He was unsuccessful at parliamentary elections in 1900 and 1902, but in 1906 was elected for Blackburn, a seat which he held until 1918. He quickly made his mark in the Commons as an eloquent, and sometimes vitriolic, speaker on national finance. He strongly supported LLOYD GEORGE's 'People's Budget', but during the First World War was a pacifist champion of conscientious objectors. He was out of Parliament from 1918 to 1922.

In 1922 he was returned for Colne Valley and, when Ramsay MACDONALD formed the first Labour Government in 1924, Snowden became Chancellor of the Exchequer and PC. He did not support the general strike of 1926 and was becoming disillusioned with the Independent Labour party. He accepted office again, however, when MacDonald, for whom he had little respect, formed his second administration in 1929. At the Hague Conference on the Young Plan, he acquired a reputation as 'the iron chancellor' by demanding changes to Britain's financial advantage, which in effect threatened the success of the conference without being of lasting benefit to the Exchequer.

By 1931 Britain was in the throes of the world depression and Snowden, faced by a serious financial crisis, brought down upon himself the wrath of his own party in trying to balance the budget by cutting public expenditure and in welcoming the findings of the May Committee which recommended further drastic economies in a report which Maynard KEYNES called 'the most foolish document I ever had the misfortune to read'.

When MacDonald formed his National Government, Snowden remained at his post to put the recommendations of the May Committee into effect. In the autumn of 1931, he was forced to suspend the gold standard. At the ensuing general election he did not stand; he accepted a seat in the House of Lords as Viscount Snowden. He remained in the Government as Lord Privy Seal until, as a free trader, he found his position to be impossible when the scheme of preferential tariffs, agreed at the Ottawa Conference, was introduced in 1932.

He resigned, and concentrated on writing his autobiography which appeared in two volumes in 1934. He died at Tilford, Surrey on 15 May 1937.

SODDY, FREDERICK (1877-1956), chemist, was born at Eastbourne on 2 September 1877, the youngest of seven sons of Benjamin Soddy, a corn merchant, and his wife, Hannah Green. He was educated at Eastbourne College, University College, Aberystwyth, and Merton College, Oxford, where he obtained a first in chemistry in 1898.

He was appointed as a demonstrator at McGill University, Montreal, and there he worked with Ernest RUTHERFORD, investigating radioactivity in thorium salts, research which led to the formation of the theory of atomic disintegration. In 1903 he returned to London, worked with Sir William RAMSAY, and with him demonstrated the production of helium from radium.

From 1904 till 1914, Soddy was lecturer in physical chemistry and radioactivity at Glasgow, and research under his supervision led to the formulation of the 'displacement law' and the conception of isotopes. In 1914 he moved to Aberdeen, but his research work was interrupted by the First World War, during which he was engaged upon scientific work in aid of the war effort.

From 1919 to 1936 Soddy was Dr Lee's Professor of Chemistry at Oxford. He had passed his peak in scientific research and spent much of his time considering more general matters, such as the Irish question and the national monetary system, subjects which often led him into controversy.

His publications include *The Interpretation of Radium* (1909) and *The Interpretation of the Atom* (1932). He was elected FRS in 1910 and received the Nobel prize for chemistry in 1921.

In 1908 he married Winifred Moller, daughter of (Sir) George Beilby; they had no children; his wife assisted him in his research and some papers were published in their joint names. Soddy died in Brighton on 22 September 1956.

SOMERVILLE, MARY (1897-1963), educationalist and broadcasting executive, was born in New Zealand on 1 November 1897, the daughter of the Revd J. A. Somerville, and his wife, Agnes Fleming. She was brought up in Scotland, and was educated at Abbey School, Melrose, Selkirk High School, and Somerville College, Oxford, where she met John REITH, who in 1927 became Director-General of the BBC.

In 1925 she was appointed Schools Assistant to J. C. Stobart, Director of Education, BBC. Since Reith regarded the function of the BBC as educational, she was able to embark on her career with good prospects of achieving her ideal of programmes of high educational quality, particularly in broadcasts to schools. In 1929 she became responsible for all such programmes and Secretary to the Central Council of School Broadcasting.

In 1947 she was promoted to Assistant Controller of the Talks Division of the BBC, and in 1950 became the first woman to become a Controller. When she retired in 1955, she was recognized as the creator of broadcasting to schools.

Basil Spence with his design for the new Coventry Cathedral, November 1951

She was appointed OBE in 1935; she became an honorary MA (Manchester) in 1943. In 1947 she lectured on school broadcasting in Australia and the USA.

In 1928 she married Ralph Penton Brown; they had a son, but she divorced her husband in 1945, and in 1962 married Eric Rowan Davies. She died at Bath a year later on 1 September 1963.

SPENCE, SIR BASIL URWIN (1907-1976), architect, was born on 13 August 1907 in Bombay, the elder son of Urwin Spence, an Indian Civil Servant, and his wife, Daisy Crisp. He was educated at George Watson's College, Edinburgh, the Edinburgh College of Art, and University College London. He qualified in 1933 and worked for a year with Sir Edwin LUTYENS on the drawings for the Viceroy's house, New Delhi. In 1934 he married Mary Joan, daughter of John Ferris, a farmer; they had one son and one daughter.

During the Second World War he served with the Royal Artillery. In 1947 he was Chief Architect for the 'Britain Can Make It' exhibition, in 1949 for the Scottish Industries Exhibition, and in 1951 designed the Sea and Ships pavilion at the Festival of Britain exhibition.

In 1951 he won first prize in the competition for a new cathedral at Coventry. He worked enthusiastically on this project, lecturing in Canada to raise money, and commissioning Graham SUTHERLAND, John Piper, and Jacob EPSTEIN to contribute tapestry, stained glass and sculpture to his plans for the new cathedral, which included his imaginative decision to use the bombed remains of the old cathedral as an approach to the new building.

This commission made his reputation, and later he designed new office buildings, schools, churches, and university buildings, including the new Sussex University (1962-72), in which his buildings were skilfully set on a magnificent downland site, making the most of their beautiful surroundings. His designs were not invariably accepted without criticism; in the case of Knightsbridge Barracks, the tower was thought, by some, to intrude upon the Hyde Park scenery.

In 1958 he became President of the Royal Institute of British Architects; he was elected ARA (1953) and RA (1960); he was appointed OBE (1948), knighted (1960), and admitted to the Order of Merit (1962). He held a number of academic posts and received honorary degrees. Spence died at Eye, Suffolk, on 19 November 1976.

SPENCER, SIR STANLEY (1891-1959), artist, was born at Cookham-on-Thames on 30 June 1891, the seventh son in a family of eleven children of William Spencer, organist and music teacher, and his wife, Anna Caroline Slack. He had no formal education but studied at the Technical School, Maidenhead in 1907 and a year later went to the Slade School. In 1912 he won the Melville Nettleship prize for a painting *The Nativity*. While still a student, he painted a series of notable pictures including *Apple Gatherers* (1912-13), which was acquired by the Tate Gallery. Most of his work was inspired by a trance-like vision of Cookham scenes and biblical stories, inter-mixed in an ecstatic fantasy in which normal everyday things were irradiated by a heavenly light.

His life in Cookham was interrupted by the First World War, in which he served in the RAMC and the 17th Royal Berkshires. After the war, he finished *Swan Upping* (Tate), which he had left uncompleted for four years, and from 1919 to 1923 painted most of his finest works, such as *The Robing*

Stanley Spencer sketching in the Clyde shipyards, October 1943

of Christ and *The Disrobing of Christ* (Tate). He held his first one-man exhibition in 1927.

In 1925 he married Hilda Anne Carline, and his daughters were born in 1925 and 1930. From this time, his personal life became confused and complicated. His wife showed signs of mental unbalance, and he was heavily in debt, his affairs inordinately disorganized. He was being maintained largely by the generosity of his friends and, when he became involved with another woman, Patricia Preece, he had to support both women and two daughters by turning out 'pot-boilers' in the form of landscapes and flower-pieces. Even though these sold well, he was frequently being sued by Hilda for maintenance, owed large sums to the income-tax authorities, whose demands he ignored, and exorcised his sexual frustration with erotic paintings, including a number of nudes of Patricia Preece, which were difficult to sell.

In 1935 he resigned from the Royal Academy, of which he had been elected ARA in 1932. Two of his pictures had been rejected for the summer exhibition. In 1937 Hilda divorced him and he married Patricia, but still professed to love Hilda and, according to Patricia, wanted all three of them to live together. In 1938 he had a breakdown and, for some months, was unable to paint. His dealer, Dudley Tooth, took over the management of his finances and contrived to create some order out of chaos.

Between 1939 and 1942 Spencer painted seven of the series of eight pictures of 'Christ in the Wilderness' and during 1940-5 painted war pictures of shipyards. While he was at Port Glasgow, the sight of a cemetery inspired him to a series of resurrection pictures, including *Resurrection: Port Glasgow* (1947-50) bought by the Tate. In 1945 he returned

to Cookham, where he continued to paint until his death. A huge altar-piece in praise of Hilda, who had died of cancer in 1950, was incomplete when he died.

Retrospective exhibitions of his work were held in Leeds in 1947 and at the Tate in 1955. Spencer was appointed CBE in 1950 and knighted in 1959. He rejoined the Academy as RA in 1950. He died at Cliveden on 14 December 1959 and was buried in Cookham churchyard. Elizabeth Rothenstein, writing in the *DNB*, described him as 'the outstanding—the most potent and fertile—imaginative painter of the English-speaking people in the first half of the twentieth century'.

SPENCER JONES, SIR HAROLD (1890-1960), astronomer, was born in London on 29 March 1890, the elder son of Henry Charles Jones, an accountant, and his wife, Sarah Ryland, formerly a schoolmistress. He was educated at Latymer Upper School, Hammersmith and Jesus College, Cambridge, where he was a scholar, and obtained firsts in both parts of the mathematical tripos (1909-11), and part ii of the natural sciences tripos (physics) in 1912. He was elected Isaac Newton student in 1912 and in 1913 was second Smith's prizeman and elected to a research fellowship at Jesus College.

In 1913 he was appointed to a post in the Royal Observatory, Greenwich, and during the First World War worked on optical instrument design for the Ministry of Munitions. During this time, he began research on the rotation of the earth and the system of astronomical constants and wrote his book *General Astronomy* published in 1922. In 1918 he married Gladys Mary, daughter of Albert Edward Owen, a civil engineer; they had two sons.

In 1923 he was appointed Astronomer at the Royal Observatory at the Cape of Good Hope, South Africa, a post which he held until 1933, when he was recalled to Greenwich to become the tenth Astronomer Royal, succeeding Sir Frank Dyson. In 1925 he had been awarded the Sc.D. (Cambridge). In 1939 he published an important paper 'The rotation of the Earth, and the secular accelerations of the Sun, Moon and planets', which demonstrated that the observed fluctuations were due to the irregularities in the rate of rotation of the earth and led directly to the adoption, in 1950, of the concept of Ephemeris Time.

Spencer Jones was responsible for the decision to remove the Royal Observatory from Greenwich to Herstmonceux Castle in Sussex, although the move was not completed until after his retirement at the end of 1955. He also played a leading part in obtaining approval for the 98-inch Isaac Newton Telescope to be erected at the new site. He made notable contributions to time-measurement and horology, and the application of geo-magnetism to navigation. He was President of the British Horological Institute from 1939 and the inaugural President of the Institute of Navigation in 1947.

After his retirement as Astronomer Royal, he took an important part in the organization of international science and was President of the International Astronomical Union from 1945 to 1948. He was Secretary-General of the International Council of Scientific Unions from 1956 to 1958 and was also one of the most active supporters of the International Geophysical Year whose *Annuals* he edited.

He became FRS in 1930 and honorary Fellow of Jesus College, Cambridge in 1933. In 1943 he was knighted and in 1955 appointed KBE. He died in London on 3 November 1960.

SPILSBURY, SIR BERNARD HENRY (1877-1947), pathologist, was born on 16 May 1877 at Leamington, the elder son of James Spilsbury, an analytical chemist, and his wife, Marion Elizabeth Joy. He was educated at schools in Leamington, London, and Manchester, and at Magdalen College, Oxford (1899). He studied medicine at St Mary's Hospital, Paddington, and qualified in 1905; before qualifying he was already an assistant demonstrator, specializing in pathology. In 1908 Spilsbury married Edith Caroline Mary, daughter of William Henry Horton, surgeon-dentist; they had three sons and a daughter.

He acquired a reputation in the lecture-room and in coroners' and criminal courts as an investigator of meticulous detail. He first came into prominence in the trial of Dr Crippen in 1910, when his evidence supported that of A. J. Pepper, with whom he had worked at St Mary's, and the identification of a scar on a piece of skin was an important element in the prosecution's case. He was appointed junior honorary pathologist to the Home Office, where another old associate (Sir) William Willcox was Senior Analyst.

Spilsbury gave specialist evidence at other famous murder trials, including those of Seddon (1912), Smith (the 'Brides in the Bath' case, 1915), Voisin and Armstrong (1923), Mahon (1924), and Thorne (1925). In all of these cases his forthright evidence, based upon his firm conviction of the validity of his findings, made a marked impression on the jury to the exasperation of defending counsel.

In 1923 he left St Mary's for St Bartholomew's Hospital and in that year was knighted. He was also a lecturer in forensic medicine at University College and St Thomas's Hospital. For thirty-five years he was a witness in almost every murder trial in the south of England, his evidence backed by long hours of careful investigation in his laboratory. The cases in which he appeared between 1930 and 1944 included those of Fox (1930), Rouse (1931), Barney (1932), Chaplin (1938), and Cummins (1942). The last case in which he gave evidence was that of the murder of de Antiquis in 1947.

The years during and immediately after the war were increasingly depressing for him. One son, a house-surgeon at St Thomas's Hospital, was killed in an air-raid (1940), one of his sisters died in 1941, and another son died of tuberculosis in 1945. Spilsbury himself, crippled by arthritis and threatened with a coronary thrombosis, committed suicide in his laboratory at University College on 17 December 1947.

SPOONER, WILLIAM ARCHIBALD (1844-1930), Warden of New College, Oxford, was born on 22 July 1844 in London, the eldest son of William Spooner, a barrister and county court judge, and his wife, Jane Lydia, daughter of John Wilson of Seacroft Hall, Leeds. He was an albino and suffered from defects of eyesight and speech. He was educated at Oswestry School and New College, Oxford, where he was a scholar and obtained firsts in Classical Mods and Greats (1864-6). He was elected a Fellow of New College (1867), lecturer (1868), tutor (1869), and held the office of dean from 1876 to 1889. He was ordained deacon in 1872 and priest in 1875, became an honorary Canon of Christ Church in 1899, and DD in 1903. In 1878 he married Frances Wycliffe, daughter of Harvey Goodwin, Bishop of Carlyle; they had two sons and five daughters.

From 1903 to 1924 Spooner was Warden of New College. He did valuable work as an examiner for Greats, but he also supported the promotion of studies in the natural sciences.

He lectured on ancient history, philosophy, and divinity, and published *The Histories of Tacitus* (1891) and small volumes on *Bishop Butler* (1901) and *William of Wykeham* (1909). He will be remembered, however, for his lapses of speech (metaphasis) which added the word 'spoonerism' to the English language. Many spoonerisms attributed to him were undoubtedly apocryphal, but the most famous genuine example is 'Kinquering kongs their titles take'. Spooner died at Oxford on 29 August 1930.

SPRY, CONSTANCE (1886-1960), artist in flower arrangement, was born in Derby on 5 December 1886, the only daughter and eldest of six children of George Fletcher, a railway clerk, and his wife, Henrietta Maria Clark. Her father became assistant secretary in the department of agriculture in Ireland, and she was educated at Alexandra School and College, Dublin. On leaving college, she helped Lady Aberdeen in her work for sick children.

In 1910 she married James Heppell Marr and they had a son, but the marriage was not a happy one. During the First World War Constance returned to England and became head of women's staff at the Department of Aircraft Production of the Ministry of Munitions; there she met Henry Ernest Spry, who had been seconded from the Indian Civil Service. After the war Constance was appointed Principal of the LCC day continuation school in Homerton. Spry retired from the ICS, both succeeded in obtaining divorces, and they married and settled at Abinger in Surrey.

She had for many years been interested in floral arrangement, and in 1928 resigned from her teaching post and, with the encouragement of her friends, Sidney L. Bernstein and Norman Wilkinson, opened her own small shop near Victoria Station called 'Flower Decorations'. Within a few years she was so successful with her artistic approach to the use of flowers, leaves, and fruit for decoration that she was able to move to the West End, and was soon in great demand for society weddings and other functions. She also became a lecturer on the new art she had invented and opened a school to train others in the work.

In 1935 she prepared the floral decorations for the wedding of the Duke of Gloucester and among her clients she was able to number the Prince of Wales (later Edward VIII) and the Duke of Kent. By this time, her fame was spreading to the United States and she visited America to lecture on her skills. She was also responsible for the flowers when the Duke and Duchess of Windsor were married. Her greatest success came when she provided the flowers for the wedding of Princess Elizabeth, and later, when the Princess became Queen, Constance Spry advised the Ministry of Works on the decorations for the coronation, and did the flowers for Westminster Abbey and for parts of the route of the procession. In 1953 she was appointed OBE.

She wrote a number of books on flower arrangement and designed vases and floral carpets and prints. She was also very active on behalf of the Royal Gardeners' Orphan Fund. She died on 3 January 1960 at Winkfield Place, near Windsor, which she had bought and turned into a residential school for young people to learn all aspects of running a home efficiently.

SPY (1851-1922), cartoonist, whose real name was Leslie Ward, was born in London on 21 November 1851, the eldest son of Edward Matthew Ward, and his wife, Henrietta Mary Ada Ward, both artists. Her father and grandfather were engravers and she was related to the portrait painter John

Spy cartoon of F. E. Smith, *Vanity Fair*, January 1907

Jackson, and George Morland. Leslie Ward was educated at Eton and exhibited at the Royal Academy while still at school. He joined the Royal Academy Schools in 1871, and from 1873 for thirty-six years contributed regularly to *Vanity Fair* under the pseudonym of 'Spy'. His cartoons of well-known people: politicians, sportsmen, judges, jockeys, authors, musicians, actors, generals, and admirals were portraits in colour, reproduced by lithography, and they appeared, not only in *Vanity Fair*, but on the walls of London clubs, college commonrooms, and in private houses.

Unlike other cartoonists such as David Low or VICKY, he did not caricature his subjects but portrayed them as they appeared to their contemporaries in real life. In 1915 he published his recollections, *Forty Years of 'Spy'*. In 1899 he married Judith Mary Topham-Watney, daughter of Major Richard Topham, 4th Hussars and 16th Bengal Cavalry; they had one daughter.

Ward was knighted in 1918 and died in London on 15 May 1922.

STANFORD, SIR CHARLES VILLIERS (1852–1924), composer, conductor, and teacher of music, was born in Dublin on 30 September 1852, the only child of John Stanford, a distinguished lawyer and keen amateur musician, and his wife, Mary, daughter of William Henn, Master in Chancery. He was educated in Dublin at Henry Tilney Bassett's School. His first music teachers, all of them able Irish musicians, introduced him to the music of Brahms, which was to influence his own compositions for the whole of his life. At the age of eighteen, he went to Queen's College, Cambridge as a choral scholar.

In 1873 he was appointed organist of Trinity College, Cambridge, a post which he held until 1892, but in the years 1874–6 he was able to spend long periods in Germany studying music with Carl H. C. Reinecke and Friedrich Kiel. By the time he was twenty-four he was attracting notice as a composer with his music for Tennyson's *Queen Mary* and his First Symphony. His reputation was established by the Cambridge production of the *Eumenides* of Aeschylus for which he composed the music (1885).

In 1878 he had married Jane Anna Maria, daughter of Henry Champion Wetton, of Shere, near Guildford; they had one son and one daughter.

From 1883 to 1924 Stanford was Professor of Composition and Orchestral Playing at the Royal College of Music, and from 1887 to 1924 Professor of Music at Cambridge. Unlike his contemporary Hubert PARRY, Stanford did not publish many books on music but as a teacher he was particularly influential, numbering among his pupils, during his forty years at the Royal College, Ralph VAUGHAN WILLIAMS, Gustav HOLST, John IRELAND, and Arthur BLISS.

Stanford was, perhaps, the most versatile British composer of his time. His efforts in the cause of opera were not so successful as his choral works, of which his *Requiem* (1897) and *Stabat Mater* (1907) are the best known. He composed seven symphonies, notably 'The Irish' (1887), his third, and 'L'Allegro ed il Penseroso' (1895), his fifth. He was also a prolific writer of chamber music and his church music during his time was highly regarded, in particular his Anglican church service known as 'Stanford in B flat' (1879). However, his best work was probably his composition of songs for solo voice and chorus such as *Songs of the Sea* (1905) and *Songs of the Fleet* (1910).

Stanford was also a notable conductor; in the 1870s he conducted the Cambridge University Music Society in some of the first English performances of the works of Brahms. From 1885 to 1902 he was Director of the Bach Choir, London, and from 1901 to 1910, Director of the Leeds Festival. He received many honorary degrees and in 1902 was knighted. He died in London on 29 March 1924, and was buried in Westminster Abbey.

STANLEY, EDWARD GEORGE VILLIERS, seventeenth EARL OF DERBY (1865–1948), was born in London on 4 April 1865, the eldest son of Frederick Arthur Stanley, who became the sixteenth earl in 1893. He was educated at Wellington, and joined the Grenadier Guards in 1885, was aide-de-camp to his father, Governor-General of Canada (1889–91), and in 1892 was elected Conservative MP for the West Houghton division of Lancashire. In 1889 he married Lady Alice Maude Olivia Montagu, daughter of the seventh Duke of Manchester; they had two sons and a daughter. In 1895 he became a junior Lord of the Treasury, and during the Boer War served as Private Secretary to the Commander-in-Chief, Lord Roberts. He was appointed CB in 1900.

From 1901 to 1906 he was a member of the Government, during 1901–3 as Financial Secretary to the War Office, and during 1903–6 as Postmaster-General. He lost his seat in 1906, and succeeded to the earldom in 1908. During the years up to the outbreak of the First World War, he was active in public work, mainly in the north of England. He was Lord Mayor of Liverpool in 1911, President of the Liverpool Chamber of Commerce (1910-43), Chairman of the Cotton Growing Association, and of the committee for the building of Liverpool Cathedral, and Chancellor of the University.

In 1914 he raised five battalions of the King's Regiment; he was in favour of conscription but agreed in 1915 to become director of recruitment and to inaugurate the 'Derby Scheme', under which men attested their readiness to enlist and to await their call to the colours. The scheme proved to be just a stepping stone to conscription.

In 1916 Derby was appointed Under-Secretary of State at the War Office, and when LLOYD GEORGE became Prime Minister, he was promoted to Secretary of State for War. In this post he found that he was a buffer between the Chief of the Imperial Staff, Sir William Robertson, and Sir Douglas HAIG on the one hand, and Lloyd George on the other. The Prime Minister had no hesitation in going behind his back, and Derby was more than once determined to resign. When Robertson was replaced, he did resign but, when it became clear that Haig would remain to work in collaboration with the War Cabinet, he withdrew his resignation. In 1918, however, he handed over to Lord MILNER and accepted appointment as Ambassador in Paris where he remained until 1920.

In 1921 he travelled incognito to Dublin to negotiate, without success, with DE VALERA. In 1922 he refused an offer of the India Office. In 1924 he retired from politics, and became Lord Lieutenant of Lancashire in 1928. In 1920 he had founded the Franco-British Society, and he was President of the Pilgrims Society during 1945-8.

Lord Derby was renowned as a popular sportsman. He won the St Leger six times and the Derby twice. He was a Steward of the Jockey Club five times. He was an intimate friend of King George V. He was appointed KCVO (1905), GCVO (1908), KG (1915), and GCB (1920).

In 1927 his daughter died in the hunting field. His elder son, Edward, died in 1938 when he was Secretary of State for the Dominions. Lord Derby died at Knowsley, his home, on 4 February 1948, and was succeeded by his grandson.

STANSGATE, first VISCOUNT (1877-1960). See BENN, WILLIAM WEDGWOOD.

STEED, HENRY WICKHAM (1871-1956), Editor of *The Times*, was born at Long Melford, Suffolk, on 10 October 1871, the son of Joshua George Steed, a solicitor's clerk, and his wife, Fanny Wickham. He was educated at Sudbury Grammar School and studied at Berlin University and the Sorbonne, Paris. Sending reports to English newspapers led in 1896 to his appointment as *The Times* correspondent in Berlin, and then in 1897 as Rome correspondent.

From 1902 to 1913 he held a similar post in Vienna, and in 1913 published *The Hapsburg Monarchy*. Lord NORTHCLIFFE appointed him head of the Foreign Department of *The Times* (1914), and throughout the First World War he was closely concerned in organizing propaganda in enemy countries.

In 1919, when Northcliffe and Geoffrey DAWSON disagreed over Northcliffe's interference with editorial policy, Steed succeeded Dawson as Editor. During his three years in the post, he tried to maintain the political independence of the paper, but he distrusted the policies of LLOYD GEORGE

and he and Northcliffe played a part in the decision of the Conservative party to withdraw from the coalition in 1922.

Later that year, however, Northcliffe sold *The Times* to John ASTOR and John Walter, and the new proprietors dismissed Steed and reinstated Dawson.

From 1923 to 1930, he edited the *Review of Reviews* which he had bought. He also published his autobiography, *Through Thirty Years* (2 vols., 1924), and lectured at home and abroad. From 1925 to 1938 he lectured on Central European history at King's College, London, and from 1937 to 1947 was a leading commentator on world affairs for the BBC. In 1937 Steed married Violet Sybille, daughter of James Francis Mason, of Eynsham Hall, Witney. He died on 13 January 1956 at Wootton-by-Woodstock.

STOCKS, MARY DANVERS, BARONESS STOCKS (1891-1975), Principal of Westfield College and broadcaster, was born in London on 25 July 1891, the daughter of Roland Danvers Brinton, MD, MRCP, and his wife, Helen Constance Rendel. She was educated at St Paul's School and the London School of Economics, where she obtained a B. Sc. (Econ.) and became an assistant lecturer (1916-19). She was also a lecturer in economics at King's College for Women (1918-19).

In 1913 she married John Leofric Stocks, Fellow and tutor of St John's College, Oxford; they had one son and two daughters. In 1924 Stocks was appointed Professor of Philosophy at Manchester and his wife became an extension lecturer and extra-mural tutor in the university (1924-37). She was also a JP (1930-6).

In 1936 her husband was appointed Vice-Chancellor of Liverpool University but he died suddenly in 1937. During 1938-9 she was General-Secretary of the London Council of Social Service. In 1939 she was appointed Principal of Westfield College, London and, until she retired in 1951, did much to enhance the reputation of the College, steering it through the difficult war years (1939-45).

She was a member of a number of Government committees and became well known to the general public by her skill as a broadcaster, particularly in the BBC's 'Any Questions' programmes. She was always interested in the work of the WEA, and in 1953 published *The Workers' Educational Association, the First Fifty Years*. She also published other works on social and educational matters, including *Eleanor Rathbone* (1949), *Ernest Simon of Manchester* (1963), and *A Hundred Years of District Nursing* (1960). Her autobiography, *My Commonplace Book*, appeared in 1970, followed by *Still More Commonplaces* (1973). She received honorary degrees from Manchester and Liverpool, and was raised to the peerage in 1966. She described one of her recreations as 'attending the House of Lords'.

She died in London on 6 July 1975.

STOLL, SIR OSWALD (1866-1942), impresario, was born at Melbourne, Australia, on 20 January 1866, the only child of Oswald James Alexander Gray, an engineer, and his wife, Adelaide, daughter of Patrick Macdonnell, a surveyor, of Dublin. His father died in 1869, and his mother married in 1879 John George Stoll, owner of the Parthenon music-hall in Liverpool, and changed her son's name to Stoll. He worked in the music-hall from the age of fourteen.

In 1889 he acquired a music-hall at Cardiff, and later bought up others, eight in all, and sought to improve the quality of the entertainment. In 1900 he merged his interests with those of (Sir) Edward Moss and his partners and the new company, Moss Empires Ltd., opened the London Hippodrome (1900) and the Coliseum (1904).

In 1892 he married Harriet, daughter of Samuel Lewis, manager of an ironworks; they had a daughter; Harriet died in 1902, and in 1903 he married Millicent, daughter of Joseph Shaw, architect and builder; they had three sons.

In 1910 Stoll broke with Moss Empires, retained control of the Coliseum, purchased the Alhambra, and in 1916, as Chairman of the Opera House Syndicate Ltd., acquired the London Opera House and turned it into a cinema, which in 1919 became the property of Stoll Picture Theatre (Kingsway) Ltd., of which Stoll remained Chairman until he died.

The Coliseum and the Alhambra during their heyday billed most of the leading variety entertainers of the time, but, with a change in public taste from the end of the First World War, variety was replaced by large musical extravaganzas.

During the war, Stoll set up the War Seal (Sir Oswald Stoll) Foundation for disabled officers, and made generous donations to this and other charitable causes. He was knighted in 1919.

Stoll died in London on 9 January 1942.

STOPES, MARIE CHARLOTTE CARMICHAEL (1880-1958), scientist and sex reformer, was born in Edinburgh on 15 October 1880, the elder daughter of Henry Stopes, and his wife, Charlotte Carmichael, a pioneer of women's university education. Marie was educated at St George's, Edinburgh, North London Collegiate School, and University College, London, where she obtained a first in botany (1902). She studied in Munich and obtained her Ph.D. (1904) and her D.Sc. (London, 1905).

In 1904 she was appointed assistant lecturer in botany at Manchester, and from 1909 to 1920 lectured in palaeobotany, first at Manchester, then in London. She became a Fellow of University College London in 1910 and published *Ancient Plants*. Her *Catalogue of the Cretaceous Flora* in the British Museum was published in two volumes (1913-15). During the First World War she did some important work on the structure of coal.

In 1911 she married a Canadian botanist, Reginald Ruggles Gates: this marriage was annulled in 1916 on her suit of non-consummation. In 1918 she married Humphrey Verdon-Roe; they were both interested in birth control, family planning, and sex education. Marie Stopes published *Married Love* in 1918. It made a great sensation and was an immediate success. It was followed by *Wise Parenthood* (1918) which was even more successful. Further publications on the same subject include *Radiant Motherhood* (1920) and *Enduring Passion* (1928). For the first time, conception and the problems of sex were brought into the open for public discussion.

In her personal relations, Marie Stopes was unfortunate. Her elder son was stillborn, and her younger son and her husband and some of her friends were alienated by her fierce partisanship and arrogant conceit in assuming the infallibility of her opinions. Nevertheless, her work was of enduring value. She died at her home, Norbury Park, near Dorking, on 2 October 1958, and bequeathed the estate to the National Trust.

STRACHEY, (EVELYN) JOHN ST LOE (1901-1963), politician and writer, was born at Newlands Corner, near Guildford, on 21 October 1901, the younger son of John St Loe Strachey, Editor of the *Spectator*, and his wife, Henrietta Mary Amy Simpson. His father was a first cousin of Lytton STRACHEY. He was educated at Eton and Magdalen College, Oxford, where he edited jointly with Robert (later Lord) Boothby the *Oxford Fortnightly Review* (1922).

On leaving Oxford, he wrote leading articles and reviews for the *Spectator*, and in 1923 joined the Labour party, stood unsuccessfully for Parliament in 1924, and, in collaboration with Oswald MOSLEY, published *Revolution by Reason* (1925). He now became Editor of the *Socialist Review* and the *Miner*, and in 1929 became Labour MP for the Aston division of Birmingham and Parliamentary Private Secretary to Mosley, Chancellor of the Duchy of Lancaster. When Mosley formed the 'New Party' in 1931, Strachey left him and then lost his seat at the general election. Although he never joined the Communist party he wrote books in support of Communism, and was a powerful influence in the Left Book Club, which he helped Victor GOLLANCZ to found in 1936. He wrote regularly in *Left News* and published *The Theory and Practice of Socialism* (1936) and similar works and pamphlets.

In 1929 he married Esther, daughter of Patrick Francis Murphy, a wealthy store owner of New York; she divorced him in 1933, and he married Celia, daughter of the Revd Arthur Hume Simpson; they had a son and a daughter.

In 1940 Strachey broke away from Communism, partly under the influence of J. M. KEYNES and partly because of the Nazi-Soviet pact of 1939. He joined the RAF and worked

Marie Stopes with her infant son, August 1924

at the Air Ministry, and made a reputation as an air commentator for the BBC. In 1945 he returned to Parliament as Labour member for Dundee and was appointed Under-Secretary of State for Air in the ATTLEE Government.

In 1946 he became Minister for Food at a difficult time, when rationing was still necessary. He had the misfortune to be involved in the costly but abortive ground-nut scheme in Tanganyika (Tanzania), which seriously damaged his reputation (1949). In 1950 he became MP for West Dundee and Secretary of State for War and, when Dr Fucks, the atomic spy, was arrested, Strachey's earlier Communism was given new publicity by the *Evening Standard*. However, he remained in the Government until it was defeated in 1951.

In 1955 he supported Hugh GAITSKELL as successor to Attlee, and produced a new series of books on politics, including *Contemporary Capitalism* (1956), *The End of Empire* (1959), and *On the Prevention of War* (1962). Harold Wilson named him as Shadow Commonwealth Secretary and he would probably have held Cabinet office in the 1964 Labour Government, but he died in London on 15 July 1963.

STRACHEY, (GILES) LYTTON (1880–1932), critic and biographer, was born in London on 1 March 1880, the fourth of the five sons of Lieutenant-General (Sir) Richard Strachey, and his second wife, Jane Maria, daughter of Sir John Peter Grant. He was educated at Leamington College, Liverpool University, and Trinity College, Cambridge, where he became friends with J. M. KEYNES, E. M. FORSTER, Leonard WOOLF, and Clive BELL. He won the Chancellor's English medal in 1902.

Failing to get elected to a fellowship, he worked in London as a journalist, contributing to the *Spectator* and the *Edinburgh* and the *New Quarterly Reviews*. He was also a prominent member of the Bloomsbury circle, which included Vanessa BELL and Virginia WOOLF, and was a frequent visitor to Ottoline MORRELL at Garsington. He soon became noted for his witty, unconventional, and often malicious conversation.

His first book *Landmarks in French Literature* was published for the 'Home University Library' in 1912. Like Bertrand RUSSELL, Lytton Strachey was a conscientious objector during the First World War. His best known work, *Eminent Victorians*, appeared in 1918 and, although it aroused the fury of conventional critics, it was the first product of a literary genre, which set out to throw light upon the follies and weaknesses of celebrities whose reputations had hitherto been unblemished by such exposure. This book was followed by a number of other biographical works, including *Queen Victoria* (1921), *Elizabeth and Essex* (1928), and *Portraits in Miniature and other Essays* (1931). He will be remembered as the leader of the reaction against the Victorians, which followed the First World War and as the first of a new school of biographers, who revealed their subjects, 'warts and all'.

Though basically homosexual, in 1912 Strachey met and fell in love with the artist, Dora Carrington. They remained intimate companions for the rest of his life, in spite of her subsequent marriage to Ralph Partridge. Strachey died at his home, Ham Spray House, near Hungerford on 21 January 1932. Soon afterwards Dora Carrington, unable to bear life without him, shot herself.

STRUTT, JOHN WILLIAM, third BARON RAYLEIGH (1842–1919), mathematician and physicist, was born at Maldon, Essex, on 12 November 1842, the eldest son of John James Strutt, second baron, and his wife, Clara Elizabeth La Touche, daughter of Capt. Richard Vicars, RE. Owing to ill health, he was educated privately until he went to Trinity College, Cambridge, in 1861 and became senior wrangler and first Smith's prizeman in 1865. In 1866 he became a Fellow of Trinity. He had to resign his fellowship when in 1871 he married Evelyn, daughter of James Maitland Balfour and sister of Arthur BALFOUR; they had three sons. In 1873 he succeeded his father as third baron and was elected FRS.

His first scientific paper, *Some electro-magnetic Phenomena considered in connexion with the Dynamical Theory*, appeared in 1869. For the next ten years, his researches were mainly concerned with electrical questions and problems of light, colour, and resonance. In 1877 he published his *Treatise on Sound*.

In 1879 he succeeded James Clerk-Maxwell as Cavendish Professor of Experimental Physics at Cambridge, and for some years concentrated research at the laboratory on the re-determination of the electrical units in absolute measure. A series of papers on this subject was published (1881–3).

After retiring from his chair in 1884, Rayleigh became Secretary of the Royal Society (1885–96), but continued research in his private laboratory at Tirling Place, Witham, Essex and, in collaboration with Sir William RAMSAY, discovered argon (1894). He also became deeply interested in physical optics.

He was appointed OM in 1902 and awarded the Nobel prize (jointly with Ramsay) in 1904. In the following year he was sworn of the Privy Council. He was Chairman of the committee which proposed the establishment of the National Physical Laboratory (1898) and President of the Advisory Committee on Aeronautics (1909). He became Chancellor of Cambridge University in 1908.

Lord Rayleigh died at Witham, Essex, on 30 June 1919 and was succeeded by his eldest son, who was a well-known physicist, elected FRS in 1905, and Foreign Secretary of the Royal Society from 1929 to 1934.

SUTHERLAND, GRAHAM VIVIAN (1903–1980), painter and print-maker, was born in London on 24 August 1903, the elder son of George Humphreys Vivian Sutherland, a civil servant, and his wife, Elsie Foster. He was educated at Epsom College, an in 1919 was apprenticed to the Midland Railway Engineering Works, Derby, but realized that he would not make a good engineer and in 1921 entered the Goldsmiths' College School of Art. He specialized in etching and was influenced by the work of Samuel Palmer; he had his first exhibition in 1924, and in 1926 went as a teacher of engraving to the Chelsea School of Art. In the same year he was received into the Roman Catholic Church. A year later he married Kathleen ('Katharine') Frances, daughter of John Barry; they had a son who died when three months old. In 1932 Sutherland began to teach composition and book illustration and to take up commercial work, particularly poster design.

It was not until this comparatively late stage of his career that he took up painting, inspired by a visit to Pembrokeshire (Dyfed) in 1934; the first one-man exhibition of his paintings took place in 1938 at the Rosenberg and Helft Gallery.

During the Second World War he was an official war artist and made a deep impression on art critics with his studies of devastation caused by bombing, and subjects such as tin mines, iron foundries, and flying-bomb sites. His meticulous studies of natural forms, roots and thorns and semi-abstract landscapes led to the commission to paint a large-scale

Graham Sutherland, with his unfinished portrait of Churchill, and other works in the background

Crucifixion for St Matthew's Church, Northampton, which he completed in 1946.

After the war, he was influenced by the work of Picasso and Matisse and, having become recognized as the leader of the avant-garde among English painters, he successfully exhibited at the Venice Biennale, the Musée d'Art Moderne, Paris in 1952, and at the Tate in 1953. In 1951 he painted another large-scale work for the Festival of Britain, *The Origins of the Land*, and in 1952 was commissioned to design the tapestry of *Christ in Glory* for the rebuilt Coventry Cathedral. This was not completed until 1962.

He had begun to paint portraits in 1949, his first being an expressionist painting of W. Somerset MAUGHAM which, when exhibited, at the Tate in 1951, was a shock to the public. Further shocks were administered by a portrait of Lord BEAVERBROOK and by that commissioned by both houses of Parliament of Winston CHURCHILL. The latter, presented in 1954, was detested by its subject and by Lady Churchill, who secretly engineered its destruction. Among other portraits which are startlingly realistic in form are those of Helena Rubinstein (1957), Konrad Adenauer (1965), and Lord Goodman (1973).

In 1962 Sutherland had an exhibition at the Marlborough Fine Art Gallery, but his chief patrons during the sixties were the Italians, after a successful show of his work in Turin in 1965. He was now concentrating more on print-making, and in 1968 produced a 'Bestiary' of twenty-six colour lithographs.

In 1976 the Graham Sutherland Gallery was opened at Picton Castle in his beloved Wales. In 1960 he had been appointed OM and in 1962 became honorary D. Litt. at Oxford. He received other academic honours abroad. He died in London on 17 February 1980.

SUTHERLAND, DAME LUCY STUART (1903–1980), historian and administrator, was born in Geelong, Australia, on 21 June 1903, the only daughter of Alexander Charles Sutherland, a mining engineer, and his wife, Margaret Mabel Goddard. She was brought up in South Africa, and educated at Roedean School, Johannesburg, and Witwatersrand University. She went on to Somerville College, Oxford, with a scholarship, obtained a first in modern history (1927), and was appointed tutor and a tutorial Fellow (1928).

During the Second World War she worked as a civil servant in Whitehall, and in 1945 was appointed Principal of Lady Margaret Hall, a post in which she had to tackle the problems of post-war Oxford. She found time, however, to be Chairman of the Board of Trade Working Party on the Lace Industry (1946), a member of the Royal Commission on Taxation of Profits and Incomes (1951), the committee dealing with grants for students (1958), and the University Grants Committee (1964-9). Between 1961 and 1969 she was the first woman to act as Pro-Vice-Chancellor of Oxford University.

When she retired in 1971, her college made her an honorary Fellow, and she received a number of honorary degrees.

She had been elected FBA in 1954, and in 1957 refused the post of Regius Professor of Modern History as she preferred to remain as Principal of Lady Margaret Hall. She co-operated with other scholars in *The Correspondence of Edmund Burke* (1960) and the *History of Parliament*. She was an authority on the eighteenth-century history of the City of London and the East India Company.

She was appointed CBE in 1947 and DBE in 1969. She died, unmarried, in Oxford on 20 August 1980.

T

TANSLEY, SIR ARTHUR GEORGE (1871-1955), plant ecologist, was born in London on 15 August 1871, the only son of George Tansley, a teacher at the Working Men's College, and his wife, Amelia Lawrence. He was educated at University College London, and Trinity College, Cambridge, where he obtained firsts in both parts of the natural sciences tripos (1893-4).

He returned to University College to work with F. W. Oliver, Quain Professor of Botany, on the subject of fern-like plants. In 1903 he married one of his student collaborators, Edith, daughter of Samuel Chick, a lace merchant; they had three daughters. In 1902 he had launched the botanical journal, *The New Phytologist*, which he edited for thirty years. He also edited and largely wrote *Types of British Vegetation*, published in 1911. He was the first President of the British Ecological Society (1913), and from 1917 to 1938 edited the Society's *Journal of Ecology*. In 1915 he was elected FRS.

From 1907 to 1923 Tansley was a lecturer in botany at Cambridge and, after an interval in which he studied psychology with Freud in Vienna (1923-4), was appointed Sherardian Professor of Botany at Oxford, a post which he held until 1937. In 1939 he published his most celebrated book, *The British Islands and their Vegetation*. He played a leading role in the foundation of the Natural Conservancy and was its first Chairman from 1949 to 1953. He was knighted in 1950 and elected an honorary Fellow of Trinity College, Cambridge in 1944.

Each of his daughters had a distinguished career, respectively in physiology, architecture, and economics. Tansley died at Grantchester on 25 November 1955.

TAWNEY, RICHARD HENRY (1880-1962), historian, was born in Calcutta on 30 November 1880, the son of Charles Henry Tawney, Principal of Presidency College, and his wife, Constance Catherine Fox. He was educated at Rugby and Balliol College, Oxford, where he was a classical scholar, obtained a first in Mods, but only a second in Greats (1903).

In 1905 he became a member of the Executive Committee of the Workers' Educational Association, during 1906-8 taught economic history at Glasgow University, and from 1908 to 1914 taught for the WEA tutorial classes under Oxford University at Rochdale and in the Potteries. His first book, *The Agrarian Problem in the Sixteenth Century* (1912), established him as an authority on economic and social history. He joined the Fabian Society in 1906 and the Independent Labour party in 1909. He had no sympathy with Marxism, his political views being based on Christian socialism, and his aim was to abolish poverty and inequality.

In 1909 he married Annette Jeanie ('Jeannette'), sister of William BEVERIDGE; they had no children.

In 1915 he enlisted in the army as a private, refused a commission, was wounded in 1916 and, on recovery, served briefly in the Ministry of Reconstruction. He stood unsuccessfully for Parliament in 1918, 1922, and 1924. He was, however, a member of the Coal Industry Commission (1919), and between 1918 and 1928 became a major political influence, his writing shaping much of the policy of the Labour movement.

From 1920 to 1949 he lectured in economic history at the London School of Economics; he was appointed Reader in 1923 and Professor in 1931. He was a member of the Executive Committee of the Fabian Society from 1921 to 1933. In 1921 he published *The Acquisitive Society*, and the Labour party manifesto of 1928, *Labour and the Nation*, was largely his work.

Tawney wrote on education as well as economics, believing that politics would be sterile without education; he was a member of the Consultative Committee of the Board of Education (1912-31) and was on the panel which produced the 'Hadow Report' of 1926, recommending the raising of the school age to fifteen. He helped to found the Economic History Society in 1926 and co-edited the *Economic History Review* with Ephraim Lipson (1927-34). He published *Religion and the Rise of Capitalism* (1926) and *Equality* (1931). In 1932, after a visit to China, he published *Land and Labour in China*. He was elected FBA in 1935.

He was a member of the University Grants Committee (1943-8) and Vice-President of the WEA (1944-8). He twice refused a peerage but accepted many academic honours. His last work, *Business and Politics under James I: Lionel Cranfield as Merchant and Minister* appeared in 1958. He died in London on 16 January 1962.

TAYLOR, JOHN HENRY (1871-1963), golfer, was born at Northam, Devon, on 19 March 1871, the son of Joshua Taylor, a labourer, and his wife, Susannah Heard, a midwife. He left school at eleven to become a caddie at the Westward Ho! Golf Club and, after working as a labourer, returned there in 1888 as groundsman, the army and navy having refused him because of his poor eyesight.

In 1891 he was appointed greenkeeper and professional at the Burnham Club in Somerset, and in 1893 competed in the Open Championship at Prestwick. In 1894 he became the first English professional to win the championship. He won again in 1895, 1900, 1909, and 1913, and finished second six times.

In 1896 Taylor married Clara Fulford, a teacher; they had three sons and six daughters.

In 1901 he became the first President of the Professional Golfers' Association, which he had helped to found. He won the French Open Championship twice and won the German Open, and came second in the United States Open (1900).

From 1899 to 1946 he was professional at the Royal Mid-Surrey Club. He was elected an honorary member of the Royal and Ancient Golf Club in 1950, and in 1957 was elected President of the Westward Ho! Club, where he had started as a caddie. Together with James Braid and Harry Vardon, he was one of the great 'triumvirate' of golf at the turn of the century. He published his autobiography *Golf: My Life's Work* in 1943. Taylor died at Northam on 10 February 1963.

TEDDER, ARTHUR WILLIAM, first BARON TEDDER (1890-1967), Marshal of the Royal Air Force, was born at Glenguin, Stirling, on 11 July 1890, the younger son of (Sir) Arthur Tedder, a civil servant, and his wife, Emily Charlotte, daughter of William Henry Bryson. He was educated at Whitgift Grammar School and Magdalene College, Cambridge, where he won the Prince Consort prize in 1914. He joined the Colonial Service and was posted to Fiji, but resigned soon afterwards and obtained a commission in the RFC. In 1917 he commanded No.70 Fighter Squadron and in 1919 received a permanent commission in the RAF. In 1915 he had married Rosalinde, daughter of William McIntyre Maclardy of Sydney, Australia; they had two sons and a daughter.

Being interested in the theory and organization of air warfare, he became an instructor at the RAF Staff College from 1929 to 1931 and group captain commanding the Air Armament School from 1931 to 1933. He was then posted as Director of Training at the Air Ministry (1934-6). For two years (1936-8) he was in Singapore as Air Officer Commanding, Far East, with the rank of air vice-marshal (1937). Then, in 1938, he was brought back to the Air Ministry as Director-General of Research and Development, concerned with the development of new fighters, radar, and improved equipment. In 1940 he came into conflict with the Air Minister, Lord BEAVERBROOK and was regarded by Winston CHURCHILL as an obstructionist.

He was sent to the Middle East as Deputy Commander, when the first choice for the post was forced down in Sicily. In 1941 he became Commander-in-Chief and, within a few months, would have been removed by Churchill but for the determined opposition of PORTAL, Chief of Air Staff. During 1941-2 Tedder proved his administrative ability by co-operating closely with the army command and building up a Desert Air Force, which provided cover for the Eighth Army throughout the campaign in North Africa. In 1941 he was promoted to air marshal and in 1942 to air chief marshal.

In 1943 he became responsible for all the Allied air forces in the Mediterranean area as deputy to General Eisenhower. By this time, Churchill had revised his opinion of Tedder's efficiency and fighting qualities, and Tedder proved to be as skilful in his co-operation with the Americans as he had been with the British army commanders; when Eisenhower was appointed to plan and command the forces for the invasion of Europe, Tedder went with him as his deputy.

The success of 'Operation Overlord' owed much to the strategy which Tedder used in the deployment of the aircraft under his command, insisting on the accurate bombing of the enemy's lines of communication and massive air support for the offensive of the Allied ground troops. By 1945 his reputation was unrivalled among Allied airmen; he was promoted to marshal of the Royal Air Force, and in 1946 appointed Chief of Air Staff and raised to the peerage as Baron Tedder. He had been appointed CB in 1937, KCB and GCB in 1942.

His first wife died in 1943, and later that year Tedder married Marie de Seton, daughter of Sir Bruce Seton, Bt., and widow of Capt. Ian Reddie Hamilton Black, RN; they had one son.

In 1948 he published his Lees Knowles lectures as *Air Power in War*, and in 1950 went to Washington as Chairman of the British Joint Services Mission and British representative on the Military Committee of the North Atlantic Treaty Alliance. When he finally retired in 1951, he received many new honours and decorations. In 1950 he became Chancellor of Cambridge University and Vice-Chairman of the Board of Governors of the BBC. From 1954 to 1960 he was Chairman of the Standard Motor Co. In 1966 he published his memoirs *With Prejudice*. Tedder died at Banstead on 3 June 1967.

TEMPEST, DAME MARIE (1864-1942), actress, was born Mary Susan, daughter of Edwin Etherington, a stationer, and his wife, Sarah Mary, daughter of Henry Castle, a draper. The details of her early life are not well authenticated. Her mother appears to have left her father and gone to Canada with her two other children, leaving Mary to be brought up by her father's mother, who was employed as a servant at the Chapel Royal and, in that capacity, knew the Gladstones. Her father was illegitimate, and it is possible that his father paid for Mary's education at the Ursuline convent at Thildonck in Belgium and at a school in Paris. She took her stage name from Lady Susan Vane-Tempest, whom she claimed to be her godmother.

After school in Paris, she studied singing at the Royal Academy of Music under Manuel Garcia, and in 1885 made her début in Suppé's *Boccaccio* at the Comedy Theatre, London. She was an immediate success and, after singing in light operas, she made her name in *Dorothy* in 1887. In the years that followed, she achieved a unique position in the English theatre by her charm and by hard work.

From 1890 to 1895 she was as popular in New York as she had been in London, and on return to England she played in a number of musical comedies. Then, in 1900, she decided to try herself out in straight plays, and had an immediate success in *Becky Sharp*, adapted from Thackeray's *Vanity Fair*. Before long, she was accepted as a great comedienne and played the lead in a number of plays by many playwrights, including Arnold BENNETT, Sir James BARRIE, A. A. MILNE, Somerset MAUGHAM, and Noël COWARD. In 1914 she went on a world tour, and after the war returned to the London stage.

She celebrated her golden jubilee on the stage in 1935 in a matinée at Drury Lane attended by King George V and Queen Mary. In 1937 she was appointed DBE.

In 1885 she married Alfred Edward Izard; they had one

William Temple, Archbishop of Canterbury, walking through the bombed streets following the raid on Canterbury, June 1942

son, her only child; the marriage ended in divorce in 1889. In 1898 she married Cosmo Charles Gordon-Lennox, the author of one of her favourite plays, *The Marriage of Kitty*. He died in 1921, and she then married William Graham Browne, an actor. She was desolate when he died in 1937, and the outbreak of war in 1939 only increased her unhappiness and loneliness. She died in London on 14 October 1942.

TEMPLE, WILLIAM (1881–1944), Archbishop of Canterbury, was born at The Palace, Exeter, on 15 October 1881, the younger son of Frederick Temple, Bishop of Exeter (later Archbishop of Canterbury), and his wife, Beatrice Blanche, daughter of William Saunders Sebright Lascelles, son of the second Earl of Harewood. He was educated as a scholar at Rugby and an exhibitioner at Balliol College, Oxford, where he obtained firsts in Mods. (1902) and Greats (1904), and was President of the Union. While at the university, he became a friend of R. H. TAWNEY and William BEVERIDGE, who aroused his interest in the welfare of working men.

In 1904 he became a Fellow of the Queen's College, Oxford, and began his association with the Workers' Educational Association, of which he was President from 1908 to 1924. He had always intended to be ordained, but the Bishop of Oxford for two years refused to accept him as a candidate because of his 'uncertain, precarious, unsteady' attitude towards the Virgin Birth and the Resurrection. In 1908, however, he appealed to Randall DAVIDSON, Archbishop of Canterbury, and became a deacon later that year and was ordained priest in 1909.

From 1910 to 1914 Temple was Headmaster of Repton, and in 1914 became Vicar of St James's, Piccadilly, where he remained until 1918, publishing in 1917 *Mens Creatrix*, his contribution to the doctrines of Christian theism. From 1915 to 1918 he edited the *Challenge* and headed the 'Life and Liberty Movement'. In 1919 he was appointed Canon of Westminster and his sermons in the Abbey drew large crowds. He also edited the *Pilgrim*.

In 1916 he had married Frances Gertrude Acland, daughter of Frederick Henry Anson; they had no children.

Temple was appointed Bishop of Manchester in 1920 and served there for eight years, publishing a number of works, including *Christ in His Church* (1925) and *Personal Religion and the Life of Fellowship* (1926). He was criticized for his attempt in 1926 to mediate between the coal miners and the owners in the dispute which led to the general strike. He strongly supported Randall Davidson in the revised Prayer Book controversy and took a leading part in the Ecumenical Movement.

In 1929 he was appointed Archbishop of York and, throughout the thirteen years he remained in that office, continued to demonstrate his concern for the well-being of working people, publishing *Nature, Man and God* (1934), *Men Without Work* (1938), and *Christianity and the Social Order* (1942), and taking a leading part in the BBC's religious broadcasts. He continued also to work for the union of the Churches, and in 1942 inaugurated the British Council of Churches.

From 1942 to 1944 Temple was Archbishop of Canterbury, his appointment having been made despite rather than because of his political faith. His assistance to the Minister of Education, R. A. (later Lord) Butler was of great importance in securing the agreement of churchmen to the 1944 Education Act, and Lord Butler has paid tribute to the astuteness with which the Archbishop persuaded the Anglican clergy to moderate their opposition to this measure.

Temple received many academic honours. He died at Westgate-on-Sea, Kent, on 26 October 1944.

TEMPLER, SIR GERALD WALTER ROBERT (1898-1979), field-marshal, was born at Colchester on 11 September 1898, the only child of (Lt.-Col.) Walter Francis Templer, of the Royal Irish Fusiliers, and his wife, Mabel Eileen, daughter of (Major) Robert Johnston, of co. Antrim, serving in the Army Pay Department, India. He was educated at Wellington College and Sandhurst, and in 1917 joined the Royal Irish Fusiliers in France. He served with the regiment in Persia (Iran), Iraq, and Egypt until 1922, during which time he gained a reputation as an athlete. In 1926 he married Ethel Margery ('Peggie'), daughter of Charles Davie, a retired solicitor; they had a son and a daughter.

In 1927 he entered the Staff College, and until 1935 served in England. In that year, he was with the Loyal Regiment in Palestine and was appointed DSO in 1936. During 1938-9 he was employed in the War Office and, when war broke out, went to France as a staff officer. After Dunkirk, he held a number of posts in England rising to the rank of lieutenant-general until in 1943, at his own request, he saw fighting in North Africa and Italy, as a major-general. He was appointed OBE in 1940 and CB in 1944.

In 1944, when he was in command of the 6th Armoured Division, he was severely wounded and, after recovery in 1945, served under Field-Marshal MONTGOMERY as Director of Civil Affairs and Military Government in Germany. In this post he ordered the dismissal of Dr Konrad Adenauer, Mayor of Cologne (later Chancellor), for his failure to deal with the conditions in which the population were living. In 1946 Templer went to the War Office as Director of Military Intelligence, and then as Vice-Chief of the Imperial General

Ellen Terry as Beatrice, c. 1882

Staff, first under Montgomery, and then under Sir William SLIM. In 1950 he was promoted to general and took over Eastern Command. He thought this would be his final post, but the work in which he was to make his name was yet to come. Early in 1952 he succeeded Sir Henry Gurney, High Commissioner in Malaya, who had been murdered by Communist terrorists in October 1951.

During 1952-4 he was in charge of the civil government and the military operation against the insurgents, and combined his strategy for defeating the Communists by strengthening the security of Malayan towns and villages with plans for the acceleration of progress towards independence. In 1954 he was able to hand over to his civilian deputy and in the following year was appointed CIGS.

His term of office in this post was not a happy one. It coincided with difficulties in the Middle East, the Suez débâcle, and the British Government's decision to reduce the size of the army. He was promoted to field-marshal in 1956, and retired in 1958. He received many honours: CMG (1946), KBE (1949), KCB (1951), GCMG (1953), GCB (1955), and KG (1963). Templer died in London on 25 October 1979.

TEMPLEWOOD, VISCOUNT (1880-1959). See HOARE.

TERRY, DAME (ALICE) ELLEN (1847-1928), actress, was born in Coventry on 27 February 1847, the third of the eleven children of Benjamin Terry, an actor, and his wife, Sarah Ballard, an actress. Three of Ellen's sisters, Kate, Marion, and Florence, and her brother, Fred, went on the stage. She first appeared as a boy in *The Winter's Tale* in 1856. In 1862 she joined the company at the Theatre Royal, Bristol, and in 1863 moved to the company at the Haymarket Theatre in London. She was not happy on the stage, and in 1864 she married the artist, George Frederick Watts; she was seventeen and he was forty-seven; they separated after a year and she returned to the stage. In 1867 she acted for the first time with Henry Irving.

She was still not happy as an actress, and from 1868 till 1974 lived in retirement with Edward William Godwin, the architect, and had a daughter, Edith, and a son, (Edward) Gordon CRAIG, who became a stage designer. She returned to the stage again in 1874 and reached the turning point of her career as Portia in *The Merchant of Venice*, staged by Sir Squire Bancroft. In 1877, having been divorced by Watts, she married Charles Clavering Wardell, the actor Charles Kelly, but that marriage was also unsuccessful, and in 1881 they separated.

In 1878 she played Ophelia in Henry Irving's production of *Hamlet* at the Lyceum Theatre and this began an association which lasted until 1902, during which time Ellen Terry played as the leading lady in all Irving's productions with outstanding success, and took part in eight American tours between 1883 and 1901. In 1902 she acted at Stratford-upon-Avon. In 1903 she went into management in London in productions staged by her son, Gordon Craig. In that year she also acted for the last time with Henry Irving. She celebrated her 'Jubilee' in 1906, playing Beatrice in *Much Ado about Nothing* at Drury Lane. In 1907 she toured the United States with *Captain Brassbound's Conversion*, and married an American actor, James Usselmann; she lived with him until 1910.

She continued to play in special performances in London, though her failing memory caused her difficulty with new parts. She now took up lecturing on Shakespearian subjects;

and, between 1910 and 1915, made lecture tours of the USA and Australia as well as Britain. From 1921 she was in failing health; she received an honorary LL D from St Andrews, and in 1925 was created GBE. She died at Small Hythe, Tenterden, Kent on 21 July 1928, and her home there was converted into an Ellen Terry museum. Her correspondence with George Bernard SHAW was published in 1931.

THOMAS, DYLAN MARLAIS (1914–1953), poet, was born in Swansea on 27 October 1914, the only son of David John Thomas, a schoolmaster, and his wife, Florence Hannah Williams. After primary school, he went to Swansea Grammar School, where his father was English master. Before he left in 1931 to become a reporter on the *South Wales Daily Post*, he had already written his early poems; he was not a very reliable journalist and, within eighteen months, he resigned to devote himself to writing poetry. His first poem to be published in the London press appeared in the *Sunday Referee* in 1933.

In the following year he published his *18 Poems*, and moved to London though, from time to time, he returned to Swansea. He had no regular income, but this did not deter him from acquiring a reputation as a roystering Bohemian and a heavy drinker. In his sober moments, he could exercise great charm, and was an amusing companion, who soon had many friends. Among them was the young Pamela Hansford Johnson (later Lady Snow), who tried to persuade him to lead a more ordered life and, as their letters show, encouraged him in his work. Edith SITWELL, who had at first ridiculed his poetry, came to admire his work, and her praise helped to establish his reputation, when she reviewed *Twenty-five Poems*, published in 1937.

Among his more bibulous friends was Augustus JOHN the painter and, through him and his family, he met Caitlin, the daughter of Francis Macnamara, who at the time was living with John. In 1937 she and Thomas married and, with the financial help of another good friend, Margaret Taylor, the first wife of A. J. P. Taylor, the historian, they settled for a time at Laugharne. Although Thomas was not always faithful to his wife and they had many difficulties, he loved her for the rest of his life; they had two sons and a daughter, and to his other money problems he added the necessity of finding school fees.

In 1939 *The World I Breathe* was published in America and in 1940 appeared *The Portrait of the Artist as a Young Dog*, in which Thomas described his boyhood in Swansea and the Carmarthenshire countryside. During the Second World War he lived mostly in London, and was employed by the BBC as an actor and reader of poetry. He had always been interested in acting and he had remarkable gifts as a reader. He continued, however, to lead a disorderly life, and in 1945 an attempt was made to murder him by a drink-crazed neighbour.

After the war, again with the help of Margaret Taylor, he and Caitlin lived in Oxfordshire. The publication in 1946 of *Deaths and Entrances* confirmed his claim to be a notable poet in the Welsh tradition. But his drinking was now creating trouble with his wife and was beginning to endanger his health. In 1948 the demands of the Inland Revenue authorities for income tax, unpaid for years, brought him further stress. His friend David Higham helped to sort out the financial chaos in which he lived, but for the rest of his life he was burdened with the debts he had accumulated.

In 1950 he undertook an extensive and exhausting lecture tour of the USA in a despairing effort to earn money but, as fast as he earned it, he spent it. In 1952 he published his *Collected Poems*, and during that year and 1953 he again visited America. Then came his fourth and final visit. He was a very sick man and Caitlin warned him that another exhausting tour would kill him. But more money had to be earned, and he was due to take part in the first performance in New York of *Under Milk Wood*, his 'play for voices'. That performance was his final appearance. He died in New York of alcoholic poisoning on 9 November 1953. *Under Milk Wood* was broadcast by the BBC on 25 January 1954.

THOMAS, JAMES HENRY (1874–1949), trade-union leader and politician, was born at Newport, Monmouthshire, on 3 October 1874, the son of Elizabeth Mary Thomas, a domestic servant. He was brought up by his grandmother, went to school in Newport up to the age of twelve, and then worked as an engine-cleaner on the Great Western Railway (1889). Five years later, he was promoted to foreman, and in 1898 attended his first trades-union annual congress. In that year he married Agnes, daughter of Joseph Hill, a boilermaker; they had three sons and three daughters. In 1901 he moved to Swindon, where he was elected to the borough council, and during 1905–6 was active in local government, while still employed as an engine-turner.

In 1905 he became President of the Amalgamated Society of Railway Servants and from 1906 to 1910 its Organizing Secretary. In 1910 he was elected Labour MP for Derby, a seat which he held until 1936. When, in 1913, the National Union of Railwaymen was formed, Thomas was elected Assistant Secretary; in 1917 he became General Secretary, and from 1919 to 1931 Parliamentary General Secretary.

During the First World War he was opposed to conscription, but accepted it when it was introduced. In 1917 he went to North America with the BALFOUR mission and was sworn of the Privy Council. In 1919 the railwaymen, coal miners, and transport workers resurrected the 'triple industrial alliance', formed in 1915, with a view to co-ordinating their industrial action, but the railwaymen went on strike against the reduction of their wages without waiting for support from the other unions. Thanks to the intervention of LLOYD GEORGE, the NUR, led by Thomas, won their case, though he was criticized by some of his fellow unionists for his moderation and readiness to negotiate.

The 'triple alliance' broke up in 1921 when Government control of the coal mines ended and both railwaymen and transport workers refused to support a strike by the miners' union. Thomas played a leading part in this decision and was, in consequence, attacked by the extremists in the Labour movement, although he had the support of his own union.

In Ramsay MAC DONALD's administration of 1924, Thomas was appointed Colonial Secretary, and in the 1929 Labour Government became Lord Privy Seal with the special responsibility for dealing with unemployment. In 1926 he was unable to prevent the general strike but helped to bring it to an end. As the country and the MacDonald Government faced an increasing economic crisis, Thomas soon discovered that he had little hope of doing anything effective to reduce the numbers of unemployed. In 1930 a new post of Dominions Secretary was created for him and, when in 1931 MacDonald formed his National Government, Thomas was one of the ministers who supported him, having been returned for Derby as a National Labour candidate.

He remained at the Dominions Office until 1935, but his loyalty to MacDonald cost him the support of his friends in the Labour party. He was attacked with exceptional

Dylan Thomas directing a rehearsal of *Under Milk Wood*, New York, May 1953 bitterness, deprived of membership of the NUR, and denied a pension for his services. His tenure of the Dominions Office did nothing to enhance his reputation, and in 1935 Stanley BALDWIN moved him back to the Colonial Office.

In the following year, Thomas met with political disaster. In the weeks leading up to the budget, unusual activity at Lloyd's appeared to suggest that there had been a leakage about the intentions of the Chancellor of the Exchequer. A judicial tribunal, set up to investigate, found that Thomas had made an 'unauthorized' disclosure of budget secrets. Baldwin thought that this had probably occurred when Thomas had had too much to drink, a weakness to which he had become prone but, although there was much sympathy for him in Parliament, this indiscretion meant the end of his political career.

In his heyday as a trade-union leader, Thomas had a reputation as a man of eloquence and humour, who deliberately cultivated, perhaps invented, a working-class accent. He was a close friend of King George V and did much to show that Labour politicians were fit to govern. He received doctorates from Oxford and Cambridge Universities. Thomas died in London on 21 January 1949.

THOMAS, (PHILIP) EDWARD (1878-1917), poet, journalist, and critic, was born in Lambeth on 3 March 1878, the eldest of five sons of Philip Henry Thomas, a civil servant at the Board of Trade, and his wife, Mary Elizabeth, daughter of Edward Thomas Townsend, of Newport, Monmouthshire. He was educated at St Paul's School and Lincoln College, Oxford, of which he was a scholar (1898-1900). In 1899 he married Helen, daughter of James Ashcroft Noble, writer and critic. They had one son and two daughters.

Thomas's father was anxious that his son should enter the Civil Service but, although he sat for the examination, Thomas decided that he preferred to earn a precarious living by writing. His first book, *The Woodland Life*, had been published in 1897. After his marriage, however, he was beset by financial difficulties, and was forced to undertake literary hack work of a kind that he found tedious and wearisome. His wife Helen has related, in *As It Was* (1926), a pathetic account of her husband's bouts of manic depression during which she feared that he might commit suicide.

Both of them felt a passionate delight in the beauty of the English countryside, and much of Thomas's work was coloured by his interest in nature. In 1912 he met the writer Eleanor FARJEON, who became a close family friend and many years later gave testimony of that friendship in *Edward Thomas: the Last Four Years* (1958). W. H. NEVINSON helped him by commissioning work for the *Daily Chronicle*, but it was not until 1913, when Thomas met the American poet, Robert Frost, that he was encouraged to pursue his efforts to write poetry. In the meantime he had to earn a living for himself and his family by reviewing books and working as a free-lance journalist.

In 1915 Thomas enlisted in the Artists' Rifles, but soon became a corporal in the Royal Garrison Artillery, being commissioned in November 1916. He was killed in action at Arras on 9 April 1917. Only after his death was his ability as a poet recognized. *Six Poems* appeared, published privately, in 1916, and his *Collected Poems*, with a foreword by his friend, Walter DE LA MARE, were published in 1920 (and republished in 1949). In his foreword De La Mare wrote: 'When Edward Thomas was killed in Flanders a mirror of England was shattered'.

Among Thomas's prose works are *The Heart of England*

(1906), *The South Country* (1909), and *In Pursuit of Spring* (1914). A selection of articles on other poets which he had written for *T. P. Weekly* was published posthumously as *A Literary Pilgrim in England* (1917). His biographical studies include *Richard Jefferies* (1909), *Maeterlinck* (1911), *Swinburne* (1912), *George Borrow* (1912), and *Walter Pater* (1913).

In his poem *In Memoriam (Easter, 1915)* Thomas wrote what might be regarded as his own epitaph:

> Ten flowers left thick at nightfall in the wood
> This Eastertide call into mind the men,
> Now far from home, who, with their sweethearts, should
> Have gathered them and will never do again.

THOMSON, SIR JOSEPH JOHN (1856-1940), physicist, was born at Cheetham Hill, near Manchester on 18 December 1856, the elder son of Joseph James Thomson, publisher and bookseller, and his wife, Emma Swindells. He was educated at the Owens College, Manchester and Trinity College, Cambridge, where he was second wrangler and second Smith's prizeman, and became a Fellow (1880). In 1881 he published a paper in the *Philosophical Magazine* (5th series, vol.xi), proving that an electric charge must possess inertia and showing how to calculate its mass. In 1882 he was appointed a lecturer in mathematics, and in 1894 succeeded Lord RAYLEIGH as Cavendish Professor of Experimental Physics at Cambridge, a post which he held until 1919.

In 1890 he married Rose Elizabeth, daughter of Sir George Edward Paget; they had a son and a daughter.

In 1893 Thomson published *Notes on Recent Researches in Electricity and Magnetism*, which gave a comprehensive account of the discharge of electricity through gases. His further experiments led him to the conclusion that the current in these discharges was carried by positively and negatively charged particles (ions) formed by the disruption of the chemical molecules of the gas. The discovery of X-rays in 1895 by Röntgen enabled Thomson to confirm his findings.

He proceeded to the next stage of his research by attempting to determine the nature of the electrical particles by measuring their masses, and found that there was a more fundamental unit than the chemical atom, an atom of pure electricity, which in due course came to be called an electron. This revolutionary finding was announced at a meeting of the Royal Institution in 1897. For the rest of his career, Thomson sought to improve the technique which had succeeded so well with the electron, and to use it to calculate the masses, energies, and electric charges of the other particles occurring in electric currents through gases. This research was important because it forecast the theory of nuclear, as well as of atomic, structure.

From 1918 to 1940 'J. J.', as he was always known, was Master of Trinity College, Cambridge. He was elected FRS in 1884 and, from 1915 to 1920, was President of the Royal Society. During the First World War he was busy on war work. He was active in the formation of the Department of Scientific and Industrial Research (1919-27). Under his guidance, the Cavendish Laboratory became the leading research school in experimental physics. He was the recipient of many honours. In 1906 he was awarded the Nobel prize for physics; he was knighted in 1908, and appointed OM in 1912; he received honorary degrees from twenty-three universities.

In addition to his books on electricity and magnetism, he published his autobiography *Recollections and Reflections* (1936). From the day he entered Trinity College, Cambridge,

Sybil Thorndike as Mrs White in *Waters of the Moon* by N. C. Hunter, Haymarket, April 1951

he never missed a term. 'J. J.' died in the Master's Lodge of Trinity on 30 August 1940 and his ashes were buried in Westminster Abbey. His son, Sir George Paget Thomson, was also a physicist.

THORNDIKE, DAME (AGNES) SYBIL (1882–1976), actress, was born on 24 October 1882 at Gainsborough, Lincolnshire, the eldest child of the Revd Arthur John Webster Thorndike, and his wife, Agnes Macdonald, daughter of John Bowers, a shipping merchant. She was educated at Rochester High School, and studied the piano at the Guildhall, London. However, after giving a recital in Rochester in 1899, she had to give up playing, owing to a disability, and sought another career on the stage.

In 1904 she joined the company of (Sir) P. B. Ben Greet and toured America, playing a large number of parts and 'learning her trade'. On return to England in 1907, she became a member of Miss Horniman's company, met and married (Sir) Lewis Casson and, with occasional breaks and visits to the USA, played with the Horniman company until the outbreak of the First World War, when her husband joined the army and she moved to the Old Vic company of Lilian BAYLIS, playing the lead in many plays of Shakespeare.

After the war, she played Hecuba in Euripedes' *The Trojan Women* and, directed by Lewis Casson, took part in a series of Grand Guignol melodramas. Then, in 1922, the Cassons set up in management at the New Theatre, and Bernard SHAW wrote *St. Joan* for her, in which she appeared

in 1924. This was the high point of her career; the play ran for 244 performances and was revived many times, her final performance in the part taking place in 1941.

Sybil Thorndike and Lewis Casson went on playing through the Second World War and after, until their final performance in a revival of *Arsenic and Old Lace* in 1966. Casson died in 1969, and his widow made her last appearance in that year at the Thorndike Theatre in Leatherhead. In 1931 she was appointed DBE, and in 1970 made a CH. She and Lewis Casson, who was knighted in 1945, had two sons and two daughters. Sybil Thorndike died in London on 9 June 1976.

TIZARD, SIR HENRY THOMAS (1885–1959), scientist and administrator, was born at Gillingham on 23 August 1885, the only son of Thomas Henry Tizard, oceanographer and hydrographic surveyor, and his wife, Mary Elizabeth Churchward. He was educated at Westminster School and Magdalen College, Oxford, where he obtained firsts in Mathematical Mods. and chemistry (1905–8). After studying in Berlin, where he met F. A. LINDEMANN, and at the Royal Institution, working on the colour changes of indicators, he returned to Oxford in 1911 as tutorial Fellow at Oriel College. In 1915 he married Kathleen Eleanor, daughter of Arthur Prangley Wilson, a mining engineer; they had three sons.

During the First World War he served in the RGA and the RFC, testing bomb-sights and aircraft, and also worked in the Ministry of Munitions. In 1919 he went back to Oxford, and in 1920 became Reader in chemical thermodynamics and carried out research on aviation fuels. Later in 1920, he was appointed Assistant Secretary to the Department of Scientific and Industrial Research to work on the co-ordination of the scientific work of the civil and defence departments. From 1927 to 1929 he was Permanent Secretary of the DSIR, and was largely responsible for the establishment of the Chemical Research Laboratory at Teddington.

He left this post in 1929 to become Rector of Imperial College, London, where he stayed until 1942. He felt strongly that Britain needed more scientists and engineers, and he did much to develop the College, but increasingly he was drawn in to consideration of the problems of defence. In 1933 he became Chairman of the Aeronautical Research Committee and gave encouragement to imaginative inventors like (Sir) Frank Whittle, with his jet engine. From 1935 to 1940 he was Chairman of the Air Defence Committee and was inadvertently led into controversy with his friend, Lindemann, who was at this time the head of the Clarendon Laboratory at Oxford, a post to which Tizard had helped to get him appointed. Lindemann had himself suggested the appointment of a sub-committee to the Committee of Imperial Defence and was affronted when he was told that the Tizard Committee already existed. Tizard was busy with such practical problems of air defence as the development of Robert WATSON-WATT's radio beam for the detection of aircraft. Lindemann, using his influence with Winston CHURCHILL, was appointed to the Tizard Committee, and quickly found himself in disagreement with his colleagues over priorities. The committee resigned and was reconstituted without Lindemann.

Tizard continued to press on with the programme for the development of radar; he succeeded in getting the first radar stations set up and supported the work that was in progress to develop airborne radar. When, however, Churchill became

Sir Henry Tizard with General Montgomery, Oxford, March 1944

Prime Minister in 1940, with Lindemann as his scientific adviser, Tizard resigned from his Air Ministry responsibilities, except for his membership of the Aeronautical Research Committee. In 1940 he headed a mission to the USA, which did invaluable work in advising the American authorities on the scientific work done in Britain on radar and other defensive devices. He continued to interest himself in the development of the jet engine and supported the work on Barnes WALLIS's dam-busting bomb. He queried the policy of bombing built-up areas of Germany, but Lord Cherwell (Lindemann) was now at the height of his influence with the Prime Minister and he was in favour of this policy.

In 1942 Tizard accepted the presidency of Magdalen College, Oxford, but his advice continued to be sought by the Service Chiefs, and in 1944 he was chairman of a committee set up to assess the probable effects of new weapons on defence policy. In 1947 he resigned from Magdalen College to become Chairman of the Defence Research Policy Committee and Advisory Council on Scientific Policy, but in post-war conditions he found this an arduous and often frustrating responsibility. His health began to fail, and in 1952 he retired from Whitehall.

Tizard received many honours; an AFC in 1918, CB in 1927, KCB in 1937 and GCB in 1949. He was elected FRS in 1926 and was Vice-President in 1940-1 and 1944-5. He received many academic honours, and in 1948 was President of the British Association. He died at Fareham on 9 October 1959 and his ashes were buried in the ante-chapel of Oriel College, Oxford.

TOLKIEN, JOHN RONALD REUEL (1892-1973), author and philologist, was born in Bloemfontein, Orange Free State, on 3 January 1892, the elder son of Arthur Reuel Tolkien, branch manager of the Bank of Africa, and his wife, Mabel, daughter of John Suffield, formerly of Birmingham.

His father died when he was three, and his mother settled with her two sons near Birmingham. Tolkien was educated at King Edward VI's School, Birmingham and Exeter College, Oxford, where he obtained a first in English language and literature (1915). His mother had died when he was twelve and he and his brother were, at her request, brought up as Roman Catholics by Father Francis Morgan of the Birmingham Oratory.

During the First World War Tolkien fought with the Lancashire Fusiliers on the Western Front, was invalided home with trench fever and, whilst in hospital, began to write *The Silmarillion,* tales of a mythological world. In 1916 he married Edith, the orphaned daughter of Francis Bratt, of Wolverhampton, with whom he had fallen in love at the age of sixteen; they had three sons and a daughter.

For a time, Tolkien worked on the staff of the *New English Dictionary* and then, in 1920, was appointed Reader in English language at Leeds University. In 1925, in collaboration with E. V. Gordon, he published an edition of *Sir Gawain and the Green Knight.* That year he was elected Rawlinson and Bosworth Professor of Anglo-Saxon at Oxford and set out to improve the 'language' side of the syllabus. In 1929 he published an essay in *Essays and Studies',* vol. xiv, on the Middle English *Ancrene Wisse.*

Although Tolkien had a career as a professional philologist, he made his name with his book for children, *The Hobbit,* published by Stanley UNWIN in 1937; this was an immediate success and was followed by *The Lord of the Rings* recording the mythological adventures of Frodo and Gandolf to free Middle-Earth from the Tyranny of Sauron, the Lord of Darkness. The first volume of this trilogy was not finished until 1949 and did not appear in print until 1954. The second volume was also published in 1954 and the third in 1955. The delay was caused by Tolkien's wish to publish *The Silmarillion* with the new book but, in fact, this was not published until 1977, four years after his death.

From 1945 till 1959 Tolkien was Merton Professor of English Language and Literature at Oxford. The success of *The Hobbit* and *The Lord of the Rings* was enhanced by their acceptance as a 'campus cult' in America and, after his retirement from his Oxford chair, Tolkien was overwhelmed by the publicity aroused by his success. In the USA a Tolkien Society was formed.

After his wife died in 1971 Tolkien lived in Merton College of which he became an honorary Fellow in 1973. He was appointed CBE in 1972, and among his academic honours was an honorary fellowship of Exeter College, Oxford. He died in Bournemouth on 2 September 1973. His *Letters* were published in 1981, edited by Humphrey Carpenter with the assistance of Christopher Tolkien, his father's literary executor.

TONKS, HENRY (1862-1937), artist and teacher of art, was born at Solihull on 9 April 1862, the second son of Edmund Tonks, a brass-founder, and his wife, Julia, daughter of Henry Johnson, a wine merchant. He was educated at Clifton and studied medicine at the Royal Sussex Hospital, Brighton and at the London Hospital (1881). He became demonstrator in anatomy and was elected FRCS in 1888. He later became Senior Medical Officer at the Royal Free Hospital.

He had always been interested in art, and from 1890 he studied part-time under Frederick Brown at the Westminster School of Art. In 1894 he became assistant to Brown on his appointment as Slade Professor of Fine Art at University

College London. Shortly afterwards, they were joined by Wilson Steer.

Tonks, while teaching Augustus JOHN, William ORPEN, and many other students who later made their names, was able to develop his own work, at first, in water-colours and, then, in oils. In 1895 he became a member of the New English Art Club and regularly contributed to its exhibitions. His painting *The Birdcage* can be seen in the Ashmolean Museum, Oxford, and some of his other pictures are in the Tate Gallery.

Tonks was particularly outstanding as a teacher. In 1917 he succeeded Brown as the Slade Professor and held that post until 1930. He was an out-and-out traditionalist, with no respect for futurism or abstract forms of art. Of necessity, this led him into fierce controversies, in which he upheld his views with vehemence. This did not preclude him from enjoying the friendship of many distinguished artists and writers. A special exhibition of his work was held at the Tate in 1936. He died, unmarried, in London on 8 January 1937.

TOYNBEE, ARNOLD JOSEPH (1889–1975), scholar and author, was born in London on 14 April 1889, the only son of Harry Valpy Toynbee, a worker for the Charity Organization Society, and his wife, Sarah Edith Marshall. He went as a scholar to Winchester and Balliol College, Oxford, where he obtained firsts in Classical Mods. and Greats (1909–11). Between then and 1915 he travelled in Greece and Asia Minor and was a student at the British School of Archaeology, Athens. In 1913 he married Rosalind, daughter of Gilbert MURRAY, the Oxford scholar; they had three sons. Unfit for military service during the First World War, Toynbee worked in the Political Intelligence Department of the Foreign Office.

He was a member of the British delegation to the Paris Peace Conference in 1919 and was appointed Koraes Professor of Byzantine and Modern Greek Language, Literature, and History at London University (1919–24). In 1925 he became Director of Studies at Chatham House (the Royal Institute of International Affairs), and was responsible for the production of the annual *Survey of International Affairs*. He was also Research Professor of International History, London University. He retired from both posts in 1955, having during the Second World War been Director of the Foreign Office Research Department.

His first marriage ended in divorce in 1946, and in that year he married Veronica Marjorie, daughter of the Revd Sidney Boulter, with whom he had worked since 1925 at Chatham House.

Toynbee's reputation as a scholar rests on *A Study of History* (12 vols., 1934–61), published by the Oxford University Press, in which he gave copious illustrations of his view that successive civilizations rose and fell according to 'challenge and response', climatic or otherwise, a theory that did not go unchallenged by other scholars of history. An abridged edition, prepared by David C. Somervell, made this compendious work more easily accessible to the general reader (1960).

Toynbee published many other learned books, as well as contributing regularly to the *Manchester Guardian* and the *Observer*, and writing many editorials for *The Economist* between 1930 and 1939. His lectures, including the Reith lecture of 1952 and the Gifford series of 1953–4, were also published in book form. Among his other works are *Hannibal's Legacy* (1965), *Acquaintances* (1967), *Experiences*

Herbert Beerbohm Tree in Clyde Fitch's *The Last of the Dandies*, Her Majesty's Theatre, 1901

(1969), *Mankind and Mother Earth* (1976), and *The Greeks and their Heritages* (1981).

He was elected FBA (1937), elected an honorary Fellow of Balliol (1957), and appointed CH (1956). He had many other academic honours, including appointment as an associate member of the French Institute (1968). Toynbee died on 22 October 1975 at York.

TREE, SIR HERBERT BEERBOHM (1852–1917), actor-manager, was born in London on 17 December 1852, the second son of Julius Ewald Beerbohm, a grain merchant and a naturalized British subject of German, Dutch, and Lithuanian extraction, and his first wife, Constantia Draper. Max BEERBOHM was his half-brother. He was educated in England and Germany, and worked in his father's business, but by 1876 was already appearing as an amateur actor under the name of Beerbohm Tree.

In 1879 he turned professional, and between 1880 and 1887 appeared in over fifty plays, showing himself to be an actor of versatile talents. In 1887 he became his own manager, and for the next ten years, as lessee and Manager of the Haymarket Theatre, London, he produced and acted in over thirty plays, including works by Shakespeare, Ibsen, Wilde, and Maeterlinck. In 1895–6 he made visits to the USA.

Tree reached the height of his fame when, from 1897 to the beginning of the First World War, he made His Majesty's

Theatre his home, and produced there works by a number of playwrights, but notably specializing in elaborate productions of Shakespeare, in which he acted as Mark Antony, Bottom, Malvolio, Falstaff, Shylock, and Macbeth, with flamboyant realism. In 1914 he made one excursion into modernism by producing SHAW's *Pygmalion*. During 1915-16 he was in the USA, fulfilling a contract with a film company.

In 1904 he founded the Academy of Dramatic Art, and in 1905 succeeded Sir Henry Irving as President of the Theatrical Managers' Association. He was knighted in 1909. In 1882 he had married Maud, daughter of William Holt; they had three daughters. He died suddenly in London on 2 July 1917.

TRENCHARD, HUGH MONTAGUE, first VISCOUNT TRENCHARD (1873-1956), Marshal of the Royal Air Force, was born at Taunton on 3 February 1873, the second son of Henry Montague Trenchard, a lawyer, and his wife, Georgiana Louisa Catherine Tower, daughter of Capt. John McDowall Skene, RN. Having little formal schooling he failed the entry examination to Dartmouth, and went instead to an army crammer. It was an unhappy time for him, principally on account of the disgrace he felt when his father became a bankrupt, but after several attempts Trenchard finally entered the army as a militia candidate and was posted to India with the 2nd battalion Royal Scots Fusiliers in 1893.

After service in India and in the Boer War, in which he was seriously wounded, he joined the Southern Nigeria Regiment and served in West Africa from 1903 to 1910, being appointed DSO in 1906. In 1912 he obtained an air pilot's certificate and was seconded to the Royal Flying Corps as an instructor, and earned the nickname 'Boom' by which he soon became generally known. By 1914 he was commandant of the Military Wing at Farnborough, responsible for the organization and equipment of a rapidly expanding force. From 1915 to 1918 he commanded the RFC in France and made his reputation as an exponent of persistent attack by air with the object of obtaining complete mastery over the enemy.

For his war services Trenchard received a baronetcy in 1919, having been appointed in 1918 KCB and first Chief of the new Air Staff. He found that he could not work with Lord ROTHERMERE, the Air Minister, and after a few months, he resigned. When, however, Winston CHURCHILL became Minister for War and Air in 1919, Trenchard returned to his post as Chief of the Air Staff and stayed there for the next ten years. He had become a legendary figure to pilots in the First World War, and he now addressed himself to the tasks of building up a modern air force in peace-time conditions and of protecting it from take-over by the War Office or the Admiralty. In 1927 he was appointed the first Marshal of the Royal Air Force, having been promoted GCB in 1924. He had married in 1920 Katharine Isabel Salvin, daughter of Edward Salvin Bowlby and widow of Capt. the Hon. James Boyle; they had two sons.

When Trenchard retired in 1929 he was regarded as the 'Father of the Royal Air Force' and Lord MORAN described him in his book on Churchill as 'a block of granite'. A. J. P. Taylor has claimed that, as a result of his experience in the First World War, Trenchard 'insisted that victory by air power alone was theoretically possible, and he riveted this doctrine on the RAF', and 'This was probably the most permanent, certainly the most disastrous, legacy of the First World War'. Nevertheless, whether or not Trenchard's advocacy of mass bombardment went too far, he could justly

claim to have created a force, both of fighters and bombers, that saved Britain in 1940.

Shortly after his retirement Trenchard was created a baron, and in 1931 he was asked to become Commissioner of the Metropolitan Police, which was thought to be in need of re-organization. Trenchard tackled this new responsibility with characteristic energy, improving training methods and creating the Police College and Forensic Laboratory at Hendon, but his activities in this post were not without their critics and, after he retired in 1935, many of his proposed reforms were quickly forgotten. For this work he was appointed GCVO (1935), and in 1936 created a viscount.

After leaving government service Trenchard was Chairman of the United Africa Company from 1936 to 1953. He was appointed OM in 1951, and granted honorary degrees by Oxford and Cambridge Universities. His elder son was killed in action in North Africa in 1943. Trenchard himself died in London on 10 February 1956; he was buried in Westminster Abbey and was succeeded by his younger son, Thomas.

TRENT, first BARON (1850-1931). See BOOT.

TREVELYAN, GEORGE MACAULAY (1876-1962), historian, was born on 16 February 1876 at Welcombe, Warwickshire, the third son of (Sir) George Otto Trevelyan, author and politician, and his wife, Caroline, daughter of Robert Needham Philips. Lord Macaulay, the historian, was his great-uncle and he was brought up to admire his work and to seek to emulate him as a literary historian. He was educated at Harrow and Trinity College, Cambridge, where he obtained a first in the historical tripos (1896), and was elected to a fellowship (1898) with a dissertation, which was published in 1899 as *England in the Age of Wycliffe*.

He lectured and taught history at Trinity until 1903, when he left Cambridge for London and, a year later, married Janet Penrose, daughter of Humphry and Mary Ward, the novelist. In the same year he published *England under the Stuarts*, a book not for scholars but for the general public. This was followed by one of his major works, the trilogy on Garibaldi (1907-11), which brought him fame. In 1913 he published *Clio, a Muse*, his plea for the acceptance of history as a branch of literature, and a *Life of John Bright*.

Poor eyesight precluded war service in 1914, but he raised and commanded an ambulance unit, which served on the Italian front; he was awarded Italian decorations, and appointed CBE in 1920. After the war he reverted to his writing, published *Lord Grey of the Reform Bill* (1920), *British History in the Nineteenth Century* (1922), and his *History of England* (1926), all remarkable for their descriptive ability and lucidity.

In 1927 Trevelyan was appointed Regius Professor of Modern History at Cambridge, and set out to write his second major work *England under Queen Anne* (3 vols., 1930-4). He also wrote a life of Lord GREY of Fallodon (1937). Then, in 1940, he became Master of Trinity College, Cambridge. His administrative responsibilities, however, did not prevent him from writing, and in 1944 his *English Social History* appeared, another readable work which had a wider circulation. This was the last of his historical studies, but he produced other works including anthologies from Carlyle (1953) and Meredith (1955), and *A Layman's Love of Letters* (1954).

In 1951 he was President of the English Association, from 1950 to 1958 he was Chancellor of Durham University, he was elected FBA (1925) and FRS (1950) and appointed OM (1930). He received many academic honours and was a Trustee of the British Museum and National Portrait Gallery.

He and his wife had two sons and a daughter, who also became a historian. Janet Trevelyan was appointed CH in 1936 for her work in London for children. G. M. Trevelyan died in Cambridge on 21 July 1962.

TURING, ALAN MATHISON (1912–1954), mathematician, was born in London on 23 June 1912, the younger son of Julius Mathison Turing, of the Indian Civil Service, and his wife, Ethel Sara, daughter of Edward Walter Stoney, chief engineer of an Indian railway. He was educated at Sherborne School and King's College, Cambridge, where he was a scholar and obtained a first in the mathematical tripos, part ii, in 1934. In the following year he was elected to a fellowship at King's, and in 1936 awarded a Smith's prize. In a paper for the London Mathematical Society in 1937, Turing demonstrated that there are classes of mathematical problems which cannot be solved by any automatic process; at the same time he produced a theoretical description of a computing machine for automatic problem-solving (later known as the Turing machine), which aroused much interest.

Turing spent two years (1936–8) at Princeton in the USA, but when the Second World War broke out he was employed by the Communications Department of the Foreign Office. For many years after his death nothing was known publicly of the work Turing did at Bletchley Park, though in 1946 he was appointed OBE for his services. The breach of the German naval codes in 1941 gave the Admiralty, for a time, immense advantages in fighting the 'Battle of the Atlantic', and Turing was one of the central figures in devising the means to bring about this achievement using his own model computer for the purpose. In the winter of 1942–3 he returned to the United States for a visit to give his American counterparts the benefits of his expertise.

After the war he decided to specialize in the field of computers and became a senior principal scientific officer in the mathematics division of the National Physical Laboratory at Teddington. There he put forward proposals, specifying the electronic requirements of a 'universal' computer of the kind he had described theoretically in 1937. When in 1948 he resigned, disappointed by the fact that the assembly of such a machine had not even been started, he accepted a readership at Manchester University and became Assistant Director of the Manchester Automatic Digital Machine. A working model of the Automatic Computing Engine he had devised at the NPL was eventually demonstrated in 1950.

At Manchester Turing became increasingly interested in the central questions concerning artificial intelligence: whether the human mind can be simulated by machine and how the success of any attempted simulation might be measured. His article 'Computing Machinery and Intelligence' in *Mind* (1950) was a major contribution to the philosophy of this new science. In the following year Turing was elected FRS. However, the Manchester computer was a slow unwieldy version of the kind of machine that Turing would have wished to see, and, disappointed once more, he turned away from the subject, and during his last few years set out on research in theoretical biology, devoting his genius to the problems of a mathematical analysis of the chemistry of growth in plants and animals.

Turing was a solitary man who enjoyed long distance running. He never married, being a homosexual. He died at Wilmslow, Cheshire on 7 June 1954, having taken poison; after inquiry, a verdict of suicide was returned.

TWEEDSMUIR, first BARON (1875–1940). See BUCHAN.

U

UNWIN, SIR STANLEY (1884–1968), publisher, was born on 19 December 1884 in London, the youngest of nine children of Edward Unwin, a printer, and his wife, Elizabeth, daughter of James Spicer, a paper manufacturer. He was brought up a devout Nonconformist and educated at the School for the Sons of Missionaries, Blackheath and Abbotsholme School (1897–9). After gaining experience of the book trade in Germany, he joined the publishing firm of his uncle, T. Fisher Unwin (1904).

Failing to agree with his relative on a joint ownership, he bought the bankrupt firm of George Allen & Co. in 1912 and quickly established himself as the spokesman of the British book trade at home and abroad. His list of authors included Bertrand RUSSELL, Benedetto Croce, August Strindberg, Albert Sorel, James Elroy Flecker, Jules Romain, and Sir J.C. Squire.

In 1914 he married (Alice) Mary, daughter of Rayner Storr, an auctioneer; they had two sons and a daughter.

During the First World War Unwin published books by conscientious objectors, including *The Framework of a Last-ing Peace*, edited by Leonard WOOLF (1917) and books about the peace by George Lansbury, G. P. GOOCH, and J. H. B. Masterman. He was not interested in fiction and, after the war, his list included Russell's *The Practice and Theory of Bolshevism* (1920) as well as the works of Arthur WALEY, Sidney WEBB, G. D. H. COLE, R. H. TAWNEY, Lowes-Dickinson, Gilbert MURRAY, H. W. NEVINSON, and Sigmund Freud. He also had strong links with the Fabian Society and published the work of Harold LASKI.

In 1936 he published the best seller *Mathematics for the Million*, followed in 1938 by *Science for the Citizen*, both by Lancelot Hogben. In 1937 he brought out J. R. R. TOLKIEN's *The Hobbit*, followed later by *The Lord of the Rings* (1954–5). One of his later successes was Thor Heyerdahl's *The Kon-Tiki Expedition* (1950).

Stanley Unwin travelled widely on business and in the interest of the Publishers' Association and the British Council. He was President of the Association in 1933. Almost up to the time of his death, he was a fanatical tennis player. He was knighted in 1946 and appointed KCMG in 1966. In

Stanley Unwin (left) with Basil Blackwell

1926 he published his own book, *The Truth about Publishing*, and in 1960 *The Truth about a Publisher*. Unwin died in London on 13 October 1968. His son, Rayner, succeeded him in the business.

UVAROV, SIR BORIS PETROVITCH (1889-1970), entomologist, was born in Russia at Uralsk on 5 November 1889, the youngest son of Petr P. Uvarov, a State Bank employee, and his wife, Alexandra. He graduated at St Petersburg (Leningrad) University with a first in biology (1910). In that year he married Anna Federova Prodanjuk;

they had one son who was educated in Britain. Uvarov held appointments in provincial departments of agriculture until, in 1915, he became Director of the Tiflis Bureau of Plant Protection. Four years later, when he was Keeper of Entomology and Zoology in the State Museum of Georgia, he met Patrick A. Buxton, medical entomologist with the British troops in Georgia and, through him, was given an appointment at the Imperial Bureau (later the Commonwealth Institute) of Entomology in London (1920).

While he worked in Russia, Uvarov had become an expert on the study of locusts and grasshoppers and had evolved the 'phase theory', which enunciated that swarming and non-swarming locusts were not different species but phases of the same insect. At the Bureau in London, he not only organized and supervised investigations into plagues of swarming locusts in south-west Asia and Africa, but he also published *Locusts and Grasshoppers* (1928), *Insect Nutrition and Metabolism* (1928), and *Insects and Climate* (1931). His small unit soon came to be recognized as the world centre for locust research.

In 1938 Uvarov initiated a plan for the international control of locusts, concentrating on their destruction in the 'outbreak' areas as a means of preventing dangerous swarming. The plan was interrupted by the Second World War, but the methods proposed were used successfully under Uvarov's direction in North Africa. In 1943 he became a naturalized British citizen, and in 1945 his unit became the Anti-Locust Research Centre under the Colonial Office and the foremost laboratory in the world for research on locusts. He retired in 1959 but continued to work as a consultant. His output of scientific articles was prodigious; his contribution to taxonomy, in which he classified and described many hundreds of species, was remarkable; and his emphasis on the importance of physiological and ecological studies was proved to be of practical value in the large-scale control of locust outbreaks.

He received many honours, notably CMG (1943), FRS (1950), and KCMG (1961). During 1959-61 he was President of the Royal Entomological Society of London. Uvarov died at Ealing on 18 March 1970.

V

VANBRUGH, DAME IRENE (1872-1949), actress, was born at Exeter on 2 December 1872, the youngest daughter of the Revd Reginald Henry Barnes, Prebendary of Exeter Cathedral, and his wife, Frances Mary Emily, daughter of William Nation, a barrister. The stage name Vanbrugh was adopted by her sister Violet, at the suggestion of Ellen TERRY. Violet, who was over five years older than Irene, entered on her stage career under J. L. Toole in 1886. Irene was then at school but, after a short spell of training under Sarah Thorue, she made her stage début in 1888 as Phoebe in *As You Like It*. She first appeared in London as the White Queen and Jack of Hearts in *Alice in Wonderland* in the same year.

For a time she appeared in a number of West End productions under J. L. Toole, and toured Australia with him

in 1890. She had her biggest successes, however, in the plays of Arthur PINERO, beginning with Rose in *Trelawny of the 'Wells'* (1898) and reaching one of her greatest triumphs as Nina Jesson in *His House in Order* (1906). She also played leading parts in BARRIE's *The Admirable Crichton* (1902), Somerset MAUGHAM's *Grace* (1910) and *The Land of Promise* (1914), and A.A. MILNE's *Mr Pim Passes By* (1920).

In 1901 she married Dion Boucicault, the younger, who in 1915 became her manager and with whom she acted until his death in 1929; they had no children.

In the thirties she appeared in plays by G. B. SHAW, and in 1934 played Mistress Page to her sister's Mistress Ford in *The Merry Wives of Windsor*.

She was appointed DBE in 1941 and during the Second World War co-operated with (Sir) Donald Wolfit, putting on lunch-time performances at the Strand Theatre. She was ready to help every theatrical good cause, and was a keen supporter of the Royal Academy of Dramatic Art, of which her brother, Sir Kenneth Barnes, was the first Director. She appeared in a number of films, although the living theatre was her main interest. In 1948 she published her autobiography, *To Tell My Story*. She died in London on 30 November 1949.

VANSITTART, ROBERT GILBERT, Baron Vansittart (1881–1957), diplomat, was born on 25 June 1881 at Farnham, the eldest son of Robert Arnold Vansittart, 7th Dragoon Guards, and his wife, Susan (Alice), daughter of Gilbert Jones Blane, of Foliejon Park, Berkshire. He was educated at Eton, where he distinguished himself in modern languages. He then visited Germany and France in preparation for the Foreign Service, which he entered as an attaché in Paris (1903).

Between 1903 and 1911 he served in Paris, Tehran, and Cairo and, in the latter year, was posted to the Foreign Office. During the First World War he was joint head of the Contraband Department and then head of the Prisoners of War Department. He attended the Paris Peace Conference, became an Assistant Secretary in 1920, and during 1928–9 was Private Secretary to the Prime Minister. In 1930 he was appointed Permanent Under-Secretary in the Foreign Office. (While he was at the Paris embassy, a play in French written by him ran for four months.)

From 1930 to 1938 Vansittart was head of the Foreign Office, through the critical years which saw the rise of Mussolini and Hitler, the incorporation of Austria in Germany, and the growing menace of another war in Europe. He saw clearly the threat which the Nazi aggression posed to Ger-many's neighbours and was a most outspoken critic of the inertia of successive British Governments in the face of this danger. He not only warned the Prime Minister and the Foreign Secretary, challenging the policy of appeasement; he passed information to Winston CHURCHILL and invoked the assistance of the press in his campaign. By 1938 foreign policy was, to all intents and purposes, in the hands of the Prime Minister, Neville CHAMBERLAIN, and Chamberlain, tired of Vansittart's warnings, removed him from his office as Permanent Under-Secretary and created a special post of 'chief diplomatic adviser', in which Vansittart would be innocuous as his advice could be ignored.

He held that post for three years and saw the outbreak of war, the fall of France, and the supersession of Chamberlain by Churchill. The proposal for union between Britain and France, which it was hoped might induce the French Government to fight on in 1940, was drafted by Vansittart, together with General de Gaulle and Jean Monnet.

When he retired in 1941 he was created a baron, having been sworn of the Privy Council in the previous year. His other honours were MVO (1906), CMG (1920), CB (1927), KCB (1929), GCMG (1931), and GCB (1938). In 1958 he published his autobiography *The Mist Procession*.

In 1921 he married Gladys, daughter of William C. Heppenheimer of the United States Army; they had one daughter; Gladys died in 1928, and in 1931 he married Sarita Enriqueta, daughter of Herbert Ward, of Paris, and widow of Sir Colville Barclay. Vansittart died at Denham on 14 February 1957 and the peerage became extinct.

VAUGHAN WILLIAMS, RALPH (1872–1958), composer, was born on 12 October 1872 at Down Ampney, Gloucestershire, the younger son of the Vicar, the Revd Arthur

Vaughan Williams conducting the band of the 2nd Battalion, Duke of Cornwall's Light Infantry at Milton Court, Dorking in the incidental music to *England's Pleasant Land* by E. M. Forster

Vaughan Williams, and his wife, Margaret, daughter of the third Josiah Wedgwood, grandson of the potter. He was educated at Charterhouse and Trinity College, Cambridge, and studied at the Royal College of Music, where he took his Mus. Bac. (1894) and, after further study with Max Bruch in Berlin, and Ravel in Paris, became Mus. D. (1901). In 1897 he married Adeline, daughter of Herbert William Fisher, and sister of H. A. L. FISHER.

His music was influenced by English folk-song and hymnody, including plainsong, to which he was led by editing *The English Hymnal* (1906). He also edited a volume of works by Purcell and Elizabethan madrigals. His earliest work consisted of songs, examples of which are 'Linden Lea' (1902) and 'Silent Noon' (1903). His collection of folk-songs led to three orchestral 'Norfolk Rhapsodies' (1906-7) and the *Fantasia on Christmas Carols* (1912). In 1910 he produced the *Sea Symphony*, with words by Walt Whitman, whose verse he had used in an earlier work, *Towards the Unknown Region* (1907).

During the First World War he served in the Royal Army Medical Corps in France and Salonika, and with the Royal Garrison Artillery.

His first purely instrumental symphony, the *London*, appeared in 1920, one of nine which also included the *Pastoral* (1922) and the *Sinfonia Antartica* (1952), which stemmed from the music he had composed for the film *Scott of the Antarctic*. Among his choral works, there was one oratorio, *Sancta Civitas* (1926). He also composed much dramatic music, including incidental music to pageants, masques, Shakespearian plays, and Greek plays, such as *The Wasps* of Aristophanes (1909). Other dramatic music included *Hugh the Drover* (1924) and *The Pilgrim's Progress* (1951). His most important chamber work is the song sequence *On Wenlock Edge* (1909).

From 1921 to 1928 Vaughan Williams conducted the Bach Choir; he taught composition at the Royal College of Music for twenty years. For many years, he was associated with the Leith Hill musical festival, having been brought up at Leith Hill Place. He received many honours including an honorary Mus. D. (Oxford, 1919) and an honorary fellowship of Trinity College, Cambridge (1935). He refused a knighthood, but was appointed OM (1935).

His first wife died in 1951, and in 1953 he married Ursula, daughter of Major-General Sir Robert Lock and widow of Lt.-Col. J. M. J. Forrester Wood. Vaughan Williams died in London on 26 August 1958 and was buried in Westminster Abbey.

VENTRIS, MICHAEL GEORGE FRANCIS (1922–1956), archaeologist, was born at Wheathampstead, Herts. on 12 July 1922, the only child of Edward Francis Vereker Ventris, Indian Army, and his wife, Dora Janasz, who was partly Polish. He was educated at Stowe School and the Architectural Association School, London. He served in the RAF during the Second World War, and then finished his architectural training with honours (1948).

He became a member of the Ministry of Education Schools Development Branch and was expected to have a brilliant career ahead as an architect. In 1956 he was awarded the first research fellowship offered by the *Architects' Journal*.

From his childhood he was keenly interested in languages and scripts and, from the age of fourteen, he was concerned with the problem of the undeciphered Minoan scripts, which Sir Arthur EVANS called Linear A and B, written on tablets by the prehistoric inhabitants of Crete and Greece. At first,

Vicky at work on one of his daily cartoons, 1951

Ventris thought they were related to Etruscan, until in 1951 publication of tablets found at Pylos in south-west Greece gave him a clue from which, by painstaking systematic analysis, he was led to the conclusion that Linear B was of Greek origin. He published his theory in the *Journal of Hellenic Studies* in 1953. At first regarded by Greek scholars with some scepticism, the theory which Ventris had formulated was confirmed by the discovery of another tablet.

In 1956 he published *Documents in Mycenaean Greek*, his only book. In 1955 he received the OBE. In 1942 he had married Lois Elizabeth, daughter of Lt.-Col. Hugh William Knox-Niven; they had a son and a daughter. Ventris was killed in a car accident near Hatfield on 6 September 1956.

VICKY (1913–1966), cartoonist, whose real name was Victor Weisz, was born in Berlin on 25 April 1913, the son of Desider Weisz and his wife, Isabella, who were Hungarian Jews. He went to the Berlin Art School and found work on the Berliners' *12 Uhr Blatt*, publishing an anti-Hitler cartoon at the age of fifteen. He made a reputation as a caricaturist of theatrical and sporting personalities, but earned the antagonism of the Nazis, lost his job, and had to escape to England.

With little knowledge of English, he failed to get work with the *Daily Herald* in 1938 but, a year later, was recruited to the *News Chronicle* by (Sir) Gerald Barry, the Editor. He set to work to make himself competent in the language and to understand the English sense of humour, studying *Hansard* and the ITMA shows of Tommy HANDLEY. After two years, his English was perfect, and in 1941 he became staff cartoonist for the *News Chronicle*, a post which he held until 1955.

In 1946 he became a British subject. He was now a notable cartoonist with decidedly left-wing views. He resigned from the *News Chronicle*, when one of his cartoons on Kenya was refused. He joined the *Daily Mirror* and in 1958 moved to the *Evening Standard*. He also produced 'profiles' for the *New Statesman*.

He had now succeeded David Low as the most brilliant cartoonist in Britain, famous for his caricatures of political figures, such as Charles de Gaulle, the totem pole, ATTLEE, the zither player, Macmillan, Supermac, and EDEN, the White Rabbit. His output was prodigious. He was not, however, a happy man. He was obsessed with disillusion about the course of world events and the indifference of politicians to disasters which seemed to him to threaten the civilized

world. Michael Foot described him as 'a twentieth-century Don Quixote'.

He was married four times, but had no children. He had a brief period of happiness with his fourth wife, Ingelore, daughter of Shosama Weltsch, a German Jewess, whom he married in 1965. He died in London on 23 February 1966, having taken an overdose of sleeping pills, and leaving behind a newly-drawn cartoon about the Labour Government's attitude to the Vietnam War. His widow committed suicide nine years later, on the anniversary of his death.

W

WADDELL, HELEN JANE (1889–1965), author and translator, was born on 31 May 1889 in Tokyo, the youngest child of the Revd Hugh Waddell, Presbyterian missionary, and his wife, Jane Martin, of Banbridge, co. Down. Her mother died when Helen was two and she was brought up in Ulster, being educated at Victoria College and Queen's University, Belfast, where she graduated with first class honours (1911) and became MA (1912).

In 1913 she published *Lyrics from the Chinese*. In 1920 she went up to Somerville College, Oxford to work for a research degree and became interested in medieval Latin lyric and medieval humanism. During 1922–3 she taught at Bedford College, London and during 1924–5 studied in Paris with a travelling scholarship from Lady Margaret Hall, where in 1926 she lectured on 'The Wandering Scholars'.

Between 1927 and 1936 she published a number of books, including *The Wandering Scholars* (1927), *Medieval Latin Lyrics* (1929), the novel *Peter Abelard* (1933), perhaps her best work, and *The Desert Fathers* (1936). She also edited *A Book of Medieval Latin for Schools* (1931) and *Cole's Paris Journal* (1931), and translated *Manon Lescaut* (1931) and a collection of stories *Beasts and Saints* (1934). She was also assistant editor of *The Nineteenth Century*.

Among her many friends she numbered Max BEERBOHM, Charles L. MORGAN, G. B. SHAW, and Siegfried SASSOON. Her last book, *Poetry in the Dark Ages*, was published in 1948. She never married. She died in London on 5 March 1965.

WAKEFIELD, CHARLES CHEERS, VISCOUNT WAKEFIELD (1859–1941), business man and philanthropist, was born in Liverpool on 12 December 1859, the youngest son of John Wakefield, a customs official, and his wife, Mary, daughter of William Cheers, of Manchester. He was educated at the Liverpool Institute and then worked for an oil-broker and travelled widely. In 1887 he married Sarah Frances, daughter of William Graham, a book-keeper of Liverpool. They had no children.

In 1899 he founded C. C. Wakefield & Co., dealing in lubricating oils and appliances. Motor vehicles were in the experimental stage and he gave his oil the trade name 'Castrol' because early engine lubricants contained castor oil. His industry and acumen soon brought Wakefield great wealth, and he became a benefactor in many charitable causes.

He was elected to the Court of Common Council of the City of London in 1904, was Sheriff in 1907–8, knighted in 1908, and was Lord Mayor in 1915–16. He became a baronet in 1917 and was appointed CBE in 1919.

He gave generous aid to the Guildhall Library and Art Gallery and to the Imperial Institute. He financed Sir Alan Cobham's and Amy JOHNSON's record flights and Sir Henry Segrave's speed trials at Daytona and Miami. He owned the three Miss England speedboats which set up world water-speed records. He was Chairman of the RAF Benevolent Fund, President of the Bethlem Royal Hospital, and Governor of St Thomas's and St Bartholomew's Hospitals. He gave lavishly to these and many other organizations.

In 1930 he became Baron Wakefield, and in 1934, Viscount. He was appointed GCVO in 1936. He published *America To-day and To-morrow* (1924) and *On Leaving School and the Choice of a Career* (1927). Wakefield died at Beaconsfield on 15 January 1941.

WALCAN-BRIGHT, GERALD (1904–1974). See GERALDO.

WALEY, ARTHUR DAVID (1889–1966), orientalist, was born at Tunbridge Wells on 19 August 1889, the second of the three sons of David Frederick Schloss, an economist, and his wife, Rachel Sophia, daughter of Jacob Waley, Professor of Political Economy at London University. Both sides of the family were Jewish. Arthur and his brother David, who became a distinguished civil servant, were educated at Rugby but, whereas David went on to Balliol College, Oxford, Arthur went to King's College, Cambridge with an open scholarship. There, he obtained a first in part i of the classical tripos in 1910, but had to abandon Cambridge when he developed defective eyesight.

Travelling abroad, he learnt German and Spanish, and on his return to England, influenced by Oswald Sickert, a brother of the painter, he joined the Sub-Department of Oriental Prints and Drawings at the British Museum. Soon he had taught himself Chinese and Japanese, though he never visited either country. When the First World War broke out, he and his brothers changed their name to Waley.

By 1917 Waley was translating Chinese poems and publishing them in the *New Statesman* and other journals. In 1918 Constable published a volume of his translations *A*

Hundred and Seventy Chinese Poems. Later Stanley UNWIN became his publisher and close friend. Waley was known to the Bloomsbury group, including the Stephen sisters, Vanessa (BELL) and Virginia (WOOLF), but he was too serious minded to be admitted to their circle and, for some reason, had incurred the hostility of Lytton STRACHEY.

He worked in the British Museum for sixteen years, but his only official publications were the index of Chinese artists (1922) and a catalogue of the paintings recovered from Tunhuang by Sir Aurel Stein (1931). In 1923, however, he published *An Introduction to the Study of Chinese Painting* and some Japanese translations of selections of classic poetry from the *Uta* and *Nō* plays were brought out in 1919 and 1921. His best-known work was his translation of the *Genji Monogatari* by Murasaki Shikibu, the tenth-century novelist of Japan (6 vols., 1925–33).

Waley lived in Bloomsbury for over forty years and for forty years, off and on from the 1920s, he was associated with Beryl de Zoete, an anthropologist and authority on Eastern dances. She was an eccentric, intelligent woman, but a little formidable in the eyes of Waley's friends and, for the last ten years of her life, the victim of an incurable hereditary disease of the nervous system. Waley was inclined to be a silent, remote figure in company, his greatest relaxation being to get away to ski on the loneliest slopes he could find in Switzerland or Norway. However, he had a brief affair with a young New Zealander, Alison Grant, at a time when his relations with Beryl de Zoete had temporarily been broken off.

Although Waley knew little of contemporary China or Japan, he was bitterly critical of the attitude of the West to the culture of the Far East, and aired his views in *The Opium War through Chinese Eyes* (1958). As a scholar, he always sought to interpret Chinese and Japanese thought with meticulous accuracy and deep seriousness and to make his translations works of literature in themselves.

In 1945 he became an honorary Fellow of King's College, Cambridge; he was elected FBA in the same year; he received the Queen's medal for poetry in 1953, and was appointed CBE in 1952 and CH in 1956. After the death in 1962 of Beryl de Zoete, whom Waley had devotedly cared for during her last ten years, Alison Grant returned to him, although since their last meeting she had been married and divorced. They went to live at Highgate and were married a month before Waley died from cancer on 27 June 1966. An anthology of his writings was edited by Ivan Morris and published as *Madly Singing in the Mountains* (1970), and a bibliography of his work was published by F. A. Johns in 1968. Alison Waley gave her account of her relationship with Waley in *A Half of Two Lives*, published in 1982.

WALLACE, (RICHARD HORATIO) EDGAR (1875–1932), novelist and playwright, was born in Greenwich on 1 April 1875, the son of an actor, Richard Horatio Edgar, and an actress, Mary Jane (Polly) Richards. He was brought up by George Freeman, a Billingsgate fish porter, and his wife. At eleven, he was selling newspapers and, when he left school at twelve, had various jobs as a printer's boy, in a shoe shop, in a mackintosh cloth factory, on a Grimsby trawler, as a milk-roundsman, and as a road-maker and builder's labourer.

At eighteen, he enlisted in the Royal West Kent Regiment and then transferred to the Medical Staff Corps and served in South Africa (1896). Then, he wrote verse and articles for the *Cape Times*, and became a correspondent for Reuters and for the *Daily Mail*. In 1902 he became the first Editor of the *Rand Daily Mail* and, on return to England, worked again for the *Daily Mail*.

The first of the thriller novels that would bring him fame was *The Four Just Men* (1905), and this was followed by a large number of other detective mystery novels, in which inventive plots and simple narration made his stories easy to read and highly popular. As an alternative to these, he published novels set in West Africa, including *Sanders of the River* (1911) and *Bones* (1915). By 1923 his thrillers, such as *The Crimson Circle* and the *Green Archer*, were being sold in hundreds of thousands. Altogether, he published more than one hundred and seventy books.

From his early days, he also produced music-hall songs and review sketches, and in 1926 he had his first dramatic stage success, *The Ringer*. At times he had two or three plays running simultaneously on the West End stage, and both his plays and novels were highly successful in the United States and in many European countries.

In 1901 he married Ivy Maud, daughter of William Shaw Caldecott, a Wesleyan minister in South Africa; they had two sons and a daughter, and the marriage ended in divorce in 1918. In 1921 he married Ethel Violet King; they had a daughter. Wallace was Chairman of the Press Club (1923–5), and inaugurated the Press Club Fund.

He died suddenly on 10 February 1932 in Hollywood, where he had been writing film scripts; one of the films, *King Kong*, was produced shortly after his death.

Edgar Wallace, the characteristic silhouette

WALLAS, GRAHAM (1858–1932), political psychologist, was born at Sunderland on 31 May 1858, the elder son of the Revd Gilbert Innes Wallas, curate at Bishopwearmouth, and his wife, Frances Talbot Peacock. He was educated at Shrewsbury and Corpus Christi College, Oxford, where he was a scholar (1878–81). On leaving Oxford, he was a schoolmaster until 1890, when he became a university extension lecturer. In 1886 he joined the Fabian Society, and three years later contributed to *Fabian Essays on Socialism*. In 1895 he was appointed lecturer at the London School of

Barnes Wallis; in the background is a picture of the dams breached by his bouncing bombs

Economics and Political Science, which he had helped to found. Two years later he married Ada, daughter of George David Radford, a draper, of Plymouth; they had one daughter. From 1914 to 1923 Wallas was Professor of Political Science at the LSE, and between 1890 and 1928 made four lecture tours to the USA.

He made his name with five books: *The Life of Francis Place* (1898), *Human Nature in Politics* (1908), *The Great Society* (1914), *Our Social Heritage* (1921), and *The Art of Thought* (1926). The first of these was a historical study; the other four were concerned with the view that contemporary political thinkers took too little account of the vagaries of human nature, and that political studies should be closely associated with psychology. He urged that the modern advances in mass production and political organization should be studied in relation to human needs and aspirations. In the last of these books, he studied the less conscious, instinctive factors in thought, drawing upon his experience as a teacher. His approach to these problems exerted a powerful influence over the thought of his generation as the importance of the issues, to which he first drew attention, became increasingly realized. Wallas died at Portloe, Cornwall on 9 August 1932.

WALLIS, SIR BARNES NEVILLE (1887–1979), inventor, was born on 26 September 1887, the son of Charles George Wallis MRCS, LRCP, and his wife, Edith Eyre Ashby. He was educated at Christ's Hospital and trained as a marine engineer at J. S. White & Co., Cowes (1905–13).

In 1913 he was appointed Designer in the Airship Department of Vickers Ltd. (1913–15). During the First World War he enlisted with the Artists' Rifles and was commissioned in the RNVR, but in 1916 he was brought back to Vickers to carry on with the design of airships.

In 1925 he married Mary Frances Bloxham; they had two sons and two daughters.

From 1923 to 1930 he was Chief Designer of the Airship Guarantee Company and, with Sir Dennistoun Burney, worked on the R100; from 1930 to 1937 he was Chief Designer, structures, for Vickers Aviation Ltd., for whom he invented the geodetic aircraft. The first of this new type of machine to enter the RAF was the Vickers Wellesley bomber which set a new world non-stop flight record in 1938.

From 1937 to 1945 Barnes Wallis was Assistant Chief Designer of the Aviation Section of Vickers–Armstrongs Ltd. and was concerned with the design of missiles. He himself suggested the bombing of the German dams, so as to cut off the power to Hitler's armaments industry. He designed the special type of bomb required to surmount the dams' defences and thus made possible the breach of the Möhne and Eder Dams by No. 617 Squadron of the RAF, led by Wing Commander Guy GIBSON. He designed other bombs, one of which was used to sink the German battleship, *Tirpitz*, and others to disrupt communications and assist the landings in Normandy in 1944.

After the war, he turned to the invention of a new type of aeroplane, incorporating variable sweep wings and variable thrust lines for the engines. His prototype, the Swallow, did not, however, secure the support of the Government and, to his disappointment and in spite of protests in Parliament, his designs were passed to the USA under a 'joint arrangement' and in the mid-sixties were developed as the F111 and the Boeing variable sweep supersonic transport planes.

Barnes Wallis was appointed CBE in 1943 and knighted in 1968. He was elected FRS in 1945, and was awarded the silver medal of the Royal Aeronautical Society in 1928 and 1937. He received a number of other honours and awards. He died on 30 October 1979.

WALPOLE, SIR HUGH SEYMOUR (1884–1941), novelist, was born in Auckland, New Zealand, on 13 March 1884, the eldest of the three children of the Revd George Henry Somerset Walpole, and his wife, Mildred Helen, daughter of Charles Barham, a physician, of Truro. He was educated at the King's School, Canterbury, Durham School, and Emmanuel College, Cambridge (1906).

Between 1909 and 1914 he published six novels, including *Mr Perrin and Mr Traill* (1911), a story of life in the common-room of a boys' school. During the First World War he served with the Russian Red Cross and used his experiences in *The Dark Forest* (1916) and *The Secret City* (1919). These books established him as a literary figure in London, a friend of Henry JAMES and Arnold BENNETT, and made him a popular lecturer in the United States.

Walpole published forty-two novels, many of them of little worth, but his Lakeland saga, *Rogue Herries* (1930), *Judith Paris* (1931), *The Fortress* (1932), and *Vanessa* (1933), reached a wide public. His *Jeremy* trilogy (1919–1927) was also very popular.

Walpole was a generous benefactor, and exercised some influence as Chairman of the selection committee of the Book Society (1929). He was appointed CBE in 1918 and knighted in 1937. He was not universally popular with his contemporaries. Somerset MAUGHAM, in a preface to his *Cakes and Ale*, said that it was inevitable that he should bear Walpole in mind when he created the character of Alroy Kear, an author eager to obtain a success which his literary merits scarcely deserved. This malicious view of Walpole was not wholly justified, but Walpole's well-known resentment of criticism made him an easy target.

He never married. He died at his home at Brackenburn, near Keswick, on 1 June 1941.

WARD, SIR LESLIE (1851-1922). See SPY.

WARNER, SIR PELHAM FRANCIS (1873-1963), cricketer and cricket writer, was born in Port of Spain, Trinidad, on 2 October 1873, the son of Charles William Warner, for many years Attorney-General of Trinidad, and his second wife, Maria, daughter of John Joseph Garcia Cadiz, a Spanish barrister. Warner was the youngest of his fathers' eighteen children. He was educated at Harrison College, Barbados, Rugby, and Oriel College, Oxford. Always known as 'Plum', he was a delicate boy but, in spite of poor health, was captain of cricket at Rugby and gained his blue at Oxford in 1895. By then, he had already played for Middlesex and, in the previous year, had had the memorable experience of playing against W. G. GRACE. In 1900 he was called to the Bar (Inner Temple), but never practised in the courts. In 1904 Warner married Agnes, daughter of Henry Arthur Blyth, of Stansted, Essex. They had two sons and one daughter.

He had made his first cricket tour abroad in 1897, when he went to the West Indies as a member of a team led by Lord Hawke; and some controversy was aroused when he was selected to captain the England test side for the 1903-4 tour to Australia. The sports writers gave England little chance of victory against the Australians but, in the event, the tour proved to be a great triumph for Warner, as his team won the rubber by three matches to two and thus recovered the Ashes. He was selected again to captain England in Australia in 1911-12 but, owing to a breakdown in health, he only played in one game and spent the rest of the tour in a nursing home. England won that series by four matches to one.

Warner had joined the Inns of Court Regiment in 1900 and served in the Territorial Army until 1912. During the First World War he was commissioned in the Inns of Court Training Corps, but ill health continued to be a serious handicap and, after an operation in 1916, he was invalided from the service.

He had been Captain of Middlesex since 1908 but his greatest success for the county did not come until 1920, his last year with the side. At the end of July, they had to win all their remaining matches if they were to win the championship. In a close contest, Middlesex succeeded in winning all of the games and, when they finally defeated Surrey with only ten minutes to spare, Warner was carried shoulder-high from the field by his jubilant team-mates.

Throughout his cricket career, Warner was beset by poor health and a frail physique. In his time the number of matches played by first-class cricketers was much less than in later years. Statistics therefore mean little but, when he retired, Warner had made nearly 30,000 runs, including 60 centuries. He was not a brilliant batsman in the class of Ranjitsinhji or HOBBS, but he could always be relied on to put up a stubborn defence on a 'sticky' wicket. The sphere in which he excelled was that of captain. He invariably showed a profound understanding of the strategy and tactics of the game and a shrewd assessment of the strengths and weaknesses of his opponents. The professionals who played with him, such as Hearne and Hendren, called him 'the General' and loved him.

Warner's career in cricket was financed mainly by his writing. He began writing for the *Sportsman* during his tour to the West Indies in 1897. In 1903 J. A. Spender invited him to write a weekly article on cricket for the *Westminster Gazette*. From 1921 to 1933 he was cricket correspondent of the *Morning Post* and in 1921 he also became Editor of the *Cricketer*. He was a prolific writer on the game and published many books including *My Cricketing Life* (1921), *Cricket Between Two Wars* (1942), *Lord's 1787-1945* (1946), and *Long Innings* (1951). After retiring from the game, Warner took a prominent part in its administration. He was Chairman of the England Test Match Selection Committee in 1926, 1931-2, and 1935-8, and was Joint-Manager of the side that toured Australia in 1932-3. That tour was marred by the 'body-line' bowling controversy and, although Warner himself considered this type of aggressive bowling to be against the spirit of the game, he preferred to leave the question of the tactics employed in the field to the England Captain, in this case, Douglas JARDINE.

He had been a member of the MCC since 1892, and was nominated President in 1950. A unique tribute was paid to him in 1958 when the new members' stand at Lord's was named after him. In 1961 he became the first life Vice-President in the history of the MCC. He was knighted in 1937, and died at Midhurst, Sussex on 30 January 1963.

WATSON-WATT, SIR ROBERT ALEXANDER (1892-1973), meteorologist and pioneer of radar, was born on 13 April 1892 at Brechin, Angus, the son of Patrick Watson Watt, and his wife, Mary Matthew. He was educated at Brechin High School and University College, Dundee, and in 1915 joined the staff of the Meteorological Office, London, where he undertook research on the radio location of thunder storms.

In 1921 he became Superintendent of the Radio Research Stations of the Department of Industrial and Scientific Research and was responsible for important work with radio direction-finders and radio beacons. He then became Superintendent of the Radio Department of the National Physical Laboratory, and later, Superintendent of the Air Ministry's Research Station at Bawdsey (1936-8). Finally, he was appointed Scientific Adviser on Telecommunications to the Air Ministry and the Ministry of Aircraft Production.

In these posts Watson-Watt was responsible for the development of radar (Radio Detection and Ranging). By 1935 he had developed a system which could detect advancing aircraft over a range of forty miles, and by the outbreak of the Second World War a network of radar stations was in place in Britain. In 1939 microwave radar was introduced and played an important part in the Battle of Britain. Later in the war, portable radar enabled fighter planes to engage enemy targets at night.

Watson-Watt earned the title of 'the father of radar'; the advantage which Britain secured with the use of this weapon was a crucial factor in winning the war. For his contribution to the development of radar installations, he was granted an ex-gratia award of £50,000, the largest sum ever recommended by the Royal Commission on Awards to Inventors for payment to one individual. He was appointed CB and elected FRS in 1941; he was knighted in 1942. His publications include *Three Steps to Victory* (1958) and *The Pulse of Radar* (1959).

In 1916 he married Margaret, daughter of Davidson Robertson of Perth; the marriage was dissolved in 1952, and in that year he married Jean, widow of Professor George M. Smith; she died in 1964, and in 1966 he married Air Chief Commandant Dame Katherine Jane Trefusis Forbes, who had been Director of the WAAF (1939–43). Watson-Watt died in Inverness on 5 December 1973.

WATTS, SIR PHILIP (1846–1926), naval architect, was born at Deptford on 30 May 1846, the son of John Watts, chief assistant shipwright at Portsmouth dockyard, and his wife, Mary Ann Featherstone. Watts's father, grandfather,

and great-grandfather were all shipwrights. He was educated in Portsmouth, and in 1860 apprenticed to the royal dockyard. From 1866 to 1870 he studied at the Royal School of Naval Architecture, South Kensington and from 1870 to 1885 worked at the Admiralty on the construction staff. In 1875 he married Elise Isabelle, daughter of Chevalier Gustave Simoneau de St Omer, of Brussels; they had two daughters.

In 1885 he left the Admiralty to become Naval Designer and General Manager to Armstrong & Co. at Elswick-on-Tyne. During the next seventeen years, the warship yard under his control became well known for its production of

Evelyn Waugh and his family at Combe Florey, where he lived unhappily as a country gentleman, January 1960

cruisers, not only for the Royal Navy, but for the navies of Japan and many other countries. He was elected FRS in 1900.

In 1902 Watts was appointed Director of Naval Construction at the Admiralty and from 1904, when Sir John FISHER became First Sea Lord, he was able to design new types of more powerful warships, culminating in the design and construction of the *Dreadnought* battleship and the *Indomitable* battle-cruiser, with heavier armament and higher speed than hitherto. Watts designed a number of battleships, including the *Iron Duke* and *Queen Elizabeth* and, when the First World War broke out, all the effective battle-cruisers in the Royal Navy were of his design. At the Battle of Jutland (1916) twenty-nine of the thirty-four British battleships and battle-cruisers had been designed by him.

In 1912 he returned to Elswick as a director of Armstrong, Whitworth & Co. He was created KCB in 1905. In 1921 he took a leading part in the restoration of Nelson's *Victory*. He also contributed a number of important papers to the *Transactions* of the Institution of Naval Architects. Watts died in London on 15 March 1926.

WAUGH, EVELYN ARTHUR ST JOHN (1903-1966), novelist, was born in London on 28 October 1903, the younger son of Arthur Waugh, publisher and author, and his wife, Catherine Charlotte, daughter of Henry Charles Biddulph Colton Raban of the Bengal Civil Service. His older brother Alec went to Sherborne School, and in 1917 published *The Loom of Youth*, a novel based on his schooldays. Consequently, another school had to be found for Evelyn: he went to Lancing and from there went with a history scholarship to Hertford College, Oxford, where he quickly acquired a reputation as a noisy drunkard, and formed a life-long antipathy to his tutor.

He left Oxford in 1924 and, for three unhappy years, worked as a schoolmaster in Wales, Buckinghamshire, and London. In Wales he was sufficiently disconsolate to make a half-hearted attempt to drown himself. But, while he was a teacher, he wrote an essay on the *Pre-Raphaelite Brotherhood*, which was printed privately in 1926. In 1927 he gave up teaching, and in 1928 published a book on Dante Gabriel Rossetti, which received good reviews but brought him little money. He was working as a journalist, but he wanted to marry and had to earn more. He set to work on *Decline and Fall*, a novel based on his experiences as a schoolmaster. The success of this when it was published in 1928, enabled him, in the same year, to marry Evelyn Gardner, daughter of Lord Burghclere, though her widowed mother was strongly opposed to the marriage.

While he was writing his next book *Vile Bodies* (1930), he spent some time at Beckley, near Oxford while his wife shared their London flat with Nancy MITFORD. She then took a lover, John Heygate, and left her husband. In 1930 Waugh obtained a divorce, but in the same year he became a Roman Catholic, precluded from re-marrying unless he could get his first marriage annulled. He sought annulment in 1933, but it was not granted until 1936. In the following year he married Laura Laetitia Gwendolen Evelyn, a cousin of his first wife, and youngest daughter of Aubrey Nigel Henry Molyneax Herbert.

By that time, he had published *Black Mischief* (1932), a novel about Abyssinia, which he had visited in 1930, and *A Handful of Dust* (1934), a novel more serious than his earlier ones, and two travel books, *Remote People* (1931) and *Waugh in Abyssinia* (1936). He also wrote a biography of Edmund

Campion (1935), for which he was awarded the Hawthornden prize. By the time the Second World War broke out he was an established author, having added *Scoop* (1938) to his novels. Laura Waugh, having borne their first child, Tessa (1938), was about to bear their second, Auberon (1939).

Waugh served with the Royal Marines and the Royal Horse Guards during the war. In 1941 he went as personal assistant to (Sir) Robert Laycock in the Middle East but, in spite of his physical courage, he was unpopular with both officers and men, and in 1943 returned to England. He found time to write the satirical novel, *Put Out More Flags* (1942), and his greatest success, *Brideshead Revisited*, published in 1945. But his military career was not over. His friend, Randolph CHURCHILL, took him to join (Sir) Fitzroy Maclean's mission to Tito's Communist partisans in Yugoslavia (1944). Waugh did not like what he saw there and reported to the Vatican the danger of the subjection of Catholic Croats and Slovenes to an atheist Communist regime; he also instigated questions in Parliament, but found that the British Government was prepared to accept the help of any partisans fighting against Hitler.

After the war, in 1947, Waugh visited Hollywood to discuss a film of *Brideshead Revisited* but, as he refused to alter the story to meet the rigid standards of decency required at the time, the film was not made, and it was not until many years later, in a more permissive era, that the novel was filmed for television. In 1950 he published a historical novel about Saint Helena, the mother of Constantine the Great, and in 1952 the first volume of his war trilogy, *Men at Arms*, which was awarded the James Tait Black memorial prize. *Officers and Gentlemen* appeared in 1955, and *Unconditional Surrender* in 1961; in 1962 all three were published together as *Sword of Honour*. In the years following the war, Evelyn Waugh was a worried, unhappy man. He had always needed to be alone to write, and now he was drinking too heavily for his health, resorting to sleeping pills in large quantities to combat insomnia, and anxious about the threatened loss of his mental faculties. In 1954 he set out for Ceylon (Sri Lanka), but his letters to his wife and to his friend, Lady Diana Cooper, caused them such uneasiness that Laura felt that she must get him back to England. In fact, he was suffering from hallucinations caused by a complete mental breakdown, an experience which he vividly described, when he had recovered, in *The Ordeal of Gilbert Pinfold* (1957).

In 1956 he and his patient wife, Laura, went to live at Combe Florey House, near Taunton, and there Waugh lived unhappily as a country gentleman, in a home furnished with Victoriana, which he much admired. Two more daughters; Harriet and Margaret, had been born during the war. In 1946 the Waughs' second son, James, was born and their third son and youngest child, Septimus, in 1950. In 1957 Waugh's close friend, Monsignor Ronald KNOX, died after a long illness, in which Waugh had shown him great solicitude; his biography of Knox was published in 1959. He also began his own autobiography, but only completed the first volume, *A Little Learning* (1964). His last years were saddened by changes, which he hated, in the Catholic liturgy and by his fears that old age would make him increasingly incapacitated. He died very suddenly on Easter Sunday 10 April 1966, after hearing Mass in the old rite. His *Diaries* were published in 1976 and his *Letters* in 1980. *Illustration p. 343.*

WAVELL, ARCHIBALD PERCIVAL, first EARL WAVELL (1883-1950), field-marshal, was born on 5 May 1883 at Colchester, the only son of Major (later Major-General)

General Wavell (left) inspecting the Singapore defences, November 1941; in the background is one of the fixed guns pointing out to sea

Archibald Graham Wavell, and his wife, Lillie, daughter of Richard N. Percival, of Springfields, Bradwall, Cheshire. He was educated at Winchester, and entered Sandhurst in 1900. He was gazetted to the Black Watch, saw service in South Africa, and in 1903 was posted to India. In 1911, after a course at the Staff College, he spent a year with the Russian Army.

During the First World War he fought first in France and lost an eye at the battle of Ypres (1915); he was awarded the MC. In that year he had married Eugénie Marie, daughter of Col. John Owen Quirk. Later in the war, he served in Turkey and Palestine. During the next twenty years (1919–39), Wavell earned a reputation as an exceptional trainer of troops; he served in the War Office and on the staff, and in July 1939 was posted to the new command of the Middle East.

During the Second World War he was, at first, very successful; with small forces at his disposal, he decisively defeated the Italians in the Western Desert and, early in 1941, held the whole of Cyrenaica. He acquiesced in the evacuation of Somaliland and, in consequence, had his first clash with Winston CHURCHILL. Having defeated the Italians in Ethiopia, he was ordered to intervene in Greece, though in his judgement he had no forces to spare for such an operation. The result was disastrous. Greece, Crete, and Cyrenaica were over-run by the Germans. He was now instructed to operate against enemy forces in Iraq and Syria, as well as against the Germans in North Africa. When he objected that he must have time to prepare for a new advance, he was superseded by Sir Claude Auchinleck and posted, in Auchinleck's place, as Commander-in-Chief, India (1941).

Wavell, who was undoubtedly a capable commander, was unfortunate in that, although he could quote Virgil and

Byron in conversation with his ADC, he was inarticulate when face to face with Winston Churchill, who could not endure what he considered to be Wavell's obstinacy and lack of drive. The posting to India was intended to be demotion.

When, however, Japan came into the war in December 1941, Wavell was again in the thick of the conflict. His reputation stood high with the Americans, and he was nominated Supreme Commander of the South-West Pacific. Once more, he found himself faced by a formidable enemy with inadequate forces under his control. He was blamed for the loss of Singapore, was wounded in Java, and had to accept responsibility for the withdrawal from Burma. In June 1943 he was appointed Viceroy of India and raised to the peerage as a viscount. In January 1943 he had been promoted to field-marshal. He was also sworn of the Privy Council.

As Viceroy, Wavell set to work with infinite patience to prepare the way for agreement between the Hindu and Muslim leaders on the future of India. In 1945 he released the Congress leaders who had been in prison since 1942. In the following year he took part in the tedious negotiations, in which Lord PETHICK-LAWRENCE and Sir Stafford CRIPPS endeavoured to obtain the agreement of Congress and the Muslim League to a constitution for a united India. The negotiations ended in failure, and Wavell urged the Labour Government to decide what action should be taken in the absence of an agreement. Early in 1947 the Government made its decision to accede to the demands for separation between India and Pakistan and announced simultaneously that Wavell would be succeeded by Lord MOUNTBATTEN OF BURMA. Wavell was created an earl.

Wavell retired, and for three years enjoyed some leisure, following the literary pursuits to which he was much attached, becoming President of the Royal Society of Litera-

Sidney and Beatrice Webb

ture, and other societies concerned with poets and poetry. His anthology *Other Men's Flowers* (1944) enjoyed considerable popularity. He also published *The Palestine Campaigns* (1928), a biography of Viscount ALLENBY, his lectures on *Generals and Generalship* (1941), and other lectures and essays, collected under the title *The Good Soldier* (1948). Wavell received many honours, both military, and academic. He was appointed CMG (1919), CB (1935), KCB (1939), GCB (1941), and GCSI and GCIE (1943).

Earl Wavell died in London on 24 May 1950. He and his wife had three daughters and one son, who succeeded his father in the titles but was killed in the Mau-Mau rebellion in Kenya in 1953 when the titles became extinct.

WAVERLEY, first VISCOUNT (1882–1958). See ANDERSON.

WEBB, (MARTHA) BEATRICE (1858–1943). See WEBB, SIDNEY JAMES.

WEBB, SIDNEY JAMES, BARON PASSFIELD (1859–1947), social reformer and historian, was born in London on 13 July 1859, the younger son of Charles Webb, a public accountant, and his wife, Elizabeth Mary, daughter of Benjamin Stacey. Elizabeth was a hairdresser. Sidney Webb was educated in Switzerland, Germany, and at the Birkbeck Institute and City of London College. From 1875 to 1878 he was employed

as a clerk; in 1878 he entered the Civil Service, and in 1881 became a first division clerk in the Colonial Office. He was called to the Bar (Gray's Inn) in 1885 and became LL B (London) in 1886.

In 1885 his friend G. B. SHAW introduced him to the Fabian Society, of which he became an influential member, writing pamphlets and contributing to *Fabian Essays in Socialism* (1889). In 1892 he resigned from the Civil Service to work for the LCC, of which he was a member for the next eighteen years.

In the same year (1892), Webb married (MARTHA) BEATRICE **POTTER,** born near Gloucester on 22 January 1858, the eighth of the nine daughters of Richard Potter, a wealthy industrialist and Liberal MP, and his wife, Laurencina, daughter of Laurence Heyworth, a Liverpool merchant. From the age of eighteen, Beatrice helped her father in his business and became interested in social problems in the East End of London in consequence of her work in rent collecting. She also studied the co-operative movement and published *The Co-operative Movement in Great Britain* (1891).

After their marriage, the Webbs joined forces in their work for social welfare; together they published *The History of Trade Unionism* (1894), *Industrial Democracy* (2 vols., 1897), and *English Local Government* (9 vols., 1906–29). In 1895 they launched the idea which led to the establishment of the London School of Economics and Political Science, of which, from 1912 to 1927, Sidney was honorary Professor of Public Administration.

At the time of the Boer War, the Webbs supported the Government and had no sympathy for the pacifism of the Independent Labour party. Sidney served on the Royal Commission reviewing trade-union law (1903) and Beatrice was a member of the Royal Commission on the Poor Laws (1905–9). Sidney became the Chairman of the first board of the *New Statesman* (1913). They had become unpopular with the Fabian Society and H. G. WELLS wrote critically of their views in the *New Machiavelli* (1911). They now saw the Labour party as the only means of continuing social reform. In 1915 Sidney became a member of its executive, and served in that capacity until 1925. He drafted the statement of policy adopted in 1918, *Labour and the New Social Order*.

In 1922 he became Labour MP for the Seaham division of Durham, a seat which he held until 1929. In 1924 he was sworn of the Privy Council and appointed President of the Board of Trade. He had decided not to contest his seat again, but in 1929 Ramsay MACDONALD persuaded him to become Secretary of State for the Dominions and Colonies (1929–30) and for the Colonies (1930–1). This involved acceptance of a barony, but Beatrice refused to use the title. Both were relieved when Sidney resigned when MacDonald formed his National Government.

They visited Russia in 1932, and published their impressions in *Soviet Communism: a New Civilisation?* (2 vols., 1935) described by A. J. P. Taylor as the most preposterous book ever written about Soviet Russia. Beatrice died at Passfield Corner, near Liphook on 30 April 1943. The story of her life with Sidney was told in her diaries, *My Apprenticeship* (1926) and *Our Partnership* (1948). She was elected FBA in 1931, and received honorary degrees from Manchester, Edinburgh, and Munich. Sidney was appointed OM in 1944, and received honorary degrees from London, Wales, and Munich. They had no children. Sidney died on 13 October 1947 also at Passfield Corner. Their ashes were buried in Westminster Abbey.

Two volumes of Beatrice Webb's diaries, edited by Norman and Jeanne MacKenzie, have been published: vol. 1 (*Glitter Around and Darkness Within*) in 1982 and vol. 2 (*All the Good Things of Life*) in 1983. The diaries, of which there are still two volumes to be published, are much more interesting than the books which Beatrice wrote with her husband.

WEBSTER, (GILBERT) TOM (1886–1962), sporting cartoonist, was born on 17 July 1886 at Bilston, Staffs., the son of Daniel Webster, an ironmonger, and his wife, Sarah Ann Bostock. He was educated at the Royal Wolverhampton School, where he learnt to draw. At fourteen, he was employed as a ticket clerk by the GWR and, when he was nineteen, he won prizes for humorous sketches offered by the Birmingham *Weekly Post*, the Manchester *Evening Chronicle* and the *Athletic News*. He then joined the staff of the Birmingham *Sports Argus*.

During the First World War he served in the Royal Fusiliers, was disabled by rheumatic fever, and nearly died (1916). After the war, he was for some time unemployed and down-and-out. But, eventually, one of his sporting cartoons was accepted by the *Evening News* and came to the notice of Lord NORTHCLIFFE, who arranged for Webster to have a staff appointment on the *Daily Mail*. By 1924 he was the highest-paid cartoonist in the world.

Chaim Weizmann is sworn in as the first President of the state of Israel, Jerusalem, 16 February 1949

He had a keen sense of the ridiculous and made the most of it in his work. One of his most famous cartoons was that of 'Tishy', the horse with her legs in a twist. Favourite for the Cesarewitch in 1921, she had fallen as a result of crossing her legs. Webster had a hand in the arrangement of the revue 'Cartoons' at the Criterion Theatre in 1924. In 1936 he was one of the artists commissioned to decorate the state rooms of the *Queen Mary*.

He retired from the *Daily Mail* in 1940, but resumed work in 1944, and in 1953 joined the *News Chronicle*, on which he worked for the next three years. Each year he published *Tom Webster's Annual*.

In 1929 he married Mae Flynn in New York; they divorced in 1933; and in 1935 he married Ida, daughter of John Rupert Michael, a master mariner. She was twenty-five years his junior; they had one son and two daughters. Webster died in London on 21 June 1962.

WEISZ, VICTOR (1913-1966). See VICKY.

WEIZMANN, CHAIM (1874-1952), Zionist leader, was born at Motol in the Jewish Pale of Settlement in Russia in November 1874, the third child of Ezer Weizmann, a timber merchant, and his wife, Rachel Leah, daughter of Michael Tzchmerinsky of Motol. He was educated at Pinsk High School and Freiburg University, where he gained his doctorate in 1899. After working as a lecturer in chemistry at Geneva, he emigrated to England in 1904. In 1906 he married Vera, daughter of Isaiah Chatzmann, of Rostov-on-Don; they had two sons.

Weizmann was appointed to lecture at Manchester University, and in 1910 became a British subject. In 1913 he was promoted to a readership in biochemistry. By 1914 he was a prominent figure in the Zionist movement. During the First World War he was useful to LLOYD GEORGE in overcoming the shortage of acetone, an important product in the manufacture of explosives. When Lloyd George became Prime Minister and Arthur BALFOUR, Foreign Secretary, Weizmann was able to influence both in the direction of Zionist claims, and in 1917 the War Cabinet agreed to the Balfour Declaration, advocating the establishment in Palestine of a national home for the Jewish people.

In 1918 he headed a Zionist Commission in Palestine and in 1919 presented the case for a Jewish national home at the Paris Peace Conference. In 1920 he was elected President of the World Zionist Organization. The hostility of the Palestine Arabs made political progress slow, but in 1929 Weizmann created a Jewish Agency for Palestine. He supported the proposals of the royal commission under Lord Peel for the partition of Palestine (1937) but, subsequently, the St James's Palace Conference collapsed and attempts at an agreed settlement failed (1939).

Throughout the Second World War, during which his younger son was killed while serving with the RAF, Weizmann maintained close contact with British politicians. In 1947 he urged the claims of Zionists in the United Nations and, when the British mandate in Palestine expired in 1948 and the establishment of a Jewish state was proclaimed, he was elected its first President. As President he helped to found the Hebrew University of Jerusalem and the Weizmann Institute of Science at Rehovoth. Weizmann died at Rehovoth on 9 November 1952.   *Illustration p. 347.*

WELLS, HERBERT GEORGE (1866-1946), author, was born at Bromley on 21 September 1866, the third son of Joseph Wells, a professional cricketer and shopkeeper, and his wife, Sarah, daughter of George Neal, an innkeeper. The family business was always on the verge of insolvency and, when Wells was fourteen, the family broke up, his mother going to Up Park, Sussex, as housekeeper where, before her marriage, she had been lady's maid. He went to a commercial school, but was virtually self-taught and, having been apprenticed to the drapery trade and to pharmacy, eventually became student assistant at Midhurst Grammar School (1883-4), and won a scholarship to the Normal School (later Royal College) of Science, South Kensington, where he studied under T. H. Huxley.

For a few years he earned his living as a teacher, and in 1890 gained his B.Sc. (London) with a first in zoology. He was already trying his hand at journalism on scientific subjects and was a keen socialist. In 1891 he became a tutor at the University Tutorial College and married his cousin, Isabel Mary Wells, but in 1893 he left her for one of his pupils, Amy Catherine (Jane) Robbins and, after divorce, he married her in 1895; they had two sons. After the birth of the second son in 1903 they ceased to be lovers, but to Wells women were a necessity, and he had many mistresses. From 1913 to 1923 Rebecca West and he were lovers and she had a son by him. He never left his wife, however. At the time of his second marriage, he was writing short stories, such as *The Stolen Bacillus* (1895), and in that year began his long series of novels, based on scientific fact, but imaginatively prophetic in scope, including *The Time Machine* (1895), *The Invisible Man* (1897), *The First Men on the Moon* (1901), and *The Shape of Things to Come* (1933), in which he foretold war in the air, the use of tanks, and splitting the atom, as well as men on the moon.

These novels were interspersed with stories of 'real' life, in which Wells drew upon his personal experiences; these included *Love and Mr Lewisham* (1900), *Kipps* (1905), *Tono-Bungay* (1909), and *The History of Mr Polly* (1910). Now recognized as an important novelist, he was living at Sandgate in Kent, with Henry JAMES and Joseph CONRAD as his neighbours. During this time he was involved in controversy with the Sidney WEBBS over the policy of the Fabian Society and resigned in 1908. In the following year he published *Ann Veronica*, a story based on his own love affair with a young student, in which he advocated free love, and brought a hornet's nest about his ears from those scandalized by his outspoken views on sex. Surprised, but unabashed by his critics, Wells continued in the same vein with *The New Machiavelli* (1911) and *Marriage* (1912).

During the First World War he worked with Lord NORTHCLIFFE at Crewe House and wrote for the Ministry of Information. His attitude to the war was made clear in *The War That Will End War* (1914) and *Mr Britling Sees It Through* (1916). He now saw himself with a mission, seeking 'The World State' in which peace would prevail and humanity would reap lasting benefits from the progress of science. In *A Modern Utopia* and *The World of William Clissold* (3 vols., 1926), he expressed these hopes for better things to come. Simultaneously, he was endeavouring to improve public education by his encyclopedic works *The Outline of History* (1920), *The Science of Life* (1931), and *The Work, Wealth and Happiness of Mankind* (1932).

In 1934 he paid two visits to Russia and became involved in controversy with G. B. SHAW regarding his estimate of the importance of Lenin and Stalin in world affairs. In that year, too, there appeared his *Experiment in Autobiography* (2 vols.). As the prospect of another world war loomed more

Bateman cartoon of H. G. Wells, entitled 'Minutes with the Mighty: Imaginary Interviews', from the *Sketch*, 29 May 1912

menacingly, the earlier optimism of Wells's work gave way to disappointment and pessimism. His health declined, and he was appalled by the outbreak of the Second World War. During the war he lived in Hanover Terrace, Regent's Park and, as David Garnett has recounted, was always ready to give shelter to young writers or artists.

During his eighty years, Wells produced over a hundred books and he was writing almost to the end of his days. He could be a fascinating conversationalist, but as a public speaker he was severely handicapped by a high-pitched voice that, when he was excited, became a squeak. He died in London on 13 August 1946 tormented by the fear that the human race was doomed to destroy itself.

WHEELER, SIR (ROBERT ERIC) MORTIMER (1890–1976), archaeologist, author, and broadcaster, was born in Glasgow on 10 September 1890, the only son of (Robert) Mortimer Wheeler, a journalist, and his wife, Emily Baynes, niece and ward of Thomas Spencer Baynes, philosopher and scholar. He was educated at Bradford Grammar School and University College London, where he was a classical scholar (1907–12). In 1913 he won the first Franks studentship.

In 1914 he married Tessa Verney, who was to be closely associated with his work as an archaeologist. During the First World War Wheeler fought in France and Italy with the Royal Field Artillery and won the MC. After the war, he returned to the Royal Commission on Historical Monuments with which he had worked before joining the army, but in 1920 he was appointed Keeper of Archaeology in the National Museum of Wales. In 1924 he was promoted to Director. He and his wife and their students worked on Roman military sites, and in 1925 he published *Prehistoric and Roman Wales*.

In the following year, he left Wales to become Director of the London Museum and, while reorganizing the collections there, set out to establish an Institute of Archaeology, which was eventually opened in 1937. He and his wife excavated at Lydney, Verulamium, and the hill fort of Maiden Castle in Dorset, until in 1936 she died. During 1938–9 Wheeler explored the hill forts of Brittany and Normandy but, when the Second World War broke out, he organized an anti-aircraft battery which expanded into the 42nd Royal Artillery Regiment, and fought in North Africa and Italy.

In 1944 he went out to India as Director-General of Archaeology. There, with characteristic energy, he set to work to revitalize the department and launched a journal, *Ancient India*. He was appointed CIE in 1947, and also served as archaeological adviser to the Government of Pakistan. He returned to London in 1948, became part-time Professor at London University and honorary Secretary to the British Academy (1949–68). He also held many other posts, including Director of the Society of Antiquaries (1940–4 and 1949–54), President (1954–9), Trustee of the British Museum (1963–73), Chairman of the Ancient Monuments Board, England (1964–6), and Professor of Ancient History to the Royal Academy (1965–76).

Among his many books are *The Indus Civilization* (1953, 1960, and 1968) and *Rome Beyond the Imperial Frontiers* (1954). He also published his autobiography *Still Digging* (1955). He became well known to the British public through his brilliance as a popular broadcaster and in 1954 was chosen television personality of the year.

He received numerous academic honours, was knighted in 1952, appointed CH in 1967, and elected FRS in 1968. He

had one son by his first wife, and in 1939 married Mavis de Vere Cole; this marriage was dissolved in 1942, and in 1945 he married Margaret Norfolk, a marriage which also failed. He spent his last years with Molly Myers, who had been his assistant during the fifties and sixties. He died at Leatherhead on 22 July 1976.

WHITEHEAD, ALFRED NORTH (1861–1947), mathematician and philosopher, was born at Ramsgate on 15 February 1861, the son of the Revd Alfred Whitehead, a headmaster, and his wife, Maria Sarah Buckmaster. He was educated at Sherborne and Trinity College, Cambridge, where he was a scholar, was bracketed fourth wrangler in the mathematical tripos of 1883, and elected a Fellow in 1884. In 1898 he published *A Treatise on Universal Algebra with Applications*, which investigated systems of symbolic reasoning and led to his election as FRS in 1903.

In 1899 Whitehead had married Evelyn Ada Maud Rice, daughter of Capt. Arthur Robert Willoughby-Wade, Seaforth Highlanders; they had one daughter and two sons.

One of Whitehead's pupils at Trinity College was Bertrand RUSSELL; in 1900 they were together in Paris where they learned of the work of Giuseppe Peano of Turin, who had invented a new ideography for use in symbolic logic. They recognized the importance of Peano's work, and decided to follow it up, in an attempt to settle the vexed question of the foundations of mathematics. For the next ten years they worked together on this project, which eventually appeared as the *Principia Mathematica* (3 vols., 1910–13), which has been described as 'the greatest single contribution to logic that has appeared in the two thousand years since Aristotle'. There was to have been a fourth volume on geometry, to be written by Whitehead, but it was never completed.

In 1910 he resigned from his post as senior lecturer in mathematics at Trinity College, and joined the staff of University College London; and from 1914 to 1924 he held a chair of applied mathematics at the Imperial College of Science and Technology. He had by this time become interested in problems of metaphysics. His younger son was killed in action in 1918. In 1919 he published *An Enquiry Concerning the Principles of Natural Knowledge*, followed in 1920 by *The Concept of Nature*. He went on to devise his own theory of relativity, which he set out in a book published in 1922; his theory was not, however, generally accepted.

From 1924 to 1937 Whitehead was Professor of Philosophy at Harvard University, and in 1927–8 he delivered the Gifford lectures at Edinburgh, which were published as *Process and Reality, an Essay in Cosmology* (1929), putting forward the doctrine that the ultimate components of reality are events which he called 'actual entities'. He regarded ordinary speech as inadequate for the purposes of logic, and even more inadequate for metaphysics, and for this reason he felt bound to use new words and to give new meanings to old words in order to describe his concepts.

In his later years, Whitehead received many academic distinctions; in 1931 he was elected FBA and in 1945 was appointed OM. His main claim to lasting fame will be his co-authorship with Bertrand Russell of the *Principia Mathematica*. On the whole their collaboration appears to have been harmonious, though their approaches were different and had to be reconciled. Russell himself wrote in his autobiography that there was hardly a page in the three volumes which could be attributed to either of them singly. Whitehead died at Cambridge, Massachusetts, on 30 December 1947.

WHITFIELD, ERNEST ALBERT, first BARON KENS-WOOD (1887–1963), professional violinist and welfare worker for the blind, was born on 15 September 1887 in London, the younger son of John Henry Christopher Whitfield, and his wife, Louisa, daughter of Michael Farren of Copenhagen. He was educated at Archbishop Tenison's and University College Schools, London, and Vienna and London Universities. He worked in a Vienna business from 1907, until his sight began to deteriorate in his early twenties. He had to prepare for a new career and decided that his ability to play the violin must determine his choice.

In 1913 he made his début as a soloist, although he was almost completely blind, but the outbreak of war in 1914 obliged him to return to England and to try to get established there as a concert artist. Through a chance meeting with Sir (Cyril) Arthur Pearson, the newspaper proprietor who founded St Dunstans', he was introduced to braille and joined the St Dunstan's Blind Musicians Concert Party.

In 1917, without revealing his disability, Whitfield became leader of the orchestra at Wyndham's Theatre, London, and remained in that post for two years. He appeared as a soloist in the Queen's Hall Promenade Concerts in 1918, and in 1920 formed the Guild of Singers and Players. In that year he married Sophie Madeline, only child of Ernest Walter Howard, of London; they had a daughter and a son.

From 1921 to 1923 he made his reputation as an accomplished violinist, but when ill health restricted his concert engagements, he took up the study of economics, political science, and philosophy. He obtained his B.Sc. (London) in 1926 and his Ph.D. in 1928. In the latter year he was elected to the Executive Council of the National Institute for the Blind. In 1935 he damaged a hand and had to abandon his musical career.

During the Second World War he worked for the blind in the USA and Canada. From 1946 to 1950 he was a Governor of the BBC. In 1951 he was created a baron, and from 1951 to 1955 was President of the National Federation of the Blind. He also served on a number of welfare committees and contributed to various periodicals on the welfare of the blind.

His first wife died in 1961, and he married in 1962 Catherine, widow of Charles Chilver-Stainer and daughter of Frank Luxton. Whitfield died in London on 21 April 1963.

WILDE, WILLIAM JAMES (JIMMY) (1892–1969), professional boxer, was born on 12 May 1892 at Pontygwarth, South Wales, the son of James Wilde, a coal miner, and his wife, Margaret Ann Evans, daughter of a coal miner. He left the local school at thirteen to work in the pit, earned some extra money by boxing at fairgrounds, and made a reputation, which encouraged him at the age of nineteen to turn professional. In 1910 he married Elizabeth Davies, daughter of Dai Davies, a miner, who had originally coached him as a boxer; they had two sons.

From 1916 till 1923 he was the undisputed flyweight champion of the world, normally boxing at 94 lb., although the weight limit for his class was 112 lb. His speed on his feet and his reach and speed with his punches gave him victory over heavier opponents, who found him difficult to hit effectively.

During his professional career (1911–23), he took part in 138 fights, including seven British or world-title contests. He won outright a Lonsdale belt. His phenomenal punching earned him the title of 'the Mighty Atom'. He was defeated only four times, including his final defence of his world-title against Pancho Villa in New York.

Jimmy Wilde died in Cardiff on 10 March 1969, having become a manager and promoter of boxing, after his retirement from the ring.

WILKINS, SIR (GEORGE) HUBERT (1888–1958), polar explorer, climatologist, and naturalist, was born at Mount Bryan East, South Australia, on 31 October 1888, the thirteenth child of Harry Wilkins, a sheep farmer, and his wife, Louisa Smith. Until he was fifteen he worked on the family sheep station, and from 1903 to 1908 studied electrical and general engineering at the Adelaide School of Mines. In 1908 he stowed away on a ship bound for Algiers, and later worked in London as a reporter and cameraman, spending some months in 1912 filming the war between the Turks and Bulgarians. He also learnt to fly.

In 1913 he went as photographer on the Canadian Arctic Expedition, and became convinced that aeroplanes could be used to explore and map the polar regions and that weather stations should be set up there to monitor weather forecasting. During the First World War he served as a war photographer in France and was awarded the MC with two bars.

In 1920–1 he was second in command of an expedition to the Antarctic, and then served as naturalist on Sir Ernest SHACKLETON's expedition in the *Quest*. He also photographed the effects of drought in Soviet Russia, and did a biological survey of Northern Australia for the British Museum (1923–5). In 1928 he published *Undiscovered Australia*. He returned to the Arctic and flew with Carl Ben Eielson from Alaska over the Arctic Ocean to Spitzbergen, recounting this experience in *Flying the Arctic* (1928).

During 1928–30 he led two expeditions to the Antarctic undertaking aerial exploration, and in 1931 he proved, in the *Nautilus* expedition to the Arctic, that a submarine could operate successfully beneath the polar ice. He continued throughout the thirties to carry on polar research in both Antarctic and Arctic regions. He published *Under the North Pole* in 1931.

During the Second World War he served as geographer and climatologist with the US Army and, after the war, served in an advisory capacity with the US Weather Bureau, and later with the Arctic Institute of North America until, in 1953, he was appointed Geographer to the Research and Development Command, specializing in the polar areas.

He was knighted in 1928, and was a Fellow of the Royal Meteorological Society and the Royal Geographical Society. He received a number of honours and medals. In 1929 he married Suzanne Bennett, an Australian actress, daughter of John Evans, a mining engineer of Victoria, Australia; they had no children. Wilkins died on 30 November 1958 at Framingham, Massachusetts and his ashes were scattered near the North Pole.

WILKINSON, ELLEN CICELY (1891–1947), trade unionist and politician, was born in Manchester on 8 October 1891, the third of the four children of Richard Wilkinson, a cotton operative, and his wife, Ellen Wood. She was educated at elementary and secondary schools in Manchester and went to Manchester University with a scholarship (1910–13). In 1913 she became an organizer of the National Union of Women's Suffrage Societies in Manchester, in 1915 was appointed a national woman organizer for the Amalgamated Union of Co-operative Employees, and from 1919 to 1925 represented the union on four trade boards.

In 1912 she joined the Independent Labour party and in

Ellen Wilkinson leading the Jarrow marchers to London, 2 November 1936

1920 joined the Communist party; from 1923 to 1926 she was a member of the Manchester City Council. In 1924 she resigned from the Communist party and from 1924 to 1931 was Labour MP for Middlesborough East. During the general strike of 1926 she worked energetically on behalf of the coal miners, and in 1932 visited India and the USA. She was quick to recognize the menace of Nazism.

In 1935 she became Labour MP for Jarrow and was soon deeply involved in work for the depressed areas of the northeast. She led the 1936 march of the unemployed from Jarrow to London, and in 1939 told Jarrow's story in *The Town that was Murdered*. She was passionately opposed to the policy of 'non-intervention' in the Spanish Civil War (1937). In 1938 she carried the Hire-Purchase Bill through the House of Commons.

In 1940 she was appointed Parliamentary Secretary to the Ministry of Pensions, and later to the Ministry of Home Security. She spent many nights in the air-raid shelters and took part in the reorganization of civil defence and the fire service. In 1945, in the ATTLEE Government, she was Minister of Education, a member of the Cabinet, and a Privy Counsellor. She fought strenuously to ensure that the Education Act of 1944 would be implemented. She died in London on 6 February 1947. Her vivid personality, her compassion, and intense loyalty to truth and justice gave her great influence with her colleagues and won great respect from her opponents.

WILLIAMS, EDWARD FRANCIS, BARON FRANCIS-WILLIAMS (1903–1970), author, journalist, and publicist, was born on 10 March 1903 at St Martin's, Shropshire, the son of John Edmund Williams, a farmer, and his wife, Sally Francis. He was educated at Queen Elizabeth's Grammar School, Middleton, and at seventeen joined the weekly *Bootle Times* (1910). He then obtained work on the Liverpool *Daily Courier* and also contributed to the *Daily Herald*.

In 1922 he obtained a part-time job on the *Sunday Express*, and came to the notice of Lord BEAVERBROOK, who appointed him financial reporter (1926). Williams had joined the Independent Labour party while he was in Liverpool, and in 1929 became City Editor of the *Daily Herald*. In 1936 he was appointed Editor of the *Daily Herald* and quickly raised its circulation; but in 1940 he resigned because Lord Southwood, Chairman of Odhams, owners of the paper, interfered with his freedom to publish foreign news as he saw it.

During the Second World War he became Controller of press and censorship in the Ministry of Information and succeeded in gaining the co-operation and respect of foreign correspondents. In 1945 he was appointed CBE for his war services. During the ATTLEE Government, he was public relations adviser to the Prime Minister until in 1947 he went to Washington as correspondent of the *Observer*. When he returned to London, he became a columnist on the *News Chronicle* and for fourteen years also ran a 'Fleet Street' column in the *New Statesman*.

He was a Governor of the BBC (1951-2) and became a notable personality in broadcasting and television. He was Regents' Professor at California University in 1961 and Kemper Knapp Professor at Wisconsin in 1967. In 1962 he became a life peer. He wrote a large number of books, including *Press, Parliament and the People* (1946), *Ernest Bevin: Portrait of a Great Englishman* (1952), *A Prime Minister Remembers* (with Earl Attlee, 1961), and *A Pattern of Rulers* (1965). His autobiography, *Nothing So Strange*, was published in 1970.

In 1926 he married Jessie Melville Hopkin, a distinguished medical psychologist; they had one son and one daughter. Williams died at Abinger, Surrey, on 5 June 1970.

WILLIAMS, IVY (1877-1966), the first woman to be called to the English Bar, was born on 7 September 1877 in Newton Abbot, Devon, daughter of George St Swithin Williams, a solicitor, and his wife, Emma Ewers. She was educated privately with her brother, Winter, and studied Latin, Greek, Italian, and Russian; she also spoke French and German fluently. At nineteen she entered the Society of Oxford Home-Students (later St Anne's College) and was taught by Edward Jenks and William S. HOLDSWORTH. She became BCL (1902) and LL D (London, 1903) but, owing to the restrictions on women students, did not receive her Oxford BA, MA, and BCL until 1920.

In 1920 women were admitted to the Inns of Court. In that year Ivy Williams joined the Inner Temple and in 1922 became the first woman to be called to the English Bar. From 1920 to 1945 she was tutor and lecturer in law to the Society of Home-Students, and worked strenuously to advance the cause of women law students. In 1923, when she published *The Sources of Law in the Swiss Civil Code*, she was awarded the DCL (Oxford), the first woman to achieve this honour. In 1925 she published *The Swiss Civil Code: English Version, with Notes and Vocabulary*.

In 1930 she was a delegate to the Hague Conference for the Codification of International Law and in 1932 was a member of the Aliens Deportation Advisory Committee. In memory of her brother, who had been killed in the First World War, she endowed two law scholarships at Oxford, one for women only. In 1956 she was elected an honorary Fellow of St Anne's College.

In her later years, with failing eyesight, she taught herself to read braille and, because of the difficulties she encountered, wrote a braille primer, which was published for the National Institute of the Blind in 1948. She died at her home in Oxford on 18 February 1966.

WILLIAMS, RALPH VAUGHAN (1872-1958). See VAUGHAN WILLIAMS.

WILSON, CHARLES MCMORAN, first BARON MORAN (1882-1977), physician, was born on 10 November 1882, the son of John Forsythe Wilson, MD, at Skipton, Yorkshire. He studied at St Mary's Hospital Medical School and qualified in 1908, proceeding to become MRCP and MD (London) with a Gold Medal in 1913.

During the First World War he served in France as medical officer to the 1st Battalion, The Royal Fusiliers, winning the MC during the Battle of the Somme; in 1917-18 he worked in a hospital at Boulogne doing research on mustard gas and its effects. In 1919 he married Dorothy, daughter of Dr S. F. Dufton, HM Inspector of Schools for the West Riding of Yorkshire; they had two sons. In the same year he joined the staff of St Mary's Hospital, and from 1920 till 1945 was Dean of the Medical School. In that office, he transformed the medical school, being responsible for the erection of new buildings and the introduction of new methods of training. He also served as an examiner in medicine for the universities of London, Cambridge, Liverpool, and Birmingham.

Having been knighted in 1938, he became well known during the war years as personal physician to Winston CHURCHILL, whom he accompanied on his visits abroad to conferences with Roosevelt, Stalin, and other war leaders. He was raised to the peerage in 1943 and in that year was in attendance on the Prime Minister when he was struck down with pneumonia while visiting General Eisenhower in North Africa.

From 1941 till 1950 Moran was President of the Royal College of Physicians at a time when great changes were taking place in the medical profession in Britain but, although he was always listened to with great attention when he spoke in the House of Lords, he was distrusted by many of his medical colleagues in spite of the fact that during his period of office as President of the College he had considerable influence with the Government.

In 1945 he published *The Anatomy of Courage*, based on lectures he had given to the Staff College, Camberley, in the years between the wars, drawing on his experience of the behaviour of soldiers under the stress of fear and anxiety in front-line conditions of danger and hardship.

In 1966 he published his controversial work *Winston Churchill: The Struggle for Survival* in which he not only recounted his own relations with the Prime Minister but commented on most of those with whom he came into contact as Churchill's personal doctor. Although this book has value as a day-by-day diary of important events of lasting historical interest it has been severely criticized for its breach of the confidential nature of information acquired by a doctor as a result of his intimate relationship with his patient. In his preface to the book Moran asserts that he was persuaded to undertake the work by the historian G. M. TREVELYAN, who told him, 'It is inevitable that everything about this man will be known in time. Let us have the truth.' Having put pen to paper, Moran inexorably pursued his purpose, into Churchill's declining years during which 'his will was sapped by old age and disease'. Moran's publication of this case-book of his experiences as Churchill's medical attendant was regarded by many critics as the greatest mistake of his career.

Moran died in London on 12 April 1977 in his ninety-fifth year.

WILSON, CHARLES THOMSON REES (1869-1959), physicist, was born at Glencorse, Midlothian on 14 February 1869, the youngest son of John Wilson, a sheep farmer, and his second wife, Annie Clark Harper. The family moved to Manchester on the death of his father, when he was four. He was educated at Owens College, where he gained his B.Sc. in 1887, and then went with a scholarship to Sidney Sussex College, Cambridge, where he obtained firsts in both parts of the natural sciences tripos (1890-2). He held the Clerk Maxwell scholarship from 1895 to 1898, and in 1900 was elected a Fellow of his college. He became university demonstrator (1900-1), lecturer (1901-19), and Reader in electrical meteorology (1919-25). From 1925 to 1934 he was Jacksonian Professor of Natural Philosophy.

From 1895 to 1899 he carried out experiments which established the main features of condensation of water droplets from a supersaturated dust-free gas, and devised a gold-leaf electroscope, in which surface leakage from the charged leaf to the case of the instrument was not possible. Between 1903 and 1910, his main interest was directed to the phenomena of atmospheric electricity and thunderstorms. In 1910 he developed a cloud chamber, and in 1911 published the first cloud chamber photographs, which provided workers in atomic physics with clear evidence of facts which previously had had to be painfully pieced together from indirect observations. These were outstanding achievements in the field of physical optics; Ernest RUTHERFORD described the cloud chamber as 'the most original apparatus in the whole history of physics'.

Wilson was elected FRS in 1900; he received many medals for scientific achievement, and in 1927 won the Nobel prize for physics, jointly with A. H. Compton. In 1937 he was appointed CH, and he received many honorary degrees.

Henry Wilson, sketch by Sheldon Williams, Johannesburg, 1900

In 1908 he married Jessie Fraser, daughter of the Revd George Hill Dick, of Glasgow; they had one son and two daughters. He died at Carlops, near Edinburgh on 15 November 1959.

WILSON, SIR HENRY HUGHES (1864-1922), field-marshal, was born at Currygrane, co Longford on 5 May 1864, the second son of James Wilson and his wife, Constance Grace Martha, daughter of James Freeman Hughes of Stillorgan, co. Dublin. He was educated at Marlborough College. He failed twice to gain admission to Woolwich and three times to Sandhurst. In 1882 he obtained a commission in the Longford Militia, and in 1884 went to India with the Rifle Brigade. He was wounded in Burma in 1887 and, after studying at the Staff College and working at the War Office, served in the Boer War for which he received the DSO (1901).

In 1891 he married Cecil Mary, daughter of George Cecil Gore Wray, of Ardnamona, co. Donegal; they had no children.

From 1901 till 1907, Wilson worked in the War Office, and in the latter year was appointed Commandant of the Staff College, where he became very popular. He made himself the leading exponent of close co-operation with the French and in the process became a friend of General (later Marshal) Foch, at that time head of the French École Supérieure de Guerre. In 1910 he was appointed Director of Military Operations at the War Office and concentrated on schemes for co-operation with France in the event of war with Germany. He had been created CB in 1908, and in 1913 he was promoted to major-general.

In 1914, as a Protestant Irishman, his sympathies were with the army officers at the Curragh, who threatened to resign rather than coerce Ulster. When the First World War broke out, he went to France as Sub-Chief of the General Staff. In 1915 he became chief liaison officer with French HQ and had no direct influence on the course of events in the field. He was appointed KCB. Later in 1915, he commanded IV Army Corps, but saw little action and, towards the end of 1916, headed a mission to Russia on the supply of war material.

In 1917 Wilson, now lieutenant-general, was posted to the Eastern command at home and this brought him into close touch with LLOYD GEORGE, with whom he went to the Rapallo Conference, at which it was decided by the Allies to set up a 'Supreme War Council', on which Wilson would be the British representative.

Friction between Lloyd George and Sir William Robertson, CIGS, had been increasing for some time and, in February 1918, Robertson was superseded by Wilson, who attended the conference at Doullens, when it was decided that Foch should assume control of the combined Allied armies, an arrangement which Wilson had advocated since the beginning of the war. When the German offensive of 1918 came to a halt and hostilities came to an end Wilson went to Paris for the peace conference. In 1919 he was promoted to field-marshal and created a baronet.

In peacetime, however, Wilson became disenchanted with Lloyd George. He was dissatisfied with the peace terms and opposed to the League of Nations. He was always in favour of military action whenever any kind of crisis arose, and his antipathy to Lloyd George grew stronger as the difficulties with the Irish increased. In 1922 he resigned from the army and was elected Conservative MP for North Down (Ireland). He became an implacable enemy of Sinn Fein, when his speeches in the Commons proclaimed his hostility to the pretensions of the Southern Irish. On 22 June 1922 he was assassinated by two members of Sinn Fein on the doorstep of his London home.

In 1927 his *Diaries* (2 vols.) were published: they disclosed that he was a man of much prejudice, who was more of a politician than a soldier, given to intrigue, and with little military talent.

WILSON, JOHN DOVER (1881–1969). See DOVER WILSON.

WINGATE, ORDE CHARLES (1903–1944), major-general, was born at Naini Tal, India, on 26 February 1903, the eldest son of Col. George Wingate, Indian Army, and his wife, Mary Ethel Stanley, daughter of Capt. Charles Orde Browne, RHA. Both parents were Plymouth Brethren. He was educated at Charterhouse as a day-boy and at the Royal Military Academy, Woolwich. He was commissioned in the Royal Artillery in 1923, and became such a skilful horseman that in 1926 he qualified as an instructor at the Army School at Weedon.

With the encouragement of his relative, Sir Reginald Wingate, who had been Governor-General of the Sudan (1899–1916), he learnt Arabic, and in 1927 went to the Sudan and was appointed to the Sudan Defence Force (1928–33). From 1933 to 1936 he served with an artillery unit in England. Then in 1936 he was posted to the intelligence staff in Palestine, where he learnt Hebrew and became a convinced Zionist, organized Jewish resistance to Arab rebels, and was appointed DSO (1938).

In 1940 he was again in Khartoum under Sir Archibald WAVELL and raised and trained forces to restore the Emperor Haile Selassie to his Abyssinian throne. In 1941 he invaded the country with a small force which, within four months, defeated the Italians and entered Addis Ababa.

When Burma was invaded by the Japanese, Wavell, who had been transferred to India as Commander-in-Chief, asked for Wingate to assist in plans for stopping the Japanese advance towards India, and Wingate put forward proposals for the training of a 'long-range penetration group' to operate behind the Japanese lines. Early in 1943, these plans were tried out and appeared to be moderately successful. Wingate had received a bar to his DSO after his Abyssinian campaign and he was now awarded a second bar.

Wingate was able to gain a hearing from Winston CHURCHILL for his unorthodox ideas on an offensive against the Japanese forces occupying Burma, and for a short time the Prime Minister appeared to regard Wingate as another T. E. LAWRENCE. Wingate accompanied Churchill to the Quebec Conference where he also impressed Roosevelt with his ideas. He was promoted to major-general, and early in 1944 his 'chindits', a force of divisional strength, were landed behind the Japanese lines and captured a large area, from which they attacked lines of communication and made themselves a nuisance to the enemy.

There have been conflicting views of the value of this exploit. General SLIM thought that it achieved little but had considerable psychological rewards. Wavell, writing in the *DNB*, paid tribute to Wingate's efficiency as well as his novel ideas, and thought that 'he had undoubtedly a high degree of military genius'. Wingate himself took little part in the 1944 expedition. On 24 March his aeroplane crashed in a tropical storm over the Naga hills between Assam and Burma and all the occupants were killed.

In 1935 he married Lorna Elizabeth Margaret, daughter

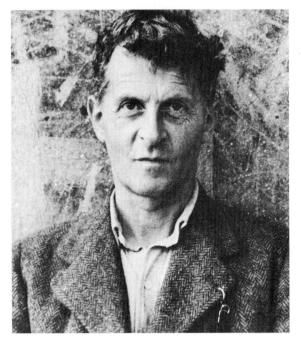

Wittgenstein

of Walter Moncrieff Paterson, of Tilliefoure, Monymusk, Aberdeenshire; they had one son who was born after his father's death.

WITTGENSTEIN, LUDWIG JOSEF JOHANN (1889–1951), philosopher, was born in Vienna on 26 April 1889, the youngest son of Karl Wittgenstein, a Jewish iron and steel magnate. He was educated at school in Linz and at the Technische Hochschule in Berlin-Charlottenburg, where he studied mechanical engineering. In 1908 he came to England as a research student in the Department of Engineering, Manchester University. He designed a jet reaction propeller, which led him to an interest in mathematics and to a study of the philosophical basis of mathematics. He was influenced by reading Bertrand RUSSELL's *Principles of Mathematics* (1903).

In 1912 he went to Trinity College, Cambridge to study philosophy with Russell, and in 1913 settled in Norway and corresponded with Russell about his work on logic. During the First World War he fought in the Austrian Army and was taken prisoner by the Italians. He returned to Vienna in 1919, gave away the fortune he had inherited from his father, and worked first as a schoolmaster in Lower Austria, and then from 1926 to 1928 as an architect in Vienna.

His work published in England in 1922 under the title *Tractatus Logico-Philosophicus* had been written in 1918 and published in German in 1921. During the years from 1919 to 1928, he did not concern himself actively with philosophical research, though he came to exercise considerable influence on the 'Vienna Circle', from which logical positivism arose. At this time he possibly thought that in the *Tractatus* he had said the last word about philosophy, in declaring that it was not concerned with theories about the foundation of knowledge or the nature of reality, but was fundamentally based on a clarification of thought through an examination

P. G. Wodehouse, 1928

of the meaning of language, and an understanding that there are limits to the possibilities of linguistic expression.

In 1929 Wittgenstein returned to Cambridge, submitted the *Tractatus* for a Ph.D., and in the following year was elected a Fellow of Trinity College. When the fellowship expired in 1936, he returned to Norway and, having in some sense revised the ideas formulated in his earlier work, began writing *Philosophical Investigations*. He came back to Cambridge in 1937, became naturalized in 1938, and in 1939 succeeded G. E. MOORE as Professor of Philosophy, a chair which he held until 1947. His teaching in the university was interrupted by the Second World War, during which he worked voluntarily as a porter at Guy's Hospital, London, and as an assistant in a medical laboratory. He lived in Ireland after retirement in 1947 and completed his *Philosophical Investigations* there. This work was published posthumously in 1953. Basically, it reinterprets Wittgenstein's original thesis about the value of language, and reaches the conclusion that philosophy does not find the answers to questions, but merely enables the philosopher to invalidate propositions which are based on a misunderstanding of the ordinary use of language.

Wittgenstein was a philosopher of unusual genius and originality, who has had a marked influence on his successors, though he thought that his work was much misunderstood. In fact, his theories questioned the nature of philosophy itself by distinguishing between the role of philosophy and the sciences and clarifying the possibilities and limitations of both.

He died at Cambridge on 29 April 1951. He never married.

WODEHOUSE, PELHAM GRENVILLE (1881–1975), writer, was born on 15 October 1881 at Guildford, the third son of Henry Ernest Wodehouse, a Hong Kong magistrate, and his wife, Eleanor, daughter of the Revd John Bathurst Deane. After he was born, his mother returned to Hong Kong, and Pelham, at the age of two, was left in England with his two brothers in the care of a Miss Roper. After a dame school in Croydon, he went to Dulwich College. Deprived of any family background, he lived in a world of his own imagination, and determined to be a writer while he was still a schoolboy. One of his brothers obtained a scholarship to Oxford but his father could not afford to send more than one son to college and 'P.G.', on leaving school, went into the Hong Kong and Shanghai Bank in work which he hated.

He left when he was offered a job writing the 'By the Way' column on the *Globe* newspaper and, from then onwards, he supported himself by writing light verse, articles, and stories for *Punch*, the *Public School Magazine*, and *The Captain*. His first book was a school story, called *The Pothunters* (1902) and this was followed by six similar books, the last of which, *Mike* (1909), included Psmith, who became one of Wodehouse's most popular characters.

In 1904 he visited the USA, and afterwards some of his novels had an American setting; in 1914 he was in America and stayed there for the duration of the First World War. In 1914 he married Ethel Newton, the widow of Leonard Rowley, of Dee Bank, Cheshire. By her first husband she had a daughter, to whom Wodehouse became devoted—they had no other children, and Ethel managed all her husband's business affairs, leaving him free to write. He was now writing the lyrics for musical comedies, in collaboration with Guy Bolton and Jerome Kern. After the war, he returned to London, but continued to spend much time in the USA until, in 1934, he and his wife settled at Le Touquet in France.

They were there when the Second World War broke out but, unlike Somerset MAUGHAM, Wodehouse did not leave France; he was interned by the Germans, and earned considerable opprobrium in Britain by making broadcasts to America when he was released in 1941. He did not intend these broadcasts to be taken seriously, but this was not accepted in London, except by a few fellow writers who defended him; he was not immune from prosecution in England and, when the war ended, he settled in the USA, becoming an American citizen in 1955.

Wodehouse's output of novels, short stories, lyrics, light verse, and articles was prolific; under his own name he wrote nearly one hundred books. His sales were phenomenal, and his work was translated into all the major languages of the world. His characters, Psmith, Jeeves, Bertie Wooster, and Lord Emsworth of Blandings Castle, delighted millions of readers and, for a time, created a cult. He also wrote amusingly on golf.

In 1939 he received an honorary Litt.D. from Oxford. In 1975, when he had been restored to favour, he was appointed KBE. He died at Long Island on 14 February 1975 with a reputation as one of the most enjoyable novelists of his time.

WOOD, EDWARD FREDERICK LINDLEY, first EARL OF HALIFAX (1881–1959), politician, was born at Powderham Castle, Devon, on 16 April 1881, the fourth son of Charles Lindley Wood, later second Viscount Halifax, and his wife, Lady Agnes Elizabeth Courtenay, daughter of the eleventh Earl of Devon. His three brothers died while he was a child, and he himself was born with a withered left arm. He was educated at Eton and Christ Church, Oxford, where he obtained a first in history (1903) and was elected a Fellow of All Souls. In 1909 he married Lady Dorothy Evelyn Augusta Onslow, daughter of the fourth Earl of Onslow; they had three sons and one surviving daughter. From an early age Wood was a devout churchman and it was his custom, before taking any important decision, to pray for guidance. At times, it would appear that he misunderstood the counsel thus revealed to him.

In 1910 he was elected Conservative MP for Ripon, a seat which he held until created a peer in 1925. In spite of his disability, he served during 1914–17 in the Yorkshire Dragoons. In 1917 he returned to England to a post in the Ministry of National Service. He held minor ministerial posts in the Coalition Government until its fall in 1922, when he entered BONAR LAW's Cabinet as President of the Board of Education and was sworn of the Privy Council. He made little mark in this post or in that of Minister of Agriculture in BALDWIN's second administration.

In 1925 he was appointed Governor-General and Viceroy of India and created Lord Irwin. In 1927 the Simon Commission was set up. Irwin and BIRKENHEAD, Secretary of State, agreed that it should consist entirely of British members of Parliament, not Indians. In consequence, the Commission was met in India with hostility, and the Viceroy realized that he had made a big mistake. By the time a Labour Government was elected in 1929, Irwin had decided that partnership must be substituted for benevolent autocracy. Without waiting for the report of the Commission, but with the support of the Secretary of State for India, William Wedgwood BENN, he announced that there would be a Round Table Conference to consider the arrangements for giving India dominion status. The vehement objections in London aroused by this declaration did nothing to convince Indian leaders of its sincerity. After an abortive meeting with

the Viceroy, GANDHI began his civil disobedience campaign. In 1930 he led his march to the sea to defy the salt laws. Irwin ordered his imprisonment.

A year later Gandhi was released and, after exhaustive discussions, he and the Viceroy reached an agreement: Indians would take part in the Round Table Conference. Irwin, having been appointed GCSI and GCIE in 1926, returned to England and was appointed KG. He refused the office of Foreign Secretary in the National Government, but in 1932 became Minister of Education again. In 1933 he was elected Chancellor of Oxford University and in 1934 succeeded his father as Lord Halifax. In 1937 he was appointed Lord President of the Council in Neville CHAMBERLAIN's Government.

He was now primarily interested in foreign policy, and in 1937 visited Germany and met Hitler, but failed to realize that the Führer was a megalomaniac and thought him 'very sincere'. Anthony EDEN resigned his post of Foreign Secretary in 1938, disgruntled by the interference of the Prime Minister in the conduct of foreign affairs. Halifax stepped into Eden's shoes, apparently prepared to subordinate his role to that of Neville Chamberlain.

He watched the invasion of Austria, the dismemberment of Czechoslovakia, and the progress of appeasement to Munich. When, in 1939, Hitler marched into Prague, it was announced that Britain had guaranteed the independence of Poland, but Halifax refused an invitation to Moscow, and whatever chance there was of an agreement with Soviet Russia disappeared with the Russo-German pact for the partition of Poland.

When, in 1940, it was clear that Neville Chamberlain had lost the confidence of Parliament, it seemed possible that Halifax would take over as Prime Minister. That eventuality was averted and he remained as Foreign Secretary and a member of the War Cabinet in Winston CHURCHILL's Government. Towards the end of the year Churchill asked him to succeed Lord LOTHIAN as Ambassador at Washington.

In 1941 he took up this post and, during the months leading up to the Japanese attack upon Pearl Harbor, discovered that he could still make mistakes which did little for his popularity with the Americans. However, once the USA was involved in the war, Halifax was able to win the confidence of Cordell Hull, the Secretary of State, and the influential Harry Hopkins. In 1942 the second of his three sons was killed in battle and the third gravely wounded. He would have liked to be relieved of his post, but Eden, Foreign Secretary again, persuaded him to stay on at Washington for a further three years. When the Japanese war ended, he assisted Lord KEYNES in the negotiation of an American loan and took part in the Dumbarton Oaks Conference. In 1944 he became Earl of Halifax and in 1946 returned to England and was admitted to the Order of Merit.

He filled his remaining years with public service in such offices as Chancellor of Oxford and Sheffield, and Chairman of the General Advisory Council of the BBC. He published his memoirs, *Fulness of Days* (1957), and died on 23 December 1959 at Garrowby in Yorkshire.

WOOD, SIR HENRY JOSEPH (1869–1944), conductor, was born in London on 3 March 1869, the only child of Henry Joseph Wood, an optician, and his wife, Martha, daughter of Evan Morris, a Welsh farmer; both parents were musical. He was educated in London, played the organ from an early age, and studied at St John's Wood and the Slade art schools. Having decided on a musical career, he studied

Sir Henry Wood, June 1938

at the Royal Academy of Music and made his début as a professional with an opera company in 1889. In 1890 he was appointed assistant conductor to the D'Oyly Carte Company.

In 1895 Robert Newman, Manager of the Queen's Hall, decided to mount a series of Promenade Concerts and engaged Wood to be his musical director. These concerts were sufficiently successful to become an annual event, but Wood was also kept busy with a number of festivals in provincial cities.

In 1898 he married Olga, daughter of Princess Sofie Ouroussoff, of Podolia, Russia, who had been one of his pupils. She died in 1909. In 1901 Robert Newman went bankrupt, but (Sir) Edgar Speyer sponsored the continuance of Promenade Concerts. Wood was knighted in 1911, and that year married Muriel Ellen, daughter of Major Ferdinand William Greatrex of the 1st (Royal) Dragoons; they had two daughters.

From 1915 to 1926 financial responsibility for the Promenade Concerts was taken over by Chappell, the lessees of the Queen's Hall. In 1926 Chappell decided that they could not continue, and Wood negotiated an agreement with the BBC, under which the Corporation took over responsibility and the concerts were broadcast. In 1930 the BBC Symphony Orchestra was formed, and Wood continued to conduct until, in 1941, the Queen's Hall was destroyed in an air raid; the concerts were given without interruption by being transferred to the Royal Albert Hall.

In 1944 he was appointed CH and it was decided that the concerts should in future be named 'The Henry Wood Promenade Concerts'. Sir Henry was the first British conductor to found a stable and permanent orchestra and to earn an international reputation, not only for his relations with foreign composers such as Strauss, Debussy, Sibelius, and Grieg, whom he invited to conduct their own music, but also for his encouragement of contemporary British composers.

Sir Henry was able to conduct on the opening night of his fiftieth promenade season, but he died on 19 August 1944. A bust of this gifted conductor is annually, on the last night of the Proms, decorated with a laurel wreath by young music-lovers anxious to honour his memory. His published works include *The Gentle Art of Singing* (4 vols., 1927-8) and *About Conducting* (1945).

WOODCOCK, GEORGE (1904-1979), General Secretary of the Trades Union Congress, was born on 20 October 1904, at Walton le Dale, Lancashire, the second son of Peter Woodcock, a cotton weaver, and his wife, Ann Baxendale. He was educated at Brownedge Roman Catholic Elementary School, and left at thirteen to become a cotton weaver. He became a minor official in the local weavers' union, and during the 1929 election was election agent for the Labour party. That year he won a TUC scholarship to Ruskin College, Oxford, and in 1931 went to New College with an extra-mural scholarship, and in 1933 obtained a first in philosophy, politics, and economics.

During 1934-6 he worked in the Civil Service and in 1936 joined the TUC as head of the Research and Economic Department. From 1946 to 1960 he was Assistant General Secretary and from 1960 to 1969 General Secretary. When he joined the TUC, the country was in the grip of depression; he was a keen exponent of the views of J. M. KEYNES, and regarded it as one of the highlights of his career when, in 1944, the Government declared that, after the war, a primary aim and responsibility would be the maintenance of a high and stable level of employment. He realized, however, that co-operation between trade unions, industry, and the Government could only be achieved if the trade unions were prepared to accept the responsibility of avoiding inflation, and to exercise their new power sensibly. He was concerned that full employment should be maintained by co-operation between the unions and Government and not by legislation.

In 1962 he persuaded the TUC to take part in the National Economic Development Council, set up by Selwyn LLOYD, Conservative Chancellor of the Exchequer; and in 1964, when a Labour Government came to power, he persuaded the TUC to accept a wages and incomes policy. He foresaw that, if the unions at any time failed to co-operate with the Government, the Government would be forced to modify the commitment to maintain a high level of employment. How right he was has, since his death in 1979, been demonstrated only too forcibly.

Woodcock served on a number of public commissions and committees. In 1969 he was appointed Chairman of the Commission on Industrial Relations, but resigned in 1971. He was succeeded as General Secretary of the TUC by Victor Feather (1908-1976), who found himself in the position forecast by Woodcock when he had to lead the unions in opposition to the Industrial Relations Act brought in by the Conservative Government of 1970.

Woodcock was appointed CBE in 1953 and PC in 1967. He received a number of honorary degrees. In 1933 he married Laura Mary, daughter of Francis McKernan, an engine

George Woodcock, speaking at a rally of post office workers, supports their action against the Government's pay-pause, Albert Hall, 29 December 1961

fitter, of Horwich, Lancashire; they had a son and a daughter, and Laura Woodcock became a magistrate and Mayor of Epsom. She was the first woman to be made a freeman of Epsom. Woodcock died there on 30 October 1979.

WOODHAM-SMITH, CECIL BLANCHE (1896–1977), historian, was born on 29 April 1896 at Tenby, Wales, daughter of Col. James FitzGerald, Indian Army officer, an Irishman, and his wife, Blanche Elizabeth Philipps, who was Welsh. She was educated at the Royal School for Officers' Daughters, Bath, and St Hilda's College, Oxford. In 1928 she married George Ivon Woodham-Smith, a London solicitor, and had a son and a daughter.

When her children were at boarding-school she began her literary career and, after nine years of research, published *Florence Nightingale* (1950), which was an immediate success, and won the James Tait Black memorial prize. This biography, in its way a masterpiece, was followed by *The Reason Why* (1953), an eminently readable account of the antagonisms, the intrigues, and the aristocratic inefficiency which resulted in the horrors of the Crimean War and the charge of the Light Brigade at Balaclava.

In *The Great Hunger* (1962), she graphically and bitterly described the bureaucratic rigidity with which the disasters of the Irish potato famine were exacerbated, and portrayed the macabre death traps of the coffin-ships conveying Irish emigrants across the Atlantic. Then, in 1972, she produced

Queen Victoria: Her Life and Times (vol. i), another remarkably vivid account of the court of the young queen, her marriage, and the calamity that befell her when the Prince Consort died. She herself died in London on 16 March 1977 before she could continue the story.

She was appointed CBE in 1960, received honorary doctorates from the National University of Ireland (1964) and St Andrews (1965), and became an honorary Fellow of St Hilda's (1967).

WOOLF, (ADELINE) VIRGINIA (1882–1941), novelist and critic, was born on 25 January 1882 in London, the second daughter of (Sir) Leslie Stephen and his second wife, Julia Prinsep, widow of Herbert Duckworth. Leslie Stephen, at the time of Virginia's birth, was Editor of the *Cornhill Magazine* and about to become the first Editor of *The Dictionary of National Biography*. He had resigned his fellowship at Trinity Hall, Cambridge, in 1862 because he had become an agnostic and could no longer conscientiously attend services in the college chapel. Virginia's mother, Julia, was a beautiful widow who had two sons and a daughter by her previous marriage. She and Leslie Stephen had two daughters, Vanessa (later BELL) and Virginia, and two sons, Thoby and Adrian.

Virginia grew up in a household in which she met many literary and artistic friends of her parents, including Henry JAMES, George Meredith, and G. F. Watts; and life in this setting is graphically described in her novel *To the Lighthouse* (1927) in which she depicts Mrs Ramsey, the warm-hearted wife with a difficult husband and a large family on a holiday set in the Hebrides. From a very early age, however, Virginia suffered from a nervous disposition which, under any kind of stress, was liable to reduce her to bouts of suicidal manic depression. The death of her mother when she was fourteen was a shattering blow and instead of going to school, she spent her girlhood in the family homes in London and Cornwall, being taught by her father and devouring rapaciously the books in his library.

Her Duckworth half-brothers, very unlike her own brothers, were young men of the world, who believed it their duty to secure good husbands for their sisters, but Virginia was already sufficiently unconventional to resist their efforts. She preferred the Cambridge friends of her brothers, Thoby and Adrian and, after her father died in 1904, they set up house together in Bloomsbury. Virginia was already writing for the *Times Literary Supplement*, and she and Vanessa, who had both inherited their mother's beauty, were soon surrounded by the circle of young writers and painters, Roger FRY, J. Maynard KEYNES, Lytton STRACHEY, E. M. FORSTER, Leonard WOOLF, and Clive BELL, who became well known as the Bloomsbury group.

Virginia was a party to a famous practical joke, thought up by Adrian, in which she, disguised as the Crown Prince of Abyssinia, was received with full naval honours by the admiral on board a *Dreadnought*, while her brothers and friends posed as members of the Prince's entourage. She and her sister were already marked out as unusual young women.

The death of her brother Thoby in 1906 was a further tragic blow, which threatened Virginia's mental stability, but she continued to live in Bloomsbury until, in 1912, she married Leonard Sidney Woolf, who had been a colonial civil servant in Ceylon (Sri Lanka), but had resigned to become a writer and publicist. For the rest of her life until she died in 1941, Leonard was her devoted protector who tried to ensure that she led a quiet life, partly in London, and partly at Rodmell in Sussex. Sir Geoffrey Keynes, in his autobiography *The Gates of Memory* (1981), has recorded how, as a young house surgeon, he and Leonard dashed to St Bartholomew's Hospital to obtain the equipment necessary to save Virginia from her first attempt at suicide in 1913.

Her first novel *The Voyage Out* was published in 1915 by her half-brother, Gerald Duckworth, followed in 1919 by *Night and Day*. *Jacob's Room*, in which she first demonstrated that she was a great writer, with a catholic interest in the world around her, was published in 1922. Her ability to abstract an idea, from some remark overheard in the street or some small item in a newspaper or a letter, showed that she was always aware of people as individuals with particular interests and motives, with the kind of psychological insight into character that Henry James had displayed. In the story, Jacob is portrayed as a young man, seen through the eyes of an old lady, as he travels with her in a railway carriage to Cambridge.

In *Mrs Dalloway*, published in 1925, she portrays a woman who, as a girl, had potentialities similar to those of Virginia herself but, unlike her, chose to follow convention and observe the snobbish prejudices and traditions of her class. Among her other novels, Virginia produced *The Waves* (1931) and *The Years* (1937); she also wrote two fantasies, *Orlando* (1928) and *Flush* (1933), books of critical and biographical essays, and a biography of Roger Fry (1940).

As each of her books was finished Virginia was threatened with a period of mental breakdown, and it was partly to give her something less exciting to do that Leonard founded the Hogarth Press in 1917, which she helped him to manage.

Virginia had a number of intimate women friends. She was often at Garsington Manor with Lady Ottoline MORRELL, where the other guests noted her remote, ethereal beauty; she was in love with Vita SACKVILLE-WEST around whom *Orlando* was written; and in her later years, she was a friend of Elizabeth BOWEN. She and Leonard never had children, and at last, his efforts to protect her from her suicidal impulses failed. As he wrote in his autobiography, she was 'half in love with easeful Death'. In 1941, under the strain imposed by the war, Virginia had a final breakdown and drowned herself on 28 March.

A number of her books, including her letters, and extracts from her diary, *A Writer's Diary* (1953), were published posthumously. Lord David Cecil in the *DNB* gave his verdict on her work: 'In Virginia Woolf the English aesthetic movement brought forth its most exquisite flower.'

WOOLF, LEONARD SIDNEY (1880–1969), author, publisher, and political worker, was born on 25 November 1880 in London, the second son of Sidney Woolf, QC, and his wife, Mary de Jongh, both Jews. His father died when he was twelve, leaving nine children, and it was necessary for the sons to win scholarships. This Leonard achieved, first at St Paul's, then at Trinity College, Cambridge, where he obtained a first in part i, and a second in part ii of the classical tripos (1902–3). He arrived at Trinity with little money and no friends but while there he became an 'Apostle' and, through his first friend Saxon Sidney-Turner, he made many other friends, including Thoby Stephen, Lytton STRACHEY, Maynard KEYNES, and G. E. MOORE. At this time Woolf also became friendly with Thoby Stephen's sisters: Virginia, his future wife, and Vanessa, who later married Clive BELL.

In 1904 he entered the Ceylon Civil Service and spent seven years as an administrator. In 1911 he returned to England and, leaving the Service, married Virginia, daughter

Virginia and Leonard Woolf

of Sir Leslie Stephen (1912). He found his Cambridge friends extended into the Bloomsbury set. Leonard and Virginia WOOLF were both writing novels, and in 1913 he published *Village in the Jungle*, followed by *The Wise Virgins* (1914).

In 1913 he became a socialist, joined the Fabian Society, and took an interest in the Co-operative Movement, which led to the publication of articles and two books on the subject. His political activities were restricted by the precarious health of Virginia, who was having periodical bouts of manic depression, during which she needed much careful attention.

During the First World War Leonard Woolf was exempted from military service on health grounds and he turned to the study of international politics and colonialism. His book, *International Government* (1916), influenced the British proposals for a League of Nations; this was followed by *Empire and Commerce in Africa* (1920). In 1919 he edited the *International Review* and the international section of the *Contemporary Review*; he was also honorary Secretary of the Labour party advisory committees on international affairs.

To give Virginia a new interest, he set up the Hogarth Press. Begun in 1917 as a hobby, it soon became an important publishing house, producing the works of E. M. FORSTER, T. S. ELIOT, Katherine MANSFIELD, Freud, Gorki, Maynard Keynes, and the Woolfs themselves. From 1931 to 1959 Woolf was Joint Editor of the *Political Quarterly* and from 1959 to 1962 Literary Editor. He was also Literary Editor of the *Nation*. His publications include *Imperialism and Civilization* (1928), *The War for Peace* (1940), and *Principia Politica* (1953).

The Second World War put paid to his hopes for international sanity, and then in 1941 Virginia, convinced that she was going mad, drowned herself. To use his own words, Woolf was 'so battered and beaten that he was like some hunted animal, which, exhausted, can only instinctively drag itself into its hole or lair'. He continued, however, to work for the Hogarth Press and for the Labour party. He also wrote five fascinating volumes of autobiography, *Sowing* (1960), *Growing* (1961), *Beginning Again* (1964), *Downhill All the Way* (1967), and *The Journey not the Arrival Matters* (1969).

He declined a CH but accepted an honorary doctorate from Sussex University (1964). He died on 14 August 1969 at Monks House, Rodmell, where he and Virginia were living when she died. They had no children.

WOOLLEY, SIR (CHARLES) LEONARD (1880–1960), archaeologist, was born on 17 April 1880, the son of the Revd George Herbert Woolley, a curate, and his wife, Sarah Cathcart. He was educated at St John's, Leatherhead and New College, Oxford, where he was a scholar and obtained a first in Greats (1903).

In 1905 he was appointed assistant to Arthur EVANS, Keeper of the Ashmolean Museum. He began his field work in 1907 in Nubia, and from 1912 to 1914 was leader of the British Museum expedition to Carchemish in Northern Syria, accompanied by T. E. LAWRENCE. This work was interrupted by the First World War, during which Woolley did intelligence work in Egypt and became a prisoner of the Turks (1916–18).

In 1922 he began his most important work at Ur, and was excavating there and making important discoveries for the next thirteen years. He described this work in a number of books including *The Sumerians* (1928), *The Development of Sumerian Art* (1935) and *Excavations at Ur, A Record of Twelve Years' Work* (1954).

During 1937–9 and 1946–9 Woolley worked at Atchana and described his discoveries there in *Alalakh, excavations at Tell Atchana* (1955). In 1938 he advised the Government of India on their programme of archaeological work. He was knighted in 1935, and elected honorary ARIBA (1926) and an honorary Fellow of New College, Oxford. He recounted his reminiscences in *Dead Towns and Living Men* (1920).

In 1927 he married Katharine Elizabeth, widow of Lt.-Col. Francis Keeling, and she took an active part in his work until her death in 1945. Woolley died in London on 20 February 1960.

WOOLTON, first EARL OF (1883–1964). See MARQUIS.

WRIGHT, SIR ALMROTH EDWARD (1861–1947), bacteriologist, was born at Middleton Tyas, near Richmond, Yorkshire, on 10 August 1861, the son of the Revd Charles Henry Hamilton Wright, and his wife, Ebba Johanna Dorothea, daughter of Nils Wilhelm Almroth, Governor of the Royal Mint, Stockholm. He was educated at the Royal Academical Institution, Belfast, and Trinity College, Dublin, where he graduated in modern literature (1882) and medicine (1883). He undertook further study in Germany and then, from 1892 to 1902, was Professor of Pathology at the Army Medical School, Netley. He introduced anti-typhoid inoculation and served on the first Indian Plague Commission (1898–1900).

In 1889 he married Jane Georgina, daughter of Robert Mackay Wilson, of Coolcarigan, co. Kildare; they had two sons and one daughter.

After a dispute with the War Office about the use of anti-typhoid vaccine in the army, he resigned, and spent the rest of his career, from 1902 till 1946, as Professor at St Mary's Hospital, London. There he developed a new school of 'therapeutic immunization'. His laboratory expanded into a research institute, and he was appointed Director of the Bacteriological Department of the Medical Research Committee (later Council). During the First World War he worked with the RAMC doing research on wound infections.

After the war, Wright returned to St Mary's and continued his work on immunization, research which produced over 130 scientific papers, and made him one of the founders of modern immunology. In 1906 he was knighted and elected FRS; he was appointed CB in 1915, and KBE in 1919. He received many academic honours and awards. Wright died at Farnham Common, Bucks., on 30 April 1947.

SHAW caricatured Sir Almroth Wright in *The Doctor's Dilemma*.

Y

YATES, DORNFORD (1885–1960), novelist, whose real name was Cecil William Mercer, was born at Upper Walmer, Kent on 7 August 1885, the only son of Cecil John Mercer, a solicitor, and his wife, Helen Wall. H. H. MUNRO was his cousin. He was educated at Harrow, and University College, Oxford, where he was President of the OUDS (1906–7). He was called to the Bar (Inner Temple), in 1909, and in 1910 assisted Travers HUMPHREYS in the Crippen case.

In the First World War he served in the 3rd County of London Yeomanry in Egypt and Salonika. After the war, with chronic rheumatism, he settled at Pau, France with his American wife, Bettine Edwards of Philadelphia, whom he married in 1919. They had one son.

Before the war he was already writing for the *Windsor Magazine* under the name of Dornford Yates. *The Brother of Daphne* was published in 1914, followed by *The Courts of Idleness* (1920), *Berry and Co.* (1921), and *Jonah and Co.* (1922), easily readable romantic comedies about 'Berry' Pleydell and his relatives, all handsome in the case of the men, beautiful in the case of the ladies, rich, witty, and adventurous.

Other less well known of his books are *She Fell Among Thieves* (1925), *The Stolen March* (1926), and *Blood Royal* (1929).

His first marriage ended in divorce in 1933. In 1934 he married Elizabeth, daughter of David Mather Bowie. By this time he had made a sizeable fortune from his books and was able to build his dream house, which he later described in *The House that Berry Built* (1945). He had to leave the house when the Second World War broke out, and he had to escape from France through Spain. Having settled in South Africa, he served for a short time with the Southern Rhodesian forces. After the war, he settled at Umtali (Mutari) and wrote more novels, including *As Berry and I Were Saying* (1952) and *B. Berry and I Look Back* (1958).

He died at Umtali on 5 March 1960.

YEATS, WILLIAM BUTLER (1865–1939), Irish poet and playwright, was born in Dublin on 13 June 1865, the eldest son of John Butler Yeats, painter, and his wife, Susan, daughter of William Pollexfen, a shipowner. His grandfather and great-grandfather had been Church of Ireland clergymen. In 1877 he went to the Godolphin School, Hammersmith, while his father was studying art in London, but in 1881 the family returned to Dublin and Yeats went to Dublin High School. Encouraged by his father, he began to write poetry at the age of sixteen and, at the Metropolitan School of Art, he was one of a group of mystics, including AE (George William Russell), who became one of his closest friends.

His first book *Mosada*, a dramatic poem, was published in

W. B. Yeats

Dublin in 1886, but in the following year he joined his parents in London, where they had settled again, and was encouraged by W. E. Henley and William Morris to continue writing lyrics and plays. He also joined a group of theosophists and spiritualists and, with E. J. Ellis, wrote *The Works of William Blake, Poetic, Symbolic, and Critical* (1893). He also published his folk-stories in *The Celtic Twilight* (1893) and his earliest *Poems* (1895), followed by *The Secret Rose* (1897) and *Wind Among the Reeds* (1899).

He never became a London-Irishman of letters, however, because on visits to Ireland he set about organizing literary societies and formed friendships with the Fenian, John O'Leary, who was prominent in Irish revolutionary politics, and with Maud Gonne (Madame Gonne MacBride), the great love of his life and the subject of his love poems. He also came under the influence of Isabella Augusta, Lady GREGORY, who, with Edward Martyn and George MOORE, arranged for the first performance in Dublin of Yeats's verse-play, *The Countess Cathleen*, which had been published in the *Poems* of 1895. The play aroused Roman Catholic suspicion and later, when the Abbey Theatre was established, he succeeded in arousing the hostility of the Fenians by his defence of J. M. Synge.

His most popular play was *Cathleen ni Houlihan*, first performed in 1902, when Maud Gonne played a leading part. His experiences in the theatre led to a more sophisticated approach to poetry, in which he seemed to repudiate the mood of the 'Celtic Twilight', and in *Responsibilities* (1914) and *The Wild Swans of Coole* (1917) he struck a new note. The Easter rising in 1916 and the subsequent executions moved him to a new mood of Irish patriotism:

> We know their dream; enough
> To know they dreamed and are dead.

Coole Park, Galway, was the home of Lady Gregory, and Yeats spent weeks there each summer. For him, Coole Park symbolized all that was best in the Irish aristocratic tradition. However, he always returned to his London friends and was sometimes to be found enjoying the hospitality of the MORRELLS at Garsington Manor. In 1917 he married an English girl much younger than he was, Georgie, only daughter of William Gilbert Hyde Lees of Pickhill Hall, Wrexham. They had a son and a daughter. For a short time they lived in Oxford, and in 1925 Yeats published *A Vision*, in which he revealed his interest and belief in the supernatural and extrasensory perception, and his preoccupation with the impact of eternity in time.

He saw something of the civil war in Ireland in 1922–3 and accepted an invitation to become a Senator, an office which he held until 1928. In 1923 he was awarded the Nobel prize for literature, and later received honorary degrees from Oxford and Cambridge as well as Dublin. He continued to be out of step, at times, with his Irish friends. In 1925 he made a passionate attack in the Senate on legislation about divorce, which he considered to be unjust to the Protestant Irish.

In 1928 he published *The Tower*, followed in the next year

by *The Winding Stair*, regarded by some critics as his greatest poems. He was by now recognized as the leading poet of English-speaking Ireland. In these years, he frequently undertook lecture tours in the United States, and in 1932 made the last of these, collecting funds for the Irish Academy of Letters, which he and G. B. SHAW and George Russell had founded. His *Collected Poems* and *Collected Plays* were published in 1933-4. In 1935 he paid a visit to Majorca with an Indian religious man, Shri Purohit Swami, who was making an English translation of the *Upanishads*. This revived his interest in the Eastern philosophies, which he had first revealed in *A Vision*. In 1938, when he was dying, he went with his wife to Cap Martin, near Méntone; he died at Roquebrune, near Monaco, on 28 January 1939.

YOUNGHUSBAND, SIR FRANCIS EDWARD (1863- 1942), soldier, diplomat, and explorer, was born at Muree, India, on 31 May 1863, the second son of Major (later Major-General) John William Younghusband and his wife, Clara Jane, daughter of Robert Grant Shaw. He was educated at Clifton and the Royal Military College, Sandhurst, and was commissioned in the 1st (King's) Dragoon Guards in 1882.

He was stationed at Meerut, and began his explorations by reconnoitering the Afghan border and visiting Manchuria. In 1887 he travelled from Peking to Rawalpindi via Chinese Turkestan, and in 1890-1 journeyed from India to Kashgar and back, exploring the northern approaches to India.

In 1889 he was transferred to the Indian Foreign Department and between 1892 and 1903 was Political Officer in Hunza, Chitral, Haraoti, and Tonk and Resident of Indore. In 1891, while travelling in the Pamirs, he was escorted by Russians from 'Russian territory', and the British Government eventually received an apology from the Russian Government and a boundary agreement was reached. Younghusband's journeys are described in *The Heart of a Continent* (1896). In 1891 he was appointed CIE.

In 1903 at the request of the Viceroy, Lord CURZON, Younghusband led a mission to Tibet in an attempt to end frontier hostility; he reached Lhasa with a military escort and obtained a treaty from the Tibetans without any fighting. He was appointed KCIE (1904). From 1906 to 1910 he was Resident, Kashmir; then retired in 1910 and published *India and Tibet*.

He was also interested in religious philosophy, on which he wrote two books: he was a mystic and a Christian but with a deep understanding of Hinduism and Buddhism. In retirement he became the first Chairman of the Mount Everest Committee and wrote *The Epic of Mount Everest* (1926) and *Everest: The Challenge* (1936). He was appointed KCSI (1917), and received a number of academic honours. In 1897 he married Helen Augusta, daughter of Charles Magniac, MP; they had a son, who died in infancy, and a daughter. Younghusband died at Lytchet Minster, near Poole, on 31 July 1942.

YPRES, First EARL OF (1852-1925). See FRENCH.

INDEX OF BIOGRAPHIES BY OCCUPATION OR SPHERE OF INTEREST

ARCHAEOLOGY

Bell, Gertrude
Carter, Howard
Evans, Sir Arthur
Mallowan, Sir Max
Murray, Margaret
Petrie, Sir Flinders
Ventris, Michael
Wheeler, Sir Mortimer
Woolley, Sir Leonard

ARCHITECTURE

Abercrombie, Sir Patrick
Baker, Sir Herbert
Howard, Sir Ebenezer
Hussey, Christopher
Lutyens, Sir Edwin
Scott, Sir Giles Gilbert
Spence, Sir Basil

ARMED FORCES

Alanbrooke, Viscount. *See* Brooke, Alan
Alexander, Harold, Earl Alexander of
    Tunis
Allenby, Edmund
Baden-Powell, Robert
Battenberg, Prince Louis of. *See*
    Mountbatten, L. A.
Beatty, David, Earl
Brooke, Alan, Viscount Alanbrooke
Bruce, Charles
Byng, Julian, Viscount
Chatfield, Alfred, Baron
Cunningham, Andrew, Viscount
Dill, Sir John
Douglas, William Sholto, Baron
Dowding, Hugh, Baron
Dyer, Reginald
Evans, Edward, Baron Mountevans
Fisher, John, Baron
French, John, Earl of Ypres
Gibson, Guy
Haig, Douglas, Earl
Hart, Sir Basil Liddell. *See* Liddell Hart
Ismay, Hastings
Jellicoe, John, Earl
Kitchener, Horatio Herbert, Earl
Lawrence, T. E.
Leigh-Mallory, T. *See* Mallory, G.
Liddell Hart, Sir Basil
Lugard, Frederick, Baron
Mallory, G. and Leigh-Mallory, T.
Maurice, Sir Frederick
Milford Haven, Marquess of. *See*
    Mountbatten, L. A.

Montgomery, Bernard, Viscount
Mountbatten, Louis Alexander,
    Marquess of Milford Haven
Mountbatten, Louis, Earl
Mountevans, Baron. *See* Evans, Edward
Portal, Charles, Viscount
Slim, William, Viscount
Smuts, J. C.
Tedder, Arthur, Baron
Templer, Sir Gerald
Trenchard, H. M., Viscount
Wavell, Archibald, Earl
Wilson, Sir Henry
Wingate, Orde
Ypres, Earl of. *See* French

ART & DESIGN

Bairnsfather, Bruce
Bateman, H. M.
Beaton, Cecil
Beatty, Chester
Beerbohm, Max
Bell, Clive. *See* Bell, V.
Bell, Vanessa & Clive
Courtauld, Samuel
Dick, Sir William Reid. *See* Reid Dick
Duveen, Joseph
Dyson Perrins, C. W.
Easton, Hugh
Epstein, Sir Jacob
Flint, Sir William Russell
Fry, Roger
Gill, Eric
Gunn, Sir James
Heath Robinson, William
Hepworth, Barbara
John, Augustus
Kennington, Eric
Knight, Dame Laura & Harold
Knight, Harold. *See* Knight, L.
Lavery, Sir John
Leach, Bernard
Lee, Arthur, Viscount Lee of Fareham
Low, David
Lowry, L. S.
Marsh, Sir Edward
Messel, Oliver
Morison, Stanley
Munnings, Sir Alfred
Nash, Paul
Orpen, Sir William
Peake, Mervyn
Perrins, C. W. Dyson. *See* Dyson Perrins
Pissarro, Lucien
Potter, Beatrix
Read, Sir Herbert

Reid Dick, Sir William
Robinson, William Heath. *See* Heath
    Robinson
Rothenstein, Sir William
Salisbury, Frank O.
Shepard, E. H.
Sheridan, Clare
Sickert, Walter
Spencer, Stanley
Spy
Sutherland, Graham
Tonks, Henry
Vicky
Ward, Sir Leslie. *See* Spy
Webster, Tom
Weisz, Victor. *See* Vicky

COMMERCE & INDUSTRY

Aberconway, 2nd Baron. *See* McLaren
Astor, John, Baron Astor of Hever
Austin, Herbert, Baron
Balcon, Sir Michael
Baylis, Lilian
Bearsted, Viscount. *See* Samuel, Marcus
Benn, Sir Ernest
Berry, Gomer & William
Boot, Jesse, Baron Trent
Burnham, Viscount. *See* Lawson
Burton, Sir Montague
Butlin, Billy
Cadbury, George
Camrose, Viscount. *See* Berry
Cape, Jonathan
Cassel, Sir Ernest
Catto, Thomas, Baron
Christie, John
Cochran, Charles
Courtauld, Samuel
Crowther, Geoffrey, Baron
Currie, Sir William
De Havilland, Sir Geoffrey
Du Cros, Arthur & Dunlop, John
Dunlop, John. *See* Du Cros
Dyson Perrins, C. W.
Elvin, Sir Arthur
Faber, Sir Geoffrey
Fleck, Alexander, Baron
Foyle, William
Fraser, Hugh
Gollancz, Victor
Handley Page, Sir Frederick
Harmsworth, Alfred, Viscount
    Northcliffe
Harmsworth, Harold, Viscount
    Rothermere
Heinemann, William

ACKNOWLEDGEMENTS

The author and publishers thank the following for permission to reproduce the copyright illustrations on the pages listed:

Gilbert Adams: 306; Allen & Unwin, *The Autobiography of Bertrand Russell*: 294; Ashmolean Museum, Oxford: 205; *Athletics Weekly*: 1; Estate of H. M. Bateman 1985: 24; BBC & Billy Smart's Circus: 312; BBC Hulton Picture Library: 3, 7, 11, 16, 20, 21, 26, 28, 41, 42, 52, 57, 60, 63, 73, 77, 79, 85, 89, 94, 122, 132, 144, 153, 162, 163, 168, 170, 176, 177, 181, 182, 184, 200, 241, 245, 266 top, 270, 272 top, 282, 283, 285, 286, 290, 296, 316, 317, 319, 323, 327, 338, 356, 358; Cecil Beaton photograph, courtesy of Sotheby's & Co., London: 223, 310; Department of Biochemistry, University of Cambridge: 148; Mrs Giovanna Bloor: 38; The Blackwell Group: 335; British Aerospace: 97; British Library & India Office Library: 91; British Library of Political & Economic Science: 346; The British Motor Industry Heritage Trust: 14; The Burton Group: 56; Business Press International: 152; Cadbury: 59; The Syndics of Cambridge University Library: 141; University of Cambridge, Cavendish Laboratory: 295; Camera Press: 244 (Tom Blau), 343 (Mark Gerson); Bob Collins: 195, 203; Culver Pictures: 190; *Daily Herald* Collection: 124; Dunlop: 104 left; The Provost and Fellows of Eton College photograph, Courtauld Institute of Art: 47; Mary Evans Picture Library © 1975 The Estate of W. Heath Robinson, *Absurdities* (Gerald Duckworth & Co.): 160; The Estate of Eleanor Farjeon: 115; House of Fraser: 126; Geraldo Entertainments: 135; Mark Gerson: 301; Grainger Museum Board, University of Melbourne: 99; Mr R. Grenfell: 142; Griffith Institute: 62; Trustees of the Thomas Hardy Memorial Collection in the Dorset County Museum, Dorchester, Dorset: 156; Michael Holroyd, *Augustus John* (William Heinemann): 188; Eric Hosking: 118; The *Illustrated London News* Picture Library: 189, 242, 255, 303, 314, 321, 349, 362; Imperial War Museum: 6, 64, 75, 103, 136, 147, 180, 214, 268, 280 top, 345; International Museum of Photography at George Eastman House: 304; Keele University Library: 31; John Lewis Partnership: 212; London Films & Kobal Collection: 198; MGM & Kobal Collection: 105 left; Angus McBean photograph, Harvard Theatre Collection: 116; © Rollie McKenna: 328; Mrs Rosemary Magnus: 237; The Raymond Mander & Joe Mitchenson Theatre Collection: 78, 264, 278, 331, 333; Mansell Collection: 53, 104 right, 133, 196, 258; Marks & Spencer: 233; Colin Middleton Murry: 260; Helen Muspratt, Swanage: 261; National Portrait Gallery, London: 70, 138, 172, 193, 263, 291, 354; University of Newcastle upon Tyne: 29; Norfolk Record Office: 146; Dr Jerrold Northrop Moore: 109; Oxford & County Newspapers: 332; Norman Parkinson: 98; Lady Percy & British Architectural Library, RIBA, London: 222; The Photo Source: 9, 12, 36, 44, 71, 95, 107, 111, 129, 137, 151, 167; Popperfoto: 18, 34, 49, 50, 67, 86, 87, 93, 101, 110, 120, 145, 159, 204, 218, 219, 225, 238, 239, 247, 252, 254, 266 bottom, 277, 299 right, 326, 347, 352; The Queen Victoria Hospital, East Grinstead, Sussex: 227; *Radio Times*: 178; Mrs Eva Reichmann & Ashmolean Museum, Oxford: 183; Rex Features: 210; Ben Richards: 335; Rolls-Royce: 292; Royal College of Music: 272 bottom; Royal Geographical Society: 231; The Royal Institution: 45; The Royal Society for the Protection of Birds: 174 right; Trustees of the Royal Victoria Hall Foundation: 25; E. H. Shepard, *Drawn from Memory* (Methuen, London), reproduced by permission of Curtis Brown, London, on behalf of the estate of E. H. Shepard: 305; *The Standard*: 230, 236; Theatre Museum, Victoria & Albert Museum: 113; Times Newspapers: 249; Topham: 82, 83, 235, 269, 275, 288, 302, 340, 359; United Artists & Kobal Collection: 69; Mrs R. Vaughan Williams: 169, 337; Vickers: 341; Board of Trustees of the Victoria & Albert Museum: 206; Mrs Julian Vinogradoff: 251, 299 left; Margaret Lane, *The Magic Years of Beatrix Potter* with the permission of Frederick Warne: 280 bottom; Warner Brothers & Kobal Collection: 209; Virginia Woolf estate: 361.

Harold Oxbury is a scholar of Trinity College, Cambridge, where he read history. He is a former Deputy Director-General of the British Council and spent many years in Burma in the Indian Civil Service. He is the principal editor of *The Concise Dictionary of National Biography 1901—1970.*